A LABORATORY TEXT IN

MICROCOMPUTERS & APPLICATIONS

Featuring DOS, WordPerfect 5.0, Lotus 1-2-3, and dBASE IV

A LABORATORY TEXT IN

MICROCOMPUTERS & APPLICATIONS

Featuring DOS, WordPerfect 5.0, Lotus 1-2-3, and dBASE IV

ERNEST S. COLANTONIO

D. C. HEATH AND COMPANY
LEXINGTON, MASSACHUSETTS TORONTO

Acquisitions Editor: John Carter Shanklin
Developmental Editor: Katherine T. Pinard
Production Editor: Kathleen A. Savage
Designer: Cornelia L. Boynton
Production Coordinator: Mike O'Dea
Composition and pre-press: Graphic Typesetting Service
Photo Researcher: Martha L. Shethar
Cover: John D. Kramer/ImageSet Design

Published simultaneously in Canada.

Printed in the United States of America.

International Standard Book Number: 0–669–21751–4

Library of Congress Catalog Card Number: 89–85748

10 9 8 7 6 5 4 3 2 1

PREFACE

The microcomputer has become standard equipment in most schools, offices, and businesses. A wealth of exceptional software is available to apply this versatile tool to a wide range of tasks. *A Laboratory Text in Microcomputers and Applications Featuring DOS, WordPerfect 5.0, Lotus 1-2-3, and dBASE IV* has been written for the novice end-user of microcomputers and application software.

Most end-users are not computer engineers; therefore, we discuss hardware only to help students understand how to use software. Most end-users are not computer programmers; we do not teach programming languages such as BASIC and Pascal. Most microcomputer users, however, do work with operating system, word processing, spreadsheet, and data base management software. They may also use communications and networking, graphics, and desktop publishing software, as well as other more specialized application programs. This text teaches students how to use such software in their everyday lives. In particular, this text concentrates on the most recent versions of DOS, WordPerfect, Lotus 1-2-3, and dBASE.

Text Content and Organization

A Laboratory Text in Microcomputers and Applications has been carefully designed for use in any first course in microcomputer application software. It should also be helpful to individuals who want to learn more about using microcomputers.

Variety The text introduces basic concepts of microcomputer hardware and software. The most commonly used software is emphasized—operating systems and word processing, spreadsheet, and data base management packages. Its comprehensive coverage also includes many other popular types of application software—from disk backup utilities to expert system shells. A chapter on computers and society discusses the role computers play in our lives, the problems they can cause, and what the future may hold. Despite this diversity, *A Laboratory Text in Microcomputers and Applications* requires no previous computer or mathematical skills beyond basic arithmetic.

Flexibility The text, which is divided into six parts, is a flexible introduction to microcomputer software. We recommend covering Part 1, The Microcomputer System, first, and then Part 2, DOS. Part 3, WordPerfect; Part 4, Lotus 1-2-3; and Part 5, dBASE IV, can be read in any order. Part 6, Special Applications, will be most meaningful if it is covered last. The chapters within each part, except for Part 6, should be read in order. The advanced chapters, which come last in Parts 2 through 5, can be omitted in courses that cover only basic software topics.

Computer Skills The text is designed for use in courses with microcomputer laboratory facilities, but Part 1 and Part 6 do not require computer access. Many commercial software products are simply presented as examples throughout these two parts. Parts 2 through 5 cover the details of using a particular software product. Specifically, the text teaches DOS 3.3 and 4.0; WordPerfect 5.0; Lotus 1-2-3 Releases 2.01, 2.2 and 3.0; and dBASE IV. We assume that students have access to these software packages and a computer that can run them.

Appendixes The text's six appendixes provide additional material that may be of interest to students and instructors. Appendix A, Data Representation, briefly discusses how computers code numbers and characters. Appendix B, Selecting a System, provides valuable tips for those individuals faced with the daunting task of purchasing hardware and software. Appendix C, Software Installation, briefly summarizes how to set up DOS, WordPerfect, Lotus1-2-3, and dBASE IV on a computer. Appendix D, Computer Careers, furnishes useful information for students seeking job opportunities in the computer industry. Appendix E, OS/2, introduces the powerful multitasking operating system for IBM and IBM-compatible microcomputers that use an Intel 80286 or 80386 microprocessor. Appendix F presents comprehensive command summaries for DOS, WordPerfect 5.0, Lotus 1-2-3, and dBASE IV.

Text Learning Aids

A Laboratory Text in Microcomputers and Applications combines a relaxed writing style with an outstanding array of pedagogical features to facilitate understanding and encourage reader enthusiasm.

Chapter Outline Each chapter opens with *In This Chapter*, an outline of the chapter's headings.

Chapter Preview Students learn more effectively if they are presented with clear learning objectives. Each chapter's *Preview* section introduces the material and provides learning objectives.

Computer Insights Chapters 1 through 4, Parts 2 through 5, and Chapters 17 through 21 each include an *Insight* box, which poses an intriguing question about microcomputers and then answers it with information obtained from computer experts.

Real World Chapters 1 through 4, Parts 2 through 5, and Chapters 17 through 21 each include a *Real World* box, a selection from a magazine, newspaper, or book about a topic covered in the chapter. This feature is designed to help the reader understand how microcomputers and application software are actually being used in today's world.

Readability The text's engaging writing style ensures that concepts are explained clearly and simply. Editors, course instructors, and reviewers have carefully monitored the reading level to maintain accessibility for students.

Design and Illustrations Students prefer a textbook that will hold their interest. We have created a design that is simple, but that effectively presents the material. Current photographs, striking line art, and high-resolution computer screen views are liberally inserted throughout each chapter to help illustrate major topics. A section of color photographs enhances the presentation of key subjects.

End-of-Chapter Materials A carefully graded set of review materials is provided at the end of each chapter. First, the *Summary* briefly reviews the information that parallels the learning objectives stated in the chapter's *Preview*. Next, the *Key Terms* presents all of the chapter's boldfaced glossary terms. In Parts 1 and 6, twenty short-answer *Review Questions* follow, providing a rote review of the chapter's major topics. Fifteen *Multiple Choice* questions provide further opportunity for students to review the chapter, and four special *Projects* encourage students to extend their learning beyond the chapter content. Parts 2 through 5, which cover specific software products, have a slightly different set of student exercises. Twenty *Multiple Choice* and twenty *Fill-In* questions test students' understanding of the material. Ten *Short Problems* and ten *Long Problems* provide computer exercises that let students apply their new skills.

Glossary and Index A complete glossary includes clear definitions for all the boldfaced terms in the text. In addition, a detailed index provides a handy reference for both student and instructor.

Command Summaries Appendix F contains comprehensive command summaries for DOS, WordPerfect 5.0, Lotus 1-2-3, and dBASE IV that serve as quick-reference guides to the software packages.

Keyboard Templates Color-coded keyboard templates for DOS, WordPerfect 5.0, Lotus 1-2-3, and dBASE IV are included just inside the back cover of the book. Designed to be detached from the book and placed on top of the keyboard, these invaluable reminders list the important keyboard commands of each software product. The color-coding indicates at a glance whether the Shift, Control, or Alternate key should be pressed in conjunction with another key to execute a command.

Supplements

Instructors' Supplements The supplements designed for instructors include an *Instructor's Guide* with transparency masters, a *Test Item File*, and HeathTest Plus (a Computerized Test Generator).

Instructor's Guide Prepared by Richard E. Morel, the *Instructor's Guide* includes the following materials for busy teachers: learning objectives, chapter overviews, annotated lecture outlines, answers to text questions, additional classroom and lecture materials, and transparency masters.

Test Item File A *Test Item File* developed by Richard E. Morel includes approximately 2,000 test questions: 40% true-false, 30% multiple choice, and 30% fill-in.

HeathTest Plus A computerized test generator for microcomputers is also available. Instructors can produce chapter tests, mid-terms, and final exams easily and accurately. Instructors can also edit existing questions or add new ones as desired, or preview questions on screen and add them to a test with a single keystroke.

Acknowledgments

Many people helped make *A Laboratory Text in Microcomputers and Applications* possible. I would like to thank Robert Hendersen and Nancy Sampson of the University of Illinois Department of Psychology Instructional Computer Laboratory for the use of various microcomputer hardware and software. Paul W. Ross of Millersville University provided many helpful suggestions throughout the development of this project. In addition to her work as copyeditor, Ann Hall helped extensively with the *Insight* and *Real World* features and wrote the *Computer Careers* appendix.

I would like to thank all of my colleagues who reviewed the manuscript:

- Professor Harvey Blessing, Essex Community College
- Professor Walter Bremer, California Polytechnic University
- Professor Frank S. Butash, University of Hartford
- Dr. William J. Engelmeyer, Anne Arundel Community College
- Professor Clinton P. Fuelling, Ball State University
- Professor C. Brian Honess, University of South Carolina
- Professor Susan Karian, Denison University
- Professor Gladys Norman, Linn-Benton Community College
- Dr. J. Douglas Robertson, Bentley College
- Professor Jerry Sitek, Southern Illinois University at Edwardsville
- Professor Karen Watterson, Shoreline Community College

Thanks also to the Lotus Development Corporation for their support of students and faculty by supplying us with copies of their new software. Thanks to Ashton-Tate and WordPerfect Corporation for their support as well.

Finally, my special gratitude and appreciation go to all the people at D. C. Heath who worked long hours and sweated endless details to make this text the best that it could be, especially Kathleen Savage, Cia Boynton, and Mike O'Dea.

E.S.C.

About the Author

Ernest S. Colantonio brings combined teaching, technical, and writing skills to this textbook. He received his undergraduate degree in psychology and completed several semesters of graduate work in computer science at the University of Illinois at Urbana-Champaign. While in graduate school, he taught introductory courses in computer science for nontechnical majors. Since 1982, Mr. Colantonio has developed microcomputer software for various organizations, including the Illinois State Geological Survey, the University of Illinois Department of Psychology, the Office of Naval Research, Psychology Software Tools Corporation, and SubLOGIC Corporation. He is the author of several data processing and microcomputer textbooks. Currently, Mr. Colantonio spends most of his time writing new textbooks from his home north of Green Bay, Wisconsin. He also develops and teaches introductory computer courses for Lakeland College and Northeast Wisconsin Technical College.

Brief Contents

PART 1 The Microcomputer System 1

1 Computer Concepts 3
2 Hardware 37
3 Software 85
4 Operating System Concepts 117

PART 2 DOS 141

5 Beginning DOS 143
6 Intermediate DOS 189
7 Advanced DOS 241

PART 3 WordPerfect 283

8 Beginning WordPerfect 285
9 Intermediate WordPerfect 337
10 Advanced WordPerfect 395

PART 4 Lotus 1-2-3 457

11 Beginning Lotus 1-2-3 459
12 Intermediate Lotus 1-2-3 509
13 Advanced Lotus 1-2-3 555

PART 5 **dBASE IV** **607**

14 Beginning dBASE IV 609
15 Intermediate dBASE IV 657
16 Advanced dBASE IV 713

PART 6 **Special Applications** **763**

17 Communications and Networking 765
18 Graphics 805
19 Desktop Publishing 845
20 Software Sidelights 877
21 Computers and Society: Future Trends 915

APPENDIX A **Data Representation** **A1**

APPENDIX B **Selecting a System** **A9**

APPENDIX C **Software Installation** **A23**

APPENDIX D **Computer Careers** **A31**

APPENDIX E **OS/2** **A43**

APPENDIX F **Command Summaries** **A49**

Glossary **A93**

Photo Credits **A108**

Index **A109**

CONTENTS

PART 1 The Microcomputer System 1

1 Computer Concepts 3

PREVIEW 4

WHY STUDY COMPUTERS? 4

INSIGHT: How Small Can Computers Get? 5
- Learning 4
- Employment 6
- Productivity 6
- Capability 7
- Fun 7

HOW COMPUTERS ARE USED 8
- Personal Productivity 8
- Information Management 9
- Communication 10
- Presentation 12
- Education 13

A TYPICAL MICROCOMPUTER SYSTEM 13
- What Is a Microcomputer? 14
- Hardware 15
- Software 17
- Users 18

TYPES OF MICROCOMPUTERS 19
- Hand-held Computers 19
- Laptop Computers 20
- Portable Computers 21
- Desktop Computers 21
- Floor Models 22

MICROCOMPUTER STANDARDS 22
Apple II 23
IBM 23
Apple Macintosh 25

OTHER TYPES OF COMPUTERS 26
Workstations 28
Minicomputers 28
Mainframes 29
Supercomputers 30

REAL WORLD: You're Smarter Than You May Have Thought 31

Summary • Key Terms • Review Questions • Multiple Choice • Projects

2 Hardware 37

PREVIEW 38

THE MICROCOMPUTER REVEALED 38

INSIGHT: What Happens When Your Computer Goes Out of Production? 41

THE MICROPROCESSOR 41
Structure 42
Register Size 43
Data Bus Size 44
Speed 45

PRIMARY STORAGE 46
RAM 46
ROM 47

SECONDARY STORAGE 47
Floppy Disks 48
Hard Disk Drives 51
Magnetic Tape Drives 53
Bernoulli Disk Drives 54
Optical Disk Drives 55

KEYBOARDS AND MICE 57

DISPLAYS 60
Monochrome Text Monitors 60
Monochrome Graphics Monitors 61
Color Graphics Monitors 62

EXPANDING THE SYSTEM 63
Expansion Slots 63
Expansion Boards 64
Interfaces 65
The Serial Interface • The Parallel Interface • The Small Computer System Interface
Printers 66
Dot-Matrix Printers 66
Daisy-Wheel Printers 68
Ink-Jet Printers 68
Laser Printers 68
Plotters 70

MODEMS 70

OTHER PERIPHERALS 73
- Joysticks 73
- Trackballs 73
- Light Pens 74
- Touch-Screens 75
- Graphics Tablets 76
- Scanners 76
- Voice Recognition Systems 77
- Speech Synthesizers 78

REAL WORLD: Changing Chips 78

Summary • Key Terms • Review Questions • Multiple Choice • Projects

3 Software 85

PREVIEW 86

COMPUTER PROGRAMS 86

INSIGHT: Do I Need to Learn a Programming Language? 86

SYSTEM SOFTWARE 88
- Operating Systems 88
- Utilities 89
- Windowing Environments 91

PROGRAMMING LANGUAGES 91
- Machine Languages 92
- Assembly Languages 93
- High-level Languages 94
  - BASIC • Pascal • C • FORTRAN • COBOL • Ada
- Fourth Generation Languages 98

APPLICATION SOFTWARE 100
- Word Processing 100
- Spreadsheet 101
- Data Base Management 102
- Communications and Networking 103
- Graphics 103
- Desktop Publishing 104
- Other Packages 105

THE USER INTERFACE 106
- Commands 106
- Prompts 107
- Static Menus 107
- Pop-up Menus 108
- Pull-down Menus 110
- Graphical User Interfaces 111

REAL WORLD: Microsoft's Phenomenon 109

Summary • Key Terms • Review Questions • Multiple Choice • Projects

4 Operating System Concepts 117

PREVIEW 118

WHAT OPERATING SYSTEMS DO 118

INSIGHT: What Causes an Operating System to Crash? 119

Control Hardware 118
Manage Software 119
Interact with Users 120

TYPES OF OPERATING SYSTEMS 120
Single-user, Single-tasking 120
Single-user, Multitasking 121
Multiuser, Single-tasking 122
Multiuser, Multitasking 123
Multiprocessing 123
Networking 125

OPERATING SYSTEM COMPONENTS 126
Hardware Interface 127
Application Interface 128
User Interface 128

IMPORTANT MICROCOMPUTER OPERATING SYSTEMS 129
CP/M 129
DOS 130
OS/2 131
UNIX 132
ProDOS 134
Apple Macintosh System 134

REAL WORLD: The Lure of UNIX 136

Summary • Key Terms • Review Questions • Multiple Choice • Projects

PART 2 DOS 141

5 Beginning DOS 143

PREVIEW 144

INSIGHT: Will PC-DOS Be Replaced by Another Operating System? 145

DOS VERSIONS 145

GETTING STARTED 146

LESSON 1: BOOTING DOS 147

LESSON 2: REBOOTING DOS 150

LESSON 3: LISTING A DISK FILE DIRECTORY 151

LESSON 4: USING SPECIAL DOS KEYS 156

LESSON 5: CHANGING THE DEFAULT DISK DRIVE 160

LESSON 6: CHECKING DISK AND MEMORY STATUS 162
LESSON 7: CLEARING THE SCREEN 163
LESSON 8: FORMATTING A DISKETTE 163
LESSON 9: FORMATTING A SYSTEM DISKETTE 165
LESSON 10: COPYING FILES 168
LESSON 11: COPYING AN ENTIRE DISKETTE 172
LESSON 12: CHANGING FILE NAMES 173
LESSON 13: ERASING FILES 175
LESSON 14: PROTECTING DISKETTES 177
LESSON 15: DISPLAYING AND PRINTING TEXT FILES 179
LESSON 16: RUNNING A PROGRAM 181
REAL WORLD: Microsoft Branches Out 182
Summary • Key Terms • Multiple Choice • Fill-In • Short Problems

6 Intermediate DOS 189

PREVIEW 190
GETTING STARTED 190
LESSON 1: USING THE DOS EDITING AND FUNCTION KEYS 190
LESSON 2: SETTING THE BREAK OPTION 193
LESSON 3: WORKING WITH SUBDIRECTORIES 194
LESSON 4: USING THE PATH AND APPEND COMMANDS 198
LESSON 5: CHANGING THE DOS PROMPT 201
LESSON 6: BACKING UP AND RESTORING DISKS AND FILES 203
LESSON 7: RECOVERING FILES FROM DAMAGED DISKS 207
LESSON 8: USING THE PROMPT OPTION WHEN ERASING FILES 209
LESSON 9: LEARNING MORE ABOUT THE COPY COMMAND 210
LESSON 10: SETTING THE VERIFY OPTION 213
LESSON 11: CHANGING FILE ATTRIBUTES 214
LESSON 12: COPYING GROUPS OF FILES 216
LESSON 13: UPDATING SETS OF FILES 219
LESSON 14: TRANSFERRING THE DOS SYSTEM FILES 221
LESSON 15: COMPARING FILES AND DISKS 223
LESSON 16: DISPLAYING AND CHANGING A VOLUME LABEL 224
LESSON 17: DISPLAYING AND CHANGING THE DATE AND TIME 226
LESSON 18: DISPLAYING A MEMORY REPORT 227
LESSON 19: REASSIGNING, JOINING, AND SUBSTITUTING DRIVES 229

LESSON 20: LEARNING MORE ABOUT THE PRINT COMMAND 232

Summary • Key Terms • Multiple Choice • Fill-In • Short Problems

7 Advanced DOS 241

PREVIEW 242

GETTING STARTED 242

LESSON 1: REDIRECTING OUTPUT AND INPUT 242

LESSON 2: USING DOS FILTERS AND PIPING 245

LESSON 3: USING BATCH FILES 249

LESSON 4: USING BATCH PROCESSING COMMANDS 252

LESSON 5: SETTING UP THE CONFIGURATION FILE 261

LESSON 6: PARTITIONING AND FORMATTING HARD DISKS 265

LESSON 7: LEARNING ABOUT OTHER DOS COMMANDS 267

LESSON 8: USING THE DOS SHELL 272

Summary • Key Terms • Multiple Choice • Fill-In • Short Problems

PART 3 WordPerfect 5.0 283

8 Beginning WordPerfect 285

PREVIEW 286

GETTING STARTED 286

INSIGHT: What Is the Secret to WordPerfect's Success? 287

LESSON 1: RUNNING WORDPERFECT 287

LESSON 2: THE EDITING SCREEN 289

LESSON 3: EXECUTING COMMANDS AND GETTING HELP 290

LESSON 4: ENTERING TEXT 292

LESSON 5: MOVING THE CURSOR 294

LESSON 6: INSERTING TEXT 297

LESSON 7: OVERWRITING MISTAKES 298

LESSON 8: DELETING MISTAKES 299

LESSON 9: SEARCHING AND REPLACING 300

LESSON 10: SAVING THE DOCUMENT 302

LESSON 11: CHECKING SPELLING 304

LESSON 12: WORKING WITH BLOCKS OF TEXT 306

LESSON 13: CANCELING COMMANDS 311

LESSON 14: FORMATTING CHARACTERS 312

LESSON 15: FORMATTING LINES 315

LESSON 16: FORMATTING PAGES 320

LESSON 17: PRINTING A DOCUMENT 325

LESSON 18: RETURNING TO DOS 325

LESSON 19: EDITING AN EXISTING DOCUMENT 327

REAL WORLD: The Men Behind WordPerfect 329

Summary • Key Terms • Multiple Choice • Fill-In • Short Problems • Long Problems

9 Intermediate WordPerfect 337

PREVIEW 338

GETTING STARTED 338

LESSON 1: MANAGING DOCUMENTS 338

LESSON 2: CREATING A LONGER DOCUMENT 346

LESSON 3: LEARNING MORE CURSOR-MOVEMENT COMMANDS 350

LESSON 4: LEARNING MORE DELETE COMMANDS 352

LESSON 5: WORKING WITH CODES 354

LESSON 6: USING THE THESAURUS 356

LESSON 7: WORKING WITH WINDOWS 360

LESSON 8: INDENTING PARAGRAPHS 364

LESSON 9: USING TAB STOPS TO CREATE TABLES 367

LESSON 10: USING THE TAB ALIGN COMMAND 371

LESSON 11: USING THE FLUSH RIGHT COMMAND 373

LESSON 12: USING THE DATE COMMAND 375

LESSON 13: CENTERING TEXT ON A PAGE 378

LESSON 14: ADDING A DOCUMENT SUMMARY 379

LESSON 15: USE THE TEXT IN/OUT COMMAND 381

LESSON 16: EXECUTE A DOS COMMAND WITHIN WORDPERFECT 383

Summary • Key Terms • Multiple Choice • Fill-In • Short Problems • Long Problems

10 Advanced WordPerfect 395

PREVIEW 396

GETTING STARTED 396

LESSON 1: USING THE PRINT MENU 396

LESSON 2: HYPHENATING WORDS 402

LESSON 3: AVOIDING ORPHANS AND WIDOWS 405

LESSON 4: USING THE CONDITIONAL END OF PAGE FEATURE 407
LESSON 5: USING THE FONT MENU 409
LESSON 6: ADDING HEADERS AND FOOTERS 413
LESSON 7: CREATING TEXT COLUMNS 415
LESSON 8: ADDING FOOTNOTES AND ENDNOTES 418
LESSON 9: SORTING TEXT 420
LESSON 10: PERFORMING MATH 422
LESSON 11: OUTLINING A DOCUMENT 424
LESSON 12: GENERATING A TABLE OF CONTENTS 426
LESSON 13: GENERATING AN INDEX 429
LESSON 14: ADDING GRAPHICS 430
LESSON 15: USING MACROS 436
LESSON 16: CREATING FORM LETTERS 438
LESSON 17: USING STYLES 443
LESSON 18: CUSTOMIZING WORDPERFECT 446
Summary • Key Terms • Multiple Choice • Fill-In • Short Problems • Long Problems

PART 4 **Lotus 1-2-3** 457

11 Beginning Lotus 1-2-3 459
PREVIEW 460
GETTING STARTED 460
INSIGHT: Which Lotus Spreadsheet Software is Right for Me? 461
LESSON 1: RUNNING 1-2-3 461
LESSON 2: CREATING A WORKSHEET 463
LESSON 3: USING 1-2-3 MENUS 469
LESSON 4: SAVING A WORKSHEET 470
LESSON 5: PRINTING A WORKSHEET 471
LESSON 6: QUITTING 1-2-3 473
LESSON 7: RETRIEVING AN EXISTING WORKSHEET 474
LESSON 8: GETTING HELP 475
LESSON 9: MOVING AROUND A WORKSHEET 478
LESSON 10: EDITING CELLS 480
LESSON 11: CHANGING COLUMN WIDTHS 481

LESSON 12: DELETING AND INSERTING COLUMNS AND ROWS 483

LESSON 13: COPYING AND MOVING CELLS 484

LESSON 14: CELL FORMATTING 486

LESSON 15: USING THE UNDO FEATURE IN RELEASES 2.2 AND 3.0 489

LESSON 16: USING FORMULAS 490

LESSON 17: USING FUNCTIONS 496

REAL WORLD: Temporaries Trained to Use Lotus 1-2-3 499

Summary • Key Terms • Multiple Choice • Fill-In • Short Problems • Long Problems

12 Intermediate Lotus 1-2-3 509

PREVIEW 510

GETTING STARTED 510

LESSON 1: CREATING A BAR GRAPH 510

LESSON 2: PRINTING A GRAPH WITH RELEASE 2.0 OR 2.2 515

LESSON 3: PRINTING A GRAPH WITH RELEASE 3.0 518

LESSON 4: NAMING A GRAPH 518

LESSON 5: CREATING A PIE CHART 520

LESSON 6: CREATING A LINE GRAPH 523

LESSON 7: CREATING A STACKED BAR GRAPH 528

LESSON 8: CREATING AN XY GRAPH 531

LESSON 9: CREATING A DATA BASE WORKSHEET 535

LESSON 10: SORTING A DATA BASE WORKSHEET 538

LESSON 11: SEARCHING A DATA BASE WORKSHEET 540

LESSON 12: EXTRACTING RECORDS FROM A DATA BASE WORKSHEET 543

LESSON 13: USING THE DATA BASE FUNCTIONS 545

Summary • Key Terms • Multiple Choice • Fill-In • Short Problems • Long Problems

13 Advanced Lotus 1-2-3 555

PREVIEW 556

GETTING STARTED 556

LESSON 1: CHANGING WORKSHEET SETTINGS 556

LESSON 2: FREEZING TITLES AND USING WINDOWS 559

LESSON 3: HIDING COLUMNS AND PROTECTING CELLS 563

LESSON 4: CHANGING RANGE FORMATS 566

LESSON 5: USING RANGE NAMES 571

LESSON 6: FILLING A RANGE WITH A SEQUENCE OF NUMBERS 572

LESSON 7: TRANSPOSING COLUMNS AND ROWS 574

LESSON 8: CONTROLLING RECALCULATION AND ITERATION 575

LESSON 9: USING RELATIVE, ABSOLUTE, AND MIXED CELL REFERENCES 579

LESSON 10: USING ADDITIONAL FUNCTIONS 582

LESSON 11: USING MACROS 584

LESSON 12: USING THE LEARN FEATURE WITH RELEASE 2.2 588

LESSON 13: USING THE RECORD FEATURE WITH RELEASE 3.0 590

LESSON 14: LINKING WORKSHEETS WITH RELEASES 2.2 AND 3.0 592

LESSON 15: USING THREE-DIMENSIONAL WORKSHEETS WITH RELEASE 3.0 595

Summary • Key Terms • Multiple Choice • Fill-In • Short Problems • Long Problems

PART 5 **dBASE IV** 607

14 Beginning dBASE IV 609

PREVIEW 610

GETTING STARTED 610

LESSON 1: STARTING dBASE IV 610

LESSON 2: USING THE CONTROL CENTER 612

INSIGHT: Large Data Base Packages vs. File Management Programs 613

LESSON 3: DESIGNING A DATA BASE FILE 617

LESSON 4: ENTERING DATA BASE RECORDS 622

LESSON 5: EXAMINING AN EXISTING DATA BASE 625

LESSON 6: ADDING NEW RECORDS 627

LESSON 7: MODIFYING EXISTING RECORDS 628

LESSON 8: DELETING RECORDS 630

LESSON 9: FINDING RECORDS 634

LESSON 10: MODIFYING THE DATA BASE DESIGN 638

LESSON 11: SORTING THE DATA BASE 641

LESSON 12: INDEXING THE DATA BASE 644

LESSON 13: GENERATING REPORTS 647

REAL WORLD: Computerizing the City Clerk 648

Summary • Key Terms • Multiple Choice • Fill-In • Short Problems • Long Problems

15 Intermediate dBASE IV 657

PREVIEW 658

GETTING STARTED 658

LESSON 1: USING MEMO FIELDS 658

LESSON 2: CREATING A SIMPLE VIEW QUERY 662

LESSON 3: CREATING A RELATIONAL DATA BASE 665

LESSON 4: LINKING FILES 671

LESSON 5: CREATING AN UPDATE QUERY 675

LESSON 6: USING CALCULATED FIELDS 679

LESSON 7: SUMMARIZING DATA 681

LESSON 8: DESIGNING CUSTOM FORMS 683

LESSON 9: DESIGNING CUSTOM REPORTS 689

LESSON 10: CREATING MAILING LABELS 695

LESSON 11: USING APPLICATIONS 699

LESSON 12: USING THE CATALOG MENU 701

LESSON 13: USING THE TOOLS MENU 704

Summary • Key Terms • Multiple Choice • Fill-In • Short Problems • Long Problems

16 Advanced dBASE IV 713

PREVIEW 714

GETTING STARTED 714

LESSON 1: ACCESSING THE DOT PROMPT 714

LESSON 2: EXAMINING A DATA BASE FILE 718

LESSON 3: ENTERING AND MODIFYING RECORDS 723

LESSON 4: DELETING RECORDS 726

LESSON 5: SORTING AND INDEXING 728

LESSON 6: FINDING DATA 730

LESSON 7: RELATING FILES 735

LESSON 8: USING OTHER dBASE IV COMMANDS 738

LESSON 9: USING dBASE IV FUNCTIONS 743

LESSON 10: CREATING A dBASE IV PROGRAM 746

LESSON 11: USING THE APPLICATIONS GENERATOR 749

LESSON 12: USING SQL COMMANDS 753

Summary • Key Terms • Multiple Choice • Fill-In • Short Problems • Long Problems

PART 6 **Special Applications** 763

17 Communications and Networking 765

PREVIEW 766

COMMUNICATIONS HARDWARE 766

INSIGHT: Unauthorized Hackers: A Serious Problem? 768

Internal Modem System 768
External Modem System 769
Other Modem Considerations 771
Speed • Hayes Compatibility

COMMUNICATIONS SOFTWARE 771
Terminal Emulation 772
File Transfer 772
Introducing CROSSTALK 774

COMMUNICATIONS PARAMETERS 776
Speed 776
Data 776
Port 776
Parity 777
Stop 777
Duplex 777
Emulate 777
Mode 777

CALLING A MAINFRAME COMPUTER 778
Determine and Set the Parameters 778
Log On to the Mainframe 778
Use the Mainframe 779
Disconnect 780

SENDING AND RECEIVING ELECTRONIC MAIL 780
Log On to the System 781
Send a Message 782
Read a Message 784

USING AN ON-LINE INFORMATION SERVICE 784
Log On to the System 786
Read the News 788
Research an Encyclopedia 789

CALLING ANOTHER MICROCOMPUTER 790

LOCAL AREA NETWORKS 792
Hardware 793
Workstations • Servers • Media • Interfaces

Topology 794
Protocols 796
Software 797
Using a Network 799

REAL WORLD: An On-Line Cornucopia 798

Summary • Key Terms • Review Questions • Multiple Choice • Projects

18 Graphics 805

PREVIEW 806

GRAPHICS HARDWARE 806

INSIGHT: Professional Artists and Microcomputers 808

Display Adapter 807
Monitor 809
Input Device 810
Hard-Copy Output Device 811

GRAPHICS SOFTWARE 812

CHARTING PROGRAMS 813
Types of Charting Programs 813
Introducing EnerGraphics 814
Creating a Pie Chart 815
Creating a Bar Graph 818

PAINTING PROGRAMS 820
Introducing MacPaint 821
The MacPaint Screen 821
The MacPaint Pointer 822
The MacPaint Tools 823
Designing a Logo with MacPaint 824

DRAWING PROGRAMS 826
Introducing MacDraw 826
The MacDraw Screen 827
The MacDraw Tools 827
The MacDraw Menus 829
Designing a Desk with MacDraw 830

COMPUTER-AIDED DESIGN PROGRAMS 830
CAD Features 832
Introducing AutoCAD 832
Designing a Floor Plan with AutoCAD 833

SLIDE SHOW PROGRAMS 836
Introducing PC Storyboard 837
Creating the Pictures 837
Editing the Slide Show 838
Presenting the Slide Show 839

REAL WORLD: Graphics Gain a Foothold 841

Summary • Key Terms • Review Questions • Multiple Choice • Projects

19 Desktop Publishing 845

PREVIEW 846
Why Desktop Publishing? 846

INSIGHT: How Can Desktop Publishing Save a Company Money? 847

DESKTOP PUBLISHING APPLICATIONS 848

COMPONENTS OF A DESKTOP PUBLISHING SYSTEM 849
Powerful Microcomputer 849
Graphics Display 850
Mouse 850
Laser Printer 851
Scanner 853
Word Processing Software 853
Graphics Software 854
Page Layout Software 854

PRINCIPLES OF PAGE DESIGN 854

INTRODUCING PAGEMAKER 855

PRODUCING A NEWSLETTER 856
Writing and Editing the Text 856
Creating or Scanning the Artwork 858
Laying Out the Pages 861
Setting Up the Pages • Turning on Rules and Column Guides • Placing the Letterhead Logo • Typing the Newsletter Title • Finishing Off the Heading • Placing the Text • Placing the Sketch and Photo • Creating the Mailer • Final Adjustments
Printing the Document 870
Making Multiple Copies 871

REAL WORLD: Desktop Publishing Looks Ahead 871

Summary • Key Terms • Review Questions • Multiple Choice • Projects

20 Software Sidelights 877

PREVIEW 878

INTEGRATED SOFTWARE 878

INSIGHT: The Future of Software Packages 879

Advantages of Integrated Software 878
Disadvantages of Integrated Software 879
Popular Integrated Software Packages 880

WINDOWING ENVIRONMENTS 882
Types of Windowing Environments 882
Popular Windowing Environments 884

DOS SHELLS 885

UTILITIES 887
Disk and File Utilities 888
Printer Utilities 890
Keyboard Utilities 891

DESK ACCESSORIES 891
ON-LINE REFERENCES 893
STATISTICAL AND MATH PACKAGES 895
PROJECT MANAGEMENT SOFTWARE 896
ACCOUNTING SOFTWARE 898
PERSONAL FINANCE AND TAX PROGRAMS 900
EDUCATIONAL SOFTWARE 902
ENTERTAINMENT SOFTWARE 902
HYPERTEXT PROGRAMS 905
ARTIFICIAL INTELLIGENCE AND EXPERT SYSTEMS 907
REAL WORLD: Breaking the Rules 908
Summary • Key Terms • Review Questions • Multiple Choice • Projects

21 Computers and Society: Future Trends 915

PREVIEW 916
COMPUTERS AND EDUCATION 916
Computer-Assisted Instruction 916
Computer-Managed Instruction 917
COMPUTERS AND THE ARTS 917
INSIGHT: How Does a Virus Infect a Computer? 918
Music 917
Art 919
Movies 919
COMPUTERS AND MEDICINE 920
Training 921
Diagnosis 921
Imaging 921
COMPUTERS AND GOVERNMENT 922
The Internal Revenue Service 922
The Department of Defense 923
COMPUTERS AND BUSINESS 923
Computer-Aided Design, Engineering, and Manufacturing 924
Management Information and Decision Support Systems 925
COMPUTERS AND THE WORKPLACE 925
Job Security 926
Performance Monitoring 927
Health Concerns 927
Ergonomics 929
Telecommuting 929
COMPUTERS AND THE LAW 931
Hackers 931
Viruses 931

White-Collar Crime 933
Software Piracy 934
Copyrights, Licenses, Trademarks, and Patents 936
Ethics 938

COMPUTERS AND PRIVACY 938
Matching 939
Legal Protection 940
Security 942

COMPUTERS AND THE FUTURE 943

REAL WORLD: A Portrait of the Artist 946
Microprocessors 943
Supercomputers 944
Artificial Intelligence 945
Neural Networks 946

Summary • Key Terms • Review Questions • Multiple Choice • Projects

APPENDIX A **Data Representation A1**

APPENDIX B **Selecting a System A9**

APPENDIX C **Software Installation A23**

APPENDIX D **Computer Careers A31**

APPENDIX E **OS/2 A43**

APPENDIX F **Command Summaries A49**

Glossary A93

Photo Credits A108

Index A109

A LABORATORY TEXT IN

MICROCOMPUTERS & APPLICATIONS

Featuring DOS, WordPerfect 5.0, Lotus 1-2-3, and dBASE IV

PART 1

The Microcomputer System

The computer has changed our world. Almost every sector of our economy and every aspect of our society have been affected by computers. It's not just the scientists, engineers, and business people who need to know how to use computers; to some extent, we all do. The simple fact is: If you work with information, sooner or later you'll have to use a computer.

Microcomputers are by far the most numerous and accessible type of computer. These small, relatively inexpensive computers have infiltrated virtually all large corporations, most schools, and many homes. Why? Because they have proven to be extremely useful, versatile, and economical. The key to their power is the tasks they have been programmed to do. These tasks, or *applications,* are the primary focus of this book.

This part of the text sets the stage for your study of microcomputer applications. Chapter 1 presents basic computer concepts. Chapter 2 describes the physical components that make up microcomputer systems. Chapter 3 introduces the instructions, or *software programs,* that make microcomputers work. Chapter 4 is a general introduction to operating systems, the special software programs that manage computers.

CHAPTER 1

COMPUTER CONCEPTS

In This Chapter

Why Study Computers?
- Learning
- Employment
- Productivity
- Capability
- Fun

How Computers Are Used
- Personal Productivity
- Information Management
- Communication
- Presentation
- Education

A Typical Microcomputer System
- What Is a Microcomputer?
- Hardware
- Software
- Users

Types of Microcomputers
- Hand-held Computers
- Laptop Computers
- Portable Computers
- Desktop Computers
- Floor Models

Microcomputer Standards
- Apple II
- IBM
- Apple Macintosh

Other Types of Computers
- Workstations
- Minicomputers
- Mainframes
- Supercomputers

Preview

Once you get past the technical terminology of computers, they're really not all that difficult to learn about and use. This chapter sets the stage for your study of microcomputers by discussing why you should learn about computers, how these machines are used, and the various types of computers. Don't be alarmed if you see unfamiliar words. Most of the technical terms in this chapter will be initially defined very briefly or in context. Important terms will be defined again more rigorously in later chapters, after you have read additional background material. You may not wind up teaching people how to use computers or running a computer business, but this text will show you how to effectively use microcomputers in our high-tech information age.

After studying this chapter, you will understand

- why you should study computers.
- some of the ways in which microcomputers are used.
- the elements of a typical microcomputer system.
- the different types of microcomputers.
- the dominant microcomputer standards.
- the various types of other computers.

Why Study Computers?

Computers have been getting a lot of attention lately. We hear about them almost every day and we see them all around us. In fact, every time you cash a check, go through a supermarket checkout, or listen to a compact disc player, computers are involved. What can they do for you? Why should you spend the time and effort to learn more about computers? Why did you take this course?

You could simply answer that this course is required by your department or perhaps it is a prerequisite for some other, more advanced course that you want to take. There are, however, more profound reasons why you should know more about computers. A few of them have to do with learning, employment, productivity, capability, and fun.

Learning

Computers affect our lives, whether we realize it or not. They are used in banks, offices, stores, factories, schools, government agencies, military installations, and just about any other organization you can think of. Tiny specialized computers are built into many modern appliances, machines, and vehicles. All kinds of advanced equipment from cameras to jet aircraft depend utterly on computer technology. Unless you learn a few fundamental computer concepts, it will be difficult to understand many of today's and tomorrow's technological issues. Just as people had to learn to use the telephone in the early twentieth century, people have to learn to use computers in order to function in our increasingly complex society.

This is especially true for college students, because computer use on campuses has been growing at a phenomenal rate. According to a report in the *Chronicle of Higher Education*, colleges spent $800 million and students spent another $1 billion on microcomputer products in 1987 alone. At many colleges, courses in a wide range of subjects now require students to use computers (see Figure 1). In some cases, faculty members are designing their own ways for students to use computers in their studies. For example, the philosophy depart-

Insight

How Small Can Computers Get?

Look in the mirror. What you see is the only restriction on the incredible shrinking computer. Your hands have to fit on the keyboard and you have to be able to see the screen. Simple.

In their infancy, computers were giant Baby Hueys that filled the whole floor of a building. They pumped out heat, regularly blew out their vacuum tubes, clattered and whirred. Some of them had to have their circuits rewired whenever their programs were changed.

Some early microcomputers, such as the Compaq and Kaypro, were about the size of a portable sewing machine and weighed around 25 to 30 pounds. They weren't exactly portable—more like luggable. The person on the go could develop back strain carrying one of these around.

But there was a big market for smaller computers, which prodded manufacturers into producing machines that were about the size of a portable typewriter. These became known as laptop computers.

Laptops have a flat screen like a pocket calculator or a digital watch. They have at least one floppy disk for storing programs and data, and the newer systems have a built-in hard drive capable of storing at least 10 million characters of information. They can be plugged into a wall outlet or they can run for a few hours from an internal, rechargeable battery pack.

Laptops are being improved all the time. Their limited space is being used more efficiently, and their memory and storage are being expanded. If a modem is used with the laptop, files can be moved back and forth from a central computer. This increases the unit's power and flexibility, making it ideal for traveling business people or for journalists filing stories.

ment at Carnegie Mellon University in Pittsburgh offers a computerized course to help students learn the principles of symbolic logic at their own pace. Students who already know how to use a computer may find it easier to adapt to these types of courses.[1]

Figure 1* *Computers in Education
Many schools now require students to use computers in some of their subjects.

1. Jack Hayes, "Do Computer Skills Make College Grads More Marketable?," *Family & Home Office Computing,* April, 1988, pp. 26–28.

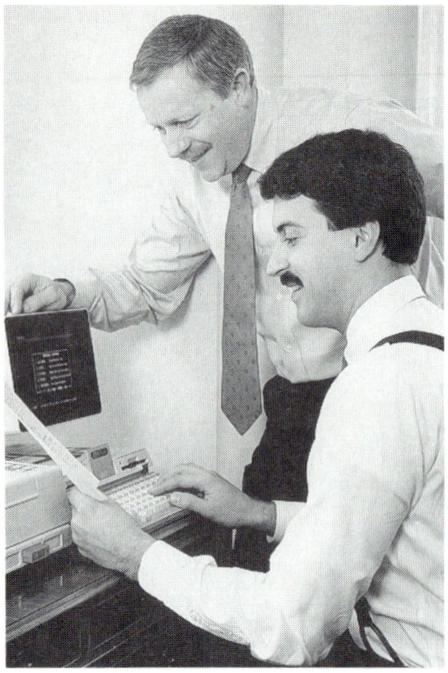

***Figure 2* Computers on the Job**
At Northwestern Mutual Life, insurance agents simply can't do business without a microcomputer.

Employment

Since most businesses and other organizations routinely use computers, employers need workers who are at least familiar with them. Knowing how to use a computer certainly won't guarantee you a job, but it can help you to be more competitive in today's labor market. At Northwestern Mutual Life, for example, microcomputers are essential tools. The company has sold more than 2000 computers to its 6000 independent insurance agents. Agents working in the same office generally share computers, so every agent has access to a computer (see Figure 2). According to Mark Lichtenberger, a technical planning officer at Northwestern Mutual, "An agent can't do business without a PC (personal computer). Without one, he or she has no access to sales-illustration charts, which are impossible to calculate manually." Some life insurance policies now offered by Northwestern Mutual are so complex that agents need a computer to demonstrate the advantages to potential customers.[2]

Another indication that students with computer skills do better in the job market comes from an informal survey done by Barbara Kurshan, former director of academic computing at Hollins College, a liberal arts school in Roanoke, Virginia. A cross section of students was questioned, including one hundred who had taken at least two computer courses at Hollins. Kurshan found that 70 percent of the students who had taken computer courses were routinely using computers in their jobs. These individuals generally thought that they got their jobs and were paid more because of their computer experience.[3]

Productivity

A compelling reason for learning to use a computer is that it can help you do certain jobs more efficiently. For example, **word processing,** a common computer application (see Figure 3), allows you to produce documents, such as letters and reports, with a computer. Once you learn how to do word processing with a

2. Craig Zarley, "PCs an Essential Tool for Insurance Sales," *PC Week*, March 15, 1988, pp. 47–53.
3. Hayes, "Computer Skills," pp. 26–28.

***Figure 3* Word Processing on a Microcomputer**
Many people use word processing to increase their personal productivity.

computer, producing documents is easier, faster, and more flexible than with an ordinary typewriter. Since you can correct errors before committing your work to paper, word processing also can produce much cleaner final documents, more efficiently. For example, a study done by R. Haider in 1979 suggests that word processing can eliminate up to 70 percent of the time spent on conventional typing.[4] Besides word processing, many other computer applications can save you a great deal of time and effort in your routine work.

Capability

Computers not only let you perform everyday tasks more efficiently, but they also allow you to tackle jobs you otherwise wouldn't be able to do at all. One example is a computer-simulated chemistry lab at the University of Illinois (see Figure 4). This lab lets students mix hazardous chemicals and see the results without endangering themselves or the building. Actually, students don't mix real chemicals; they just tell the computer what they would mix. The computer then displays on a screen prerecorded video sequences of the results that would occur if those chemicals were actually combined. Although computer-simulated explosions aren't quite as exciting as the real thing, they are much safer for students and less destructive to equipment and facilities.

Fun

Once they learn to use a computer, most people find that they enjoy it. It's fun to work with such an interactive and attentive device. Give the computer the correct command and it will leap into action, often completing the task much

4. R. Haider, "New Frontiers in Office Automation," *Proceedings of the Infotech State of the Art Conference*, Vienna, 1979.

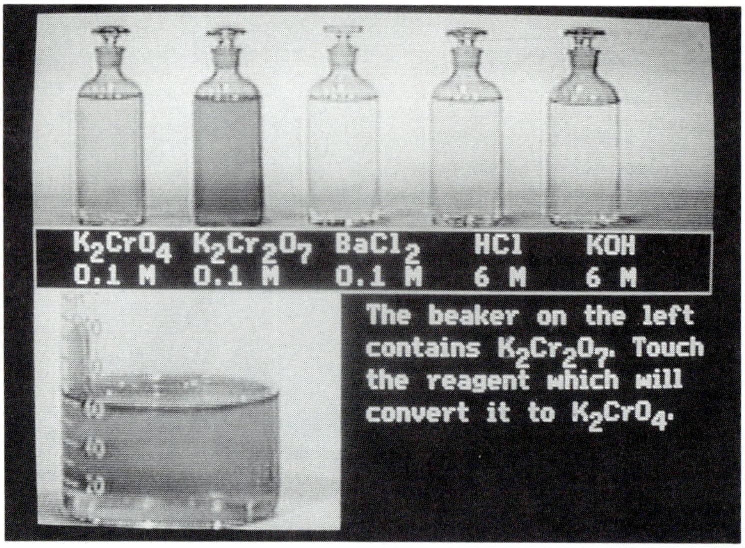

***Figure 4* Computer Chemistry Lab**
At the University of Illinois, computers enable students to simulate mixing dangerous chemicals without blowing themselves up.

more quickly than you thought possible. Some people even seem to get a greater feeling of accomplishment after successfully performing a task with a computer than if they did it by hand. Besides, there are many computer games available—from simulations of traditional board games such as chess and Monopoly, to exciting arcade games such as Pac Man and Dark Castle (see Figure 5). The computer opens whole new worlds of information, communication, productivity, and entertainment.

How Computers Are Used

Computers are tools; they help people perform many different kinds of tasks. One way to gain an appreciation for computers is to see how some people use them in their daily lives. The sections following in this chapter describe a few specific examples of people using computers to improve their personal productivity, to manage information, to communicate with others, to make presentations, and to help them learn.

Personal Productivity

Dr. Robert Hendersen, a professor in the Psychology Department at the University of Illinois at Urbana-Champaign, uses microcomputers nearly every day. Dr. Hendersen has an IBM Personal Computer AT in his office on campus and an identical system at home. When he travels to conferences he often takes a small, battery-operated IBM Convertible. Dr. Hendersen probably uses his microcomputers most frequently for word processing. He uses a program called WordPerfect to prepare scientific articles, classroom lectures, student handouts, and research specifications. Many of the graphs and figures Dr. Hendersen includes in his articles and lectures are prepared on his computer with graphics programs such as Energraphics and AutoCAD. He even used AutoCAD to design the landscaping of his yard at home.

Figure 5 Computer Entertainment *Microcomputers are often used to play games and to pursue other entertaining activities.*

Dr. Hendersen also uses his computers for much of his routine correspondence with colleagues. From home with his Personal Computer AT or from a hotel room with his Convertible, Dr. Hendersen can call up and tap into the large computer housed in the Psychology Building on campus. He can read messages sent to him by other faculty members and send them immediate replies. For regular phone correspondence, Dr. Hendersen maintains a list of associates' telephone numbers with a program called SideKick (see Figure 6). This same program also provides an on-screen calculator, an appointment calendar, and a notepad for jotting down ideas. Finally, since many psychology classes and research projects require microcomputers, Dr. Hendersen uses his machines to test and demonstrate software that is developed by teaching assistants, research assistants, and other faculty members. In short, Dr. Hendersen would probably be much less productive in his everyday work if he didn't use microcomputers.

Information Management

Computers are excellent tools for managing large quantities of information (see Figure 7). Just ask Ron Wubker, a partner at Western Freezers, a Fremont, California-based company that sells ice cream machines. Wubker uses an IBM Personal Computer and a program called Prodex to keep track of staff, suppliers, and other contacts. Once he had entered the name, address, phone number, and a few brief notes about each of his 200 contacts into the computer, Wubker was able to maintain and retrieve this information much more efficiently than he could with a Rolodex file. The Prodex program allows him to organize his list of contacts by last name, first name, company, or recall date. If he wants to make a call to one of his contacts, Wubker can tell the program to have the computer automatically dial the phone. Instead of taking a card file of contacts with him on business trips, Wubker simply prints out the entire list on paper. It's a lot less frustrating, Wubker claims, than spending half the night in a hotel room reorganizing his card file after accidentally spilling the cards all over the floor.[5]

5. Sam Diamond, "People Tracking," *Personal Computing*, December, 1987, pp. 133–139.

Figure 6 Personal Productivity Software
SideKick, from Borland International, is one example of personal productivity software. This program provides functions such as a notepad, calculator, calendar, and phone dialer.

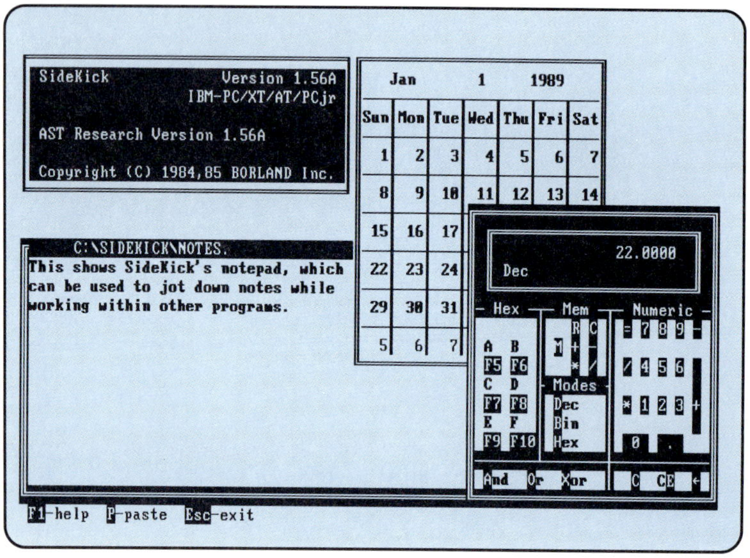

Communication

The telephone and the computer are two of our most useful tools. Combine them and you end up with a powerful communication system. Many people use their computers together with their telephones to call **on-line information services.** These services allow computer users access to vast quantities of information. They can read the latest news, shop, bank, buy stocks, make travel arrangements, and communicate with other users all over the world. Many information services allow users who share special interests to participate in electronic forums, or **teleconferences.** For example, CompuServe is the largest on-line information service in the world. One of its many special interest groups is MedSIG, the Medical Special Interest Group (see Figure 8). MedSIG recently sponsored an on-line conference about an anti-inflammatory drug called Zomax. According to Dr. John Sheppard, a general practitioner in Vermont who operates MedSIG, one of the members of the group started the conference because "he believed people were dying from the drug, and he wanted to see what kinds of experiences other doctors were having after prescribing the drug for their patients." This electronic conference was one of the first organized discussions about problems with the drug Zomax. Other doctors, it seemed, were also having bad results with Zomax. One of the conference participants happened to be a member of the Food and Drug Administration. Eventually, Zomax was withdrawn from the market. The FDA was so impressed with the MedSIG conference that it is investigating ways to use an internal on-line information service.[6]

6. Henry Fersko-Weiss, "On-line Contacts," *Personal Computing,* January, 1987, pp. 83–91.

Figure 7 ***Information Managers***
Microcomputers are frequently used to manage information, such as lists of personal contacts and their addresses and phone numbers.

Records **Fields** **Go To** **Exit** 11:48:46 am

LAST_NAME	FIRST_NAME	ADDRESS	CITY	STATE	ZIP_CODE	COMM
Skubic	Mike	321 Gregory	Champaign	IL	61820	MEMO
Griffith	Oscar	805 Florida	Urbana	IL	61801	MEMO
Carver	George	906 Busey	Brainerd	MN	56401	memo
Banks	David	604 Armory	Green Bay	WI	54035	memo
Young	Susan	1104 Grand	Anchorage	AK	99502	memo
Mitchell	Dan	310 Paddock	Flagstaff	AZ	86001	memo
Hudson	Henry	1007 Barclay	Akron	OH	44309	memo
Becker	Molly	402 Main	Ann Arbor	MI	48106	memo
Franklin	Melissa	2012 Anderson	Big Bear	CA	92314	memo
Savage	Julian	2209 Philo	Cedar City	UT	84720	memo
Prorok	Brian	502 Chalmers	Fairfax	VA	22030	memo
Underwood	Rhonda	701 Dover	Las Vegas	NV	89114	memo
Hall	Robert	1721 Valley	Ogallala	NE	69153	memo
Davis	Becky	7822 Kostner	Chicago	IL	60652	memo
Alexander	Barbara	102 White	Baltimore	MD	21233	memo
Walden	Roxanne	1010 Bridle	Denver	CO	80202	memo
Quinlan	Kerry	311 Southmoor	Homestead	FL	33030	memo

Browse | C:\lessons\MAILING | Rec 1/25 | File

View and edit fields

Figure 8 ***Computer Communications***
Microcomputers are often used to tie into on-line information services and participate in special interest group teleconferences, such as this one on CompuServe's MedSIG.

```
There are 2 Replies.

Press <CR> for next or type CHOICES !

#: 51852 S1/General/Profess.
    17-Jun-88  19:54:53
Sb: #51845-virus
Fm: Neil Lombardi, M.D. 74236,1744
To: will nielsen 72467,1256 (X)

Will, The virus is Cytomegalic Inclusion Disease Virus (CMV). This virus is
endemic in the human population (carried by many if not most people). In most
instances when first contacted it produces a flu-like illness (nasal
congestion, cough, fever, swollen glands) and the person becomes immune to the
infection or a carrier of the virus. Unfortunately, if a woman who is pregnant
is exposed to the virus for the first time it can cause serious problems for
the fetus, depending on when the exposure occurs. The baby can be born with any
number of problems from life threatening illness in the newborn period to brain
damage, mental retardation, deafness, or just mild learning problems or even no
symptoms at all. For more information GO PCH (Paperchase) or try HealthNet (GO
HEALTH). I hope this was helpful. Neil

Press <CR> for next or type CHOICES !
 Esc for ATtention, Home to SWitch |     Capture Off     | On: 00:05:08
```

Figure 9 Microcomputer Presentations
Secretary of the Interior Donald Hodel used an Apple Macintosh II and a program called Hypercard to present his 1989 budget proposal.

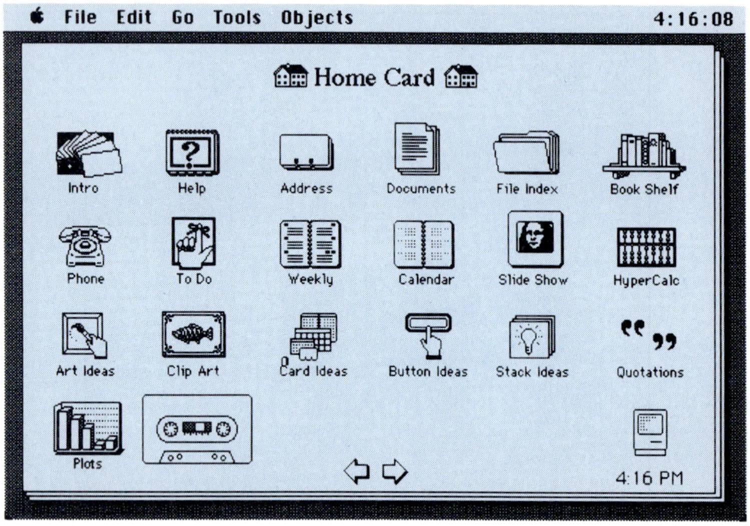

Presentation

Microcomputers are frequently used to present graphs, charts, and other figures at meetings, lectures, and demonstrations (see Figure 9). For example, when U.S. Secretary of the Interior Donald Hodel presented his $5 billion 1989 budget proposal at a press conference, he used a microcomputer to project images on a 20-foot screen. The secretary began his presentation by saying, "To those of you who are cost-conscious and think this looks sophisticated, it's an off-the-shelf technology using a $49.95 software package called Hypercard on the Macintosh II." Hodel went on to describe his department's annual budget proposal for managing park lands, Indian reservations, and wildlife protection programs. Sue Masica, budget analyst for the Department of the Interior, controlled the projected images from the Apple Macintosh II sitting next to the podium. "Budget numbers are always changing at the last minute," said Masica, who had just learned to use the Macintosh three months before. "Hypercard is wonderful in that it gives us the ability to make sure things are correct right up until the last minute. We didn't have to send out to get our slides made. We had complete control of the process right here in the office." As Hodel said to his audience, "We're using a new technique, different from slides. Not only can we show images in sequence, but if a question arises, we can go back or pick out images to help answer them." Apparently, the presentation was a success. According to *New York Times* correspondent Phil Shabbacoff, who was in the audience, "[Hodel] could push a button and go immediately to a line item that someone was asking about. I had never seen that before. I found his ability to flash those numbers on the screen very impressive."[7]

7. Stuart Silverstone, "Hypercard Helps Hodel Present Budget Proposal," *MacWeek*, March 8, 1988, pp. 42–44.

Figure 10 Microcomputers on Campus
The Molecular Editor was developed by Allan Smith of Drexel University to allow students to build molecules on the Apple Macintosh screen and rotate them in three dimensions.

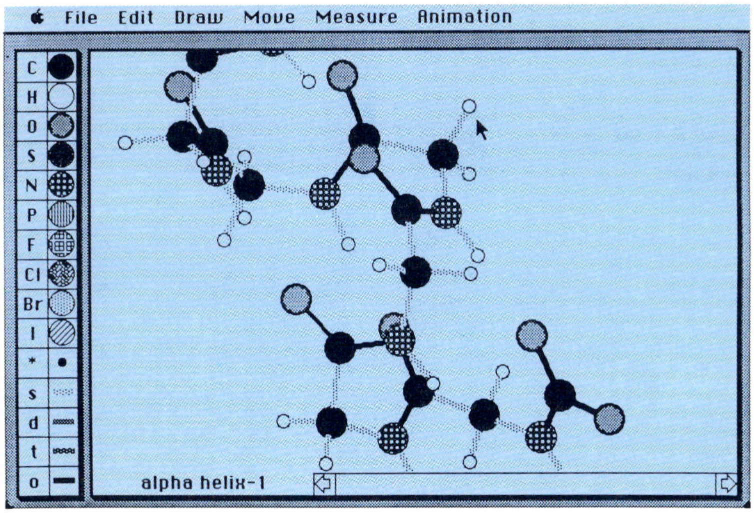

Education

You know by now that microcomputers are widely used in schools. This is especially true at colleges and universities. Drexel University in Philadelphia, for example, made an early commitment to microcomputers. Starting in 1984, all freshmen were required to have access to an Apple Macintosh, and most students bought their own from Drexel at less than half the retail price. Students were enthusiastic, and the program has continued with each incoming freshman class. Today there are more than 12,000 Macintoshes on the Drexel campus.

Many faculty members at Drexel create Macintosh programs to help their students learn difficult subjects. Allan Smith of the chemistry department, for example, developed the Molecular Editor, which students can use to build complex molecules on the screen (see Figure 10). Atoms of any element in the periodic table can be combined, manipulated, and analyzed without using expensive laboratory equipment. The Molecular Editor includes an animation of a chemical reaction in three dimensions and ready-made samples of organic molecules, inorganic molecules, and crystals. Undoubtedly, the Molecular Editor has made chemistry more understandable to students at Drexel.[8]

A Typical Microcomputer System

Now that you've seen some examples of how microcomputers are used, let's define exactly what we mean by the term *microcomputer* and examine the three basic elements that make up a microcomputer system: hardware, software, and users (see Figure 11).

8. Donna Osgood, "The Difference in Higher Education," *BYTE*, February, 1987, pp. 165-178.

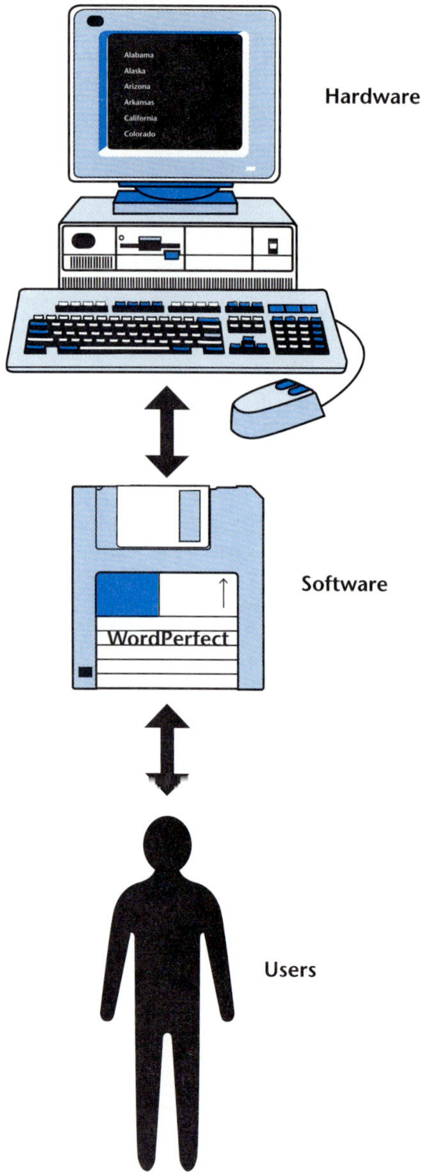

Figure 11 The Microcomputer System
A microcomputer consists of three basic elements: hardware, software, and users.

What Is a Microcomputer?

Its very name tells us that a **microcomputer** is a small computer. As you will see, several types of computers are classified as microcomputers. Most people think of a microcomputer as being small enough to fit on a desktop. In addition, although some powerful models can serve several users simultaneously, most microcomputers are used by only one person at a time. For this reason, microcomputers are also often called **personal computers.**

Another characteristic of microcomputers is that their "brain" or **central processing unit** (CPU) consists of a single electronic device known as a **microprocessor.** This device, a marvel of miniature engineering, controls the microcomputer, performs its calculations, and processes information. We'll have more to say about microprocessors and other internal components of microcomputers in the next chapter.

One way to define microcomputers is by what they do. We've already discussed some real-life examples of the tasks microcomputers can accomplish. Fundamentally, however, a microcomputer performs the same basic operations as all computers. First, a **program** is needed to tell the computer what to do. This is a set of instructions that controls a computer's operation. The program lets you enter **data,** which can consist of numbers, text, pictures, and even sounds. This data entered into the computer is called **input.** The program instructs the computer to process the data by doing calculations, comparisons, and other manipulations. The final result is **information,** which should be a more organized and useful form of the original input. This information produced by the computer is called **output.** Keep in mind that there is no magic here—a program is needed to tell the computer what to do, and the output information is only as valid as the original input data.

Although microcomputers perform the same basic operations as larger computers, they differ in speed and capacity. Larger computers generally can process data faster than microcomputers. They also can internally store more data at a time than microcomputers. These factors make larger computers better for performing lots of extremely complex and time-consuming computations. Microcomputers are also less adept than larger computers at handling several different users or tasks at the same time. On the other hand, microcomputers are superbly adapted to help with many work-a-day tasks like typing papers, figuring taxes, maintaining mailing lists, sending messages, drawing charts, managing finances, and even playing games.

Finally, microcomputers generally fall within a given price range. They can cost as little as $100 or as much as $15,000. Today the average price of a typical microcomputer used in business is around $2500. This is, however, a good deal less than the many thousands or even millions of dollars typical of much more powerful computers. We'll give some specific prices later in this chapter when we describe the various kinds of larger computers. Although microcomputers are by no means cheap, their prices have been consistently dropping even as their capabilities have increased. For example, in late 1983 the list price of a basic IBM Personal Computer XT was $5675. The list price of its successor, a similarly equipped IBM Personal System/2 Model 30, was only $2545 when first released in mid 1987. Even though the newer Model 30 cost less than half as much as the old XT, it still had more than twice the speed and storage capacity, along with many other improvements.

Hardware

The **hardware** of a computer system is the electronic and mechanical equipment that makes it work. Like a stereo system, microcomputer hardware generally consists of several distinct components connected by cables. Figure 12(a) shows a typical microcomputer system, which has four major parts:

- *Display.* Similar in many ways to an ordinary television, the **display,** or **monitor,** is the screen that presents text and **graphics** (any kind of pictures, drawings, charts, or plots).
- *System Unit.* The **system unit** is the central component that houses the computer's microprocessor, control circuitry, memory, and disk drives. **Memory,** a computer's internal storage, temporarily holds programs and data. A **disk drive** reads and writes programs and data on magnetic disks. A **magnetic disk** is a semipermanent storage medium that can be erased and rewritten over and over again. From the outside, the system unit looks like a shallow box about the size of a portable typewriter.

Figure 12 Typical Microcomputers
(a) An IBM Personal System/2 Model 30 with a mouse. (b) An Apple Macintosh SE.
(c) Toshiba T3100.

(a)

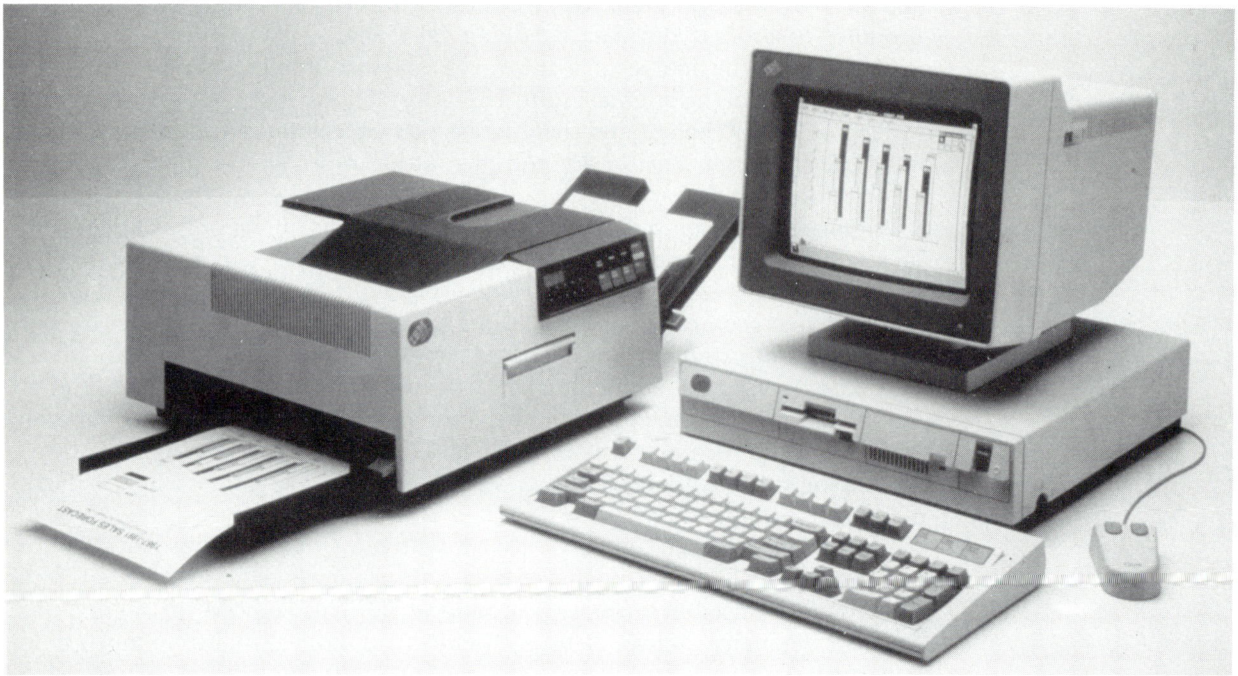

(b)

(c)

- *Keyboard.* Descended from the typewriter, the **keyboard** is the primary device for entering text and telling the computer what to do. Many microcomputers also have an auxiliary input device known as a **mouse.** This little box, which is slid across the table top, allows the user to manipulate objects on the display screen and select actions to be performed by pressing one or more buttons.
- *Printer.* The **printer** is an auxiliary component that produces permanent copies of text and graphics on paper.

There are, of course, several common variations to the typical arrangement of these four computer parts. For example, sometimes the system unit and display are joined in a single housing. The Apple Macintosh SE has this arrangement, shown in Figure 12(b). In other cases, the system unit and keyboard are combined. As Figure 12(c) shows, this arrangement is used in the Toshiba T3100. Finally, you can often mix and match some components from different manufacturers and add devices to expand your system's capabilities. In the next chapter, we'll examine the different microcomputer hardware components in a bit more detail.

Software

By itself, computer hardware is useless. Programs and people are needed to operate the hardware. As we mentioned before, a program is simply a sequence of instructions that tells a computer what to do. **Software** is a general term that refers to any single program or group of programs. In contrast to hardware, which is constructed from physical materials like metal and plastic, software is built from knowledge, planning, and testing. A person who creates programs is called a **programmer.** Programmers use their knowledge of how a computer works to plan sets of instructions that accomplish useful tasks. These instructions are entered into the computer and repeatedly tested and modified until they achieve the desired results. You will recall that programs and data generally are kept on storage media such as magnetic disks, where they can be retrieved and used over and over again. One common type of magnetic disk, the **floppy disk,** is quite inexpensive and can be removed from the computer's disk drive when not in use (see Figure 13). Note that the disks themselves aren't the software, they're just the medium on which software and data are stored.

For an analogy, think of a stereo system. The stereo receiver/amplifier, compact disc player, and speakers are the hardware. The receiver/amplifier is like the central processing unit and memory, the compact disc player is like the disk drive, and the speakers are like the display, except they present audio instead of video output. The music, which is stored on compact discs, is like software, which is stored on floppy disks. Just as you can amass a huge music collection by buying more compact discs, you can build a bigger software library by purchasing additional programs on floppy disks. The stereo system is of little use without the compact discs, and the compact discs are useless without the stereo system. Similarly, a computer system is useless without software, and software is useless without a computer system on which to run.

Just as there are different types of hardware, there are also different types of software. We'll have much more to say about software in Chapter 3 and the rest of this book, but for now you should realize that there are three basic categories:

- *System Software.* **System software** handles the many details of managing a computer system. One example of system software is a program that identifies

Figure 13 The Floppy Disk *The floppy disk is a commonly used medium for storing computer programs and data.*

which key you've pressed, determines the character that corresponds to that key, and forms that character on the display screen. Another example is a program that lets you erase the contents of a magnetic disk. Some system software is built into the computer, while other system software comes on magnetic disks and must be purchased separately.

- *Programming Languages.* Computer programs are developed with **programming languages,** which are simply sets of symbols and rules used to direct the operations of a computer. Many different programming languages are in common use, each designed to develop certain types of programs. As we will discuss in Chapter 3, a few of the most popular programming languages are BASIC, Pascal, C, FORTRAN, COBOL, and Ada.
- *Application Software.* **Application software** applies the computer to useful tasks like helping you write letters, figure your taxes, maintain mailing lists, and draw charts. Also called **application packages** or simply **applications,** these programs are the real reason most people buy and use microcomputers. As we said before, a word processor is an application package, one that helps you prepare documents. Other examples of application software include: **spreadsheet packages,** which help you manipulate tables of numbers; **data base management packages,** which help you organize and retrieve large quantities of information; **communications packages,** which let your computer "talk" to other computers; **graphics packages,** which let you use your computer to produce pictures and charts; and **desktop publishing packages,** which allow you to combine the results of word processing and graphics to produce near-typeset-quality documents. We'll have much more to say about these and the many other types of application software in later chapters.

Users

It might seem obvious, but hardware and software don't do anything without users. A **user,** sometimes called an **end user,** is simply a person who runs software on a computer to accomplish some task. Just as there are different kinds of hardware and software, there are also different kinds of users. A beginning user is often called a **novice.** Somewhat unfamiliar with computers, novices need a little extra help to perform some tasks. Many computer programs are developed with the novice in mind. These easy-to-learn programs are sometimes described as **user friendly** because they can be run by people who don't necessarily have a lot of computer experience.

At the other end of the user spectrum are those who have a great deal of computer experience. An **expert,** sometimes called a **power user,** is someone who feels quite at home using computers. While programmers are generally experts, every expert is not necessarily a programmer. A person can become an expert at running particular application programs without knowing how those applications were actually developed in the first place. A race car driver, as an analogy, is certainly an expert automobile user. A good race car driver, however, need not be an auto mechanic or engineer.

Types of Microcomputers

We've described the typical microcomputer system, but in fact there are many different types of microcomputers sold today. An obvious way to classify them is by physical size, or how easy they are to pick up and carry around. Although a few models are difficult to classify, most microcomputers easily fall into one of the following size categories: hand-held, laptop, portable, desktop, and floor model.

Hand-held Computers

At first glance, the smallest microcomputers resemble large hand-held calculators (see Figure 14). Upon closer examination, however, several important differences appear. Typically smaller than a paperback book and weighing less than a pound, a **hand-held computer** has a complete alphabetic keyboard in addition to the number keys you find on ordinary calculators. The screen is usually a one- or two-line **liquid crystal display (LCD)** that can hold anywhere from twelve to sixty-four characters at once. Most LCD screens present black characters against

Figure 14 Hand-held Computer
This is a typical hand-held computer, the Tandy PC-6 Pocket Computer.

Figure 15 Laptop Computer
This NEC MultiSpeed HD is a typical laptop microcomputer.

a grey background and are commonly used in watches, clocks, and calculators. Hand-held computers generally have very limited memory capacities and run on built-in rechargeable batteries. Some hand-held computers can be connected to a wide range of optional devices, such as printers, disk drives, and larger display screens. The model shown in Figure 14 is a typical hand-held computer. This Tandy PC-6 Pocket Computer sells for about $120, has a twenty-four character LCD, and folds up to around six square inches.

Hand-held microcomputers are ideal for on-the-go engineers, business people, and students who need more computing power than pocket calculators provide. Their small screen sizes, tiny keyboards, and minimal memory, however, make hand-held computers inappropriate for the most commonly used application software. They are usually used for simple financial formulas, statistics, engineering math, and games.

Laptop Computers

The **laptop computer,** also called a **briefcase computer,** is to some people perhaps the most alluring of all types of microcomputers. It's a full-fledged microcomputer crammed into a 4- to 15-pound package smaller than most briefcases (see Figure 15). Laptops have an LCD or other type of flat display screen, usually around 5 by 9 inches in size, that normally can accommodate as much text and graphics as larger microcomputer monitors can. The keyboard is like that of full-size microcomputers, except that it may be without a separate numeric keypad and have fewer special-purpose keys. Many laptops have memory capacities and disk drives similar to that of larger desktop models. Most laptop computers can run on built-in rechargeable batteries, some for as long as twenty hours at a time. The NEC MultiSpeed HD shown in Figure 15 is a typical laptop microcomputer. This model is compact enough to fit in a knapsack, weighs a little more than 14 pounds, can run on batteries for almost 2 hours of average use, and offers much of the functionality of a desktop computer.

Laptop computers have become increasingly popular in recent years thanks to the many technological improvements that have been made. Except for their small screens, laptops are in many ways just as good as full-size microcomputers. They are easy to carry and are a boon to travellers who can't do without a computer.

Portable Computers

Of course, hand-held and laptop computers are portable in the sense that they're easily carried about. The term **portable computer,** however, has come to mean a microcomputer that's more or less the size of a small suitcase (see Figure 16). These rugged machines, which typically weigh from 20 to 30 pounds, are designed to be moved, but not to be used in transit. Portable computers aren't battery powered, so they can only be used near an electrical socket. For the most part, portable computers are just as capable as comparably priced desktop models. They usually have a small screen, say 5 by 9 inches, that can display as much text and graphics as the larger monitors used with desktop computers can. Many portables can have as much memory as similar desktop computers and are also equipped with disk drives. Basically, a portable computer is a complete microcomputer you can fold up and take with you, just as you would a portable electric typewriter. The Compaq Portable 386 shown in Figure 16, for example, is an extremely powerful state-of-the-art microcomputer. Faster and more advanced than most desktop computers, this model from Compaq weighs just over 21 pounds and lists for about $8000.

In general, the portable computers on the market today are as well-designed and useful as their desktop relatives. As long as you don't have to carry one too far and you don't mind the slightly smaller screen, a portable computer may be ideal for taking your work home with you for an evening or away for a weekend.

Desktop Computers

The **desktop computer** is the most common type of microcomputer (see Figure 17). It's small enough to fit on top of a table or desk, and that's where it's generally kept, although some users set their system unit on its side on the floor to clear

Figure 16 Portable Computer
This Compaq Portable 386 is one of the most advanced microcomputers you can buy, even if it does come in a relatively small package.

more table space. As we said before, some of these microcomputers have a separate system unit, monitor, and keyboard, while others combine the system unit and monitor, or the system unit and keyboard, into a single housing. Despite the growing popularity of laptop models, desktop computers are still by far the most common type of microcomputer. The IBM Personal System/2 Model 50 shown in Figure 17 is a good example of a typical desktop microcomputer.

Floor Models

Some microcomputers are specifically designed to stand upright on the floor. A **floor model** is usually a powerful, expensive microcomputer. The system unit of a floor model is often larger than the typical desktop system unit and is designed to accommodate more add-in hardware components. Some floor models are set up to serve several users or are used to coordinate several individual microcomputers connected together. The IBM Personal System/2 Model 80 shown in Figure 18, for example, is a powerful floor model microcomputer that can be used alone or connected to other computers in a large information system.

Microcomputer Standards

We've just described how microcomputers can be classified according to their physical size. Perhaps a more meaningful approach is to categorize them by microcomputer standards. A **microcomputer standard** is a generally accepted set of rules by which hardware and software operate. One way to establish a standard is to get a formal agreement between manufacturers on how to develop hardware and software. In most cases, however, standards emerge from the leadership of a few powerful manufacturers. One manufacturer may make a computer, hardware component, or software package that becomes so popular that other manufacturers follow. Even though no formal agreement has been reached, a *de facto* standard exists because other manufacturers voluntarily make products that will work together. Today, there are three dominant microcomputer standards: the Apple II, IBM, and the Apple Macintosh.

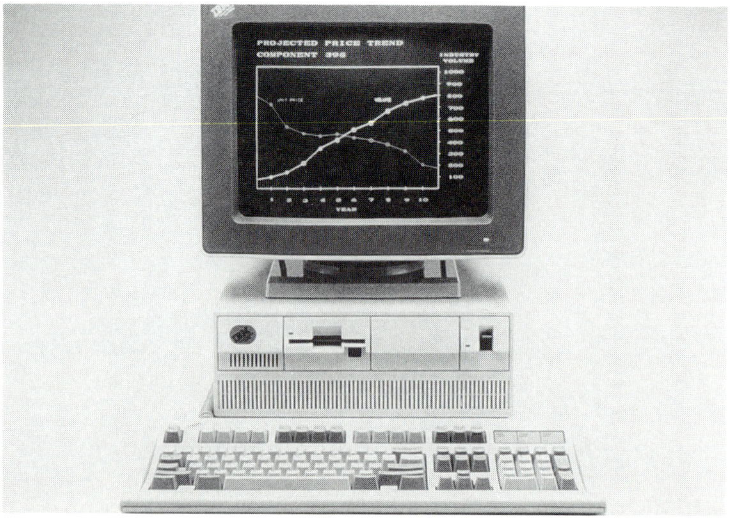

Figure 17 Desktop Computer
The IBM Personal System/2 Model 50 is a typical desktop microcomputer.

Apple II

You've probably heard the rags-to-riches story of how Apple Computer was formed in 1976 by Steven Jobs and Stephen Wozniak, who built their prototype, the Apple I, in a garage for $1300. By the end of 1977, the Apple II had emerged as one of the most popular microcomputers on the market. One of the major reasons for its widespread acceptance was that Apple encouraged many hardware and software manufacturers to develop products that worked with the Apple II. When Dan Bricklin and Bob Frankston developed VisiCalc, the first spreadsheet program, for the Apple II in 1979, microcomputers began to attract serious business users. Even after the introduction of more powerful microcomputers by IBM and Apple itself, the Apple II family of computers remained very popular, especially in homes and schools. Today, the Apple II family of computers still sells well, thanks to continual improvements by Apple and a huge base of available software. The current line of Apple II computers includes the Apple IIe, the Apple IIc, and the Apple IIGS (see Figure 19).

IBM

International Business Machines, by far the most successful seller of large, powerful computers, didn't enter the microcomputer market until August of 1981. Its first model, the IBM Personal Computer, quickly became the world's best-selling microcomputer (see Figure 20). Although it wasn't especially innovative from an engineering standpoint, the solidly built IBM PC triggered the overwhelming acceptance of microcomputers by business, government, and educational institutions.

IBM's handling of the PC was somewhat unorthodox. The company ignored many of its time-honored traditions and released a machine that primarily consisted of off-the-shelf parts. Furthermore, IBM readily distributed the technical specifications of its new microcomputer. Instead of developing its own system

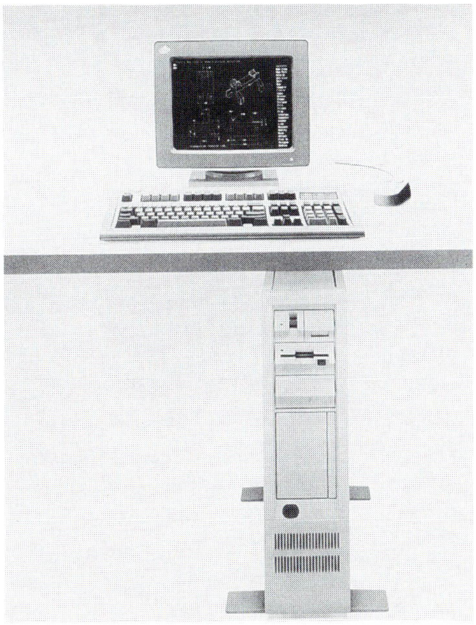

Figure 18 Floor Model
The IBM Personal System/2 Model 80 is a powerful microcomputer designed to stand upright on the floor. It has more room inside than a desktop model to accommodate more add-in hardware components.

Figure 19 The Apple II Family
Even though there are more powerful machines on the market, the Apple II family remains a very popular microcomputer standard.

(a)

(b)

(c)

software for the PC, IBM selected Microsoft Corporation to do it. Microsoft was also allowed to sell this system software to anyone who wanted to buy it. These factors, combined with IBM's reputation as one of the biggest and most stable companies in the world, encouraged many independent hardware and software manufacturers to develop products that worked with the IBM Personal Computer.

Soon companies such as Compaq Computer Corporation developed the first **clones** of the IBM Personal Computer. Also called **IBM-compatibles,** these machines worked just like (or in some ways even better than) the original IBM Personal Computer and usually sold at a lower price. When IBM released its more powerful PC-XT in 1983 and the more advanced PC-AT in 1984, the clone makers followed suit and produced compatibles for these machines as well. Eventually, the clone makers together sold more IBM-compatibles than IBM itself sold.

IBM-compatible computers offer varying degrees of speed and storage capacity but all are able to use the same software and hardware components as real IBM Personal Computers. Computers compatible with the original IBM PC, PC-XT, and PC-AT are currently the most popular types of microcomputers in the world, with tens of millions of machines in offices, factories, schools, and homes. Hundreds of companies now sell IBM-compatible microcomputers.

In 1987, IBM introduced its new Personal System/2 line of microcomputers. Today, the IBM PS/2 line is made up of several basic models, including the Model

Figure 20 The Original IBM Personal Computer
The original IBM Personal Computer was released in August, 1981 and quickly became a runaway best seller.

25, the Model 30, the Model 50, the Model 55 SX, the Model 60, the Model 70, and the Model 80 (see Figure 21). These computers are different from their predecessors in several important ways. Although they can run virtually all of the previously written IBM PC software, the PS/2 computers have different floppy disk drives. Most PS/2 models cannot use many of the internal hardware components that work with their PC predecessors. They have a different underlying circuit design known as the **Micro Channel Architecture.** These Personal System/2 computers offer significantly higher performance than previous computers. A new generation of software is required, however, to take full advantage of the Personal System/2 computers. A few hardware manufacturers, such as Tandy, offer clones of the Personal System/2 computers, which suggests that the IBM Personal System/2 family has spawned a new, slightly different IBM microcomputer standard.

Apple Macintosh

The Apple II was the best-selling microcomputer from 1978 until 1982, when the IBM Personal Computer overwhelmed the market. By mid-1983, after the unenthusiastic reception of Apple's two new models, the Lisa and the Apple III, market analysts began to wonder if Apple would survive as a major microcomputer manufacturer. Amid corporate infighting, Steven Jobs himself took over the division of Apple that was building its last, best hope—the Macintosh. Released in early 1984 amid the ballyhoo of a $20-million advertising scheme, the Apple Macintosh was hailed as "the computer for the rest of us."

Many of the easy-to-use features incorporated into the Apple Lisa and the Macintosh were actually developed by Xerox in the early 1970s at the Palo Alto Research Center. Xerox's 8010 Star Information System was the first commercial

Figure 21 The IBM Personal System/2 Family
IBM's line of Personal System/2 microcomputers has replaced the earlier IBM PCs, PC-XTs, and PC-ATs.

computer to use concepts later popularized by the Apple Macintosh. These features included the use of a sharp black-on-white graphics screen, a mouse, menus, windows, and icons. You already know what a mouse is: a device for manipulating objects on the screen and selecting activities to be performed. A **menu** is simply a list of activities you can select to perform. A **window** is a boxed-in area on the screen that shows the activity of a particular software program. Several windows may be on the screen at the same time. Finally, an **icon** is a small pictorial symbol that represents some activity. For example, to erase a disk on a computer that uses icons you might move a little picture of a floppy disk on top of a little picture of a trash can. Apple certainly didn't invent the mouse, menus, windows, and icons. Nevertheless, the Macintosh was the first affordable microcomputer that did a good job of incorporating all of these user-friendly features.

The Apple Macintosh is a **proprietary** system. This means that Apple holds and tightly controls the patents for many of the Macintosh hardware components and the copyrights for the system software. Apple has not licensed these patents and copyrights to other manufacturers, so there are no legal Macintosh clones. This allows Apple to maintain a higher profit margin, but it also means that the Macintosh standard is not nearly as widespread as the IBM-PC standard. Many more IBM and IBM-compatible microcomputers are in use than Apple Macintoshes. Nevertheless, Apple has sold millions of Macintosh computers. Several models are available, including the Macintosh Plus, Macintosh SE, Macintosh SE/30, Macintosh II, Macintosh IIx, Macintosh IIcx, the Macintosh IIci, and the Macintosh Portable (see Figure 22).

Other Types of Computers

This textbook emphasizes microcomputers, but several other types of computers also play very important roles in many businesses and organizations. Nowadays, computers of all types are frequently connected in **networks** to share hardware,

Figure 22 The Apple Macintosh Family
Apple's Macintosh family represents a microcomputer standard totally different from the Apple II and all of the IBM machines.

software, and data. Although there is considerable overlap between categories, computers can be classified according to their physical size, storage capacity, speed, number of simultaneous users, and cost. At the low end are microcomputers. Continuing up the hierarchy in order of increasing power and cost are workstations, minicomputers, mainframes, and supercomputers, which we will examine in more detail shortly.

Table 1 compares specific examples of these various types of computers according to the number of simultaneous users, speed, and cost. Keep in mind, however, that the values in this table are approximations. The actual number of simultaneous users can vary depending on how the system is equipped and set up. The speeds, given in units of **million instructions per second,** or **MIPS,** are also estimates. Theoretically, a computer that operates at 1 MIPS executes one million

Table 1 Computer Types

Type	Example	Users	Speed (MIPS)	Approx. Cost ($)
Microcomputer	IBM PS/2 50	1	1.6	3,000
Workstation	Sun-3/60	1	3.0	12,900
Minicomputer	DEC VAX 8200	1 to 30	2.0	100,000
Mainframe	IBM 3090/600E	1 to 500	73.4	10,300,000
Supercomputer	Cray Y-MP	1 to 500	2000.0	20,000,000

instructions per second. Many experts downplay the significance of measuring computer performance in MIPS because different instructions accomplish different tasks on different computers. Nevertheless, MIPS do give some basis for comparing the performance of computers. Finally, the actual cost of a particular computer depends on the exact way in which it is equipped. Despite these qualifications, Table 1 should give you some idea of the differences between computers. The microcomputer used for comparison is the IBM Personal System/2 Model 50, shown previously in Figure 17.

Workstations

A **workstation,** sometimes called a **supermicro,** is a small, yet powerful computer generally used by only one person at a time (see Figure 23). Similar to microcomputer floor models with large graphics screens, workstations have been traditionally used by scientists and engineers as tools for drafting, design, and mapmaking. They are superior to most microcomputers in their ability to perform complex calculations, display sharp and colorful graphics, and communicate with other computers. Ranging in price from around $4000 to $100,000, workstations are also faster than most microcomputers and can typically run several different programs at the same time. Although many workstations use the same microprocessors found in powerful microcomputers, others employ more specialized types of central processing units. Figure 23 shows a typical workstation, the Sun-3/60 from Sun Microsystems. This computer, with its sharp 16-inch color screen, can execute around three million instructions per second and costs about $12,900.

Minicomputers

The term **minicomputer** generally describes medium-sized computers that simultaneously serve several users or control complex equipment (see Figure 24). In the past, minicomputers were easier to distinguish from other types of computers than they are today. Powerful microcomputers and workstations approach, and in some cases surpass, the capabilities and speed of some contemporary minicomputers. Powerful minicomputers, sometimes called **superminis,** approach

***Figure 23* Workstation**
The Sun-3/60 is a typical workstation.

the capabilities of some larger systems. The smallest minicomputers are about the same size as floor model microcomputers, while the largest may be as big as one or two file cabinets. Minicomputer prices range from about $15,000 to $500,000. Most general-purpose minicomputers are set up to serve multiple users, usually fewer than one hundred at the same time.

Minicomputers are commonly used in small businesses and organizations for routine office tasks such as accounting, billing, order entry, inventory, and word processing. More specialized minicomputers are also used to monitor instruments in laboratories and to control automated manufacturing equipment in factories. Some minicomputers are used to control networks of interconnected computers. A good example of a typical minicomputer is the VAX 8200 from Digital Equipment Corporation, shown in Figure 24. This computer can simultaneously serve up to 30 users, runs at about 2 MIPS, and costs around $100,000.

Mainframes

A **mainframe** is a big, powerful, fast, expensive computer. Mainframes typically serve hundreds of users at the same time, execute many millions of instructions per second, and cost anywhere from $100,000 to $20 million. A mainframe computer may be as small as one or two file cabinets or large enough to fill an entire room. Some mainframes must be kept in carefully controlled environments to keep them cool and as dust free as possible. Mainframe computers are generally used by large businesses and organizations for high-volume data processing, such as the preparation of thousands or even millions of paychecks, bills, orders, and mailing labels. Mainframe computers are also used to maintain huge **data bases** or collections of facts, such as Social Security and income tax records. In addition, large networks of computers often require mainframes to manage the connections and communications. A typical mainframe computer is the IBM 3090/600, shown in Figure 25, which operates at around 73.4 MIPS, can serve hundreds of users at the same time, and costs $10.3 million.

Figure 24 Minicomputer *Digital Equipment Corporation's VAX 8200 is a good example of a typical minicomputer.*

***Figure 25* Mainframe**
The IBM 3090/600 is a powerful mainframe computer.

Supercomputers

A **supercomputer** is an extremely fast mainframe. These computers typically execute *billions* of instructions per second, can serve hundreds of users simultaneously, and cost between $5 million and $25 million each. Although there are only a few hundred supercomputers operating today in the world, they perform many vital tasks that would be impossible with ordinary mainframes. Supercomputers are used mostly in scientific and military research. There are eleven supercomputers at Los Alamos Scientific Laboratory in New Mexico, for example, where they are used for top-secret weapons research. The National Security Agency in Fort Mead, Maryland, uses supercomputers to crack military codes

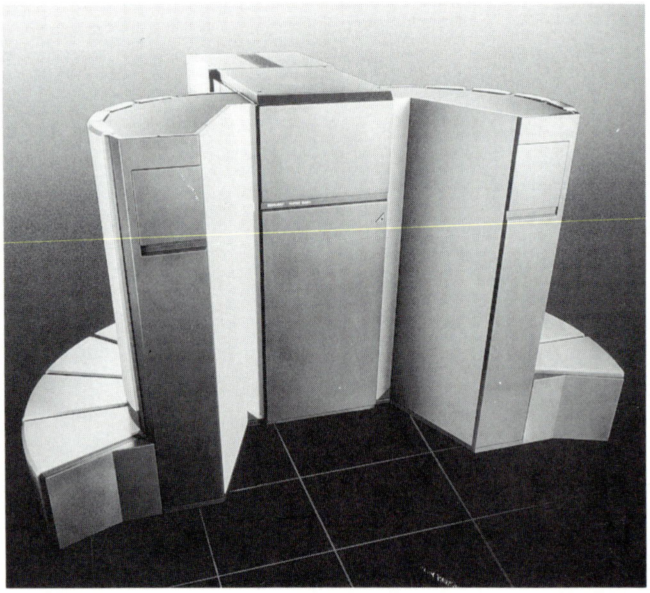

***Figure 26* Supercomputer**
The Cray Y-MP is one of the most powerful supercomputers in the world.

Real World

You're Smarter Than You May Have Thought

There was a lady who sort of thought she might like to find out what computers were all about. But she kept putting it off because she felt intimidated before she even began her quest. Some of what she had read and heard had led her to believe that she lacked the manual dexterity to interact successfully with a computer.

(On the day she had that thought, she successfully and single-handedly took command of a 4000-pound machine whose proper operation required her to coordinate and synchronize independent activities of her left hand, her right hand, her left foot and her right foot, and to monitor, with eye and ear, various gauges and sounds, while looking over her left shoulder. She backed her car out of her garage.)

She had read just enough computer ads to be able to fret about the apparently incomprehensible vocabulary of bits and bytes and modems not to mention peripherals and programming and other concepts that made "learning computers" sound like an academic enterprise well beyond her mental abilities.

(On *that* day, she utilized the concepts of accounts payable and receivable, cash flow management, double entry bookkeeping, information storage and retrieval, mathematics, and inference. She balanced her checkbook.)

She tentatively set foot in her neighborhood computer store. She felt uncomfortable and out of place in the sleek high-tech environment. She *did* find it impossible to communicate with the young man who was on duty at the store, who looked at her with a mixture of pity and disdain when she apparently failed his initial vocabulary test.

She left the computer store in confusion and mounting despair. While shopping at the supermarket that very afternoon, she impulsively bought a Commodore VIC-20 computer off the shelf, between the paper towels and the photographic film, took it home, read the manual, hooked it up, plugged it in, turned it on, started enjoying herself, bought a couple of other books to supplement the not-always-great manual, played games, started in on a home bookkeeping system, made a few tentative stabs at learning programming, took a class in programming, wrote programs, bought a larger and more sophisticated computer, helped automate her husband's business, gave lectures on overcoming computer fear, taught classes in computerization, and finally opened her own computer service bureau in the storefront vacated by the bankruptcy of the computer store she had first visited.

Source: John Bear, *Computer Wimp*, Ten Speed Press, Berkeley, California, 1983, pp. 134–136.

and manage the flood of intelligence data the agency collects every day. At the University of Illinois, a Cray X-MP supercomputer is used to simulate and display colorful animations of natural phenomenon, from the swirling birth of a tornado to the turbulent activity of a black hole at the center of a galaxy. On the lighter side, Digital Productions, a Hollywood film company, uses a Cray X-MP supercomputer to produce special effects for movies.

Although several companies now produce supercomputers, Cray Research dominates the market. This single company accounts for approximately 60 percent of all supercomputers sold in the world. The Cray Y-MP, introduced in 1988, is a good example of a supercomputer (see Figure 26). It succeeds the popular Cray X-MP supercomputer and is two to three times as powerful. Under ideal conditions, the eight processing units of the Cray Y-MP work together to execute two billion to four billion instructions per second. This is roughly equivalent to the computing power of 1250 IBM Personal System/2 Model 50s. The Y-MP can serve hundreds of users at the same time and costs around $20 million.

Summary

- *Why you should study computers.* A knowledge of computers may help you to complete your education, to get a job, to increase your productivity, to increase your capabilities, and to have fun.
- *Some of the ways in which microcomputers are used.* Microcomputers are used to increase personal productivity, to manage information, to communicate with others, to make presentations, and to help learn difficult subjects.
- *The elements of a typical microcomputer system.* Hardware (display, system unit, keyboard, and printer), software (system software, programming languages, and application software), and users are the three basic ingredients of a microcomputer system.
- *The different types of microcomputers.* Classified by size, they are hand-held, laptop, portable, desktop, and floor model.
- *The dominant microcomputer standards.* Apple II, IBM-compatible, and Apple Macintosh are the three most widely used microcomputer standards.
- *The various types of other computers.* In addition to microcomputers, there are workstations, minicomputers, mainframes, and supercomputers.

Key Terms

As an extra review of this chapter, try defining the following terms.

application software
  (application package, application)
central processing unit (CPU)
clone
communications package
data
data base
data base management package
de facto standard
desktop computer
desktop publishing package
disk drive
display (monitor)
expert (power user)
floor model
floppy disk
graphics
graphics package
hand-held computer
hardware
IBM-compatible
icon
information
input
keyboard
laptop (briefcase) computer
liquid crystal display (LCD)
magnetic disk
mainframe
memory
menu
Micro Channel Architecture
microcomputer (personal computer)
microcomputer standard
microprocessor
million instructions per second
  (MIPS)
minicomputer
mouse
network
novice
on-line information service
output
personal computer
portable computer
printer
program
programmer
programming language
proprietary
software
spreadsheet package

supercomputer
supermini
system software
system unit
teleconference
user (end user)
user friendly
window
word processing
workstation (supermicro)

Review Questions

1. Give a specific example of how computers are used in education.
2. Why do employers need workers who are familiar with computers?
3. What common application of computers allows you to produce documents such as letters and reports?
4. List some of the activities you can do with an on-line information service.
5. How are microcomputers often used at meetings, lectures, and demonstrations?
6. What electronic device is the central processing unit of a microcomputer?
7. What is the difference between data and information?
8. In what ways do microcomputers differ from larger computers?
9. What is the average price of a typical microcomputer used in business?
10. List four major microcomputer hardware components.
11. List three basic categories of software.
12. List six types of application software.
13. What are hand-held microcomputers typically used for?
14. What is the difference between a laptop and a portable microcomputer?
15. What is the most common size of microcomputers?
16. What are the three dominant microcomputer standards?
17. List four features in the Apple Macintosh previously introduced commercially in Xerox's 8010 Star Information System.
18. How are workstations superior to most microcomputers?
19. What is the fastest type of computer?
20. List two common uses of minicomputers.

Multiple Choice

1. A microcomputer's CPU consists of a single
   (a) display. (b) microprocessor.
   (c) keyboard. (d) printer.
2. A computer processes data to form
   (a) input. (b) programs.
   (c) information. (d) hardware.
3. A computer's internal storage, used to temporarily hold programs and data, is called
   (a) a system unit. (b) memory.
   (c) a keyboard. (d) a mouse.

4. What type of software processes keypresses and forms characters on the display screen?
   (a) system software (b) programming language
   (c) application software (d) word processor
5. A spreadsheet program is a type of
   (a) system software. (b) programming language.
   (c) application software. (d) printer software.
6. Which of the following can usually be operated on batteries?
   (a) laptop (b) portable
   (c) desktop (d) floor model
7. The most common microcomputer size is the
   (a) laptop. (b) portable.
   (c) desktop. (d) floor model.
8. Which of the following is most likely to be a powerful, expensive microcomputer?
   (a) laptop (b) portable
   (c) desktop (d) floor model
9. Which company developed the system software for the IBM Personal Computer and its descendants?
   (a) IBM (b) Apple
   (c) Microsoft (d) Compaq
10. Which of the following is not considered to be a popular microcomputer standard?
    (a) Apple II (b) Sun-3/60
    (c) Apple Macintosh (d) IBM PC
11. Which one of the following commercial computers was the first to incorporate user-friendly features such as a mouse, menus, windows, and icons?
    (a) Apple II (b) IBM Personal Computer
    (c) Xerox 8010 Star Information System (d) Apple Macintosh
12. The Apple Macintosh is a
    (a) Micro Channel Architecture system. (b) proprietary system.
    (c) operating system. (d) mainframe system.
13. What type of computer has been traditionally used by individual scientists and engineers as a tool for drafting, design, and map-making?
    (a) workstation (b) minicomputer
    (c) mainframe (d) supercomputer
14. Mainframe computers are generally used by
    (a) hobbyists. (b) students.
    (c) small businesses. (d) large businesses.
15. How many instructions can the typical supercomputer execute per second?
    (a) hundreds (b) thousands
    (c) millions (d) billions

Projects

1. Why do you want to learn about computers? Write a brief essay specifying the reasons you have for taking this course. How do you think a microcomputer could help you with your studies or work?
2. Does anyone you know use a microcomputer? If not, try to find an article in a magazine or book about a real person who uses a microcomputer in his or her daily life. Write a brief report describing how the computer is used. What kind of microcomputer does the person have and what kind of software? How does using a microcomputer make a difference in the user's life?
3. Find out if there are any computer clubs or users groups in your area. You don't actually have to go to any meetings (unless you want to, of course), but try to learn a little bit about these organizations. How many members do they have, and what kinds of microcomputers do they use?
4. Get a recent issue of a popular computer magazine at a newsstand, bookstore, or library. Find a review of some hardware or software product. Read the article carefully and "review" the review. How helpful do you think this review would be if you were shopping for that particular type of hardware or software?

CHAPTER 2

HARDWARE

In This Chapter

The Microcomputer Revealed

The Microprocessor
- Structure
- Register Size
- Data Bus Size
- Speed

Primary Storage
- RAM
- ROM

Secondary Storage
- Floppy Disk Drives
- Hard Disk Drives
- Magnetic Tape Drives
- Bernoulli Disk Drives
- Optical Disk Drives

Keyboards and Mice

Displays
- Monochrome Text Monitors
- Monochrome Graphics Monitors
- Color Graphics Monitors

Expanding the System
- Expansion Slots
- Expansion Boards
- Interfaces

Printers
- Dot-Matrix Printers
- Daisy-Wheel Printers
- Ink-Jet Printers
- Laser Printers
- Plotters

Modems

Other Peripherals
- Joysticks
- Trackballs
- Light Pens
- Touch-Screens
- Graphics Tablets
- Scanners
- Voice Recognition Systems
- Speech Synthesizers

Preview

Advances in technology are a primary reason for the growing role microcomputers now play in our society. Hardware determines the software that can be run, and hence profoundly influences how computers are used. You needn't become a computer engineer, but it is important to have a basic understanding of the hardware components that make up a typical system. In this chapter, we examine the physical parts of a microcomputer and see how they work. We discuss what makes the newest microprocessors so powerful. Memory, disk drives, displays, keyboards, mice, expansion boards, printers, and modems are all covered. Learning about these devices will help you realize what computers can do, given the right software. Once you become familiar with the hardware of microcomputer systems, you can then concentrate on the software that puts it to work.

After studying this chapter, you will understand

- the components inside the system unit.
- the key features that affect a microprocessor's power.
- the difference between RAM and ROM.
- commonly used secondary storage devices.
- the primary input device.
- the basic types of displays.
- how microcomputer systems can be expanded.
- the basic types of printers.
- how computers communicate with modems.
- alternate input and output devices.

The Microcomputer Revealed

Let's take the cover off a typical microcomputer and look at its internal structure. Figure 1 shows the system unit of an IBM Personal System/2 Model 50 taken apart. Inside we find that there are several major components. We'll briefly examine each of these parts, and then go on to delve into the ones that are most important for understanding how a computer processes data. Afterwards, we'll cover the input, output, and other devices that are commonly connected to the system unit of a microcomputer. The components you see in Figure 1 include:

- *Chassis.* The **chassis** is a frame, constructed of metal and high-impact plastic, that houses all of the internal components of a computer. This particular computer also has a plastic *subchassis,* which helps secure the disk drives and extra circuit boards. When all the parts are assembled, the chassis is covered by a plastic case coated on the inside with conductive silver paint to reduce radio frequency emissions.
- *Motherboard.* The **motherboard** or **system board** is the main circuit board of a computer (see Figure 2). Among other components, the motherboard holds the computer's CPU, some memory, and much of its control circuitry. Although not all computers are constructed with a motherboard in this fashion, it's a popular arrangement used in most microcomputers.
- *Memory.* In this particular computer, most of the memory, or **primary storage,** is made up of chips mounted on their own small circuit boards that plug

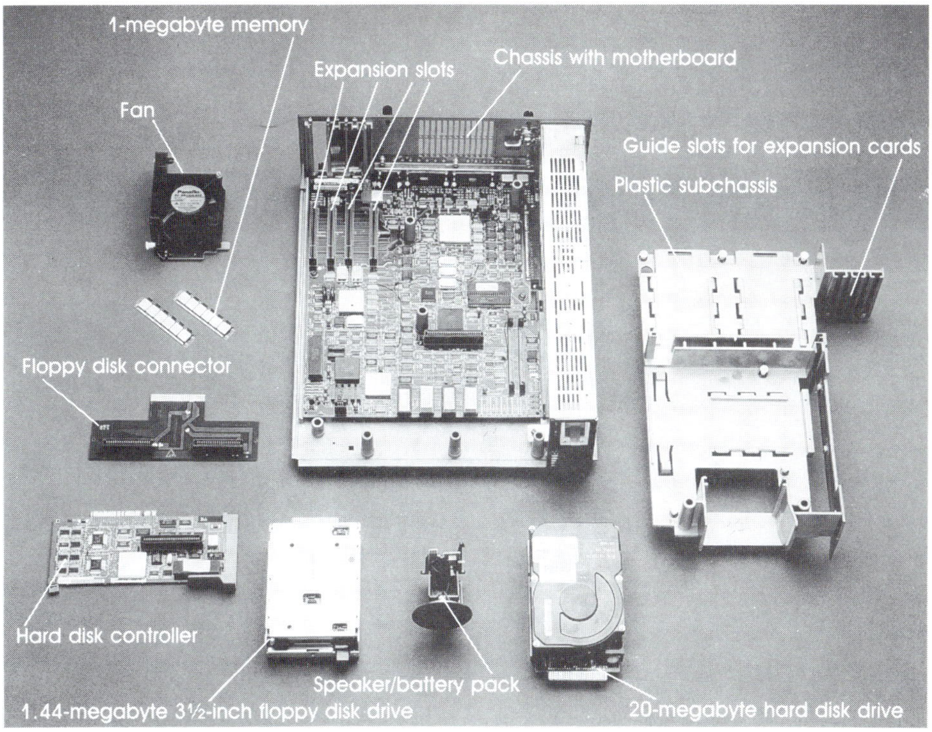

Figure 1 Inside the System Unit
Here are the components of the system unit of an IBM PS/2 Model 50.

into special sockets on the motherboard. Many computers, however, have their memory chips plugged or soldered directly into the motherboard.

- *Power Supply.* The delicate circuits that make up any computer require a refined source of electrical power. The **power supply** plugs into an ordinary outlet, but contains a transformer to lower and regulate the voltage level of the electricity provided to the computer. Relatively large and heavy, the power supply in the IBM Personal System/2 Model 50 extends the entire right-side length of the chassis (see Figure 1). The red toggle at the front end is the power switch that turns the computer on and off.
- *Expansion Slots.* An **expansion slot** is an internal connector that allows you to plug an additional circuit board into the motherboard. This particular computer has four expansion slots, although some computers come with eight or more. A circuit board that plugs into an expansion slot is called an **expansion board, card,** or **adapter.** Such circuit boards make it possible to connect a wide variety of auxiliary peripheral equipment to a computer, thus expanding its capability. We'll have more to say about expansion slots and boards later in this chapter.
- *Disk Drives.* As we said in Chapter 1, a disk drive is a piece of equipment that can read and write programs and data on disks. Most microcomputers now have two basic kinds of disk drives. A **floppy disk drive** works with *floppy disks,* which are inexpensive flexible magnetic disks encased in plastic. Floppy disks can be inserted and removed from their disk drives. This computer also comes with a hard disk drive. Unlike floppy disk drives, a **hard disk drive,** or **fixed disk drive,** usually has its magnetic disks permanently sealed inside. The magnetic disks inside a hard disk drive are rigid, much faster, and have much greater capacity than a floppy disk. We'll have more to say about both floppy and hard disk drives later in this chapter.

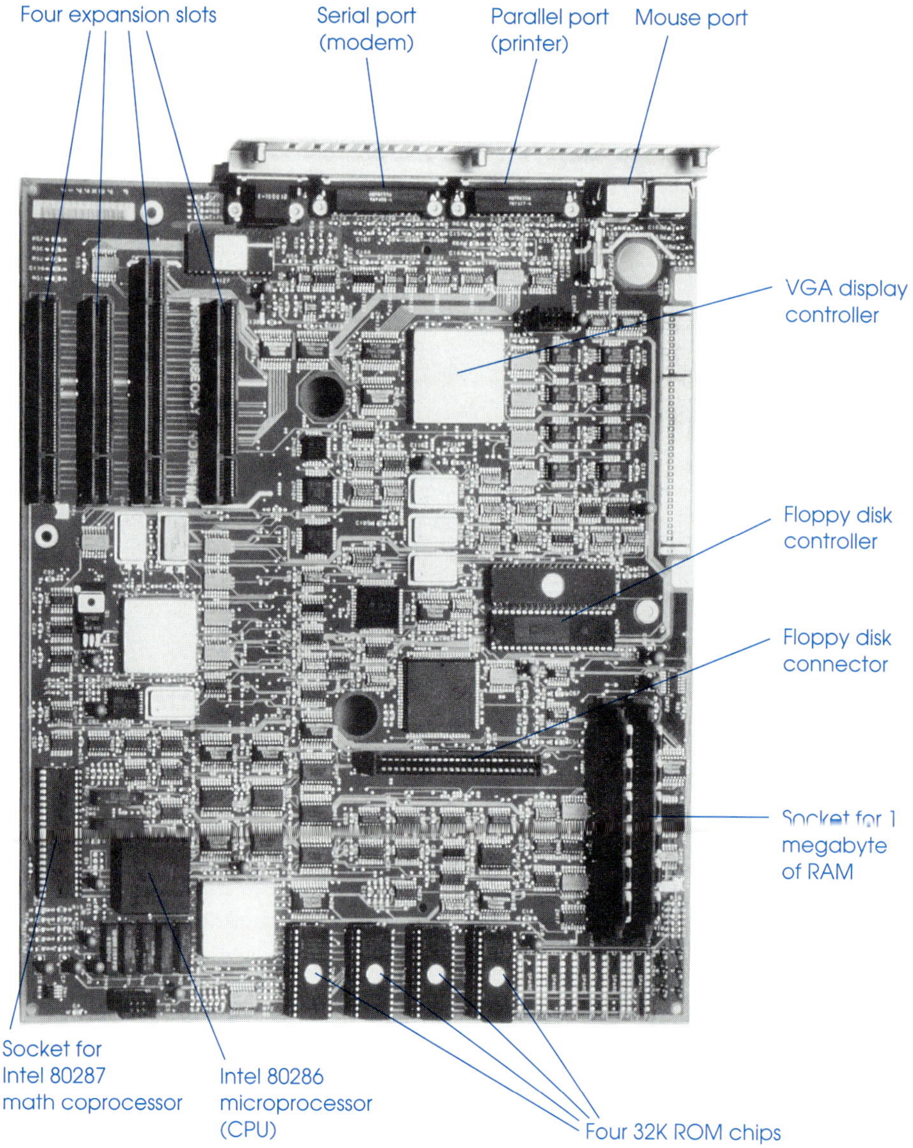

Figure 2 The Motherboard *Here is the motherboard of an IBM PS/2 Model 50 with its principal components labeled.*

- *Device Controllers.* A **device controller** is a set of chips or a circuit board that operates a piece of computer equipment such as a disk drive, display, keyboard, mouse, or printer. Some device controllers are so complex that they are, in actuality, small computers unto themselves. Recently, there has been a trend toward building device controllers onto microcomputer motherboards. In this IBM Personal System/2 Model 50, for example, the device controllers for the display, keyboard, mouse, and floppy disk drives are made up of chips mounted on the motherboard (see Figure 2). The *hard disk controller,* on the other hand, is a separate circuit board that plugs into one of the expansion slots. By having the hard disk controller on a removable expansion board, the computer can be easily upgraded later with a faster or higher capacity hard disk.
- *Other Components.* Most computers have various other components inside the system unit. This particular computer, for example, also has a speaker, battery

Insight

What Happens When Your Computer Goes Out of Production?

You just spent $1500 on a new computer. You have unpacked it. You have finally figured out how to get it working.

The next morning, the headline is on the front page: Your new computer is being replaced by a newer, more powerful, less expensive model. Your new computer is a dinosaur.

Or, it could be that the manufacturer has stopped producing your model, which means parts are no longer available and service will be difficult. In either case, you are allowed a predictable and understandable childish reaction. Then you have to sit down and think.

Businesses face this sort of problem all the time. It can be especially hard on companies that have a lot of money tied up in hardware and software or on businesses that rely heavily on their computers.

Businesses have a special way of dealing with the financial impact of obsolescence. The cost of major assets such as computers is amortized, or spread out over the useful life of the equipment. This is based on the assumption that after maybe five to seven years, the machine or system will be worn out and will have to be replaced. The way things are changing in the computer field, this useful lifetime may become even shorter.

Both you and business have several ways to handle this problem.

First, you can always hope that parts and service will be available from the manufacturer for two or three years. If the company also goes out of business, you'll have to track down the company that bought up its stock or parts.

The second possibility is to trade in or sell your computer and move your applications and files to another system. This often is the best idea, because the useful life of software is at most three or four years. By then, your needs or the needs of your business may have changed, and you'd have to replace your software anyway.

Finally, you can run the system as long as you can, salvaging parts from other computers. This works well for the business that is upgrading its system and has enough old machines to supply the parts.

pack, fan, and floppy disk connector. The *speaker* is used for emitting "beeps," musical tones, and other sounds. The *battery pack* is used to maintain power to a few special memory chips that hold the current date, time, and various equipment settings. The *fan* is an important piece of equipment needed to keep the sensitive computer circuits from overheating. In this particular computer, the *floppy disk connector* is needed to plug floppy disk drives into their device controller on the motherboard.

The Microprocessor

As we said in Chapter 1, the brain of a computer is called the *central processing unit*, or *CPU*. The CPU of a microcomputer is a single microprocessor, which is a small processor. What does it process? Data. In the computer world, all data are essentially numbers. Even alphabetic letters, pictures, and sounds are encoded as numbers by computers. Computers process data by performing arithmetic operations, comparing, moving, and copying data from one place to another. In fact, all computers really have only three basic functions: they receive numbers as input, process them in some fashion, and present the results as output. Every component of a computer system performs one or more of these three basic functions. For example, a keyboard is an input device; a display is an output device. The system unit, which contains the microprocessor, control circuitry, and storage devices, performs all three functions.

Structure

Figure 3 shows what a typical microprocessor looks like. This one is an Intel 8088, the CPU used in the original IBM Personal Computer and many other similar microcomputers. It's about two inches long, a half inch wide, and a quarter of an inch thick. The forty pins sticking out and bent down from the two longer sides are electrical connections that plug into a socket or are soldered into a larger circuit board. In fact, the black rectangle you see is not actually the microprocessor itself, but rather a ceramic or plastic case within which the microprocessor is permanently and completely sealed. The actual microprocessor is an extremely complex integrated circuit chip.

An **integrated circuit chip** is a thin slice of semiconductor material, such as pure silicon crystal, impregnated with carefully selected impurities. A **semiconductor** is a substance that conducts electricity poorly at low temperatures, but pretty well at high temperatures. The impurities, such as boron and phosphorus, enhance its ability to transmit electricity. These impurities are laid out into intricate patterns that define the electronic and logical properties of the chip. Amazingly, this design enables a single solid chip to behave as if it were constructed of many extremely tiny electronic circuits known as *gates*. Each one of these gates is like a switch that can be turned off or on. As simple as these off/on gates are in their operation, they can be arranged into complex circuits that are capable of storing, adding, subtracting, multiplying, dividing, and comparing numbers. A microprocessor is an especially complex chip that contains thousands of gates. Table 1 examines some of today's most popular microprocessor chips.

Besides the main microprocessor, some microcomputers contain other chips designed to perform certain specialized tasks. Such chips are called **coprocessors**

Figure 3 Microprocessor
The Intel 8088 microprocessor chip is a popular CPU, used in the original IBM Personal Computer and many other similar microcomputers.

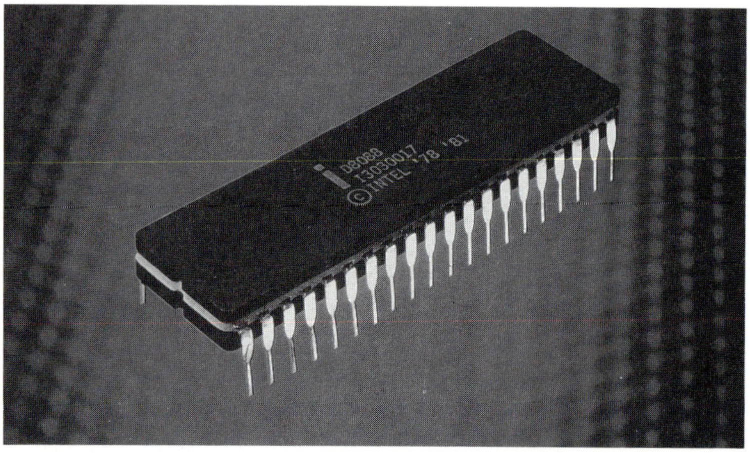

Table 1 Popular Microprocessors

This table presents some of today's most popular microprocessor chips. Each chip is listed along with its register size in bits, its data bus size in bits, its maximum speed in megahertz, its maximum addressable memory, and an example of a computer that uses the chip.

Chip	Reg. Size (Bits)	Data Bus Size (Bits)	Max. Speed (MHz)	Max. Memory (Bytes)	Example Microcomputer
MOS Technology 6502	8	8	1	64K	Apple IIe
Intel 8088	16	8	10	1M	IBM Personal Computer
Intel 8086	16	16	10	1M	IBM PS/2 Model 30
Intel 80286	16	16	20	16M	IBM PS/2 Model 50
Intel 80386SX	32	16	16	4G	IBM PS/2 Model 55SX
Intel 80386	32	32	33	4G	IBM PS/2 Model 80
Motorola 68000	32	16	12.5	16M	Apple Macintosh SE
Motorola 68020	32	32	25	4G	Apple Macintosh II
Motorola 68030	32	32	25	4G	Apple Macintosh IIx

1K (kilobyte) = 1,024 bytes
1M (megabyte) = 1,048,576 bytes
1G (gigabyte) = 1,073,741,824 bytes

because they work along with the main microprocessor. Coprocessors often help speed up microcomputers by taking over certain types of time-consuming operations. For example, many microcomputers use separate coprocessors for certain complex mathematical calculations, input/output operations, and the display of graphic images. Since they're specialized, coprocessors can do their jobs more efficiently than the general-purpose main microprocessor. Furthermore, the main microprocessor is relieved from having to do these tasks. The result can be a significant increase in overall computer performance.

Register Size

The power of a particular computer depends upon several characteristics of its CPU. Although there are many ways to evaluate a particular processor's power and some of them can be quite involved, one convenient measure is the size of a computer's registers. A **register** is essentially a storage compartment inside the CPU for temporarily holding numbers that are currently being manipulated. You can think of registers as scratch pads for the computer. The larger the registers, the larger the numbers they can hold. Register size is usually expressed in terms of bits, which we will examine now.

As we said before, computer circuitry is made up of gates that can turn off or on. Electrically, off is represented by the absence of current and on is the presence of some predefined level of current. Numerically, *off* is symbolized by 0 and *on* is symbolized by 1. Because of this, most computers use the binary number system. Instead of the ten digits of our familiar decimal system, there are only two digits in the binary number system: 0 and 1. A single binary digit

Figure 4 Bits and Bytes
A bit is a zero or a one. A byte is a group of eight bits. This particular byte holds the number 65 in binary form, which is also the code representing an uppercase A in most computers.

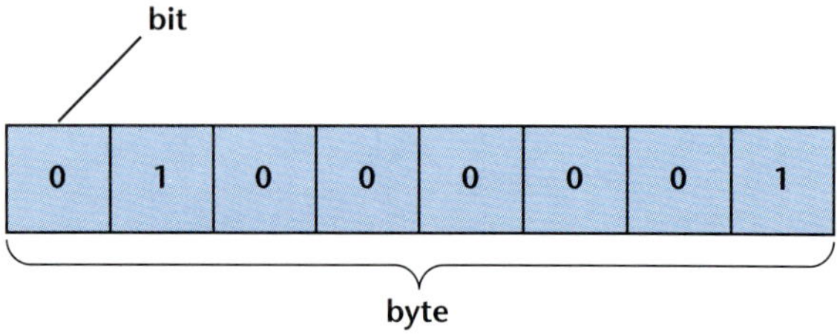

is called a **bit,** which can only be 0 or 1. Larger numbers are constructed from strings of zeros and ones representing successive powers of two. A commonly used grouping of bits is the **byte,** which consists of eight bits (see Figure 4). This is the amount of storage used to hold a number between 0 and 255, or a single character, such as A, b, or $.

The more bits a computer can work with at a time, the faster and more efficiently it can get the job done. For example, a computer with 32-bit registers can usually process data at least twice as fast as a computer with 16-bit registers. In general, the bigger the register size, the more powerful the computer.

Virtually all of the microprocessors in microcomputers today use 8-bit, 16-bit, or 32-bit registers. The 8-bit microprocessors are the oldest and least powerful of the bunch. They are still used in some low-end Apple, Atari, and Commodore computers. Microprocessors with 16-bit registers are currently the most common. The Intel 8088 you see in Figure 3 is a good example of a 16-bit microprocessor because it's used in so many IBM Personal Computers and similar machines. Finally, 32-bit microprocessors have become increasingly popular since their choice by Apple for the Macintosh line of computers. Other powerful 32-bit microcomputers are also available from several manufacturers, including Compaq, IBM, Tandy, and Zenith.

Data Bus Size

Register size isn't the only measure of a CPU's ability to process data. Another important factor is the size of the **data bus.** This is the pathway connecting the microprocessor to memory. We said before that the main circuit board of a microcomputer is called the motherboard and is housed inside the system unit. The microprocessor, memory, and various other chips and circuits are all plugged, soldered, or embedded in the motherboard. The main circuit connecting all of these components is called the **bus** (see Figure 5). Basically, the bus can be likened to a group of wires that connects the internal and external devices of a computer to the CPU. The wires are divided into three groups: address lines, data lines, and control lines. Address lines carry signals that indicate which memory locations are to be read or written for a particular operation. Data lines, or the data bus, carry program instructions and data from memory to the CPU and back. Control lines convey directives from the CPU to other computer components.

How does the size of the data bus affect computer performance? Basically, it determines how much data can be moved, and thus processed, at a time. Imagine

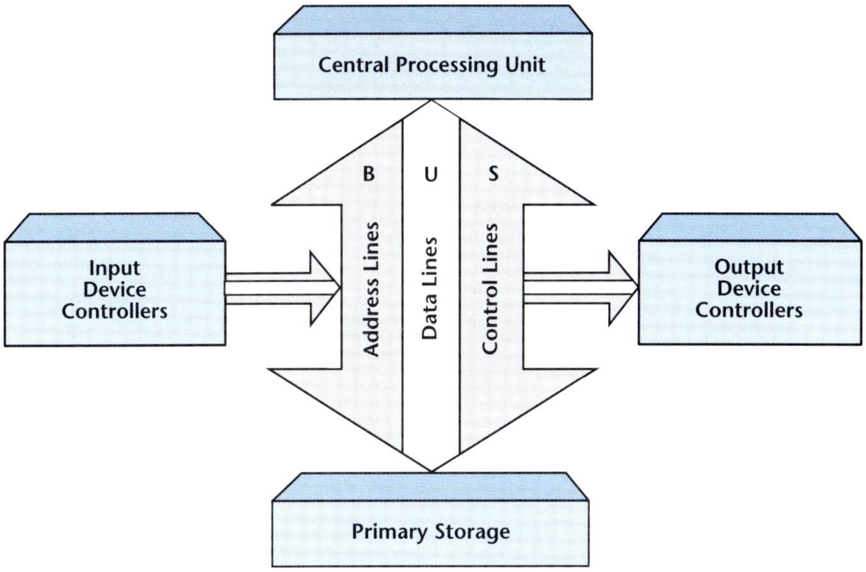

Figure 5 The Bus
The bus connects the CPU to memory and to input and output device controllers.

that you had a big jar of jelly beans and you had to move them to another jar. Let's say that you couldn't pour them from one jar to the other and you had to move just eight jelly beans at a time. If there were 1024 jelly beans in the first jar, it would take you 128 transfers to get the job done. On the other hand, if you could move 32 jelly beans at a time it would only take you 32 transfers. In the analogy, you are like the computer, a jelly bean is like a data bit, and the number of jelly beans you can transfer at one time is like the size of the computer's data bus. In general, the larger the data bus, the more powerful the computer.

Speed

Another way to evaluate the performance of a particular microprocessor is to look at the speed with which it operates. This speed is dependent upon two factors. The first is the microprocessor design, since manufacturers specify a range of possible speeds for each type of microprocessor they make. The second factor is the speed of the **system clock.** This clock is a crystal that oscillates, or "ticks" at a certain frequency. This frequency is typically several million times per second. The system clock is connected to the microprocessor and other electronic circuits of the computer. It synchronizes the internal operations of these computer components. In some respects, the system clock acts like a musician's metronome by pacing the work of the microprocessor and the devices connected to it.

Since all computer operations require a certain number of clock ticks to be completed, the faster the clock operates, the faster the work gets done. As microcomputers have become more advanced, we have come to expect them to perform more complex tasks faster and faster. So, manufacturers have constantly tried to increase the clock speeds of their microprocessors. Consequently, many modern microcomputers are significantly faster than much bigger computers of the previous decade.

The speed of a system clock, and hence of the microprocessor connected to it, is measured by the number of ticks or cycles per second. This is usually expressed in a unit of frequency known as the *hertz*. One hertz (Hz) equals one cycle per second. Since most system clocks tick several million times per second, their speeds are usually given in **megahertz.** One megahertz (MHz) equals one million cycles per second. Today's microcomputers have a wide range of clock rates. Some of the low-end 8-bit computers have clock rates between 1 and 2 megahertz, while expensive 32-bit models can run at 33 megahertz. The 8088 chip you see in Figure 3 was used with a 4.77 megahertz system clock in the original IBM Personal Computer. These days, it's common for mid-range microcomputers to run at clock rates between 8 and 16 megahertz.

Primary Storage

As we said before, computers process data in the form of numbers. They also need numerically coded instructions to tell them specifically what to do with the data. Ultimately, all programs and data are just numbers. For computers to achieve the speed and efficiency they do, programs and data must be presented to the CPU very rapidly when needed. A good way to do this is to compile programs and data beforehand and hold them temporarily in some quickly accessible storage area. Although a CPU's registers do store numbers, there simply isn't enough room to hold all the data and instructions for a typical task. For example, the Intel 8088 microprocessor has only fourteen 16-bit registers. Clearly, more storage than this is needed.

To solve the problem of program and data storage, computers are given memories. This memory, or primary storage, consists of an array of specialized integrated circuit chips that have the ability to hold numbers. Directly connected to the CPU, primary storage is an essential component of every computer system. The overall performance of a computer depends as much on the speed and amount of its primary storage as it does on the speed and power of its CPU. In general, the total amount of memory a particular computer can have is dependent upon the capabilities of its CPU. Table 1, for example, lists the maximum memory that can be used with various microprocessors under ordinary circumstances. In microcomputers, two basic types of primary storage are used: random access memory (RAM) and read-only memory (ROM).

RAM

A computer's memory consists of a sequence of individual storage locations. Each storage location has a unique identifying number. This number is called an **address,** just like the addresses that identify the individual mail boxes in a post office. When a number is placed in storage at a particular address, it is said to be *written* to memory. When a number is looked up in storage, it is said to be *read* from memory. **Random access memory** or **RAM** is storage in which all addresses are equally accessible. In other words, any location can be written to or read from in the same amount of time.

That's the technically correct definition of RAM. RAM, however, has come to mean the memory in a computer that can be freely written to and read from. Sometimes called *read-write memory,* it's the storage that's used by the computer to hold both programs and data as needed. The amount of RAM is another measure of a computer's power. The more RAM a computer has, the more complex the programs it can run and the more data it can have quickly accessible.

As we said before, computers deal with binary numbers, which consist of strings of bits (zeros and ones). A convenient grouping of bits is the byte, which is eight bits long. Since the byte is the smallest unit of storage that can be directly addressed by most computers, memory is measured in bytes. How much memory a computer has is usually expressed in units of 1024 bytes. This number, which is 2 to the 10th power, is somewhat imprecisely called 1 **kilobyte (K)**, because *kilo* is a Greek prefix meaning thousand. When we refer to a computer as having 640K of RAM, we really mean it has 640 times 1024 or 655,360 bytes of memory. Some computers have so much memory that even bigger units are used, such as **megabyte (M)** and **gigabyte (G).** One megabyte (*mega* stands for million) is equal to 2 to the 20th power, or 1,048,576 bytes; and one gigabyte (*giga* stands for billion) is equal to 2 to the 30th power, or 1,073,741,824 bytes.

The maximum amount of RAM a microcomputer can have is determined by the microprocessor it uses. Today's microcomputers exhibit a wide range of possible memory capacities. For example, while the original Apple II computer could have no more than 64K of RAM, the Apple Macintosh II can theoretically handle up to 4 gigabytes. In reality, memory is also limited by cost and space considerations. Most microcomputers these days have somewhere between 512K and 4 megabytes of RAM. For example, the IBM PS/2 Model 50 comes with 1 megabyte of RAM (see Figure 1).

ROM

In almost all microcomputers, RAM is used for the temporary storage of programs and data. This is because the most commonly used RAM chips lose their contents when the power is shut off. Most computers have a small set of programs and data that are used very frequently, yet never have to be changed. For these, **read-only memory,** or **ROM,** is used.

ROM is like RAM in that every location has its own address and every address can be read in the same amount of time. The difference is that ROM chips are manufactured with programs and data permanently written in their storage locations. When the power is turned off, ROM chips retain their contents. Hence the programs and data can be read and used, but they cannot be altered. Manufacturers must be very careful to make sure programs and data are correct before they are placed into ROM chips. Despite the extra precautions that must be taken, ROM chips are used because they are simple, inexpensive, fast, and reliable. Most microcomputers contain at least one ROM chip as part of their primary storage. For example, the IBM Personal System/2 Model 50 computer uses four 32K ROM chips to store essential programs and data (see Figure 2).

Secondary Storage

In order to do any processing, a computer must have a program and any necessary data in primary storage. But a computer also must have some kind of secondary storage system. **Secondary storage** supplements primary storage by providing a place to keep programs and data when they are not needed at the moment. Although secondary storage generally takes longer to access than primary storage, it is used for the following reasons:

- *Secondary storage is unlimited.* Even though new computers are continually being developed with more and more primary memory, there still isn't enough for users to store all of their programs and data. Secondary storage systems typically involve disks or tapes. Since you can always buy more of these, there's no limit to the amount of secondary storage a computer system can have.

- *Secondary storage is economical.* Although technological advances are steadily reducing the cost of primary storage, secondary storage still costs less.
- *Secondary storage is stable.* The contents of RAM, which makes up most of primary storage, are lost when the power is turned off. The contents of most secondary storage systems remain intact until you direct the computer to change them.
- *Secondary storage is portable.* The programs and data in one computer's RAM cannot be transferred to another computer unless a direct communication link exists between the two computers. Many forms of secondary storage can be easily transported between computers.

Floppy Disk Drives

Floppy disks or *diskettes* are the most common secondary storage medium used with microcomputers. They are called *floppy* because the disk itself is a circular sheet of thin, flexible plastic. Thinly coated with a magnetic film, floppy disks store binary numbers in the form of tiny magnetic spots arranged in concentric circles.

Microcomputer floppy disks generally come in two sizes: 5¼ inches and 3½ inches. The 5¼-inch floppies are encased in a square, flexible plastic jacket that leaves the enclosed disk exposed in a couple of places. Because of this exposure, 5¼-inch floppies are usually stored in a protective paper sleeve when they aren't being used. Floppy disks of the 3½-inch variety look considerably different (see Figure 6). Besides being smaller, 3½-inch floppies are completely enclosed in a square case of rigid plastic. Access to the disk inside is through a sliding metal door that remains closed until the floppy is slipped inside the computer. Currently, the older, 5¼-inch floppies are still more popular, mainly because there is a huge installed base of computers that use them. This situation is gradually changing, however, because newer microcomputers tend to use the 3½-inch format. Although the 3½-inch floppies are generally faster, more rugged, more durable, and more compact than the 5¼-inch diskettes, they also cost more.

In addition to the two sizes, other differences distinguish floppy disks. All disks, of course, have two sides: a top and a bottom. If only one of these sides is used for storage, that disk is called *single-sided*. Predictably enough, floppy

***Figure 6* Floppy Disks**
The two most common types of floppies are: left, 3½-inch diskettes and right, 5¼-inch diskettes.

Table 2 Popular Floppy Disk Types

Size (Inches)	Sides	Density	Capacity (Bytes)	Example Microcomputer
5¼	single	single	140K	Apple II
5¼	double	double	360K	IBM Personal Computer
5¼	double	high	1.20M	IBM Personal Computer AT
3½	single	double	400K	Apple Macintosh
3½	double	double	800K	Apple Macintosh SE
3½	double	double	720K	IBM PS/2 Model 30
3½	double	high	1.44M	IBM PS/2 Model 50

1K (kilobyte) = 1024 bytes
1M (megabyte) = 1,048,576 bytes

disks that use both sides for storage are called *double-sided.* Variations also exist in the density of the magnetic coating that cover diskettes. The denser the coating, the more bytes a floppy disk can store. *Single-density, double-density,* and *high-density* are commonly used terms that reflect how much data can be stored on a particular diskette. To get an idea of the types and storage capacities of the floppy disks used in several popular microcomputers, examine Table 2.

A *floppy disk drive,* or *floppy drive,* is a device that reads and writes the data stored on floppy disks (see Figure 7). Most microcomputers have at least one floppy disk drive, and some can even accommodate four. One or two floppy drives are the most common, however, and they're usually enclosed inside the system unit. Some computers, such as the Apple IIe, have external floppy drives

Figure 7 Floppy Disk Drive
The floppy disk drive reads and writes programs and data on floppy disks.

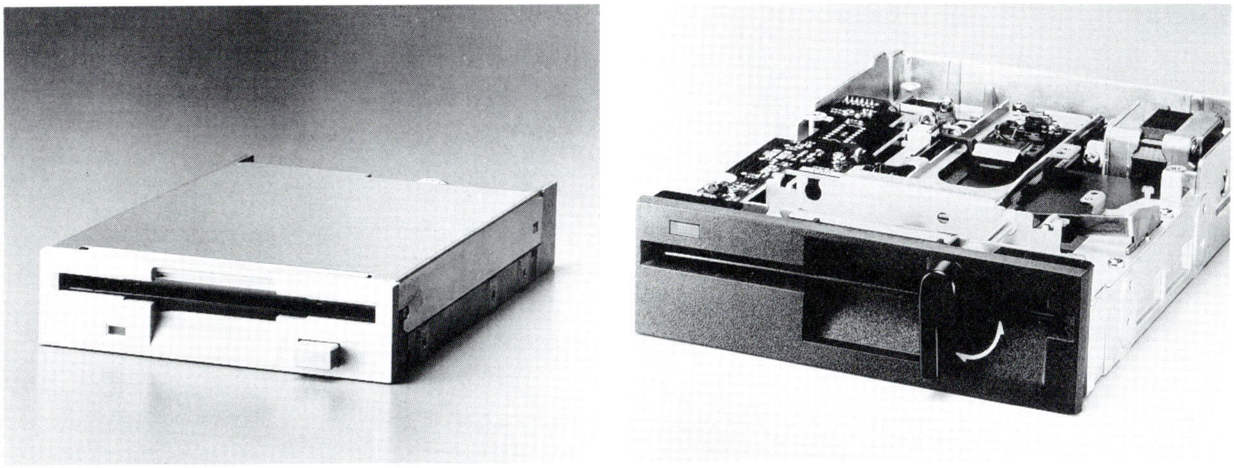

Figure 8 Inside a Floppy Disk Drive
This diagram shows the major internal components of a floppy disk drive.

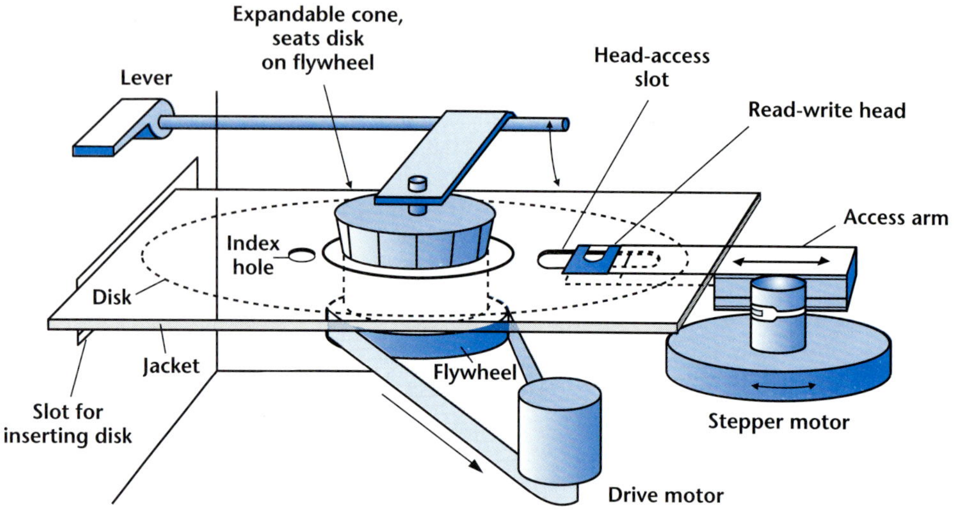

in their own separate little cabinets. From the outside, there's an open slot into which you put a single floppy disk at a time. Most 5¼-inch floppy drives also have a door or lever you close after you put a diskette inside. Disk drives for 3½-inch floppies may only have a slot visible from the outside, or they may have a slot and a button that you can press to eject the disk.

The disk drive operates by spinning the disk under a read-write head mounted on the tip of an access arm (see Figure 8). This **read-write head** is a tiny electromagnet that can create or erase minuscule magnetic spots on the disk directly below. The **access arm** is a mechanical extension that can move the read-write head toward or away from the center of the disk. The combination of rotating the disk and moving the access arm enables the read-write head to be placed above any spot on the disk. Double-sided disk drives have forked access arms that hold a read-write head for each of the two disk surfaces.

In general, you must know what kind of floppy disk drive your computer has so that you can select the correct diskettes. Obviously, a 3½-inch floppy disk drive cannot accommodate 5¼-inch floppy disks, nor can a 5¼-inch drive accept 3½-inch floppies. Although most double-sided disk drives can use single-sided diskettes, this doesn't utilize the disk drive's full potential. The density of the floppy disk magnetic coating also must be considered. The best approach is to carefully read your computer's user manual so that you understand what kind of floppy disks it requires.

As we said before, floppy disks are the most common form of secondary storage and most microcomputers have at least one floppy drive. There are several reasons for this. First, floppy disk drives are relatively inexpensive. The typical price range is between $80 and $500 for a single disk drive. Second, floppy disk drives are reliable. Like any other mechanical device, floppy drives do occasionally break down, and some models require periodic cleaning and adjustment. But in most cases, floppy disk drives provide years of service without any problems whatsoever. Finally, they are now a very important means for distributing and copying programs and data. Most programs that are purchased come on floppy disks. Because floppies are fairly durable, lightweight, compact, thin, and inexpensive, they can be easily packaged and mailed. People who are using similar computers can very easily trade data with each other. For example, this textbook was written with a microcomputer and the individual chapters were sent to the publisher on floppy disks. Floppy disks are also very easy to reproduce. This makes them an important medium for keeping extra copies of programs and data. Because it's so easy and cheap to make extra or **backup** copies of vital programs and data, computer users are encouraged to do so. This gives them something to fall back on if the original copy is accidentally lost, destroyed, or erased.

Hard Disk Drives

Despite the advantages of floppy disks, many microcomputer users need still more storage. In one sense, floppy disk storage is unlimited because you can always buy more diskettes. But if you have only one floppy disk drive, you can only gain access to the storage of one floppy disk at a time. Perhaps your microcomputer can accommodate additional floppy drives. The upper limit is usually four, however. For very large programs and huge amounts of data, the capacity of even four floppy disks isn't sufficient.

The *hard disk drive* was developed to meet this need for ever increasing amounts of storage (see Figure 9). It's a very fast device that can hold much more data than a single floppy disk. Although the basic operating principles of hard disk drives are similar to those of floppy disk drives, there are some important differences. A **hard disk** is a circular platter of rigid metal or glass covered with a thin magnetic coating. Just like floppy drives, a hard disk drive has a read-write head mounted on an access arm for each surface of the disk. It's common, however, for hard disk drives to have more than one disk mounted inside on the same spindle, like records stacked on a turntable. Because hard disks are rigid, they can be spun much faster than floppy disks. The movement of the access arms in hard disk drives is much more precisely controlled than in floppy drives. Hard disks are also covered with a very high quality, dense magnetic coating. These factors combine to make hard disk drives much faster at transferring data

Figure 9 Hard Disk Drive
The hard disk drive is a fast, high-capacity secondary storage device.

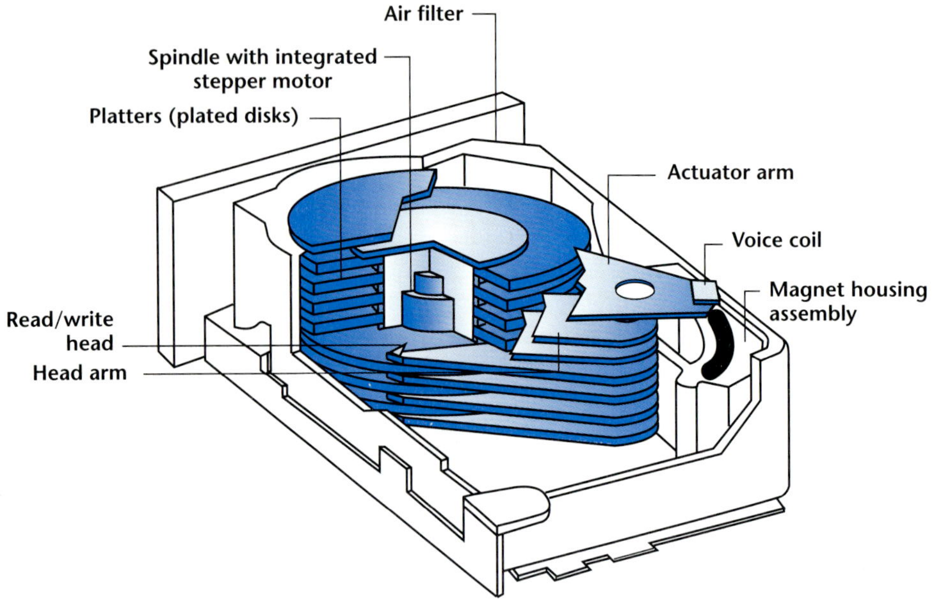

Figure 10 Inside a Hard Disk Drive
This diagram shows the major internal components of a hard disk drive.

than floppy drives, while at the same time providing a much higher storage capacity.

Most hard disk drives consist of hard disks, spinning motors, access arms, and read-write heads completely enclosed in a sealed, airtight housing (see Figure 10). This arrangement minimizes vibration and keeps out dust, dirt, smoke, and other contaminants. Hard disks spin so quickly (more than 100 miles per hour), and read-write heads are positioned so closely to disk surfaces (about 20 millionths of an inch), that sharp vibrations and foreign matter such as dust can cause considerable damage. The read-write head can collide with a minute obstruction or actually hit the disk surface itself. This **head crash** can destroy the read-write head and data stored at the point of collision on the disk surface. Fortunately, such disasters are quite rare with the hard disk drives now used in microcomputers. Nevertheless, hard disk drives still tend to be less rugged than floppy disk drives.

Like floppy drives, hard disk drives are usually enclosed inside the system unit, but they are sometimes found in their own external housings. As we said before, most hard disk drives used with microcomputers have their hard disks permanently sealed inside. This is the reason the term *fixed disk drive* is often used to refer to a hard disk drive. You can't buy additional hard disks to increase the storage capacity of most hard disk drives. Many users find that this isn't a problem because hard disk drives already have such a high capacity. For example, a typical microcomputer hard disk drive can hold at least 20 megabytes and may cost as little as $250. The capacity of this hard disk drive is equal to that of almost 57 floppy disks that hold 360K each. If you still need more storage, you can usually purchase a hard disk drive with an even higher capacity. Some microcomputer hard disk drives can hold hundreds of megabytes. Although most microcomputers seldom have more than a single hard disk drive, it's often possible to connect an additional one.

A microcomputer with one or two floppy disk drives and a hard disk drive has a truly powerful secondary storage system. Most people who have this arrangement store all the programs and data they use daily on the hard disk.

This provides faster access and high capacity for those large programs and huge sets of data. The floppy drive is used to copy programs and data to and from the hard disk. Infrequently used programs and data can be copied to floppy disks and taken off the hard disk instead of being completely abandoned. Finally, the floppy disk drive also can be used to make backup copies of important programs and data normally kept on the hard disk.

Magnetic Tape Drives

In the early days of microcomputers, floppy disk drives were quite expensive and no sane hobbyist would even think of using a hard disk drive for secondary storage. The most common secondary storage device for microcomputers at that time was the cassette tape recorder. Instead of storing music, cassettes were used in early microcomputers to store programs and data in an inexpensive and reliable form. The process of reading and writing data was rather slow, but cassette tape recorders were perfectly adequate for the simple microcomputers of the time. Although they are still used for secondary storage in some very inexpensive microcomputers, cassette tape recorders are rarely seen today in the more powerful systems found in most schools, offices, and homes. They are, however, one example of a class of secondary storage devices that now serves an important specialized function in some modern microcomputers.

A **magnetic tape drive** is a secondary storage device that uses magnetic tape to store programs and data. **Magnetic tape** consists of a long strip of thin plastic covered with a magnetic coating. Just like disks, read-write heads are used to read and write data in the form of magnetic spots on these tapes. Unlike disks, however, magnetic tape is a **sequential access medium.** This means that numbers are recorded one after another along the length of the tape. Consequently, the farther away it is on the tape the longer it takes to reach a number. If the read-write head is positioned at the beginning of the tape and the number you want is at the end of the tape, the computer has to skip through all the numbers that are in between. A familiar example of this is the way songs are recorded on cassette tape. If you want to listen to a song at the end of a tape, you have to push the fast-forward button until you get to it. Disks, on the other hand, are a **direct access medium** because you can go directly to any piece of data on the disk in a very short time.

Although magnetic tape drives have been used with computers for years, they have taken on a specialized function in some modern microcomputer systems. Their sequential access nature makes them poorly suited to the routine storage of programs and data used daily. Magnetic tape drives, however, work very well as backup systems for hard disk drives. Data can be stored very compactly on magnetic tape, and the sequential reading and writing of data can be done very rapidly. For example, some magnetic tape backup systems can copy in about five minutes the entire contents of a 20-megabyte hard disk onto a tape that looks very much like a cassette tape. Systems such as these can play an important role in preventing the loss of valuable programs and data.

Some microcomputers come with built-in magnetic tape backup systems. In most cases, however, the magnetic tape drive is purchased separately and installed into the system unit or externally connected to the microcomputer with a cable (see Figure 11). Tape backup systems are only used with microcomputers that have hard disk drives. In fact, only a minority of hard disk users get magnetic tape backup systems. Most people can get by with keeping extra copies of their programs and data on floppy disks. For some groups of users who need to make periodic backup copies of their entire hard disks, a magnetic tape drive is worth

Figure 11 Tape Backup System
Magnetic tape drives, such as these systems shown, are now used primarily for making backup copies of hard disks.

the added expense. Since the tape drive is only used every so often, it can be shared among several microcomputers if it is an external model. This also helps to justify the cost of the tape backup system, which can be anywhere from $300 to several thousand dollars.

Bernoulli Disk Drives

Floppy disk and hard disk drives are by far the most commonly used secondary storage devices for microcomputers. They are, almost always, the only types of secondary storage that come as standard equipment with microcomputers. Some companies, however, have developed alternatives to these devices. One such alternative is the **Bernoulli disk drive,** sometimes called the **Bernoulli box** (see Figure 12). It's a secondary storage device that, in a sense, combines the advantages of both floppy and hard disk drives.

The Bernoulli disk drive is like a high performance, high capacity floppy disk drive (see Figure 13). It uses a special type of floppy disk that's sealed inside in a hard plastic case. The disk is spun at about 3000 revolutions per minute. This is fast enough to subject the flexible disk to an aerodynamic effect first described by the Swiss mathematician Daniel Bernoulli in the eighteenth century. Basically, the Bernoulli effect causes the disk to be lifted close to the read-write head and stabilized by the air currents generated when it is rotated at high speeds. If a dust particle gets in the way, or a sharp vibration occurs, the rotation slows and the disk temporarily falls safely away from the read-write head, thus preventing a head crash. The air flow also tends to purge contaminating particles from the disk.

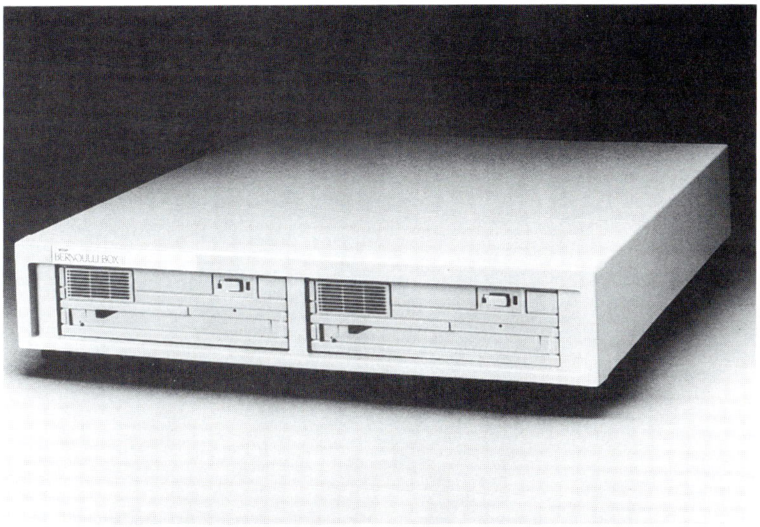

Figure 12 The Bernoulli Box
The Bernoulli Box combines some of the advantages of both floppy and hard disk drives.

The Bernoulli disk drive is often housed in its own separate cabinet, connected to the microcomputer system unit with a cable. Currently, Bernoulli disks generally come in two capacities: 20 and 44 megabytes. This type of secondary storage device operates at about the same speed as a slow hard disk drive, but costs significantly more. Nevertheless, Bernoulli drives offer a distinct advantage: the disks are rugged and removable like floppy disks, yet they have the capacity of hard disks. So, if you need more storage, you can purchase additional disks. Bernoulli disks cost between $50 and $90, but each one can store a large amount of data. Some Bernoulli units have two drives built into one cabinet so you can use two disks at the same time and easily make backup copies. They are a viable alternative to hard disk drives for some users, despite the added expense.

Optical Disk Drives

In the last few years, an entirely new class of secondary storage devices has emerged that is based on light. The **optical disk drive** uses a laser to read or write data on a disk. Currently, three basic types of optical disk drives are sometimes used with microcomputers: CD-ROM drives, WORM drives, and erasable optical drives.

Compact Disc Read-Only Memory, or **CD-ROM,** is a specialized form of secondary storage that only allows you to read previously recorded data, not record it yourself. CD-ROM drives use compact discs (CDs) that look just like the digital audio disks first introduced by Sony in 1983. When used to store data, these 12-centimeter (4.72-inch) disks of molded plastic can each hold an amazing 550 megabytes—the equivalent of several hundred books. Just like audio CDs, CD-ROM disks can be written only at the factory by special equipment. Since the appearance of the first CD-ROM drives early in 1985, many businesses have published encyclopedias, reference works, professional directories, and other

Figure 13 Inside the Bernoulli Box
This diagram shows the major internal components of a Bernoulli disk drive.

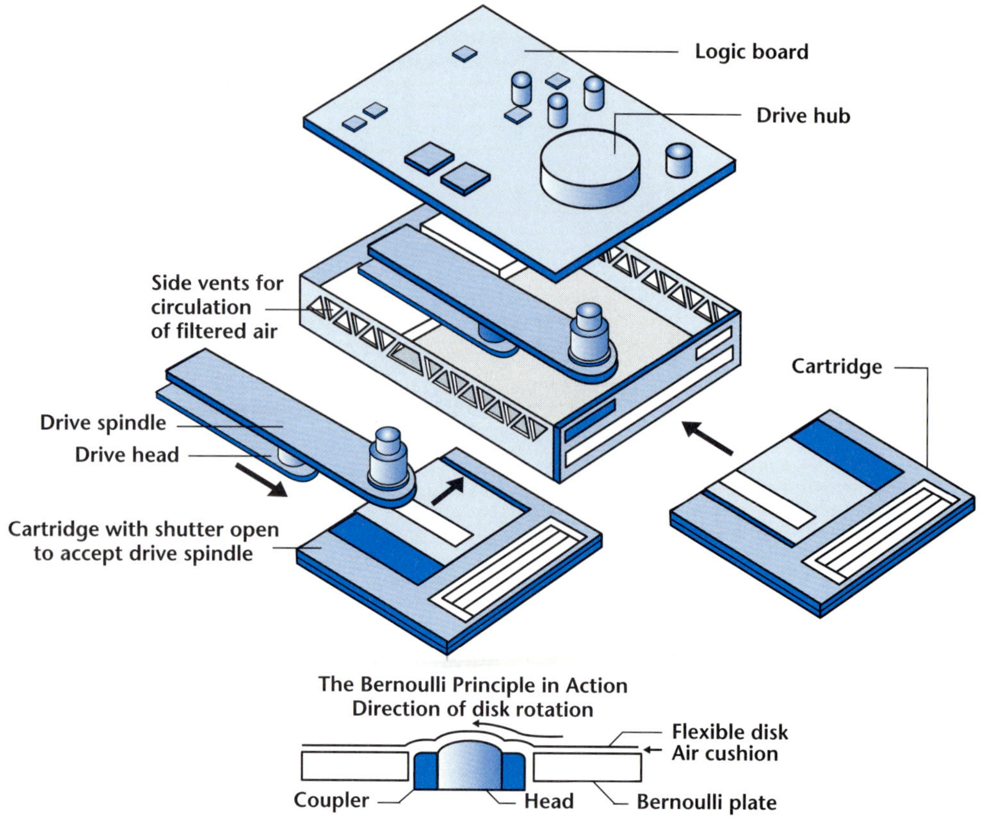

large sets of data on CDs. Some CD-ROM drives can be installed inside a microcomputer's system unit, while other models are housed in their own external cabinets (see Figure 14).

Write Once, Read Many (times), or **WORM,** is a slightly different type of optical disk storage that allows users to record their own programs and data. Once programs and data have been copied onto a WORM disk, they can be used but never changed or deleted. WORM disks typically hold between 100 and 400 megabytes each. WORM disk drives are similar to CD-ROM drives except that they include a more powerful laser used to record data by melting little depressions in the recording surface. Since these pits are irreversible physical changes in the disk, once data is written on WORM disks it cannot be erased. Despite this limitation and the fact that they are still rather expensive (between $2000 and $10,000), WORM disk drives can be invaluable to users who need to create huge, permanent collections of data.

The **erasable optical disk drive** works with removable optical disks that can be written to and read from any number of times. An erasable optical disk can hold much more data than a typical hard disk, but cannot access it as fast. A good example is the optical drive included with the NeXT computer, a workstation developed by NeXT, Incorporated, the company Steve Jobs started when he left Apple Computer. The drive built into the NeXT computer accepts cartridges that contain an optical platter resembling a compact disc. Each cartridge, which

Figure 14 CD-ROM Drive
The CD-ROM drive reads the contents of previously recorded compact discs, each of which can hold around 550 megabytes of programs and data.

costs around $50, can hold 256 megabytes of programs and data. A single laser performs both read and write operations by using principles of optics and magnetism. Consequently, this type of device is sometimes called a read/write magneto-optical drive. Still new on the market and quite expensive ($1500 to $15,000), erasable optical drives are not yet common in microcomputers. Nevertheless, they offer advantages that may become irresistible once prices come down. Erasable optical disk drives provide an effective means of backing up programs and data, maintaining huge libraries of secondary storage, and letting a user keep all of his or her work on a single disk that can be removed from the computer and carried away or locked up for security purposes.

Keyboards and Mice

The primary input device of every microcomputer is a keyboard, used to enter data and tell the computer what to do. Like typewriters, microcomputer keyboards have keys for alphabetic letters, numbers, mathematical symbols, and punctuation marks. These keys are almost always in the same positions on most keyboards. In addition to this basic set of keys, microcomputer keyboards have other, special-purpose keys. Some popular microcomputers, like IBM's Personal System/2 series, come with keyboards that have more than 100 keys (see Figure 15), twice that of most typewriters. Different types of computers have distinct keyboard designs for the additional keys. Other differences also exist, such as how the keys feel and sound when they are pressed, and the relative sizes of certain keys. Most modern microcomputers have a detachable keyboard that is connected to the system unit with a coiled cable. This gives you the freedom to alter the position of your keyboard or even type with it in your lap. For more comfort, many keyboards also can be adjusted to lie flat on the table or be tilted a bit toward you.

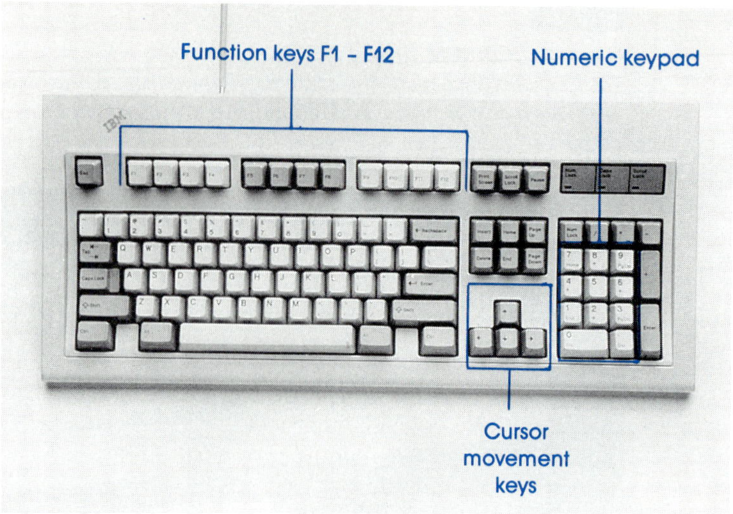

Figure 15 Microcomputer Keyboard
IBM's Enhanced Keyboard has 101 keys.

Computer keyboards work by constantly scanning themselves to see if any keys are currently depressed. Every key is assigned its own code number. When a key is pressed, its code is sent to the computer. If the computer is busy or if keys are pressed more quickly than the computer can process them, key codes may be temporarily stored by the keyboard in its own memory chips and sent when the computer is ready. As you can imagine, microcomputer keyboards have become rather sophisticated devices. In fact, many keyboards are so complex that they contain their own microprocessor to handle the work of decoding and storing keystrokes. It's important to realize that the keyboard merely passes on key codes to the computer; it is the computer that actually decodes the keypresses and interprets the actions to be taken. Thus, computer programs may assign different meanings to different keys, especially the special-purpose keys we mentioned.

Since special-purpose keys are found on many microcomputer keyboards, let's go into a bit more detail and describe what some of these keys are and what they're typically used for:

- *Enter or Return Key.* Analogous to the carriage return on a typewriter, this key is used to signal the end of an entry. When pressed, it tells the computer to go ahead and process what was just typed.
- *Escape Key.* This key is often used to cancel a previously typed entry or to prematurely end a program.
- *Break Key.* This key is much like the Escape key and is used by some programs in a similar fashion.
- *Control Key.* Somewhat like a shift key, the Control key is pressed in conjunction with other keys. It's used to control a program's actions by sending certain codes to the computer.
- *Alternate Key.* Very similar to the Control key, the Alternate key is also pressed in conjunction with other keys. It's used to give an alternate meaning to the keys pressed along with it.
- *Insert Key.* This key is often used to insert a new entry between existing entries.
- *Delete Key.* This key is often used to erase an entry or a single character.
- *Function Keys.* These keys are pressed to activate frequently used operations within a program. They are used differently by different programs. Micro-

computers that have function keys typically have between two and twelve of them.

- *Cursor Movement Keys.* Most programs use these keys to let you move the cursor (a little blinking underscore or box) around the screen. In a word processing program, for example, the cursor marks the place where text is to be inserted, deleted, or otherwise manipulated. Cursor movement keys usually include Up Arrow, Down Arrow, Left Arrow, Right Arrow, Home, End, Page Up, and Page Down keys.
- *Numeric Keypad.* This is an array of keys at the right side of a keyboard that resembles the layout of a calculator's keys. It includes the ten digits and other symbols that facilitate the entry of numbers and formulas.

Early microcomputers usually didn't have all these keys. The original Apple Macintosh computer, for example, had a keyboard with only 58 keys. In an effort to keep their microcomputers as easy to use as possible, Apple purposely minimized the number of keys on its keyboards. To help compensate for the elimination of most special-purpose keys, Apple included with its Macintosh computers a little device known as the *mouse.* This device is a small box with at least one button that the user holds in his or her hand and rolls about on the table top (see Figure 16). The mouse is connected to the computer with a thin cable through which it sends signals indicating its movement. The computer uses these signals to similarly move a cursor or arrow on the screen. Thanks to clever computer programming, the mouse is quite a versatile tool. It can be used to point the cursor at symbols (also called *icons*) that represent activities to be performed. By pressing a button on the mouse, the user tells the computer to go ahead and complete the activity depicted by the icon at which the cursor is currently pointing. In addition to its use in moving the cursor and selecting options, a mouse also can be used to draw figures. Although Apple certainly didn't invent the mouse, the company did popularize this useful accessory by making it an essential component of the Macintosh computers. Because the mouse has proven so useful, other computer manufacturers have jumped on the bandwagon. Now, most microcomputers can accommodate a mouse as an optional input device, even if they have many special-purpose keys on their keyboards.

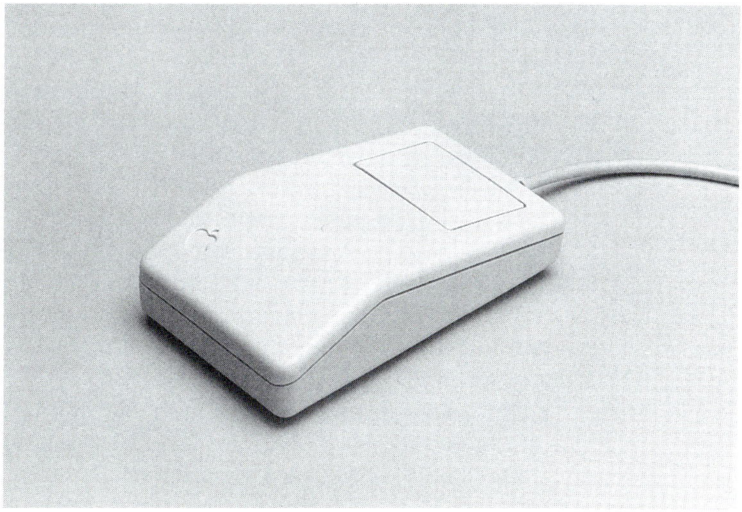

Figure 16 Mouse
The mouse is the most popular alternate input device, used for pointing, selecting, and drawing.

Incidentally, Apple has abandoned the very simple keyboard of its original Macintosh. Modern Macintoshes are equipped with one of two keyboard designs: the 81-key Apple Keyboard, or the 105-key Extended Keyboard, which is similar to the IBM Enhanced Keyboard shown in Figure 15.

Displays

As we said in Chapter 1, a computer display, or monitor, is an output device that has a screen on which text and graphic images are presented to the user. Virtually every microcomputer has some type of display. This essential component is used by the computer to echo back the characters you type at the keyboard and to show the results of the programs you run.

Most computer displays are similar to ordinary television screens. They consist of a **cathode ray tube,** or **CRT,** that uses an electron gun to paint images on a phosphor-coated glass screen. Screen sizes of CRTs typically range from nine to nineteen inches, measured diagonally. CRT screens are by far the oldest and most commonly used type of computer display.

In addition to CRT screens, several kinds of flat-panel displays are used, primarily with small portable computers. These screens are relatively small, thin, and lightweight. Currently, the most popular and inexpensive of these flat-panel screens is the **liquid crystal display,** or **LCD.** Smaller versions of this type of display have been used in watches, calculators, tiny televisions, and other electronic devices for years. They consist of a thin layer of liquid crystalline substance sandwiched between two sheets of glass. Very thin wires are embedded horizontally in one glass sheet and vertically in the other sheet. When electricity is passed through a wire in each sheet, the crystals at the intersection line up to produce a dark dot. Images are constructed from these tiny dots.

Besides these technological differences, we've mentioned before that some microcomputer models have the display built into the same cabinet as the system unit, while others have a separate display connected to the system unit by a cable. There also are differences in the type of images that displays can present. Most displays fall into one of the following classifications: monochrome text monitors, monochrome graphics monitors, and color graphics monitors.

Monochrome Text Monitors

A **monochrome text monitor** displays characters such as letters and numbers in a single color (see Figure 17). Sometimes these characters include symbols that can be combined to form lines, boxes, bar graphs, and even primitive pictures, but these images are limited. Consequently, microcomputers with monochrome text monitors can only run programs that generate rather simple output. They are completely useless for programs that must display complex graphic images such as drawings, figures, charts, and maps.

The display color may vary from model to model. Currently, the most common colors for monochrome monitors are green, amber, or white characters on a black background, and black on a white background. Most monochrome monitors can highlight by brightening or dimming text, underlining text, and causing characters to blink.

The characters presented on a monochrome text monitor are arranged into rows and columns. Each character takes up the same amount of space as every other character, so the rows are perfectly aligned horizontally and the columns

Figure 17 ***Monochrome Text Monitor***
This monochrome text monitor, used with IBM's original line of Personal Computers, can display only 256 different types of characters.

are perfectly aligned vertically. The most common arrangement is to have 25 lines (or rows) of 80 characters (or columns) each. The characters themselves are made up of little dots. The more dots used per character, the more sharply defined those characters appear. A monitor with sharply defined characters is much more pleasant to work with because eyestrain is minimized. This sharpness, or **resolution,** of a character is expressed in terms of the width and height of the box that contains the character. For example, many monochrome text monitors have a 9 by 14 character box. In other words, every character displayed by these monitors fits into a box that is 9 dots wide and 14 dots high. Other common character resolutions are 8 by 8, 8 by 14, 8 by 16, and 9 by 16.

Monochrome text monitors are the simplest and least expensive type of microcomputer display. Some monochrome text monitors sell for as little as $70. Although they are limited to rather simple output, monochrome text monitors are still used in many microcomputer systems, such as the original IBM Personal Computer shown in Figure 17.

Monochrome Graphics Monitors

Computer graphics is the presentation of images such as figures, charts, graphs, maps, diagrams, and other pictures on a display screen. A **monochrome graphics monitor,** therefore, presents such pictures in a single color, usually green, amber, white, or black (see Figure 18). It also can display ordinary characters, just like a text monitor. In fact, a monochrome graphics monitor may differ from a monochrome text monitor only in the electronic circuit board that controls it. We'll have more to say about these circuit boards later in this chapter when we discuss the expansion capabilities of microcomputers. For now, let's just say that graphics monitors have the electronic circuitry to allow the computer to individually control every dot on the screen.

***Figure 18* Monochrome Graphics Monitor**
The monitor built into Apple's Macintosh SE can display graphics as well as text, but only in black and white.

Each dot, also called a **pixel** or **pel** (for *picture element*), can be turned on or off to construct images. The effect produced is somewhat like the pictures you see in black and white newspapers, which also are made up of dots. Most monochrome graphics monitors only have the ability to turn pixels on or off, but some also can vary the intensity of each pixel and make them blink, too.

One of the most important factors to consider with graphics monitors is resolution, since this determines not only how sharp characters can be, but also the ultimate definition of pictures produced. The resolution of graphics monitors is given as the total number of horizontal dots by the total number of vertical dots. For example, the Apple Macintosh SE screen you see in Figure 18 is a monochrome graphics display with a resolution of 512 by 342 pixels. In other words, there are 342 rows and 512 columns of dots. There are quite a few different screen resolutions used with microcomputer graphics monitors. Some monitors can even use different resolutions at different times. Occasionally, you'll see the terms *low-resolution, medium-resolution,* and *high-resolution* used in describing the capabilities of a graphics monitor. No standard values define these terms, but in IBM microcomputers, for example, low-resolution is 160 by 200 pixels, medium-resolution is 320 by 200 pixels, and high-resolution may mean 640 by 200, or more.

Color Graphics Monitors

A **color graphics monitor** can present text and pictures in more than one color. It's like a monochrome graphics monitor except that each pixel may be any one of several possible colors. Most color graphics monitors can display different resolutions at different times. The number of different colors that can be displayed on the screen at one time is related to the resolution. In general, the greater the resolution, the fewer the colors that can be displayed at one time. This combination of screen resolution and number of colors that can be used at one time is often called a **video mode.** For example, many color graphics monitors can only display two colors when they are used in their high-resolution video mode. If the color used for the background is black, and the other color used for text or pictures is white, the color graphics monitor may look just like a monochrome graphics monitor. The difference is that the color graphics monitor can vary these two colors, while in the monochrome monitor the background and foreground colors cannot be changed.

The total number of colors you have to choose from in a particular video mode is called the **palette.** On some monitors, the palette can be quite large. For example, the color graphics monitors available for IBM's Personal System/2 microcomputers have a palette that consists of 262,144 colors. On these computers, in the medium-resolution video mode (320 by 200 pixels), you can choose 256 colors out of this palette of 262,144 to be present on the screen at the same time. With monitors such as these, the picture quality can approach that of ordinary color television.

Color graphics monitors are the cream of the crop when it comes to microcomputer displays, but they are significantly more expensive than monochrome text or graphics monitors. Prices can range from $200 up to several thousand dollars. Even so, many computer owners find that the advantages of a color graphics monitor are well worth the cost.

Expanding the System

One of the best features microcomputers have to offer is that most of them can be easily expanded and upgraded. This means that additional devices can be connected to a system, and existing devices can be replaced with better models. Microcomputer manufacturers generally encourage other companies to build equipment that can be added to their systems. Consequently, all kinds of devices have been designed to work with microcomputers, so that buyers can start simply and gradually add more capabilities to their systems. With these individually tailored additions, the microcomputer can become an extremely versatile machine, as reflected by its widespread use in not only offices, but also in homes, schools, laboratories, factories, and just about every business imaginable. The hardware components that make this versatility possible are expansion slots, expansion boards, and interfaces.

Expansion Slots

Previously in this chapter we said that a computer's *bus* is a group of wires that connects the internal and external components to the CPU. In many microcomputers, the bus is extended to a set of one or more connectors on the motherboard. Each of these connectors, called an *expansion slot,* lets you plug in an additional circuit card known as an *expansion board* (see Figure 19). Many of the external devices that can be connected to a microcomputer require an expansion board to control their functions and connect them to the bus. Expansion slots make it easy to expand and upgrade a microcomputer system. In many cases, all you have to do to add a new hardware component is open the system unit's case and simply plug in an expansion board. On some microcomputers, you don't even need a screwdriver to do this.

Figure 19 Expansion Board
This multifunction board combines several different capabilities on a single circuit card. The connector along the bottom edge plugs into an expansion slot on the microcomputer's motherboard.

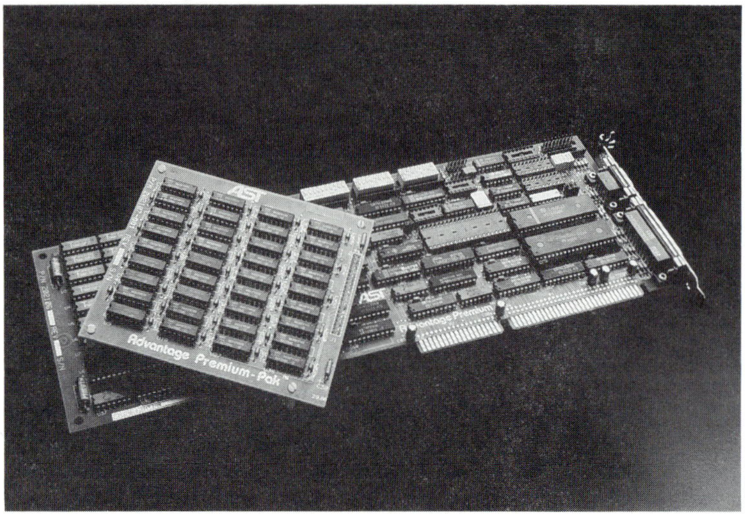

Expansion Boards

Expansion slots and expansion boards make it possible to add a host of optional hardware components and devices to an existing computer system. Here are a few of the more common types of expansion boards:

- *Additional memory.* Many microcomputers can accommodate more RAM than will fit on the motherboard. In these cases, expansion boards that contain additional memory can be installed to run bigger programs or handle more data.
- *Display adapters.* Some microcomputers have the control circuitry for their displays built onto their motherboards. On quite a few other models, displays must be plugged into a special type of expansion board called a **display adapter.** It's not just the type of monitor, but also the type of display adapter that determines whether your computer can present monochrome text, monochrome graphics, or color graphics.
- *Disk drive controllers.* Some microcomputers also have their floppy and hard disk drives controlled by expansion boards. This is especially true for external disk drives, which usually plug into an expansion board via a cable.
- *Real-time clocks.* As we said before, all computers have a system clock that acts as a metronome for the CPU. Most of them also have another type of clock, known as a real-time clock, that is used to keep the date and time-of-day. Some expansion boards contain a real-time clock run by a battery that keeps time even when the computer is turned off.
- *Game adapters.* There are both computer games and more serious programs that require the use of certain alternate input devices. We'll be discussing these devices, such as joysticks and trackballs, later in this chapter. For now, suffice it to say that on some microcomputers, these devices are controlled by a type of expansion board called a **game adapter.**

- *Network adapters.* A **local area network** (**LAN**) is an arrangement in which two or more microcomputers are connected by cables for the purpose of sharing programs, data, and hardware devices such as printers and high-capacity hard disks. A **network adapter** is a sophisticated expansion board that's used to connect a microcomputer to a local area network.
- *Multifunction boards.* Microcomputers only have so many expansion slots. While some computers have as many as eight, other models may have only one. An option like a real-time clock, however, doesn't take up enough space to fill an entire expansion board. So, this prompted the idea of putting several different options on a single expansion board. Thus the **multifunction board** was born (see Figure 19). There are now all kinds of multifunction boards sold that include every conceivable combination of add-on options, including memory, real-time clocks, game adapters, display adapters, and serial and parallel interfaces.

Interfaces

An **interface** is a connection between a computer's CPU and an external device operated under its control. Such devices, sometimes called *peripherals,* perform input, output, and storage functions. We've already discussed several examples of peripherals: external disk drives, monitors, and keyboards. The three most popular interfaces used to connect peripheral devices to microcomputers are the serial interface, the parallel interface, and the Small Computer System Interface.

The Serial Interface A **serial interface** or **serial port** transmits bytes of data, one bit at a time, between a computer and an external device. Each bit in a byte is sent serially, one by one. Serial interfaces are often used to connect computers to graphic input devices such as a mouse. They also are used to connect computers to modems (devices that transmit data over telephone lines, which we'll be discussing later in this chapter). Less frequently, serial interfaces are used to connect computers to printers. The serial interface is reliable and inexpensive, but is limited in speed because it only transmits one bit of data at a time.

The *RS-232C standard* is one type of serial interface used with many microcomputers. It specifies the functions and voltage levels of 25 wires attached to pins on a standardized plug or holes in a standardized socket. Thanks to this standardization, many external devices and computers from different manufacturers use the RS-232C serial interface.

Some computers have at least one serial interface built onto the motherboard that connects to a plug emerging from the back of the system unit. Other computers may have one or more serial interfaces on expansion boards. One or two serial interfaces are often included on multifunction boards.

The Parallel Interface A **parallel interface** or **parallel port** transmits data, an entire byte at a time, between a computer and an external device. The eight bits in each byte are sent simultaneously, in parallel, with a single wire carrying each bit. Ten wires are needed to send data in parallel: one for each of the eight bits in a byte, a ground (electrical reference) line, and a control line. Parallel interfaces are most commonly used to connect printers to microcomputers.

The *Centronics standard* is perhaps the most popular type of parallel interface used with microcomputer printers. It's based on the connector first used in the printers manufactured by Centronics Data Computer Corporation. Subsequently, many printer and microcomputer manufacturers have adopted this standard.

As with serial interfaces, some computers have a parallel interface built onto the motherboard while others provide it on an expansion board.

The Small Computer System Interface The **Small Computer System Interface** or **SCSI** (pronounced *scuzzy*) provides high-speed access to peripheral devices. It's most often used to connect hard disk drives and magnetic tape backup systems to microcomputers. Although the SCSI is not as common as the RS-232C and Centronics standard interfaces, it has been gaining popularity lately. Apple uses the SCSI in its Macintosh computers for both internal and external hard disks.

Printers

A printer is a device that prints text and possibly graphics onto paper. Although a printer is not an absolutely essential component of a microcomputer system, most microcomputers have one connected to them. This is because computers are commonly used to produce letters, reports, books, tables, figures, charts, graphs, diagrams, maps, and pictures. Paper output, or *hard copy* as it's also called, is a convenient medium for distributing and communicating this work to others.

Virtually all printers are connected to microcomputers through a serial or parallel interface or a network. Despite this common bond, there are many types of microcomputer printers. They differ in how they operate, which also affects the type and quality of their output. The four kinds of printers most frequently used with microcomputers are dot-matrix printers, daisy-wheel printers, ink-jet printers, and laser printers. In addition, a special class of paper output devices, called plotters, is also important.

Dot-Matrix Printers

A **dot-matrix printer** is an output device that uses tiny dots to create text and graphics on paper. Just as graphics monitors use pixels to construct characters and pictures on a screen, dot-matrix printers similarly use dots of ink on pages of paper. Inside the dot-matrix printer a *printhead* is moved across the paper from left to right, and sometimes also from right to left. This printhead may contain anywhere from 7 to 27 pins arranged in a vertical column. While most dot-matrix printers use 9 pins, more expensive printers with 18 or 24 pins are also common. As the printhead moves horizontally, it constructs a character by repeatedly striking these pins against an inked ribbon and the paper (see Figure 20). Electrical signals cause the appropriate pins to be thrust out at the proper moment to form the successive columns of dots that make up a character's image. Each column of the character is struck in turn against the ribbon and paper until the complete image has been formed. Dot-matrix printers are more frequently used for text, but this printing mechanism allows most models to produce graphics, too.

Dot-matrix printers are by far the most popular type of microcomputer printer. They are reasonably priced, fairly quick, and pretty reliable. Prices range between $150 and $3000, but the typical cost of an average 9-pin dot-matrix printer is about $500. The speed of a dot-matrix printer depends upon what print mode it is using. The fastest mode is called **draft mode,** in which characters are formed by just a single pass of the print head. Some expensive dot-matrix printers are able to achieve speeds of 400 characters per second in draft mode. Many dot-matrix printers also have a **near letter-quality** or **NLQ** mode. In this mode, the printhead makes two or more passes over each character, slightly shifting its

Figure 20 Dot-Matrix Printer
(a) Dot-matrix characters are formed by striking a column of pins against an inked ribbon and the paper. (b) A popular dot-matrix printer.

(a)

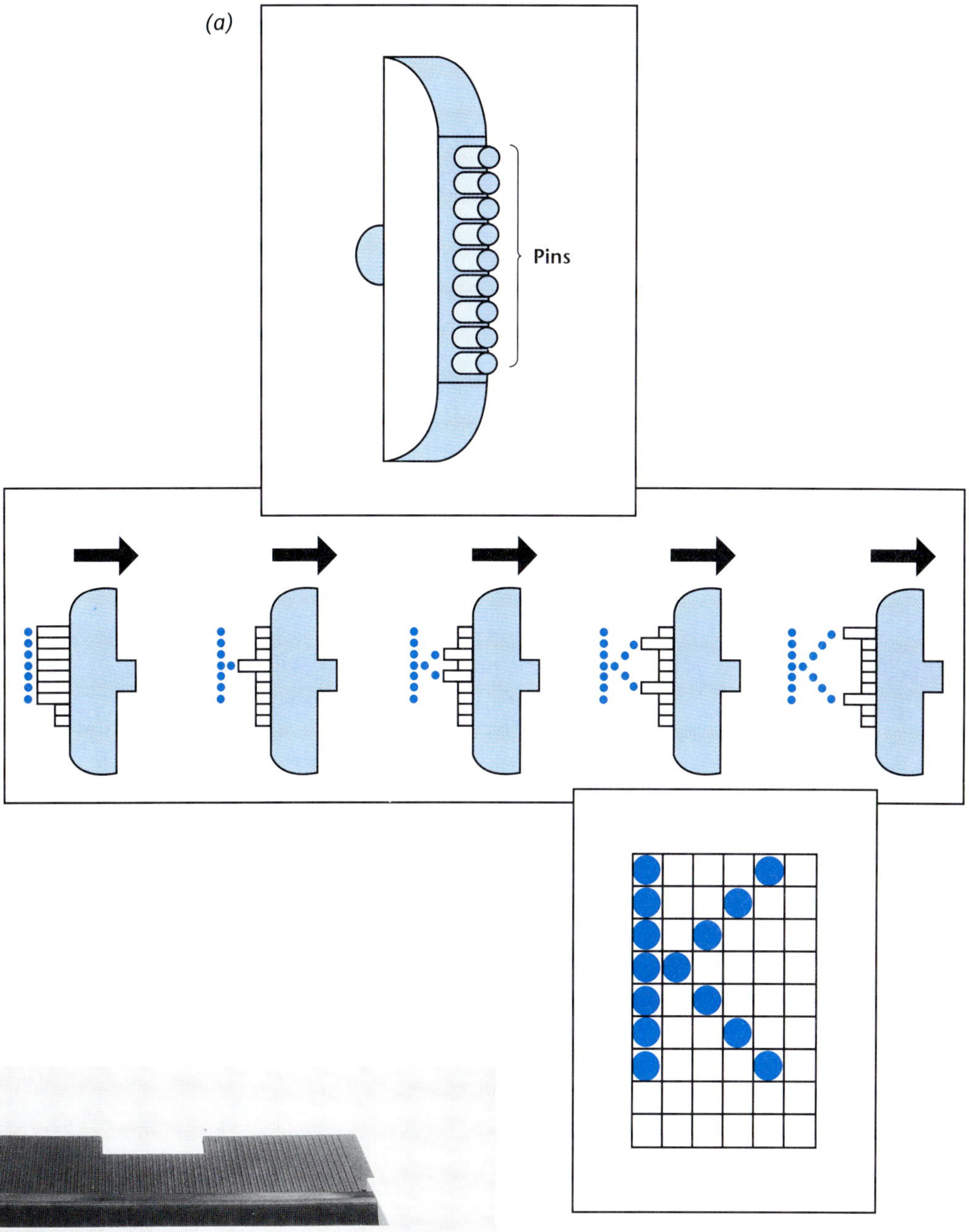

(b)

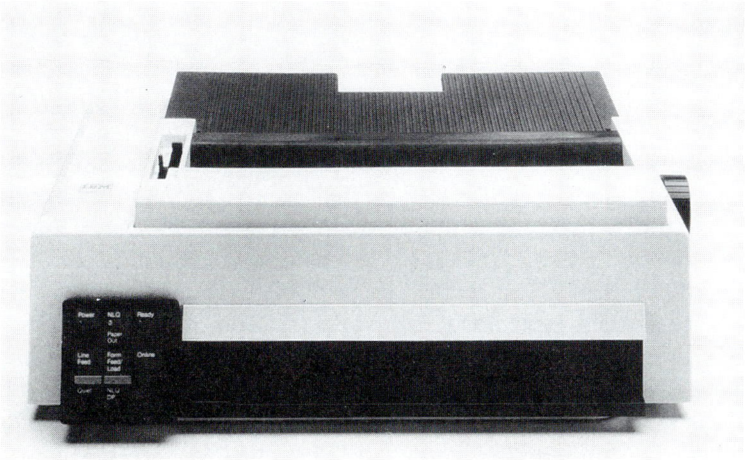

position each time. This tends to fill in the gaps between the dots and makes text appear more like the printing of an electric typewriter. Using NLQ mode may slow some printers down to only 15 characters per second. Generating graphics with a dot-matrix printer also can be time-consuming. Depending upon how dark the images are, it may take several minutes per page to produce graphics on a dot-matrix printer.

Daisy-Wheel Printers

A **daisy-wheel printer** is an output device with solid, raised characters embossed on the ends of little arms arranged like the spokes of a wheel or the petals of a daisy. As the wheel spins, a tiny hammer strikes the back of the proper character when it passes (see Figure 21). This impact drives the character pattern, which is embossed in reverse, against an inked ribbon and the paper. Daisy-wheel printers are true **letter-quality** printers because they produce well-defined text just like electric typewriters. Their prices are comparable to those of dot-matrix printers. Unlike dot-matrix printers, however, daisy-wheel printers cannot produce graphics. They also are noisier and slower than dot-matrix printers. The typical daisy-wheel printer can only print about 10 characters per second, and even the most expensive models generally cannot do better than one hundred characters per second. Daisy-wheel printers are still common, but they are gradually being supplanted by 24-pin dot-matrix printers and laser printers.

Ink-Jet Printers

An **ink-jet printer** has a mechanism that squirts tiny, electrically-charged droplets of ink out of a nozzle and onto the paper (see Figure 22). Ink-jet printers are fast, quiet, and can produce high-quality print, but they are slightly more expensive than dot-matrix printers. Some ink-jet printers have a tendency to clog their nozzle with ink and smear characters on paper. Many ink-jet printers, however, have the capability to print in color, a capability most other types of printers lack.

Laser Printers

A **laser printer** is an output device that uses tightly focused beams of light to transfer images to paper (see Figure 23). A tiny laser emits pulsating pinpoint bursts of light that are reflected off a special spinning mirror. This mirror reflects light onto a rotating drum. Light striking the drum causes it to become charged with electricity. An ink-like toner is attracted to the drum in these electrically charged spots. When the drum is rolled over a piece of paper, the toner is transferred to the paper and an image is permanently fixed through a combination of heat and pressure. This image transfer process is similar to that found in a standard copy machine. The result is high-quality text and graphics that almost look as if they were typeset.

Laser printers represent a very advanced printing technology. Although the images they produce are made up of dots, these dots are much smaller and more densely packed than the dots created with a dot-matrix printer. The typical microcomputer laser printer is capable of printing at a resolution of 300 dots per inch, both horizontally and vertically. This means 90,000 dots per square inch. Besides printing high-quality images, laser printers are also fast and quiet. The average speed of most laser printers is eight pages per minute. This is equivalent to about 400 characters per second. Because laser printers don't use impact methods like dot-matrix and daisy-wheel printers, they are very quiet by comparison. The

Figure 21 Daisy-Wheel Printer
(a) The daisy-wheel printing mechanism works somewhat like a typewriter to produce letter-quality text. (b) A popular daisy-wheel printer.

(a)

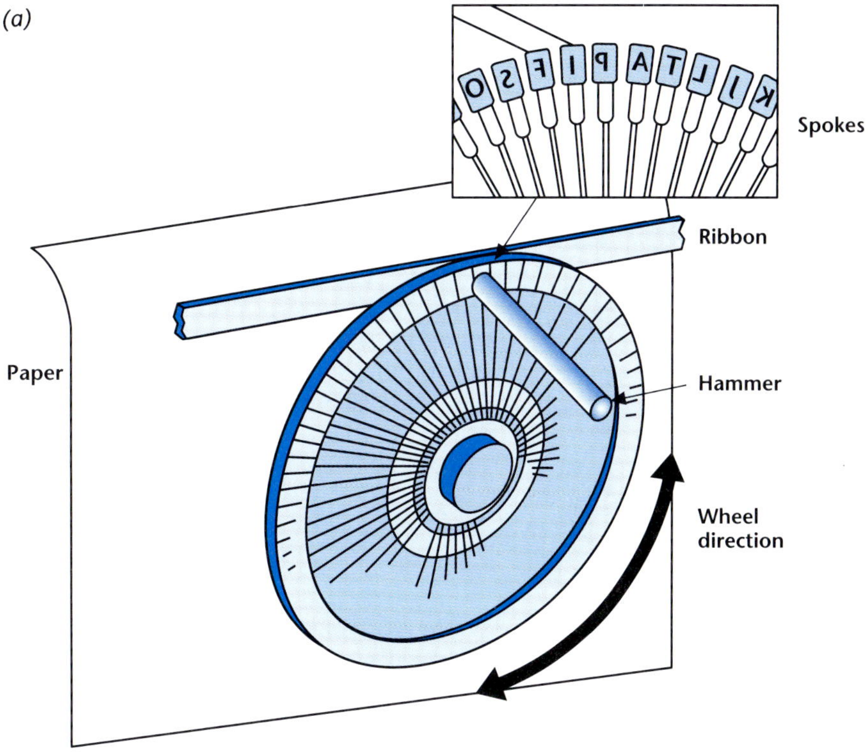

(b)

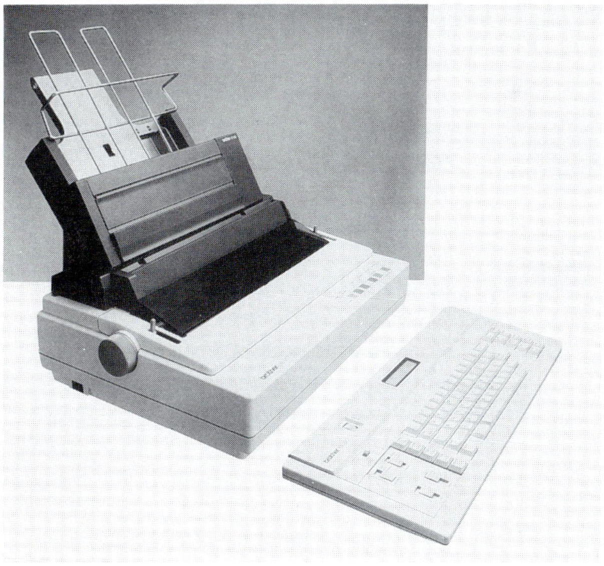

Figure 22 Ink-Jet Printer
(a) A stream of tiny ink drops are shot out of a nozzle and guided onto the paper by electrically charged deflection plates. (b) A popular ink-jet printer.

(a) *(b)*

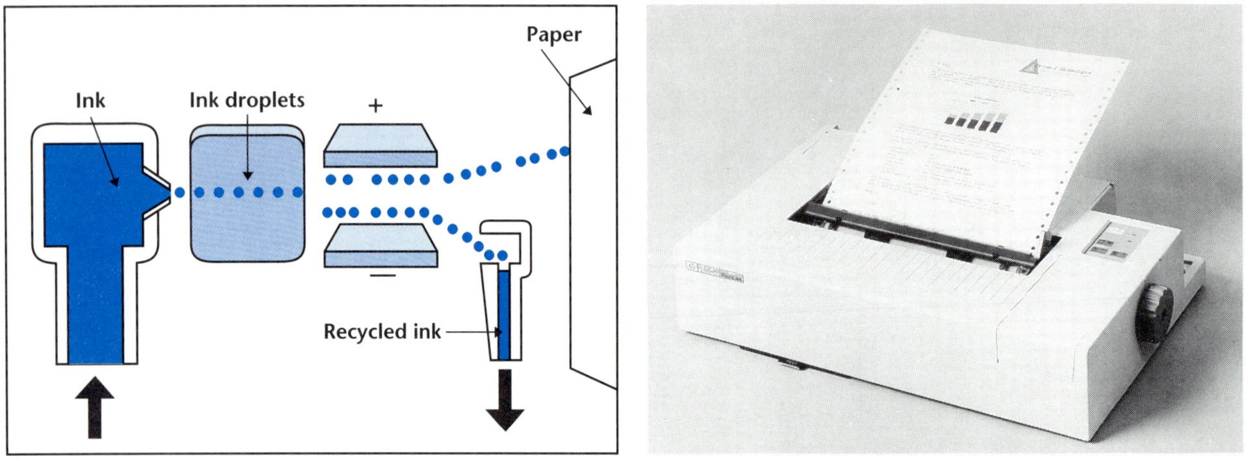

major disadvantage of laser printers is their cost. Prices generally start at about $1500. Despite the cost, more and more laser printers are being used with microcomputers every year. They are especially popular in offices where the printer can be shared among several users.

Plotters

A **plotter** is an output device that uses one or more pens to draw on paper (see Figure 24). Plotters are especially well-suited to producing high-quality graphs, charts, diagrams, maps, and blueprints. Although they are much slower than printers, plotters are quiet and can generate extremely accurate, well-defined drawings. Plotters with several pens can even create multicolored drawings. They are, however, inappropriate for producing textual documents such as formal letters, reports, and manuscripts. Consequently, plotters are used much less frequently than printers.

Modems

One of the most useful tasks microcomputers can perform is communicating with other computers. In some cases where the computers are in the same building, this communication takes place through a local area network, which we briefly described when we discussed expansion boards. When the computers are far apart, the connection is often made through telephone lines. Since the telephone system is a world-wide network, it's technically feasible for one computer to communicate with almost any other computer on earth. This opens up a whole range of possibilities as microcomputers tap into huge quantities of data and complex programs that exist only on much larger and more expensive computers. For example, information services have sprung up that cater to microcomputer users. These services allow users to "chat" with one another, post messages, join

*Figure 23 **Laser Printer***
(a) A laser printer uses light to transfer images to paper.
(b) A popular laser printer.

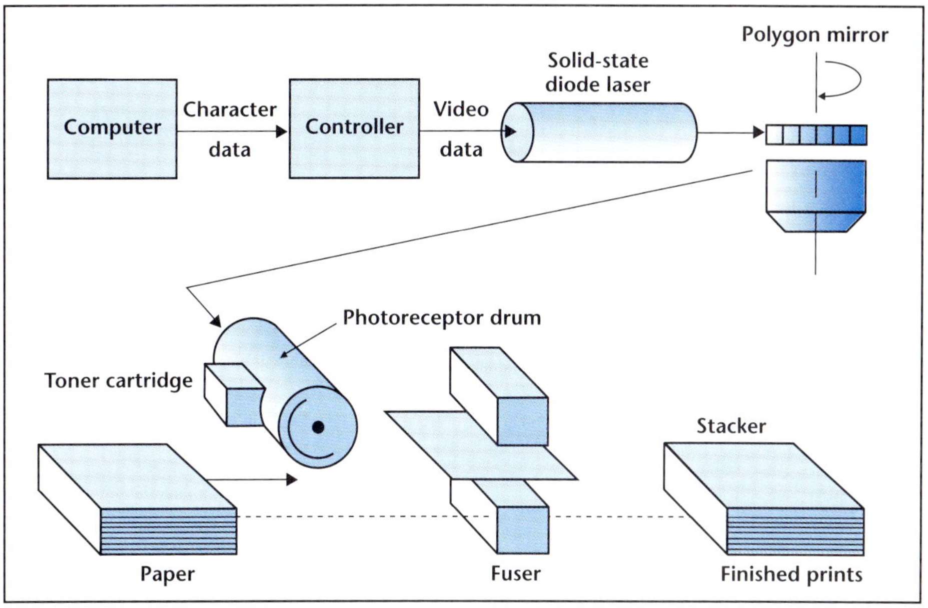

(a)

(b)

special interest groups, hold electronic forums, get stock market data, make travel reservations, read the latest news, shop and bank by computer, and gain access to all kinds of compiled data. An individual microcomputer owner can even set up a mini-information service in the form of an electronic bulletin board that can be read by other computer users. Recently, many people are even using microcomputers to **telecommute,** or work at home using a microcomputer that is connected to a computer at their office.

The electronic device that makes all of this possible is the **modem,** which allows a computer to transmit and receive data over telephone lines. Modems are necessary because computers use digital signals while most telephone lines are designed to carry analog signals. *Digital signals* are the discrete low and high voltages that represent zeros and ones. In contrast, *analog signals* are continuous

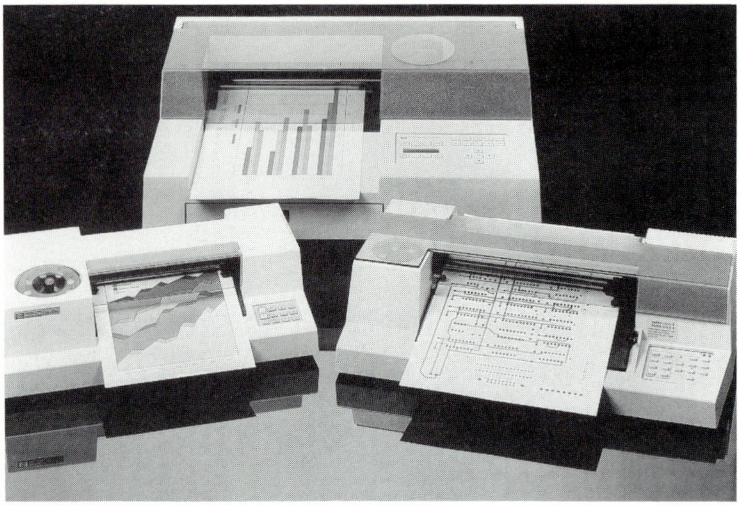

Figure 24 Plotters
A plotter is a computer output device that draws with one or more pens.

voltage ranges, which in the case of the telephone, are used to represent the sounds of human voices. Digital signals must be converted to analog signals before they can be transmitted over most phone lines. This conversion is called *modulation.* At the other end, where data transmissions are received, the analog signals must be reconverted into digital signals again. This is called *demodulation.* A modem, therefore, is a *modulator/demodulator.*

Microcomputer modems are relatively inexpensive options with prices that range from about $80 to $600. An average modem usually costs around $120. The price differential is based mainly on the speed with which modems can transmit and receive data. This speed is usually expressed in terms of **bits per second,** or **bps.** For example, nowadays most microcomputer modems can operate at 1200 bps. This means that they can transfer between 120 and 150 bytes per second. In other words, the contents of a single-spaced typed page can be transmitted in about 20 seconds. Some microcomputer modems operate as slowly as 300 bps, while other high-speed models can transmit and receive at up to 9600 bps. The most popular speeds for microcomputer modems are currently 1200 bps and 2400 bps.

Besides speed, there are other differences that distinguish microcomputer modems. Two basic types of modems are commonly used: internal and external.

An **internal modem** is either built onto the motherboard of a computer or is a circuit board that fits into an expansion slot. It's generally less expensive than an external modem because it needs no separate cabinet or power supply. Internal modems are convenient because they take up no desk space and don't have to be plugged into an electrical socket. A telephone cord is plugged right into the back of the computer or expansion board. The only disadvantages to internal modems are that they require an expansion slot and are specifically designed for particular computers. For example, you can't use an internal modem designed for an IBM Personal System/2 computer in an Apple Macintosh computer.

An **external modem,** or **direct-connect modem,** is built into a box about the size of a paperback book (see Figure 25). It plugs right into a phone set or telephone wall jack and usually requires a power supply consisting of an AC adapter that plugs into an electrical socket. The external modem also requires a serial interface to connect it to the computer. So, if your computer has a serial interface already built in, an external modem doesn't take up an expansion slot. It does,

Figure 25 External Modem
Any computer with a serial interface can use a device such as this direct-connect modem to communicate with other computers over ordinary telephone lines.

however, take up desk space and usually an electrical socket. The major advantage to an external modem is that you can use the same modem with any computer that has a serial interface. External modems generally cost $10 to $30 more than internal modems of comparable speed.

Other Peripherals

Thanks to serial and parallel interfaces and expansion slots, a wide variety of devices can be attached to most microcomputers. Although we couldn't possibly discuss every type of peripheral device on the market, a few are worth mentioning.

Joysticks

Anybody who's played video games is familiar with the joystick. Fashioned after the control mechanism used in early airplanes, the **joystick** is a vertical lever that can be tilted forward and backward, left and right, and every direction in between (see Figure 26). With computers, joystick movements are used to control a cursor or steer a simulated vehicle. Most computer joysticks also have one or more buttons, often used to fire missiles on the display screen. Although joysticks are mostly used for computer games, they are sometimes used like a mouse.

Trackballs

Basically, a **trackball** is like a mouse turned upside-down. It's a box that contains a protruding ball, often similar to a billiard ball, that can be freely rotated in any direction (see Figure 27). Also like a mouse, a trackball generally has one or more buttons, which are mounted beside or in front of the ball on top of the box.

Figure 26 Joystick
The joystick is an alternate input device often used for computer games.

When first used with microcomputers, trackballs were primarily intended for game control. Increasingly, however, they are being touted as a stationary alternative to the mouse. The Apple Macintosh Portable, for example, comes with a built-in trackball instead of a mouse. A trackball can do everything a mouse can do, yet it takes up less desk space because only the ball is moved, not the whole trackball box. Some optional keyboards on the market even have a trackball built in. Many people find moving a cursor around the screen is easier with a trackball. On the other hand, most people think drawing is easier with a mouse.

Light Pens

A **light pen** is a rod that's used to point at or draw on a computer display screen (see Figure 28). Most light pens have a cord that plugs into the graphics adapter, but some cordless models are also available. The light pen works by detecting

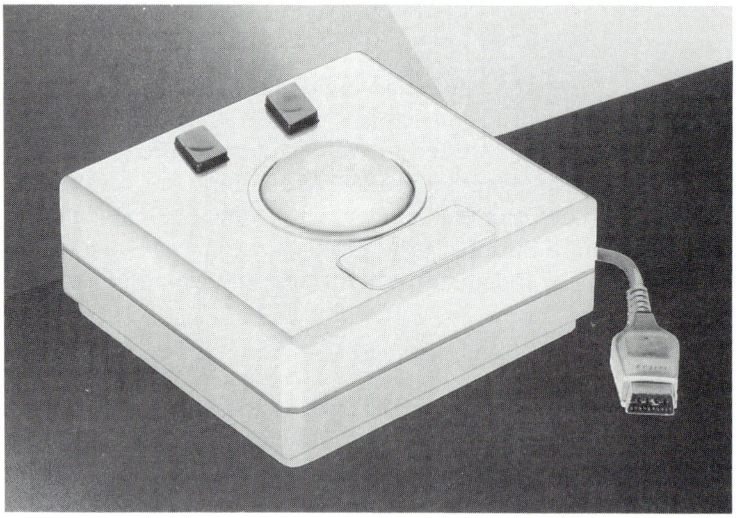

Figure 27 Trackball
The trackball is an alternative to the mouse.

***Figure 28* Light Pen**
A light pen lets you draw and manipulate objects right on the display screen.

where its point is positioned on the screen, then passing this positional data to the computer through the graphics adapter. This information is then handled by computer programs especially designed to work with light pens. Light pens are sometimes used in microcomputer systems that handle order entry in warehouses and in some sophisticated cash registers. They are also used by some computer drawing and design programs.

Touch-Screens

Eliminate the light pen and just use your finger to point, and you have the basic concept of the touch-screen. More precisely, a **touch-screen** is an input device that's built into or fits over a display screen (see Figure 29). It uses infrared light beams or an electrically conductive surface to identify the position of your finger as it touches the screen. Touch-screens are simple to use, but they have several

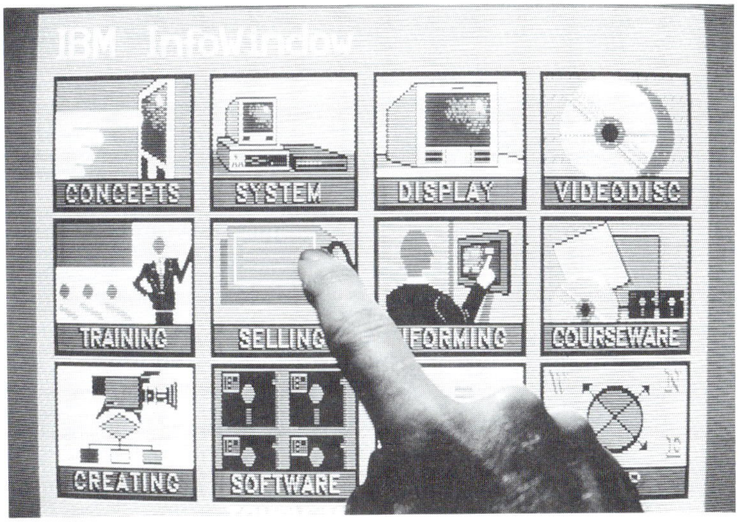

***Figure 29* Touch-Screen**
A touch-screen lets you use your fingers to point to objects on the display.

Figure 30 Graphics Tablet
The graphics tablet is an alternate input device well-suited to drawing and computer-aided design.

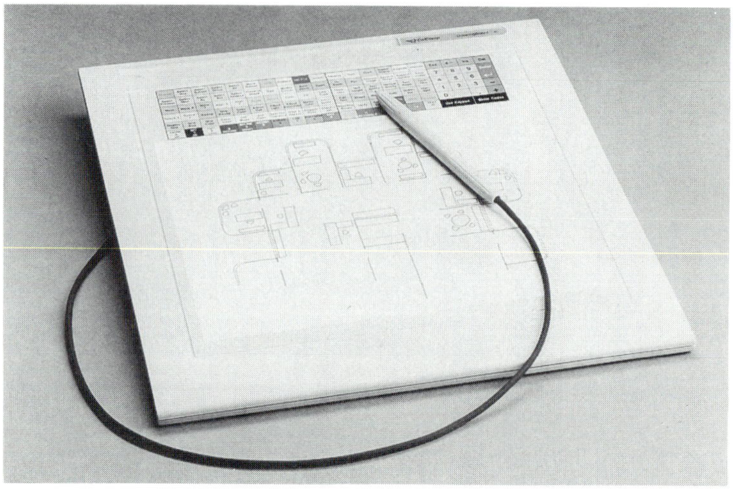

drawbacks. Fingers are, after all, rather wide pointers. So, the number of different positions on a screen that can be distinguished by a pointing finger is somewhat limited. Also, having to lift your arm to point at the screen over and over again can become tiresome. Finally, fingerprints tend to accumulate on touch-screens which increases glare and generally looks messy. Despite these problems, touch-screens are being successfully used in specialized situations, such as in shopping center kiosks, public information displays, museums, and automated teller machines.

Graphics Tablets

A **graphics tablet,** also called a **digitizer,** is a flat surface on which the user draws with a stylus, pen, or some other pointing device (see Figure 30). The tablet senses where it is touched and communicates this positional data to the computer. Some graphics tablets are capable of very high resolutions and can be extremely accurate. Consequently, they are often used in map-making and computer-aided design applications.

Scanners

In many offices, secretaries often must enter previously typed or printed information into computers. In other situations, workers must laboriously enter maps, blueprints, and other figures into computers by hand with graphics tablets. Imagine being able to feed a sheet of paper containing text or graphics into a machine that automatically reads the contents and enters it into the computer for you. A **scanner,** like the one in Figure 31, can do just that. These devices, relative newcomers on the microcomputer scene, are becoming increasingly common. Although full-page scanners are rather expensive ($1000 to $40,000), many organizations and even some individuals find that they save so much time, they are well worth

Figure 31 Scanner
A scanner enables the computer to read text and graphics directly from a source document.

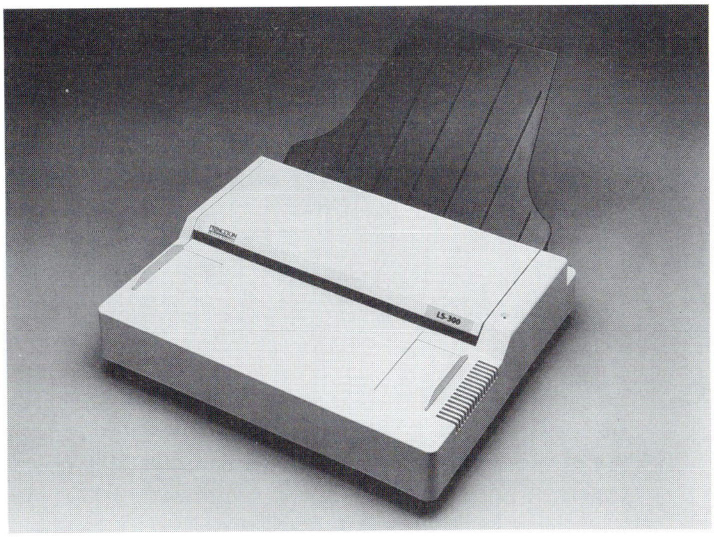

the money. Besides, there are now a number of small, hand-held scanners on the market that perform almost as well as full-page scanners for as little as $200.

Voice Recognition Systems

Why can't you just talk to your computer? After all, this would clearly be the most natural method of communication with computers for most people. Unfortunately, technology is not yet sufficiently advanced to make true conversation with computers possible. Nevertheless, several devices on the market can, in a limited sense, understand some human speech. A **voice recognition system** is an input device that can recognize a finite number of isolated sounds, words, and phrases (see Figure 32). Currently, the most advanced microcomputer voice recognition systems have a maximum vocabulary of about 1000 words. Furthermore, most systems must be "trained" by having each user initially pronounce every word to be recognized. The voice recognition system analyzes each word's sound waveform, encodes this waveform as a series of numbers, and stores these numbers in memory. Subsequently, it recognizes words by comparing their waveforms as they are spoken with the previously stored waveforms. If a match is found, the word is understood. Most manufacturers of voice recognition systems claim an accuracy rate of better than 90 percent. Unless your voice is distorted by a cold, sore throat, or some other affliction, this means that the system should recognize the words you have trained it to understand nine times out of ten. Although voice recognition systems are expensive, have limited vocabularies, and must be trained by each user, they are being used successfully in several unique applications. For example, some are currently being used to help busy factory workers control their assembly lines, to answer simple phone requests automatically, and to help the physically disabled control appliances in their homes.

Figure 32 Voice Recognition System
This diagram illustrates how voice recognition systems work.

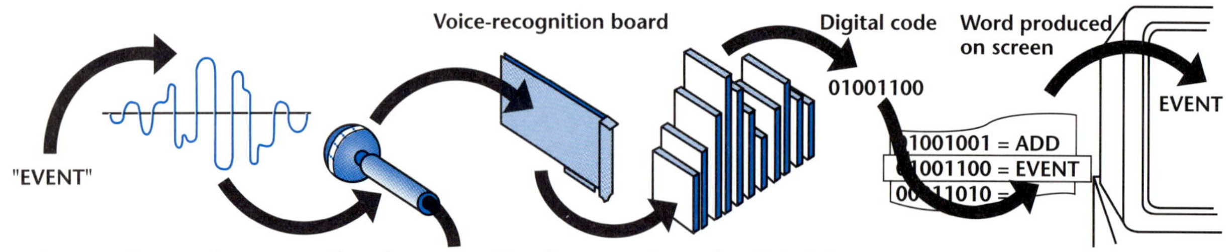

Speech Synthesizers

Making computers talk is quite a bit easier than making them listen. Computer-generated voice output has been possible for quite some time and has even become commonplace. A **speech synthesizer** is a device that either mimics human speech or constructs it out of prerecorded sounds. These devices have been crafted onto integrated circuit chips and are now quite inexpensive. Thanks to this technology, we now have talking cash registers, kitchen appliances, auto-

Real World

Changing Chips

A new generation of computer chips is changing the face of the computer industry.

The new chips, such as Motorola's 68030 and Intel's 80486, may make the microcomputer the dominant force in the computer business. Edward M. Esber, Jr., chief executive of PC software supplier Ashton-Tate, believes microcomputers will become "the core of computing—more important than minis or mainframes." Mainframes have ruled the computer roost for roughly 30 years because of their considerable power.

How can tiny components the size of a fingernail have such a huge impact? Compared with the complex circuitry in larger computers, microprocessor chips have always been considerably cheaper. But they have been less powerful, as well. Now, a new generation of chips has hit the market with astounding impact.

The newest microchips have double the information-processing capacity of their ancestors. This means they can transmit data in 32-bit chunks, the same as Digital Equipment Corp. minicomputers. The main difference is that the new desktop microcomputers using Intel's 80486 chip can cost as little as $3000 and Digital's minicomputers cost $500,000. IBM claims that its PS/2 Model 80 with an 80386 chip, which sells for around $7000, has the processing speed of a 1975 mainframe that cost $3.5 million.

Intel officials speculate that more than 100 computer companies are designing machines that will use the 80486 microchip. They predicted that perhaps 5 million of these computers will be sold annually by 1992.

Source: John W. Verity and Geoff Lewis, "Computers: The New Look," *Business Week*, November 30, 1987, pp. 112–123.

mobiles, vending machines, greeting cards, airport trains, video games, and, of course, computers. Microcomputer speech synthesizers typically plug into a serial port or are built onto an expansion board. They may use a speaker inside the microcomputer or require an external one. Speech synthesizers operate by taking text and translating it into spoken words. One of the most useful applications is a microcomputer-controlled reading machine for the blind that scans printed text and pronounces the words aloud.

Summary

- *The components inside the system unit.* A typical microcomputer system unit contains a chassis, motherboard, memory, power supply, expansion slots, disk drives, and device controllers.
- *The key features that affect a microprocessor's power.* Important features include its register size, data bus size, and speed.
- *The difference between RAM and ROM.* RAM is used for temporary storage, while ROM holds programs and data that never change.
- *Commonly used secondary storage devices.* The most commonly used devices for secondary storage are floppy disk drives, hard disk drives, magnetic tape drives, Bernoulli disk drives, and optical disk drives.
- *The primary input device.* Every microcomputer has a keyboard as its primary input device, but many also have a mouse.
- *The basic types of displays.* Three types of displays are monochrome text monitors, monochrome graphics monitors, and color graphics monitors.
- *How microcomputer systems can be expanded.* Expansion slots, expansion boards, and interfaces make it possible to add a host of optional hardware components to most microcomputers.
- *The basic types of printers.* Among the types of output devices are dot-matrix, daisy-wheel, ink-jet, and laser printers. Plotters are a special type of output device that draws with pens.
- *How computers communicate with modems.* A computer with a modem can transmit and receive programs and data to similarly equipped computers over ordinary telephone lines.
- *Alternate input and output devices.* Other commonly used peripherals include joysticks, trackballs, light pens, touch-screens, graphics tablets, scanners, voice recognition systems, and speech synthesizers.

Key Terms

As an extra review of this chapter, try defining the following terms.

access arm
address
backup
Bernoulli disk drive (Bernoulli Box)
bit
bits per second (bps)
bus
byte
cathode ray tube (CRT)
chassis

color graphics monitor
Compact Disc Read-Only Memory (CD-ROM)
computer graphics
coprocessors
daisy-wheel printer
data bus
device controller
direct access medium
display adapter
dot-matrix printer
draft mode
erasable optical disk drive
expansion board (card, adapter)
expansion slot
external modem (direct-connect modem)
floppy disk drive
game adapter
gigabyte (G)
graphics tablet (digitizer)
hard disk
hard disk drive (fixed disk drive)
head crash
ink-jet printer
integrated circuit chip
interface
internal modem
joystick
kilobyte (K)
laser printer
letter-quality
light pen
liquid crystal display (LCD)
local area network (LAN)
magnetic tape
magnetic tape drive
megabyte (M)
megahertz (MHz)
modem
monochrome graphics monitor
monochrome text monitor
motherboard (system board)
multifunction board
near letter-quality (NLQ)
network adapter
optical disk drive
palette
parallel interface (parallel port)
pixel (pel)
plotter
power supply
primary storage
random access memory (RAM)
read-only memory (ROM)
read-write head
real-time clock
register
resolution
scanner
secondary storage
semiconductor
sequential access medium
serial interface (serial port)
Small Computer System Interface (SCSI)
speech synthesizer
system clock
telecommute
touch-screen
trackball
video mode
voice recognition system
Write Once, Read Many (times) (WORM)

Review Questions

1. Where is the CPU located on many microcomputers?
2. What are the two basic kinds of magnetic disk drives?
3. What type of material is used to make integrated circuit chips?
4. List the three register sizes used by microcomputer microprocessors.
5. How does the size of the data bus affect computer performance?
6. How is the speed of the system clock related to the operation of a microprocessor?
7. What is the function of primary storage in a computer?
8. RAM and ROM are both used to store programs and data. What is the major difference between these two kinds of memory?

9. Why is secondary storage a necessary supplement to primary storage?
10. What is the most common secondary storage medium used with microcomputers?
11. How do hard disk drives differ from floppy disk drives?
12. What is the primary use for magnetic tape drives in microcomputer systems?
13. In what sense do Bernoulli drives combine the advantages of both floppy and hard disk drives?
14. What are the three basic types of optical disk drives used with microcomputers?
15. List some special-purpose keys found on microcomputer keyboards.
16. What are some uses of a mouse?
17. List the three basic types of microcomputer displays.
18. What hardware components make it possible to expand and upgrade most microcomputers?
19. What type of printer uses tightly focused bursts of light to transfer images to paper?
20. Why are modems needed to enable computers to send data over phone lines?

Multiple Choice

1. Which of the following computer components is not usually built onto the motherboard?
   (a) CPU (b) memory
   (c) control circuitry (d) monitor
2. Which of the following register sizes describes the most powerful microprocessor?
   (a) 2-bit (b) 8-bit
   (c) 16-bit (d) 32-bit
3. Which of the following microcomputer components synchronizes the internal operations of the microprocessor and other electronic circuits?
   (a) real-time clock (b) system clock
   (c) chassis (d) ROM
4. Which of the following units represents the largest amount of memory?
   (a) byte (b) kilobyte
   (c) gigabyte (d) megabyte
5. What type of memory chip holds programs and data that are used very frequently, yet can never be changed?
   (a) RAM (b) ROM
   (c) CRT (d) LCD
6. What is the most common form of secondary storage?
   (a) floppy disks (b) magnetic tape
   (c) Bernoulli disks (d) WORM disks
7. What type of disk drive uses circular platters of rigid metal or glass covered with a thin magnetic coating?
   (a) floppy (b) hard
   (c) CD-ROM (d) Bernoulli

8. Which of the following is a sequential access medium?
   (a) floppy disk (b) hard disk
   (c) magnetic tape (d) CD-ROM
9. Which of the following storage media does not allow you to record your own programs and data?
   (a) floppy disk (b) hard disk
   (c) WORM (d) CD-ROM
10. What is the primary input device of every microcomputer?
    (a) keyboard (b) mouse
    (c) trackball (d) display
11. What type of display mechanism is used by most computer screens?
    (a) CRT (b) LCD
    (c) RAM (d) WORM
12. Which of the following terms describes a screen with the sharpest picture?
    (a) no-resolution (b) low-resolution
    (c) medium-resolution (d) high-resolution
13. A multifunction board plugs into a(n)
    (a) monitor. (b) expansion slot.
    (c) serial interface. (d) display adapter.
14. An external modem plugs into a(n)
    (a) display adapter. (b) parallel interface.
    (c) serial interface. (d) expansion slot.
15. What is the most common type of microcomputer printer?
    (a) dot-matrix (b) daisy-wheel
    (c) ink-jet (d) laser

Projects

1. Select a microcomputer system that you have access to at home, school, or work. Read the user manual or talk to someone familiar with that particular system's configuration. Try to answer the following questions about the microcomputer:

   What company makes this computer?
   What model is it?
   What kind of microprocessor does it use?
   What is the speed of the system clock?
   How much ROM does this computer have?
   How much RAM does this computer have?
   What is the maximum RAM it can have?
   How many expansion slots are there?
   What expansion boards are currently installed?
   What kind of floppy disk drive(s) does it use?
   If there is a hard disk, what is its capacity?
   What type of display is used?
   If there is a graphics display, what is its resolution?
   What kind of printer, if any, is connected?

What kind of interfaces does it have?
List any other peripheral devices it has.

2. To get a better idea of how much data can be held in secondary storage, figure out *approximately* how many bytes of information are in a well-known set of encyclopedias. Assume that each character of text requires one byte of storage. How many 360K, 5¼-inch floppies would this encyclopedia take up? How many 800K, 3½-inch floppies? How many megabytes would it require? Would it fit on a single 550-megabyte CD-ROM disk?
3. The length of time it takes to retrieve a piece of data from computer storage is often referred to as *access time*. Frequently, this is expressed in milliseconds, or thousandths of a second. Investigate the typical access times of RAM and ROM, as well as of various secondary storage devices like floppy disks, hard disks, and optical disks. Prepare a table that compares these values.
4. Even if you don't own a computer, you've probably used some kind of keyboard. But have you ever used a mouse? If not, try to experience its use. Perhaps there is an Apple Macintosh computer you can use at home, school, or work. You may be able to try a mouse at a local computer store. After you've tried using one, write a brief report presenting your opinion of this alternate input device. List the advantages and disadvantages of using a mouse versus depending completely on a keyboard. Finally, do you think a trackball would be better than a mouse? In discussing your opinion, describe the situations in which one is superior to the other.

CHAPTER 3

SOFTWARE

In This Chapter

Computer Programs

System Software

- Operating Systems
- Utilities
- Windowing Environments

Programming Languages

- Machine Languages
- Assembly Languages
- High-level Languages
- Fourth Generation Languages

Application Software

- Word Processing
- Spreadsheet
- Data Base Management
- Communications and Networking
- Graphics
- Desktop Publishing
- Other Packages

The User Interface

- Commands
- Prompts
- Static Menus
- Pop-up Menus
- Pull-down Menus
- Graphical User Interfaces

Preview

In the previous chapter, we spent a lot of time discussing the various hardware components of a typical microcomputer system. With all the talk of microprocessors, RAM, ROM, disk drives, monitors, expansion slots, printers, and other devices, you might get the impression that hardware is the most important aspect of a computer. This simply isn't so. You must understand hardware to some extent because it determines the ultimate potential of a computer system. But computer hardware by itself is utterly useless. Software is what makes the computer the indispensable helper it has become in our society. People determine the task and run the software; software operates the hardware. For most computer users, software issues far outweigh hardware concerns. This is why software is the major focus of the rest of this book.

After studying this chapter, you will understand

- how programs tell computers what to do.
- how system software helps you use a computer.
- the major types of programming languages.
- the major types of application software.
- the major types of user interfaces.

Computer Programs

We've already said that a computer *program* is a set of instructions that tells a computer what to do. *Software* is a general term that refers to any single program or group of programs. In contrast with hardware, which is made from physical

Insight

Do I Need to Learn a Programming Language?

Learning a high-level programming language like BASIC, Pascal, or COBOL can take a lot of time and effort. Don't do it unless you have to.

Most people use their computers for word processing or for keeping track of their finances with spreadsheets. Learning to use a word processor is only a little harder than learning to use a typewriter. The spreadsheet is the computer equivalent of the accountant's ruled pad. A simple knowledge of math and elementary algebra is all that you need to use one.

The need to learn a programming language starts to stir when you get into more advanced spreadsheet use. For example, it becomes tedious to type in long and involved command sequences. The Lotus 1-2-3 spreadsheet program lets you use a special form of notation called macros to record these keystroke sequences. That's very simple programming.

Learning a programming language is more important when you are using a data base, since the tasks involved in producing a report or searching a data base for information can become very involved. Most data base systems have some sort of programming language to help with this. You may want to learn more about programming languages if you will be working heavily with data bases.

materials such as metal and plastic, software is constructed solely from knowledge, thinking, planning, and testing. You can't really touch a computer program because it's an expression of the ideas of the people who designed it.

Despite the amazing accomplishments of a well-programmed computer, it's really just a machine. Every computer is only capable of a limited set of simple tasks. Each of these simple tasks is represented by a single instruction, and each instruction is encoded as a number. A computer's **instruction set** consists of all of those simple tasks that it can do when it receives a single instruction. Take the Intel 8088 microprocessor, for example. You may recall that this is the microprocessor used in millions of IBM Personal Computers and similar machines. The 8088 instruction set consists of only about 100 basic instructions. Table 1 shows a few of the more commonly used instructions.

To a computer, programs are just lists of numbers, like the code numbers you see in Table 1. These numbers represent simple instructions that tell the central processing unit what to do with other numbers. Computers can store and manipulate programs just as they do data. In a sense, programs are data too. Computers can be instructed to perform operations on the very numbers that make up other programs. This is the key to the power of the computer. Starting from a very simple set of instructions, more complex operations can be built; then operations can be put together like building blocks to perform abstract tasks. No one need start from scratch because programs can be permanently stored. Every person who uses computers uses some programs written by others. In fact, most people who use computers don't write any programs at all. Some programs control the various hardware components of a computer. Others help people manage their computer systems. Some even help people write other programs. Finally, there are programs that help people with their daily activities, such as writing reports, figuring budgets, and maintaining business accounts. All these different types of programs can be divided into three basic categories: system software, programming languages, and application software.

Table 1 Selected 8088 Instructions

Instruction	Numeric Code	Operation
MOV	139	Copies contents of one register to another
XCHG	147	Exchanges contents of two registers
IN	228	Inputs a byte from some external device
OUT	230	Outputs a byte to some external device
INC	64	Increments (adds 1 to) a register's contents
DEC	72	Decrements (subtracts 1) from a register
ADD	3	Adds the contents of two registers
SUB	43	Subtracts one register's contents from another
MUL	247	Multiplies contents of two registers
CMP	59	Compares the contents of two registers
JZ	116	Jumps to another instruction if result is zero
AND	35	Logically combines contents of two registers
LOOP	226	Repeats one or more instructions
CALL	255	Carries out some other group of instructions
RET	195	Returns when finished with a CALL instruction

System Software

Computer systems are complicated equipment. We've seen that they consist of several sophisticated components: microprocessors, memory chips, circuits, displays, keyboards, disk drives, and printers. All of these devices are controlled by programs designed to accomplish very specific tasks. As we said in Chapter 1, the programs that deal most intimately with a computer's hardware are called *system software*.

System software handles the very basic details of managing a computer's hardware and software resources. Some system software is not obvious to the user, such as the programs that interpret keypresses or form characters on the display screen. The user directly invokes other programs to perform "housekeeping" activities, such as erasing a disk or changing a printer from draft mode to near-letter-quality mode. Still other system software is essential to people who develop application programs, allowing them to both write and test the programs. Finally, other system software helps people who aren't necessarily computer experts manage and use their software.

As you can see, a wide variety of programs can be called system software. Although the categories overlap somewhat, there are several different types of system software: operating systems, utilities, and alternative operating environments.

Operating Systems

An **operating system** is a set of programs that controls a computer's hardware and manages the use of software. It is the heart and soul of a computer. Besides providing valuable services for other software, it's the main channel through which you tell the computer what to do. An operating system also enables the various parts of a computer to work together. Every general-purpose computer can be run by at least one operating system. This essential software basically determines what you can accomplish with a particular computer and how easy that computer is to use.

Turn on your computer and the operating system is automatically brought into action (see Figure 1). It tests and sets up various hardware components and then waits for your command. Do you want to use your word processing program? Just enter the name of your program or perhaps select its symbol with a mouse-controlled pointer. The operating system interprets your command, loads the word processing program from disk into primary storage, and instructs the CPU to run the program. From that point, until you're done with the word processor, the operating system silently works in the background, helping the word processor use hardware devices and other software. When you're finished with your word processing program, control is returned to the operating system. Again, it patiently waits to help you with some other task. Constantly, tirelessly, the operating system works to bridge the gaps between you and your software, and between your software and the computer hardware. Under normal circumstances, the operating system ceases its chores only when the computer is turned off.

Besides its work with other programs, the operating system provides a set of services that you can use directly to help with certain frequently performed activities. For example, operating systems typically include programs that let you set up new floppy disks, copy programs and data, erase programs and data, display information on your screen, send information to your printer, reset the

Figure 1 The Operating System
Turn on the computer and the operating system of the Apple Macintosh automatically tests various hardware components and then waits for you to tell it what programs you want to run.

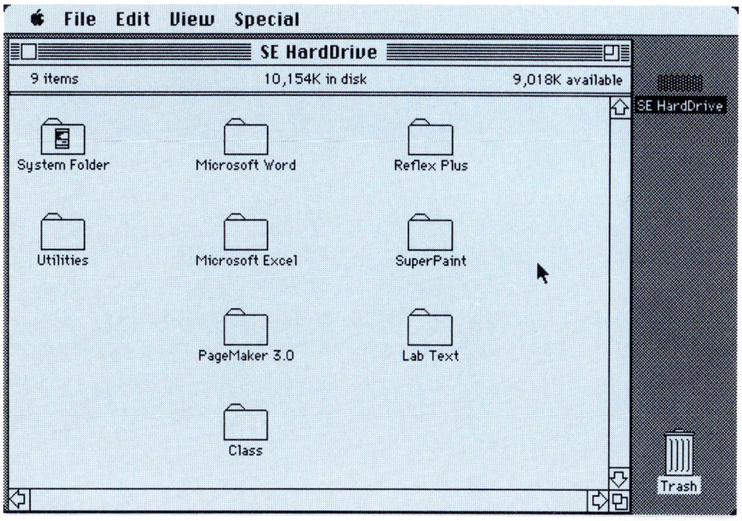

real-time clock, indicate which disk drive to use, organize your secondary storage, and specify certain hardware settings. To a large extent, the type of work you do with your computer determines how much you will directly interact with the operating system. Some users, especially novices, tend to use operating system services as little as possible. They try to get by with functions that are built into the programs they use. For instance, many word processing programs let you copy, delete, and print documents without having to exit and return to the operating system. Other users, especially computer experts, try to take full advantage of the services provided by the operating system. They can almost tell you what every command does and how you might use it. Most people find that they are somewhere between these two extremes. Every computer user must interact with the operating system to some extent, so learning a few of the basics can help you work much more efficiently. We will have more to say about the specifics of operating systems and present some examples of microcomputer operating systems in Chapter 4 and Part 2 of this book.

Utilities

Despite all the services operating systems provide, computer users always seem to need more programs to help them manage their hardware and software resources. A **utility** is a program that fills some very specific need. Such programs tend to be fairly small and quite limited in scope. Utilities perform all kinds of different but very useful tasks. In one sense, utility programs are like accessories to operating systems. They fill in gaps by doing little jobs not easily accomplished by the operating system's services. Some utility programs come packaged with operating systems, but many are offered by other software producers. Quite often, a programmer develops a utility for his or her own use and offers it free or at a very nominal cost to others. If the utility becomes popular, it might even be the basis for a new software company.

Utility programs, by their very nature, can be somewhat difficult to classify. There are so many different types of utilities that it might seem strange to group them together. Often, if a program performs one or more very specific tasks and doesn't fit into any other particular category, it's called a utility.

Some utilities are designed to help average users in commonly encountered situations. For example, the operating system used with most IBM microcomputers has no provision for letting you recover programs and data you've accidentally erased. As a result, several companies offer programs that, in many cases, can help users who find themselves in such predicaments. Other utility programs enhance the capabilities of certain hardware devices. Some printer utilities, for example, let you change print modes, print mailing labels and envelopes, and even print very wide tables so that they appear sideways across several pages. Keyboard enhancement utilities allow you to customize the way your keyboard works by redefining keys and assigning several keystrokes to certain control and function keys. Some utility programs provide desktop accessories like simulated calculators, calendars, notepads, appointment books, and telephone books (see Figure 2). Hardware-related utilities help you diagnose potential problems, as well as maintain, adjust, and even repair devices such as disk drives, displays, and printers. Finally, a whole group of utilities is designed to assist programmers in their development of software. These utilities compare programs, sort and merge programs, help isolate and correct errors, cross reference memory locations, and manage updates of new program versions. In Chapter 20, we'll have more to say about some of the most popular types of utility programs.

Figure 2 Utility Program
SideKick is a popular utility program that provides various desktop accessories, including a calculator, calendar, and notepad.

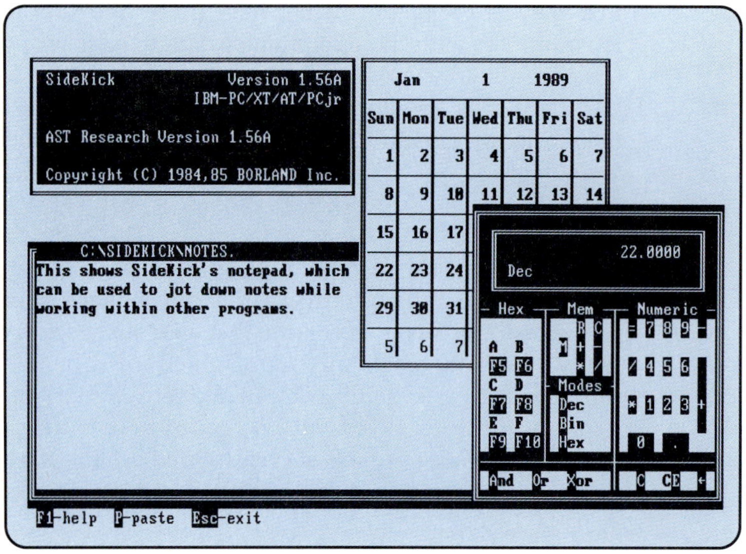

Windowing Environments

Even with extra utilities and the ability to write additional programs, some operating systems still leave much to be desired. Most people find that operating systems such as that of the Apple Macintosh are visually pleasing, intuitively understandable, and easy to use. Other operating systems, such as that of the original IBM Personal Computer and compatible machines, seem inadequate to some people by comparison. So, a few software developers have come up with windowing environments that work along with such operating systems.

A **windowing environment,** sometimes called an **alternate operating environment,** is a type of system software that surrounds a basic operating system with a shell that displays a simulated desktop (see Figure 3). This desktop, which appears on the display screen, contains menus and enclosed boxes, called *windows,* that pop up and allow you to select the programs that you want to run. You can even execute several programs seemingly at the same time. These windowing programs are designed to improve the way the operating system interacts with the user, while at the same time give the user more power to do several tasks at once. Basically, windowing environments try to make rather difficult operating systems easier to use. We'll have more to say about windows later in this chapter when we talk about the user interface, and we'll discuss windowing environments in Chapter 20.

Programming Languages

A language, as you know, is a means of communicating. People use spoken and written languages to convey ideas, feelings, and requests to one another. As we said in Chapter 1, a computer *programming language* is a set of symbols and rules

Figure 3 Windowing Environment
Microsoft Windows is a popular windowing environment for IBM-compatible microcomputers.

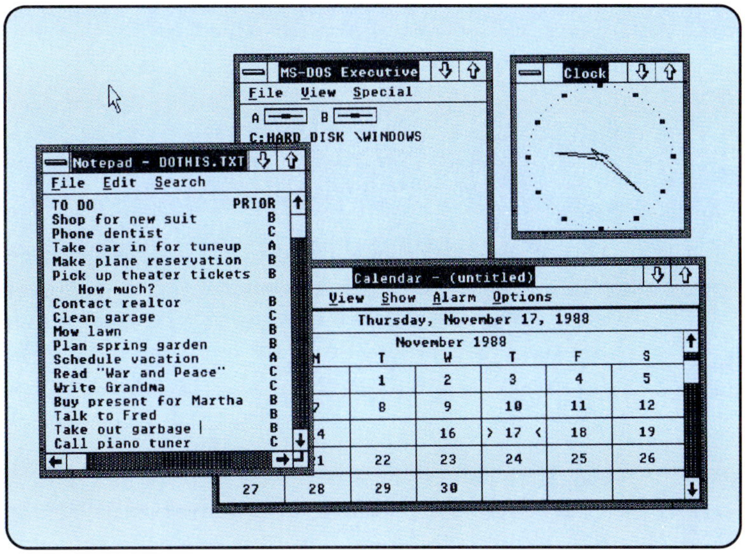

used to direct the operations of a computer. As such, programming languages are a very limited, yet precise form of communication. You can't write a love sonnet in a programming language, but you can use a programming language to write a word processing program.

As with human languages, dozens of computer programming languages are in common use. Each one was primarily designed to solve certain kinds of problems. The purpose of every programming language, however, is to create programs that direct the operations of a computer. So, they all have certain types of instructions in common. Although instructions for the computer may be expressed in vastly different ways, all programming languages, in general, perform the following tasks:

- *Input and Output.* These instructions tell the computer to get data from the user or some input device and to present information on a display screen or printer.
- *Calculation.* These instructions direct the computer to perform mathematical operations such as addition, subtraction, multiplication, and division.
- *Comparison.* These instructions tell the computer to examine a number to see if it's less than, greater than, or equal to another number.
- *Data Movement, Storage, and Retrieval.* These instructions direct the computer's use of primary and secondary storage.
- *Transfer of Control.* The normal sequence of computer operation is to execute program instructions in order, one after another. Transfer of control instructions tell the computer to deviate from this sequential processing. So, the computer can be instructed to jump (or *branch*) back to previous instructions or ahead to skip instructions. These are perhaps the most powerful types of instructions because they enable computers to perform different operations given different input. They also let computers repeat sequences of instructions by jumping back and *looping* through those instructions again and again.

Although there are many different programming languages, the most common microcomputer languages can be put into one of four categories. These categories can be ranked by their relative level of abstraction. In other words, low-level languages are not at all abstract because they are similar to the simple numeric codes all computers ultimately use as instructions. High-level languages are much more abstract because they're closer to the languages people use, such as English. Going from lowest to highest, the microcomputer programming language classifications are: machine languages, assembly languages, high-level languages, and fourth generation languages.

Machine Languages

The only programming language that can be directly used by a particular computer is its own machine language. A **machine language** program consists of binary numbers that represent the CPU instructions, memory addresses, and data needed to solve a particular problem. So, every machine language is just numbers expressed in binary form. The exact numbers and their arrangement, however, generally differ from one computer model to the next. For example, the machine language of IBM Personal Computers is quite different from the machine language of Apple Macintosh computers. Both machine languages are just binary numbers, but a program in the IBM Personal Computer machine language would not work correctly, if at all, on an Apple Macintosh.

Machine language instructions are basically composed of two parts. The first part is called the **operation code** or **opcode** because it's a numeric code for the operation to be performed. You've already seen examples of some opcodes in decimal form in Table 1. In microcomputers, opcodes are basically microprocessor instructions in binary number form. The second part of a machine language instruction is called the **operand,** or the number on which the operation is to be performed. An operand may be a piece of data or a memory address that specifies the location of a piece of data. For example, the following two binary numbers make up a machine language instruction for computers that use the Intel 8088 family of microprocessors:

```
00000101 00001101
  ADD       13 (in binary)
```

This instruction tells the computer to add 13 to the number currently in a special register known as the accumulator.

In the very early days of computers, all programming was done with machine languages. Every instruction, memory location, and data value had to be specified in strings of zeros and ones. This made machine language programming exceedingly tedious, time-consuming, and error-prone. Although computers work perfectly well with binary numbers, people aren't particularly happy, efficient, or accurate when they have to write zeros and ones all day. Consequently, other programming languages have since been developed that are much easier for people to use. Now people write programs using these more abstract languages, enter them into the computer, and run a program that translates the more abstract language into machine language.

No one programs directly in machine languages anymore. It's important to realize, however, that no matter which language is used, programs somehow must be translated into machine language before they can be executed by a computer.

Assembly Languages

The next level up from machine languages are assembly languages. An **assembly language** substitutes meaningful abbreviations for the numerically coded instructions of a machine language. You can see some examples of these easy-to-remember abbreviations, called **mnemonics,** in Table 1. Even the relatively simple concept of using mnemonics such as ADD instead of 00000101 to represent computer operations makes assembly languages vastly superior to machine languages. In addition to mnemonic abbreviations for CPU instructions, most assembly languages also allow the use of words to represent memory addresses and data values. This **symbolic addressing** lets a programmer call a memory location TOTAL, for example, instead of some meaningless numeric address such as 01001010. Symbolic addressing enables programmers to name and use memory locations like variables in algebraic equations. Furthermore, constant data values can also be named to lend even more meaning to programs. For instance, in several places a program might compare input values against a maximum value to make sure that no outrageous data is entered. Naming that value MAXIMUM instead of expressing it as a number helps make the program easier to understand, check for errors, and update if necessary. Finally, assembly languages generally allow programmers to express numbers in bases other than base two. More familiar or convenient number systems such as decimal (base 10), octal (base 8), and hexadecimal (base 16) can also be used. All of these factors make assembly languages much easier to use than machine languages for programming computers.

Figure 4 shows a very simple assembly language program for IBM microcomputers. Like machine languages, assembly languages are specific to particular types of computers. So, this assembly language program won't run on an Apple Macintosh computer. Another similarity between machine and assembly languages is that individual instructions aren't very powerful. In fact, there is generally a one-to-one correspondence between machine language and assembly language instructions. Assembly language is primarily a more convenient way of expressing machine language. Because each individual instruction has a very specific and limited function, it usually takes many, many instructions to get the computer to perform even the simplest tasks.

Unlike machine languages, assembly languages must be translated before they can direct computer operations. After a program is written in assembly language, it's run through a special program called an **assembler** that translates assembly language instructions into the binary numbers of machine language. Software in assembly language (or any higher-level language) prior to this translation process is often called **source code.** Once the program has been converted to machine language, it may be referred to as **object code.**

As we said, assembly language is a definite improvement over machine language, but it still requires manipulating very low-level computer operations. A good deal of knowledge concerning the inner workings of a particular computer is needed in order to write assembly language programs. The process of developing software with assembly language remains fairly tedious, time-consuming, and error-prone. Nevertheless, assembly language programming is often worth the extra effort in some special situations. Expert programmers who must deal with the unique characteristics of a particular computer usually work in assembly language. Because assembly languages afford a great deal of control over individual computer operations, they are often used for programs that must be extremely fast, efficient, or compact. For these reasons, assembly languages are frequently used to develop system software such as operating systems, utilities, and programming language translators.

High-level Languages

The two main disadvantages of assembly languages are that they are difficult even for experts to use and they are machine-specific. Although assembly languages have their uses, it became apparent that another type of programming language would be needed to help more people develop complex computer software. High-level languages were devised to make programs easier to write and easier to adapt to different computers. A **high-level language** is an abstract programming language that facilitates the expression of complex data processing operations. Such languages are often called *procedure-oriented* or *problem-oriented* because they allow programmers to concentrate on the task to be performed rather than worry about the specific details of how their particular computers operate. Because individual high-level language instructions may correspond to many machine language instructions, powerful programs are much easier to develop. Complex operations can often be expressed in just a few high-level language statements.

Like assembly language programs, high-level language programs must be translated into machine language before they can be run by a computer. Nevertheless, high-level languages are generally *machine-independent.* This means that a program written in a high-level language can easily be adapted to any computer that has the applicable translator program. There are two basic types of translators: compilers and interpreters.

Figure 4 Assembly Language Program
This simple assembly language program displays a short message on the screen.

```
;*****************************************************************************
;  HELLO Program
;
;  This program writes the message "Hello There!" to the display screen at
;  the current cursor location.
;
;  Author:  Ernest Colantonio              Computer:  IBM Personal Computer
;  Date:    September 25, 1990             Language:  IBM 8088 Macro Assembler
;
;*****************************************************************************
;-----------------------------------------------------------------------------
stack           SEGMENT PARA STACK 'stack'          ; Set up stack area.
                DB      256 DUP (0)                 ; Reserve 256 bytes.
stack           ENDS
;-----------------------------------------------------------------------------
data            SEGMENT PARA PUBLIC 'data'          ; Set up data area.
message         DB      'Hello There!'              ; Define message bytes.
n_characters    EQU     12                          ; Number of characters.
data            ENDS
;-----------------------------------------------------------------------------
code            SEGMENT PARA PUBLIC 'code'          ; Set up code area.
                ASSUME CS:code, SS:stack, DS:data   ; Associate segment registers.

program         PROC    FAR                         ; Program procedure.

start:          PUSH    DS                          ; Initialize stack for
                MOV     AX,0                        ;   return to
                PUSH    AX                          ;   operating system.

                MOV     AX,data                     ; Initialize
                MOV     DS,AX                       ;   the data registers.

                LEA     SI,message                  ; Load message address.
                MOV     CX,n_characters             ; Load number of characters.

next_character: MOV     AH,2                        ; Load display output code.
                MOV     DL,[SI]                     ; Load character to display.
                INT     33                          ; Operating system service.
                INC     SI                          ; Increment character pointer.
                LOOP    next_character              ; Do the next character.

                RET                                 ; Return from procedure.
program         ENDP                                ; End of procedure.

code            ENDS                                ; End of code area.
;-----------------------------------------------------------------------------
                END     start                       ; End of program.
;*****************************************************************************
```

Most high-level languages are translated into machine language by special programs called compilers. A **compiler** is like an assembler, except it translates a particular high-level language instead of an assembly language. Compilers and assemblers translate an entire program all at once, producing a complete machine language program. Another type of high-level language translator, called an **interpreter,** works a little differently. An interpreter translates and runs one program instruction at a time as it's entered into the computer. This interactive environment allows a programmer to test ideas or modify programs and see the results almost instantly. Interpreters often make programming easier and hasten the software development process, but interpreted programs generally run slower than compiled programs once they're finished. Some high-level languages have both compilers and interpreters available for program translation.

High-level languages offer many advantages over assembly languages. In general, high-level languages are much easier to learn and use. Instructions are expressed in words and mathematical symbols, making high-level languages more understandable than assembly languages. Consequently, it's easier to write, correct, and revise programs in high-level languages. Since programmers can ignore most machine-specific details, they can concentrate on problem solving. Thanks to their greater degree of abstraction, high-level languages are much better suited than assembly languages to the development of large, complex programs. Programming errors are easier to avoid when you work with high-level languages, and easier to find and correct when they do occur. Finally, because high-level languages are machine-independent, programs can be used on different types of computers without having to be completely rewritten in different assembly languages. For these reasons, most people use high-level languages instead of assembly languages to program computers.

Many high-level languages are used on microcomputers, but a few clearly stand out as the most popular. These commonly used microcomputer programming languages are BASIC, Pascal, C, FORTRAN, COBOL, and Ada.

BASIC **BASIC,** an acronym for Beginners' All-purpose Symbolic Instruction Code, was developed by Dr. John Kemeny and Dr. Thomas Kurtz at Dartmouth College in 1965. It was originally designed as a simple interactive language to teach students about computer programming. Although BASIC was first used on large multiuser computers, it has become the most popular programming language for microcomputers. In fact, BASIC was the first high-level programming language to be adapted for use on microcomputers. William Gates and Paul Allen developed a version of BASIC in 1975 to run on the first commercially available microcomputer, the Altair 8800. With this product, Gates and Allen founded Microsoft Corporation, which has become perhaps the single most important microcomputer software company in the world.

BASIC is a simple language that most people find easy to learn and easy to use. Although BASIC compilers are commonly available, most versions of this language are translated by interpreters. Because BASIC is so simple, it's extremely well suited for use on small computers. BASIC is often included on a disk along with the other system software when you purchase a microcomputer. Some microcomputers, like those from IBM, even have a simple version of BASIC embedded in a ROM chip. Microcomputer users who decide that they want to learn a programming language usually wind up choosing BASIC. Figure 5 shows an example BASIC program.

Pascal **Pascal** is a modern programming language named in honor of the seventeenth-century French philosopher and mathematician Blaise Pascal. It was developed by Swiss computer scientist Niklaus Wirth. Introduced in 1971, Pascal

Figure 5 BASIC Program
This simple BASIC language program displays a table of squares and square roots of the numbers 1 through 20.
(a) Source code of the program.

```
010 REM ************************************************************************
020 REM  SQUARE Program
030 REM
040 REM  This program prints a table of the squares and square roots of the
050 REM  numbers from 1 to 20.
060 REM
070 REM   Author:  Ernest Colantonio          Computer:  IBM Personal Computer
080 REM   Date:    September 25, 1990         Language:  IBM BASIC
090 REM
100 REM ************************************************************************
110 LPRINT " N          N Squared      Square Root of N"
120 LPRINT "==========================================="
130 FOR N = 1 TO 20
140    LPRINT N, N*N, SQR (N)
150    NEXT N
160 END
999 REM ************************************************************************
```

(b) Printed output of the program.

```
N           N Squared       Square Root of N
===========================================
1           1               1
2           4               1.414214
3           9               1.732051
4           16              2
5           25              2.236068
6           36              2.44949
7           49              2.645751
8           64              2.828427
9           81              3
10          100             3.162278
11          121             3.316625
12          144             3.464102
13          169             3.605551
14          196             3.741657
15          225             3.872984
16          256             4
17          289             4.123106
18          324             4.242641
19          361             4.358899
20          400             4.472136
```

was originally intended as a general-purpose, high-level language for teaching principles of good programming design. Simplicity, elegance, and structure made Pascal immediately popular with computer scientists and students, scientific programmers, and microcomputer users. Although not quite as simple as BASIC, Pascal is a well-designed language that is straightforward and fairly easy to learn. Furthermore, it imposes rules that encourage sound programming habits. Pascal has become an inexpensive, compact, yet powerful alternative to BASIC for small computers.

C C is a concise, yet powerful, programming language originally developed at Bell Laboratories by Dennis Ritchie in 1972. Similar in some ways to Pascal, C was intended as an alternative to assembly languages for the development of system software. It can perform many low-level operations normally achievable only with assembly languages. C has become popular with more expert microcomputer programmers who use it to develop software that's compact, efficient, and fast. Consequently, C is now considered the language of choice for programmers who develop system and application software.

FORTRAN **FORTRAN,** a contraction of FORmula TRANslator, was one of the very first high-level computer programming languages. Developed by IBM and introduced in 1957, FORTRAN was designed to fulfill the computational needs of scientists, engineers, and mathematicians. It originally ran on large computer systems but was adapted for use on microcomputers when they became widespread. Because of its facility at expressing complex computations, FORTRAN is still the most widely used programming language in the scientific community.

COBOL **COBOL,** which stands for COmmon Business Oriented Language, is also a relatively old programming language. It was introduced in 1960, after having been developed by the Conference On DAta SYstems Languages (CODASYL), a committee of U.S. government and industry representatives called together by the Department of Defense. COBOL was designed especially for business data processing. Because its use was greatly encouraged by the U.S. government, COBOL has been extensively applied throughout business and industry. It's probably still the single most widely known and used computer language in the world. When businesses started acquiring microcomputers in large numbers, COBOL was inevitably adapted so that existing software could still be used.

Ada **Ada** is a relatively new high-level programming language, first introduced in 1980. It was named for Countess Augusta Ada Lovelace, a mathematician considered to be the first computer programmer. In 1842, she described how to program Charles Babbage's Analytical Engine, a general-purpose, mechanical computer designed in 1833 but never built. The programming language Ada was commissioned by the U.S. Department of Defense, the world's largest software consumer. Similar in some ways to Pascal, Ada is a powerful, comprehensive language applicable to a wide range of problems. It is now used on all kinds of computers, by all kinds of organizations (not just the Department of Defense).

Fourth Generation Languages

Fourth generation languages or **4GLs** are the most abstract type of programming language. They are also known as *application generators, very high-level languages,* and *nonprocedural languages.* Fourth generation languages are designed to make it as easy as possible for users to tell the computer what to do. They eliminate many of the strict rules characteristic of most high-level programming languages. With a fourth generation language, the user typically concentrates on specifying the necessary input and the desired output instead of giving the computer explicit procedural instructions on how to convert input to output.

Some fourth generation languages are like human languages, such as English, but with very limited vocabularies. Others are like traditional high-level programming languages, such as Pascal, but have fewer rules. Still others guide you through the entire software development process and let you easily design your own data files, menus, output screens, and printed reports. Figure 6, for example, shows Clarion Professional Developer, a popular application generator for IBM-compatible microcomputers.

Fourth generation languages are becoming more popular as computer hardware and software systems become more sophisticated. They offer many advantages, especially to users who aren't trained as programmers. Even professional programmers often find fourth generation languages easier to use than traditional high-level programming languages. One particularly important advantage of fourth generation languages is that they can often significantly reduce the time it takes to develop new application software. In some cases, reducing development time can be more important than any other consideration. Some industry experts predict that fourth generation languages will gradually replace conventional high-level programming languages as tools for software development.

For now, however, there are still some disadvantages to fourth generation languages. Most of them are proprietary systems, developed and sold by a single company for a particular type of computer. This means that there is little industry-wide standardization. No fourth generation language has achieved the popularity and versatility of high-level languages such as BASIC and Pascal. Furthermore, fourth generation languages are typically not suitable for the

Figure 6 Application Generator
The main menu of CLARION Professional Developer, a popular application generator for IBM-compatible microcomputers.

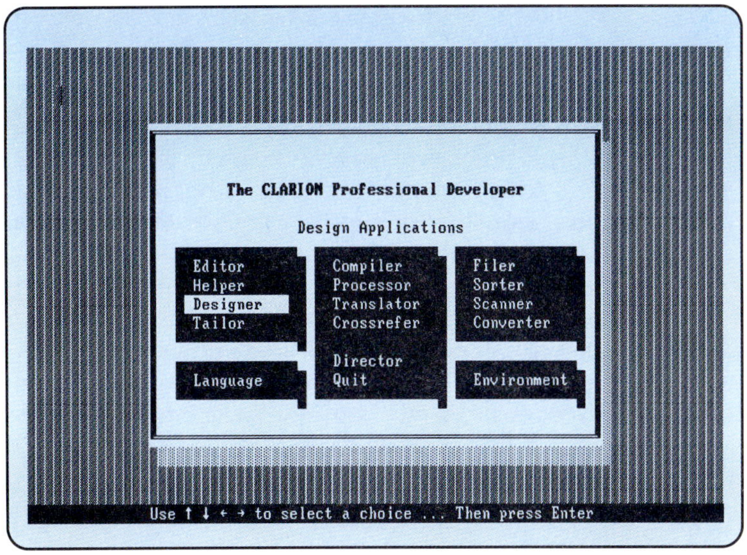

development of system software. In many cases, application programs created with fourth generation languages run slower and use more memory than equivalent programs written in high-level languages. Fourth generation languages are often more expensive and require more memory and disk space than high-level language compilers. Finally, high-level languages are still widely used to develop the great majority of application packages. This means that most programmers and many users are already familiar with conventional high-level languages. They may be hesitant to learn a fourth generation language, even if it would ultimately prove easier to use and cut software development time.

Application Software

System software deals with the management and effective use of a computer's hardware and software resources. The tasks performed by system software are quite specific and somewhat incidental to what most people really want their computers to do. *Application software* puts computers to practical use. These programs, sometimes called *application packages,* are designed to help people do all kinds of workaday jobs such as writing letters and planning budgets. Application software has been central to the computer revolution. By making computers work for people who perhaps aren't programmers themselves, application packages have become the primary reason why most individuals, businesses, and organizations purchase computers.

Application software is generally bought separately when the computer is purchased. Since the advent of microcomputers, the number of companies developing application software has increased dramatically. Consequently, literally thousands of different programs are on the market. One way to classify application software is by what it does. Three categories of microcomputer software stand out as clearly the most prevalent: word processing, spreadsheet, and data base management. In addition, communications and networking, graphics, desktop publishing, and some other packages are also commonly used with microcomputers.

Word Processing

Word processing packages are perhaps the most popular of all types of application software (see Figure 7). It's been estimated that more than 90% of all microcomputer owners have at least one word processing program. Simply stated, a word processing package helps you enter, store, modify, format, copy, and print text. Such software gives a microcomputer and printer the power to do much more than an ordinary typewriter. Many of the tedious and time-consuming tasks associated with typing can be done automatically by word processing packages. For example, most word processors can start a new line when you reach the margin, start a new page when you reach the bottom of a page, center titles, copy sections of text, alter line spacing, and even check for spelling errors. You can type, correct, and format your entire document on the computer display screen. Once you're satisfied that everything looks just right, you can print out any number of perfect copies on paper. Not only do word processors make it easy to initially enter and print text, they allow you to store and update documents as well. We'll have more to say about this amazing tool in Part 3 of this book.

Figure 7 Word Processing Package
This screen shows WordPerfect 5.0 for IBM-compatible microcomputers being used to create a letter.

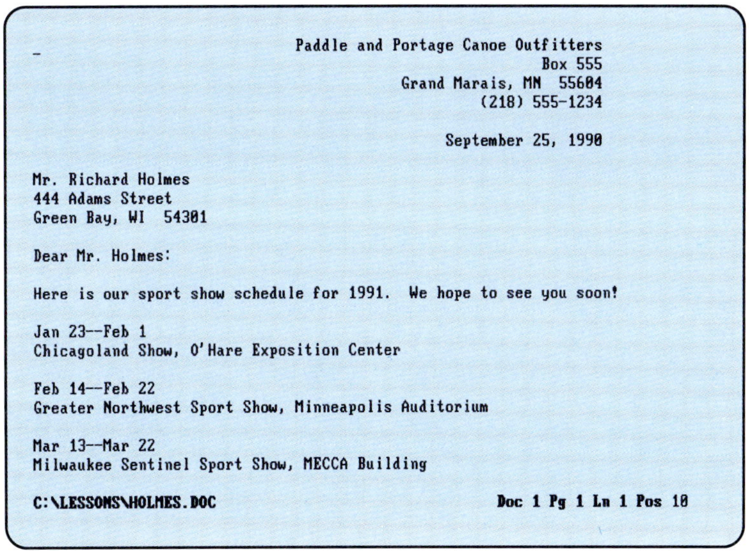

Paddle and Portage Canoe Outfitters
Box 555
Grand Marais, MN 55604
(218) 555-1234

September 25, 1990

Mr. Richard Holmes
444 Adams Street
Green Bay, WI 54301

Dear Mr. Holmes:

Here is our sport show schedule for 1991. We hope to see you soon!

Jan 23--Feb 1
Chicagoland Show, O'Hare Exposition Center

Feb 14--Feb 22
Greater Northwest Sport Show, Minneapolis Auditorium

Mar 13--Mar 22
Milwaukee Sentinel Sport Show, MECCA Building

C:\LESSONS\HOLMES.DOC Doc 1 Pg 1 Ln 1 Pos 10

Spreadsheet

Spreadsheet packages are a relatively new type of application software initially designed especially for microcomputers. In 1978, an MIT graduate named Dan Bricklin, who was enrolled in Harvard Business School, felt that he was spending too much time laboring over the financial worksheets required for his accounting classes. **Worksheets,** also called **spreadsheets,** are basically tables of rows and columns of numerical data. Bricklin had only two choices at the time: perform the many worksheet computations with a pocket calculator, or use the school's mainframe computer. Neither of these alternatives particularly suited Bricklin. Because he couldn't store intermediate results except by writing them down, using a pocket calculator would be too time-consuming and error prone. Gaining access to and programming the school's mainframe would be inconvenient. So Bricklin devised a microcomputer program that could easily manipulate tables of numbers. He and fellow MIT alumni Bob Frankston and Daniel Flystra formed a company called Software Arts in 1979. They sold the first spreadsheet program, called VisiCalc (short for Visible Calculator), which ran on Apple microcomputers. Although VisiCalc is no longer sold, it paved the way for a whole new class of microcomputer software.

The spreadsheet program is an extremely flexible tool that can be applied to a wide range of common problems (see Figure 8). Adept at manipulating tables of numbers, spreadsheet software is most often used to handle typical business accounting chores such as cash flow projections, depreciation calculations, balance sheets, and income statements. Spreadsheet programs also can be used to monitor investments, balance checkbooks, and work out home budgets. One of their most valuable features is that they allow users to ask "what if" questions about their data. This is possible because spreadsheet programs can automatically recalculate all entries whenever any single figure is changed. Once a worksheet

Figure 8 ***Spreadsheet Program***
This screen shows Lotus 1-2-3 Release 2.2 being used to create a budget.

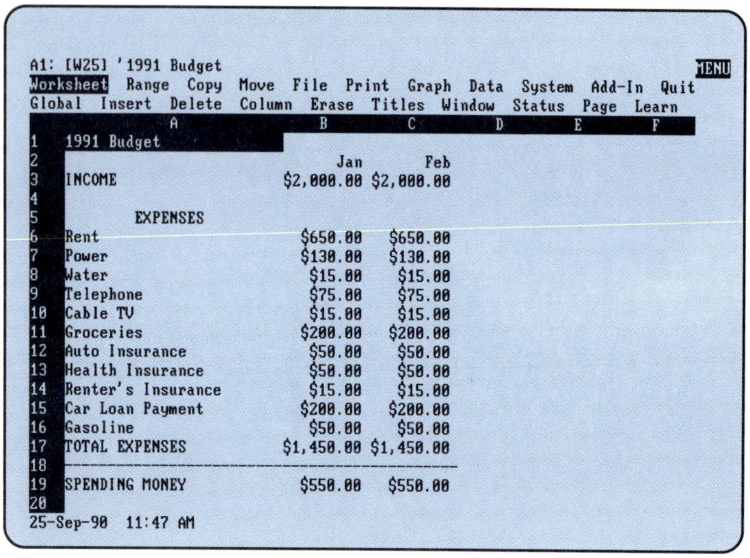

has been set up, it's easy to try different values just to see what the results would be. The potential uses of spreadsheet programs are almost endless. In addition to the applications we've already mentioned, spreadsheet programs also have been used to create conversion tables, statistical analyses, financial models, and even games. Part 4 will cover spreadsheet packages in more detail.

Data Base Management

One of the major jobs we delegate to computers is that of managing huge quantities of data. Sometimes we don't need computers to actually compute anything—just store, sort, retrieve, print, or in some manner manipulate information. Large computers were doing this long before microcomputers came on the scene. Once microcomputers became so popular, however, it was only natural that they also be put to work managing data bases.

A *data base* is an organized collection of one or more files of interrelated data. A **file** is simply a mass of individual data items kept together in secondary storage. Computer files may contain programs, numerical data, or text. In general, data bases are made up of files containing numbers and text compiled for some specific purpose. For example, data bases are often used to store mailing lists, phone numbers, personnel files, customer accounts, credit records, inventories, bibliographies, and even entire reference works. *Data base management packages* enable people to create, add to, delete from, update, sort, rearrange, select from, print out, and otherwise administer data files (see Figure 9). We'll have more to say about these sophisticated information storage and retrieval systems in Part 5.

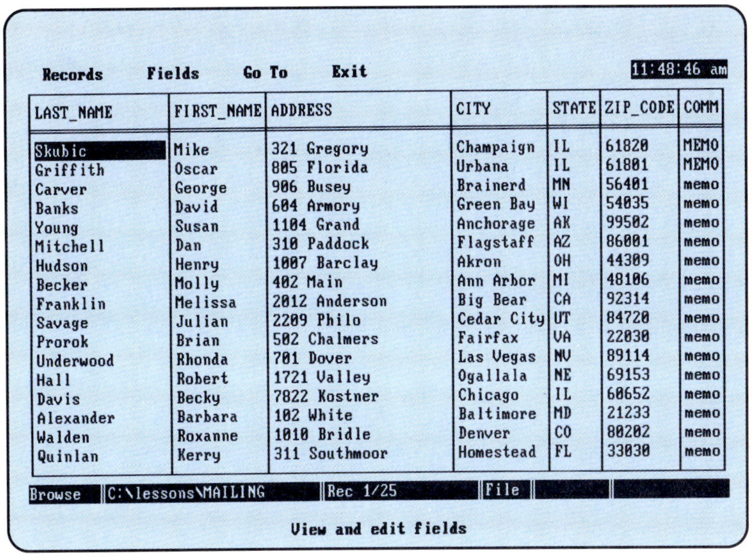

Figure 9 Data Base Management Package
Here dBASE IV is being used to maintain a mailing list.

Communications and Networking

In the previous chapter we saw how modems enable microcomputers to transmit and receive data over telephone lines. Communications software is just as important as hardware in the process of exchanging data and accessing remote computers. Communications packages perform essential tasks such as coordinating the manner and speed in which data are transmitted and received, dialing phone numbers, capturing incoming data in secondary storage, and sending messages, files, and commands over transmission lines (see Figure 10).

As we briefly mentioned in Chapter 2, a local area network (LAN) is an arrangement that connects several microcomputers and peripherals together, usually in the same building or in nearby buildings. This allows people to easily exchange data, share files, and take turns using expensive peripherals like laser printers and high-capacity hard disks. Along with special hardware like network adapters and cables, LANs also require network software to control the flow of data and manage the use of peripheral devices. Communications and networking are two far-reaching microcomputer applications about which we'll have more to say in Chapter 17.

Graphics

Graphics packages let users create pictures with their computers. (You know what they say about a picture being worth a thousand words.) Computer-generated graphics can transform dull data into eye-catching, informative images. Several different types of graphics application packages are available for microcomputers. Some are used to produce graphs, charts, maps, simulated slide shows, and animated presentations. Others are freehand painting and drawing programs often used to create illustrations (see Figure 11). Even more sophisticated packages are used for precise computer-aided design and drafting applications. Chapter 18 covers graphics packages in more detail.

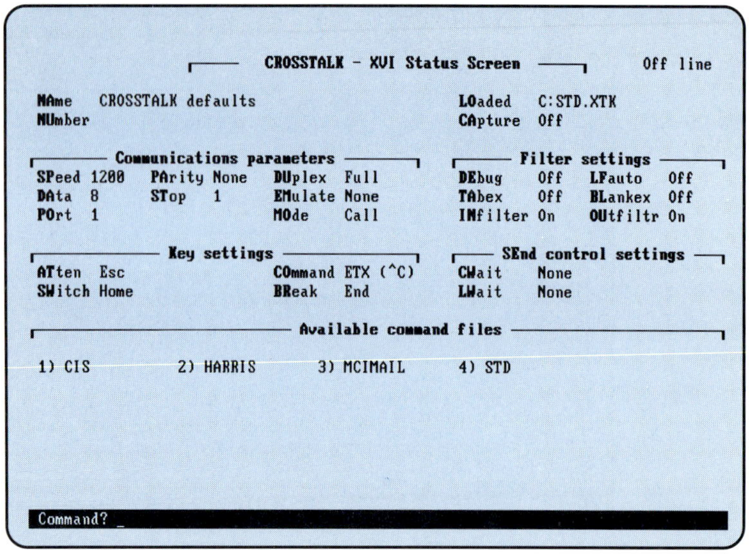

***Figure 10* Communications Program**
CROSSTALK XVI is a popular communications program for IBM-compatible microcomputers.

Desktop Publishing

Combine word processing and graphics capabilities with the beautiful output of a laser printer and you have the essence of *desktop publishing*. This type of application package can produce near-typeset-quality printed material complete with illustrations using microcomputers and laser printers at relatively low cost (see Figure 12). All kinds of organizations, from small clubs to multinational corporations, are using desktop publishing packages to produce their own newsletters, advertisements, memos, contracts, documents, and even books. Chapter 19 will examine further the recent phenomenon of desktop publishing.

***Figure 11* Graphics Program**
Programs such as MacPaint for the Apple Macintosh can be used to create freehand illustrations.

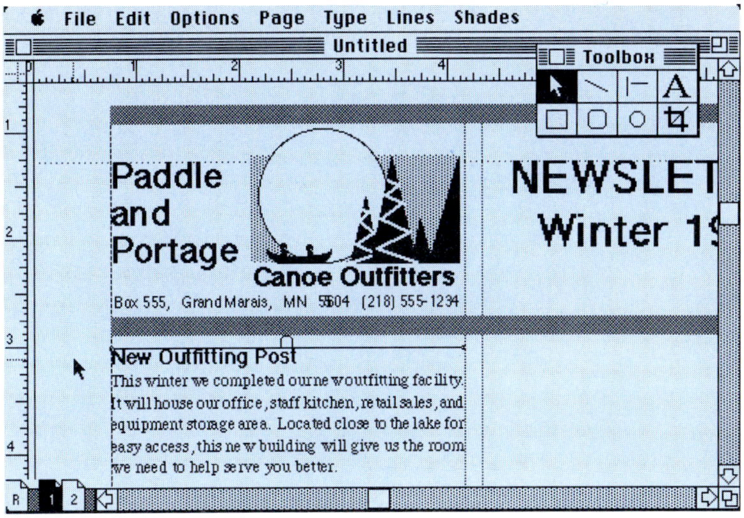

Figure 12 Desktop Publishing
Programs such as PageMaker let you create documents with both text and pictures.

Other Packages

In addition to the major types of software we've just discussed, still more packages are often used with microcomputers. These include the following (which will be covered in Chapter 20):

- *Integrated software.* These large programs typically include several different applications in the same packages. For example, a single integrated package might include word processing, spreadsheet, data base management, graphics, and communications capabilities.
- *On-line references.* Imagine having a dictionary, thesaurus, book of quotations, zip code listing, stock market table, or census information in your computer's secondary storage.
- *Statistical and math packages.* These types of software, long available on large computers, have become increasingly popular for use on microcomputers. These packages are especially attractive to business analysts, mathematicians, and engineers, as well as physical, biological, and social scientists.
- *Project management packages.* These applications are used to help managers plan and coordinate huge multitask projects.
- *Accounting packages.* Many applications have been developed especially for business accounting to help boost profits, cut costs, improve cash flow, pay bills, calculate earnings, assemble marketing information, and explore operational alternatives.
- *Personal finance and tax packages.* These applications can do everything from balancing your checkbook to managing your investments and figuring your income taxes.
- *Educational packages.* A wide range of topics and skills can be taught with microcomputer software, from the alphabet to experimental physics.
- *Entertainment packages.* Games, simulators, and music-makers are but a few of the many types of entertainment software available for microcomputers.
- *Hypertext packages.* These programs let you store, organize, and present unstructured information.

- *Artificial Intelligence and Expert Systems.* These programs, pioneers on the software frontier, attempt to enable computers to learn, deduce, diagnose, and advise.

The User Interface

System software and application software tell computers what to do. But to perform most tasks with computers, people must tell software what to do. The way people interact with software—how you direct the actions of software and how that software responds to your requests—is often called the **user interface.** Since most people who now use computers are not necessarily technical experts, the user interface has become an increasingly important aspect of software and even hardware design.

In the early days of computers, little attention was paid to making computers easy to use. User interfaces were primarily determined by programmers, who believed that the tasks performed by computers were of paramount importance. How people interacted with software was considered incidental, so whatever was easiest to program became the user interface. Since most computer users were scientists and engineers, and the tasks themselves required little interaction, user interfaces were pretty primitive. People just had to adapt to the software.

Then along came microcomputers. People who programmed them and people who used them were for the most part ordinary folks, not rocket scientists. It became evident that software would have to be easier to use. Instead of designing user interfaces for ease of programming, software developers began to really think about making programs more *user friendly.* Nowadays, user interfaces are foremost in the minds of those who create software. There are operating systems and application packages with sophisticated user interfaces that are almost intuitively understood by most people. Computer software has at last begun to adapt to people.

A wide range of user interfaces is still found in today's microcomputer software, however. Going from primitive to more sophisticated, let's take a look at some of the ways software interacts with people.

Commands

A **command** is a directive that you issue to a program and is perhaps the simplest type of user interface. Commands are quick and efficient, but they require a substantial initial learning and memorization process. For example, the operating system used with most IBM microcomputers requires you to issue the PRINT command to send a text file to the printer (see Figure 13). Perhaps this seems easy enough, but there may be many, many commands and their names may not all be so memorable. How do you know when you can print files? Is the printer turned on or even connected? How do you tell the operating system which file to print? If you forget the name of a command or don't know exactly how it operates, you may have to look it up in a reference manual.

Using commands isn't completely negative, however. Once you memorize the commands you need and know how they work, you can often get things done very quickly. The real problem comes when you try to use some other command-driven software. Its commands might be totally different or, worse, similar in name but different in function. For instance, in some word processors you erase the character to the left of the cursor by pressing the Backspace key. In other word processors, the Delete key does the same job. Little differences like

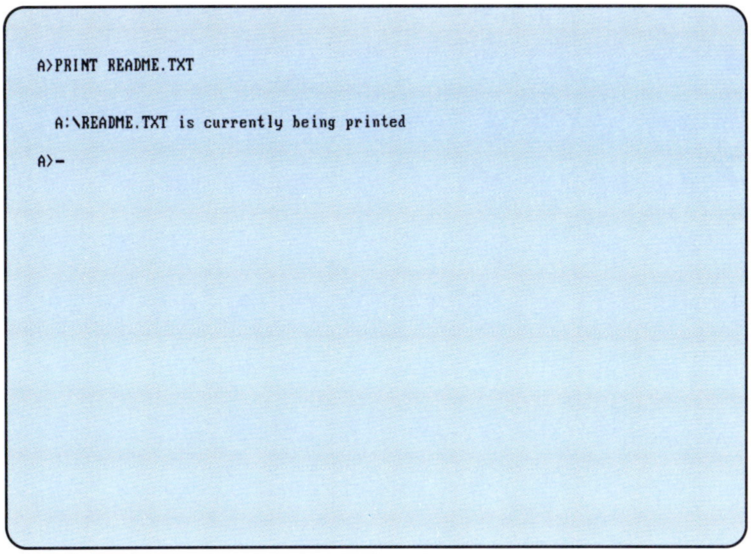

Figure 13 ***Command***
On an IBM-compatible microcomputer, one way to print the contents of a file is to issue a PRINT command.

this can be very annoying if you have to use several programs with conflicting commands.

Prompts

One step up from commands are prompts. A **prompt** generally provides information or instructions about how to do something and then waits for your response. For example, a prompt familiar to users of IBM microcomputers is

```
Current date is Tue 1-01-1980
Enter new date (mm-dd-yy):_
```

In some cases, a prompt may take the form of a question. If you issue the ERASE command to tell the IBM Personal Computer operating system to delete every file on a disk, it uses a prompt to confirm this drastic action (see Figure 14):

```
Are you sure (Y/N)?_
```

Prompts, generally easy to understand, are occasionally used by most software. But prompts can only be used when software is waiting for some very specific response from you. They can't be used too often, because software has no way of determining when you might want to initiate some action on your own.

Static Menus

One of the major problems with commands is that they may be difficult to memorize. This deficiency can be addressed through the use of menus. As we said in Chapter 1, a *menu* is a list of available alternatives that's displayed on the screen. A **static menu** is one that remains on the screen in a fixed position (see Figure 15). In some respects, menus combine prompts and commands. By providing information about which commands are available and how to invoke them, menus are much easier to use than commands by themselves and much more versatile than individual prompts. Unfortunately, static menus take up valuable screen space, and complex actions may require several levels of submenus.

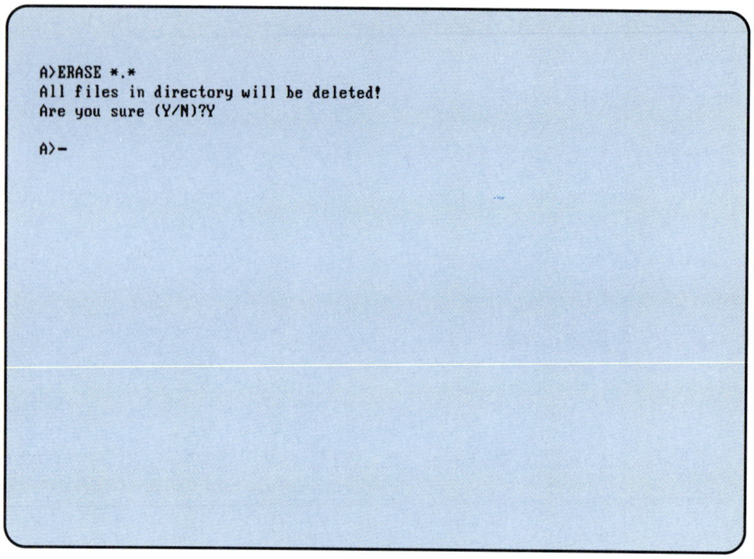

Figure 14 Prompt
After you issue an ERASE command that will delete all files, the operating system of IBM-compatible microcomputers presents a prompt asking you if you are sure this is what you want to do.

On balance, however, menus are a significant improvement over commands and prompts.

Pop-up Menus

In general, static menus stay on the screen in one place. Some programs allow you to remove their static menus from the screen with a special command. An even more flexible type of menu, the **pop-up menu,** has become very popular lately. This type of menu is generally kept off the screen until you issue a special command that causes the menu to pop up. Some clever programs can position their pop-up menus so that information currently on the screen is not covered,

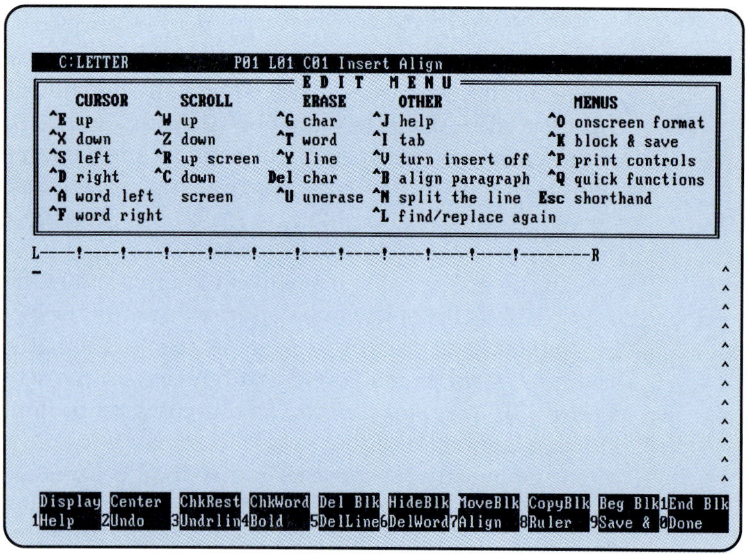

Figure 15 Static Menu
The WordStar classic menus are static menus that provide information about the available commands and how to invoke them.

Real World

Microsoft's Phenomenon

William H. Gates III is 33 years old and worth $1 billion. He didn't inherit the money and he didn't win the lottery. What Gates did was found one of the world's largest software companies—Microsoft Corp. Consider this: Gates and partner Paul Allen began Microsoft in 1975, after Gates had dropped out of Harvard. In 1986, when the company offered stock to the public, Gates's share was worth roughly $300 million. Two years later the stock had more than quadrupled. He was a billionaire.

Many people believe that Microsoft is the leading software designer in the $35 billion personal computer industry. It supplies programming language translators and applications programs, but it is perhaps best known as the creator of MS-DOS, the operating system chosen by IBM for its personal computer line. After IBM made its choice, Tandy, Compaq, and all the IBM clone-makers followed. By 1986, DOS was being used in 58 percent of the 7.1 million personal computers installed in the United States.

Microsoft's new operating system, OS/2, runs on high-end IBM-compatible machines, enabling them to perform several tasks at once, and making them easier to use.

In many ways, Gates is a typical young computer entrepreneur. He is precocious, shrewd, visionary, and a perfectionist. And he won't take "no" for an answer. When IBM executives balked at buying his Windows software in favor of developing their own, Gates calmly sat down and convinced them to change their minds.

Microsoft, like its founder, is striving to maintain its entrepreneurial spirit as well, with company meetings, flexible hours, and weekly parties.

Source: Richard Brandt, "The Billion-Dollar Whiz Kid," *Business Week*, April 13, 1987, pp. 68–76.

if there's empty space. Other programs actually let you move the menu around so you can see what's beneath. Once the menu is up, what you type goes toward selecting an alternative and doesn't appear in the application below. In a sense, you are temporarily disconnected from the normal action of the program when the pop-up menu is in place. When you've made a selection, the pop-up menu automatically disappears, leaving your screen as it was before.

Pop-up menus are a definite improvement over static menus. Their most obvious benefit is that they take up screen space only when in actual use. Pop-up menus are out of sight when you don't need them, thereby reducing clutter and confusion. Another benefit is that certain actions can only be performed when the menu is up on the screen. This helps prevent accidentally invoking some command by inadvertently pressing its keys. Keypresses can have different meanings when a pop-up menu is present, yielding more possible commands. Pop-up menus are often cited as the beginning of truly friendly user interfaces.

A good example of pop-up menus can be found in the extremely successful Lotus 1-2-3 spreadsheet package (see Figure 16). To invoke the main menu, you press the / (forward slash) key. A list of words appears that represent actions to be taken. In the Lotus 1-2-3 program, these words are listed horizontally across one or two lines, but the same basic concept has been used in other programs that list options vertically.

A choice is made in one of two ways. The first method involves a brightly lit or colored bar that's used to highlight one of the alternatives. This highlight bar can be moved from one option to the next by pressing arrow keys. Sometimes

Figure 16 Pop-up Menu
Lotus 1-2-3 uses a pop-up menu system that you invoke by pressing the / (forward slash) key. The Main Menu then appears at the top of the screen with the Worksheet option highlighted.

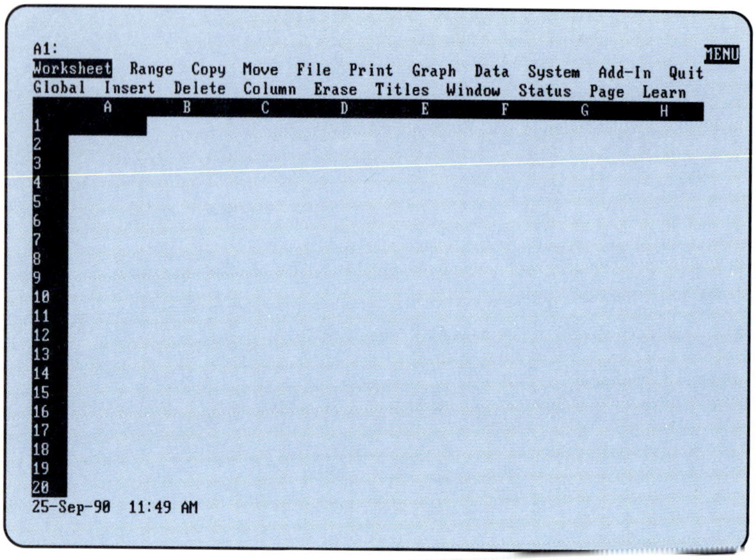

this highlight bar is called a *cursor* or *pointer.* When it's positioned on top of the desired selection, the Enter key is usually pressed to confirm and execute that alternative. The other method of selection is quicker. All the options listed in this type of menu begin with a different letter. To select an option, all you have to do is press the key that matches its first letter. This type of menu is now used in a wide range of different software packages.

Pull-down Menus

Pop-up menus are generally completely absent from the screen until you press the key that activates them. A **pull-down menu** is usually activated by selecting a name from a list of menu names, called a *menu bar,* arranged horizontally across the top of the screen. Some pull-down menus are activated by holding down the Alternate key and typing the first letter of the menu's name. Frequently, a mouse is used to activate a pull-down menu. The mouse controls a little pointer, shaped like an arrow or index finger, so that it can be moved anywhere on the screen. When the pointer is positioned on top of a name in the menu bar, a mouse button can be pressed to pull down the menu (see Figure 17). Once the menu is on the screen, the pointer is used to drag a highlight bar up or down the list of options. When the desired option is highlighted, the mouse button is released, the menu disappears, and the selected alternative is executed. Most people find it very natural to use a mouse to position a pointer. This can make pull-down menus even easier to use than pop-up menus.

Figure 17 Pull-down Menu
This screen shows a pull-down menu in MacWrite, a popular word processing program for the Apple Macintosh. The Style menu has been pulled down and the Bold option is currently highlighted.

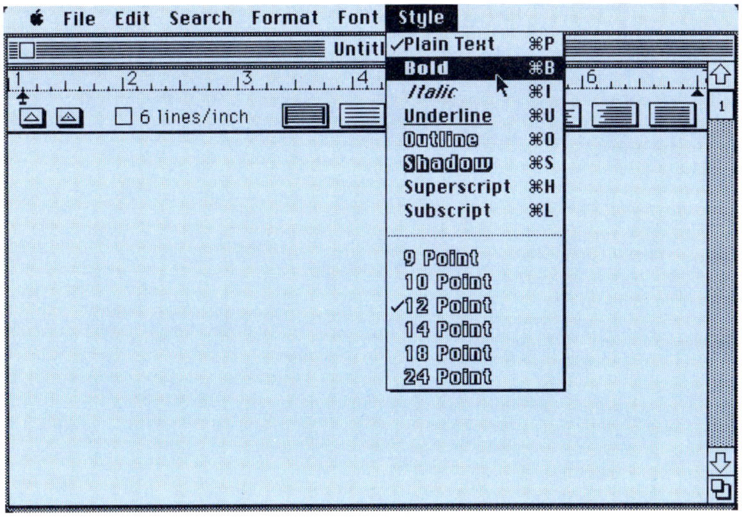

Graphical User Interfaces

The most sophisticated and easiest to use of all types of microcomputer user interfaces is the **graphical user interface (GUI),** which includes pull-down menus, icons, and windows and arranges the display screen into a simulated desktop. A mouse and a graphics display screen are almost always used with a graphical user interface. Perhaps the best example of a graphical user interface can be seen in the system and application software of the Apple Macintosh (see Figure 18). *Icons,* as we said in Chapter 1, are graphic symbols used to represent hardware devices, programs, data files, and actions to be performed. Computer concepts and devices are represented pictorially as familiar office items. Actions are indicated graphically. For example, instead of typing a command to erase a file, you discard data by using the mouse to drag a file folder over to a trash can. Instead of issuing typewritten commands, the computer is directed by manipulating objects on the screen with a mouse-controlled pointer. The screen becomes a familiar desktop. The contents of storage devices, data files, and documents are displayed inside their own individual windows that pop up on that desktop. System utilities and application software have similar windows displayed while they are running. Windows can be superimposed on the screen just as you can lay several file folders on your desk at the same time. The one on top is currently active.

On computers such as the Apple Macintosh, most software presents the same basic graphical user interface. This means that a person who masters one program can use many of those same skills in running some completely different type of software. The graphical user interface has proven so effective, especially

Figure 18 Macintosh Graphical User Interface
This screen shows the graphical user interface of the Apple Macintosh operating system with several windows open on the desktop.

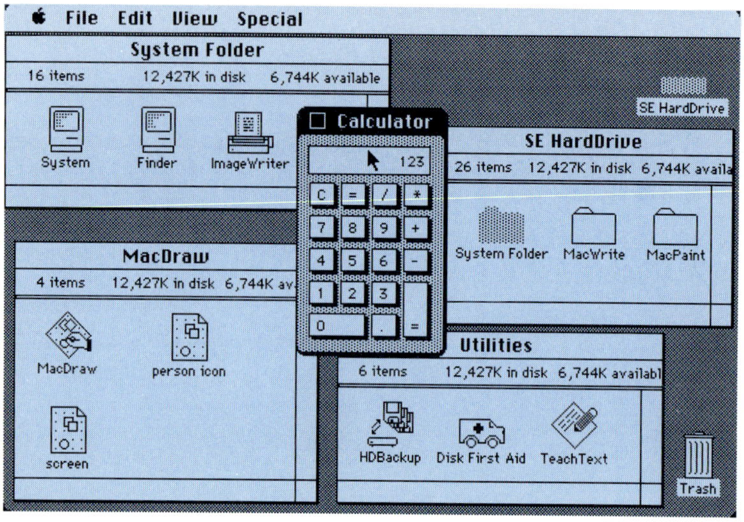

for novices, that it is being adapted for all kinds of computers. For example, several graphical user interfaces are now available for IBM-compatible microcomputers as well.

There are some drawbacks, however, to this sophisticated type of user interface. In general, it takes a great deal of computer power and memory to make such schemes work. Graphical user interfaces run only on computers equipped with high-resolution graphics displays. User-friendly software is difficult and more expensive to develop. Some people find the cute user interface tiresome once they become experts. Critics argue that after you master a command-oriented system, such as the IBM Disk Operating System, you can work faster and more efficiently. Proponents on both sides of the issue have made good points, but what's important is that users now have more options than ever in the way they interact with computers.

Summary

- *How programs tell computers what to do.* Every computer is only capable of a limited set of simple tasks, each represented by a single instruction. A program is a group of instructions that tells a computer what to do.
- *How system software helps you use a computer.* System software handles the details of managing a computer's hardware and software resources, and includes operating systems, utilities, and alternative operating environments.
- *The major types of programming languages.* Arranged from less abstract to more abstract, the major types of programming languages are machine languages, assembly languages, high-level languages, and fourth generation languages.

- *The major types of application software.* Three categories stand out as clearly the most prevalent: word processing, spreadsheet, and data base management. Communications and networking, graphics, and desktop publishing software packages are also very popular.
- *The major types of user interfaces.* The types of user interfaces, listed from simple to more complex include commands, prompts, static menus, pop-up menus, pull-down menus, and graphical user interfaces.

Key Terms

As an extra review of this chapter, try defining the following terms.

Ada
assembler
assembly language
BASIC
C
COBOL
command
compiler
file
FORTRAN
fourth generation languages (4GLs)
graphical user interface (GUI)
high-level language
instruction set
interpreter
machine language
mnemonics
object code
operand
operating system
operation code (opcode)
Pascal
pop-up menu
prompt
pull-down menu
source code
static menu
symbolic addressing
user interface
utility
windowing environment (alternate operating environment)
worksheets (spreadsheets)

Review Questions

1. What is a group of instructions that tells a computer what to do?
2. How are instructions encoded by computers?
3. List some tasks performed by system software.
4. What software is immediately brought into action when you turn on a computer?
5. What kinds of tasks are performed by utility programs?
6. What are the basic types of instructions included in all programming languages?
7. Explain the distinction between low- and high-level computer programming languages.
8. What is the only programming language that can be directly used by a computer?
9. What advantages do assembly languages have over machine languages?
10. What are some of the disadvantages of using assembly languages?
11. What are the two basic types of programs used to translate high-level language source code into object code?
12. What advantages do high-level languages have over assembly languages?

13. List the most commonly used microcomputer high-level programming languages.
14. What kind of software improves the way an operating system interacts with the user, while often affording the power to do several tasks at once?
15. What kind of software has primarily motivated people to buy computers?
16. What is perhaps the most popular of all types of application packages?
17. List some of the applications of spreadsheet software.
18. What kinds of tasks does a data base management package perform?
19. List some other popular types of microcomputer application software.
20. Briefly describe six of the interaction methods found in the user interfaces of today's microcomputer application software.

Multiple Choice

1. Every computer is only capable of a limited set of simple tasks, each represented by a single
   (a) bit. (b) byte.
   (c) instruction. (d) operating system.
2. Programs that deal most intimately with a computer's hardware are called
   (a) programming languages. (b) system software.
   (c) application software. (d) user interfaces.
3. Which of the following tasks is usually performed by the operating system?
   (a) setting up new floppy disks (b) drawing pie charts
   (c) creating documents (d) sorting mailing lists
4. A small program that lets you recover accidentally erased files would usually be categorized as a(n)
   (a) application package. (b) operating system.
   (c) data base manager. (d) utility.
5. Which of the following types of instructions is not normally included in a programming language?
   (a) input and output (b) boot up
   (c) calculation (d) comparison
6. Which type of low-level programming language is characterized by the use of mnemonics and symbolic addressing?
   (a) machine language (b) assembly language
   (c) Pascal (d) fourth generation language
7. Which type of programming language is generally machine-independent?
   (a) machine language (b) assembly language
   (c) high-level language (d) system language
8. Which type of programming language translator program translates and runs one program instruction at a time as it's entered into the computer?
   (a) assembler (b) compiler
   (c) interpreter (d) converter

9. Which was the first high-level programming language to be adapted for use on microcomputers?
   (a) BASIC (b) Pascal
   (c) FORTRAN (d) COBOL
10. Which type of programming language generally makes it easiest for the user to tell the computer what to do?
   (a) machine language (b) assembly language
   (c) high-level language (d) fourth generation language
11. Which is probably the most popular of all types of application software?
   (a) word processing (b) spreadsheet
   (c) data base management (d) communications and networking
12. Which type of software is best for manipulating tables of numbers?
   (a) word processing (b) spreadsheet
   (c) data base management (d) accounting
13. Which type of software would you use to store mailing lists, phone numbers, personnel files, inventories, and bibliographies?
   (a) word processing (b) spreadsheet
   (c) data base management (d) on-line references
14. Which is the most primitive type of user interface?
   (a) command (b) static menu
   (c) pull-down menu (d) graphical user interface
15. Which type of user interface almost always uses a mouse?
   (a) command (b) prompt
   (c) pop-up menu (d) graphical user interface

Projects

1. A computer program is really just a detailed list of the steps required to accomplish some task. In your own words, write a "program" that describes how to prepare your favorite meal.
2. Investigate a few of the other high-level programming languages also used with microcomputers. Write a short description of each one. Be sure to mention under which circumstances each of these languages is typically used.
3. In this chapter we've tried to mention the most popular types of application software. An almost infinite variety of packages is available for microcomputers, however. Using computer magazines, newspapers, and books, compile a list of some of these other types of applications.
4. One way to see if software is easy to learn and use is to observe how many books are published about it. An operating system that novices find difficult to understand generally spawns a whole school of supplementary books on the subject. Go to a local bookstore and see how many books you can find about the IBM Personal Computer operating system (called PC-DOS or MS-DOS) versus the number you see covering the Apple Macintosh system.

CHAPTER 4

OPERATING SYSTEM CONCEPTS

In This Chapter

What Operating Systems Do

- Control Hardware
- Manage Software
- Interact with Users

Types of Operating Systems

- Single-user, Single-tasking
- Single-user, Multitasking
- Multiuser, Single-tasking
- Multiuser, Multitasking
- Multiprocessing
- Networking

Operating System Components

- Hardware Interface
- Application Interface
- User Interface

Important Microcomputer Operating Systems

- CP/M
- DOS
- OS/2
- UNIX
- ProDOS
- Apple Macintosh System

Preview

An operating system is the "heart and soul" of a computer. It is the foundation on which all application software rests. The operating system takes care of low-level details, such as interpreting your keypresses, reading data from a disk, and erasing the display screen. Application packages handle more abstract tasks, such as helping you create a document, draw a graph, or compute statistics. The computer user, operating system, and application packages must work together as a team to process data into information.

Many different types of operating systems are used with computers today. Some are specific to a particular computer, while others have been adapted to run on many very different computers. This chapter emphasizes microcomputer operating systems, but sometimes we will mention features mainly found on much larger and more powerful machines. This will help you understand operating systems in general and suggest the capabilities of future microcomputer operating systems.

After studying this chapter, you will understand

- what operating systems do.
- the basic types of computer operating systems.
- the fundamental components of an operating system.
- several important microcomputer operating systems.

What Operating Systems Do

In Chapter 3, we introduced the operating system as a set of programs that controls a computer's hardware and manages the use of software. Operating systems perform several essential chores, which can be divided into three broad categories: controlling hardware, managing software, and interacting with users.

Control Hardware

Many of the operations of a computer system's internal components and peripheral devices are controlled by built-in electronic circuits. Software, however, controls many other important operations. Operating systems include programs that direct the actions of many hardware devices, including displays, keyboards, printers, real-time clocks, serial and parallel interfaces, and especially disk drives. These programs are extremely valuable to programmers developing application software for computers. They provide a standard, readily accessible method of using the various hardware devices of a computer system, thereby saving programmers a great deal of work. Some of the specific hardware-control tasks performed by operating systems include

- automatically and periodically updating the current time of day based on the ticking of the real-time clock.
- erasing the display screen.
- drawing a dot at a given location on a graphics display.
- given its code, drawing a character on the screen.
- changing background and foreground colors on a color display.
- when a key on the keyboard is pressed, temporarily halting the current program to acknowledge and store the code that identifies that key.

Insight

What Causes an Operating System to Crash?

It may not be as bad as skidding off a rain-slick road and wrapping your VW around a tree, but an operating system crash can be pretty painful.

You might lose work or miss a deadline, or an entire connected computer network might grind to a halt. When a computer crashes, it usually just stops dead. Nothing seems to revive it, including pounding on the keyboard. Sometimes, random characters glare at you from the screen, or the disk drives keep spinning aimlessly.

Why does this happen? First, remember that an operating system consists of the programs that manage the computer and run application software. The operating system makes its home in the computer's memory. When it's in control, the computer taps into this memory for the step-by-step instructions it needs to work.

One of the most common causes for an operating system crash is that a program inadvertently overwrites an area of memory occupied by the operating system. For example, suppose a poorly written spreadsheet program accidentally stores data in a critical area of memory used by the operating system. This area might contain the program for gaining access to the disk drive. When the application program you're running tries to read or write data to the disk drive, the system crashes.

Obvious programming errors like this are rare because the software is usually tested before it's released.

Unfortunately, however, large programs can become so complex that it's almost impossible to detect every potential bug. This means that if you routinely use a computer, you'll have the displeasure of an operating system crash sooner or later.

In most cases, the only way to revive the system is to restart, or *reboot*, it. Sometimes you can do this by pressing a certain combination of keys, but you may have to turn off the computer and then turn it on again. Any programs you were running will have to be rerun. Worse yet, you'll probably have to reenter any data you were working on at the time of the crash, because rebooting an operating system erases the entire contents of the computer's memory. An operating system crash may also scramble programs and data stored on disk drives. Not a good way to start the day.

- constantly noting the current location of the mouse and updating the corresponding pointer or cursor on the screen.
- reading and writing data to and from floppy and hard disks.
- sending data through a parallel interface to a printer.
- transmitting and receiving data through a serial interface connected to a modem.
- generating sounds through the computer's speaker.
- automatically testing memory and internal circuits, and reporting problems.

Although these activities may sound simple enough, in actuality they may require many computer instructions each. In order to write programs to perform these tasks, a programmer would have to know a great deal about the low-level internal workings of computer hardware. For maximum efficiency, programs such as these must usually be written in assembly language. If all programmers had to write their own programs in assembly language to do each one of these common tasks, they would require more training and the development of application software would be even more time consuming and expensive.

Manage Software

Operating systems manage software by controlling how programs are run and what computer resources they can utilize. Among other activities, this includes loading a program from its disk into memory, getting the computer ready to run the program, initiating the program, providing built-in software resources for the program to use, watching for and reporting any grave errors that might occur, and, after the program is finished, preparing the computer to run the next program. In some cases, operating systems must place restrictions on the memory and disk storage to which a particular program has access. This is especially true for operating systems on computers that can run more than one program at a time or serve several users simultaneously. For example, two users or two programs cannot use the same memory locations, disk space, printer, or input device without conflicts occurring. It's the operating system's job to facilitate the execution of programs, while preventing such conflicts.

Interact with Users

The third major function of an operating system is to help average users, not necessarily programmers, put their computers to work. When you first turn on a microcomputer, the operating system is activated and awaits your instruction. You might type a command or use a mouse to select an activity from a menu. In either case, the operating system processes your directive and initiates some program. Some of these programs are part of the operating system itself. They allow users to change settings, examine or print files, check the contents of disks, reorganize disk storage, or otherwise manage their computers. Most of the time, however, users are just interested in running their application software. The operating system is simply the vehicle through which application software is activated. It allows users to see what programs they have stored on their disks and select which one they want to run. In some cases, this selection process can be automated by the operating system for those users who want to run a particular application every time they turn on their computer. Still, just about everyone who uses a computer eventually has some direct interaction with its operating system. Most people who use computers on a regular basis find it worth the effort to become familiar with this essential system software.

Types of Operating Systems

Several different types of operating systems are in common use; they are classified according to the number of people who can use the system simultaneously, the number of programs (also referred to as *tasks*) that can be run at the same time, and the number of processing units that are being controlled.

Single-user, Single-tasking

The simplest and most common type of operating system accommodates a single user and is **single-tasking.** In other words, only a single program is run at a time (see Figure 1). That program generally has access to all of the computer's resources, such as memory, disk storage, keyboard input, display output, and printer output. Once initiated, a program usually runs until it's finished or the user stops it. While running, however, the program may be frequently interrupted for very short periods of time by the operating system to handle activities such as updating the time of day and processing keyboard input. On some computers, the operating system's ability to temporarily interrupt processing to handle some critical task has been put to some rather ingenious uses. **Memory-resident** (also called **RAM resident**) programs have been developed for some operating systems that allow the user to temporarily suspend an activity and

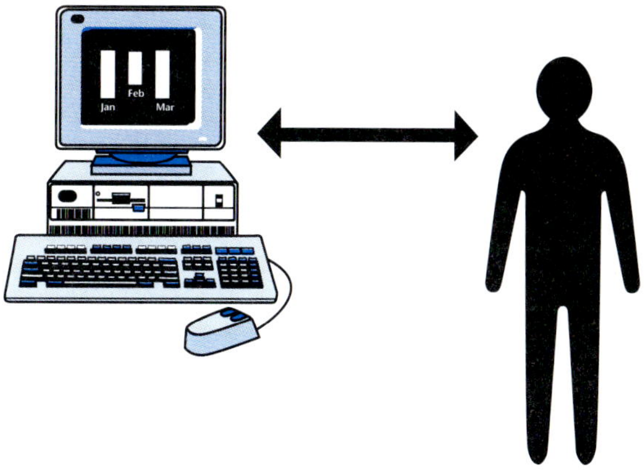

Figure 1 Single-user, Single-tasking Operating System
The simplest type of operating system lets a single user run a single program at a time.

switch to some other one. For example, one such program that simulates a hand-held calculator may be loaded into memory but not executed when the computer is turned on. By pressing some key combination, the user can activate this calculator. So, if you are using a word processing program and you need to add several numbers, you can activate the calculator, temporarily suspend the word processor, compute your sum, and then deactivate the calculator and return to word processing. It may be possible to have several different memory-resident programs installed and switch among them at will, but the computer is still only running a single program at a time. Most microcomputers have single-user, single-tasking operating systems.

Single-user, Multitasking

The majority of microcomputer users probably get along quite well running only a single program at a time. In several instances, however, running a single program at a time doesn't utilize the computer's full potential. For example, most printers print characters much more slowly than computers can send them over the cable. Depending upon the word processor or printing program, you might not be able to use your computer for other tasks while it prints a document. For long documents, this can tie up your computer for quite a while. This and many similar problems can be solved by multitasking operating systems.

Multitasking is the ability to run more than one program concurrently, or seemingly at the same time. This is similar to what a juggler does. First one ball is thrown up into the air, then another is caught and thrown up into the air, and so on. The juggler works so quickly that all the balls seem to be in the air at once. A single-user, multitasking operating system can juggle the execution of several programs (see Figure 2). The central processing unit very rapidly takes turns attending to each task so that it seems as if the programs are running simultaneously. For programs that use different computer resources, this works very well. For example, a spreadsheet program would probably run just as fast while a document is printing as it would if the printer were idle. Unless the CPU is powerful, however, running several applications that draw on the same

Figure 2 Single-user, Multitasking Operating System
A multitasking operating system lets you run several programs concurrently.

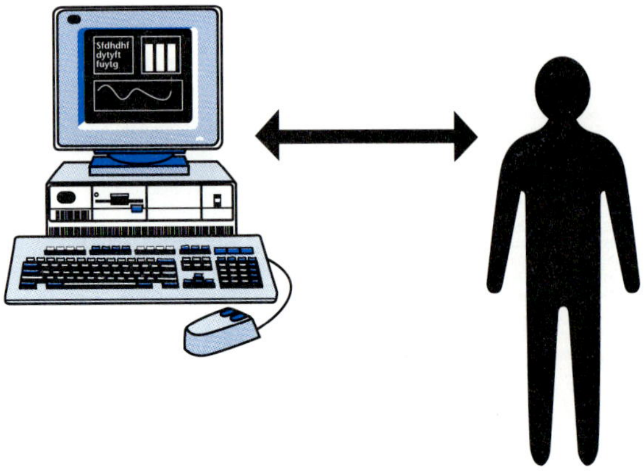

computer resources usually results in some decrease in performance. A spreadsheet program would probably run slower, for instance, while a statistics program is also running because both programs involve substantial numeric processing. For this reason, multitasking operating systems are generally implemented on computers with fairly sophisticated CPUs.

Multiuser, Single-tasking

A single-user, single-tasking operating system under-utilizes the resources of a powerful computer. Single-user, multitasking operating systems are one way to more fully exploit a computer's potential. Another approach is to let several people use the same computer at the same time. Multiuser, single-tasking operating systems let several people each run one program at a time (see Figure 3). Each user is equipped with his or her own **terminal,** which is an input/output station consisting of a keyboard and display. The terminal is connected to the central computer. This arrangement is also called **time-sharing,** because the operating system instructs the computer to rapidly switch among users at fixed intervals of time. These intervals, called *time slices,* are so small (typically a few thousandths of a second) that each user gets the illusion of having the computer's complete attention. As long as the CPU isn't saddled with more users than it can handle, its *response time* is quick enough to maintain this illusion. Consequently, time-sharing operating systems are generally implemented on computers with fast, powerful, and sophisticated CPUs. Although they are predominantly found on large computer systems, there are a few multiuser, single-tasking operating systems for some microcomputers.

Besides allowing several users to share the resources of a single computer, multiuser operating systems offer some other benefits, too. The cost per user for expensive hardware devices and software packages is reduced. Multiuser systems enable people to easily share data bases and send messages to one another. This can be especially useful in an office. One disadvantage of multiuser systems, however, is that if the central computer breaks down, everyone's work is brought to a halt.

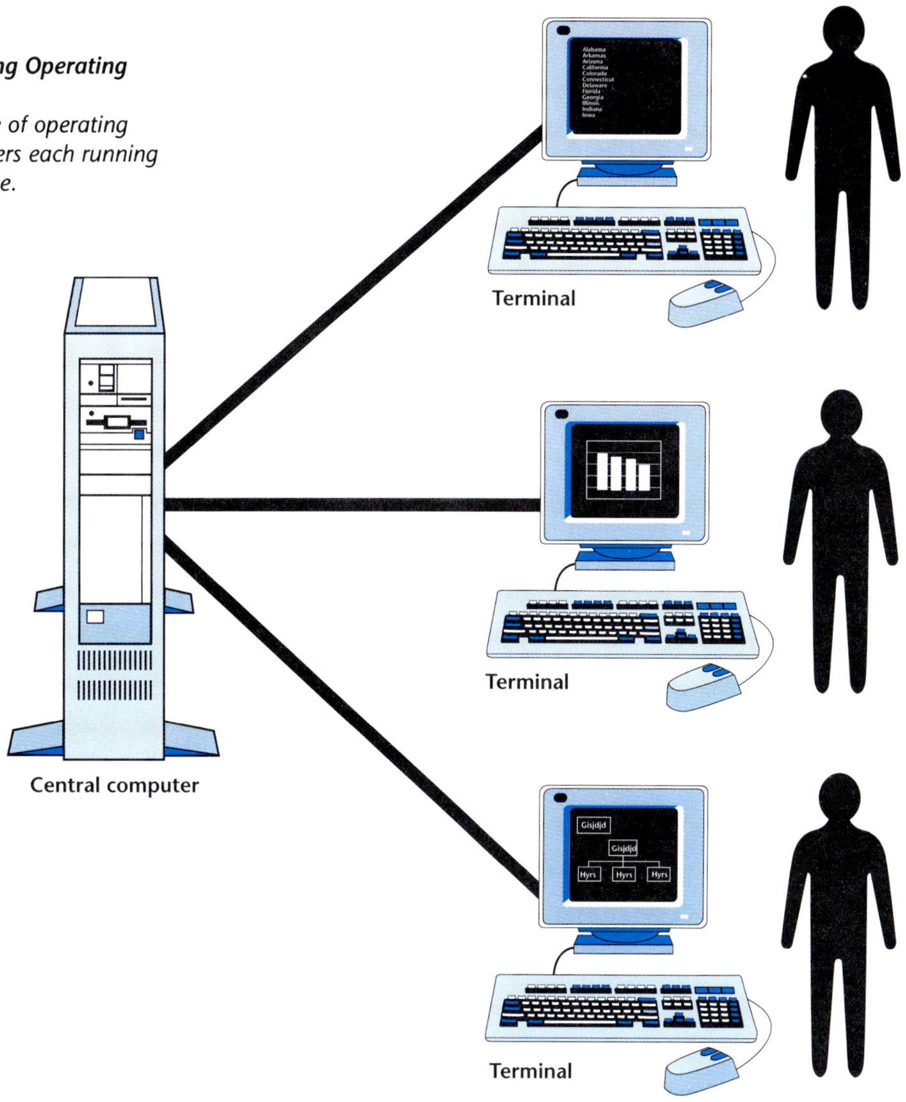

***Figure 3* Multiuser, Single-tasking Operating System**
Also called time-sharing, this type of operating system accommodates several users each running a single program at the same time.

Multiuser, Multitasking

Some sophisticated operating systems combine the concepts of time-sharing and multitasking (see Figure 4). This allows several users to each have more than one activity in progress at once. As you can imagine, multiuser, multitasking operating systems are quite sophisticated and generally require powerful computers. Nevertheless, such operating systems are currently available for 16-bit and 32-bit microcomputers. As microcomputer technology advances, it's likely that multiuser, multitasking operating systems will become increasingly popular.

Multiprocessing

Time-sharing and multitasking operating systems work by rapidly switching the computer's single CPU between several active users or programs. The primary goal is to get more work done in a given amount of time. Another way computer designers have approached this problem is to construct systems that use more

***Figure 4* Multiuser, Multitasking Operating System**
This is a sophisticated operating system that can serve several users each running several concurrent programs.

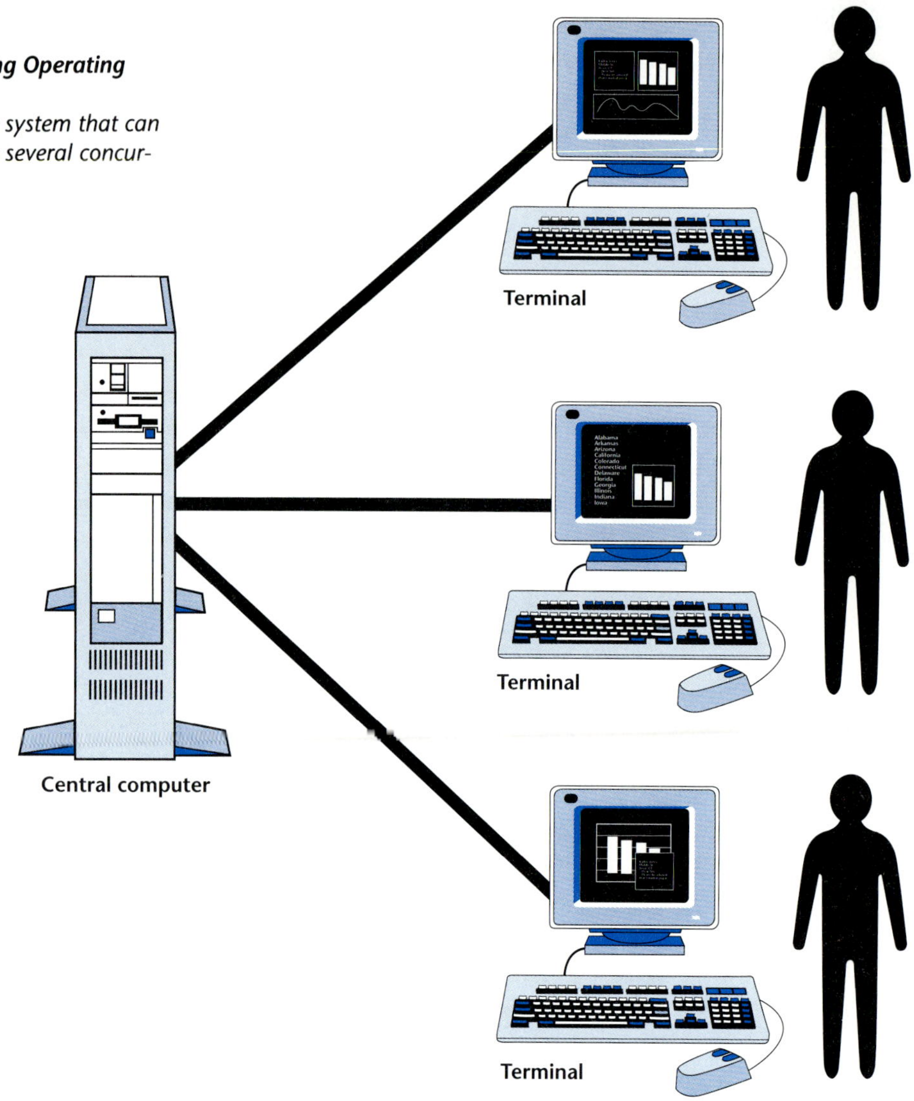

than one processing unit. So, instead of one central processing unit, there may be several equally capable processing units. **Multiprocessing** is the term used to describe such computers and the operating systems that run them (see Figure 5). Some multiprocessing systems assign a separate processing unit to each user or program, while others switch the processing units from user to user or program to program. Unlike time-sharing and multitasking operating systems, multiprocessing systems truly serve several users or programs simultaneously. Sometimes programs are broken down into steps that can be accomplished at the same time, and these steps are completed in parallel by the multiprocessing computer. Such *parallel processing* often can perform complex mathematical computations much more quickly than the sequential processing method of computers that have a single CPU. Multiprocessing systems are also generally more reliable than single CPU computers. If one processor fails, multiprocessing computers are usually constructed so that the other processors can automatically take over without the system grinding to a halt.

Figure 5 Multiprocessing Operating System
A true multiprocessing operating system can run only on a computer with several processing units.

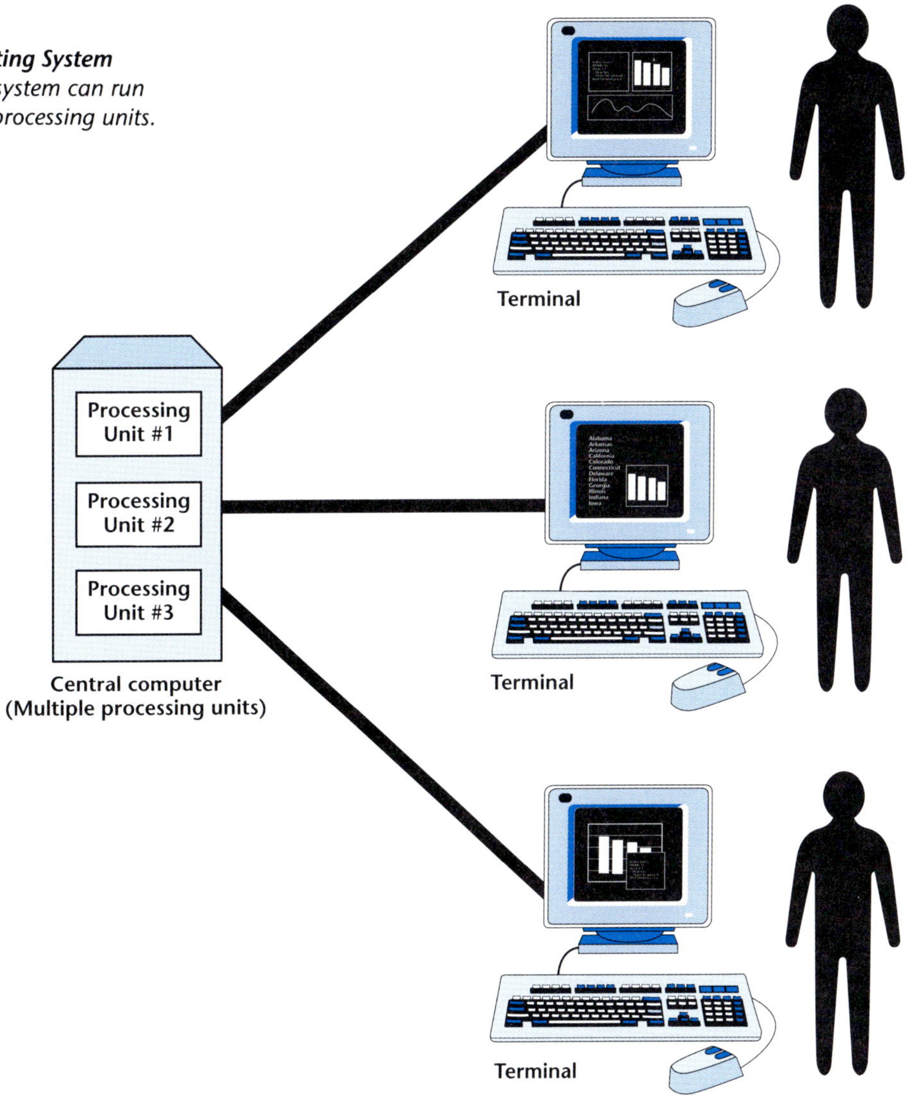

Multiprocessing operating systems are used primarily on mainframes and supercomputers. There are, however, a few microprocessor-based computers that use multiprocessing. The **Transputer,** for example, is a microprocessor that can be connected with other Transputers to construct a very fast and powerful computer. The T800-20 from INMOS Limited is a 32-bit parallel processing Transputer chip. Many T800-20 chips can be connected together in a box the size of a desktop microcomputer to yield near supercomputer performance. For example, Cogent Research in Beaverton, Oregon has developed the XTM, a desktop supercomputer that uses IMMOS T800 transputers. Although microcomputer multiprocessing systems are just beginning to appear in the marketplace, their use is expected to increase as Transputer technology advances.

Networking

A multiprocessing system may have many processing units, but it's still considered a single computer. A networking operating system connects many individual computers (see Figure 6). This gives users the advantages of having their

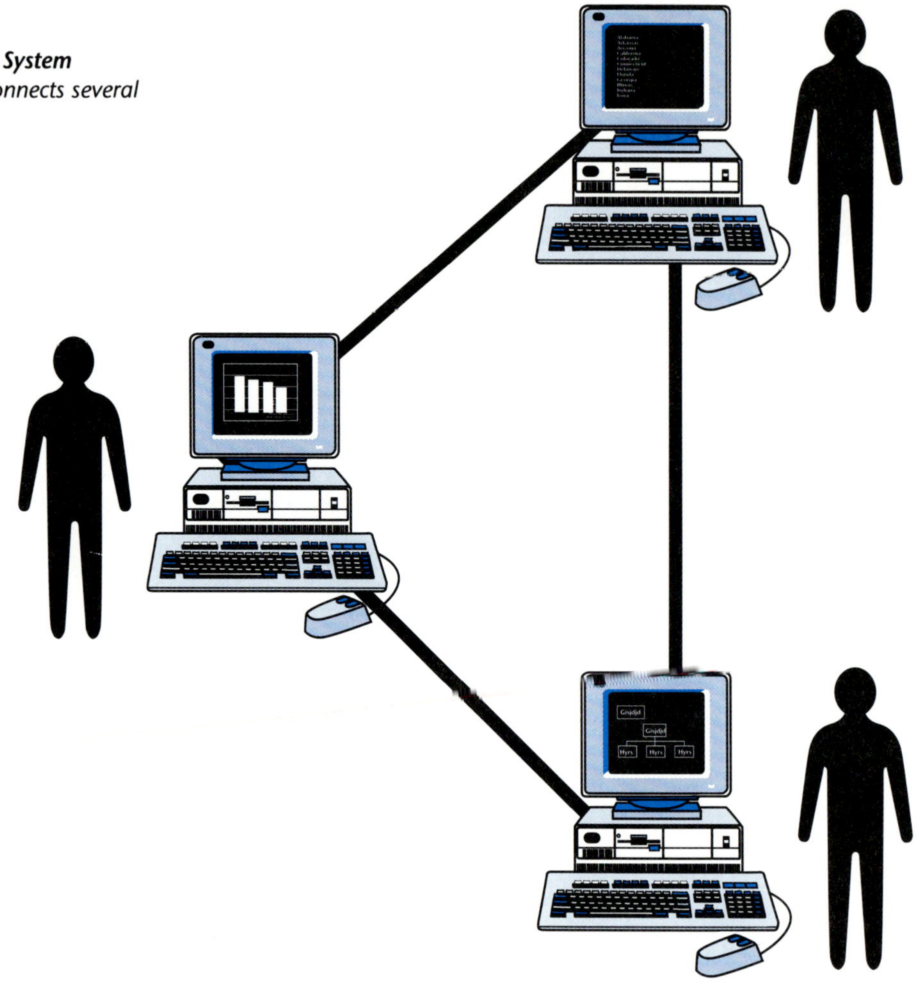

***Figure 6* Networking Operating System**
A networking operating system connects several independent computers.

own stand-alone computers, while allowing them to share software, data bases, and hardware devices such as disk drives and laser printers. Users can also transmit and receive messages to others on the network. Networking all kinds of computers, especially microcomputers, has become extremely popular lately. Most major microcomputer operating systems either allow networking directly or they can be equipped with additional software that allows individual computers to be connected. Because microcomputer networking is such an important topic, we'll have more to say about it in Chapter 17.

Operating System Components

Even simple operating systems are complex software, painstakingly developed by an elite corps of professional programmers. You've seen in this chapter that there are several different classes of operating systems. Most are comprised of several levels or layers of software, each of which performs some specified set of tasks. The innermost layer of an operating system deals with the intimate details of controlling hardware, while the outermost layer handles communication with the computer user. The middle layer performs tasks that help appli-

Figure 7 Operating System Layers
An operating system is made up of three basic layers of software: the hardware interface, the application interface, and the user interface.

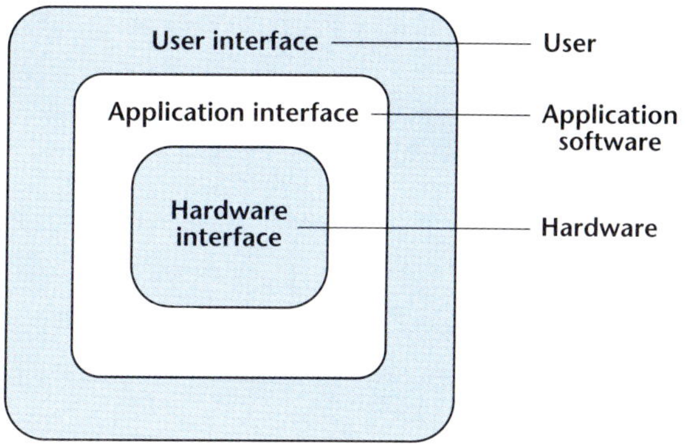

cation software deal with both hardware and the user. We call these layers the hardware interface, the application interface, and the user interface (see Figure 7).

Hardware Interface

The innermost layer of an operating system is the hardware interface. This is the software that controls the physical components, devices, and peripherals of the computer system such as the disk drives, monitor, keyboard, and printer. In many cases, part or all of this software is permanently encoded onto one or more ROM chips installed in the computer. Its job is to accommodate the immediate needs of the computer's hardware so that higher-level software need not be concerned with the details of how this hardware works. On some computers, this hardware interface is called the **BIOS,** or **Basic Input/Output System.**

Fundamentally, the BIOS acts as a connector and translator between the physical components of a computer and the other system software and application packages run on that computer. The BIOS is really software, but because it deals so intimately with computer hardware and is often stored on ROM chips, it's sometimes called **firmware.** The programs that make up the BIOS perform all kinds of essential activities. Some involve automatically checking components to see if they are working correctly. For example, the BIOS in most microcomputers makes sure that every memory location can be read, checks to see how many and what kind of disk drives are attached, and sends special codes to set up devices such as printers and keyboards. If all the equipment appears functional, the BIOS then loads the rest of the operating system from disk into memory and begins its execution. While the computer is running, programs in the BIOS automatically handle incoming signals from components such as keyboards and modems. These signals, called **interrupts** because they break into the program currently running, tell the CPU that some critical event has occurred, such as a keypress or data transmission. Besides these automatic programs, the BIOS also contains **service programs,** or **system calls,** that can be invoked by other software to perform hardware-related tasks. For example, BIOS services often include programs to erase the display, write a character or draw a dot on the screen, read data from a disk, and send characters to the printer.

Application Interface

The services performed by the hardware interface of an operating system are low-level tasks that deal with the physical aspects of computer components. At a higher, more abstract level are the services provided by the application interface of an operating system. These application services perform more complex activities that deal with the computer in a logical, rather than simply physical, fashion. For example, the BIOS provides programs that merely read and write data bytes anywhere on a disk. Most application software, however, cannot deal with data stored randomly on a disk; data must be organized into files. So, the application interface of an operating system provides programs that allow other software to create, write, read, copy, delete, and rename data files in the same fashion no matter which physical storage device is actually being used. Similarly, programs are provided that allow application packages to ignore the particular type of display connected to a computer. While the BIOS may have separate programs for writing a character on a monochrome text display and writing a character on a color graphics display, the application interface takes care of automatically deciding which one to use.

Application packages call upon the services provided by the application interface, which in turn call upon the services provided by the hardware interface. The primary purpose of the application interface of an operating system is to further isolate application software from the hardware specifics of the computer. The practical result of this approach is that the same application software can run on all different computer configurations with the same operating system. A wide variety of monitors, disk drives, and printers can be connected to most computers. Software that effectively uses an operating system's application interface can run on most combinations of this equipment.

User Interface

Unless you're a computer designer or programmer, you probably will never directly use the programs that make up the hardware and application interfaces of an operating system. To be sure, any application packages you run use these programs, but you can probably get along just fine without knowing the details of how they operate. If you use computers at all, however, you'll definitely deal with an operating system's user interface. As we said in Chapter 3, the user interface defines the manner in which people interact with software. The user interface of an operating system specifies how you will tell the computer to run system software and invoke application packages. It also sets the tone for how application packages will interact with users. For example, operating systems that have a graphical user interface generally breed application software with similar features (see Figure 8).

The user interface of an operating system is what actually processes the commands you type or the activities you select with a mouse. It translates your directives into the computer instructions necessary to load and run the programs you choose. While an application package is running, the operating system's user interface generally remains dormant. When you're finished with the package, it regains control and awaits your next command or selection.

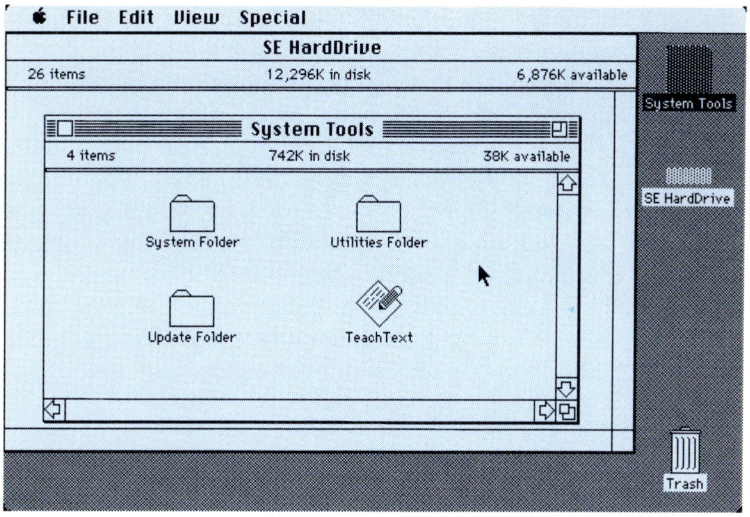

Figure 8 User-friendly Operating System
The operating system of the Apple Macintosh microcomputer uses menus, icons, windows, and desktops.

Important Microcomputer Operating Systems

A number of operating systems are commonly used on microcomputers. Some of these are classified as **generic operating systems** because they can be adapted to run on diverse computers. Generic operating systems are typically marketed by software companies that don't have a stake in any one particular brand of computer. **Proprietary operating systems,** on the other hand, usually are developed by a hardware manufacturer or a software firm contracted by a hardware manufacturer. These operating systems are designed specifically for use on computers sold by that hardware manufacturer. Proprietary operating systems are not often licensed by the manufacturer for use on other companies' computers. Both generic and proprietary operating systems are found on microcomputers. Some of the most noteworthy of these operating systems are CP/M, DOS, OS/2, UNIX, ProDOS, and the Apple Macintosh System. Let's briefly examine these operating systems now.

CP/M

CP/M stands for *Control Program/Monitor* or *Control Program for Microcomputers.* It was developed in 1973 by Gary Kildall, a software consultant then working for Intel Corporation. The operating system is now sold by Digital Research, a company Kildall founded in 1976. CP/M was the first popular microcomputer operating system sold by an independent software firm. Subsequent microcomputer operating systems have largely replaced CP/M, but it is still used by some loyal devotees. CP/M is noteworthy mainly as the predecessor and early rival of the much more popular DOS, which we will be discussing shortly. Originally designed as a single-user, single-tasking operating system for computers with 8-bit microprocessors such as the Intel 8080 and Zilog Z80 chips, CP/M has been constantly revised and upgraded. There is a version called CP/M-86 that runs on microcomputers that use the 16-bit 8086 family of microprocessors and even a multiuser, multitasking version called MP/M.

CP/M is a relatively simple operating system that can be easily adapted to run on different computers. Kildall isolated all of the machine-specific portions of the operating system and put them into a single BIOS module. No matter which computer the operating system is running on, the remaining parts of the operating system are basically the same. This adaptability coupled with its small size made CP/M the preeminent generic operating system used on many early microcomputers. CP/M has few commands that the user need memorize, but these commands were carefully chosen for their power. Although by today's standards CP/M isn't considered to be particularly user-friendly, it paved the way for the more sophisticated operating systems to come. A large collection of application software packages is still available for machines that run under this "grandfather" of microcomputer operating systems.

DOS

PC-DOS, which stands for *Personal Computer Disk Operating System,* was developed in 1981 by Microsoft Corporation for IBM. Microsoft also kept the right to sell the operating system under its own name, **MS-DOS.** Although there are a few very minor differences, PC-DOS and MS-DOS are basically the same operating system. The major distinction is that PC-DOS is sold by IBM for IBM microcomputers, and MS-DOS is sold by Microsoft for IBM-compatible microcomputers. Starting with version 4.0, IBM began calling the operating system *IBM DOS.* Since they are so similar, from now on we'll refer to all of these operating systems generically as **DOS** (see Figure 9).

Since the original IBM Personal Computer was introduced in 1981, DOS has become the dominant operating system for 16-bit computers that use the Intel 8088, 8086, and 80286 chips. At this time, it's also still the most popular operating system for powerful 32-bit microcomputers that use the Intel 80386 micropro-

Figure 9 IBM DOS
This screen shows IBM DOS version 4.00 after the CHKDSK (Check Disk) command has been executed.

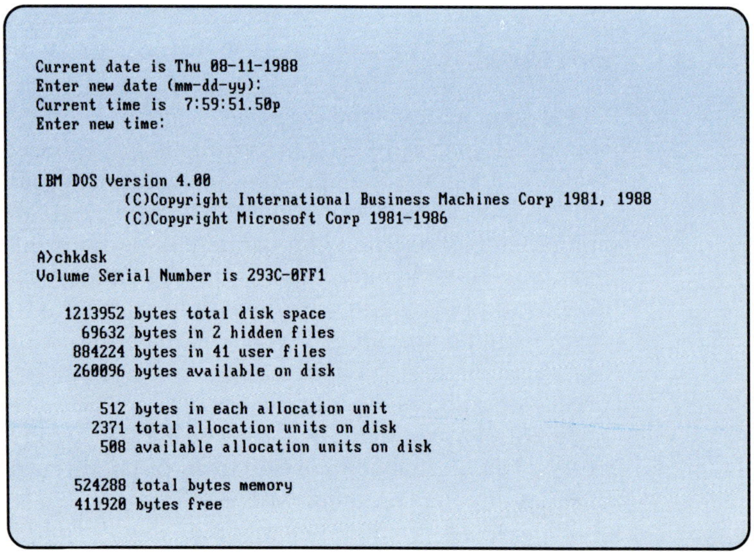

cessor. More microcomputers use DOS than any other operating system, and there are literally thousands of application packages available that run under it. According to *Forrester's Professional Automation Report,* an estimated 3.3 million copies of DOS were sold in 1988 alone. IBM estimates that around 20,000 different application packages have been developed to run under DOS.

Microsoft did not develop DOS on its own, however. In 1981, it purchased an operating system called QDOS (short for *Quick and Dirty Operating System*) from Seattle Computer Products and revised the system for IBM. IBM offered it as PC-DOS, the standard operating system on its first family of microcomputers. When IBM-compatibles appeared in the marketplace, Microsoft sold the operating system under the MS-DOS label. When IBM and IBM-compatible microcomputers became runaway bestsellers, DOS gained its immense popularity in home, school, and especially business markets.

Conceptually similar in some ways to CP/M, DOS also borrows concepts from the UNIX operating system, which we'll be discussing shortly. Although DOS was originally designed to have the same general "feel" as CP/M, it was equipped with some important improvements. Working together, IBM and Microsoft have continually upgraded DOS since 1981. Today, DOS is a powerful single-user, single-tasking operating system equipped to handle the latest hardware developments. Although it's not particularly easy for novices to fully master, DOS is a fairly straightforward operating system with a huge following of devoted users. Because DOS runs on many different brands of computers, it's not classified as a proprietary operating system. It is, however, basically limited to the Intel 8086 family of microprocessors. For this reason, DOS is not a fully generic operating system either. Nevertheless, because of the continuing popularity of IBM-compatible microcomputers, DOS will likely remain the most widely used operating system for some time.

OS/2

IBM and Microsoft joined forces again in 1987. They announced **OS/2,** a single-user, multitasking operating system designed for IBM and IBM-compatible microcomputers that use the Intel 80286 and 80386 microprocessors (see Figure 10). OS/2 does not run on IBM and IBM-compatible machines that use the 8088 and 8086 chips. This long-awaited operating system, however, more fully utilizes the power of the 80286 and 80386 chips in ways that DOS never could. OS/2 is a complex operating system that allows programs direct access to almost 16 megabytes of memory and provides true multitasking. Although it requires a new generation of application packages to make full use of this power, OS/2 can run most existing DOS programs in its *DOS Compatibility Box.* This is a special environment that can run a single DOS application at a time. Other applications designed especially for OS/2 can be concurrently run as separate tasks while a DOS program executes in the DOS Compatibility Box.

At its most basic level, OS/2 appears to be very similar to DOS. It has the same command-oriented user interface and duplicates many of the existing DOS commands. Software applications are run from OS/2 just like they are from DOS: by typing their name and pressing the Enter key. The difference is that with a special combination of keypresses you can switch the entire display screen to a different task and begin a new program before the other program is finished. Each of these different *screen groups,* as they are called, can run a single program or a group of programs. OS/2 can maintain as many as sixteen simultaneous screen groups, each running different programs. One special screen group is reserved for the DOS Compatibility Box we mentioned before, which can only run a single DOS program at a time.

Figure 10 OS/2
Here you see OS/2, the advanced operating system for high-end IBM and IBM-compatible microcomputers.

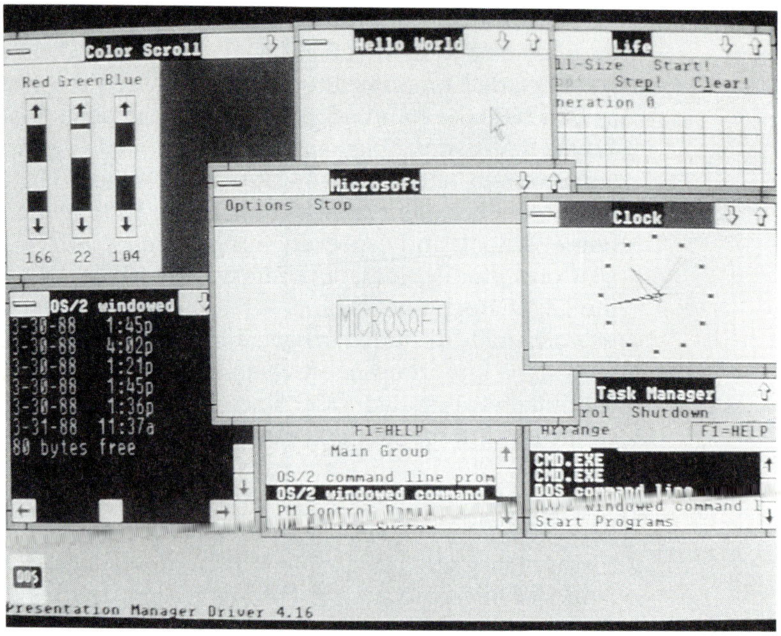

The first version of OS/2 was released with only this basic command-oriented user interface. Subsequent versions of OS/2, however, include a graphics-based windowing environment called the *Windows Presentation Manager.* The Presentation Manager is itself a separate screen group that can run multiple programs. Although the simple command-oriented user interface is fine for full-screen programs that do not use graphics, the Windows Presentation Manager is much better for graphics applications.

A disadvantage of OS/2 is that it is a new operating system, so relatively few applications have been written especially for it. It's also more expensive and requires more memory than DOS. However, OS/2 does provide some compatibility with the huge base of existing DOS applications. It also has the potential to run extremely powerful application software. IBM and Microsoft hope that OS/2 will become the standard operating system on 80286 and 80386 computers. The foundations established by OS/2 could carry such microcomputers through to almost the end of this century.

UNIX

UNIX is a multiuser, multitasking operating system originally developed at AT&T's Bell Laboratories in the early 1970s. Ken Thompson, a staff member at Bell Labs, led the group that developed the first assembly language version of UNIX in 1969. In 1972 Dr. Dennis Ritchie rewrote the operating system in his new high-level programming language C. At the time, before the advent of microcomputers, UNIX was designed to run on PDP-7 and PDP-11 minicomputers made by Digital Equipment Corporation. Since then, UNIX has been adapted to run on

Figure 11 UNIX
This screen shows a typical session with UNIX, a popular operating system for multiuser computers.

```
login: ernie
Password:
You have mail.
$
$ date
Mon Jan 02 09:25:52 CST 1989
$ who
jcd       tty0    Jan 02 08:13
ernie     tty2    Jan 02 09:25
fred      tty4    Jan 02 08:22
ellen     tty5    Jan 02 09:01
vulcan    tty7    Jan 02 07:14
rah       tty8    Jan 02 09:14
$ mail
From vulcan Mon Jan 02 08:01 CST 1989
Call me sometime today about the documentation for STATUS.

?
From ellen Mon Jan 02 09:10 CST 1989
How about lunch today at Garcia's?

? d
$
$ mail ellen
Sounds good.  I haven't had pizza all week!  I'll meet you there at noon.
```

all kinds of computers, large and small. It's perhaps the best example of a truly generic operating system (see Figure 11).

At first, UNIX was used internally at Bell Labs. In 1973 it was licensed to nonprofit organizations. This made UNIX available to many educational institutions. By 1975 UNIX had become very popular at colleges and universities. As students and faculty members left school, they took their enthusiasm for UNIX with them. Consequently, UNIX has become increasingly popular with both scientists and business people. Today, more than 10 percent of all the computers in the world run some version of UNIX. The market research firm International Data Corporation estimates that 22 percent of computers worldwide will be running UNIX by 1991.

About 95 percent of the UNIX operating system is written in the high-level programming language C. The rest is written in assembly language. As a result, UNIX can be easily adapted to run on almost any computer. This is a major attraction, but UNIX also has many other desirable features. It can accommodate multiple users, each of whom can run several concurrent tasks. UNIX is ideal for software developers because it generally comes with hundreds of utility programs that perform many useful chores and can be easily incorporated into programs being developed. In fact, many UNIX applications can be entirely constructed from this rich set of ready-made, built-in utilities.

Although UNIX is loved and cherished by many computer scientists and software developers, it also has its drawbacks as a microcomputer operating system. Computer novices often find UNIX difficult to learn, but the operating system is so flexible that it can be enhanced to present a more friendly user interface. Perhaps the biggest problem some people have with UNIX is that several different versions are in common use, none of them completely compatible. Even AT&T has a few distinct varieties of UNIX. One popular microcomputer version of UNIX, called XENIX, is sold by Microsoft for IBM and IBM-compatible machines that use the 80286 and 80386 microprocessors. Apple also has a version of UNIX called A/UX for the Macintosh II. Some versions of UNIX were designed primarily for educational and scientific uses, so they may lack features important for business use. Another drawback is that fewer application packages are available for UNIX systems than there are for other popular operating systems such as DOS. Nevertheless, UNIX is an extremely influential operating system whose use is expected to become even more widespread.

ProDOS

In 1983 Apple introduced **ProDOS,** a new single-user, single-tasking proprietary operating system for the Apple II family of microcomputers. It's faster and represents a significant improvement over previous Apple II operating systems, such as Apple DOS 3.3. ProDOS offers advanced features such as a hierarchical file system that allows subdirectories, a maximum file size of 16 megabytes, support for high-capacity hard disk drives, and the ability to handle interrupt signals from hardware devices. These capabilities allow software developers to write advanced and highly interactive applications such as word processors, spreadsheets, data base managers, graphics programs, and communications and networking packages.

Although many Apple II owners still use the older Apple DOS 3.3 operating system, ProDOS is now the preferred operating system. Most new Apple II application software runs under ProDOS. Because ProDOS disks are formatted differently than DOS 3.3 disks, there are some incompatibilities between the two operating systems. This means that some programs and data files created under Apple DOS 3.3 won't work under ProDOS. Apple does include a utility to convert programs and data files between the two systems, but some Apple DOS 3.3 programs may not be convertible. Since March of 1984, ProDOS has been the standard operating system shipped with new computers of the Apple II family. Because so many Apple II computers are in current use, ProDOS has become a popular microcomputer operating system.

Apple Macintosh System

The original Apple Macintosh microcomputer, introduced in 1984, utilized the powerful 32-bit Motorola 68000 microprocessor. This microcomputer, which evolved from the earlier Apple Lisa line, was revolutionary in design and achieved a high degree of user friendliness. Most of this was due to its specially designed operating system, which had little in common with DOS or any other existing microcomputer operating system. The advanced Macintosh operating system had its roots in the Smalltalk programming language developed at Xerox's Palo Alto Research Center in the 1970s and borrowed many easy-to-use features originally included in the Xerox 8010 Star Information System. Early versions of the Macintosh operating system were strictly single-user, single-tasking. More recent versions, however, include an accessory called the **MultiFinder** that adds some multitasking capabilities to the newer Macintosh computers (see Figure 12).

The Macintosh operating system is made up of several levels. At the top level are the MultiFinder and the **Finder.** Both of these are system programs, each stored in its own disk file. They manage the Macintosh "desktop" (see Figure 8) by letting you run application programs, set up disks, and organize, copy, and delete files. Older Macintoshes came with just the Finder, which allows you to run only one application program at a time. The newest Macintoshes also include

Figure 12 MultiFinder
The MultiFinder is a multitasking accessory to the Apple Macintosh operating system that lets you switch between several programs on your screen at the same time.

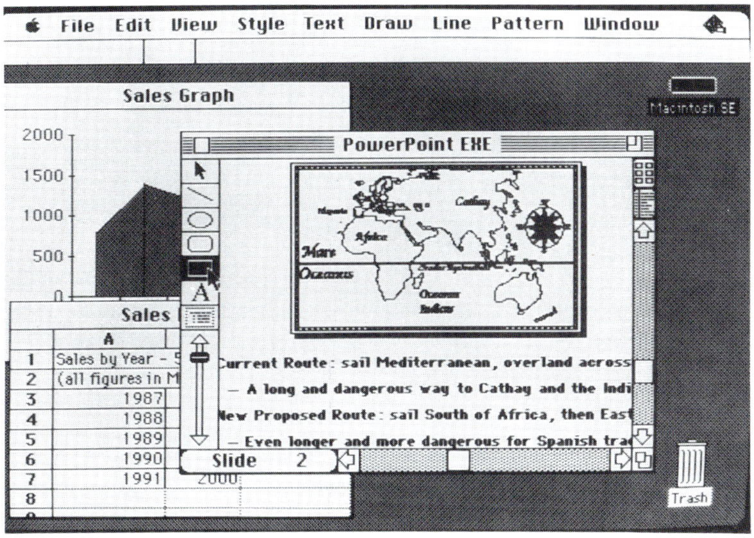

the MultiFinder, which lets you open up several windows with a different program running in each one and lets you rapidly switch between these windows. Although this sounds like multitasking, the current version of the MultiFinder isn't a true multitasking system. Only the program in the currently selected window is fully active. Certain specially designed programs can run in the background, however, and perform unattended, time-consuming tasks such as printing documents and making backup copies of disks.

Below the MultiFinder and the Finder is an accompanying file, called the System file. The System file contains typefaces, graphic images, text messages, and some of the program code that makes up the Macintosh operating system. At the lowest level of the Macintosh operating system is a powerful set of subprograms permanently encoded in a ROM chip that is built into the computer.

The main idea underlying the Macintosh operating system is that the computer should adapt to the user instead of the other way around. It has an exceptional user interface that allows you to perform many tasks quickly and easily. You instruct the computer to perform tasks by using a mouse to manipulate graphic objects on the screen and select options from pull-down menus. These graphic objects, called **icons,** are symbols for files, file folders, actions to be performed, or application programs to be run. For example, to delete a file from a disk, you simply point to the icon representing that file, hold down the mouse button to capture the icon, drag the file icon over to a trash can symbol, and release the mouse button. With little instruction, most users can quickly learn to operate the Macintosh. This friendly operating system encourages experimentation and is just plain fun to use.

The Apple Macintosh and its operating system are a proprietary system. Apple holds and tightly controls the patents for many of the Macintosh hardware components and the copyrights for the system software. Apple has not licensed

Real World

The Lure of UNIX

Gary D. Handler, the executive in charge of computer systems for Shearson, Lehman Brothers' trading floor, is a UNIX convert. After considerable reluctance, he agreed to base his company's computerized trading operations on this much-ballyhooed operating system. Now he believes he's ready for the future.

Operating system software provides basic instructions for a computer's operation. AT&T's UNIX is one of the stars of the operating system market. The 1986 market for UNIX-based computers was valued at $3.7 billion, up 37 percent from 1985, according to industry analysts.

What makes UNIX so popular is that it can run on computers of different sizes and brands, although sometimes slight modifications are necessary. Users can build networks of many kinds of computers. By contrast, proprietary systems, such as those of Digital Equipment Corp. and Apple, run only on machines built by those companies.

The Air Force was so taken by UNIX that it announced a $4.5 billion contract recently for computers that use the operating system. The company that won the contract would provide more than 20,000 mid-size computers, printers, and maintenance to the Air Force, Army, and defense agencies around the world. The contract's goal was to cut costs and increase efficiency by using the UNIX standard for all computer purchases.

Source: John Wilke, "Digital, Wang Drop Bid for Air Force Contract," *The Boston Globe*, January 6, 1988, p. 57.

these patents and copyrights to other manufacturers, so there are no legal Macintosh clones. There are some modified Macintoshes sold by a few companies, but these are just Apple Macintoshes that have been taken apart and reassembled in a different form, for example as a laptop computer. By keeping such tight controls over its microcomputers, Apple can maintain a high profit margin, but this means that the use of the Macintosh operating system is not nearly as widespread as other operating systems, such as DOS and UNIX. Nevertheless, there are still several million Apple Macintoshes currently in use.

Summary

- *What operating systems do.* Operating systems control hardware, manage software, and interact with users.
- *The basic types of computer operating systems.* The types of operating systems include single-user, single-tasking; single-user, multitasking; multiuser, single-tasking; multiuser, multitasking; multiprocessing; and networking.
- *The fundamental components of an operating system.* An operating system is composed of layers of software including the hardware interface, the application interface, and the user interface.
- *Several important microcomputer operating systems.* The major microcomputer operating systems include CP/M, DOS, OS/2, UNIX, ProDOS, and the Apple Macintosh System.

Key Terms

As an extra review of this chapter, try defining the following terms.

BIOS (Basic Input/Output System)
CP/M
DOS (PC-DOS, MS-DOS)
Finder
firmware
generic operating system
interrupt
memory-resident (RAM resident)
MultiFinder
multiprocessing
multitasking
OS/2
ProDOS
proprietary operating system
service program (system call)
single-tasking
terminal
time-sharing
UNIX

Review Questions

1. List three broad categories of activities performed by operating systems.
2. List five specific hardware-control tasks performed by operating systems.
3. List five specific software-control tasks performed by operating systems.
4. How might you tell an operating system to run a program?
5. What are some factors used in the classification of operating systems?
6. What is the simplest and most common type of operating system?
7. Describe one instance in which multitasking might be useful.
8. What are some advantages of time-sharing operating systems?
9. What kind of operating systems allow users to each run several different programs concurrently?
10. What kind of computers and operating systems serve several users and/or several programs in a truly simultaneous fashion?
11. What is the difference between multiprocessing and networking?
12. What are the basic component layers of an operating system?
13. Where is an operating system's BIOS often stored?
14. What is the difference between the hardware and application interfaces?
15. What was the first popular microcomputer operating system sold by an independent software firm?
16. Besides DOS, what operating system has been developed jointly by IBM and Microsoft?
17. What multiuser, multitasking operating system was developed at AT&T's Bell Laboratories in the early 1970s?
18. Name the preferred single-user, single-tasking operating system for Apple II computers.
19. Which operating system has its roots in the Smalltalk programming language and features from the Xerox 8010 Star Information system?
20. What is currently the single most popular microcomputer operating system?

Multiple Choice

1. Which of the following tasks is not performed by operating systems?
   (a) controlling disk drives
   (b) loading programs into memory
   (c) processing user commands
   (d) calculating statistics
2. What is the simplest and most common type of operating system for microcomputers?
   (a) single-user, single-tasking
   (b) single-user, multitasking
   (c) multiuser, single-tasking
   (d) multiprocessing
3. Which of the following types of operating systems is also called time-sharing?
   (a) single-user, single-tasking
   (b) single-user, multitasking
   (c) multiuser, single-tasking
   (d) multiprocessing
4. Which type of operating system connects many individual, stand-alone computers?
   (a) single-user, single-tasking
   (b) multiuser, multitasking
   (c) multiprocessing
   (d) networking
5. What is the innermost layer of an operating system?
   (a) hardware interface
   (b) application interface
   (c) user interface
   (d) serial interface
6. Which operating system layer allows software to create, write, read, copy, delete, and rename files in the same fashion no matter which storage device is being used?
   (a) hardware interface
   (b) application interface
   (c) user interface
   (d) serial interface
7. Which operating system layer processes commands and menu selections?
   (a) hardware interface
   (b) application interface
   (c) user interface
   (d) serial interface
8. What is the most common use of an operating system?
   (a) maintaining mailing lists
   (b) running application packages
   (c) creating application packages
   (d) controlling modems
9. What type of program allows the user to temporarily suspend an activity and switch to some other one?
   (a) BIOS
   (b) spreadsheet
   (c) memory-resident
   (d) utility
10. Which word best describes the execution of programs on a multitasking system?
    (a) simultanteous
    (b) sequential
    (c) parallel
    (d) concurrent
11. What type of operating system can execute two programs truly simultaneously?
    (a) multitasking
    (b) multiprocessing
    (c) single-tasking
    (d) time-sharing
12. Which was the first popular generic operating system for microcomputers?
    (a) CP/M
    (b) DOS
    (c) OS/2
    (d) UNIX

13. Which operating system runs on the original IBM Personal Computer?
    (a) ProDOS (b) DOS
    (c) OS/2 (d) Apple Macintosh System
14. Which of the following operating systems is designed especially for IBM and IBM-compatibles that use the Intel 80286 and 80386 microprocessors?
    (a) CP/M (b) DOS
    (c) OS/2 (d) Apple Macintosh System
15. Which of the following is a multiuser, multitasking operating system that has been adapted to run on all kinds of computers, large and small?
    (a) CP/M (b) ProDOS
    (c) OS/2 (d) UNIX

Projects

1. Several popular microcomputers have a variety of operating systems available for them. For example, an IBM Personal System/2 Model 80 can run DOS, OS/2, CP/M-86, XENIX, and several other less popular systems not mentioned in this chapter. Investigate the various operating systems for a computer such as the IBM PS/2 Model 80. Write a report that enumerates some of the major differences between these operating systems. If you owned such a computer, which operating system would you choose? Why?
2. Most operating systems are constantly upgraded by the manufacturer. It's not uncommon for a new version of a particular operating system to be released every year or so. In most cases, the upgrade is prompted by advancements in computer hardware. Choose one of the operating systems discussed in this chapter and research its history. Write a report that lists each major release and the reason for the upgrade. Computer books and past issues of computer magazines such as *PC Magazine, BYTE, A+,* and *MacWorld* are good sources of information.
3. As microcomputer hardware becomes more advanced, the trend is toward more sophisticated operating systems. Many newer computers either already have multitasking operating systems or have programmers working furiously to develop them. No doubt the expert "power users" will find ample opportunity to apply multitasking to their everyday work, but what about average users? Is it really that helpful to be able to run sixteen different programs at once? Or are single-tasking operating systems already powerful enough for most people? Look through some computer magazines for reviews of multitasking operating systems. Write a report that presents the pros and cons of multitasking operating systems as compared to single-tasking operating systems.
4. Choose one of the specific operating systems we've discussed in this chapter and try to find out more about it. Prepare a report that details the system's most important features. If you can gain access to a computer that runs the system, learn how to use it. Discuss how easy or difficult you found it to use and why.

PART 2

DOS

DOS, sold by both IBM and Microsoft, is the world's most popular operating system. It is run on millions of IBM and IBM-compatible microcomputers. You must learn at least the basics of DOS to effectively use these microcomputers, which are now common in schools, businesses, and even homes. Part 2 will teach you how to use DOS. Chapter 5 covers the basics, the bare essentials you need to run the computer. Chapter 6 presents lessons that will increase your understanding of DOS. Chapter 7 examines more advanced DOS topics, including the new DOS Shell.

CHAPTER 5

BEGINNING DOS

In This Chapter

DOS Versions

Getting Started

Lesson 1: Booting DOS
Lesson 2: Rebooting DOS
Lesson 3: Listing a Disk File Directory
Lesson 4: Using Special DOS Keys
Lesson 5: Changing the Default Disk Drive
Lesson 6: Checking Disk and Memory Status
Lesson 7: Clearing the Screen
Lesson 8: Formatting a Diskette
Lesson 9: Formatting a System Diskette
Lesson 10: Copying Files
Lesson 11: Copying an Entire Diskette
Lesson 12: Changing File Names
Lesson 13: Erasing Files
Lesson 14: Protecting Diskettes
Lesson 15: Displaying and Printing Text Files
Lesson 16: Running a Program

Preview

According to *Business Week,* some 10 million IBM and IBM-compatible microcomputers were being used in businesses around the world by the middle of 1987. Joseph R. (Rod) Canion, president of Compaq Computer Corporation, figures that customers have spent $80 billion on IBM PCs, IBM-compatibles, and the hardware and software that work with them. IBM sold approximately 2.7 million microcomputers in 1988. Compaq, the leading "clone" manufacturer and number 2 business computer maker in the United States, sold around 500,000 that same year. The number 3 business computer manufacturer is Apple, which makes machines that are not IBM-compatible unless they are fitted with special equipment. Frederic E. Davis, editor-in-chief of *MacUser* magazine, estimates that IBM and IBM-compatibles outnumber Apple Macintoshes in the marketplace six to one. Clearly, IBM and IBM-compatibles are by far the most popular class of microcomputer. The overwhelming majority of these machines are running DOS.

After the original IBM Personal Computer was unveiled in 1981, DOS quickly became popular in offices, large corporations, and other businesses where IBM has traditionally wielded a great deal of influence. As soon as various hardware manufacturers started selling lower cost IBM-compatible computers, DOS also began popping up in small businesses, organizations, and institutions, as well as in schools, libraries, and homes. Because of this "hardware explosion," many software developers began to write application packages to run under DOS. This attracted even more users, who attracted still more software developers. At the same time, hardware manufacturers began to develop expansion boards and peripheral devices to be used with computers that run DOS. Today, a huge body of application software and a multitude of hardware devices are devoted to DOS microcomputers. Despite more advanced operating systems, such as OS/2 and XENIX, designed for high-end IBM and IBM-compatible machines, DOS is still the most popular microcomputer operating system in the world. In 1988 alone, IBM and Microsoft shipped 9.8 million copies of DOS, and approximately 75 percent of all microcomputers sold used DOS. This percentage is expected to increase until at least 1991.

After studying this chapter, you will know how to

- start up DOS with the computer turned off.
- start up DOS with the computer turned on.
- obtain a directory of the files on a disk.
- use the special DOS keys.
- change the default disk drive.
- obtain a disk and memory status report.
- clear the display screen.
- format a diskette.
- format a system diskette.
- copy files.
- copy an entire diskette.
- change file names.
- erase files.
- protect a diskette from accidental erasure.
- display on the screen and print text files.
- run an application package.

Insight

Will PC-DOS Be Replaced by Another Operating System?

Watch out, PC-DOS—there are a couple of hounds nipping at your heels.

PC-DOS (or MS-DOS) has been enjoying a fairly safe and secure life as a leader of the operating system pack since the microcomputer population explosion of the 1980s. But time is taking its toll, and the gray hairs are starting to show.

DOS was originally designed to be a single-user, single-tasking operating system, allowing only one program to be run at a time. Today, there are some clever applications packages that seem to let you do two things at once, such as print a file in the background while you're still working with the word processor. DOS doesn't handle this well.

When you want to perform more involved tasks, such as processing a large number of accounting transactions while still working on a spreadsheet, DOS is definitely inadequate. In large business, scientific, and engineering applications, these kinds of tasks are almost required today.

More elaborate *multitasking* operating systems can run several programs at the same time. Actually, they switch back and forth between tasks, giving each program a small slice of time. The switching is so fast that it's not apparent to the user.

People who use their IBM-compatible microcomputers for multitasking have two main choices in operating systems today—UNIX and OS/2. UNIX is a very powerful and flexible operating system that was developed by Bell Laboratories and originally ran on minicomputers. OS/2 was developed jointly by Microsoft and IBM. It is a memory-hungry system that runs only on the more powerful IBM-compatible microcomputers that use the Intel 80286, 80386, and 80486 processors.

UNIX and OS/2 are being groomed as the operating system leaders of the next generation of powerful microcomputers. But it's unlikely that DOS will just slink off into the woods. DOS has a huge, installed base and many devoted users. For many simple computing needs, it will undoubtedly remain on top.

DOS Versions

DOS stands for **Disk Operating System.** It was originally written for IBM by Microsoft, which kept the right to sell DOS under its own name. Today, DOS is developed jointly by both IBM and Microsoft. When it is sold by IBM for IBM microcomputers, it is called PC-DOS or IBM DOS. When it is sold by Microsoft for IBM-compatibles, such as those made by Compaq, Tandy, or Zenith, it is called MS-DOS. Although a few minor differences exist between the system software sold by IBM and Microsoft, from the user's standpoint PC-DOS and MS-DOS are almost identical. So, they are often both referred to generically as DOS.

Computer technology advances quickly. To remain popular, an operating system must be continually upgraded to accommodate new computers and new capabilities for existing models. Several versions of DOS have been released by IBM and Microsoft. In each release, bugs have been worked out and improvements have been made to previous versions. The driving force behind each new version of DOS, however, has been new hardware capabilities, usually related to disk drives.

It is important to know which version of DOS you are using, because some hardware and software can only be used with more recent releases. Fortunately, each new DOS version is **upwardly compatible** with former versions. This means, at least in theory, that every official command that worked with previous versions should work with the new version. In most cases, this is so. However, there always seems to be at least one command that doesn't work quite the same in the new release. Nevertheless, for the most part you probably don't have to change the way you did things before unless you want to take advantage of the added capabilities of a new DOS version.

If you don't need these additional capabilities, you don't have to buy the latest version of DOS each time a new release is issued. As long as the version you have works well with your hardware and software, you can continue using it. Keep in mind that although a new DOS version may add certain capabilities, you must pay for the upgrade and that new DOS versions typically use more memory and more disk space. In many cases, upgrading is simply not worth it. Unless you're buying a new machine or adding a different disk drive, you may not need the latest DOS version.

DOS versions are identified by numbers such as 1.00, 3.30, and 4.01. The number to the left of the decimal point reflects a major classification; the numbers to the right represent more minor differences. The larger the number, the more recent the version. This table summarizes the major DOS versions that have been released so far, along with the primary reason for each upgrade:

Version	Date	Reason for Upgrade (New Capabilities)
1.00	8/81	5¼" 160K single-sided floppy disk drives
1.10	5/82	5¼" 320K double-sided floppy disk drives
2.00	3/83	5¼" 360K floppy, 10M hard disk drives
2.10	10/83	5¼" 360K half-height floppy drives
3.00	8/84	5¼" 1.2M floppy, bigger hard disk drives
3.10	3/85	Network disks and file sharing
3.20	12/85	3½" 720K floppy disk drives
3.30	3/87	3½" 1.44M floppy disk drives
4.00	7/88	Hard disks larger than 35M, DOS Shell
4.01	10/88	Corrected errors in version 4.00

Throughout Part 2 we will be using MS-DOS 4.01 for the examples. Most of what we cover, however, also applies to DOS 2.00 and newer versions. Versions 1.00 and 1.10 are now considered obsolete. If you are using a version of DOS other than 4.01, the screens you see on your computer may be slightly different than the ones shown in this book.

Getting Started

Although DOS is a powerful microcomputer operating system, you can easily learn its most commonly used features. DOS might be set up at your particular computer site in any of several different ways. You are most likely to use DOS in one of the following arrangements:

1. On a microcomputer with two floppy disk drives and DOS installed on one or more diskettes.

2. On a microcomputer with a hard disk drive and DOS installed on the hard disk.
3. On a microcomputer connected to a local area network with DOS installed on the network file server. Some DOS commands do not work over a network, as we will point out.

You may need additional direction from your instructor to run DOS at your computer installation. You should then be able to complete the following lessons. If DOS has not already been installed on your hard disk (with a path to the DOS subdirectory) or on floppy disks for you, see Appendix C.

Lesson 1: Booting DOS

DOS stands for Disk Operating System. Although some low-level parts of the operating system programs are stored in ROM chips, the higher level programs of the operating system are kept on a floppy or hard disk. Like any program, the operating system must be loaded into the computer's memory before it can start working. The operating system, however, is what loads programs into memory and sets up the computer to execute them. If this is so, how does the operating system itself get started? Does it load itself? In a way, yes. Basically, a small program in ROM is automatically invoked every time the computer is turned on or reset. After loading itself into memory, this program then loads the rest of the operating system into memory and begins execution. In a sense, the computer pulls itself up by its own bootstraps. The process of initially loading and executing the operating system is often called **booting up.** In the particular case of IBM and IBM-compatibles, this is also called booting DOS, loading DOS, or simply starting DOS. At this point, your computer should be turned off.

Step 1: Insert the DOS Startup Disk

If your computer has a hard disk, skip this step and go directly to Step 2. If your computer is connected to a local area network, you may have to complete this step. If your computer does not have a hard disk and is not connected to a network, you must insert a diskette containing DOS before you can turn it on. In most cases, this diskette will be labeled "DOS Startup."

If your computer has two or more floppy disk drives, the A drive is the one on top or to the left. This is the floppy disk drive from which you boot DOS.

If drive A accepts 5¼-inch diskettes, grasp the DOS Startup disk by the label and remove it from the paper sleeve. Be careful not to touch the exposed parts around the oval slot and circular hole. Hold the disk with the label side up and the oval slot pointing toward the computer. Slide the diskette all the way into the drive slot, where it may click into place, and close the door or lever (see Figure 1).

If drive A accepts 3½-inch diskettes, grasp the DOS Startup disk with the label up and the metal shield pointing toward the computer. The arrow embossed or printed on the disk should point toward the computer. Slide the diskette all the way into the drive slot, where it will click and drop into place (see Figure 1).

Figure 1 Inserting and Removing Diskettes

3 1/2 - inch diskette

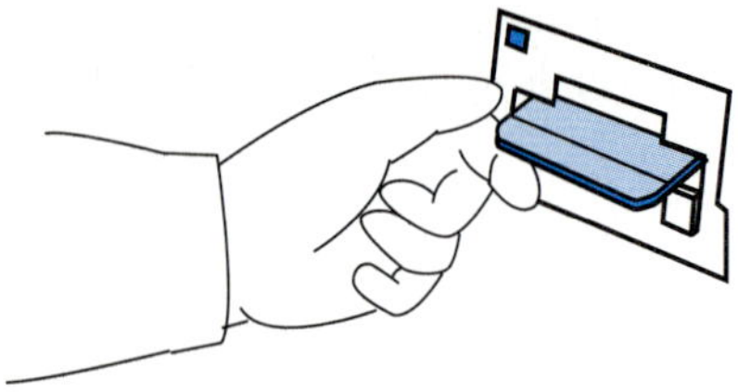

Insert diskette with arrow side up and arrow pointing to diskette drive. Press gently on diskette until it clicks and drops into place.

Remove by pressing eject button on lower right of diskette drive.

5 1/4 - inch diskette

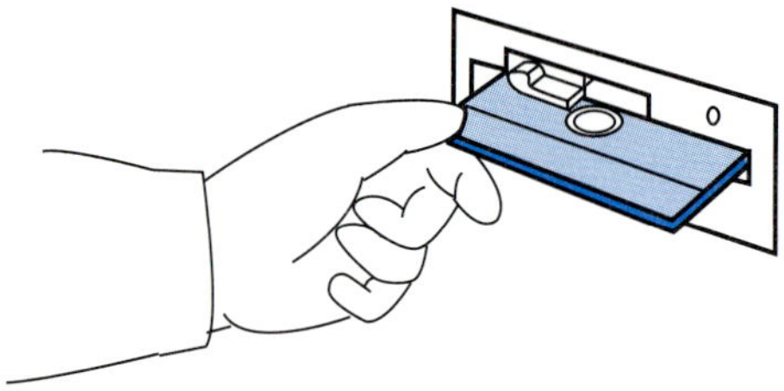

Insert diskette into drive until it clicks into place; label must be facing up with write-protect notch on left. Close drive door.

Remove by opening drive door and gently pulling out diskette.

Step 2: Turn On the Computer

If your display has its own power switch, turn it on first. Then turn on the computer. Older IBM microcomputers have a big red toggle switch on the right side of the system unit toward the rear; the newer Personal System/2 models have the switch right up in front (see Figure 2). Some IBM-compatibles have the power switch on the back side of the system unit. Flip the power switch. On many computers you will hear the cooling fan begin to hum.

Step 3: Watch the Display and Wait

After the power has been turned on, the computer completes some self-tests to ensure that it is working properly. One of these tests checks out all of the memory installed in the computer. This test could take several minutes, so don't be alarmed if nothing seems to be happening. After the power-on self-tests are complete, the computer will beep and check drive A to see if it contains the DOS Startup disk. If your computer has a hard disk and no diskette in drive A, it will boot up from the hard disk. Assuming the computer is in working order, the Startup diskette has been inserted correctly (if you need it), and DOS has been correctly installed on the Startup diskette or hard disk, you will see a message on the display screen. The exact contents of this message will depend on the type of computer and the way DOS was installed on the disk. If your computer does not have a built-in battery-maintained clock, DOS may ask you to enter the current date and time.

Step 4: Enter the Date and Time

If you don't see the following message on your screen, skip this step:

```
Current date is Tue 01-01-1980
Enter new date (mm-dd-yy):
```

Type today's date in the form of mm-dd-yy or mm/dd/yy. In other words, type in the month number, a dash or slash, the day of the month, another dash or slash, and the last two digits of the year.

Figure 2 The Power Switch

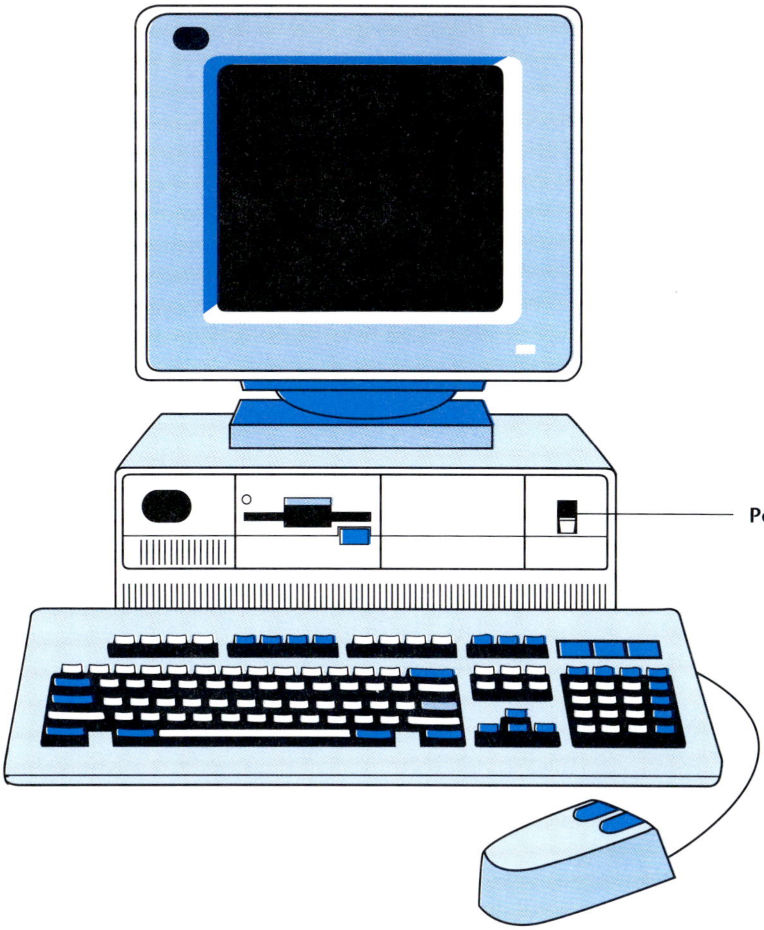

Press **Enter**

Next, a message like this may appear:

```
Current time is 12:00:39.05a
Enter new time:
```

Type the hour, a colon, and the minute. If it is afternoon, add twelve to the hour as in the 24-hour clock format. For example, if it is 2 P.M., you would enter 14:00. You can also enter the second and hundredths of a second if you happen to carry a stop watch and feel so inclined. Just the hour and minute are sufficient, however.

Press **Enter**

At this point, your screen may look like Figure 3. The C> on the last line is the **DOS prompt.** In this case, it indicates that disk drive C, the hard disk, is the default drive. The **default drive** is the disk drive that DOS assumes you want to use unless you specify otherwise. If you booted up from drive A, then drive A would be your default drive and the DOS prompt would be A>. The prompt tells you that DOS is waiting for a command.

Practice

Turn off the computer. Wait ten seconds. Turn it back on again. If it asks you to enter a new date, just press **Enter** without typing a date. If it asks you to enter

Figure 3 Booting Up

```
Current date is Tue 01-01-1980
Enter new date (mm-dd-yy): 7-10-89
Current time is 12:00:39.05a
Enter new time: 12:42

Microsoft(R) MS-DOS(R) Version 4.01
             (C)Copyright Microsoft Corp 1981-1988

C>_
```

a new time, just press **Enter** without typing a time. You don't have to enter a new date and time, but if your computer doesn't have a battery-maintained clock, it is best to enter the correct date and time when you boot up.

Lesson 2: Rebooting DOS

Occasionally, something goes wrong in a program and the computer may seem to be "stuck." Or after working with a program you may have to "reinitialize," or bring the computer back to the way it was when you first turned it on. You could, of course, just turn off the computer and boot it up as you learned in Lesson 1. There is another way to reboot the computer without shutting it off, however.

Step 1: Press Ctrl-Alt-Del

DOS has a special combination of keypresses that will reboot the computer without having to shut it off first. All you have to do is press the keys marked Control (or Ctrl), Alternate (or Alt), and Delete (or Del), and hold them down at the same time for a moment.

Press **Ctrl-Alt-Del**

Step 2: Watch the Display and Wait

In most cases, the screen will go blank, the computer will beep, and the disk drive will spin and blink its red access light just as it did when you first turned it on. If all this doesn't happen, a serious program error has probably overwritten a crucial part of DOS in memory, and you will have to turn off the computer and boot it up as you did in Lesson 1. If all is well, DOS will again ask you to supply the date and time if your computer does not have a battery-maintained clock.

Step 3: Enter the Date and Time

If DOS asks you to enter a new date and time, do so as you did in Lesson 1. DOS will once again display its copyright message and the prompt, as shown in Figure 3.

Practice

Reboot your computer without turning it off. Enter the correct date and time if asked to do so.

Lesson 3: Listing a Disk File Directory

In most cases, you tell DOS what to do by entering commands or responding to prompts that ask you to supply more information. Some DOS commands are loaded into memory when the computer is booted up and kept there until the power is turned off. These **internal commands,** also called **resident routines,** are kept in memory because they are the most essential or most frequently used parts of the operating system. For example, one of the simplest and most commonly used DOS internal commands is DIR, which displays a file directory. After you boot up, internal commands are always available from any disk. The remaining DOS commands are called **external commands** or **transient routines,** because they are kept in disk storage and temporarily loaded into memory only when they are needed or specifically requested. CHKDSK, for example, is an external DOS command that displays information about a disk and the memory installed in your computer.

Programs, data, and text are kept on disks in files. Every file has a name, size, creation date, and creation time associated with it. The DIR command lets you see what files you have on a particular disk or in a particular subdirectory. A **subdirectory** is a group of files on a disk organized under a single name.

Step 1: Enter DIR

To execute the DIR command:

Type **dir**
Press **Enter**

It doesn't matter whether you type DOS commands in lowercase letters, uppercase letters, or a combination of both. For example, DIR, dIr, and Dir are all equivalent.

DIR, which is short for DIRectory, displays information about the files on a disk or in a subdirectory. When the command is entered by itself, it will produce a directory listing on the screen of the default disk or current subdirectory. Figure 4 shows the screen after executing the DIR command. Your screen is probably different because your default disk most likely has different files on it.

Step 2: Examine the Directory Listing

Examine the screen in Figure 4. First it reveals the volume label of the disk. The volume label is just the name of the disk, which in this case is HARD DISK. Next is the volume serial number, which is just a code number assigned to the disk when it is formatted. DOS versions prior to 4.00 do not have volume serial numbers. Then DOS says that this is a directory of the disk in drive C, and it

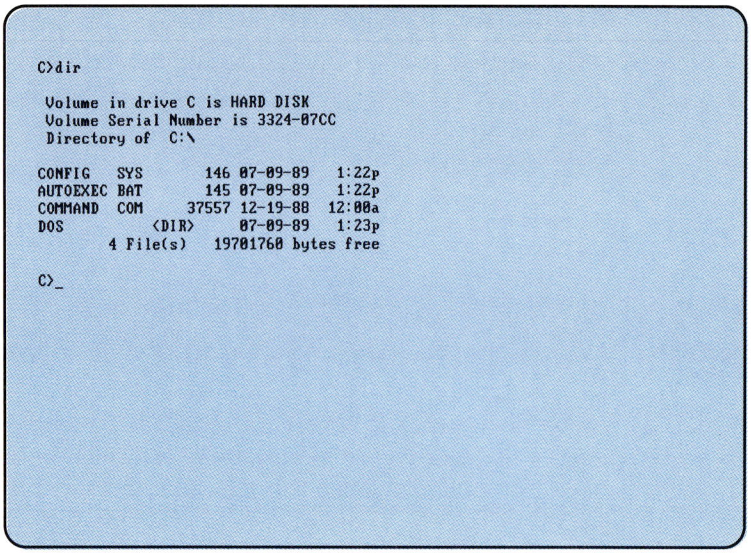

***Figure 4* Listing a Directory**

lists the names, sizes, dates, and times of the files. Notice that the first three file names have two parts. We'll have more to say about this file name format shortly. The last file name in the list, DOS, is the name of a subdirectory. The <DIR> designation next to the name tells you that it is a subdirectory and not an ordinary file. This subdirectory, which we'll look at later, contains the files that make up most of DOS. It was created when DOS was installed on the hard disk.

Each file name, except for the DOS subdirectory, has a number to its immediate right. This is the size of that file in bytes. A byte, you'll recall, is basically equivalent to a single character. Finally, listed to the right of each file size is the date and then the time at which the file was created or last changed. The first file in the list, for example, is named CONFIG.SYS, occupies 146 bytes, and was created on July 9, 1989, at 1:22 P.M.

At the bottom of the listing, the DIR command tells you that four files are in this directory and there are 19,701,760 "bytes free." This means that 19,701,760 bytes of storage are still unused on the disk. Since it's important to know what files are on a disk and how much room is left, DIR is one of the most frequently used DOS commands.

Step 3: Examine Another Disk's Directory

The DIR command can also be used to list the directory of a disk in a drive other than the current default drive. You can do this by specifying the disk drive letter after DIR. For example, if your computer has a hard disk, you can examine the directory of a disk in floppy drive A. If you have a diskette with files on it, insert the diskette into drive A.

Type **dir a:**
Press **Enter**

The **a:** is the designation for the A disk drive. If you have a computer with two floppy drives, you can examine a disk in the second drive by entering DIR B:. Note that the hard disk is usually referred to as the C drive, regardless of whether a B floppy drive is installed.

Step 4: Examine the Contents of a Subdirectory

The DIR command can also be used to list the files in a subdirectory. All you have to do is type the name of the subdirectory after the DIR. For example, if your computer has a hard disk with a subdirectory named DOS, try the following command:

Type **`dir dos`**
Press **Enter**

Figure 5 shows the result. Since 68 files are in this directory listing but only 25 lines can be shown on the screen, many of the names have moved up and disappeared off the top of the screen. Figure 5, therefore, shows only the bottom part of the listing. For the rest of this chapter, we will assume you have a computer with a hard disk that has a DOS subdirectory.

Step 5: Look For a Specific File

Frequently, you'd like to be able to check if a particular file is on a disk or in a subdirectory without having to look at the entire directory listing. The DIR command can do this for you if you give it the name of the file you're looking for. All you have to do is enter the name of the file after the DIR. If you want to look in a subdirectory, type the subdirectory name, a backward slash (\), and then the name of the file. DOS will either list an abbreviated directory with only that file in it or tell you the file is not there. For example, if your computer has a DOS subdirectory, execute this command:

Type **`dir dos\format.com`**
Press **Enter**

This command tells DOS to look in the DOS subdirectory for a file named FORMAT.COM. Figure 6 shows the result. If your computer doesn't have a DOS subdirectory, try this command instead:

Type **`dir format.com`**
Press **Enter**

Figure 5 Looking at a Subdirectory

```
GRAPHICS COM     16693 10-06-88  12:00a
GRAPHICS PRO      9397 10-06-88  12:00a
HIMEM    SYS      6261 10-06-88  12:00a
MODE     COM     22960 10-06-88  12:00a
NLSFUNC  EXE      6878 10-06-88  12:00a
PRINTER  SYS     18914 10-06-88  12:00a
RECOVER  COM     10588 10-06-88  12:00a
4201     CPI      6404 10-06-88  12:00a
4208     CPI       720 10-06-88  12:00a
5202     CPI       370 10-06-88  12:00a
README   TXT     14148 10-12-88   9:13p
BACKUP   COM     36880 10-06-88  12:00a
EGA      CPI     49068 10-06-88  12:00a
LCD      CPI     10703 10-06-88  12:00a
RESTORE  COM     36946 10-06-88  12:00a
PCIBMDRV MOS       263 10-06-88  12:00a
SHELL    CLR      4406 10-06-88  12:00a
SHELL    HLP     66527 10-06-88  12:00a
SHELL    MEU      4588 10-06-88  12:00a
SHELLB   COM      3894 10-06-88  12:00a
SHELLC   EXE    153855 10-06-88  12:00a
DOSUTIL  MEU      6660 10-06-88  12:00a
        68 File(s)  19701760 bytes free

C>_
```

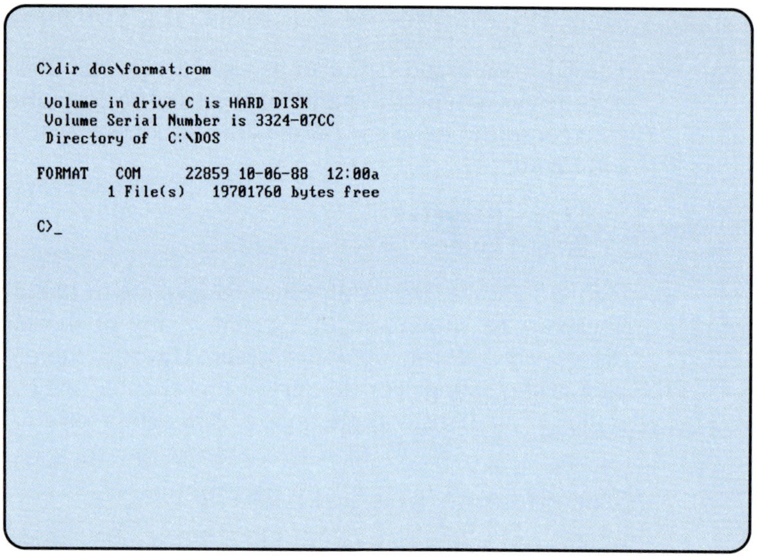

Figure 6 Looking for a Specific File

For the rest of this chapter, we will assume you have a DOS subdirectory on your default disk. If you do not, omit the dos or dos\ designations from the instructions given.

DOS File Names This is a good time to digress a bit and discuss DOS file names in more detail. First of all, notice that each file in the directory you listed has a unique name. No two files in the same directory can have the same name because DOS wouldn't be able to tell them apart. Two files on different disks or in different subdirectories, however, can have the same name. A file name can consist of two parts: a primary filename and an optional extension. The first part, or **filename** as IBM calls it, can be from one to eight characters long. It can include any of the characters you see on the keyboard except for the following, which are considered invalid in filenames:

. " / \ [ ] : | < > + = ; ,

The second part, an optional short name, is called an **extension.** It is separated from the primary filename by a period and has from one to three characters in it. These characters also can be any of the keyboard characters except those we just listed. If a file's name does have an extension, you may have to use both parts when telling DOS to do something with that file. Extensions are most often used to classify files. For example, here are some of the more common file name extensions, along with the types of files they usually designate:

COM	DOS external command or an executable program
EXE	DOS external command or an executable program
BAT	Batch file
SYS	System setup file
ASM	Assembly language program
BAS	BASIC language program
PAS	Pascal language program
TXT	Text file
BAK	Backup copy of some other file
DOC	Document file of some word processing programs
WKS	Worksheet file of some spreadsheet programs
DBF	Data base file of some data base managers

Finally, a file name can be prefaced with the designation of its disk drive and subdirectory. For example, C:\DOS\FORMAT.COM is the full specification for the file FORMAT.COM on the hard disk C in the DOS subdirectory. Note that the colon must be used after the disk drive letter and the backslash must be used before and after the subdirectory name. If you don't enter part of the specification, such as the disk drive letter or subdirectory, DOS will assume you mean the default drive or current subdirectory.

Step 6: Look for a Specific Group of Files

Not only can the DIR command find a single file on a disk, it can also be used to list a group of files if their names have some characters in common. The DOS **global file name characters,** * and ?, can be included in a filename or extension to give you greater flexibility in designating DOS files. The * character can be used in a file specification to symbolize any character or group of characters. For example, *.SYS means "any file with an extension of SYS." The ? character is used to symbolize any single character. For example, MO?E.COM means "any file that has an extension of COM and a four-letter filename beginning with MO and ending with an E." Both global file name characters can be used together in the same specification, too. For example, ????.* means "any file with at most four characters in its first part." Try each of the following commands:

Type	**dir dos*.sys**
Press	**Enter**
Type	**dir dos\mo?e.com**
Press	**Enter**
Type	**dir dos\????.***
Press	**Enter**

Figure 7 shows what you should see on your screen after entering the command DIR DOS*.SYS.

```
C>dir dos\*.sys

 Volume in drive C is HARD DISK
 Volume Serial Number is 3324-07CC
 Directory of  C:\DOS

COUNTRY  SYS     12806 10-06-88  12:00a
DISPLAY  SYS     15692 10-06-88  12:00a
KEYBOARD SYS     23328 10-06-88  12:00a
EMM386   SYS     87776 10-06-88  12:00a
RAMDRIVE SYS      8235 10-06-88  12:00a
SMARTDRV SYS     10224 10-06-88  12:00a
XMA2EMS  SYS     29211 10-06-88  12:00a
ANSI     SYS      9105 10-06-88  12:00a
DRIVER   SYS      5241 10-06-88  12:00a
HIMEM    SYS      6261 10-06-88  12:00a
PRINTER  SYS     18914 10-06-88  12:00a
       11 File(s)   19701760 bytes free

C>_
```

Figure 7 Looking for a Group of Files

Practice

1. List a directory of your default disk drive.
2. List a directory of the DOS subdirectory.
3. Try this command:

   Type **dir *.***
   Press **Enter**

   What does it do?
4. Try this command:

   Type **dir dos*.exe**
   Press **Enter**

   What does it do?
5. Create a listing of the DOS subdirectory that shows only those files that begin with the letter S.
6. Create a listing of the DOS subdirectory that shows only those files with primary filenames less than four characters long.
7. Notice that subdirectory names have no extensions. Try this command (follow the asterisk with a period):

   Type **dir *.**
   Press **Enter**

   What does it do?

Lesson 4: Using Special DOS Keys

Like most software, DOS assigns special meanings to certain keys and combinations of keypresses. You've already learned some of these. For example, you know that you must press the Enter key after typing in a command. This tells DOS to go ahead and process that command. The Backspace key can be used to correct typing errors on a line before the Enter key has been pressed. In Lesson 2 you learned that pressing the Control (Ctrl), Alternate (Alt), and Delete (Del) keys at the same time will reboot DOS without having to shut off the power and turn it back on. Let's explore some of the other keys DOS uses (see Figure 8).

Step 1: Press the Escape Key to Cancel a Line

As you've probably already discovered, it's pretty easy to make typing mistakes when using a keyboard. If the command you're typing is short and you haven't pressed the Enter key yet, the easiest way to fix a mistake is to backspace over it and retype it. If the command is long or if you really messed it up, you can cancel the entire line and start over. To do this, press the Escape (Esc) key. For example, type the following line at the DOS prompt (but don't press the Enter key):

Type **This line is really messed up!**

Suppose what you really meant to type in was DIR DOS, and you realized your mistake before you pressed the Enter key.

Press **Escape**

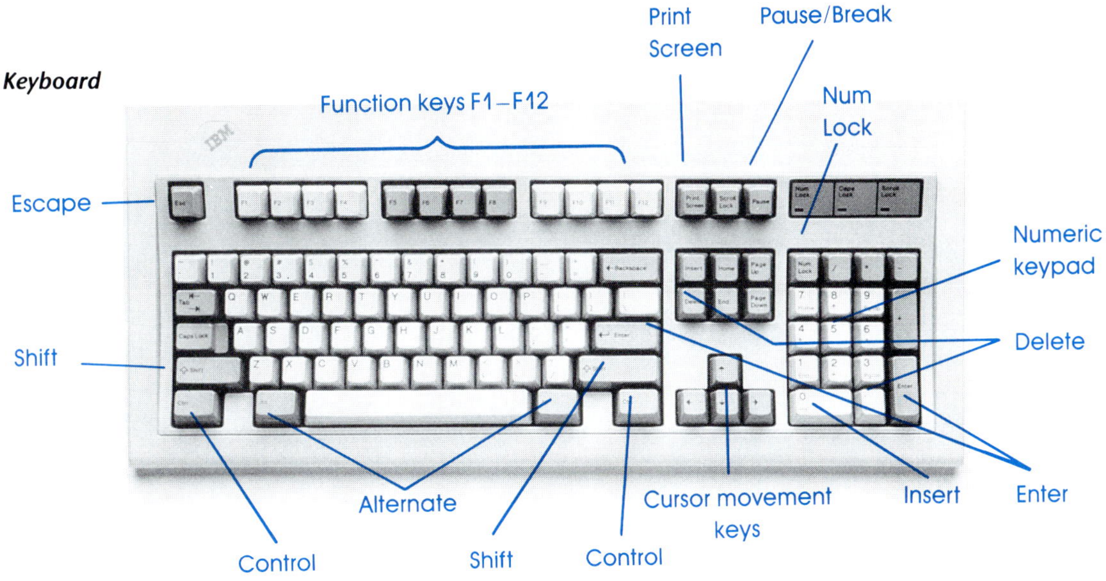

Figure 8 The Keyboard

Pressing the Escape key cancels the current line. When you do this, DOS will display a / (slash) to signal that the line has been canceled, and it will skip down to the next line so you can start over. Now execute the following command to see the familiar DOS directory:

Type **dir dos**
Press **Enter**

Step 2: Press Ctrl-Num Lock to Pause Screen Scrolling

As you watch the DOS directory scroll by on the screen, the first part of it disappears off the top. Sometimes, information scrolls by before you get a chance to read it all. It would be nice if you could temporarily stop the screen so that you wouldn't have to take speed-reading lessons to use the computer. Fortunately, DOS will pause for you if you hold down the Control key and press the Num Lock key. On the newer IBM Enhanced-style keyboards, you press the Pause key instead of Ctrl-Num Lock. In either case, this action will immediately pause any screen that is scrolling by. To resume scrolling, press any key (except a Shift, Lock, Ctrl, or Alt key). For example, execute the following commands:

Type **dir dos**
Press **Enter**
Press **Ctrl-Num Lock** (or **Pause**)

Figure 9 shows what can happen. You can pause and resume scrolling as many times as you wish.

Step 3: Press Ctrl-Break to Cancel a Command

Suppose that you've entered DIR DOS or DIR by mistake and you don't want to wait for the whole directory to scroll by on the screen. Or perhaps you've seen enough and you just want to stop it. You can cancel a DOS command by pressing

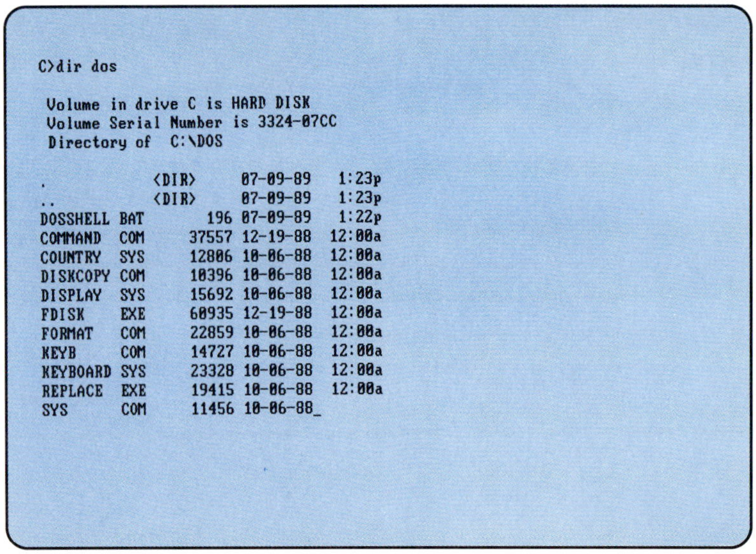

Figure 9 Pausing Screen Scrolling

the Control and Break keys at the same time. This stops a command from finishing its job. In many cases, Ctrl-Break will also terminate programs other than just DOS commands. To see how this works, follow these directions:

Type **dir dos**
Press **Enter**
Press **Ctrl-Break**

Pressing Ctrl-Break will terminate the directory command before it finishes. Figure 10 shows how this might appear on your screen. The ^C at the bottom stands for Ctrl-C, which means that the command has been canceled.

On IBM PC- and AT-style keyboards, the Break key is right next to the Num Lock key, and is also labeled Scroll Lock. On the newer IBM Enhanced-style keyboards, the Break key is the same as the Pause key. On all types of keyboards, you can also cancel a command by holding down the Control key and typing a C. Note that Ctrl-Break (or Ctrl-C) is different from the Escape key. Escape will cancel a line typed at the DOS prompt before the Enter key is pressed. Ctrl-Break cancels a command after the Enter key has been pressed and while the command is executing.

Step 4: Press Shift-PrtSc to Print the Screen

Frequently there is a sequence of commands or some information on the screen that you would like to save. If you have a printer connected to your computer, DOS can produce a hard copy of everything that is currently on the display screen. On IBM PC- and AT-style keyboards, you press one of the Shift keys along with the key marked PrtSc (Print Screen). On the newer IBM Enhanced-style keyboards, you simply press the key labeled Print Screen. If you have a printer, make sure it's turned on.

Press **Shift-PrtSc** (or **Print Screen**)

You should get a copy of what's on your screen right now.

Figure 10 Canceling a Command

```
DOSSHELL BAT      196 07-09-89   1:22p
COMMAND  COM    37557 12-19-88  12:00a
COUNTRY  SYS    12806 10-06-88  12:00a
DISKCOPY COM    10396 10-06-88  12:00a
DISPLAY  SYS    15692 10-06-88  12:00a
FDISK    EXE    60935 12-19-88  12:00a
FORMAT   COM    22859 10-06-88  12:00a
KEYB     COM    14727 10-06-88  12:00a
KEYBOARD SYS    23328 10-06-88  12:00a
REPLACE  EXE    19415 10-06-88  12:00a
SYS      COM    11456 10-06-88  12:00a
ASSIGN   COM     5753 10-06-88  12:00a
ATTRIB   EXE    18263 10-06-88  12:00a
CHKDSK   COM    17787 10-06-88  12:00a
COMP     COM     9459 10-06-88  12:00a
DEBUG    COM    21574 10-06-88  12:00a
DISKCOMP COM     9857 10-06-88  12:00a
EDLIN    COM    14069 10-06-88  12:00a
FC       EXE    15807 10-06-88  12:00a
FILESYS  EXE    11129 10-06-88  12:00a
FIND     EXE     5941 10-06-88  12:00a
IFSFUNC  EXE    21739 10-06-88  12:00a
^C

C>_
```

Step 5: Press Ctrl-PrtSc to Echo to the Printer

The printout you got from the previous step contains only one screen of text. This output would not help much if you wanted a hard copy of the entire DOS directory, because the whole directory doesn't fit on the screen at once. Pressing Control and PrtSc (or Control and Print Screen on the Enhanced-style keyboards), however, will cause whatever you type and the computer's responses to be displayed both on the screen and sent to the printer. This echoing will continue until you press Ctrl-PrtSc again. So, you could, for example, get a hard copy of your entire computer session.

To get a hard copy of the DOS disk directory, follow these directions:

Press **Ctrl-PrtSc**
Type **dir**
Press **Enter**

You should see the directory information being displayed on the screen a bit slower as it is also being sent to the printer. When it's finished and you see the DOS prompt, execute this command again to turn off printer echoing:

Press **Ctrl-PrtSc**

Practice

1. Create a hard copy listing of this Practice session if you have a printer.

   Press **Ctrl-PrtSc** (or **Ctrl-Print Screen**)

2. Start typing a command, but don't press the Enter key:

   Type **dir a:**

   Suppose you meant to type just **dir**, but made a mistake. Cancel the command:

   Press **Escape**

   Now execute the command you meant to enter:

   Type **dir**
   Press **Enter**

3. Generate a directory listing of your DOS subdirectory or Startup disk. Pause and restart the screen scrolling at least twice before the command is finished.
4. Again, generate a directory listing of your DOS subdirectory or Startup disk. This time, however, cancel the command before it finishes by using Ctrl-Break or Ctrl-C.
5. Turn off printer echoing.
6. If you have a printer, make sure it is turned on.

   Type **dir**
   Press **Enter**

   Create a hard-copy listing of just the current contents of your screen.

Lesson 5: Changing the Default Disk Drive

IBM and IBM-compatible computers without hard disks boot up from the diskette in drive A, which is the default disk drive. Computers that have a hard disk with DOS installed on it boot up from drive C, which is considered the default drive. You will recall that the current default drive is indicated by the DOS prompt, for example, A> or C>. This means that whenever you enter a command that doesn't explicitly specify a particular disk drive, the current default drive is assumed. For example, when you enter DIR by itself, you get the directory of the current default drive. If your computer has more than one disk drive, like most IBM and IBM compatible computers, you may occasionally want to change your default drive from A or C to another installed drive. This is a common procedure, sometimes called **switching drives.** Let's look at how and why you would change the default disk drive.

Step 1: Enter the Designation of the New Default Drive

If you have a computer with a hard disk and one floppy drive, put a disk with files on it into drive A. Then execute this command to change your default drive from C to A:

Type **a:**
Press **Enter**

If you have a computer with two floppy disk drives, put a disk with files on it into drive B. Then execute this command to change your default drive to B:

Type **b:**
Press **Enter**

DOS will respond with a prompt indicating the new default drive.

Step 2: Use the New Default Drive

Now when you execute a command, DOS will assume you are referring to the new default drive unless you specify otherwise. For example, try this command:

Type **dir**
Press **Enter**

You will get a directory listing of the new default drive, A or B (see Figure 11). Although this might not seem terribly exciting at the moment, being able to

Figure 11 Changing the Default Disk Drive

```
A>dir

 Volume in drive A has no label
 Volume Serial Number is 0E1E-1BE0
 Directory of  A:\

COMMAND  COM     37557 12-19-88  12:00a
AUTOEXEC BAT        39 10-06-88  12:00a
CONFIG   SYS        96 10-06-88  12:00a
COUNTRY  SYS     12806 10-06-88  12:00a
DISKCOPY COM     10396 10-06-88  12:00a
DISPLAY  SYS     15692 10-06-88  12:00a
FDISK    EXE     60935 12-19-88  12:00a
FORMAT   COM     22859 10-06-88  12:00a
KEYB     COM     14727 10-06-88  12:00a
KEYBOARD SYS     23328 10-06-88  12:00a
REPLACE  EXE     19415 10-06-88  12:00a
SELECT   COM      3642 10-06-88  12:00a
SELECT   HLP     28695 10-06-88  12:00a
SELECT   PRT      1329 10-06-88  12:00a
SYS      COM     11456 10-06-88  12:00a
       15 File(s)      18432 bytes free

A>_
```

change the default drive enables you to make full use of all of your installed disk drives. As you become more proficient with DOS and application packages, you'll find yourself switching disk drives often. For example, on systems with two floppy drives, you may leave the DOS Startup disk in drive A and a disk containing a particular application package in drive B. Then, after booting up, you could switch to drive B to run your application program.

Step 3: Switch Back to the Original Default Disk Drive

If your computer has a hard disk, execute this command to switch back to it:

Type **c:**
Press **Enter**

If your computer has no hard disk, execute this command to make A your default drive:

Type **a:**
Press **Enter**

Practice

1. If your computer has a hard disk, put a diskette with files on it in drive A. If your computer has no hard disk, put a diskette with files on it in drive B. Change your default disk drive to A or B. Use the DIR command to generate a directory listing. Now switch back to your original drive.
2. Try switching to a disk drive that doesn't exist, such as Z. What happens?
3. Try switching to your current drive. For example, if C is your default drive, do this:

   Type **c:**
   Press **Enter**

   What happens?

Lesson 6: Checking Disk and Memory Status

You've already learned how one DOS command, DIR, can be used to list information about the files on a disk or in a subdirectory. Another DOS command, CHKDSK, can be used to display further information about a disk and the memory installed in your computer. CHKDSK is an external command, which means that it is kept in a separate file named CHKDSK.COM in the DOS subdirectory on a hard disk. External commands are available only when they are located on your default disk or in your current subdirectory, or when a path has been set up to the subdirectory that contains them. You will learn about paths in the next chapter. If DOS has been installed correctly on your hard disk, a path should already be set up to the DOS subdirectory so that the DOS external commands are always available. Note: the CHKDSK command does not operate when DOS is running on a local area network.

Step 1: Enter CHKDSK

To check the disk in your default drive, execute this command:

Type **chkdsk**
Press **Enter**

Your screen should look like Figure 12, although the numbers probably will be different.

Step 2: Examine the Status Report

The CHKDSK status report supplies several useful items of information. First, it tells you that the total capacity of the hard disk is 21,204,992 bytes (a little more than 20 megabytes). This is roughly equivalent to about 6,575 pages of single-spaced typewritten text. **Hidden files** are special files used by DOS and some other programs. They're hidden because they do not appear in the disk directory so that you won't rename, change, or delete them. Next the CHKDSK command tells you how many subdirectories and ordinary user files are on the disk and how much space they occupy. It will also say whether any bytes on the disk are in "bad sectors," although there aren't any on the disk shown in Figure 12. Bad sectors occur when some of the disk is unusable due to manufacturing flaws—a fairly common occurrence with hard disks. The unusable areas are discovered when the disk is formatted and are marked so that DOS won't use them. The disk shown in Figure 12 has 19,701,760 bytes of empty space.

The CHKDSK command also reveals information about **allocation units,** which relate to how DOS assigns disk space to files. This is technical information that most users don't really need to know. Finally, CHKDSK reports that this particular computer has 655,360 bytes (or 640K) of RAM installed, of which 521,248 bytes are free to be used by application programs. The difference between these two figures, 134,112 bytes, is the amount of RAM taken up by the parts of DOS that remain in memory, such as the internal commands, and any memory-resident programs that have been loaded.

Practice

Like many DOS commands, CHKDSK can be used on a disk other than the default disk. Put a diskette with files on it into drive A. Then execute this command:

Type **chkdsk a:**
Press **Enter**

Figure 12 The CHKDSK Report

```
C>chkdsk

Volume HARD DISK   created 01-01-1980 12:28a
Volume Serial Number is 3324-07CC

  21204992 bytes total disk space
     73728 bytes in 3 hidden files
      4096 bytes in 1 directories
   1425408 bytes in 69 user files
  19701760 bytes available on disk

      2048 bytes in each allocation unit
     10354 total allocation units on disk
      9620 available allocation units on disk

    655360 total bytes memory
    521248 bytes free

C>_
```

Lesson 7: Clearing the Screen

By now, you've probably accumulated quite a collection of commands and directory listings on your screen. Although this does no harm, it can be a bit distracting. Or, perhaps you want to type a sequence of commands and then do a print screen, and you would like to start off with a clean slate. It's easy to tell DOS to clear the screen with an internal command called CLS.

Step 1: Enter CLS

To clear the screen, execute the clear screen command:

Type **cls**
Press **Enter**

DOS will erase everything from the screen and start you off again with the system prompt on the first line in the upper left corner.

Practice Use the DIR command to generate a directory listing of your default disk drive. Now clear the screen.

Lesson 8: Formatting a Diskette

Every new disk must undergo an initial preparation known as formatting before it can be used to store programs and data files. Many manufacturers and retailers format the hard disks that are installed in the computers they sell. This initialization for diskettes, however, is not commonly done at the factory, so generally you must format each new floppy you're going to use with your own computer. You also can reformat a previously formatted disk to completely erase all the files that are stored on it. But you should be very careful whenever you format a previously used disk. Make sure that it doesn't hold any files that you want to save. Basically, DOS performs the following procedures when you format a disk:

- Checks the disk for bad or damaged spots that cannot reliably store data and marks these as unusable
- Completely erases any programs and data that might be on the disk
- Builds a directory to hold information about the files that eventually will be stored on the disk
- Marks off the empty space on the disk into equal-sized portions called **sectors**
- Creates a DOS startup disk if instructed to do so

The DOS FORMAT command, which is an external command, performs all of these functions. Note: the FORMAT command does not operate when running DOS on a local area network. This is a safety precaution to prevent users from reformatting shared hard disks.

Step 1: Get a Floppy Disk to Format

The most common and simplest use of the FORMAT command is to set up diskettes that will not be used to boot up the computer. Since the operating system is not installed on these diskettes, they can devote all of their space to holding programs and data files. For this lesson you'll need a new floppy disk or a previously used disk that can be completely erased. If you are going to format a diskette that's not new, double-check to make sure it doesn't have any programs or data files on it that you want to keep. Formatting a disk erases everything on it.

Step 2: Enter the FORMAT Command

To format a diskette in the A drive, execute the following command:

Type **`format a:`**
Press **Enter**

Step 3: Insert the Disk to Be Formatted

The FORMAT command will then tell you to insert the new diskette into drive A. Insert the disk as indicated, and then press the Enter key.

Press **Enter**

Step 4: Enter a Volume Label

The procedure takes about a minute for a 5¼-inch double-sided, double-density diskette, during which time DOS displays a percentage that shows how much it has formatted so far. When it is finished, the FORMAT command will prompt you to enter a volume label, or name, for the newly formatted disk. (Older versions of DOS don't automatically ask you to do this.) You can choose any name you like, but it must be no longer than eleven characters. If you don't want to enter a name, you can just press the Enter key. Name your disk like this:

Type **`my disk`**
Press **Enter**

Step 5: Examine the Screen

After you enter a volume label, FORMAT will tell you how much room is on the disk and whether it contains any bad sectors (see Figure 13). If the diskette has no bad sectors and DOS has not been installed on it, these two numbers will be the same: 362,496 bytes for a 5¼-inch double-sided, double-density diskette. The FORMAT command also displays information about the disk's allocation units and reports the volume serial number.

Step 6: Terminate the FORMAT Command

Finally, the FORMAT command asks you if you want to format another diskette. You can answer "no" like this:

Type **n**
Press **Enter**

You'll then get the DOS prompt back again, as shown in Figure 13.

Practice Format another blank diskette or reformat the disk you have just formatted. This time, however, press **Enter** without typing a volume label.

Lesson 9: Formatting a System Diskette

The diskette you formatted in Lesson 8 can be used to store programs and data files. It cannot, however, be used to boot up the computer, because it doesn't have DOS installed on it. If you want to format a DOS startup diskette that can be used to boot up your computer from drive A, you must follow a slightly different procedure.

Figure 13 Formatting a Diskette

```
C>format a:
Insert new diskette for drive A:
and press ENTER when ready...

Format complete

Volume label (11 characters, ENTER for none)? my disk

    362496 bytes total disk space
    362496 bytes available on disk

      1024 bytes in each allocation unit
       354 allocation units available on disk

Volume Serial Number is 354B-0BD4

Format another (Y/N)?n
C>_
```

Step 1: Use the /S Parameter

A **parameter** is a specification that designates an alternate action for a command. Many DOS commands can be given one or more parameters to specify a slightly different way of performing their tasks. The FORMAT command, for example, can be instructed to install the operating system on the disk it's preparing. To do this, you add the /S parameter after the specification of the disk to be formatted. The /S tells FORMAT to put the DOS internal commands and the command processor on the disk being formatted. You can try this out by reformatting the disk you formatted in Lesson 8. To prepare a DOS startup disk, execute this command:

Type **`format a:/s`**
Press **Enter**

Step 2: Insert the Disk to Be Formatted

The FORMAT command will then tell you to insert the new diskette into drive A. Insert the disk you formatted in Lesson 8 into drive A and then press the Enter key.

Press **Enter**

Step 3: Enter a Volume Label

When the formatting procedure is complete, the FORMAT command will report that the system has been transferred to the disk. It will then prompt you to enter a volume label for the disk. Name your disk like this:

Type **`startup`**
Press **Enter**

Step 4: Examine the Screen

After you enter a volume label, FORMAT will tell you how much room is on the disk, whether the disk contains any bad sectors, and how much space is being used by DOS. Figure 14 shows a 5¼-inch double-sided, double-density diskette with MS-DOS 4.01 installed on it. The disk holds 362,496 bytes, DOS takes up 109,568 bytes, and 252,928 bytes of empty space are available. The FORMAT command also displays information about the disk's allocation units and reports the volume serial number.

Step 5: Terminate the FORMAT Command

Finally, the FORMAT command asks you if you want to format another diskette. You can answer "no" like this:

Type **n**
Press **Enter**

You'll then get the DOS prompt back again.

Step 6: Examine the Disk's Directory

Now, let's look at the directory of the disk you just formatted. Execute this command:

Figure 14 Formatting a System Diskette

```
C>format a:/s
Insert new diskette for drive A:
and press ENTER when ready...

Format complete
System transferred

Volume label (11 characters, ENTER for none)? startup

    362496 bytes total disk space
    109568 bytes used by system
    252928 bytes available on disk

      1024 bytes in each allocation unit
       247 allocation units available on disk

Volume Serial Number is 0308-07D1

Format another (Y/N)?n
C>_
```

Type **dir a:**
Press **Enter**

Your screen should look like Figure 15. Notice that only the file COMMAND.COM is on the new system disk. It does not contain any of the external command files that are on the DOS disk. So, although you could boot up with this new disk and you could execute internal commands such as DIR, you could not use any external commands such as CHKDSK or FORMAT unless you copied their command files onto it.

Hard Disks The FORMAT command also works for hard disks. Once a hard disk is initially formatted, however, it may seldom, if ever, be formatted again. Since computers with hard disks often have many important and sometimes irreplaceable files on them, you should be extremely cautious with them. Don't

Figure 15 Directory of the New System Diskette

```
C>dir a:

 Volume in drive A is STARTUP
 Volume Serial Number is 0308-07D1
 Directory of  A:\

COMMAND  COM     37557 12-19-88  12:00a
        1 File(s)     252928 bytes free

C>_
```

attempt to format a hard disk unless you know exactly what you're doing and you're sure that all files on the hard disk have backup copies on other disks. As we said, many computers now come with their hard disks already formatted by the manufacturer or retailer.

Practice

1. Try booting up from your new system diskette. Make sure the newly formatted diskette is in drive A. If the drive has a door or lever, make sure it is closed.

   Press **Ctrl-Alt-Del**

   Skip entering the date and time:

   Press **Enter**
   Press **Enter**

2. Use DIR to list a directory of your default disk, which should be the new system diskette in drive A. As you can see, internal commands like DIR always work after you boot up because they are kept in a hidden DOS file and automatically loaded into memory, where they remain.
3. Use CHKDSK to try to get a status report of your default disk. DOS will say "Bad command or file name." CHKDSK does not work on your new system disk because it is an external command, stored in its own file named CHKDSK.COM, and it has not been copied to the new disk. Similarly, FORMAT will not work from your new system disk either unless its file is copied to the disk first.
4. Remove the new system diskette from drive A. If your computer does not have a hard disk, put the original DOS Startup diskette back into drive A. Reboot your computer:

   Press **Ctrl-Alt-Del**

   Enter the correct date and time if necessary.

Lesson 10: Copying Files

One of the reasons computers are so useful is that they make it simple to copy programs and data. Once information is entered into a computer, any number of copies usually can be made very easily and quickly. An important function of any operating system is duplicating files. DOS provides several methods of copying files. One of the most popular DOS commands is COPY, which reproduces one or more individual files.

Step 1: Copy a Single File (the Long Way)

Once a diskette has been formatted, it can be used to store program and data files. Let's use the COPY command to copy a single file from the DOS subdirectory onto your newly formatted diskette. First, we'll do it the longhand way, and then we'll show you a shortcut. To copy the file FORMAT.COM from the DOS subdirectory onto your formatted diskette, make sure the diskette is in drive A. Then execute this command:

Type **`copy c:\dos\format.com a:format.com`**
Press **Enter**

The first file specification after the COPY command is the **source,** or what you're copying from—the file FORMAT.COM on the hard disk C in the DOS subdirectory. The second file specification is the **target,** or what you're copying to—a file named FORMAT.COM on the diskette in drive A. The source and the target can have the same name because they are on separate disks. After you execute the COPY command, DOS will tell you that one file was copied. Now execute this command to see the contents of the diskette:

Type **`dir a:`**
Press **Enter**

You should see the file FORMAT.COM in the directory of the diskette in drive A, as shown in Figure 16.

Step 2: Copy a Single File (the Short Way)

In most cases, if you omit certain information from a command, DOS will make an assumption about what you mean. For example, if you don't supply a disk drive or subdirectory designation in front of a file name, DOS will assume that you mean the default drive and current directory. Similarly, if you don't specify a name for the target file, the COPY command will assume that it is to use the same name as the source. This assumption will work as long as the source and the target files are on different disks or in different subdirectories. Now try this shorter command to copy FORMAT.COM to the diskette:

Type **`copy dos\format.com a:`**
Press **Enter**

This command tells DOS to copy the file FORMAT.COM on the default disk in the DOS subdirectory to the diskette in drive A and give it the same name.

Note that you have just copied the FORMAT.COM in the DOS subdirectory to the FORMAT.COM that already existed on the diskette in drive A from the copy operation performed in Step 1. If you choose a name that already exists on the target, DOS will simply copy over it, destroying whatever was in that file

***Figure 16** Copying a File*

```
C>copy c:\dos\format.com a:format.com
        1 File(s) copied

C>dir a:

 Volume in drive A is STARTUP
 Volume Serial Number is 0308-07D1
 Directory of  A:\

COMMAND  COM     37557 12-19-88  12:00a
FORMAT   COM     22859 10-06-88  12:00a
        2 File(s)     229376 bytes free

C>_
```

before. Since you copied the same file, there's no problem here. As a rule, however, you should be very careful about the name you choose for a target file. If it already exists on the disk you're copying to, the original version will be overwritten. Make sure you no longer need any file on the target disk or subdirectory with the same name as a copy to be created.

Step 3: Copy a Group of Files

By using the global file name characters * and ? introduced in Lesson 3, you can copy several files at once with a single COPY command. For example, execute this command:

Type **copy dos*.com a:**
Press **Enter**

This command will try to copy every file in the DOS subdirectory with an extension of COM to the diskette in drive A. If you have only a 360K diskette in drive A, it will probably run out of room, as shown in Figure 17. Nevertheless, DOS will copy as many files as it can to the diskette.

Step 4: Copy a File to the Same Directory

You cannot have two files in the same directory with identical names. The COPY command simply will not allow you to duplicate a file in the same directory unless you provide a different name for the target file. So, the COPY command can reproduce a file on the same disk or in the same subdirectory, but the source and the target must have different names.

A common reason for duplicating a file in the same directory is for backup purposes. Let's say that you're going to change an existing file. If that file is especially important, you might want to keep a copy of the original version before you make any alterations. Then if some problem occurs, you will still have the original version intact. So, before you change a file, it might be a good idea to make a copy of it, but with a slightly different name. For example, suppose you

Figure 17 Copying a Group of Files

```
C>copy dos\*.com a:
DOS\COMMAND.COM
DOS\DISKCOPY.COM
DOS\FORMAT.COM
DOS\KEYB.COM
DOS\SYS.COM
DOS\ASSIGN.COM
DOS\CHKDSK.COM
DOS\COMP.COM
DOS\DEBUG.COM
DOS\DISKCOMP.COM
DOS\EDLIN.COM
DOS\LABEL.COM
DOS\MORE.COM
DOS\TREE.COM
DOS\PRINT.COM
DOS\GRAFTABL.COM
DOS\GRAPHICS.COM
DOS\MODE.COM
DOS\RECOVER.COM
DOS\BACKUP.COM
Insufficient disk space
        19 File(s) copied

C>_
```

wanted to somehow change the file AUTOEXEC.BAT, but wanted to keep a copy of the original. You could make a backup copy of the original version on the same disk if you change its name slightly. For example, execute these commands:

Type **copy autoexec.bat autoexec.bak**
Press **Enter**
Type **dir**
Press **Enter**

The COPY command creates a copy of the AUTOEXEC.BAT file on the default disk and names it AUTOEXEC.BAK (the BAK is for backup), as shown in Figure 18. Now you could go ahead and safely make modifications to AUTOEXEC.BAT, because you've retained a copy of the original file in AUTOEXEC.BAK.

Practice

1. You can use the COPY command to duplicate every non-hidden file on a disk or in a subdirectory. For example, execute this command:

   Type **copy dos*.* a:**
   Press **Enter**

   You will probably quickly run out of room on the diskette in drive A, but this command would work if the target disk were large enough.

2. To see how the COPY command will not allow you to duplicate a file with the same name in the same directory, try this command:

   Type **copy autoexec.bak**
   Press **Enter**

   Because you omitted the target file name, DOS assumed you meant the same name as the source. Since two files in the same directory cannot have the same name, DOS aborts the command and displays the error message, "File cannot be copied onto itself."

Figure 18 Copying a File to the Same Directory

```
C>copy autoexec.bat autoexec.bak
        1 File(s) copied

C>dir

 Volume in drive C is HARD DISK
 Volume Serial Number is 3324-07CC
 Directory of  C:\

CONFIG   SYS       146 07-09-89   1:22p
AUTOEXEC BAK       256 01-01-80   5:52a
COMMAND  COM     37557 12-19-88  12:00a
DOS          <DIR>     07-09-89   1:23p
AUTOEXEC BAT       256 01-01-80   5:52a
        5 File(s)   19699712 bytes free

C>_
```

3. You should be careful with the COPY command. It is up to you to make sure you are copying the file you want and that the target name is correct. For example, execute this command (be sure you type *.bak* and not *.bat*):

   Type **copy command.com autoexec.bak**
   Press **Enter**

   DOS will copy the file COMMAND.COM to the file AUTOEXEC.BAK, overwriting the previous contents of AUTOEXEC.BAK. It does not ask you if this is really what you want to do.

Lesson 11: Copying an Entire Diskette

DOS has a more specific copy command that lets you duplicate an entire diskette all at once. The DISKCOPY command formats the target diskette, if necessary, and copies all files, hidden or otherwise, exactly as they are on the original source diskette. DISKCOPY may be used to duplicate only floppy disks, not hard disks. Furthermore, DISKCOPY works only if the source and target are the same type of diskette. For instance, you cannot use the DISKCOPY command to duplicate the contents of a 5¼-inch diskette on a 3½-inch diskette. Fortunately, you can use DISKCOPY even if you have only one floppy drive. To see how the DISKCOPY command works, you can make an exact copy of the formatted system diskette you've been working with. You will need another diskette of the same type, either new and unformatted, or containing files you are sure you no longer need. Note: the DISKCOPY command does not operate when running DOS on a local area network.

Step 1: Execute the DISKCOPY Command

If your computer has two identical floppy disk drives, execute this command:

Type **diskcopy a: b:**
Press **Enter**

If your computer has only one floppy drive or two drives that are of different types, such as a 5¼-inch drive and a 3½-inch drive, execute this command instead:

Type **diskcopy a: a:**
Press **Enter**

Step 2: Follow the Directions

The DISKCOPY command will tell you which drive to put your source and target diskettes into and when to do so. Remember: the diskette you want to copy is the source, and the new diskette is the target. If your computer has only one floppy drive, you may have to swap the source and target diskettes in drive A several times, depending on how much memory is installed.

Step 3: Terminate the DISKCOPY Command

When it is finished, DISKCOPY will ask you if you want to copy another diskette. If the answer is no, do this:

Type **n**
Press **Enter**

If you have only one floppy drive, Figure 19 shows what you should see on your screen when DISKCOPY is finished.

DISKCOPY is a very useful command for making backup copies of important diskettes. In fact, the documentation that comes with many software packages suggests that you use the DISKCOPY command to duplicate all of your original diskettes as soon as you get them. Furthermore, you should put the originals away for safekeeping and only use your copies. Then, if you accidentally erase something or if a diskette you use daily becomes damaged or wears out, you will still have your original diskettes from which to make additional copies. These are good suggestions, and DISKCOPY will work fine as long as your software is not copy-protected.

Practice Use DISKCOPY to duplicate some other diskette that you have.

Lesson 12: Changing File Names

When you create a file, either using a DOS command such as COPY or from within an application package such as a word processor, you assign it a name. This name need not be permanent, however. DOS lets you change file names very easily. There are several reasons why you might want to change an existing file name. Perhaps you've thought of a more appropriate name or maybe you would like to shorten the name. You may want to copy a file onto a disk that already contains another file with the same name. In this case, you could change the name of the file already on the disk so that its contents will not be overwritten by the file you want to copy. The RENAME command, which is an internal command, lets you change the name of one or more files.

Step 1: Rename a Single File

Changing a single file's name is quite easy. Just type RENAME (or its abbreviation, REN), followed by the file name you want to change and then the new

Figure 19 Copying an Entire Diskette

```
C>diskcopy a: a:

Insert SOURCE diskette in drive A:

Press any key to continue . . .

Copying 40 tracks
9 Sectors/Track, 2 Side(s)

Insert TARGET diskette in drive A:

Press any key to continue . . .

Volume Serial Number is 08E3-3224

Copy another diskette (Y/N)? n

C>
C>_
```

name that file is to have. For example, suppose you want to copy a new version of the file FORMAT.COM to the system diskette you created in Lesson 9, but you want to keep a copy of the original FORMAT.COM. You could rename the original FORMAT.BAK and then copy the new FORMAT.COM to your disk. Make sure your formatted system diskette is in drive A. Then execute these commands:

Type **a:**
Press **Enter**
Type **rename format.com format.bak**
Press **Enter**
Type **dir format.***
Press **Enter**

Your screen should look like Figure 20. The directory shows that you've successfully changed the name of FORMAT.COM to FORMAT.BAK.

Before you go on, change FORMAT.BAK back to FORMAT.COM to restore your disk to the way it was. This time, however, try using the abbreviated form of the RENAME command:

Type **ren format.bak format.com**
Press **Enter**

Step 2: Rename Several Files at Once

Using the global file name characters * and ?, you can rename several files at once. For example, with a single command you can rename each file on your system diskette with an extension of COM and give it an extension of BAK. Make sure the system diskette you formatted in Lesson 9 is in drive A and that drive A is your default drive. Then execute this command:

Type **ren *.com *.bak**
Press **Enter**

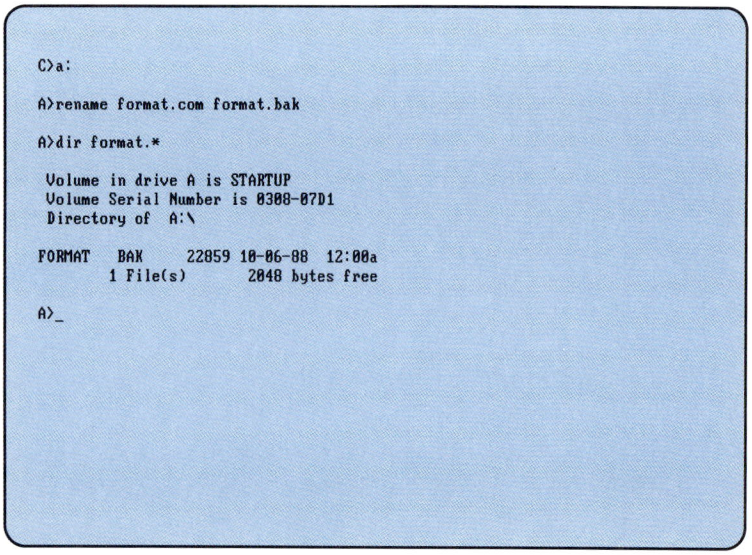

Figure 20 Renaming a File

Now execute this directory command to see what you've done:

Type **dir *.bak**
Press **Enter**

Your screen should look something like Figure 21. There are now no files on your disk with COM extensions. They all have BAK extensions instead. Before you go on, change them all back to the way they were with this command:

Type **ren *.bak *.com**
Press **Enter**

Practice Change the name of the file AUTOEXEC.BAK, which you created in Lesson 10, to JUNK. Remember, this file is on your hard disk or DOS Startup disk.

Lesson 13: Erasing Files

Just as you accumulate old memos, notes, letters, clippings, and other scraps of paper on your desk, disks also can become cluttered with files that are no longer needed. Occasionally, you may have to clean up a disk and discard unnecessary files. Once you erase a file, however, it may be difficult or even impossible to retrieve its contents. In fact, DOS includes no utility for "unerasing" files, although such programs are sold by some independent software publishers. Before you erase any file, make sure you no longer need it. DOS makes it very easy to erase files, so you should be careful. Many instances of people losing files can be attributed to accidents or carelessness with the DOS ERASE command, also known as DEL. ERASE (or DEL) is an internal command.

Step 1: Erase a Single File

To erase a single file, just type ERASE or DEL (for delete) and follow it with the name of the file you want to erase. Make sure that the system diskette you

Figure 21 Renaming a Group of Files

```
 Volume Serial Number is 0308-07D1
 Directory of  A:\

COMMAND  BAK     37557 12-19-88  12:00a
FORMAT   BAK     22859 10-06-88  12:00a
DISKCOPY BAK     10396 10-06-88  12:00a
KEYB     BAK     14727 10-06-88  12:00a
SYS      BAK     11456 10-06-88  12:00a
ASSIGN   BAK      5753 10-06-88  12:00a
CHKDSK   BAK     17787 10-06-88  12:00a
COMP     BAK      9459 10-06-88  12:00a
DEBUG    BAK     21574 10-06-88  12:00a
DISKCOMP BAK      9857 10-06-88  12:00a
EDLIN    BAK     14069 10-06-88  12:00a
LABEL    BAK      4458 10-06-88  12:00a
MORE     BAK      2134 10-06-88  12:00a
TREE     BAK      6302 10-06-88  12:00a
PRINT    BAK     14131 10-06-88  12:00a
GRAFTABL BAK     10239 10-06-88  12:00a
GRAPHICS BAK     16693 10-06-88  12:00a
MODE     BAK     22960 10-06-88  12:00a
RECOVER  BAK     10588 10-06-88  12:00a
       19 File(s)       2048 bytes free

A>_
```

formatted in Lesson 9 is in drive A and that drive A is your default drive. Because you know this diskette holds only copies of DOS files that you have on the hard disk or on the original DOS Startup disk, you can safely erase files from it. Nevertheless, you should always be careful when erasing files. Data and programs are more frequently lost as the result of an accidentally or carelessly entered ERASE command than from any other cause. Suppose you want to erase the file FORMAT.COM from the diskette. Execute this command:

Type **erase format.com**
Press **Enter**

Now execute this directory command to see what you've done:

Type **dir format.com**
Press **Enter**

The file is now gone, so your screen should look like Figure 22.

Step 2: Erasing Several Files All at Once

By using the global file name characters * and ?, you can tell DOS to erase several files with a single ERASE command. In fact, you can even wipe out every file on a disk. Although this is often done to clear off a disk, it should be used with care. Make sure that the system diskette you formatted in Lesson 9 is in drive A and that drive A is your default drive. Then execute this command:

Type **erase *.***
Press **Enter**

Because this is a potentially disastrous command if entered by mistake, DOS will ask if you are sure you want to do this. If you answer yes, DOS will go ahead and erase everything. If you answer no, DOS will immediately cancel the ERASE command. You will get this chance to back out, however, only if you use the *.* designation. If you enter ERASE *.EXE, for example, DOS will not ask if you are sure and will immediately delete all files with an extension of EXE. So again, *be*

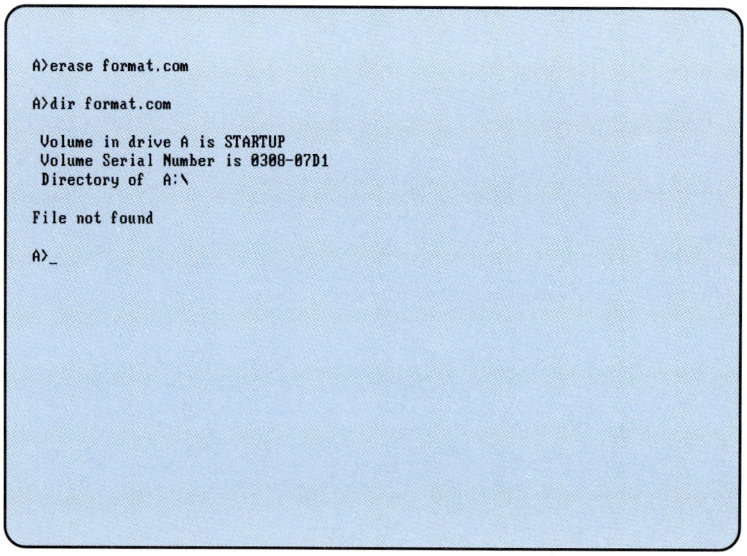

Figure 22 Erasing a File

careful with the ERASE command! Answer yes and then list a directory to see what you have done:

Type **y**
Press **Enter**
Type **dir**
Press **Enter**

Your screen should look like Figure 23.

Practice

Switch back to the hard disk or the DOS Startup disk you used to boot up the computer. Remember the AUTOEXEC.BAK file you created in Lesson 10 and that you renamed JUNK in the Practice section of Lesson 12? Erase it, but this time use DEL instead of ERASE. DEL and ERASE are two names for the same DOS command.

Lesson 14: Protecting Diskettes

In certain situations, commands such as FORMAT, COPY, DISKCOPY, RENAME, and ERASE won't work. Most diskettes have a feature that prevents them from being altered. This feature, called **write-protection,** is similar to the tabs on audio and video cassette tapes that you can remove to prevent accidentally recording over material you want to save.

Step 1: Write-Protect a 5¼-inch Diskette

Most 5¼-inch diskettes have a small rectangle cut out of one side, called the **write-protect notch** (see Figure 24(a)). This notch can be covered with a gummed tab or tape to write-protect the diskette. Files on a diskette protected in this manner can be read but not written or altered as long as the notch remains covered. Diskettes that are write-protected cannot be formatted, have files renamed

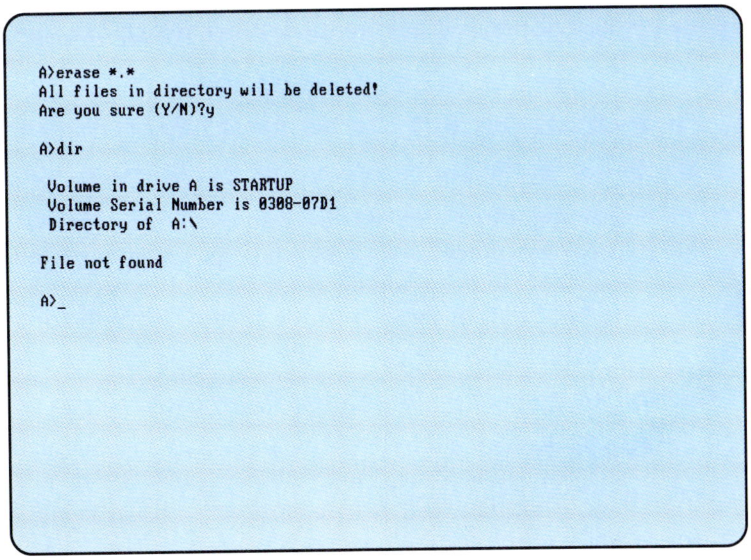

Figure 23 Erasing All the Files

Figure 24 Write-Protecting Diskettes

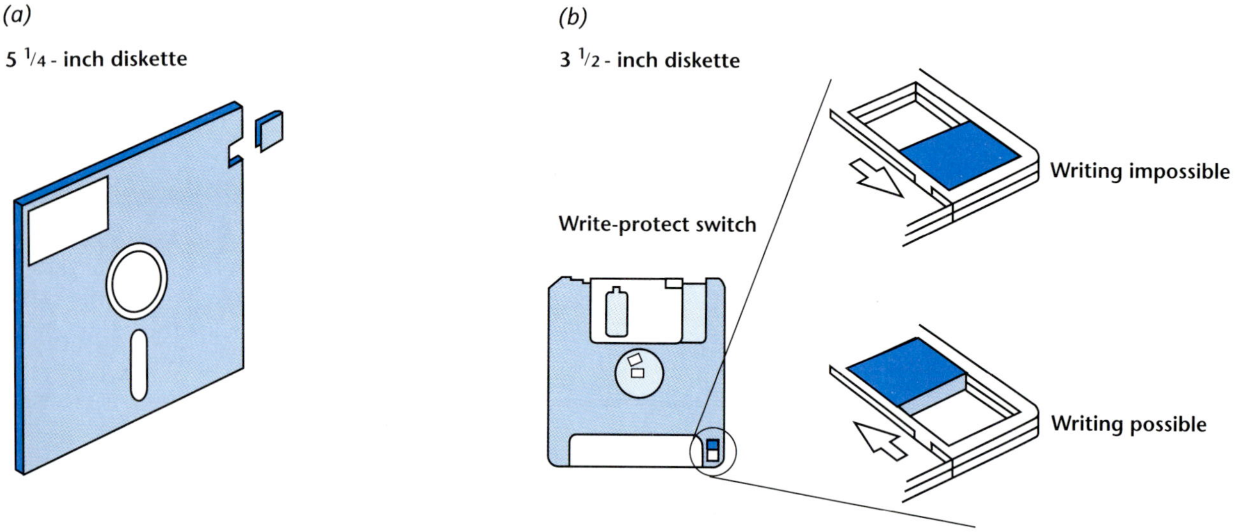

on them, have files copied onto them, or have files erased from them. If you attempt to do so, DOS simply issues a write-protect error message. Some 5¼-inch diskettes don't have a write-protect notch. These diskettes are permanently write-protected.

If you have a gummed tab or piece of tape, try write-protecting a 5¼-inch diskette. Then try copying a file to the diskette, or renaming or erasing a file already on the diskette.

Step 2: Write-Protect a 3½-inch Diskette

The smaller, 3½-inch diskettes also can be write-protected, but the mechanism is slightly different. These diskettes have a **write-protect switch** on the reverse side in the lower right corner (see Figure 24(b)). This switch is a tab that can be slid to open or close a little hole in the disk's plastic case. When the hole is open, the diskette is write-protected. When it is closed, files can be written and altered on the diskette.

If your computer uses 3½-inch diskettes, try write-protecting one. Then try copying a file to the diskette, or renaming or erasing a file already on the diskette.

Copy-Protection With write-protection, you can safeguard programs and data that are stored on diskettes from accidental erasure. Some software developers use **copy-protection** to discourage you from duplicating their packages and illegally selling or giving away copies. Copy-protected diskettes are prepared in a manner that makes it difficult or impossible to copy them with ordinary DOS commands such as COPY and DISKCOPY. Since it is so easy to duplicate diskettes, some manufacturers feel that they must copy-protect their software to prevent widespread distribution to people who don't rightfully pay for it. Unfortunately, copy-protected software is often inconvenient for rightful owners to use or back up. Although manufacturers of most major application packages have since dropped copy-protection from their products, many game programs are still copy-protected.

6. To boot DOS with the power off
   (a) insert the DOS Startup disk (if necessary) and turn on the power.
   (b) hold down the Control, Alternate, and Delete keys at the same time.
   (c) turn the power on and issue the boot command.
   (d) turn the power on and kick the computer.
7. Pressing Ctrl-Alt-Del will
   (a) invoke a DOS transient routine.
   (b) delete a file.
   (c) reboot DOS without having to shut off the computer.
   (d) execute an application program.
8. The DOS directory command is
   (a) DIRECT.
   (b) LIST.
   (c) DIR.
   (d) CATALOG.
9. The two parts of a DOS file name are
   (a) a disk drive designation and a disk sector number.
   (b) a primary filename and an optional extension.
   (c) a primary filename and a creation date.
   (d) a primary extension and the size in bytes.
10. Files with COM and EXE extensions usually designate
    (a) external commands and executable program files.
    (b) command files and extension files.
    (c) configuration files and batch files.
    (d) BASIC and FORTRAN files.
11. Pressing Ctrl-Num Lock or Pause will
    (a) echo input and output to the printer.
    (b) print the screen.
    (c) cancel a command.
    (d) temporarily halt screen scrolling.
12. To change the default disk drive
    (a) put a new disk in drive A.
    (b) type the new disk drive designation and press Enter.
    (c) open up the computer and replace the faulty drive.
    (d) issue the DIR command.
13. To display a disk and memory status report, use
    (a) STATUS.
    (b) DIR.
    (c) CHKDSK.
    (d) DISKCOPY.
14. Formatting a diskette does not do the following:
    (a) check the diskette for bad sectors.
    (b) wipe out all data on the diskette.
    (c) mark off the space into sectors.
    (d) sort files in the directory.
15. To format a system diskette you must
    (a) reboot the system.
    (b) use the /S parameter with the FORMAT command.
    (c) enter the COPY command.
    (d) purchase a master diskette from IBM.

16. Which command would you use to copy every file from disk drive A to B?
    (a) COPY A:*.* B: (b) DIR A: B:
    (c) COPY A: B: (d) REN
17. To make an exact copy of an entire diskette, use
    (a) COPY.   (b) DISKCOPY.
    (c) DIR.   (d) Ctrl-Alt-Del.
18. Entering the command DEL *.* will
    (a) reboot the system.   (b) copy all files to the disk in the default drive.
    (c) rename all files on the disk in the default drive.   (d) erase all files from the disk in the default drive.
19. To display a text file on your screen, use the
    (a) PRINT command.   (b) DISKCOPY command.
    (c) TYPE command.   (d) Ctrl-Num Lock key.
20. To run a program you must
    (a) type its filename and press the Enter key.   (b) reboot DOS.
    (c) press Ctrl-Break.   (d) first make a backup copy.

Fill-In

1. A disk operating system has many utilities for dealing with the ______ that are stored on disks.
2. ______ is usually used with IBM computers while ______ is usually used with compatible computers such as those made by Compaq, Tandy, and Zenith.
3. Booting DOS refers to the process of loading the disk operating system into ______.
4. In some cases, when you first boot DOS it asks you to enter the ______ and the ______.
5. The ______ command can be used to list the names, sizes, and creation dates and times of all the files on a disk.
6. A file's primary filename can have from one to ______ characters in it.
7. File name extensions are often used to ______ files.
8. You can press the ______ key to cancel a command if you haven't pressed the Enter key yet.
9. You can press ______ to cancel a command before it finishes executing.
10. The DOS ______ indicates the current default disk drive.
11. The ______ command can tell you how much memory is installed in your computer.
12. A diskette must be ______ before it can be used to store program and data files.
13. The ______ command can be used to duplicate one or more files on the same or on different disks.
14. ______ file name characters can be used to refer to several files at the same time.

15. The DISKCOPY command will automatically ______ the target diskette if it's brand new.
16. The REN command can be used to ______ one or more file names.
17. To remove a file from a disk, you would enter ______ or ______ followed by the file's name.
18. The TYPE command lets you display ______ files on your screen.
19. You could use the ______ command to produce a hard copy of a text file.
20. To run a program, you must type its ______ and then press ______.

Short Problems

1. If you have access to a diskette other than DOS Startup, produce a directory listing of the files on it. If you have a printer, try using Ctrl-PrtSc to turn on printer echoing before you issue the directory command so that you can get a hard copy.
2. When you booted DOS, you may have been asked to supply the date and time. Two DOS commands, DATE and TIME, tell you the current date and time and let you change these settings. Try the DATE and TIME commands. If you don't want to change the date and time settings, just press the Enter key when asked for the new date or time. Notice how DOS automatically figures out and displays the day of the week.
3. Use the * global file name character to produce a directory listing of all the files in the DOS subdirectory or on the DOS Startup disk with an EXE extension.
4. Use the * global file name character to produce a directory listing of all the files in the DOS subdirectory or on the DOS Startup disk whose names begin with the letter K.
5. Use the ? global file name character to produce a directory listing of all the files in the DOS subdirectory or on the DOS Startup disk that have an *E* as the second letter of their primary filename.
6. DOS versions 3.0 and newer have a command that lets you supply or change a volume label without having to reformat a disk. If you have DOS 3.0 or newer try using the LABEL command on a diskette that you have formatted for a lesson in this chapter.
7. If you don't know what DOS version you have, enter **ver**. This command displays the number of the DOS version you are using.
8. Another way to find out the volume label of a disk is to use the VOL command. Enter **vol**. This command displays the volume label (if there is one) of the default disk.
9. It is possible to display a text file on your screen by using the COPY command instead of the TYPE command. In certain cases, DOS can refer to its peripheral devices as if they were files. There are several file names that have a special meaning to DOS. These are called DOS device names. For example, CON refers to the console, or the keyboard and screen. If your disk has a file named AUTOEXEC.BAT on it, execute this command:

   Type **copy autoexec.bat con**
   Press **Enter**

   You should see the text of file AUTOEXEC.BAT displayed on your screen just as if you used the TYPE command.

10. Just as CON is a DOS device name that refers to the keyboard and screen, PRN is a DOS device name that refers to the printer. Try using the COPY command to get a printout of the AUTOEXEC.BAT file.
11. The DIR command has two optional parameters that can be useful when looking at disks with lots of files on them. The /P parameter will automatically pause the display when the screen is full and let you press a key to continue. The /W parameter will display the directory in a wide format across the screen, omitting the sizes and creation dates and times so that more file names will fit at once. Obtain a directory listing of the DOS subdirectory or DOS Startup disk using these options:

    Type **dir /p**
    Press **Enter**
    Type **dir /w**
    Press **Enter**

CHAPTER 6

INTERMEDIATE DOS

In This Chapter

Getting Started
Lesson 1: Using the DOS Editing and Function Keys
Lesson 2: Setting the BREAK Option
Lesson 3: Working with Subdirectories
Lesson 4: Using the PATH and APPEND Commands
Lesson 5: Changing the DOS Prompt
Lesson 6: Backing Up and Restoring Disks and Files
Lesson 7: Recovering Files from Damaged Disks
Lesson 8: Using the Prompt Option When Erasing Files
Lesson 9: Learning More About the COPY Command
Lesson 10: Setting the VERIFY Option
Lesson 11: Changing File Attributes
Lesson 12: Copying Groups of Files
Lesson 13: Updating Sets of Files
Lesson 14: Transferring the DOS System Files
Lesson 15: Comparing Files and Disks
Lesson 16: Displaying and Changing a Volume Label
Lesson 17: Displaying and Changing the Date and Time
Lesson 18: Displaying a Memory Report
Lesson 19: Reassigning, Joining, and Substituting Drives
Lesson 20: Learning More About the PRINT Command

Preview

In the previous chapter you learned the basics of DOS, the operating system used on millions of IBM and IBM-compatible microcomputers. This chapter continues your exploration of DOS with slightly more advanced topics.

After studying this chapter, you will know how to

- use the DOS editing and function keys.
- set the BREAK option.
- work with subdirectories.
- use the PATH and APPEND commands.
- change the DOS prompt.
- back up and restore disks and files.
- recover files from damaged disks.
- use the prompt option when erasing files.
- append files and copy files to devices.
- set the VERIFY option.
- change file attributes.
- copy groups of files.
- update sets of files.
- transfer the DOS system files.
- compare files and disks.
- change volume labels.
- change the current date and time.
- display a memory report.
- reassign, join, and substitute drives.
- print multiple files.

Getting Started

You've already learned how to start DOS and use its most common features and commands. This chapter assumes you have completed all of the lessons and exercises in Chapter 5. Furthermore, it assumes that you have a computer with a hard disk and DOS 3.30, 4.00, or 4.01 installed on it in a subdirectory named DOS. All of the screens in the following lessons were created with MS-DOS 4.01. To work the following lessons, boot up or reboot your computer if you have not already done so.

Lesson 1: Using the DOS Editing and Function Keys

As you learned in Chapter 5, DOS assigns special meanings to certain keys. By now you should know how to use Enter, Ctrl-Alt-Del, Escape, Ctrl-Num Lock (or Pause), Ctrl-Break, Shift-PrtSc (or Print Screen), and Ctrl-PrtSc. In addition, DOS has other key presses that can help you enter commands and save time. These are known as the DOS editing and function keys.

Step 1: Retrieve the Previous Command

Every time you enter a command, DOS saves what you have typed in a special area of memory. You can retrieve the previous command by pressing the F3 function key. For example, follow these instructions:

Type **dir**
Press **Enter**
Press **F3**

When the directory command is finished, DOS will copy the previous command, which was DIR, to your screen at the cursor location, as if you had typed it again.

Press **Enter**

DOS will execute the DIR command again. The F3 command is especially convenient for repeating the same command several times in a row, or for repeating an especially long command.

Step 2: Edit the Command Line

When you press F3, DOS only copies the previous command to the command line. You still have to press Enter to actually execute the command. You can, however, alter the command line if you like. For example:

Press **F3**
Press **Space Bar**
Type **c:**
Press **Enter**

This sequence of actions will retrieve the previous command, which was DIR, and add the disk drive specification C: onto the end. Once the previous command is retrieved, you can also use the Backspace or Left Arrow key to delete characters to the left of the cursor.

Step 3: Copy the Next Character from the Previous Command

Pressing F3 retrieves all of the previous command and presents it on your screen. You can also retrieve one character at a time from the previous command by pressing the F1 key. For example:

Press **F1** (3 times)
Press **Enter**

This sequence of commands will retrieve and then execute only the first three characters (DIR) of the previous command. The F1 key allows you to retrieve some of the previous command or make modifications to it.

Step 4: Retrieve Some of the Previous Command

Put a formatted diskette in drive A if it does not already contain one. Execute this command:

Type **dir a:**
Press **Enter**

Suppose you now want to examine disk drive C or B.

Press **F2**
Type **a**

This tells DOS to retrieve the previous command, but only up to the *a* character you've specified. So, now you can type a different end to the command:

Type **c:**
Press **Enter**

Step 5: Examine the Other Editing Keys

The editing and function keys we have discussed are probably the most frequently used. A few other keys, however, are available. The following table lists all of the DOS editing keys.

Key	*Action*
F1	Retypes one character at a time from the previous command.
F2	Retypes all characters up to the next character you type from the previous command.
F3	Retypes all of the previous command.
F4	Deletes all the characters from the previous command up to the next character you type.
F5	Saves the contents of your current command line as if it were the previous command.
F6	Inserts an end-of-file code (Ctrl-Z).
Delete	Skips over a character from the previous command.
Insert	Switches insert/overwrite mode in the command line.
Escape	Cancels the current line.

Practice

1. Try the F4 function key.

   Type **garbage dir**
   Press **Enter**

   Don't worry about the error message. To throw out the garbage, and execute the remaining DIR command, do this:

   Press **F4**
   Type **d**
   Press **F3**
   Press **Enter**

2. Try the F5 function key. Suppose you are typing a long command and realize you have made an error. You have not yet pressed the Enter key. For example, do this (but don't press Enter):

   Type **ytpe autoexec.bat**
   Press **F5**

   Pressing F5 will save what you have typed as if it were the previous command. Now, follow these instructions to correct your error, retrieve the rest of the command, and execute the correct TYPE command:

   Type **ty**
   Press **F3**
   Press **Enter**

3. Try the Del editing key.

   Type **xxdir**
   Press **Enter**

Suppose you meant to type *dir.* To fix your mistake, do this:

Press **Del** (2 times)
Press **F3**
Press **Enter**

4. Try the Ins editing key.

Type **dir os**
Press **Enter**

Suppose you meant to type *dir dos*. To fix your mistake, follow these instructions:

Press **F1** (4 times)
Press **Ins**
Type **d**
Press **F3**
Press **Enter**

Lesson 2: Setting the BREAK Option

In Chapter 5 you learned that you can press Ctrl-Break to cancel a program that is running. Normally, Ctrl-Break works only when DOS is checking the keyboard or sending characters to the screen or printer. You can also tell DOS to check whether Ctrl-Break has been pressed during disk reads and writes.

Step 1: Execute the BREAK Command

The BREAK command allows you to check or change the status of the BREAK option, which controls when Ctrl-Break will cancel a program. To see the current setting of the BREAK option, execute this command:

Type **break**
Press **Enter**

DOS will tell you whether BREAK is on or off.

Step 2: Change the BREAK Option

You can change the current setting of BREAK by entering the BREAK command followed by ON or OFF. For example, if BREAK is OFF, turn it on with this command:

Type **break on**
Press **Enter**

Now check what you have done:

Type **break**
Press **Enter**

Your screen should look like Figure 1.

Practice Switch the BREAK option back to the way it was before you changed it.

Figure 1 Setting the BREAK Option

```
C>break
BREAK is off

C>break on

C>break
BREAK is on

C>_
```

Lesson 3: Working with Subdirectories

As you can imagine, people who use microcomputers extensively often generate large numbers of files. Before hard disks became common, users stored their files in many different floppy disks. Organizing files meant physically organizing diskettes by keeping them well-labeled and storing them in subdivided boxes, racks, or cabinets. Once hard disks became common, however, operating systems had to devise a better method of organizing large numbers of files. Even a modest 20-megabyte hard disk can store thousands of different files. Looking for a particular file among hundreds or thousands of files is time consuming and tedious. Consequently, most microcomputer operating systems, including DOS, have evolved a **hierarchical** method of organizing files into groups. A hierarchical system allows you to cluster files into orders or ranks, each subordinate to the one above. These groups of files, called subdirectories, are like file folders that can be nested within one another. Disks can be organized into subdirectories, each of which can contain files and other subdirectories.

Subdirectories are an invaluable tool for organizing programs and data files on high-capacity storage devices. In addition, subdirectories make it easier for the operating system to locate a particular file, because large numbers of files are divided into smaller groups. Although subdirectories are most often, indeed almost always, found on hard disks, they are occasionally used on floppy disks, too. DOS includes commands that let you create, access, and remove subdirectories.

With DOS, every disk has a single main directory, known as the **root directory.** DOS automatically creates a root directory on every disk you format. This is the directory you are in when you first boot up DOS or when you first change your default drive. The root directory itself has no name, but it's represented by a backslash (\).

Step 1: Create a Subdirectory

The internal DOS command MD or MKDIR (short for "make directory") is used to create a new subdirectory. It is followed by the **path** of the new subdirectory. A path is an optional disk drive specifier followed by a list of subdirectory names, separated by backslashes. The rules for naming subdirectories are the same as the rules for naming files. The simplest path is a single backslash \, which represents the root directory of your current default drive. Let's create a new subdirectory on your hard disk. Execute this command:

Type **md c:\myfiles**
Press **Enter**

The command you just entered creates a subdirectory named MYFILES on the hard disk C. This subdirectory is one level below the root directory. To see the result, execute this command:

Type **dir**
Press **Enter**

You should see MYFILES followed by the <DIR> designation in the directory listing as shown in Figure 2.

Step 2: Change to the Subdirectory

Think of the subdirectory as a separate "sub-disk" on your disk. You use the change directory (CD or CHDIR) command, which is an internal command, to move into your new subdirectory. Execute these commands:

Type **cd c:\myfiles**
Press **Enter**
Type **dir**
Press **Enter**

Your screen should look like Figure 3, showing the directory listing inside the MYFILES subdirectory.

Figure 2 Using MD to Create the MYFILES Subdirectory

```
C>md c:\myfiles

C>dir

 Volume in drive C is HARD DISK
 Volume Serial Number is 3324-07CC
 Directory of  C:\

CONFIG   SYS       146 07-09-89   1:22p
MYFILES      <DIR>     07-12-89   2:10p
COMMAND  COM     37557 12-19-88  12:00a
DOS          <DIR>     07-09-89   1:23p
AUTOEXEC BAT       256 01-01-80   5:52a
        5 File(s)   19699712 bytes free

C>_
```

Figure 3 Using DIR Inside the MYFILES Subdirectory

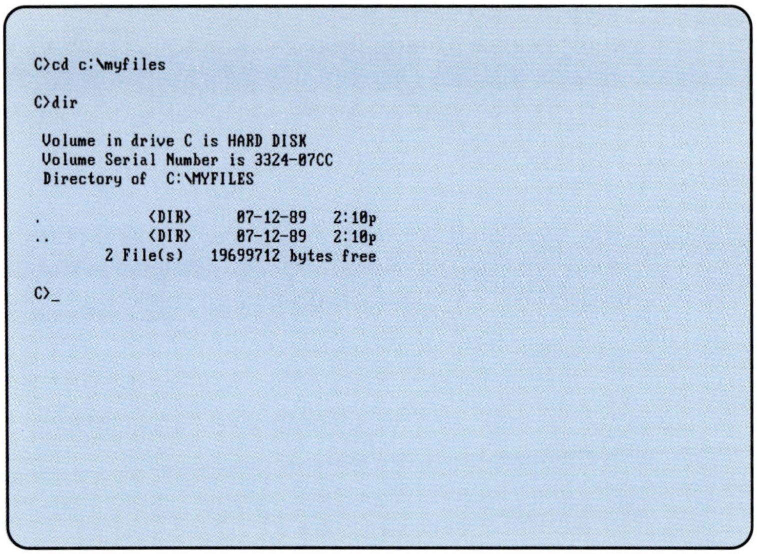

Step 3: Copy a File to the Subdirectory

Right now, the MYFILES subdirectory has no ordinary user files in it. You can, however, copy files into this subdirectory just as if it were a separate disk. For example, let's copy the AUTOEXEC.BAT file from the root directory into the MYFILES subdirectory. Execute this command:

Type **copy c:\autoexec.bat**
Press **Enter**

This command copies the file AUTOEXEC.BAT from the root directory of the hard disk C into your current subdirectory, which happens to be MYFILES. Execute this command to see the contents of your subdirectory:

Type **dir**
Press **Enter**

A copy of AUTOEXEC.BAT now also exists in the MYFILES subdirectory. It's important to realize that there are two separate copies of AUTOEXEC.BAT now on the disk: one in the root directory and one in the MYFILES subdirectory.

Step 4: Display the Directory Structure

A hard disk can hold a great many subdirectories and files. DIR will list the subdirectories and files of only one directory at a time; it cannot show the structure beneath that level. TREE, an external DOS command, can list all of the subdirectories on a disk. It can also list all of the files in each subdirectory. With DOS versions 4.00 and newer, TREE depicts the structure of the disk graphically. Older DOS versions simply list the paths and subdirectories. Execute this command to get a TREE listing of the root directory of your hard disk:

Type **tree c:**
Press **Enter**

Figure 4 shows the result. You can also tell the TREE command to list all files in all directories by using the /F parameter. Execute this command to see how it works:

Type **tree c:\ /f**
Press **Enter**

Step 5: Remove the Subdirectory

Once you are in a subdirectory, you can almost think of it as a separate disk. You can run programs from within a subdirectory. Many DOS commands that deal with files will operate only on the files in your current subdirectory unless you specify otherwise. For example, you can delete every file in a subdirectory without affecting any of the files in the root directory or any other subdirectory. For example, make sure you are in the MYFILES subdirectory and then execute these commands:

Type **erase *.***
Press **Enter**
Type **y**
Press **Enter**
Type **dir**
Press **Enter**

DOS will erase every file in your current directory, the MYFILES subdirectory. The DIR command should reveal that this is true. Now change back to the root directory and check its contents by executing these commands:

Type **cd c:**
Press **Enter**
Type **dir**
Press **Enter**

As you can see, the AUTOEXEC.BAT file in the root directory is still intact.

Figure 4 Using TREE to Display the Directory Structure

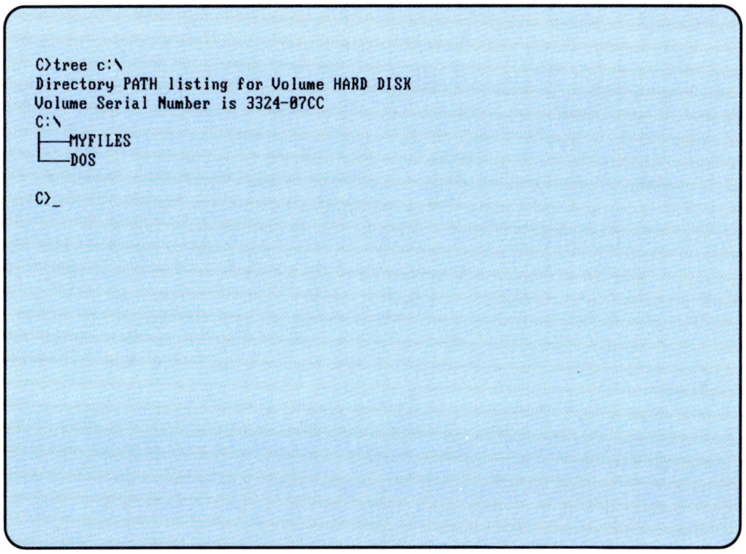

Just as you must occasionally delete unneeded files, sometimes you must remove subdirectories too. Suppose that you are finished with the MYFILES subdirectory and you want to remove it from your disk. To do this you must first erase any files inside the subdirectory and move out of the subdirectory. You have already done this. Now execute the remove directory command (RD or RMDIR) to remove the empty MYFILES subdirectory from your disk:

Type **rd c:\myfiles**
Press **Enter**
Type **dir**
Press **Enter**

You will see that the MYFILES subdirectory has indeed been removed, and your disk is the same as it was when you began this lesson. Like MD and CD, RD is an internal DOS command.

Practice

1. Create a new subdirectory on your disk and name it after yourself (eight characters or less). Change to your new subdirectory. Now create three additional subdirectories inside your new subdirectory and name them ONE, TWO, and THREE. Change to the ONE subdirectory and copy the AUTOEXEC.BAT file from the root, or some other file from the DOS subdirectory into the ONE subdirectory.
2. Use the DIR command to examine the contents of your ONE subdirectory. Notice the first two entries in the directory listing. The . (single period) is a special DOS designation that symbolizes your current directory. The .. (double period) symbolizes the directory above your current directory. For example:

   Type **dir .**
   Press **Enter**

   See what happens. Now try this command:

   Type **dir ..**
   Press **Enter**

   You will get a listing of the directory above ONE.
3. DOS pros often use the . and .. designations as shortcuts. The . is equivalent to *.*. Use it to erase all the files in your current subdirectory, which should be ONE. Now, change back to the subdirectory above ONE, the subdirectory you named after yourself:

   Type **cd ..**
   Press **Enter**

   Try using the .. designation again to return to the root directory.
4. Remove the ONE, TWO, and THREE subdirectories and then remove the subdirectory you named after yourself, leaving your disk the way it was before this practice session.

Lesson 4: Using the PATH and APPEND Commands

In many ways, a subdirectory is like a separate disk. Unless you give DOS special instructions, you can access the files within a subdirectory only when you have switched to that subdirectory with the CD command. In order to fully realize the benefits of DOS subdirectories, you must also understand the PATH and APPEND commands.

Step 1: Execute the PATH Command

By default, you cannot gain access to the programs or data files in a subdirectory unless you are in that subdirectory. Alternatively, you can precede the name of every command or data file with its full path. For example, if you want to use the CHKDSK command (which is an external command kept in the file CHKDSK.COM), and you are not in the DOS subdirectory on the hard disk C, you could enter the command this way:

Type **c:\dos\chkdsk**
Press **Enter**

Typing the disk drive and path before every command, however, can be tiresome. Fortunately, the PATH command can eliminate the need to do this.

Use the PATH command to tell DOS which subdirectories to search through if it cannot find a program or batch file you request in your current directory. (You will learn about batch files later in this chapter.) For example, in most cases you want the commands in the DOS subdirectory to be accessible no matter which disk or directory you are using. Usually, DOS is installed so that a PATH command granting access to the DOS subdirectory is executed every time the computer is booted up. As you will learn later in this chapter, this is typically done by putting a PATH command in the AUTOEXEC.BAT file.

Execute the following command to see the current command search path that has been set up for you:

Type **path**
Press **Enter**

You can also use the PATH command to change the command search path. For example, suppose you want programs and batch files in the root directory and the DOS subdirectory to be accessible from any disk or directory. To set this up, execute the following PATH command:

Type **path c:\;c:\dos**
Press **Enter**

The PATH command is followed by a list of paths you want DOS to search whenever it cannot find the command you have entered. The paths are separated by semicolons. This PATH command has two search paths, c:\, the root directory of the hard disk C, and c:\dos, the DOS subdirectory beneath the root directory on the hard disk C. To see what you have done, execute this command again:

Type **path**
Press **Enter**

Your screen should look like Figure 5.

You need only enter the PATH command once, unless you want to change the list of subdirectories. Consequently, it is usually placed in the AUTOEXEC.BAT file to be executed every time you boot up your computer.

Step 2: Execute the APPEND Command

The PATH command works only for files with extensions of BAT, COM, or EXE. In other words, PATH will allow DOS to find only programs and batch files in other directories. Users of DOS 3.3 and newer versions, however, can use the APPEND command, which can find other types of files.

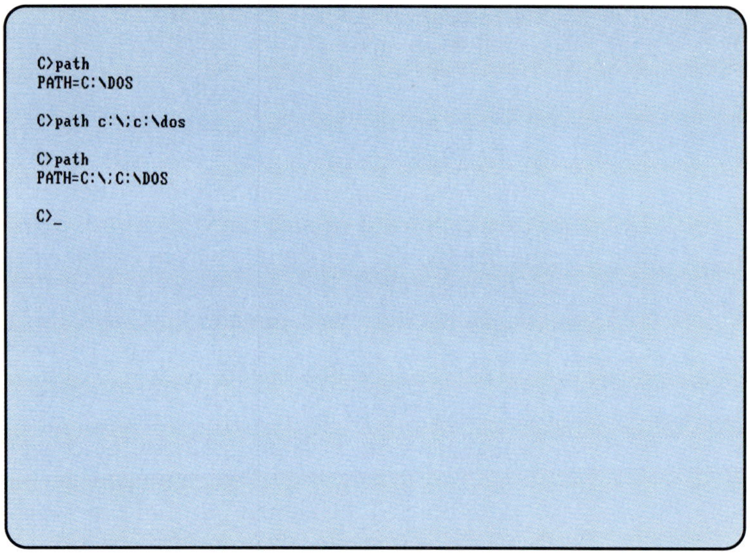

Figure 5 Using the PATH Command

For example, create a subdirectory called LESSONS on your hard disk and change to it with these commands:

Type **`md c:\lessons`**
Press **Enter**
Type **`cd c:\lessons`**
Press **Enter**

Now, execute these commands to create a sample text file you can use:

Type **`copy con sample.txt`**
Press **Enter**
Type **`This is a sample text file.`**
Press **Enter**
Press **F6**
Press **Enter**

To see what you have created, execute this command:

Type **`type sample.txt`**
Press **Enter**

The text file you have just created should be presented on your screen. As you can see, it is accessible from within the LESSONS subdirectory. Now, move back to the root directory and try to type the file by executing these commands:

Type **`cd c:\`**
Press **Enter**
Type **`type sample.txt`**
Press **Enter**

DOS should say "File not found," as shown in Figure 6, because you are at the root and the file SAMPLE.TXT is in the LESSONS subdirectory.

Now suppose that you want data files in the root directory, the DOS subdirectory, and the LESSONS subdirectory to be accessible from all other disks and directories. Like the PATH command, APPEND can be followed by a list of sub-

Figure 6 SAMPLE.TXT Is Not Found in the Root Directory

```
C>md c:\lessons

C>cd c:\lessons

C>copy con sample.txt
This is a sample text file.
^Z
        1 File(s) copied

C>type sample.txt
This is a sample text file.

C>cd c:\

C>type sample.txt
File not found - SAMPLE.TXT

C>_
```

directories separated by semicolons. Execute the following APPEND command:

Type **append c:\;c:\dos;c:\lessons**
Press **Enter**

This command tells DOS the directories you want to search for files that have extensions other than BAT, COM, and EXE. Now try this command again:

Type **type sample.txt**
Press **Enter**

The file should be displayed on your screen, as shown in Figure 7. DOS was able to find SAMPLE.TXT because the APPEND command you entered told it where to search.

Like PATH, the APPEND command is usually put in the AUTOEXEC.BAT file to set up the search paths for data files every time the computer is turned on.

Practice

1. You can also use the APPEND command to see the current search path for data files.

   Type **append**
   Press **Enter**

   If you enter this command without a list of subdirectories, DOS will display the search paths, if any, that have been established by the most recent APPEND command on your computer.
2. Use the TYPE command to examine the AUTOEXEC.BAT file in the root directory of your disk. Does it contain a PATH and APPEND statement?

Lesson 5: Changing the DOS Prompt

By default, the DOS prompt consists of the current drive letter followed by a > (greater than sign). For example, if hard disk C is your current drive, then the default DOS prompt is

C>

floppy disks until it copies all of the files. Furthermore, the BACKUP command of DOS versions 3.3 or newer will even format the backup floppy disks if necessary.

Suppose you want to make a backup copy of your entire hard disk. Assume that you have never backed up your hard disk before. First, you would switch back to the root directory and use DIR or CHKDSK to estimate how many floppy disks you will need. For example, if your hard disk contains 10 megabytes of files, you would need 29 or 30 360K floppy disks. Don't do this on your computer (it might require too many diskettes and take too long), but here is the command you would enter:

backup c: a: /s

This command tells DOS to back up the C drive onto the floppy disks that you will put into drive A. The /S parameter tells DOS to back up all the subdirectories as well. If you are using DOS 4.00 or newer, the BACKUP command can automatically format new diskettes if necessary. If you are using DOS 3.3, you should tell the BACKUP command to format new diskettes (if yours are not already formatted) by including the /F parameter after the /S parameter. Finally, if you are using a DOS version previous to 3.3, you have to format all of your backup diskettes *before* you execute the BACKUP command.

The BACKUP command will then beep and present the message shown in Figure 8. It is up to you to make sure that the floppy disks you use for the backup do not contain any files you need. You would insert the first diskette into drive A, close the door, and press any key. DOS will then list the files as it copies them to the first diskette. When no more room is left on the diskette, DOS will beep and prompt you to enter the second diskette. This will continue until all the files are backed up. As DOS fills the diskettes, you should label them consecutively as backup disk 1, backup disk 2, and so on.

Step 2: Do an Incremental Backup

If you make it a practice of backing up your hard disk at regular intervals, say every day or week, there is no need to copy those files that have not changed. You do, however, want to make sure that you back up any new or modified files.

Figure 8 Using the BACKUP Command

```
C:\>backup c: a: /s

Insert backup diskette 01 in drive A:

WARNING! Files in the target drive
A:\ root directory will be erased
Press any key to continue . . .
```

Figure 6 SAMPLE.TXT Is Not Found in the Root Directory

```
C>md c:\lessons

C>cd c:\lessons

C>copy con sample.txt
This is a sample text file.
^Z
        1 File(s) copied

C>type sample.txt
This is a sample text file.

C>cd c:\

C>type sample.txt
File not found - SAMPLE.TXT

C>_
```

directories separated by semicolons. Execute the following APPEND command:

Type **append c:\;c:\dos;c:\lessons**
Press **Enter**

This command tells DOS the directories you want to search for files that have extensions other than BAT, COM, and EXE. Now try this command again:

Type **type sample.txt**
Press **Enter**

The file should be displayed on your screen, as shown in Figure 7. DOS was able to find SAMPLE.TXT because the APPEND command you entered told it where to search.

Like PATH, the APPEND command is usually put in the AUTOEXEC.BAT file to set up the search paths for data files every time the computer is turned on.

Practice

1. You can also use the APPEND command to see the current search path for data files.

   Type **append**
   Press **Enter**

   If you enter this command without a list of subdirectories, DOS will display the search paths, if any, that have been established by the most recent APPEND command on your computer.
2. Use the TYPE command to examine the AUTOEXEC.BAT file in the root directory of your disk. Does it contain a PATH and APPEND statement?

Lesson 5: Changing the DOS Prompt

By default, the DOS prompt consists of the current drive letter followed by a > (greater than sign). For example, if hard disk C is your current drive, then the default DOS prompt is

C>

Figure 7 APPEND Enables DOS to Find SAMPLE.TXT

```
C>md c:\lessons

C>cd c:\lessons

C>copy con sample.txt
This is a sample text file.
^Z
        1 File(s) copied

C>type sample.txt
This is a sample text file.

C>cd c:\

C>type sample.txt
File not found - SAMPLE.TXT

C>append c:\;c:\dos;c:\lessons

C>type sample.txt
This is a sample text file.

C>_
```

You can, however, change the appearance of the DOS prompt with the PROMPT command.

Step 1: Change the Prompt to a Text String

Suppose you want your DOS prompt to be Hello> instead of A> or C>. Execute this command:

Type **prompt Hello$g**
Press **Enter**

As soon as you enter this command, the DOS prompt will be changed to Hello>. The $g in the command is a special code that stands for the > (greater than sign).

Step 2: Change the Prompt to Show the Disk and Directory

You can probably think of any number of cute prompts such as Hello>. A more useful prompt would show your current disk drive and directory. This is especially handy if you frequently use subdirectories, because it's easy to forget your current path. To change your prompt to display your current path, execute this command:

Type **prompt pg**
Press **Enter**

If you are at the root directory of your hard disk, the prompt will immediately change to C:\>. Now change to your LESSONS subdirectory by executing this command:

Type **cd \lessons**
Press **Enter**

Your DOS prompt should now be C:\LESSONS>.

Step 3: Explore the Other Prompt Options

The PROMPT command allows several options besides $g and $p. The following table lists all of the special codes you can use with the PROMPT command. These codes can be combined and mixed with text to create an unlimited number of prompts.

Prompt Code	*Action*
$q	Presents the = (equal sign) character.
$$	Presents the $ (dollar sign) character.
$t	Presents the current time of day.
$d	Presents today's date.
$p	Presents the current path.
$v	Presents the version of DOS being used.
$n	Presents the current drive letter.
$g	Presents the > (greater than sign) character.
$l	Presents the < (less than sign) character.
$b	Presents the | (vertical bar) character.
$_	Starts a new line.
$e	Presents a left arrow symbol.
$h	Performs a Backspace.

Practice

Try as many of the prompt options in the preceding table as you like. When you are finished experimenting, execute the following command to change the DOS prompt to the current disk drive and directory:

Type **prompt pg**
Press **Enter**

Lesson 6: Backing Up and Restoring Disks and Files

Floppy disks and hard disks, though quite reliable, are not infallible. Eventually, every disk or disk drive will fail. In addition, almost every computer user mistakenly erases important programs or data on occasion. It is essential, therefore, to keep backup copies of all files that may be difficult, if not impossible, to replace. DOS includes two external commands, BACKUP and RESTORE, that help you keep extra copies of your software and data files.

Step 1: Back Up the Entire Hard Disk

Although the DOS BACKUP command can be used to make extra copies of floppy disks on other floppy disks, it is most often used to back up all or part of a hard disk onto floppy disks. BACKUP is better than using the COPY command to back up a hard disk, because most hard disks contain too many files to fit on a single floppy disk. Unlike COPY, the BACKUP command will automatically use as many diskettes as needed to save the files from a hard disk. The BACKUP command will fill each diskette as much as possible, even if it means splitting a single file between two disks. Then, BACKUP will prompt you to insert additional floppy disks until it copies all of the files. Furthermore, the BACKUP command of DOS versions 3.3 or newer will even format the backup floppy disks if necessary.

Suppose you want to make a backup copy of your entire hard disk. Assume that you have never backed up your hard disk before. First, you would switch back to the root directory and use DIR or CHKDSK to estimate how many floppy disks you will need. For example, if your hard disk contains 10 megabytes of files, you would need 29 or 30 360K floppy disks. Don't do this on your computer (it might require too many diskettes and take too long), but here is the command you would enter:

backup c: a: /s

This command tells DOS to back up the C drive onto the floppy disks that you will put into drive A. The /S parameter tells DOS to back up all the subdirectories as well. If you are using DOS 4.00 or newer, the BACKUP command can automatically format new diskettes if necessary. If you are using DOS 3.3, you should tell the BACKUP command to format new diskettes (if yours are not already formatted) by including the /F parameter after the /S parameter. Finally, if you are using a DOS version previous to 3.3, you have to format all of your backup diskettes *before* you execute the BACKUP command.

The BACKUP command will then beep and present the message shown in Figure 8. It is up to you to make sure that the floppy disks you use for the backup do not contain any files you need. You would insert the first diskette into drive A, close the door, and press any key. DOS will then list the files as it copies them to the first diskette. When no more room is left on the diskette, DOS will beep and prompt you to enter the second diskette. This will continue until all the files are backed up. As DOS fills the diskettes, you should label them consecutively as backup disk 1, backup disk 2, and so on.

Step 2: Do an Incremental Backup

If you make it a practice of backing up your hard disk at regular intervals, say every day or week, there is no need to copy those files that have not changed. You do, however, want to make sure that you back up any new or modified files.

Figure 8 Using the BACKUP Command

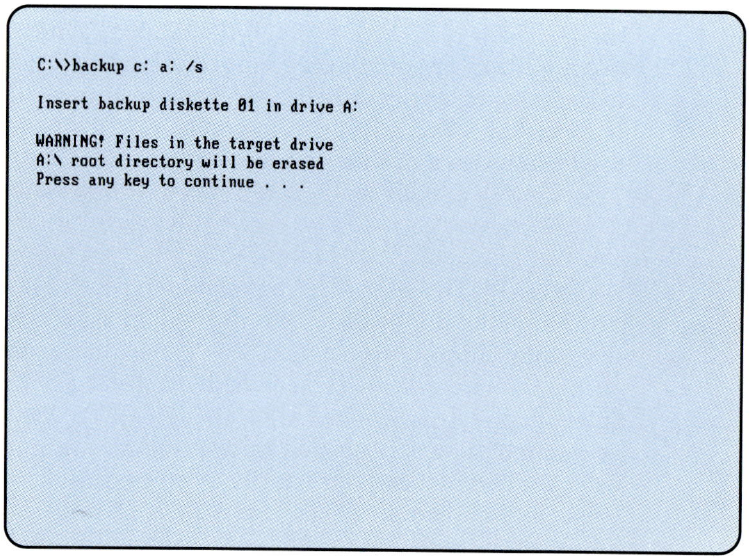

This is known as an **incremental backup.** Fortunately, you can tell DOS to do an incremental backup with two additional parameters to the BACKUP command. The /M parameter tells the BACKUP command to copy only new or changed files. The /A parameter tells the BACKUP command to add the selected files to the existing backup diskettes and not erase their contents. So, this would be the command you enter to do an incremental backup (don't do it now):

backup c: a: /s/m/a

DOS would then tell you to insert the last backup diskette into drive A and press any key when you are ready. Any new or changed files would then be added to this diskette, and additional diskettes, if needed.

In addition to /S, /M, /A, and /F (for DOS 3.3), the BACKUP command also accepts the following parameters:

/D:*date*	Backs up only those files that were created or modified on or after the specified *date*.
/T:*time*	Backs up only those files that were created or modified at or after the specified *time*.
/L:*file*	Creates a backup log in the specified *file*.

Step 3: Restore the Backed Up Disk

Hopefully, you'll never have to use the backup diskettes of your hard disk. Suppose the worst has happened, however, and you must copy the files from your backup diskettes back onto your hard disk. This is done with the RESTORE command. First, you would make sure that you are at the root directory of the hard disk. Again, don't do this now, but the command to restore the entire hard disk would be:

restore a: /s

This command will restore the files from the backup diskettes in drive A to your current directory, which should be the root directory of the hard disk C. It will prompt you to insert the backup diskettes in the same order in which they were created. The /S parameter tells DOS to restore subdirectories as well.

Step 4: Back Up a Subdirectory

It is also possible to use the BACKUP command to save a copy of a single subdirectory. This is often done when the contents of a hard disk subdirectory will not fit on a single floppy disk. Although your LESSONS subdirectory is very small, let's create a backup of it to illustrate the procedure. Get a formatted floppy disk that is either empty or contains files that can be erased. Then execute this command:

Type **backup c:\lessons a: /s**
Press **Enter**

Insert the floppy disk into drive A and press any key. DOS will back up the contents of the LESSONS subdirectory onto the diskette in drive A. Your screen should look like Figure 9.

Figure 9 Backing Up the LESSONS Subdirectory

```
C:\>backup c:\lessons a: /s

Insert backup diskette 01 in drive A:

WARNING! Files in the target drive
A:\ root directory will be erased
Press any key to continue . . .

*** Backing up files to drive A: ***
Diskette Number: 01

\LESSONS\SAMPLE.TXT

C:\>_
```

Step 5: Restore a Subdirectory

Suppose that you accidentally erased the contents of the LESSONS subdirectory. Simulate this accident by executing this command:

Type **`erase c:\lessons\*.*`**
Press **Enter**
Type **y**
Press **Enter**

Now, execute the following command to restore the LESSONS subdirectory from the backup diskette:

Type **`restore a: c:\lessons\*.* /s`**
Press **Enter**

DOS will ask you to insert backup diskette 1 in drive A and press any key when you are ready. After you do this and the RESTORE command is finished, your screen should look like Figure 10.

In addition to /S, which ensures the restoration of subdirectories, the RESTORE command also accepts the following parameters:

/P	Prompts you for permission to restore files.
/B:*date*	Restores only those files that were last modified on or before the specified *date*.
/A:*date*	Restores only those files that were last modified on or after the specified *date*.
/E:*time*	Restores only those files that were last modified at or earlier than the specified *time*.
/L:*time*	Restores only those files that were last modified at or later than the specified *time*.
/M:*file*	Restores only those files modified since the last BACKUP.
/N	Restores only those files that no longer exist on the target disk.

Figure 10 Restoring the LESSONS Subdirectory

```
C:\>restore a: c:\lessons\*.* /s

Insert backup diskette 01 in drive A:
Press any key to continue . . .

*** Files were backed up 07-13-1989 ***

*** Restoring files from drive A: ***
Diskette: 01
\LESSONS\SAMPLE.TXT

C:\>_
```

Step 6: Back Up and Restore One or More Files

BACKUP and RESTORE can also be used for individual files and groups of files specified with the DOS global file name characters ? and *. Simply insert the file specification instead of just the drive letter or subdirectory of the disk to be backed up. For example, suppose you wanted to back up only those files with an extension of TXT on your hard disk. Make sure you are at the root directory of hard disk C and execute this command:

Type **`backup c:*.txt a: /s`**
Press **Enter**

Insert your floppy disk into drive A and press **Enter** again. All TXT files in all subdirectories on disk C will be backed up to drive A. To restore the files, enter this command:

Type **`restore a: c:*.txt /s`**
Press **Enter**

Practice

1. If you have several blank diskettes you can use, backup the DOS subdirectory from your hard disk onto them. If you have only one diskette available, back up only one file or a group of files (such as *.SYS) that will fit on a single diskette.
2. Use the DIR command to examine the backup diskette you have created.

Lesson 7: Recovering Files from Damaged Disks

Every hard disk and floppy disk will eventually wear out or become physically damaged or magnetically corrupted in some way. When one of these unfortunate events occurs, DOS may not be able to read the files stored in or around the bad spots. This is one reason why you should try to maintain up-to-date backup copies of all of your important files and disks. If you don't do this, however, and DOS cannot read one of your files or perhaps even an entire disk, the RECOVER command may be able to help. This external command should be used only as a last resort. RECOVER does not work when DOS is run from a local area network.

Step 1: Recover a Single File

Suppose you try to retrieve a file from a floppy disk in drive A and DOS reports that it cannot read that file. You may get one of the following messages from DOS:

```
Disk error reading drive A:
General failure reading drive A:
Read fault error reading drive A:
Sector not found error reading drive A:
Track 0 bad - disk unusable
Unrecoverable read error on drive A:
```

First, take out the disk, make sure it is inserted correctly, and close the disk drive door or lever again. Then try using the CHKDSK command on that disk. If the CHKDSK command reports that a sector on the disk is bad, RECOVER might be able to read all or part of the file by skipping over the bad spots. Suppose the file you are trying to read is SAMPLE.TXT. You would enter this command (don't do this now):

recover a:sample.txt

RECOVER would then try to read SAMPLE.TXT, part by part, ignoring the bad spots. Then it would try to rewrite the file without the bad spots, possibly allowing you to read at least some of the original SAMPLE.TXT.

Step 2: Recover an Entire Disk

If you cannot gain access to any files on a disk, then you can tell the RECOVER command to try and reconstruct the entire disk. Again, this should only be done as a last resort. Here is the command you would enter to recover all the files on the disk in drive A (don't do it now):

recover a:

Practice

1. Take a diskette with files on it that you don't need, such as the backup diskette you created in Lesson 6, and insert it into drive A. Suppose that it is a damaged disk. Execute the following command to try to get back readable information on the damaged disk:

   Type **recover a:**
   Press **Enter**

   Press any key when the RECOVER command asks you to do so. When it is finished, RECOVER will report how many files it recovered.

2. RECOVER is to be used only as a last resort. When it recovers files, it changes their names to FILE0001.REC, FILE0002.REC, and so on. So, you have to examine and rename the recovered files to get them into usable form again. You don't need the files you recovered on the diskette in drive A, so reformat it:

Type **format a:**
Press **Enter**

Lesson 8: Using the Prompt Option When Erasing Files

You have already learned how to use the ERASE (or DEL) command to remove files from a disk. If you try to erase every file on a disk or in a subdirectory, DOS will ask you if you are sure this is what you want to do before it discards the files. The ERASE command, however, does not automatically ask this question when you erase several files at once with the global file name characters * or ?. Fortunately, an optional parameter is available that lets you have DOS prompt you before erasing each file. This option is also handy for selectively erasing some files from a group of many.

Step 1: Specify the /P Parameter

Copy some files from the DOS subdirectory into your LESSONS subdirectory so that you have some files you can erase safely. Execute the following commands:

Type **cd c:\lessons**
Press **Enter**
Type **copy c:\dos*.com**
Press **Enter**

Use the DIR command to make sure that you are in the LESSONS subdirectory. Execute this command to erase the COM files from your LESSONS subdirectory with a prompt before erasing each file:

Type **erase *.com /p**
Press **Enter**
Type **y**
Press **Enter**

As Figure 11 shows, DOS will prompt you with "Delete (Y/N)?" before it actually deletes each file. For the remaining files, answer yes for some files and no for others. When the ERASE command has finished, execute this command to examine the LESSONS subdirectory:

Type **dir**
Press **Enter**

The files for which you answered no will still be present.

Step 2: Don't Specify the /P Parameter

To delete the remaining COM files from your LESSONS subdirectory, execute this command:

Type **erase *.com**
Press **Enter**

Practice Make sure you are in your LESSONS subdirectory. Use the ERASE command with the /P parameter to tell DOS to delete every file in the subdirectory, but to prompt you first. Answer **n** for no to each prompt so that you don't erase any

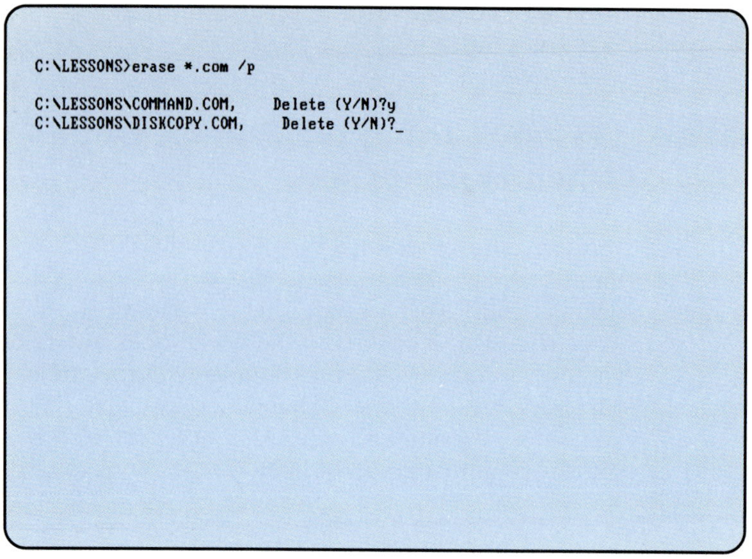

Figure 11 Using the /P Parameter When Erasing Files

files. To be extra safe, you can make it a practice to always use the /P parameter with the ERASE or DEL command.

Lesson 9: Learning More About the COPY Command

COPY is a versatile command that can be used in several different ways. You have already learned how to use COPY to duplicate one or more files from one disk or subdirectory to another. By specifying different names for the source and the target files, you can also duplicate files in the same subdirectory.

Step 1: Copy from the Console to Create a Text File

The COPY command can create a new text file without using a word processing or text editing program. Actually, you already did this in Lesson 4, but let's go over it again.

DOS can refer to certain hardware devices as if they were files. These devices are given special file names called DOS device names. For example, CON refers to the console, or the keyboard and the screen. Similarly, PRN refers to the printer. You can use device names such as CON and PRN as if they were file names in commands such as COPY. Make sure you are in your LESSONS subdirectory and then execute this command:

Type **copy con sample2.txt**
Press **Enter**

This command tells DOS to take every character you now type at the keyboard and copy it into a new file named SAMPLE2.TXT. Type the following text, pressing **Enter** at the end of each line:

```
A text file contains only letters, numbers,
punctuation marks, and other symbols that
appear on the keyboard.
```

An end-of-file mark is the Ctrl-Z character; it is the last character in a text file. When you are finished entering the text, you must insert an end-of-file mark into the file by doing this:

Press **F6**
Press **Enter**

To see what you have done, execute these commands:

Type **`dir`**
Press **Enter**
Type **`type sample2.txt`**
Press **Enter**

Your screen should look like Figure 12.

Step 2: Use COPY to Append Files

The COPY command is sometimes used to append or combine files. Suppose you wanted to create a new file named SAMPLE3.TXT that contained the contents of SAMPLE.TXT followed by the contents of SAMPLE2.TXT. Execute this command:

Type **`copy sample.txt+sample2.txt sample3.txt`**
Press **Enter**

Any number of source files can be combined by listing their names separated by plus signs. The last file name in the COPY command is the target file that will contain the combination of the source files. If you omit the name of a target file, DOS will combine the source files and copy them to the first source file listed. To see what you have done, enter these commands:

Type **`dir`**
Press **Enter**
Type **`type sample3.txt`**
Press **Enter**

Your screen should look like Figure 13.

Figure 12 Using COPY to Create a Text File

```
C:\LESSONS>copy con sample2.txt
A text file contains only letters, numbers,
punctuation marks, and other symbols that
appear on the keyboard.
^Z
        1 File(s) copied

C:\LESSONS>dir

 Volume in drive C is HARD DISK
 Volume Serial Number is 3324-07CC
 Directory of  C:\LESSONS

.            <DIR>      07-15-89  11:06a
..           <DIR>      07-15-89  11:06a
SAMPLE   TXT         29 07-15-89  11:06a
SAMPLE2  TXT        113 07-15-89  11:08a
        4 File(s)   19691520 bytes free

C:\LESSONS>type sample2.txt
A text file contains only letters, numbers,
punctuation marks, and other symbols that
appear on the keyboard.

C:\LESSONS>_
```

Figure 13 Using COPY to Append Files

```
C:\LESSONS>copy sample.txt+sample2.txt sample3.txt
SAMPLE.TXT
SAMPLE2.TXT
        1 File(s) copied

C:\LESSONS>dir

 Volume in drive C is HARD DISK
 Volume Serial Number is 3324-07CC
 Directory of  C:\LESSONS

.            <DIR>      07-15-89  11:06a
..           <DIR>      07-15-89  11:06a
SAMPLE   TXT        29 07-15-89  11:06a
SAMPLE2  TXT       113 07-15-89  11:08a
SAMPLE3  TXT       143 07-15-89  11:09a
        5 File(s)   19689472 bytes free

C:\LESSONS>type sample3.txt
This is a sample text file.
A text file contains only letters, numbers,
punctuation marks, and other symbols that
appear on the keyboard.

C:\LESSONS>_
```

Step 3: Use the /V Parameter

The COPY command has three optional parameters, /V, /B, and /A. The /V parameter tells DOS to verify that the copy has been made successfully with no errors. Each time data is written to the disk, a confirmation procedure will be performed to ensure that data can be read without error. The /V parameter is used only when making copies to disk files, not device names. Verifying a copy takes longer and is usually not necessary, but you may want to do it when copying especially important files, such as programs in which the scrambling of a single byte can cause a bug. For example, try this command:

Type **copy c:\command.com command.bak /v**
Press **Enter**

You won't see any difference on the screen when the COPY command is used with the /V parameter, except that it works a little slower.

Step 4: Use the /B and /A Parameters

By default, the COPY command creates a target file that is the same type of file as the source. If you copy a text file, COPY produces a text file. Another term for text file is **ASCII file.** ASCII, which stands for American Standard Code for Information Interchange, is the most common scheme used to encode characters as numbers so that they can be manipulated by computers. A **binary file** is a file that contains programs or data that are not encoded as ASCII characters. Files with extensions of EXE and COM, for example, are binary files. If you copy a binary file, COPY normally produces a binary file.

The other two parameters of the COPY command, /B and /A, are used when the type of file you want to produce is different than the source. The /B parameter, when specified after a source file name, tells DOS to copy the entire file, including any end-of-file marks. When used with a target file name, the /B parameter tells DOS not to add an end-of-file mark to the end of the file. The /A parameter tells

DOS to treat the file as an ASCII file. If a source file name is followed by /A, only data up to and including the first end-of-file mark will be copied. If a target file name is followed by /A, an end-of-file mark will be added as the last character of the file.

In most cases, you don't have to use /B or /A. You can, however, use the /B command to view the entire contents of a binary file on your screen. First, try the following COPY command without the /B parameter:

Type **`copy command.bak con`**
Press **Enter**

Remember, COMMAND.BAK is a copy of COMMAND.COM, the DOS command processor, which is a binary file. When you copy it to the screen, the display will stop when the first end-of-file mark is encountered. Now, try this command to display the entire COMMAND.BAK binary file on your screen (the computer will beep quite a bit, so skip this command if you don't want to disturb others around you):

Type **`copy command.bak /b con`**
Press **Enter**

Don't be alarmed if your computer seems to be going crazy. All the strange characters and beeps occur because binary programming code is being displayed on the screen. Occasionally, you will see words or phrases that you can read, usually messages embedded in the command processor. It will take a couple of minutes for the entire COMMAND.BAK file to be copied to the screen, and Ctrl-Break won't stop it, so just be patient and wait.

Practice

1. Use the COPY command with the CON device name to display the contents of SAMPLE2.TXT on your screen.
2. Use the COPY command with the PRN device name to send SAMPLE2.TXT to your printer.
3. Use the COPY command with the /B parameter and CON device name to examine an EXE or COM file from the DOS subdirectory on your hard disk.

Lesson 10: Setting the VERIFY Option

In Lesson 9 you learned that the COPY command's optional /V ensures that files copied to the disk can be read without error. The VERIFY command lets you turn this option on or off whenever any files are copied to a disk, not just for a single COPY command like the /V parameter.

Step 1: Execute the VERIFY Command

To see the current setting of the VERIFY option, execute this command:

Type **`verify`**
Press **Enter**

The default setting of the VERIFY option is off.

Step 2: Change the VERIFY Option

You can change the current setting of the VERIFY option by following the command with ON or OFF. For example, execute these commands:

Type **verify on**
Press **Enter**
Type **verify**
Press **Enter**

Practice Turn the VERIFY option off again.

Lesson 11: Changing File Attributes

A **file attribute** is a characteristic of a file. DOS has several attributes that can be associated with files. The two most commonly encountered by the average user are the read-only and the archive attributes.

When a file's **read-only attribute** is turned off, the default state, it can be read, written, modified, or deleted. If the file's read-only attribute is turned on, it cannot be changed in any way. The only way to modify or delete the file is to turn the read-only attribute back off again.

The **archive attribute** indicates whether a file has been changed since it was last saved with the BACKUP command. The archive attribute is turned on whenever a file is rewritten to disk (that is, changed in some way). When the BACKUP command saves a file, its archive attribute is turned off. This is how DOS can tell if a file has been changed since you last backed it up.

Step 1: Change the Read-only Attribute

Suppose the SAMPLE.TXT file was an extremely important file that you did not want to accidentally delete. One way to help ensure that it would not be deleted would be to turn on its read-only attribute. This can be done with the ATTRIB command.

Make sure you are in the LESSONS subdirectory, and then execute this command:

Type **attrib +r sample.txt**
Press **Enter**

This command turns on the read-only attribute for the file SAMPLE.TXT. Now, this file cannot be changed or deleted. Try the following three commands:

Type **type sample.txt**
Press **Enter**
Type **erase sample.txt**
Press **Enter**
Type **dir**
Press **Enter**

As you can see from Figure 14, you can read the file, but you cannot delete it after the read-only attribute has been turned on. DOS replies with "Access denied" when you try to delete a read-only file. Entering the DIR command confirms that the file SAMPLE.TXT has not been deleted.

Figure 14 Using ATTRIB to Set the Read-only Attribute

```
C:\LESSONS>attrib +r sample.txt

C:\LESSONS>type sample.txt
This is a sample text file.

C:\LESSONS>erase sample.txt
Access denied

C:\LESSONS>dir

 Volume in drive C is HARD DISK
 Volume Serial Number is 3324-07CC
 Directory of  C:\LESSONS

.            <DIR>      07-15-89  11:06a
..           <DIR>      07-15-89  11:06a
SAMPLE   TXT         29 07-15-89  11:06a
SAMPLE2  TXT        113 07-15-89  11:08a
SAMPLE3  TXT        143 07-15-89  11:09a
COMMAND  BAK      37557 12-19-88  12:00a
        6 File(s)   19650560 bytes free

C:\LESSONS>_
```

Step 2: Change the Archive Attribute

The ATTRIB command can also be used to change the archive attribute. You could, for example, turn off the archive attribute for a file, even though it has been changed, to prevent it from being saved by the next BACKUP command. Execute the following command:

Type **attrib -a sample.txt**
Press **Enter**

This turns off the archive attribute for the SAMPLE.TXT file. Unless you change the file or the attribute again, it will not be saved by the next BACKUP command.

The ATTRIB command can also be used to view the current attributes of a file. Execute the following command:

Type **attrib sample.txt**
Press **Enter**

As Figure 15 shows, if you omit the R and A switches between the ATTRIB and the file name, DOS will report which attributes are turned on for that file. Since the read-only attribute is turned on and the archive attribute is turned off, DOS replies with only R before the full file name C:\LESSONS\SAMPLE.TXT.

You can also set both attributes at once with a single ATTRIB command. Turn the read-only attribute back off and the archive attribute back on by executing this command:

Type **attrib -r +a sample.txt**
Press **Enter**

Practice

1. Use the ATTRIB command to examine the file attributes of SAMPLE2.TXT.
2. Turn on the read-only attribute of SAMPLE2.TXT and then try to delete the file.
3. Turn off the read-only attribute of SAMPLE2.TXT.

Figure 15 Using ATTRIB to Display a File's Attributes

```
C:\LESSONS>attrib -a sample.txt

C:\LESSONS>attrib sample.txt
      R     C:\LESSONS\SAMPLE.TXT

C:\LESSONS>_
```

Lesson 12: Copying Groups of Files

In Chapter 5 you learned that you can copy groups of files with the COPY command by using the global file name characters ? or * in your file specifications. Starting with version 3.2, however, DOS included XCOPY, a more sophisticated command for copying files. While the COPY command reads and then writes a single file at a time, XCOPY reads as many files as it can into memory first and then writes them. This makes XCOPY faster than COPY in some cases. In addition, XCOPY accepts more optional parameters, making it more flexible than COPY. On the other hand, unlike COPY, XCOPY is an external command. This means that XCOPY must be accessible on your disk if you want to use it.

Step 1: Copy a Group of Files with XCOPY

To see how XCOPY works, make sure you are in the LESSONS subdirectory on your hard disk and put a formatted diskette in drive A. Then execute this command:

Type **xcopy *.* a:**
Press **Enter**

Your screen should look like Figure 16. XCOPY read all of the files in the LESSONS subdirectory into memory first, and then copied them to the diskette in drive A.

Step 2: Copy Subdirectories

Unlike the COPY command, XCOPY can be instructed to copy files from all the subdirectories in the source disk or directory. In the process, it will create new subdirectories on the target disk if necessary. For example, change to the root directory of your hard disk and try the following XCOPY command:

Type **cd **
Press **Enter**
Type **xcopy sample.* a: /s**
Press **Enter**

Figure 16 Using XCOPY to Duplicate a Group of Files

```
C:\LESSONS>xcopy *.* a:
Reading source file(s)...
SAMPLE.TXT
SAMPLE2.TXT
SAMPLE3.TXT
COMMAND.BAK
        4 File(s) copied

C:\LESSONS>_
```

XCOPY will look for all files with a primary filename of SAMPLE no matter what subdirectory they might be in. It will create corresponding subdirectories on the floppy disk in drive A and copy the files into the appropriate subdirectories. Execute the following two commands to see what you have done to your floppy disk:

Type **dir a:**
Press **Enter**
Type **dir a:\lessons**
Press **Enter**

Your screen should look like Figure 17.

Figure 17 Using XCOPY to Duplicate a Subdirectory

```
C:\>dir a:

 Volume in drive A has no label
 Volume Serial Number is 1A3F-12C9
 Directory of  A:\

SAMPLE   TXT        29 07-15-89  11:06a
SAMPLE2  TXT       113 07-15-89  11:08a
SAMPLE3  TXT       143 07-15-89  11:09a
COMMAND  BAK     37557 12-19-88  12:00a
LESSONS      <DIR>     07-15-89  11:39a
        5 File(s)    319488 bytes free

C:\>dir a:\lessons

 Volume in drive A has no label
 Volume Serial Number is 1A3F-12C9
 Directory of  A:\LESSONS

.            <DIR>     07-15-89  11:39a
..           <DIR>     07-15-89  11:39a
SAMPLE   TXT        29 07-15-89  11:06a
        3 File(s)    319488 bytes free

C:\>_
```

Step 3: Examine the Other XCOPY Parameters

Several other parameters can be used with the XCOPY command in addition to /S. The following table lists all of them.

Parameter	*Action*
/A	Copies only those files whose archive attribute is turned on. Does not change the archive attribute after copying.
/D:*date*	Copies only those files created or last modified on or after the specified *date*.
/E	Copies any subdirectories beneath the specified source disk or directory, even if they contain no files. This parameter, if used, must be used with /S.
/M	Same as /A, but turns off the archive attribute after copying.
/P	Prompts you for confirmation before each file is copied.
/S	Copies nonempty subdirectories beneath the specified source disk or directory.
/V	Verifies each copy to be identical to the original.
/W	Waits for you to press a key before copying files.

Practice

1. Try each of the following commands and explain exactly what they do. Answer **n** for no to each prompt to leave your diskette in drive A unchanged.

   Type **xcopy *.* a: /p /a**
   Press **Enter**
   Type **xcopy *.* a: /p /d:01-01-89**
   Press **Enter**
   Type **xcopy *.* a: /w /p /m**
   Press **Enter**

2. The XCOPY command can copy an entire diskette to another diskette, even if the source and target diskettes are different types, as long as the target diskette has enough room. For example, if you have a 5¼-inch floppy drive A and a 3½-inch floppy drive B, you would have to use XCOPY instead of DISKCOPY to duplicate a 5¼-inch diskette on a 3½-inch diskette. Even if you have only one floppy drive, you can use XCOPY to duplicate an entire diskette. Unlike DISKCOPY, however, XCOPY cannot automatically format a diskette. To copy an entire diskette with XCOPY, get an extra formatted diskette and execute the following command:

   Type **xcopy a: b: /s /e**
   Press **Enter**

   Note that this command will work even if you don't have a floppy drive B installed in your computer. DOS has the ability to "pretend" that drive A is temporarily drive B to complete such commands. It will prompt you when to insert the diskette for drive A or for drive B. Just swap the source and target diskettes in drive A. When you are finished, use DIR to examine the disk in drive A.

Lesson 13: Updating Sets of Files

Suppose you have identical copies of the file SAMPLE.TXT in various subdirectories on your hard disk and you want to update them all with a new copy of SAMPLE.TXT stored on a floppy disk. Although you cannot do this with a single COPY command, you can use a single REPLACE command. REPLACE is an external DOS command that is used to update previous versions of files.

Step 1: Prepare the Floppy Disk

Let's create an updated version of the file SAMPLE.TXT on the diskette in drive A. Then execute the following command to create a new SAMPLE.TXT:

Type **`copy con a:sample.txt`**
Press **Enter**

Now, do the following to add the text to SAMPLE.TXT in drive A:

Type **`This is the new sample text file.`**
Press **Enter**
Press **F6**
Press **Enter**

Step 2: Replace the Hard Disk Files

Suppose you had several copies of SAMPLE.TXT on the hard disk in different subdirectories. (You don't, but it doesn't matter for this example.) Execute the following command to replace all copies of SAMPLE.TXT on the hard disk with the new version from the floppy disk in drive A:

Type **`replace a:sample.txt c:\ /s`**
Press **Enter**

The /S parameter tells the REPLACE command to search through all subdirectories of the target for files to replace. To see what you have done, execute this command:

Type **`type c:\lessons\sample.txt`**
Press **Enter**

Your screen should look like Figure 18.

Step 3: Add Files to the Target Disk

The REPLACE command can also be used to copy files that exist on the source disk, but not on the target disk, to the target disk. Execute the following commands to move back into the LESSONS subdirectory on the hard disk and rename a few of the files:

Type **`cd lessons`**
Press **Enter**
Type **`ren sample.txt part1.txt`**
Press **Enter**
Type **`ren sample2.txt part2.txt`**
Press **Enter**
Type **`ren sample3.txt example.txt`**
Press **Enter**

Figure 18 Replacing Files on the Hard Disk

```
C:\>replace a:sample.txt c:\ /s

Replacing C:\LESSONS\SAMPLE.TXT

1 file(s) replaced

C:\>type c:\lessons\sample.txt
This is the new sample text file.

C:\>_
```

Now your LESSONS subdirectory on the hard disk contains the files PART1.TXT, PART2.TXT and EXAMPLE.TXT. The floppy disk in drive A does not contain files with these three names. Suppose you wanted to copy *only* those files with different names from C to A. Execute this command:

Type **replace *.* a: /a**
Press **Enter**

The /A is a parameter that tells the REPLACE command to add files from the source to the target, but only those that don't already exist in the target. To see the result, execute this command:

Type **dir a:**
Press **Enter**

Your screen should look like Figure 19.

Step 4: Examine the Other REPLACE Parameters

Several other parameters can be used with the REPLACE command. The following table lists all of them.

Parameter	*Action*
/A	Adds new files to the target instead of replacing existing files. Cannot be used with /S or /U.
/P	Prompts you for confirmation before each file is replaced.
/R	Replaces read-only files as well as regular files.
/S	Searches all subdirectories on the target disk to replace matching files. Cannot be used with /A.
/U	Replaces only those target files that are older than their matching source files. Cannot be used with /A.
/W	Waits for you to press a key before replacing or adding files.

Figure 19 Using REPLACE to Add Files

```
Adding A:\PART1.TXT

Adding A:\PART2.TXT

Adding A:\EXAMPLE.TXT

3 file(s) added

C:\LESSONS>dir a:

 Volume in drive A has no label
 Volume Serial Number is 1A3F-12C9
 Directory of  A:\

SAMPLE   TXT        35 07-15-89  11:45a
SAMPLE2  TXT       113 07-15-89  11:08a
SAMPLE3  TXT       143 07-15-89  11:09a
COMMAND  BAK     37557 12-19-88  12:00a
LESSONS      <DIR>     07-15-89  11:39a
PART1    TXT        35 07-15-89  11:45a
PART2    TXT       113 07-15-89  11:08a
EXAMPLE  TXT       143 07-15-89  11:09a
        8 File(s)     316416 bytes free

C:\LESSONS>_
```

Practice Make sure you are in the LESSONS subdirectory on the hard disk and execute the following command to change the EXAMPLE file:

Type **copy part1.txt+part2.txt example.txt**
Press **Enter**

Execute this command and explain what it does:

Type **replace *.* a: /w /p /r /u**
Press **Enter**

Press any key to continue and answer **y** for yes to the prompt.

Lesson 14: Transferring the DOS System Files

When you format a system diskette with the /S parameter as you learned in Lesson 9 of Chapter 5, DOS copies two hidden system files to the newly formatted disk. These files, along with the command processor, COMMAND.COM, let you boot up your computer from that disk. It is also possible to format a diskette and leave space for the system files to be transferred later. This is sometimes done by individuals and companies that transfer software or data to others. It is not legal to give away or sell DOS without a license from IBM or Microsoft, so you are not supposed to distribute boot-up disks. You can, however, format a disk so that the recipient can transfer his or her own copy of DOS to that disk. The SYS command makes this possible. The SYS command is also used for upgrading to a new version of DOS. SYS, which is an external command, will not work if you are running DOS from a network.

Step 1: Format a Diskette with the /B Parameter

Execute this command to format a diskette to which DOS can be transferred later:

Type **format a: /b**
Press **Enter**

Insert the diskette you have been using into drive A and press the **Enter** key. When the format procedure is finished, press **Enter** to skip typing a volume label and enter **n** for no in response to the prompt asking if you want to format another disk. As you can see from Figure 20, DOS reserved 73,728 bytes for the system. The hidden system files, however, have not yet been transferred to this space.

Step 2: Transfer the Hidden System Files

To transfer the hidden system files, execute this command:

Type **sys a:**
Press **Enter**

When DOS is finished, it will display the message "System transferred," but if you examine the disk with the DIR command, no files will appear in the directory. This is because the system files are hidden.

Step 3: Copy the File COMMAND.COM

One more step is necessary in order to be able to boot up your computer from this diskette. Execute the following command to copy the DOS command processor from the root directory of your hard disk to the diskette in drive A:

Type **copy c:\command.com a:**
Press **Enter**

The diskette in drive A can now be used to boot up the computer.

Practice

1. Reboot your computer from the system diskette you just created. Enter the current date and time. Use DIR to examine the directory of your diskette. The procedure you followed in this lesson achieves the same result as using the /S parameter with the FORMAT command.

Figure 20 Using the /B Parameter with FORMAT

```
C:\LESSONS>format a: /b
Insert new diskette for drive A:
and press ENTER when ready...

Format complete

Volume label (11 characters, ENTER for none)?

    362496 bytes total disk space
     73728 bytes used by system
    288768 bytes available on disk

      1024 bytes in each allocation unit
       282 allocation units available on disk

Volume Serial Number is 283D-13CC

Format another (Y/N)?n
C:\LESSONS>_
```

2. Now, reboot your computer from the hard disk. Enter the date and time if necessary. Change the DOS prompt so it displays the current drive and directory, if it does not already do so.

Lesson 15: Comparing Files and Disks

Keeping one or more copies of important files or disks is prudent. After you make a copy of an especially important file or diskette, you might want to check it to make sure that it is identical to the original. Although errors are rare, a bit or byte can get scrambled during the copy procedure if the VERIFY option is turned off. DOS has two external commands, COMP and DISKCOMP, that compare files and diskettes, respectively. These commands can also be used if you forget whether two files or disks are identical. Note: DISKCOMP will not work if you are running DOS from a network.

Step 1: Compare Two Files

Change to your LESSONS subdirectory if you are not already there. Use the directory command to examine the files inside LESSONS. It should contain a file named COMMAND.BAK, which you created in Lesson 9. Let's see if COMMAND.BAK in the LESSONS subdirectory is identical to COMMAND.COM in the root directory of your hard disk. Execute this command:

Type **comp command.bak c:\command.com**
Press **Enter**

Your screen should look like Figure 21. The files are identical, so DOS reports that the "Files compare OK." Press **n** for no in response to the prompt asking if you want to compare more files. If the files had been different sizes or if any bytes had been different, DOS would have told you.

Figure 21 Using COMP to Compare Two Files

```
C:\LESSONS>comp command.bak c:\command.com


C:COMMAND.BAK and C:\COMMAND.COM

EOF mark not found
Files compare OK
Compare more files (Y/N) ?_
```

Step 2: Compare Two Diskettes

The DISKCOMP command is used to compare the contents of two diskettes. For example, if your computer has two floppy drives, A and B, that are the same type, put a diskette in each one and compare them with this command:

Type **diskcomp a: b:**
Press **Enter**

If your computer has only one floppy disk drive, like many hard disk systems, try this command instead:

Type **diskcomp a: a:**
Press **Enter**

DOS will then prompt you when to insert each diskette. If the two diskettes are identical, then DOS will display "Compare OK." Otherwise, "Compare error" messages will be displayed that report where mismatches were found. When it is finished, DISKCOMP will ask you if you want to compare another diskette. Type **n** for no.

Practice

1. Let's see what COMP does if two files are different. Try this command:

   Type **comp part1.txt part2.txt**
   Press **Enter**

   The COMP command determines immediately that the files are different sizes, so they cannot be identical. It doesn't examine them any further.

2. Now let's try comparing two files that are the same size, but different in some other way. Follow these instructions to create a file similar, but not identical, to PART1.TXT:

   Type **copy con partx.txt**
   Press **Enter**
   Type **This is the old sample text file.**
   Press **Enter**
   Press **F6**
   Press **Enter**

   Compare PART1.TXT with PARTX.TXT with this command:

   Type **comp part1.txt partx.txt**
   Press **Enter**

   Since COMP is typically used by programmers, the results are given in hexadecimal (base 16) ASCII codes. For example, the letter "n" is represented as 6E and "o" is 6F. COMP shows three differences between the two files: the letters "n e w" versus "o l d."

Lesson 16: Displaying and Changing a Volume Label

DOS calls the name of a disk the **volume label.** This name, which is optional, can be helpful when trying to identify a disk.

Step 1: Display a Volume Label

One way to see the volume label of a disk is to use the DIR command. Another way is to use the internal command VOL. Try this:

Type **vol**
Press **Enter**

DOS will display the volume label of the disk in your default drive. You can get the volume label of a disk other than the one in your default drive by specifying the disk drive letter. For example, put a formatted diskette into drive A and execute this command:

Type **vol a:**
Press **Enter**

DOS will respond with the volume label of the diskette in drive A.

Step 2: Change a Volume Label

DOS versions 4.0 and newer automatically ask you to supply a volume label whenever you format a disk. With earlier DOS versions, you can use the /V parameter to have the FORMAT command prompt you for a volume label. You can also specify a new volume label or change an existing one with the LABEL command. LABEL is an external command; it does not work if you are running DOS from a network. To see how it works, put a formatted diskette in drive A and execute this command:

Type **label a:**
Press **Enter**

DOS will report the current volume label and allow you to enter a new name, which can be up to 11 characters long.

Type **sample**
Press **Enter**

To see the new volume label of the diskette, execute this command:

Type **vol a:**
Press **Enter**

Figure 22 shows the result.

Practice

1. If you specify the new volume label right after the LABEL command, DOS won't prompt you. Try this command:

   Type **label a:example**
   Press **Enter**

   Use DIR or VOL to examine the new volume label.
2. You can also delete an existing volume label. Try the following:

   Type **label a:**
   Press **Enter**
   Press **Enter**
   Type **y**

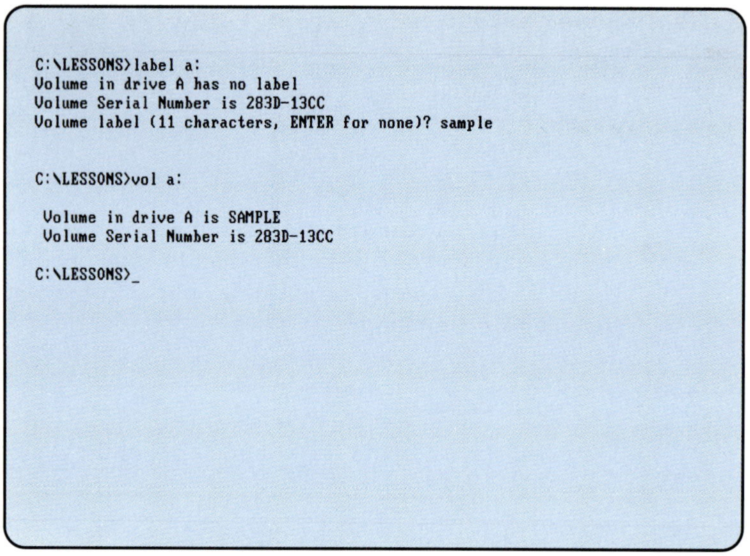

Figure 22 Using LABEL to Change a Disk's Name

3. VER is an internal DOS command similar to VOL. It is used to find out the version of DOS you are using, in case you don't know or forget. Try it:

   Type **ver**
   Press **Enter**

Lesson 17: Displaying and Changing the Date and Time

If no AUTOEXEC.BAT file is present in the root directory of the startup disk, DOS will prompt you to enter the new date and time whenever you boot up or reboot the computer. If an AUTOEXEC.BAT file is present, DOS will not prompt you for the date and time unless the commands DATE and TIME are in AUTOEXEC.BAT. DATE and TIME are internal commands that let you see and change the current date and time kept by the computer's real-time clock. Most microcomputers sold today have a battery that keeps the real-time clock operating even when the computer is off, so you don't need to execute DATE and TIME every time you boot up. Nevertheless, you can still use DATE and TIME to see the current date and time. In addition, DATE and TIME are sometimes needed to correct the internal clock, such as when changing to or from daylight saving time. It is important to set your computer to the correct date and time so that you know when files were created or last changed.

Step 1: Execute the DATE Command

To see the current date kept by your computer, without changing it, execute this command:

Type **date**
Press **Enter** (2 times)

Step 2: Change the Date

One way to change the current date is to execute the DATE command without any parameters. DOS will prompt you to enter the new date. Another way to change the date is to specify the new date after the DATE command before you press Enter. For example, execute this command:

Type **`date 1-1-90`**
Press **Enter**

Now, use the DATE command without any parameters to see the date you set. Notice how DOS automatically figures out the correct day of the week.

When you specify a new date, you must use only numbers: 1–12 for the month, 1–31 for the day, and 80–79 or 1980–2079 for the year. The month, day, and year entries may be separated with hyphens (-) or slashes (/).

Step 3: Execute the TIME Command

To see the current time kept by your computer, without changing it, execute this command:

Type **`time`**
Press **Enter** (2 times)

Step 4: Change the Time

One way to change the current time is to execute the TIME command without any parameters. DOS will prompt you to enter the new date. Another way to change the time is to specify the new time after the TIME command before you press Enter. For example, execute this command:

Type **`time 14:22:13.45`**
Press **Enter**

Now, use the TIME command without any parameters to see the time you set (see Figure 23). Notice that the new time starts ticking as soon as you enter it.

When you specify a new time, you must use the 24-hour format. If you like, you can specify a new time accurate to hundredths of seconds. The command you just executed sets the time to 22 minutes, 13.45 seconds past 14 hundred hours (2 P.M.). You don't have to enter the seconds or hundredths of seconds. If the time is exactly on the hour, you don't have to enter the minutes. Any portion of the time you omit will be set to zero.

Practice

1. Use the DATE command to reset the correct date.
2. Use the TIME command to reset the correct time.
3. Check the current date and time again.

Lesson 18: Displaying a Memory Report

Starting with version 4.0, DOS includes MEM, an external command that presents a memory report. This report displays the amount of memory used and free. It can also specify the location, size, and name of each program or data area

Figure 23 Displaying and Changing the Date and Time

```
C:\>date
Current date is Sun 07-16-1989
Enter new date (mm-dd-yy):

C:\>date 1-1-90

C:\>date
Current date is Mon 01-01-1990
Enter new date (mm-dd-yy):

C:\>time
Current time is 10:41:11.84a
Enter new time:

C:\>time 14:22:13.45

C:\>time
Current time is  2:22:15.09p
Enter new time:

C:\>_
```

currently loaded into memory. MEM can provide more detailed and technical information about memory usage than CHKDSK.

Step 1: Execute the MEM Command

If you don't have DOS 4.00 or newer, you cannot use MEM. Otherwise, execute this command:

Type **mem**
Press **Enter**

Figure 24 shows the result, although your report may have different numbers, depending on the amount of RAM installed and the programs that have been loaded in your computer.

Figure 24 Using MEM to Display a Memory Report

```
C:\>mem


    655360 bytes total memory
    655360 bytes available
    521248 largest executable program size

C:\>_
```

Step 2: Use the /PROGRAM Parameter

The MEM command has an optional parameter that will also display the programs loaded into memory. Execute this command:

Type **mem /program**
Press **Enter**

The resulting report will be longer and contain technical details concerning the location, name, and size of each program and data area in memory.

Practice

MEM has one other optional parameter, /DEBUG, that provides even more detailed information than the /PROGRAM parameter. The /DEBUG parameter presents technical facts of interest mainly to assembly language programmers, but you can still try it. Execute this command:

Type **mem /debug**
Press **Enter**

The /PROGRAM and /DEBUG parameters cannot be used at the same time.

Lesson 19: Reassigning, Joining, and Substituting Drives

DOS has three external commands that influence the use of disk drives and subdirectories, namely ASSIGN, JOIN, and SUBST. These commands can be handy when working with programs that require certain disks to be in certain drives, when programs don't allow you to specify paths, or when paths get too long. JOIN and SUBST do not work when running DOS from a network.

Step 1: Execute the ASSIGN Command

The ASSIGN command lets you change the drive letter associated with a disk drive. It is sometimes used with application programs developed before hard disks were common. A program, for example, may only work with diskette drives A and B. With ASSIGN, however, you may be able to trick the program into thinking that your hard disk is drive A. Make sure you are at the root directory of your hard disk and then execute this command:

Type **assign a = c**
Press **Enter**

To see the result, execute this command:

Type **dir a:**
Press **Enter**

DOS will present the directory of the hard disk, not the diskette in drive A. It "thinks" the hard disk is drive A, even though the DOS prompt still reports your current drive and directory as C:\ (see Figure 25).

To change all drives back to their original assignments, execute this command:

Type **assign**
Press **Enter**

Figure 25 Using ASSIGN to Change a Drive's Letter

```
C:\>assign a = c

C:\>dir a:

 Volume in drive A is HARD DISK
 Volume Serial Number is 3324-07CC
 Directory of  A:\

CONFIG   SYS       146 07-09-89   1:22p
COMMAND  COM     37557 12-19-88  12:00a
DOS          <DIR>     07-09-89   1:23p
LESSONS      <DIR>     07-12-89   4:01p
AUTOEXEC BAT       256 01-01-80  12:03a
        5 File(s)   19652608 bytes free

C:\>_
```

In practice, you should avoid using ASSIGN if at all possible because it disguises the true type of the disk drive. Microsoft suggests that you use an equivalent SUBST command instead, which we will discuss shortly, because ASSIGN may not be compatible with future versions of DOS.

Step 2: Execute the JOIN Command

The JOIN command lets you treat an entire disk as if it were a subdirectory on another disk. You can then work with files on multiple disks as if they were part of one subdirectory on one disk. Let's try an example. Make sure you are at the root directory of your hard disk. Create a new subdirectory by executing this command:

Type **md diska**
Press **Enter**

Put a formatted diskette in drive A. Then execute this command:

Type **join a: diska**
Press **Enter**

To see the result, execute these commands:

Type **join**
Press **Enter**
Type **dir diska**
Press **Enter**

Figure 26 shows the result. When the JOIN command is entered without any parameters, it displays the current drives and subdirectories that are joined. The DIR command presents the files on the floppy disk, in this case just COMMAND.COM, as if they were in the DISKA subdirectory on the hard disk.

You use the /D parameter to undo a previous JOIN command. Execute the following commands to disconnect the join and remove the DISKA subdirectory:

Type **join a: /d**
Press **Enter**

Figure 26 Using JOIN to Treat a Disk as a Subdirectory

```
C:\>md diska

C:\>join a: diska

C:\>join
A: => C:\DISKA

C:\>dir diska

 Volume in drive C is HARD DISK
 Volume Serial Number is 3324-07CC
 Directory of  C:\DISKA

COMMAND  COM     37557 12-19-88  12:00a
        1 File(s)   19650560 bytes free

C:\>_
```

Type **rd diska**
Press **Enter**

Step 3: Execute the SUBST Command

SUBST is the opposite of the JOIN command; it lets you treat a subdirectory as if it were a disk in a separate drive. For example, let's substitute the imaginary drive letter D for your LESSONS subdirectory. If you have a real disk drive D in your computer, choose a different letter. Make sure you are at the root directory of your hard disk and execute these commands:

Type **subst d: lessons**
Press **Enter**
Type **subst**
Press **Enter**
Type **dir d:**
Press **Enter**

SUBST entered without any parameters reports the substitutions that have been made. As Figure 27 shows, the subdirectory C:\LESSONS can now be referred to as simply D:.

You use the /D parameter to cancel a previous substitution. For example, execute the following command:

Type **subst d: /d**
Press **Enter**

Note that the following DOS commands do not work on drives used in the JOIN or SUBST commands: BACKUP, CHKDSK, DISKCOMP, DISKCOPY, FDISK, FORMAT, LABEL, RECOVER, RESTORE, and SYS.

Practice

The MS-DOS 4.01 *User's Reference* manual suggests that you use the SUBST command instead of ASSIGN. Repeat Step 1 of this lesson, except execute the following command instead of the ASSIGN command:

Type **subst a: c:**
Press **Enter**

Figure 27 Using SUBST to Treat a Subdirectory as a Disk

```
C:\>subst d: lessons

C:\>subst
D: => C:\LESSONS

C:\>dir d:

 Volume in drive D is HARD DISK
 Volume Serial Number is 3324-07CC
 Directory of  D:\

.            <DIR>      07-15-89  11:06a
..           <DIR>      07-15-89  11:06a
PART1    TXT         35 07-15-89  11:45a
PART2    TXT        113 07-15-89  11:08a
EXAMPLE  TXT        149 07-15-89  11:48a
COMMAND  BAK      37557 12-19-88  12:00a
PARTX    TXT         35 07-15-89   2:49p
        7 File(s)   19652608 bytes free

C:\>_
```

When you are finished examining the directory, use the SUBST command with the /D parameter to restore the original drive assignments.

Lesson 20: Learning More About the PRINT Command

PRINT is a sophisticated command that can print one or more files in the background while you continue your work with DOS. This limited multitasking ability is called **spooling.** Several PRINT parameters allow you to fine-tune this spooling capability on your computer.

Step 1: Examine the First Time PRINT Parameters

Several of the PRINT parameters may be used only the first time you execute the PRINT command after booting up. These parameters set the stage for the way PRINT will work for the rest of your DOS session. You have already used the PRINT command since you booted up, so don't try the following parameters. Just read and try to understand the explanations.

Parameter	*Action*
/D:*device*	Specifies the device name of the printer to be used by PRINT. The default is PRN or LPT1, the printer connected to the first parallel port on your computer. LPT2, LPT3, and COM1 through COM4 are device names of other parallel ports and serial ports to which a printer might be connected. If you don't specify the /D parameter, DOS will prompt you for the device name the first time you use the PRINT command.
/B:*size*	Sets the size in bytes of the memory buffer to be used for data to be printed. The minimum and default value is 512. The maximum value is 1634. Larger values enable PRINT to work faster, but use more memory.

/U:*ticks* — Specifies how long in clock ticks PRINT should wait before giving up for a printer that is still busy. The minimum and default value is 1. The maximum value is 255.

/M:*ticks* — Specifies the number of clock ticks it can take to print a character. The value can range from 1 to 255. The default value is 2.

/S:*time* — Specifies the time interval PRINT must wait before getting the attention of the CPU. The value can range from 1 to 255. The default value is 8.

/Q:*number* — Specifies the number of files that can be held in the **print queue,** the list of files to be printed in the background. The number can range from 4 to 32. The default number is 10.

Step 2: Print Several Files

The remaining parameters to the PRINT command can be used any time, not just the first time PRINT is executed for a given DOS session. Change to your LESSONS subdirectory on the hard disk. If you have a printer, turn it on, but take it off line. In other words, press the On Line button so that the On Line light turns off. This will simulate a busy printer. Execute the following commands:

Type **`print part1.txt`**
Press **Enter**
Type **`print part2.txt`**
Press **Enter**
Type **`print example.txt`**
Press **Enter**

Figure 28 shows the result. Each time you execute a PRINT command, the file is placed in the queue and the DOS prompt returns.

Figure 28 Placing Files in the Print Queue

```
C:\LESSONS>print part1.txt

  C:\LESSONS\PART1.TXT is currently being printed

C:\LESSONS>print part2.txt

  C:\LESSONS\PART1.TXT is currently being printed
  C:\LESSONS\PART2.TXT is in queue

C:\LESSONS>print example.txt
Errors on list device indicate that it
may be off-line. Please check it.

  C:\LESSONS\PART1.TXT is currently being printed
  C:\LESSONS\PART2.TXT is in queue
  C:\LESSONS\EXAMPLE.TXT is in queue

C:\LESSONS>_
```

Step 3: Use the /C Parameter

The /C parameter removes a file from the print queue. Execute this command:

Type **print part2.txt /c**
Press **Enter**

PART2.TXT will not be printed.

Step 4: Use the /T Parameter

To remove all the files from the print queue, use the /T parameter like this:

Type **print /t**
Press **Enter**

Step 5: Use the /P Parameter

Press your printer's On Line button. The final PRINT parameter /P adds a file to the print queue. This default option is assumed if you don't specify any parameters. For example, try this command:

Type **print example.txt /p**
Press **Enter**

Executing the above command is the same as executing this command:

Type **print example.txt**
Press **Enter**

In either case, the file EXAMPLE.TXT will be printed.

Summary

- *Using the DOS editing and function keys.* Delete, Insert, Escape, and F1 through F6 perform various editing functions on the DOS command line.
- *Setting the BREAK option.* The BREAK command changes the status of the BREAK option, OFF or ON, which controls when Ctrl-Break will cancel a program.
- *Working with subdirectories.* MD or MKDIR creates a new subdirectory, CD or CHDIR moves into a subdirectory, TREE displays the structure of a disk, and RD or RMDIR removes an empty subdirectory.
- *Using the PATH and APPEND commands.* PATH sets up a directory search path for BAT, COM, and EXE files. APPEND sets up a directory search path for all other files.
- *Changing the DOS prompt.* PROMPT followed by one or prompt codes, such as pg, changes the DOS prompt.
- *Backing up and restoring disks and files.* BACKUP backs up all or part of a hard disk onto floppy diskettes. RESTORE copies files from backup diskettes onto a hard disk.
- *Recovering files from damaged disks.* RECOVER attempts to salvage data from a damaged disk.

- *Using the prompt option when erasing files.* The ERASE (or DEL) command's /P parameter causes DOS to ask for confirmation before erasing each file.
- *Appending files and copying files to devices.* The COPY command can be used to append two or more files together. It can also be used to copy data directly to devices such as displays and printers.
- *Setting the VERIFY option.* The VERIFY command changes the status of the VERIFY option OFF or ON, which controls error checking whenever writing data to a disk.
- *Changing file attributes.* The ATTRIB command can change the status of a file's read-only and archive attributes.
- *Copying groups of files.* XCOPY is often faster and more flexible than COPY for duplicating files, subdirectories, and disks.
- *Updating sets of files.* REPLACE is used to update existing files or add new files from one disk to another.
- *Transferring the DOS system files.* If a disk has been formatted with the /B parameter, SYS can transfer the hidden DOS system files to that disk.
- *Comparing files and disks.* COMP checks two files to see if they are identical. DISKCOMP checks two diskettes to see if they are identical.
- *Changing volume labels.* LABEL can display or change the name of a disk.
- *Changing the current date and time.* DATE and TIME can display or change the current date and time kept by the computer.
- *Displaying a memory report.* MEM can present a more detailed and technical memory report than CHKDSK.
- *Reassigning, joining, and substituting drives.* ASSIGN can change the drive letter associated with a disk drive. JOIN can tell DOS to treat an entire disk as if it were a subdirectory on another disk. SUBST can tell DOS to treat a subdirectory as if it were a disk in a separate drive.
- *Printing multiple files.* PRINT can print one or more files in the background. The /P, /C, and /T parameters add or remove files from the print queue.

Key Terms

As an extra review of this chapter, try defining the following terms.

archive attribute
ASCII file
binary file
file attribute
hierarchical
incremental backup
path
print queue
read-only attribute
root directory
spooling
volume label

Multiple Choice

Choose the best selection to complete each statement.

1. Which keys would you press to repeat the previous DOS command?
   (a) F1 and then Enter
   (b) F2 and then Enter
   (c) F3 and then Enter
   (d) Escape and then Enter
2. Which key would you press to skip over a character from the previous DOS command?
   (a) Insert
   (b) Delete
   (c) Escape
   (d) F1
3. What keypresses are influenced by the BREAK command?
   (a) Alt-Break
   (b) Ctrl-Break
   (c) Alt-Num Lock
   (d) Ctrl-Num Lock
4. Which item cannot be contained in a subdirectory?
   (a) file
   (b) subdirectory
   (c) DOS external command
   (d) disk
5. Every disk has a single main directory known as the
   (a) root directory
   (b) prime directory
   (c) subdirectory
   (d) master directory
6. Which expression is a valid path?
   (a) c: hard disk lessons
   (b) a:\lessons/c:
   (c) c:\lessons\part1
   (d) c:/lessons/part1
7. Which DOS command is used to create a new subdirectory?
   (a) MD
   (b) CD
   (c) RD
   (d) TREE
8. Which DOS command displays the subdirectory structure of a disk?
   (a) MD
   (b) CD
   (c) RD
   (d) TREE
9. What must be done before you can remove a subdirectory?
   (a) execute DIR
   (b) execute TREE
   (c) delete all files in the subdirectory
   (d) delete all files in the root directory
10. Which command is used to establish a subdirectory search path for BAT, COM, and EXE files?
    (a) APPEND
    (b) PATH
    (c) TREE
    (d) SEARCH
11. Which prompt codes would you use with the PROMPT command to have the DOS prompt always display the current path?
    (a) Hello
    (b) pg
    (c) dg
    (d) vq
12. Which command would back up the entire contents of the hard disk to diskettes in drive A?
    (a) backup c: a: /s
    (b) backup c:\lessons*.* a: /s
    (c) backup a: c: /s
    (d) backup hard disk a:

13. Which command is used to salvage files from damaged diskettes?
    (a) RESTORE (b) RECOVER
    (c) COPY (d) SYS
14. Of the following commands, which is the safest to use?
    (a) del *.* (b) erase *.*
    (c) erase ????????.* (d) erase *.* /p
15. Which device name stands for the keyboard or display screen?
    (a) CON (b) PRN
    (c) LPT1 (d) COM1
16. Which command appends two files to form a third?
    (a) append file1 + file2 file3 (b) copy file1 + file2 file3
    (c) xcopy file1 + file2 file3 (d) diskcopy file1 + file2 file3
17. Which command makes it impossible to delete the file SAMPLE.TXT?
    (a) attrib +r sample.txt (b) attrib +a sample.txt
    (c) attrib −r sample.txt (d) attrib −a sample.txt
18. Which command will read as many files as it can into memory first, before copying them?
    (a) copy a:*.* c: (b) xcopy a:*.* c:
    (c) copy a:*.* c: /all (d) mem a:*.* c:
19. Which command will copy only those files from the disk in drive A that don't already exist on the disk in drive C?
    (a) copy a:*.* c: /a (b) xcopy a:*.* c: /a
    (c) append a:*.* c: /a (d) replace a:*.* c: /a
20. What command must have been used on a diskette before you can use the SYS command to copy the DOS system files to it?
    (a) TREE (b) APPEND
    (c) FORMAT /S or FORMAT /B (d) FORMAT /V

Fill-In

1. The simplest path is ______, which represents the root directory of the default drive.
2. You can copy files into a ______ just as if it were a separate disk.
3. The ______ command tells DOS the directories to be searched for files that have extensions other than BAT, COM, or EXE.
4. The ______ command lets you change the DOS prompt.
5. Unlike COPY, the ______ command can automatically use as many diskettes as needed to save the files from a hard disk.
6. The ______ command reinstates files that have been saved with the BACKUP command.
7. The ______ parameter of the ERASE (or DEL) command tells DOS to ask for confirmation before erasing each file.
8. You can use ______ names such as CON and PRN as if they were file names in commands such as COPY.

9. The _______ parameter of the COPY command tells DOS to verify that the copy has been made successfully with no errors.
10. Another term for text file is _______ file.
11. A _______ file is a file that contains programs or data that are not encoded as ASCII characters.
12. The _______ attribute indicates whether a file has been changed since it was last saved with the BACKUP command.
13. Unlike the COPY command, _______ can be instructed to copy files from all the subdirectories in the source disk or directory.
14. The _______ command is used to update previous versions of files.
15. The _______ command is used to compare the contents of two diskettes.
16. The _______ command lets you change the name of a disk.
17. Starting with version 4.0, DOS included _______, an external command that can present a memory report more detailed than CHKDSK.
18. The ASSIGN command lets you change the drive _______ associated with a disk drive.
19. The _______ command, which is the opposite of the JOIN command, lets you treat a subdirectory as if it were a disk in a separate drive.
20. The /T parameter of the PRINT command removes all files from the print _______.

Short Problems

1. Change to your LESSONS subdirectory on the hard disk if you are not already there. Use the ATTRIB command to turn on the read-only attribute for every file in the subdirectory. Hint: you can use the global file name character * to do this with a single command. Now try to erase every file in the LESSONS subdirectory. When you are finished, turn off the read-only attributes of all the files in the LESSONS subdirectory.
2. Put a formatted floppy disk in drive A. Back up the contents of the LESSONS subdirectory using the /L parameter to create a log file. Don't specify a file name after the /L. When the BACKUP command is finished, a file named BACKUP.LOG will exist in the root directory of your hard disk. Examine this file with the TYPE command. As you can see, BACKUP.LOG lists the date and time of the backup, as well as the backup disk number and full path and name of each backed-up file.
3. You can create many interesting and useful DOS prompts with the PROMPT command. For example, try the following command:

   Type **`prompt Date = $d Time = $t$_$p$g`**
   Press **Enter**

   Press **Enter** a few times to see the result. When you are finished, change the DOS prompt back to the way it was.
4. Insert a formatted floppy disk into drive A. If the LESSONS subdirectory isn't your current directory, change to it. Now, use the DIR command to see a directory listing of the LESSONS subdirectory. Notice that . and .. appear as the first two entries in the listing. These are special DOS designations for your current directory and the parent of your current directory. For example,

execute the following command to see a listing of the directory immediately above your current directory, which, in this case, happens to be the root directory of hard disk C:

Type **dir ..**
Press **Enter**

The . designation is equivalent to *.*, meaning your entire directory. Execute this command to see how it works:

Type **xcopy . a:**
Press **Enter**

This command will copy all of the files in your current directory, which happens to be LESSONS, to the disk in drive A.

5. Use the COPY command to copy all the files in your DOS subdirectory to a diskette in drive A. It doesn't matter if they all won't fit. Try to time, either with a watch or by counting, approximately how long this takes. Now, turn on the VERIFY option and then repeat the same COPY operation, timing the procedure in the same way. Does turning verification on cause the COPY command to take longer? Turn off the VERIFY option when you are finished.
6. Use the DATE command to find out what day of the week July 4, 2026 will fall on.
7. Create a new subdirectory named TEXT inside your LESSONS subdirectory. Copy all files with an extension of TXT from your LESSONS subdirectory to the LESSONS\TEXT subdirectory. Use the TREE command to display the structure of the LESSONS subdirectory. Then change to the LESSONS\TEXT subdirectory.
8. Make sure you are inside the LESSONS\TEXT subdirectory. You should have the files PART1.TXT, PART2.TXT, PARTX.TXT, and EXAMPLE.TXT inside the subdirectory. Create a new EXAMPLE.TXT file with the COPY command by appending PART2.TXT to PARTX.TXT. Use the TYPE command to examine the new EXAMPLE.TXT file.
9. Erase every file inside the LESSONS\TEXT subdirectory. Use the /P parameter to have DOS prompt you before erasing each file. Answer **y** for yes each time.
10. Use DIR to confirm that the LESSONS\TEXT subdirectory is empty. Move back to its parent subdirectory, LESSONS, by using the .. designation with the CD command. Remove the LESSONS\TEXT subdirectory, but leave the LESSONS subdirectory intact. Use DIR to confirm what you have done.

CHAPTER 7

ADVANCED DOS

In This Chapter

Getting Started
Lesson 1: Redirecting Output and Input
Lesson 2: Using DOS Filters and Piping
Lesson 3: Using Batch Files
Lesson 4: Using Batch Processing Commands
Lesson 5: Setting Up the Configuration File
Lesson 6: Partitioning and Formatting Hard Disks
Lesson 7: Learning About Other DOS Commands
Lesson 8: Using the DOS Shell

Preview

Chapters 5 and 6 taught you most of what the average computer user needs to know about DOS. This chapter proceeds to more advanced DOS topics. You may not need all of the commands and features presented in this chapter, but many of them can make your work easier, faster, and less tedious. The more you learn about DOS, the better you will understand and use your microcomputer hardware and application software.

After studying this chapter, you will know how to

- redirect output and input.
- use DOS filters and piping.
- use batch files.
- use batch processing commands.
- set up a configuration file.
- partition and format a hard disk.
- execute several other DOS commands.
- use the DOS Shell.

Getting Started

You've already learned how to start DOS and use its most common features and commands. This chapter assumes you have completed all of the lessons and exercises of Chapters 5 and 6. It also assumes that you have a computer with a hard disk and DOS 3.30, 4.00, or 4.01 installed on it in a subdirectory named DOS. The screens in this chapter were created with MS-DOS 4.01. To work the following lessons, boot up or reboot your computer if you have not already done so.

Lesson 1: Redirecting Output and Input

An interesting and useful aspect of DOS is its ability to redirect input or output information. Input usually comes from the keyboard or a file. Output usually goes to the display screen, printer, or a file. Some DOS commands that work with files can also receive input from or send output to peripheral devices, such as the keyboard, display, or printer. This can be done by using DOS device names such as CON and PRN in place of file names. CON stands for the console, which refers to the keyboard and display screen, and PRN refers to the printer.

Step 1: Redirect Output to the Printer

Redirection lets you change the normal source or destination of information processed by a DOS command. For example, the DIR command normally sends its output to the display screen. You can, however, instruct DOS to have DIR send its output to the printer. If you have a printer, turn it on, make sure it is on line and loaded with paper, and execute this command:

Type **dir >prn**
Press **Enter**

The directory should print instead of being displayed on your screen. The > (greater than sign) is the DOS symbol for redirecting output. It tells the DIR command to send its output to the device or file whose name follows, which, in this case, is the printer.

Redirecting the output to the printer works for most DOS commands. As another example, try this command:

Type **chkdsk >prn**
Press **Enter**

Step 2: Redirect Output to a File

You can also redirect the output of a DOS command to a text file instead of the display screen or printer. Simply type a valid file name after the redirection symbol. Change to your LESSONS subdirectory if you are not already in it and execute this command:

Type **dir >dirlist**
Press **Enter**

This time, the output of the DIR command goes to a file named DIRLIST. Since this file did not already exist in your LESSONS subdirectory, DOS created it. If a file of that name had existed, however, DOS would have overwritten its contents with the directory listing. Now, execute the following two commands to see a list of the files in your subdirectory and to display the contents of the DIRLIST file:

Type **dir**
Press **Enter**
Type **type dirlist**
Press **Enter**

Your screen should look like Figure 1. The directory listing in the file DIRLIST contains an entry for DIRLIST with a size of 0 bytes because DOS created the file before it actually performed the DIR.

Figure 1 Output of DIR Redirected to DIRLIST

```
PART1    TXT        35 07-15-89  11:45a
PART2    TXT       113 07-15-89  11:08a
EXAMPLE  TXT       149 07-15-89  11:48a
COMMAND  BAK     37557 12-19-88  12:00a
PARTX    TXT        35 07-15-89   2:49p
DIRLIST            471 07-18-89  10:36a
        8 File(s)  19650560 bytes free

C:\LESSONS>type dirlist

 Volume in drive C is HARD DISK
 Volume Serial Number is 3324-07CC
 Directory of  C:\LESSONS

.            <DIR>      07-12-89   4:01p
..           <DIR>      07-12-89   4:01p
PART1    TXT        35 07-15-89  11:45a
PART2    TXT       113 07-15-89  11:08a
EXAMPLE  TXT       149 07-15-89  11:48a
COMMAND  BAK     37557 12-19-88  12:00a
PARTX    TXT        35 07-15-89   2:49p
DIRLIST              0 07-18-89  10:35a
        8 File(s)  19650560 bytes free

C:\LESSONS>_
```

Step 3: Redirect and Append Output to a File

The > redirection symbol creates a new file or overwrites an existing file if it is followed by a file name. You can, however, tell DOS to append the output of a command to an existing file instead of overwriting its contents. Execute these commands:

Type **chkdsk >>dirlist**
Press **Enter**
Type **type dirlist**
Press **Enter**

Your screen should look like Figure 2. The >> redirection symbol adds the output of the CHKDSK command to the end of the DIRLIST file instead of overwriting it. If DIRLIST did not already exist, however, the >> symbol would tell DOS to create it.

Step 4: Redirect Input to a Command

DOS can also redirect the input to a command or program, but this is less common than redirecting output. Several DOS commands and many programs require the user to enter responses to prompts. In some cases, you can avoid having to enter these responses every time by putting them all in a text file and then redirecting that text file as input to the command or program.

For example, suppose that you want DOS to display the time, but you don't want to change it. If you don't specify a new time on the command line when you execute TIME, DOS will prompt you for the new time. You must press Enter to go on even if you don't want to change the time. You can, however, put your response in a text file beforehand and then redirect the input from that file to the TIME command. First, create a text file containing the carriage return generated by the Enter key. Execute these commands:

Type **copy con enter.txt**
Press **Enter**

Figure 2 Output of CHKDSK Redirected and Appended to DIRLIST

```
PART1    TXT         35 07-15-89  11:45a
PART2    TXT        113 07-15-89  11:08a
EXAMPLE  TXT        149 07-15-89  11:48a
COMMAND  BAK      37557 12-19-88  12:00a
PARTX    TXT         35 07-15-89   2:49p
DIRLIST               0 07-18-89  10:35a
        8 File(s)   19650560 bytes free

Volume HARD DISK   created 01-01-1980 12:28a
Volume Serial Number is 3324-07CC

  21204992 bytes total disk space
     73728 bytes in 3 hidden files
      6144 bytes in 2 directories
   1474560 bytes in 75 user files
  19650560 bytes available on disk

      2048 bytes in each allocation unit
     10354 total allocation units on disk
      9595 available allocation units on disk

    655360 total bytes memory
    521248 bytes free

C:\LESSONS>_
```

Figure 3 Input Redirected from ENTER.TXT

```
C:\LESSONS>copy con enter.txt

^Z
        1 File(s) copied

C:\LESSONS>time <enter.txt
Current time is 10:58:13.35a
Enter new time:

C:\LESSONS>_
```

Press **Enter**
Press **F6**
Press **Enter**

The file ENTER.TXT now contains the carriage return character. To use ENTER.TXT as input to TIME, execute this command:

Type **`time <enter.txt`**
Press **Enter**

The < (less than sign) is the DOS symbol for redirecting input. After you enter this command, your screen should look like Figure 3. The TIME command displays the current time, but instead of waiting for you to enter the new time, it takes its input from the file ENTER.TXT and immediately returns to the DOS prompt.

Because it eliminates the need for you to enter responses, redirecting input is most often used for commands and programs that are run automatically from batch files.

Practice

1. If you are using DOS 4.00 or newer and have a printer, execute the MEM command with the /PROGRAM parameter, but redirect its output to the printer.
2. If you have a printer, change to the root directory and execute the TREE command with the /F parameter, but redirect its output to the printer. Change back to the LESSONS subdirectory.
3. You can use the ENTER.TXT file you created in this lesson as input to other commands. For example, redirect it as input to the DATE command.

Lesson 2: Using DOS Filters and Piping

A DOS **filter** is a command that normally reads input from the keyboard, changes it in some way, and then presents it as output to the display screen. Three DOS commands act as filters: FIND, MORE, and SORT. These commands work only with text. If you redirect the input, a filter can also accept input from a text file or a program. Similarly, you can redirect the output from a filter to a printer, file, or program.

In addition to redirection, DOS has a feature called piping that can be used with filter commands. **Piping,** symbolized by the | (vertical bar), allows you to take the output of one command, which would normally go to the display screen, and feed it as input to another command.

Step 1: Searching Files for Lines of Text

The DOS FIND filter searches a file for lines that contain a specified word or phrase and presents them as output. For example, suppose you want to find all the lines that contain the word "bytes" in the file DIRLIST. Execute the following command:

Type **`find "bytes" dirlist`**
Press **Enter**

Figure 4 shows the result. Note that the FIND command will locate only those lines with exact matches of the word or phrase you specify. In other words, uppercase and lowercase letters are considered different.

The FIND command has three parameters that can be useful:

Parameter	*Action*
/V	Displays only those lines *not* containing the specified word or phrase.
/C	Displays only the number of lines that contain a match, not the actual lines themselves.
/N	Precedes each line it finds with its relative line number in the file.

Figure 4 The FIND Command

```
C:\LESSONS>find "bytes" dirlist

---------- DIRLIST
       8 File(s)   19650560 bytes free
  21204992 bytes total disk space
     73728 bytes in 3 hidden files
      6144 bytes in 2 directories
   1474560 bytes in 75 user files
  19650560 bytes available on disk
      2048 bytes in each allocation unit
    655360 total bytes memory
    521248 bytes free

C:\LESSONS>_
```

Step 2: Displaying Output One Screen at a Time

The MORE command accepts input and then presents it as output, but only one screen at a time. This filter is almost always used with redirected or piped input from another command or file.

For example, some directories contain so many files that they scroll by too quickly to read when you use the DIR command. If your hard disk has a DOS subdirectory, execute this command:

Type **dir c:\dos | more**
Press **Enter**

Your screen should look like Figure 5. The output of the DIR command has been piped into the MORE filter instead of being displayed directly on the screen. MORE presents the same output, but pauses after a screen is full and displays the message "-- More --" at the bottom of the screen. Press a key, such as **Enter** or **Space Bar,** when you are ready to continue. MORE will present the rest of the directory, one screen at a time. Press a key to continue until you see the DOS prompt again.

The MORE filter can receive its input from a text file as well as from a command. Try this command to display DIRLIST and pause after each screen:

Type **more <dirlist**
Press **Enter**

The text file DIRLIST is redirected as the input to the MORE filter. Press a key to continue.

Step 3: Sorting Text

SORT is another DOS filter. This command receives input text, sorts the lines alphabetically or numerically, then displays the sorted text as output. SORT is often used with redirection, piping, and other DOS commands. The SORT filter

Figure 5 Output Piped into the MORE Filter

```
 Volume in drive C is HARD DISK
 Volume Serial Number is 3324-07CC
 Directory of  C:\DOS

.            <DIR>     07-09-89   1:23p
..           <DIR>     07-09-89   1:23p
DOSSHELL BAT       196 07-09-89   1:22p
COMMAND  COM     37557 12-19-88  12:00a
COUNTRY  SYS     12806 10-06-88  12:00a
DISKCOPY COM     10396 10-06-88  12:00a
DISPLAY  SYS     15692 10-06-88  12:00a
FDISK    EXE     60935 12-19-88  12:00a
FORMAT   COM     22859 10-06-88  12:00a
KEYB     COM     14727 10-06-88  12:00a
KEYBOARD SYS     23328 10-06-88  12:00a
REPLACE  EXE     19415 10-06-88  12:00a
SYS      COM     11456 10-06-88  12:00a
ASSIGN   COM      5753 10-06-88  12:00a
ATTRIB   EXE     18263 10-06-88  12:00a
CHKDSK   COM     17787 10-06-88  12:00a
COMP     COM      9459 10-06-88  12:00a
DEBUG    COM     21574 10-06-88  12:00a
DISKCOMP COM      9857 10-06-88  12:00a
-- More --_
```

is often used to present an alphabetical directory listing. If you have a DOS subdirectory on your hard disk, execute this command:

Type **dir c:\dos | sort | more**
Press **Enter**

Figure 6 shows the result. The output of the DIR command is piped into the SORT filter, which rearranges the lines alphabetically. The output of the SORT filter is then piped into the MORE filter, which presents the sorted listing one screen at a time.

SORT is also used to rearrange text files. Let's create a sorted copy of the file DIRLIST in another file named DIRSORT. Execute these commands:

Type **sort <dirlist >dirsort**
Press **Enter**
Type **type dirsort**
Press **Enter**

Figure 7 shows the result. The lines from the file DIRLIST were redirected as input to the SORT filter. The sorted listing was redirected as output to the newly created file DIRSORT.

The SORT command has two useful parameters:

Parameter	*Action*
/R	Sorts the input in descending order (from Z to A, then from 9 to 0).
/+*n*	Sorts the input beginning with the character in column *n*, where *n* is some number. If you do not use this parameter SORT assumes column 1.

Practice

1. Execute each of the following commands and explain what it does:

   Type **find /v "bytes" dirlist**
   Press **Enter**

Figure 6 Output Piped into SORT and MORE

```
        68 File(s)   19644416 bytes free
 Directory of  C:\DOS
 Volume in drive C is HARD DISK
 Volume Serial Number is 3324-07CC
.            <DIR>      07-09-89    1:23p
..           <DIR>      07-09-89    1:23p
4201     CPI       6404 10-06-88   12:00a
4208     CPI        720 10-06-88   12:00a
5202     CPI        370 10-06-88   12:00a
ANSI     SYS       9105 10-06-88   12:00a
APPEND   EXE      11154 10-06-88   12:00a
ASSIGN   COM       5753 10-06-88   12:00a
ATTRIB   EXE      18263 10-06-88   12:00a
BACKUP   COM      36880 10-06-88   12:00a
CHKDSK   COM      17787 10-06-88   12:00a
COMMAND  COM      37557 12-19-88   12:00a
COMP     COM       9459 10-06-88   12:00a
COUNTRY  SYS      12806 10-06-88   12:00a
DEBUG    COM      21574 10-06-88   12:00a
DISKCOMP COM       9857 10-06-88   12:00a
DISKCOPY COM      10396 10-06-88   12:00a
DISPLAY  SYS      15692 10-06-88   12:00a
-- More --_
```

Figure 7 Redirected Input and Output for SORT

```
      2048 bytes in each allocation unit
      6144 bytes in 2 directories
      9595 available allocation units on disk
     10354 total allocation units on disk
     73728 bytes in 3 hidden files
    521248 bytes free
    655360 total bytes memory
   1474560 bytes in 75 user files
  19650560 bytes available on disk
  21204992 bytes total disk space
 Directory of  C:\LESSONS
 Volume in drive C is HARD DISK
 Volume Serial Number is 3324-07CC
.            <DIR>      07-12-89   4:01p
..           <DIR>      07-12-89   4:01p
COMMAND  BAK     37557 12-19-88  12:00a
DIRLIST              0 07-18-89  10:35a
EXAMPLE  TXT       149 07-15-89  11:48a
PART1    TXT        35 07-15-89  11:45a
PART2    TXT       113 07-15-89  11:08a
PARTX    TXT        35 07-15-89   2:49p
Volume HARD DISK   created 01-01-1980 12:28a
Volume Serial Number is 3324-07CC

C:\LESSONS>_
```

Type **find /c "bytes" dirlist**
Press **Enter**
Type **find /n "bytes" dirlist**
Press **Enter**
Type **find /v/c "bytes" dirlist**
Press **Enter**
Type **find /v/n "bytes" dirlist**
Press **Enter**

2. Change to the root directory. Try the following command and explain what it does:

   Type **tree /f | find ".EXE"**
   Press **Enter**

   How is it different from DIR *.EXE? Change back to the LESSONS subdirectory.

3. Execute each of the following commands and explain what it does:

   Type **sort /r < dirlist**
   Press **Enter**
   Type **dir c:\dos | sort /+14 | more**
   Press **Enter**

   Hint for the second command: the file size appears in the directory listing after column 14.

Lesson 3: Using Batch Files

A **batch file** is a text file that contains a list of commands or programs to be run. Batch files are usually created with a text editor or word processing program, but you can easily create short ones using the COPY command and the CON device name. Every batch file must have an extension of BAT. A batch file is invoked by typing its filename, without the extension, and pressing the Enter key. When this is done, DOS executes each command or program listed in the batch file, one at a time. DOS includes features that enable experienced users to construct complex and very helpful batch files. Even if you never make your own batch files, you will undoubtedly use some made by others or included with application packages. As an example, let's create and use a simple batch file.

Step 1: Create the Batch File

Batch files are usually created with a text editor or word processor. Short ones, however, can be easily created with the COPY command. Make sure LESSONS is your current subdirectory. Execute these commands to create a simple batch file named SHOW.BAT:

Type **copy con show.bat**
Press **Enter**
Type **cls**
Press **Enter**
Type **dir *.txt**
Press **Enter**
Type **type example.txt**
Press **Enter**
Press **F6**
Press **Enter**

Note that the CLS, DIR, and TYPE commands were not executed when you pressed Enter because they are text in the file SHOW.BAT. They were not passed to the DOS command processor.

Step 2: Execute the Batch File

Running a batch file is the same as executing a command or running an application program. You type its filename (without the extension) and press the Enter key. To run your newly created batch file, execute this command:

Type **show**
Press **Enter**

Figure 8 shows the result. The commands inside the file SHOW.BAT were executed as if you had entered them directly from the keyboard.

Most commands and programs that you can run directly from the DOS prompt can be put inside a batch file. Batch files allow you to automate frequently executed series of commands. They also allow experts to set up complex sequences of commands to be run by novices. For example, many new application programs must be installed on your system before you can use them. In some cases, this installation process can be quite involved. Most software developers, therefore, include one or more batch files that make the installation process easier for users.

Step 3: Examine the AUTOEXEC.BAT File

The most commonly used batch file is a special one named AUTOEXEC.BAT—the auto-execute batch file. Each time you boot up your computer, DOS searches the root directory of the default drive for this AUTOEXEC.BAT file. If no AUTOEXEC.BAT is file present, DOS simply asks you to supply the current date and time, and then displays its prompt. If, on the other hand, AUTOEXEC.BAT is found, that batch file is automatically executed. DOS will not prompt you for the

Figure 8 The SHOW Batch File

```
C:\LESSONS>dir *.txt

 Volume in drive C is HARD DISK
 Volume Serial Number is 3324-07CC
 Directory of  C:\LESSONS

PART1    TXT        35 07-15-89  11:45a
PART2    TXT       113 07-15-89  11:08a
EXAMPLE  TXT       149 07-15-89  11:48a
PARTX    TXT        35 07-15-89   2:49p
ENTER    TXT         2 07-18-89  10:57a
        5 File(s)   19644416 bytes free

C:\LESSONS>type example.txt
This is the new sample text file.
A text file contains only letters, numbers,
punctuation marks, and other symbols that
appear on the keyboard.

C:\LESSONS>
C:\LESSONS>_
```

date and time if it finds AUTOEXEC.BAT, unless the DATE and TIME commands appear in AUTOEXEC.BAT.

Since the AUTOEXEC.BAT file is automatically invoked every time you boot up your computer, it is ideal for listing commands and programs you always run when you first turn on your machine. PATH, APPEND, and PROMPT, for example, are often put into the AUTOEXEC.BAT file to be executed each time the computer is booted. Most DOS users eventually set up their own AUTOEXEC.BAT files or have someone else help them do so. You can examine the contents of the AUTOEXEC.BAT file on your computer by executing this command:

Type **type c:\autoexec.bat**
Press **Enter**

Figure 9 shows a typical AUTOEXEC.BAT file; yours might be different. Some of the commands, such as VERIFY, PATH, APPEND, PROMPT, VER, and PRINT, should be familiar to you. You will learn about the other commands shown in Figure 9 in this chapter.

Practice

1. Create a batch file named NOW.BAT that displays the current date and time and immediately returns to the DOS prompt without prompting you to enter a new date and time. Hint: redirect input from the ENTER.TXT file you created in Lesson 1. Execute NOW.BAT a couple of times to see that it works.
2. Create a batch file named WHAT.BAT that displays the DOS version and the volume label of the default disk. Execute WHAT.BAT a couple of times to see that it works.
3. Although AUTOEXEC.BAT is executed automatically every time you boot up the computer, you can also execute it manually like any other batch file. Change to the root directory and execute AUTOEXEC.BAT. Then change back to the LESSONS subdirectory.

Figure 9 A Typical AUTOEXEC.BAT File

```
C:\LESSONS>type c:\autoexec.bat
@ECHO OFF
SET COMSPEC=C:\DOS\COMMAND.COM
VERIFY OFF
PATH C:\DOS
APPEND /E
APPEND C:\DOS
PROMPT $P$G
C:\DOS\GRAPHICS
VER
PRINT /D:LPT1

C:\LESSONS>_
```

Lesson 4: Using Batch Processing Commands

Any command or program you can invoke from the keyboard can be executed from inside a batch file. In addition, DOS has a special set of internal commands known as **batch processing commands** that can add power and flexibility to batch files. Batch processing commands are normally executed only from within batch files. Let's examine batch files in more detail and demonstrate the batch processing commands designed especially for them.

Step 1: Use Replaceable Parameters

Most computer users find that they occasionally repeat the same, or nearly the same, command sequence over and over. In some cases, you can reduce repetitive typing by creating a batch file with a very short name that contains the command sequence. For example, make sure you are in your LESSONS subdirectory, and execute these commands:

Type **copy con d.bat**
Press **Enter**
Type **dir | sort | more**
Press **Enter**
Press **F6**
Press **Enter**

You have created a batch file named D.BAT that contains the DIR | SORT | MORE sequence of commands. To execute this batch file:

Type **d**
Press **Enter**

This batch file can save you a lot of typing if you often execute the commands it contains, but what if you want to use it on some other directory? You can make this batch file much more flexible by using a **replaceable parameter.** This is a special code you insert into your batch file that lets you pass information to that batch file while it is running. To demonstrate, let's redo the D.BAT file. Execute these commands:

Type **copy con d.bat**
Press **Enter**
Type **dir %1 | sort | more**
Press **Enter**
Press **F6**
Press **Enter**

The %1 you have typed into the batch file is a replaceable parameter. When you execute the batch file, the %1 will be replaced by whatever you type on the command line after the D. For example, execute this command:

Type **d c:\dos**
Press **Enter**

The computer will display a sorted listing of the DOS subdirectory on your hard disk, one screen at a time. The C:\DOS you typed after the D replaced the %1 in the batch file. Now you can use your D.BAT file to list any directory on any disk, simply by typing a different path after the D. You can even type nothing after the D to get a listing of your current directory. DOS allows you to use up to nine such replaceable parameters, from %1 to %9, in any single batch file command.

Step 2: Use the CALL Batch Command

A batch file can contain any command you can type at the DOS prompt, even the name of another batch file. For example, execute the following commands to create a new batch file named DO_D.BAT:

Type **copy con do_d.bat**
Press **Enter**
Type **type d.bat**
Press **Enter**
Type **d**
Press **Enter**
Type **type d.bat**
Press **Enter**
Press **F6**
Press **Enter**

Now, execute your new batch file:

Type **do_d**
Press **Enter**

Your screen should look like Figure 10. If you look closely, you will see that DO_D.BAT did not do what you might have expected. It did the first TYPE D.BAT and then executed D.BAT all right, but it did not execute the second TYPE D.BAT. This is because when D.BAT ended, so did DO_D.BAT. It appears that invoking one batch file from within another only works when the inside one is at the end. This is sometimes called **chaining** batch files.

The CALL batch file command, however, allows you to invoke one batch file from within another batch file without ending the first batch file. This is some-

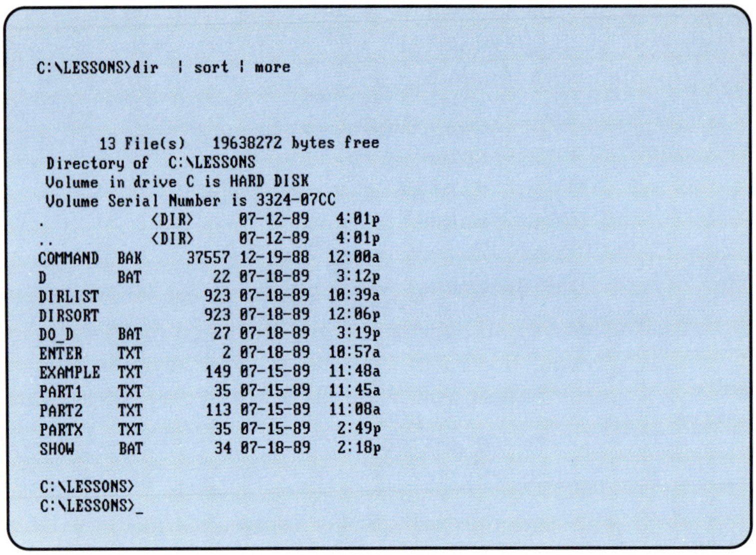

Figure 10 Chained Batch Files

times known as **nesting** batch files. Let's redo DO_D.BAT. Execute the following commands:

Type **copy con do_d.bat**
Press **Enter**
Type **type d.bat**
Press **Enter**
Type **call d**
Press **Enter**
Type **type d.bat**
Press **Enter**
Press **F6**
Press **Enter**

Now, execute your new DO_D.BAT file:

Type **do_d**
Press **Enter**

This time, DO_D.BAT will execute the second TYPE D.BAT as well, as shown in Figure 11.

Step 3: Use the ECHO Batch Command

Normally, the commands in a batch file are displayed, or echoed, to the screen just as if you had entered them from the command line. The ECHO command lets you turn this echoing off and back on again. It can also be used to display a message on the screen from within a batch file. To demonstrate the ECHO command, execute the following commands to create a new batch file named E.BAT:

Type **copy con e.bat**
Press **Enter**
Type **@echo off**
Press **Enter**
Type **echo Your current directory:**

Figure 11 CALL Used to Nest Batch Files

```
      13 File(s)   19638272 bytes free
 Directory of  C:\LESSONS
 Volume in drive C is HARD DISK
 Volume Serial Number is 3324-07CC
.            <DIR>      07-12-89   4:01p
..           <DIR>      07-12-89   4:01p
COMMAND  BAK      37557 12-19-88  12:00a
D        BAT         22 07-18-89   3:12p
DIRLIST             923 07-18-89  10:39a
DIRSORT             923 07-18-89  12:06p
DO_D     BAT         32 07-18-89   3:22p
ENTER    TXT          2 07-18-89  10:57a
EXAMPLE  TXT        149 07-15-89  11:48a
PART1    TXT         35 07-15-89  11:45a
PART2    TXT        113 07-15-89  11:08a
PARTX    TXT         35 07-15-89   2:49p
SHOW     BAT         34 07-18-89   2:18p

C:\LESSONS>
C:\LESSONS>type d.bat
dir %1 | sort | more

C:\LESSONS>
C:\LESSONS>_
```

Press **Enter**
Type **dir**
Press **Enter**
Press **F6**
Press **Enter**

Now, try the batch file you have just created:

Type **e**
Press **Enter**

Figure 12 shows the result. The @ (at-sign) preceding the first ECHO command tells DOS not to display that batch file line on the screen. The second ECHO

Figure 12 The ECHO Batch Command

```
        1 File(s) copied

C:\LESSONS>e
Your current directory:

 Volume in drive C is HARD DISK
 Volume Serial Number is 3324-07CC
 Directory of  C:\LESSONS

.            <DIR>      07-12-89   4:01p
..           <DIR>      07-12-89   4:01p
PART1    TXT         35 07-15-89  11:45a
PART2    TXT        113 07-15-89  11:08a
EXAMPLE  TXT        149 07-15-89  11:48a
COMMAND  BAK      37557 12-19-88  12:00a
PARTX    TXT         35 07-15-89   2:49p
DIRLIST             923 07-18-89  10:39a
ENTER    TXT          2 07-18-89  10:57a
DIRSORT             923 07-18-89  12:06p
SHOW     BAT         34 07-18-89   2:18p
D        BAT         22 07-18-89   3:12p
DO_D     BAT         32 07-18-89   3:22p
E        BAT         46 07-18-89   3:28p
       14 File(s)   19638272 bytes free
C:\LESSONS>_
```

does not need to be preceded by a @ because echoing has already been turned off by the previous command. Note that with echoing turned off, only the output of the DIR command is presented on the screen, not the DIR command itself.

Step 4: Repeat a Command On a Set of Files

DOS has a batch command that lets you repeat an action on a set of files. The FOR command is similar to the counted loop commands found in high-level programming languages, such as BASIC and Pascal. Suppose you want to display the contents of every batch file in your current directory. Let's create a batch file that can do this. Execute the following commands:

Type **`copy con type_all.bat`**
Press **Enter**
Type **`for %%f in (*.bat) do type %%f`**
Press **Enter**
Press **F6**
Press **Enter**

Now, try this batch file:

Type **`type_all`**
Press **Enter**

Figure 13 shows the result. DOS has repeated the TYPE command on every batch file in your current directory. The %%f symbol in the TYPE_ALL.BAT file is like a variable that holds a different file name each time the FOR command repeats. It repeats for each file that matches the *.BAT file specification and uses the TYPE command to display the contents of that file on the screen.

Step 5: Use the IF and GOTO Batch Commands

The IF and GOTO commands allow you to alter the order in which batch file commands are executed, based on the result of a condition. This is sometimes called **branching.** Like the FOR command, IF and GOTO are similar to statements

Figure 13 The FOR Batch Command

```
C:\LESSONS>type SHOW.BAT
cls
dir *.txt
type example.txt

C:\LESSONS>type D.BAT
dir %1 | sort | more

C:\LESSONS>type DO_D.BAT
type d.bat
call d
type d.bat

C:\LESSONS>type E.BAT
@echo off
echo Your current directory:
dir

C:\LESSONS>type TYPE_ALL.BAT
for %%f in (*.bat) do type %%f


C:\LESSONS>
C:\LESSONS>_
```

found in high-level programming languages, such as BASIC and Pascal. Complex and extremely useful batch files can be set up with these commands, but let's keep our example simple. Suppose you wanted to create a batch file that just tells you if any TXT files are in a directory. Execute the following commands:

Type **copy con any_txt.bat**
Press **Enter**
Type **@echo off**
Press **Enter**
Type **if not exist %1*.txt goto notfound**
Press **Enter**
Type **echo At least one .TXT file is in %1.**
Press **Enter**
Type **goto end**
Press **Enter**
Type **:notfound**
Press **Enter**
Type **echo No .TXT files are in %1.**
Press **Enter**
Type **:end**
Press **Enter**
Press **F6**
Press **Enter**

Let's discuss what this batch file does before you try it. First, it turns off echoing. Notice that it has one replaceable parameter, %1, that is used in two places. This parameter will be the path of the directory to be checked; it must be typed by the user when ANY_TXT.BAT is executed. The IF command tells DOS to branch to the "notfound" label if no .TXT files exist in the specified directory. In this context, a **label** is simply a place for a GOTO command to branch to; it must be present later in the batch file on its own line preceded by a : (colon). If at least one .TXT file is present in the specified directory, the first ECHO message will be displayed, the batch file will branch to the "end" label, and then it will terminate. If no .TXT files were found, only the second ECHO message will be displayed.

Now, execute the following commands to try your ANY_TXT.BAT file:

Type **any_txt \lessons**
Press **Enter**
Type **any_txt \dos**
Press **Enter**
Type **any_txt **
Press **Enter**

Figure 14 shows the result.

Step 6: Use the PAUSE Batch Command

In some batch files, it may be necessary for the user to change disks or perform some other action. The PAUSE command lets you suspend the execution of a batch file until the user is ready and presses a key to continue. Execute the following commands to create a simple example:

Type **copy con dir_a.bat**
Press **Enter**

Figure 14 The IF and GOTO Batch Commands

```
C:\LESSONS>copy con any_txt.bat
@echo off
if not exist %1\*.txt goto notfound
echo At least one .TXT file is in %1.
goto end
:notfound
echo No .TXT files are in %1.
:end
^Z
        1 File(s) copied

C:\LESSONS>any_txt \lessons
At least one .TXT file is in \lessons.
C:\LESSONS>any_txt \dos
At least one .TXT file is in \dos.
C:\LESSONS>any_txt \
No .TXT files are in \.
C:\LESSONS>_
```

Type **@echo off**
Press **Enter**
Type **echo Please put a disk into drive A.**
Press **Enter**
Type **pause**
Press **Enter**
Type **dir a:**
Press **Enter**
Press **F6**
Press **Enter**

To try your new batch file, execute this command and follow the directions:

Type **dir_a**
Press **Enter**

Figure 15 shows the result, but your screen may be different, depending on the diskette you inserted into drive A.

Step 7: Use the REM Command to Add Comments

In some ways, a batch file is like a program created with a high-level language, such as BASIC or Pascal. Most programming languages provide a way for you to document your programs by adding comments. These statements don't tell the computer to do anything; they just let you describe how your program works. Adding comments can help you identify and remember what you did when you created your program. They are also invaluable to anyone who may be trying to understand your work. REM is the DOS batch file comment command. To see how it works, execute the following commands:

Type **copy con r.bat**
Press **Enter**
Type **rem This batch file demonstrates the REM command.**
Press **Enter**

Figure 15 The PAUSE Batch Command

```
C:\LESSONS>copy con dir_a.bat
@echo off
echo Please put a disk into drive A.
pause
dir a:
^Z
        1 File(s) copied

C:\LESSONS>dir_a
Please put a disk into drive A.
Press any key to continue . . .


 Volume in drive A has no label
 Volume Serial Number is 283D-13CC
 Directory of  A:\

COMMAND  COM     37557 12-19-88  12:00a
        1 File(s)     252928 bytes free
C:\LESSONS>_
```

Type **rem Remarks (comments) are displayed if ECHO is ON.**
Press **Enter**
Type **@echo off**
Press **Enter**
Type **rem If ECHO is turned OFF, remarks won't be displayed.**
Press **Enter**
Press **F6**
Press **Enter**

Now, execute your new batch file:

Type **r**
Press **Enter**

Your screen should look like Figure 16. Note that even if remarks aren't displayed, they are still in the batch file and can be viewed if you TYPE it or examine it with a text editor or word processor. REM commands are also sometimes used to **comment out,** or temporarily shut off, batch file commands that you may want to activate again later.

Step 8: Use the SHIFT Batch Command

You have learned that you can pass information to a batch file by using replaceable parameters. Usually, batch files are limited to handling a maximum of ten replaceable parameters, symbolized by %0 through %9. The SHIFT command, however, lets you have more than ten replaceable parameters in the unlikely event you would ever need that many. Every time the SHIFT command is executed in a batch file, all parameters on the command line are shifted one position to the left. In other words, the %1 parameter will replace the %0 parameter, the %2 parameter will replace the %3 parameter, and so on. Once SHIFT is executed, you cannot go backward and retrieve the former %0 parameter. SHIFT is a some-

Figure 16 The REM Batch Command

```
C:\LESSONS>copy con r.bat
rem This batch file demonstrates the REM command.
rem Remarks (comments) are displayed if ECHO is ON.
@echo off
rem If ECHO is turned OFF, remarks won't be displayed.
^Z
        1 File(s) copied

C:\LESSONS>r

C:\LESSONS>rem This batch file demonstrates the REM command.

C:\LESSONS>rem Remarks (comments) are displayed if ECHO is ON.
C:\LESSONS>_
```

what exotic command that is rarely needed. Nevertheless, here is an example of its use. Execute the following commands:

Type **copy con supert.bat**
Press **Enter**
Type **@echo off**
Press **Enter**
Type **:again**
Press **Enter**
Type **for %%f in (%1 %2 %3 %4 %5 %6 %7 %8 %9) do type %%f**
Press **Enter**
Type **for %%x in (1 2 3 4 5 6 7 8 9) do shift**
Press **Enter**
Type **if not "%1"=="" goto again**
Press **Enter**
Press **F6**
Press **Enter**

This rather complex batch file, named SUPERT.BAT, is essentially a super TYPE command that can accept any number of individual file names on the command line, as long as the total length of the command line does not exceed 127 characters. The first FOR command reads in each of the first nine replaceable parameters and tries to TYPE it out as a file name. The second FOR command performs nine SHIFT commands in a row to load in the next nine file names. The IF statement branches to the "again" label if the first file name is not blank, in which case the entire process is repeated again. SUPERT.BAT ends when no more file names are on the command line.

Suppose you have 20 files named A, B, C, and so on to T. You can use SUPERT to type them all out with one command. Execute the following command even though you don't have files named A to T. (The TYPE command will just say "File not found" for each file.)

Type **supert a b c d e f g h i j k l m n o p q r s t**
Press **Enter**

Your screen should look like Figure 17. If you did have 20 files named A through T, SUPERT.BAT would have displayed them all on the screen, one after the other. SUPERT.BAT can handle any number of replaceable parameters. If it weren't for the SHIFT command, it could handle no more than ten.

Practice

1. Use your D.BAT file to generate a directory listing of the root directory. Use it again on your current subdirectory.
2. Try the TYPE_ALL.BAT file again, now that you have more batch files in your LESSONS subdirectory.
3. Use DIR to get a directory of your LESSONS subdirectory. Then use SUPERT.BAT in one command to type out any three batch files and any three text files in the LESSONS subdirectory. Remember: a command line can take up more than one line (just keep typing) as long as it contains no more than 127 characters. Notice how SUPERT.BAT runs all the files together on the screen.

Lesson 5: Setting Up the Configuration File

The configuration file CONFIG.SYS is a special text file that DOS looks for in the root directory of the default disk when you boot up. It contains special commands that set up your system in a certain way and is usually created when you install DOS or a new application package. You may, however, have to create or modify the CONFIG.SYS file yourself if you ever add new hardware or software to your system.

Step 1: Examine Your CONFIG.SYS File

Change back to the root directory of your hard disk and examine the contents of your CONFIG.SYS file by executing these commands:

Type **cd **
Press **Enter**

Figure 17 The SHIFT Batch Command

```
C:\LESSONS>supert a b c d e f g h i j k l m n o p q r s t
File not found - A
File not found - B
File not found - C
File not found - D
File not found - E
File not found - F
File not found - G
File not found - H
File not found - I
File not found - J
File not found - K
File not found - L
File not found - M
File not found - N
File not found - O
File not found - P
File not found - Q
File not found - R
File not found - S
File not found - T
C:\LESSONS>_
```

Type **type config.sys**
Press **Enter**

Figure 18 shows a typical CONFIG.SYS file, but yours is probably different. If DOS replies with the message "File not found," then you do not have a CONFIG.SYS file. This means that when DOS boots up on your computer, it uses the default configuration settings.

Step 2: Explore the Configuration Commands

You are not going to change your CONFIG.SYS file in this lesson. If you have one already set up on your computer, it contains the commands you need for your particular arrangement of hardware and software. Usually, CONFIG.SYS is created or modified with a text editor or word processor. It can also be created by copying the output of the console to the file CONFIG.SYS.

Instead of actually changing your CONFIG.SYS file, let's just briefly discuss the special commands that can be put there. Note that the following commands (except for BREAK) cannot be entered from the DOS prompt; they work only in the CONFIG.SYS file when the computer boots up. Some configuration commands are often used, while others are more technical and are rarely used on most systems. The DOS configuration commands are as follows.

Command	*Action*
BREAK = *x*	This command controls whether or not DOS will stop a command or program from completing its task if Ctrl-Break (or Ctrl-C) is pressed. BREAK = OFF tells DOS to terminate a program only during screen, keyboard, and printer reads and writes if Ctrl-Break is pressed. BREAK = ON tells DOS to terminate a program also during disk reads and writes.
BUFFERS = *n*	A **disk buffer** is an area of memory DOS uses to temporarily hold data being read from or written to a disk. Increasing the number of buffers may increase performance, but it uses more memory. There is no definite rule for what *n* should be; use a value suggested by the documentation of the software package you use most often.
COUNTRY = *xxx*	DOS can be set up to use international conventions for date, time, currency, and character set. This command can be omitted if you want to use the settings for the United States. Otherwise, enter the country code *xxx*, which you can look up in the DOS reference manual.
DEVICE = *file*	A **device driver** is a file that contains the programming code needed to attach and use a special device such as a nonstandard disk drive, memory board, mouse, monitor, or printer. This file is usually provided by the manufacturer of the device. The *file* name, which has an extension of SYS, must be specified along with any parameters indicated by the manufacturer.

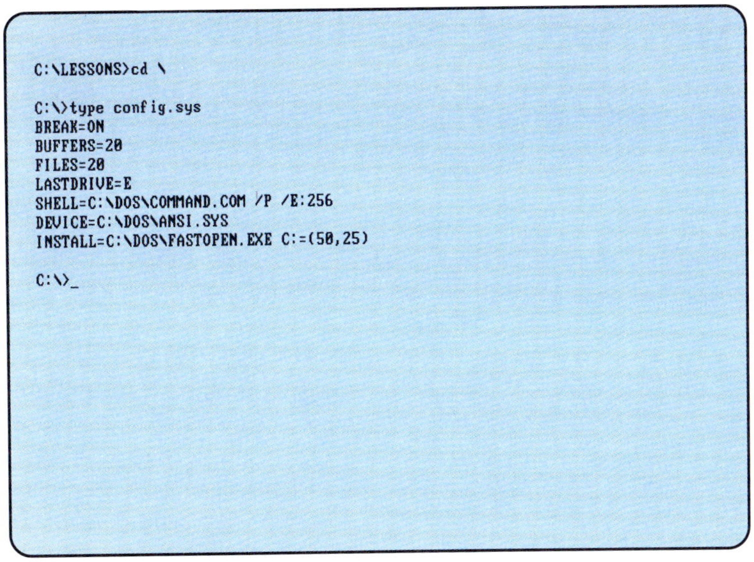

```
C:\LESSONS>cd \

C:\>type config.sys
BREAK=ON
BUFFERS=20
FILES=20
LASTDRIVE=E
SHELL=C:\DOS\COMMAND.COM /P /E:256
DEVICE=C:\DOS\ANSI.SYS
INSTALL=C:\DOS\FASTOPEN.EXE C:=(50,25)

C:\>_
```

***Figure 18** A Typical CONFIG.SYS File*

Command	*Action*
DRIVEPARM = */x*	This command allows you to define parameters for disk or tape drives when you start DOS, overriding the default device settings. You can specify the drive number, type of drive, number of read/write heads, number of sectors, and number of tracks. For example, suppose you want to set up an internal tape drive as drive D configured to write 20 tracks of 40 sectors per track. Here is the command you would use: DRIVEPARM = /D:3 /F:6 /H:1 /S:40 /T:20 The /D:3 specifies the tape drive as drive D. The /F:6 specifies that the device is a tape drive. The /H:1 specifies one read/write head. The /S:40 and /T:20 specify 40 sectors and 20 tracks.
FCBS = *x,y*	A **file control block** (**FCB**) is a data structure used by early versions of DOS to manage open files. If you have an old application program that requires file control blocks, you can use the FCBS command in CONFIG.SYS to specify the number of files that can be open at one time (*x*) and the number of opened files that DOS cannot close automatically (*y*).
FILES = *n*	By default, DOS can have only eight files open at a time. But many sophisticated software packages, especially data base managers, must have more than eight files open at a time. The FILES command lets you increase the maximum number of open files by specifying a larger *n*, such as 20.
INSTALL = *file*	This command can be used to execute certain DOS commands that should be executed only once. It is preferable to put these commands in CONFIG.SYS

Command	*Action*
	rather than in AUTOEXEC.BAT because AUTOEXEC.BAT can be executed more than once after the computer is booted up. The *file* name after INSTALL must be one of the following: FASTOPEN.EXE, KEY.EXE, NLSFUNC.EXE, or SHARE.EXE. You will learn what these DOS commands do later in this chapter.
LASTDRIVE = *x*	By default, DOS supports only five drives, A through E. In order to create and access drives with letters beyond E, you must put the LASTDRIVE command in CONFIG.SYS and specify *x*, where *x* is the letter of the last drive you wish to access. For example, suppose you want to use the SUBST command to treat a subdirectory as if it were disk drive Z. You would have to put the command LASTDRIVE = Z in your CONFIG.SYS file and then reboot before you could execute the SUBST command to create the virtual drive Z.
REM	The CONFIG.SYS file can be cryptic, especially to DOS novices. Fortunately, DOS versions 4.0 and newer include a REM configuration command. The REM configuration command allows you to add comments to CONFIG.SYS, just as the REM batch command allows you to add comments to batch files. REM is also handy for temporarily commenting out commands in CONFIG.SYS that you expect to reinstate later. To comment out a command in CONFIG.SYS, you simply insert REM and a space in front of it and then reboot. DOS will ignore that command as a comment.
SHELL = *file*	COMMAND.COM is the program that processes the DOS commands you enter. The SHELL configuration command lets you install an alternate command processor program. It also lets you install COMMAND.COM as your command processor, but with certain additional parameters specified. For example, examine the SHELL command that appears in Figure 18. It tells DOS to install the COMMAND.COM in the DOS subdirectory as the command processor with an environment size of 256 bytes. (You will learn about environment size later in this chapter.)
STACKS = *n,s*	When a hardware interrupt occurs, such as a keypress, the computer saves what it was doing in a data structure known as a **stack.** The STACKS configuration command lets you set the number (*n*) and size (*s*) of the internal stacks DOS will use when handling hardware interrupts. A hardware or software situation that causes many interrupts in a short period of time might necessitate increasing the number and size of the internal stacks with the STACK command.

Practice

1. Type out the CONFIG.SYS file in the root directory of your startup disk and explain what each command does. Skip Practice exercise 2 if you already have a CONFIG.SYS file.
2. If you already have a CONFIG.SYS file in your root directory, do NOT do this exercise. Only if no CONFIG.SYS file is present in your root directory, create one by following these instructions:

Type	**copy con config.sys**
Press	**Enter**
Type	**break=on**
Press	**Enter**
Type	**buffers=20**
Press	**Enter**
Type	**files=20**
Press	**Enter**
Type	**lastdrive = z**
Press	**F6**
Press	**Enter**

Reboot your computer to execute the configuration commands in the new CONFIG.SYS file.

Lesson 6: Partitioning and Formatting Hard Disks

A **partition** is a separate section of a hard disk that may contain its own operating system. Every hard disk must contain at least one partition and may contain as many as four. A DOS partition must be created on a hard disk before DOS can be installed on it and before it can be formatted as a startup disk. This procedure has already been done on your computer. Partitioning and formatting the hard disk is often done by computer retailers, so you may not have to do it even if you buy a new computer. Nevertheless, you should be familiar with this process if you ever have to reconfigure your hard disk.

Step 1: Use the FDISK Command

FDISK is an external command that presents a series of menus to help you partition a hard disk for DOS. FDISK does not work if you are running DOS from a network. You must use FDISK if you want to do one of the following procedures:

- Create a primary DOS partition
- Create an extended DOS partition
- Create a logical DOS drive
- Set the active partition
- Delete a DOS partition or logical drive
- Display information about a partition
- Configure an additional hard drive

The primary DOS partition is the part of the hard disk where DOS is installed. You boot up from the primary DOS partition. In most cases, one DOS partition, the primary partition, will be on a hard disk. Very large hard disks, however, may contain extended DOS partitions configured as extra logical drives. This was common before DOS 4.00, which first allowed hard disks larger than 32 megabytes to be used as a single drive. For example, if you have an 80-megabyte hard disk and you want to run DOS 3.3, you would need to set up a primary DOS partition and two extended DOS partitions. The primary DOS partition of 32 megabytes would be set up as drive C. The extended DOS partitions, each of 24 megabytes, would be set up as logical drives D and E. They are called logical because they are treated as different drives even though they are actually part of the same drive. DOS versions 4.00 and newer allow partitions to be larger than 32 megabytes, so using extended partitions is optional.

After the DOS partitions have been created, you also use FDISK to select the active partition. The active partition is the one that contains the operating system and the files you access when you turn on or reboot your computer. For example, you could set up a large hard disk with a partition for DOS and a partition for XENIX, a variant of the UNIX operating system. Only one of these partitions could be active at a time, however. The XENIX partition would have to be set up after booting up the computer from a XENIX startup diskette.

Let's use FDISK to display partition information about your hard disk.

Type **fdisk**
Press **Enter**

Figure 19 shows the FDISK menu that appears on the screen. Do NOT choose options 1, 2, or 3 unless you are absolutely sure of what you are doing. Creating or changing DOS partitions destroys all existing files on a hard disk. You should reconfigure a hard disk with FDISK only if it is a new, empty disk or if you have backup copies of all the files on the disk. Choose option 4 to display partition information:

Type **4**
Press **Enter**

The FDISK command will present a screen that reveals information about the partitions on your hard disk. Figure 20 shows a computer that has only one DOS

Figure 19 The FDISK Menu

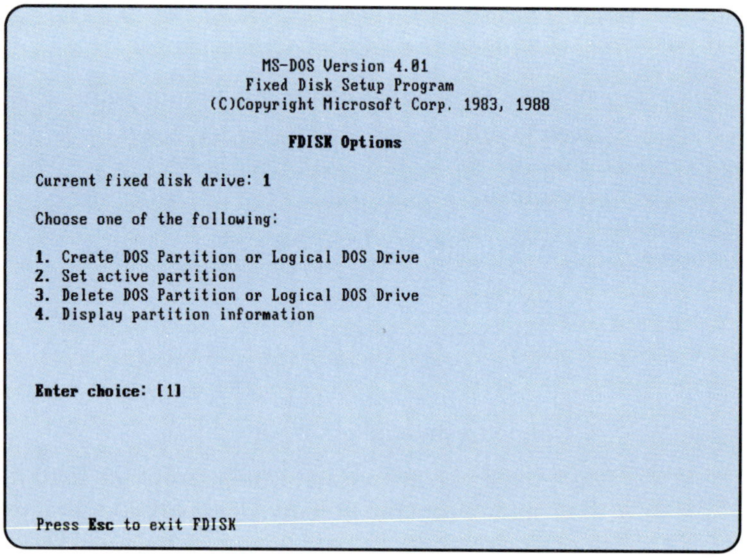

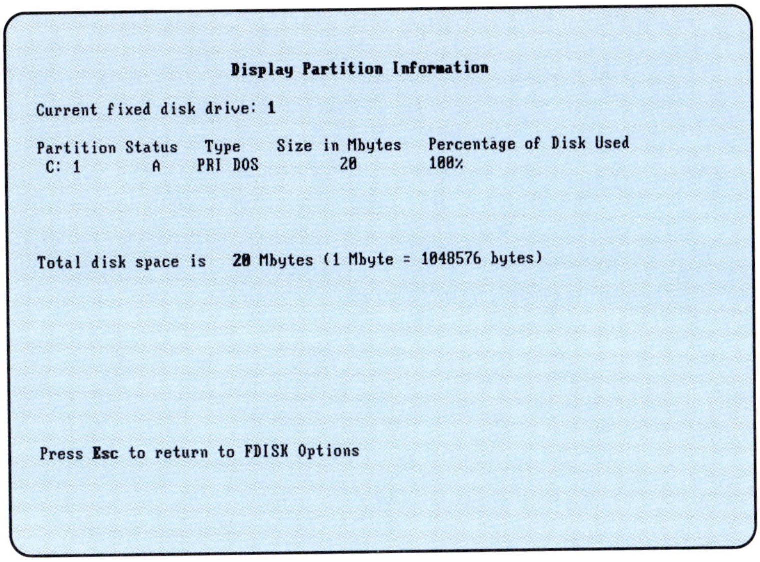

Figure 20 Partition Information Displayed by FDISK

partition, the primary and active partition, with a size of 20 megabytes. Now, do the following to leave FDISK and return to the DOS prompt:

Press **Escape** (2 times)

Step 2: Use the FORMAT Command

If you were setting up a new hard disk or reconfiguring an old one, you would still have to format each partition you created with FDISK. DON'T do this now, but you would use the FORMAT command with the /S parameter on hard disk C to create the startup disk. Then you would format any extended DOS partitions configured as logical drives.

Warning: you should not use the FDISK and FORMAT commands on a hard disk unless you know *exactly* what you are doing because you can lose all the files on the disk.

Practice Use the DIR and CHKDSK commands to examine the root directories of all the DOS partitions set up as hard drives on your computer.

Lesson 7: Learning About Other DOS Commands

In Chapters 5 and 6 and in the previous lessons of this chapter, you have examined the most commonly used DOS commands. There are other DOS commands, however, we have not yet covered. Some of the remaining ones are rarely used by most people; some are quite technical. Let's briefly discuss these other DOS commands.

Step 1: Examine the CHCP Command

DOS versions 3.30 and newer use code pages to determine which country's character set is to be displayed on the screen or sent to the printer. A **code page** is a conversion table that tells DOS how to translate data stored as numeric values into letters, numbers, punctuation, and other symbols to be displayed or printed. Each country's code page is assigned a different number. The United States' code page, number 437, is the default. Unless you live in a country other than the United States or speak a language other than English, you don't have to worry about code pages. You can, however, see or change your code page number with the internal command CHCP. For example, execute this command:

Type **chcp**
Press **Enter**

DOS will respond with the message

```
Active code page: 437.
```

Step 2: Examine the COMMAND Command

The DOS command processor is the program that translates and acts on the commands you enter. COMMAND.COM is the command processor that comes with DOS. It is automatically invoked when you boot up DOS and includes all internal commands, such as DIR and COPY. COMMAND is an external command that lets you invoke a second command processor or load a customized command processor. For example, for security purposes you can create a version of COMMAND.COM that does not include the ERASE (or DEL) command, and load this modified command processor with the COMMAND command. Most people seldom use the COMMAND command directly, but it is sometimes used by application programs to let the user execute a DOS command from within the program. For example, try this command:

Type **command /c chkdsk**
Press **Enter**

This command starts a new command processor under the current program, executes the CHKDSK command, and returns to the first command processor.

Step 3: Examine the CTTY Command

The internal command CTTY lets you change your terminal, the device from which you issue DOS commands and see the results. Normally, your terminal is the console, which consists of your computer's keyboard and display screen. The CTTY command can be used, for example, to transfer control of your computer to a separate terminal or workstation connected to the serial port. Most people rarely use CTTY.

Step 4: Examine the EXE2BIN Command

You may have noticed that two kinds of files can be executed as commands besides batch files: EXE files and COM files. The differences between these two kinds of files are somewhat technical. A COM file may load slightly faster than an equivalent EXE file, but it can be no larger than 64K. The external command EXE2BIN allows a skilled assembly language programmer to convert an EXE file to a COM file.

Step 5: Examine the EXIT Command

The EXIT command allows you to terminate a second command processor installed with the COMMAND command and return to the primary command processor. As you will learn later in this chapter, EXIT is also used to return from the DOS Shell to the DOS prompt.

Step 6: Examine the FASTOPEN Command

FASTOPEN is an external command that decreases the amount of time needed to gain access to frequently used files and directories. It works only on hard disks, but will not work when running DOS from a network.

DOS can take a long time to search for a file if your hard disk contains many levels of subdirectories. FASTOPEN maintains a list in memory of your most recently used directory and file locations. If you repeatedly reference a particular file or directory, DOS will be able to find it more quickly by looking up its location in memory instead of checking the disk. If FASTOPEN has not already been executed in your AUTOEXEC.BAT file or INSTALLed in the CONFIG.SYS file, you can improve the performance of your hard disk C by doing this:

Type **`fastopen c:`**
Press **Enter**

Step 7: Examine the GRAFTABL Command

Many older IBM-compatible computers are equipped with a relatively low-resolution Color Graphics Adapter (CGA). These machines display certain graphics characters poorly in graphics modes unless you use the external command GRAFTABL. Executing GRAFTABL will load an extended character set that looks better in programs that use the CGA graphics modes.

Step 8: Examine the GRAPHICS Command

In Chapter 5, you learned that pressing the Print Screen key (or Ctrl-PrtSc on older IBM PC and AT keyboards) will send a copy of your current screen to the printer. By default, this works only with text screens. You can also print graphics screens, however, if you first execute the external command GRAPHICS. This will load the instructions DOS needs to be able to reproduce a graphics screen on your printer. GRAPHICS should be executed only once, so it is often put in the AUTOEXEC.BAT file.

Step 9: Examine the KEYB Command

The external command KEYB is used to load a keyboard translation table for a specific country. It should be executed only once, so it generally appears in the AUTOEXEC.BAT file or is run with the INSTALL command in CONFIG.SYS. If you live in the United States or speak English, you will probably never have to use this command.

Step 10: Examine the MODE Command

The external command MODE can be used to control certain aspects of the printer, serial interface, and display screen. It has many parameters and many possible variations. Fortunately, most of today's application software takes care of setting up these devices, so you probably won't have to use MODE. If you have a color graphics display, however, you can easily demonstrate one aspect of the MODE command.

Type **mode co40**
Press **Enter**

This command tells DOS to display 40 characters across your color screen. Use the DIR command to see how this looks. When you are finished, execute the following command to change your display back to 80 columns:

Type **mode co80**
Press **Enter**

Step 11: Examine the NLSFUNC Command

NLSFUNC is another external command that is used to load country-specific information for DOS. It supports international language features and code pages. Again, if you live in the United States or speak English, you will probably never use this command.

Step 12: Examine the SELECT Command

With DOS 4.00 and newer versions, the external command SELECT is an easy-to-use menu-driven facility for installing DOS on a hard or floppy disk and creating the AUTOEXEC.BAT and CONFIG.SYS files (see Appendix C, Software Installation). With earlier DOS versions, SELECT is a more limited command that uses prompts to let you install DOS with country-specific keyboard layout, date, and time formats.

Step 13: Examine the SET Command

There is a special area in memory called the **DOS environment** that contains variables, values, and text used by some programs. It is sort of like a scratch pad for DOS. The internal command SET lets you view and change the contents of the DOS environment. For example, execute the following command:

Type **set**
Press **Enter**

Figure 21 shows a typical result. The COMSPEC line displays the full path and file specification of your default command processor. The PATH, APPEND, and PROMPT lines should be familiar; the DOS environment stores the current settings.

You can also use the SET command to change items in the DOS environment, such as new settings for PATH or PROMPT. For example, execute the following command:

Type **set prompt=Hello$g**
Press **Enter**

This changes the DOS prompt just as the PROMPT command does. Change the prompt back to the way it was before with this command:

Type **set prompt=pg**
Press **Enter**

Figure 21 The DOS Environment Displayed by SET

```
C:\>set
COMSPEC=C:\DOS\COMMAND.COM
PATH=C:\DOS
APPEND=C:\DOS
PROMPT=$P$G

C:\>_
```

Step 14: Examine the SHARE Command

SHARE is an external command that instructs DOS to allow file sharing and locking. **File sharing** is when two or more people or programs are using the same file at the same time. **File locking** is the opposite of file sharing—only one person or program can use a file or part of a file at a time. The SHARE command is generally used only on local area networks.

Practice

1. Have DOS display your current code page number on the screen.
2. Check the amount of memory you have free by executing the CHKDSK or MEM command. Then start a new command processor by executing this command:

   Type **command**
   Press **Enter**

   Check the amount of memory you have free again by executing CHKDSK or MEM. The amount should be less than before because a secondary command processor is now loaded into memory. Return to the previous command processor by executing this command:

   Type **exit**
   Press **Enter**

   Use CHKDSK or MEM once again to see that you now have the original amount of memory free.
3. Make sure you are at the root directory of your hard disk. Use the SET command to examine the current DOS environment. Then use SET to change your search PATH to just the root directory of the hard disk. Try to execute the CHKDSK command. Why doesn't it work? Use SET to change the search path back to the DOS subdirectory. Try the CHKDSK command again.

Lesson 8: Using the DOS Shell

Starting with DOS version 4.00, IBM and Microsoft included an enhancement to the operating system's user interface called the **DOS Shell.** This feature allows you to complete common DOS tasks by selecting options from menus instead of entering commands at the DOS prompt. Novices sometimes find it easier to use the DOS Shell than ordinary DOS commands.

We have not used the DOS Shell in this book so far. It wasn't offered with previous versions of DOS, and most people are still using regular DOS commands. Nevertheless, it is worthwhile to take a brief look at this new user interface. If you have DOS 4.00 or a newer version, you might find that you prefer using the DOS Shell. If you don't have DOS 4.00 or a newer version, skip this lesson.

Step 1: Invoke the DOS Shell

The DOS Shell is an option; you can choose whether or not to use it. DOS can be installed so that the DOS Shell is activated every time you turn on the computer. This is done by putting the DOSSHELL command in the AUTOEXEC.BAT file. DOSSHELL.BAT is a batch file created when DOS is installed that starts the DOS Shell. If DOS is installed without putting DOSSHELL in the AUTOEXEC.BAT file, you can still use the DOS Shell by entering this command yourself. Execute the following command to activate the DOS Shell from the DOS prompt:

Type **dosshell**
Press **Enter**

Figure 22 shows the first screen you see in the DOS Shell—the Start Programs screen. (Note: Your screens may look slightly different if your computer has a color graphics display.)

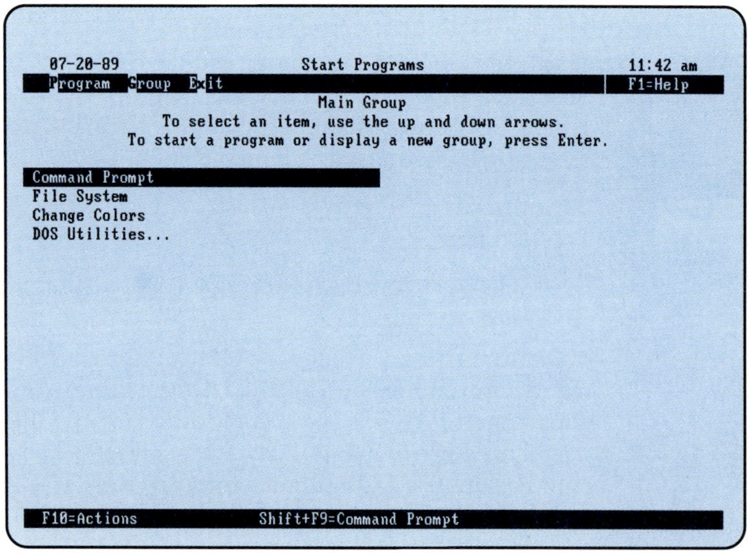

Figure 22 The Start Programs Screen

Step 2: Examine the DOS Utilities Menu

From the Start Programs screen you can run programs, customize the DOS Shell menus, change the screen colors, and manage your files and subdirectories. For example, several common DOS tasks are available under the heading DOS Utilities. To position the reverse-video highlight bar on this heading and select it, do this:

Press **Down Arrow** (3 times)
Press **Enter**

Figure 23 shows the new screen that appears—the DOS Utilities menu. The options that appear in this menu correspond to some DOS commands. If you want to copy a diskette, for instance, you would position the highlight bar on the second option in this menu and press the Enter key. The DOS Shell would then prompt you for more information about making the copy. Although this menu contains only a few DOS functions, other commands can be added as options or appear as options inside other menus.

Step 3: Examine the File System Screen

Now, let's go back to the Start Programs screen.

Press **Escape**

Your screen should look like Figure 22 again. The File System option in the Main Group is another useful feature of the DOS Shell. To select this option, follow these directions

Press **Up Arrow** (2 times to highlight File System)
Press **Enter**

DOS will read information from the disk. Then the File System screen will show your current disk and subdirectory path (see Figure 24). The left side of the screen presents a chart that shows the structure of the current disk. The right side of

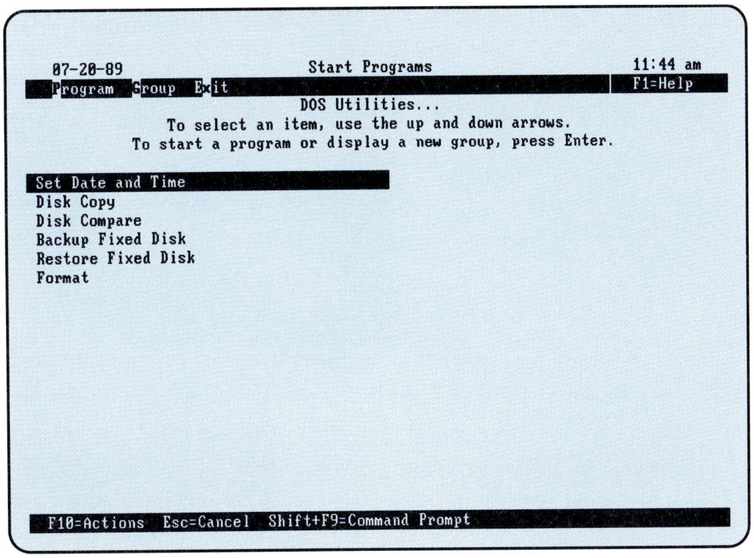

Figure 23 The DOS Utilities Menu

Figure 24 The File System Screen

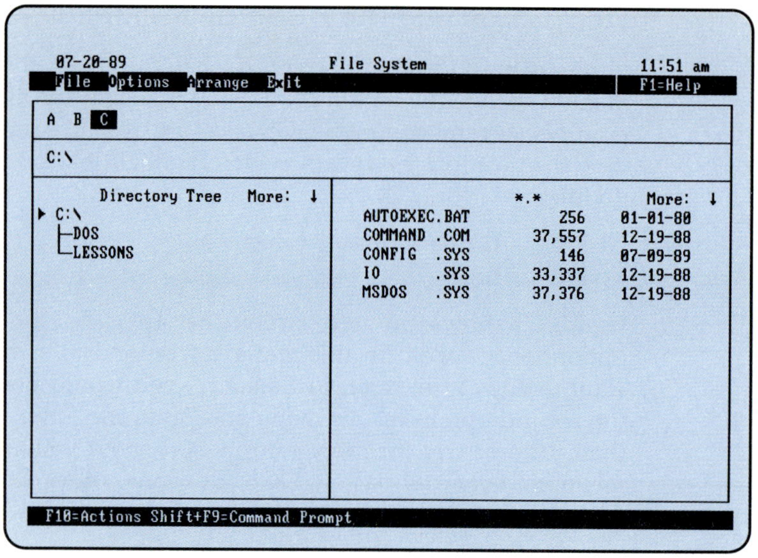

the screen shows the files in the currently selected directory, including the hidden files. Right now, the root directory of hard disk C is depicted. You should recognize the files AUTOEXEC.BAT, COMMAND.COM, and CONFIG.SYS. The two additional entries, IO.SYS and MSDOS.SYS, are the hidden MS-DOS system files in the root directory of the hard disk. (If you are running IBM DOS, the two hidden system files will be named IBMBIO.COM and IBMDOS.COM instead.)

Step 4: View the Contents of a Different Subdirectory

Changing to another subdirectory and viewing its contents is very easy. For example, let's look at the DOS subdirectory.

Press **Tab**
Press **Down Arrow**
Press **Enter**

Pressing the Tab key moves the highlight bar from the disk drive letter to the directory tree chart. Pressing the Down Arrow key moves the highlight to the DOS subdirectory. Pressing the Enter key actually selects the highlighted option. Figure 25 shows the resulting screen. The right side lists the files in the DOS subdirectory in alphabetical order. If you press the Tab key again, the highlight bar will move to this directory listing. You can execute any program in the subdirectory simply by highlighting it and pressing the Enter key.

Step 5: Switch to the DOS Prompt

Some people prefer to use a menu-oriented system like the DOS Shell, while others would rather enter commands from the DOS prompt. Fortunately, it's easy to switch back and forth between the DOS prompt and the DOS Shell. For example, to activate the DOS prompt, do this:

Press **Shift-F9**

Figure 25 The Files in the DOS Subdirectory

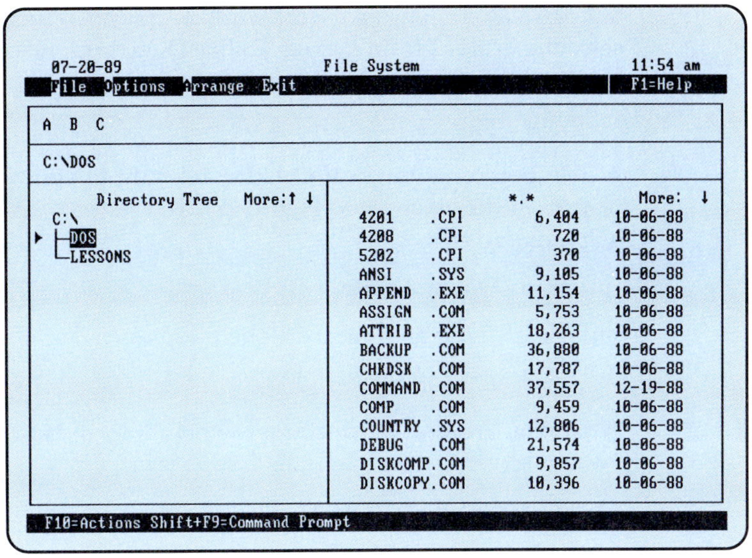

As Figure 26 shows, the DOS Shell disappears and the DOS prompt appears. You can now use DOS the way you have learned in previous lessons, without the DOS Shell. When you want to return to the DOS Shell from the DOS prompt, execute the EXIT command:

Type **exit**
Press **Enter**

Step 6: Try Other DOS Shell Features

Although we've only briefly introduced the DOS Shell, you should see that it can be an easy system for novices to use. There are many features of the DOS Shell we have not covered. For example, the DOS Shell can be set up to present more attractive screens if your computer has a high-resolution graphics adapter

Figure 26 The DOS Prompt Activated from the DOS Shell

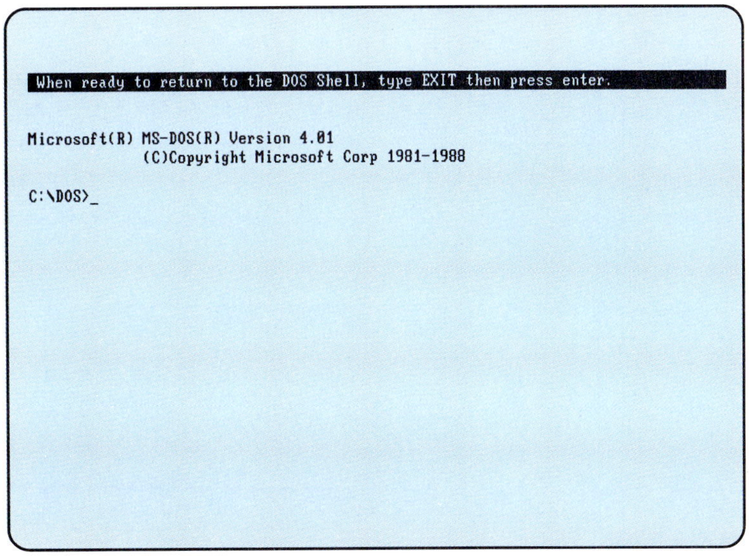

and display. It can also work with a mouse, which simplifies the process of selecting options from menus. Unlike DOS from the command prompt, the DOS Shell provides comprehensive help information. To get help at any time, do this:

Press **F1**

A help box containing information relevant to your current activity will be displayed on the screen (see Figure 27). To see the next page of information in the help box, do this:

Press **Down Arrow**

You can also see an index of all help topics:

Press **F11** (or **Alt-F1**)

When you are finished reading the help information, you can return to the File System screen by pressing the Escape key:

Press **Escape** (2 times)

The DOS Shell is very flexible, since it allows you to create new menus and add any programs you like as options. Existing menus can be modified by adding options, deleting options, and copying options from other menus. So although the DOS Shell can make it easier for a novice to use the operating system at a very basic level, it also offers complex features for more advanced users.

Practice

1. The DOS Shell File System should be on your screen. Change to the LESSONS subdirectory:

   Press **Down Arrow** to highlight LESSONS
   Press **Enter**

   Move the highlight bar to the right side of the screen, where the files inside the LESSONS subdirectory are listed:

   Press **Tab**

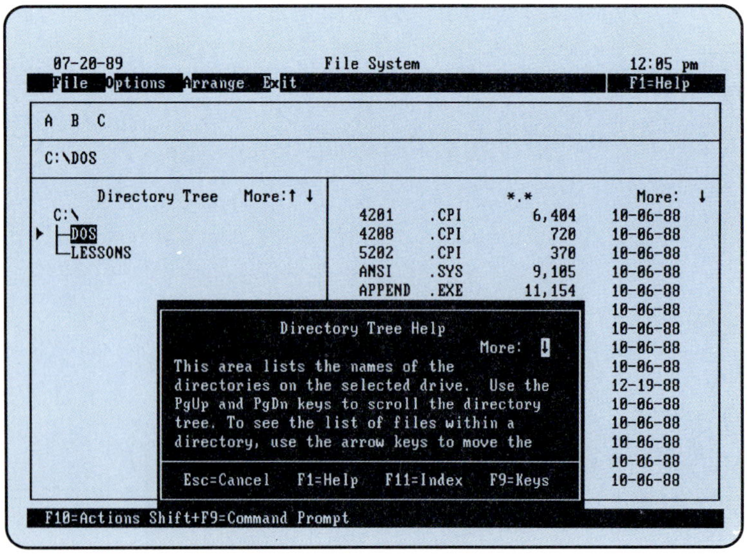

Figure 27 The DOS Shell Help Box

From the DOS Shell File System, you can execute any batch file, external command, or other program by highlighting its file name and pressing Enter. For example, execute the D.BAT batch file:

Highlight **D.BAT**
Press **Enter** (2 times)

When the D.BAT file is finished (you may have to press any key to continue from the MORE command), you press **Enter** again to return to the DOS Shell File System.

2. Highlight the file COMMAND.BAK in the LESSONS subdirectory listing on the right side of the File System screen. Then follow these instructions to delete this file:

   Press **Space Bar** (to select COMMAND.BAK)
   Press **F10** (to move to the menu bar)
   Press **Down Arrow** (to activate the File menu)
   Press **Down Arrow** (5 times to highlight Delete)
   Press **Enter** (to activate the Delete command)
   Press **Enter** (to proceed)
   Press **2** (to execute the Delete option)

   The file COMMAND.BAK will be deleted from the LESSONS subdirectory.

3. Highlight the file ANY_TXT.BAT in the LESSONS subdirectory listing on the right side of the File System screen. Then follow these instructions to view the contents of this file:

   Press **Space Bar** (to select ANY_TXT.BAT)
   Press **F10** (to move to the menu bar)
   Press **Down Arrow** (to activate the File menu)
   Press **Down Arrow** (8 times to highlight View)
   Press **Enter** (to execute the View command)

   When you are finished examining the file's contents:

   Press **Escape** (to return to the File System)

4. Use the DOS Shell help facility to read about all the options in all of the menus. Remember, you press the F10 key to move to the menu bar and the arrow keys to move between and within menus. Pressing F1 will bring up a help box about the currently selected item.

Summary

- *Redirecting output and input.* The > symbol redirects output from the screen to a device or file. The >> symbol redirects and appends output. The < symbol redirects input from a file instead of from the keyboard.
- *Using DOS filters and piping.* FIND, MORE, and SORT are filters that work with text input. The | symbol pipes output from one program into another program.
- *Using batch files.* A batch file is a text file with a BAT extension that contains DOS commands to be run. AUTOEXEC.BAT is a special batch file automatically executed every time the computer is booted.

- *Using batch processing commands.* Replaceable parameters, CALL, ECHO, FOR, IF, GOTO, PAUSE, REM, and SHIFT can greatly enhance the flexibility and power of batch files.
- *Setting up a configuration file.* CONFIG.SYS is a special text file in the root directory that contains configuration commands to set up the computer.
- *Partitioning and formatting a hard disk.* The FDISK command presents a series of menus to divide a hard disk into sections called partitions. A hard disk must be formatted after it has been partitioned.
- *Executing other DOS commands.* Other DOS commands include CHCP, COMMAND, CTTY, EXE2BIN, EXIT, FASTOPEN, GRAFTABL, GRAPHICS, KEYB, MODE, NLSFUNC, SELECT, SET, and SHARE.
- *Using the DOS Shell.* The DOS Shell, included with DOS versions 4.00 and newer, is a user-friendly interface that presents options in menus instead of requiring commands to be entered at the DOS prompt. It is invoked by executing the DOSSHELL.BAT file.

Key Terms

As an extra review of this chapter, try defining the following terms.

batch file
batch processing commands
branching
chaining
code page
comment out
device driver
disk buffer
DOS environment
DOS Shell
file control block (FCB)
file locking
file sharing
filter
label
nesting
partition
piping
redirection
replaceable parameter
stack

Multiple Choice

Choose the best selection to complete each statement.

1. Which of the following characters tells DOS to redirect the output of a command to a file or device?

   (a) > (b) <
   (c) | (d) $

2. Which of the following characters tells DOS to pipe the output of one command into another command?

   (a) > (b) <
   (c) | (d) $

3. Which of the following commands is NOT a filter?

   (a) FIND (b) MORE
   (c) COPY (d) SORT

4. What is the name of the DOS configuration file?
   (a) AUTOEXEC.BAT (b) CONFIG.SYS
   (c) VDISK.SYS (d) CONFIG.BAT
5. Which of the following commands may appear only in the configuration file?
   (a) DEVICE (b) ASSIGN
   (c) JOIN (d) APPEND
6. Which command would you use to nest batch files?
   (a) EXIT (b) CALL
   (c) COMMAND (d) JOIN
7. Every batch file must have an extension of
   (a) BAK. (b) BAT.
   (c) COM. (d) EXE.
8. Which of the following commands is usually found only in batch files?
   (a) DEVICE (b) COMMAND
   (c) ECHO (d) DIR
9. Which batch file command repeats an action on a set of files?
   (a) MORE (b) IF
   (c) APPEND (d) FOR
10. Which of the following commands basically does nothing?
    (a) DIR (b) CHKDSK
    (c) PROMPT (d) REM
11. Which of the following configuration commands may increase disk performance, but use more memory?
    (a) BREAK (b) BUFFERS
    (c) COUNTRY (d) DEVICE
12. Which configuration command is used to install device drivers?
    (a) DEVICE (b) INSTALL
    (c) DRIVEPARM (d) FCBS
13. Which command must you use in CONFIG.SYS before you can create and access disk drive Z?
    (a) FILES (b) LASTDRIVE
    (c) DRIVEPARM (d) STACKS
14. A separate section of a hard disk that may contain its own operating system is called a
    (a) partition. (b) sector.
    (c) track. (d) cylinder.
15. Which command must be used on a new hard disk before it is formatted?
    (a) ASSIGN (b) BACKUP
    (c) FDISK (d) SELECT
16. Which command presents the current code page number?
    (a) CHCP (b) DIR
    (c) CHKDSK (d) NLSFUNC

17. Which command terminates a second command processor or returns from the DOS Shell to the DOS prompt?
    (a) CALL (b) EXIT
    (c) JOIN (d) REPLACE
18. Which command displays the contents of the DOS environment?
    (a) DIR (b) CHKDSK
    (c) MEM (d) SET
19. What is the name of the first screen you see after starting the DOS Shell?
    (a) Start Programs (b) DOS Utilities
    (c) File System (d) Exit Program
20. Which key do you press to get help from within the DOS Shell?
    (a) Alternate (b) Enter
    (c) F1 (d) F10

Fill-In

1. The ______ symbol is used to redirect and append the output of a command to a file.
2. The ______ filter accepts input and then presents it as output, one screen at a time.
3. The SORT filter is often used with piping and ______.
4. The ______ command is used in CONFIG.SYS to set the maximum number of files that can be open at a time.
5. You can pass information to a running batch file by using a ______ parameter.
6. Chaining is when you invoke a ______ file as the last command in a batch file.
7. The ______ and ______ commands are used to branch within a batch file.
8. You can suspend the execution of a batch file until the user presses a key by inserting the ______ command.
9. To insert a comment in a batch file or CONFIG.SYS, you precede the line with ______.
10. The FDISK command is used to set up DOS ______.
11. If you want the Print Screen key to work on graphics screens, you must first execute the ______ command.
12. ______ is the command processor that comes with DOS.
13. The ______ command can be used to transfer control of your computer to a separate terminal connected to a serial port.
14. The ______ command decreases the amount of time needed to gain access to frequently used files and directories.
15. The ______ command is a menu-driven facility for installing DOS on a disk and creating AUTOEXEC.BAT and CONFIG.SYS.
16. The ______ command is generally used only on local area networks to prevent two programs from using the same file at the same time.
17. To start the DOS Shell, you type ______ and press the Enter key.
18. The DOS Shell was first introduced with DOS version ______.

19. The DOS Shell's ______ System screen shows the structure of the default disk and lists the files in the current directory.
20. You can switch to the DOS ______ from within the DOS Shell by pressing Shift-F9.

Short Problems

1. Use the DIR command, piping, and the FIND filter with the /V parameter to display a directory listing of all the files in the LESSONS subdirectory that do NOT have the extension BAT.
2. Use the DIR command, piping, and the FIND filter with the /C parameter to display a count of the number BAT files in the LESSONS subdirectory.
3. Use the DIR command, piping, and the SORT filter to display a listing of the current directory, with the files arranged in order of increasing file size.
4. Create a batch file named T.BAT that will clear the screen and then TYPE the file specified on the command line. (Hint: Use a replaceable parameter for the file name.) Try T.BAT a few times.
5. Create a batch file named HELP.BAT that turns echoing off, clears the screen, and then uses ECHO commands to present a brief description of how to execute a batch file.
6. Use the COPY command to create a text file called NAMES1.TXT containing the last names of ten of your friends. Type each name on a separate line and enter the names in random order. When you are finished, redirect NAMES1.TXT into the SORT filter and redirect the output to create a new file called NAMES2.TXT, which will contain the names arranged in alphabetical order. Compare the contents of NAME1.TXT and NAME2.TXT with the TYPE command.
7. Create a batch file named REPEAT.BAT that repeats the DIR command forever. (Hint: use the GOTO command to branch to a label placed before the DIR command in the batch file.) Execute the REPEAT batch file. You can stop it at any time by pressing Ctrl-Break and then answering yes when DOS prompts you to terminate the batch job.
8. The MODE command can display the status of all devices installed in your system. Execute the MODE command without any parameters and examine the output.
9. If you have the DOS Shell, invoke it and then format a diskette by using the Format option from the DOS Utilities menu.
10. If you have the DOS Shell, invoke it and delete all the files in your LESSONS subdirectory. Then remove the LESSONS subdirectory.

PART 3

WordPerfect 5.0

Next to operating systems, which all microcomputers require, word processing packages are undoubtedly the most commonly used type of software. It has been estimated that over 90 percent of all microcomputer owners have at least one word processing program. This means that tens of millions of word processing packages are available, ready to produce all kinds of documents. A word processing package is the first application package most novices learn to use. Whether you need to create a brief memo or an entire book, word processing software, along with a microcomputer and printer, can help you do the job faster, easier, and more neatly.

WordPerfect is the leader in microcomputer word processing software. Since its introduction in October 1982, the package has received high praise from both reviewers and users. WordPerfect Corporation has significantly enhanced its product with every new release. Although WordPerfect is considered one of the most feature-laden word processing packages on the market, it is also known for its simple, well-designed user interface.

In Part 3, we examine the benefits and techniques of word processing with WordPerfect 5.0. Chapter 8 covers the basics, the bare essentials you need to produce a document with WordPerfect. Chapter 9 presents lessons that will increase your understanding and control of WordPerfect. Chapter 10 helps you explore more advanced WordPerfect topics, including desktop publishing features such as multiple columns, graphics, and page preview.

CHAPTER 8

BEGINNING WORDPERFECT

In This Chapter

Getting Started
Lesson 1: Running WordPerfect
Lesson 2: The Editing Screen
Lesson 3: Executing Commands and Getting Help
Lesson 4: Entering Text
Lesson 5: Moving the Cursor
Lesson 6: Inserting Text
Lesson 7: Overwriting Mistakes
Lesson 8: Deleting Mistakes
Lesson 9: Searching and Replacing
Lesson 10: Saving the Document
Lesson 11: Checking Spelling
Lesson 12: Working with Blocks of Text
Lesson 13: Canceling Commands
Lesson 14: Formatting Characters
Lesson 15: Formatting Lines
Lesson 16: Formatting Pages
Lesson 17: Printing a Document
Lesson 18: Returning to DOS
Lesson 19: Editing an Existing Document

Preview

A word processor is a computer system that helps you type, edit, store, and print documents. Memos, letters, term papers, reports, contracts, articles, and book chapters are all examples of documents that can be produced with a word processing package. The typical word processor consists of a microcomputer, printer, and word processing software package. Systems of this type are common today and are helping all kinds of people with their daily writing chores. Students, educators, authors, scientists, business people, professionals, and office workers are some of the people who use word processing systems. Word processing packages, also called word processors, are perhaps the most popular type of software used on microcomputers. And WordPerfect is the most popular word processing package, with versions sold for most major microcomputers, including IBMs and IBM-compatibles, Apple IIs and Apple Macintoshes, Commodore Amigas, and Atari STs. In this chapter and the next two chapters, you will learn to use WordPerfect 5.0 for IBM and IBM-compatible microcomputers.

After studying this chapter, you will know how to

- start WordPerfect.
- use the editing screen.
- execute commands and get help.
- enter text into a document.
- move the cursor.
- insert new text.
- overwrite mistakes.
- delete mistakes.
- search for and replace text.
- save a document in a disk file.
- check spelling.
- mark, move, copy, and delete blocks of text.
- cancel commands and restore deletions.
- underline, boldface, and otherwise format characters.
- set margins, tab stops, justification, line spacing, and line height.
- center text.
- format pages.
- print a document.
- edit an existing document.
- exit WordPerfect.

Getting Started

Although WordPerfect is a large and sophisticated software package, it is not difficult to learn to use it for basic word processing tasks. WordPerfect might be set up at your particular computer installation several different ways. You're most likely to use the package in one of three possible arrangements:

1. on a microcomputer with two floppy drives and WordPerfect installed on several diskettes.
2. on a microcomputer with a hard disk and WordPerfect installed in a subdirectory named WP50 or WP.
3. on a microcomputer connected to a local area network with WordPerfect installed on the network file server.

Insight

What is the Secret to WordPerfect's Success?

Even though you've read and re-read the manual, pressed every key combination you can think of, and asked all your friends, your new word processing software is laughing at you. You haven't even managed to set it up, much less write your term paper. What do you do now?

WordPerfect Corporation, maker of WordPerfect word processing software, has an answer: lifetime, toll-free support for everyone who buys its products. The company has a fleet of support operators on the payroll who answer phoned-in questions Monday through Friday from 7 a.m. to 6 p.m and Saturday from 8 a.m to noon, Mountain Standard Time. The monthly telephone tab for this service tops $300,000.

"It's truly unlimited support," says Stan Mackay, head of WordPerfect's support group. "We don't even ask for user numbers. We want to help them, unhassled."

Each support worker specializes in either installation; features; printers; the company's other software, including DataPerfect, Library, and PlanPerfect; the Amiga and Atari versions; the Apple Macintosh version; or general questions. Callers hear three levels of recordings, and the goal is to answer the phone in two minutes and never to let anyone languish on hold for more than 45 minutes. That's not exactly lightning fast, but apparently OK to the people who make the 80,000 calls that come in every month.

Of course, no system is perfect. When WordPerfect 5.0 and WordPerfect for the Macintosh were released within days of one another, so many people called in that all toll-free lines into Utah were knocked out, disabling the telemarketing centers for American Express, Delta Air Lines, and others.

This extensive customer support is a major reason for the astonishing success of the Orem, Utah-based company. Other reasons are its marketing savvy and, as is often the case with software stars, a measure of good timing.

Sources: Christine Strehlo, "What's So Special About WordPerfect?" *Personal Computing,* March 1988, pp. 100–116. Daniel J. Rosenbaum, "Evolutionary Strategy Pays Off for WordPerfect," *PC World*, December 1988, pp. 82–86.

You may need some additional direction from your instructor on how to start WordPerfect, but once you get situated you should be able to do the following lessons.

Lesson 1: Running WordPerfect

You're all ready to start word processing, but first you must boot up your computer and run WordPerfect.

Step 1: Boot Up the Computer

Start up your computer as you learned in Lesson 1 of Chapter 5.

Step 2: Prepare Diskette or Subdirectory for Documents

The WordPerfect program is stored on its own diskettes or in its own subdirectory on a hard disk or network. It is best to prepare a separate diskette or subdirectory for the document files you will create in the following lessons. If your computer has only floppy drives, obtain a formatted diskette with room for your files. If your computer has a hard disk, create a subdirectory called LESSONS, if you don't already have one, that you can use to store your files. If you are running on a network, your instructor may have other directions for you to follow.

Step 3: Insert the WordPerfect 1 Disk or Switch to the WordPerfect Subdirectory

If you have a system with only floppy drives, remove the DOS startup diskette from drive A and replace it with the diskette labeled "WordPerfect 1."

If you have a microcomputer with a hard disk, WordPerfect should already be installed in its own subdirectory named WP50 or WP (see Appendix C, Software Installation). Switch to the WordPerfect subdirectory by executing the appropriate DOS command:

Type **cd c:\wp50**
Press **Enter**

If your computer is connected to a local area network, you may have to follow some other directions from your instructor before actually starting the WordPerfect program.

Step 4: Invoke WordPerfect

Once you get situated in the proper disk drive directory, running WordPerfect is easy.

Type **wp**
Press **Enter**

It will take a few seconds for WordPerfect to be loaded from the disk into memory. Then your screen will look like Figure 1, which displays the copyright information for WordPerfect. If you are running the program from the WordPerfect 1 diskette in drive A, this message will also appear:

```
Insert diskette labeled "WordPerfect 2" and press any key
```

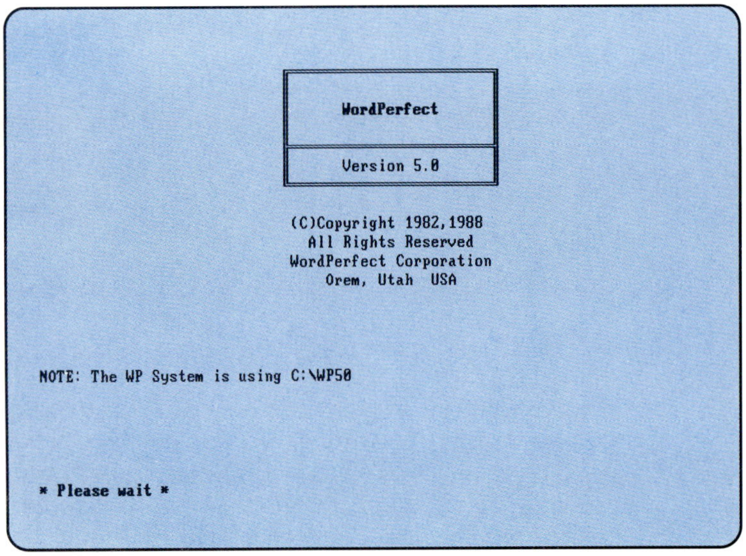

Figure 1 The WordPerfect Copyright Screen

Follow the directions. It will take a few more seconds for the rest of WordPerfect to be loaded from the disk into memory.

Practice

Reboot your computer:

Press **Ctrl-Alt-Del**

Follow the steps of this lesson to start up WordPerfect again.

Lesson 2: The Editing Screen

The copyright notice will disappear after a few moments, and WordPerfect will display the almost empty screen shown in Figure 2. This is WordPerfect's editing screen, where you enter, view, and modify text.

Step 1: Examine the Cursor

Look at the upper left corner of the screen. You should see the blinking underscore, known as the **cursor,** which marks your current position within the document. The cursor indicates where text will be inserted, deleted, or changed in some way.

Step 2: Examine the Status Line

The **status line,** shown at the bottom of the screen, displays messages and warnings from WordPerfect. Right now, the status line indicates that you are working on document one (of a possible two) and that your position within the document is 1 inch from the left edge and 1 inch from the top edge of page 1. WordPerfect already has default margins, tab stops, and line spacing set up. To create a document, all you have to do is begin typing.

Figure 2 The Editing Screen

Step 3: Examine the Text Area

The rest of the screen, from the cursor down to the status line, is the **text area.** This is the space in which you will enter text and edit your document.

Practice

Follow these instructions and notice how the status line changes:

Type **Hello**
Press **Backspace** (5 times)

Lesson 3: Executing Commands and Getting Help

Most WordPerfect commands and menus are executed either by pressing a function key alone or by pressing the Shift, Control, or Alternate key with a function key.

Step 1: Invoke the Help Command

As an example, let's execute the Help command. WordPerfect has an on-line help facility that you can use to answer many questions about the package without having to refer to the manual. To invoke the Help command, do this:

Press **F3**

WordPerfect will present the screen shown in Figure 3. Simply type a letter of the alphabet (A–Z) to see a list of all the features that begin with that letter. For example, to view the WordPerfect features that begin with the letter B, do this:

Type **b**

Figure 4 shows the result. When you are finished with the help facility, you can press either the Enter key or the Space Bar to return to the editing screen.

Press **Enter**

Figure 3 The Help Screen

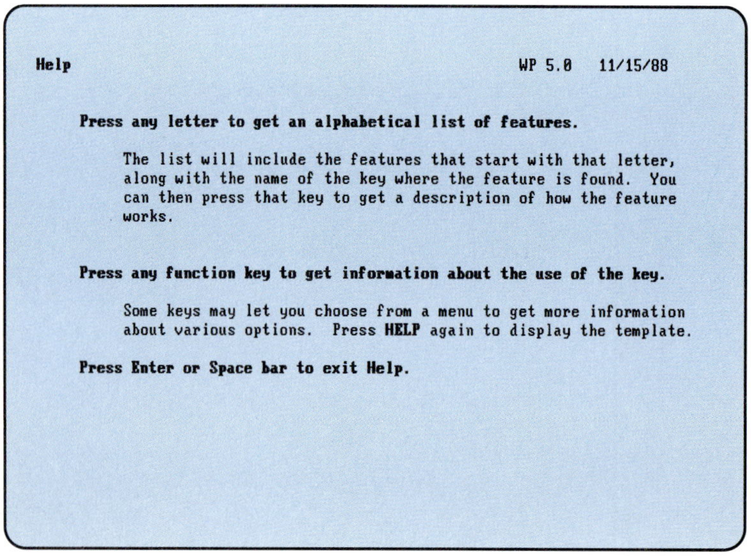

Figure 4 List of WordPerfect Features Beginning with B

Key	Feature	Key Name
Backspace	Backspace (Delete)	Backspace
Shft-F1	Backup Files, Automatic	Setup,1
Shft-F1	Backup Directory Location	Setup,7
Shft-F2	Backward Search	<-Search
Ctrl-F8	Base Font	Font
Shft-F1	Beep Options	Setup,5
Shft-F7	Binding Width	Print
Shft-F1	Black and White, View Doc. in	Setup,3
Alt-F4	Block	Block
Ctrl-F4	Block, Append (Block On)	Move
Shft-F6	Block, Center (Block On)	Center
Ctrl-F5	Block, Comment (Block On)	Text In/Out
Del	Block, Delete (Block On)	Del
Ctrl-F4	Block, Move (Block On)	Move
Shft-F7	Block, Print (Block On)	Print
Shft-F8	Block Protect (Block On)	Page Format
Ctrl-F8; F6	Bold	Font,2; Bold
Alt-F9	Box (Figure, Table, Text, Users)	Graphics

Step 2: Display the Keyboard Template

When you purchase WordPerfect, you get a **keyboard template** that lists the most common commands. This plastic guide fits over or near the function keys on the keyboard and is invaluable for beginning users. (A cardboard keyboard template is included inside the back cover of this book.) If you don't have the keyboard template, however, you can see an on-screen version by doing this:

Press **F3** (2 times)

Figure 5 shows the result. While the help facility is active, you can get additional information about any function key simply by pressing the key. For example, do this:

Press **F7**

Figure 5 On-Screen Keyboard Template

WordPerfect 5.0 Template (IBM Layout)

Key	Ctrl + Function Key	SHIFT + FUNCTION KEY	Alt + Function Key	Function Key alone
F1	Shell	SETUP	Thesaurus	Cancel
F2	Spell	<-SEARCH	Replace	Search->
F3	Screen	SWITCH	Reveal Codes	Help
F4	Move	->INDENT<-	Block	->Indent
F5	Text In/Out	DATE/OUTLINE	Mark Text	List Files
F6	Tab Align	CENTER	Flush Right	Bold
F7	Footnote	PRINT	Math/Columns	Exit
F8	Font	FORMAT	Style	Underline
F9	Merge/Sort	MERGE CODES	Graphics	Merge R
F10	Macro Define	RETRIEVE	Macro	Save

Legend:
Ctrl + Function Key
SHIFT + FUNCTION KEY
Alt + Function Key
Function Key alone

Figure 6 shows the help screen presented when you press the F7 key, referred to by WordPerfect as the Exit key. This is the command you use to exit WordPerfect and return to DOS. When you are finished with the help facility, return to the editing screen by doing this:

Press **Enter**

Practice

1. Invoke the Help facility and display the commands that begin with the letter F. When you are finished reading the list, return to the editing screen.
2. Invoke the Help facility and display the on-screen keyboard template. When you are finished reading the list, return to the editing screen.
3. Execute the Exit command. Answer No to the two prompts that follow, which ask whether you want to save the document and whether you want to exit WordPerfect.

Lesson 4: Entering Text

The process of entering the text with a word processor is similar to typing on a typewriter. There are, however, a few important differences that make using a word processor much easier. To illustrate how to use WordPerfect, let's create a memo. This memo, from the personnel department of a company to its employees, will explain company policy on employee sick leave.

Step 1: Type the Heading

As we said before, WordPerfect initially places the cursor in the first column of the first line of the first page. To create a new document, simply type the words and punctuation. Don't be concerned if you make some typing errors. You will learn how to fix mistakes later. To start out, follow these instructions:

Type **`To: All Employees`**
Press **Enter**
Type **`From: Personnel Department`**
Press **Enter**
Type **`Re: Sick Leave`**
Press **Enter**

At this point, your screen should look like Figure 7.

Step 2: Type the Body of the Memo

If you had to press Enter at the end of every line typed with a word processor, it wouldn't be all that much better than typing text with an electric typewriter. All word processing programs, however, have a feature called **word wrap** that eliminates having to press Enter most of the time. The word processing program detects when you are approaching the right margin. If you type a word that extends beyond the right margin, that word is automatically shifted, or wrapped around, to the beginning of the next line. In other words, the word processing program inserts a **soft return** just before the wrapped word. You can then continue typing on the new line without having to press the Enter key. Word wrap significantly speeds up typing because it eliminates having to constantly check the screen to make sure you don't overrun the right margin. You need only press

Figure 6 Help Screen for F7

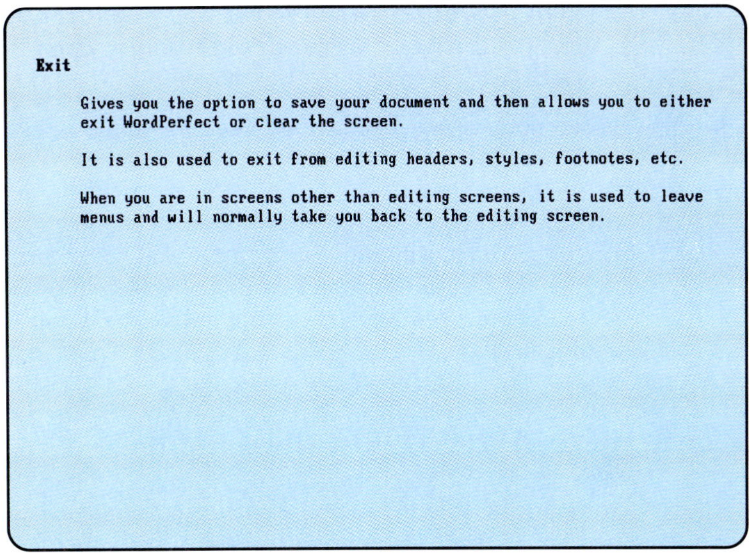

the Enter key when you want to insert a **hard return,** which forces a new line or begins a new paragraph. For example, insert a hard return to space down a line by doing this:

Press **Enter**

Now, to see how word wrap works, type the rest of the memo without pressing the Enter key:

`Full-time employees are entitled to twelve working days of sick leave each year. Time taken off is charged against these twelve days and at the end of the year the unused balance is carried forward. Sick leave should only be used for an employee's illness or doctor's appointments. It is essential that accurate records are`

Figure 7 Memo Heading

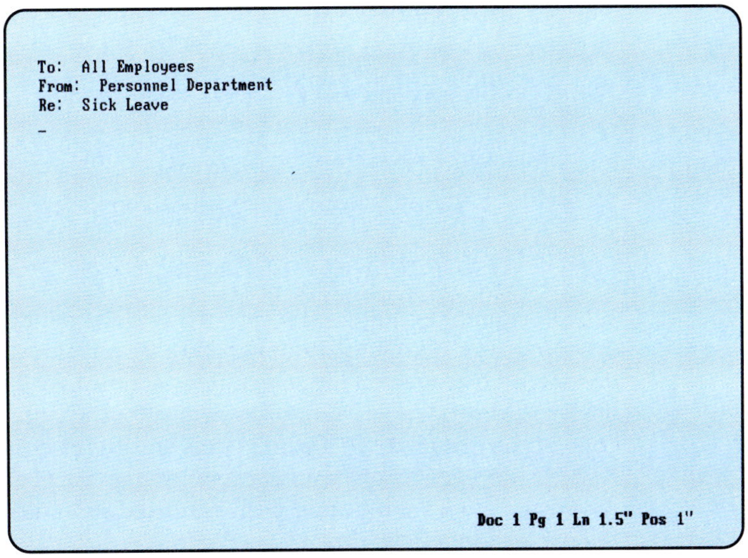

```
kept because employees are entitled to payment for one-
half of their unused sick days when they resign or
retire.
```

When you are finished, your screen should look like Figure 8.

Practice

Use the Backspace key to erase the last sentence of the memo. Notice how the cursor automatically moves up to the end of the previous line when necessary. Retype the last sentence, watching the screen to see what happens when a word wrap occurs. Remember: do not press the Enter key. The words will wrap automatically.

Lesson 5: Moving the Cursor

You must be able to move the cursor to change existing text and to see different parts of a long document. Fortunately, there are many ways to move the cursor, the most common of which are quick, direct, and easy.

Step 1: Use the Arrow Keys

All IBM and IBM-compatible keyboards have at least one set of arrow keys. In many programs, including WordPerfect, the simplest way to move the cursor is to press an arrow key. For example, try the following actions:

Press **Up Arrow** (to move up one line)
Press **Down Arrow** (to move down one line)
Press **Left Arrow** (to move back one space)
Press **Right Arrow** (to move forward one space)

To move the cursor rapidly, you can simply hold down an arrow key for more than a second without releasing it. The computer will simulate repeating the key press ten times per second. Try these actions:

Press **Left Arrow** (and hold for 5 seconds)
Press **Right Arrow** (and hold for 5 seconds)

You can also hold down the Control key and press Left Arrow or Right Arrow to move the cursor a word at a time. Try these key presses to move the cursor to the beginning of the word to the left, and then to the beginning of the word to the right:

Press **Ctrl-Left Arrow**
Press **Ctrl-Right Arrow**

Step 2: Use Scrolling and Paging

Your document is quite short, but many documents are too long to fit entirely on the screen. Scrolling and paging commands let you change the part of your document displayed on the screen. One simple way to scroll the screen is to press the Up Arrow or Down Arrow key even after the cursor reaches the top or bottom edge of the text area. This won't work on your document because all of it fits on a single screen. If there were more lines above or below, however, pressing Up Arrow or Down Arrow after reaching the edge would scroll the screen and move the cursor to the next line.

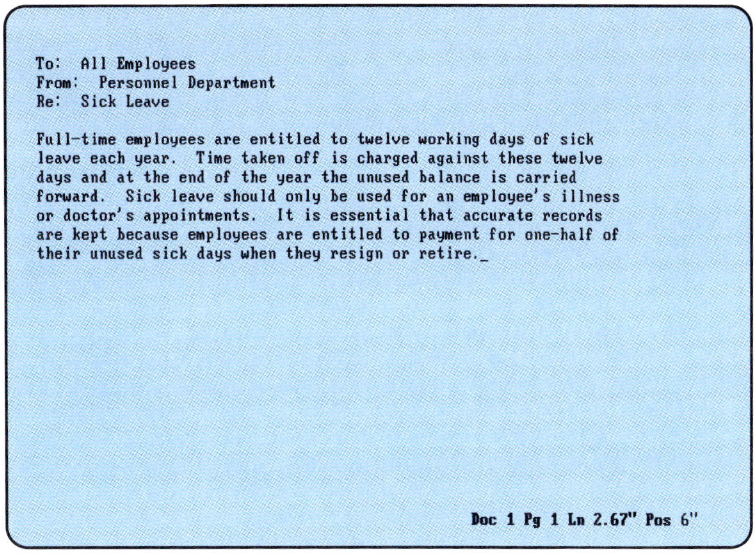
To: All Employees
From: Personnel Department
Re: Sick Leave

Full-time employees are entitled to twelve working days of sick leave each year. Time taken off is charged against these twelve days and at the end of the year the unused balance is carried forward. Sick leave should only be used for an employee's illness or doctor's appointments. It is essential that accurate records are kept because employees are entitled to payment for one-half of their unused sick days when they resign or retire._

Doc 1 Pg 1 Ln 2.67" Pos 6"

Figure 8 Word Wrap Automatically Begins New Lines

The Grey Plus (+) and Grey Minus (−) keys on the numeric keypad are used to move the cursor an entire screen at a time. Try this:

Press **Grey Plus**

Grey Plus moves the cursor down to the last line of the current screen. If your document were too long to entirely fit on the screen, pressing the Grey Plus key again would move the cursor down through the next screen. Now try this:

Press **Grey Minus**

Grey Minus moves the cursor up to the first line of the current screen. If you had more text above your current screen, pressing the Grey Minus key again would move the cursor up through the previous screen.

Paging is like scrolling an entire page at a time. The Page Down and Page Up keys are used to move between pages. Try this:

Press **Page Down**

The cursor will move to the first line of the next page. Since your document has only one page, pressing Page Down merely moves the cursor to the end of the document. Now try this:

Press **Page Up**

The Page Up key moves the cursor to the first line of the previous page. Again, since your document has only one page, pressing Page Up simply moves the cursor to the beginning of the document.

Step 3: Use the End and Home Keys

End and Home are the two other cursor movement keys on all IBM-compatible keyboards. Try this:

Press **End**

The End key moves the cursor to the end of the current line.

In WordPerfect, the Home key is used with other keys to perform various cursor movements. For example, follow these directions:

Press **Home**
Press **Left Arrow**

Home followed by Left Arrow moves the cursor to the left edge of the current screen—in other words, the beginning of the current line. Now try this:

Press **Home**
Press **Right Arrow**

Home followed by Right Arrow moves the cursor to the right edge of the current screen. You can also use the Home key and the Down Arrow or Up Arrow key to move the cursor to the end or beginning of your document. Follow these directions:

Press **Home** (2 times)
Press **Down Arrow**
Press **Home** (2 times)
Press **Up Arrow**

Pressing Home twice followed by the Down Arrow key moves the cursor to the end of the document. Pressing Home twice followed by the Up Arrow key moves the cursor to the beginning of the document.

Step 4: Use the Go To Command

Another sequence of keypresses lets you move to a particular page number in a WordPerfect document. Since your current document fits entirely on a single page, the Go To command would be of little use. Nevertheless, you can still try it:

Press **Ctrl-Home**

WordPerfect will display the prompt "Go to" on the status line. Then you enter the page number to which you want to go:

Type **1**
Press **Enter**

WordPerfect will move the cursor to the top of that page.

Practice Try the following keypresses and explain what each one does:

Up Arrow	**Down Arrow**
Left Arrow	**Right Arrow**
Ctrl-Left Arrow	**Ctrl-Right Arrow**
Grey Plus	**Grey Minus**
Page Up	**Page Down**
Home, Left Arrow	**Home, Right Arrow**
Home, Home, Up Arrow	**Home, Home, Down Arrow**
Ctrl-Home	**End**

Lesson 6: Inserting Text

WordPerfect, like most word processing software, has two basic typing modes: insert and typeover. By default, WordPerfect has insert mode turned on when you open a document. This means that to insert new material into a document, you just move the cursor to the location where you want the insertion to occur and begin typing. The new characters you type push any existing characters to the right. As an example, let's insert some new text into the memo you've typed.

Step 1: Move the Cursor

Suppose you want to insert the word "cumulative" between the words "twelve" and "working" in the first line of the memo. Use any of the cursor movement keys described in Lesson 5 to put the cursor beneath the "w" in the word "working."

Step 2: Type the New Text

Since WordPerfect uses insert mode by default, all you have to do is type the new text to be inserted.

Type **cumulative**
Press **Space Bar**
Press **Up Arrow**

Notice how WordPerfect automatically reforms the paragraph and wraps words to fit within the margins when you move the cursor. Your screen should now look like Figure 9.

Practice Insert the word "mistake" anywhere in the document. Then use the Backspace key to remove it.

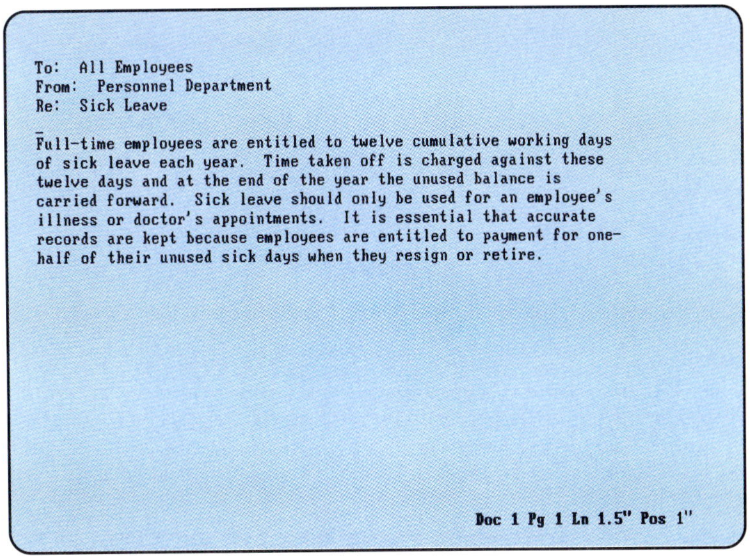

Figure 9 Text Inserted in a Document

Lesson 7: Overwriting Mistakes

One of the benefits of using a word processor is the ease with which you can make corrections. Since no one is perfect, typing errors are bound to occur—as you may have already discovered. In addition, you may have to go back and change a word or phrase that you already entered. One way to make corrections is by typing over existing text.

Step 1: Move the Cursor

Suppose that employees are only entitled to eleven days of sick leave. You must change the word "twelve" to "eleven" in the memo. Using the cursor movement keys described in Lesson 5, put the cursor beneath the "t" in the first "twelve."

Step 2: Change to Typeover Mode

Insert mode is on by default. To switch, or toggle, between insert and typeover mode, you use the Insert key.

Press **Insert**

When you change to typeover mode, WordPerfect displays the word "Typeover" in the status line. Now, any characters you type will replace the existing characters in the same positions.

Step 3: Make the Correction

With the cursor at the beginning of the word "twelve," do this:

Type **eleven**

Your screen should now look like Figure 10.

Figure 10 Word Corrected in Typeover Mode

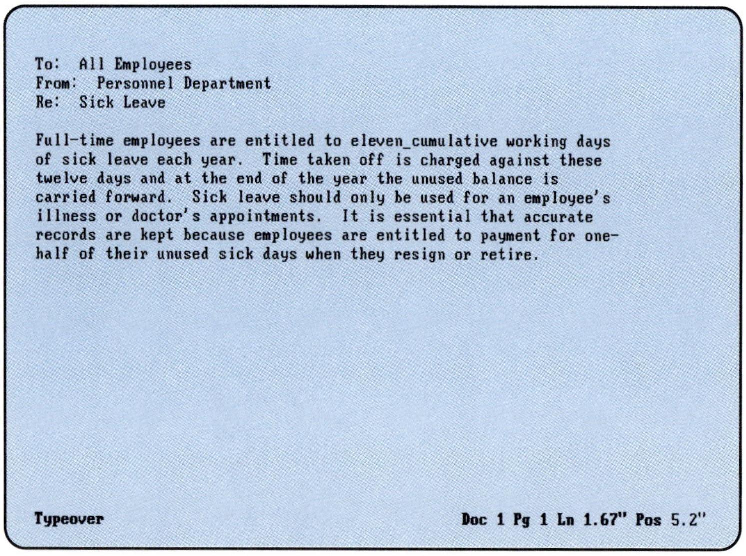

Practice Change from typeover mode to insert mode. Change back to typeover mode.

Lesson 8: Deleting Mistakes

Another common way to make corrections and modifications is to delete text.

Step 1: Move the Cursor

Before text can be deleted, the cursor must be moved to the first character to be erased. Let's change the eleven sick days to ten. The first three letters of "eleven" can simply be overwritten with "ten." Move the cursor to the first "e" in "eleven" and do this:

Type **ten**

The cursor should now be at the "v." Change to insert mode by doing this:

Press **Insert**

Step 2: Use the Delete Key

The Delete (Del) key removes the character at the cursor and shifts all characters to the right of the cursor to the left one space. To remove the characters "ven," do this:

Press **Delete** (3 times)

Your screen should now look like Figure 11.

Figure 11 Characters Erased with the Delete Key

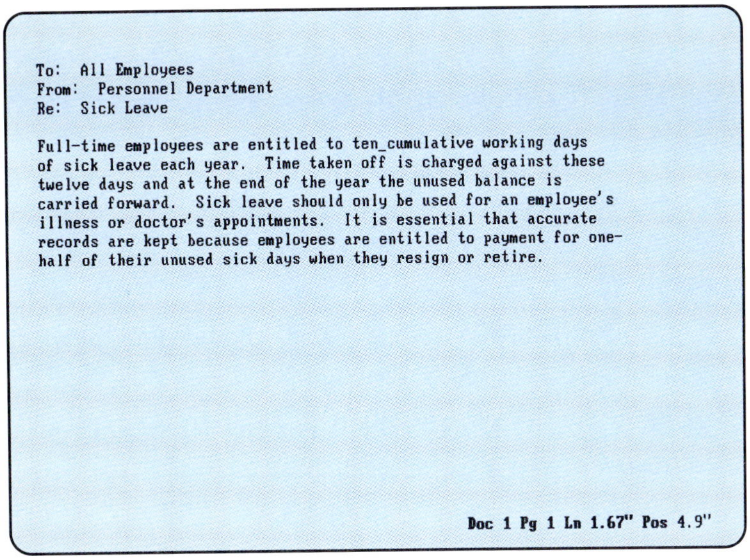

To: All Employees
From: Personnel Department
Re: Sick Leave

Full-time employees are entitled to ten_cumulative working days
of sick leave each year. Time taken off is charged against these
twelve days and at the end of the year the unused balance is
carried forward. Sick leave should only be used for an employee's
illness or doctor's appointments. It is essential that accurate
records are kept because employees are entitled to payment for one-
half of their unused sick days when they resign or retire.

Doc 1 Pg 1 Ln 1.67" Pos 4.9"

Step 3: Use the Backspace Key

The Delete key removes the character at the current cursor location. Another way to erase text is to use the Backspace key. This key removes the character to the immediate left of the cursor. For example, erase the "ten" like this:

Press **Backspace** (3 times)

Make sure insert mode is turned on and restore the memo to its original state:

Type `twelve`

Step 4: Delete an Entire Word

WordPerfect also makes it easy to erase an entire word. Position the cursor on the first character of the word "twelve." To delete the entire word and the following space, do this:

Press **Ctrl-Backspace**

Now, make sure insert mode is turned on and put the word back again:

Type `twelve`
Press **Space Bar**

Step 5: Delete an Entire Line

WordPerfect has an even more drastic command that lets you erase an entire line all at once. Move the cursor up to the beginning of the third line in the memo, the one that reads "Re: Sick Leave."

Press **Ctrl-End**
Press **Delete**

All the text from the current cursor location to the end of the line will be deleted. Pressing the Delete key erases the hard return and causes the lines of text below to move up to fill in the empty space, as shown in Figure 12.

Needless to say, Ctrl-End should be used carefully. Unfortunately, you need the deleted line for the remaining lessons, so do this:

Type `Re: Sick Leave`
Press **Enter**

Although WordPerfect has several other commands for deleting text, Delete, Backspace, Ctrl-Backspace, and Ctrl-End are the most frequently used.

Practice Use each of the following keys to remove text from the memo: Delete, Backspace, Ctrl-Backspace, and Ctrl-End. Then restore the memo to its original state.

Lesson 9: Searching and Replacing

The memo you've typed is fairly short, so making corrections throughout the entire document isn't too difficult. But you may have to modify much longer documents. In some cases, the same mistake is made in several places in the document. Most word processors have features that help you locate specific portions of text and change them if necessary.

Figure 12 An Entire Line Deleted

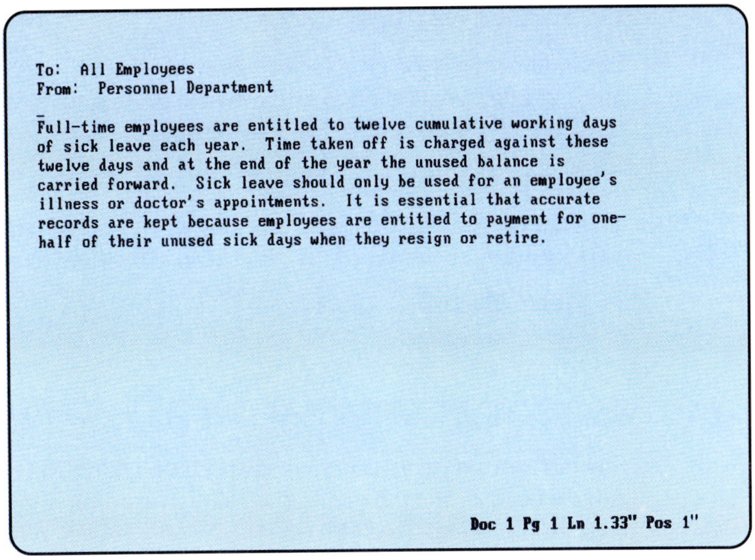

```
To:  All Employees
From:  Personnel Department

Full-time employees are entitled to twelve cumulative working days
of sick leave each year.  Time taken off is charged against these
twelve days and at the end of the year the unused balance is
carried forward.  Sick leave should only be used for an employee's
illness or doctor's appointments.  It is essential that accurate
records are kept because employees are entitled to payment for one-
half of their unused sick days when they resign or retire.

                                     Doc 1 Pg 1 Ln 1.33" Pos 1"
```

Step 1: Find Text

You may have noticed that the word "twelve" is used twice in the memo. If you found out that employees are really entitled to only eleven days of sick leave, you would have to change both instances of "twelve" to "eleven." In this case, you could simply look through the memo to make sure there are no more occurrences of "twelve" to change. If the document were much longer, however, you would have to scan through many pages of text, and you might miss a "twelve" or two. Fortunately, WordPerfect has a search command that can find text quickly and accurately. This feature can be used to make corrections or merely to locate every place in a document where a certain word or phrase is mentioned.

Execute the following commands to move the cursor to the beginning of the document and then search for the word "twelve":

Press **Home** (2 times)
Press **Up Arrow**
Press **F2**
Type **twelve**
Press **F2**

The Search command will advance the cursor just past the next location of the word "twelve." If it cannot find the word you tell it to search for, WordPerfect will display "* Not Found *" on the status line.

Step 2: Modify the Text

In many cases, you search for a piece of text because you want to change it or some text around it. Now that you've found "twelve," change it to "eleven" like this:

Press **Backspace** (6 times)
Type **eleven**

Step 3: Repeat the Search

Particular words or phrases are often repeated, especially in a long document. You can tell WordPerfect to find the next occurrence of the word or phrase without having to redo the entire Search command.

Press **F2** (2 times)

This action repeats the previous search operation, advancing the cursor to the next location of the word "twelve." Change this "twelve" to "eleven" too.

Press **Backspace** (6 times)
Type **eleven**

Step 4: Find and Replace Text

Since it is often necessary to find and then change a word or phrase, WordPerfect can do both at once. Execute the following commands to find each "eleven" and change it back to "twelve":

Press **Home** (2 times)
Press **Up Arrow**
Press **Alt-F2**
Press **Enter**
Type **eleven**
Press **F2**
Type **twelve**
Press **F2**

Pressing Alt-F2 executes the Replace command, which displays the message shown in Figure 13. Here WordPerfect is asking if you want to confirm or cancel each replacement. If you answer yes, WordPerfect will prompt you before replacing each occurrence of the text. If you answer no, or just press Enter, WordPerfect will automatically replace every occurrence of the text without confirmation. This is known as a **global search and replace.** Since you indicated a global search and replace, WordPerfect changed every "eleven" to "twelve" throughout the entire document, without stopping for confirmation.

Practice

1. Move the cursor to the beginning of the document. Use the Search command to locate each occurrence of the word "sick."
2. Move the cursor to the beginning of the document. Use the Replace command with confirmation to change each occurrence of the word "sick" to "ill." Now, use the Replace command without confirmation to change each "ill" back to "sick." Notice how WordPerfect is clever enough to preserve capitalization.

Lesson 10: Saving the Document

Word processing programs are useful not only because they make it easier to enter and edit text, but also because they let you save documents on disks. While you are editing a document, it is kept in the computer's primary memory, which gives the software quick access. The contents of primary memory are lost when the computer is turned off, so you should periodically save a document to disk

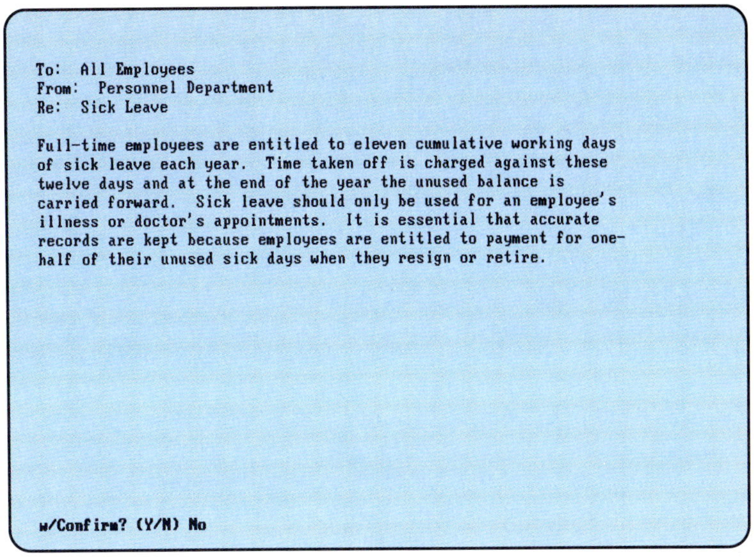

Figure 13 Prompt to Confirm Each Replacement

as you work on it, even if it is not finished yet. This guards against losing all of your work if the power should fail or if you make a drastic mistake. Saving a document in a disk file gives you a more permanent copy of your work that can be stored for future reference, printed out later, or retrieved and modified. A long document, such as an article or a book chapter, can be created and edited a little at a time. Corrections, updates, and new versions can be made without having to retype everything. A document stored on a disk is much more compact and useful than the same document printed on paper. So, before we go on, let's save the memo in a disk file.

Step 1: Invoke the Save Command

Execute WordPerfect's Save command:

Press **F10**

This command allows you to copy the memo to a disk file, yet continue working on it. If you are using a computer with two floppy drives and no hard disk, you may want to put your document file on a separate diskette. If so, insert a formatted floppy disk into drive B.

Step 2: Enter the File Name

WordPerfect will prompt you for the name of the document to be saved, as shown in Figure 14. You can enter any valid DOS file name. If you are working from a hard disk and want to save the memo in your LESSONS subdirectory, do this:

Type **\lessons\memo.doc**
Press **Enter**

If you are using a computer with two floppy drives and want to save your document in a file on the diskette in drive B, do this instead:

Type **b:memo.doc**
Press **Enter**

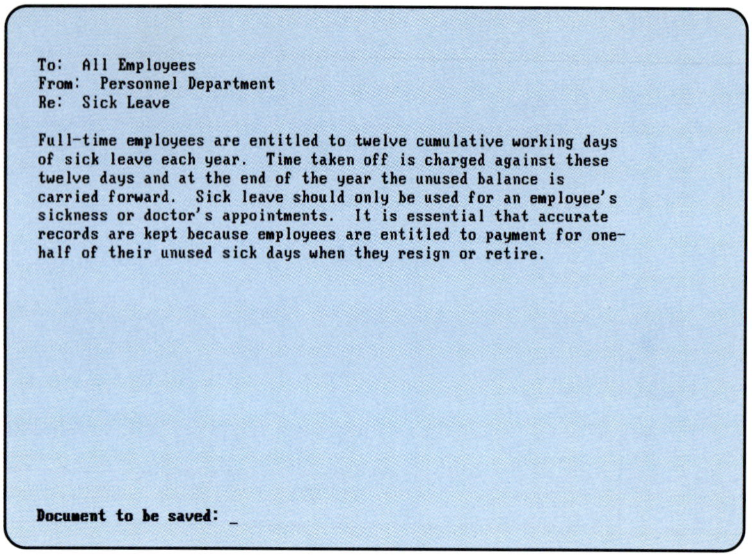
To: All Employees
From: Personnel Department
Re: Sick Leave

Full-time employees are entitled to twelve cumulative working days of sick leave each year. Time taken off is charged against these twelve days and at the end of the year the unused balance is carried forward. Sick leave should only be used for an employee's sickness or doctor's appointments. It is essential that accurate records are kept because employees are entitled to payment for one-half of their unused sick days when they resign or retire.

Document to be saved: _

***Figure 14* Name the Document to be Saved**

The document will then be copied to the disk under the name MEMO.DOC and WordPerfect will return to the editing screen. Notice that the left side of the status line now displays the path and name of your document file.

Practice

You can save a document as many times as you like while you are working on it, even if you are not finished creating it. Each time you save a document, the version on the screen and in memory will replace the version on the disk. Execute the Save command again:

Press **F10**
Press **Enter**
Type **y**

Notice how WordPerfect suggests the file name you used last time, so you don't have to retype the name every time you save the document. For safety, the program also prompts you before replacing the old version.

Lesson 11: Checking Spelling

One of WordPerfect's most useful features is its spelling checker. Let's put a misspelled word in the memo to use as an example. Go to the second line and remove an "n" from the word "Personnel."

Step 1: Invoke the Spelling Checker

If you are using WordPerfect on a microcomputer with no hard disk, then you must now put the diskette labeled "Speller" in drive B. If your computer has a hard disk, the spelling checker is probably already installed on it.

Execute this command to invoke the spelling checker:

Press **Ctrl-F2**

WordPerfect will present the Check menu shown in Figure 15. To check the entire memo, select the Document option:

Type **d**

Note that you can select an option from a WordPerfect menu either by typing its number or an easy-to-remember letter, usually the first letter of the option, shown in boldface.

After the dictionary has been loaded from the disk into memory, the spelling checker begins to examine each word in your document to see if it is in the dictionary.

Step 2: Correct Spelling Mistakes

When WordPerfect finds a word it doesn't recognize, it highlights the word, suggests possible replacements, and displays the Not Found menu at the bottom of the screen, as shown in Figure 16. To automatically replace "personel" with the second suggested correction, "personnel," do this:

Type **b**

WordPerfect will then check the rest of the memo, find it to be correct, and give you a word count. Press any key to return to the editing screen.

In most longer documents, WordPerfect would likely encounter several more words not in its dictionary. Not all of these would necessarily be misspellings. The spelling checker, for example, cannot recognize many proper names, technical terms, and slang. Nor can it recognize some forms of correctly spelled words. In these cases, you can choose the Skip Once option or the Skip option from the Not Found menu. If you choose Skip Once, WordPerfect will leave the word intact and go on, but it will stop at the next occurrence of the word. If you choose Skip, the program will ignore all occurrences of the word for the rest of the document.

If the spelling checker cannot suggest a correction for a misspelled word, you can choose the Edit option from the Not Found menu and correct the word yourself.

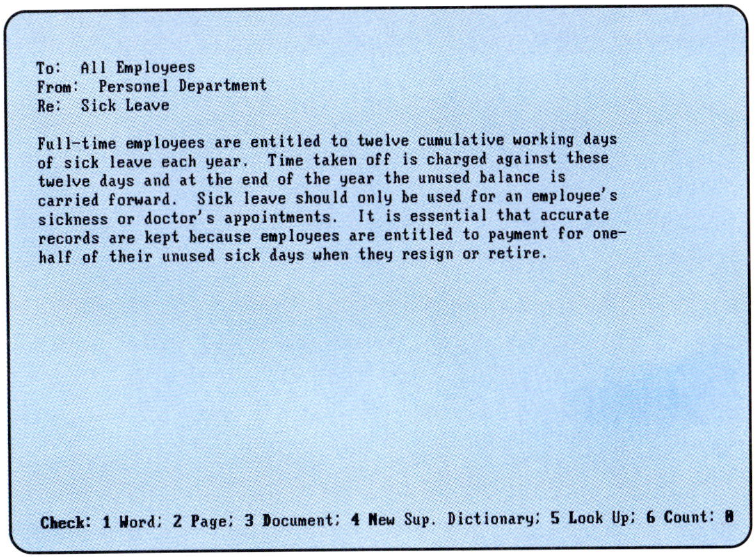

Figure 15 The Spelling Check Menu

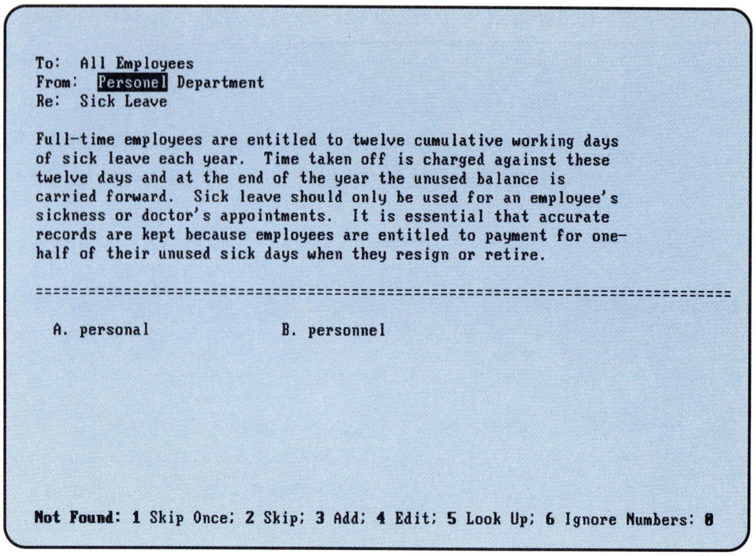

Figure 16 The Not Found Menu

Practice

1. A spelling checker cannot find in its dictionary every correctly spelled word, especially names. Insert your last name somewhere in the document. Then execute a spelling check. Select the Skip option from the Not Found menu. Delete your name after you are finished.
2. The spelling checker can be used to check an individual word in your document. Move the cursor to the word "Department." Invoke the spelling checker, but this time select the Word option from the Check menu. If the word is spelled correctly, WordPerfect will simply advance the cursor to the next word. You can continue to check the words one by one. Exit the spelling checker and return to the editing screen:

   Press **F7**

3. You can also use the spelling checker to look up a word that is not in the document. Invoke the spelling checker, but this time select the Look Up option. Enter a purposely misspelled word and see if WordPerfect can suggest the appropriate correction. Try another misspelled word if you like. When you are finished, exit the spelling checker and return to the editing screen:

   Press **F7**

Lesson 12: Working with Blocks of Text

In addition to individual characters, words, and lines, most word processing packages let you specify and manipulate blocks of text. In WordPerfect, a **block** is a section of text that can be of any size—from a single character to an entire document. Once a block is designated, or marked, it can be moved, copied, or deleted.

Step 1: Mark a Block

You're going to need more text in your document to better illustrate WordPerfect's block commands. Move the cursor to the end of the document and insert a blank line:

Press **Home** (2 times)
Press **Down Arrow**
Press **Enter** (2 times)

Now, type this paragraph without pressing Enter:

Full-time employees earn twenty-four working days of vacation per year. These are in addition to official company holidays and must be used by the end of each year. Accurate records of vacation leave taken must be kept because employees will be paid for their unused days when they resign or retire.

Leave a blank line at the end of the document:

Press **Enter** (2 times)

The paragraph you just typed is the block you're going to work with. To mark the block, move the cursor to the first character in the paragraph and execute the Block command:

Press **Up Arrow** (6 times)
Press **Alt-F4**

The message "Block on" will flash on and off in the status line. Move the cursor to the last character to be included in the block, in this case, the end of the document:

Press **Home** (2 times)
Press **Down Arrow**

As the cursor moves, the text in the block will change to reverse video (dark characters against a light background) as shown in Figure 17. You can increase or reduce the size of the marked block by simply moving the cursor.

Step 2: Move a Block

Once a block has been marked, it's easy to move it to another position in the document. Suppose you want to put the vacation leave paragraph before the sick leave paragraph. First, activate the Move menu, shown in Figure 18:

Press **Ctrl-F4**

To move the marked block, select the Block option:

Type **b**

Another menu appears, as shown in Figure 19. Choose the Move option, move the cursor to the first character in the sick leave paragraph, and press Enter:

Type **m**
Press **Up Arrow** (8 times)
Press **Enter**

Figure 17 A Marked Block

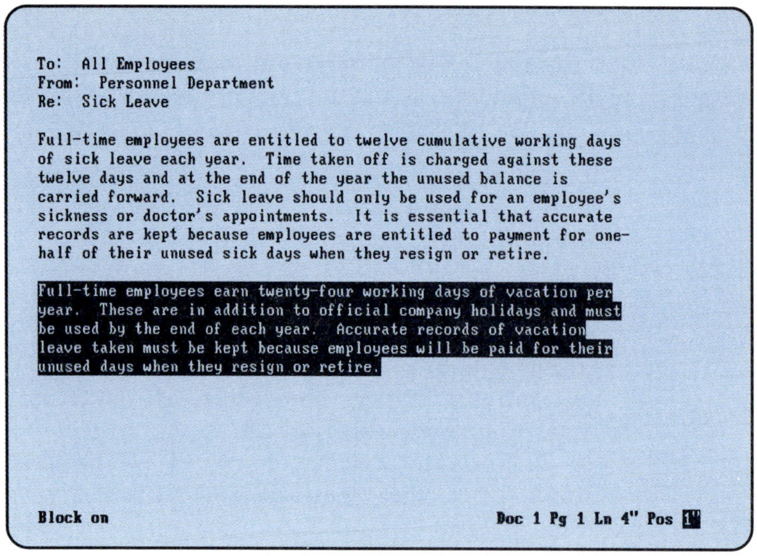

The marked block will be removed from its original position and inserted in the new location.

Step 3: Copy a Block

Sometimes it's useful to copy text from one location to another. You might need an exact duplicate or a version that's only slightly different. Instead of retyping the text in the new location, you can mark a block, copy the text, then make any necessary modifications. This can save time when you are working on documents that contain repeated sections of text.

Just for practice, let's make a copy of the vacation leave paragraph and put it at the end of the memo. Although the duplicate paragraphs won't make sense in your particular document, the exercise will demonstrate how to copy a block.

Figure 18 The Move Menu

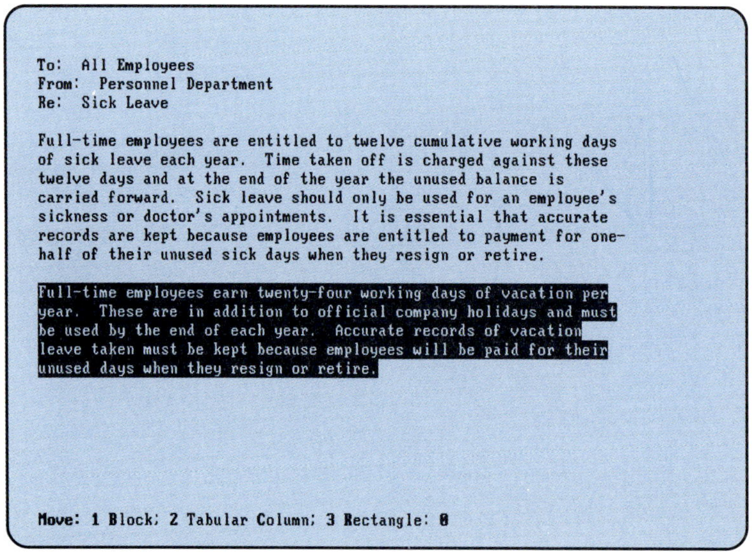

Figure 19 The Move-Block Menu

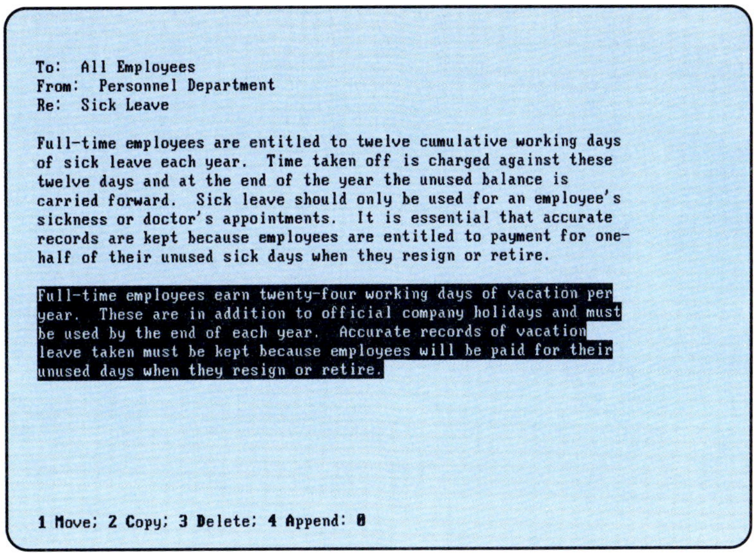

First, mark the block to be copied, in this case the first paragraph. If the cursor is not already at the first character of the paragraph, move it there. Then do this:

Press **Alt-F4**
Press **Down Arrow** (6 times)

Now, activate the Move menu, select the Block option, select the Copy option, move the cursor to the end of the document, and press Enter:

Press **Ctrl-F4**
Type **b**
Type **c**
Press **Home** (2 times)
Press **Down Arrow**
Press **Enter**

WordPerfect will duplicate the vacation leave paragraph at the end of the document, as shown in Figure 20.

Step 4: Delete a Block

You now have two copies of the vacation leave paragraph, but you need only one for this memo. This is a good opportunity to try deleting a block. Instead of deleting every character, word, or line in a paragraph, you can erase the whole thing at once. For example, mark the first vacation leave paragraph and then delete it:

Press **Home** (2 times)
Press **Up Arrow**
Press **Down Arrow** (4 times)
Press **Alt-F4**
Press **Down Arrow** (6 times)
Press **Delete**

Figure 20 First Paragraph Copied at End of Document

```
To:  All Employees
From:  Personnel Department
Re:  Sick Leave

Full-time employees earn twenty-four working days of vacation per
year.  These are in addition to official company holidays and must
be used by the end of each year.  Accurate records of vacation
leave taken must be kept because employees will be paid for their
unused days when they resign or retire.

Full-time employees are entitled to twelve cumulative working days
of sick leave each year.  Time taken off is charged against these
twelve days and at the end of the year the unused balance is
carried forward.  Sick leave should only be used for an employee's
sickness or doctor's appointments.  It is essential that accurate
records are kept because employees are entitled to payment for one-
half of their unused sick days when they resign or retire.

Full-time employees earn twenty-four working days of vacation per
year.  These are in addition to official company holidays and must
be used by the end of each year.  Accurate records of vacation
leave taken must be kept because employees will be paid for their
unused days when they resign or retire.
C:\LESSONS\MEMO.DOC                          Doc 1 Pg 1 Ln 4" Pos 1"
```

WordPerfect will display the prompt

```
Delete block? (Y/N) No
```

Since you are sure that you want to delete the marked block, answer yes:

Type **y**

Figure 21 shows the result.

Practice

1. Mark the heading of the memo (the first three lines) as a block.
2. Copy the marked block to the end of the memo.
3. Mark the lines you just copied as a block and then delete it.

Figure 21 Paragraph Deleted

```
To:  All Employees
From:  Personnel Department
Re:  Sick Leave

Full-time employees are entitled to twelve cumulative working days
of sick leave each year.  Time taken off is charged against these
twelve days and at the end of the year the unused balance is
carried forward.  Sick leave should only be used for an employee's
sickness or doctor's appointments.  It is essential that accurate
records are kept because employees are entitled to payment for one-
half of their unused sick days when they resign or retire.

Full-time employees earn twenty-four working days of vacation per
year.  These are in addition to official company holidays and must
be used by the end of each year.  Accurate records of vacation
leave taken must be kept because employees will be paid for their
unused days when they resign or retire.

C:\LESSONS\MEMO.DOC                       Doc 1 Pg 1 Ln 1.67" Pos 1"
```

Lesson 13: Canceling Commands

At one time or another, everyone who uses a word processing package makes a mistake deleting text or executing some other command. Fortunately, WordPerfect has a Cancel command that can restore accidentally erased text or stop an executing command. The Cancel command, which is invoked by pressing the F1 function key, can do the following:

- Return from a WordPerfect menu or cancel your response to a WordPerfect prompt before the response is final
- Turn off, or unmark a marked block
- Restore any of the three most recently deleted text items

Whenever you erase text, whether a single character or an entire block, WordPerfect temporarily stores that text in a special area of memory. Up to three deletions are saved, allowing you to reverse a delete command. For example, suppose you accidentally delete the last paragraph in the memo.

Step 1: Delete the Paragraph

Mark the last paragraph as a block and delete it by following these instructions:

Press **Home** (2 times)
Press **Down Arrow**
Press **Up Arrow** (6 times)
Press **Alt-F4**
Press **Down Arrow** (6 times)
Press **Delete**
Type **y**

Step 2: Set the Cursor

Now, suppose you realize your mistake and want the deleted paragraph back. First, you would move the cursor to the place where you want to insert the restored text. In this case, the cursor is already at the correct location, so you don't have to move it.

Step 3: Invoke the Cancel Command

Execute the Cancel command to activate WordPerfect's Undelete menu (see Figure 22) and restore the most recently deleted item at the current cursor location:

Press **F1**
Type **r**

The deleted text will be reinstated. To restore a previously deleted item, you would type 2 or P to select Previous Deletion, until the text you want to restore is displayed in reverse video.

Practice

Execute the Cancel command. Select the second option from the Undelete menu to examine the previous deletion. You don't want to insert this text back into your document, so cancel the Cancel command:

Press **F7**

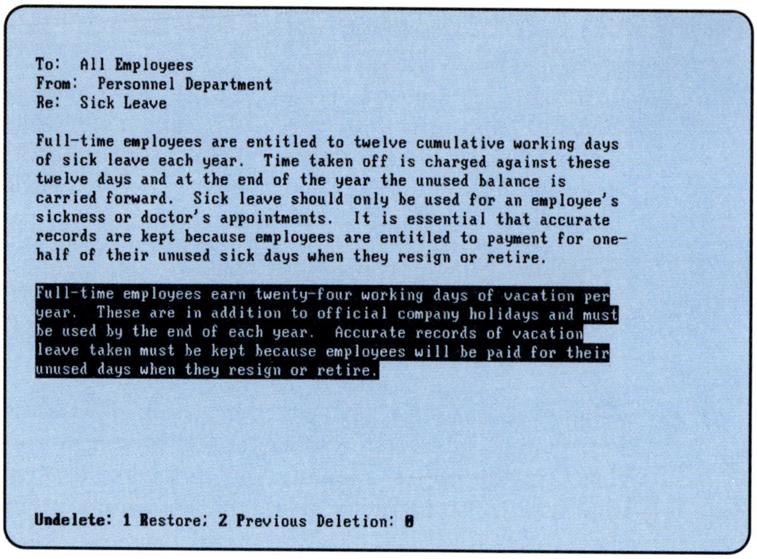

Figure 22 The Undelete Menu

Lesson 14: Formatting Characters

Formatting a document means specifying how it will look when it is printed. True what-you-see-is-what-you-get (WYSIWYG) word processing software has an exact correspondence between the screen and the printed page. WordPerfect is not a WYSIWYG word processing package; some formatting specifications show up on the display screen, but others only become evident when the document is printed. WordPerfect has many features that let you format characters, lines, and entire pages. Let's start with the character formatting options.

Step 1: Underline Text

WordPerfect offers several ways to emphasize characters in a document. Let's add an underlined heading before the sick leave paragraph. First, make sure insert mode is turned on. Then follow these instructions:

Press **Home** (2 times)
Press **Up Arrow**
Press **Down Arrow** (4 times)
Press **F8**
Type **Sick Leave**
Press **F8**
Press **Enter** (2 times)

The F8 key turns underline on and off. On the screen, underlined text may appear underlined, highlighted, or in a different color, depending on the type of monitor you have and the way that WordPerfect has been set up (see Figure 23). When the document is printed, however, the heading "Sick Leave" will be underlined.

Step 2: Boldface Text

WordPerfect makes it just as easy to boldface text. Follow these directions to add a boldfaced heading before the vacation leave paragraph:

Press **Home** (2 times)
Press **Down Arrow**

Figure 23 Underlined Text

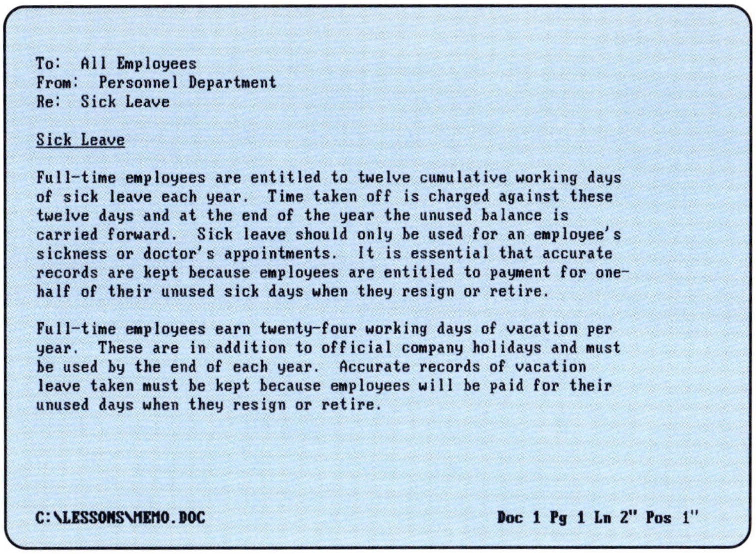

To: All Employees
From: Personnel Department
Re: Sick Leave

Sick Leave

Full-time employees are entitled to twelve cumulative working days of sick leave each year. Time taken off is charged against these twelve days and at the end of the year the unused balance is carried forward. Sick leave should only be used for an employee's sickness or doctor's appointments. It is essential that accurate records are kept because employees are entitled to payment for one-half of their unused sick days when they resign or retire.

Full-time employees earn twenty-four working days of vacation per year. These are in addition to official company holidays and must be used by the end of each year. Accurate records of vacation leave taken must be kept because employees will be paid for their unused days when they resign or retire.

C:\LESSONS\MEMO.DOC Doc 1 Pg 1 Ln 2" Pos 1"

Press **Up Arrow** (6 times)
Press **F6**
Type **`Vacation Leave`**
Press **F6**
Press **Enter** (2 times)

The F6 key turns boldface on and off. On the screen, boldfaced text appears in brighter characters, in a different color, or in reverse video, depending on your monitor and the way in which WordPerfect has been set up (see Figure 24). When the document is printed, however, the "Vacation Leave" heading will be boldfaced.

Figure 24 Boldfaced Text

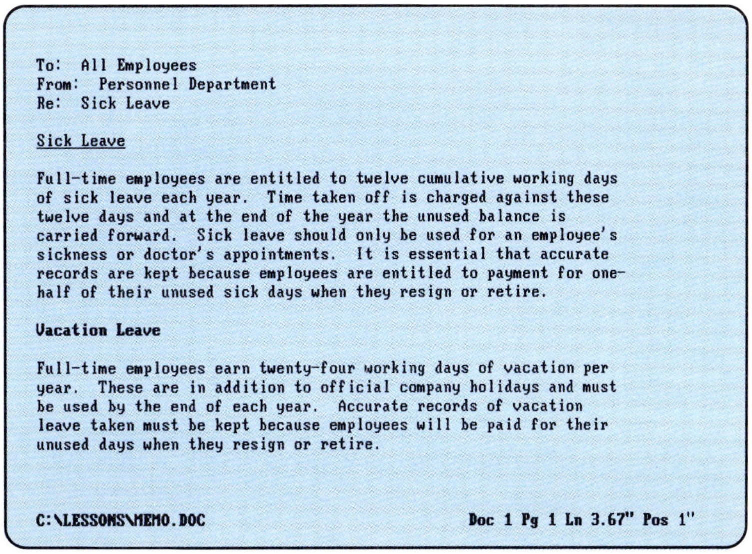

To: All Employees
From: Personnel Department
Re: Sick Leave

Sick Leave

Full-time employees are entitled to twelve cumulative working days of sick leave each year. Time taken off is charged against these twelve days and at the end of the year the unused balance is carried forward. Sick leave should only be used for an employee's sickness or doctor's appointments. It is essential that accurate records are kept because employees are entitled to payment for one-half of their unused sick days when they resign or retire.

Vacation Leave

Full-time employees earn twenty-four working days of vacation per year. These are in addition to official company holidays and must be used by the end of each year. Accurate records of vacation leave taken must be kept because employees will be paid for their unused days when they resign or retire.

C:\LESSONS\MEMO.DOC Doc 1 Pg 1 Ln 3.67" Pos 1"

Step 3: Using other Character Formats

Underline and boldface are the two most commonly used character formats, but WordPerfect also provides other options. Follow these directions to activate the Font menu and select the Appearance option:

Press **Ctrl-F8**
Type **a**

The menu shown in Figure 25 will appear on the screen. In addition to boldface and underline, this menu also lists double underline, italics, outline, shadow, small capitals, redline, and strikeout character formats. Exit the menu when you are finished examining it:

Press **F7**

Practice

1. In Steps 1 and 2, you formatted new characters as you typed them. You can also format existing text. Find the word "essential" in the first paragraph of the memo and move the cursor to the beginning of the word. Mark this word as a block. Now underline the word:

   Press **F8**

2. Certain combinations of character formats are allowed. For example, text can be underlined and boldfaced. Mark the word "essential" in the first paragraph as a block again. This time, boldface the word:

   Press **F6**

   The word "essential" should now appear underlined and boldfaced.

3. Choose some other word in the memo and mark it as a block. Activate the Font menu and select the Appearance option:

   Press **Ctrl-F8**
   Type **a**

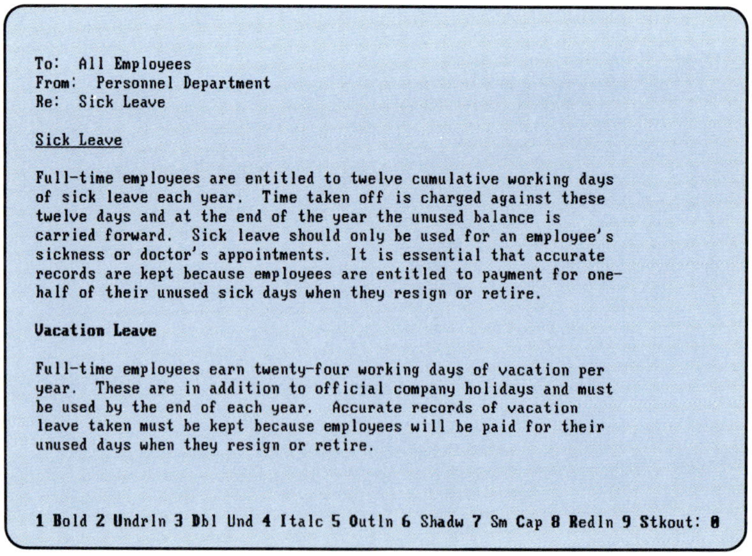
To: All Employees
From: Personnel Department
Re: Sick Leave

Sick Leave

Full-time employees are entitled to twelve cumulative working days of sick leave each year. Time taken off is charged against these twelve days and at the end of the year the unused balance is carried forward. Sick leave should only be used for an employee's sickness or doctor's appointments. It is essential that accurate records are kept because employees are entitled to payment for one-half of their unused sick days when they resign or retire.

Vacation Leave

Full-time employees earn twenty-four working days of vacation per year. These are in addition to official company holidays and must be used by the end of each year. Accurate records of vacation leave taken must be kept because employees will be paid for their unused days when they resign or retire.

1 Bold 2 Undrln 3 Dbl Und 4 Italc 5 Outln 6 Shadw 7 Sm Cap 8 Redln 9 Stkout: 0

Figure 25 The Font-Appearance Menu

Select a character format option other than underline or boldface for the marked word. The appearance of the word may or may not change on the screen, depending on the type of monitor you have. It will be printed in the format you selected, however, if your printer is capable of producing it.

4. In WordPerfect, character formatting is indicated by hidden codes stored before and after the formatted text. You turn off character formatting by deleting these codes. Let's turn off the formatting you turned on in the previous Practice exercises. Move the cursor to the space just before the word "essential" in the first paragraph, and do this:

   Press **Right Arrow**
   Press **Delete**

   WordPerfect will ask you if you want to delete the underline code.

   Type **y**

   Now, turn off the boldface:

   Press **Delete**
   Type **y**

   Use what you have learned to turn off the character format you turned on in Practice exercise 3.

Lesson 15: Formatting Lines

Like most word processing packages, WordPerfect has a number of features that control the appearance of lines, paragraphs, and other sections of text. The most common formatting operations allow you to change margins, set tab stops, turn justification on or off, set line spacing, set line height, and center text.

Step 1: Change Margins

WordPerfect initially sets both the left and right margins of a document at one inch from the edge of the paper. Although these margins are usually adequate, you may need to change them for some documents. Let's change the left and right margins of the memo to 1.25 inch. First, move the cursor to the beginning of the document, where you want the new margins to begin:

Press **Home** (2 times)
Press **Up Arrow**

Next, activate the Format menu (see Figure 26) and select the first option to display the Line menu (see Figure 27):

Press **Shift-F8**
Type **L**

Select the Margins option and enter the new left and right margin measurements:

Type **m**
Type **1.25"**
Press **Enter**
Type **1.25"**
Press **Enter**

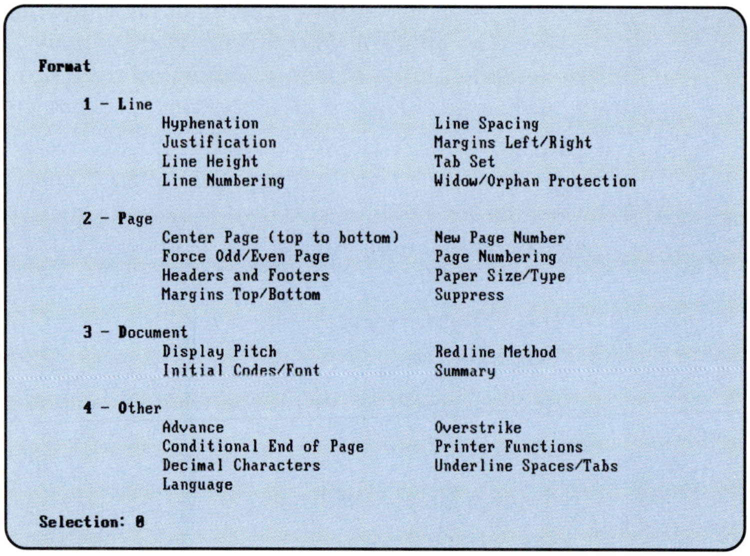

Figure 26 The Format Menu

Execute the Exit command to leave the Line menu and return to the editing screen:

Press **F7**

The new margins will be established, as shown in Figure 28. They will remain in effect in this document unless you change them later.

Step 2: Set Tab Stops

Like typewriters, computer keyboards have at least one Tab key. When this key is pressed, the cursor advances to some preset location. By default, WordPerfect initially sets tab stops at half-inch intervals. For example, move the cursor to the next tab stop:

Press **Tab**

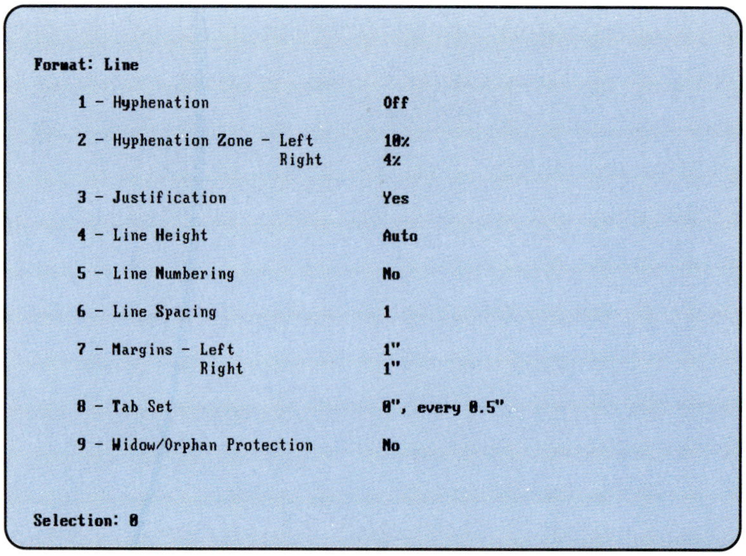

Figure 27 The Line Menu

Figure 28 New Margins Have Been Set

```
To:  All Employees
From:  Personnel Department
Re:  Sick Leave

Sick Leave

Full-time employees are entitled to twelve cumulative working days
of sick leave each year.  Time taken off is charged against these
twelve days and at the end of the year the unused balance is
carried forward.  Sick leave should only be used for an employee's
sickness or doctor's appointments.  It is essential that accurate
records are kept because employees are entitled to payment for one-
half of their unused sick days when they resign or retire.

Vacation Leave

Full-time employees earn twenty-four working days of vacation per
year.  These are in addition to official company holidays and must
be used by the end of each year.  Accurate records of vacation
leave taken must be kept because employees will be paid for their
unused days when they resign or retire.

C:\LESSONS\MEMO.DOC                              Doc 1 Pg 1 Ln 1" Pos 1.25"
```

If insert mode is turned on, pressing the Tab key pushes any existing characters to the right; if typeover mode is turned on, the Tab key moves the cursor over existing text. If Insert mode was turned on when you pressed Tab, remove the Tab:

Press **Backspace**

To view or change the current tab settings, activate the Format menu, select the Line option, and then select the Tab Set option:

Press **Shift-F8**
Type **L**
Type **t**

Figure 29 shows the Tab Set menu. The dotted line near the bottom of the screen is a **ruler line** showing the current tab stops. Each "L" denotes a left-justified tab

Figure 29 The Tab Set Menu

```
  To:  All Employees
  From:  Personnel Department
  Re:  Sick Leave

  Sick Leave

  Full-time employees are entitled to twelve cumulative working
  days of sick leave each year.  Time taken off is charged
  against these twelve days and at the end of the year the
  unused balance is carried forward.  Sick leave should only be
  used for an employee's sickness or doctor's appointments.  It
  is essential that accurate records are kept because employees
  are entitled to payment for one-half of their unused sick days
  when they resign or retire.

  Vacation Leave

  Full-time employees earn twenty-four working days of vacation
  per year.  These are in addition to official company holidays
  and must be used by the end of each year.  Accurate records
L....L....L....L....L....L....L....L....L....L....L....L....L....L....L....L...
|    ^    |    ^    |    ^    |    ^    |    ^    |    ^    |    ^    |    ^
1"        2"        3"        4"        5"        6"        7"        8"
Delete EOL (clear tabs); Enter Number (set tab); Del (clear tab);
Left; Center; Right; Decimal; .= Dot Leader; Press Exit when done.
```

stop. You can use the Left Arrow and Right Arrow keys to move the cursor within the ruler line, and delete existing tab stops with the Delete key. You can add a new tab stop at any position by typing one of the following characters:

L	Inserts a left-justified tab stop, which aligns text along the left side at the tab stop.
C	Inserts a centered tab stop, which centers text at the tab stop.
R	Inserts a right-justified tab stop, which aligns text along the right side at the tab stop.
D	Inserts a decimal tab stop, which aligns numbers by their decimal points at the tab stop.

If you like, you can also delete the existing tab stops in the ruler line by pressing Ctrl-End and insert all new tab stops. For now, just leave the tab stops where they are. Exit the Tab Stop menu and return to the editing screen:

Press **F7** (2 times)

Step 3: Turn Off Justification

When a document is justified, text is aligned exactly to both the left and right margins. If necessary, **soft spaces** are automatically generated by the word processor and inserted between words to give the text a block look. (**Hard spaces** are inserted only when you press the Space Bar.) By default, WordPerfect's justification feature is turned on, but the on-screen text is not displayed as justified. Justification becomes evident only when the document is printed. Justified text looks best when it is produced by a printer that can do **proportional spacing,** which allots different amounts of space for different characters. The combination of justification and proportional spacing produces text similar to the typeset material in this book.

If your printer cannot do proportional spacing, it is better to turn off justification. The resulting text will have a ragged right margin similar to that of typewritten text. To turn off justification for the memo, follow these directions:

Press **Home** (2 times)
Press **Up Arrow**
Press **Shift-F8**
Type **L**
Type **j**
Type **n**
Press **F7**

These actions move the cursor to the beginning of the document, activate the Format menu, select the Line option, select the Justification option, turn off justification, and return to the editing screen. Justification will then be turned off from the cursor position to the end of the document, but the appearance of text on the screen will not change.

Step 4: Set Line Spacing

Word processing packages allow you to determine the line spacing for documents. By default, WordPerfect's line spacing is set to 1. In other words, lines are automatically single spaced. This means that no blank lines are left between successive lines of text whenever a word wrap occurs or whenever you press the Enter key. Double spacing leaves one blank line between successive lines of text, triple spacing leaves two blank lines, and so on.

Suppose you want your document to be double spaced. First you move the cursor to where you want double spacing to begin. Then you activate the Format menu, select the Line option, select the Line Spacing option, and specify the line spacing. Follow these directions:

Press **Home** (2 times)
Press **Up Arrow**
Press **Shift-F8**
Type **L**
Type **s**
Type **2**
Press **Enter**
Press **F7**

The memo will be double spaced, as shown in Figure 30. Any new text you type from the current cursor location to the end of the document will also be double spaced.

Since memos are usually single spaced, change the line spacing from 2 back to 1:

Press **Shift-F8**
Type **L**
Type **s**
Type **1**
Press **Enter**
Press **F7**

Step 5: Set Line Height

In WordPerfect, the distance between lines of printed text is called **line height.** This is not the same as line spacing. *Line height* is measured from the bottom of one line to the bottom of the next line below. *Line spacing* is one plus the number of blank lines left between successive lines of text. In practice, line height is

Figure 30 Double-Spaced Memo

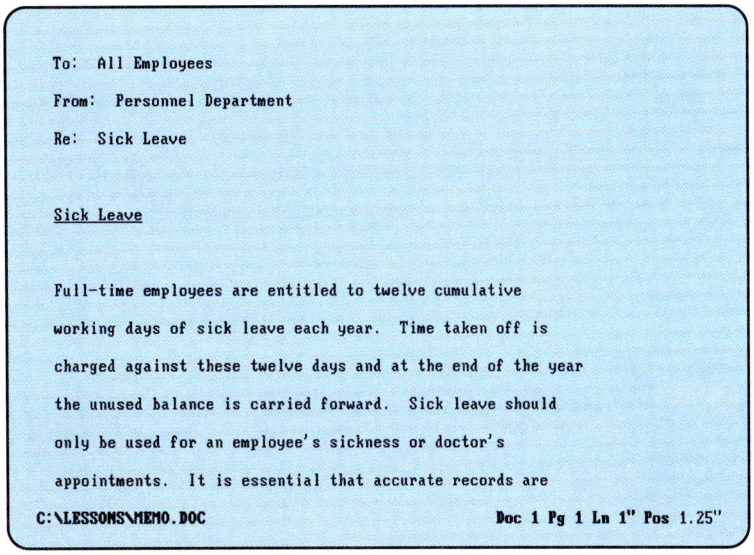
To: All Employees

From: Personnel Department

Re: Sick Leave

Sick Leave

Full-time employees are entitled to twelve cumulative

working days of sick leave each year. Time taken off is

charged against these twelve days and at the end of the year

the unused balance is carried forward. Sick leave should

only be used for an employee's sickness or doctor's

appointments. It is essential that accurate records are

C:\LESSONS\MEMO.DOC Doc 1 Pg 1 Ln 1" Pos 1.25"

seldom changed. WordPerfect's default line height yields 6 lines of text per vertical inch, which is the standard line height of most typewriters. To change line height, you activate the Format menu, select the Line option, select the Line Height option, select the Fixed option, and then enter a new line height measurement. Follow these directions:

Press **Shift-F8**
Type **L**
Type **h**
Type **f**

WordPerfect will then display the current line height in inches. Let's just leave it at 0.17", which is 1/6-inch. Return to the editing screen:

Press **F7** (2 times)

Step 6: Center Text

Many documents require certain headings or other text to be centered between the left and right margins. To do this manually is tedious. Fortunately, WordPerfect, like most word processing packages, can automatically center text.

Let's center the headings above the two paragraphs in our memo. Follow these instructions to center the heading "Sick Leave":

Press **Home** (2 times)
Press **Up Arrow**
Press **Down Arrow** (4 times)
Press **Shift-F6**
Press **Left Arrow**

Now, center the "Vacation Leave" heading:

Press **Down Arrow** (11 times)
Press **Shift-F6**
Press **Down Arrow**

Your screen should look like Figure 31.

You can also center a new line of text as you type it. You would simply move the cursor to the left margin of the new line, press Shift-F6 to move the cursor to the center of the line, type the text, and press Enter.

Practice

1. Move the cursor to the beginning of the document. Change the left and right margins to 2 inches. See how the text is automatically reformatted within the new margins. Change them back to 1.25 inches.
2. Triple space your entire document and see how it looks. Then change line spacing back to 1.
3. Type the heading "Unpaid Leave" at the end of the memo, centering it as you type it. When you are finished, delete the heading from the document.

Lesson 16: Formatting Pages

Page formatting features affect entire pages of text. WordPerfect has several commands that let you specify how pages are laid out. Although you don't need to change any of the default page format settings for our simple memo, you may

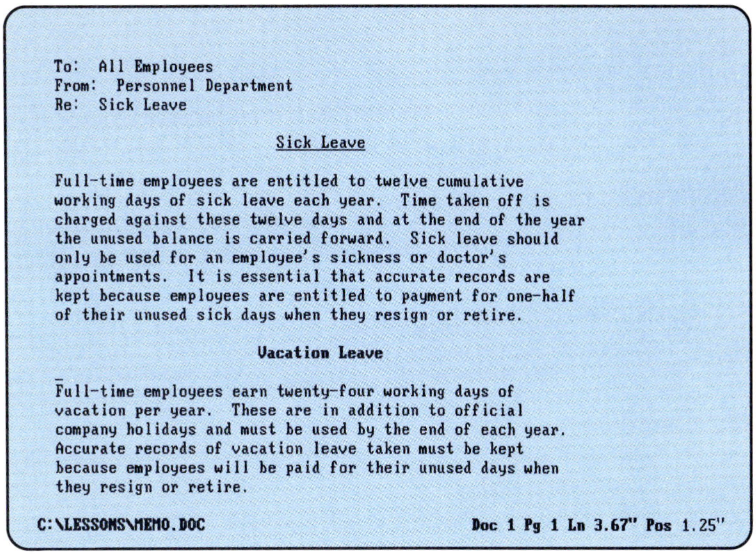
To: All Employees
From: Personnel Department
Re: Sick Leave

Sick Leave

Full-time employees are entitled to twelve cumulative working days of sick leave each year. Time taken off is charged against these twelve days and at the end of the year the unused balance is carried forward. Sick leave should only be used for an employee's sickness or doctor's appointments. It is essential that accurate records are kept because employees are entitled to payment for one-half of their unused sick days when they resign or retire.

Vacation Leave

Full-time employees earn twenty-four working days of vacation per year. These are in addition to official company holidays and must be used by the end of each year. Accurate records of vacation leave taken must be kept because employees will be paid for their unused days when they resign or retire.

C:\LESSONS\MEMO.DOC Doc 1 Pg 1 Ln 3.67" Pos 1.25"

Figure 31 Centered Headings

need to change them for other documents. Let's look at the commands that control paper size and type, top and bottom margins, page breaks, and page numbering.

Step 1: Set the Paper Size and Type

Standard letter-size paper is 8½ inches wide and 11 inches long. Given a standard line height of 6 lines per inch, the number of lines on letter-size paper is 6 times 11, or 66. WordPerfect's default paper size is 8½ by 11 inches, but this can be changed. First, activate the Format menu and then select the Page option:

Press **Shift-F8**
Type **p**

WordPerfect will display the Page menu (see Figure 32). Now, select the Paper Size option:

Type **s**

Here you could select a different paper size (see Figure 33). Let's leave it at 8½ by 11 inches.

Press **F7**

Next, the Paper Type menu appears, shown in Figure 34. Here you could select a paper type. Let's leave it as Standard. Return to the editing screen:

Press **F7** (2 times)

Step 2: Set the Top and Bottom Margins

Most documents are printed with some blank space at the top and bottom of every page. By default, WordPerfect leaves one-inch top and bottom margins. You can change these settings from the Page Format menu:

Press **Shift-F8**
Type **p**
Type **m**

Figure 32 The Page Menu

```
Format: Page

     1 - Center Page (top to bottom)    No

     2 - Force Odd/Even Page

     3 - Headers

     4 - Footers

     5 - Margins - Top                  1"
                   Bottom               1"

     6 - New Page Number                1
           (example: 3 or iii)

     7 - Page Numbering                 No page numbering

     8 - Paper Size                     8.5" x 11"
               Type                     Standard

     9 - Suppress (this page only)

Selection: 0
```

Here you could enter new top and bottom margin measurements. Let's leave them at one inch. Return to the editing screen.

Press **F7** (3 times)

Step 3: Start a New Page

The actual number of lines of text printed on a page depends on several factors. For example, WordPerfect's default line height is 1/6 inch. The default page length is 11 inches (66 lines), with a top margin of 1 inch (6 lines) and a bottom margin of 1 inch (6 lines). That leaves 66 minus 12, or 54, as the default number of lines of text printed on a page.

Figure 33 The Paper Size Menu

```
Format: Paper Size

     1 - Standard                 (8.5" x 11")

     2 - Standard Landscape       (11" x 8.5")

     3 - Legal                    (8.5" x 14")

     4 - Legal Landscape          (14" x 8.5")

     5 - Envelope                 (9.5" x 4")

     6 - Half Sheet               (5.5" x 8.5")

     7 - US Government            (8" x 11")

     8 - A4                       (210mm x 297mm)

     9 - A4 Landscape             (297mm x 210mm)

     0 - Other

Selection: 1
```

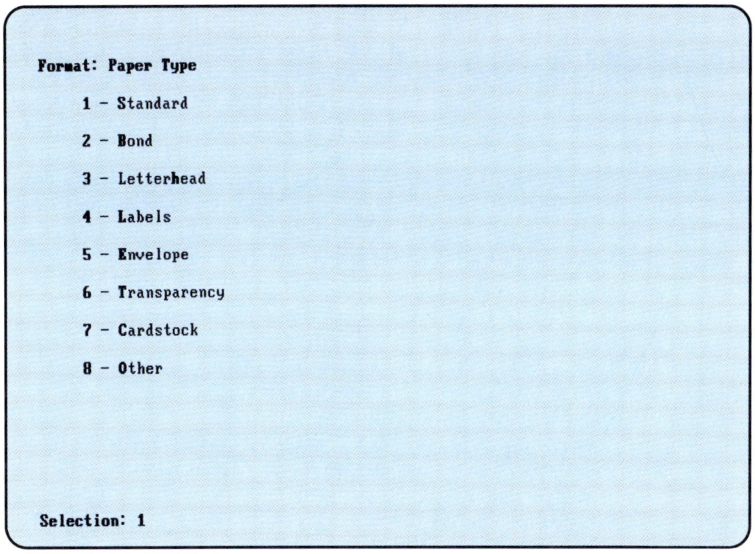

Figure 34 The Paper Type Menu

As you type text with WordPerfect, the word wrap feature automatically starts new lines. WordPerfect also automatically starts new pages. Assuming the default page-format settings are in effect, a soft page break is inserted after every 54 lines you type. A **soft page break** is a division between two pages automatically generated by the word processing software. It is symbolized on the screen by a horizontal line of dashes. This line is not actually printed on paper; it simply indicates the place where a new page will begin.

Although WordPerfect's automatic page-break feature is convenient, you may sometimes want to have a page with fewer than 54 lines. A new page can be forced by pressing Ctrl-Enter to insert a **hard page break.** This is a division between two pages that is manually generated by the user. It is symbolized on the screen by a horizontal line of equal signs. You can begin a new page at any point within a document simply by pressing Ctrl-Enter. For example, let's insert a hard page break between the two paragraphs in the memo:

Press **Home** (2 times)
Press **Up Arrow**
Press **Down Arrow** (15 times)
Press **Ctrl-Enter**

Your screen should look like Figure 35. If this document were printed, the text below the line of equal signs would begin on a new page.

A hard page break can be removed from a document with the Delete or Backspace key. Let's remove the hard page break you just inserted. Make sure the cursor is still at the beginning of the line with the "Vacation Leave" heading.

Press **Backspace**

The page break will disappear.

Step 4: Set the Page Numbering

WordPerfect automatically keeps track of page numbers while you work on a document and displays the current page number on the screen in the status line (see Figure 35). But WordPerfect does not print page numbers unless you tell it

Figure 35 A Hard Page Break

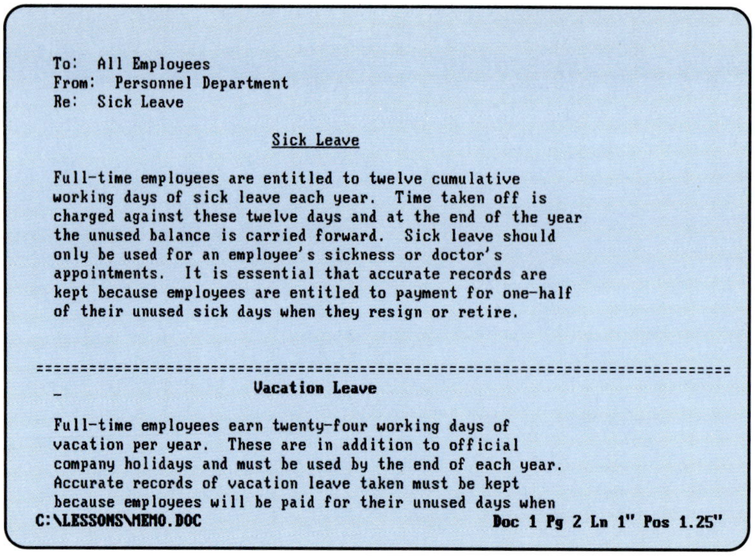

to do so. Although we don't need a page number on our single-page memo, let's see how you would turn on printed page numbering.

Press **Shift-F8**
Type **p**
Type **p**

WordPerfect will display the Page Numbering menu on the screen as shown in Figure 36. Here you would select a page numbering option. For example, if you wanted a page number to appear in the top right corner of every page, you would type 3 and then press F7. Since you don't need page numbering in the memo, return to the editing screen:

Press **F7**

Figure 36 The Page Numbering Menu

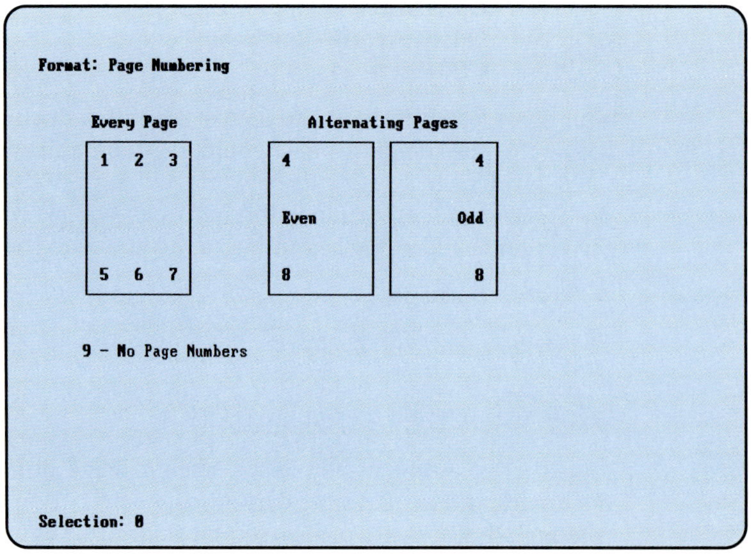

Practice

1. Change the paper size to Legal. Then change it back to Standard.
2. Change the top and bottom margins to 2 inches. Then change them back to 1 inch.
3. Insert a page break in the memo before the first paragraph. Now, remove the page break.

Lesson 17: Printing a Document

You've entered, formatted, proofread, and corrected your document. You're satisfied with your work and now it's time to produce the final product. You're ready to print your document on paper.

Step 1: Save the Document

It is a good idea to save your document before printing.

Press **F10**
Press **Enter**
Type **y**

Step 2: Prepare the Printer

Make sure the printer is connected to the computer and turned on. Also, make sure that paper is loaded and aligned to the top of a new page. Finally, make sure that the printer's On Line light is lit. (If it isn't, press the On Line button.)

Step 3: Invoke the Print Command

Activate the Print menu (see Figure 37) and select the Full Document option:

Press **Shift-F7**
Type **f**

When WordPerfect is finished printing the document, it will return to the editing screen.

Lesson 18: Returning to DOS

When you are finished working with WordPerfect, you will exit the program and return to DOS.

Step 1: Invoke the Exit Command

Execute the Exit command to tell WordPerfect that you either want to work on a different document or return to DOS:

Press **F7**

Figure 37 The Print Menu

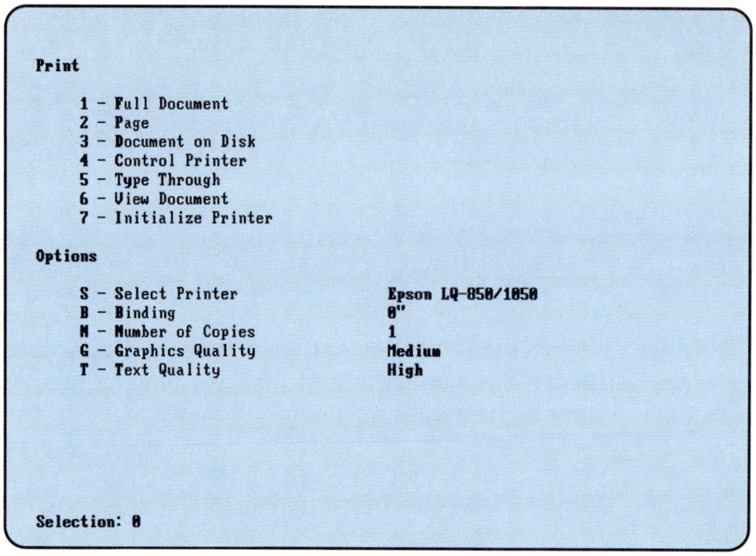

Step 2: Save the Document

WordPerfect will ask you if you want to save the document. Unless you are just viewing a document that you don't want to change, you should answer yes. If you have never saved this document before, you must enter a file name. If you have saved this document before, as we have done twice in this chapter, WordPerfect will suggest the current name. You can press Enter to choose this name, or type a new name if you want to save the document to a different file. If you choose the same name, WordPerfect will ask if you want to replace the existing document file with the version on your screen, and you should answer yes.

Type **y**
Press **Enter**
Type **y**

Step 3: Confirm the Exit

WordPerfect will copy the document to the disk and then display the prompt

```
Exit WP? (Y/N) No            (Cancel to return to document)
```

Here the program is asking you if you really want to return to DOS, and it assumes you do not. If you press F1, the Cancel key, you can return to editing your document. If you type N or press Enter, you can begin a new document. Exit WordPerfect:

Type **y**

You should see the DOS prompt on your screen.

Practice Start up WordPerfect. Then exit to DOS.

Lesson 19: Editing an Existing Document

Word processors make it so easy to store documents in disk files that editing an existing document is a common procedure. Any time you want to examine, modify, or update a previously stored document, all you have to do is tell WordPerfect to retrieve the file.

Step 1: Specify the Document When Loading WordPerfect

At this point you should be at the DOS prompt because you exited WordPerfect at the end of the last lesson. Before you can edit an existing document, you must make sure its file is stored on an accessible disk. The location of the document file depends on your default directory or the path and name you chose when you last saved the document. Your document may be on the diskette in drive B, on your hard disk C, or on a network file server disk.

If you know the name and location of the document file you want to edit, you can start WordPerfect and load the document at the same time. If you are using a computer with a hard disk and MEMO.DOC is stored in the LESSONS subdirectory, execute this command:

Type **wp \lessons\memo.doc**
Press **Enter**

If you are running WordPerfect on a computer with no hard disk and you saved the memo on the diskette in drive B, execute this command instead:

Type **wp b:memo.doc**
Press **Enter**

Your document will be loaded into memory along with WordPerfect, where you can view or edit it.

Step 2: Use the List Files Menu

Another way to edit an existing document is to retrieve its file from within WordPerfect. Exit WordPerfect and return to DOS. Start WordPerfect again with this command:

Type **wp**
Press **Enter**

Now, activate the List Files menu:

Press **F5**

WordPerfect will suggest your current drive and directory. If your computer has a hard disk and your document is in the LESSONS subdirectory, do this:

Type **\lessons**
Press **Enter**

If your document is on the diskette in drive B, do this instead:

Type **b:**
Press **Enter**

A screen like the one in Figure 38 will appear. This screen shows the files in the specified directory and presents the List Files menu. Your screen may look somewhat different, depending on the drive or directory you specified.

To load an existing document, use the arrow keys to move the reverse video highlight bar to its file name. Locate MEMO.DOC and highlight it. Then select the Retrieve option:

Type **r**

WordPerfect will load the file into memory and present the memo on the editing screen.

Step 3: Edit the Document

Sometimes you load an existing document file just to read it. Other times you actually want to correct, update, or modify the contents. Let's make a couple of additions to the memo:

Press **Enter**
Press **Up Arrow**
Type **`Date:`** `(today's date)`
Press **Down Arrow** (3 times)
Press **Space Bar**
Type **`and Vacation Leave`**

Except for the date, your screen should look like Figure 39.

Step 4: Exit WordPerfect and Save the File

Execute the Exit command and save the updated memo document:

Press **F7**
Type **y**
Press **Enter**

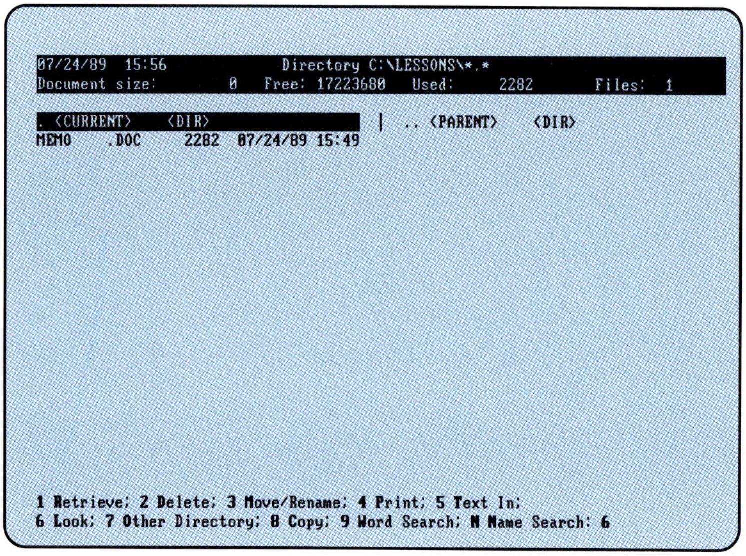

Figure 38 The List Files Menu

Real World

The Men Behind WordPerfect

Alan Ashton was so happy with his company's profits in 1987 that he took everyone—the whole company—to Hawaii for a week.

Ashton's goal was that his WordPerfect Corporation would make $100 million in profits, double the 1986 figure. On December 22, 1987, the figure stood at $100.3 million in sales. What's more, the company he cofounded has achieved record sales and profits every year since it was created in 1980.

Its success in large part is due to the success of its WordPerfect word processing software. WordPerfect is currently the world's best-selling word processing program. The White House, Congress, and law offices all over the world use it.

Who are the people who took a company to such dizzying heights in just seven years?

Ashton, president and chief executive officer, owns 49.9 percent of the stock in this private company. A former Brigham Young University professor, he is a Mormon who brings strong values and a sense of family to work with him. He is, according to employees, a father figure so down-to-earth that he recently only reluctantly traded in his pickup truck for a Cadillac. But he's a father figure with incredible drive—a tough combination to beat.

Bruce Bastian founded the company along with Ashton and is now an equal partner with him. Also a Mormon and a former college professor, Bastian now serves as chairman of the board and president of WordPerfect's highly successful international division.

The man who holds the tie-breaking 0.2 percent of the company stock is Pete Peterson. Back when the company was called Satellite Software International, Peterson was hired to keep the books. He quit the next day because there were no books.

There were also other problems, including no business license and very sketchy records. But when Ashton and Bastian realized that this man with a psychology degree knew what he was doing, they hired him back. Peterson uses a South American saying to describe the situation: "In the land of the blind, the one-eyed man is king."

Source: Christine Strehlo, "What's So Special About WordPerfect?" *Personal Computing,* March 1988, pp. 100–116.

Figure 39 The Completed Memo

```
Date:  July 24, 1989
To:  All Employees
From:  Personnel Department
Re:  Sick Leave and Vacation Leave_

                    Sick Leave

Full-time employees are entitled to twelve cumulative
working days of sick leave each year.  Time taken off is
charged against these twelve days and at the end of the year
the unused balance is carried forward.  Sick leave should
only be used for an employee's sickness or doctor's
appointments.  It is essential that accurate records are
kept because employees are entitled to payment for one-half
of their unused sick days when they resign or retire.

                  Vacation Leave

Full-time employees earn twenty-four working days of
vacation per year.  These are in addition to official
company holidays and must be used by the end of each year.
Accurate records of vacation leave taken must be kept
because employees will be paid for their unused days when
they resign or retire.
C:\LESSONS\MEMO.DOC                    Doc 1 Pg 1 Ln 1.5" Pos 4.65"
```

Type **y**
Type **y**

You should see the DOS prompt again.

Practice

1. Start WordPerfect and load your MEMO.DOC file. Change the date to tomorrow's date. Exit WordPerfect, saving the updated file.
2. Start WordPerfect without loading MEMO.DOC. Execute the List Files command and examine your WordPerfect subdirectory or diskette. Look at other subdirectories or diskettes from the List Files menu. When you are finished, exit WordPerfect and return to DOS.

Summary

- *Starting WordPerfect.* From DOS, type WP and press Enter.
- *The editing screen.* The cursor marks the place where text will be inserted. The status line indicates the document, page number, and line and column position.
- *Executing commands and getting help.* Most commands are executed by pressing a function key alone or by pressing the Shift, Control, or Alternate key with a function key. Help is obtained by pressing F3.
- *Entering text.* Simply type the text, pressing Enter only to force a new line or start a new paragraph.
- *Moving the cursor.* Arrow keys move up, down, left, and right. Ctrl-Left Arrow and Ctrl-Right Arrow move an entire word at a time. Grey Plus and Grey Minus move an entire screen at a time. Page Up and Page Down move an entire page at a time. End moves to the end of a line. Home, Left Arrow moves to the beginning of a line and Home, Right Arrow moves to the end of a line. Home, Home, Up Arrow moves to the beginning of the document and Home, Home, Down Arrow moves to the end of the document. Ctrl-Home moves to a particular page number.
- *Inserting new text.* Set the cursor, make sure insert mode is on, and type the text.
- *Overwriting mistakes.* Switch to typeover mode by pressing Insert and type over mistakes.
- *Deleting mistakes.* The Delete key removes the character at the cursor. The Backspace key removes the character to the left of the cursor. Ctrl-Backspace deletes an entire word. Ctrl-End deletes an entire line.
- *Searching for and replacing text.* Press F2 to execute the Search command. Press Alt-F2 to execute the Replace command.
- *Saving a document.* Press F10 to save a document to a disk file.
- *Checking spelling.* Press Ctrl-F2 to invoke the spelling checker.
- *Working with blocks of text.* Press Alt-F4 to mark a block. Press Ctrl-F4 to activate the Move menu and then select the Block option to move or copy a marked block. Press Delete to erase a marked block.

- *Canceling commands.* Press F1 to cancel a command in progress or restore a deletion.
- *Formatting characters.* Press F8 to underline text. Press F6 to boldface text. Press Ctrl-F8 to activate the Font menu, then select the Appearance option to choose other character formats.
- *Formatting lines.* Press Shift-F8 to activate the Format menu, then select the Line option to set left and right margins, tab stops, justification, line spacing, and line height. Press Shift-F6 to center text.
- *Formatting pages.* Press Shift-F8 to activate the Format menu, then select the Page option to set paper size and type, top and bottom margins, and page numbering. Press Ctrl-Enter to force a page break.
- *Printing a document.* Press Shift-F7 to activate the Print menu, then select the Full Document option.
- *Editing an existing document.* Type the document name on the command line when starting WordPerfect or press F5 to activate the List Files menu to load an existing document.
- *Exiting WordPerfect.* Press F7 and answer the prompts to return to DOS.

Key Terms

As an extra review of this chapter, try defining the following terms.

block	proportional spacing
cursor	ruler line
global search and replace	soft page break
hard page break	soft return
hard return	soft space
hard space	status line
keyboard template	text area
line height	word wrap

Multiple Choice

Choose the best selection to complete each statement.

1. When you start WordPerfect without loading a document, the only thing on the editing screen, except for the cursor, is the
   (a) Start Up menu. (b) ruler line.
   (c) status line. (d) Help facility.
2. Which keys would you press to see an on-screen version of the WordPerfect function key template?
   (a) F1, F1 (b) F3, F3
   (c) F3, F7 (d) Alt-F3
3. What is inserted into your document when you press the Enter key?
   (a) hard return (b) soft return
   (c) hard page break (d) soft page break

4. What feature eliminates having to press Enter at the end of every line?
   (a) justification
   (b) proportional spacing
   (c) word wrap
   (d) auto-hyphenation
5. Which keys would you press to move the cursor to the beginning of the next word to the right?
   (a) Right Arrow
   (b) Shift-Right Arrow
   (c) Ctrl-Right Arrow
   (d) Home-Right Arrow
6. You can move the cursor to the beginning of a document by pressing
   (a) Ctrl-End.
   (b) End, End, Down Arrow.
   (c) Ctrl-PgDn.
   (d) Home, Home, Up Arrow.
7. Pressing the Insert key toggles the
   (a) delete mode.
   (b) insert mode.
   (c) line spacing.
   (d) tab settings.
8. Pressing the Delete key deletes the character
   (a) at the current cursor location.
   (b) to the immediate right of the cursor.
   (c) to the immediate left of the cursor.
   (d) farthest from the cursor.
9. Pressing Ctrl-Backspace
   (a) deletes the word to the left of the cursor.
   (b) deletes the word at the cursor.
   (c) moves the cursor to the beginning of the line.
   (d) moves the cursor to the end of the line.
10. One operation that WordPerfect cannot do to a marked block is
    (a) copy it.
    (b) reverse it.
    (c) delete it.
    (d) move it.
11. Which keys would you press to repeat the previous search operation?
    (a) F2, F2
    (b) Alt-R
    (c) F3, F3
    (d) Ctrl-R
12. To force a page break, you must press
    (a) Alt-P.
    (b) Ctrl-Enter.
    (c) Ctrl-PgDn.
    (d) Alt-End.
13. Power failures, voltage fluctuations, system crashes, and unknown WordPerfect bugs are all good reasons to periodically
    (a) print your document.
    (b) edit your document.
    (c) retrieve your document.
    (d) save your document.
14. Including a file name after the WP when you start WordPerfect
    (a) prints that file.
    (b) automatically loads that file.
    (c) periodically saves that file.
    (d) deletes that file.

15. Which key would you press to restore the most recently deleted word or phrase?
    (a) Ctrl-U (b) F1
    (c) Ctrl-End (d) Escape

16. Which two character-formatting options can each be used by pressing a single function key?
    (a) italics and outline (b) shadow and strikeout
    (c) underline and boldface (d) double underline and small capitals

17. What are the default WordPerfect settings for left and right margins?
    (a) 1″ and 1″ (b) 1.25″ and 1″
    (c) 1″ and 2″ (d) 0″ and 1″

18. How many blank lines are left between double-spaced lines?
    (a) 0 (b) 1
    (c) 2 (d) 3

19. What keys do you press to activate the Print menu?
    (a) Shift-F7 (b) Ctrl-P
    (c) Ctrl-F1 (d) Shift-PrtSc

20. What key do you use to exit WordPerfect and return to DOS?
    (a) F1 (b) F3
    (c) F5 (d) F7

Fill-In

1. To start WordPerfect, you type ______ and press Enter.
2. The line at the bottom of the WordPerfect editing screen is called the ______.
3. Pressing ______ and then ______ moves the cursor to the left edge of the screen.
4. Pressing F3 brings up WordPerfect's ______ facility.
5. ______ is the key you press to move the cursor to the end of the current line.
6. When a document is formatted so that all of the lines line up at the right margin, it is ______.
7. Word processors have a feature called ______ that eliminates having to press Enter at the end of each line.
8. Pressing Enter generates what's known as a ______ return.
9. The ______ keys include the Home, End, Page Up, Page Down, and arrow keys.
10. If insert mode is turned on, pressing the Insert key switches to ______ mode.
11. To overwrite mistakes, you must first turn insert mode ______.
12. Backspace, Delete, Ctrl-Backspace, and Ctrl-End are all examples of commands that ______ text.

13. Existing text can be centered between the left and right margins by pressing ______.
14. A ______ is any section of text, from a single character to a whole document, that can be marked and treated as a single entity.
15. A global ______ and ______ operation is used to automatically change every occurrence of a word or phrase.
16. By default, WordPerfect sets both the top and bottom page margins to ______.
17. When justification is not used, you get a ______ right margin.
18. If the spelling checker stops on a word that is not misspelled, you can use the ______ or ______ option to continue.
19. When you ______ a document, WordPerfect copies it from primary memory to a disk file.
20. In WordPerfect, page numbering is turned ______ by default.

Short Problems

1. Start up WordPerfect without loading an existing document. Type the following text. Press **Enter** only once, after the last line.

   The next meeting of the EZ Systems Board of Managers will be held at 7:00 P.M on November 19, 1989 in Room 217 of Champaign Federal Savings. This is an important meeting, so please try to attend.

2. Move the cursor to the top of the document and type the following lines. Press **Enter** after each line.

   To: Board of Managers
   From: David Franklin, Secretary
   Re: Next meeting

3. Press the **Enter** key again to leave a blank line before the paragraph. Move the cursor to the top of the document, and do this:

   Type **M E M O**
   Press **Enter**

   Boldface, underline, and center this title.

4. Move the cursor to the last line of the memo and delete it with a single command. Restore the text you've deleted with the Cancel command.
5. Mark "EZ Systems" as a block of text and copy it before the "Board of Managers" after the "To:."
6. Move the cursor to the top of the file. Use the search and replace command to change "Managers" to "Directors" throughout the entire document.
7. Move the cursor to the beginning of the document and set the left and right margins to 1½ inches.
8. Change the tab stops so that they occur at 1-inch intervals.
9. Turn off justification for this memo.
10. Go back and double space the entire document (use the Line Spacing option from the Line Format menu).
11. Save the document in a disk file named MEETING.DOC, but don't exit WordPerfect.

12. If your computer is equipped with a printer, make sure it is turned on and on-line, and print this memo.
13. Use WordPerfect's on-line help facility to get a list of all the features that begin with A. Select a different letter and try it again. Now try learning more about the function keys.

Long Problems

1. Use WordPerfect to create a letter to be sent to three different software companies requesting information about the word processor they sell. Use the same basic letter, but tailor it to each company and its product. Save each version in its own disk file and print out all three. If you have no word processors in mind, use these three:

WordPerfect WordPerfect Corp. 1555 No. Technology Way Orem, UT 84057	WordStar WordStar International Corp. 33 San Pablo Ave. San Rafael, CA 94903	Microsoft Word Microsoft Corp. 16011 N.E. 36th Way Redmond, WA 98073

2. Use WordPerfect to write a paper for one of your classes or a report for your company. Be sure to follow any format guidelines specified.
3. Look in a newspaper or placement office listing for a position you might apply for. Prepare a realistic resume and cover letter for this job with WordPerfect. Be sure to use underlining and boldface where appropriate.
4. Investigate three different word processing programs. Use WordPerfect to prepare a report that compares their features.
5. Use WordPerfect to create your academic schedule for this semester. List the days, times, classes, buildings, rooms, and instructors.
6. Create a weekly appointment calendar with WordPerfect. Print out several copies for the next few weeks.
7. Write a letter with WordPerfect to a company praising or criticizing their product or service.
8. Use WordPerfect to write a letter to WordPerfect Corporation detailing some of the things you like or dislike about their word processing package. You can use the address given in Problem 1.
9. Create an address and phone listing of your friends and acquaintances using WordPerfect.
10. Create a quick reference guide to DOS with WordPerfect. In other words, list each DOS command along with a brief description of what it does and how to invoke it.
11. Use WordPerfect to create a quick reference guide to WordPerfect. List the commands and operations that you think are most important to remember.
12. Take a week's worth of notes from a class you are taking and redo them with WordPerfect. Try to do more than just type them as is. Organize, rearrange, and reword the material if you can. Do you think using a word processor can improve your notes?
13. As you redo your notes for Problem 12, keep in mind any questions you might have about the material. Write a letter to your professor in which you

outline your questions. If possible, copy sections or even direct quotes from your notes and include them in your letter.

14. Perhaps you have an item that you would like to sell through a newspaper ad, such as a musical instrument, bicycle, car, couch, television, stereo, or computer. You might be looking for a roommate or have an apartment to sublet. Use WordPerfect to design a classified ad to place in your school or local newspaper.
15. Choose a current event or local news item that interests you and use WordPerfect to write a letter expressing your views on it to the editor of your school or town newspaper.

CHAPTER 9

Intermediate WordPerfect

In This Chapter

Getting Started
Lesson 1: Managing Documents
Lesson 2: Creating a Longer Document
Lesson 3: Learning More Cursor-Movement Commands
Lesson 4: Learning More Delete Commands
Lesson 5: Working with Codes
Lesson 6: Using the Thesaurus
Lesson 7: Working with Windows
Lesson 8: Indenting Paragraphs
Lesson 9: Using Tab Stops to Create Tables
Lesson 10: Using the Tab Align Command
Lesson 11: Using the Flush Right Command
Lesson 12: Using the Date Command
Lesson 13: Centering Text on a Page
Lesson 14: Adding a Document Summary
Lesson 15: Use the Text In/Out Command
Lesson 16: Execute a DOS Command within WordPerfect

Preview

In Chapter 8 you learned the basics of WordPerfect, the most popular microcomputer word processing package. This chapter continues your exploration of WordPerfect with slightly more advanced topics.

After studying this chapter, you will know how to

- manage documents with the List Files menu.
- create longer documents.
- use additional cursor movement commands.
- use additional delete commands.
- work with formatting codes.
- use the built-in thesaurus.
- split the screen into two windows.
- indent paragraphs.
- create tables with tab stops.
- align numbers to tab stops.
- move text flush right.
- insert the current date automatically.
- center text on a page.
- create a document summary.
- retrieve and save text files.
- execute a DOS command within WordPerfect.

Getting Started

You've already learned how to start WordPerfect and use its most common features and commands. This chapter assumes you have completed all of the lessons and exercises in Chapter 8. Furthermore, it assumes that you have a computer with a hard disk and WordPerfect 5.0 installed on it in a subdirectory named WP50. It also assumes you have a subdirectory named LESSONS in which to store your document files.

Lesson 1: Managing Documents

WordPerfect makes it easy to create new documents, retrieve existing documents, save and search for documents, as well as delete, rename, copy, and print documents. You can also change the default directory and examine the contents of a directory or file. All of these features are available either as a function key command or as an option in the List Files menu.

Step 1: Start WordPerfect

If you are not already running WordPerfect, switch to the proper subdirectory and start the program:

Type **cd c:\wp50**
Press **Enter**
Type **wp**
Press **Enter**

Step 2: Retrieve a Document By Name

In the previous chapter, you learned how to load an existing document file by specifying the file name on the command line when starting WordPerfect or by selecting the file from the List Files screen and executing the Retrieve option. If you know the location and name of the document file you want, a third method exists to retrieve it. Suppose you want to work on the MEMO.DOC file in the LESSONS subdirectory. Execute the Retrieve command:

Press **Shift-F10**

WordPerfect will display the prompt

`Document to be retrieved:`

Enter the path and name of the document file:

Type **`c:\lessons\memo.doc`**
Press **Enter**

The document will be loaded into memory and displayed on the screen in the text area.

Step 3: Starting a New Document

If you are finished looking at or working on a document, you can clear the screen to start a new document without actually exiting WordPerfect and restarting the program. Suppose you have either already saved the current document or don't want to save it. Execute the Exit command and answer "no" to both prompts:

Press **F7**
Type **n**
Type **n**

WordPerfect will not save the file and will not return to DOS, but will clear the screen so you can start a new document.

Step 4: Execute the List Files Command

The screen and menu presented by the List Files command provide many options for managing your documents. This command lets you see the names of the files stored on a disk or in a subdirectory. It also lets you retrieve, delete, rename, copy, and print files. Execute the List Files command to examine your default directory, which should be the subdirectory C:\WP50:

Press **F5**
Press **Enter**

As Figure 1 shows, WordPerfect will display the directory of C:\WP50 and present the List Files menu at the bottom of the screen.

Step 5: Select the Other Directory Option

You can look at any disk or subdirectory from the List Files menu. Select the Other Directory option:

Type **o**

Figure 1 The List Files Menu

```
07/23/89  08:44                 Directory C:\WP50\*.*
Document size:          0   Free: 16783360   Used:  2049550        Files:  62

. <CURRENT>     <DIR>                     .. <PARENT>     <DIR>
LEARN    .      <DIR>   07/21/89 09:21    8514A    .WPD    3476  09/16/88 15:57
AIRPLANE.WPG     8484  09/16/88 15:57    AND      .WPG    1978  09/16/88 15:57
ANNOUNCE.WPG     5388  09/16/88 15:57    APPLAUSE.WPG    1522  09/16/88 15:57
ARROW1  .WPG      366  09/16/88 15:57    ARROW2  .WPG     738  09/16/88 15:57
AWARD   .WPG     1746  09/16/88 15:57    BADNEWS .WPG    3750  09/16/88 15:57
BOOK    .WPG     1800  09/16/88 15:57    BORDER  .WPG   13518  09/16/88 15:57
CHECK   .WPG     1074  09/16/88 15:57    CLOCK   .WPG    6234  09/16/88 15:57
CONFIDEN.WPG     3226  09/16/88 15:57    EGA512  .FRS    3584  09/16/88 15:57
EGAITAL .FRS     3584  09/16/88 15:57    EGASMC  .FRS    3584  09/16/88 15:57
EGAUND  .FRS     3584  09/16/88 15:57    EPLQ850 .PRS    8612  07/21/89 09:34
FLAG    .WPG      730  09/16/88 15:57    GAVEL   .WPG     856  09/16/88 15:57
GENIUS1 .WPD     4692  09/16/88 15:57    GENIUS2 .WPD    4735  09/16/88 15:57
GOODNEWS.WPG     4242  09/16/88 15:57    GRAB    .COM   15334  09/16/88 15:57
HAND    .WPG     1054  09/16/88 15:57    HOURGLAS.WPG    1834  09/16/88 15:57
HRF12   .FRS    49152  09/16/88 15:57    HRF6    .FRS   49152  09/16/88 15:57
KEY     .WPG     1578  09/16/88 15:57    KEYS    .MRS    4800  11/15/88 16:51
MAPSYMBL.WPG     2450  09/16/88 15:57    NEWSPAPR.WPG    1388  09/16/88 15:57
NO1     .WPG     3234  09/16/88 15:57 ▼  PC      .WPG    2586  09/16/88 15:57

1 Retrieve; 2 Delete; 3 Move/Rename; 4 Print; 5 Text In;
6 Look; 7 Other Directory; 8 Copy; 9 Word Search; N Name Search: 6
```

WordPerfect will display the prompt

New directory = C:\WP50

Here the program is presenting the current path and is asking you to enter the path of the other directory you want to examine. Specify the LESSONS subdirectory:

Type **c:\lessons**
Press **Enter** (2 times)

The list of files will change to reveal the contents of the LESSONS subdirectory.

Step 6: Select the Look Option

Look is the default option of the List Files menu. This option lets you examine the contents of a directory, which you have just done. The Look option also allows you to examine the contents of a file without actually loading that file into the editing screen. Let's look at the file MEMO.DOC. Highlight the file name and select the Look option:

Press **Down Arrow**
Type **L**

Your screen should look like Figure 2. The file MEMO.DOC is presented, but you can only look at it, not edit it. If the file is too long to fit on a single screen, you can use the cursor movement keys to see the rest of it. When you are finished examining the file, execute the Exit command:

Press **F7**

Step 7: Select the Retrieve Option

You have already learned to use the Retrieve option, but let's try it again. The file name MEMO.DOC should already be highlighted, so just select the Retrieve option:

Type **r**

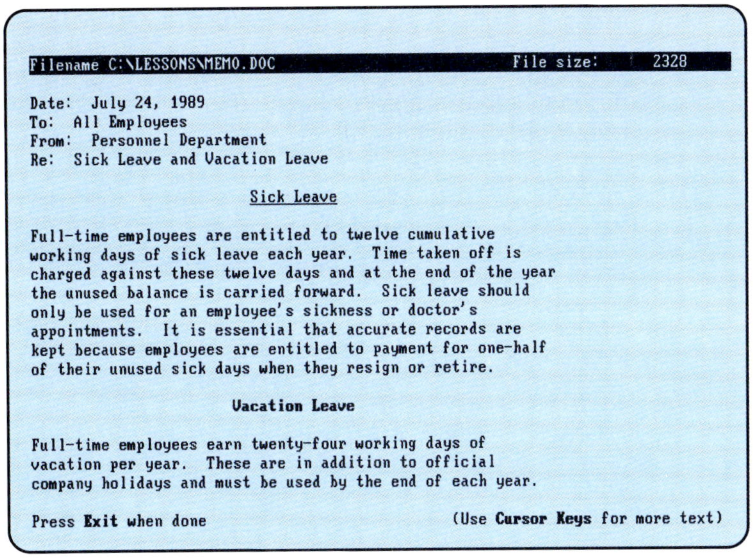

Filename C:\LESSONS\MEMO.DOC File size: 2328

Date: July 24, 1989
To: All Employees
From: Personnel Department
Re: Sick Leave and Vacation Leave

Sick Leave

Full-time employees are entitled to twelve cumulative working days of sick leave each year. Time taken off is charged against these twelve days and at the end of the year the unused balance is carried forward. Sick leave should only be used for an employee's sickness or doctor's appointments. It is essential that accurate records are kept because employees are entitled to payment for one-half of their unused sick days when they resign or retire.

Vacation Leave

Full-time employees earn twenty-four working days of vacation per year. These are in addition to official company holidays and must be used by the end of each year.

Press **Exit** when done (Use **Cursor Keys** for more text)

Figure 2 ***MEMO.DOC Presented with the List Files Look Option***

WordPerfect will load the file into memory and present it on the editing screen. Unlike using the Look option, using the Retrieve option lets you edit the document.

Now, clear the screen and execute the List Files command again:

Press **F7**
Type **n**
Type **n**
Press **F5**
Press **Enter**

Step 8: Select the Copy Option

You can use the Copy option of the List Files menu to duplicate a file. The duplicate can be created either in the same directory or in a different directory. If it is in the same directory as the original, the duplicate must be given a different name. Let's copy the file MEMO.DOC and name the duplicate MEMO.BAK. First, highlight the file MEMO.DOC and then select the Copy option:

Press **Down Arrow**
Type **c**

WordPerfect will display the prompt

```
Copy this file to:
```

Simply enter the name of the duplicate to be created:

Type **memo.bak**
Press **Enter**

The file MEMO.BAK will be created in the current directory. Unfortunately, the List Files screen isn't updated, so highlight the current directory and execute the Look option to see what you have done:

Press **Up Arrow**
Type **L**
Press **Enter**

The file MEMO.BAK will now appear in the directory listing shown on the screen.

Step 9: Select the Move/Rename Option

The Move/Rename option of the List Files menu can be used to move a file to a different subdirectory or change the name of a file. Let's rename MEMO.BAK to MEMO.OLD. First, highlight MEMO.BAK. Then select the Move/Rename option:

Type **m**

WordPerfect will display the prompt

```
New name: C:\LESSONS\MEMO.BAK
```

To move the file, you would edit the path. To rename the file, simply enter the new name:

Type **memo.old**
Press **Enter**

The file MEMO.BAK will become MEMO.OLD in the LESSONS subdirectory.

Step 10: Select the Print Option

In the previous chapter you learned how to print a document from the editing screen. You can also print a document that is not currently loaded into memory from the List Files menu. Let's print MEMO.OLD. Make sure your printer is turned on, loaded with paper, and on-line. Highlight the file to be printed. Then select the Print option from the List Files menu:

Type **p**

WordPerfect will display the prompt

```
Page(s): (All)
```

Select the default option to print all of the pages:

Press **Enter**

The document will be sent to the printer.

Step 11: Select the Text In Option

WordPerfect documents are files that contain various formatting codes in addition to the actual text. ASCII files, also known as text files, contain only letters, numbers, punctuation marks, and other symbols you can produce from the keyboard. Batch files, CONFIG.SYS, programming language source code, and certain data files are examples of ASCII files. The Text In option of the List Files menu lets you load and edit ASCII files. Let's use this option to load AUTOEXEC.BAT, the auto-execute batch file in the root directory of the hard disk. First, use the Other Directory option to change to the root directory:

Type **o**
Type **c:**
Press **Enter** (2 times)

Use the arrow keys to highlight the file AUTOEXEC.BAT. Then select the Text In option:

Type **t**

AUTOEXEC.BAT will be retrieved from the disk and displayed on the editing screen (see Figure 3). There the text can be edited, but without formatting features such as margins, page breaks, underlining, and so on.

Now, clear the screen, execute the List Files command, and change to the WP50 subdirectory:

Press **F7**
Type **n**
Type **n**
Press **F5**
Type **c:\wp50**
Press **Enter**

Step 12: Select the Name Search Option

The Name Search option of the List Files menu allows you to highlight a file name by typing its name instead of using the arrow keys to move through the list. When you type the first letter of the file name, the highlight moves to the first file name that begins with that letter. As you type more letters of the file name, the highlight moves to the next file name that matches what you have typed so far. You can usually highlight the file name you want by typing just a few characters.

The WordPerfect subdirectory displayed on your screen contains many files. Suppose you want to find the file named WP.EXE. Instead of scrolling through the long list with the arrow keys to highlight WP.EXE, use the Name Search option:

Type **n**
Type **wp.e**

Each file name character you type moves the highlight to the next matching file name. By the time you type the "e," the file WP.EXE is highlighted (see Figure 4). Return to the List Files menu:

Press **Enter**

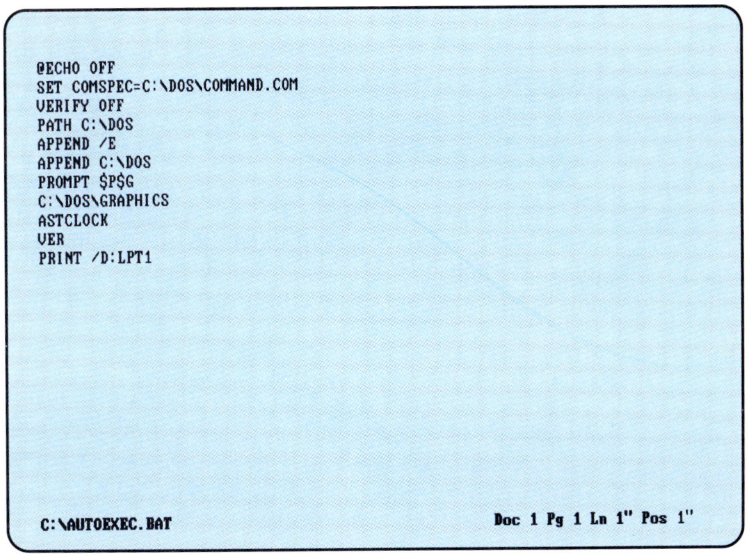

Figure 3 The Text File AUTOEXEC.BAT Retrieved

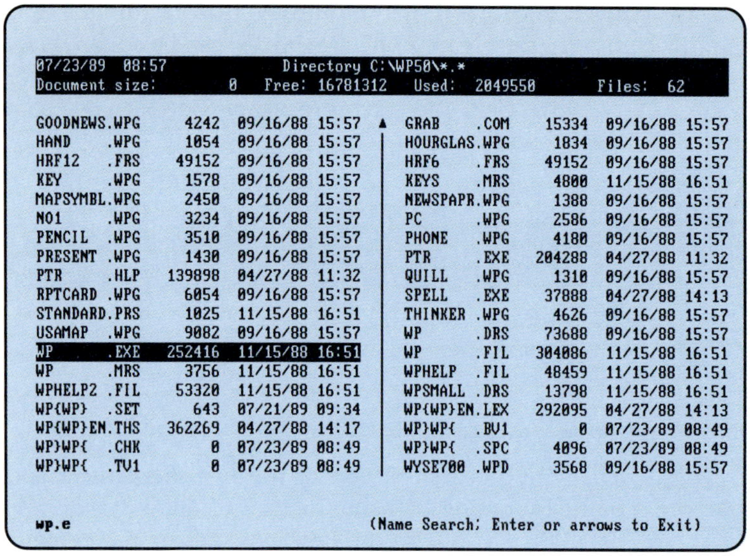

Figure 4 The Name Search Option of the List Files Menu

Now, change to the LESSONS subdirectory:

Type **o**
Type **c:\lessons**
Press **Enter** (2 times)

Step 13: Mark Files

In some cases it is necessary to perform an operation on a group of files. For example, you may want to copy, delete, or print several files at once. WordPerfect allows you to mark each file you want on the List Files screen with an asterisk (*). After the files are marked, you can select Copy, Delete, or Print from the List Files menu. Let's see how to mark and unmark files. First, move the highlight to the file MEMO.OLD. Then mark the file with an asterisk:

Type *****

An asterisk will appear in the directory listing just after the file size. Now mark MEMO.DOC too. If you have a printer connected to your computer, select the Print option:

Type **p**
Type **y**

Both files will be printed.

To unmark a file, simply repeat the process by highlighting the file name and typing another asterisk. The asterisk will disappear from the directory listing. Unmark MEMO.DOC and MEMO.OLD.

Step 14: Select the Word Search Option

Word Search is a powerful List Files option that lets you mark files that meet specific conditions. For example, you can mark all those files that contain the word "vacation." Select the Word Search option:

Type **w**

WordPerfect will present a menu that lists four types of searches:

- **1 Doc Summary** This option searches document summaries for the specified word pattern. A *document summary* is a collection of information about a document. You will learn how to create document summaries later in this chapter.
- **2 First Page** This option searches only the first page or the first 4000 characters of documents for the specified word pattern.
- **3 Entire Doc** This option searches entire documents for the specified word pattern.
- **4 Conditions** This option allows you to enter criteria to conduct a more detailed search.

Let's use the Entire Document option:

Type **e**

WordPerfect will display the prompt

`Word pattern:`

Now you specify the text you want to search for. You can use a question mark (?) to represent any single character and an asterisk (*) to represent any group of characters. These **wild-card characters** work just like the DOS global file name characters ? and *. In our simple example, however, you don't need wild-card characters because you are just searching for documents that contain the word "vacation." Specify the word pattern:

Type **vacation**
Press **Enter**

WordPerfect will search through all the documents in the current directory and mark with an asterisk those documents that contain the word "vacation." Since MEMO.DOC and MEMO.OLD are duplicates that both contain the word "vacation," both files are marked with asterisks.

Now, unmark both files. You can unmark every file on the List Files screen with a single command:

Press **Home**
Type *

Step 15: Select the Delete Option

The Delete option in the List Files menu lets you erase files. Let's delete MEMO.OLD. First, highlight MEMO.OLD. Then select the Delete option:

Type **d**

WordPerfect will display the prompt

`Delete C:\LESSONS\MEMO.OLD? (Y/N) No`

If you are sure you want to delete the file, answer yes:

Type **y**

The file will be erased from the disk and removed from the List Files screen.

Now, exit the List Files screen and return to the editing screen:

Press **F7**

Practice

1. Execute the List Files command. Put a formatted diskette in drive A. Select the Other Directory option and examine the contents of the diskette in drive A.
2. Use the Other Directory option to switch to the root directory of the hard disk. Use the Text In option to load the file CONFIG.SYS. Use the Exit command to clear the screen without saving the file and without leaving WordPerfect.
3. Execute the List Files command and specify the LESSONS subdirectory. Copy the file MEMO.DOC and name the duplicate NOTE.DOC.
4. Use the Look option to examine the contents of NOTE.DOC.
5. Retrieve NOTE.DOC into the editing screen. Make a change to the file and then save it. Execute the List Files command again.
6. Rename NOTE.DOC to NOTE.OLD.
7. Print NOTE.OLD.
8. Delete NOTE.OLD. Exit the List Files screen and return to the editing screen.

Lesson 2: Creating a Longer Document

To illustrate more of WordPerfect's capabilities, you need a more substantial document. In this lesson, you will create a simple newsletter for a fictional business, Paddle and Portage Canoe Outfitters.

Step 1: Type the Heading

The top of the newsletter will present the centered address and phone number of the business. Follow these instructions:

Press **Shift-F6**
Type **Paddle and Portage Canoe Outfitters**
Press **Enter**
Press **Shift-F6**
Type **Box 555**
Press **Enter**
Press **Shift-F6**
Type **Grand Marais, MN 55604**
Press **Enter**
Press **Shift-F6**
Type **(218) 555-1234**
Press **Enter** (2 times)

Step 2: Type the Title

The title of the newsletter will also be centered. Follow these instructions:

Press **Shift-F6**
Type **NEWSLETTER**
Press **Enter**
Press **Shift-F6**
Type **1991**
Press **Enter** (2 times)

Step 3: Type the First Section

Each section of the newsletter will have an underlined heading.

Press **F8**
Type **New Outfitting Post**
Press **F8**
Press **Enter**

Type the paragraph without pressing Enter at the end of each line:

This winter we completed our new outfitting facility. It will house our office, staff kitchen, retail sales, and equipment storage area. Located close to the lake for easy access, this new building will give us the room we need to help serve you better.

Space down for the next section:

Press **Enter** (2 times)

Step 4: Type the Next Section

Follow these directions:

Press **F8**
Type **Sport Shows**
Press **F8**
Press **Enter**
Type **This year we will be attending the following sport shows:**
Press **Enter** (2 times)
Type **Jan 23-Feb 1**
Press **Enter**
Type **Chicagoland Show, O'Hare Exposition Center**
Press **Enter** (2 times)
Type **Feb 14-Feb 22**
Press **Enter**
Type **Greater Northwest Sport Show, Minneapolis Auditorium**
Press **Enter** (2 times)
Type **Mar 13-Mar 22**
Press **Enter**
Type **Milwaukee Sentinel Sport Show, MECCA Building**
Press **Enter** (2 times)
Type **If you can, stop by and say "Hi." Remember our SPECIAL BONUS RATES for sport show reservations.**
Press **Enter** (2 times)

Step 5: Save the Document So Far

It is a good idea to periodically save your document on a disk as you are creating it, even if it is not yet finished. Save the document in the LESSONS subdirectory and name it NEWS.DOC:

Press **F10**
Type **c:\lessons\news.doc**
Press **Enter**

Step 6: Type the Rest of the Document

Follow these directions to type the rest of the newsletter:

Press **F8**
Type **New Regulations**
Press **F8**
Press **Enter**

Type this paragraph:

Only Ontario's Quetico Provincial Park has changed regulations for this season. Reservations for Quetico camping permits will be accepted no sooner than January 19. Written reservations may be made 21 days in advance of trip departure. Phone reservations may be made from 21 days prior to and up to the date of departure. As always, we will handle all permit reservations for our guests.

Press **Enter** (2 times)
Press **F8**
Type **Equipment Improvements**
Press **F8**
Press **Enter**

Type this paragraph:

Our most exciting equipment addition this year is a new Super-Lite Badger canoe. It weighs, believe it or not, slightly over 40 pounds. We feel that this new 17-foot Badger canoe is ideal for wilderness tripping. It's stable, safe, and much easier to paddle and portage.

Press **Enter**
Press **Tab**

Type this paragraph:

Last year we field tested several nylon packs and found one in particular that offered several advantages. Lighter and dryer than canvas Duluth packs, we will be incorporating these new nylon packs into our equipment line beginning this year. The Super-Lite Badger canoes and nylon packs will be available on a first-come, first-serve basis.

Press **Enter** (2 times)
Press **F8**
Type **Trail Food Improvements**
Press **F8**
Press **Enter**

Type this paragraph:

We have replaced the Ham and Potatoes with Meatballs and Gravy, the Beef Stromboli with Chicken Stew 'N Dumplings, and the Buttermilk Pancakes with Blueberry Pancakes. These are all taste improvements, not cost savings, so our Trail Food will be even better this year.

Press **Enter** (2 times)
Press **F8**
Type **Trips**
Press **F8**
Press **Enter**

Type this paragraph:

This fall we took a trip into the Cherry Lake area for some lake trout fishing. We had our usual quota of rain, but did enjoy two beautiful crisp autumn days. Mornings we awoke to clear, deep blue skies with heavy, white steam rising from Cherry Lake. It was almost like being in a shaving commercial. On shore we could look up into the blue sky, but as we paddled into the steam we disappeared into white nothingness. It was a trip we'll long remember.

Press **Enter**
Press **Tab**

Type this paragraph:

We extended our camping into winter this year with several overnight trips in December. From our house we have easy access to about 15 kilometers of cross-country ski trails that lead to Boundary Waters Canoe Area campsites. After setting up a base camp, we would typically venture out for exploring and ice fishing. Nothing like twenty below temperatures to get you moving in the morning!

Press **Enter** (2 times)
Press **F8**
Type **A Final Note...**
Press **F8**
Press **Enter**

Type this paragraph:

After having our best year ever, we want to thank all of you for your friendship and patronage and wish you a happy and prosperous New Year. We look forward to seeing you this spring, summer, or fall.

Press **Enter** (2 times)
Type **Becky and Bob Johnson, owners/operators**
Press **Enter**
Type **Paddle and Portage Canoe Outfitters**
Press **Enter**

Step 7: Check Your Work

Read over the document you have created and make sure it contains no errors. Use what you have learned in the previous chapter to correct any typographical errors you may have made.

Step 8: Save the Completed Document

Now that the document is finished, you must save it on a disk. Execute the Save command and replace your previous version of NEWS.DOC:

Press **F10**
Press **Enter**
Type **y**

Step 9: Move to the Beginning

Move the cursor up to the beginning of the document:

Press **Home** (2 times)
Press **Up Arrow**

Your screen should look like Figure 5.

Practice

1. Use the spelling checker to further inspect the newsletter for typographical errors. Tell the spelling checker to skip proper names that are not in the dictionary, such as Marais, Chicagoland, O'Hare, Quetico, Stromboli, and Becky.
2. Move the cursor back to the beginning of the document.

Lesson 3: Learning More Cursor-Movement Commands

In the previous chapter you learned several ways to move the cursor within a WordPerfect document. This lesson covers a few other cursor movement commands.

Step 1: Move to the Bottom and Top of the Screen

Pressing Home once followed by an arrow key moves the cursor to that end of the text on the screen. Home, Left Arrow moves the cursor to the left edge of the screen and Home, Right Arrow moves the cursor to the right edge of the screen. You can also move to the bottom edge and top edge of the current screen. Execute this command:

Press **Home**
Press **Down Arrow**

The cursor will jump to the bottom edge of the current screen in the same column, or close to the same column, as its original position. If you repeat the command, the cursor will advance to the bottom of the next screen. Pressing Home, Down Arrow is the same as pressing Grey Plus. Now, execute the opposite command:

Press **Home**
Press **Up Arrow**

The cursor will jump to the top of the current screen. Pressing Home, Up Arrow is the same as pressing Grey Minus.

Figure 5 The Completed Newsletter

```
                 Paddle and Portage Canoe Outfitters
                               Box 555
                        Grand Marais, MN  55604
                           (218) 555-1234

                             NEWSLETTER
                                1991

New Outfitting Post
This winter we completed our new outfitting facility.  It will
house our office, staff kitchen, retail sales, and equipment
storage area.  Located close to the lake for easy access, this new
building will give us the room we need to serve you better.

Sport Shows
This year we will be attending the following sport shows:

Jan 23--Feb 1
Chicagoland Show, O'Hare Exposition Center

Feb 14--Feb 22
Greater Northwest Sport Show, Minneapolis Auditorium

Mar 13--Mar 22
C:\LESSONS\NEWS.DOC                             Doc 1 Pg 1 Ln 1" Pos 1"
```

Step 2: Move a Specified Number of Lines

WordPerfect lets you move up or down a specified number of lines. Suppose you want to move the cursor down 12 lines. Follow these instructions:

Press **Escape**
Type **12**
Press **Down Arrow**

The cursor will move down 12 lines, just as if you had pressed Down Arrow 12 times. Now, move up 6 lines with this command:

Press **Escape**
Type **6**
Press **Up Arrow**

Repeat this command to move the cursor up another 6 lines.

Step 3: Move a Specified Number of Characters

In fact, the Escape key can be used in this manner with other cursor movement keys as well. Suppose you want to move the cursor right 20 characters. Execute this command:

Press **Escape**
Type **20**
Press **Right Arrow**

The cursor will move to the right 20 characters just as if you had pressed Right Arrow 20 times. Now, try the opposite command:

Press **Escape**
Type **20**
Press **Left Arrow**

Step 4: Move a Specified Number of Screens or Pages

The Escape key can also be used to rapidly scroll or page. For example, try this command:

Press **Escape**
Type **3**
Press **Grey Plus**

The cursor will move down three screens, just as if you had pressed Grey Plus three times. Now, try a repeated paging command:

Press **Escape**
Type **2**
Press **Page Up**

The cursor will move up two pages, in this case to the top of the document.

Step 5: Move to a Specific Character

A variation of the Go To feature, executed by pressing Ctrl-Home, lets you position the cursor to the immediate right of the first occurrence of a particular character. For example, move the cursor to the beginning of the first line of the newsletter. Suppose you want to advance the cursor just past the "C" in the word "Canoe." Execute this command:

Press **Ctrl-Home**
Type **C**

The cursor will be placed on the "a" following the "C" in the word "Canoe."

Practice

1. Move the cursor to the beginning of the document.
2. Advance the cursor 10 characters to the right, then move the cursor 5 characters to the left. (Don't press the arrow keys repeatedly.)
3. Move the cursor down 10 lines without repeatedly pressing Down Arrow.
4. Advance the cursor to the next occurrence of the letter R.
5. Move the cursor down 4 screens, then move the cursor back up 4 screens. Now, move the cursor to the beginning of the line.

Lesson 4: Learning More Delete Commands

WordPerfect provides several commands for deleting text. You have already learned the most common methods in the previous chapter.

Step 1: Delete to Word Boundary

Suppose you want to delete just part of a word. WordPerfect lets you erase characters from the current cursor location to the beginning or end of a word. For example, move the cursor to the letter "f" in the word "Outfitters" in the first line of the newsletter. Delete the first part of the word:

Press **Home**
Press **Backspace**

The "Out" part of the word will be deleted. Now, restore what you have deleted:

Press **F1**
Type **r**

This time, try deleting the latter part of the word:

Press **Home**
Press **Delete**

The "fitters" part of the word will be deleted. Restore what you have deleted:

Press **F1**
Type **r**

Step 2: Delete Several Lines

You can use the Escape key to repeat the Delete to End of Line command and erase several lines at once. For example, move the cursor to the beginning of the paragraph beneath the title "New Outfitting Post." Delete four lines by executing this command:

Press **Escape**
Type **4**
Press **Ctrl-End**

The four lines will disappear from the screen. Now, restore the lines you have deleted:

Press **F1**
Type **r**

Step 3: Delete to End of Page

WordPerfect provides an even more drastic command that lets you delete the text from the current cursor position to the end of the page. Execute this command:

Press **Ctrl-PgDn**
Type **y**

After you answer yes to the prompt (see Figure 6), WordPerfect will delete the rest of the text on the current page. Now, restore what you have erased:

Press **F1**
Type **r**

Practice

1. Select a long word in the newsletter. Move the cursor into the middle of the word. Delete the first half of the word. Restore what you have deleted. Then delete the second half of the word. Again, restore what you have deleted.
2. Delete ten lines of text from the newsletter with one command. Restore the lines you have deleted.
3. Delete half of the second page of the newsletter. Restore what you have deleted. Move the cursor to the beginning of the document.

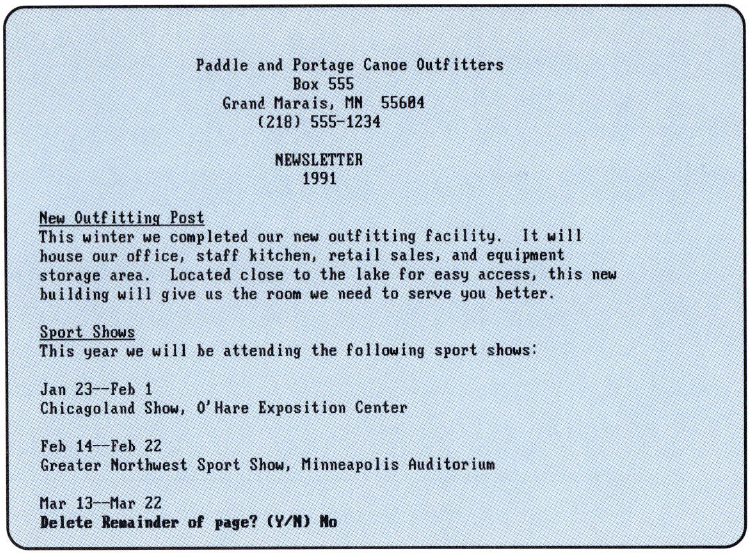

Figure 6 The Delete to End of Page Prompt

Lesson 5: Working with Codes

Whenever you press the Enter key, WordPerfect inserts a **code** in your document that tells the display or printer to start a new line. Although this code does not appear on the screen, it is stored in your document like any other character. WordPerfect has many such hidden formatting codes. Codes are inserted whenever you press the Tab key, underline text, center text, change margins, or execute any of a number of commands that change a document's appearance. Codes not only control how the document should look on the screen, they tell the printer how to print the document. Learning about codes helps you understand and control the way in which WordPerfect formats text.

Step 1: Reveal Codes

By default, codes are hidden from view to simplify the editing screen. You can display codes along with the text at any time, however, by executing the Reveal Codes command. Do this now:

Press **Alt-F3**

Your screen should look like Figure 7. The top part of the screen is the normal view of the document with codes hidden. The bar across the middle of the screen is a ruler line that indicates the current left margin (open brace {), the tab stops (triangles), and the right margin (close brace }). The portion of the screen below the ruler line reveals the codes, which are bright characters enclosed in square brackets, and the text in ordinary characters. For example, [Und] is the code that turns underlining on and off. It appears in uppercase [UND] when turned on and lowercase [und] when turned off.

WordPerfect has nearly 120 different formatting codes. The following table lists a few of the most common codes.

Figure 7 Formatting Codes Revealed

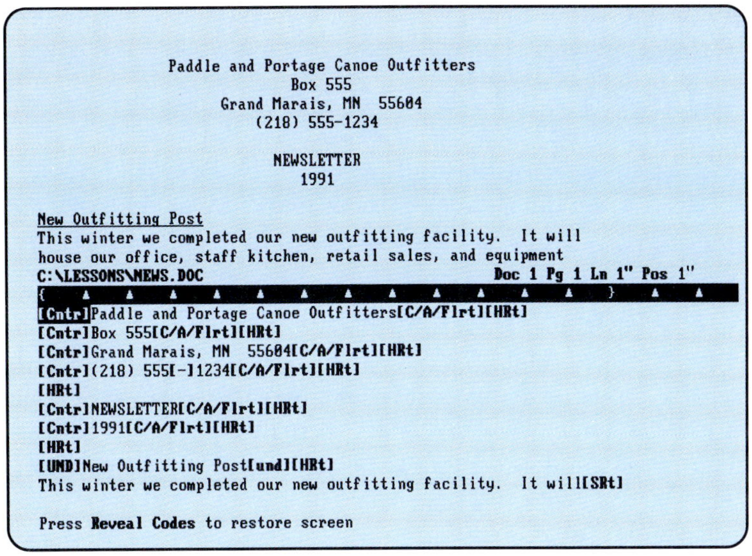

Code	Description
[-]	Hard hyphen inserted by pressing - key
[Bold]	Boldface on or off
[Cntr]	Begin centering text
[C/A/Flrt]	End centering, Align, or Flush Right text
[HPg]	Hard page break inserted by Ctrl-Enter
[HRt]	Hard return inserted by pressing Enter
[SPg]	Soft page break inserted by WordPerfect
[SRt]	Soft return inserted by word wrap
[Tab]	Advance to next tab stop
[Und]	Underline on or off

Step 2: Examine the Document

With Reveal Codes turned on, use the Down Arrow key to examine the document. Notice how the Reveal Codes cursor, a reverse video block, moves as you press the Down Arrow key. Look up the codes you see in the previous table and try to understand what they mean.

Step 3: Delete Codes

Codes are special characters that you can insert and delete. For example, to remove centering or underlining, you simply delete the appropriate codes. Although you don't have to reveal codes to delete them, revealing codes does make it easier to see what is happening. For example, let's uncenter the first line in the newsletter. Move the cursor to the first [Cntr] code in the file and then delete it:

Press **Delete**

The [C/A/Flrt] code that symbolizes the end of centering will also be removed and the text will shift to the left edge of the screen. Now, restore the code you have deleted:

Press **F1**
Type **r**

You can also delete codes to remove underlining and remove hard returns [HRt] to join lines or paragraphs.

Step 4: Hide Codes

Revealing codes displays two views of the same document, but you can see only about ten lines at a time. You can leave codes revealed for as long as you like, but most users prefer to turn them on only when needed. When you are finished working with codes, you can hide them again:

Press **Alt-F3**

The editing screen will return to full size, the ruler line will disappear, and codes will be hidden again.

Practice

1. Reveal codes.
2. Remove the underline from the heading "New Outfitting Post." Restore the underline by marking the heading as a block and then pressing the underline key (F8).
3. Move the cursor down to the end of the first paragraph after the heading "Equipment Improvements." Remove the hard return and the following tab to join the two paragraphs. Restore the hard return and tab. Move the cursor to the beginning of the document.
4. Use the help facility to read more about the Reveal Codes command:

   Press **F3**
   Press **Alt-F3**

   When you are finished reading the help screen, return to the document:

   Press **Enter**
5. Hide codes.

Lesson 6: Using the Thesaurus

Like most modern word processing packages, WordPerfect includes a built-in thesaurus program that can help you select just the right word for a situation. The WordPerfect thesaurus can examine a word already in your document or a word that you enter and display a list of synonyms (words with the same or similar meaning) and antonyms (words with the opposite meaning).

Step 1: Move the Cursor to the Desired Word

The thesaurus feature is very easy to use. For example, suppose you want to see alternatives to the word "house" in the second sentence of the New Outfitting Post paragraph. First, move the cursor anywhere within the word "house."

Step 2: Execute the Thesaurus Command

After you have selected the word you want to look up, simply execute the thesaurus command:

Press **Alt-F1**

Step 3: Examine the Thesaurus Screen

Your screen should look like Figure 8. In this case, "house" is the **headword,** a word that can be looked up in the thesaurus. The words under the headword, called references, are divided into nouns (n), verbs (v), adjectives (a), and antonyms (ant). No adjectives are available for "house." References preceded by a dot are other headwords that can also be looked up in the thesaurus. The references are collected into numbered groups of words with the same meaning. Six groups of references are available for "house." The Reference menu is the column of capital letters preceding the references. The Thesaurus menu is the list of four options across the bottom of the screen. Presently, the Reference menu is on the first column of words: abode, dwelling, home, residence, and so on. You can move the Reference menu from column to column by pressing Right Arrow and Left Arrow. For example, move the Reference menu to the second column of references:

Press **Right Arrow**

The column of capital letters will move over so that the word "accommodate" is A, "lodge" is B, "quarter" is C, and so on.

Step 4: Replace the Word

If you find a word in the list of references that you like, you can tell WordPerfect to replace the word you have looked up. Suppose you want to replace "house" with "accommodate." Select the Replace Word option from the Thesaurus menu and then type the letter of the word you want:

Type **1**
Type **a**

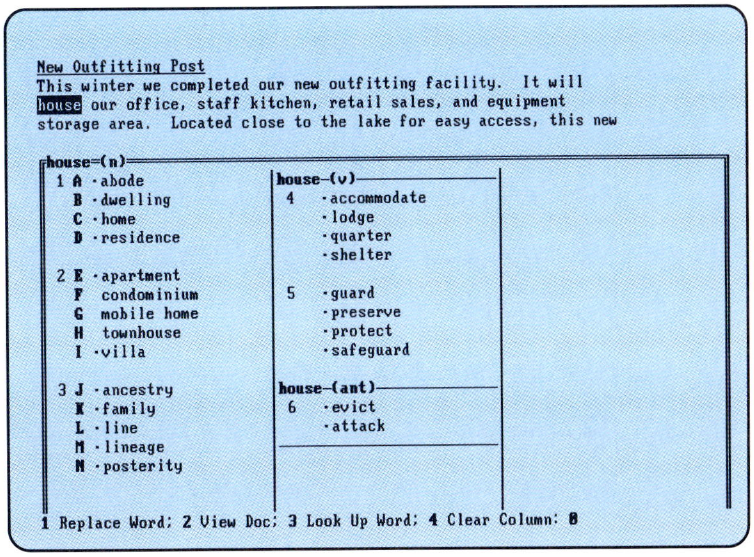

Figure 8 The Thesaurus Screen

The word "house" will automatically be replaced with "accommodate."

Step 5: Look Up Other Words

Invoke the thesaurus again:

Press **Alt-F1**

This time, "accommodate" is the headword. While the thesaurus is on the screen, you can use three methods to look up other words. The first method is to select the Look Up Word option and enter the word you want. Suppose you want to look up the word "lodge."

Type **3**
Type **lodge**
Press **Enter**

WordPerfect will display references for "lodge" in addition to the references for "accommodate" already on the screen (see Figure 9).

Step 6: Specify a Letter

Another way to look up a word while in the thesaurus is to type the letter next to a headword marked with a dot. Suppose you want to look up the word "board," which is preceded by the letter "M."

Type **m**

WordPerfect will display references for "board" in addition to the references for "lodge" and "accommodate" already on the screen (see Figure 10). You can move down or up within columns to see more references by pressing the Down Arrow or Up Arrow keys.

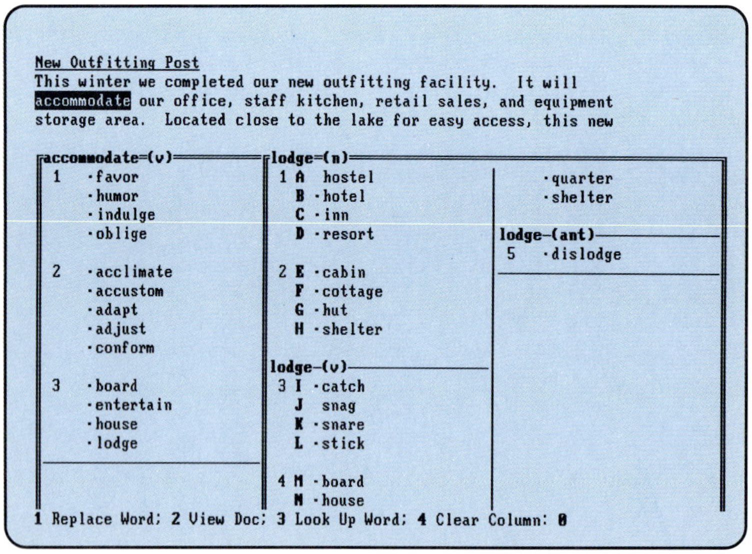

Figure 9 References for Two Headwords Displayed

Figure 10 References for Three Headwords Displayed

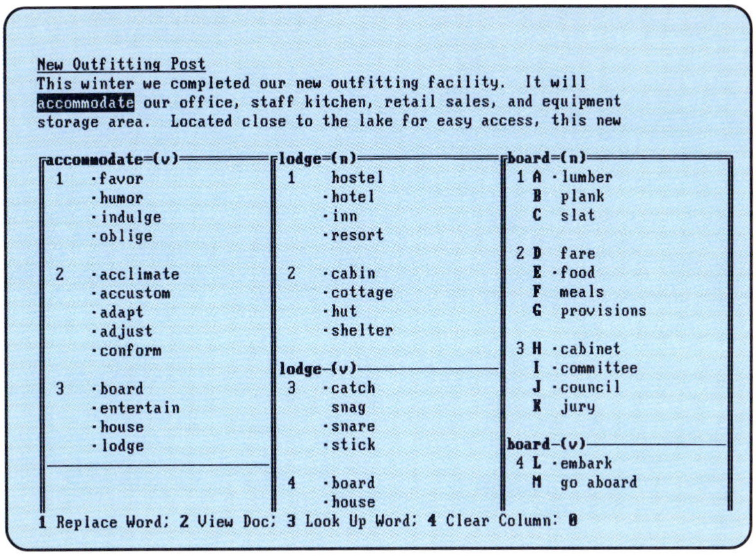

Step 7: Use the View Doc Option

The third way to look up other words while using the thesaurus is to select the View Doc option, move the cursor to another word in the document, and execute the Thesaurus command.

Type **2**

The cursor will move to the top of the screen where four lines of the document are displayed. You can now move the cursor within the document while the thesaurus remains on the screen. Move the cursor to the word "office" and then execute the Thesaurus command:

Press **Alt-F1**

The thesaurus screen will clear to reveal only the references for "office."

Step 8: Clear a Column

One more option is in the Thesaurus menu at the bottom of the screen: Clear Column. This option is handy for clearing the contents of a column to make room for the references of another word.

Type **4**

The column of references for the headword "office" will clear. You now have three empty columns in the thesaurus screen for looking up other words.

Step 9: Exit the Thesaurus

If you replace a word from the thesaurus, WordPerfect will automatically return to the editing screen. You can also exit the thesaurus without replacing a word.

Press **F7**

Practice

1. Move the cursor to the word "room" in the New Outfitting Post paragraph and invoke the thesaurus.
2. Tell the thesaurus to replace the word "room" with "space."
3. Invoke the thesaurus again. Use the Look Up Word option to look up any words you like. When you are finished, exit the thesaurus and move the cursor to the beginning of the document. Save the document to preserve any changes you have made.

Lesson 7: Working with Windows

WordPerfect's Window feature allows you to split the display into two separate document editing screens, each with its own status line. You can then show two different areas of the same document or work on two different documents at the same time. The Window feature is especially handy for referring to one part of a document while working on another part or for copying text from one document to another.

Step 1: Split the Screen

Suppose you want to create a new document while looking at an existing document. You can split the screen into two windows. Execute the Screen command, select the Window option, and specify the number of lines to be in the window:

Press **Ctrl-F3**
Type **w**
Type **11**
Press **Enter**

Figure 11 shows the result. The top window, which is eleven lines, contains the NEWS.DOC document. It has its own status line at the bottom. A ruler line

Figure 11 Split-Screen Windows

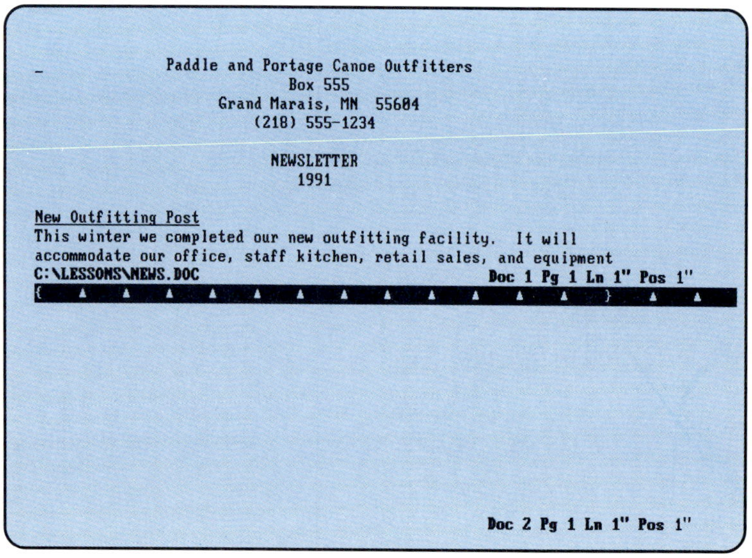

showing the current margin and tab stop settings separates the two windows. The bottom window, also eleven lines, is empty. In it you can create a new document. Notice that the bottom status line indicates that it is for document number 2.

Step 2: Switch Windows

The top window, which contains the cursor, is the active window. The ruler line reflects the settings in this window and the tab stop triangles point up. The commands you execute and the text you enter affect only this window. Before you can work in the bottom window, you must switch to it. Execute the Switch command:

Press **Shift-F3**

The cursor will move into the bottom window and the tab stop arrows in the ruler line will point down. Any text you enter or commands you execute will now affect only the bottom window. To go back up to the first window, execute the Switch command again:

Press **Shift-F3**

Step 3: Copy the Letterhead

Let's create a new document in the bottom window that will be a letter to a customer who inquired about Paddle and Portage Canoe Outfitters' sport show schedule. Fortunately, some of the text can be copied from the newsletter instead of being retyped.

Mark the letterhead at the top of the newsletter as a block of text:

Press **Home** (2 times)
Press **Up Arrow**
Press **Alt-F4**
Press **Down Arrow** (4 times)

Execute the Move Block Copy command:

Press **Ctrl-F4**
Type **b**
Type **c**

Position the cursor in the bottom window where you want to copy the block by executing the Switch command and then pressing Enter:

Press **Shift-F3**
Press **Enter**

The letterhead will be copied from NEWS.DOC in the top window to the new document in the bottom window (see Figure 12).

Step 4: Type the Letter

Follow these instructions to type the letter in the bottom window:

Press **Home** (2 times)
Press **Down Arrow**
Press **Enter**
Type **January 2, 1990**

Figure 12 The Letterhead Copied to the Bottom Window

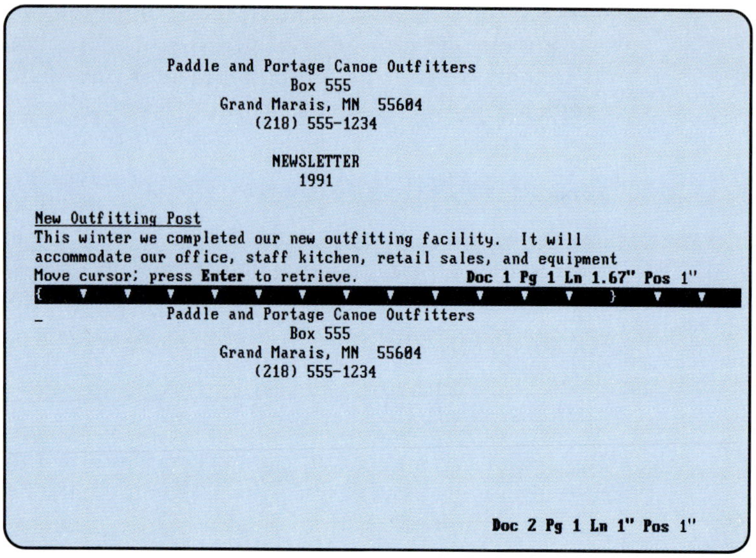

Press **Enter** (2 times)
Type **Mr. Richard Holmes**
Press **Enter**
Type **444 Adams Street**
Press **Enter**
Type **Green Bay, WI 54301**
Press **Enter** (2 times)
Type **Dear Mr. Holmes:**
Press **Enter** (2 times)
Type **Here is our sport show schedule for 1991.**
Type **We hope to see you soon!**
Press **Enter** (5 times)
Type **Sincerely,**
Press **Enter** (4 times)
Type **Bob Johnson**
Press **Enter**

Step 5: Copy the Schedule

Notice that the sport show schedule was purposely omitted from the letter. Instead of retyping the sport show schedule, you can copy it from the newsletter. Follow these directions:

Press **Up Arrow** (8 times)
Press **Shift-F3**
Press **Home** (2 times)
Press **Up Arrow**
Press **Down Arrow** (17 times)
Press **Alt-F4**
Press **Down Arrow** (11 times)
Press **Ctrl-F4**
Type **b**
Type **c**
Press **Shift-F3**
Press **Enter**

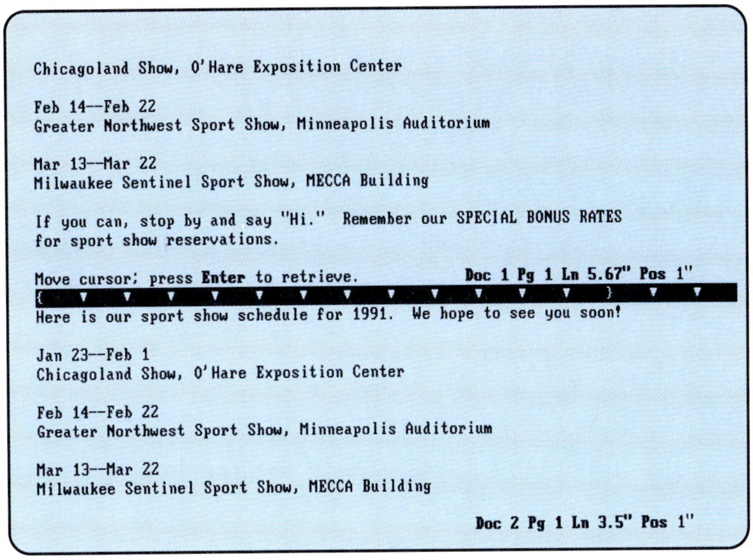

Figure 13 More Text Copied to the Bottom Window

The sport show schedule and the two sentences that follow it will be copied to the letter in the bottom window (see Figure 13).

Step 6: Save the Letter

Move the cursor to the top of the letter and examine it for typographical errors. After you are sure that it is correct, save the file on the hard disk in the LESSONS subdirectory and name it HOLMES.DOC.

Press **F10**
Type **c:\lessons\holmes.doc**
Press **Enter**

Step 7: Clear the Bottom Window

After the letter has been saved, you can clear the bottom window and use it to view some other document. Execute the Exit command:

Press **F7**
Type **n**
Type **y**

The bottom window will be cleared and the cursor will be moved into the top window. Move the cursor to the beginning of the document:

Press **Home** (2 times)
Press **Up Arrow**

Step 8: View the Same Document in the Bottom Window

The Window feature can also be used to view two different parts of the same document. This capability is especially handy for long documents if you have to refer to distant sections at the same time. Follow these directions to switch to the bottom window and retrieve NEWS.DOC:

Press **Shift-F3**
Press **Shift-F10**
Type **c:\lessons\news.doc**
Press **Enter**

The newsletter will be loaded into the bottom window. Now you can look at two different parts of the same document. Move to the end of the newsletter in the bottom window:

Press **Home** (2 times)
Press **Down Arrow**

As Figure 14 shows, the beginning of the newsletter appears in the top window and the end of the newsletter appears in the bottom window.

Step 9: Close a Window

Suppose you are finished working on two different sections of the same document or two different documents and want to close one of the windows. First, switch to the window you want to close, if the cursor is not already there, and execute the Exit command:

Press **F7**
Type **y**
Press **Enter**
Type **y**
Type **y**

The document will be saved and disappear from the window, but the screen will still be split. The cursor will move to the window containing text. To remove the empty window, expand the other window to 24 lines so that it fills the entire screen:

Press **Ctrl-F3**
Type **w**
Type **24**
Press **Enter**

A single window will expand to fill the entire screen.

Practice

1. Split the screen into two windows of equal size.
2. Retrieve the document MEMO.DOC into the bottom window.
3. Switch back and forth between the windows, examining their contents.
4. Exit and close the second window. The document NEWS.DOC should be on your screen. Move the cursor to the beginning of the newsletter.

Lesson 8: Indenting Paragraphs

Indenting refers to moving text away from the margin toward the center of the page. Several types of paragraph indentation are commonly used in documents. WordPerfect lets you use the first line indent, left indent, left and right indent, and hanging indent.

Figure 14 The Same Document In Two Windows

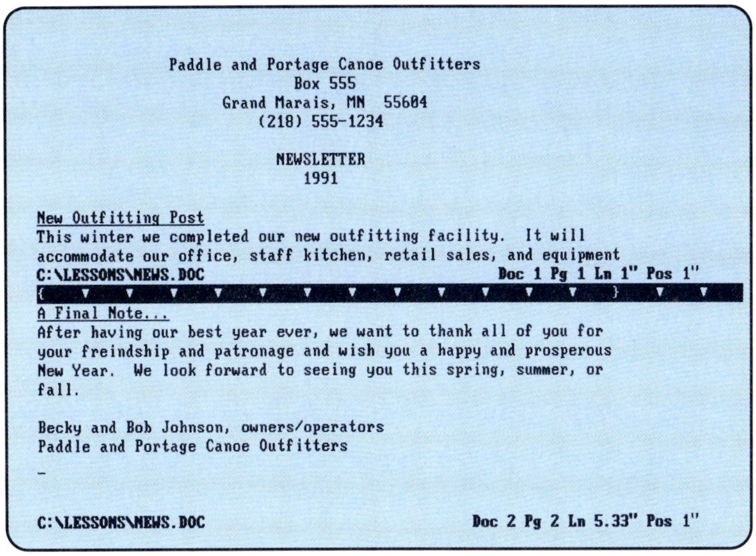

Step 1: Start a New Document

To illustrate paragraph indentation with WordPerfect, exit NEWS.DOC and create a new document:

Press **F7**
Type **n**
Type **n**

Your editing screen should now be empty.

Step 2: Indent the First Line of a Paragraph

The **first line indent** moves only the first line of the paragraph in from the left margin. This is done by pressing the Tab key before typing the paragraph.

Press **Tab**

Now type the text:

`This paragraph illustrates the first line indent. Only the first line of the paragraph is moved from the left margin toward the center of the page.`

Press **Enter** (2 times)

Step 3: Indent Paragraphs from the Left Margin

The **left indent** moves all lines of the paragraph in from the left margin. This is done by executing the Left Indent command.

Press **F4**

Now type the text:

`This paragraph illustrates the left indent, in which all lines are moved from the left margin toward the center`

of the page. Pressing F4 creates a temporary left margin one tab stop in from the permanent left margin. Words will automatically wrap to the indented left margin.

Press **Enter** (2 times)
Press **F4** (2 times)

Type this text:

Each time you press F4, the temporary left margin moves in another tab stop toward the center of the page.

Press **Enter** (2 times)

Step 4: Indent Paragraphs from Both Margins

A paragraph can be indented from both the left and right margins. This is done by executing the Left and Right Indent command.

Press **Shift-F4**

Now type the text:

This paragraph is indented from both the left and right margins. All lines are moved in from both margins toward the center of the page.

Press **Enter** (2 times)
Press **Shift-F4** (2 times)

Type this text:

Each time you press Shift-F4, the temporary left and right margins move in another tab stop toward the center of the page.

Press **Enter** (2 times)

Step 5: Create a Hanging Indent

A **hanging indent** occurs when all lines of a paragraph except for the first are indented from the left margin. It is created by executing both the Left Indent and Margin Release commands.

Press **F4**
Press **Shift-Tab**

Now type the text:

This paragraph illustrates the hanging indent. The first line of the paragraph stays at the left margin, while all of the remaining lines are moved toward the center of the page.

Your screen should look like Figure 15.

Step 6: Save the Document

Save the new document you have created in a file named INDENT.DOC in the LESSONS subdirectory.

Figure 15 Paragraph Indentation

```
     This paragraph illustrates the first line indent.  Only the
first line of the paragraph is moved from the left margin toward
the center of the page.

     This paragraph illustrates the left indent, in which all lines
     are moved from the left margin toward the center of the page.
     Pressing F4 creates a temporary left margin one tab stop in
     from the permanent left margin.  Words will automatically wrap
     to the indented left margin.

          Each time you press F4, the temporary left margin moves
          in another tab stop toward the center of the page.

     This paragraph is indented from both the left and right
     margins.  All lines are moved in from both margins toward
     the center of the page.

          Each time you press Shift-F4, the temporary
          left and right margins move in another tab stop
          toward the center of the page.

This paragraph illustrates the hanging indent.  The first line of
     the paragraph stays at the left margin, while all of the
     remaining lines are moved toward the center of the page._
                                        Doc 1 Pg 1 Ln 4.83" Pos 7.1"
```

Press **F10**
Type **c:\lessons\indent.doc**
Press **Enter**

Practice

1. Move the cursor to the beginning of the INDENT.DOC document. Then execute the Reveal Codes command:

   Press **Alt-F3**

   Scroll through the document and examine the indentation codes. You should be able to understand what they mean. Try deleting one of the indentation codes and see what happens. Then restore the deleted code. Execute the Reveal Codes command again to return to the regular editing screen.

2. Use the help facility to read about the Left Indent command:

   Press **F3**
   Press **F4**

   Then use the help facility to read about the Left and Right Indent (Shift-F4) and the Margin Release (Shift-Tab) commands.

Lesson 9: Using Tab Stops to Create Tables

Tab stops allow you to position text precisely within a line. They are often used for aligning text or numbers in a table. Tab stops should always be used instead of pressing the Space Bar to vertically align items in a table because the size of a space varies from font to font. To align items in a table, you press the Tab key to insert a tab code and move the cursor to the next tab stop.

Initially, WordPerfect has a tab stop set at every half-inch position. But you can change these tab stop settings by executing the Format command, selecting the Line option, and then selecting the Tab Set option.

To illustrate the use of tab stops, let's add a short table to NEWS.DOC that presents the current outfitting rates.

Step 1: Retrieve NEWS.DOC

Clear the editing screen and retrieve the newsletter document by executing these commands:

Press **F7**
Type **n**
Type **n**
Press **Shift-F10**
Type **c:\lessons\news.doc**
Press **Enter**

Step 2: Move the Cursor

Let's insert the new table between the Trail Food Improvements paragraph and the Trips paragraph. A quick way to move the cursor is to use the Search command:

Press **F2**
Type **Trips**
Press **F2**
Press **Up Arrow**

The cursor should now be on the blank line just before the Trips paragraph.

Step 3: Insert the Heading

The table will be entitled "Current Outfitting Rates," so insert this underlined heading:

Press **Enter**
Press **F8**
Type **Current Outfitting Rates**
Press **F8**
Press **Enter**

Step 4: Change the Tab Stop Settings

A left-aligned tab stop lines up the left edge of text to the tab stop. This is the default and most commonly used type of tab stop. Let's insert left-aligned tab stops at the 2-inch and 4-inch positions. These tab stops will then affect all text at and below the cursor. Follow these directions:

Press **Shift-F8**
Type **L**
Type **t**
Press **Ctrl-End**
Type **2"**
Press **Enter**
Type **L**
Type **4"**
Press **Enter**
Type **L**

At this point, your screen should look like Figure 16. Pressing Ctrl-End deletes all of the default tab stops. Left-aligned tab stops are inserted by entering the desired line position and typing L. You can also press Right Arrow or Left Arrow

Figure 16 The New Tab Stop Settings

```
Beaver canoes and nylon packs will be available on a first-come,
first-serve basis.

Trail Food Improvements
We have replaced the Ham and Potatoes with Meatballs and Gravy, the
Beef Stromboli with Chicken Stew 'N Dumplings, and the Buttermilk
Pancakes with Blueberry Pancakes.  These are all taste
improvements, not cost savings, so our Trail Food will be even
--------------------------------------------------------------------
better this year.

Current Outfitting Rates

Trips
This fall we took a trip into the Cherry Lake area for some lake
trout fishing.  We had our usual quota of rain, but did enjoy two
beautiful crisp autumn days.  Mornings we awoke to clear, deep blue
skies with heavy, white steam rising from Cherry Lake.  On shore
we could look up into the blue sky, but as we paddled into the
steam we disappeared into white nothingness.  It was a trip we'll
..........L...................L............................................
|    ^    |    ^    |    ^    |    ^    |    ^    |    ^    |    ^    |    ^
1"        2"        3"        4"        5"        6"        7"        8"
Delete EOL (clear tabs); Enter Number (set tab); Del (clear tab);
Left; Center; Right; Decimal; .= Dot Leader; Press Exit when done.
```

to move the cursor within the ruler line to select the desired tab stop position. Now execute the Exit command twice to finalize your new tab stops and return to the editing screen:

Press **F7** (2 times)

Step 5: Enter the Table

Follow these directions to enter the Current Outfitting Rates table:

Press **Tab**
Type **`Number In Party`**
Press **Tab**
Type **`Rate Per Person Per Day`**
Press **Enter**
Press **Tab**
Type **`1 to 3 persons`**
Press **Tab**
Type **`$31.00`**
Press **Enter**
Press **Tab**
Type **`4 to 6 persons`**
Press **Tab**
Type **`$29.25`**
Press **Enter**
Press **Tab**
Type **`7 to 9 persons`**
Press **Tab**
Type **`$28.50`**
Press **Enter**

Your screen should look like Figure 17.

Figure 17 The Current Outfitting Rates Table

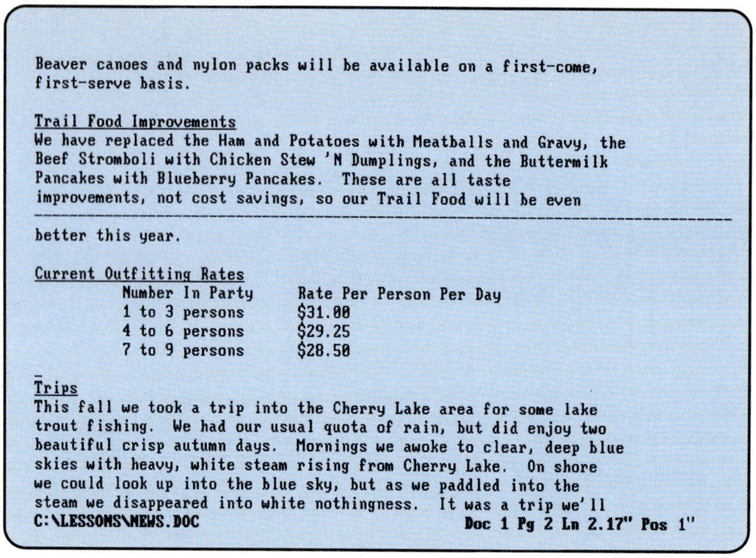

```
Beaver canoes and nylon packs will be available on a first-come,
first-serve basis.

Trail Food Improvements
We have replaced the Ham and Potatoes with Meatballs and Gravy, the
Beef Stromboli with Chicken Stew 'N Dumplings, and the Buttermilk
Pancakes with Blueberry Pancakes.  These are all taste
improvements, not cost savings, so our Trail Food will be even
------------------------------------------------------------------------
better this year.

Current Outfitting Rates
           Number In Party        Rate Per Person Per Day
           1 to 3 persons         $31.00
           4 to 6 persons         $29.25
           7 to 9 persons         $28.50

Trips
This fall we took a trip into the Cherry Lake area for some lake
trout fishing.  We had our usual quota of rain, but did enjoy two
beautiful crisp autumn days.  Mornings we awoke to clear, deep blue
skies with heavy, white steam rising from Cherry Lake.  On shore
we could look up into the blue sky, but as we paddled into the
steam we disappeared into white nothingness.  It was a trip we'll
C:\LESSONS\NEWS.DOC                                Doc 1 Pg 2 Ln 2.17" Pos 1"
```

Step 6: Reset Default Tab Stops Below the Table

Changing tab stops affects all text at and below the current cursor location. But you don't want the rest of the document to have the same tab stops as the table. So, you must reset the default tab stops below the table. Follow these directions:

Press **Shift-F8**
Type **L**
Type **t**
Type **0,0.5**
Press **Enter**
Press **F7** (2 times)

This will set a tab stop at every half inch position beginning at position 0, the left edge of the page.

Step 7: Save the Document

Save the document to the disk to preserve the changes you have made:

Press **F10**
Press **Enter**
Type **y**

Practice

1. Use the Reveal Codes command to examine the Tab Set codes that appear before and after the Current Outfitting Rates table. When you are finished, execute the Reveal Codes command again to return to the full editing screen.
2. Using tabs is better than using spaces to align text and numbers in columns. One reason is that different characters are different widths in some fonts, so columns may not line up when the document is printed if you have used the Space Bar to align text on the screen. Another reason to use tabs is that they make it easy to change the position of columns later. For example, move the

cursor to the beginning of the line just below the heading "Current Outfitting Rates." Activate the Tab Set menu:

Press **Shift-F8**
Type **L**
Type **t**

Delete the tab stop at the 2-inch position by moving the cursor there and pressing the Delete key. Insert a new tab stop at the 2.5-inch position. Delete the tab stop at the 4-inch position and insert a new one at the 4.5-inch position. Exit the Tab Set menu and return to the editing screen. The entire table will be shifted a half inch to the right.

3. Execute the Reveal Codes command again. Note that WordPerfect simply inserted a new Tab Set code for the new tab stop settings you created in the previous exercise. You can remove that Tab Set code and revert to the previous tab stop settings:

   Press **Left Arrow**
   Press **Delete**

   The table will shift back to the left a half inch. Execute the Reveal Codes command again to return to the full editing screen. Move the cursor to the beginning of the document.

Lesson 10: Using the Tab Align Command

The numbers in the Current Outfitting Rates table line up nicely, but only because they all have the same number of characters. Numbers with fewer or more digits would not line up on the decimal points. In such cases, you can use a decimal tab stop instead of a left-aligned tab stop. Another alternative is to use the Tab Align command. To illustrate this command, let's insert another table that lists the Paddle and Portage 1990 fishing records.

Step 1: Move the Cursor

Let's insert the new table after the Current Outfitting Rates table. Move the cursor to the end of the last line of the table. By inserting the new table here, you use the same tab stop settings as the Current Outfitting Rates table.

Step 2: Insert the Heading

The table will be entitled "1990 Fishing Records," so do this:

Press **Enter** (2 times)
Press **F8**
Type **`1990 Fishing Records`**
Press **F8**
Press **Enter**

Step 3: Enter the Table

Now, enter the table as follows:

Press **Tab**
Type **`Bluegill`**

Figure 18 The Numbers Aligned with the Tab Align Command

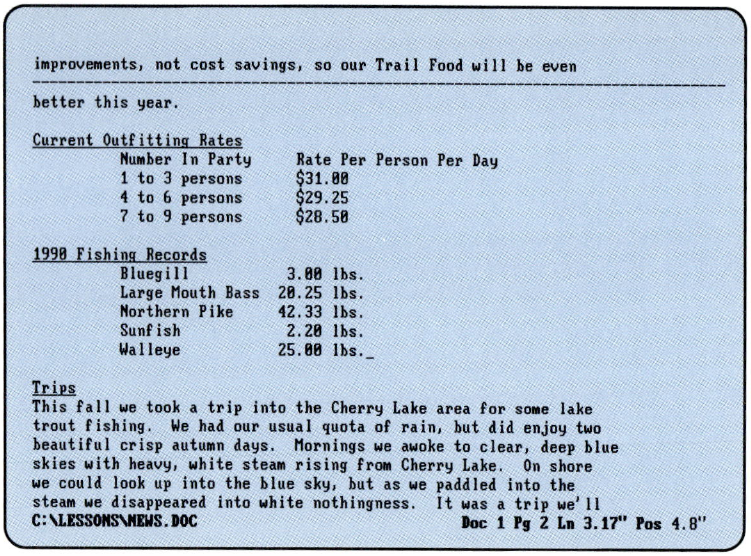

```
improvements, not cost savings, so our Trail Food will be even
--------------------------------------------------------------------------------
better this year.

Current Outfitting Rates
          Number In Party       Rate Per Person Per Day
          1 to 3 persons        $31.00
          4 to 6 persons        $29.25
          7 to 9 persons        $28.50

1990 Fishing Records
          Bluegill             3.00 lbs.
          Large Mouth Bass    20.25 lbs.
          Northern Pike       42.33 lbs.
          Sunfish              2.20 lbs.
          Walleye             25.00 lbs._

Trips
This fall we took a trip into the Cherry Lake area for some lake
trout fishing.  We had our usual quota of rain, but did enjoy two
beautiful crisp autumn days.  Mornings we awoke to clear, deep blue
skies with heavy, white steam rising from Cherry Lake.  On shore
we could look up into the blue sky, but as we paddled into the
steam we disappeared into white nothingness.  It was a trip we'll
C:\LESSONS\NEWS.DOC                                 Doc 1 Pg 2 Ln 3.17" Pos 4.8"
```

Press **Ctrl-F6**
Type **3.00 lbs.**
Press **Enter**
Press **Tab**
Type **Large Mouth Bass**
Press **Ctrl-F6**
Type **20.25 lbs.**
Press **Enter**
Press **Tab**
Type **Northern Pike**
Press **Ctrl-F6**
Type **42.33 lbs.**
Press **Enter**
Press **Tab**
Type **Sunfish**
Press **Ctrl-F6**
Type **2.20 lbs.**
Press **Enter**
Press **Tab**
Type **Walleye**
Press **Ctrl-F6**
Type **25.00 lbs.**

Your screen should look like Figure 18. In each line of the table, you pressed Ctrl-F6 instead of Tab before typing the number. This keypress executes the Tab Align command, which lines up text or numbers on an alignment character. The default alignment character is the period or decimal point. When you press Ctrl-F6, the cursor moves to the next tab stop and WordPerfect displays the prompt

```
Align char=.
```

This prompt tells you the default alignment character and lets you change it. For entering numbers, you want the period to be the alignment character so you can ignore the prompt. Characters you type at the tab stop move left until the alignment character is typed, or until Ctrl-F6, Tab, or Enter are pressed. Characters typed after the alignment character move to the right, as they normally do. The result is that all numbers line up on their decimal points at the tab stop.

Step 4: Save the Document

Save the document to the disk to preserve the changes you have made:

Press **F10**
Press **Enter**
Type **y**

Practice

1. Execute the Reveal Codes command and examine the table you have just entered. The [Align] code indicates the execution of a Tab Align command and the [C/A/Flrt] code indicates the end of a Tab Align command. Return to the normal editing screen.
2. Invoke the help facility and read about the Tab Align command:

   Press **F3**
   Press **Ctrl-F6**

   When you are finished, return to the editing screen:

   Press **Space Bar**
3. Insert another line in the 1990 Fishing Records table:

   `Lake Trout 50.00 lbs.`

   Save the document to the disk. Move the cursor to the beginning of the document.

Lesson 11: Using the Flush Right Command

The Flush Right command lets you easily align text to the right margin. This feature is especially handy for typing the return address and date in a letter. Let's see how this feature works in the HOLMES.DOC letter you created in Lesson 7.

Step 1: Clear the Screen

Exit NEWS.DOC and clear the screen:

Press **F7**
Type **n**
Type **n**

Step 2: Retrieve the Letter

Execute the Retrieve command to load the document HOLMES.DOC and display it on the editing screen:

Press **Shift-F10**
Type **`c:\lessons\holmes.doc`**
Press **Enter**

Step 3: Type a New Line Flush Right

The letterhead at the top of the document HOLMES.DOC is centered. Let's delete the first line and retype it flush right. The cursor should already be at the beginning of the first line of HOLMES.DOC. Delete to the end of the line:

Press **Ctrl-End**

Now, execute the Flush Right command and retype the line:

Press **Alt-F6**
Type **`Paddle and Portage Canoe Outfitters`**

Notice how the cursor moves to the right margin when you press Alt-F6 and how the text you type moves to the left. Since a hard return already exists at the end of the line, move to the beginning of the next line without pressing Enter:

Press **Right Arrow** (2 times)

You have to press Right Arrow twice to skip over the end flush right code and the hard return code.

Step 4: Move an Existing Line Flush Right

The Flush Right command can also move an existing line of text to the right margin. Let's move the second line of the letterhead flush right. First, uncenter the line by deleting the Center code:

Press **Delete**

Now, move the line flush right:

Press **Alt-F6**
Press **Down Arrow**

The end of the second line will be aligned to the right margin.

Step 5: Move a Block Flush Right

You can move several lines of text flush right by first marking them as a block. Execute the following commands:

Press **Home**
Press **Left Arrow**
Press **Alt-F4**
Press **Down Arrow** (4 times)
Press **Alt-F6**
Type **y**

The rest of the letterhead and date will move flush right as shown in Figure 19.

Step 6: Save the Document

Save the document to the disk to preserve the changes you have made:

Press **F10**
Press **Enter**
Type **y**

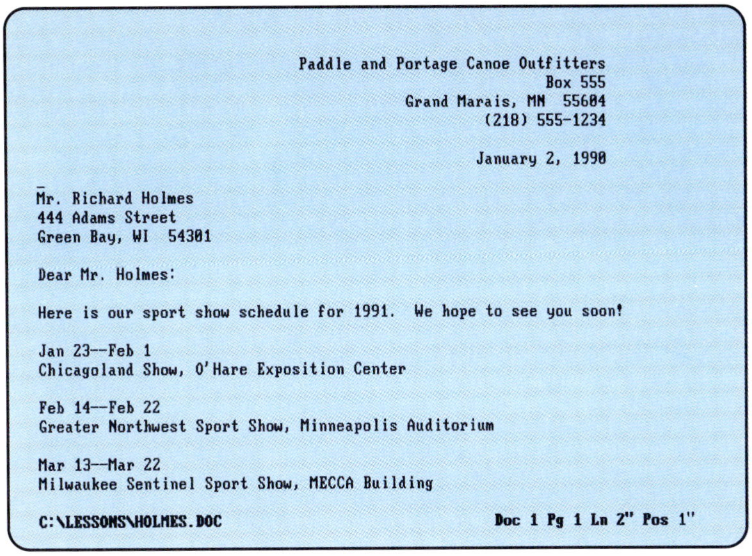

Paddle and Portage Canoe Outfitters
Box 555
Grand Marais, MN 55604
(218) 555-1234

January 2, 1990

Mr. Richard Holmes
444 Adams Street
Green Bay, WI 54301

Dear Mr. Holmes:

Here is our sport show schedule for 1991. We hope to see you soon!

Jan 23--Feb 1
Chicagoland Show, O'Hare Exposition Center

Feb 14--Feb 22
Greater Northwest Sport Show, Minneapolis Auditorium

Mar 13--Mar 22
Milwaukee Sentinel Sport Show, MECCA Building

C:\LESSONS\HOLMES.DOC Doc 1 Pg 1 Ln 2" Pos 1"

Figure 19 Letterhead and Date Moved Flush Right

Practice

1. Execute the Reveal Codes command and examine the text you have just moved. The [Flsh Rt] code indicates the start of a flush right line and the [C/A/Flrt] indicates the end.
2. Move the cursor to the [Flsh Rt] code before the date and delete it. See how the date moves back to the left margin. Move the date flush right again:

   Press **Alt-F6**
   Press **Down Arrow**

   Execute the Reveal Codes command to return to the normal editing screen.
3. Execute the Help command and read about the Flush Right command:

   Press **F3**
   Press **Alt-F6**

   When you are finished reading the description, return to the editing screen:

   Press **Space Bar**

Lesson 12: Using the Date Command

WordPerfect's Date command lets you insert the current date into your document as text or as a code that is automatically updated and converted to text whenever the document is retrieved or printed. This feature is handy for letters, memos, and other documents that must display the current date. As an example, let's use the Date command to insert the date into the HOLMES.DOC letter. Note that in order for the Date command to work, your computer's clock must be set to the correct date. If the current date is not maintained by a built-in battery, you must use the DOS DATE command to specify the correct date when you boot up.

Step 1: Delete the Existing Date

First, delete the date that you have already typed into the document. Move the cursor to the line that contains the date and delete to the end of the line:

Press **Ctrl-End**

Step 2: Execute the Flush Right Command

The Flush Right codes were deleted in the previous step, so execute the Flush Right command before inserting the date:

Press **Alt-F6**

Step 3: Select the Date Text Option

Activate the Date/Outline menu:

Press **Shift-F5**

Your screen should look like Figure 20. To insert the current date as text, just as you would type it yourself, select the Date Text option:

Type **t**
Press **Down Arrow**

The current date will be inserted into the document, flush against the right margin.

Step 4: Select the Date Code Option

The date you inserted in the previous step is ordinary text. It will not change to reflect the current date if you retrieve or print the letter tomorrow. If you want the date in the letter to be current whenever it is retrieved or printed, you must

Figure 20 The Date/Outline Menu

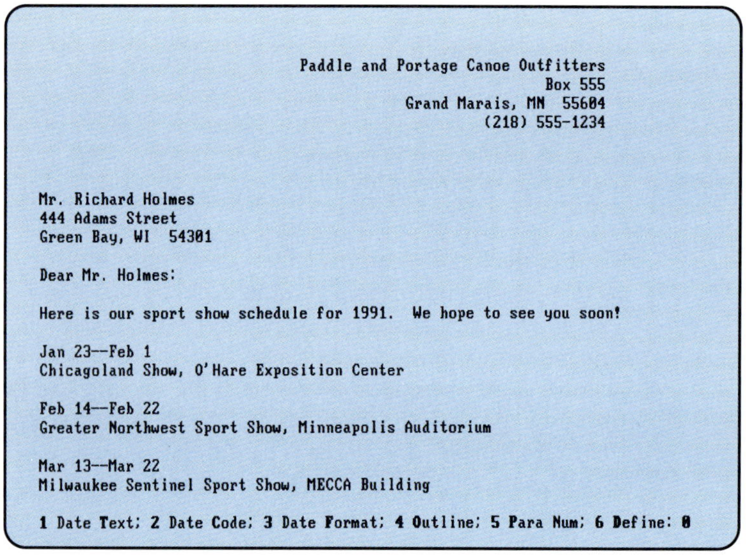

use the Date Code option from the Date/Outline menu. Follow these directions to delete the date text and insert the date code instead:

Press **Up Arrow**
Press **Ctrl-End**
Press **Alt-F6**
Press **Shift-F5**
Type **c**
Press **Down Arrow**

The result looks the same as in the previous step, but the date you see will change if you retrieve or print the letter in the future.

Step 5: Select the Format Option

The Format option in the Date/Outline menu lets you change the way the date is displayed. Activate the Date/Outline menu and select the Format option:

Press **Shift-F5**
Type **f**

The Date Format menu will appear on the screen (see Figure 21). The default date format is presented at the bottom of the screen. The format code 3 1, 4 means the month (word) followed by the day of the month, a comma, and all four digits of the year. The date format menu gives you a great deal of flexibility in specifying how the date is to appear when you execute the Date command. Return to the editing screen without changing the date format:

Press **F7** (2 times)

Step 6: Save the Document

Save the document to the disk to preserve the changes you have made:

Press **F10**
Press **Enter**
Type **y**

Figure 21 The Date Format Menu

```
Date Format

     Character   Meaning
         1       Day of the Month
         2       Month (number)
         3       Month (word)
         4       Year (all four digits)
         5       Year (last two digits)
         6       Day of the Week (word)
         7       Hour (24-hour clock)
         8       Hour (12-hour clock)
         9       Minute
         0       am / pm
         %       Used before a number, will:
                   Pad numbers less than 10 with a leading zero
                   Output only 3 letters for the month or day of the week

     Examples:  3 1, 4        = December 25, 1984
                %6 %3 1, 4    = Tue Dec 25, 1984
                %2/%1/5 (6)   = 01/01/85 (Tuesday)
                8:90          = 10:55am

Date format: 3 1, 4
```

Practice

1. Execute the Reveal Codes command to examine the date code. Note that no text is actually stored in the document, just the code [Date:3 1, 4], which specifies the format in which to present the current date. Return to the full editing screen.
2. Try moving the cursor within the date. You will find that WordPerfect treats the date as a single character because it is really a date code. You can delete it, but not change it.
3. Delete the date code in the letter. Execute the Date/Outline command and select the Format option. Change the date format and insert a new date code:

   Type **2/1/5**
   Press **Enter**
   Type **c**

   Observe the new date format. Now delete the date code, change the date format back to the way it was, and insert a new date code.

Lesson 13: Centering Text on a Page

Short letters and memos often look better when they are centered from top to bottom on a page. Centering from top to bottom is also used for title pages. The Center Page feature makes it easy to center text on a page when it is printed.

Step 1: Move Cursor Before All Codes

To center text on a page, you must move to the very beginning of the document, before any codes that may be hidden. Pressing the Home key three times followed by an Up Arrow or Left Arrow key moves the cursor ahead of any codes at the beginning of a document or line. Execute this command:

Press **Home** (3 times)
Press **Up Arrow**

Step 2: Select the Center Page Option

Execute the Format command, select the Page option, select the Center Page option, and then execute the Exit command:

Press **Shift-F8**
Type **p**
Type **c**
Press **F7**

The document will not look any different on the screen, but it will be centered vertically on the page when it is printed.

Step 3: Print the Document

To see the result of using the Center Page option, print the letter:

Press **Shift-F7**
Type **f**

Practice

1. Execute the Reveal Codes command. The first code in the document is [Center Pg], which tells WordPerfect to center the text vertically on the page when printed. Return to the full editing screen.
2. Turn off the Center Page option for this document. You can either delete the Center Page code or select the Center Page option from the Page menu of the Format command.
3. Execute the Help command and read about the Center Page option:

   Press **F3**
   Press **Shift-F8**
   Type **p**
   Type **c**

   When you are finished reading the description, return to the editing screen:

   Press **Space Bar**

Lesson 14: Adding a Document Summary

DOS file names, such as HOLMES.DOC, are limited to eight characters plus a three-character extension. Even if you try to use mnemonic file names, remembering important details about your documents can become difficult, especially if you collect a large number of documents over a long period of time. Fortunately, WordPerfect lets you create a summary for each document that contains a descriptive file name, the subject, the author, the typist, and comments. Although a document summary is never printed, you can look at it on the screen. Document summaries may also be searched by the Word Search option of the List Files menu. As an example, let's add a document summary to HOLMES.DOC.

Step 1: Select the Summary Option

A document summary can be created or edited from any place in a document. Simply execute the Format command, select the Document option, and then select the Summary option:

Press **Shift-F8**
Type **d**
Type **s**

WordPerfect will display the Document Summary screen, as shown in Figure 22.

Step 2: Enter the Descriptive Filename

The System Filename and Date of Creation have already been entered for you by WordPerfect. In addition, the first 400 characters of the document are automatically inserted in the Comments box. To enter the Descriptive Filename, select the first option and type the name:

Type **d**
Type `Letter to Richard Holmes`
Press **Enter**

You are limited to 40 characters for each item in the document summary except comments, which can contain up to 780 characters.

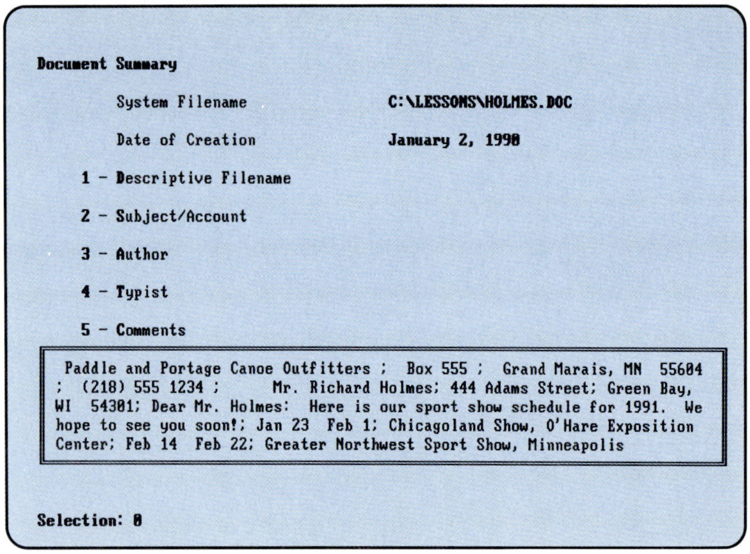

Figure 22 The Initial Document Summary Screen

Step 3: Enter the Subject

To enter the subject of the document, select the second option and enter the information:

Type **s**
Type **Sport Show Schedule**
Press **Enter**

Step 4: Enter the Author

To enter the author's name, select the third option:

Type **a**
Type **Bob Johnson**
Press **Enter**

In this case, you are pretending to be Bob Johnson. There is no other typist, so you can leave the Typist section blank. You can also leave the Comments box unchanged. Your screen should look like Figure 23.

Step 5: Exit the Document Summary Screen

To save the document summary and return to the editing screen, execute the exit command:

Press **F7**

Step 6: Save the Document

Save the document, along with its summary, to the disk to preserve the changes you have made:

Press **F10**
Press **Enter**
Type **y**

Figure 23 The Completed Document Summary Screen

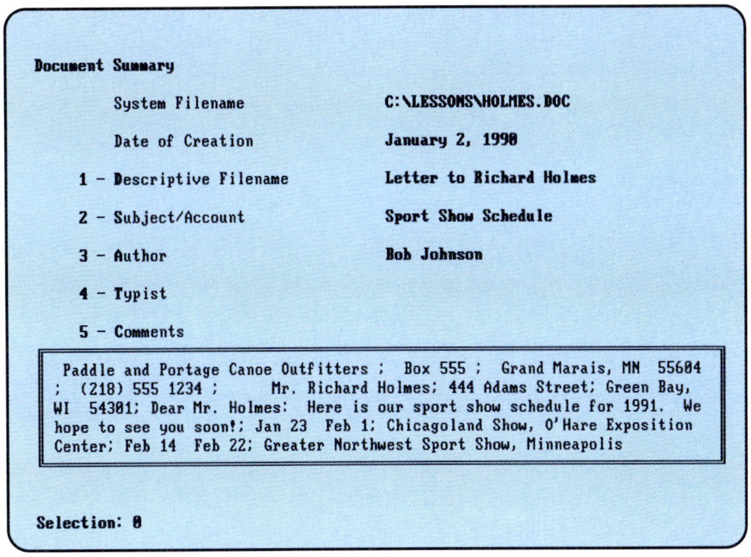

Practice

1. Display the document summary for HOLMES.DOC on your screen. Then return to the editing screen.
2. Execute the List Files command and specify the subdirectory C:\LESSONS. Select the Word Search option from the List Files menu and then select the Doc Summary option. Specify the following word pattern:

   Type **Schedule**
   Press **Enter**

   WordPerfect should highlight the file HOLMES.DOC and mark it with an asterisk. Unmark the file and exit the List Files screen.

Lesson 15: Use the Text In/Out Command

A text file or ASCII file is a file that contains no special formatting codes—only letters, numbers, punctuation marks, spaces, tabs, and carriage returns. Text files are used for DOS batch files, the CONFIG.SYS file, programming language source code files, and some types of data files. In addition, text files are sometimes used to store documents in a format that can be read by other programs and word processing packages. The Text In/Out command lets you work with text files in WordPerfect. More specifically, it can perform the following procedures:

- Save the current document as a text file.
- Retrieve a text file to be edited with WordPerfect.
- Save the current document in a generic word processing format.
- Save the current document as a WordPerfect version 4.2 file.

Let's examine the Text In/Out command more closely.

Step 1: Clear the Editing Screen

Exit your current document and clear the editing screen:

Press **F7**
Type **n**
Type **n**

Step 2: Retrieve a Text File

Suppose you want to change the AUTOEXEC.BAT file in the root directory of the hard disk. In Lesson 1, you learned that you can retrieve a text file with the Text In option of the List Files menu. You can also retrieve a text file with the Text In/Out command.

Press **Ctrl-F5**

WordPerfect will display the Text In/Out menu (see Figure 24). To load a text file, select the first option:

Type **t**

Another menu will be presented with three options. The first option is for saving a text file. The second option will retrieve a text file and convert carriage return and line feed pairs into hard returns. The third option retrieves a text file and converts carriage return/line feeds into soft returns. You use the second option for editing text files that will not be converted into WordPerfect documents. Select the Retrieve option and specify the file:

Press **r**
Type **c:\autoexec.bat**
Press **Enter**

The file AUTOEXEC.BAT will be loaded into the editing screen.

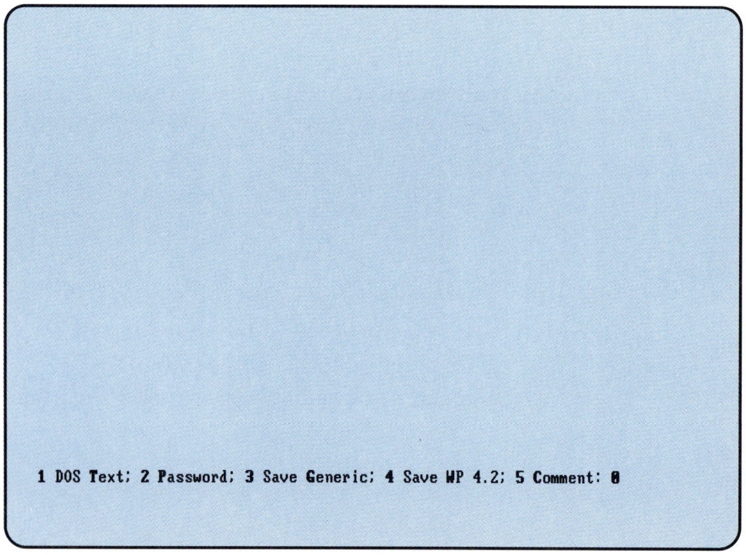

***Figure 24** The Text In/Out Menu*

Step 3: Save a Text File

You can now edit the file AUTOEXEC.BAT with WordPerfect. Since it is not a document, you should not use formatting features such as margins, underlining, flush right, and so on. You can, however, insert, typeover, and delete text. Suppose you are finished editing the file. You save it to the disk with the Text In/Out command.

Press **Ctrl-F5**
Type **t**
Type **s**
Press **Enter**
Type **y**

Step 4: Examine the Other Text In/Out Options

Execute the Text In/Out command again to display the menu:

Press **Ctrl-F5**

The Password option allows you to protect a document so that no one will be able to retrieve or print it without knowing the password. This option works with WordPerfect document files, not text files. It seems out of place in the Text In/Out menu.

The Save Generic option lets you save a document so that the general format is preserved without WordPerfect-specific codes. For example, spaces would be used to center, indent, and flush right text instead of WordPerfect formatting codes. This option might be used to save a WordPerfect document in a file to be read by some other word processing package.

The Save WP 4.2 option lets you save a document in a file that can be read by WordPerfect version 4.2.

Finally, the Comment option is used to insert or edit comments in a document. Comments can be displayed on the screen, but are never printed with a document. They can be used for reminders, notes, and suggestions that are not actually part of the document. Like the Password option, the Comment option has nothing to do with text files. Who knows why it is in the Text In/Out menu?

Practice

1. Execute the Help command and read about the Text In/Out command and all of its options.
2. Clear the editing screen. Use the Text In/Out command to retrieve the text file CONFIG.SYS from the root directory of the hard disk. Without changing the file, save it to the disk with the Text In/Out command.

Lesson 16: Execute a DOS Command within WordPerfect

Like many of today's application packages, WordPerfect lets you execute one or more DOS commands without actually exiting the program. The Shell command keeps WordPerfect in memory while control is passed to a secondary DOS command processor. When you are finished performing DOS commands, you execute the DOS EXIT command and return to WordPerfect, which is still in memory. This handy feature, for example, can be used to check a disk, format a diskette, or copy files without exiting WordPerfect.

Step 1: Execute the SHELL Command

Suppose you want to execute CHKDSK or some other DOS command without exiting WordPerfect. Execute the WordPerfect Shell command:

Press **Ctrl-F1**
Type **g**

WordPerfect will load a secondary DOS command processor and display a message telling you how to get back to the program (see Figure 25).

Step 2: Execute the DOS Commands

You are now at the DOS prompt and can execute any DOS commands, but WordPerfect is still dormant in memory. Execute the following DOS commands:

Type **chkdsk**
Press **Enter**
Type **dir**
Press **Enter**

Step 3: Execute the EXIT Command

When you are finished with DOS, you execute the EXIT command to return to WordPerfect:

Type **exit**
Press **Enter**

The computer will immediately return to the editing screen, just where you left off when you executed the Shell command.

Practice

1. Execute the Shell command and return to DOS. Theoretically, you can now execute any DOS command and even start an application package. In reality,

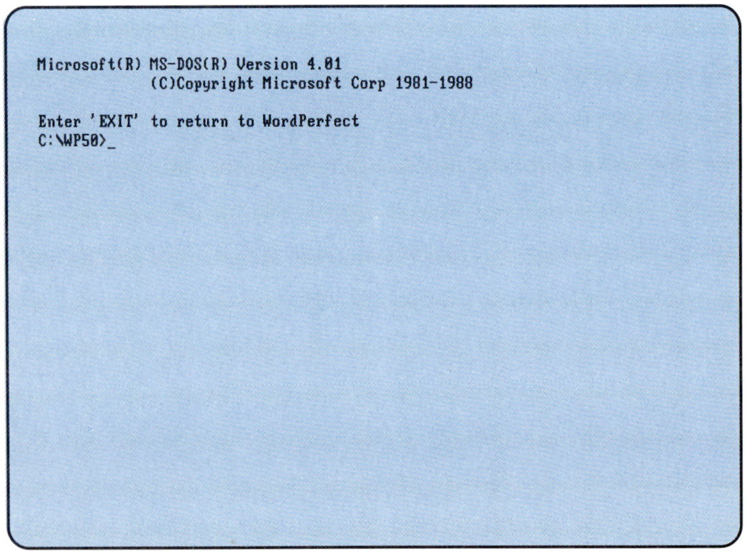

Figure 25 The Secondary DOS Command Processor Prompt

you are limited by the amount of memory installed in your computer. Try running WordPerfect from the secondary command processor. You will probably get the DOS error message:

```
Program too big to fit in memory
```

The reason is that you already have WordPerfect in memory along with a secondary DOS command processor.

2. If you are running DOS version 4 or newer, execute this command:

   Type **mem /program**
   Press **Enter**

   You should see WP, which stands for WordPerfect, in the list of programs in memory.

3. Execute the DOS EXIT command to return to WordPerfect. This will discard the secondary DOS command processor. Exit WordPerfect the usual way and return to the primary DOS command processor.

Summary

- *Managing documents with the List Files menu.* Press F5 to activate the List Files menu. Then select an option to change the directory, look at a file, retrieve a file, copy a file, move or rename a file, print a file, load a text file, select a file name, search for files, or delete a file.
- *Using additional cursor movement commands.* Pressing Home, Down Arrow moves the cursor to the bottom edge of the screen. Home, Up Arrow moves to the top edge. Pressing Escape, typing a number, and then pressing a cursor movement key repeats that key the specified number of times. Pressing Ctrl-Home and then typing a character advances the cursor just past the next occurrence of that character.
- *Using additional delete commands.* Pressing Home, Backspace deletes to the beginning of a word. Home, Delete erases to the end of a word. Pressing Escape, typing a number, and pressing Ctrl-End deletes the specified number of lines. Ctrl-PgDn deletes to the end of the page.
- *Working with formatting codes.* Press Alt-F3 to reveal or hide formatting codes. Press the Delete key to remove a code.
- *Using the built-in thesaurus.* Move the cursor to the word to be looked up and press Alt-F1 to invoke the thesaurus.
- *Splitting the screen into two windows.* Press Ctrl-F3, select the Window option, and specify the number of lines to split the screen into two windows. Press Shift-F3 to move the cursor into the other window.
- *Indenting paragraphs.* Press Tab for a first-line indent, press F4 for a left indent, press Shift-F4 for a left and right indent, and press F4 followed by Shift-Tab for a hanging indent.
- *Creating tables with tab stops.* Press Shift-F8 to execute the Format command, select the Line option, and then select the Tab Set option to change the default tab stops.

- *Aligning numbers to tab stops.* Press Ctrl-F6 to execute the Tab Align command, which advances to the next tab stop and aligns text or numbers on an alignment character, usually the period.
- *Moving text flush right.* Press Alt-F6 to execute the Flush Right command, which lets you type new text or move existing text flush against the right margin.
- *Inserting the current date automatically.* Press Shift-F5 to activate the Date/Outline menu and then select the Date Text or Date Code option.
- *Centering text on a page.* Move the cursor before all codes, press Shift-F8 to activate the Format menu, select the Page option, and then select the Center Page option to center text vertically on a page.
- *Creating a document summary.* Press Shift-F8 to activate the Format menu, select the Document option, and then select the Summary option to enter or edit document summary information.
- *Retrieving and saving text files.* Press Ctrl-F5 to activate the Text In/Out menu, select the DOS Text option, and then select the Retrieve or Save option.
- *Executing a DOS command within WordPerfect.* Press Ctrl-F1 to execute the Shell command. Then execute one or more DOS commands. Use the EXIT command to return to WordPerfect.

Key Terms

As an extra review of this chapter, try defining the following terms.

code
first line indent
hanging indent
headword
indenting
left indent
wild-card characters

Multiple Choice

Choose the best selection to complete each statement.

1. Which command do you execute to clear the screen to start work on a new document?
   (a) Retrieve
   (b) Save
   (c) Cancel
   (d) Exit
2. Which command would you execute to examine the files in a subdirectory, retrieve a file, copy a file, or delete a file?
   (a) Switch
   (b) Search
   (c) List Files
   (d) Format
3. ASCII files, also known as text files, differ from document files in that they contain no
   (a) carriage returns.
   (b) special formatting codes.
   (c) punctuation marks.
   (d) numbers.

4. Which key or character do you type to mark a file on the List Files screen?
   (a) asterisk (*) (b) F1
   (c) F10 (d) ampersand (&)
5. Which sequence of keypresses will move the cursor to the top edge of the current screen?
   (a) Ctrl-Home (b) Ctrl-Up Arrow
   (c) Home, Up Arrow (d) Home, Left Arrow
6. Which sequence of keystrokes will move the cursor down five lines?
   (a) Down Arrow, 5 (b) Escape, 5, Down Arrow
   (c) F1, 5, Down Arrow (d) Home, Home, Home, Home, Home, Down Arrow
7. Which sequence of keystrokes will advance the cursor just past the next occurrence of the letter *x*?
   (a) Ctrl-Home, x (b) Home, Home, x
   (c) Right Arrow, x (d) F3, x
8. Which sequence of keypresses will delete characters from the cursor to the end of the word?
   (a) Home, Backspace (b) Home, Delete
   (c) Home, Right Arrow (d) Delete-Right Arrow
9. What do you press to reveal or hide formatting codes?
   (a) Alt-C (b) Alt-PgDn
   (c) Alt-F3 (d) Ctrl-F3
10. To use the thesaurus, move the cursor to the word you want to look up and then press
    (a) Alt-F1. (b) Alt-T.
    (c) F1. (d) F3.
11. Which command do you execute to display two windows?
    (a) Format (b) Help
    (c) Screen (d) Exit
12. Which type of paragraph indentation moves all lines toward the center of the page except for the first line?
    (a) first line indent (b) left indent
    (c) left and right indent (d) hanging indent
13. By default, WordPerfect has a tab stop set every
    (a) half inch. (b) inch.
    (c) inch and a half. (d) two inches.
14. Which command is an alternative to using decimal tab stops?
    (a) Tab (b) Tab Align
    (c) Indent (d) Flush Right
15. Which command is used to type text aligned to the right margin?
    (a) Tab (b) Tab Align
    (c) Indent (d) Flush Right

16. Which code indicates the end of a Center, Tab Align, or Flush Right command?
    (a) [HRt] (b) [SRt]
    (c) [C/A/Flrt] (d) [Und]
17. Which option from the Date/Outline menu do you select to insert a date that will always show the current date whenever the document is retrieved or printed?
    (a) Date Text (b) Date Code
    (c) Format (d) Outline
18. Which command do you execute first to create a document summary?
    (a) Screen (b) Shell
    (c) Format (d) List Files
19. Which command do you execute to retrieve an ASCII file, such as AUTOEXEC.BAT or CONFIG.SYS?
    (a) Retrieve (b) Search
    (c) Switch (d) Text In/Out
20. Which command do you execute to temporarily return to DOS while keeping WordPerfect loaded in memory?
    (a) Exit (b) Text In/Out
    (c) Shell (d) Cancel

Fill-In

1. The ______ option of the List Files menu lets you examine the contents of a file or subdirectory.
2. The Word Search option of the List Files menu lets you ______ files that meet specific conditions.
3. The ______ key lets you repeat a cursor-movement command a number of times.
4. A WordPerfect document contains special ______ that specify how the document is to be formatted.
5. The built-in ______ can examine a word in your document or a word that you enter, and display a list of synonyms and antonyms.
6. The ______ option of the Screen command lets you split the display into two separate document-editing screens, each with its own status line.
7. The ______ command, executed by pressing Shift-F3, allows you to move the cursor from one window to the other.
8. ______ refers to moving text away from the margin toward the center of the page.
9. A hanging indent is created by executing both the Left Indent and ______ commands.
10. The default and most commonly used type of tab stop is the ______ tab stop.
11. The Tab Align command, executed by pressing Ctrl-F6, lines up text or numbers on an ______ character, usually the period.
12. The ______ command is especially handy for typing the return address and date against the right margin in a letter.

13. You can move several lines of text against the right margin at once by pressing Alt-F4 if you first mark the lines as a ______.
14. If you want the date in a document to be updated whenever it is retrieved or printed, you must use the Date ______ option from the Date/Outline menu.
15. The ______ option in the Date/Outline menu lets you change the way the date is displayed.
16. Press the ______ key three times and then press Up Arrow to move the cursor ahead of any codes at the beginning of a document.
17. Adding a Document ______ lets you maintain detailed information about a document, including a descriptive file name, the subject, the author, the typist, and other comments.
18. The ______ command lets you save a document in a generic format that can be used by word processors other than WordPerfect.
19. Press Ctrl-F1 to execute the ______ command, which lets you temporarily return to the DOS prompt.
20. The DOS ______ command is used to return to WordPerfect from a secondary command processor.

Short Problems

1. Start WordPerfect if you are not already running the program.

   The Escape key can be used to repeat a character or some WordPerfect features a specified number of times. The default number is 8, but you can change this value. You have already learned to use the Escape key to repeat certain cursor movements. Now use the Escape key to type the letter A twenty times:

   Press **Escape**
   Type **20**
   Type **a**

   The Escape key can also be used with the Delete key. Move the cursor to the beginning of the line and use the Escape key with Delete to remove the first ten letters.

2. Normally, WordPerfect displays only the status line below the text area on the editing screen. Some people like to have a ruler line also displayed on the screen to see the current margins and tab stop settings. You can use the Window option of the Screen command to present a ruler line at the bottom of the screen.

   Press **Ctrl-F3**
   Type **w**
   Type **23**
   Press **Enter**

   Setting the window size to 23 lines displays the ruler line below the status line at the bottom of the screen. Note that you have really opened two windows, but only one window fits on the screen at a time. You can move to the other window with the Switch command (Shift-F3), and edit a different document or view a different part of the same document.

3. The Date command can insert the current time as well as the date into your document. Execute the Date/Outline command and select the Format option. Examine the Date Format menu and change the format to

   `3 1, 4 8:90`

   Select the Date Text or Date Code option and observe the result.

4. WordPerfect has four styles of tabs you can set: left, center, right, and decimal. In addition, the program has a dot leader feature that can fill in the blank space preceding a tab stop with periods. Execute the Format command, select the Line option, and then select the Tab Set option to display the Tab Set menu on your screen. Clear the default tab settings by deleting to the end of the line. Set a left tab stop at 2 inches and a right tab stop at 7 inches. With the cursor still at the 7-inch position, type a period to specify a dot leader for the right tab stop. Return to the editing screen. Enter these lines:

   Press **Tab**
   Type **John Anderson**
   Press **Tab**
   Type **555-1234**
   Press **Enter**
   Press **Tab**
   Type **Melissa Smith**
   Press **Tab**
   Type **555-2408**
   Press **Enter**

5. Now try the center and decimal tab styles. Activate the Tab Set menu and clear the current tab stops. Set a center tab stop at 4 inches and a decimal tab stop at 6 inches. Enter these lines:

   Press **Tab**
   Type **Advertising**
   Press **Tab**
   Type **$1,236.22**
   Press **Enter**
   Press **Tab**
   Type **Office Supplies**
   Press **Tab**
   Type **$287.15**
   Press **Enter**

6. Execute the Thesaurus command and select the Look Up Word option. (If the cursor is at the beginning of a new line, the Look Up Word option will be selected automatically.) Look up the word "wonderful." Select the Look Up Word option again and try these words: "powerful" and "unusual."

7. Obtain a new diskette or one that can be reformatted. Execute the Shell command to temporarily return to DOS without exiting WordPerfect. Put the diskette in drive A. Execute the FORMAT A: command to format the diskette. Copy the file NEWS.DOC from the LESSONS subdirectory to the diskette. Execute the EXIT command to return to WordPerfect.

8. Clear the screen and retrieve MEMO.DOC. Center the document vertically on the page. Print MEMO.DOC by executing the Print command and selecting the Full Document option.

9. Use the Print option from the List Files menu to print the document INDENT.DOC.

10. You have already created a document summary for HOLMES.DOC. Now create document summaries for the files MEMO.DOC, INDENT.DOC, and NEWS.DOC. Note that you have to retrieve a document into the editing screen before you can add a document summary.

Long Problems

1. Use what you have learned about the Date and Right Flush commands to create a letter of complaint to a company about inadequate service you may have received or an inferior product you may have purchased.
2. Create a table of contents for this chapter, using a right tab stop with a dot leader to align all the page numbers at the right margin.
3. Reproduce a page from the Glossary in this book, using ½-inch hanging indents. Each term along with its definition should be a single paragraph. Remember to boldface the terms.
4. Reproduce the following table of information about the United States. Use tab stops, not spaces, to align the columns. Use left tab stops for the State and Capital columns, a center tab stop for the Admitted column, and a right tab stop for the Size Rank column.

State	Capital	Admitted	Size Rank
Alabama	Montgomery	1819	29
Alaska	Juneau	1959	1
Arizona	Phoenix	1912	6
Arkansas	Little Rock	1836	27
California	Sacramento	1850	3
Colorado	Denver	1876	8
Connecticut	Hartford	1788	48
Delaware	Dover	1787	49
District of Columbia	Washington	—	51
Florida	Tallahassee	1845	22
Georgia	Atlanta	1788	21
Hawaii	Honolulu	1959	47
Idaho	Boise	1890	13
Illinois	Springfield	1818	24
Indiana	Indianapolis	1816	38
Iowa	Des Moines	1846	25
Kansas	Topeka	1861	14
Kentucky	Frankfort	1792	37
Louisiana	Baton Rouge	1812	31
Maine	Augusta	1820	39
Maryland	Annapolis	1788	42
Massachusetts	Boston	1788	45
Michigan	Lansing	1837	23
Minnesota	St. Paul	1858	12
Mississippi	Jackson	1817	32
Missouri	Jefferson City	1821	19
Montana	Helena	1889	4
Nebraska	Lincoln	1867	15

State	Capital	Admitted	Size Rank
Nevada	Carson City	1864	7
New Hampshire	Concord	1788	44
New Jersey	Trenton	1787	46
New Mexico	Santa Fe	1912	5
New York	Albany	1788	30
North Carolina	Raleigh	1789	28
North Dakota	Bismarck	1889	17
Ohio	Columbus	1803	35
Oklahoma	Oklahoma City	1907	18
Oregon	Salem	1859	10
Pennsylvania	Harrisburg	1787	33
Rhode Island	Providence	1790	50
South Carolina	Columbia	1788	40
South Dakota	Pierre	1889	16
Tennessee	Nashville	1796	34
Texas	Austin	1845	2
Utah	Salt Lake City	1896	11
Vermont	Montpelier	1791	43
Virginia	Richmond	1788	36
Washington	Olympia	1889	20
West Virginia	Charleston	1863	41
Wisconsin	Madison	1848	26
Wyoming	Cheyenne	1890	9

5. Use the Text In/Out command to create the following DOS batch file for starting WordPerfect. Name the file W.BAT when you save it.

```
cd c:\wp50
wp
cd c:\
```

6. Create an inventory of your personal property. Use tab stops to arrange the data into columns. Use a decimal tab stop for the column listing the cost of each item.

7. Use successively nested left and right indentation to reproduce the following paragraphs. Turn on justification for this document and print it when you are finished.

   Supercomputers are extremely fast mainframes that execute billions of instructions per second and can serve hundreds of users simultaneously. They cost between $5 million and $20 million each. Only a few hundred supercomputers are operating in the world today.

   > Mainframes are big, powerful, fast, expensive computers. They execute many millions of instructions per second, can serve hundreds of users at the same time, and cost between $100,000 and $20 million. A mainframe computer may be as small as one or two file cabinets or large enough to fill an entire room.
   >
   > > Minicomputers are medium-sized computers that serve several users simultaneously or control complex equipment. The smallest minicomputers are about the same size as floor-standing microcomputers; the largest may be as big as one or two file cabinets. Minicomputers cost between $15,000 and $500,000.

Workstations are small, powerful computers generally used by only one person at a time. They are superior to microcomputers in their ability to perform complex calculations, display sharp and colorful graphics, and communicate with other computers. Workstations range in price from $4000 to $100,000.

Microcomputers are small enough to fit on a desk and are almost always used by one person at a time. The CPU usually consists of a single micro-processor chip. Prices range from $100 to $15,000.

8. Create a list of all the college courses you have taken, when you took them, the instructor (if you remember), and the grade you received. Use tab stops to align the columns.
9. Create a list of the LP records, cassette tapes, and compact discs you own. Include the title, artist, and type of media. Use tab stops to align the columns.
10. Create a document that lists the 10 or 12 function keys on your computer and the WordPerfect commands that correspond to these keys. Include columns for the key pressed alone, and the key pressed with Shift, Alternate, and Control. Use tab stops to align the columns.

CHAPTER 10

ADVANCED WORDPERFECT

In This Chapter

Getting Started
Lesson 1: Using the Print Menu
Lesson 2: Hyphenating Words
Lesson 3: Avoiding Orphans and Widows
Lesson 4: Using the Conditional End of Page Feature
Lesson 5: Using the Font Menu
Lesson 6: Adding Headers and Footers
Lesson 7: Creating Text Columns
Lesson 8: Adding Footnotes and Endnotes
Lesson 9: Sorting Text
Lesson 10: Performing Math
Lesson 11: Outlining a Document
Lesson 12: Generating a Table of Contents
Lesson 13: Generating an Index
Lesson 14: Adding Graphics
Lesson 15: Using Macros
Lesson 16: Creating Form Letters
Lesson 17: Using Styles
Lesson 18: Customizing WordPerfect

Preview

Chapters 8 and 9 taught you most of what the average user needs to know about WordPerfect. This chapter proceeds to more advanced word processing topics. You may not need all of the commands and features presented in this chapter, but many of them can make your work easier, quicker, and less tedious. Learning more about WordPerfect can help you create more complex and attractive documents.

After studying this chapter, you will know how to

- use the Print menu.
- hyphenate words.
- avoid orphans and widows.
- avoid splitting paragraphs between pages.
- use the Font menu.
- add headers and footers.
- create text columns.
- add footnotes and endnotes.
- sort text.
- perform math.
- outline a document.
- generate a table of contents.
- generate an index.
- add graphics.
- use macros.
- create form letters.
- use styles.
- customize WordPerfect.

Getting Started

You've already learned how to start WordPerfect and use its most common features and commands. This chapter assumes you have completed all of the lessons and exercises in Chapters 8 and 9. Furthermore, it assumes that you have a computer with a hard disk and WordPerfect 5.0 installed on it in a subdirectory named WP50 and you have a subdirectory named LESSONS that contains your document files. To work the following lessons, boot up your computer, change to the WP50 subdirectory, and start WordPerfect.

Lesson 1: Using the Print Menu

In the two previous chapters you used the Full Document option of the Print menu to print your documents. Full Document is the most commonly used option, but the Print menu's other options can be handy in some circumstances.

Step 1: Retrieve NEWS.DOC

Retrieve the newsletter document:

Press **Shift-F10**
Type **c:\lessons\news.doc**
Press **Enter**

Step 2: Execute the Print Command

Activate the Print menu:

Press **Shift-F7**

Your screen should look like Figure 1.

Step 3: Prepare the Printer

Make sure the printer is connected to the computer and turned on. Also, make sure that paper is loaded and aligned to the top of a new page. Finally, make sure that the printer's On Line light is lit. (If it isn't, press the On Line button.)

Step 4: Select the Page Option

You already know how to use Full Document, the first option in the Print menu. The second option, Page, lets you print the single page in which the cursor is located. At this point, the cursor should be in the first page of NEWS.DOC. Print the current page:

Type **p**

Only the first page will be printed. WordPerfect will then return to the editing screen.

Step 5: Select the Document on Disk Option

When you choose the Full Document or Page option, the document currently on the editing screen is printed. The Document on Disk option lets you print a document other than the one you are editing. Suppose you want to print MEMO.DOC without retrieving it. Activate the Print menu, select the Document on Disk option, and enter the name of the document to be printed:

Press **Shift-F7**
Type **d**

Figure 1 The Print Menu

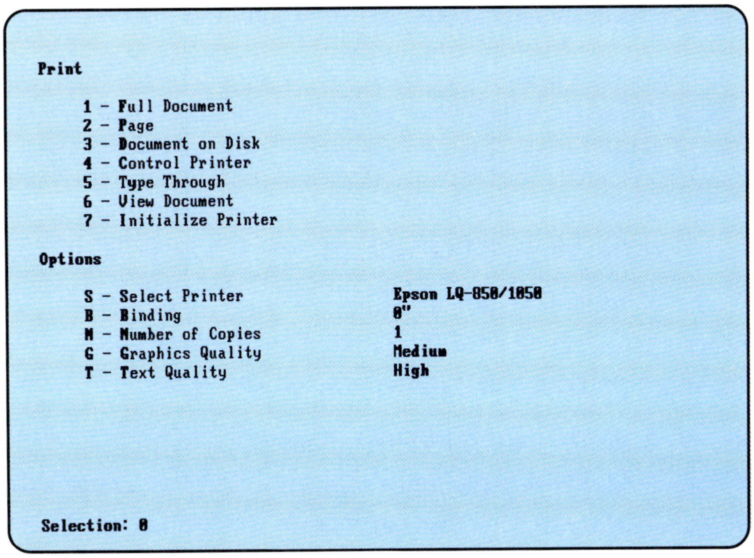

Type **c:\lessons\memo.doc**
Press **Enter**

WordPerfect displays the prompt

`Page(s): (All)`

You can enter a page number or range of pages, or simply press the Enter key to print the entire document.

Press **Enter**

The document MEMO.DOC will be printed and the Print menu will remain on the screen.

Step 6: Select the Control Printer Option

If you use the Full Document option, WordPerfect returns to the editing screen and lets you work while the document is printing. You can also return to the editing screen from the Print menu after selecting the Document on Disk option. In fact, you can choose Document on Disk several times and specify several documents to be printed. WordPerfect stores the names of the documents you have sent to the printer in a **print queue,** or waiting line of print jobs. The Printer Control option of the Print menu lets you manage these print jobs. Let's see how it works.

Press your printer's On Line button to take it off line (the On Line light should be off). This will prevent the printer from printing while you examine the print queue. The Print menu should be displayed on your screen. Follow these instructions to load two files into the print queue and then select the Control Printer option:

Type **d**
Type **c:\lessons\memo.doc**
Press **Enter** (2 times)
Type **d**
Type **c:\lessons\news.doc**
Press **Enter** (2 times)
Type **c**

Information about your print jobs and the Printer Control menu will appear on the screen (see Figure 2). The messages displayed on the screen can diagnose most printing problems and help you solve them. The menu provides options for controlling your print jobs. The Cancel option lets you terminate one or more print jobs. The Rush Job option changes the priority of a document in the print queue. The Display Jobs option presents all of the print jobs if they are not already shown on the screen. The Go (start printer) option restarts the printer after it has been halted to change a cartridge or after using the Stop option. The Stop option halts the printer, without canceling any print jobs, to let you handle a paper jam, ribbon change, or some other problem.

Cancel all of the print jobs and return to the editing screen:

Type **c**
Type *****
Type **y**
Press **F7**

Figure 2 The Printer Control Menu

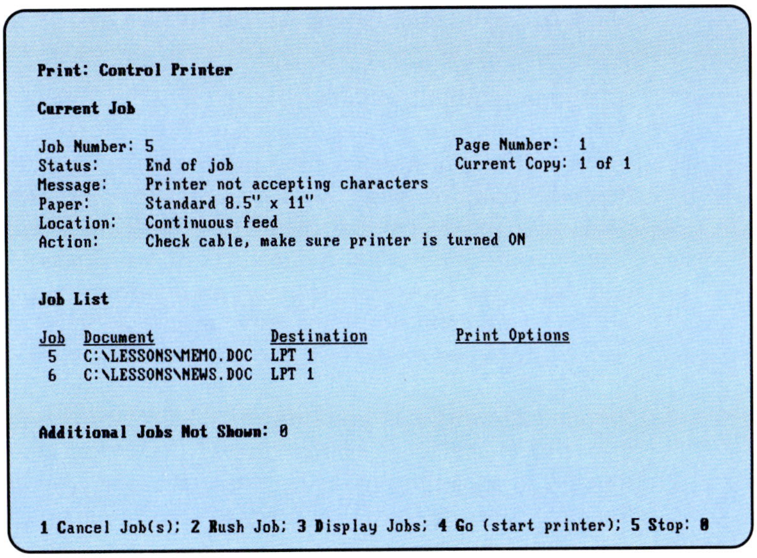

Press your printer's On Line button again. Part of the first document may still be printed, because many printers have their own internal memory buffer. WordPerfect cannot control text that has already been sent to a printer's buffer. You can, however, shut off the printer while it is still off-line to clear the buffer, wait a few seconds, and then turn it on again.

Step 7: Select the Type Through Option

The Type Through option of the Print menu allows you to use your computer and printer as if they were a typewriter. Each character or line you type is sent immediately to the printer. This feature is sometimes used for creating short memos or filling in a pre-printed form. Execute the Print command and select the Type Through option:

Press **Shift-F7**
Type **y**

Two Type Through options are available: Line and Character. The Line option lets you correct mistakes on a line with the Backspace and Delete keys. The line you type is not sent to the printer until you press Enter. The Character option sends each character you type immediately to the printer, just like a typewriter. Some printers, however, will not work with the Character option. Make sure your printer is on line and select the Line option:

Type **L**
Type **`Hello there!`**
Press **Enter**

The message you typed will then be printed. When you are finished with the Type Through option, execute the Exit command to return to the Print Menu:

Press **F7**

Step 8: Select the View Document Option

The View Document option lets you see how your document will look when it is printed, without actually printing it. This option works best on a computer with a graphics adapter and display. A graphics screen can show as closely as possible the appearance of the printed page, including the position of text on the page, margins, page numbers, and character formats such as underline and boldface. View Document can be useful in the preparation of documents that include some of the advanced features we will discuss later in this chapter, including headers and footers, footnotes and endnotes, columns, and graphics.

The Print menu should be on your screen. Select the View Document option:

Type **v**

If your computer has graphics capability, WordPerfect will present a full-page view of the first page of the current document (see Figure 3). Although it is difficult to read the tiny text, called **greeking,** you can easily see the layout of the page. Use the Page Down key to see the next page in the document:

Press **Page Down**

Now, return to the first page:

Press **Page Up**

The View Document menu at the bottom of the screen presents several options for showing a page. The default option, Full Page, shows an entire page of the document on the screen, using greeking to represent text. Try the 100% option, which presents the page in the actual size it would be if it were printed:

Type **1**

Figure 4 shows the result. The entire page does not fit on the screen, but you can use the arrow keys to see other parts of the page:

Press **Right Arrow**
Press **Down Arrow** (4 times)

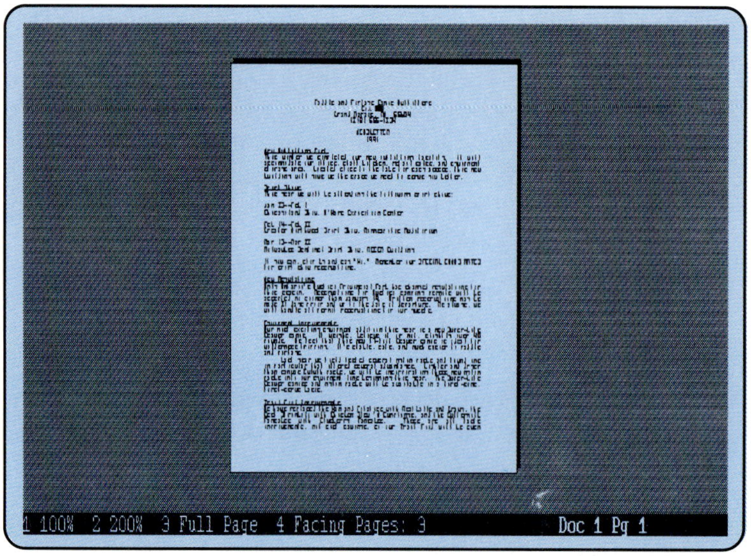

Figure 3 View Document Showing the Full Page

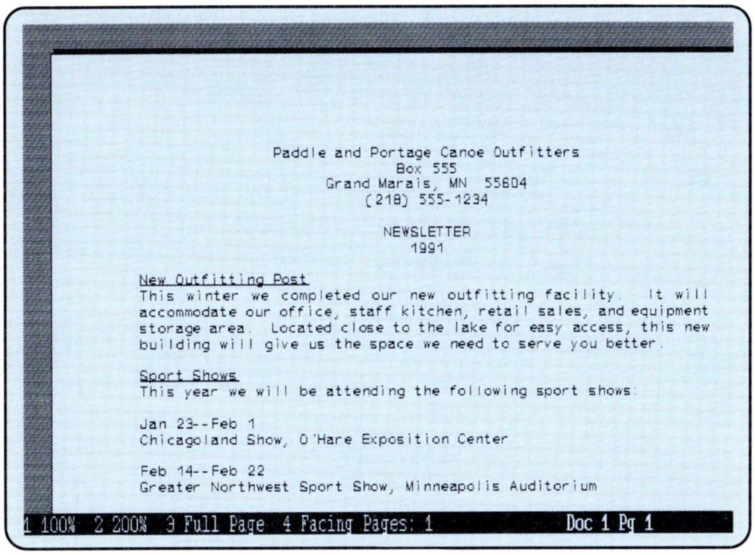

Figure 4 View Document Showing the Actual Size Page

Now, return to the top of the document:

Press **Home** (2 times)
Press **Up Arrow**

The 200% option presents a page twice its actual size.

Type **2**
Press **Right Arrow** (5 times)

Your screen should look like Figure 5. The last option in the View Document menu, Facing Pages, is used to display odd-numbered pages on the right and even-numbered pages on the left. Note that you cannot edit text in the View

Figure 5 View Document Showing the Page Twice Actual Size

Document screen, only examine it. Use the Exit command to return to document editing screen:

Press **F7**

Step 9: Examine the Other Print Options

Execute the Print command again:

Press **Shift-F7**

Several other options are available in the Print menu. Option number 7, Initialize Printer, is normally used only with certain laser printers to load software fonts. The Select Printer option is used to connect a new printer to your computer or choose another connected printer. The Binding option lets you leave space along the edges of pages that are to be bound into a book. You can print several copies of the same document with the Number of Copies option. The last two options, Graphics Quality and Text Quality, allow you to control the resolution and speed of printing. High quality looks the best, but it also takes the longest to print. In addition to High and Medium quality settings, WordPerfect also has Draft, which prints a fast, rough copy. The Do Not Print option is also available for printing text and graphics separately.

Practice

1. With NEWS.DOC on your editing screen, print HOLMES.DOC from the LESSONS subdirectory.
2. Use the Type Through option to print the following message:

   `A computer is a rather expensive typewriter.`

3. Use the View Document option to examine the bottom half of the second page of NEWS.DOC. Use the 200% option to magnify the page.
4. Change the Number of Copies option to print two copies of MEMO.DOC with the Document on Disk option.

Lesson 2: Hyphenating Words

By default, word wrap moves an entire word to the next line whenever that word extends past the right margin. WordPerfect will not split words between lines unless you turn on the hyphenation feature. **Hyphenation** is the division of certain words at the ends of lines to improve the appearance of text. Hyphenation is most useful when text is justified. If hyphenation is turned off for justified text, large gaps may appear between the words on some lines. These gaps occur when a long word at the end of a line is wrapped to the next line. Hyphenation can make justified text more attractive by splitting long words at the ends of lines, which reduces large gaps between words. It can also improve the appearance of unjustified text by reducing the raggedness of the right margin.

Step 1: Move the Cursor

Before turning on hyphenation, you must move the cursor to the place where you want hyphenation to begin. In most cases, this place will be the beginning of the document.

Press **Home** (2 times)
Press **Up Arrow**

Step 2: Turn On Justification

You can use hyphenation with justification turned off, but hyphenation is most often used with justification turned on. Turn on justification for the newsletter:

Press **Shift-F8**
Type **L**
Type **j**
Type **y**
Press **F7**

The appearance of text on the screen will not change, but the text will be justified when it is printed or examined with View Document.

Step 3: Turn On Manual Hyphenation

WordPerfect offers two types of hyphenation: Manual and Automatic. **Manual hyphenation** requires you to confirm the splitting of each word as you scroll through the document. **Automatic hyphenation** uses a set of built-in rules to attempt splitting words without confirmation. If the rules cannot be applied to a particular word, WordPerfect reverts to manual hyphenation for that word only. Let's try manual hyphenation first. Execute the Format command, select the Line option, select the Hyphenation option, and then select the Manual option:

Press **Shift-F8**
Type **L**
Type **y**
Type **m**
Press **F7**

Step 4: Scroll Through the Document

In order to hyphenate an existing document, you must scroll through it. WordPerfect will beep and display a prompt when it finds a word that should be hyphenated. Use the Down Arrow key to move the cursor through the document:

Press **Down Arrow** (until WordPerfect beeps)

The first hyphenation will occur in the Trail Food Improvements paragraph. WordPerfect will beep and display the prompt shown in Figure 6. It presents the word "improvements" and suggests where to insert the hyphen. You can press the Left Arrow or Right Arrow key to change the position of the hyphen. When the hyphen is where you want it, you press the Escape key. In this case, the hyphen is fine.

Press **Escape**

The word will be hyphenated in the text. In this manner, you could scroll through the rest of the document and confirm each of WordPerfect's hyphenation suggestions.

Step 5: Turn On Automatic Hyphenation

Now, let's try automatic hyphenation.

Press **Shift-F8**
Type **L**
Type **y**

Figure 6 The Manual Hyphenation Prompt

```
New Regulations
Only Ontario's Quetico Provincial Park has changed regulations for
this season.  Reservations for Quetico camping permits will be
accepted no sooner than January 19.  Written reservations may be
made 21 days prior and up to the date of departure.  As always, we
will handle all permit reservations for our guests.

Equipment Improvements
Our most exciting equipment addition this year is a new Super-Lite
Beaver canoe.  It weighs, believe it or not, slightly over 40
pounds.  We feel that this new 17-foot Beaver canoe is ideal for
wilderness tripping.  It's stable, safe, and much easier to paddle
and portage.
     Last year we field tested several nylon packs and found one
in particular that offered several advantages.  Lighter and dryer
than canvas Duluth packs, we will be incorporating these new nylon
packs into our equipment line beginning this year.  The Super-Lite
Beaver canoes and nylon packs will be available on a first-come,
first-serve basis.

Trail Food Improvements
We have replaced the Ham and Potatoes with Meatballs and Gravy, the
Beef Stromboli with Chicken Stew 'N Dumplings, and the Buttermilk
Pancakes with Blueberry Pancakes.  These are all taste
Position hyphen; Press ESC improve-ments,
```

Type **a**
Press **F7**

Hyphenation also works while you are entering new text. To see it in action, delete the word "improvements".

Press **Ctrl-Backspace**

Retype the word and see how it is automatically hyphenated:

Type **`improvements,`**
Press **Space Bar**

Step 6: View the Document

The best way to see the full result of hyphenation and justification is to print the document or use the View Document feature.

Press **Shift-F7**
Type **v**
Type **1**

You may have to use the arrow keys to bring the Trail Food Improvements paragraph into view. Your screen should look like Figure 7. When you are finished examining the page, return to the editing screen:

Press **F7**

Step 7: Turn Off Hyphenation

You turn off hyphenation by selecting the first option in the Hyphenation menu. Move the cursor to the beginning of the document and turn off hyphenation:

Press **Home** (2 times)
Press **Up Arrow**
Press **Shift-F8**

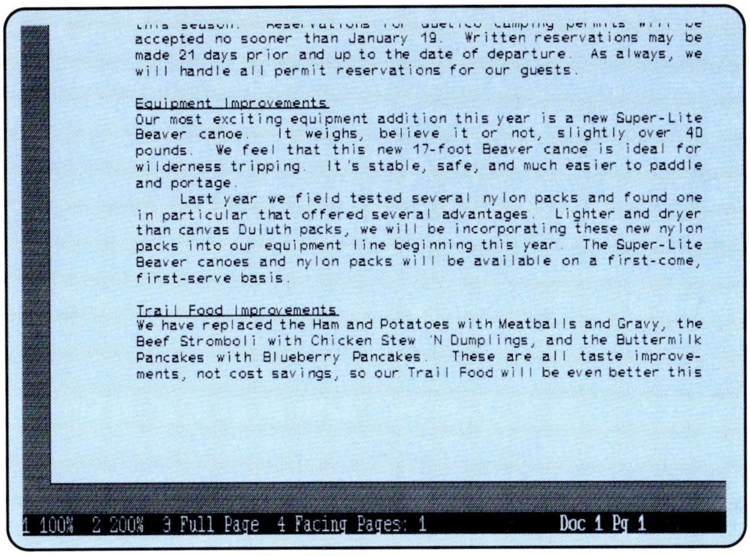

Figure 7 Hyphenation and Justification

Type **L**
Type **y**
Type **f**
Press **F7**

Practice

1. Move the cursor to the beginning of the document and turn on automatic hyphenation.
2. Use the Down Arrow key to scroll through the entire document.
3. Use the View Document feature to examine the document. Return to the editing screen, move the cursor to the beginning of the document, and leave automatic hyphenation turned on.

Lesson 3: Avoiding Orphans and Widows

The page formatting settings determine how many lines of text will appear on a page. WordPerfect simply counts the number of lines and inserts a soft page break wherever necessary. Some paragraphs, however, may be divided inappropriately between pages. An **orphan** is the last line of a paragraph that appears at the top of a page. A **widow** is the first line of a paragraph that appears at the bottom of a page. Both orphans and widows are considered poor form because they can confuse the reader. It is better to have two lines from a paragraph at the top or bottom of a page. Fortunately, WordPerfect can automatically eliminate orphans and widows.

Step 1: Examine the Document

The document NEWS.DOC contains a good example of an orphan. A single-word line from the end of a paragraph appears at the top of the second page. To see it on the screen, follow these directions:

Press **Home** (2 times)
Press **Up Arrow**

Figure 8 An Orphan at the Top of the Second Page

```
ments, not cost savings, so our Trail Food will be even better this
----------------------------------------------------------------------------------
year.

Current Outfitting Rates
          Number In Party      Rate Per Person Per Day
          1 to 3 persons       $31.00
          4 to 6 persons       $29.25
          7 to 9 persons       $28.50

1990 Fishing Records
          Bluegill              3.00 lbs.
          Large Mouth Bass     20.25 lbs.
          Northern Pike        42.33 lbs.
          Sunfish               2.20 lbs.
          Walleye              25.00 lbs.
          Lake Trout           50.00 lbs.

Trips
This fall we took a trip into the Cherry Lake area for some lake
trout fishing.  We had our usual quota of rain, but did enjoy two
beautiful crisp autumn days.  Mornings we awoke to clear, deep blue
skies with heavy, white steam rising from Cherry Lake.  On shore
we could look up into the blue sky, but as we paddled into the
C:\LESSONS\NEWS.DOC                                 Doc 1 Pg 1 Ln 9.83" Pos 1"
```

Press **Page Down**
Press **Up Arrow**

The word "year" is all by itself at the top of the page (see Figure 8). This is the worst kind of orphan and it should not appear in the final document.

Step 2: Move the Cursor

Before eliminating orphans and widows from an entire document, you must move the cursor to the beginning.

Press **Home** (2 times)
Press **Up Arrow**

Step 3: Turn On Widow and Orphan Protection

To avoid orphans and widows, execute the Format command, select the Line option, and then select the Widow/Orphan Protection option:

Press **Shift-F8**
Type **L**
Type **w**
Type **y**
Press **F7**

Step 4: Examine the Document

Examine the document again to see if the orphan has been eliminated.

Press **Page Down**
Press **Up Arrow**

As you can see from Figure 9, the page break has been inserted one line earlier so that two lines from the end of the paragraph appear at the top of the second page.

Figure 9 The Orphan Has Been Eliminated

```
Pancakes with Blueberry Pancakes.  These are all taste improve-
---------------------------------------------------------------------
ments, not cost savings, so our Trail Food will be even better this
year.

Current Outfitting Rates
          Number In Party      Rate Per Person Per Day
          1 to 3 persons       $31.00
          4 to 6 persons       $29.25
          7 to 9 persons       $28.50

1990 Fishing Records
          Bluegill              3.00 lbs.
          Large Mouth Bass     20.25 lbs.
          Northern Pike        42.33 lbs.
          Sunfish               2.20 lbs.
          Walleye              25.00 lbs.
          Lake Trout           50.00 lbs.

Trips
This fall we took a trip into the Cherry Lake area for some lake
trout fishing.  We had our usual quota of rain, but did enjoy two
beautiful crisp autumn days.  Mornings we awoke to clear, deep blue
skies with heavy, white steam rising from Cherry Lake.  On shore
C:\LESSONS\NEWS.DOC                          Doc 1 Pg 1 Ln 9.67" Pos 1"
```

Step 5: Save the Document

Save the document to the disk to preserve the changes you have made:

Press **F10**
Press **Enter**
Type **y**

Practice

1. Move the cursor to the beginning of NEWS.DOC and execute the Reveal Codes command. Note the [Hyph On] code, which indicates that hyphenation is turned on, and the [W/O On] code, which indicates that widow and orphan protection is turned on. Return to the full editing screen.
2. Execute the Help command and read about widow and orphan protection:

   Press **F3**
   Press **Shift-F8**
   Type **L**
   Type **w**

   When you are finished reading, return to the editing screen:

   Press **Space Bar**

Lesson 4: Using the Conditional End of Page Feature

Widow and orphan protection keeps the two lines at the beginning or end of a paragraph from being split between pages. The Conditional End of Page feature is another way to protect text from being split between pages. This feature is handy for keeping titles or headings together with their first paragraphs or for preventing tables from being split between pages.

Step 1: Move the Cursor to the Line Above

Suppose you want to keep the three lines at the end of the paragraph from being split between pages. The first step is to move the cursor to the line before the lines you want to keep together.

Press **Home** (2 times)
Press **Up Arrow**
Press **Page Down**
Press **Up Arrow** (2 times)

Step 2: Select the Conditional End of Page Option

Execute the Format command, select the Other option, and then select the Conditional End of Page option:

Press **Shift-F8**
Type **o**
Type **c**

Step 3: Enter the Number of Lines

WordPerfect will prompt you for the number of lines to keep together (see Figure 10). Enter the number and exit the menu:

Type **3**
Press **Enter**
Press **F7**

Step 4: Move the Cursor

The page break will not actually change position until you move the cursor.

Press **Down Arrow** (2 times)

Figure 10 Conditional End of Page Prompt

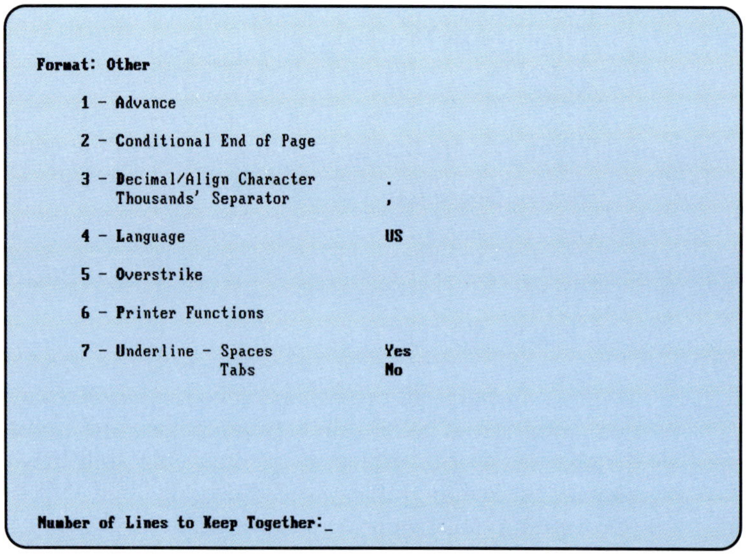

The last three lines of the paragraph will be kept together after the page break (see Figure 11).

Practice

1. Execute the Reveal Codes command. Note the code [Cndl EOP:3], which indicates the Conditional End of Page option has been set for the three lines below the current line. Delete this code to turn the option off. Return to the full editing screen and move the cursor to the beginning of the document.
2. Execute the Help command and read about the Conditional End of Page option. When you are finished, return to the editing screen.

Lesson 5: Using the Font Menu

WordPerfect has the ability to use different fonts and change the size, appearance, and color of text. Whether or not you can actually use these features depends on your computer and printer. Nevertheless, let's examine the options of the Font menu.

Step 1: Clear the Editing Screen

Exit NEWS.DOC and start a new document to illustrate the capabilities of the Font menu:

Press **F7**
Type **n**
Type **n**

Step 2: Activate the Font Menu

Execute the Font command:

Press **Ctrl-F8**

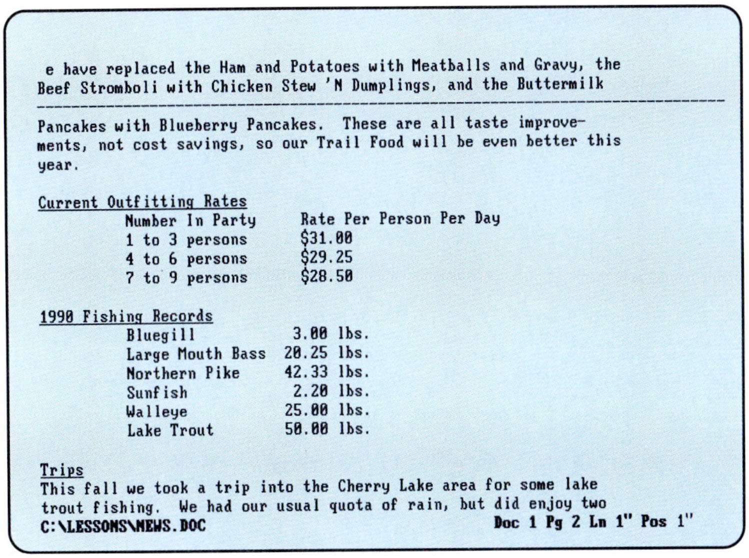

```
e have replaced the Ham and Potatoes with Meatballs and Gravy, the
Beef Stromboli with Chicken Stew 'N Dumplings, and the Buttermilk
--------------------------------------------------------------------
Pancakes with Blueberry Pancakes.  These are all taste improve-
ments, not cost savings, so our Trail Food will be even better this
year.

Current Outfitting Rates
          Number In Party      Rate Per Person Per Day
          1 to 3 persons       $31.00
          4 to 6 persons       $29.25
          7 to 9 persons       $28.50

1990 Fishing Records
          Bluegill            3.00 lbs.
          Large Mouth Bass   20.25 lbs.
          Northern Pike      42.33 lbs.
          Sunfish             2.20 lbs.
          Walleye            25.00 lbs.
          Lake Trout         50.00 lbs.

Trips
This fall we took a trip into the Cherry Lake area for some lake
trout fishing.  We had our usual quota of rain, but did enjoy two
C:\LESSONS\NEWS.DOC                          Doc 1 Pg 2 Ln 1" Pos 1"
```

Figure 11 Last Three Lines of the Paragraph Kept Together

Five options will be listed in a menu across the bottom of the screen: Size, Appearance, Normal, Base Font, and Print Color.

Step 3: Select the Size Option

The Size option of the Font menu deals with the height of characters or their relative position in a line. Select the Size option:

Type **s**

Seven options will be listed in a new menu across the bottom of the screen: Superscript, Subscript, Fine, Small, Large, Very Large, and Extra Large. While these options do not change the appearance of text on the screen, they do allow you to change the size of text in the printed document. The Superscript and Subscript options also change the position of text. Superscript characters are small and raised, like ^{this}, and subscript characters are small and lowered, like $_{\text{this}}$. Follow these directions to try all of the Size options:

Type **p**
Type **Superscript**
Press **Right Arrow**
Type **characters**
Press **Enter**
Press **Ctrl-F8**
Type **s**
Type **b**
Type **Subscript**
Press **Right Arrow**
Type **characters**
Press **Enter**
Press **Ctrl-F8**
Type **s**
Type **f**
Type **Fine characters**
Press **Right Arrow**
Press **Enter**
Press **Ctrl-F8**
Type **s**
Type **s**
Type **Small characters**
Press **Right Arrow**
Press **Enter**
Press **Ctrl-F8**
Type **s**
Type **L**
Type **Large characters**
Press **Right Arrow**
Press **Enter**
Press **Ctrl-F8**
Type **s**
Type **v**
Type **Very Large characters**
Press **Right Arrow**
Press **Enter**

Press **Ctrl-F8**
Type **s**
Type **e**
Type `Extra Large characters`
Press **Right Arrow**
Press **Enter**

Selecting a Size option inserts size codes into the document before and after the text you type, just like the Underline command. Pressing the Right Arrow key after typing text in a particular size moves the cursor past the second size code and returns to the default size. To see what you have done, print the document:

Press **Shift-F7**
Type **f**

You can also use the View Document feature to examine the results. Note that some of the sizes turn out the same, depending upon your printer. A dot-matrix printer, for example, may have only two or three different sizes. A laser printer, on the other hand, can probably produce all of the different character sizes.

Step 4: Select the Appearance Option

Activate the Font menu and select the Appearance option:

Press **Ctrl-F8**
Type **a**

WordPerfect will display the Appearance menu, which has nine options: Bold, Underline, Double Underline, Italic, Outline, Shadow, Small Caps, Redline, and Strikeout. This menu allows you to change character formats, as you learned in the Beginning WordPerfect chapter. Execute the Exit command:

Press **F7**

Step 5: Select the Normal Option

The Normal option of the Font menu turns off all size and appearance attributes for the next characters you type. It returns to the default character size and format.

Press **Ctrl-F8**
Type **n**

Step 6: Select the Base Font Option

The Base Font option of the Font menu displays the fonts available with your printer and allows you to change the font you are using.

Press **Ctrl-F8**
Type **f**

Figure 12 shows the result for an Epson LQ-850 dot-matrix printer. The list you see on your screen may be different. The font highlighted and marked with an asterisk is the base font, the default typeface used for normal characters. If more fonts are available than fit on the screen, they can be viewed by pressing Up Arrow or Down Arrow to scroll through the list. The list presents the name of each font and its size. Sizes are given in points (pt) or characters per inch (CPI).

Figure 12 The Base Font Menu for the Epson LQ-850 Printer

```
Base Font

 Roman (10 CPI)
 Roman (12 CPI)
 Roman (15 CPI)
 Roman (17 CPI)
 Roman (20 CPI)
 Roman 12pt (PS)
 Roman 12pt (PS) Condensed
 Roman 12pt (PS) Dbl-Wide
 Roman 12pt (PS) Italic
 Roman Italic ( 5 CPI)
 Roman Italic ( 6 CPI)
 Roman Italic ( 7 CPI)
 Roman Italic (10 CPI)
 Roman Italic (12 CPI)
 Roman Italic (15 CPI)
 Roman Italic (17 CPI)
 Roman Italic (20 CPI)
 San Serif ( 5 CPI)
 San Serif ( 6 CPI)
 San Serif ( 7 CPI)
* San Serif (10 CPI)

1 Select; N Name search: 1
```

A **point** is a typographic measure equal to about 1/72-inch. Ten characters per inch (10 CPI), the most common default size, is equivalent to the type produced by pica typewriters. Elite typewriters produce 12-CPI type. The abbreviation PS stands for "proportionally spaced," which refers to fonts that use different amounts of horizontal space for each character.

The two options at the bottom of the screen allow you to select a different base font or search through the list for a particular font name. Let's just leave the base font the same. Execute the Exit command to leave the Base Font menu:

Press **F7**

Step 7: Select the Print Color Option

If you have a color printer, you can use the Print Color option to change the color of printed text.

Press **Ctrl-F8**
Type **c**

Most printers cannot produce colors, only black and white. If you have a color printer, however, the table presented by the Print Color option lets you compose print colors by specifying the mixture percentages of the primary colors red, green, and blue. Leave the table the same and return to the editing screen:

Press **F7**

Practice

1. Move the cursor to the beginning of the document and execute the Reveal Codes command. Note the following codes for character sizes: [SUPRSCPT], [SUBSCPT], [FINE], [SMALL], [LARGE], [VRY LARGE], and [EXT LARGE]. Return to the editing screen.
2. Reproduce these expressions in your document:

   H_2O
   2×10^3
   $e = mc^2$

3. Use the Help facility to read about all of the Font menu options. When you are finished, return to the editing screen.
4. Change the base font, type some new text, and print out the document to see the result. Then change the base font back to what it was before. Clear the screen without saving the document:

   Press **F7**
   Type **n**
   Type **n**

Lesson 6: Adding Headers and Footers

A **header** is one or more lines of text printed at the top of every page. A **footer** is one or more lines of text printed at the bottom of every page. Headers and footers are most often used to print titles, chapters, page numbers, or other identification on every page. WordPerfect makes it easy to create headers and footers.

Step 1: Retrieve NEWS.DOC

As an example, let's add a header to the document NEWS.DOC. Your editing screen should be empty. If it is not, use the Exit command to clear it. Then retrieve NEWS.DOC from the LESSONS subdirectory:

Press **Shift-F10**
Type **c:\lessons\news.doc**
Press **Enter**

Step 2: Select the Headers Option

To create a header, execute the Format command, select the Page option, and then select the Header option:

Press **Shift-F8**
Type **p**
Type **h**

Step 3: Select the Header

Another menu will appear with two options: Header A and Header B. WordPerfect lets you create up to two headers. Select Header A:

Type **a**

Step 4: Select the Pages

Another menu will appear with five options: Discontinue, Every Page, Odd Pages, Even Pages, and Edit. Select the Every Page option to have the header printed at the top of every page:

Type **p**

Step 5: Enter the Header Text

The screen will temporarily clear so you can enter the text of the header. Suppose you want the header to be "Newsletter" followed by the page number. Follow these instructions:

Type **Newsletter**
Press **Space Bar**
Press **Ctrl-b**
Press **F7** (2 times)

The Ctrl-b is a code that tells WordPerfect to insert the current page number.

Step 6: Print or View the Document

Headers show up only when the document is printed or examined with View Document. If you have a printer, you can print the document:

Press **Shift-F7**
Type **f**

Or you can use the View Document feature:

Press **Shift-F7**
Type **v**

The header will appear in the upper left corner of every page (see Figure 13).

Step 7: Examine the Other Options

The process for creating footers is the same, except you choose the Footers option from the Page menu of the Format command. The Discontinue option allows you to remove an existing header or footer. The Edit option allows you to make changes to an existing header or footer.

Figure 13 The Header Has Been Inserted

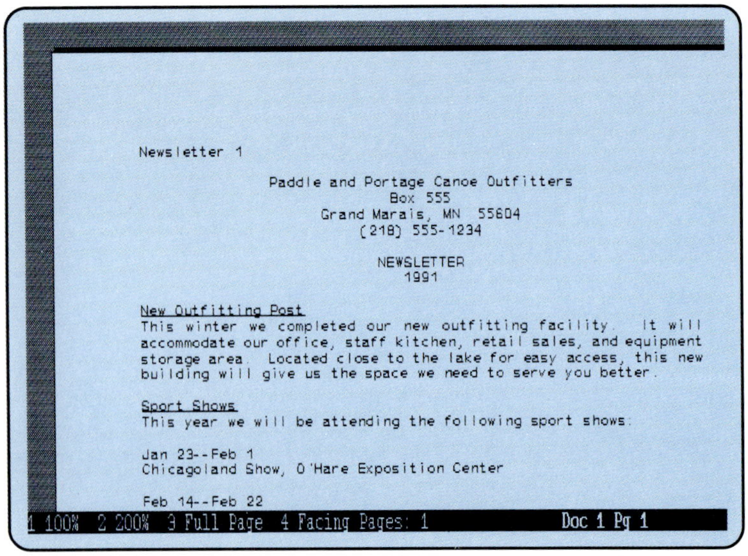

Practice

1. Discontinue the header you have created for NEWS.DOC.
2. Create a footer for NEWS.DOC. Print the document or examine it with View Document.
3. Use the Edit option to alter the footer in some way.
4. Discontinue the footer.

Lesson 7: Creating Text Columns

WordPerfect can create two types of text columns in a printed document: newspaper-style and parallel. **Newspaper-style columns** contain text that continues from the bottom of one column on the left to the top of the next column on the right on the same page. **Parallel columns** contain text that continues in the same column on the next page. Columns are often used in newsletters, magazines, newspapers, and for narrow lists of items in books. As an example, let's reformat NEWS.DOC so that it contains two newspaper-style columns.

Step 1: Move the Cursor

The first step is to move the cursor to the place in the document where columns are to begin. In NEWS.DOC, columns should begin on the line that contains the title "New Outfitting Post."

Press **Home** (2 times)
Press **Up Arrow**
Press **Down Arrow** (8 times)

Step 2: Turn On Automatic Hyphenation

It is usually necessary to hyphenate some words when text is arranged in columns. Turn on automatic hyphenation:

Press **Shift-F8**
Type **L**
Type **y**
Type **a**
Press **F7**

Step 3: Define the Columns

Next, you must tell WordPerfect the number of columns you want and their spacing on the page. Execute the Math/Columns command and select the Column Definition option:

Press **Alt-F7**
Type **d**

WordPerfect will display the Text Column Definition menu, as shown in Figure 14. The default type of columns is newspaper-style, with two three-inch-wide columns spaced ½-inch apart. These default settings are fine for our example, so tell WordPerfect to accept them:

Press **Enter**

Figure 14 The Text Column Definition Menu

```
Text Column Definition

     1 - Type                                  Newspaper

     2 - Number of Columns                     2

     3 - Distance Between Columns

     4 - Margins

     Column    Left     Right     Column    Left     Right
       1:      1"       4"        13:
       2:      4.5"     7.5"      14:
       3:                         15:
       4:                         16:
       5:                         17:
       6:                         18:
       7:                         19:
       8:                         20:
       9:                         21:
      10:                         22:
      11:                         23:
      12:                         24:

Selection: 0
```

Step 4: Turn On Columns

The columns are now defined, but you still have to turn them on. Select the Column On/Off option from the Math/Columns menu:

Type **c**

After you turn on columns, any new text you type will automatically be arranged in columns. You can turn off columns at any time by executing the Column On/Off command again. Then you can type text that you don't want split into columns.

Step 5: Scroll Through the Text

Now that columns are turned on, you can use the Down Arrow key to scroll through the text and WordPerfect will create the columns on your screen.

Press **Down Arrow** (to the end of the document)

The program will prompt you to manually hyphenate words that it cannot hyphenate automatically. If you cannot hyphenate the word correctly, execute the Cancel command (press F1) to wrap the entire word to the next line.

Step 6: Move to the Other Column

The normal cursor movement commands work only within the current column. You must use a variation of the Go To command to move to another column. Execute this command to move to the right column:

Press **Ctrl-Home**
Press **Right Arrow**

Now, move back to the left column:

Press **Ctrl-Home**
Press **Left Arrow**

Step 7: Print or View the Document

The screen shows the two columns, but you can see the document better by printing it or using the View Document feature. If you have a printer, you can print the document:

Press **Shift-F7**
Type **f**

Or you can use the View Document feature:

Press **Shift-F7**
Type **v**

The newsletter will appear in two newspaper-style columns (see Figure 15). Don't worry about the tables, which do not line up or are split between the pages. The tab stops were set too wide for the narrow columns. If this were an actual newsletter, you would have to fix the tables and any other minor formatting problems.

Step 8: Exit and Retrieve NEWS.DOC

Let's abandon the columns you have created and leave NEWS.DOC the way it was before this lesson. Exit the file without saving it and then retrieve NEWS.DOC again:

Press **F7**
Type **n**
Type **n**
Press **Shift-F10**
Type **c:\lessons\news.doc**
Press **Enter**

Practice Invoke the Help facility and read about the commands and options you have used in this lesson.

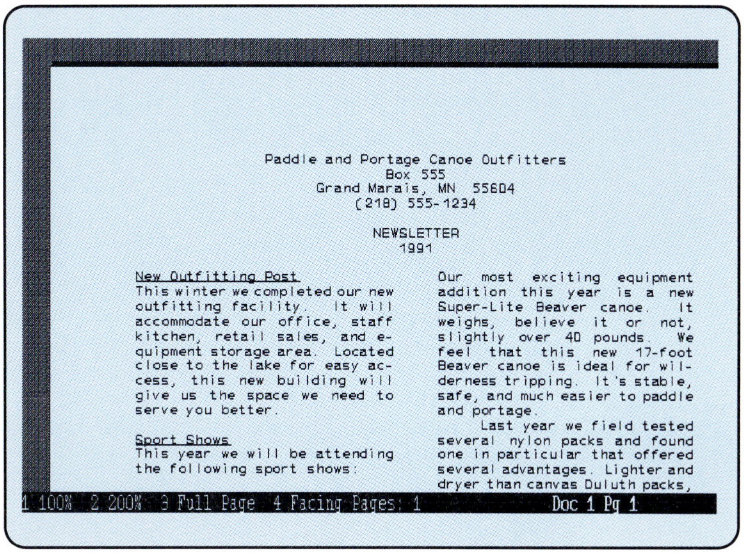

Figure 15 Two Newspaper-Style Text Columns

Lesson 8: Adding Footnotes and Endnotes

Anyone who has written a term paper or technical report has faced the problem of placing footnotes. A **footnote** is a numbered comment or explanation at the bottom of a page. Footnotes are used to list sources or provide more detailed information about items in the text. A footnote must appear at the bottom of the page that contains its number. Placing footnotes at the bottom of the appropriate pages is difficult with a typewriter and some word processing programs. If text is added or deleted, existing footnotes may have to be moved to a different page. Fortunately, WordPerfect automatically numbers footnotes and keeps them at the bottom of the appropriate page. An **endnote** is similar to a footnote, except that comments are collected and placed at the end of the document instead of at the bottom of each page. You can have footnotes and endnotes in the same document. Although newsletters usually don't have footnotes or endnotes, let's add a footnote to NEWS.DOC just to see how they work.

Step 1: Move the Cursor

The cursor must be moved to the location in the document where the note number is to be inserted. Let's put a footnote number at the end of the New Outfitting Post paragraph.

Press **Home** (2 times)
Press **Up Arrow**
Press **Down Arrow** (12 times)
Press **End**

Step 2: Execute the Footnote Command

Footnotes and endnotes are created by executing the Footnote command.

Press **Ctrl-F7**

WordPerfect will present a menu at the bottom of the screen with three options: Footnote, Endnote, and Endnote Placement. Select the Footnote option:

Type **f**

Step 3: Create the Footnote

The Footnote menu will appear at the bottom of the screen with four options: Create, Edit, New Number, and Options. Select the Create option to begin creating the footnote:

Type **c**

WordPerfect will present a special screen for editing footnotes. The footnote number, in this case 1, is automatically created. Simply type the text of the footnote:

Type **`See last year's newsletter for a photo.`**

Your screen should look like Figure 16. Execute the Exit command to save the footnote and return to the document editing screen:

Press **F7**

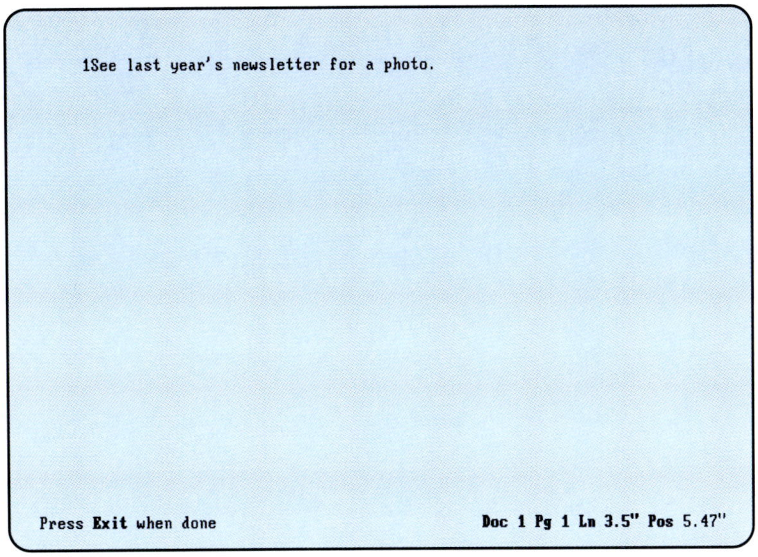

Figure 16 The Footnote Text

Step 4: View the Document

When you return to the editing screen, you can immediately see the footnote number WordPerfect placed at the end of the first paragraph. The footnote text, however, only appears when the document is printed or examined with View Document. Use the View Document feature to look at the footnote you have created:

Press **Shift-F7**
Type **v**
Type **1**
Press **Grey Plus** (2 times)

Your screen should look like Figure 17. The footnote appears at the bottom of the first page beneath a line separating it from the document text. Return to the editing screen:

Press **F7**

Step 5: Examine Other Options

Creating endnotes is just like creating footnotes, except that you select the Endnote option instead of the Footnote option after you execute the Footnote command. In addition, you have to tell WordPerfect where you want the endnotes placed in the document. This is done by moving the cursor to the desired location, executing the Footnote command, and then selecting the Endnote Placement option.

To edit existing footnotes or endnotes, you select the Edit option from the Footnote or Endnote menu. The New Number option lets you start numbering notes with a new number. This option is useful when you have a document broken up between two files and you want the note numbers in the second file to continue after the numbers in the first file instead of starting from 1. The Options option in the Footnote or Endnote menu lets you specify attributes such as footnote spacing and the numbering style.

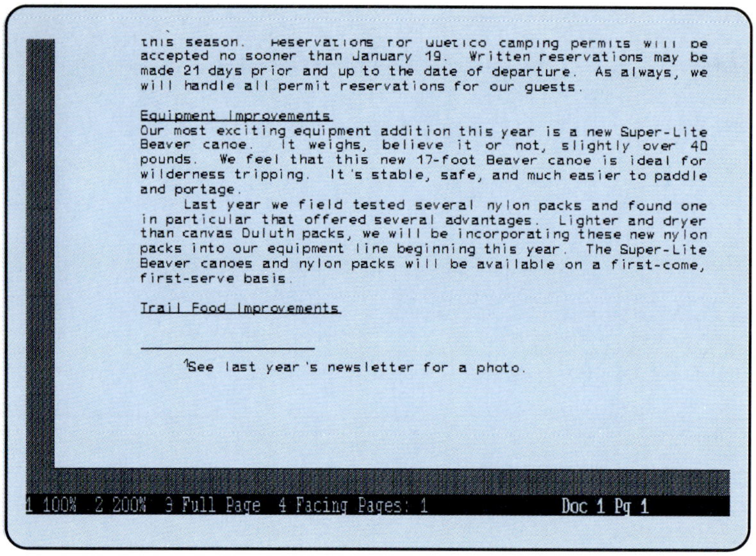

this season. Reservations for Quetico camping permits will be accepted no sooner than January 19. Written reservations may be made 21 days prior and up to the date of departure. As always, we will handle all permit reservations for our guests.

Equipment Improvements
Our most exciting equipment addition this year is a new Super-Lite Beaver canoe. It weighs, believe it or not, slightly over 40 pounds. We feel that this new 17-foot Beaver canoe is ideal for wilderness tripping. It's stable, safe, and much easier to paddle and portage.
Last year we field tested several nylon packs and found one in particular that offered several advantages. Lighter and dryer than canvas Duluth packs, we will be incorporating these new nylon packs into our equipment line beginning this year. The Super-Lite Beaver canoes and nylon packs will be available on a first-come, first-serve basis.

Trail Food Improvements

[1]See last year's newsletter for a photo.

1 100% 2 200% 3 Full Page 4 Facing Pages: 1 Doc 1 Pg 1

Figure 17 The Footnote Has Been Added at the Bottom

Practice

1. Add the following footnote at the end of the New Regulations paragraph:

   `Write to the Ontario Ministry of Natural Resources for more information.`

2. Add a couple of endnotes and place them at the end of the document. Use the View Document feature to examine the endnotes you have created.
3. Delete all of the footnotes and endnotes you have created by deleting each note number in the document text. Answer "yes" to the confirmation prompt displayed by WordPerfect each time you delete a note number. Move the cursor to the beginning of the document.

Lesson 9: Sorting Text

Sorting is arranging items in some particular order. WordPerfect makes it easy to sort lines of text or paragraphs. This feature is handy for alphabetizing names or any list of words or phrases. Sorting is also used to arrange numbers, such as dates and ZIP codes, into ascending or descending order. As an example, let's sort the list of fishing records on the second page of NEWS.DOC.

Step 1: Mark the Lines As a Block

The first step is to mark the lines of text to be sorted as a block. Follow these directions to move the cursor with the Search command and then mark the fishing records as a block:

Press **Home** (2 times)
Press **Up Arrow**
Press **F2**
Type **`Bluegill`**
Press **F2**

Figure 18 The Sort Menu

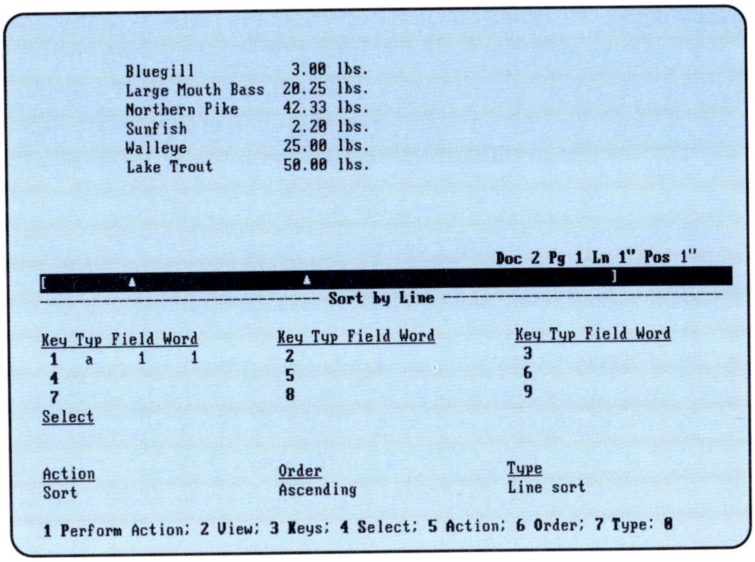

Press **Home**
Press **Left Arrow**
Press **Alt-F4**
Press **Down Arrow** (6 times)

The table of fishing records will be marked as a block and displayed in reverse video.

Step 2: Execute the Merge/Sort Command

The table of fish names and records is almost sorted. The only name out of order is Lake Trout. Let's sort the table by fish name. Execute the Merge/Sort command:

Press **Ctrl-F9**

WordPerfect will display the Sort menu shown in Figure 18. Each line in the marked block is a **record** to be sorted. Each word separated by tabs or spaces is a **field.** The **key** is a field on which the records are to be sorted. WordPerfect lets you specify up to nine keys, but in most cases you need only one. The key in this case will be the first word of the fish names. But because all of the lines in this table begin with a tab, you must tell WordPerfect that the second field in each record is to be the key. Select the Keys option and change the key field from 1 to 2:

Type **k**
Press **Right Arrow**
Type **2**
Press **F7**

The default sort order is Ascending, which will sort items in alphabetical order from A to Z. Select the Perform Action option to complete the sort:

Type **p**

The table will be rearranged, with Lake Trout coming after Bluegill.

Practice

1. Sort the Fishing Records table in descending order. Select the Order option from the Sort menu and then select the Descending option.
2. Sort the Fishing Records table in ascending order again. Save NEWS.DOC to the disk to preserve the changes you have made. Move the cursor to the beginning of the document.

Lesson 10: Performing Math

WordPerfect has a Math feature that lets you perform calculations in your documents. The most common use of the Math feature is to add up a column of numbers. As an example, let's add up the weights in the Fishing Records table. Although adding these numbers does not make much sense in the context of this table, it will serve as a useful illustration of the Math feature.

Step 1: Move the Cursor

The first step is to move the cursor to the line that contains the first number to be totaled. Follow these directions to move to the beginning of the Fishing Records table.

Press **Home** (2 times)
Press **Up Arrow**
Press **F2**
Type **Bluegill**
Press **F2**
Press **Home**
Press **Left Arrow**

Step 2: Define the Math Columns

You already have the numbers arranged in a column created with tab stops. The next step is to define the math columns. Execute the Math/Columns command:

Press **Alt-F7**

WordPerfect will display the Math/Columns menu at the bottom of the screen. Select the Math Definition option:

Type **e**

WordPerfect will then display the Math Definition menu. By default, all columns are assumed to be math columns, negative numbers will appear in parentheses, and two digits will appear to the right of the decimal point. The default settings are fine, so just execute the Exit command:

Press **F7**

Step 3: Turn On Math

WordPerfect will return to the Math/Columns menu at the bottom of the screen. Select the Math On option to turn on the Math feature:

Type **m**

WordPerfect will return to the editing screen, and the word "Math" will appear in the status line to remind you that the Math feature is turned on.

Step 4: Insert the Math Operator

You must insert the math operator + below the numbers to tell WordPerfect to compute their total. Move the cursor to the end of the last line in the table:

Press **Down Arrow** (5 times)
Press **End**

Now, insert a label and the operator to compute the total:

Press **Enter**
Press **Tab**
Type **Total**
Press **Tab**
Type +

Note that the Tab key acts like the Tab Align command (Ctrl-F6) when the Math feature is turned on. This ensures that the total will line up with the numbers above.

Step 5: Select the Calculate Option

Execute the Math/Columns command and select the Calculate option to actually compute the total:

Press **Alt-F7**
Type **a**

The total will be computed and inserted before the plus sign. You can now delete the operator:

Press **Backspace**

Your screen should look like Figure 19.

Figure 19 The Computed Total

```
          1 to 3 persons        $31.00
          4 to 6 persons        $29.25
          7 to 9 persons        $28.50

1990 Fishing Records
          Bluegill               3.00 lbs.
          Lake Trout            50.00 lbs.
          Large Mouth Bass      20.25 lbs.
          Northern Pike         42.33 lbs.
          Sunfish                2.20 lbs.
          Walleye               25.00 lbs.
     Total                     142.78_

Trips
This fall we took a trip into the Cherry Lake area for some lake
trout fishing.  We had our usual quota of rain, but did enjoy two
beautiful crisp autumn days.  Mornings we awoke to clear, deep blue
skies with heavy, white steam rising from Cherry Lake.  On shore
we could look up into the blue sky, but as we paddled into the
steam we disappeared into white nothingness.  It was a trip we'll
long remember.
     We extended our camping into winter this year with several
overnight trips in December.  From our house we have easy access
to about 15 kilometers of cross-country ski trails that lead to
Math                                        Doc 1 Pg 2 Ln 4.17" Pos 4.3"
```

Step 6: Turn Off Math

After you have performed the calculation, you should turn off the Math feature.

Press **Alt-F7**
Type **m**

The word "Math" will disappear from the status line, indicating that the Math feature is now off for the text below the table.

Step 7: Delete the Total Line

Computing a total of the weights in the Fishing Records table makes little sense. It was done just to illustrate the use of the Math feature. So delete the Total line to restore the table to the way it was before:

Press **Home**
Press **Left Arrow**
Press **Ctrl-End**
Press **Delete**

Practice Use the Help facility to read more about the Math feature.

Lesson 11: Outlining a Document

An outline is an invaluable tool for organizing topics before you type the text of a document. Many word processing programs include outlining facilities to help you plan your documents. WordPerfect's Outline feature is simple and easy to use. Let's illustrate this helpful feature by creating part of the outline of a quick reference guide to WordPerfect.

Step 1: Clear the Screen

Exit and save NEWS.DOC to clear the editing screen:

Press **F7**
Type **y**
Press **Enter**
Type **y**
Type **n**

Step 2: Select the Outline Option

Execute the Date/Outline command and then select the Outline option:

Press **Shift-F5**
Type **o**

WordPerfect will display the word "Outline" on the status line to indicate the Outline feature is turned on.

Step 3: Enter the Outline

The default outline style used by WordPerfect can be summarized as follows: I., A., 1., a., (1), (a), 1), and a). In other words, the first level headings are assigned Roman numerals, the second level headings are assigned capital letters, the third level headings are assigned Arabic numerals, and so on. Up to eight heading levels can be used. The first level headings begin at the left margin. You press the Tab key to move in to the next level heading. Headings are automatically numbered or lettered by WordPerfect. Follow these directions to enter part of the outline of our quick reference guide:

Press **Enter**
Press **Space Bar**
Type **`Function Key Commands`**
Press **Enter**
Press **Tab**
Press **Space Bar**
Type **`F1 Key Commands`**
Press **Enter**
Press **Tab** (2 times)
Press **Space Bar**
Type **`Cancel (F1)`**
Press **Enter**
Press **Tab** (2 times)
Press **Space Bar**
Type **`Thesaurus (Alt-F1)`**
Press **Enter**
Press **Tab** (2 times)
Press **Space Bar**
Type **`Shell (Ctrl-F1)`**
Press **Enter**
Press **Tab** (2 times)
Press **Space Bar**
Type **`Setup (Shift-F1)`**
Press **Enter**
Press **Tab**
Press **Space Bar**
Type **`F2 Key Commands`**
Press **Enter**

Your screen should look like Figure 20. You can edit an outline and add or delete headings. You can press Shift-Tab to move back to a previous heading level after pressing Tab too many times.

Step 4: Turn Off the Outline Feature

When you are finished creating your outline, execute the Date/Outline command and select the Outline option again to turn off the feature:

Press **Shift-F5**
Type **o**

WordPerfect will remove the word "Outline" from the status line, indicating that the Outline feature has been turned off.

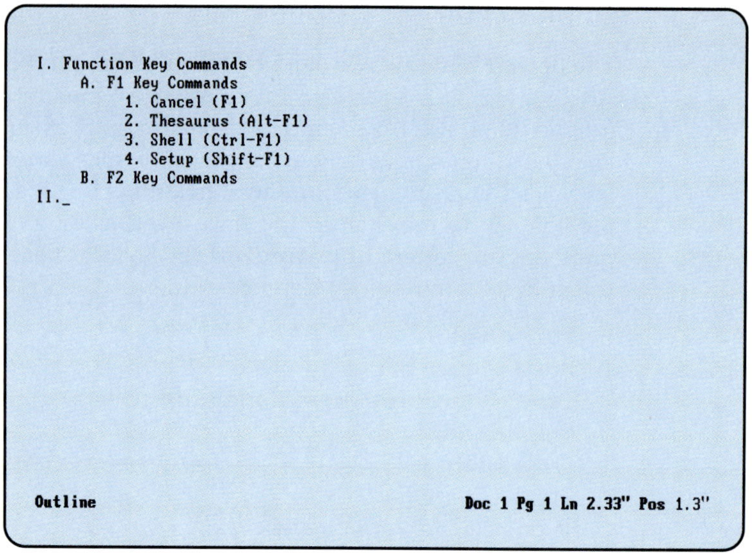

Figure 20 An Outline Has Been Created

Practice

1. Turn on the Outline feature again and enter headings that go below "F2 Key Commands":

    Search Forward (F2)
    Replace (Alt-F2)
    Spell (Ctrl-F2)
    Search Backward (Shift-F2)

2. Turn off the Outline feature. Save the document in a file named OUTLINE.DOC in the LESSONS subdirectory.

Lesson 12: Generating a Table of Contents

Many long documents, such as reports and books, require a table of contents. The purpose of a table of contents is to list the chapter titles and other headings along with their page numbers. WordPerfect, like many advanced word processing packages, can automatically generate a table of contents. All you have to do is mark the headings to be included in the table of contents, define a numbering style for the table, and tell WordPerfect to generate the table. The headings will be copied from the existing text and the correct page numbers will be inserted by the program. Although it is rather short, let's generate a table of contents for the document NEWS.DOC.

Step 1: Retrieve NEWS.DOC

Clear the editing screen and retrieve the document NEWS.DOC:

Press **F7**
Type **n**
Type **n**
Press **Shift-F10**
Type **c:\lessons\news.doc**
Press **Enter**

Step 2: Mark the Heading as a Block

Each title or heading from the document to be included in the table of contents must be marked as a block and then flagged as a table entry. Follow these steps to mark the "New Outfitting Post" heading as a block:

Press **Down Arrow** (8 times)
Press **Alt-F4**
Press **End**

Step 3: Select the ToC Option

Now, flag the marked block as a table of contents entry by executing the Mark Text command and selecting the ToC option:

Press **Alt-F5**
Type **c**

WordPerfect will display the prompt

```
ToC Level:
```

Up to five levels of headings can be created in the table of contents. In this simple document, all of the table of contents entries will be at the first level.

Type **1**

Step 4: Mark the Remaining Headings

Repeat the two previous steps for the remaining headings in the document. First, mark each heading as a block. Then execute the Mark Text command, select the ToC option, and type 1 as the level.

Step 5: Insert a New Page for the Table

The table of contents will come before the text of the document. So, move the cursor to the beginning of the document, insert a new page, and type a title for the table:

Press **Home** (2 times)
Press **Up Arrow**
Press **Ctrl-Enter**
Press **Up Arrow**
Type **`Paddle and Portage Newsletter`**
Press **Enter**
Type **`Table of Contents`**
Press **Enter** (2 times)

Step 6: Define the Table

After the headings have been marked and a page has been inserted for the table of contents, you must define a numbering style. Follow these directions to execute the Mark Text command and specify the default settings for defining the table of contents:

Press **Alt-F5**
Type **d**

Figure 21 The Generated Table of Contents

```
Paddle and Portage Newsletter
Table of Contents

New Outfitting Post. . . . . . . . . . . . . . . . . . . . . 2

Sport Shows. . . . . . . . . . . . . . . . . . . . . . . . . 2

New Regulations. . . . . . . . . . . . . . . . . . . . . . . 2

Equipment Improvements . . . . . . . . . . . . . . . . . . . 2

Trail Food Improvements. . . . . . . . . . . . . . . . . . . 2

Current Outfitting Rates . . . . . . . . . . . . . . . . . . 3

1990 Fishing Records . . . . . . . . . . . . . . . . . . . . 3

Trips. . . . . . . . . . . . . . . . . . . . . . . . . . . . 3

A Final Note.... . . . . . . . . . . . . . . . . . . . . . . 3

==============================================================
              Paddle and Portage Canoe Outfitters
C:\LESSONS\NEWS.DOC                     Doc 1 Pg 1 Ln 1" Pos 1"
```

Type **c**
Press **Enter**

When the table is generated, WordPerfect will use one level of headings and present page numbers flush right with dot leaders.

Step 7: Generate the Table

The final step is to tell WordPerfect to generate the table of contents. Follow these directions to execute the Mark Text command and generate the table:

Press **Alt-F5**
Type **g**
Type **g**
Type **y**
Press **Home** (2 times)
Press **Up Arrow**

Your screen should look like Figure 21.

Practice

1. Use the Help facility to read about the Mark Text command and its various options.
2. Move the cursor to the "New Outfitting Post" heading in the document on page 2. Execute the Reveal Codes command and examine the codes that mark the heading as a table of contents entry.
3. You can remove a heading from the table of contents as follows. Delete the code [Mark:ToC,1] in front of the heading "New Outfitting Post." Execute the Reveal Codes command again to return to the full editing screen. Move the cursor to the beginning of the document. Repeat Step 7 in this lesson to regenerate the table of contents. The new table of contents will omit the heading "New Outfitting Post."
4. Mark the heading "New Outfitting Post" as a table of contents entry again. Then regenerate the table of contents.

Lesson 13: Generating an Index

An index lists important terms and their page numbers in alphabetical order at the end of a document. Generating an index with WordPerfect is similar to generating a table of contents. As an example, let's create an index containing a few terms for the document NEWS.DOC.

Step 1: Move the Cursor to a Term

If a term to be included in the index is a single word, you can simply move the cursor to the word. If the term is a phrase, it must be marked as a block. Move the cursor to the word "building" in the New Outfitting Post paragraph:

Press **F2**
Type **`building`**
Press **F2**
Press **Left Arrow**

Step 2: Select the Index Option

To flag the word as an index entry, execute the Mark Text command and select the Index option:

Press **Alt-F5**
Type **i**

WordPerfect will display the prompt

```
Index heading: Building
```

At this point, you can enter a more descriptive index entry or simply press the Enter key twice to accept the entry as is and without a subheading:

Press **Enter** (2 times)

Step 3: Mark the Remaining Index Entries

To create a comprehensive index, you would have to go through the entire document and mark all the significant terms. For the purpose of this example, however, just mark each of the following terms by moving the cursor to the term and repeating Step 2:

Shows
Regulations
Equipment
Food
Rates
Fishing
Trips

Step 4: Insert a New Page for the Index

The index will come after the text of the document. So, move the cursor to the end of the document, insert a new page, and type a title for the index:

Press **Home** (2 times)
Press **Down Arrow**
Press **Ctrl-Enter**
Type **`Newsletter Index`**
Press **Enter** (2 times)

Step 5: Define the Index

After the entries have been marked and a page has been inserted for the index, you must define a numbering style. Follow these directions to execute the Mark Text command and specify that page numbers are to be flush right with dot leaders:

Press **Alt-F5**
Type **d**
Type **i**
Press **Enter**
Type **L**

Step 6: Generate the Index

The final step is to tell WordPerfect to generate the index. Follow these directions to execute the Mark Text command and generate the index:

Press **Alt-F5**
Type **g**
Type **g**
Type **y**
Press **Home** (2 times)
Press **Down Arrow**

Your screen should look like Figure 22.

Practice

1. Mark a few more terms as index entries. Try some phrases instead of single words. Remember that you must mark a phrase as a block before you can mark it as an index entry. Also, try entering a slightly different entry when WordPerfect prompts you for the index heading.
2. Move the cursor to a term you have marked as an index entry. Execute the Reveal Codes command and examine the code that designates a term as an index entry. You can delete the index code to unmark the term as an index entry. Return to the full editing screen.
3. Regenerate the index. Save the document to preserve the changes you have made.

Lesson 14: Adding Graphics

With WordPerfect you can incorporate horizontal and vertical lines, boxes, and pictures in documents. These features can greatly improve the appearance of documents such as newsletters, reports, ads, and tutorials. This lesson will intro-

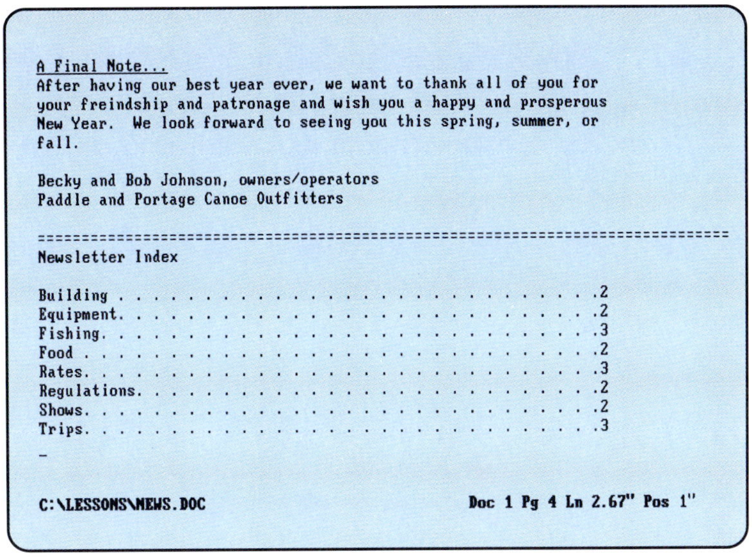

Figure 22 The Generated Index

duce some of WordPerfect's graphics capabilities. In order to use them, however, you will need a computer with a graphics display or a dot-matrix or laser printer.

Step 1: Insert a Horizontal Line

The simplest application of graphics in a document is to add horizontal or vertical lines. Even basic elements such as lines can improve the appearance of a document. Horizontal lines are often used to separate sections of text. Let's insert a horizontal line between the heading and first paragraph of the newsletter. First, move the cursor to the proper position and insert a blank line:

Press **Home** (2 times)
Press **Up Arrow**
Press **Page Down**
Press **Down Arrow** (7 times)
Press **Enter**
Press **Up Arrow**

The cursor is now where you want the horizontal line to go. Next, execute the Graphics command, select the Line option, and then select the Horizontal Line option:

Press **Alt-F9**
Type **L**
Type **h**

WordPerfect will present the Horizontal Line menu, which lets you specify the position, length, width, and gray shading of the line. The default settings are for a thin black line extending from the left margin to the right margin. Accept these settings and return to the editing screen:

Press **Enter**

The line will be inserted, but you can see it only if you print the document or use the View Document feature.

Press **Shift-F7**
Type **v**

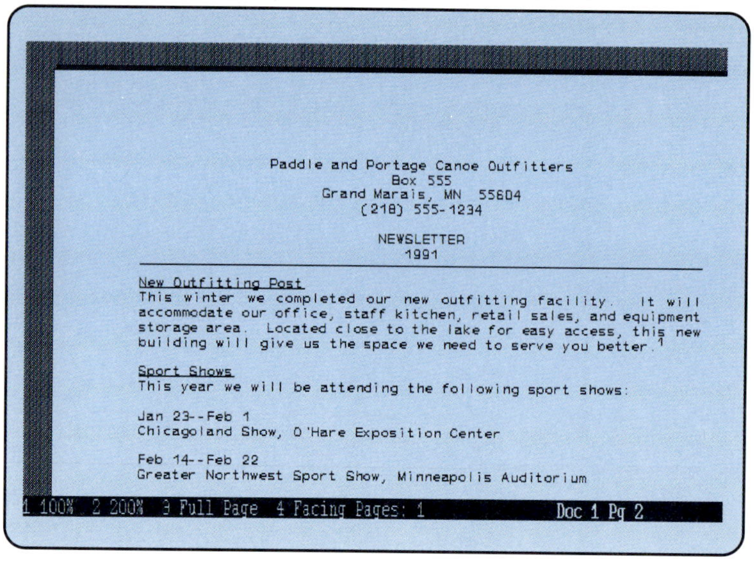

Figure 23 ***The Horizontal Line***

Your screen should look like Figure 23. When you are finished examining your work, return to the editing screen.

Press **F7**

Step 2: Insert a Vertical Line

Vertical lines are often used to separate columns of text. Let's insert a vertical line between the columns of the Current Outfitting Rates table. Move the cursor between the columns in the first line of the table:

Press **F2**
Type **`Number In Party`**
Press **F2**

Look in the status line. The cursor is 3.5 inches from the left edge of the paper. The next column begins 4 inches from the left edge of the paper. So, 3.75 inches from the left edge would be a good place to put the vertical line. Since the table is only four lines long and six lines equals an inch, the line should be about 0.67 inches long. Execute the Graphics command, select the Line option, and then select the Vertical Line option:

Press **Alt-F9**
Type **L**
Type **v**

WordPerfect will present the Vertical Line menu on the screen. Follow these directions to specify a vertical line 0.67 inches long positioned 3.75 inches from the left edge of the paper:

Type **h**
Type **s**
Type **`3.75`**
Press **Enter**
Type **v**

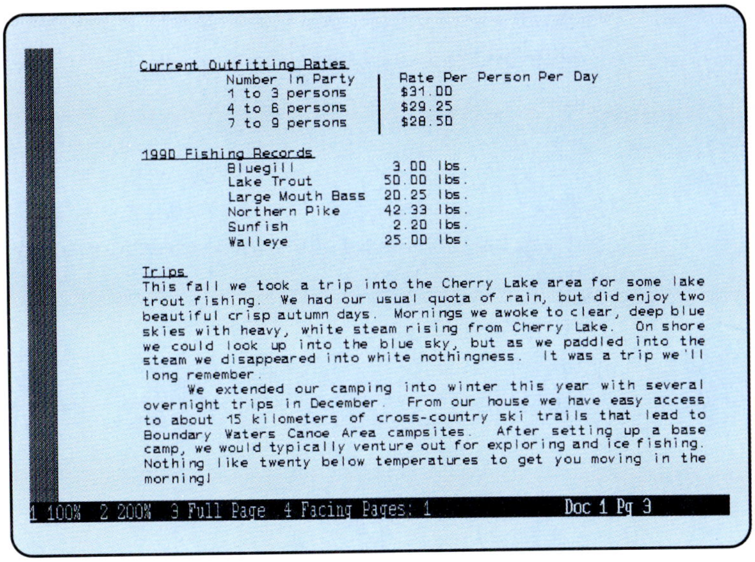

***Figure 24** The Vertical Line*

Type **s**
Press **Enter**
Type **L**
Type **0.67**
Press **Enter** (2 times)

To see the vertical line you have created, use the View Document feature:

Press **Shift-F7**
Type **v**

Your screen should look like Figure 24. When you are finished examining your work, return to the editing screen:

Press **F7**

Step 3: Insert a Box Around Text

Text is often enclosed in a box to draw the reader's eye. As an example, let's enclose the letterhead of the newsletter in a box. First, move the cursor to the first line of the letterhead and insert a blank line:

Press **Home** (2 times)
Press **Up Arrow**
Press **Page Down**
Press **Enter**

Insert another blank line after the letterhead and move back up to the top of the page:

Press **Down Arrow** (4 times)
Press **Enter**
Press **Grey Minus**

Execute the Graphics command, select the Text Box option, and then select the Options option:

Press **Alt-F9**
Type **b**
Type **o**

WordPerfect will display a menu of options for designing a text box. By default, a text box has no sides. Follow these directions to add thick lines to the sides of the box:

Type **b**
Type **t**
Type **t**
Press **F7** (2 times)

Execute the Graphics command again, select the Text Box option, and then select the Create option:

Press **Alt-F9**
Type **b**
Type **c**

WordPerfect will display the Text Box Definition menu. Specify the type, position, and size of the box as follows:

Type **t**
Type **a**
Type **h**
Type **s**
Type **2.25**
Press **Enter**
Type **s**
Type **b**
Type **4**
Press **Enter**
Type **1**
Press **Enter**
Type **w**
Type **n**
Press **F7**

WordPerfect will return to the editing screen, but you will not see the box. You must print the document or use the View Document feature to see the box you have created:

Press **Shift-F7**
Type **v**

Figure 25 shows the result. Note that the inside of the box is lightly shaded, due to the default Gray Shading setting of 10%. When you are finished examining your work, return to the editing screen:

Press **F7**

Step 4: Insert a Picture

You cannot create pictures with WordPerfect, but you can import images created with many painting, drawing, and graphing packages. In fact, WordPerfect comes with a number of sample graphics files on the diskette labeled Graphics. These

***Figure 25** The Text Box*

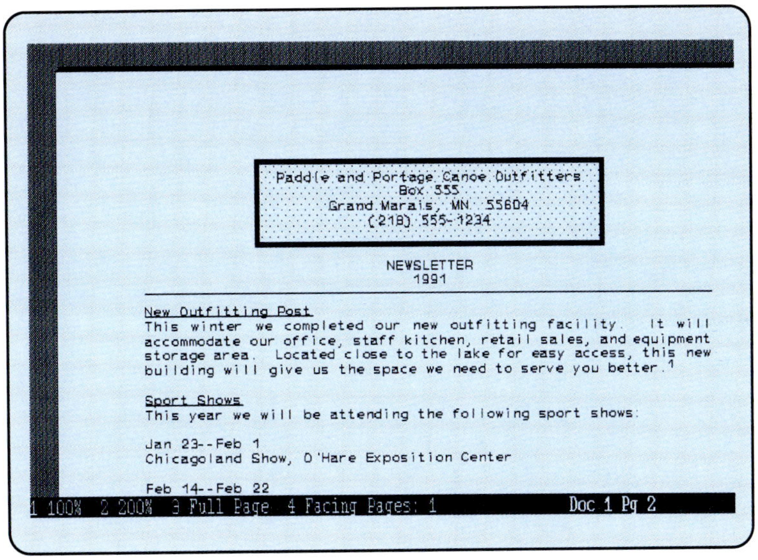

files are identified by the extension WPG, which stands for WordPerfect Graphics format. This lesson assumes that you have at least one of these WPG files on your hard disk in the WP50 subdirectory. As an example, let's insert a picture on a new page before the index. The graphics file we will use is USAMAP.WPG, which contains a line drawing map of the United States. If you like, you can substitute another WPG file or a picture file from some other program, such as PC Paintbrush, Microsoft Windows Paint, or Lotus 1-2-3. Use the List Files command to examine your disk to find the name of a graphics file if you are not going to use USAMAP.WPG in the WP50 subdirectory.

Move the cursor to the end of the page before the index and insert a new page:

Press **Home** (2 times)
Press **End**
Press **Page Up**
Press **Ctrl-Home**
Press **Down Arrow**
Press **Ctrl-Enter**

Next, execute the Graphics command, select the Figure option, and then select the Create option:

Press **Alt-F9**
Type **f**
Type **c**

WordPerfect will display the Figure Definition screen. All of the default settings are fine for our example, but you must specify the name of the graphics file.

Type **f**
Type **usamap.wpg**
Press **Enter**
Press **F7**

If you do not have USAMAP.WPG in your WP50 subdirectory, type the path and name of a graphics file you do have. When WordPerfect returns to the editing

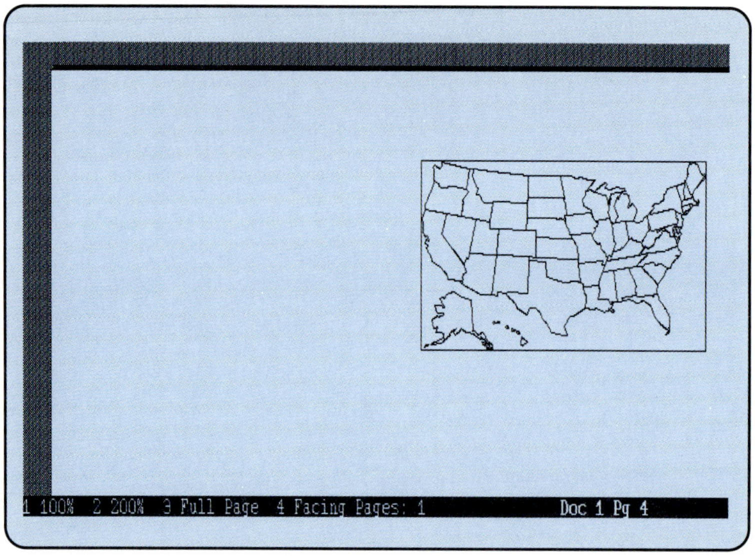

***Figure 26** The Picture from USAMAP.WPG*

screen, you will not see the picture. You must print the document or use the View Document feature to see the picture you have inserted.

Press **Shift-F7**
Type **v**

Your screen should look like Figure 26. When you are finished examining your work, return to the editing screen:

Press **F7**

WordPerfect has many other options for inserting graphics into your documents. You can resize pictures, specify their exact position on the page, and wrap text around them. You can also automatically number figures and create captions for them.

Practice

1. Insert a horizontal line in the newsletter after the line "Becky and Bob Johnson."
2. Insert a vertical line in the newsletter separating the columns of the Fishing Records table.
3. Use the List Files command to see the names of any WPG files you may have in your WP50 subdirectory. Choose a name and insert this picture file into the newsletter. Print the document or examine it with the View Document feature.
4. Use the Reveal Codes command to examine the document. Graphic elements such as lines, boxes, and pictures can be removed by deleting their codes. Delete the code for the picture you just inserted and examine the newsletter with the View Document feature.

Lesson 15: Using Macros

A **macro** is a sequence of keystrokes that can be recorded, stored, and replayed. The keystrokes may include function keys, menu selections, and ordinary text. Macros are handy for automating frequent actions that require many keystrokes. For instance, suppose you must often type the phrase "Paddle and Portage Canoe

Outfitters" in a document. WordPerfect lets you assign this entire phrase to an abbreviated command, such as Alt-P. Once you define the macro, you can simply press Alt-P instead of typing the phrase. Instead of having to type 35 characters, you need only press two keys at the same time. The phrase will be automatically inserted at the current cursor location. You can use the macro as often as you like. As an example, let's create such a macro.

Step 1: Move the Cursor

When you create a macro, the keys you press will be executed. So, you must first move the cursor to the place where you want to perform the action the first time. In this case, you can move the cursor to the end of the document:

Press **Home** (2 times)
Press **Down Arrow**

Step 2: Name the Macro

Before you can use a macro, you must name it and then record it. Execute the Macro Define command:

Press **Ctrl-F10**

WordPerfect will display the prompt:

```
Define Macro:
```

This is where you choose a name for the macro. You can enter a name up to eight characters long, press Enter to have WordPerfect choose a name for you, or hold down the Alternate key and type any letter from A to Z. The last method is the easiest to use, but you get only a single letter with which to name your macro. Name your macro Alt-P, for Paddle and Portage:

Press **Alt-P**

Step 3: Describe the Macro

WordPerfect will display the prompt

```
Description:
```

Now you can enter an optional explanation of the function of your macro. A description is helpful for complex macros, but our simple example hardly requires a comment. Leave the description blank:

Press **Enter**

Step 4: Record the Macro

The macro recorder will be turned on and WordPerfect will display a blinking "Macro Def" message on the status line. Now you press the keys that will make up the macro—the keystrokes that will be activated when you press Alt-P later. To specify our simple macro, type the phrase and then execute the Macro Define command again:

Type **`Paddle and Portage Canoe Outfitters`**
Press **Ctrl-F10**

Step 5: Use the Macro

The macro can now be used anywhere in the document. To see how it works, move down a line and execute the macro:

Press **Enter**
Press **Alt-P**

The phrase "Paddle and Portage Canoe Outfitters" will be inserted at the current cursor location. Try it again:

Press **Enter**
Press **Alt-P**

This simple macro merely inserts text, but it can save you a lot of time if you must type the same phrase over and over again. Remember that macros can record any series of keys, including commands and menu selections. They can be a powerful tool for repeating complex sequences of commands.

Practice

1. Create a macro named Alt-N to type your name. Try the macro a number of times.
2. Create a macro named Alt-B to move the cursor to the beginning of the document and then execute the List Files command on the current directory. Exit the List Files menu, move the cursor to the end of the document, and try the macro you have created.

Lesson 16: Creating Form Letters

WordPerfect's Merge feature allows you to print form letters or other personalized text by combining a document with a data file. This feature, sometimes called **mail-merge,** is very useful to businesses and organizations that send letters or bills to various individuals. As an example, let's modify the document HOLMES.DOC, which you created in the previous chapter, so that it can be used to print personalized form letters to a number of different customers.

Step 1: Create the Address File

Form letters are generated by combining names and addresses from a data file with a generic letter. The letter contains codes that indicate where the names and addresses are to go. The data file is sometimes called the **secondary merge file** or **address file.** Let's create the address file first. Execute the Exit command and save the current file to clear the screen:

Press **F7**
Type **y**
Press **Enter**
Type **y**
Type **n**

Suppose form letters are to be sent to four customers. The address file will consist of one record for each customer. Each record consists of five fields: the name, street address, city, state, and ZIP code. Each field is typed on its own line and is terminated by pressing F9 to insert a Merge R code. A record is terminated by pressing Shift-F9 and then selecting the Merge E code option. Follow these directions to enter the four customer records:

Type **Oscar Griffith**
Press **F9**
Type **805 Florida**
Press **F9**
Type **Urbana**
Press **F9**
Type **IL**
Press **F9**
Type **61801**
Press **F9**
Press **Shift-F9**
Type **e**
Type **George Carver**
Press **F9**
Type **906 Busey**
Press **F9**
Type **Brainerd**
Press **F9**
Type **MN**
Press **F9**
Type **56401**
Press **F9**
Press **Shift-F9**
Type **e**
Type **David Banks**
Press **F9**
Type **604 Armory**
Press **F9**
Type **Green Bay**
Press **F9**
Type **WI**
Press **F9**
Type **54305**
Press **F9**
Press **Shift-F9**
Type **e**
Type **Susan Young**
Press **F9**
Type **1104 Grand**
Press **F9**
Type **Anchorage**
Press **F9**
Type **AK**
Press **F9**
Type **99502**
Press **F9**
Press **Shift-F9**
Type **e**

At this point, your screen should look like Figure 27. Save the document in the LESSONS subdirectory in a file named CUSTOMER:

Press **F10**
Type **c:\lessons\customer**
Press **Enter**

Step 2: Create the Primary File

The **primary file** is the text of the form letter containing special merge codes. In this case, you can simply modify the existing document HOLMES.DOC to create the primary file. Clear the screen and retrieve HOLMES.DOC:

Press **F7**
Type **n**
Type **n**
Press **Shift-F10**
Type **c:\lessons\holmes.doc**
Press **Enter**

Move the cursor to the line that contains "Mr. Richard Holmes" and delete to the end of the line:

Press **Down Arrow** (7 times)
Press **Ctrl-End**

Instead of an explicit name, you will insert the merge code ^F1^. This code stands for the first field of the data file, which contains the customer's name. Follow these directions to execute the Merge Codes command, select the ^F merge code, and then enter the field number.

Press **Shift-F9**
Type **f**
Type **1**
Press **Enter**

When the letter is merged with the address file, the ^F1^ codes will be replaced with customer names. Now, follow these directions to delete the remaining address items and replace them with the appropriate merge codes:

Press **Home**
Press **Left Arrow**
Press **Down Arrow**
Press **Ctrl-End**
Press **Shift-F9**
Type **f**
Type **2**
Press **Enter**
Press **Home**
Press **Left Arrow**
Press **Down Arrow**
Press **Ctrl-End**
Press **Shift-F9**
Type **f**
Type **3**
Press **Enter**
Type **,**

Figure 27 The Address File

```
^E
===============================================================================
George Carver^R
906 Busey^R
Brainerd^R
MN^R
56401^R
^E
===============================================================================
David Banks^R
604 Armory^R
Green Bay^R
WI^R
54305^R
^E
===============================================================================
Susan Young^R
1104 Grand^R
Anchorage^R
AK^R
99502^R
^E
===============================================================================
_
                                               Doc 1 Pg 5 Ln 1" Pos 1"
```

Press **Space Bar**
Press **Shift-F9**
Type **f**
Type **4**
Press **Enter**
Press **Space Bar** (2 times)
Press **Shift-F9**
Type **f**
Type **5**
Press **Enter**
Press **Home**
Press **Left Arrow**
Press **Down Arrow** (2 times)
Press **Right Arrow** (5 times)
Press **Ctrl-End**
Press **Shift-F9**
Type **f**
Type **1**
Press **Enter**
Type **:**

When you are finished, your screen should look like Figure 28. Save the document in the LESSONS subdirectory and name the file LETTER.DOC:

Press **F10**
Type **c:\lessons\letter.doc**
Press **Enter**

Step 3: Merge the Primary File and Address File

The address file and primary file are now complete. When they are merged, WordPerfect will substitute items from the address file for the ^F1^ through ^F5^ merge codes in the letter. A new document will be created containing four separate letters, each one addressed to a different customer. Clear the screen, execute

Figure 28 The Primary File

```
                                Paddle and Portage Canoe Outfitters
                                                            Box 555
                                              Grand Marais, MN  55604
                                                     (218) 555-1234

                                                    January 2, 1990

^F1^
^F2^
^F3^, ^F4^  ^F5^

Dear ^F1^:_

Here is our sport show schedule for 1991.  We hope to see you soon!

Jan 23--Feb 1
Chicagoland Show, O'Hare Exposition Center

Feb 14--Feb 22
Greater Northwest Sport Show, Minneapolis Auditorium

Mar 13--Mar 22
Milwaukee Sentinel Sport Show, MECCA Building

C:\LESSONS\HOLMES.DOC                         Doc 1 Pg 1 Ln 2.83" Pos 2"
```

the Merge/Sort command, select the Merge option, enter the names of the primary and secondary merge files, and move to the beginning of the document:

Press **F7**
Type **n**
Type **n**
Press **Ctrl-F9**
Type **m**
Type **c:\lessons\letter.doc**
Press **Enter**
Type **c:\lessons\customer**
Press **Enter**
Press **Home** (2 times)
Press **Up Arrow**

Your screen should look like Figure 29. Examine the other three letters:

Press **Page Down**
Press **Page Down**
Press **Page Down**

You could now save the new document or print it to produce the four separate letters.

Practice

1. Clear the screen without saving the document containing the four form letters. Retrieve the CUSTOMER file and add another record:

   Richard Holmes
   444 Adams Street
   Green Bay
   WI
   54301

   Save the updated CUSTOMER file and clear the screen. Note that you can add any number of records to the address file.

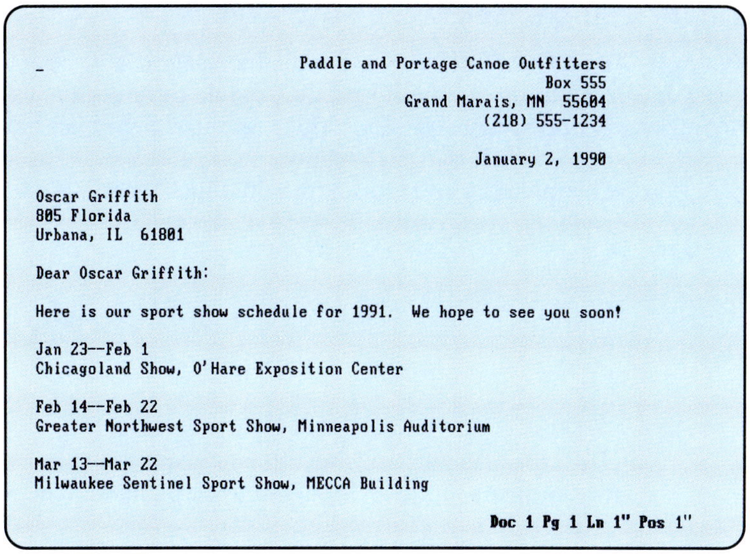

Paddle and Portage Canoe Outfitters
Box 555
Grand Marais, MN 55604
(218) 555-1234

January 2, 1990

Oscar Griffith
805 Florida
Urbana, IL 61801

Dear Oscar Griffith:

Here is our sport show schedule for 1991. We hope to see you soon!

Jan 23--Feb 1
Chicagoland Show, O'Hare Exposition Center

Feb 14--Feb 22
Greater Northwest Sport Show, Minneapolis Auditorium

Mar 13--Mar 22
Milwaukee Sentinel Sport Show, MECCA Building

Doc 1 Pg 1 Ln 1" Pos 1"

***Figure 29** A Generated Form Letter*

2. Merge LETTER.DOC with the new CUSTOMER file to create five form letters.
3. Print the full document to output the five form letters.

Lesson 17: Using Styles

A **style** is a collection of formatting codes and possibly text that can be created, saved, and inserted into documents to automate formatting and provide a consistent appearance to documents. Styles are often used for book chapters, newsletters, and other long documents whose format settings are used over and over again. For example, three styles might be used for a book. One style could include the margin and tab stop settings and be inserted at the beginning of each chapter. Another style could contain formatting codes for the chapter headings. A third style could include formatting codes for the multiple choice questions that appear at the end of each chapter. As an example, let's create a style that sets margins, justification, and tab stops.

Step 1: Clear the Screen

Clear your current editing screen:

Press **F7**
Type **n**
Type **n**

Step 2: Name the Style

Execute the Style command, select the Create option, select the Name option, and then enter a name for the style:

Press **Alt-F8**
Type **c**
Type **n**
Type **`Settings`**
Press **Enter**

Step 3: Select the Style Type

Two types of styles are available, paired and open. A **paired style** type has a beginning and ending code. A style to underline text, for example, would be a paired style because a code is required before and after the underlined text. An **open style** has just a beginning code and is often used to set formats for an entire document. A style to set margins, justification, and tab stops would be an open style. Select Open as the type of the style:

Type **t**
Type **o**

Step 4: Describe the Style

The style description is text that explains the purpose of the style. This description appears in the Styles menu to help you remember what the style does. Enter a description for the style:

Type **d**
Type **Margins, justification, and tab stop settings**
Press **Enter**

Step 5: Enter the Codes

A style can contain WordPerfect codes and text. To include codes in a style, you select the Codes option and then execute the commands to create those codes. Follow these directions to enter the codes to set margins, justification, and tab stops:

Type **c**
Press **Shift-F8**
Type **L**
Type **m**
Type **1.25**
Press **Enter**
Type **1.25**
Press **Enter**
Type **j**
Type **n**
Type **t**
Press **Home** (2 times)
Press **Left Arrow**
Press **Ctrl-End**
Type **L**
Type **0,1**
Press **Enter**
Press **F7** (4 times)

WordPerfect will return to the Styles menu, shown in Figure 30. The Settings style that you have created will set the left and right margins to 1.25 inches, turn off justification, and set tab stops at 1-inch intervals beginning at the left edge of the page.

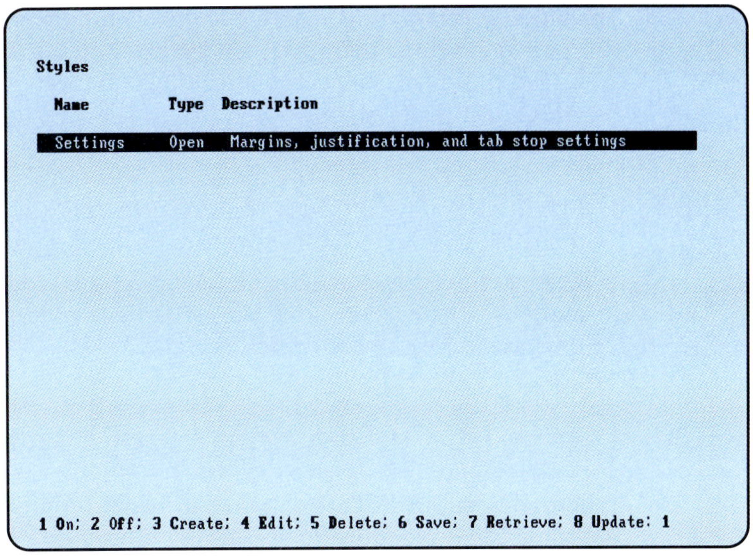

Figure 30 The Styles Menu

Step 6: Save the Style

By default, a style is saved with the document in which it was created. You can, however, save the styles you create separately and use them in any document. Select the Save option and then enter a file name to hold your styles:

Type **s**
Type **c:\lessons\styles**
Press **Enter**

The style Settings is now saved in a file named STYLES in the LESSONS subdirectory. Return to the editing screen:

Press **F7**

Step 7: Use the Style

After you have created and saved a style, you can use it in any document. Move the cursor to the place where the style is to be inserted, execute the Style command, and retrieve the style file:

Press **Home** (2 times)
Press **Up Arrow**
Press **Alt-F8**
Type **r**
Type **c:\lessons\styles**
Press **Enter**
Type **y**

WordPerfect will present the Styles menu. In this case, only one style is listed. You can, however, create and save a number of different styles. Then you would use Up Arrow or Down Arrow to highlight the style you want to use. When the style is highlighted, select the On option:

Type **o**

The Settings style is now inserted at the beginning of the current document. You don't have to set the margins, justification, and tab stops individually. Any time you need these particular format settings, you can simply retrieve the STYLES file and select the Settings style.

Practice

1. Execute the Reveal Codes command to confirm that the Settings style has indeed been inserted. When you are finished, return to the full editing screen.
2. Execute the Format command and select the Line option to confirm that the margins, justification, and tab stops have indeed been set. When you are finished, return to the editing screen.

Lesson 18: Customizing WordPerfect

When you start WordPerfect, you can begin typing immediately. The program has already been set up for speed and efficiency. The default settings in effect are adequate for most users. You can, however, tailor WordPerfect to your specific needs by using the Setup command to change various settings. These changes will then remain in effect each time you start WordPerfect. Let's examine the settings you can change with the Setup command.

Step 1: Execute the Setup Command

To examine or change various WordPerfect options, execute the Setup command:

Press **Shift-F1**

The program will display the Setup menu, shown in Figure 31.

Figure 31 The Setup Menu

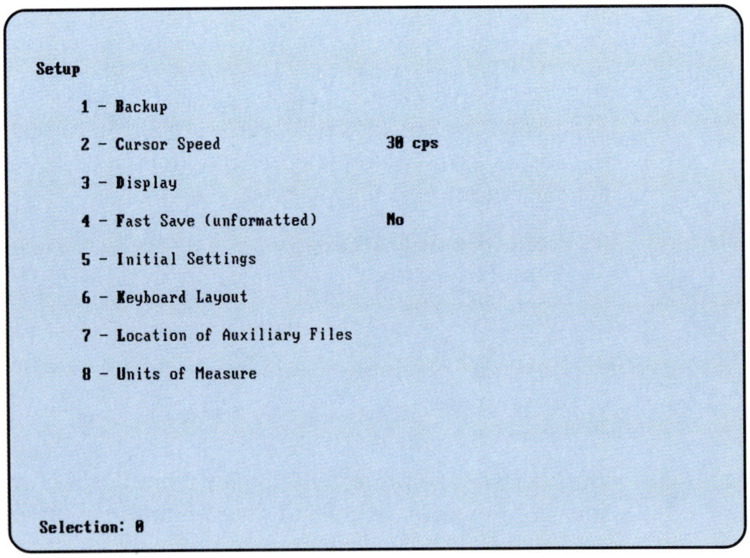

Step 2: Examine the Backup Option

Select the Backup option:

Type **b**

Two automatic Backup options will be described on the screen. The Timed Document Backup option will automatically save your document to the disk without you having to execute the Save command. The default interval for Timed Document Backup is every 30 minutes. The Original Document Backup option will save the original document in a file with the extension BK! whenever you replace it during a Save or Exit command. Both of these Backup options can help safeguard against power failures and mistakes, but they are no substitute for saving your documents frequently as you edit them. Return to the Setup menu:

Press **F1**

Step 3: Examine the Cursor Speed Option

Most keys repeat when you hold them down for more than a second. The Cursor Speed option lets you change the rate at which a key repeats when it is held down. The speed is given in characters per second (cps). Note that many computers can repeat keys no faster than ten times per second, even if the Cursor Speed option is set higher.

Step 4: Examine the Display Option

Select the Display option:

Type **d**

A menu of display options will appear on the screen. These options let you change the way in which WordPerfect displays text and graphics on the screen. Return to the Setup menu:

Press **F1**

Step 5: Examine the Fast Save Option

When the Fast Save option is turned on, WordPerfect saves a document to the disk without formatting it. Although this option saves time, it prevents you from printing a document from the disk unless that document is currently on your editing screen.

Step 6: Examine the Initial Settings Option

Select the Initial Settings option:

Type **i**

The Initial Settings menu allows you to change a number of default settings to be in effect each time you start WordPerfect. For example, you can specify whether WordPerfect will beep when error messages are displayed and whether the program will prompt you for a document summary whenever you save or exit a document. Return to the Setup menu:

Press **F1**

Step 7: Examine the Keyboard Layout Option

Select the Keyboard Layout option:

Type **k**

This option lets you change the commands and even the characters assigned to keys. For example, you can create a keyboard layout that makes the F1 key execute the Help command instead of the Cancel command. You can use the Keyboard Layout feature to make WordPerfect simulate some other word processing program by executing its commands. You can even reassign the letter keys if you want to try an alternate keyboard arrangement, such as the Dvorak system. Unlike the more popular QWERTY arrangement, the Dvorak keyboard layout places the most frequently used letters in the center for use by the strongest fingers to increase speed and comfort, while reducing errors. Return to the Setup menu:

Press **F1**

Step 8: Examine the Location of Auxiliary Files Option

Select the Location of Auxiliary Files option:

Type **L**

Auxiliary files are files that WordPerfect needs for features such as the spelling checker, thesaurus, macros, printer, and so on. The Location of Auxiliary Files option lets you specify the disk drives and subdirectories of these various files. Return to the Setup menu:

Press **F1**

Step 9: Examine the Units of Measure Option

Select the Units of Measure option:

Type **u**

The Units of Measure option lets you specify the units for the presentation of cursor position, margins, tab stops, and other measurements. The default unit of measure is inches, but WordPerfect can use centimeters, points, or line and column numbers instead. Return to the Setup menu:

Press **F1**

Step 10: Exit the Program

This concludes the WordPerfect lessons. Exit the program and return to DOS:

Press **F7** (2 times)
Type **n**
Type **y**

Practice Use the Help facility to read more about the various Setup command options.

Summary

- *Using the Print menu.* Press Shift-F7 to activate the Print menu and then select Full Document, Page, Document on Disk, Control Printer, Type Through, View Document, Initialize Printer, Select Printer, Binding, Number of Copies, Graphics Quality, or Text Quality.
- *Hyphenating words.* Press Shift-F8 to activate the Format menu, select Line, select Hyphenation, and then select Manual or Automatic.
- *Avoiding orphans and widows.* Press Shift-F8 to activate the Format menu, select Line, and then select Widow/Orphan Protection.
- *Avoiding splitting paragraphs between pages.* Press Shift-F8 to activate the Format menu, select Other, and then select Conditional End of Page.
- *Using the Font menu.* Press Ctrl-F8 to activate the Font menu and then select Size, Appearance, Normal, Base Font, or Print Color.
- *Adding headers and footers.* Press Shift-F8 to activate the Format menu, select Page, and then select Header or Footer.
- *Creating text columns.* Press Alt-F7 to activate the Math/Columns menu, select Column Definition, specify the column settings, select Column On/Off, and type the text. Press Ctrl-Home followed by an arrow key to move to another column.
- *Adding footnotes and endnotes.* Press Ctrl-F7 to activate the Footnote menu, select Footnote or Endnote, select Create, and type the note.
- *Sorting text.* Mark the lines to be sorted as a block, press Ctrl-F9 to activate the Sort menu, specify the keys, specify the sort order, and select Perform Action.
- *Performing math.* Press Alt-F7 to activate the Math/Columns menu, select Math Definition, specify the settings, select Math On, insert the operator, press Alt-F7 again, select Calculate.
- *Outlining a document.* Press Shift-F5 to activate the Date/Outline menu, select, Outline, and enter the headings. Press Tab to move in to the next level heading.
- *Generating a table of contents.* Mark each heading as a block, press Alt-F5 to activate the Mark Text menu, select the ToC option, and enter the heading level. Press Alt-F5 again, select Define, and select Table of Contents. Press Alt-F5 again, select Generate, and then select Generate Tables.
- *Generating an index.* Move the cursor to each word to be in the index, press Alt-F5 to activate the Mark Text menu, and select Index. Press Alt-F5 again, select Define, and select Index. Press Alt-F5 again, select Generate, and then select Generate Tables.
- *Adding graphics.* Press Alt-F9 to activate the Graphics menu, and then select Line, Text Box, or Figure.
- *Using macros.* Press Ctrl-F10 to execute the Macro Define command, name the macro, describe the macro, and record the macro. Use the macro by pressing Alternate along with its key.
- *Creating form letters.* Create the address file, separating fields with Merge R codes and records with Merge E codes. Create the primary file containing

merge codes ^F1^, ^F2^, ^F3^, and so on to represent field contents. Press Ctrl-F9 to activate the Merge/Sort menu, select Merge, and enter the names of the primary and address files to generate the form letters.

- *Using styles.* Press Alt-F8 to activate the Style menu, select Create, specify the name, type, description, and codes of the style, and then save the style. Press Alt-F8 again, select Retrieve, enter the file name, highlight the style name, and select On.
- *Customizing WordPerfect.* Press Shift-F1 to activate the Setup menu and then select Backup, Cursor Speed, Display, Fast Save, Initial Settings, Keyboard Layout, Location of Auxiliary Files, or Units of Measure.

Key Terms

As an extra review of this chapter, try defining the following terms.

automatic hyphenation
endnote
field
footer
footnote
greeking
header
hyphenation
key
macro
mail-merge
manual hyphenation
newspaper-style columns
open style
orphan
paired style
parallel columns
point
primary file
print queue
record
secondary merge file (address file)
sorting
style
widow

Multiple Choice

Choose the best selection to complete each statement.

1. WordPerfect lets you specify several documents to be printed by using a
   (a) display adapter. (b) function key.
   (c) print queue. (d) View Document feature.
2. Which feature do you use to see how your document will look when it is printed?
   (a) Setup (b) Reveal Codes
   (c) Screen (d) View Document
3. Which feature can make justified text more attractive by reducing large gaps between words?
   (a) hyphenation (b) indentation
   (c) mail-merge (d) word wrap
4. What term is used to describe the last line of a paragraph that appears at the top of a page?
   (a) orphan (b) widow
   (c) header (d) footer

5. Which feature is handy for keeping titles or headings together with their first paragraphs?
   (a) Merge (b) Block
   (c) Mark Text (d) Conditional End of Page
6. Which command would you use to change the size of characters?
   (a) Bold (b) Macro
   (c) Font (d) Screen
7. One or more lines of text printed at the top of every page is called a(n)
   (a) orphan. (b) widow.
   (c) header. (d) footer.
8. Which type of column continues text from the bottom of one column on the left to the top of the next column on the right on the same page?
   (a) parallel (b) newspaper style
   (c) horizontal (d) vertical
9. A numbered comment or explanation at the bottom of a page is a(n)
   (a) footnote. (b) endnote.
   (c) header. (d) footer.
10. Which of the following sequences is an example of descending sort order?
    (a) A to Z (b) Z to A
    (c) 0 to 9 (d) X, Y, Z
11. What is the most common use of the WordPerfect Math feature?
    (a) computing π (pi) (b) computing square roots
    (c) adding columns of numbers (d) multiplying columns of numbers
12. After the Outline feature is turned on, which key do you press to move in to the next level heading?
    (a) Enter (b) Shift
    (c) Space Bar (d) Tab
13. After a phrase has been marked as a block, what command do you execute to flag it as a table of contents or index entry?
    (a) Text In/Out (b) Merge/Sort
    (c) Macro Define (d) Mark Text
14. How do you remove a term from an index?
    (a) Execute the Cancel command. (b) Execute Reveal Codes and delete the index code.
    (c) Execute the Macro command and delete the line. (d) Execute the Merge R command.
15. Which command do you use to insert lines and boxes into a document?
    (a) Underline (b) Graphics
    (c) Date/Outline (d) Format
16. Which file name extension identifies the sample graphics files that come with WordPerfect?
    (a) GRA (b) DOC
    (c) PIX (d) WPG

17. Which key, along with a letter key, is often used to name and execute WordPerfect macros?
    (a) Alternate (b) Control
    (c) Shift (d) Tab
18. Which feature allows you to create personalized form letters?
    (a) List Files (b) Macro
    (c) Merge (d) Style
19. Which term describes a collection of formatting codes that can be created, saved, and inserted into documents to provide a consistent appearance?
    (a) Format (b) Macro
    (c) Outline (d) Style
20. What command would you use to have WordPerfect automatically back up your current document every 30 minutes?
    (a) Date (b) Replace
    (c) Save (d) Setup

Fill-In

1. The View Document option of the _______ menu allows you to see on the screen how your document will look when it is printed.
2. WordPerfect offers two types of hyphenation: _______ and _______.
3. To avoid orphans and widows, execute the _______ command, select the Line option, and then select the Widow/Orphan Protection option.
4. The Conditional End of Page feature is a way to keep text from being _______ between pages.
5. The _______ option of the Font menu displays the fonts available with your printer and allows you to change the font you are using.
6. A _______ or _______ is often used to print a title, chapter number, page number, or other identification on every page.
7. Press _______ and then Right Arrow to move the cursor to the right column in a document set up with newspaper-style or parallel columns.
8. An _______ is similar to a footnote, except that comments are collected and placed at the end of the document instead of at the bottom of each page.
9. The _______ command is handy for alphabetizing names or any list of words or phrases.
10. After math columns have been defined and the math feature has been turned on, the math operator _______ is inserted below a column of numbers to tell WordPerfect to compute their total.
11. An _______ is an invaluable tool for organizing topics before you type the text of a document.
12. A table of contents entry is flagged by executing the Mark Text command and selecting the _______ option.
13. Generating an _______ with WordPerfect is similar to generating a table of contents.
14. Text may be enclosed in a box by executing the _______ command and selecting the _______ option.

15. The Figure option of the Graphics menu lets you insert a previously created _______ in your document.
16. A macro is a sequence of _______ that can be recorded, stored, and replayed.
17. The Merge command allows you to combine a primary file, containing text and merge codes, with an address file, containing fields and records, to create _______ letters.
18. An _______ style has just a beginning code and is often used to set formats for an entire document.
19. You can tailor WordPerfect to your specific needs by using the _______ command to change various default settings.
20. You would use the _______ option from the Setup menu to have the cursor position on the status line reported in column and line numbers.

Short Problems

1. Start WordPerfect and retrieve the file MEMO.DOC from the LESSONS subdirectory. Activate the Print menu and change the Text Quality option to Draft. Print the file and compare its quality to previous printouts of the memo. Change the Text Quality option back to High.
2. Clear the screen and retrieve NEWS.DOC from the LESSONS subdirectory. Use the Conditional End of Page feature to ensure that no headings are separated from their paragraphs.
3. Clear the screen. Use the Base Font option of the Font menu to create a document that demonstrates at least five different fonts available with your printer. Print the document to see the results.
4. Clear the screen. Type the following words, pressing **Enter** after each one:

   ```
   couch
   zebra
   donkey
   turtle
   frog
   apple
   gate
   vine
   ball
   uncle
   horse
   whistle
   elephant
   x-ray
   ivy
   reindeer
   kangaroo
   parrot
   lobby
   neighbor
   soda
   melody
   ```

   Use the Sort feature to alphabetize this list of words.

5. Clear the screen. Use the Graphics Line options to create a sheet for playing Tic-Tac-Toe. Print two copies using the Number of Copies option in the Print menu.
6. Clear the screen. Use the Graphics Figure option to import one or two WPG files from the WP50 subdirectory or the WordPerfect Graphics diskette. Examine the pictures with View Document. Activate the Print menu, set Graphics Quality to High, and print the document.
7. Clear the screen. Use the math feature to add up the following column of numbers:

   16.34
   25.00
   127.35
   57.70
   50.00
   75.00
   22.00
   19.97
   906.51
   209.12
8. Create a macro named Alt-D that will move the cursor to the end of the document and execute the Reveal Codes command. Return to the full editing screen, move the cursor to the beginning of the document, and try your new macro.
9. Create a style named Letterhead that will set the left and right margins to 1.5 inches. In addition, have the style insert a centered letterhead containing your name and address, and the current date flush right two lines below the letterhead. Save the style in the file LHEAD in the LESSONS subdirectory. Clear the screen, execute the Style command, retrieve LHEAD from LESSONS, and apply the Letterhead style to your new document.
10. Execute the Setup command, select the Units of Measure option, and change the status line display so that it reports the current cursor position in line and column numbers. Return to the editing screen, move the cursor, and observe the status line. Now, change the setting back to inches.

Long Problems

1. Create a quick reference guide to WordPerfect that includes all of the commands covered in this chapter and the previous two chapters.
2. Use WordPerfect's Outline feature to organize the topics of a term paper, report, speech, or presentation you must do for school or work.
3. Use WordPerfect to type a term paper or report, complete with footnotes or endnotes, for school or work.
4. Use the Line options of the Graphics command to create a calendar page for the month of January.
5. Create an address file containing ten friends' names and addresses. Remember to separate the fields with Merge R codes and the records with Merge E codes. Create a primary file that contains the text and appropriate merge codes of an invitation to your birthday party. Use the Merge feature to generate and print the form letters for all ten friends.

6. Suppose you are moving. Create a form letter informing your friends of your new address. You can use the address file you created in the previous exercise.
7. Select an article from a newspaper or magazine. Reproduce this article in a WordPerfect document with two newspaper-style columns.
8. Create a document that demonstrates how text can wrap around a picture. Import a WPG file from the WP50 subdirectory or WordPerfect Graphics diskette. Examine the picture with View Document. Make up a couple of paragraphs to go with the picture and type the text so that it wraps around the picture. Print the document when you are finished.
9. Suppose you want to sell your stereo, bike, car, or some other possession. Use what you have learned about drawing lines and text boxes and changing character sizes to create an attractive and eye-catching flyer to put up on bulletin boards.
10. Use what you have learned about drawing boxes and lines to create a chart showing your family tree going back at least two generations.

PART 4

LOTUS 1-2-3

If you could learn only one spreadsheet program, which should it be? For IBM-compatible microcomputers, Lotus 1-2-3 is the likely choice. This program, without a doubt the best-selling spreadsheet, is probably the world's most popular application package as well. Millions of copies are sold every year. Lotus Development Corporation, the company that created 1-2-3, is second only to Microsoft in microcomputer software sales. Consequently, 1-2-3, with its massive installed base, is the spreadsheet against which all others are measured, and it will continue to be a force to contend with for the foreseeable future. Learning something about using 1-2-3 is almost a prerequisite for computer literacy.

CHAPTER 11

Beginning Lotus 1-2-3

In This Chapter

Getting Started
Lesson 1: Running 1-2-3
Lesson 2: Creating a Worksheet
Lesson 3: Using 1-2-3 Menus
Lesson 4: Saving a Worksheet
Lesson 5: Printing a Worksheet
Lesson 6: Quitting 1-2-3
Lesson 7: Retrieving an Existing Worksheet
Lesson 8: Getting Help
Lesson 9: Moving Around a Worksheet
Lesson 10: Editing Cells
Lesson 11: Changing Column Widths
Lesson 12: Deleting and Inserting Columns and Rows
Lesson 13: Copying and Moving Cells
Lesson 14: Cell Formatting
Lesson 15: Using the Undo Feature in Releases 2.2 and 3.0
Lesson 16: Using Formulas
Lesson 17: Using Functions

Preview

The original 1-2-3 program was conceived by Mitch Kapor, founder of Lotus Development Corporation, in 1982. By that time Kapor had already teamed up with a programmer named Jonathan Sachs, who helped develop the software. Lotus 1-2-3 was first released in the fall of 1982. One year later, its sales had reached 53 million dollars. Designed specifically for the then new IBM Personal Computer, 1-2-3 was a best-seller because of its power, flexibility, and ease of use. The second major version of 1-2-3, which was released in 1985, sold extremely well. In 1989, after a long wait by computer industry standards, Lotus finally delivered two new releases of its venerable software: Lotus 1-2-3 Release 2.2 for low-end IBM-compatible microcomputers that use the 8088 or 8086 chip, and Lotus 1-2-3 Release 3.0 for more powerful machines that use the 80286 or 80386 chip. Despite increased competition from other powerful spreadsheet packages, such as Microsoft Excel and SuperCalc5, Lotus 1-2-3 remains the best-selling spreadsheet package, with at least 65 percent of the market. In this chapter and the next two chapters, you will learn to use Lotus 1-2-3. Most of the lessons can be completed with any version of 1-2-3, Release 2.0 or newer. A few lessons address special and advanced features introduced with Lotus 1-2-3 Release 2.2 and Release 3.0.

After studying this chapter, you will know how to

- start 1-2-3.
- create a worksheet.
- use 1-2-3 menus.
- save a worksheet.
- print a worksheet.
- quit 1-2-3.
- retrieve an existing worksheet.
- get help.
- move around a worksheet.
- edit cells.
- change column widths.
- delete and insert columns and rows.
- copy and move cells.
- format cells.
- undo commands.
- use formulas.
- use functions.

Getting Started

Although Lotus 1-2-3 is a large and sophisticated software package, it is easy to learn to use for basic spreadsheet tasks. Lotus 1-2-3 might be set up several different ways at your particular computer installation. You are most likely to use the package in one of three possible arrangements:

1. On a microcomputer with two floppy drives and 1-2-3 installed on several diskettes
2. On a microcomputer with a hard disk and 1-2-3 installed in a subdirectory named 123 or 123R3 (for Release 3.0)
3. On a microcomputer connected to a local area network with 1-2-3 installed on the network file server

Insight

Which Lotus Spreadsheet Software is Right for Me?

The release of Lotus 1-2-3's new 2.2 and 3.0 versions has created an embarrassment of riches for Lotus customers.

Spreadsheet users who, in the past, automatically reached for Lotus 1-2-3 now have to decide which Lotus version to use, or whether to drop Lotus and head for Microsoft's or some other company's product.

"It's a complex and difficult decision," said one spreadsheet user. "Before, it was much simpler. Then your choices were: stay put, change to release 3.0, or go to a third product. Now, you've got four choices. It makes the decision either very complex or very easy. If all you've got is 8088 machines, it's pretty easy. For those who don't, it's much more complex. Most of us are in that boat."

Which version to use depends on the customer's microprocessor and graphics adapter support. Lotus designed release 3.0 for computers using Intel's 80286 and 80386 chips. Release 2.2 was designed for first-generation computers, which have smaller memory capabilities. But what about companies with different generations of computers?

There are other considerations as well. Version 2.2 is a direct descendant of 2.01. Release 3.0, written in C language, has a new format that prevents it from being used with existing 1-2-3 add-in packages. To further complicate matters, there is some confusion about how easy it is to upgrade from 2.2 to 3.0.

Many customers are taking a wait-and-see attitude about the new Lotus releases. Changing software is too expensive to base on a snap judgement, and in many cases, may also require an even more costly hardware upgrade.

Source: Bob Francis, "Muddy Waters," *Datamation*, July 15, 1989, pp. 31–32.

You may need some additional direction from your instructor on how to start Lotus 1-2-3, but once you get situated, you should be able to do the following lessons.

Lesson 1: Running 1-2-3

You are all ready to start working with spreadsheets, but first you must boot up your computer and run 1-2-3.

Step 1: Boot Up the Computer

If your computer is not already turned on and running DOS, boot it up as you learned to do in the Beginning DOS chapter.

Step 2: Prepare Diskette or Subdirectory for Files

The Lotus 1-2-3 software is stored on its own diskettes or in its own subdirectory on a hard disk or network. It is best to prepare a separate diskette or subdirectory for the files you will create in the following lessons. If your computer has only floppy drives, obtain a formatted diskette with room for your files and insert it into drive B. If your computer has a hard disk, create a subdirectory called LESSONS, if you don't already have one, that you can use to store your files. If you are running on a network, your instructor may have other directions for you to follow.

Step 3: Insert the System Disk or Switch to the LESSONS Subdirectory

If you have a system with only floppy drives, remove the DOS startup diskette from drive A and replace it with the Lotus 1-2-3 diskette labeled "System Disk." The diskette to hold your data files should be in drive B. Go on to Step 4.

If you have a microcomputer with a hard disk, 1-2-3 should already be installed in its own subdirectory, named 123 or 123R3 for Release 3.0 (see Appendix C, Software Installation). The following lessons assume that a path has been set up so that you can run 1-2-3 from any subdirectory and that you have a LESSONS subdirectory on the hard disk for your files. Switch to the LESSONS subdirectory with this DOS command:

Type **cd c:\lessons**
Press **Enter**

If your computer is connected to a local area network, you may have to follow other directions from your instructor before actually starting 1-2-3.

Step 4: Invoke 1-2-3

Once you are in the proper disk drive directory, running 1-2-3 is easy.

Type **123**
Press **Enter**

It will take a few moments for 1-2-3 to be loaded from the disk into memory. A screen presenting the 1-2-3 logo and copyright information will appear (see Figure 1).

Most of the Lotus 1-2-3 figures you will see in this book have been created with Release 2.2. Some figures have been created with Release 3.0 to illustrate features available only in that version of 1-2-3. Except where indicated, all of the spreadsheet lessons can be completed with any version of 1-2-3, Release 2.0 or newer, although your screen may differ slightly from the figures you see in this book.

Figure 1 Lotus 1-2-3 Copyright Screen

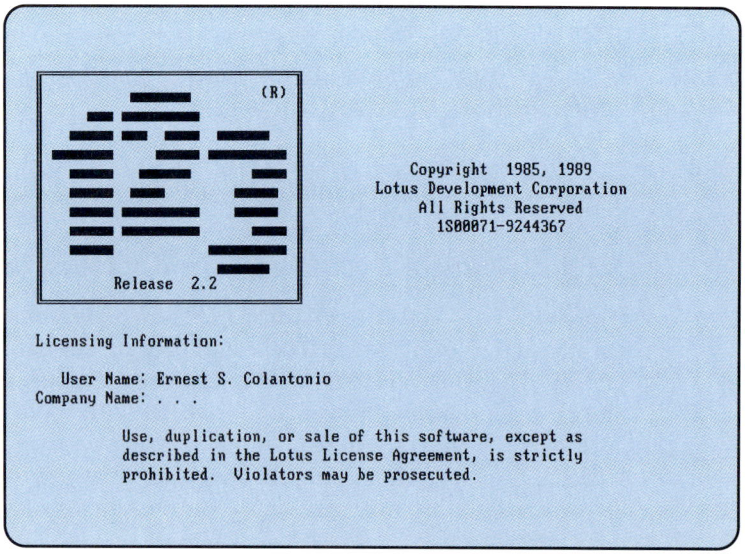

Practice Reboot your computer and start 1-2-3 again.

Lesson 2: Creating a Worksheet

As a simple example, let's use Lotus 1-2-3 to create a small budget worksheet. A **worksheet** is simply a table of data arranged into rows and columns. In the context of a spreadsheet program, **data** can be numbers, labels, or formulas. A **number** is a numeric quantity, such as 100, 52.34, or 0.05. A **label** is any kind of text, such as a title, heading, name, or address. A **formula** is an expression that tells the spreadsheet program to perform a calculation, such as 100 + 200.

Step 1: Examine the Worksheet Screen

After the copyright screen disappears, 1-2-3 presents the empty worksheet screen shown in Figure 2. The letters A through H across the top represent columns. The numbers 1 through 20 along the left side represent rows. Although you can see only 8 columns and 20 rows at the moment, the whole worksheet is actually much larger than this. Imagine the columns continuing out beyond the right edge of the screen and the rows continuing down below the bottom. A Lotus 1-2-3 worksheet has a maximum of 256 columns and 8,192 rows. The first 26 columns are labeled A through Z. The next 26 are labeled AA through AZ, the next 26 are labeled BA through BZ, and so on up to IV. The rows are simply numbered 1 through 8192.

Each intersection of a row and a column is called a cell. The **cell** is the basic unit of storage in a worksheet—where you put a number, label, or formula. Each cell is designated by its column letter(s) and row number. For example, A1 refers to the cell located at the intersection of the first column and the first row. This column-row designation is known as the **cell address** or **cell reference** because it uniquely identifies and locates each storage unit.

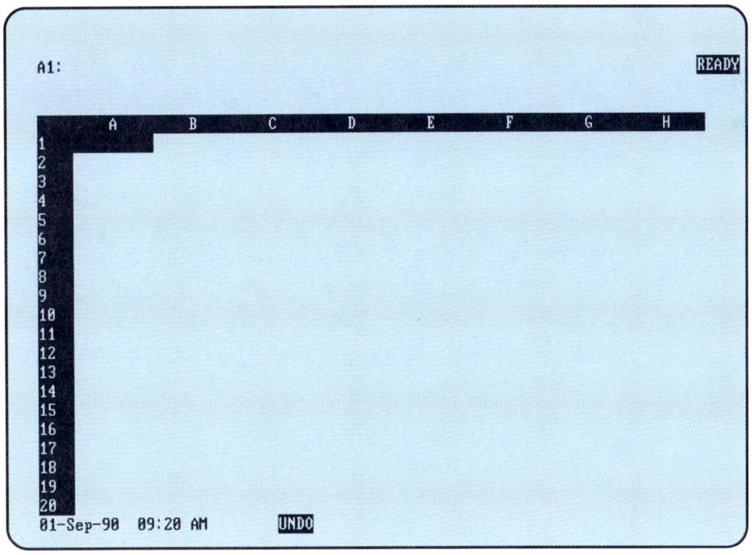

Figure 2 The Empty Worksheet Screen

Lotus 1-2-3 can refer to 256 × 8,192 or 2,097,152 cells, but you cannot actually store data in all of these cells at once. The absolute number of cells you can fill depends on the amount of memory installed in your computer and several other factors. For example, on a microcomputer equipped with 640K of memory, you can fill around 40,000 cells with numbers before you run out of memory. Lotus 1-2-3 addresses more cells than you can possibly fill so that you can place your data in convenient locations.

As you can see in Figure 2, all of the cells are initially blank. The **cell pointer** is the highlighted bar that indicates the **current cell,** the place in the worksheet where you can enter data, perform a calculation, or initiate a command. The blinking underscore within the cell pointer is the cursor. When you start a new worksheet, A1 is the current cell.

The space at the top of the screen above the column letters is known as the **control panel.** It displays cell information, command choices, command descriptions, messages, and the mode in which 1-2-3 is operating. The address of the current cell appears in the upper left corner of the control panel. The blank space to the right of the current cell address indicates that the cell is empty. The highlighted block in the upper-right corner of the control panel is the **mode indicator,** which describes the current operating mode. Right now, the mode indicator displays READY, telling you that 1-2-3 is waiting for you to enter data or initiate a command.

Now look at the bottom of the screen. The lower left corner of the screen displays the current date and time. Lotus 1-2-3 Release 2.2 also shows the UNDO indicator, which tells you that you can use the Undo feature to cancel the last operation you performed. You will learn more about the Undo feature later in this chapter.

Step 2: Enter the Labels

Our simple budget worksheet will have text labels in column A and numbers in column C. Any text you enter that does not resemble a number or formula is assumed by 1-2-3 to be a label. To be more precise, a label is any text that does not begin with one of the following characters:

0 1 2 3 4 5 6 7 8 9 . + - ($ # @

If you want to begin a label, such as an address or phone number, with one of these characters, you must precede it with a **label prefix character.** This is a symbol, such as an apostrophe ('), that tells 1-2-3 to treat the characters that follow it as a label, not as a number or formula. You will learn more about label prefix characters later in this chapter.

To enter a label, type its characters, then press the Enter key or move the cell pointer. As you type, the characters will appear in the control panel. The characters are not actually stored in the cell until you press the Enter key or move the cell pointer. If you make a mistake before you press the Enter key or move the cell pointer, you can press the Backspace key to erase the characters, then retype them. Follow these directions to enter the labels into your worksheet:

Type **Monthly Budget**
Press **Down Arrow** (2 times)
Type **INCOME**
Press **Down Arrow** (2 times)
Type **EXPENSES**
Press **Down Arrow**

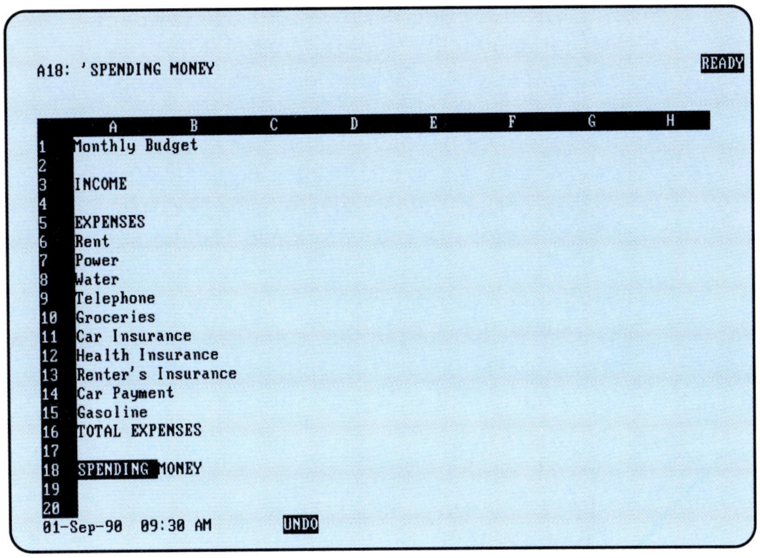

***Figure 3** Labels Entered into the Worksheet*

Type **Rent**
Press **Down Arrow**
Type **Power**
Press **Down Arrow**
Type **Water**
Press **Down Arrow**
Type **Telephone**
Press **Down Arrow**
Type **Groceries**
Press **Down Arrow**
Type **Car Insurance**
Press **Down Arrow**
Type **Health Insurance**
Press **Down Arrow**
Type **Renter's Insurance**
Press **Down Arrow**
Type **Car Payment**
Press **Down Arrow**
Type **Gasoline**
Press **Down Arrow**
Type **TOTAL EXPENSES**
Press **Down Arrow** (2 times)
Type **SPENDING MONEY**
Press **Enter**

Your screen should look like Figure 3.

Step 3: Enter the Numbers

Lotus 1-2-3 assumes an entry to be a number if it begins with one of the following characters:

0 1 2 3 4 5 6 7 8 9 . + - $ (

You may enter numbers without decimal points (like 10, −22, or 1234) or with decimal points (like .5, −0.12, or 11.123). You may not include spaces or commas in a number. You may precede a number with + or $, or enclose it in parentheses, but these characters will not be displayed in the worksheet. In addition to normal decimal notation, you may also enter numbers in scientific (exponential) notation. For example, 4.32E+05 (which equals 432,000) and −2.54E−05 (which equals −0.0000254) are both valid number entries. Using scientific notation lets you include very large and very small numbers in your worksheet.

Entering numbers is just like entering labels; type them and press the Enter key or move the cell pointer. If you make a mistake before you press the Enter key or move the cell pointer, you can press the Backspace key to erase the number, then retype it. Follow these directions to move the cell pointer to C3, then enter the numbers into your worksheet:

Press **Home**
Press **Right Arrow** (2 times)
Press **Down Arrow** (2 times)
Type **2000**
Press **Down Arrow** (3 times)
Type **650**
Press **Down Arrow**
Type **125**
Press **Down Arrow**
Type **15**
Press **Down Arrow**
Type **75**
Press **Down Arrow**
Type **200**
Press **Down Arrow**
Type **50**
Press **Down Arrow**
Type **50**
Press **Down Arrow**
Type **15**
Press **Down Arrow**
Type **200**
Press **Down Arrow**
Type **50**
Press **Down Arrow**

Your screen should look like Figure 4.

Step 4: Enter the Formulas

A formula is an expression that tells the spreadsheet program to perform a calculation. It can include arithmetic operators (such as + and −), cell addresses, and functions. A **function** is a predefined formula that performs a useful operation, such as computing a sum or a square root. Lotus 1-2-3 has many functions, some of which we will discuss later in this chapter.

Our budget worksheet needs two formulas: one to compute the total expenses and the other to compute the spending money. At this point, C16 should be the current cell. Enter this formula to compute the total expenses:

Type **@sum(c6..c15)**
Press **Enter**

Figure 4 Numbers Entered into the Worksheet

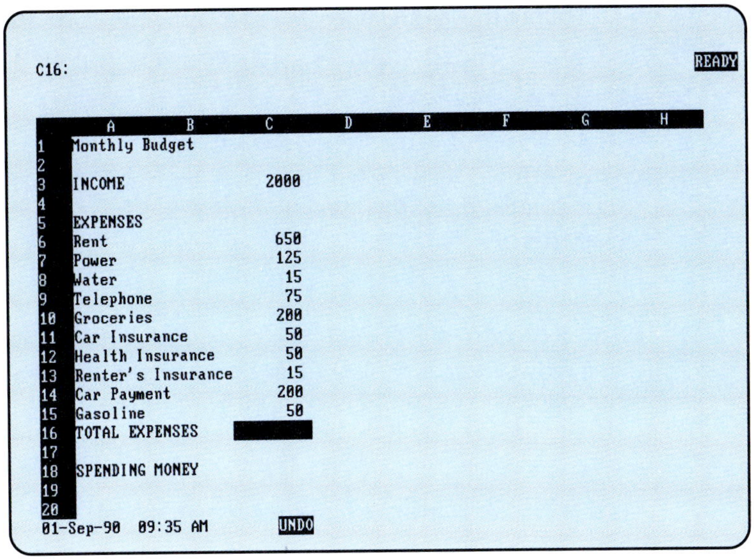

The @ character, which must begin every function name, tells 1-2-3 that the following word is a function, not a label. The @SUM function adds the contents of a range of cells. A **range** is simply a block of adjacent cells, indicated by the address of the upper left cell, two periods, and the address of the lower right cell. The range C6..C15, for example, refers to cells C6, C7, C8, C9, C10, C11, C12, C13, C14, and C15. Note that function names and cell addresses may be entered in either uppercase or lowercase letters.

Your screen should look like Figure 5. The control panel reports that cell C16 actually contains the formula @SUM(C6..C15), but the computed result of that formula, the value 1430, is displayed in the worksheet.

Figure 5 A Formula Entered into the Worksheet

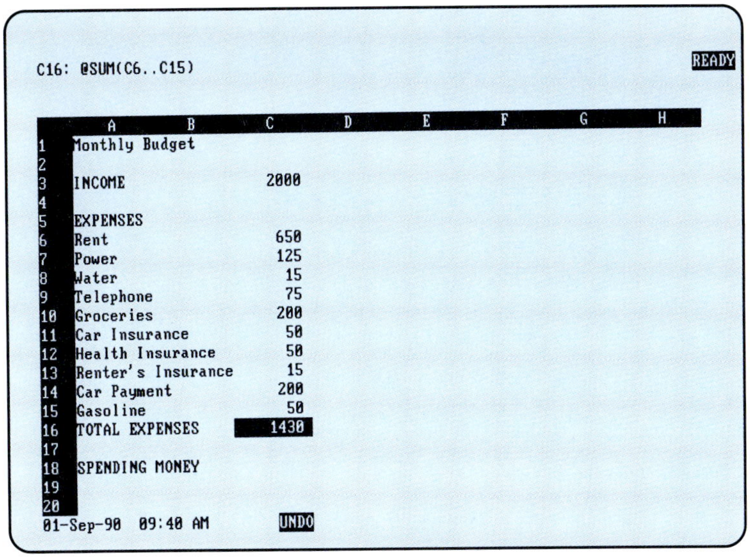

Follow these directions to enter the other formula for this worksheet:

Press **Down Arrow** (2 times)
Type **+c3-c16**
Press **Enter**

This formula tells 1-2-3 to subtract the total expenses result from the income figure. It begins with a plus sign because a formula must begin with one of these characters:

0 1 2 3 4 5 6 7 8 9 . + - (@ # $

The cell address C3 begins with a C. If you don't begin the formula with one of the above characters, 1-2-3 will assume the entry is a label and will not perform the calculation. The plus sign in front of the C3 does not change the result, it simply enables 1-2-3 to recognize the entry as a formula.

Step 5: Check and Correct Your Work

Check your screen against Figure 6 to see if you made any mistakes entering labels, numbers, or formulas. To correct a mistake, move the cell pointer with the arrow keys to the erroneous cell, retype the entry, and press the Enter key.

Practice

1. Move the cell pointer to a formula. Compare the contents of the control panel with the result you see displayed in the worksheet cell.
2. Move the cell pointer to a label. Notice the label prefix character displayed in front of the label in the control panel. The apostrophe (') is the default label prefix character automatically put in front of the label by 1-2-3. It appears in the control panel but not in the worksheet cell.

Figure 6 The Completed Worksheet

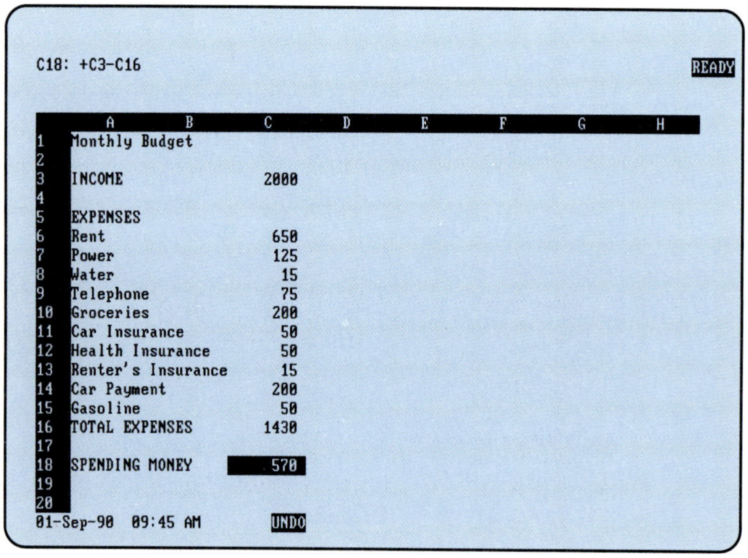

Lesson 3: Using 1-2-3 Menus

To accomplish many tasks in 1-2-3, you must select commands from menus. Commands allow you to work with, rearrange, and otherwise manipulate data stored in worksheet cells. In addition, you use commands to control the appearance, disk storage, and output of 1-2-3 worksheets. This lesson will briefly describe how to use the 1-2-3 command menus. Other lessons in this chapter and the next two chapters will cover the most important commands in more detail.

Step 1: Activate the Main Menu

Lotus 1-2-3 uses a system of pop-up menus that appear in the control panel only when activated. No menu appears in Figure 6, because 1-2-3 is in READY mode. Switch to MENU mode and display the Main menu in the control panel:

Type /

Typing a forward slash key activates the Main menu of commands, shown in Figure 7. The mode indicator changes to MENU, and the second line of the control panel displays a list of commands. A highlighted block, known as the **menu pointer,** shows the command that will be invoked if you press the Enter key. The third line of the control panel displays information relevant to the highlighted command. In many cases this information is a list of additional options available when you invoke the highlighted command. For example, Worksheet is the command currently highlighted. If you press the Enter key, 1-2-3 will present the list of options in the third line of the control panel: Global, Insert, Delete, Column, Erase, Titles, Window, Status, Page, and Learn.

Step 2: Highlight a Command and Press Enter

One way to select a command from a menu is to position the menu pointer on the command you want and press the Enter key. For example, select the File command:

Press **Right Arrow** (4 times)
Press **Enter**

The menu of File commands will be activated. This method of selecting commands is often preferred by beginners because they can see information about a command on the third line of the control panel before they choose it.

Step 3: Return From a Menu

In many cases, you can return to a previous menu without executing a command. Suppose you have changed your mind about executing a command from the File menu. You can return to the Main menu from the File menu by pressing the Escape key.

Press **Escape**

You can exit the Main menu and return to READY mode by pressing the Escape key again.

Press **Escape**

The Main menu will disappear and the second and third lines of the control panel will be cleared.

Figure 7 The Main Menu

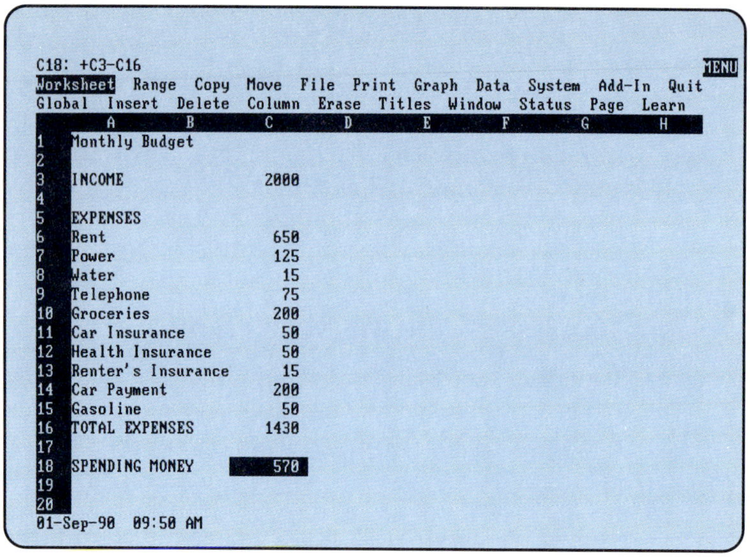

Step 4: Type the First Letter of a Command

Activate the Main menu again:

Type /

The second way to select a command from a menu is to type the first letter of the command. Each 1-2-3 menu is carefully designed so that every command begins with a different letter. Select the File option by typing its first letter:

Type **f**

Typing the first letter of a command is usually faster than moving the menu pointer and pressing the Enter key, but you don't get a chance to read the description of the command in the third line of the control panel. Users who are familiar with 1-2-3 menus often prefer to select commands this way. Now, exit the File menu and the Main menu and return to READY mode:

Press **Escape** (2 times)

Practice

1. Activate the Main menu.
2. Select the Print command by moving the menu pointer and pressing the Enter key, then exit the Print menu without executing a command.
3. Select the Range command by typing its first letter, then exit the Range menu and the Main menu to return to READY mode.

Lesson 4: Saving a Worksheet

The worksheet you see on the screen is held temporarily in memory. If you shut off your computer or the power goes out, the worksheet will be lost. To avoid losing your work, you must save your worksheet in a disk file. Saving a worksheet creates a more permanent copy of your work that can be later printed or retrieved and modified. You can create large worksheets a little at a time and make corrections, updates, and new versions without having to retype all of the entries.

You must save your worksheet before you leave 1-2-3 to use another application package. It is also prudent to save your worksheet every fifteen minutes or so as you work. By periodically saving your worksheet, you will guard against losing all of your work if you make a drastic mistake or a power failure occurs.

Step 1: Execute the File Save Command

The File Save command copies the current worksheet to a disk file. Execute the File Save command:

Type **/fs**

Step 2: Enter the File Name

Lotus 1-2-3 will prompt you to enter the name of the file to save. Let's name the worksheet file BUDGET. If your computer has a hard disk and you are working from the LESSONS subdirectory, enter the file name:

Type **budget**
Press **Enter**

If your computer has only floppy disk drives and you want to store the worksheet on the diskette in drive B, follow these directions instead:

Press **Escape**
Type **b:budget**
Press **Enter**

Lotus 1-2-3 Release 2.0 and Release 2.2 will store the worksheet in a file named BUDGET.WK1. The WK1 file name extension identifies worksheet files. Lotus 1-2-3 Release 3.0 will add the extension WK3 instead of WK1.

Practice

You can save your worksheet as many times as you like. After you name and save the worksheet the first time, 1-2-3 will remember the name, so the next time you save the worksheet you won't have to enter it again. Execute the File Save command and press Enter without typing the file name again. Lotus 1-2-3 will present a menu with three options: Cancel, Replace, and Backup. Select the Replace command to replace the file on the disk with the current worksheet. Note: Lotus 1-2-3 Release 2.0 does not present the Backup option.

Lesson 5: Printing a Worksheet

In many cases, a spreadsheet program is used to produce a finished worksheet printed on paper. Now that you have saved your worksheet, you may want to print it. If your computer is not connected to a printer, read this lesson and examine the figure without actually performing the steps.

Step 1: Execute the Print Command

The first step is to execute the Print command from the Main menu.

Type **/p**

Step 2: Choose Printer or File

The Print command provides two options: Printer and File. Lotus 1-2-3 Release 3.0 has a few other options as well. The Printer option will send the output directly to the printer. The File option will create a text file that can be printed later or used in another application, such as a word processing package. If you have a printer, select the Printer option:

Type **p**

Step 3: Specify the Range

The program will display the Print Printer menu shown in Figure 8. Lotus 1-2-3 Release 2.2 will also present the Print Settings sheet, which shows the current values of various parameters, such as margins and page length. Before you can print a worksheet, you must tell 1-2-3 the range of cells you want to print. Select the Range option:

Type **r**

The program will prompt you to enter the print range. You can specify a range two ways. The first method is to type the range and press the Enter key. For example, to specify your entire worksheet

Type **a1..c18**
Press **Enter**

The other way to specify the range is to use POINT mode to highlight the range. To use POINT mode, move the cell pointer to the first cell in the range, type a period to anchor the cell pointer, move to the last cell in the range, then press the Enter key. If you would like to try the pointing method, follow these directions:

Type **r**
Press **Home**
Type **.**
Press **Right Arrow** (2 times)
Press **Down Arrow** (17 times)
Press **Enter**

Most 1-2-3 commands accept either of these two methods of specifying a range.

Step 4: Prepare the Printer

Make sure the printer is connected to the computer and turned on. Also, make sure that paper is loaded and aligned to the top of a new page. Finally, make sure that the printer's On Line light is lit. (If it isn't, press the On Line button.)

Step 5: Select the Go Option

To begin printing, select the Go option from the Print Printer menu:

Type **g**

The worksheet will be printed.

Figure 8 The Print Printer Menu and Print Settings Sheet

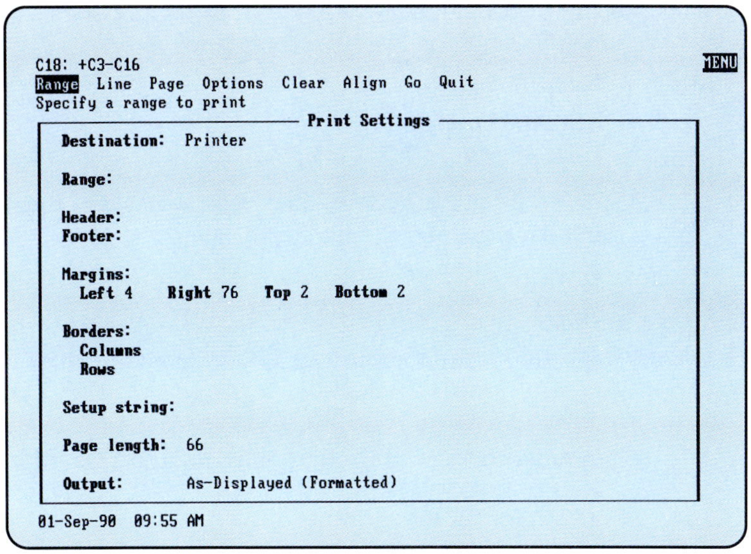

Step 6: Select the Page Option

If you like, you can tell 1-2-3 to have the printer advance to the top of the next page. Select the Page option from the Print Printer menu:

Type **p**

Step 7: Select the Quit Option

When you are finished printing, select the Quit option to exit the Print Printer menu and return to READY mode:

Type **q**

Practice

1. Print only this range from your worksheet: A1..A18.
2. Select the File option of the Print menu to produce a text file of your entire worksheet instead of sending it directly to the printer. Enter BUDGET as the file name. Precede the filename with B: if you have only floppy drives and want to put the file on the diskette in drive B. Lotus 1-2-3 will automatically add the file name extension PRN, indicating that it is a file to be printed.

Lesson 6: Quitting 1-2-3

You have entered, saved, and printed a worksheet. Suppose you are finished with Lotus 1-2-3 for now and want to return to DOS.

Step 1: Save the Worksheet

Although you have already saved your worksheet, you should save it again before you quit 1-2-3. This preserves the page settings created when you printed the worksheet. In addition, saving your worksheet before quitting records any changes you might have made since the previous save, and it is a good habit to form. Execute the File Save command:

Type **/fs**
Press **Enter**
Type **r**

Since you have already named your worksheet the first time you saved it, you don't have to enter the file name again.

Step 2: Execute the Quit Command

Activate the Main menu and execute the Quit command:

Type **/q**

You must confirm the quit by selecting the Yes option:

Type **y**

The computer will exit 1-2-3 and return to DOS.

Practice

Start Lotus 1-2-3. Enter a number in cell A1. Do not save the worksheet. Execute the Quit Yes command. If you are running Lotus 1-2-3 Release 2.0, the program will immediately return to DOS. You are out of luck if you intended to save the worksheet but forgot to do so. If you are running Release 2.2 or 3.0, however, the program will display the prompt

`WORKSHEET CHANGES NOT SAVED! End 1-2-3 anyway?`

This warning is a welcome safety feature that tells you when you are attempting to quit without having saved your worksheet. If you really do want to save your worksheet, you can select No and then execute the File Save command. In this case, you do not want to save your worksheet, so select Yes and return to DOS.

Lesson 7: Retrieving an Existing Worksheet

Retrieving an existing worksheet is a very common procedure. You can easily examine, modify, or update a previously saved worksheet. Let's start 1-2-3 again and retrieve the BUDGET worksheet.

Step 1: Start 1-2-3

In the previous lesson, you quit 1-2-3 and returned to DOS. Start the program again:

Type **123**
Press **Enter**

Lotus 1-2-3 will display a new worksheet screen.

Step 2: Execute the File Retrieve Command

To load a previously saved worksheet, execute the File Retrieve command:

Type **/fr**

Step 3: Select the File

Lotus 1-2-3 will prompt you for the name of the file to retrieve. The mode indicator will change to FILES, and the names of the worksheet files and the subdirectories in your current directory will be listed across the third line of the control panel (see Figure 9). If the file you want to retrieve is in the current directory, the easiest way to retrieve it is to use Left Arrow or Right Arrow to highlight it and press the Enter key. Alternatively, you can type the name of the file and press Enter. If you want to retrieve a file from a different disk or directory, press the Escape key twice, then enter the entire path and file name.

Highlight **BUDGET.WK1** (or **BUDGET.WK3** for Release 3.0)
Press **Enter**

The worksheet will be loaded from the disk into memory and presented on the screen. The cell pointer will appear in the position it occupied when the worksheet was saved.

Practice Change any cell in the BUDGET worksheet, but do not save the worksheet. Then execute the File Retrieve command and select the BUDGET worksheet. Lotus 1-2-3 Releases 2.0, 2.2, and 3.0 will all retrieve the file and overwrite the worksheet you have in memory without issuing a warning or confirmation prompt. You will lose the worksheet on the screen if you have not saved it whenever you retrieve an existing worksheet. Unfortunately, the designers of Lotus 1-2-3 did not add a safety feature for this situation. Always make sure you have either saved or will not need the worksheet on your screen before you retrieve an existing worksheet.

Lesson 8: Getting Help

Lotus 1-2-3 has an excellent on-line help facility that lets you retrieve information about the current command or choose from an index of topics. In many cases, using the help facility is faster and easier than consulting the printed reference manual.

Step 1: Highlight a Command

The Lotus 1-2-3 help system is **context-sensitive,** which means that it will provide information relevant to your current operation. For example, activate the Main menu:

Type /

The Worksheet command should be highlighted.

Step 2: Insert Help Disk If Necessary

If you are running Lotus 1-2-3 from a hard disk or a network, skip this step. If your computer has only two floppy drives and the file 123.HLP is not on the System Disk, remove the System Disk from drive A and replace it with the Help Disk.

Figure 9 The File Retrieve Command

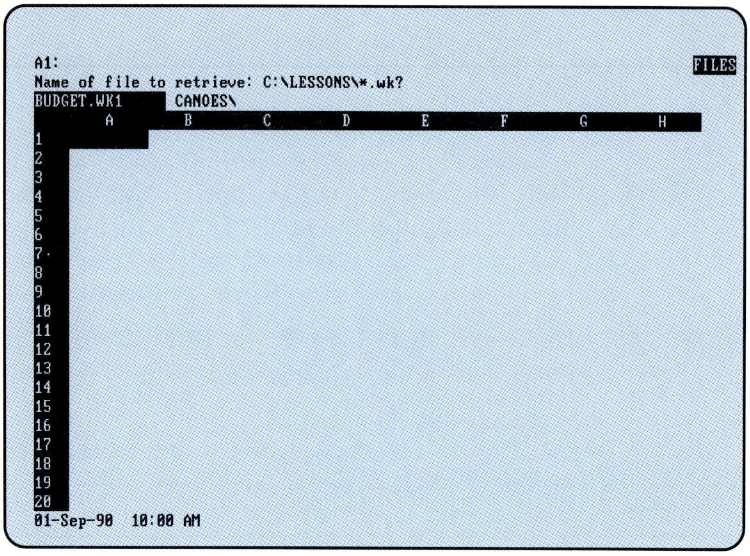

Step 3: Press the F1 Key

The help facility is activated by pressing the F1 function key.

Press **F1**

Figure 10 shows the result. The screen provides information about the Main menu and selecting commands. The topic Worksheet Commands is highlighted. You can use the arrow keys to highlight another topic or press the Enter key to read about the highlighted topic.

Press **Enter**

Lotus 1-2-3 will display another help screen with more detailed information about the topic you selected (see Figure 11).

Figure 10 Main Menu Help Screen

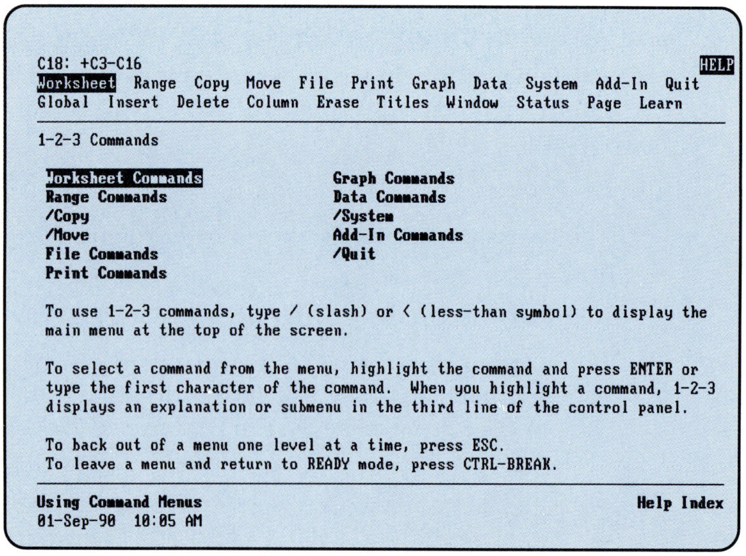

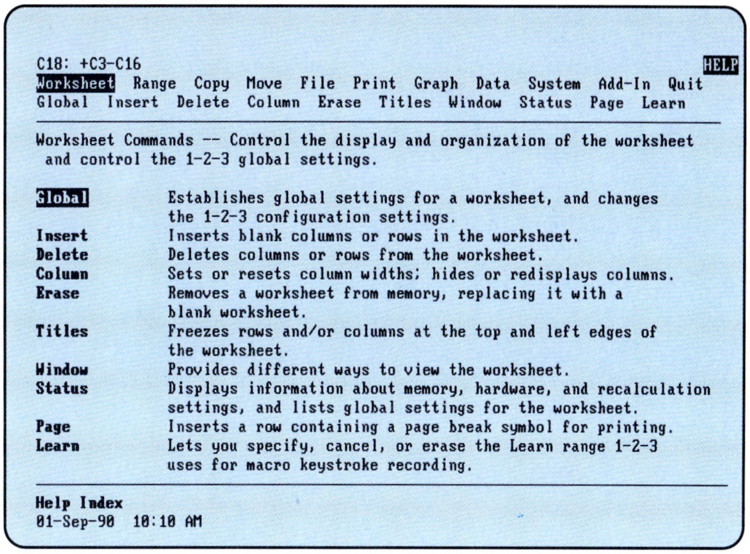

Figure 11 Worksheet Command Help Screen

Step 4: View the Help Index

You can see an index of the available help topics at any time. Highlight the Help Index topic at the bottom of the screen and press Enter:

Press **Up Arrow**
Press **Enter**

Figure 12 shows the Help Index. You can highlight any topic in this index and press the Enter key to see more information about it.

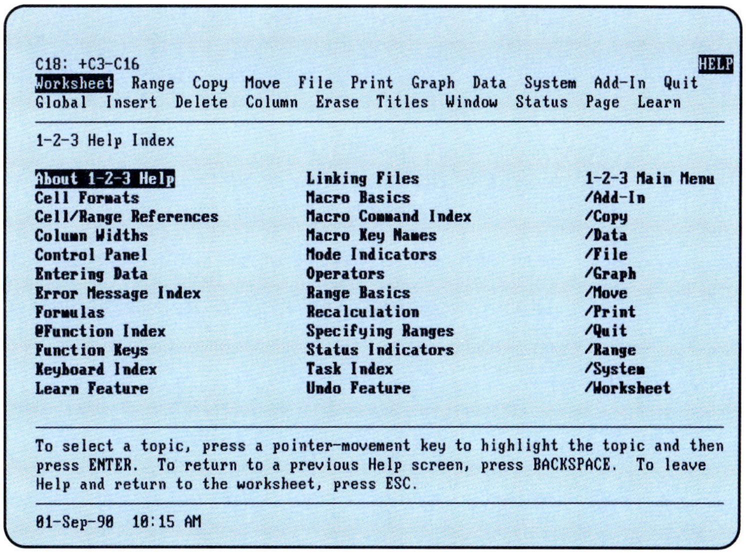

Figure 12 The Help Index

Step 5: Exit Help

When you are finished with the help facility, press the Escape key to return to what you were doing:

Press **Escape**

The Main menu should be on your screen with the Worksheet option highlighted. Return to READY mode:

Press **Escape**

If your computer has only two floppy drives, remove the Help Disk from drive A and replace it with the System Disk.

Practice

1. Activate the help facility, display the help index, and select the topic entitled "About 1-2-3 Help." Return to READY mode when you are finished.
2. Activate the Main menu and execute the File command. Activate the Help facility and read about the commands in the File menu. Return to READY mode when you are finished.

Lesson 9: Moving Around a Worksheet

Lotus 1-2-3 lets you move the cell pointer easily to any of the more than 2 million cells it can address. You have already used a few of the **pointer movement keys** that move the cell pointer. Let's examine the pointer movement keys in more detail.

Step 1: Move the Cell Pointer One Cell at a Time

The arrow keys move the cell pointer one cell at a time. Try each arrow key:

Press **Right Arrow**
Press **Left Arrow**
Press **Down Arrow**
Press **Up Arrow**

If you hold down an arrow key for more than a second, its action will be repeated about ten times a second. Try this action:

Press **Right Arrow** (hold for about two seconds)

The cell pointer will rapidly travel to the right. When it goes past the left edge of the screen into column I, the screen will scroll to reveal more columns. Now try rapidly moving the cell pointer down:

Press **Down Arrow** (hold for about five seconds)

The screen will scroll to reveal more rows when the cell pointer moves into row 21.

Step 2: Move the Cell Pointer Several Cells at a Time

Other pointer movement keys let you move the cell pointer several cells at a time. For example, try each of the following pointer movement keys:

Press **Home**

The Home key always moves the cell pointer to A1.

Press **Page Down**
Press **Page Up**

The Page Up and Page Down keys move the cell pointer an entire screen (usually 20 rows) up or down at a time.

Press **Tab** (or **Ctrl-Right Arrow**)
Press **Shift-Tab** (or **Ctrl-Left Arrow**)

The Tab and Ctrl-Right Arrow keys both move the cell pointer an entire screen to the right. The Shift-Tab and Ctrl-Left Arrow keys both move the cell pointer an entire screen to the left.

Press **End**
Press **Down Arrow**
Press **End**
Press **Right Arrow**
Press **End**
Press **Up Arrow**
Press **End**
Press **Left Arrow**

Pressing and releasing the End key followed by an arrow key moves the cell pointer to the next intersection of a blank cell and a nonblank cell in that direction.

Press **End**
Press **Home**

Pressing End followed by pressing Home moves the cell pointer to the lowest rightmost nonblank cell in the worksheet.

Step 3: Move to a Particular Cell

Lotus 1-2-3 also provides an easy way to move to a particular cell address. Suppose you want to move to cell AB2015.

Press **F5**

The F5 function key invokes the Go To feature. The program will display the prompt

```
Enter address to go to:
```

And it will suggest the current cell address. Enter the address of the cell to which you want to move:

Type **ab2015**
Press **Enter**

The cell pointer will move immediately to that cell.

Practice

1. With a single keypress, move the cell pointer to A1.
2. Move the cell pointer right two screens.
3. In the most direct manner, move the cell pointer to the lowest rightmost cell possible in a 1-2-3 worksheet, cell IV8192.

Lesson 10: Editing Cells

Suppose you make a typing error but don't discover your mistake until after you have pressed the Enter key or moved the cell pointer. Or suppose you want to modify or update the existing contents of a cell. Lotus 1-2-3 makes it easy to edit cells.

Step 1: Retype an Entry

One way to edit the existing contents of a cell is to retype the entire entry. Suppose the power bill is $130 instead of $125. Move the cell pointer to C7 and retype the entry:

Press **F5**
Type **c7**
Press **Enter**
Type **130**
Press **Enter**

Notice how the worksheet recomputes the formula results automatically. Total expenses increases by 5 and spending money decreases by 5 as soon as you change 125 to 130 for the power bill.

Step 2: Edit an Existing Entry

If an existing entry is long or complex and you don't need to change it entirely, retyping it can be tedious and can introduce errors. Fortunately, you can edit the contents of a cell without retyping the entire entry. As an example, let's change the label in cell A14 to *Car Loan Payment*. Follow these directions:

Press **F5**
Type **a14**
Press **Enter**
Press **F2**
Press **Left Arrow** (7 times)
Type **Loan**
Press **Space Bar**
Press **Enter**

First, you move the cell pointer to the cell you want to edit. Then you activate the EDIT mode by pressing the F2 key. Lotus 1-2-3 will display the existing entry in the second line of the control panel with a cursor at the end. You can use the Left Arrow, Right Arrow, Backspace, and Delete keys to move the cursor and erase characters. By default, any character you type will be inserted into the entry. To type over existing characters, you must press the Insert key. When you are finished editing the entry, press the Enter key to store it in the cell and return to READY mode. The following table summarizes the actions of certain keys in EDIT mode.

Key	*Action*
Enter	Stores entry and returns to READY mode
Backspace	Erases character to left of cursor
Delete	Erases character at cursor
Escape	Erases entire entry

Insert	Toggles insert/overwrite mode
Home	Moves cursor to first character of entry
End	Moves cursor to last character of entry
Left Arrow	Moves cursor left one character
Right Arrow	Moves cursor right one character
Tab	Moves cursor right five characters
Ctrl-Right Arrow	Moves cursor right five characters
Shift-Tab	Moves cursor left five characters
Ctrl-Left Arrow	Moves cursor left five characters
Up Arrow	Stores entry and moves up one row
Down Arrow	Stores entry and moves down one row
Page Up	Stores entry and moves up one screen
Page Down	Stores entry and moves down one screen

Step 3: Save the Worksheet

After you edit a worksheet, you should save it to preserve your changes. Execute the File Save command:

Type **/fs**
Press **Enter**
Type **r**

Practice

1. Use EDIT mode to change the entry in cell A11 from *Car Insurance* to *Auto Insurance.*
2. Move the cell pointer to C18. Use EDIT mode to change the formula to (C3 − C16). Can you explain why this formula is equivalent to +C3 − C16?

Lesson 11: Changing Column Widths

The default width of columns in Lotus 1-2-3 is nine characters. Although this width is fine in many cases, you may have to change the width of a column. In the BUDGET worksheet, some of the labels in column A appear to have overlapped into column B. This overlapping does not present a problem, since column B is empty. Keep in mind, however, that the labels really are in column A. Although characters appear to be in column B on the screen, column B is still empty. You can confirm this by moving the cell pointer to cell A13 then B13 and viewing the contents of the cells displayed in the control panel. Let's widen column A so that it can hold all of the labels in the BUDGET worksheet.

Step 1: Move the Cell Pointer into the Column

Move the cell pointer to a cell in the column to be widened or narrowed. Move to cell A1:

Press **Home**

Step 2: Execute the Worksheet Column Set-Width Command

The width of a single column can be changed with the Worksheet Column Set-Width command:

Type **/wcs**

Step 3: Enter the Width In Characters

Lotus 1-2-3 will prompt you to enter the column width, which must be between 1 and 240 characters, and it will suggest the current width of 9 characters. Change the column width to 25:

Type **25**
Press **Enter**

Column A will widen to 25 characters, as shown in Figure 13. Notice that the width of the column now appears in square brackets in the control panel, between the current cell address and the contents of the current cell.

Step 4: Save the Worksheet

After you modify a worksheet, you should save it to preserve your changes. Execute the File Save command:

Type **/fs**
Press **Enter**
Type **r**

Practice

1. Execute the Worksheet Column Reset-Width command to change the width of column A back to the default width.
2. Execute the Worksheet Column Set-Width command to change the width of column A to 25 again.

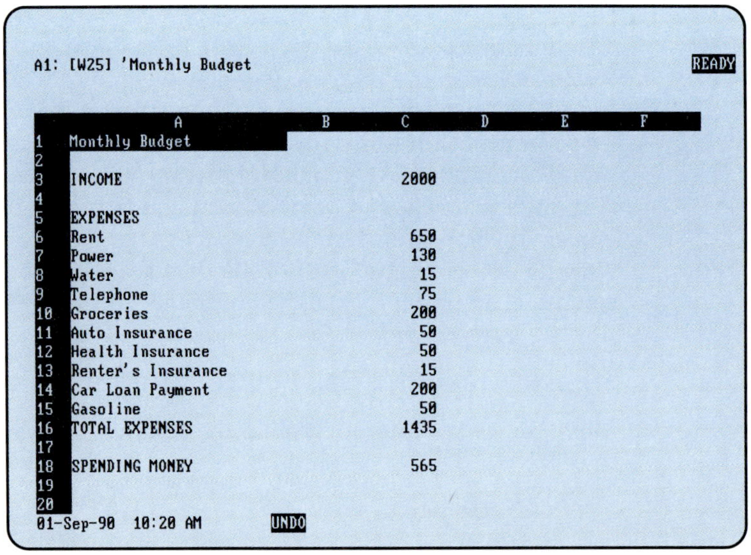

Figure 13 Column A Widened to 25 Characters

Lesson 12: Deleting and Inserting Columns and Rows

Lotus 1-2-3 provides commands for deleting and inserting columns and rows. As examples, let's delete a column and insert a row in the BUDGET worksheet.

Step 1: Delete a Column

Since you widened column A, you no longer need a blank column B. You can easily delete it. Move the cell pointer to column B and execute the Worksheet Delete Column command:

Press **Home**
Press **Right Arrow**
Type **/wdc**

Lotus 1-2-3 will prompt you for the range of columns to delete, and it will suggest the current column. Since you want to delete only the current column

Press **Enter**

The contents of column B will disappear and all the columns to the right will be shifted over to the left. The former column C is now column B. Note that the cell addresses in formulas are automatically adjusted to account for this move. For example, move to cell B16 and examine the formula to compute total expenses in the control panel:

Press **F5**
Type **b16**
Press **Enter**

Before you deleted column B, the formula in C16 was @SUM(C6..B15). After you deleted column B, 1-2-3 shifted the contents of column C into column B, and it changed the formula to @SUM(B6..B15). If you examine the formula in cell B18, you will see a similar adjustment.

The process for deleting a row is similar. Move the cell pointer to the row to be removed and then execute the Worksheet Delete Row command.

Step 2: Insert a Row

Suppose you forgot to include the cable television bill in your budgeted expenses. You can easily insert a new row and then enter the data. Move the cell pointer to the row where you want the inserted row to appear, then execute the Worksheet Insert Row command:

Press **F5**
Type **a10**
Press **Enter**
Type **/wir**
Press **Enter**

The former row 10 and all the rows below it will be shifted down. A blank row now appears as row 10. Enter the new data for this row:

Type **Cable TV**
Press **Right Arrow**
Type **15**
Press **Enter**

The new row occurs between the first and last cells in the range specified in the total expenses formula. So, the range in the formula is automatically changed to B6..B16 from B6..B15, which it was before the row was inserted. The total expenses increase by 15, and the spending money decreases by 15. Move to cell B17 to see the adjusted formula:

Press **F5**
Type **b17**
Press **Enter**

Your screen should look like Figure 14.

The process for inserting a column is similar. You move the cell pointer to the column where the new column is to be added, then execute the Worksheet Insert Column command.

Step 3: Save the Worksheet

After you modify a worksheet, you should save it to preserve your changes. Execute the File Save command:

Type **/fs**
Press **Enter**
Type **r**

Practice

1. Insert a new column B.
2. Insert a new row 13.
3. Delete the blank column B.
4. Delete the blank row 13.

Lesson 13: Copying and Moving Cells

Lotus 1-2-3 makes it easy to copy the contents of cells. The Copy command can reduce repetitive typing. As an example, let's copy a range of cells in the BUDGET worksheet. A Practice exercise will illustrate the use of the Move command, which is very similar to the Copy command.

Step 1: Execute the Copy Command

Examine your BUDGET worksheet. Suppose column B contains the numbers and formulas for a single month and you want to show another month in column C. Most of the numbers will be the same, so the easiest way to enter the data in column C is to copy the contents of column B. Execute the Copy command:

Type **/c**

Step 2: Specify the Source Range

Lotus 1-2-3 will prompt you to enter the range of cells to copy from. Specify the source range:

Type **b3..b19**
Press **Enter**

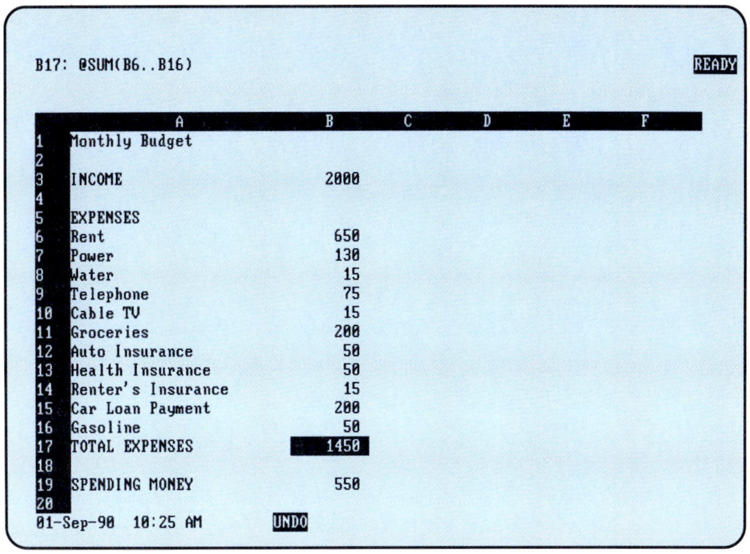

***Figure 14** Column B Deleted and Row 10 Inserted*

Step 3: Specify the Target Range

Next the program will prompt you to enter the range of cells to copy to. Specify the target range:

Type **c3..c19**
Press **Enter**

Lotus 1-2-3 will copy the cells from B3 through B19 to cells C3 through C19.

Step 4: Examine the Screen

Move the cell pointer to C17:

Press **F5**
Type **c17**
Press **Enter**

Your screen should look like Figure 15. Examine the formula in cell C17. When 1-2-3 copies formulas, it automatically adjusts the cell references. So, the formula in cell C17 sums the numbers in cells C6 through C16.

Step 5: Save the Worksheet

After you modify a worksheet, you should save it to preserve your changes. Execute the File Save command:

Type **/fs**
Press **Enter**
Type **r**

Practice

1. Copy the contents of cells A1 through A19 to cells D1 through D19, then delete column D.
2. The Move command is like the Copy command, except that the source cells are erased. Activate the Main menu, execute the Move command, and move

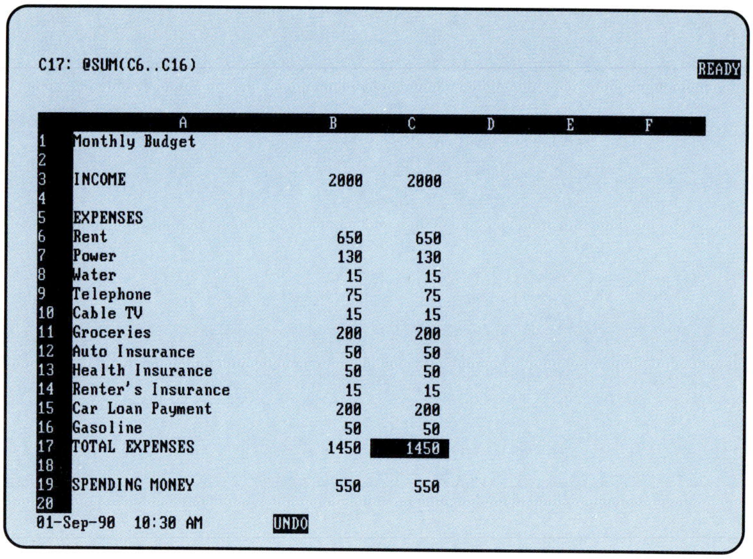

***Figure 15** Cells From Column B Copied to Column C*

the contents of cells C3 through C19 to cells E3 through E19, then move them back to column C.

Lesson 14: Cell Formatting

Lotus 1-2-3 offers an assortment of cell formatting options for tailoring the appearance of a worksheet. For example, you can left justify, center, or right justify labels within their columns. Numbers and formula results can be displayed as currency values, as percentages, with a fixed number of decimal places, or in scientific notation. In this lesson, you will learn how to use label prefix characters and how to format numbers as currency values.

Step 1: Left Justify a Label

The default label prefix character is the apostrophe ('), which aligns labels with the left edge of the cell. Whenever you type an entry that 1-2-3 recognizes as a label, an apostrophe is automatically inserted at the beginning. For example, move to cell A1 and examine the control panel:

Press **Home**

The label *Monthly Budget* is preceded by an apostrophe.

In most cases, you don't have to type the apostrophe, because it will be added automatically by 1-2-3. But if a label must begin with one of these characters, you must type the label prefix character yourself:

0 1 2 3 4 5 6 7 8 9 . + - ($ # @

For example, enter a new left-justified label in cell A1:

Type **'1991 Budget**
Press **Enter**

Step 2: Center a Label

The caret (^) label prefix character centers a label within its cell. For example, center the label *EXPENSES* in cell A5:

Press **F5**
Type **a5**
Press **Enter**
Type **^EXPENSES**
Press **Enter**

The label *EXPENSES* will be centered in cell A5.

Step 3: Right Justify a Label

The quotation mark (") label prefix character aligns a label with the right edge of its cell. For example, enter right-justified labels in cells B2 and C2:

Press **F5**
Type **b2**
Press **Enter**
Type **"Jan**
Press **Right Arrow**
Type **"Feb**
Press **Enter**

Step 4: Fill a Cell

The backslash (\) label prefix character fills a cell with the characters that follow it. It is often used to fill cells with hyphens (-), equal signs (=), or underscores (_) as dividing lines in a worksheet. For example, create a horizontal line of hyphens across cells A18 through C18:

Press **F5**
Type **a18**
Press **Enter**
Type **\-**
Press **Right Arrow**
Type **\-**
Press **Right Arrow**
Type **\-**
Press **Enter**

Your screen should look like Figure 16. Note that cells A18 through C18 appear filled with hyphens, even though each cell contains only \-.

Step 5: Format a Range as Currency

Lotus 1-2-3 offers several ways to format numbers and formula results. The default format is General, which displays no trailing zeros to the right of the decimal point, displays no commas separating thousands, and uses a minus sign to indicate negative values. A common numeric format for financial worksheets is Currency. This format displays the currency symbol, separates thousands with commas, and uses parentheses to indicate negative values. Let's format the numbers in columns B and C as currency values. Execute the Range Format Currency

Figure 16 The \ Label Prefix Character

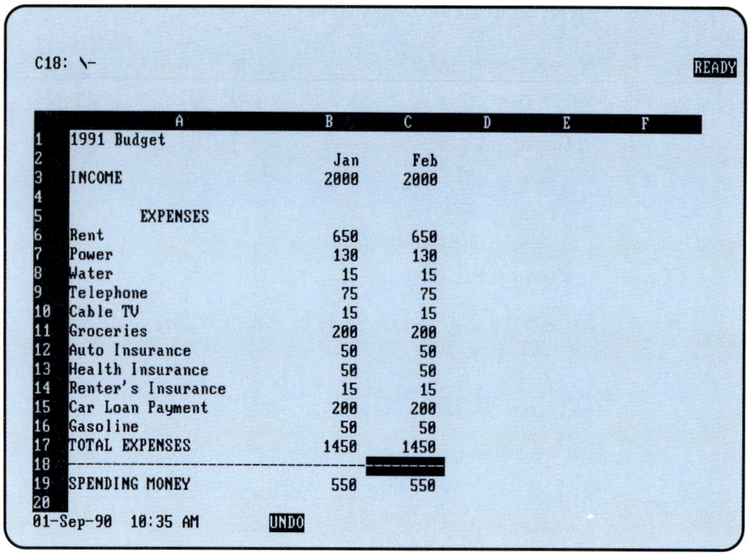

command, specify the number of decimal places as two, and then specify the range of cells to be formatted:

Type **/rfc**
Press **Enter**
Type **b3..c19**
Press **Enter**

Examine the screen. Cells B3, C3, B17, and C17 are filled with asterisks. This means that the cells are not wide enough to hold the numbers in the format you specified. Widen columns B and C:

Press **F5**
Type **b1**
Press **Enter**
Type **/wcs**
Type **10**
Press **Enter**
Press **Right Arrow**
Type **/wcs**
Type **10**
Press **Enter**
Press **Home**

Your screen should now look like Figure 17.

Step 6: Save the Worksheet

After you modify a worksheet, you should save it to preserve your changes. Execute the File Save command:

Type **/fs**
Press **Enter**
Type **r**

Figure 17 Values Formatted as Currency

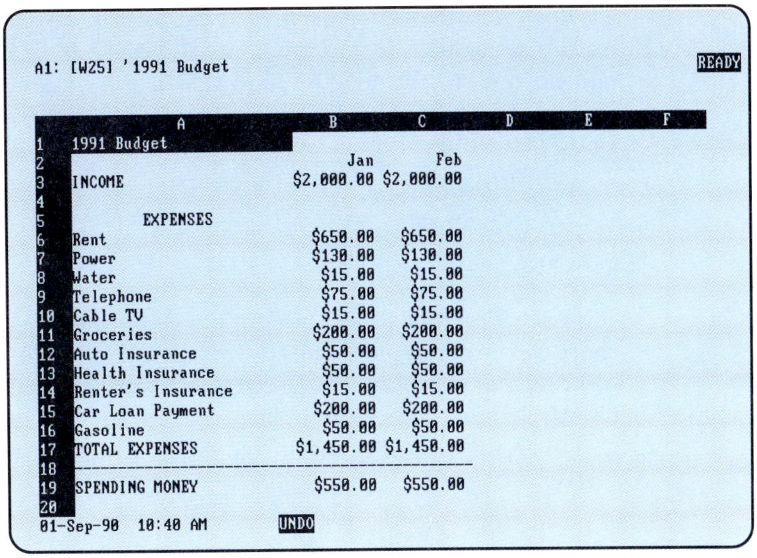

A1: [W25] '1991 Budget READY

	A	B	C	D	E	F
1	1991 Budget					
2		Jan	Feb			
3	INCOME	$2,000.00	$2,000.00			
4						
5	EXPENSES					
6	Rent	$650.00	$650.00			
7	Power	$130.00	$130.00			
8	Water	$15.00	$15.00			
9	Telephone	$75.00	$75.00			
10	Cable TV	$15.00	$15.00			
11	Groceries	$200.00	$200.00			
12	Auto Insurance	$50.00	$50.00			
13	Health Insurance	$50.00	$50.00			
14	Renter's Insurance	$15.00	$15.00			
15	Car Loan Payment	$200.00	$200.00			
16	Gasoline	$50.00	$50.00			
17	TOTAL EXPENSES	$1,450.00	$1,450.00			
18	-------------------------	----------	----------			
19	SPENDING MONEY	$550.00	$550.00			
20						

01-Sep-90 10:40 AM UNDO

Practice

1. Move to cell B3 and examine the control panel. The cell actually contains 2000 but the value $2,000.00 is displayed in the worksheet. Changing a cell's format changes the way the number is displayed in the worksheet, not the data itself. For example, execute the Range Format Currency command and specify zero decimal places for the current cell. Enter the value 1250.25 in B3. Lotus 1-2-3 will display 1250.25 as $1,250, but it still stores the value as 1250.25 and uses the fractional part in calculations. Notice that the value in cell C19 now appears in parentheses because it is a negative value.
2. Change the format of cell B3 back to Currency with two decimal places. Enter 2000 as the value in B3.

Lesson 15: Using the Undo Feature in Releases 2.2 and 3.0

It is easy to make mistakes when using a computer. Fortunately, you can correct typing errors by retyping or editing entries. If you begin to execute a command and then change your mind, you can usually back out of the operation by pressing the Escape key. Recovering accidentally deleted data, however, can be more difficult. A good way to guard against losing data is to regularly save your worksheet to a disk file.

Lotus 1-2-3 Release 2.2 and Release 3.0 also include an Undo feature that lets you reverse the effects of the most recent operation that changed data or worksheet settings. Let's demonstrate this feature by deleting some cells and recovering them with the Undo feature. Note that the Undo feature is not available in Lotus 1-2-3 Release 2.0. If you have Release 2.0, read this lesson without performing the steps.

Step 1: Enable the Undo Feature

Lotus 1-2-3 Release 2.2 has the Undo feature turned on by default. If you see the UNDO indicator at the bottom of the screen, you know that the Undo feature is enabled. Lotus 1-2-3 Release 3.0 has the Undo feature disabled by default. Release

3.0 does not display an UNDO indicator on the screen to tell you if the Undo feature is enabled. If you are using Release 3.0, or if you are using Release 2.2 and do not see the UNDO indicator at the bottom of the screen, execute the Worksheet Global Default Other Undo Enable Quit command to turn on the Undo feature and return to READY mode:

Type **/wgdoueq**

Step 2: Erase a Range

You have already learned how to delete entire rows or columns with the Worksheet Delete command. The Range Erase command lets you delete the contents of a range of cells. You can use the Range Erase command to erase a single cell, part of a column or row, or a block of adjacent cells in several columns and rows. Use the Range Erase command to delete the contents of cells B6 through C16:

Type **/re**
Type **b6..c16**
Press **Enter**

Cells B6 through C16 will be erased.

Step 3: Use the Undo Feature

Suppose you made a mistake or changed your mind about erasing that data. To invoke the Undo feature, hold down the Alternate key and press the F4 key.

Press **Alt-F4**

If you are using Lotus 1-2-3 Release 2.2, the data you deleted will be reinstated immediately. If you are using Lotus 1-2-3 Release 3.0, the program will ask you to confirm the Undo operation. Select the Yes option to tell the program to perform the Undo operation:

Type **y**

Practice

The Undo feature can be used to reverse a command that changes a worksheet setting but does not delete data. For example, use the Range Format command to select the General format for cells B3 through C19, then invoke the Undo feature to reverse your action.

Lesson 16: Using Formulas

As you know, a formula is an expression stored in a cell that tells 1-2-3 to perform a calculation. You have used formulas in this chapter to sum a column of numbers and to subtract one number from another. In fact, formulas can do much more than add and subtract numbers. In this lesson, we will discuss Lotus 1-2-3 formulas in more detail.

Step 1: Create a New Worksheet

To illustrate some of the properties of formulas, let's set up a simple worksheet. First, save the BUDGET worksheet:

Type **/fs**

Press **Enter**
Type **r**

Execute the Worksheet Erase Yes command to clear the worksheet screen and move the cell pointer to A1:

Type **/wey**

Follow these directions to create a simple worksheet:

Type **One**
Press **Down Arrow**
Type **Two**
Press **Down Arrow**
Type **Three**
Press **Home**
Press **Right Arrow**
Type **100**
Press **Down Arrow**
Type **200**
Press **Down Arrow**
Type **300**
Press **Down Arrow**

Your screen should look like Figure 18. This new worksheet is only a place for you to try out formulas for this lesson and the next lesson. You do not have to save it to a disk file when you are finished.

Step 2: Enter a Numeric Formula

Lotus 1-2-3 lets you create three basic types of formulas: numeric, string, and logical. A **numeric formula** is a mathematical expression that calculates using numeric values and produces a numeric result. Numeric formulas may include built-in functions and arithmetic operations, such as addition, subtraction, mul-

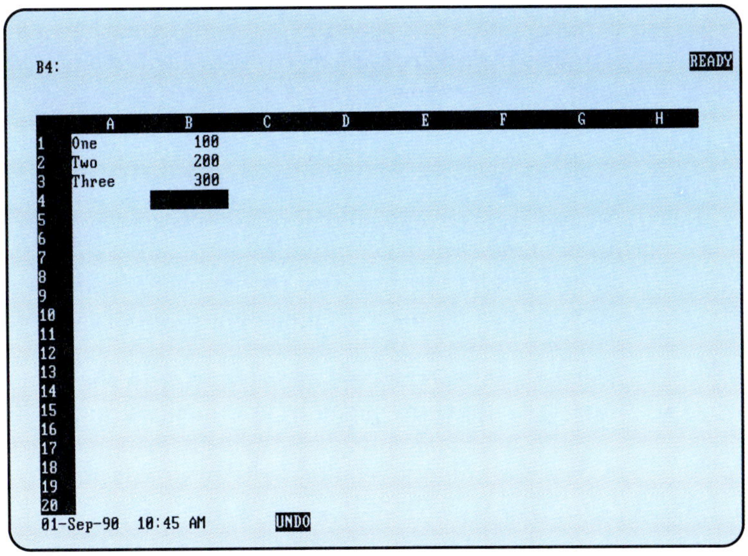

Figure 18 A Simple Worksheet

tiplication, and division. The formulas you have used so far in this chapter have all been numeric formulas. Try another numeric formula:

Type **+b1+b2+b3**
Press **Enter**

You should see the sum 600 displayed in cell B4.

Step 3: Enter a String Formula

A **string formula** manipulates labels. It may include the **string combination operator** (&), which joins two labels, and certain built-in functions. Although string formulas are used less frequently than numeric and logical formulas, they can be handy in worksheets that manipulate text. Move the cell pointer to C1 and enter a text formula:

Press **Up Arrow** (3 times)
Press **Right Arrow**
Type **+a1&" Hundred"**
Press **Enter**

This formula tells 1-2-3 to take the label in A1 and combine it with the label in quotation marks. The result is *One Hundred* in cell C1.

Step 4: Enter a Logical Formula

A **logical formula** compares values and produces the result of TRUE, symbolized by the value 1, or FALSE, symbolized by the value 0. Logical formulas may include certain built-in functions and logical operations, such as greater than, less than, and equal to. For example, suppose you want to know if the value in cell B3 is greater than the value in cell B1. Move the cell pointer to C2 and enter a logical formula:

Press **Down Arrow**
Type **+b3>b1**
Press **Enter**

Since 300 is in B3 and 100 is in B1, the result of the logical formula is 1, or TRUE (see Figure 19). Logical comparisons can be combined with logical functions to perform different operations depending on the values in specific cells. Logical formulas make it possible for a worksheet to choose between alternative sets of computations when solving a problem.

Step 5: Try the Arithmetic Operators

An **operator** is a symbol that represents an action to be performed in a formula. An **operand** is a value on which an action is to be performed. The + operator, for example, is a symbol that represents the addition of two numbers, which are the operands. While most operators act on two operands, some operators act on only one operand. In the expression −3, for instance, the − operator stands for negation, not subtraction, and acts on only one operand, the 3. Lotus 1-2-3 has three basic types of operators: arithmetic, string, and logical.

Arithmetic operators perform mathematical operations on numeric operands to produce numeric results. Let's enter a formula to illustrate each arithmetic

Figure 19 A Logical Formula

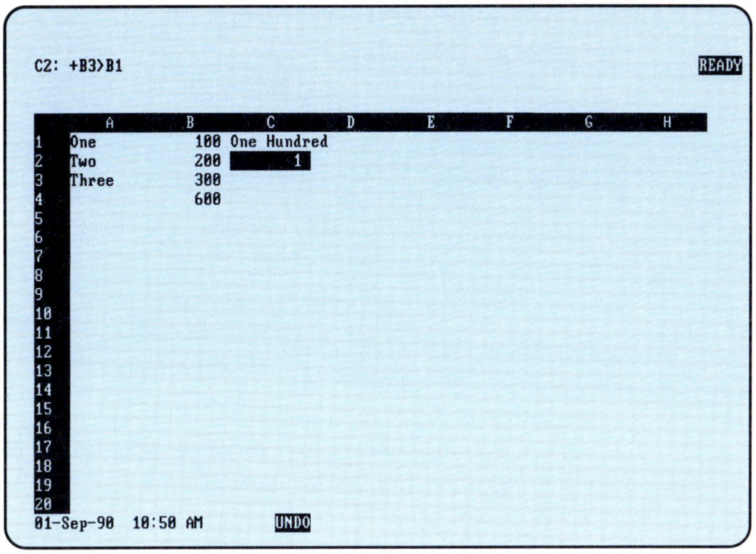

operator. After you enter each formula, examine the screen and make sure you understand the result. First, move the cell pointer to C4:

Press **F5**
Type **c4**
Press **Enter**

The addition operator (+) adds two values.

Type **25+b1**
Press **Enter**

The subtraction operator (−) subtracts one value from another.

Type **450-b3**
Press **Enter**

The negation operator (−) makes a value negative.

Type **-b1**
Press **Enter**

The multiplication operator (*) multiplies two values.

Type **15*b1**
Press **Enter**

The division operator (/) divides one value by another.

Type **+b3/b1**
Press **Enter**

The exponentiation operator (^) takes a value to a power.

Type **2^3**
Press **Enter**

This formula takes 2 to the 3rd power, which is 8.

Step 6: Try the String Operator

Lotus 1-2-3 has only one string operator, the string combination operator &. Try an example of a formula that uses the string combination operator:

Type **+a1&" "&a2&" "&a3**
Press **Enter**

You should see *One Two Three* in the current cell.

Step 7: Try the Logical Operators

Logical operators produce the result 1 for TRUE or 0 for FALSE. Let's try an example of each logical operator. After you enter each formula, examine the screen and make sure you understand the result.

The = operator produces a result of 1 for TRUE only if its two operands are equal. Otherwise it produces 0 for FALSE.

Type **+b1=100**
Press **Enter**

The < operator produces a result of 1 for TRUE only if its first operand is less than its second operand. Otherwise it produces 0 for FALSE.

Type **100<b1**
Press **Enter**

The <= operator produces a result of 1 for TRUE only if its first operand is less than or equal to its second operand. Otherwise it produces 0 for FALSE.

Type **100<=b1**
Press **Enter**

The > operator produces a result of 1 for TRUE only if its first operand is greater than its second operand. Otherwise it produces 0 for FALSE.

Type **+b1>100**
Press **Enter**

The >= operator produces a result of 1 for TRUE only if its first operand is greater than or equal to its second operand. Otherwise it produces 0 for FALSE.

Type **+b1>=100**
Press **Enter**

The <> operator produces a result of 1 for TRUE only if its two operands are not equal. Otherwise it produces 0 for FALSE.

Type **+b1<>100**
Press **Enter**

The #NOT# operator negates a logical result. It produces 1 for TRUE if its operand was FALSE, or 0 for FALSE if its operand was TRUE.

Press **Down Arrow**
Type **#not#c4**
Press **Enter**

The #AND# operator produces 1 for TRUE only if both of its operands are TRUE. Otherwise it produces 0 for FALSE.

Type **+c4#and#1**
Press **Enter**

The #OR# operator produces 0 for FALSE only if both of its operands are FALSE. Otherwise it produces 1 for TRUE.

Type **+c4#or#1**
Press **Enter**

Step 8: Understand the Order of Operations

When more than one operator is used in a formula, the operations are executed in a specific order. For example, try this formula:

Type **+b1+b2/b3**
Press **Enter**

You might expect the 100 in B1 to be added to the 200 in B2, and the result to be divided by the 300 in B3 to yield 1. In this case, however, the operations do not proceed from left to right. The division is performed before the addition, so the result is 100.6666.

You must understand the order of operations to construct formulas that execute correctly. The table below lists the Lotus 1-2-3 operators in order of priority or precedence. In other words, the ^ operator is executed first and the #AND#, #OR#, or & operator is executed last. Operators that appear on the same line in the table have equal precedence and are executed from left to right in a formula.

Order of Operations

Precedence	Operators	Operations
1	^	Exponentiation
2	–	Negation
3	* /	Multiplication and division
4	+ –	Addition and subtraction
5	= < <= > >= <>	Logical comparisons
6	#NOT#	Logical NOT
7	#AND# #OR# &	Logical AND, logical OR, and string combination

Step 9: Use Parentheses

Although it is important to understand the order of operations, you can eliminate much confusion by using parentheses in your formulas. Expressions in parentheses are evaluated first, regardless of the order of operations. When in doubt about the order of operations, use parentheses to force the order you want. For example, try this formula:

Type **(b1+b2)/b3**
Press **Enter**

First, the 100 in B1 is added to the 200 in B2. The sum, 300, is then divided by the 300 in B3 to yield a result of 1 (see Figure 20).

Expressions in parentheses can be nested within other parentheses. The expression inside the innermost set of parentheses is evaluated first. Evaluation

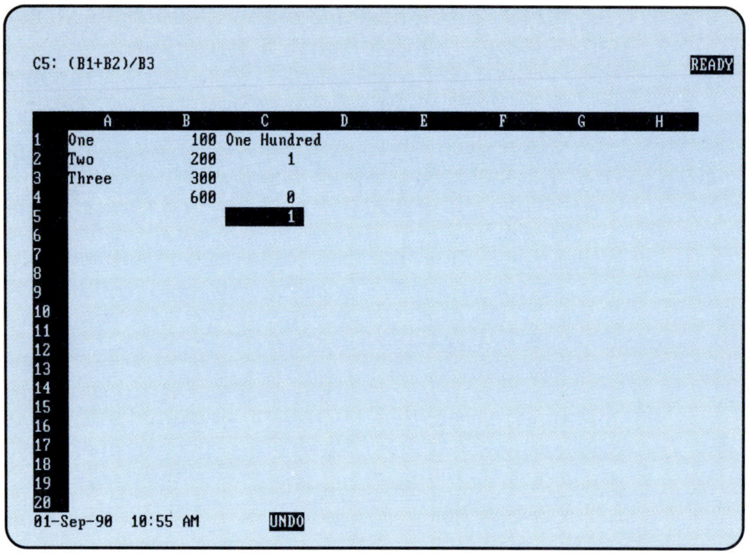

Figure 20 A Formula that Uses Parentheses

then proceeds progressively outward. Expressions within parentheses at the same level of nesting are evaluated from left to right.

Practice

1. Enter a formula to divide the result in cell B4 by 3.
2. Enter a formula to test whether the contents of cell B3 is greater than the sum of cells B1 and B2.
3. Enter a formula to add the contents of cells B1, B2, and B3 and divide the sum by 10.

Lesson 17: Using Functions

Lotus 1-2-3 functions are ready-made procedures that you can use to perform complex or common operations. For example, the @SUM function, which you have already used in this chapter, adds the contents of any range of cells. Lotus 1-2-3 provides built-in functions, like those in high-level programming languages such as BASIC or Pascal, so that users don't have to "reinvent the wheel" whenever they need to perform certain routine calculations. Functions make it easier to manipulate data in a worksheet because they provide convenience and accuracy. The built-in functions include many operations users may not know how to do on their own. For instance, do you remember how to compute a square root? Could you figure out how to compute a square root with a Lotus 1-2-3 formula? Fortunately, 1-2-3 has the @SQRT function, which will compute a square root for you.

Some functions perform operations that may be difficult or even impossible to do in any other way. For example, if you had to tally the values in 1,000 cells, you could not do it by adding the individual cells. Even if you wanted to enter all 1,000 cell addresses and plus signs, Lotus 1-2-3 would not let you, because 240 is the maximum number of characters you can enter into a cell. The @SUM function, however, lets you add up the contents of 1,000 cells as easily as 3 cells.

Lotus 1-2-3 has more than 90 different built-in functions. This lesson will introduce only a few of the most commonly used functions. You will learn more functions later. The Lotus 1-2-3 Command Summary appendix at the end of this book lists all of the Lotus 1-2-3 functions.

Step 1: Try Some Mathematical Functions

Mathematical functions compute a numeric result given one or more other numeric values. Let's try a few examples.

Type **@abs(-25)**
Press **Enter**

The result should be 25. The @ABS function computes the absolute value of a number. In other words, it converts a negative value to a positive value.

Type **@int(2.667)**
Press **Enter**

The result should be 2. The @INT function converts a value to an integer by truncating the fractional part.

Type **@log(100)**
Press **Enter**

The result should be 2. The @LOG function computes the base 10 logarithm of a value.

Type **@mod(7,3)**
Press **Enter**

The @MOD function returns the remainder (modulus) from a division operation. In this case, the result should be 1, the remainder you get when 7 is divided by 3.

Type **@rand**
Press **Enter**

The result could be any number between 0 and 1. The @RAND function returns a random number between 0 and 1. Random numbers are sometimes used in statistics and games.

Type **@round(2.2468,3)**
Press **Enter**

The result should be 2.247. The @ROUND function rounds a value to a specified number of decimal places, in this case 3.

Type **@sqrt(9)**
Press **Enter**

The result should be 3. The @SQRT function computes the square root of a value.

Step 2: Try Some Trigonometric Functions

Trigonometric functions are mathematical functions that deal with angles. Let's try a few examples.

Type **@pi**
Press **Enter**

The result should be 3.141592. The @PI function returns the value of π, the ratio of the circumference of a circle to its diameter.

Type **@sin(@pi/2)**
Press **Enter**

The result should be 1. The @SIN function returns the sine of an angle assumed to be expressed in radians. Notice how functions are combined in the above formula.

Type **@cos(0)**
Press **Enter**

The result should be 1. The @COS function returns the cosine of an angle assumed to be expressed in radians.

Type **@tan(@pi/4)**
Press **Enter**

The result should be 1. The @TAN function returns the tangent of an angle assumed to be expressed in radians.

Step 3: Try Some Statistical Functions

Statistical functions perform calculations on lists of values. These lists may be single values, ranges, or combinations of both. Let's try a few examples. The following examples assume you still have the values 100, 200, and 300 in cells B1, B2, and B3.

Type **@avg(b1..b3)**
Press **Enter**

The result should be 200. The @AVG function computes the average (or mean) of a list of values.

Type **@count(b1..b3)**
Press **Enter**

The result should be 3. The @COUNT function returns the number of nonblank cells in a list of cells.

Type **@max(b1..b3)**
Press **Enter**

The result should be 300. The @MAX function returns the maximum value in a list of values.

Type **@min(b1..b3)**
Press **Enter**

The result should be 100. The @MIN function returns the minimum value in a list of values.

Type **@sum(b1,b1..b3,200)**
Press **Enter**

The result should be 900. The @SUM function computes the sum of a list of values. This example shows how a list of values can contain individual cells, ranges, and constant values separated by commas.

Step 4: Try Some Financial Functions

Spreadsheet programs are used extensively in accounting, business, and finance. Lotus 1-2-3 provides functions for calculations concerning loans, annuities, and cash flows. Let's try a few examples.

Type **@pmt(9000,1%,48)**
Press **Enter**

The @PMT function computes the payment on a loan per payment period for a given principal amount, interest rate, and number of periods. The above formula could represent the monthly payment on a new car loan of $9,000 (the principal), at 1% per month (12% annual) interest rate, for 48 monthly payment periods. If you round the result to two decimal places, the monthly payment would be $237.

Type **@pv(2000,8%,10)**
Press **Enter**

The @PV function computes the present value of an investment, given the payment amount, discounted interest rate, and number of periods. Suppose that you have the opportunity to make an investment that will return $2,000 per year for the next ten years. To receive this fixed yearly payment or annuity of $2,000, you must invest $10,000. Is it wise to spend $10,000 today to earn $20,000 over the next ten years? You must compute the present value of the $2000 payments you will receive to decide if the investment is sound. Assume that as an alternative to this annuity, you can earn 8% investing your money in certificates of deposit. This 8% will be the discounted interest rate of the investment. The above

Real World

Temporaries Trained to Use Lotus 1-2-3

Kelly Services, one of the largest agencies of temporary workers in the United States, now provides employees who are spreadsheet literate. Because of the increase in the number of requests for temporary workers with spreadsheet skills, the agency has instituted a nationwide program to teach and certify its qualified employees in the use of programs such as Lotus 1-2-3.

"Depending on the mix of skills identified by our branch offices, we train to meet those needs," explained Carolyn Fryar, senior vice president of Kelly Services. "Software skills include setting the column width and cell display, retrieving a spreadsheet, activating calculations, sending to print, and storing a spreadsheet."

This program, the Kelly PC-Pro System for spreadsheet training, is now available in all 700 Kelly offices in the United States. Trainees receive detailed reference guides for selected spreadsheet programs and a toll-free hotline that they can call to get on-the-job help. Kelly temporaries who qualify for spreadsheet training include those who already have secretarial and word processing skills, or ledger and bookkeeping experience.

As more businesses and organizations acquire microcomputers and spreadsheet programs, their need for skilled employees grows. It seems that familiarity with spreadsheet programs is almost a necessity in today's business world.

Source: Daniel Sommer, "Kelly Trains Temps to Use Spreadsheets," *InfoWorld*, September 28, 1987, p. 48.

formula evaluates this situation. The result of 13,420.16 means that you should be willing to spend $13,420.16 now to receive $20,000 over the next ten years. Since your initial payment is only $10,000, this investment is sound.

Type **@fv(2000,8%,35)**
Press **Enter**

The @FV function computes the future value of an investment, based on a given payment, interest rate, and number of periods. Suppose you plan to deposit $2,000 at the end of each year into your Individual Retirement Account (IRA) for the next 35 years. The average rate of return on your IRA is 8% per year. How much money will you have in your IRA at the end of 35 years? The above formula answers this question. Your nest egg will be worth around $344,633 at the end of 35 years.

Type **@term(2000,8%,500000)**
Press **Enter**

The @TERM function computes the number of payment periods in the term of an investment, given a payment amount, interest rate, and future value amount. Given the scenario presented in the @FV example, how long will it take you to accumulate $500,000 in your IRA? The result of the above formula indicates that it would take a little over 39 and a half years (see Figure 21).

Practice

1. Calculate the square root of 65536.
2. Calculate the cosine of 2π.
3. Calculate the average of these three numbers: 25.67, 89.46, and 65.32.
4. Calculate the monthly payment on a $50,000 loan with an interest rate of 12% per year (1% per month) and a term of 30 years (360 months).

Figure 21 The @TERM Function

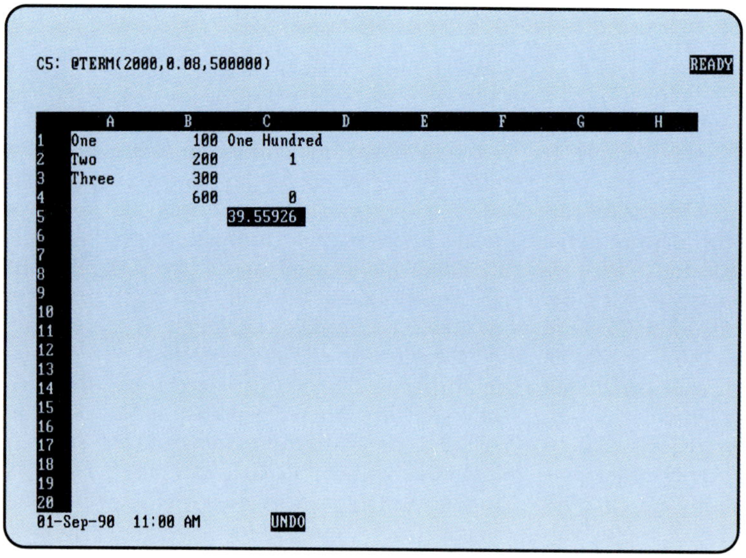

Summary

- *Starting 1-2-3.* Boot up the computer, switch to the proper disk or directory, and enter 123 from DOS.
- *Creating a worksheet.* Enter labels, numbers, and formulas into worksheet cells.
- *Using 1-2-3 menus.* Press / to activate the Main menu. Highlight a command and press Enter or type the command's first letter. Press Escape to return from a menu.
- *Saving a worksheet.* Execute the File Save command and enter the file name.
- *Printing a worksheet.* Execute the Print command, choose Printer or File, specify the range to print, and select the Go option.
- *Quitting 1-2-3.* Save the worksheet, then execute the Quit command from the Main menu.
- *Retrieving an existing worksheet.* Execute the File Retrieve command, then type or select the file name.
- *Getting help.* Press the F1 function key to activate the help facility. Press Escape to exit the help facility.
- *Moving around an existing worksheet.* The pointer movement keys include the arrow keys, Home, Page Up, Page Down, Tab, Ctrl-Right Arrow, Shift-Tab, and Ctrl-Left Arrow. Pressing End followed by an arrow key moves to the next intersection of a blank cell and nonblank cell in that direction. Pressing End followed by Home moves to the lowest rightmost nonblank cell. Pressing F5 prompts you for a cell address to go to.
- *Editing cells.* Retype an entire entry or press F2 to edit an existing entry.
- *Changing column widths.* Move to the column, execute the Worksheet Column Set-Width command, and enter the width.
- *Deleting and inserting columns and rows.* Move to the column or row and execute Worksheet Delete Column, Worksheet Delete Row, Worksheet Insert Column, or Worksheet Insert Row.
- *Copying and moving cells.* Execute the Copy or Move command, specify the source range, and specify the target range.
- *Formatting cells.* The label prefix characters include ' (left justify), ^ (center), " (right justify), and \ (fill a cell). Execute the Range Format command and select an option to format numbers and formula results.
- *Undoing commands.* Press Alt-F4 to invoke the Undo feature (not available in Lotus 1-2-3 Release 2.0).
- *Using formulas.* Three types of formulas can be used: numeric, string, and logical. The arithmetic operators are + (addition), − (subtraction and negation), * (multiplication), / (division), and ^ (exponentiation). The only string operator is &, which combines labels. The logical operators are =, <, >, <=, >=, <>, #NOT#, #AND#, and #OR#. Expression evaluation follows the order of operations unless parentheses are used.
- *Using functions.* Commonly-used mathematical functions include @ABS, @INT, @LOG, @MOD, @RAND, @ROUND, and @SQRT. Trigonometric functions include @PI, @SIN, @COS, and @TAN. Statistical functions include @AVG, @COUNT, @MAX, @MIN, and @SUM. Financial functions include @PMT, @PV, @FV, and @TERM.

Key Terms

As an extra review of this chapter, try defining the following terms.

- cell
- cell address (cell reference)
- cell pointer
- context-sensitive
- control panel
- current cell
- data
- formula
- function
- label
- label prefix character
- logical formula
- menu pointer
- mode indicator
- number
- numeric formula
- operand
- operator
- pointer movement keys
- range
- string combination operator
- string formula
- worksheet

Multiple Choice

Choose the best selection to complete each statement.

1. Which command do you enter to start Lotus 1-2-3 from the DOS prompt?
   (a) START (b) 1-2-3
   (c) 123 (d) CALC
2. A cell is a
   (a) worksheet row. (b) worksheet column.
   (c) column-row intersection. (d) piece of data.
3. How are the columns labeled in a 1-2-3 worksheet?
   (a) A to IV (b) 1 to 256
   (c) 1 to 8192 (d) A to Z
4. What are the three types of data that can be entered into worksheet cells?
   (a) headings, text, and labels (b) numbers, labels, and formulas
   (c) sums, products, and quotients (d) commands, operators, and operands
5. What is an expression that tells 1-2-3 to perform a calculation?
   (a) cell (b) address
   (c) formula (d) operand
6. Which key do you press to edit the existing contents of a cell?
   (a) Escape (b) Delete
   (c) F1 (d) F2
7. Which key do you press or character do you type to activate the Main menu?
   (a) / (b) M
   (c) Escape (d) F1
8. How many cells can Lotus 1-2-3 address?
   (a) 256 (b) 8192
   (c) 10,000 (d) 2,097,152

9. Which label prefix character do you use to center a label within its cell?
   (a) ′ (b) ^
   (c) ″ (d) \
10. Which of the following numbers is not a valid 1-2-3 entry?
   (a) 0.5 (b) 100,000
   (c) 4.32E+05 (d) −11.123
11. What is a predefined formula that performs a useful operation, such as computing a sum or a square root?
   (a) command (b) operator
   (c) function (d) operand
12. Which of the following expressions is a range?
   (a) A1..B10 (b) +A1−B10
   (c) @RAND (d) /wey
13. Which keys would you press or letters would you type to execute the File Save command?
   (a) Alt-F4 (b) /fs
   (c) Escape-Home (d) \save
14. Which key(s) do you press or letters do you type to invoke the help facility?
   (a) F1 (b) F2
   (c) /h (d) Alt-F4
15. Which key will always move the cell pointer to A1?
   (a) Escape (b) Up Arrow
   (c) Shift-Tab (d) Home
16. The three basic types of 1-2-3 formulas are
   (a) mathematical, statistical, and financial. (b) numeric, string, and logical.
   (c) additive, multiplicative, and exponential. (d) micro, mini, and macro.
17. If all of the following operators were in the same formula without parentheses, which operator would be executed first?
   (a) + (b) −
   (c) * (d) ^
18. Which expression evaluates to 1?
   (a) 100+200/300 (b) (100+200)/300
   (c) 1/100−99 (d) 10^1−1
19. Which operator combines two labels?
   (a) + (b) *
   (c) & (d) @
20. Three examples of financial functions are
   (a) @ABS, @INT, and @LOG. (b) @AVG, @MAX, and @SUM.
   (c) @SIN, @COS, and @TAN. (d) @PMT, @FV, and @TERM.

Fill-In

1. A worksheet is a table of ______ and ______ of entries.
2. The ______ is the basic unit of storage in a worksheet—where you enter numbers, labels, and formulas.
3. Lotus 1-2-3 can address over two ______ cells.
4. The three lines at the top of the 1-2-3 screen are known as the ______.
5. To move the cell pointer one cell at a time, you would press one of the ______ keys.
6. To move the cell pointer to a particular address, you would press the ______ key.
7. The three types of data you can enter into worksheet cells are numbers, labels, and ______.
8. You can change the existing contents of the current cell by pressing F2 to invoke the ______ mode.
9. Type ______ to activate the Main menu of commands.
10. To select an option from a menu, type its first letter, or move the menu pointer on top of it and press ______.
11. A rectangular block of one or more adjacent cells is called a ______.
12. The ______ command is just like the Copy command, except that it erases the contents of the source range.
13. The ______ copies the worksheet on the screen to a disk file.
14. Press ______ to activate the help facility.
15. ______ formulas produce either TRUE (symbolized by a 1) or FALSE (symbolized by a 0).
16. An ______ is a symbol that represents an action to be performed in a formula.
17. Expressions inside ______ are evaluated first, regardless of the order of operations.
18. As do high-level programming languages, Lotus 1-2-3 provides a set of ______ to perform certain routine calculations.
19. The ______ function truncates the fractional part of a value.
20. The ______ function computes the payment on a loan per payment period for a given principal, interest rate, and term.

Short Problems

1. If you are not already running 1-2-3, start the program. Create and print a simple multiplication table for the numbers 1 through 6. Use these numbers as your row and column labels. Enter only the value 1. All other values in the table should be calculated using formulas.
2. Create a table of the cube root, square root, square, and cube for each whole number value from 1 to 25. List the number in column A, the cube root in column B, the square root in column C, the square in column D, and cube in column E. Enter only the numbers in column A. All other values should be calculated using formulas. Hint: use the exponentiation operator.
3. Use the @RAND function and the Copy command to put random numbers between 0 and 1 into cells A1 through A10. Notice how a different random

number appears in each cell. Move the cell pointer to B1 and enter a formula using the @INT function to convert the random number in cell A1 to an integer between 1 and 6 inclusive. Hint: Try @INT(A1*6)+1. Copy the formula from B1 to cells B2 through B10. This worksheet simulates the throwing of a die ten times.

4. Use the @RAND function and the Copy command to simulate 100 coin tosses. Do this by generating random numbers in cells A1 through A100. Then convert these random numbers into either 0 (for heads) or 1 (for tails). Hint: Try @INT(A1*2) in B1 and copy this formula to cells B2 through B100. Use the @AVG function to compute the mean of the zeros and ones, which will be the probability of getting a tail. It should be near 0.5.
5. Make up twenty exam grades from 0 to 100 and enter them into cells A1 through A20. Use the @MAX function to find the highest grade and the @MIN function to find the lowest grade. Use the @AVG function to calculate the mean grade.
6. Use the @PMT function to calculate the monthly mortgage payment on a $100,000 home loan that has an interest rate of 10% per year and a term of 20 years.
7. You can calculate the number of periods to pay back a loan with the @TERM function if you use a negative value as the future value and take the absolute value of the result. Try the following formula to calculate the number of months it will take to pay back a $100,000 loan with an interest rate of 10% per year making monthly payments of $965.02:

   @ABS(@TERM(965.02,10%/12,−100000))

8. You just won $20 million in the new MegaBucks state lottery. You are given two payment options. You can receive 20 annual payments of $1 million at the end of each year, or you can receive an immediate lump sum payment of $8 million. Which option is worth more in today's dollars? Assume that if you accept the 20 annual payments of $1 million, you would invest the money at an interest rate of 8%, compounded annually. Hint: Try @PV(1000000,8%,20). The result will show that the $20 million paid over 20 years is worth $9,818,147.41 in today's dollars. Take the 20 annual payments.
9. Create a worksheet that will compute automobile gas mileage. Put the mileage when the tank is first filled in cell A1, the mileage when the tank is filled the second time in cell A2, and the number of gallons it took to refill the tank in cell A3. Enter a formula to compute the miles per gallon in cell A4.
10. Reproduce the following table in a 1-2-3 worksheet. You will need to use the Worksheet Column Set-Width and the Range Format commands to set up the worksheet to display such large numbers. Use formulas to compute the two totals.

```
ACCOUNT       THIS YEAR         LAST YEAR
------------------------------------------
Cash on hand  344,584,904.50    235,452,143.60
Receivables   655,473,321.08    527,004,321.97
Inventories   315,733,211.95    130,982,021.80
Real estate       894,992.20        864,389.10
Equipment     448,993,406.00    406,894,600.00
Sales         772,345,236.75    652,945,870.25
------------------------------------------
TOTAL
```

Long Problems

1. Create a worksheet that lists your major expenditures for the past 12 months. Include items like rent, room and board, or mortgage payments; tuition; power bills; telephone bills; health, automobile, and property insurance; travel expenses; credit card purchases; and so on. Be sure to compute both the row and column totals. Try to use the Copy command to reduce repetitive typing. Use appropriate labels and numeric formatting to improve the clarity and appearance of your worksheet.
2. Create a worksheet listing all of the courses you are taking this semester, along with the number of credit hours and the grade you expect. Also include a column showing the numerical equivalent for each grade you expect (A = 4.0, B = 3.0, C = 2.0, D = 1.0, and F = 0.0). Have your worksheet total your number of hours and your grade points and calculate your grade point average.
3. Suppose you have decided to purchase a new microcomputer system. List eight or ten components and supplies you'll need (computer, display adapter, monitor, disk drives, expansion boards, printer, cables, diskettes, paper, and so on). Enter these headings into column A and estimate an amount for each item in column B. Using ads from computer magazines or information from a local retailer, enter the actual costs for these items into column C. Enter a formula and use the Copy command to calculate the differences between your budgeted and actual costs in column D. Include column totals for each of the numeric columns, and add appropriate column headings.
4. In a small local newspaper the fee for classified advertising is a function of the price charged for the item. The fee is collected only if the item sells. The fee is 10% of the first $100.00 of the advertised price, plus 3% of the second $100.00, plus 2% of the third $100.00, plus 1% of the amount of the advertised price over $300.00. Create a worksheet that will accept the advertised price as input and calculate the advertising fee. Test your worksheet using prices of $140.00 (fee = $11.20) and $750.00 (fee = $19.50).
5. Once upon a time, a king won great acclaim from his subjects by abolishing all taxes. In their place, he told the people that they would have to place one grain of wheat in one square of a checkerboard at the end of the first year. At the end of the second year, they would owe him two grains, placed in the second square. At the end of the third year, they would owe four grains, placed in the third square, and at the end of the fourth year, eight grains in the fourth square, and so on up to the sixty-fourth square of the checkerboard. After that, they would own their land outright and wouldn't have to give up any more wheat. Update this problem using pennies instead of wheat, and produce a worksheet that shows each of the sixty-four years, the amount paid that year, and the total amount paid to date. Does this worksheet help explain the revolt that deposed the king several years later?
6. Assume you own 200 individual student apartments now renting for $110.00 a month. Since all your apartments are currently occupied, your gross is $22,000.00 per month. A real estate agent tells you your rent is way too low, but he further states that if you decide to raise the rent, you would lose one tenant for every $7.50 rent increase. In other words, you would be able to rent only 199 of the apartments at $117.50, 198 apartments at $125.00, and so on. Prepare a worksheet that will list in one column the number of apartments rented, in the second column the rent per apartment, and in the third

column the gross income for that particular combination of number rented and rent per apartment. What does your table suggest the rent should be?

7. Suppose you start a savings account that pays interest at a rate of 6% per year, and interest is paid monthly. In other words, you will receive 0.5% per month on your balance. You decide to begin a systematic savings plan in which you will deposit $10.00 per month. Create a worksheet that will show the amount of interest earned each month and the ending balance each month for a period of five years.
8. Consider the expenses of a typical traveling business person (airline tickets, automobile rental, mileage, meals, lodging, supplies, and so on). Construct a worksheet that keeps track of such expenses for each month of the year. Total all rows and columns and do a grand total.
9. Create a worksheet to maintain and balance your checkbook. Have column A contain the check number, column B the date, column C the payment or withdrawal amount, column D the deposit amount, column E an "x" if the transaction has cleared, and column F a description of the transaction. Leave a few blank rows at the top of the worksheet. In one of these cells, compute the current balance by subtracting the sum of the payments from the sum of the deposits. The first entry in the check register should be a deposit with the beginning balance. Enter at least twenty transactions into your checkbook worksheet and verify the computed balance.
10. Create a worksheet to track your income and taxes. For each month of the past year, list your gross income, federal income taxes withheld, state income taxes withheld, any other withholdings, and your net income. Then total the columns.

CHAPTER 12

INTERMEDIATE LOTUS 1-2-3

In This Chapter

Getting Started

Lesson 1: Creating a Bar Graph

Lesson 2: Printing a Graph with Release 2.0 or 2.2

Lesson 3: Printing a Graph with Release 3.0

Lesson 4: Naming a Graph

Lesson 5: Creating a Pie Chart

Lesson 6: Creating a Line Graph

Lesson 7: Creating a Stacked Bar Graph

Lesson 8: Creating an XY Graph

Lesson 9: Creating a Data Base Worksheet

Lesson 10: Sorting a Data Base Worksheet

Lesson 11: Searching a Data Base Worksheet

Lesson 12: Extracting Records From a Data Base Worksheet

Lesson 13: Using the Data Base Functions

Preview

In Chapter 11 you learned the basics of Lotus 1-2-3, the top-selling microcomputer spreadsheet package. This chapter teaches you how to create graphs and manage worksheet data bases using Lotus 1-2-3.

After studying this chapter, you will know how to

- create a bar graph.
- print a graph.
- name a graph.
- create a pie chart.
- create a line graph.
- create a stacked bar graph.
- create an XY graph.
- create a data base worksheet.
- sort a data base worksheet.
- search a data base worksheet.
- extract data from a worksheet.
- use the data base functions.

Getting Started

You've already learned how to start Lotus 1-2-3 and use its most basic features and commands. This chapter assumes you have completed the lessons and exercises of Chapter 11. Furthermore, it assumes that you have a computer with a hard disk and Lotus 1-2-3 installed on it in a subdirectory named 123 or 123R3. A DOS PATH should be set up so that you can run Lotus 1-2-3 from within any subdirectory. You should have a subdirectory named LESSONS in which to store your worksheet files.

Lesson 1: Creating a Bar Graph

VisiCalc, the first spreadsheet program, originally developed for the Apple II computer in 1979, could not produce graphs. Since the introduction of Lotus 1-2-3 for the IBM Personal Computer in 1982, however, graphics capability has been considered an essential component of any serious spreadsheet package. Lotus 1-2-3 can produce several different types of graphs from worksheet data.

Let's create a bar graph that will show a company's sales over a period of years. A **bar graph** is a chart in which numeric values are represented by evenly spaced, thick vertical lines. Bar graphs are useful for comparing different sets of data, such as the sales figures for several different years.

Step 1: Start 1-2-3

If you are not already running Lotus 1-2-3, switch to your LESSONS subdirectory and start the program:

Type **cd c:\lessons**
Press **Enter**
Type **123**
Press **Enter**

Step 2: Set Up a New Worksheet

In a spreadsheet program, a graph is created from data in a worksheet. So, you must first create the worksheet that contains the data for the graph. Widen column A to 16 characters:

Type **/wcs16**
Press **Enter**

Change the numeric format of the range B2 to E2 so that numbers are presented as currency values with no decimal places:

Type **/rfc0**
Press **Enter**
Type **b2..e2**
Press **Enter**

Step 3: Enter the Data

Follow these directions to enter the data for the graph into the worksheet:

Press **Right Arrow**
Type **1988**
Press **Right Arrow**
Type **1989**
Press **Right Arrow**
Type **1990**
Press **Right Arrow**
Type **1991**
Press **Home**
Press **Down Arrow**
Type **Sales (millions)**
Press **Right Arrow**
Type **55**
Press **Right Arrow**
Type **115**
Press **Right Arrow**
Type **150**
Press **Right Arrow**
Type **210**
Press **Home**

Your screen should look like Figure 1. Check your work against Figure 1 and correct any mistakes you made.

Step 4: Save the Worksheet

It is a good idea to save your worksheet in a disk file before you generate a graph. Execute the File Save command and name the worksheet file SALES:

Type **/fs**
Type **sales**
Press **Enter**

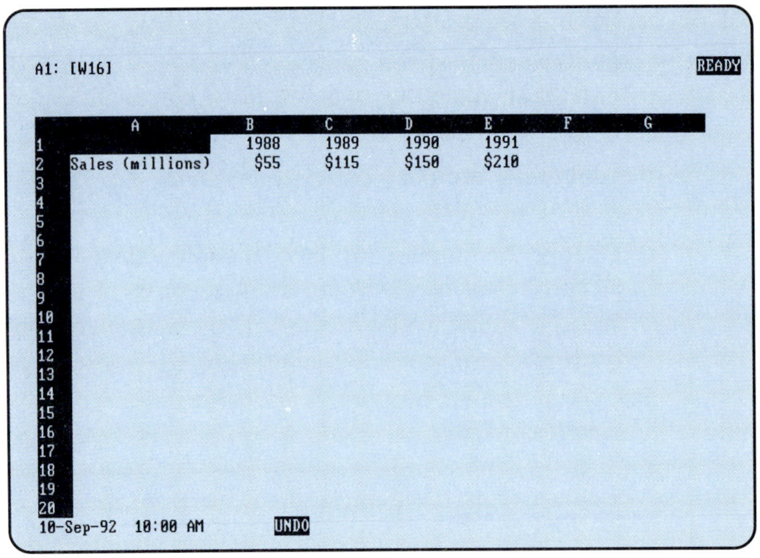

Figure 1 The SALES Bar Graph Worksheet

Step 5: Execute the Graph Command

To create a graph, you must execute the Graph command from the Main menu:

Type **/g**

The Graph menu will appear across the top of the screen (see Figure 2). If you are running Lotus 1-2-3 Release 2.2, the Graph Settings sheet will also appear. Release 2.0 and Release 3.0 do not display a Graph Settings sheet.

Step 6: Select the Type of Graph

Examine the third line of the control panel. Since the Type command is highlighted, the third line of the control panel displays the submenu of options available if you select the Type command. Lotus 1-2-3 Release 2.0 and Release 2.2 let you create five basic types of graphs. Lotus 1-2-3 Release 3.0 lets you create seven basic types of graphs. Select Bar as the type of graph you want to create:

Type **tb**

Step 7: Specify the X Data Range

In bar, line, and stacked bar graphs, the X data range contains the values or labels that will appear along the horizontal x-axis. In the SALES bar graph, the years should be presented along the x-axis, so select B1 to E1 as the X data range:

Type **x**
Type **b1..e1**
Press **Enter**

Step 8: Specify the A Data Range

Next you must specify the cells that contain the actual numeric data to be graphed along the y-axis. Some graphs may contain as many as six data ranges. In Lotus 1-2-3, these data ranges are specified as A, B, C, D, E, and F. For your simple

Figure 2 The Graph Menu and Graph Settings Sheet

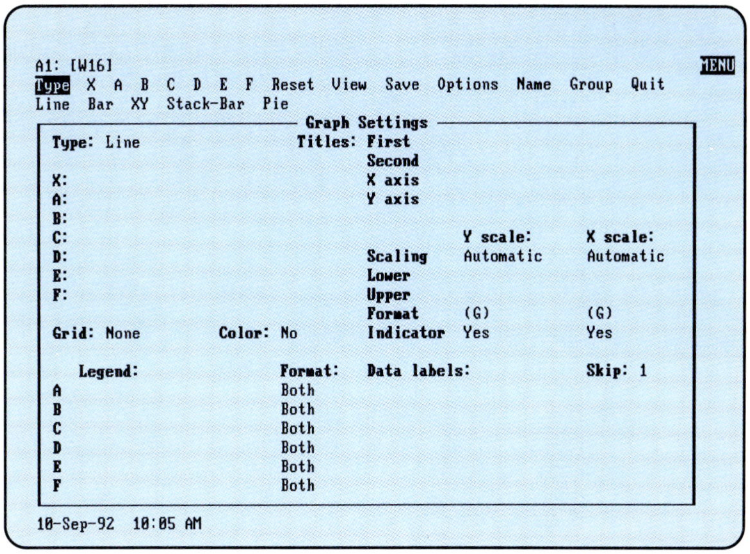

SALES bar graph, only one data range is necessary. Specify the A data range as B2 to E2:

Type **a**
Type **b2..e2**
Press **Enter**

Step 9: Add Titles

Most graphs make little sense unless they have a main title and titles along the axes. Select Options, Titles, and First, and then enter the first line of the graph title:

Type **otf**
Type **Beaver Canoe Company**
Press **Enter**

Enter the second line of the graph title:

Type **ts**
Type **Yearly Sales of Aluminum Canoes**
Press **Enter**

Enter a title for the x-axis:

Type **tx**
Type **Year**
Press **Enter**

Enter a title for the y-axis:

Type **ty**
Type **Sales (millions)**
Press **Enter**

Quit the Options submenu and return to the Graph menu:

Type **q**

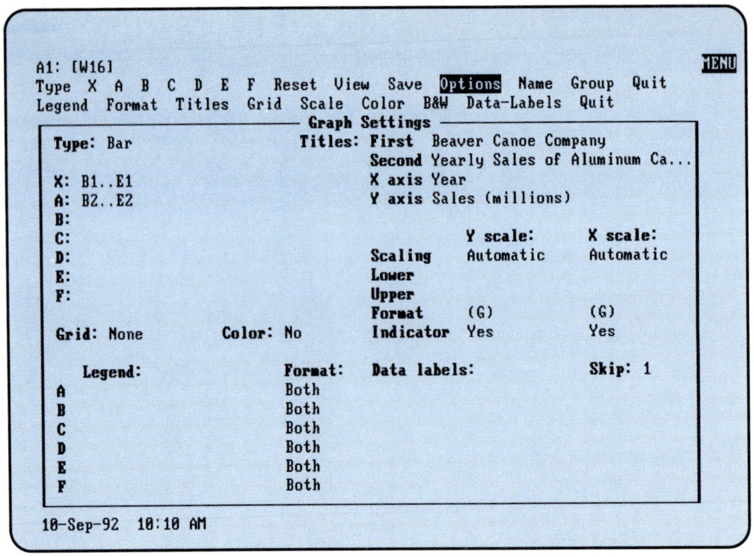

Figure 3 The Completed Graph Settings Sheet

If you are running Lotus 1-2-3 Release 2.2, the graph settings you have specified will be summarized in the Graph Setting sheet on the screen (see Figure 3).

Step 10: View the Graph

If your computer is equipped with a graphics adapter and monitor, you can view the graph you have specified. Select the View option from the Graph menu:

Type **v**

Your screen should look like Figure 4. When you are finished looking at the graph, you can press any key to return to the Graph menu:

Press **Escape**

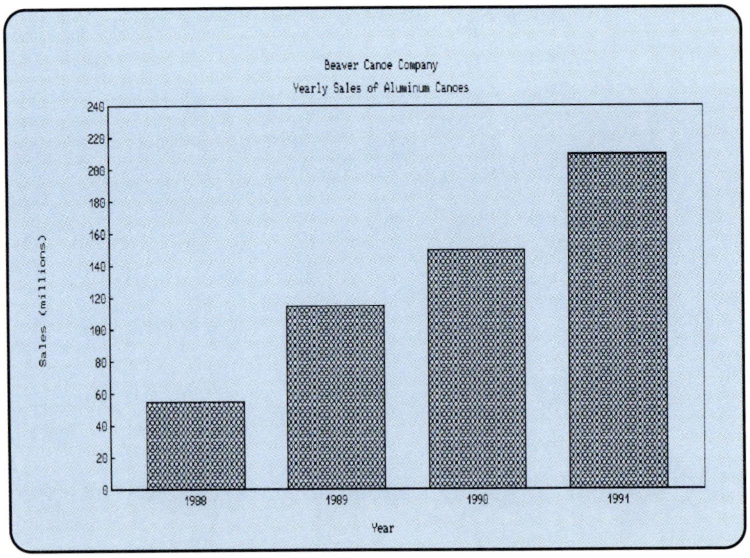

Figure 4 The SALES Graph Displayed on the Screen

Step 11: Save the Graph

Examine the Graph menu on your screen. The Save option lets you save the graph you have created in a file with a PIC extension. This type of graph file can be printed later with the Lotus PrintGraph program or loaded by another application package, such as a word processor or a graphics program that can accept Lotus PIC files. Select the Save option from the Graph menu to save your graph in a file named SALES.PIC:

Type **s**
Type **sales**
Press **Enter**

Quit the Graph menu and return to READY mode:

Type **q**

Step 12: Save the Worksheet

You have saved the graph to a file named SALES.PIC, but you must also save the worksheet to preserve the graph settings you have specified. Execute the File Save command and replace the worksheet file on the disk:

Type **/fs**
Press **Enter**
Type **r**

Practice

1. When you create a graph, you must view it the first time by selecting the View option from the Graph menu. After that, you can use a shortcut from READY mode to view the graph:

   Press **F10**

   The F10 key presents the current graph on the screen. Press any key to return to READY mode.
2. Lotus 1-2-3 provides many options for altering the appearance of a graph. For example, you can add horizontal grid lines to your SALES graph to make it easier to determine the exact heights of the bars:

   Type **/goghqv**

   Press any key to return to the graph menu.
3. Save the new graph with grid lines to SALES.PIC and save the SALES worksheet as well.

Lesson 2: Printing a Graph with Release 2.0 or 2.2

If you are running Lotus 1-2-3 Release 2.0 or Release 2.2, you must use a separate program called PrintGraph to print your graphs. Skip this lesson if you are running Lotus 1-2-3 Release 3.0.

Step 1: Exit 1-2-3

Before you can start PrintGraph, you must exit 1-2-3. Make sure that you have saved your worksheet, then

Type **/qy**

You should see the DOS prompt on your screen.

Step 2: Start PrintGraph

To run the PrintGraph program, execute the PGRAPH command from the DOS prompt:

Type **pgraph**
Press **Enter**

The PrintGraph screen will appear (see Figure 5).

Step 3: Change the Hardware Settings

Examine the Hardware Settings on the right side of the screen. You may have to change these settings. If your computer has a hard disk, the Graphs directory should be C:\LESSONS, and the Fonts directory should be C:\123. In addition, a printer should be selected. Follow these directions to change the hardware settings if necessary:

Type **shg**
Press **Escape**
Type **c:\lessons**
Press **Enter**
Type **f**
Press **Escape**
Type **c:\123**
Press **Enter**

Figure 5 The PrintGraph Screen

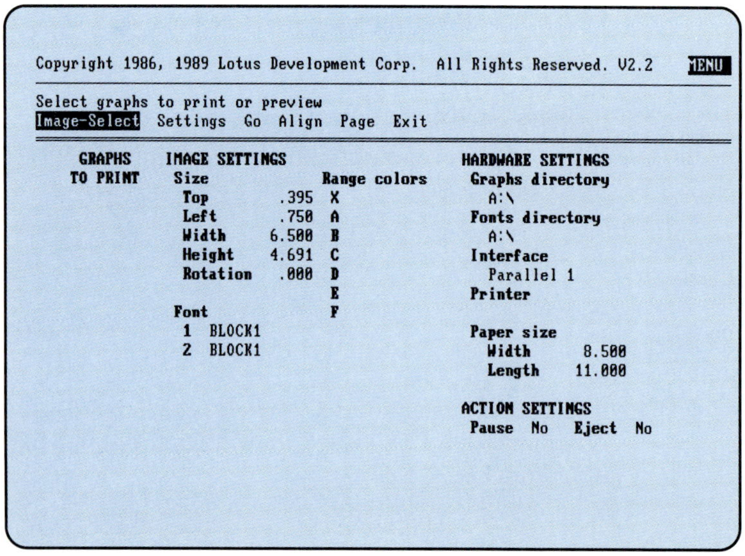

Now select the printer:

Type **p**

A list of the printers connected to your computer will appear, with two options for each printer: Low density and High density. Low density will produce quick, low-quality printouts. High density will produce slow, high-quality printouts. Highlight the printer and density you want to use.

Press **Space Bar**
Press **Enter**

Quit the Hardware Settings menu and the Settings menu:

Type **qq**

Step 4: Select the Image

Execute the Image-Select option from the Main PrintGraph menu:

Type **i**

A list of graph (PIC) files will be displayed on the screen.

Highlight **SALES**
Press **Space Bar**
Press **Enter**

Step 5: Prepare the Printer

Make sure the printer is connected to the computer and turned on. Also, make sure that paper is loaded and aligned to the top of a new page. Finally, make sure that the printer's On Line light is lit. (If it isn't, press the On Line button.)

Step 6: Select the Go Option

After you have specified all of the PrintGraph settings you want to use and have prepared the printer, select the Go option to actually print the graph.

Type **g**

The graph will be printed.

Step 7: Exit PrintGraph and Start 1-2-3

After the graph has been printed, exit the PrintGraph program, return to DOS, and start 1-2-3 again:

Type **ey**
Type **123**
Press **Enter**

Practice

Use the PrintGraph program to print the SALES graph at the other density setting. If you like, try changing some of the image settings, such as graph size, colors, and font. When you are finished experimenting with PrintGraph, exit the program and start 1-2-3 again.

Lesson 3: Printing a Graph with Release 3.0

If you are running Lotus 1-2-3 Release 3.0, you do not need to use a separate program to print out your graphs. Skip this lesson if you are running Lotus 1-2-3 Release 2.0 or Release 2.2.

Step 1: Execute the Print Printer Image Current Go Command

Printing a graph with Lotus 1-2-3 Release 3.0 is much easier than printing a graph with Release 2.0 or 2.2. You can print the current graph with the Print Printer Image Current Go command without leaving the 1-2-3 program.

Type **/ppicg**

The graph will be produced by the printer.

Step 2: Return to READY Mode

Select the Quit option from the Print menu to return to READY mode:

Type **q**

Practice

You can print the SALES graph to a file instead of directly to the printer, but you must use the Encoded option instead of the File option. Follow these directions to create an encoded file named SALES.ENC that can be printed later from DOS:

Type **/pe**
Type **sales**
Press **Enter**
Type **icg**
Type **q**

To print SALES.ENC from DOS, exit 1-2-3 and execute this command:

Type **copy sales.enc prn**
Press **Enter**

When the printer is finished, start 1-2-3 again.

Lesson 4: Naming a Graph

If you change the graph settings in the SALES worksheet, 1-2-3 will produce a different graph. Suppose you want to create a different type of graph from the same worksheet without losing the previous graph. Fortunately, 1-2-3 lets you have several graphs associated with the same worksheet. All you have to do is name your graphs.

Step 1: Retrieve the SALES Worksheet

If the SALES worksheet is not already on your screen, retrieve it from the disk:

Type **/fr**
Highlight **SALES.WK1** (or **SALES.WK3**)
Press **Enter**

Step 2: View the Graph

Make sure that the current graph is the one you want to name. In this case, only one graph is associated with the SALES worksheet, but it cannot hurt to check.

Press **F10**

You should see the bar graph on the screen. Return to READY mode:

Press **Escape**

Step 3: Execute the Graph Name Create Command

To associate a name with an existing graph, execute the Graph Name Create command:

Type **/gnc**

Step 4: Enter a Graph Name

Lotus 1-2-3 will prompt you to enter a graph name. You can specify a name up to 15 characters long (14 characters long in Release 2.0).

Type **sales_bar**
Press **Enter**

Return to READY mode:

Type **q**

Step 5: Use a Named Graph

The Graph Name Use command retrieves a named graph and makes it the current graph.

Type **/gnu**

Lotus 1-2-3 will present a menu of graph names. Currently, only one name exists for the SALES worksheet: SALES_BAR. Select this graph:

Highlight **SALES_BAR**
Press **Enter**

The program will display the bar graph on the screen. Press any key to return to the Graph menu, then quit to READY mode:

Press **Escape**
Type **q**

Practice

If you modify a named graph after you retrieve it, and want to save the changed settings, you must use the Graph Name Create and File Save commands again. Follow these directions:

Type **/gnc**
Highlight **SALES_BAR**
Press **Enter**
Type **q**
Type **/fs**
Press **Enter**
Type **r**

Lesson 5: Creating a Pie Chart

A **pie chart** represents values as wedges of a circle. Pie charts are used to show the parts of a whole. For example, a pie chart might be used to break down total sales into various categories. Let's make a pie chart for Beaver Canoe Company that shows its canoe sales at sport shows, camping stores, boat stores, department stores, and the factory outlet.

Step 1: Create the Worksheet

Let's enter the data for the pie chart in an empty area of the SALES worksheet. Move the cell pointer to A5 and enter the following data:

Press **F5**
Type **a5**
Press **Enter**
Type **Sport Show**
Press **Right Arrow**
Type **10**
Press **Down Arrow**
Type **40**
Press **Left Arrow**
Type **Camping Store**
Press **Down Arrow**
Type **Boat Store**
Press **Right Arrow**
Type **60**
Press **Down Arrow**
Type **70**
Press **Left Arrow**
Type **Department Store**
Press **Down Arrow**
Type **Factory Outlet**
Press **Right Arrow**
Type **30**
Press **Enter**

The numbers you have entered represent the sales in millions of dollars at each of the outlets. Your screen should look like Figure 6. Check your work against Figure 6 and correct any mistakes you find.

Step 2: Save the Worksheet

It is a good idea to save your worksheet before you generate the graph. Execute the File Save command:

Type **/fs**
Press **Enter**
Type **r**

Step 3: Execute the Graph Reset Graph Command

Since you already have a graph defined as the current graph, execute the Graph Reset Graph command to clear the settings.

Type **/grg**

Figure 6 The Pie Chart Data

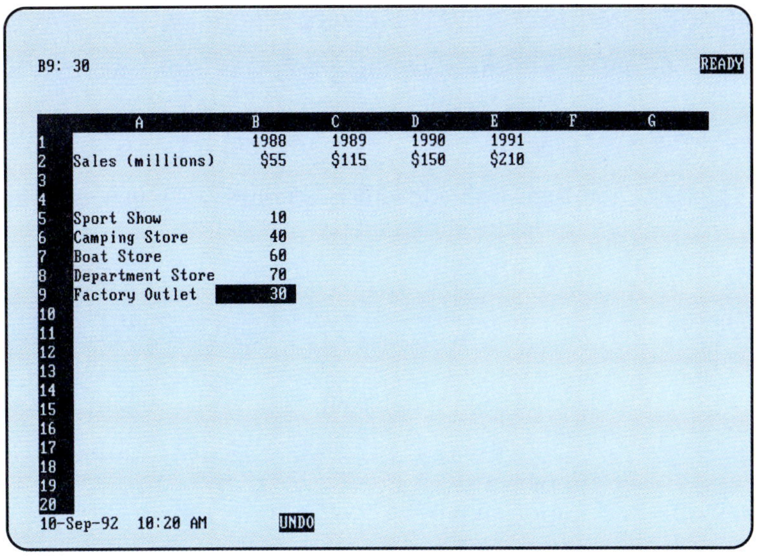

Step 4: Specify the Type Pie Option

Now tell 1-2-3 that you want to create a pie chart:

Type **tp**

Step 5: Specify the X Data Range

In a pie chart, the X data range contains the labels for the slices of the pie. Specify the X data range as cells A5 to A9:

Type **x**
Type **a5..a9**
Press **Enter**

Step 6: Specify the A Data Range

In a pie chart, the A data range contains the values that will be represented as slices. Specify the A data range as cells B5 to B9:

Type **a**
Type **b5..b9**
Press **Enter**

Step 7: Add Titles

Use the Options Titles command to add a two-line title to the pie chart:

Type **otf**
Type **Beaver Canoe Company**
Press **Enter**
Type **ts**
Type **1991 Sales to Various Outlets**
Press **Enter**

Quit the Options submenu and return to the Graph menu:

Type **q**

Step 8: View the Graph

Now you can view the graph you have specified. Select the View option from the Graph menu:

Type **v**

Your screen should look like Figure 7. When you are finished looking at the graph, return to the Graph menu:

Press **Escape**

Step 9: Save the Graph

Select the Save option from the Graph menu to save your pie chart in a file named PIE.PIC:

Type **s**
Type **pie**
Press **Enter**

Step 10: Name the Graph

Since you now have two graphs associated with the SALES worksheet, you should name the pie chart. Execute the Name Create option and specify SALES_PIE as the name of the graph:

Type **nc**
Type **sales_pie**
Press **Enter**

Quit the Graph menu and return to READY mode:

Type **q**

Step 11: Save the Worksheet

You have saved the graph to a file named PIE.PIC and named the graph SALES_PIE, but you must also save the worksheet to preserve the graph settings you have specified. Execute the File Save command and replace the worksheet file on the disk:

Type **/fs**
Press **Enter**
Type **r**

Practice

1. If your computer has a monochrome monitor, the pie chart you have created appears quite plain. You can, however, tell 1-2-3 to use different hatch patterns for the pie slices. You can even explode, or pull out, one or more slices for emphasis. These settings are specified by creating a B data range. Follow these directions:

   Press **F5**
   Type **c5**
   Press **Enter**
   Type **1**
   Press **Down Arrow**

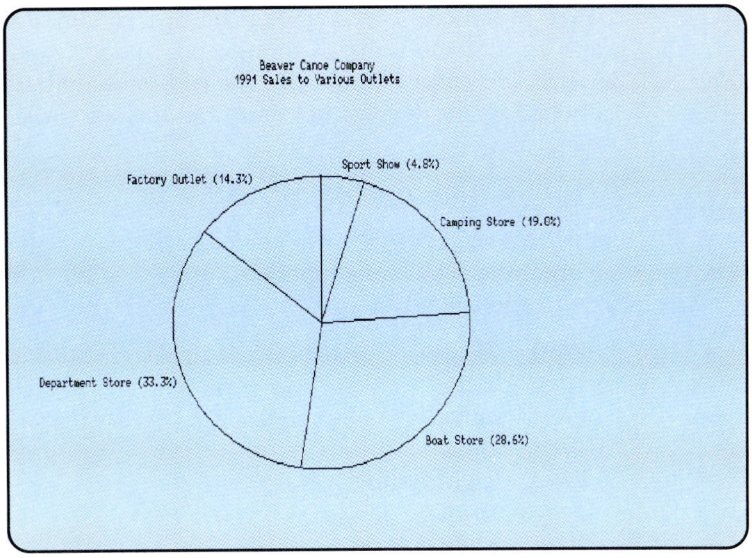

Figure 7 ***The Sales Pie Chart***

Type **2**
Press **Down Arrow**
Type **103**
Press **Down Arrow**
Type **4**
Press **Down Arrow**
Type **5**
Press **Enter**
Type **/gb**
Type **c5..c9**
Press **Enter**
Type **v**

Each slice now has a different pattern, and the Boat Store slice is exploded. Eight different hatch patterns, numbered 1 through 8, are available in Lotus 1-2-3 Releases 2.0 and 2.2. Release 3.0 has fourteen different hatch patterns. These are the numbers entered in the B data range. To explode a slice, you add 100 to the hatch pattern number in the B data range. So, the Boat Store cell in the B data range signifies hatch pattern 3 added to the 100 that indicates the slice is to be exploded from the pie.

Note that if you have a color monitor and the Graph Options Color option is set, each slice will have a different color instead of a different hatch pattern. You can select the Graph Options B&W option to display a black and white graph and see the hatch patterns.

2. Use the Name Create option to save SALES_PIE again and execute the File Save command to update the worksheet on the disk.
3. Print the new pie chart you have created.

Lesson 6: Creating a Line Graph

A **line graph** represents each data value by a point at an appropriate distance above the horizontal axis. Related points are designated by the same symbol and are connected by line segments. Line graphs are useful for plotting values that change over time. For example, the Beaver Canoe Company could use a line graph to plot the units of three canoe models sold over the past five years. Because line graphs emphasize the continuity of data over time, they are especially handy for identifying trends and making projections.

Step 1: Create the Worksheet

Let's create the line graph we just described for the Beaver Canoe Company. You can enter the data in an empty area of the SALES worksheet. Follow these directions to enter the data:

Press **F5**
Type **b12**
Press **Enter**
Type **1987**
Press **Right Arrow**
Type **1988**
Press **Right Arrow**
Type **1989**
Press **Right Arrow**
Type **1990**
Press **Right Arrow**
Type **1991**
Press **Down Arrow**
Press **End**
Press **Left Arrow**
Type **Beaver Canoe**
Press **Right Arrow**
Type **10000**
Press **Right Arrow**
Type **8000**
Press **Right Arrow**
Type **7000**
Press **Right Arrow**
Type **6500**
Press **Right Arrow**
Type **6000**
Press **Down Arrow**
Press **End**
Press **Left Arrow**
Type **Mohawk Canoe**
Press **Right Arrow**
Type **4500**
Press **Right Arrow**
Type **5500**
Press **Right Arrow**
Type **6000**
Press **Right Arrow**
Type **5200**
Press **Right Arrow**
Type **5500**
Press **Down Arrow**
Press **End**

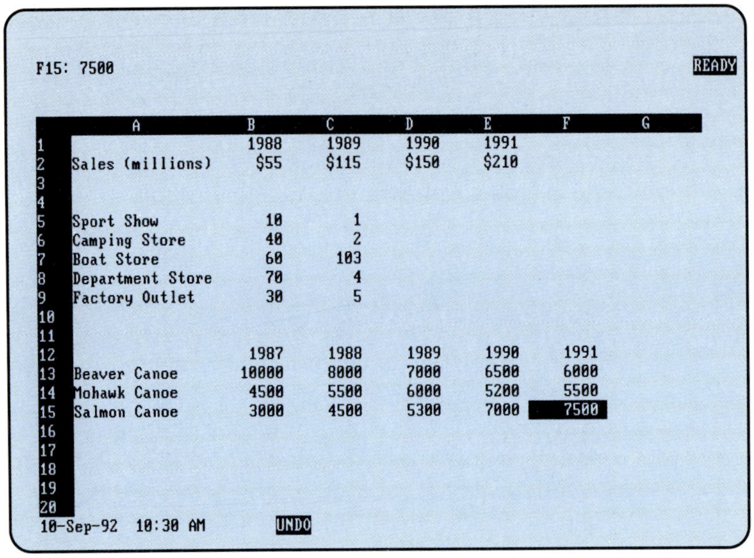

F15: 7500 READY

	A	B	C	D	E	F	G
1		1988	1989	1990	1991		
2	Sales (millions)	$55	$115	$150	$210		
3							
4							
5	Sport Show	10	1				
6	Camping Store	40	2				
7	Boat Store	60	103				
8	Department Store	70	4				
9	Factory Outlet	30	5				
10							
11							
12		1987	1988	1989	1990	1991	
13	Beaver Canoe	10000	8000	7000	6500	6000	
14	Mohawk Canoe	4500	5500	6000	5200	5500	
15	Salmon Canoe	3000	4500	5300	7000	7500	
16							
17							
18							
19							
20							

10-Sep-92 10:30 AM UNDO

Figure 8 The Line Graph Data

Press **Left Arrow**
Type **Salmon Canoe**
Press **Right Arrow**
Type **3000**
Press **Right Arrow**
Type **4500**
Press **Right Arrow**
Type **5300**
Press **Right Arrow**
Type **7000**
Press **Right Arrow**
Type **7500**
Press **Enter**

The numbers you have entered represent the units sold of each type of canoe for each year. Your screen should look like Figure 8. Check your work against Figure 8 and correct any mistakes you find.

Step 2: Save the Worksheet

It is a good idea to save your worksheet before you generate the graph. Execute the File Save command:

Type **/fs**
Press **Enter**
Type **r**

Step 3: Execute the Graph Reset Graph Command

Since you already have a graph defined as the current graph, execute the Graph Reset Graph command to clear the settings.

Type **/grg**

Step 4: Specify the Type Line Option

Now tell 1-2-3 that you want to create a line graph:

Type **tL**

Incidentally, Line is the default type of graph. If you do not select a graph type, 1-2-3 assumes you want to do a line graph.

Step 5: Specify the Data Ranges

This line graph will have four data ranges: X, A, B, and C. The X data range will contain the years 1987 through 1991. The A data range will contain the unit sales of Beaver canoes, B will contain the unit sales of Mohawk canoes, and C will contain the unit sales of Salmon canoes. The Group option from the Graph menu lets you specify several data ranges at once if they are in consecutive rows or columns. Follow these directions to specify all of the data ranges for the line graph:

Type **g**
Type **b12..f15**
Press **Enter**
Type **r**

B12 to F12 is now the X data range, B13 to F13 is the A data range, B14 to F14 is the B data range, and B15 to F15 is the C data range.

Step 6: Add Titles

Use the Options Titles command to add titles to the line graph:

Type **otf**
Type **Beaver Canoe Company**
Press **Enter**
Type **ts**
Type **Canoe Model Sales Comparison**
Press **Enter**
Type **tx**
Type **Year**
Press **Enter**
Type **ty**
Type **Number of Units Sold**
Press **Enter**

Step 7: Specify Lines and Symbols

Let's have the line graph display each point as a symbol and connect the points with lines. A different symbol will be used for each data range. Select the Format Graph Both Quit option:

Type **fgbq**

Figure 9 The Line Graph

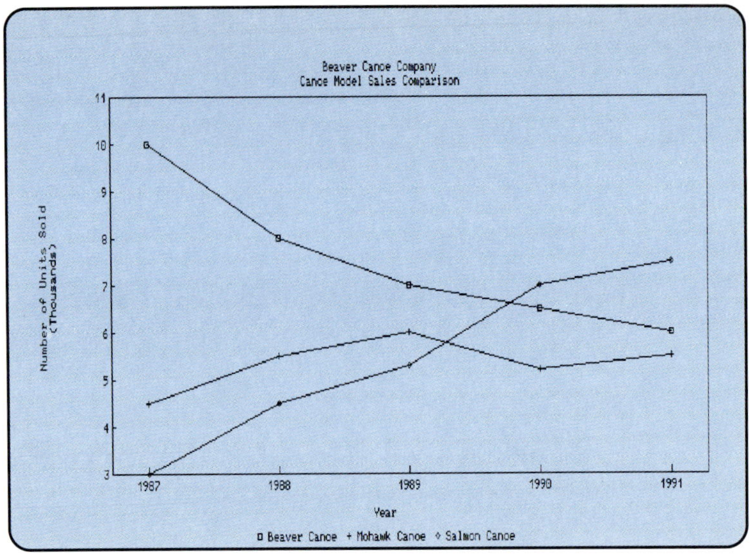

Step 8: Add a Legend

A legend identifies the data range represented by each symbol in the graph. Follow these directions to use the labels in cells A13 through A15 as the legend:

Type **Lr**
Type **a13..a15**
Press **Enter**

Quit the Options submenu and return to the Graph menu:

Type **q**

Step 9: View the Graph

Now you can view the graph you have specified. Select the View option from the Graph menu:

Type **v**

Your screen should look like Figure 9. When you are finished looking at the graph, return to the Graph menu:

Press **Escape**

Step 10: Save the Graph

Select the Save option from the Graph menu to save your line graph in a file named LINE.PIC:

Type **s**
Type **line**
Press **Enter**

Step 11: Name the Graph

Since you now have three graphs associated with the SALES worksheet, you should name the line graph. Execute the Name Create option and specify SALES_LINE as the name of the graph:

Type **nc**
Type **sales_line**
Press **Enter**

Quit the Graph menu and return to READY mode:

Type **q**

Step 12: Save the Worksheet

You have saved the graph to a file named LINE.PIC and named the graph SALES_LINE, but you must also save the worksheet to preserve the graph settings you have specified. Execute the File Save command and replace the worksheet file on the disk:

Type **/fs**
Press **Enter**
Type **r**

Practice

1. You can tell Lotus 1-2-3 to label the points in the line graph with their actual values. Labeling the points lets the viewer easily see their exact values. Follow these directions to place labels above the points in the line graph:

   Type **/godg**
   Type **b13..f15**
   Press **Enter**
   Type **raqqv**

   When you are finished looking at the graph, press any key to return to the Graph menu.
2. Use the Name Create option to save SALES_LINE again and execute the File Save command to update the worksheet on the disk.
3. Print the new line graph you have created.

Lesson 7: Creating a Stacked Bar Graph

A **stacked bar graph** is a variation of the basic bar graph that shows components and total amounts for each category. For example, you could present the unit sales of the three types of canoes for five years in a stacked bar graph. Each bar would represent the total number of units sold in a year. Each bar would be divided into three stacked sections, one section for each type of canoe. Let's create such a graph. You don't have to enter the data because it already exists in the table you created for Lesson 6.

Step 1: Execute the Graph Reset Graph Command

Since you already have a graph defined as the current graph, execute the Graph Reset Graph command to clear the settings.

Type **/grg**

Step 2: Specify the Type Stack-Bar Option

Now tell 1-2-3 that you want to create a stacked bar graph:

Type **ts**

Step 3: Specify the Data Ranges

This stacked bar graph will have the same four data ranges as the line graph you created in Lesson 6. Use the Group option to specify the four data ranges:

Type **g**
Type **b12..f15**
Press **Enter**
Type **r**

Step 4: Add Titles

Use the Options Titles command to add titles to the stacked bar graph:

Type **otf**
Type **Beaver Canoe Company**
Press **Enter**
Type **ts**
Type **Five Year Unit Sales**
Press **Enter**
Type **tx**
Type **Year**
Press **Enter**
Type **ty**
Type **Number of Units Sold**
Press **Enter**

Step 5: Add a Legend

A legend identifies the stack pattern that goes with each canoe model. Follow these directions to use the labels in cells A13 through A15 as the legend:

Type **Lr**
Type **a13..a15**
Press **Enter**

Quit the Options submenu and return to the Graph menu:

Type **q**

Step 6: View the Graph

Now you can view the graph you have specified. Select the View option from the Graph menu:

Type **v**

Your screen should look like Figure 10. When you are finished looking at the graph, return to the Graph menu:

Press **Escape**

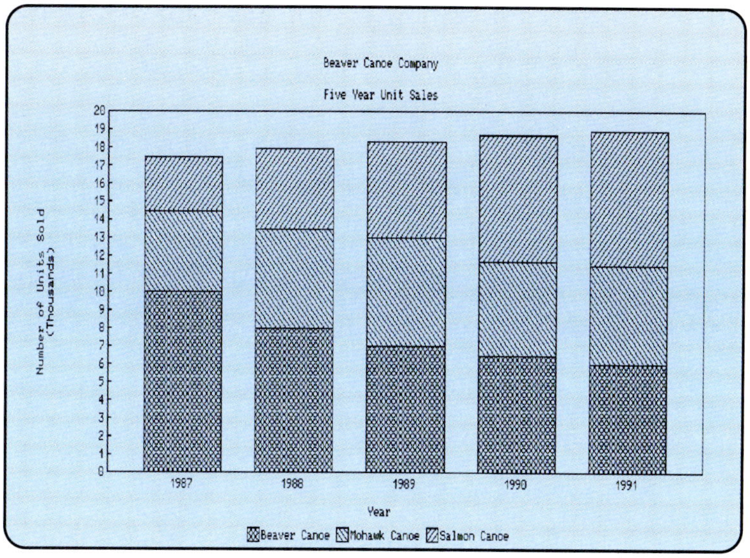

Figure 10 The Stacked Bar Graph

Step 7: Save the Graph

Select the Save option from the Graph menu to save your stacked bar graph in a file named STACK.PIC:

Type **s**
Type **stack**
Press **Enter**

Step 8: Name the Graph

Since you now have four graphs associated with the SALES worksheet, you should name the stacked bar graph. Execute the Name Create option and specify SALES_STACK as the name of the graph:

Type **nc**
Type **sales_stack**
Press **Enter**

Quit the Graph menu and return to READY mode:

Type **q**

Step 9: Save the Worksheet

You have saved the graph to a file named STACK.PIC and named the graph SALES_STACK, but you must also save the worksheet to preserve the graph settings you have specified. Execute the File Save command and replace the worksheet file on the disk:

Type **/fs**
Press **Enter**
Type **r**

Practice

1. You can easily create a bar graph from the same data that will show a separate bar for each canoe model. Execute the Graph Type Bar command, then view the graph you have created. This is a good example of a bar graph with multiple data ranges. When you are finished viewing the graph, change it back to a stacked bar graph, then return to READY mode.
2. Print the stacked bar graph you have created.

Lesson 8: Creating an XY Graph

An **XY graph,** sometimes called a **scatterplot,** shows the relationship between two or more variables. For example, XY graphs can be used to show correlations between sales and profits, price and the number of units sold, and per capita income and life expectancy. Let's create an XY graph that shows the relationship between the price of a canoe and the number of units sold for the Beaver Canoe Company.

Step 1: Create the Worksheet

You can enter the data for this new graph in an empty area of the SALES worksheet. Follow these directions to enter and format the data:

Type **/rfc0**
Press **Enter**
Type **b20..b28**
Press **Enter**
Press **F5**
Type **a19**
Press **Enter**
Type **"Units Sold**
Press **Right Arrow**
Type **"Price**
Press **Down Arrow**
Type **100**
Press **Down Arrow**
Type **200**
Press **Down Arrow**
Type **300**
Press **Down Arrow**
Type **400**
Press **Down Arrow**
Type **500**
Press **Down Arrow**
Type **600**
Press **Down Arrow**
Type **700**
Press **Down Arrow**
Type **800**
Press **Down Arrow**
Type **900**
Press **Enter**
Press **F5**

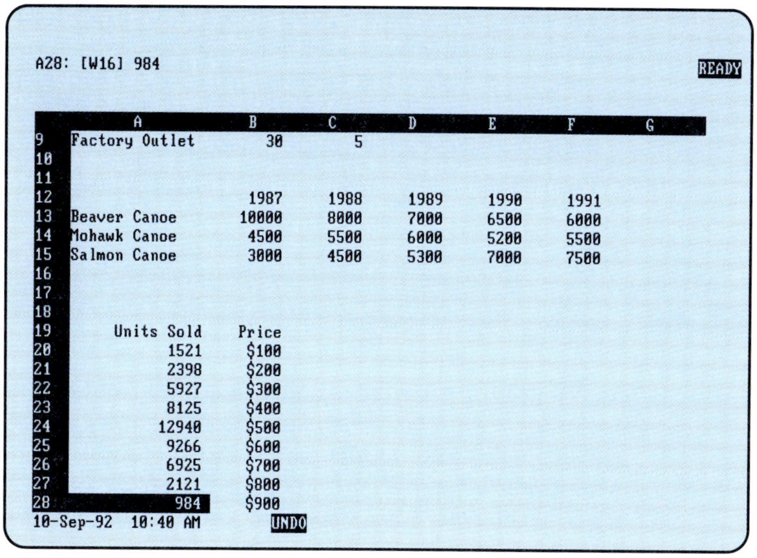

***Figure 11* The XY Graph Data**

Type **a20**
Press **Enter**
Type **1521**
Press **Down Arrow**
Type **2398**
Press **Down Arrow**
Type **5927**
Press **Down Arrow**
Type **8125**
Press **Down Arrow**
Type **12940**
Press **Down Arrow**
Type **9266**
Press **Down Arrow**
Type **6925**
Press **Down Arrow**
Type **2121**
Press **Down Arrow**
Type **984**
Press **Enter**

Your screen should look like Figure 11. Check your work against Figure 11 and correct any mistakes you find.

Step 2: Save the Worksheet

It is a good idea to save your worksheet before you generate the graph. Execute the File Save command:

Type **/fs**
Press **Enter**
Type **r**

Step 3: Execute the Graph Reset Graph Command

Since you already have a graph defined as the current graph, execute the Graph Reset Graph command to clear the settings.

Type **/grg**

Step 4: Specify the Type XY Option

Now tell 1-2-3 that you want to create an XY graph:

Type **tx**

Step 5: Specify the Data Ranges

This XY graph will have two data ranges: X and A. The X data range will contain the values for canoe prices. The A data range will contain the number of units sold at that price. Follow these directions to specify the data ranges for the XY graph:

Type **x**
Type **b20..b28**
Press **Enter**
Type **a**
Type **a20..a28**
Press **Enter**

Step 6: Add Titles

Use the Options Titles command to add titles to the line graph:

Type **otf**
Type **Beaver Canoe Company**
Press **Enter**
Type **ts**
Type **Canoe Price vs. Units Sold**
Press **Enter**
Type **tx**
Type **Price per Canoe (dollars)**
Press **Enter**
Type **ty**
Type **Number of Units Sold**
Press **Enter**

Step 7: Specify Lines and Symbols

Let's have the line graph display each point as a symbol and connect the points with lines. Select the Format Graph Both Quit option:

Type **fgbq**

Quit the Options submenu and return to the Graph menu:

Type **q**

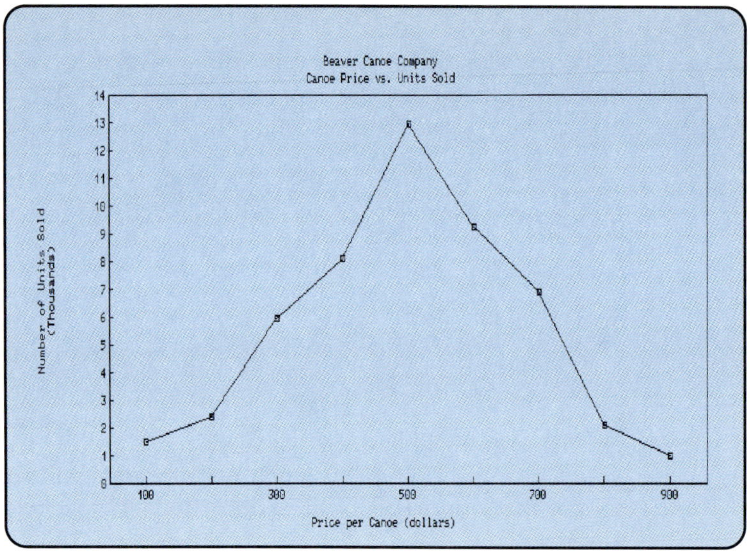

Figure 12 The XY Graph

Step 8: View the Graph

Now you can view the graph you have specified. Select the View option from the Graph menu:

Type **v**

Your screen should look like Figure 12. This graph suggests that people buy more canoes when the price is around $500. Perhaps if they are priced too low, people will think the canoes are poorly constructed and not buy them. If they are priced too high, people cannot afford them. When you are finished looking at the graph, return to the Graph menu:

Press **Escape**

Step 9: Save the Graph

Select the Save option from the Graph menu to save your line graph in a file named XY.PIC:

Type **s**
Type **xy**
Press **Enter**

Step 10: Name the Graph

Since you now have five graphs associated with the SALES worksheet, you should name the XY graph. Execute the Name Create option and specify SALES_XY as the name of the graph:

Type **nc**
Type **sales_xy**
Press **Enter**

Quit the Graph menu and return to READY mode:

Type **q**

Step 11: Save the Worksheet

You have saved the graph to a file named XY.PIC and named the graph SALES_XY, but you must also save the worksheet to preserve the graph settings you have specified. Execute the File Save command and replace the worksheet file on the disk:

Type **/fs**
Press **Enter**
Type **r**

Practice

1. Change the XY graph so that it displays symbols, but not line segments. Now change the graph to display line segments, but not symbols. Finally, change the XY graph so that it displays both symbols and lines again.
2. Print the XY graph you have created.

Lesson 9: Creating a Data Base Worksheet

A data base is an organized collection of one or more files of related data. A worksheet, which stores data in a table format, can be used as a simple data base. Although a spreadsheet package is no match for a true data base management system such as dBASE IV, you can store, sort, find, and extract data in a worksheet. As an example, let's use Lotus 1-2-3 to set up a personal property inventory.

Step 1: Erase the Worksheet

If the SALES worksheet is still on your screen, execute the Worksheet Erase command to clear it from memory and start with a blank worksheet:

Type **/wey**

Step 2: Set Up the Worksheet for the Data Base

The data base will be a list of personal property, which you might create for insurance purposes. Column A will hold short item descriptions, column B will hold the purchase dates, and column C will hold the amounts paid. Column C will also be summed, so you can maintain a property value total.

Since column A will hold item descriptions, you should widen it. Execute the Worksheet Column Set-Width command to widen column A to 40 characters:

Type **/wcs40**
Press **Enter**

Column B will hold dates; widen it to 10 characters and format it to display dates:

Press **Right Arrow**
Type **/wcs10**
Press **Enter**
Type **/rfd**
Press **Enter**
Type **b1..b100**
Press **Enter**

Column C will hold dollar amounts. Widen it to 11 characters and format it to display currency values:

Press **Right Arrow**
Type **/wcs11**
Press **Enter**
Type **/rfc**
Press **Enter**
Type **c1..c100**
Press **Enter**

Step 3: Enter the Field Names

Each row in a data base worksheet represents a record, which contains all the data about a particular item. Each column in a data base worksheet represents a field, which contains an individual data value for each record. The first row in a data base worksheet must contain the names of the fields. Follow these directions to enter the field names:

Type **"AMOUNT**
Press **Left Arrow**
Type **^DATE**
Press **Left Arrow**
Type **^ITEM**
Press **Down Arrow**

Step 4: Enter the Data

Enter the data from the following table into the worksheet. The items go in column A, the date formulas go in column B, and the amounts go in column C. Note that each date is entered as a formula made up of the @DATE function. This function converts the year, month, and day numbers into a single number that 1-2-3 uses to keep track of dates. You will learn more about date numbers in the next chapter.

Personal Property Data

Item	Date	Amount
Guitar, Yamaha	@date(86,04,13)	363.50
Tent, Eureka	@date(87,06,18)	99.95
Lamp, K-Mart	@date(85,01,15)	39.97
Microwave Oven, Sears	@date(86,03,12)	386.64
Answering Machine, Panasonic	@date(88,03,17)	127.47
Backpack, L.L. Bean	@date(89,08,08)	94.50
Walkman, Sony	@date(88,03,10)	82.31
Television, Sony	@date(89,04,29)	524.75
Skis, Trak Cross Country	@date(88,01,05)	113.45
Ski Boots, Salomon	@date(88,01,05)	81.50
Telephone, AT&T	@date(87,04,15)	87.70
CD Player, Sony	@date(87,10,17)	169.00
Stereo Receiver, JVC	@date(86,10,27)	199.00
Speakers, Avid	@date(86,10,27)	156.00
VCR, Magnavox	@date(86,01,04)	318.74
Popcorn Popper, Westbend	@date(88,01,02)	22.15
File Cabinet, Sears	@date(86,11,19)	78.45

Step 5: Enter the Formula

When you use a worksheet as a data base, you can take advantage of the computational abilities of the spreadsheet program. Adding up the amounts spent on each item in the property inventory is easy.

Press **F5**
Type **c20**
Press **Enter**
Type **@sum(c2..c19)**
Press **Enter**

If you have entered the amounts and the formula correctly, the sum will be $2,945.08. Now enter a label for the total:

Press **Left Arrow**
Press **Left Arrow**
Type **"TOTAL**
Press **Enter**

Your screen should look like Figure 13.

Step 6: Save the Worksheet

Save the worksheet in a disk file before you go on to use the data.

Type **/fs**
Type **property**
Press **Enter**

The worksheet will be saved in a file named PROPERTY.WK1 (or PROPERTY.WK3 if you are using Lotus 1-2-3 Release 3.0).

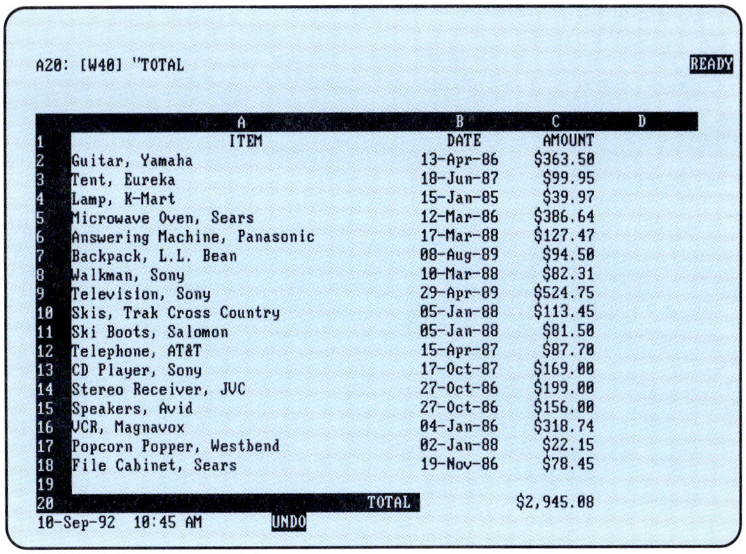

A20: [W40] "TOTAL READY

	A	B	C	D
1	ITEM	DATE	AMOUNT	
2	Guitar, Yamaha	13-Apr-86	$363.50	
3	Tent, Eureka	18-Jun-87	$99.95	
4	Lamp, K-Mart	15-Jan-85	$39.97	
5	Microwave Oven, Sears	12-Mar-86	$386.64	
6	Answering Machine, Panasonic	17-Mar-88	$127.47	
7	Backpack, L.L. Bean	08-Aug-89	$94.50	
8	Walkman, Sony	10-Mar-88	$82.31	
9	Television, Sony	29-Apr-89	$524.75	
10	Skis, Trak Cross Country	05-Jan-88	$113.45	
11	Ski Boots, Salomon	05-Jan-88	$81.50	
12	Telephone, AT&T	15-Apr-87	$87.70	
13	CD Player, Sony	17-Oct-87	$169.00	
14	Stereo Receiver, JVC	27-Oct-86	$199.00	
15	Speakers, Avid	27-Oct-86	$156.00	
16	VCR, Magnavox	04-Jan-86	$318.74	
17	Popcorn Popper, Westbend	02-Jan-88	$22.15	
18	File Cabinet, Sears	19-Nov-86	$78.45	
19				
20	TOTAL		$2,945.08	

10-Sep-92 10:45 AM UNDO

Figure 13 The Completed Data Base Worksheet

Practice Invoke the Help facility and read about the @DATE function.

Lesson 10: Sorting a Data Base Worksheet

The records in the PROPERTY data base worksheet are arranged in the order in which they were entered. Records would be easier to find if they were sorted into some predictable order. Let's tell 1-2-3 to sort the PROPERTY records by the contents of the ITEM field.

Step 1: Execute the Data Sort Command

Commands for manipulating a data base worksheet are in the Data menu. The Sort command is used to rearrange the records in a data base.

Type **/ds**

Lotus 1-2-3 will present the Data Sort menu, shown in Figure 14. If you are running Release 2.2, the program will also present the Sort Settings sheet, which displays the current settings of the Sort command.

Step 2: Specify the Data Range to be Sorted

The range to be sorted is called the data range. It should include all the records in the data base, but not the row of field names or the row with the formula for summing the AMOUNT field. Invoke the Data-Range option and specify the range of cells to be sorted:

Type **d**
Type **a2..c18**
Press **Enter**

Lotus 1-2-3 will return to the Sort menu.

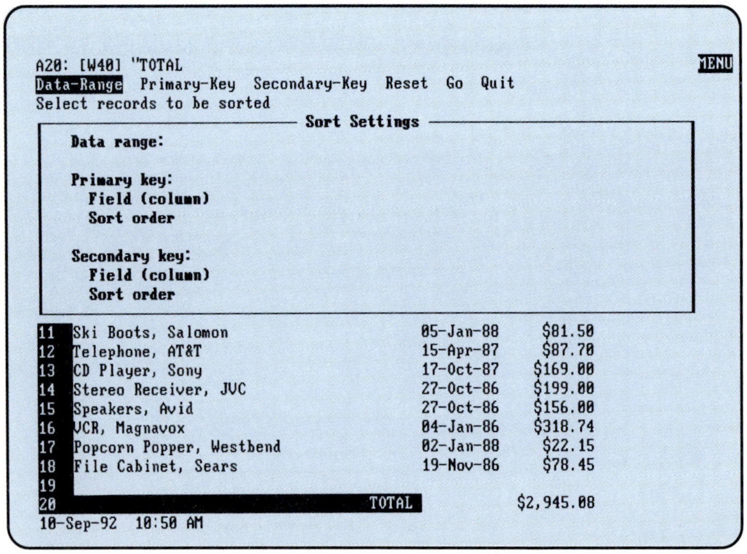

Figure 14 The Data Sort Menu

Step 3: Specify a Sort Key

A **key** is a field in a data base used to sort the records. If you want to sort the records on the basis of the contents of the ITEM field, then the ITEM field would be the key. Lotus 1-2-3 lets you specify two keys: the primary key and a secondary key. The **primary key** determines the first sort order. If you want to sort a data base on the basis of only one field, then this field is the primary key. An optional **secondary key** may be specified to determine the order of records after they are sorted first on the primary key. For example, suppose you had a mailing list data base that contained records in which several of the last names were identical. You would probably use the LAST NAME field as the primary key and the FIRST NAME field as the secondary key to sort the records. In the PROPERTY data base worksheet, you need only specify the column containing the ITEM field as the primary key.

Type **p**
Type **a1**
Press **Enter**

Note that you could have specified any cell in the ITEM column to indicate the key.

Step 4: Specify the Sort Order

Lotus 1-2-3 will prompt you to indicate the sort order. You have two choices: descending and ascending. For text, ascending order is alphabetical order from A to Z. Specify the sort order as ascending:

Type **a**
Press **Enter**

The program will return to the Sort menu.

Step 5: Execute the Sort

Now you are ready to tell 1-2-3 to sort the records. Invoke the Go option to execute the sort:

Type **g**

The records will be rearranged on the basis of the contents of the ITEM field, as shown in Figure 15.

Step 6: Save the Worksheet

If you want to keep the data base sorted in this order, you must save it to the disk.

Type **/fs**
Press **Enter**
Type **r**

Practice

1. Sort the PROPERTY data base worksheet by AMOUNT, with the most expensive item listed first. Do not save the worksheet when you are finished.
2. Sort the PROPERTY data base worksheet by DATE and then by AMOUNT. In other words, DATE should be the primary key and AMOUNT should be

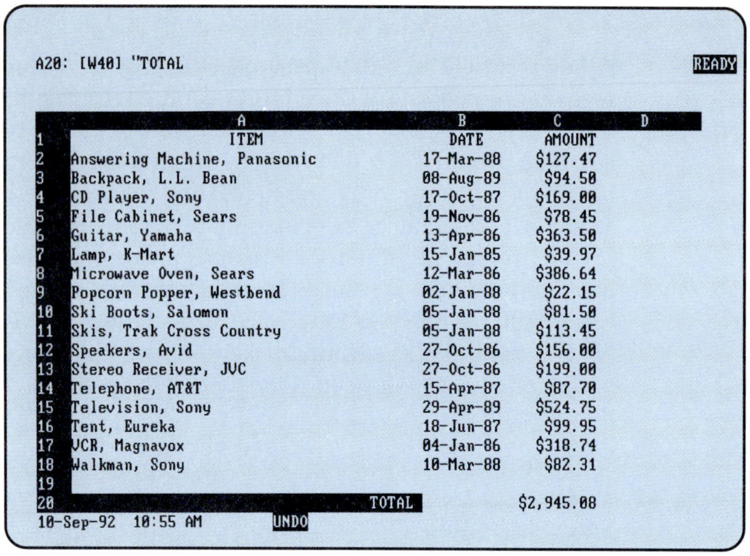

A20: [W40] "TOTAL READY

	A	B	C	D
1	ITEM	DATE	AMOUNT	
2	Answering Machine, Panasonic	17-Mar-88	$127.47	
3	Backpack, L.L. Bean	08-Aug-89	$94.50	
4	CD Player, Sony	17-Oct-87	$169.00	
5	File Cabinet, Sears	19-Nov-86	$78.45	
6	Guitar, Yamaha	13-Apr-86	$363.50	
7	Lamp, K-Mart	15-Jan-85	$39.97	
8	Microwave Oven, Sears	12-Mar-86	$386.64	
9	Popcorn Popper, Westbend	02-Jan-88	$22.15	
10	Ski Boots, Salomon	05-Jan-88	$81.50	
11	Skis, Trak Cross Country	05-Jan-88	$113.45	
12	Speakers, Avid	27-Oct-86	$156.00	
13	Stereo Receiver, JVC	27-Oct-86	$199.00	
14	Telephone, AT&T	15-Apr-87	$87.70	
15	Television, Sony	29-Apr-89	$524.75	
16	Tent, Eureka	18-Jun-87	$99.95	
17	VCR, Magnavox	04-Jan-86	$318.74	
18	Walkman, Sony	10-Mar-88	$82.31	
19				
20	TOTAL		$2,945.08	

10-Sep-92 10:55 AM UNDO

Figure 15 Records Sorted by ITEM

the secondary key. Arrange the records so that the oldest item is first. Within each date, list the most expensive item last. Do not save the worksheet when you are finished. Instead, retrieve the PROPERTY worksheet on the disk, which is sorted by ITEM.

Lesson 11: Searching a Data Base Worksheet

Creating a data base is a way to store and organize large quantities of information. One of the most common operations performed on a data base is searching it for one or more records. The PROPERTY data base worksheet contains only 17 records, so finding a particular record would not be difficult. Most data bases, however, have many more records. Imagine trying to find a particular record in a data base with hundreds or even thousands of records. Fortunately, Lotus 1-2-3 has a command that can locate records for you.

Step 1: Set Up the Criteria Range

Suppose you want to search PROPERTY for all items that cost $300 or more. In 1-2-3 you must set up a **query** to search a data base worksheet. The first step is to set up a range in which to enter the **criteria,** which are the search requirements. The criteria range consists of at least two rows: the first row must include one or more field names and the second row must include one or more expressions that specify the field values you want to find. To set up the criteria range, you can copy the field names from the first row to a blank portion of the worksheet. It is a good idea to copy all of the field names, even if you don't need them all at the moment, so that you can easily change the criteria later. Follow these directions to copy the field names to a blank area of the worksheet:

Press **Home**
Type **/ca1..c1**
Press **Enter**
Type **j1**
Press **Enter**

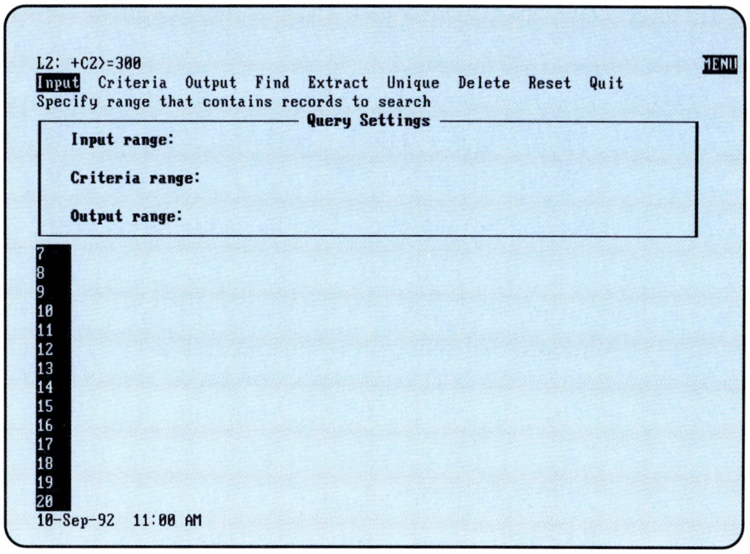

Figure 16 The Data Query Menu

Press **F5**
Type **j1**
Press **Enter**

Note that when you use the Copy command, 1-2-3 copies only the cell contents, not cell widths. Consequently, the widths of cells J1 through L1 do not match the widths of cells A1 through C1.

Step 2: Enter the Criterion

You want to search for those records with AMOUNT values equal to at least $300. In this case, the single criterion would be a logical formula that determines if a number in the AMOUNT field is greater than or equal to 300. Follow these directions to enter the criterion in the cell beneath the AMOUNT field name:

Press **Right Arrow**
Press **Right Arrow**
Press **Down Arrow**
Type **+c2>=300**
Press **Enter**

Note that you use the cell address of the first entry in the AMOUNT field for the criterion. Lotus 1-2-3 will display 0 in cell L2 as the result of that formula because the value in cell C2 is less than 300.

Step 3: Execute the Data Query Command

To search a data base worksheet, you use options from the Data Query menu.

Type **/dq**

Lotus 1-2-3 will display the Data Query menu. If you are running Release 2.2, it will also display the Query Settings sheet (see Figure 16).

Step 4: Specify the Criteria Range

Now you must tell 1-2-3 to use the criteria range you have set up. Select the Criteria option and specify the location of the cells that make up the criteria range:

Type **cj1..L2**
Press **Enter**

The program will return to the Data Query menu.

Step 5: Specify the Input Range

The range of cells you want to search is called the input range. Unlike the data range for a sort command, the input range must include the field names in addition to the data records. Select the Input option and specify the input range:

Type **ia1..c18**
Press **Enter**

The program will return to the Data Query menu.

Step 6: Begin the Search

Now that the criteria and input ranges have been specified, you can begin the search for the records that match your criterion. Select the Find option from the Data Query menu:

Type **f**

The mode indicator will change to FIND, and 1-2-3 will highlight the first record in the input range that matches the criterion in the criteria range (see Figure 17).

Step 7: Continue the Search

When 1-2-3 is in FIND mode, you simply press the Down Arrow key to advance to the next matching record.

Press **Down Arrow**

You can also use the Up Arrow key to see the previous record that matches the criterion.

Press **Up Arrow**

Keep pressing the Down Arrow key to see the rest of the records with an AMOUNT greater than or equal to $300:

Press **Down Arrow** (4 times)

Lotus 1-2-3 will beep if you press Down Arrow or Up Arrow when no more matching records are found.

Note that you can edit cell contents when 1-2-3 is in FIND mode. This is handy for updating only those records that match certain criteria.

Step 8: End the Search

Follow these directions to end the search and move to A1 when you are finished looking at the records:

Press **Enter**
Type **q**
Press **Home**

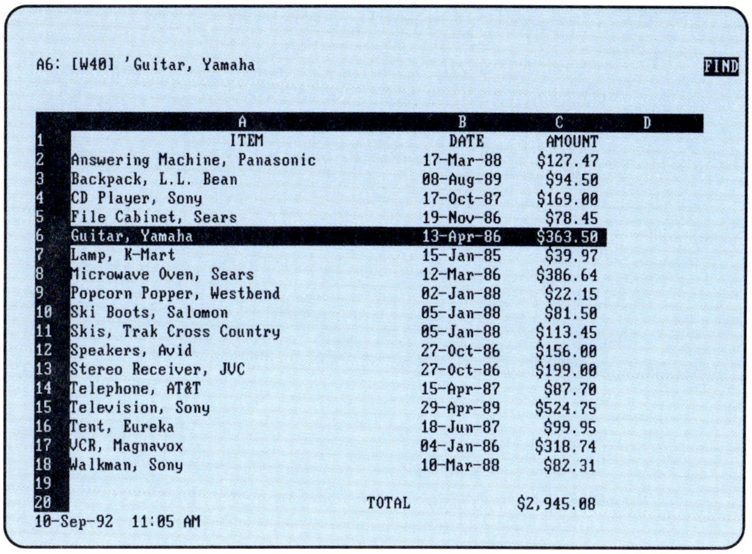

A6: [W40] 'Guitar, Yamaha FIND

	A	B	C	D
1	ITEM	DATE	AMOUNT	
2	Answering Machine, Panasonic	17-Mar-88	$127.47	
3	Backpack, L.L. Bean	08-Aug-89	$94.50	
4	CD Player, Sony	17-Oct-87	$169.00	
5	File Cabinet, Sears	19-Nov-86	$78.45	
6	Guitar, Yamaha	13-Apr-86	$363.50	
7	Lamp, K-Mart	15-Jan-85	$39.97	
8	Microwave Oven, Sears	12-Mar-86	$386.64	
9	Popcorn Popper, Westbend	02-Jan-88	$22.15	
10	Ski Boots, Salomon	05-Jan-88	$81.50	
11	Skis, Trak Cross Country	05-Jan-88	$113.45	
12	Speakers, Avid	27-Oct-86	$156.00	
13	Stereo Receiver, JVC	27-Oct-86	$199.00	
14	Telephone, AT&T	15-Apr-87	$87.70	
15	Television, Sony	29-Apr-89	$524.75	
16	Tent, Eureka	18-Jun-87	$99.95	
17	VCR, Magnavox	04-Jan-86	$318.74	
18	Walkman, Sony	10-Mar-88	$82.31	
19				
20		TOTAL	$2,945.08	

10-Sep-92 11:05 AM

Figure 17 The First Matching Record Has Been Found

Step 9: Save the Worksheet

If you will want to use your criteria range and criterion again, you must save the PROPERTY worksheet.

Type **/fs**
Press **Enter**
Type **r**

Practice

1. Lotus 1-2-3 offers three special characters that can be used in criteria when searching for text: *, ?, and ~. The * (asterisk) matches any number of characters. For example, *Ski** matches *Ski lodge, Skis, Skit,* and *Skipper.* The ? (question mark) matches any single character. For example, *Ski?* matches *Skis* and *Skit,* but not *Ski lodge* and *Skipper.* The * and ? operate just like the DOS global filename characters. The ~ (tilde) matches any label except the label that follows it. For example, *~Ski* matches every label that does not begin with *Ski.* Use one of these special characters to search PROPERTY for all records that begin with *Ski* in the ITEM field.
2. Search PROPERTY for all records of items purchased after January 1, 1988.

Lesson 12: Extracting Records from a Data Base Worksheet

The Extract option of the Data Query menu lets you copy records that meet your criteria and place them in a range outside the data base. Although the term Extract implies that the records are removed from the original data base, this is not so. The Extract option merely copies the records, leaving the originals intact. This option is handy for working with a subset of a data base. For example, you could extract all records with an AMOUNT greater than or equal to $300, then print only those records.

Step 1: Specify the Criterion

In the previous lesson, you already set up the criteria range as J1 through L2 and the input range as A2 through C18. Enter the criterion again in cell L2:

Press **F5**
Type **L2**
Press **Enter**
Type **+c2>=300**
Press **Enter**

Step 2: Set Up the Output Range

The output range is the cells where 1-2-3 will copy the records that match your criteria. The first row of the output range must contain the names of the fields that you want to extract. You do not have to extract all of the fields in the original data base. For example, you can extract only the ITEM and AMOUNT, and not the DATE. Move to a blank area of the worksheet, widen the columns, and enter the names of the fields you want to extract:

Press **F5**
Type **j10**
Press **Enter**
Type **/wcs40**
Press **Enter**
Type **^ITEM**
Press **Right Arrow**
Type **/wcs11**
Press **Enter**
Type **"AMOUNT**
Press **Enter**

Step 3: Specify the Output Range

In most cases, you will not know exactly how many records 1-2-3 will find. If you specify the single row containing the field names as the output range, 1-2-3 will use as many rows as necessary for the extracted records. You should make sure you have no existing data below the row you specify. Execute the Data Query Output command and specify the output range:

Type **/dqoj10..k10**
Press **Enter**

The program will return to the Data Query menu.

Step 4: Extract the Records

You are now ready to extract the items and amounts of records with amounts greater than or equal to $300. Select the Extract option and then quit the Data Query menu:

Type **e**
Type **q**

Your screen should look like Figure 18. At this point, you could print only these records or use them for other calculations.

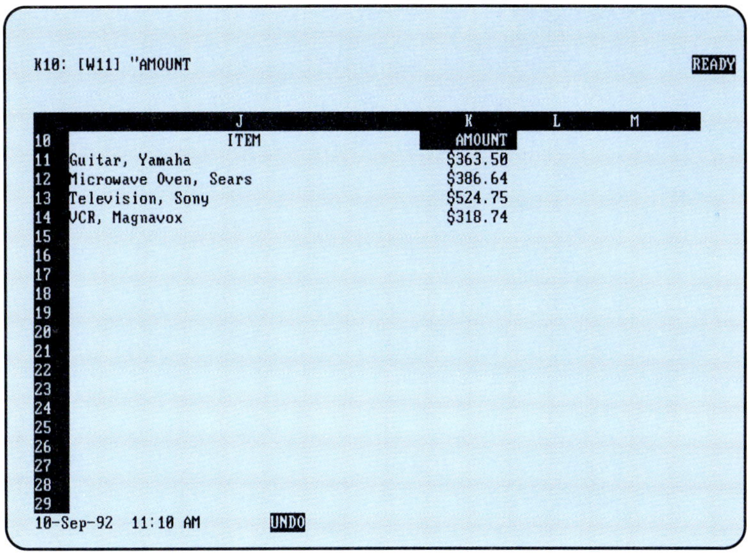

Figure 18 Records Extracted from the Data Base

Practice Extract the items and amounts of records with a DATE of January 1, 1988, or later. You can use the same output range.

Lesson 13: Using the Data Base Functions

Lotus 1-2-3 has a set of functions designed especially for data base worksheets. The data base functions scan a data base, select the records that match the criteria in the criteria range, then perform calculations on only the selected values. Let's briefly examine the Lotus 1-2-3 data base functions.

Step 1: Try the @DCOUNT Function

Suppose you want to know how many PROPERTY records have an AMOUNT value greater than or equal to $300. The @DCOUNT function counts the non-blank cells in a field of a data base. It considers only those records that meet the specified criteria. Follow these directions to see how @DCOUNT works:

Press **F5**
Type **m10**
Press **Enter**
Type **@dcount(a1..c18,0,j1..L2)**
Press **Enter**

The result should be 4 (see Figure 19). The first parameter of the @DCOUNT function is the input range, which in this case is A1 to C18. The second parameter is the field number. For the data base functions, fields are numbered from the left starting at zero. In this case, it does not matter which field is checked; the 0 refers to the ITEM field. The third parameter of the @DCOUNT function is the criteria range, which is J1 to L2.

Figure 19 The @DCOUNT Function

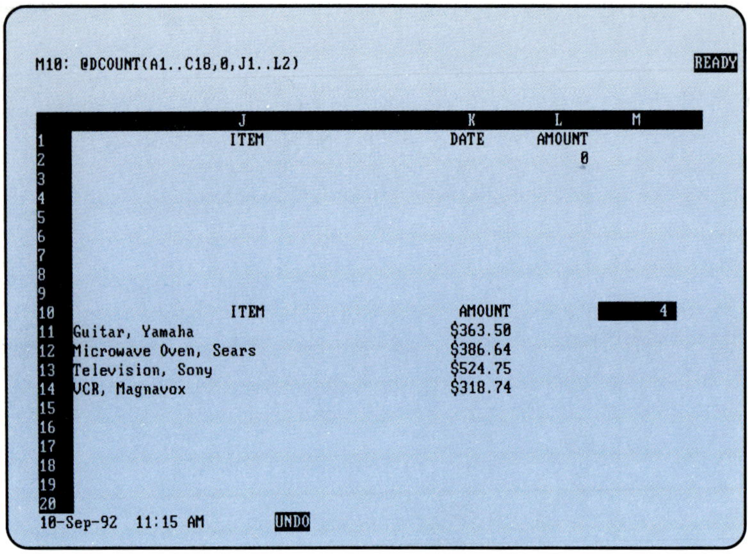

Step 2: Try the Other Data Base Functions

Lotus 1-2-3 has six other data base functions. Let's try some of them.

Type **@davg(a1..c18,2,j1..L2)**
Press **Enter**

The @DAVG function computes the average value of the specified field, in this case field 2, which is the AMOUNT field. It uses only those records that meet the specified criteria. Hence, the average you see is that of records with amounts greater than or equal to $300.

Type **@dmax(a1..c18,2,j1..L2)**
Press **Enter**

The @DMAX function returns the largest value of the specified field given the criteria.

Type **@dmin(a1..c18,2,j1..L2)**
Press **Enter**

The @DMIN function returns the smallest value of the specified field given the criteria.

Type **@dsum(a1..c18,2,j1..L2)**
Press **Enter**

The @DSUM function computes the sum of the values in the specified field given the criteria.

Two other data base functions are available in Lotus 1-2-3 for computing statistics: @DSTD and @DVAR. The @DSTD function computes the population standard deviation of the values in the specified field given the criteria. The @DVAR function computes the population variance of the values in the specified field given the criteria.

Practice Change the criterion and use a data base function to compute the average amount of PROPERTY items that cost less than $300.

Using Microcomputer Hardware

Advances in microprocessor technology are a primary reason for the growing role microcomputers now play in our society. Hardware determines the software that can be run, and hence profoundly influences how computers are used. You needn't become a computer engineer, but it is important to have a basic understanding of the hardware components that make up a typical system. In this section, we examine the physical parts of a microcomputer and see how they work. We discuss what makes the newest microprocessors so powerful. Memory, disk drives, displays, keyboards, mice, expansion boards, printers, and modems are all covered. Learning about these devices will help you realize what computers can do, given the right software. Once you become familiar with the hardware of microcomputer systems, you can then concentrate on the software that puts it to work.

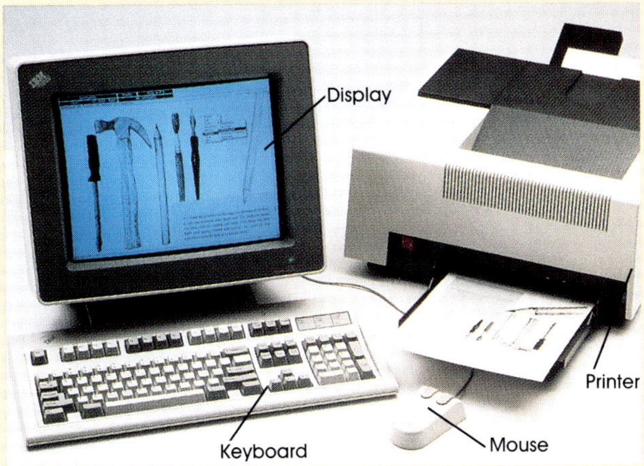

The four basic hardware components of a microcomputer system are the display, system unit, keyboard, and printer. The display is a screen to present text and graphics. The system unit contains the central processing unit (CPU), control circuitry, memory, and disk drives. The keyboard is the primary device for entering commands and data, but many microcomputers also use a mouse. Finally, the auxiliary printer is used to produce text and graphics on paper. *(IBM)*

IBM's PS/2 family. *(IBM)*

The Macintosh SE. *(Apple Computer, Inc.)*

The Mac II. *(Apple Computer, Inc.)*

Lap-top and portable computers offer portability and power in a package that can weigh less than 10 pounds. *(Toshiba, below; Compaq, right)*

(b)

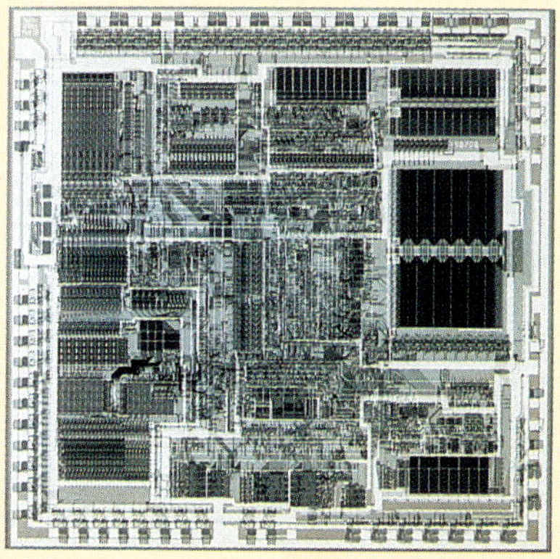

(a) The Intel 4004, the first microprocessor. (b) The Intel 80286 chip. (c) The Intel 80386 chip. *(Intel Corp.)*

(a)

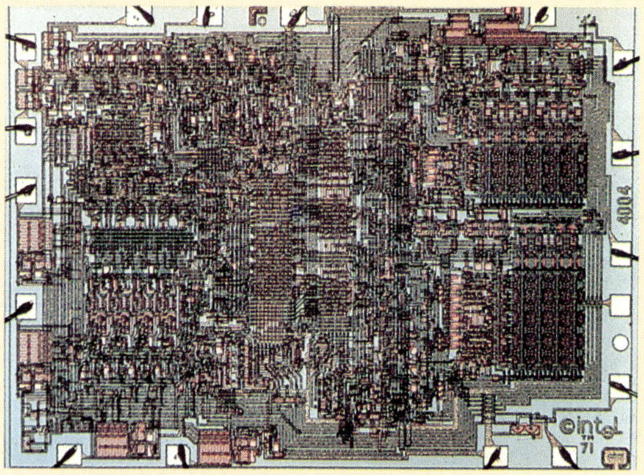

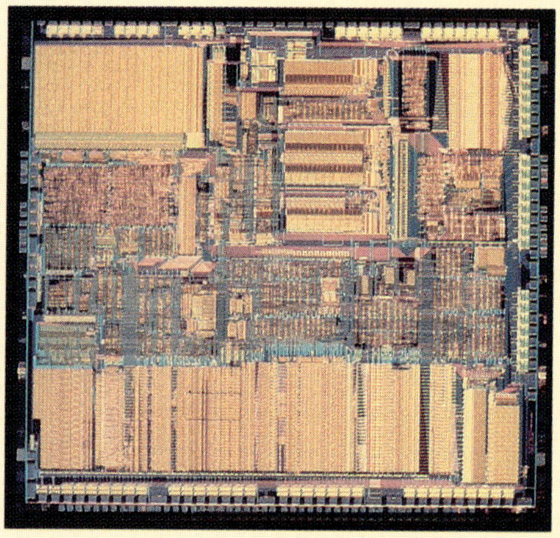

(c)

(a) This photograph shows the system unit of an IBM Personal System/2 Model 50 broken down into its major components. *(Thom O'Connor)*
(b) Here is a closeup of the motherboard. *(IBM)*

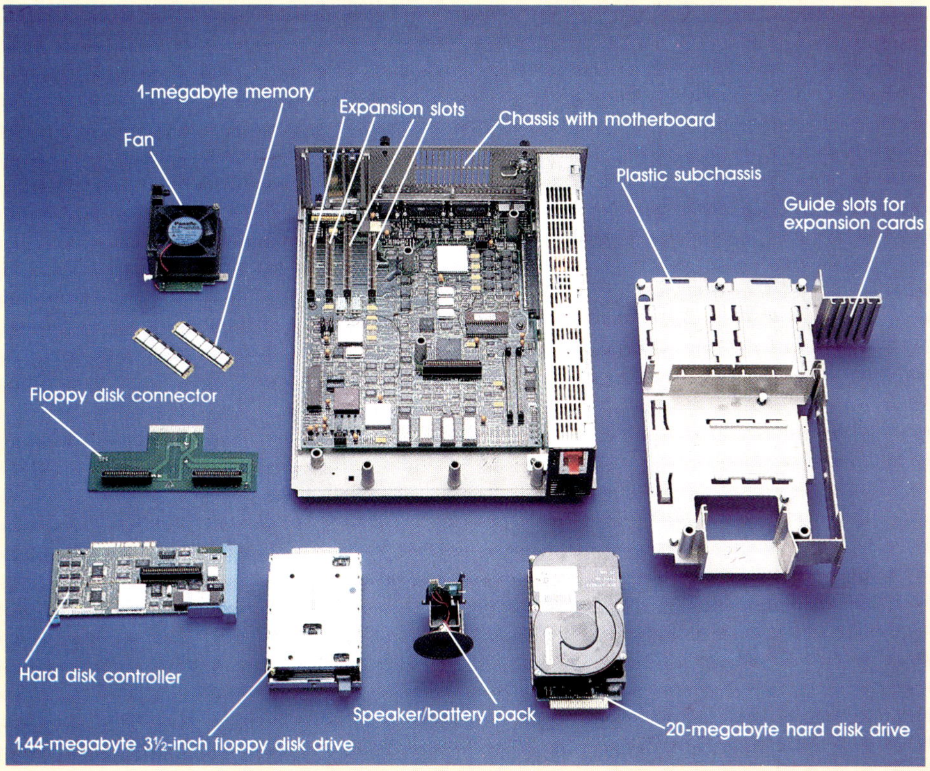

(a)

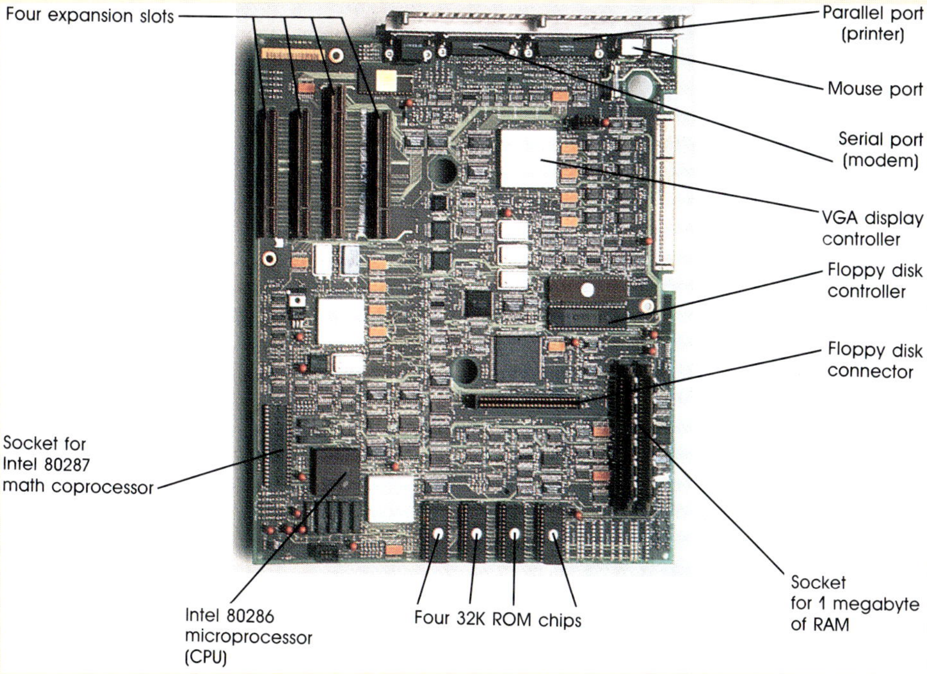

(b)

The floppy disk is a commonly used medium for storing computer programs and data. The two most commonly used sizes are (left) 5¼-inch and (right) 3½-inch disks. *(IBM)*

Seagate Technology hard disk drive. *(Seagate Technology)*

A page scanner turns artwork and photographs into digital images which can be enlarged, enhanced, and cropped by computer and later incorporated directly into printed output. *(Hewlett Packard)*

Each of these CD-ROM optical disks can store an amazing 550 megabytes—equivalent to nearly 170,000 single-spaced, typewritten pages of text. *(3M)*

The Laser Jet Series II printer from Hewlett-Packard offers publication quality printing for the office environment. This fast, quiet, high-quality office printer can merge text and graphics for desktop publishing needs. *(Hewlett Packard)*

A direct-connect modem can send information at up to 19,200 bits per second by using data compression techniques. *(Hayes Microcomputer)*

Using Lotus 1-2-3

Spreadsheet packages help users store, manipulate, analyze, and present data, most often numeric data. Many different kinds of tasks can be performed with a spreadsheet program. To give you an idea of what it's like to use this type of application software, in this section we'll create a simple income statement with Lotus 1-2-3, which is by far the most popular microcomputer spreadsheet package. An *income statement* is simply a report that lists the sources of income and expenses of a business over a given time period. The *bottom line* of an income statement shows the net profit earned, calculated by subtracting the total expenses from the total income. After we set up the income statement with Lotus 1-2-3 Release 3.0, we will make a bar graph that shows the income for each quarter of the year.

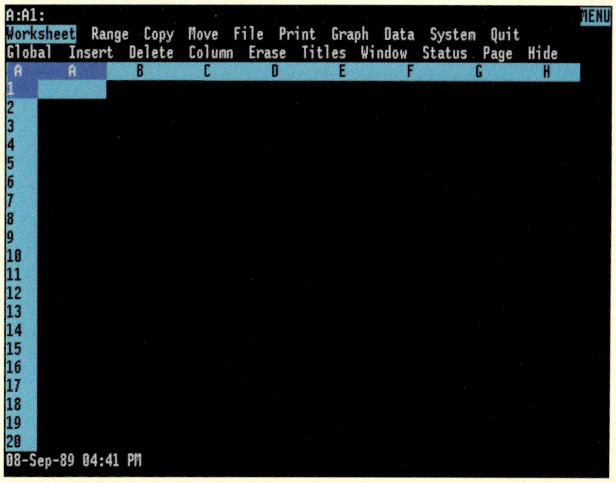

1. Lotus 1-2-3, Main menu and blank worksheet.

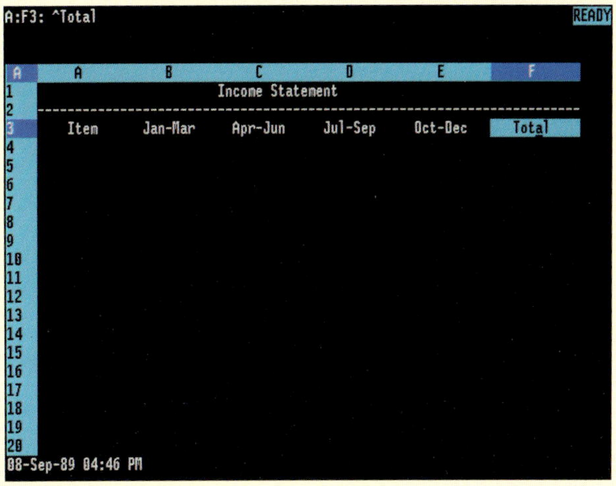

2. Most people begin by entering the text labels that will annotate the contents.

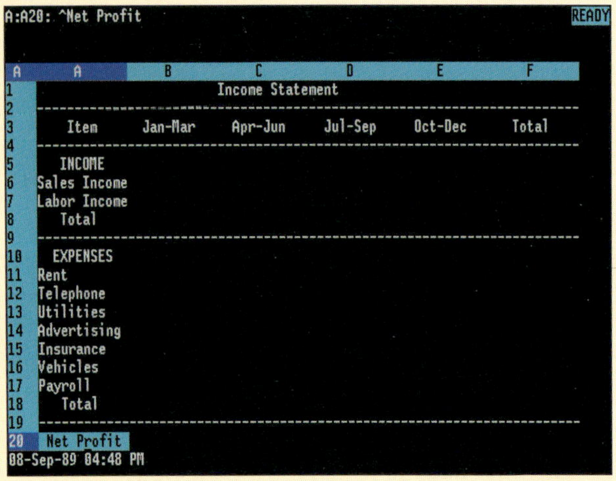

3. After you're finished entering all of the labels, the worksheet looks like this.

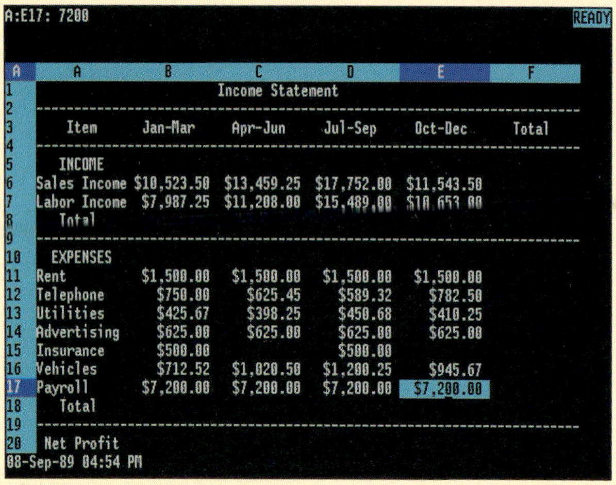

4. The next step is to enter the actual data, the numbers that represent the various income and expense figures for the four quarters of the year.

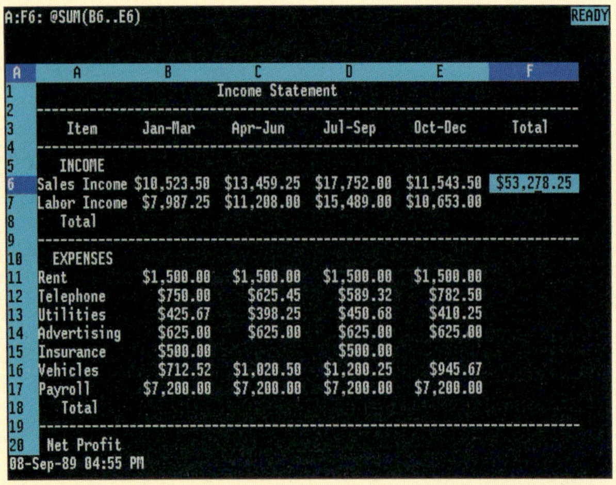

5. Once the data values are entered, you can put in the formulas that will compute totals and the net profit.

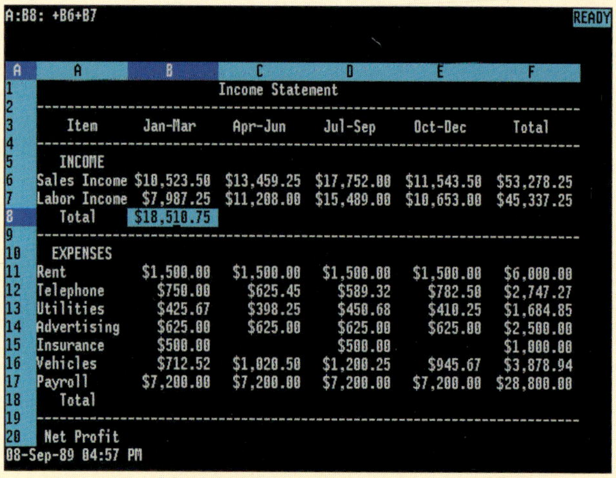

6. The next set of formulas you must enter will sum the two income figures for each quarter.

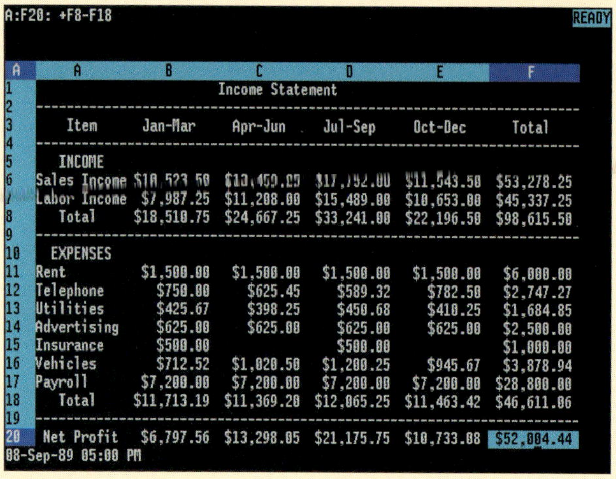

7. When you are finished with all of the formulas, the worksheet looks like this.

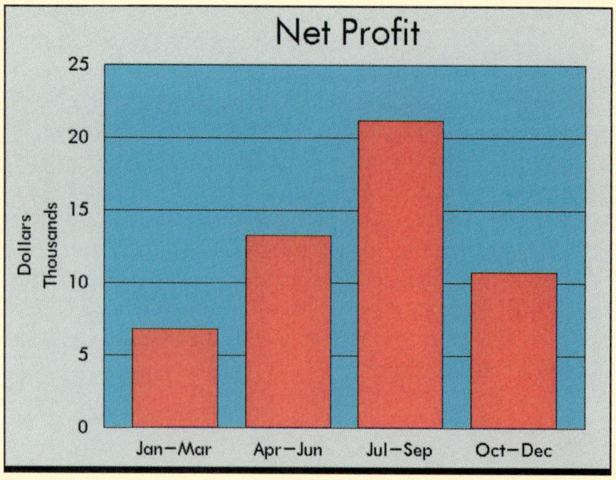

8. As a final sample of what you can do with a spreadsheet program, here is a bar graph of the net profit values.

Using dBASE IV

Data base management packages basically let users create, add to, delete from, update, sort, rearrange, select from, print out, and otherwise manipulate data files. Since managing data is one of the most common tasks performed by computers, especially in businesses, data base management packages are an extremely important type of application software. To give you an idea of what it's like to use this type of software, in this section we'll create a simple parts inventory data base for an imaginary small business with dBASE IV, one of the most popular microcomputer data base management packages.

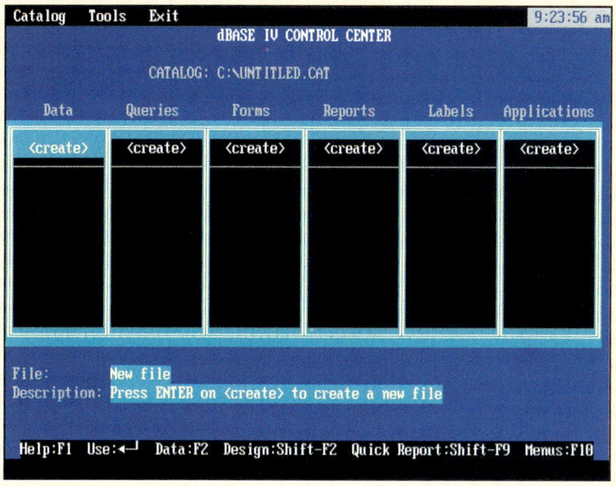

1. The dBASE IV Control Center, a menu-driven user interface.

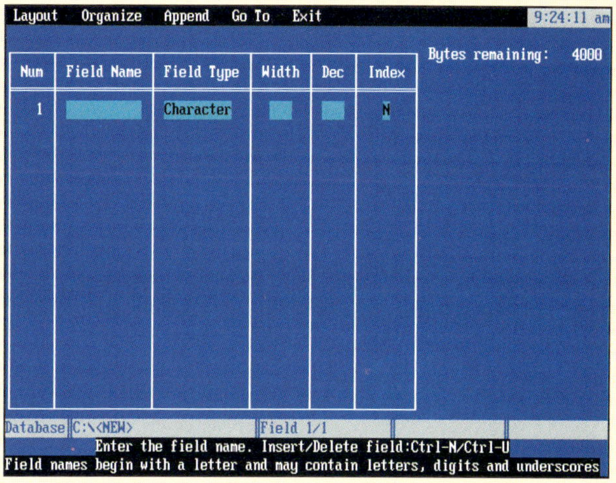

2. After you select the Create option from the Data panel, dBASE IV displays an empty data base file structure table on the screen.

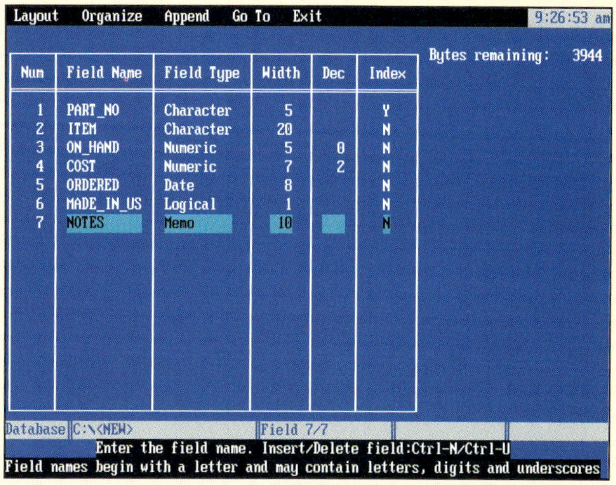

3. Here is the completed design of the example PARTS data base file.

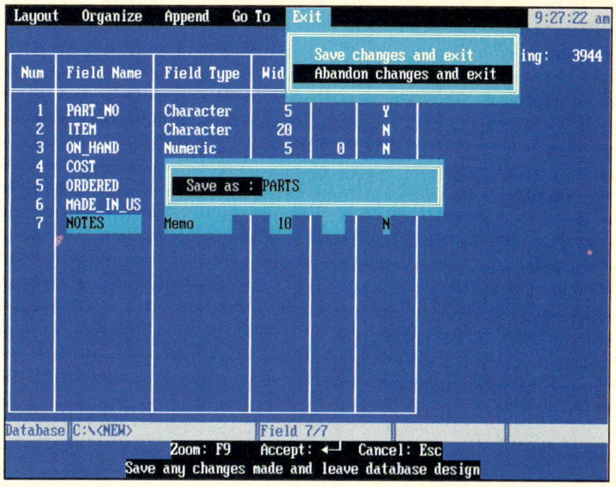

4. Pull down the Exit menu and select the Save Changes and Exit option to save the design and create the new PARTS data base file.

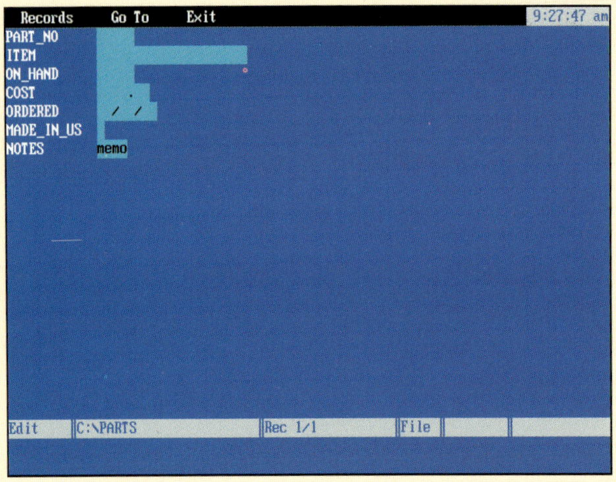

5. After you press the Data Key (F2), dBASE IV presents a blank data entry form on the screen.

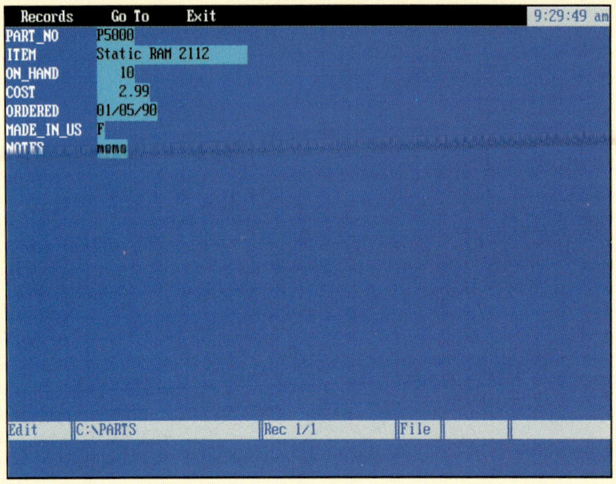

6. You simply enter the data for each field in a record, like this.

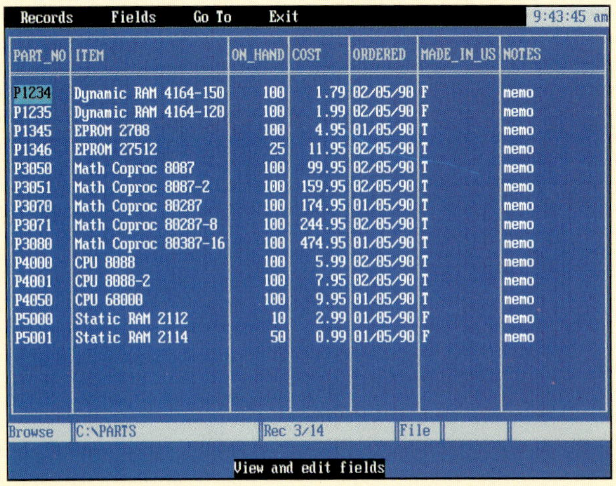

7. Press the Data Key (F2) again to display the Browse screen.

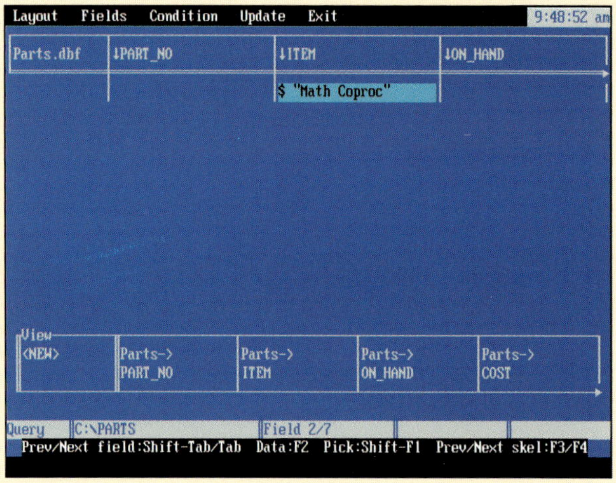

8. Select the Create option from the Queries panel to design a view query for displaying selected records.

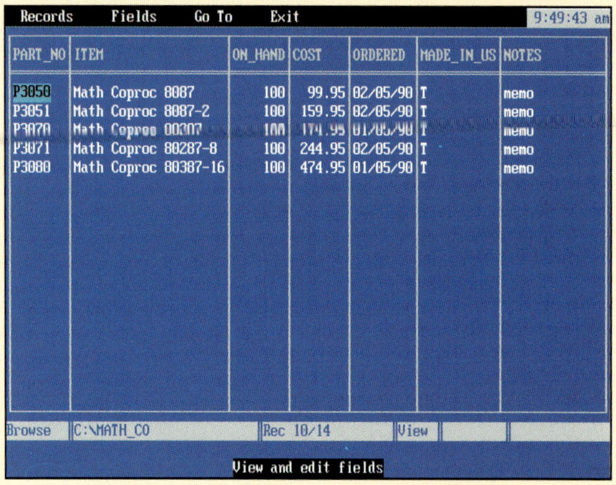

9. Press the Data Key (F2) after creating a view query to display selected records.

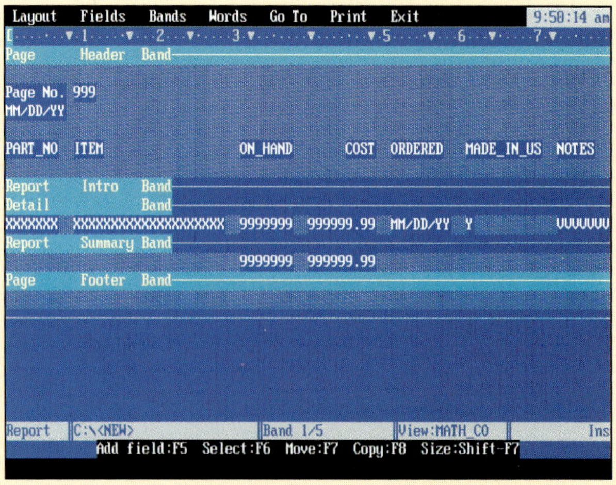

10. You can select the Create option from the Reports panel to custom design a report layout.

Using WordPerfect

The most common word-processing system consists of a general-purpose microcomputer running a word-processing application package. Simply stated, a word-processing package helps you enter, store, modify, format, copy, and print text. Most contemporary word-processing software goes beyond these basic functions to offer features such as a built-in spelling checker, an on-line thesaurus, and the ability to incorporate graphics in a document. To give you an idea of what it's like to use a modern word-processing program, in this section we'll create a simple report about the U.S. space shuttle, using WordPerfect 5.0 on an IBM-compatible microcomputer. We cannot, of course, demonstrate every feature of this popular, powerful program. Nevertheless, we can go through the basic procedure of creating, editing, formatting, and printing a document that includes both text and graphics. Although WordPerfect is not a page layout program, it can be used for simple desktop publishing applications in which previously created charts, drawings, or diagrams appear inside documents.

1. The WordPerfect document editing screen.

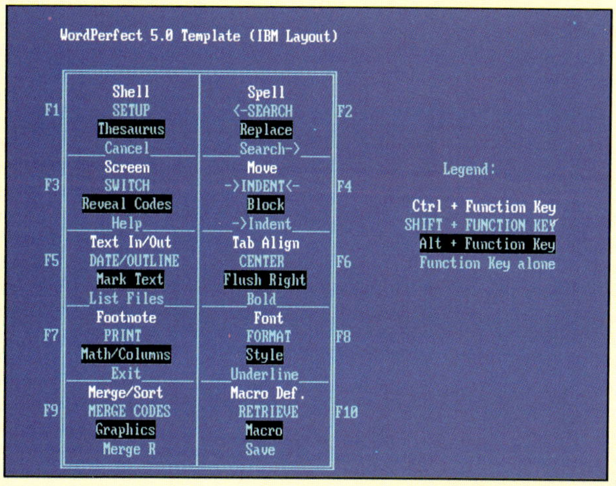

2. On-screen version of WordPerfect's keyboard template.

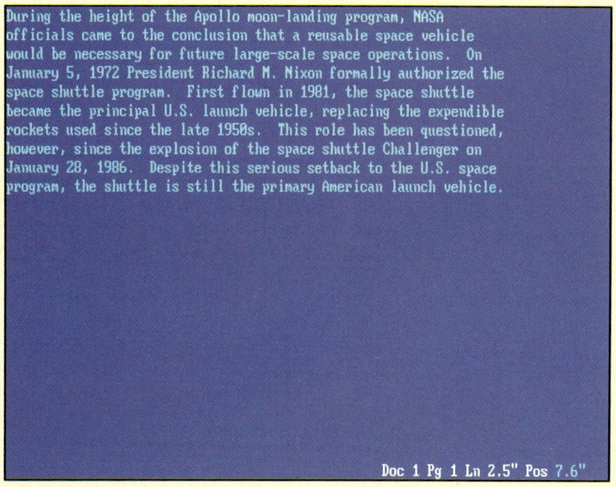

3. It's actually very easy to use WordPerfect. Once you start up the program, you can simply begin typing.

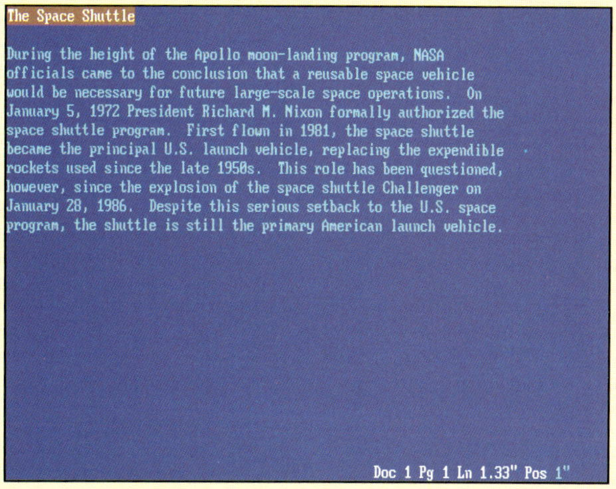

4. With a word processor, it's easy to go back and insert text at any place in an existing document.

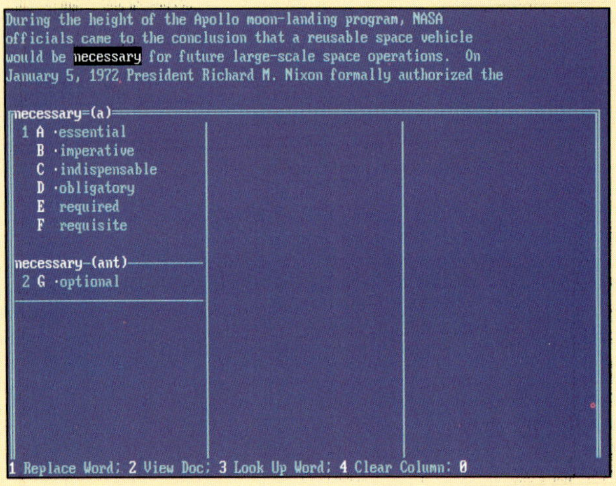

5. The WordPerfect thesaurus.

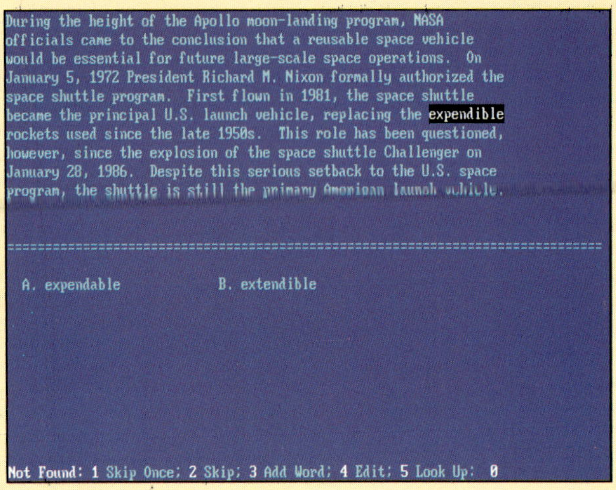

6. The WordPerfect spelling checker.

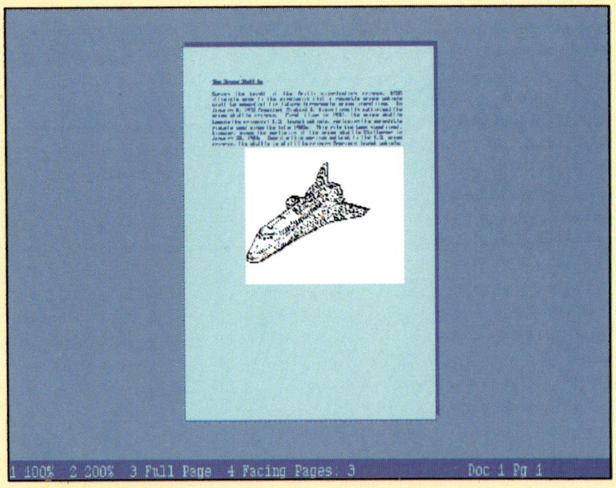

7. WordPerfect 5.0 is one of the best word-processing packages for mixing text and graphics together, without having to use a page layout program.

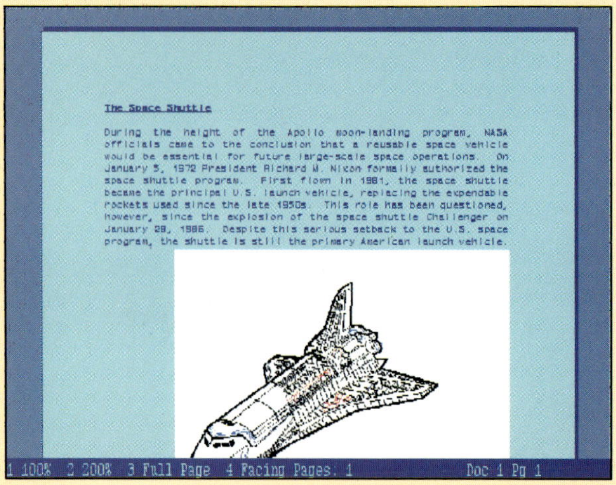

8. You can see an actual-size view of your document.

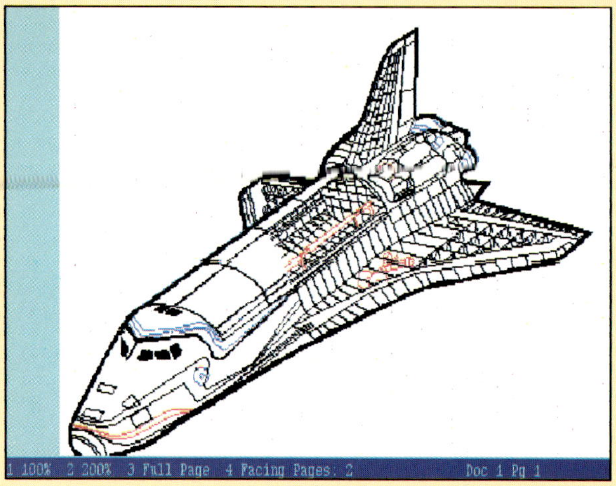

9. You can also zoom in to see a 200% view.

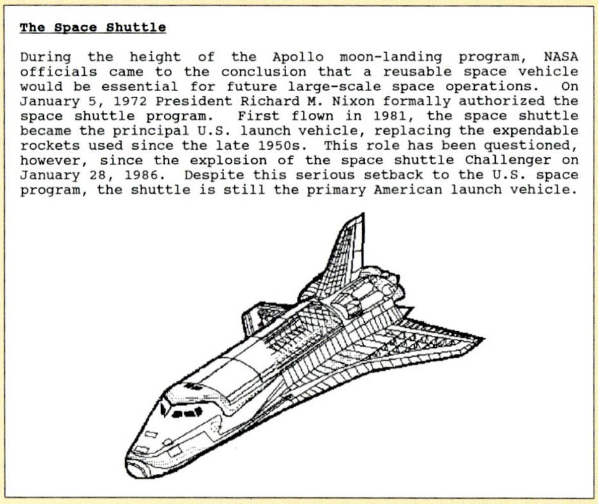

10. If you are satisfied with the way your document looks, you can proceed to print it.

Using Microcomputers

The most striking feature of our time is not so much the wonderful scientific and technological advances that have occurred, but the rate at which they continue to occur and the profound impact they have on our lives. These photos show some remarkable ways to use microcomputers.

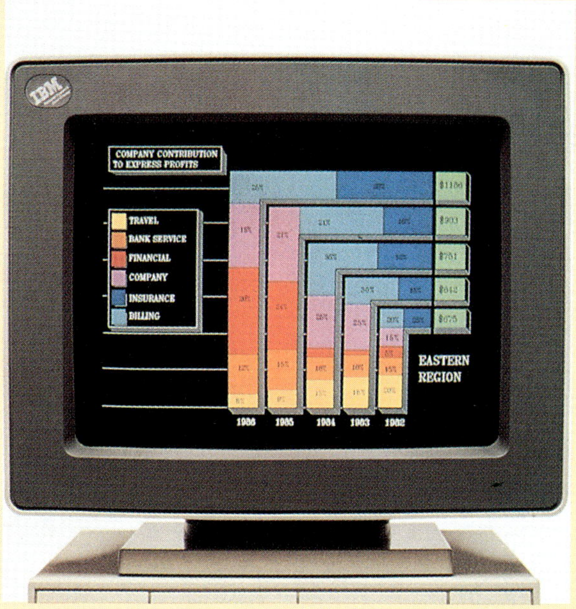

Graphics software is increasingly used in the automated office environment to produce all types of graphs, charts, and drawings. *(IBM)*

Secretary of the Interior Donald Hodel used an Apple Macintosh II microcomputer and a program called Hypercard to present his 1989 budget proposal. This is an example of presentation graphics.

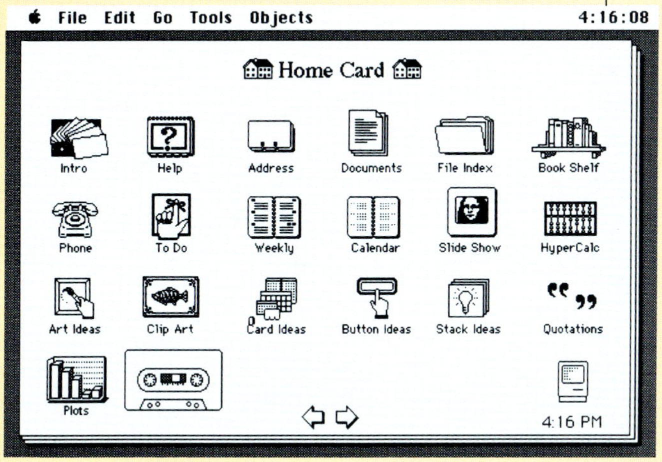

Programmers and animators at Omnibus Computer Graphics created this animated conception of a building under construction in Toronto. Based on detailed architectural input, the images were generated in order to attract companies to buy office space in the uncompleted building.

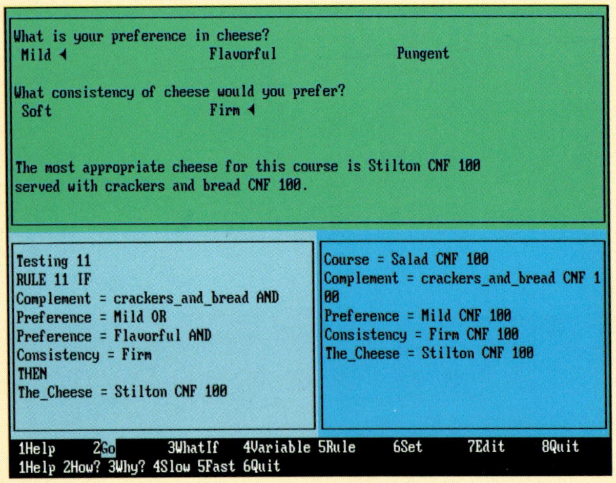

An expert system is a computer program that gives advice, emulating certain aspects of human problem-solving abilities.

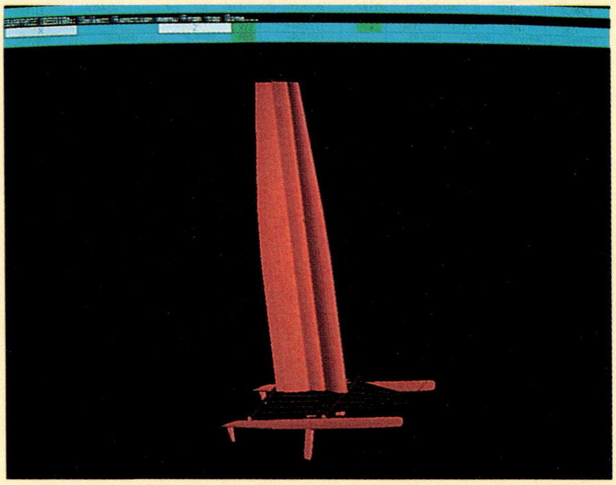

A computer-aided design (CAD) software package called *Fast Yacht* was used to design 1988's winning America's Cup Yacht. *(Dan Nerney/Dot)*

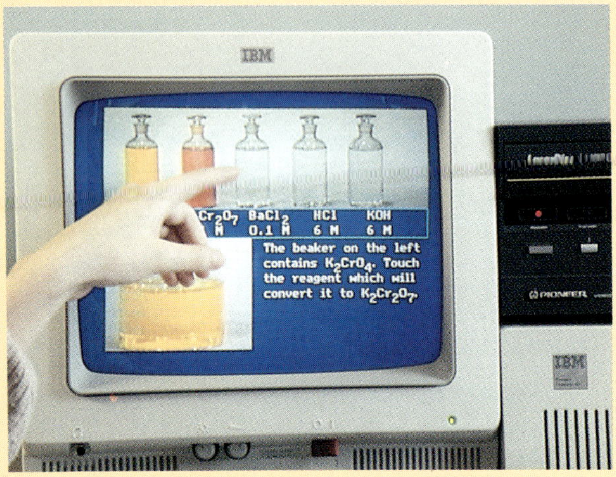

At the University of Illinois, computers enable students to simulate mixing dangerous chemicals without the danger of real injury. *(Stan Smith, Univ. of Ill.)*

Computer enhanced musicianship, with the aid of a microcomputer-based system. *(IBM)*

Microcomputers are often used to play games and pursue other entertaining activities. This screen shows Microsoft Corporation's popular Flight Simulator.

Summary

- *Creating a bar graph.* Set up the worksheet, select Bar as the graph type, and specify the data ranges.
- *Printing a graph.* Use the PrintGraph program with Lotus 1-2-3 Release 2.0 or 2.2. Execute the Print Printer Image Current Go command with Lotus 1-2-3 Release 3.0.
- *Naming a graph.* Execute the Graph Name Create command to associate a name with the current graph. The Graph Name Use command retrieves a named graph and makes it the current graph.
- *Creating a pie chart.* Set up the worksheet, select Pie as the graph type, and specify the data ranges.
- *Creating a line graph.* Set up the worksheet, select Line as the graph type, and specify the data ranges.
- *Creating a stacked bar graph.* Set up the worksheet, select Stack-Bar as the graph type, and specify the data ranges.
- *Creating an XY graph.* Set up the worksheet, select XY as the graph type, and specify the data ranges.
- *Creating a data base worksheet.* Set up the worksheet so that each column is a field and each row is a record, except for the first row, which must contain the field names.
- *Sorting a data base worksheet.* Execute the Data Sort command, specify the data range, specify one or two keys, specify the sort order, and select the Go option.
- *Searching a data base worksheet.* Set up the criteria range, enter the criteria, execute the Data Query command, specify the criteria and input ranges, and select the Find option to begin the search. Press the Down Arrow key to continue the search and the Enter key to end the search.
- *Extracting data from a worksheet.* Specify the criteria, specify the output range, and execute the Extract option from the Data Query menu.
- *Using the data base functions.* @DCOUNT, @DSUM, @DAVG, @DMIN, @DMAX, @DSTD, and @DVAR are data base functions that scan a data base, select the records that match the specified criteria, and then perform calculations on only the selected values.

Key Terms

As an extra review of this chapter, try defining the following terms.

bar graph
criteria
line graph
pie chart
primary key
query
secondary key
stacked bar graph
XY graph (scatterplot)

Multiple Choice

Choose the best selection to complete each statement.

1. What is a chart in which numeric values are represented by evenly spaced, thick vertical lines?
   (a) bar graph (b) pie chart
   (c) line graph (d) XY graph
2. In a spreadsheet program, a graph is created from data in a
   (a) data entry form. (b) settings sheet.
   (c) worksheet. (d) separate file.
3. In bar, line, and stacked bar graphs, the X data range contains the values or labels that will appear along which axis?
   (a) horizontal (b) vertical
   (c) diagonal (d) rotational
4. After you have viewed a graph the first time with the View option from the Graph menu, which key can you press to display the current graph on the screen?
   (a) Escape (b) Enter
   (c) F1 (d) F10
5. If you have Lotus 1-2-3 Release 2.0 or 2.2, what must you do to print a graph?
   (a) execute /PPICG (b) use the PrintGraph program
   (c) press Print Screen (d) press Ctrl-Alt-Del
6. Which command retrieves a named graph and makes it the current graph?
   (a) Graph Name Create (b) Graph Name Reset
   (c) Graph Name Use (d) Graph Name Delete
7. Which type of graph would you use to show the parts of a whole?
   (a) bar graph (b) pie chart
   (c) line graph (d) XY graph
8. In a pie chart, which data range contains the values that will be represented as slices?
   (a) A (b) B
   (c) C (d) X
9. In a pie chart, which optional data range can be used to specify hatch patterns and whether slices are to be exploded?
   (a) A (b) B
   (c) C (d) X
10. Which type of graph is often used to plot values that change over time as points at appropriate distances above the horizontal axis?
    (a) bar graph (b) pie chart
    (c) line graph (d) stacked bar graph
11. What graph feature identifies the data represented by each different symbol, type of line, or pattern in a graph?
    (a) legend (b) title
    (c) axis label (d) data label

12. Which type of graph shows components and total amounts for each category?
    (a) bar graph (b) line graph
    (c) XY graph (d) stacked bar graph
13. Which type of graph is often used to show the correlation between two variables?
    (a) bar graph (b) line graph
    (c) XY graph (d) stacked bar graph
14. Each row in a data base worksheet represents a
    (a) field. (b) record.
    (c) file. (d) character.
15. Each column in a data base worksheet represents a
    (a) field. (b) record.
    (c) file. (d) character.
16. The first row in a data base worksheet must contain the
    (a) first record. (b) first field.
    (c) field names. (d) record numbers.
17. Which Lotus 1-2-3 menu contains commands for manipulating a data base worksheet?
    (a) Worksheet (b) Data
    (c) File (d) Range
18. The first sort order is determined by the
    (a) primary key. (b) secondary key.
    (b) primary record. (d) secondary record.
19. In Lotus 1-2-3, what must you set up to search a data base worksheet?
    (a) data range (b) sort order
    (c) query (d) output range
20. Which function is not a data base function?
    (a) @DSUM (b) @AVG
    (c) @DCOUNT (d) @DVAR

Fill-In

1. A ______ graph is a chart in which numeric values are represented by evenly spaced, thick vertical lines.
2. Before you can create a graph, you must first create the ______ that contains the data for the graph.
3. Lotus 1-2-3 Release ______ does not require you to use PrintGraph to print out your graphs.
4. Lotus 1-2-3 lets you have several graphs associated with the same worksheet, if you ______ your graphs.
5. The Graph Name ______ command retrieves a named graph and makes it the current graph.
6. A ______ chart represents values as wedges of a circle.
7. A ______ graph is useful for plotting values that change over time.

8. A _______ bar graph is a variation of the basic bar graph that shows components and total amounts for each category.
9. A(n) _______ graph can be used to show a correlation between price and the number of units sold.
10. The _______ function converts the year, month, and day numbers into a single number that 1-2-3 uses to keep track of dates.
11. The Data _______ command is used to rearrange the records in a worksheet data base.
12. A _______ is a field in a data base used to sort the records.
13. For text, _______ order is simply alphabetical order from A to Z.
14. In 1-2-3, you must set up a _______ to search a data base worksheet.
15. In a query, the _______ range consists of at least two rows: the first row must include one or more field names and the second row must include one or more expressions that specify the field values you want to find.
16. Before you can search for records in a worksheet data base, you must specify the criteria and _______ ranges.
17. When 1-2-3 is in FIND mode, you press the _______ key to advance to the next matching record.
18. The three special characters *, ?, and ~ can be used in criteria when _______ for text.
19. The _______ option of the Data Query menu lets you copy records that meet your criteria and place them in a range outside the data base.
20. The _______ function counts the nonblank cells in a field of a data base worksheet, considering only those records that meet the specified criteria.

Short Problems

1. Retrieve the SALES worksheet you created in Lesson 1. Execute the Graph Name Use command and tell 1-2-3 that you want to use the SALES_BAR graph. Return to the Graph menu and select Options Data-Labels. For the A data range, assign B2..E2 as the range of data labels. Then select the Above option. Return to the Graph menu and view the graph. Assigning data labels in this manner presents the actual value of each bar.
2. If you are running Lotus 1-2-3 Release 2.0 or 2.2, use the PrintGraph program to print the new SALES_BAR graph. Try printing it in a different font.

   If you are running Lotus 1-2-3 Release 3.0, execute the Graph Options Advanced Text First Font command. Then select 2, 4, 5, 6, 7, or 8 to change the font of the first line of the graph title. Repeat the process for the Second and Third graph text groups, then print the graph.
3. Move the cell pointer to a blank area of the SALES worksheet below all data. Execute the Graph Name Table command and use the current cell as the range. Return to READY mode and examine the worksheet. The Graph Name Table command creates a three-column table that lists all named graphs in the worksheet, along with their graph types and titles.
4. View the SALES_PIE graph you created in Lesson 5. Modify the chart so that all slices are exploded. Save and print the new pie chart.
5. View the SALES_LINE graph you created in Lesson 6. Add horizontal and vertical grid lines to the graph. Save and print the new line graph.

6. View the SALES_STACK graph you created in Lesson 7. Add data labels above each bar for all three data ranges. Save and print the new stacked bar graph.
7. View the SALES_XY graph you created in Lesson 8. Add horizontal and vertical grid lines to the graph. Save and print the new XY graph.
8. Erase the current worksheet from the screen and retrieve the PROPERTY data base worksheet you created in Lesson 9. Make up at least ten more records and add them to the worksheet. If you add new records after the last record, you may have to change the range to include the new rows in the formula that computes the sum of the amounts.
9. Sort the PROPERTY worksheet by DATE, with the oldest item appearing first.
10. Set up a query and use a data base function to compute the average amount of PROPERTY items that cost more than $100.

Long Problems

1. Create a worksheet and bar graph to compare tape rentals of movies of various categories for the month of March for Valley Video. Use the following movie categories and numbers of rentals:

Adventure	222
Comedy	179
Foreign	65
Horror	130
Mystery	205

   Be sure to create a two-line title for the graph and label both axes. Save the worksheet and print the graph.
2. Create a worksheet and multiple data range line graph to plot the sales of three computer magazines for the years 1985 to 1990. Use different symbols for each magazine, connect the points with line segments, and have 1-2-3 generate a legend. Use the following data for the numbers of thousands of magazines sold per year:

	1985	1986	1987	1989	1990
Megabytes Magazine	200	160	140	130	120
Number Cruncher	90	110	120	104	110
Hardware User	60	90	106	140	150

   Be sure to create a two-line title for the graph and label both axes. Save the worksheet and print the graph.
3. Create a worksheet and pie chart to show the cost-per-unit breakdown for a Beaver Canoe. Use the following data:

Advertising	$69.99
Labor	$99.99
Materials	$219.98
Packaging	$30.00
Service	$79.99

   Be sure to create a two-line title for the chart and label the pie slices. Save the worksheet and print the chart.

4. Suppose Beaver Canoe Company went public in 1988. Create a worksheet and stacked bar graph to compare the components of total capitalization. Use the following data, in millions of dollars, for each fiscal year:

	1988	1989	1990
Stockholder Equity	9	11	14
Long-Term Debt	5	4	4
Short-Term Debt	1	2	3

Be sure to create a two-line title for the graph, generate a legend, and label both axes. Save the worksheet and print the graph.

5. Create a pie chart from the 1990 data in Long Problem 4. Be sure to create a two-line title for the chart and label the pie slices. Save the worksheet and print the chart.

6. Create a worksheet and XY graph to depict the relationship between per capita income (in U.S. dollars) and male life expectancy (in years). Plot per capita income along the X axis and life expectancy along the Y axis. Use the following data:

Country	Per Capita Income	Male Life Expectancy
Afghanistan	$168	40
Australia	$9,914	70
Belgium	$9,827	69
Brazil	$1,523	61
Cambodia	$90	44
Canada	$10,193	69
Denmark	$12,956	71
Ecuador	$1,050	55
Ethiopia	$117	37
France	$7,179	70
West Germany	$11,142	67
Guatemala	$1,083	48
Haiti	$300	47
Honduras	$822	53
India	$150	52
Iran	$2,160	58
Israel	$3,332	72
Italy	$6,914	70
Jamaica	$1,340	65
Japan	$8,460	73
Kenya	$196	56
Kuwait	$11,431	67
Laos	$85	39
Libya	$6,335	51
Mexico	$1,800	62
Nicaragua	$804	51
Norway	$12,432	73
Pakistan	$280	54
Poland	$4,670	66
Singapore	$4,100	68

Country	Per Capita Income	Male Life Expectancy
Spain	$5,500	70
Sweden	$14,821	73
Turkey	$1,300	57
USSR	$2,600	64
USA	$11,675	71

Be sure to create a two-line title for the graph, connect the points with line segments, and label both axes. Save the worksheet and print the graph.

7. Retrieve the worksheet you created in Long Problem 6. Save it in a file with a different name to create a copy of the worksheet and graph. Examine the data and the printed graph. Eliminate those data points that deviate significantly from the pattern. Modify the graph so that Lotus 1-2-3 labels each point. Save the worksheet and print the graph. The moral of this problem: data can be carefully selected and graphs designed to enhance or distort the facts.
8. Create an "electronic Rolodex" with Lotus 1-2-3. Set up the columns and enter the records of a worksheet data base to hold the information you keep in your personal address book. Include fields for last name, first name, address, city, state, ZIP code, and phone number. Sort the data base by last name and then by first name. Print the worksheet when you are finished.
9. Create a data base worksheet to hold the following expense records:

No	Date	Category	Amount	Description
13	03-Mar-90	Freight	$8.75	UPS
4	09-Jan-90	Publications	$3.95	PC Magazine
1	04-Jan-90	Freight	$8.50	Federal Express
3	09-Jan-90	Freight	$2.79	Postage
15	16-Mar-90	Supplies	$5.05	Envelopes
6	14-Jan-90	Supplies	$40.98	Diskettes
20	28-Mar-90	Freight	$13.50	Federal Express
8	02-Feb-90	Software	$49.88	Reflex Plus upgrade
2	04-Jan-90	Freight	$8.50	Federal Express
10	11-Feb-90	Freight	$4.79	Postage Stamps
16	20-Mar-90	Freight	$8.50	Federal Express
11	13-Feb-90	Freight	$9.50	Federal Express
18	22-Mar-90	Publications	$19.95	Using PageMaker
14	04-Mar-90	Publications	$12.70	The Well-Connected PC
5	14-Jan-90	Publications	$3.00	CD-ROM Magazine
9	10-Feb-90	Utilities	$10.04	Telephone calls
17	21-Mar-90	Freight	$8.50	Federal Express
12	21-Feb-90	Freight	$14.50	Federal Express
19	24-Mar-90	Supplies	$35.66	Computer Paper
7	02-Feb-90	Hardware	$18.01	IBM Modem Cable

Sort the records by No or Date and sum the amounts.

10. Use the data base worksheet you created in Long Problem 9. In a blank part of the worksheet, set up queries and use the @DSUM function to compute subtotals for the following expense categories: Freight, Hardware, Publications, Software, Supplies, and Utilities.

CHAPTER 13

ADVANCED LOTUS 1-2-3

In This Chapter

Getting Started
Lesson 1: Changing Worksheet Settings
Lesson 2: Freezing Titles and Using Windows
Lesson 3: Hiding Columns and Protecting Cells
Lesson 4: Changing Range Formats
Lesson 5: Using Range Names
Lesson 6: Filling a Range with a Sequence of Numbers
Lesson 7: Transposing Columns and Rows
Lesson 8: Controlling Recalculation and Iteration
Lesson 9: Using Relative, Absolute, and Mixed Cell References
Lesson 10: Using Additional Functions
Lesson 11: Using Macros
Lesson 12: Using the Learn Feature with Release 2.2
Lesson 13: Using the Record Feature with Release 3.0
Lesson 14: Linking Worksheets with Releases 2.2 and 3.0
Lesson 15: Using Three-Dimensional Worksheets with Release 3.0

Preview

The previous two chapters taught you most of what the average user needs to know about Lotus 1-2-3. This chapter proceeds to more advanced spreadsheet topics, including powerful new features found in Lotus 1-2-3 Release 2.2 and Release 3.0. You may not need all of the commands and features presented in this chapter, but many of them can make your work easier, quicker, and less tedious. Learning more about Lotus 1-2-3 can help you create more complex and powerful worksheets.

After studying this chapter, you will know how to

- change worksheet settings.
- freeze titles and use windows.
- hide columns and protect cells.
- change range formats.
- use range names.
- fill a range with a sequence of numbers.
- transpose columns and rows.
- control recalculation and iteration.
- use relative, absolute, and mixed cell references.
- use additional functions.
- use macros.
- use the Release 2.2 Learn feature.
- use the Release 3.0 Record feature.
- use file linking with Release 2.2 and 3.0.
- use three dimensional worksheets with Release 3.0.

Getting Started

You've already learned how to start Lotus 1-2-3 and use its most basic features and commands. This chapter assumes you have completed the lessons and exercises in Chapters 11 and 12. Furthermore, it assumes that you have a computer with a hard disk and Lotus 1-2-3 installed on it in a subdirectory named 123 or 123R3. A DOS path should be set up so that you can run Lotus 1-2-3 from within any subdirectory. You should have a subdirectory named LESSONS in which to store your worksheet files.

Lesson 1: Changing Worksheet Settings

Worksheet is the first option in the Main menu of Lotus 1-2-3. Selecting Worksheet activates a submenu of options for changing worksheet settings. The Worksheet Global options affect the entire worksheet. Other Worksheet options let you insert and delete columns and rows, set column widths, hide columns, erase the entire worksheet, freeze titles on the screen, split the display into windows, show the current worksheet settings, and insert page breaks into the worksheet. Let's explore some of these options.

Step 1: Start 1-2-3

If you are not already running Lotus 1-2-3, switch to your LESSONS subdirectory and start the program:

Type **cd c:\lessons**
Press **Enter**
Type **123**
Press **Enter**

Step 2: Set the Global Format

The Worksheet Global Format command lets you specify the way numeric values are to appear for the entire worksheet. We will discuss the various types of formatting later in this chapter when we cover the Range Format command. For now, let's just change the global format of the worksheet to Currency.

Type **/wgfc**
Press **Enter**

The default number of decimal places is two. Enter a number into any cell and you will see it formatted as a currency value.

Type **100**
Press **Enter**

Step 3: Set the Global Label-Prefix

The Worksheet Global Label-Prefix command lets you set the alignment of labels for the entire worksheet. The default label alignment is Left, which means that the apostrophe (') is the default global label-prefix character. Suppose you want all labels to be centered unless you explicitly specify otherwise. Set the global label-prefix to Center, which will automatically use the caret (^) as the label-prefix character.

Type **/wglc**

Now move the cell pointer and enter a label into any cell.

Press **Right Arrow**
Type **One**
Press **Enter**

The label will be centered automatically within its cell.

Step 4: Set the Global Column-Width

You already know how to set the column width for the entire worksheet, but let's try it once more. Use the Worksheet Global Column-Width command to set the width of every column to 15 characters.

Type **/wgc15**
Press **Enter**

Every column will widen to 15 characters.

Step 5: Set the Global Default Directory

By default, 1-2-3 will search the current disk drive directory for files that you want to retrieve and it will place files that you save in that same directory. If you have a DOS PATH statement set up so that you can run 1-2-3 from within any subdirectory, you probably will not have to change this default directory setting. But suppose you want Lotus 1-2-3 to use C:\LESSONS as its default directory for saving and retrieving files, no matter which directory you are in when you start the program. Execute the Worksheet Global Default Directory command and enter the path of the directory you want 1-2-3 to use.

Type **/wgdd**
Press **Escape**
Type **c:\lessons**
Press **Enter**
Type **q**

For the rest of your 1-2-3 session, the LESSONS subdirectory will be the default directory. If you want to make this the default directory every time you use 1-2-3, you would execute the Worksheet Global Default Update command.

Step 6: Set the Display of Zero Values

By default, 1-2-3 displays values of zero, whether they are entered as numbers or are the results of formulas. For example, move the cell pointer and enter a zero into a cell.

Press **Down Arrow**
Type **0**
Press **Enter**

As you can see, $0.00 is displayed in cell B2. Suppose you want to suppress the display of zero values. Execute the Worksheet Global Zero Yes command.

Type **/wgzy**

Examine cell B2. In the worksheet, the cell appears to be empty, but the control panel shows that the cell contains the number 0.

To turn on the display of zero values, execute the Worksheet Global Zero No command.

Lotus 1-2-3 Release 2.2 and Release 3.0 also let you display a label instead of zero values in the worksheet. For example, if you are running Release 2.2 or 3.0, try the Worksheet Global Zero Label command:

Type **/wgzl**
Type **(zero)**
Press **Enter**

The label *"(zero)* will appear instead of zero values in the worksheet.

Step 7: Display the Worksheet Status

The Worksheet Status command displays information about memory use, current global settings, and various hardware options.

Type **/ws**

Figure 1 shows the result. When you are finished examining the status screen, press any key to return to ready mode.

Press **Enter**

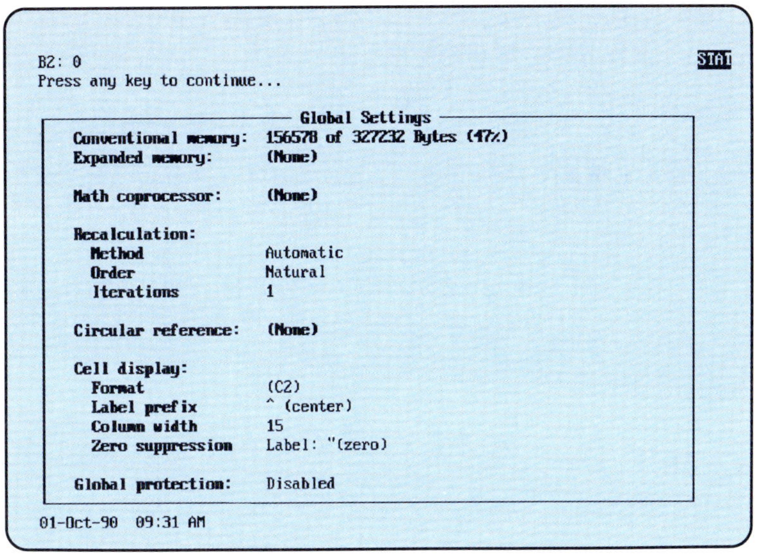

Figure 1 The Worksheet Status Screen

Step 8: Insert Page Breaks

The Lotus 1-2-3 Worksheet Page command lets you insert page breaks into a worksheet. Then when you print the worksheet, a new page will begin after each page break. For example, follow these directions to have row 11 begin at the top of a new page when the worksheet is printed:

Press **F5**
Type **a10**
Press **Enter**
Type **/wp**

A double colon (::) will appear in column A of the row that contains the page break. The rest of the worksheet will move down. No entries should appear in the row containing the page break, because 1-2-3 does not print anything in that row.

You can remove a page break by using the Range Erase command or by overwriting the cell that contains the double colon.

Practice

1. Change the Worksheet Global Format to General.
2. Change the Worksheet Global Label-Prefix to Left.
3. Change the Worksheet Global Column-Width to 12.
4. Turn on the display of zero values.
5. Delete the page break in row 10.

Lesson 2: Freezing Titles and Using Windows

The Worksheet Titles command lets you freeze rows, columns, or both on the screen so you can see them when you scroll the worksheet. Use this command to keep row and column labels on the screen when you work with long or wide worksheets. The Worksheet Windows command lets you split the screen into two horizontal or vertical windows. You can synchronize scrolling in the two windows or scroll them independently. Let's examine these two useful commands.

Step 1: Retrieve the PROPERTY Worksheet

Retrieve the PROPERTY worksheet, which you created in the previous chapter, so that you have a more substantial worksheet on the screen.

Type **/fr**
Highlight **PROPERTY.WK1** (or **PROPERTY.WK3**)
Press **Enter**
Press **Home**

Step 2: Freeze Horizontal Titles

The PROPERTY worksheet contains only 20 rows. Suppose it were much longer. When you scroll down, the column labels ITEM, DATE, and AMOUNT will disappear off the top of the screen. For example, move the cell pointer down 20 rows.

Press **Down Arrow** (20 times)

The column labels disappear. The Worksheet Titles Horizontal command lets you freeze these labels on the screen. Move the cell pointer one row below the rows you want to freeze and then execute the Worksheet Titles Horizontal command.

Press **Home**
Press **Down Arrow**
Type **/wth**

The top row is now frozen. It will always remain on the screen. You cannot move the cell pointer into the frozen row with the pointer-movement keys, but you can do so with F5, the Go To key. Try moving the cell pointer with the top row frozen.

Press **Up Arrow**
Press **Down Arrow** (25 times)

Notice how row 1 always remains on the screen even as the worksheet scrolls.

Step 3: Freeze Both Titles

The Worksheet Titles command also lets you freeze the vertical titles or both the horizontal and vertical titles. For example, move the cell pointer to B2 and freeze both titles.

Press **Home**
Press **Right Arrow**
Type **/wtb**

Row 1 and column A are now frozen. To see how they remain on the screen, scroll down and right.

Press **Down Arrow** (25 times)
Press **Right Arrow** (3 times)

Rows 2 through 8 and column B disappear, but row 1 and column A remain on the screen (see Figure 2).

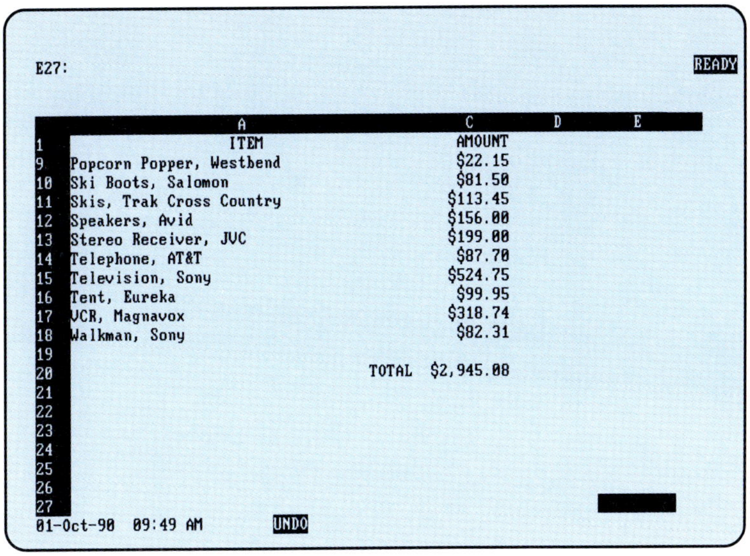

***Figure 2** Row 1 and Column A Frozen as Titles*

Step 4: Clear the Titles

The Worksheet Titles Clear command lets you unfreeze all existing titles.

Type **/wtc**
Press **Home**

You can now move to row 1 or column A, and they will disappear when the worksheet is scrolled.

Step 5: Split the Screen Into Two Windows

The Worksheet Windows command lets you split the screen into two horizontal or vertical windows so you can view two different parts of the same worksheet. Suppose you want two horizontal windows. Move the cell pointer to the row that you want to be the top of the bottom window, say row 11, and then execute the Worksheet Window Horizontal command.

Press **Down Arrow (10 times)**
Type **/wwh**

Figure 3 shows the result. The top of the second window is marked by the second column border across the middle of the screen. The top window is active and the cell pointer is in A10.

Step 6: Move Between Windows

Right now, you are in the top window. Any vertical pointer movement keys will act only within this window. For example, move the cell pointer down ten cells.

Press **Down Arrow** (10 times)

Notice that the top window scrolls while the bottom window remains still.

Figure 3 Two Horizontal Windows

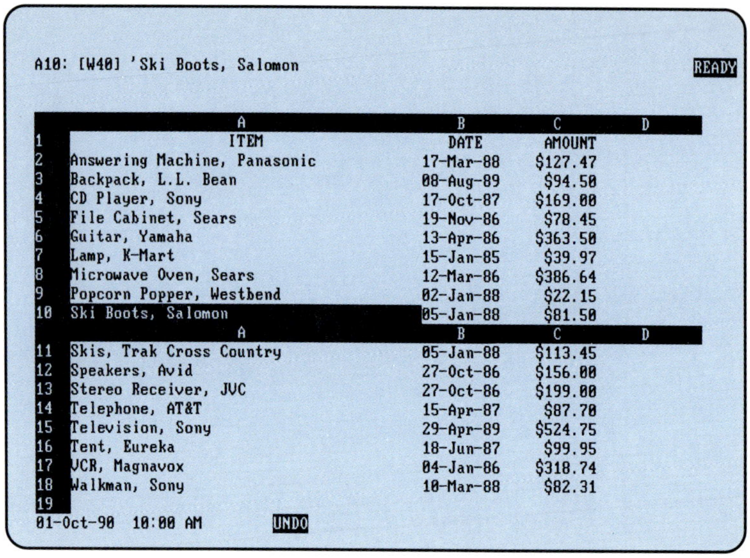

Suppose you want to move to the bottom window. The F6 function key lets you move to the other window. Switch to the bottom window, and move the cell pointer up ten rows.

Press **F6**
Press **Up Arrow** (10 times)

This time, the bottom window will scroll while the top window remains still. Switch to the top window again and move the cell pointer to A1.

Press **F6**
Press **Home**

Step 7: Unsynchronize Windows

By default, windows are synchronized. For vertical windows, this means that the same rows are kept on the screen in both windows when you scroll up or down. For horizontal windows, this means that the same columns will remain on the screen in both windows when you scroll right or left. For example, move the cell pointer to the right.

Press **Right Arrow** (4 times)

The screen will scroll so that the same columns appear in both windows.

You can tell 1-2-3 to allow windows to scroll independently in all directions by executing the Worksheet Window Unsync command.

Type **/wwu**

Now move the cell pointer to the left in the top window.

Press **Left Arrow** (4 times)

Only the top window will scroll to the left. The bottom window will remain still.

Step 8: Clear Windows

When you are finished using windows, you can restore the screen to a single window by executing the Worksheet Window Clear command.

Type **/wwc**

The contents and settings of the window that was on the top or the left will expand to occupy the entire screen.

Practice

1. Freeze column A as a vertical title. Move the cell pointer to the right and see how column A always remains on the screen. When you are finished, clear worksheet titles.
2. Move the cell pointer to column B and split the screen into two vertical windows. Tell 1-2-3 to synchronize the windows. Move the cell pointer down 25 rows and see how the two vertical windows scroll together. When you are finished, clear worksheet windows and move the cell pointer to A1.

Lesson 3: Hiding Columns and Protecting Cells

Worksheets often contain sensitive data, such as salaries and grades, that you may not want anyone to see. Lotus 1-2-3 lets you hide columns without erasing the data they contain. Worksheets may also contain data that should not be changed by the average user. Lotus 1-2-3 lets you protect ranges of cells to prevent them from being changed.

Step 1: Hide a Column

Suppose you want to keep the AMOUNT values in the PROPERTY worksheet private. The Worksheet Column Hide command lets you conceal the contents of one or more columns. Move to column C and execute the Worksheet Column Hide command.

Press **Home**
Press **Right Arrow** (2 times)
Type **/wch**
Press **Enter**

Figure 4 shows the result. Column C appears to have been removed from the worksheet. In fact, it is only hidden.

Step 2: Display a Column

Now suppose you want to see the hidden column. Execute the Worksheet Column Display command and enter a cell address from the hidden column.

Type **/wcd**
Type **c1**
Press **Enter**

The hidden column will reappear in the worksheet.

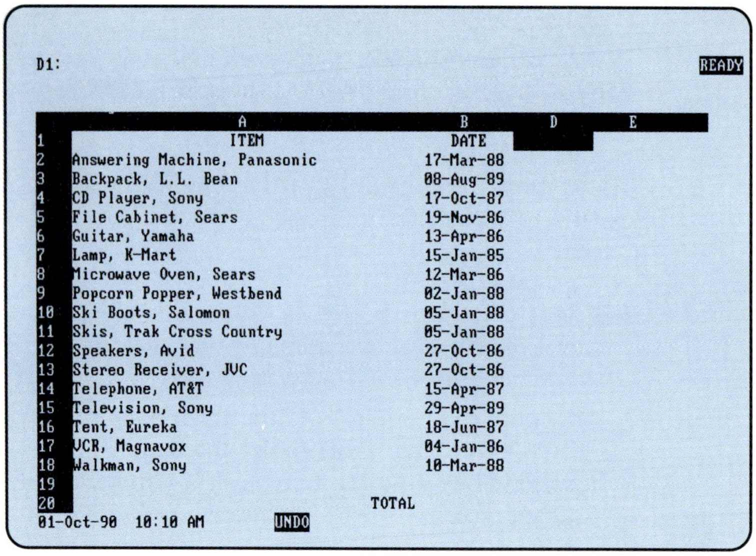

Figure 4 Column C Has Been Hidden

Step 3: Create a Template

A **template** is a general-purpose worksheet in which the user fills in the blanks or changes selected entries to perform a well defined task. The person who creates the template enters the labels, formulas, and perhaps some constant numbers. The person who uses the template supplies the variables. The template generates the result. For example, you could create a template to compute the monthly payment on a loan, given the principal, interest rate, and term. Follow these directions to create such a template:

Type **/wey**
Type **/wgfc**
Press **Enter**
Type **/wgc15**
Press **Enter**
Press **Right Arrow**
Type **'<-- Enter the amount of the loan**
Press **Down Arrow**
Type **'<-- Enter the annual interest rate**
Press **Down Arrow**
Type **'<-- Enter the term in months**
Press **Down Arrow**
Type **'<-- This is the monthly payment**
Press **Left Arrow**
Type **@pmt(a1,a2/12,a3)**
Press **Up Arrow**
Type **/rfga2..a3**
Press **Enter**

The ERR message you see in cell A4 indicates a division by zero in the formula. It will disappear as soon as numbers are entered into cells A1, A2, and A3.

Step 4: Try the Template

The template is now set up for a user to enter values in cells A1, A2, and A3. Let's try the template.

Press **Home**
Type **4500**
Press **Down Arrow**
Type **12%**
Press **Down Arrow**
Type **24**
Press **Enter**

The template will calculate the monthly payment to be $211.83.

Step 5: Protect the Worksheet

In this template, only cells A1, A2, and A3 should be changed by the user. The user should not change the labels or the formula. The Worksheet Global Protection Enable command prevents changes being made to all cells. The Range Unprot command can then be used to turn off protection for those cells the user is supposed to change.

Type **/wgpe**

Now try changing a cell.

Type **hello**
Press **Enter**

Lotus 1-2-3 will beep and display the message

```
Protected cell
```

Cancel your attempted change.

Press **Escape**

Step 6: Unprotect Selected Cells

The template is worthless if no cells can be changed. You must use the Range Unprot command to turn off protection for cells A1 through A3.

Type **/rua1..a3**
Press **Enter**

Now, try changing the amount of the loan to $9,000.

Press **Home**
Type **9000**
Press **Enter**

Cells A1 through A3 can be changed, but all other cells in the worksheet are protected.

Step 7: Save the Worksheet

Save the template you have created in a worksheet file named LOAN so that you can use it in the future.

Type **/fs**
Type **loan**
Press **Enter**

Practice

1. The Range Protect command lets you protect one or more cells you have unprotected with the Range Unprot command. For example, suppose the interest rate will never change and you don't want users to alter it. Use the Range Protect command to prevent cell A2 from being changed. Try to change it and see what happens.
2. Protection for the entire worksheet can be turned off with the Worksheet Global Protection Disable command. Use this command to allow changes to all cells in the worksheet.

Lesson 4: Changing Range Formats

Lotus 1-2-3 lets you set the numeric format of one cell, a range of cells, or every cell in the worksheet. So far, you have used General format, which is the default, and Currency format, which is used for dollar amounts. Let's examine each of the formats you can set with the Range Format command.

Step 1: Set Up a New Worksheet

Erase the worksheet from your screen and widen all columns to 15 characters.

Type **/wey**
Type **/wgc15**
Press **Enter**

Step 2: Use the General Format

General format displays negative numbers with a leading minus sign, does not use commas to separate thousands, and suppresses trailing zeros after the decimal point. If the number is too large to fit within the column width, scientific notation is used to express the number. When the number of digits to the right of the decimal point exceeds the column width, 1-2-3 displays as many digits as it can. General format is the default numeric format used for all cells unless you specify otherwise. Try General format.

Type **General**
Press **Right Arrow**
Type **12345.678**
Press **Down Arrow**
Press **Left Arrow**

Step 3: Use the Fixed Format

Fixed format lets you specify how many decimal places to display, from 0 to 15. Values are rounded or filled out with zeros to fit the exact number of decimal places you specify. Negative numbers have a leading minus sign and commas are not used to separate thousands. Values between −1 and 1 are expressed with a leading zero before the decimal point. Enter a number and use the Range Format Fixed command with two decimal places.

Type **Fixed**
Press **Right Arrow**
Type **12345.678**
Press **Enter**

Type **/rff**
Press **Enter**
Press **Enter**
Press **Down Arrow**
Press **Left Arrow**

Notice that 12345.678 is rounded to 12345.68 to fit the Fixed format with two decimal places.

Step 4: Use the Scientific Format

Scientific format expresses numbers in exponential notation. It is useful for very large or very small numbers. A number in scientific format has three parts: the mantissa, the letter E, and the exponent. The **mantissa** is the decimal part of the number. The letter E indicates exponential format and separates the mantissa from the exponent. The **exponent** indicates the power of ten to be multiplied by the mantissa to yield the number. For example, 1.5E+02 is equal to 1.5×10^2 or 150. Either the mantissa or the exponent can be negative. For example, −1.5E−02 is equal to -1.5×10^{-2} or −0.015. The mantissa can have up to 15 decimal places and the exponent can be any number from −99 to 99. Enter a number and use the Range Format Scientific command with two decimal places.

Type **Scientific**
Press **Right Arrow**
Type **12345.678**
Press **Enter**
Type **/rfs**
Press **Enter**
Press **Enter**
Press **Down Arrow**
Press **Left Arrow**

Notice that 12345.678 is expressed in scientific format as 1.23E+04 with the mantissa rounded to two decimal places.

Step 5: Use the Currency Format

You have already used Currency format, but let's try it again. Numbers are displayed with a currency symbol, such as $, thousands are separated by commas, and up to 15 decimal places can be specified. Negative values are enclosed in parentheses, a common convention in financial worksheets. However, the currency symbol and the expression of negative values in parentheses can be changed with the Worksheet Global Default Other International command. Enter a number and use the Range Format Currency command with two decimal places.

Type **Currency**
Press **Right Arrow**
Type **12345.678**
Press **Enter**
Type **/rfc**
Press **Enter**
Press **Enter**
Press **Down Arrow**
Press **Left Arrow**

The number will be rounded to two decimal places and expressed as $12,345.68.

Step 6: Use the Comma Format

Comma format is essentially the same as Currency format except it does not display the leading currency symbol. Enter a number and use the Range Format , (comma) command with two decimal places.

Type **Comma**
Press **Right Arrow**
Type **12345.678**
Press **Enter**
Type **/rf,**
Press **Enter**
Press **Enter**
Press **Down Arrow**
Press **Left Arrow**

The number will be expressed as 12,345.68.

Step 7: Use the +/− Format

The +/− format displays a horizontal bar of plus signs or minus signs, or a period. It is used to generate crude bar graphs. The number of plus signs or minus signs equals the whole-number value of the entry rounded to the nearest integer. For example, if you enter 5 into a cell in +/− format, five plus signs will be displayed. If you enter −5 instead, five minus signs will be displayed. If the number is between −1 and 1, a period will be displayed. Enter a number and use the Range Format +/− command.

Type **'+/-**
Press **Right Arrow**
Type **5**
Press **Enter**
Type **/rf+**
Press **Enter**
Press **Down Arrow**
Press **Left Arrow**

You should see five plus signs instead of the number 5 in cell B6.

Step 8: Use the Percent Format

Percent format displays numbers as percentages with up to 15 decimal places and a trailing percent sign. In other words, a number expressed in Percent format is multiplied by 100. Enter a number and use the Range Format Percent command with two decimal places.

Type **Percent**
Press **Right Arrow**
Type **0.678**
Press **Enter**
Type **/rfp**
Press **Enter**
Press **Enter**
Press **Down Arrow**
Press **Left Arrow**

You should see the number expressed as 67.80%.

Step 9: Use the Date and Time Formats

Lotus 1-2-3 maintains dates and times as numbers that can be used in calculations. Each day between January 1, 1900 and December 31, 2099 is assigned a sequential date number. January 1, 1900 is 1; January 2, 1900 is 2; and so on up to December 31, 2099, which is 73050. The total time in each day is represented by the number 1. The time number for midnight is 0.0; noon is 0.5; and just before midnight is 0.99999. Although these date and time numbers might seem strange, you can perform calculations with them, and 1-2-3 can easily express them in the format you are used to seeing. The Date option of the Range Format menu lets you express date numbers as dates, such as 21-Jun-90, and time numbers as times, such as 02:38:24 PM. Enter a number and use the Range Format Date 1 (DD-MM-YY) command.

Type **Date**
Press **Right Arrow**
Type **33045**
Press **Enter**
Type **/rfd1**
Press **Enter**
Press **Down Arrow**
Press **Left Arrow**

You should see the date number 33045 expressed as the date 21-Jun-90 in cell B8. Now, enter a number and use the Range Format Date Time 1 (HH:MM:SS AM/PM) command.

Type **Time**
Press **Right Arrow**
Type **0.61**
Press **Enter**
Type **/rfdt1**
Press **Enter**
Press **Down Arrow**
Press **Left Arrow**

You should see the time number 0.61 expressed as the time 02:38:24 PM in cell B9.

Step 10: Use the Text Format

Text format displays formulas in worksheet cells instead of their computed results. This format can be handy for checking formulas in a complex worksheet. Numbers in cells formatted as Text are displayed in General format. Enter a formula and use the Range Format Text command to display that formula instead of its computed result in the worksheet.

Type **Text**
Press **Right Arrow**
Type **+b1+b2**
Press **Enter**
Type **/rft**
Press **Enter**
Press **Down Arrow**
Press **Left Arrow**

You should see the formula +B1+B2 in cell B10 instead of the computed result 24691.356.

Step 11: Use the Hidden Format

Hidden format allows you to conceal the contents of one or more cells in the worksheet. The contents of a hidden cell still exist and can be viewed in the control panel unless the cell is protected and global protection is turned on. Enter a number and use the Range Format Hidden command to conceal it.

Type **Hidden**
Press **Right Arrow**
Type **12345.678**
Press **Enter**
Type **/rfh**
Press **Enter**

As Figure 5 shows, cell B11 appears to be empty in the worksheet, but its contents are visible in the control panel.

To reveal hidden cells, you can change their format to anything but Hidden. You can also use the Range Format Reset command to restore the global cell format for those cells.

Step 12: Save the Worksheet

Save the worksheet you have created in a file named FORMATS in case you want to use it again.

Type **/fs**
Type **formats**
Press **Enter**

Practice

1. Change the format of cell B2 to Fixed format with 0 decimal places. Notice how the number is rounded to 12346.
2. Change the number in cell B6 to −5 and observe the result. Change the number to 0.5 and see what happens. Finally, try entering 50 into the cell. The asterisks indicate that the contents cannot fit within the specified column width. Change the number back to 5.

Figure 5 Cell B11 is Hidden

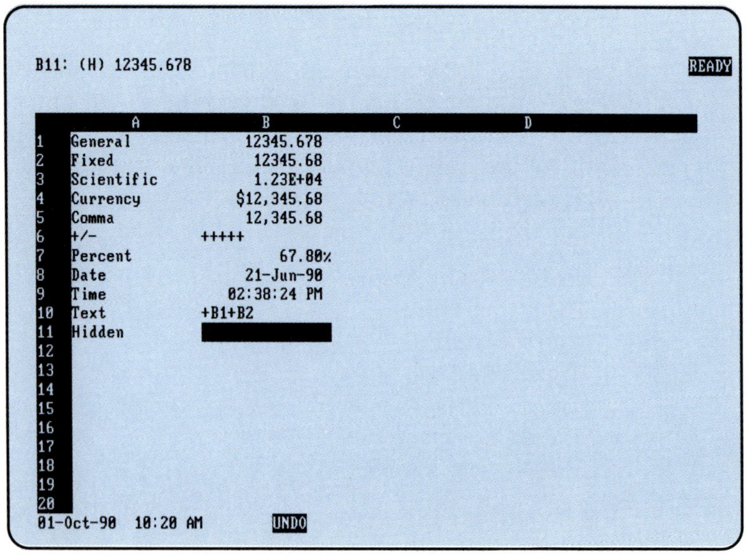

Lesson 5: Using Range Names

You have learned that a range of cells is designated like this: A1..B10. Lotus 1-2-3 also lets you assign a name to a range of cells. Range names can make it much easier to specify ranges in formulas and commands. Let's retrieve the BUDGET worksheet and see how to use range names.

Step 1: Retrieve the BUDGET Worksheet

Execute the File Retrieve command and select the BUDGET worksheet.

Type	**/fr**
Highlight	**BUDGET.WK1** (or **BUDGET.WK3**)
Press	**Enter**

Step 2: Name a Range

The expenses for January are in the range B6..B16. Let's name this range. A range name can be up to 15 characters long. It should not start with a number or resemble a cell address, such as B5. A range name cannot contain spaces or any of these characters:

, ; + * - / & < > { @ #

You can, however, use the underscore (_) character in range names. Execute the Range Name Create command, enter a name, and specify the range.

Type	**/rnc**
Type	**jan_expenses**
Press	**Enter**
Type	**b6..b16**
Press	**Enter**

Step 3: Use the Range Name in a Command

Let's use the range name JAN_EXPENSES to copy the expenses from column B to column D.

Type	**/c**
Type	**jan_expenses**
Press	**Enter**
Type	**d6**
Press	**Enter**

If you don't remember or don't want to type the range name you want to use, you can press the F3 function key to display a menu of range names. For example, follow these directions.

Type	**/c**
Press	**F3**
Highlight	**JAN_EXPENSES**
Press	**Enter**
Type	**e6**
Press	**Enter**

The contents of the JAN_EXPENSES range have been copied to columns D and E.

Step 4: Examine the Other Range Name Options

Activate the Range Name menu and examine the other Range Name options.

Type **/rn**

Figure 6 shows the Range Name menu. The Create option lets you change an existing range name as well as create a new one. The Delete option lets you remove a range name. The Labels option lets you assign range names to single-cell ranges, using the labels in adjacent cells as the range names. The Reset option deletes all range names. The Table option creates a two column table that lists all your range names and their corresponding ranges.

Practice

1. Move the cell pointer to B17 and examine the formula. Lotus 1-2-3 automatically replaced the B6..B16 in the formula with the range name JAN_EXPENSES.
2. Create range names for the February, March, and April expenses.
3. Move to an empty portion of the worksheet and execute the Range Name Table command. Return to READY mode.

Lesson 6: Filling a Range with a Sequence of Numbers

Sometimes, it is useful to fill a range of cells with a sequence of numbers. For example, suppose you wanted to number each item in your PROPERTY inventory. The Data Fill command makes it easy to generate sequences of numbers.

Step 1: Retrieve the PROPERTY Worksheet

Make PROPERTY your current worksheet.

Type **/fr**
Highlight **PROPERTY.WK1** (or **PROPERTY.WK3**)

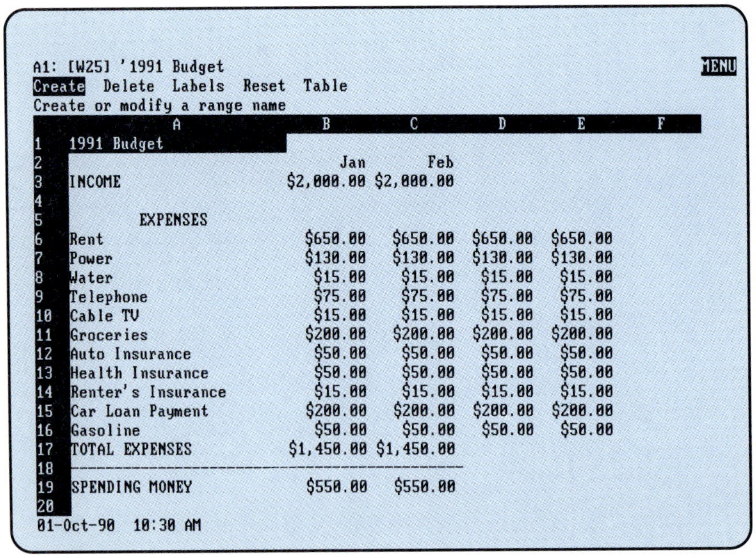

Figure 6 The Range Name Menu

Figure 7 The Data Fill Command Has Numbered the Items

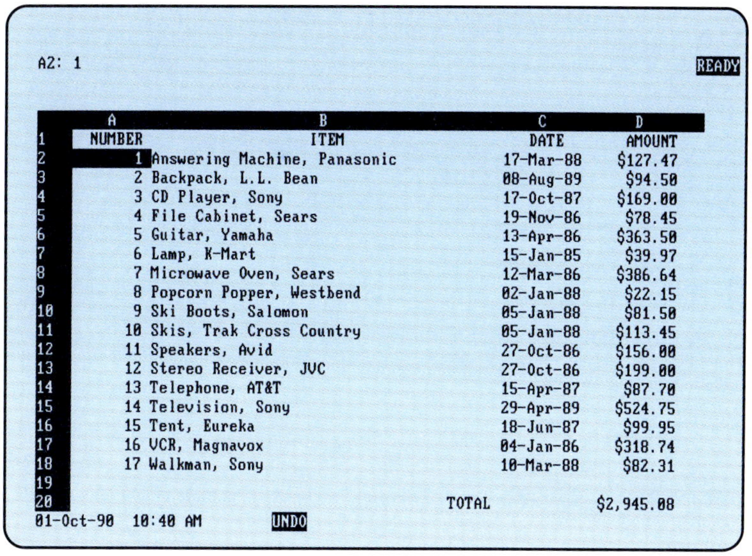

A2: 1 READY

	A	B	C	D
1	NUMBER	ITEM	DATE	AMOUNT
2	1	Answering Machine, Panasonic	17-Mar-88	$127.47
3	2	Backpack, L.L. Bean	08-Aug-89	$94.50
4	3	CD Player, Sony	17-Oct-87	$169.00
5	4	File Cabinet, Sears	19-Nov-86	$78.45
6	5	Guitar, Yamaha	13-Apr-86	$363.50
7	6	Lamp, K-Mart	15-Jan-85	$39.97
8	7	Microwave Oven, Sears	12-Mar-86	$386.64
9	8	Popcorn Popper, Westbend	02-Jan-88	$22.15
10	9	Ski Boots, Salomon	05-Jan-88	$81.50
11	10	Skis, Trak Cross Country	05-Jan-88	$113.45
12	11	Speakers, Avid	27-Oct-86	$156.00
13	12	Stereo Receiver, JVC	27-Oct-86	$199.00
14	13	Telephone, AT&T	15-Apr-87	$87.70
15	14	Television, Sony	29-Apr-89	$524.75
16	15	Tent, Eureka	18-Jun-87	$99.95
17	16	VCR, Magnavox	04-Jan-86	$318.74
18	17	Walkman, Sony	10-Mar-88	$82.31
19				
20			TOTAL	$2,945.08

01-Oct-90 10:40 AM UNDO

Press **Enter**
Press **Home**

Step 2: Insert a New Column A

To number the items in the first column, you must insert a new column A. Execute the Worksheet Insert Column command.

Type **/wic**
Press **Enter**

A new blank row A, nine characters wide, will be inserted in the worksheet. Enter a label for the column.

Type **"NUMBER**
Press **Down Arrow**

Step 3: Execute the Data Fill Command

We want to fill the range A2..A18 with the numbers 1 through 17. Execute the Data Fill command, specify the fill range, specify the start value, specify the step value, and specify the stop value.

Type **/df**
Type **a2..a18**
Press **Enter**
Type **1**
Press **Enter**
Press **Enter**
Press **Enter**

Lotus 1-2-3 will fill the range with a sequence of numbers that starts with 1 and increases by 1 in each successive cell (see Figure 7).

Step 4: Save the Worksheet

To preserve the changes you have made, save the PROPERTY worksheet to its disk file.

Type **/fs**
Press **Enter**
Type **r**

Practice

Execute the Worksheet Erase Yes command to clear the PROPERTY worksheet. Use the Data Fill command to load the range A1 to Z1 with the numbers 2, 4, 6, 8, 10, 12, and so on.

Lesson 7: Transposing Columns and Rows

Lotus 1-2-3 has many commands for rearranging existing data. For example, you already know how to use commands such as Move, Copy, Worksheet Insert, and Worksheet Delete. Range Trans is a more specialized command that lets you transpose data from a horizontal arrangement to a vertical arrangement, or vice versa. As an example, let's transpose a table in the SALES worksheet you created in the previous chapter.

Step 1: Retrieve the SALES Worksheet

Make SALES your current worksheet.

Type **/fr**
Highlight **SALES.WK1** (or **SALES.WK3**)
Press **Enter**
Press **Home**

Step 2: Transpose a Range

The sales figures in rows 1 and 2 are arranged horizontally, with a year in each column. Let's transpose this table and make a new copy in which the sales figures are arranged vertically. Execute the Range Trans command, specify the FROM range, then specify the first cell of the TO range.

Type **/rt**
Type **a1..e2**
Press **Enter**
Type **e5**
Press **Enter**

Figure 8 shows the result. The original sales table in cells A1..E2 has been transposed and copied to cells E5..F9.

Practice

Transpose another table in the SALES worksheet. Be sure to specify a TO range in an empty part of the worksheet.

Figure 8 The Transposed Sales Table

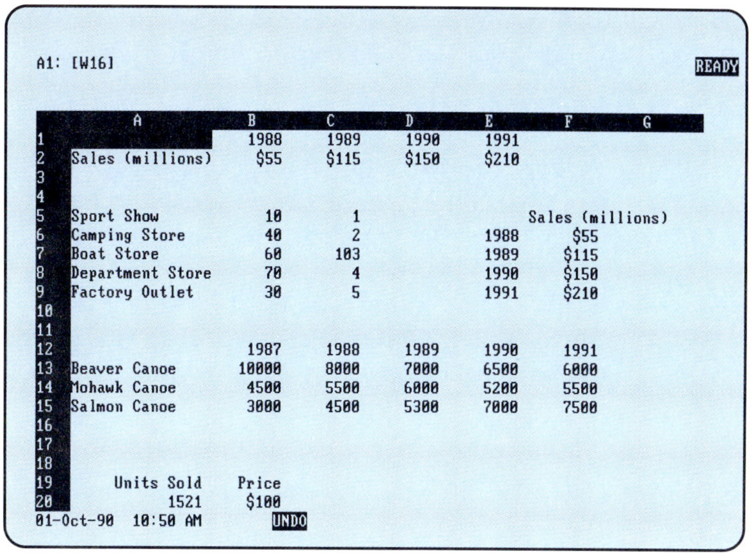

Lesson 8: Controlling Recalculation and Iteration

Spreadsheet programs are useful tools because you can easily change data and recalculate worksheets. Usually, recalculation occurs automatically, and you don't have to worry about it. In some cases, however, you must exercise control over the method and order of recalculation. Lotus 1-2-3 lets you do both.

Most formulas need only be calculated once, unless their data are changed. Some special formulas, however, may have to be recalculated many times to achieve a final result. This repeated recomputation is called **iteration.** It can also be controlled with 1-2-3.

Step 1: Set Up a New Worksheet

Erase the screen and start with a new worksheet.

Type **/wey**

Step 2: Change the Method of Recalculation

Lotus 1-2-3 has two recalculation methods: Automatic and Manual. **Automatic recalculation** is the default method, used unless you specify otherwise. In Lotus 1-2-3 Release 2.01, automatic recalculation means that every formula in the entire worksheet is recalculated every time any cell is changed. Lotus 1-2-3 Release 2.2 and Release 3.0 use a more sophisticated type of automatic recalculation known as **minimal** or **optimal recalculation.** This feature increases speed by recalculating only those cells that have changed, and the cells that depend on them, since the worksheet was last recalculated.

Even with minimal recalculation, very large worksheets can take a long time to recalculate. The delays can be annoying. Fortunately, Lotus 1-2-3 lets you turn off automatic recalculation and use **manual recalculation** instead. When manual recalculation is turned on, the worksheet is recalculated only when you press

F9, the CALC key. For example, execute the Worksheet Global Recalculation Manual command and create a simple worksheet.

Type **/wgrm**
Type **100**
Press **Down Arrow**
Type **200**
Press **Down Arrow**
Type **+a1+a2**
Press **Enter**

The formula will be calculated because it was just entered. Try changing cell A2 and see what happens.

Press **Up Arrow**
Type **100**
Press **Enter**

The result in cell A3 remains 300, even though it should be 200. You must press F9, the CALC key, to tell 1-2-3 to recalculate the worksheet.

Press **F9**

The result in cell A3 will change to 200.

Step 3: Change the Order of Recalculation

Lotus 1-2-3 can perform only one calculation at a time, so it must begin recalculating with a single cell and then proceed throughout the worksheet in some particular order. Early spreadsheet programs, such as VisiCalc, gave you a choice between two orders: column-wise and row-wise recalculation. **Column-wise recalculation** begins with cell A1 and proceeds down column A, goes on to cell B1 and proceeds down column B, and so on. **Row-wise recalculation** also starts at cell A1, but then proceeds to go across row 1, then row 2, and so on. The problem with both of these methods is that they can lead to incorrect results if you are not careful about how you set up your worksheet. For example, erase the worksheet, execute the Worksheet Global Recalculation Columnwise command, and enter the following worksheet.

Type **/wey**
Type **/wgrc**
Type **100+a3**
Press **Down Arrow**
Type **200**
Press **Down Arrow**
Type **100+a2**
Press **Enter**

As soon as you finish entering the worksheet, the formulas are calculated for the first time, and you see 100 in A1, 200 in A2, and 300 in A3. Already there is a problem. Cell A1 is supposed to contain 100 plus the value in cell A3. It should contain 400, but it contains only 100. Since the cells were evaluated in the order A1, A2, and A3, nothing was in A3 when cell A1 was originally evaluated. That is why A1 contains only 100. Now, change the contents of cell A2 to 222.

Press **Up Arrow**
Type **222**
Press **Enter**

With either column-wise or row-wise recalculation, the results will be 400 in A1, 222 in A2, and 322 in A3. This is *still* not right. Cell A1 should contain 422. It now contains 400 because 1-2-3 added 100 to the formula result of 300 left in cell A3 after the previous change. Clearly, in some instances neither column-wise nor row-wise recalculation work correctly.

Lotus 1-2-3 solves this problem by using **natural recalculation** unless you specify otherwise. This method recalculates a cell only after evaluating any cells on which it depends. For example, natural recalculation would evaluate our worksheet in this order: A2, A3, then A1. Execute the Worksheet Global Recalculation Natural command and then change cell A2 back to 200.

Type **/wgrn**
Type **200**
Press **Enter**

The results are now computed correctly. Cell A1 displays 400, cell A2 displays 200, and cell A3 displays 300.

Although natural recalculation is best for most worksheets, Lotus 1-2-3 lets you change to column-wise or row-wise so that you can create worksheets in which you have explicit control over the order of recalculation.

Step 4: Create a Direct Circular Reference

As you have just seen, formulas can refer to cells that contain other formulas. In the previous step, cell A1 contains a formula that refers to cell A3, but A3 also contains a formula. Although this might seem unusual and perhaps even a bit confusing, it is really quite common for worksheets to contain formulas that refer to other formulas. As long as natural recalculation is used, there is seldom a problem. One potential difficulty, however, can occur. A **circular reference** results when a formula in a cell is either directly or indirectly dependent on the value in that very same cell. The most obvious example is when you use a formula that refers to the same cell in which it is stored. This is a direct circular reference. For example, move to A1 and enter the following formula.

Press **Home**
Type **100+a1**
Press **Enter**

Lotus 1-2-3 cannot evaluate this formula correctly. It displays the value 100 in A1 because it calculated the formula only once. The CIRC error message appears at the bottom of the screen to indicate the presence of a formula containing a circular reference. Although you could tell Lotus 1-2-3 to recalculate the formula several times, every time it would try to evaluate 100 + A1, the value in A1 would change. No matter how many times it would try, the program could not compute a final result for this formula.

Step 5: Use Iteration

Certain *indirect* circular references, however, can be resolved eventually. An absolute final answer may not be reached, but an approximate result can often be obtained by recalculating the formulas a number of times. This method is called iterative recalculation, or simply iteration, and it can be used to solve certain kinds of problems. For example, just about everyone knows what a square root is, but do you know how to calculate one? We seldom figure square roots by hand anymore because most calculators, spreadsheet packages, and programming languages have built-in functions to compute square roots. Before these tools were available, people looked up square roots in printed tables in math books. So, although you will probably never have to know how to compute a square root, let's demonstrate an interesting way to do it with 1-2-3 without using the built-in @SQRT function.

One method to compute the square root of a number is to repeatedly make better and better estimates until you finally arrive at the correct answer. Follow these directions to create a template that will simulate this method of computing a square root:

Type **/wey**
Type **16**
Press **Right Arrow**
Type **'<-- Enter the number**
Press **Down Arrow**
Type **'<-- "Fudge factor" to avoid division by 0**
Press **Left Arrow**
Type **0.000001**
Press **Down Arrow**
Type **+a4**
Press **Right Arrow**
Type **'<-- Contains the formula +A4**
Press **Down Arrow**
Type **'<-- Here is the square root**
Press **Left Arrow**
Type **@round((a3+a1/(a3+a2))/2,2)**
Press **Enter**

Obviously, the square root of 16 is not 8,000,000. By default, 1-2-3 recalculates circular references only once. Execute the Worksheet Global Recalculation Iteration command and enter 50 as the number of times to recalculate circular references. Then press the F9 key to recalculate the worksheet.

Type **/wgri50**
Press **Enter**
Press **F9**

Figure 9 shows the result. This worksheet simulates the process of repeatedly making better square root estimates until an answer close enough to the correct answer is obtained. The formula in cell A3 displays the current result of the formula in cell A4, and the formula in cell A4 uses the current result of the formula in cell A3. This is an indirect circular reference. Each time these formulas are recalculated, the result in cell A4 gets closer to the true square root of the number in cell A1. After many iterations, a final answer is obtained.

Step 6: Save the Worksheet

Save the square root template in case you would like to use it again.

Type **/fs**
Type **sqrt**
Press **Enter**

Practice Use the template to compute the square roots of some numbers other than 16. For example, try 9, 81, 144, and any other numbers you like.

Figure 9 Iteration Used to Compute a Square Root

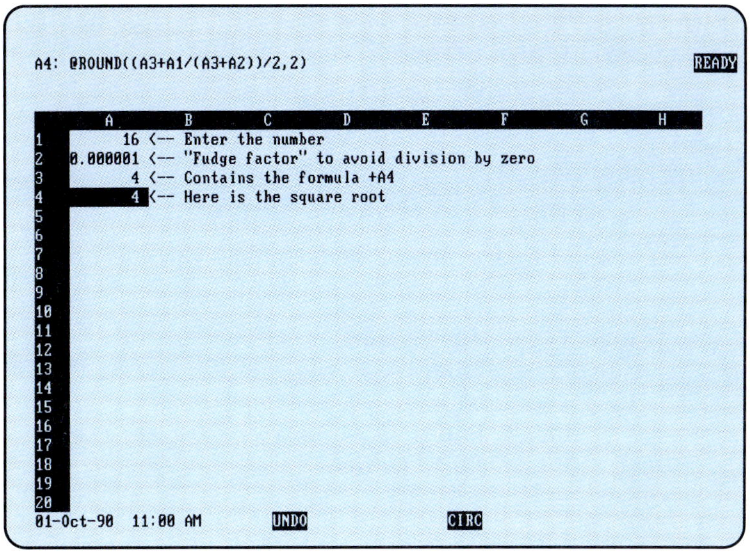

Lesson 9: Using Relative, Absolute, and Mixed Cell References

Three types of cell references can be used in a formula: relative, absolute, and mixed. A **relative reference** is a cell address that pertains to a cell's position relative to the current cell. For example, if the current cell is A3 and it contains the formula +A1+A2, the A1 in the formula refers to the cell located two cells above the formula. Lotus 1-2-3 assumes all cell references to be relative unless you specify otherwise. Relative cell references are automatically changed to reflect their new locations when they are moved or copied.

An **absolute reference** is a cell address that does not change when it is moved or copied. This type of cell address is specified by preceding the column and row designations with dollar signs. For example, the absolute reference A1 always refers to cell A1, even if a formula that contains it is moved or copied.

A **mixed reference** is half-relative and half-absolute, in which either a column or a row is absolute, but not both. For example, $A1 is a mixed reference that always means column A, but the row might be changed if this reference is copied or moved. Similarly, A$1 is a mixed cell reference that keeps the row constant.

Let's demonstrate each type of cell reference.

Step 1: Set Up a New Worksheet

Erase the screen and start with a new worksheet.

Type **/wey**

Step 2: Use Relative References

Cell addresses without dollar signs are assumed to be relative references. For example, follow these directions to create a formula that contains relative references:

Type **100**
Press **Down Arrow**
Type **200**

Press **Down Arrow**
Type **+a1+a2**
Press **Enter**

The cell references in the formula in cell A3 are relative references.

Step 3: Copy Relative References

The Copy command demonstrates the effect of using relative references. Copy cells A1 through A3 to column B.

Type **/ca1..a3**
Press **Enter**
Type **b1**
Press **Enter**
Press **Right Arrow**

Examine the formula in cell B3. The original formula was +A1+A2; it was changed to +B1+B2 when it was copied. In most cases, you want cell references to be changed in this manner when formulas are copied or moved.

Step 4: Use an Absolute Reference

In certain situations, however, you may not want a cell reference to be changed when it is copied or moved. For example, you may use a constant value, such as the current interest rate, in several formulas in different places. But you need only store the interest rate once, in a single cell. If you are going to copy or move cells containing formulas that refer to this interest rate, you should use an absolute reference for the cell containing the interest rate. Change the formula in B3 so that it contains an absolute reference to cell A1.

Type **+a1+b2**
Press **Enter**

Now change the value in B1 and see how the result of the formula in B3 remains the same because it adds A1 instead of B1 to B2.

Press **Up Arrow**
Press **Up Arrow**
Type **200**
Press **Enter**

The value displayed in cell B3 should still be 300.

Step 5: Copy An Absolute Reference

Let's see what happens when you copy a formula containing an absolute reference. Copy cells B1 through B3 to column C, then move to cell C3.

Type **/cb1..b3**
Press **Enter**
Type **c1**
Press **Enter**
Press **Down Arrow**
Press **Down Arrow**
Press **Right Arrow**

Examine the formula in C3 (see Figure 10). The absolute cell reference A1 was not changed, but the relative cell reference was changed to C2.

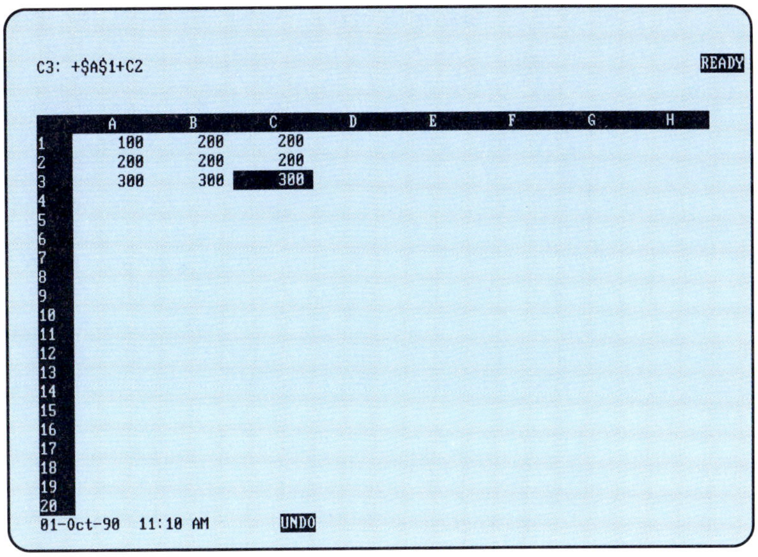

Figure 10 Absolute and Relative References in a Formula

Step 6: Use Mixed Cell References

If you want part of a cell address to remain the same and part to change when you copy or move a formula, you must use a mixed reference. Let's create a small multiplication table of the numbers 0 through 5 to demonstrate the use of mixed cell references. Follow these directions to erase the worksheet and use the Data Fill command to enter the column and row headings of the multiplicands (the numbers to be multiplied):

Type /**wey**
Type /**dfb1..g1**
Press **Enter** (4 times)
Type /**dfa2..a7**
Press **Enter** (4 times)

The numbers 0 through 5 should appear in cells B1 through G1 and A2 through A7. Move to cell B2 and enter the multiplication formula containing mixed references.

Press **Down Arrow**
Press **Right Arrow**
Type +**$a2*b$1**
Press **Enter**

When this formula is copied to the rest of the table, the $A2 mixed reference will keep column A constant, but vary the row. The B$1 mixed reference will vary the column, but keep row 1 constant. To see how these mixed references work, copy the formula in B2 to cells B3 through B7 and C2 through G7, then move to cell G7.

Type /**c**
Press **Enter**
Type **b3..b7**
Press **Enter**
Type /**c**
Press **Enter**

Figure 11 Mixed References in a Multiplication Table

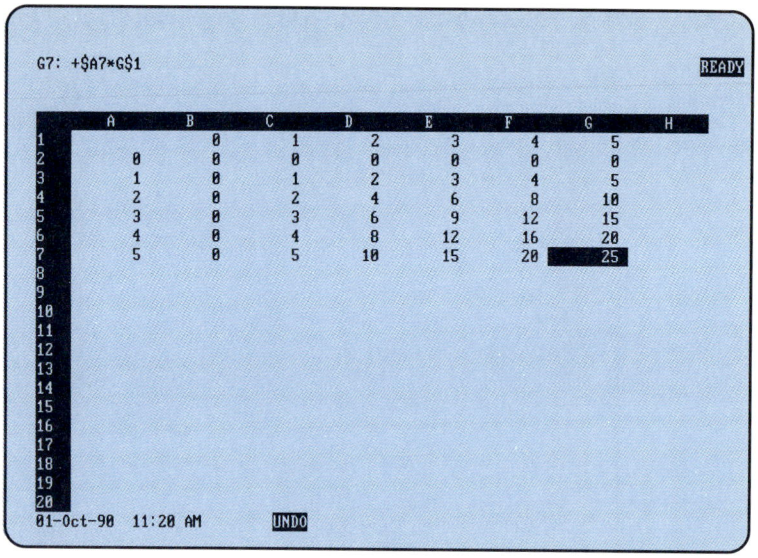

Type **c2..g7**
Press **Enter**
Press **F5**
Type **g7**
Press **Enter**

Your screen should look like Figure 11. The rest of the multiplication table is easily created with the Copy command, because you used mixed references to keep column A constant for the first multiplicand and row 1 constant for the second multiplicand.

Practice See what happens if you use relative references instead of mixed references in the multiplication table. Change the formula in B2 to +A2*B1. Then copy this formula to cells B3..B7 and C2..G7. Examine some of the copied formulas and try to understand why mixed references are necessary in this case.

Lesson 10: Using Additional Functions

You have already learned to use some of the mathematical, trigonometric, statistical, and financial functions of Lotus 1-2-3. Now let's examine some of the date and time, logical, and string functions.

Step 1: Set Up a New Worksheet

Erase the screen and start with a new worksheet.

Type **/wey**

Step 2: Try Some Date and Time Functions

Date and time functions help you work with the Lotus 1-2-3 date and time numbers. Let's try a few examples.

Type **@date(90,12,31)**
Press **Enter**

The result should be 33238. The @DATE function returns the sequential date number, given the year, month, and day.

Press **Down Arrow**
Type **@day(a1)**
Press **Enter**

The result should be 31. The @DAY function returns the day, given a date number. The @MONTH and @YEAR functions work similarly.

Press **Down Arrow**
Type **@time(14,10,20)**
Press **Enter**

The result should be 0.590509, the time number for 2:10:20 PM. The @TIME function returns the 1-2-3 time number, given an hour (0-23), minute (0-59), and second (0-59).

Press **Down Arrow**
Type **@hour(a3)**
Press **Enter**

The result should be 14. The @HOUR function returns the hour (0-23), given a time number. The @MINUTE and @SECOND functions work similarly.

Press **Down Arrow**
Type **@now**
Press **Enter**

The @NOW function returns the full serial number for the current date and time.

Step 3: Try Some Logical Functions

Logical functions return values that are dependent on the results of conditional expressions. They essentially allow you to compare values in cells and perform different actions based on the results of those comparisons. Let's try a few examples.

Press **Down Arrow**
Type **@isnumber(a1)**
Press **Enter**

The result should be 1, which stands for TRUE. The @ISNUMBER function returns 1 (TRUE) if the given value is numeric and 0 (FALSE) if it is a label. The @ISSTRING function is the opposite of @ISNUMBER.

Press **Home**
Press **Right Arrow**
Type **100**
Press **Down Arrow**
Type **@if(b1>100,"Big","Small")**
Press **Enter**

You should see "Small" in cell B2. The @IF function evaluates the given logical expression as TRUE or FALSE, and returns the first value if it is TRUE, or the second value if it is FALSE. Since the number in B1 is not greater than 100, the @IF function returns "Small," the second value after the logical expression.

Step 4: Try Some String Functions

String functions manipulate labels. Let's try a few examples.

Press **Down Arrow**
Type **@length(b2)**
Press **Enter**

The result should be 5, the number of characters in "Small," the label in cell B2. The @LENGTH function returns the length of the given string.

Press **Down Arrow**
Type **@left(b2,3)**
Press **Enter**

The result should be "Sma," the first three characters in the label in cell B2. The @LEFT function returns the first *n* characters in a string. The @RIGHT function works similarly, except that it returns the last *n* characters in a string. The @MID function returns *n* characters from the middle of a string, starting at the specified position.

Press **Down Arrow**
Type **@upper(b2)**
Press **Enter**

The result should be "SMALL." The @UPPER function converts the given string to all uppercase characters. The @PROPER function works similarly, except that it capitalizes only the first character in each word in the string.

Press **Down Arrow**
Type **@repeat("Hello ",10)**
Press **Enter**

The result should be "Hello" repeated ten times. The @REPEAT function repeats the given string a specified number of times.

Practice To see how you might use @NOW, try the following formulas: @YEAR(@NOW), @MONTH(@NOW), @DAY(@NOW), @HOUR(@NOW), @MINUTE(@NOW), @SECOND(@NOW).

Lesson 11: Using Macros

A **macro** is a sequence of keystrokes and special commands that you can create to automate a task. Any task that 1-2-3 can perform can be automated with a macro. When you run a macro, 1-2-3 performs the instructions much faster than you could do them manually. Once a macro has been created, you can use it over and over again. Creating a macro takes planning and time to develop, but it can save a great deal of time in the long run. Macros are used to automate repetitive tasks, reduce keystrokes, simplify complex procedures, guide novices who are unfamiliar with 1-2-3, increase accuracy, and ensure consistency in a worksheet. Let's start with a simple macro that will automatically enter labels into a worksheet.

Step 1: Plan the Macro

A macro is a sequence of keystrokes that you can store, name, and play back over and over again. The first step in creating a macro is to decide what you want it to do. Suppose you want to create a macro that will enter the names of the months of the year across the columns. To plan the macro, think of how you would do this procedure manually. First, you would type *January* and press the Right Arrow key. Then you would type *February* and press the Right Arrow key. After entering the twelve months in this fashion, you would move the cell pointer down to the beginning of the next row. For now, clear the current worksheet and widen all columns to 12 characters.

Type **/wey**
Type **/wgc12**
Press **Enter**

Step 2: Enter the Macro Definition

Before you can use a macro, you must define it. This definition tells 1-2-3 what keystrokes to execute when you run the macro. A macro definition is basically a series of labels stored in an empty part of the worksheet. Usually, a macro definition is stored in cells far below or to the right of the area the actual worksheet is expected to occupy. For this example, move the cell pointer to A100.

Press **F5**
Type **a100**
Press **Enter**

You may type the label entries of a macro definition in any column of cells. Furthermore, you may type more than one macro instruction in any cell, as long as you don't try to enter more than 240 characters in a single cell. Every cell entry in a macro definition must be a label; numbers and formulas will be translated when the macro is run. The entries in a macro definition may consist of any characters you can type on the keyboard. In addition, keys that perform actions instead of displaying characters can also be included in macro definitions. These special keys are specified by entering a symbol or a name enclosed in braces ({ and }). For example, to include a Right Arrow keystroke in a macro definition, you would enter {*right*}. The following table shows the macro instructions for some common keys.

Macro Instructions for Common Keys

Key	Macro Instruction
Enter	~(the tilde character)
Down Arrow	{down}
Up Arrow	{up}
Left Arrow	{left}
Right Arrow	{right}
Home	{home}
End	{end}
Page Up	{pgup}
Page Down	{pgdn}
Ctrl-Right Arrow	{bigright}

Macro Instructions for Common Keys (continued)

Key	Macro Instruction
Ctrl-Left Arrow	{bigleft}
F2	{edit}
F5	{goto}
Escape	{esc}
Backspace	{bs}
Delete	{del}

Now, follow these directions to enter the definition of a macro that will enter the months of the year across the columns.

Type **^January {right}**
Press **Down Arrow**
Type **^February {right}**
Press **Down Arrow**
Type **^March {right}**
Press **Down Arrow**
Type **^April {right}**
Press **Down Arrow**
Type **^May {right}**
Press **Down Arrow**
Type **^June {right}**
Press **Down Arrow**
Type **^July {right}**
Press **Down Arrow**
Type **^August {right}**
Press **Down Arrow**
Type **^September {right}**
Press **Down Arrow**
Type **^October {right}**
Press **Down Arrow**
Type **^November {right}**
Press **Down Arrow**
Type **^December {down}**
Press **Down Arrow**
Type **{end} {left}**
Press **Enter**

Step 3: Name the Macro

Before you can use a macro, a range name must be assigned to the cells that hold the macro definition. This range name will serve as the macro name. Two types of macro names can be used: a backslash followed by a single letter (such as \A or \M) or a name of up to 15 characters (such as HEADING or MONTHS). The type of name you choose determines how you run the macro. (Note: Lotus 1-2-3 Release 2.01 allows only macro names that consist of a backslash and a single letter.) Follow these directions to name your macro \M:

Type **/rnc**
Type **\m**

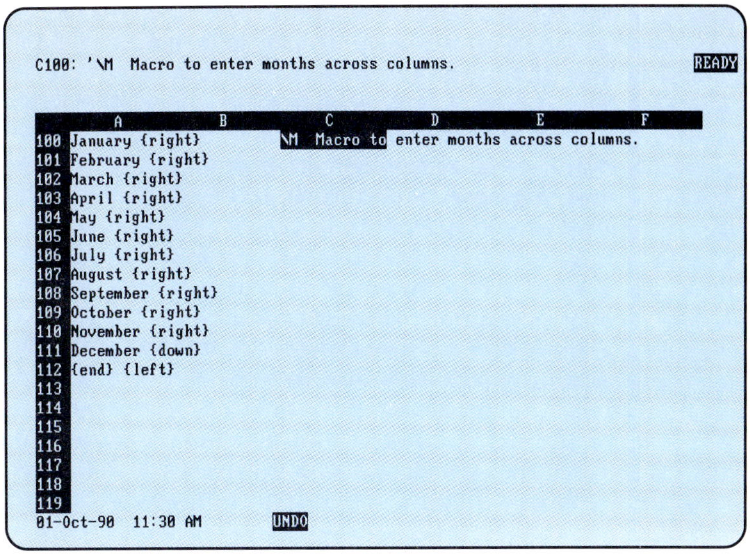

Figure 12 The Completed Macro Definition

Press **Enter**
Type **`a100..a112`**
Press **Enter**

Step 4: Document the Macro

It is a good idea to enter the macro name and a brief description beside the macro definition to document the macro for yourself and other users. Complex macros may also have a brief comment beside each macro instruction. Follow these directions to document your macro:

Press **F5**
Type **`c100`**
Press **Enter**
Type **`'\M Macro to enter months across columns.`**
Press **Enter**

The completed macro is shown in Figure 12.

Step 5: Run the Macro

Now you can use the macro you have created. A macro named with a backslash and a letter is invoked by holding down the Alternate key and typing the letter. Move to cell A2 and run the macro:

Press **Home**
Press **Down Arrow**
Press **Alt-M**

Wasn't that fun? All twelve month labels are entered automatically and the cell pointer returns to the beginning of the next row. Try it again:

Press **Alt-M**

Your screen should look like Figure 13. You can use the \M macro in any row and as many times as you like.

Figure 13 The Macro Has Been Run Twice

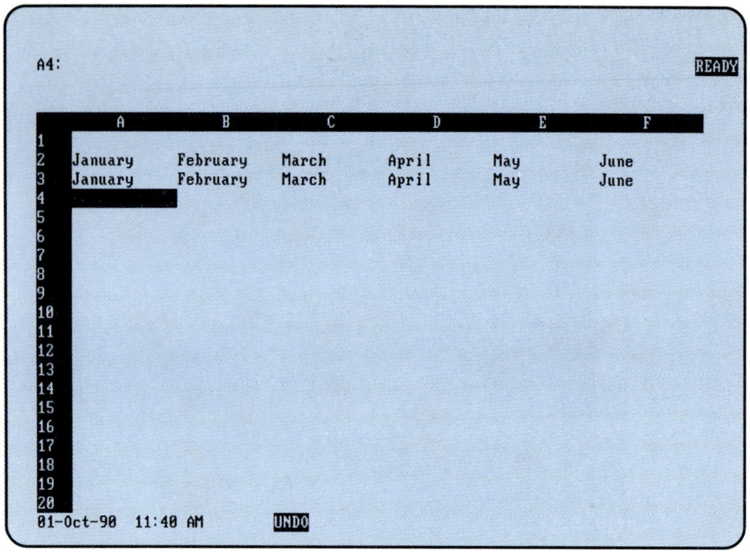

Note: a macro with a long name, such as HEADING or MONTHS, created with Lotus 1-2-3 Release 2.2 or 3.0, is run by pressing Alt-F3, the RUN key, to display a menu of macro names. You then highlight the name of the macro you want to run and press the Enter key.

Step 6: Save the Worksheet

To save the macro you have created, you must save the worksheet.

Type **/fs**
Type **months**
Press **Enter**

Practice Modify the \M macro so that it always moves the cell pointer to A1 when it is finished entering the months. Test the modified macro to make sure it works correctly.

Lesson 12: Using the Learn Feature with Release 2.2

Lotus 1-2-3 Release 2.2 has an easier way to create macros. (If you are not running Lotus 1-2-3 Release 2.2, just read this lesson without performing its steps.) The **learn feature** lets you have 1-2-3 record your keystrokes as you perform the task you want to automate in order to generate the macro definition. Let's use this method to create a macro to enter today's date in the current cell. This lesson assumes that the global column width has been set to 12 characters.

Step 1: Specify the Learn Range

The **learn range** is the single-column range of cells in your worksheet where 1-2-3 will record your keystrokes and create the macro definition. Since you cannot always be certain how many cells your macro will require, you should reserve more cells than you think you might need. The date macro should require no more than five cells. Execute the Worksheet Learn Range command and specify cells A50 to A55 as the learn range.

Type **/wlr**
Type **a50..a55**
Press **Enter**

Step 2: Turn On the Learn Feature

You must turn on the learn feature so that 1-2-3 knows what keystrokes to record. First, make sure that the cell pointer is not in the learn range. Alt-F5, the LEARN key, is used to turn on the learn feature.

Press **Alt-F5**

The LEARN indicator will appear at the bottom of the screen.

Step 3: Perform the Task

To record the macro, you perform the task you want to automate. Follow these directions to enter the @NOW function and format the current cell as a date:

Type **@now**
Press **Enter**
Type **/rfd1**
Press **Enter**

Note that the keystrokes you execute are performed as they are recorded in the learn range.

Step 4: Turn Off the Learn Feature

After you have executed the keystrokes you want to automate, you must turn off the learn feature. Alt-F5, the LEARN key, also turns off the learn feature.

Press **Alt-F5**

The LEARN indicator will disappear from the bottom of the screen.

Step 5: Name the Macro

The macro definition must be named before you can use it. Move to the learn range:

Press **F5**
Type **a50**
Press **Enter**

Notice cells A50 and A51 are filled with the keystrokes you executed while the learn feature was turned on. Remember that the ~ (tilde) character symbolizes the Enter key. Execute the Range Name Create command to name the macro \D:

Type **/rnc**
Type **\d**
Press **Enter**
Type **a50..a51**
Press **Enter**

Step 6: Document the Macro

Move to cell B50 and enter the macro name and a brief description.

Press **Right Arrow**
Type **'\D Macro to enter today's date.**
Press **Enter**

Your screen should look like Figure 14.

Step 7: Run the Macro

Move to cell A5 and run the new macro.

Press **F5**
Type **a5**
Press **Enter**
Press **Alt-D**

Today's date number will be entered into cell A5 and the cell will be formatted as a date.

Practice

Modify the macro definition so that the cell is formatted to display only the day and month. Hint: use date format number 2.

Lesson 13: Using the Record Feature with Release 3.0

Lotus 1-2-3 Release 3.0 has a feature similar to the Learn feature of Release 2.2 for easily creating macros. (If you are not running Lotus 1-2-3 Release 3.0, just read this lesson without performing its steps.) The **record feature** lets you create a macro by copying keystrokes saved in the **record buffer,** a 512-byte area of

Figure 14 Macro to Enter Today's Date

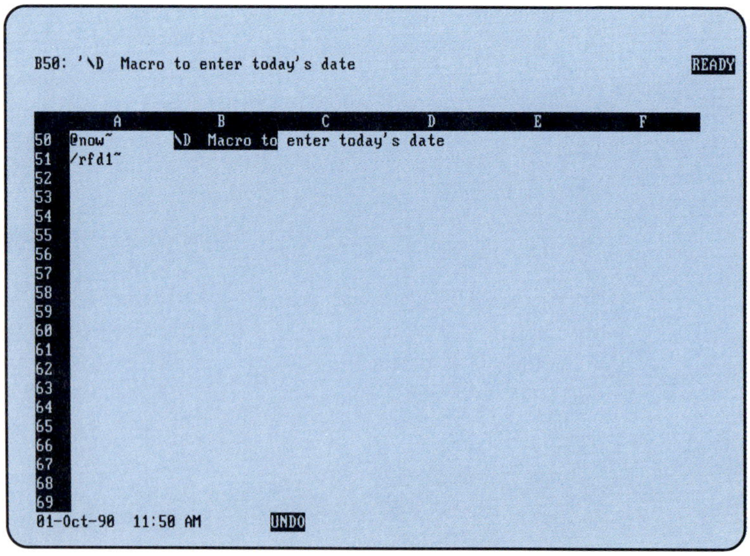

memory in which Lotus 1-2-3 Release 3.0 stores your most recent keystrokes. Let's use this method to create a macro to enter today's date in the current cell. This lesson assumes that the global column width has been set to 12 characters.

Step 1: Erase the Record Buffer

Press Alt-F2, the RECORD key, and select the Erase option to clear the current contents of the record buffer.

Press **Alt-F2**
Type **e**

Step 2: Perform the Task

Move the cell pointer to the cell where you want to start the task, and execute the keystrokes you want to automate.

Type **@now**
Press **Enter**
Type **/rfd1**
Press **Enter**

Today's date number will be entered in the current cell and it will be formatted as a date.

Step 3: Copy the Keystrokes from the Record Buffer

The next step is to copy the keystrokes you just executed from the record buffer to the range in which you want to store the macro definition. Let's store the macro definition in cell A50. Press the RECORD key, select the Copy option, highlight the keystrokes in the buffer, and specify the destination cell.

Press **Alt-F2**
Type **c**
Press **Home**
Press **Tab**
Press **End**
Press **Enter**
Type **a50**
Press **Enter**

The recorded keystrokes will be copied into cell A50.

Step 4: Name the Macro

The macro definition must be named before you can use it. Move to the cell containing the macro definition and name it \D:

Press **F5**
Type **a50**
Press **Enter**
Type **/rnc**
Type **\d**
Press **Enter**
Press **Enter**

Step 5: Document the Macro

Move to cell B50 and enter the macro name and a brief description.

Press **Right Arrow**
Type **'\D Macro to enter today's date.**
Press **Enter**

Step 6: Run the Macro

Move to cell A5 and run the new macro.

Press **F5**
Type **a5**
Press **Enter**
Press **Alt-D**

Today's date number will be entered into cell A5, and the cell will be formatted as a date.

Practice Modify the macro definition so that the cell is formatted to display only the day and month. Hint: use date format number 2.

Lesson 14: Linking Worksheets with Releases 2.2 and 3.0

Lotus 1-2-3 Releases 2.2 and 3.0 include a linking feature that allows you to use values from other worksheets in your current worksheet. (If you are running Lotus 1-2-3 Release 2.01, just read this lesson without performing its steps.) Linking is often used to consolidate data from a number of worksheets in a summary worksheet. As an example, let's create a worksheet that uses values from three other worksheets.

Step 1: Create the Three Sales Worksheets

Suppose a business has offices in three cities: New York, Chicago, and Los Angeles. Sales figures from each office are kept in separate worksheets. Follow these directions to create the three sales worksheets:

Type **/wey**
Type **/wgc12**
Press **Enter**
Type **/wgfc**
Press **Enter**
Type **New York**
Press **Right Arrow**
Type **Sales**
Press **Down Arrow**
Type **99600**
Press **Enter**
Type **/fs**
Type **ny**
Press **Enter**

Type **/wey**
Type **/wgc12**
Press **Enter**
Type **/wgfc**
Press **Enter**
Type **Chicago**
Press **Right Arrow**
Type **Sales**
Press **Down Arrow**
Type **88466**
Press **Enter**
Type **/fs**
Type **ch**
Press **Enter**

Type **/wey**
Type **/wgc12**
Press **Enter**
Type **/wgfc**
Press **Enter**
Type **Los Angeles**
Press **Right Arrow**
Type **Sales**
Press **Down Arrow**
Type **90800**
Press **Enter**
Type **/fs**
Type **la**
Press **Enter**

Step 2: Create the Summary Worksheet

Now create a worksheet that will summarize the sales figures from New York, Chicago, and Los Angeles.

Type **/wey**
Type **/wgc12**
Press **Enter**
Type **/wgfc**
Press **Enter**
Type **Sales Summary**
Press **Down Arrow**
Type **New York**
Press **Down Arrow**
Type **Chicago**
Press **Down Arrow**
Type **Los Angeles**
Press **Down Arrow**
Type **TOTAL**
Press **Right Arrow**
Type **@sum(b2..b4)**
Press **Up Arrow**

Step 3: Enter Linking Formulas

You create a link between two files by entering a linking formula in the current worksheet that refers to a cell in the other worksheet file. The cell in the other worksheet is called the source cell and the cell in the current worksheet is called the target cell. Once the two files are linked, 1-2-3 copies the value from the source cell to the target cell. A linking formula must have the following format:

+<<*file name*>>*cell reference*

For example, follow these directions to enter the linking formulas into the summary worksheet:

Type +<<**la.wk1**>>**b2**
Press **Up Arrow**
Type +<<**ch.wk1**>>**b2**
Press **Up Arrow**
Type +<<**ny.wk1**>>**b2**
Press **Enter**

Note: if you are running Lotus 1-2-3 Release 3.0, you should enter LA.WK3, CH.WK3, and NY.WK3 as the worksheet file names.

Your screen should look like Figure 15. Cell B2 contains the sales figure from cell B2 in the worksheet file NY.WK1, cell B3 contains the sales figure from cell B2 in the worksheet file CH.WK1, and cell B4 contains the sales figure from cell B2 in the worksheet file LA.WK1. The formula in cell B5 computes the sum of these values from three different worksheets.

Step 4: Save the Summary Worksheet

Save the summary worksheet in a disk file.

Type **/fs**
Type **summary**
Press **Enter**

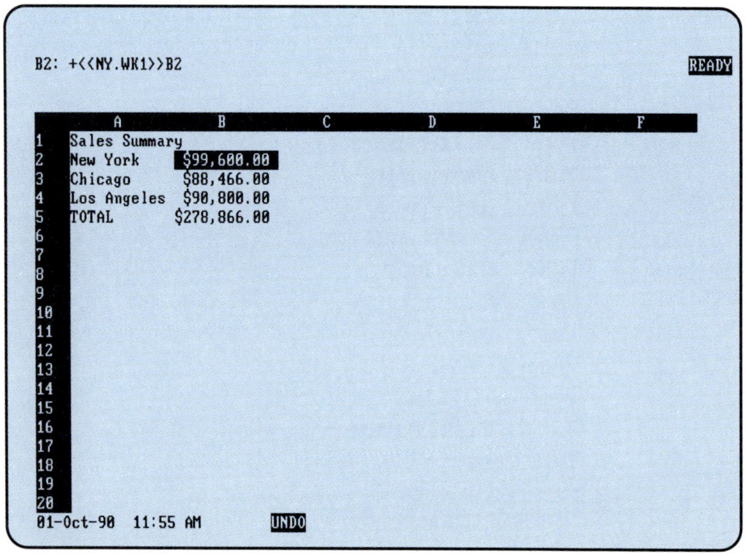

Figure 15 Linking Formulas in the Summary Worksheet

Practice Retrieve NY.WK1, change the sales figure, and save the updated file. Then retrieve SUMMARY.WK1 and see the result. If the source files are changed, values in target cells are automatically updated when the target file is retrieved.

Lesson 15: Using Three-Dimensional Worksheets with Release 3.0

Three-dimensional worksheets carry linking to its logical extreme: every cell in a worksheet can be linked to corresponding cells in other worksheets. A third dimension creates a kind of "super-worksheet" that is like a stack of conventional worksheets. Perhaps the easiest way to envision a three-dimensional worksheet is as a sequence of pages, each of which is a table of rows and columns. Lotus 1-2-3 Release 3.0 lets you create such multiple-sheet worksheet files. (If you are not running Lotus 1-2-3 Release 3.0, just read this lesson without performing its steps.) Let's create a simple three-dimensional worksheet.

Step 1: Set Up a New Worksheet

The worksheets we will create will hold sales figures for two different years and a summary statement. First, clear your current worksheet and set up the first sales worksheet.

Type **/wey**
Type **/wgc12**
Press **Enter**
Type **/wgfc**
Press **Enter**
Type **Sales 1989**
Press **Down Arrow**
Press **Down Arrow**
Press **Right Arrow**
Type **^Jan-Mar**
Press **Right Arrow**
Type **^Apr-Jun**
Press **Right Arrow**
Type **^Jul-Sep**
Press **Right Arrow**
Type **^Oct-Dec**
Press **Right Arrow**
Type **^TOTAL**
Press **End**
Press **Left Arrow**
Press **Left Arrow**
Press **Down Arrow**
Type **Sales**
Press **Right Arrow**
Type **4200**
Press **Right Arrow**
Type **5000**
Press **Right Arrow**

Figure 16 The First Sales Worksheet

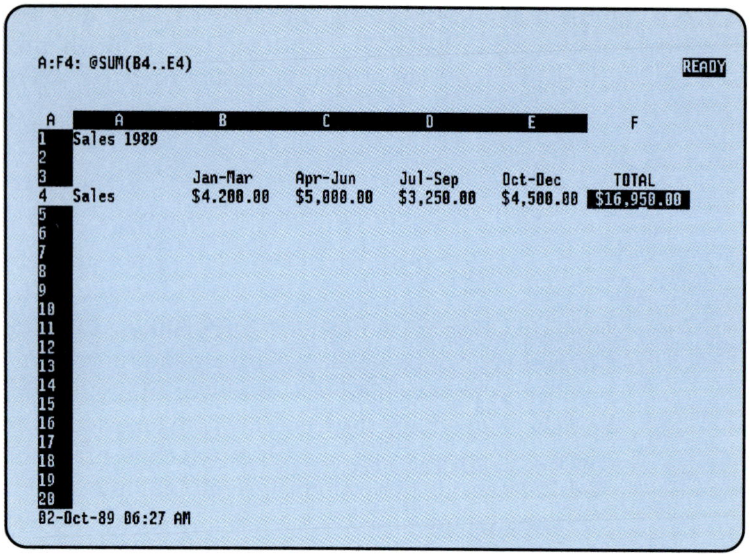

Type **3250**
Press **Right Arrow**
Type **4500**
Press **Right Arrow**
Type **@sum(b4..e4)**
Press **Enter**

Your screen should look like Figure 16.

Step 2: Add New Worksheets to a File

Lotus 1-2-3 always starts with a single worksheet on the screen. You can add up to 255 additional worksheets, depending on how much memory is installed in your computer. When multiple worksheets are loaded into memory, you can work with any one of them or with several at the same time. You can move between multiple worksheets like flipping pages in a notebook. Worksheets are designated by letters. The first worksheet is A, the second is B, and so on up to IV. Examine the upper left corner of the control panel. The full address of the current cell is A:F4, which means row 4 of column F of worksheet A.

You are going to add two new worksheets to the file. The second worksheet will hold the sales figures for 1990, and the third worksheet will summarize the first two worksheets. Execute the Worksheet Insert Sheet After 2 command to add two new worksheets after the current worksheet.

Type **/wisa2**
Press **Enter**

Worksheet B will appear on the screen.

Step 3: Change to Perspective View

Lotus 1-2-3 lets you display three consecutive worksheets on your screen at the same time stacked in an upward slope. Execute the Worksheet Window Perspective command.

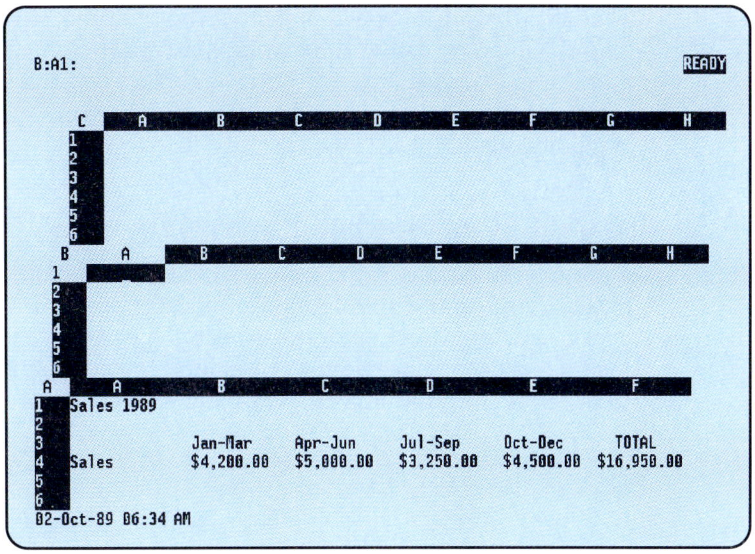

Figure 17 ***Perspective View of Three Worksheets***

Type /**wwp**

Your screen should look like Figure 17.

Step 4: Move Among Worksheets

Right now, worksheet B is your current worksheet. Several keys allow you to move among the multiple worksheets you have loaded. Move to the previous worksheet:

Press **Ctrl-PgDn**

Move to the next worksheet:

Press **Ctrl-PgUp**

Use the GOTO key to move to a particular cell in a particular worksheet:

Press **F5**
Type **c:d4**
Press **Enter**

Move to cell A:A1:

Press **Ctrl-Home**

Step 5: Format Worksheets Simultaneously

In many cases, you want all of the worksheets in the same file to be formatted the same way. You could format each worksheet individually, but by using GROUP mode, you can format all of the worksheets at once. When you turn on GROUP mode, 1-2-3 changes the format of all the worksheets in the file to match the format of the current worksheet. Make sure A is your current worksheet and execute the Worksheet Global Group Enable command.

Type /**wgge**

The GROUP indicator will appear at the bottom of the screen and worksheets B and C will be formatted like worksheet A. The global column width is now 12 and the global format is Currency for all three worksheets. The GROUP mode remains turned on until you disable it, and the worksheets will continue to format simultaneously.

Step 6: Copy Between Worksheets

You can easily create the second and third worksheets by copying the first worksheet, then making any necessary modifications. To copy the contents of worksheet A to the other two worksheets, specify a three-dimensional range that includes the worksheet letter. For example, execute the following Copy command to duplicate the contents of worksheet A in worksheets B and C.

Type **/c**
Type **a:a1.a:f4**
Press **Enter**
Type **b:a1..c:f4**
Press **Enter**

The contents of worksheet A will be copied to worksheets B and C.

Step 7: Modify Worksheet B

Worksheet B will contain the sales figures for 1990. Follow these directions to make the necessary modifications:

Press **Ctrl-PgUp**
Press **Home**
Type **Sales 1990**
Press **Down Arrow** (3 times)
Press **Right Arrow**
Type **4750**
Press **Right Arrow**
Type **5200**
Press **Right Arrow**
Type **5050**
Press **Right Arrow**
Type **6100**
Press **Right Arrow**

The TOTAL sales for 1990 should be $21,100.00.

Step 8: Modify Worksheet C

Worksheet C will summarize the figures in worksheets A and B. Instead of numbers, worksheet C will contain formulas that sum cells in worksheets A and B. Follow these directions to create the summary worksheet.

Press **Ctrl-PgUp**
Press **Home**
Type **Sales Summary 1989 - 1990**
Press **Down Arrow** (3 times)
Press **Right Arrow**
Type **@sum(a:b4..b:b4)**

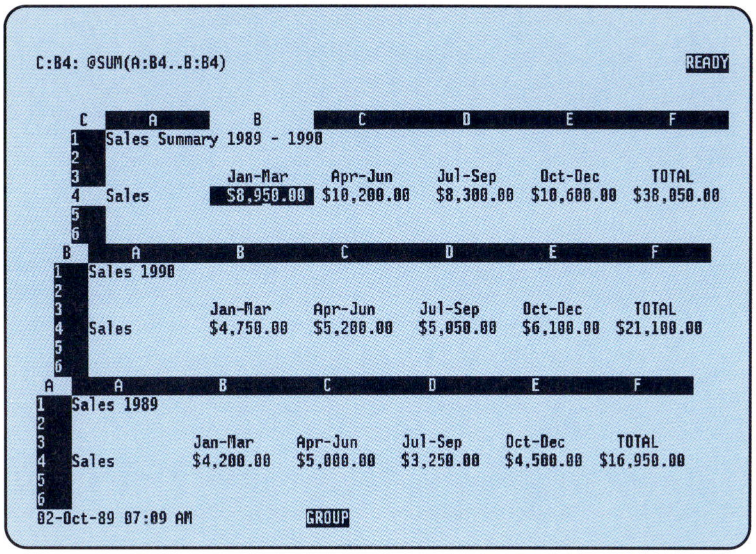

Figure 18 The Completed Summary Worksheet

Press **Enter**
Type **/c**
Press **Enter**
Type **c4..f4**
Press **Enter**

Figure 18 shows the result. Worksheet C summarizes worksheets A and B.

Step 9: Save the File

You must save the file to preserve the worksheets you have created.

Type **/fs**
Type **three_d**
Press **Enter**

All three worksheets will be saved in the file THREE_D.WK3.

Practice Print all three worksheets at the same time by specifying a three-dimensional print range.

Summary

- *Changing worksheet settings.* The Worksheet Global options affect the entire worksheet. You can change the format, label-prefix, column width, default directory, and the display of zero values. You can also display the worksheet status and insert page breaks.
- *Freezing titles and using windows.* The Worksheet Titles command lets you keep certain rows, columns, or both always on the screen. The Worksheet Windows command lets you split the screen into two horizontal or vertical windows.
- *Hiding columns and protecting cells.* The Worksheet Column Hide command lets you conceal the contents of one or more columns. The Worksheet Global

Protection Enable command prevents changes from being made to any cells. The Range Unprot command can then be used to turn off protection for selected cells.

- *Changing range formats.* The Range Format command lets you set Fixed, Scientific, Currency, Comma, General, +/−, Percent, Date, Text, and Hidden formats for one or more cells.
- *Using range names.* The Range Name Create lets you assign names to ranges to be used in commands and formulas.
- *Filling a range with a sequence of numbers.* The Data Fill command lets you fill a range of cells with a sequence of numbers.
- *Transposing columns and rows.* The Range Trans command lets you rearrange columns as rows or rows as columns.
- *Controlling recalculation and iteration.* The Worksheet Global Recalculation command lets you specify Natural, Columnwise, Rowwise, Automatic, or Manual recalculation. It also lets you set the iteration count for circular references.
- *Using relative, absolute, and mixed cell references.* Relative references change when cells are copied or moved. Absolute references, indicated by a $ in front of both the column letter and row number, always refer to the same address, even if they are copied or moved. Mixed references are half-relative and half-absolute.
- *Using more functions.* Date and time functions include @DATE, @DAY, @MONTH, @YEAR, @TIME, @HOUR, @MINUTE, @SECOND, and @NOW. Logical functions include @ISNUMBER, @ISSTRING, and @IF. String functions include @LENGTH, @LEFT, @RIGHT, @MID, @UPPER, @PROPER, and @REPEAT.
- *Using macros.* Plan the macro, enter the macro definition, and name the macro. Macros named with a \ (backslash) and a letter are run by holding down the Alternate key and typing the letter.
- *Using the Release 2.2 Learn feature.* Lotus 1-2-3 Release 2.2 lets you create a macro definition by specifying the learn range, pressing Alt-F5 to turn on the learn feature, and executing the actions to be automated.
- *Using the Release 3.0 Record feature.* Lotus 1-2-3 Release 3.0 lets you create a macro definition by copying keystrokes saved in the record buffer.
- *Using file linking with Release 2.2 and 3.0.* Lotus 1-2-3 Release 2.2 and 3.0 let you use values from other worksheets in your current worksheet.
- *Using three-dimensional worksheets with Release 3.0.* Lotus 1-2-3 Release 3.0 lets you create multi-page worksheets in a single file.

Key Terms

As an extra review of this chapter, try defining the following terms.

absolute reference
automatic recalculation
circular reference
column-wise recalculation
exponent
iteration
learn feature
learn range

macro
mantissa
manual recalculation
minimal (optimal) recalculation
mixed reference
natural recalculation
record buffer
record feature
relative reference
row-wise recalculation
template

Multiple Choice

Choose the best selection to complete each statement.

1. What options affect the entire worksheet?
   (a) Worksheet Global (b) Range Format
   (c) File Save (d) Data
2. What command lets you set the alignment of labels for the entire worksheet?
   (a) Worksheet Global Format (b) Worksheet Global Column-Width
   (c) Worksheet Global Label-Prefix (d) Worksheet Global Protection
3. Which command lets you freeze rows or columns or both on the screen so you can see them even if you scroll the worksheet?
   (a) Worksheet Global Zero (b) Worksheet Titles
   (c) Worksheet Window (d) Worksheet Page
4. Which command lets you split the screen horizontally or vertically?
   (a) Worksheet Global Zero (b) Worksheet Titles
   (c) Worksheet Window (d) Worksheet Page
5. Which command lets you conceal the contents of one or more columns?
   (a) Worksheet Global Protection (b) Worksheet Global Default
   (c) Worksheet Column Hide (d) Range Format Text
6. A general-purpose worksheet in which the user fills in the blanks or changes selected entries to perform a well-defined task is called a
   (a) macro. (b) iteration.
   (c) template. (d) circular reference.
7. The Worksheet Global Protection Enable command prevents changes being made to
   (a) all cells. (b) selected cells.
   (c) cells marked with the Range Prot command. (d) no cells.
8. Which Range Format would you use to display a number this way: 25,246.00?
   (a) Fixed (b) Scientific
   (c) Currency (d) , (comma)
9. Which Range Format would you use to generate crude bar graphs?
   (a) General (b) +/−
   (c) Percent (d) Text
10. In a Lotus 1-2-3 time number, the total time in each day is represented by the number
    (a) 1. (b) 12.
    (c) 24. (d) 360.

11. Which command would you use to enter the numbers 1 to 100 in cells A1 to A100?
    (a) Copy (b) Move
    (c) Data Fill (d) Range Format
12. What is the default method of recalculation?
    (a) Automatic (b) Manual
    (c) Column-wise (d) Row-wise
13. What is the default order of recalculation?
    (a) Automatic (b) Natural
    (c) Column-wise (d) Row-wise
14. A formula either directly or indirectly dependent on the value in the same cell results in a(n)
    (a) manual recalculation. (b) circular reference.
    (c) absolute reference. (d) iteration.
15. Which term describes the repeated recalculation of formulas containing circular references?
    (a) minimal recalculation (b) automatic recalculation
    (c) iteration (d) absolute reference
16. A cell address that does not change when it is moved or copied is called a(n)
    (a) relative reference. (b) absolute reference.
    (c) mixed reference. (d) circular reference.
17. The cell address A$1 is an example of a(n)
    (a) relative reference. (b) absolute reference.
    (c) mixed reference. (d) circular reference.
18. Which function returns the full serial number for the current date and time?
    (a) @DATE (b) @TIME
    (c) @NOW (d) @HOUR
19. What key(s) would you press to execute a macro named \B?
    (a) Alt-B (b) Ctrl-B
    (c) Shift-B (d) F5
20. Which of the following expressions is a valid linking formula that refers to cell B5 from the worksheet file NY.WK1?
    (a) +B5<<NY.WK1>> (b) +(NY.WK1)B5
    (c) +<<NY.WK1>>B5 (d) B5{NY.WK1}

Fill-In

1. The Worksheet ______ options affect the entire worksheet.
2. The Range Format ______ command displays formulas in worksheet cells instead of their computed results.
3. Range ______ can make it much easier to specify ranges in formulas and commands.
4. Lotus 1-2-3 Release 2.2 and 3.0 use ______ recalculation to increase speed by recalculating only those cells that have changed, and the cells that depend on them, since the worksheet was last recalculated.

5. A(n) ______ reference results when a formula in a cell is either directly or indirectly dependent on the value in that very same cell.
6. Certain indirect circular references can be eventually resolved through ______.
7. Lotus 1-2-3 assumes all cell addresses to be ______ unless you specify otherwise.
8. The cell address A1 is an example of a(n) ______ reference.
9. If you want part of a cell address to remain the same and part to change when you copy or move a formula, you must use a(n) ______ reference.
10. The ______ function returns the sequential date number, given the year, month, and day.
11. The ______ function evaluates the given logical expression as TRUE or FALSE, and returns the first value if TRUE, or the second value if FALSE.
12. The ______ function lets you repeat the given string a specified number of times.
13. A ______ is a sequence of keystrokes and special commands that you can create to automate a task.
14. In a macro definition, the macro instruction ______ performs the same action as pressing the Right Arrow key.
15. A macro named with the ______ and a letter is executed by holding down the Alternate key and typing that letter.
16. To facilitate the creation of macros, Lotus 1-2-3 Release 2.2 has the ______ feature and Release 3.0 has the ______ feature.
17. The range of cells containing a macro definition must be ______ before the macro can be run.
18. In Lotus 1-2-3 Release 2.2 and 3.0, you can create a ______ between two files by entering a formula in the current worksheet that refers to a cell in the other worksheet file.
19. One way to envision a three-dimensional worksheet is as a sequence of ______, each of which is a table of rows and columns.
20. In Lotus 1-2-3 Release 3.0, multiple worksheets in the same file are designated by ______, like columns.

Short Problems

1. Erase the current worksheet from the screen. Change the Worksheet Global Format to Fixed with two decimal places, the Worksheet Global Label-Prefix to Center, and the Worksheet Global Column-Width to 12 characters.
2. Retrieve the PROPERTY worksheet. Freeze the first row as a horizontal title. Then try scrolling the worksheet down.
3. Split the screen at row 11 into two horizontal windows. Switch to the other window and scroll the worksheet down. When you are finished, clear worksheet windows.
4. Turn on worksheet global protection. Try changing the contents of a cell. When you are finished, disable global protection.
5. Erase the current worksheet from the screen. Change the range format of cells A1 through A5 to scientific notation with two decimal places. Then enter the following numbers into cells A1 through A5: 156,000,000, −25,200, 0.000000381, −0.000000000752, and 4,321,123,321.

6. Erase the current worksheet from the screen. Fill cells A1 through A4095 with only even numbers from 2 through 8190.
7. Erase the current worksheet from the screen. Enter the names of the months of the year in columns B through M, then transpose these names into cells A2 through A13.
8. Retrieve the SQRT worksheet. Enter the formula @SQRT(A1) into cell A10 to check the iterative square root calculation method against the built-in SQRT function. Calculate the square root of 123456. Enter other values to try to "stump" the iterative method. Now try an obviously invalid value of −1 and see what happens.
9. Retrieve the MONTHS worksheet you created in Lesson 11. Modify the \M macro so that it enters the names of the months down a column instead of across a row. Run the macro to make sure it works correctly.
10. If you have Lotus 1-2-3 Release 2.2 or 3.0, retrieve the SUMMARY worksheet you created in Lesson 14 to demonstrate linking. You may want to see the list of linked files when you are working on a summary worksheet. Fortunately, Lotus 1-2-3 lets you do this. Execute the File List Linked command. Press the Enter key when you are finished viewing the list.

Long Problems

1. Suppose you are an instructor who uses 1-2-3 to track your students' grades. You want to post the final grades without displaying the students' names, only their social security numbers. Create the following grades worksheet and hide the names column. Then print the worksheet.

```
Name          SSN            Grade

Abel          324-32-9974    A
Alexander     322-93-2854    B
Banks         495-89-9832    C
Becker        123-93-8237    A
Calhoon       324-58-9245    D
Carver        258-11-3848    B
Crawford      429-29-2847    C
Daily         199-23-9382    A
Davis         342-21-9284    C
Diamond       415-28-3018    B
Eaton         321-45-8294    B
Edwards       312-29-9285    A
```

2. A company uses Lotus 1-2-3 to store employee salary information. Create the following worksheet and hide the salary column. Enter a formula in cell C1 to sum the salaries. Although cells may be hidden, they can still be referenced in formulas.

```
Name          Salary

Abel          $32,500.00
Alexander     $25,000.00
Banks         $30,000.00
Becker        $45,000.00
```

Name	Salary
Calhoon	$25,000.00
Carver	$20,000.00
Crawford	$35,000.00
Daily	$45,000.00
Davis	$25,000.00
Diamond	$32,250.00
Eaton	$20,000.00
Edwards	$35,000.00

3. Enter the following worksheet. Then transpose the columns and rows.

Year	Sales
1987	$32,500.00
1988	$25,000.00
1989	$30,000.00
1990	$45,000.00
1991	$25,000.00

4. Indirect circular references and iteration are sometimes used in business calculations. For example, suppose you want to calculate a bonus that is ten percent of net profit, and net profit is defined as gross profit minus the bonus. Create a worksheet that contains the following data and formulas:

	A	B
1	Gross Profit	$1,000.00
2	Bonus	10%*B3
3	Net Profit	+B1-B2

Set the Worksheet Global Recalculation Iteration to 50 and recalculate the worksheet to get final answers. The Bonus should be $90.91 and the Net Profit should be $909.09.

5. Create an addition table for the numbers 0 through 5. Enter the numbers 0 through 5 in cells B1 through G1 and cells A2 through A7. Enter a formula that adds the column and row header using mixed references. Use the Copy command to fill out the rest of the table.
6. Create a formula using the @NOW and @DATE functions to calculate the number of days since you were born.
7. Create a macro to widen all columns to 12 characters, set the worksheet global label prefix to Center, and enter the names of the days of the week in columns A through G. If you have Lotus 1-2-3 Release 2.2, use the Learn feature. If you have Lotus 1-2-3 Release 3.0, use the Record feature.
8. Create a macro to format the current cell to display the time in Lotus standard long form (for example 10:22:05 AM) and then enter the time of day.
9. If you have Lotus 1-2-3 Release 2.2 or 3.0, create a separate worksheet for each of the following income statements from different cities. Use formulas to compute the Income figures. Then create a summary worksheet that uses linking to import and sum the Income figures from the three cities.

Boston	
Net Sales	$12,000.00
Expenses	$7,350.00
Income	$4,650.00

St. Louis	
Net Sales	$11,000.00
Expenses	$6,050.00
Income	$4,950.00

San Diego	
Net Sales	$15,000.00
Expenses	$9,250.00
Income	$5,750.00

10. If you have Lotus 1-2-3 Release 3.0, create a multiple-worksheet file that puts each of the following income statements in a separate worksheet. Use formulas to compute the Income figures. Add another worksheet to summarize the data from the three income statements. Save and print your multiple-worksheet file.

Income Statement 1989	
Net Sales	$10,000.00
Expenses	$6,350.00
Income	$3,650.00

Income Statement 1990	
Net Sales	$13,000.00
Expenses	$8,050.00
Income	$4,950.00

Income Statement 1991	
Net Sales	$16,000.00
Expenses	$10,250.00
Income	$5,750.00

PART 5

dBASE IV

In January 1981, a new company called Ashton-Tate introduced its first product, dBASE II. There was no dBASE I, there was no Ashton, and cofounder George Tate didn't develop the program. Nevertheless, Tate and his partner, Hal Lashlee, along with Los Angeles advertising man Hal Pawluk, are credited with the merchandising flair that helped make *dBASE* synonymous with *data base management*. It was Pawluk who coined the name Ashton-Tate, simply because he liked the way it sounded.

The original program was called *Vulcan*, named after the home planet of *Star Trek's* Mr. Spock. It was developed for early microcomputers by Wayne Ratliff, an engineer then working for NASA's Jet Propulsion Laboratory. Vulcan was a versatile data base management program, but Ratliff sold only fifty copies the first year from an ad in the back of *BYTE* magazine. Tate and Lashlee heard about the program, contacted Ratliff, and signed him to an exclusive contract. The sales of that program, renamed dBASE II, and of its successors would ultimately make all three of them multimillionaires.

Ashton-Tate and dBASE have come a long way since the early 1980s. In Part 5, we examine data base management with dBASE IV. Chapter 14 covers the basics, the bare essentials you need to create and use data bases. Chapter 15 presents lessons that will increase your understanding and control of dBASE IV. Chapter 16 helps you explore more advanced dBASE IV topics, including Structured Query Language and data base programming.

CHAPTER 14

BEGINNING dBASE IV

In This Chapter

Getting Started
Lesson 1: Starting dBASE IV
Lesson 2: Using the Control Center
Lesson 3: Designing a Data Base File
Lesson 4: Entering Data Base Records
Lesson 5: Examining an Existing Data Base
Lesson 6: Adding New Records
Lesson 7: Modifying Existing Records
Lesson 8: Deleting Records
Lesson 9: Finding Records
Lesson 10: Modifying the Data Base Design
Lesson 11: Sorting the Data Base
Lesson 12: Indexing the Data Base
Lesson 13: Generating Reports

Preview

The original dBASE II program ran on 8-bit CP/M systems and the Apple II family of microcomputers. A version for the IBM Personal Computer soon followed and by 1983 dBASE II had sold more than 200,000 copies. In May 1984, Ashton-Tate released dBASE III, a more powerful successor to dBASE II designed especially for 16-bit computers like the IBM PC family. A year and a half later, dBASE III PLUS was introduced, offering a friendlier menu-driven user interface and local area network support for IBM-compatible microcomputers. A powerful and easy-to-use version for the Apple Macintosh computer, called dBASE Mac, was released in 1987. Finally, in the last quarter of 1988 dBASE IV for IBM-compatibles was unveiled. It boasted a new user interface, more than 300 new commands and functions, and support for Structured Query Language (SQL). Despite increased competition from other software packages, dBASE remains a leading programmable relational data base management system. It is the system against which all others are compared.

After studying this chapter, you will know how to

- start dBASE IV.
- use the Control Center.
- design a data base file.
- enter data base records.
- examine a data base.
- add new records to a data base.
- modify existing data base records.
- delete data base records.
- find data base records.
- modify the data base design.
- sort a data base.
- index a data base.
- generate a data base report.

Getting Started

Although dBASE IV is a large and sophisticated software package, it is not difficult to learn how to use for basic data base management tasks. You are most likely to use the package in one of two possible arrangements:

1. on a microcomputer with a hard disk and the single-user version of dBASE IV installed in a subdirectory named DBASE
2. on a microcomputer connected to a local area network with the multi-user version of dBASE IV installed on the network file server

The dBASE IV package cannot be run unless you have a hard disk or are connected to a local area network. Furthermore, it requires at least 640K of memory. If you are going to run dBASE IV from a network, you may need some additional directions from your instructor on how to start the program.

Lesson 1: Starting dBASE IV

This chapter and the following two chapters assume that dBASE IV has already been installed on your computer and a path has been set up so that you can run the package from any subdirectory.

Step 1: Boot Up the Computer

If your computer is not already on, you must boot it up.

Step 2: Prepare a Subdirectory for Data Files

The dBASE IV package is stored in its own subdirectory on a hard disk or network. It is best to prepare a separate subdirectory for the data files you will create in the following lessons. Create a subdirectory called LESSONS, if you don't already have one, that you can use to store your files. If you are running on a network, your instructor may have other directions for you to follow.

Step 3: Switch to the LESSONS Subdirectory

The dBASE IV package is normally installed so that it can be run from within any subdirectory. Switch to your LESSONS subdirectory:

Type **cd c:\lessons**
Press **Enter**

Step 4: Invoke dBASE IV

Once you get situated in the desired subdirectory, simply execute the DBASE command:

Type **dbase**
Press **Enter**

The program will present the Ashton-Tate logo for a moment (see Figure 1). Then you will see a screen that identifies the program and the owner and displays Ashton-Tate's License Agreement (see Figure 2). The screen will disappear in a few moments, or you can press Enter to continue:

Press **Enter**

Figure 1 The dBASE IV Opening Screen

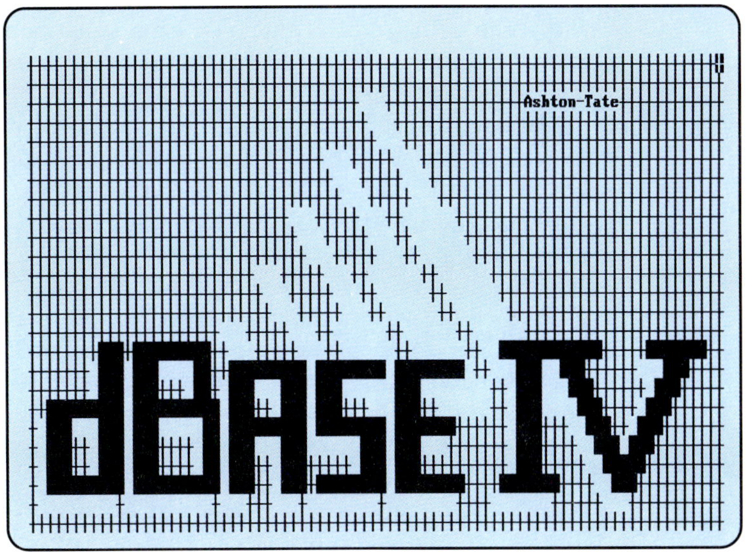

Figure 2 The dBASE IV Copyright and License Screen

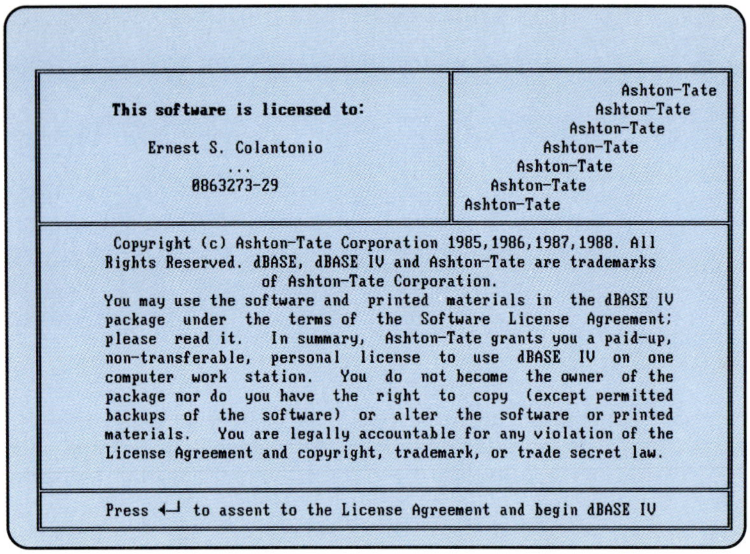

Practice

Reboot your computer:

Press **Ctrl-Alt-Del**

Follow the steps of this lesson to start up dBASE IV again.

Lesson 2: Using the Control Center

The Control Center is the menu system of dBASE IV. It is the means by which you select files and choose the actions you want to perform.

Step 1: Examine the Control Center Screen

Figure 3 shows the Control Center screen you see when you start the program. The top line of the screen contains the menu bar on the left and the time-of-day clock on the right. The **menu bar** contains the names of the menus currently available: Catalog, Tools, and Exit.

A **catalog** is a list of files in dBASE IV. Catalogs help you organize your work. For example, you could have different catalogs for separate offices, departments, or projects. When you start dBASE IV, the Control Center automatically loads the catalog you used last. If you have not created any catalogs yet, dBASE IV creates the first catalog, named UNTITLED.CAT, for you. The Control Center names the current catalog and presents the files it contains in the six panels displayed on the screen. Since you have not yet created any files, the panels are all empty. You cannot choose any existing files, only create new ones.

The six panels correspond to the six types of files you can create with dBASE IV. The Data panel lists data base files, which contain data. The Queries panel lists query files, which contain instructions for viewing or updating data base files. The Forms panel lists form files, which contain custom screen displays for entering, editing, and viewing data. The Reports panel lists report files, which print data in a specified format. The Labels panel lists label files, which print

Insight

Large Data Base Packages vs. File Management Programs

It's like using an elephant gun to kill a flea. Hauling out dBASE IV to solve a simple problem sometimes isn't worth the time or effort.

Anyone who has worked with large-scale data base programs realizes they aren't particularly easy to use. To solve elaborate problems, dBASE IV requires that you develop actual programs in the dBASE language. These programs can be as complex as programs written in BASIC, COBOL, or Pascal.

For simple applications, dBASE IV may be more powerful than necessary. Experts ignore dBASE IV, first, when the problem needs only one file that is not linked to any other files and, second, when the computations are simple and limited to operations such as summing fields or deriving a new field based on calculations of other fields.

A number of flat-file manager programs can provide excellent solutions for situations such as this. Unlike dBASE IV, flat-file manager programs can't link the fields in different files. All the information has to be in a single file. Simple address or customer lists and client billing files are examples.

Two typical file manager programs that meet these needs are PFS:Professional File and PC-File Plus. Each allows the user to define simple file structures, enter and edit data, sort records, search for information, do simple computations, and generate reports, without complex and time-consuming programming.

mailing labels. The Applications panel lists programs that can perform a variety of data base management tasks.

The last line you see in Figure 3 is the **navigation line,** which lists important keystrokes that can be used on the current screen.

Step 2: Activate the Menu Bar

The menu bar contains the titles of the currently available menus. The menus stay out of sight until you want to use them. You press the F10 key to activate the menu bar.

Press **F10**

As Figure 4 shows, "Catalog" will be highlighted in the menu bar, and the Catalog menu will appear below. The menu lists options. The first option is highlighted and a description of its function is given in the **message line,** which appears below the navigation line.

Step 3: Consider a Different Option

To consider a different option, move the highlight bar with the Up Arrow or Down Arrow keys.

Press **Down Arrow**

Notice how the highlight bar moves down and the message line changes. Try it again:

Press **Up Arrow**

Figure 3 The Control Center Screen

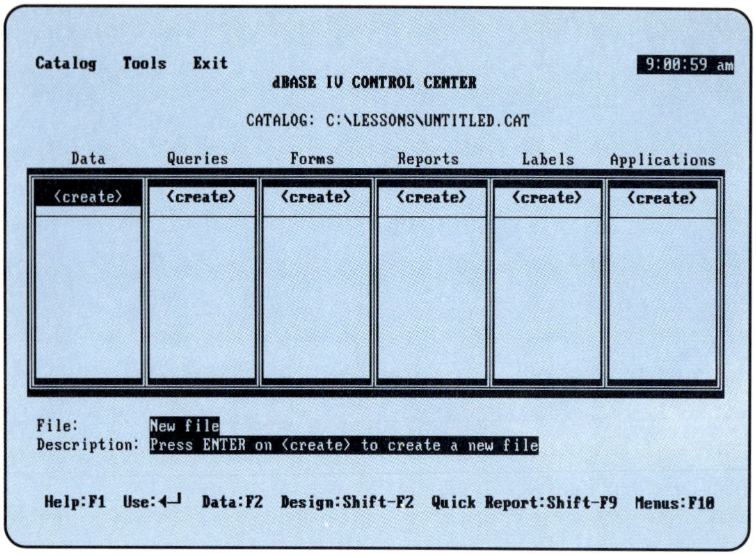

Step 4: Activate a Different Menu

Suppose you want to see the Tools menu. You can move between the titles in the menu bar by pressing the Right Arrow or Left Arrow key.

Press **Right Arrow**

Now, go back to the Catalog menu:

Press **Left Arrow**

Another way to activate a menu is to hold down the Alternate key and type the first letter of the menu title. Activate the Exit menu:

Press **Alt-E**

Figure 4 The Catalog Menu

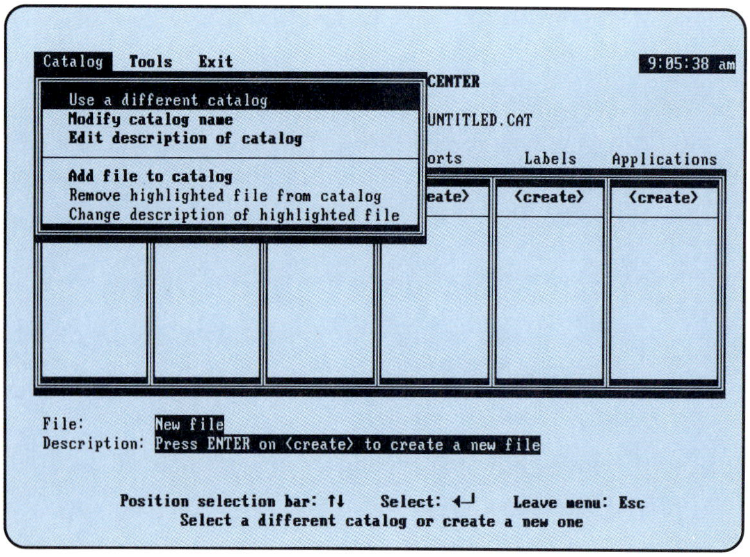

Step 5: Execute a Menu Option

To actually execute a menu option, highlight it and then press the Enter key. For example, execute the Quit to DOS option from the Exit menu on your screen:

Press **Down Arrow**
Press **Enter**

The dBASE IV program will terminate and you will return to the DOS prompt. Start up the program again:

Type **dbase**
Press **Enter**

You can also select and execute a menu option at once when the menu is active by typing the option's first letter. For example, follow these instructions to activate the Exit menu and execute the Quit to DOS option:

Press **Alt-E**
Type **q**

Start up dBASE IV again:

Type **dbase**
Press **Enter**

Step 6: Deactivate a Menu

Suppose you activate a menu and then change your mind. You can close a menu and make it disappear by pressing the Escape key. For example, activate the Tools menu and then remove it from the screen:

Press **Alt-T**
Press **Escape**

Step 7: Explore the Help System

The dBASE IV package has a comprehensive Help system that can provide on-screen information about any menu, command, or function. You can get Help at any time by pressing the F1 key.

Press **F1**

The program will present a Help box relevant to your current activity (see Figure 5). Since the highlight bar was on the <create> option in the Data panel, the Help box describes the procedure for creating data base files. If the information does not fit in a single box, you can see more by pressing the F4 key.

Press **F4**

You can reread a previous box screen by pressing the F3 key.

Press **F3**

Several options are listed across the bottom of the Help box: CONTENTS, RELATED TOPICS, BACKUP, and PRINT. The CONTENTS option presents a nested table of contents for the Help system. The CONTENTS option should be highlighted, so execute it:

Press **Enter**

Figure 5 The Help Box

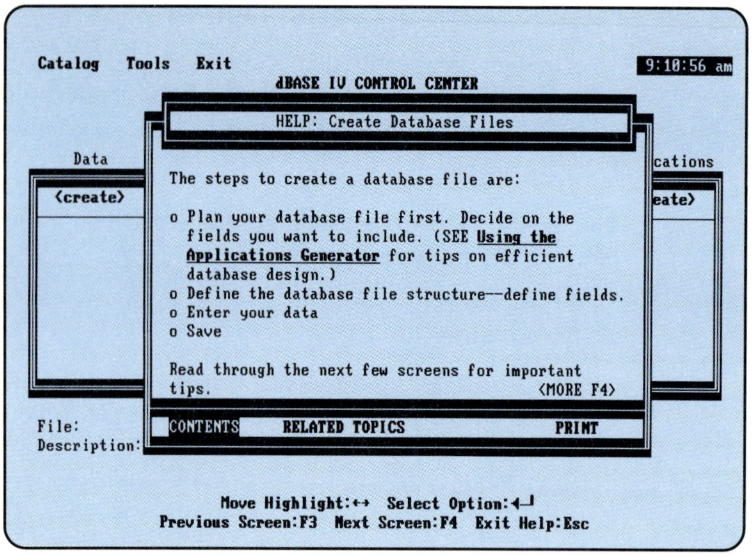

The program will present a table of contents of topics about data base files (see Figure 6). Return to the Help box entitled Create Database Files:

Press **Enter**

The RELATED TOPICS option presents a list of associated Help boxes.

Press **Right Arrow**
Press **Enter**

Remove the Related Topics box:

Press **Escape**

Figure 6 The Help System Table of Contents

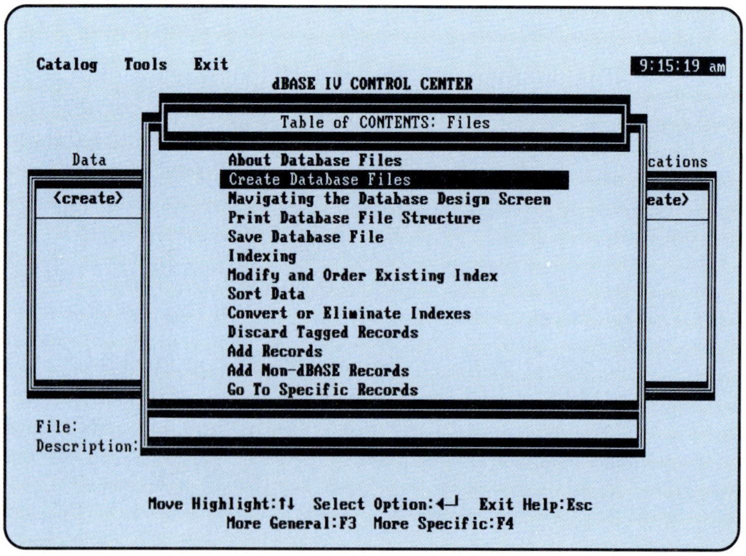

The BACKUP option lets you retrace your steps through the Help system. You can explore related topics or read about unrelated topics from the table of contents and still get back to your original Help box.

Press **Right Arrow**
Press **Enter**

PRINT is the last option in the Help box. This option lets you print the current Help box for future reference. Exit the Help system:

Press **Escape**

Practice

1. Activate the Exit menu.
2. Execute the Quit to DOS command. Restart dBASE IV.
3. Invoke the Help system. Execute the CONTENTS option and select the About Database Files topic. Execute the BACKUP option to return to your original screen. If you have a printer connected to your computer, make sure it is turned on, on-line, and contains paper. Then print the current Help box. When it is finished, exit the Help box and return to the Control Center.

Lesson 3: Designing a Data Base File

A **data base** is one or more related files. A **file** is a collection of records. A **record** is a sequence of fields. And a **field** is simply a single data item, such as a number, character, word, or phrase. As an example, let's create a data base file to contain the Paddle and Portage Canoe Outfitters mailing list of customer names and addresses, shown in Figure 7. Each record in the file will store the data about a single customer. Each field in a record will hold the individual data items, including the customer's first name, last name, address, city, state, and ZIP code. Before you can enter any data, however, you must specify the structure of the records that will make up the data base file. This is called designing the data base.

Step 1: Execute the Create Option in the Data Panel

When you start dBASE IV with the Control Center, a highlight bar is automatically placed on the <create> option in the Data panel. This is the option you execute to design a new data base file.

Press **Enter**

Step 2: Examine the Data Base Design Screen

The Data Base Design screen will appear after you press the Enter key (see Figure 8). This is where you specify the structure of the new file. Note the new menu bar across the top of the screen containing the titles Layout, Organize, Append, Go To, and Exit. In addition, the reverse video **status bar** now appears as the third line from the bottom, just above the navigation line. It provides information about the operation you have chosen or are about to choose. The status bar lists the type of screen you are in (Database), the path and name of the current file (C:\lessons\<NEW>), and the location of the cursor (Field 1/1).

The table in the center of the screen is where you enter information about the fields that make up the records of the data base file you are designing. The message

```
Bytes remaining: 4000
```

Figure 7 Paddle and Portage Canoe Outfitters Mailing List

Last Name	First Name	Address	City	State	ZIP
Skubic	Mike	321 Gregory	Champaign	IL	61820
Griffith	Oscar	805 Florida	Urbana	IL	61801
Carver	George	906 Busey	Brainerd	MN	56401
Banks	David	604 Armory	Green Bay	WI	54035
Young	Susan	1104 Grand	Anchorage	AK	99502
Mitchell	Dan	310 Paddock	Flagstaff	AZ	86001
Hudson	Henry	1007 Barclay	Akron	OH	44309
Becker	Molly	402 Main	Ann Arbor	MI	48106
Franklin	Melissa	2012 Anderson	Big Bear	CA	92314
Savage	Julian	2209 Philo	Cedar City	UT	84720
Prorok	Brian	502 Chalmers	Fairfax	VA	22030
Underwood	Rhonda	701 Dover	Las Vegas	NV	89114
Hall	Robert	1721 Valley	Ogallala	NE	69153
Davis	Becky	7822 Kostner	Chicago	IL	60652
Alexander	Barbara	102 White	Baltimore	MD	21233
Walden	Roxanne	1010 Bridle	Denver	CO	80202
Quinlan	Kerry	311 Southmoor	Homestead	FL	33030
Irving	Judith	1329 Grandview	Cairo	GA	31728
Diamond	Jim	142 Hazelwood	Belmar	NJ	07719
Kelley	Joyce	805 Randolf	Albany	NY	12207
Garret	Gerald	135 Cedar	Boone	NC	28607
Weaver	Sally	700 Elm	Madison	WI	53705
Tudor	Anthony	909 Crestwood	Duluth	MN	55806
Jenkins	Alfred	605 Willis	Hometown	IL	60456
Calhoon	Carrie	809 Maple	Superior	WI	54880

Figure 8 The Blank Data Base Design Screen

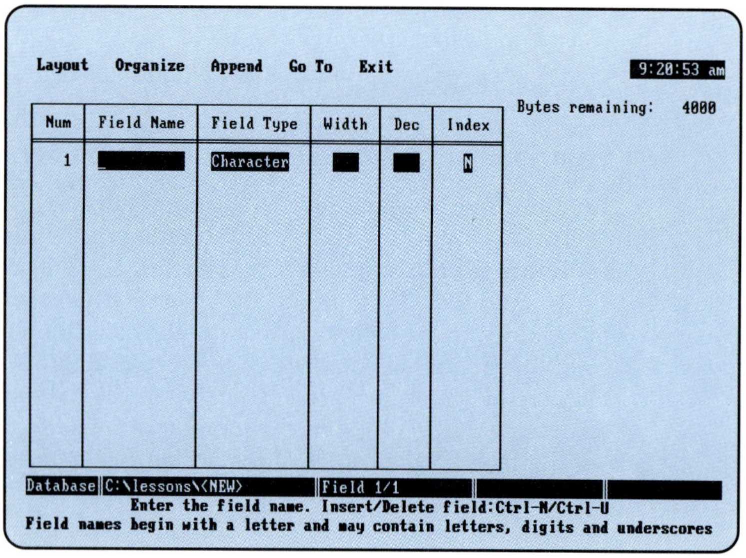

tells you how much room you have left for the record definition. A byte is equivalent to a single character. The maximum size of a single data base record is 4000 bytes.

Each row in the table corresponds to a field and each column specifies an attribute of that field. The Num column gives the field's number, which is automatically generated by dBASE IV and reflects the position of the field within the record.

The Field Name column contains the name you choose for the field. Field names can have up to ten letters, digits, or underscores (_), but the first character must always be a letter. No blanks can be embedded in field names; underscores are often used instead, like this: FIRST_NAME. You can type field names in lowercase letters, but dBASE IV translates all the letters to uppercase.

The Field Type column specifies the type of field to be created. Six types of fields are available:

Character	up to 254 letters, digits, or punctuation marks
Numeric	numbers used for counting or exact calculations
Float	very small or large numbers for calculations
Date	dates of the form mm/dd/yy, such as 01/15/91
Logical	T for True, or F for False
Memo	pointer to a file containing up to 512K of text

The Width column specifies the maximum number of characters or digits that can be stored in the field. Character fields can have a maximum width of 254. Numeric and Float fields can be up to 20 digits wide. The widths for Date, Logical, and Memo fields are entered automatically by dBASE IV. Date fields are 8 characters wide, Logical fields are 1 character wide, and Memo fields are 10 characters wide.

The Dec column is relevant only to Numeric and Float fields. It specifies the number of digits, from 0 to 18, to appear to the right of the decimal point. The width specified for a Numeric or Float field must be at least two greater than the number of decimal places to accommodate the decimal point and a possible minus sign.

The Index column specifies whether the field is to be used to index the file. Indexing, a method of arranging the records in a data base, will be discussed later in this chapter.

Step 3: Decide on the Field Attributes

Before you can actually specify the data base design, you must decide what fields to include. Then for each field you have to choose its name, type, and width. If the field is a numeric value, you must also decide the number of digits to appear to the right of the decimal point. Examine the mailing list in Figure 7. There are six fields: last name, first name, address, city, state, and ZIP code. Naming the fields after the contents is a good idea. More thought must be applied to choosing field widths: you want widths that are not too large because that will waste storage space, yet you want the fields to be wide enough to hold the necessary data. Deciding on the field type is pretty straightforward.

The Paddle and Portage Canoe Outfitters mailing list is a fairly simple example. All of its fields are Character fields. Note that although the fields for address and ZIP code will contain numbers, these numbers are classified as characters because they don't represent quantities and won't be used in calculations. The following field names, field types, and widths can be used for the mailing list:

Field Name	*Field Type*	*Width*
LAST_NAME	Character	15
FIRST_NAME	Character	10
ADDRESS	Character	20
CITY	Character	10
STATE	Character	5
ZIP	Character	5

The Dec column will be blank for all fields, and the Index entries will all be N for No.

Step 4: Fill In the Data Base Design Table

Once you have decided on the field names, types, and widths, you can enter them into the empty data base design table. Follow these instructions to fill in the table:

Type **last_name**
Press **Enter** (2 times)
Type **15**
Press **Enter** (2 times)
Type **first_name**
Press **Enter**
Type **10**
Press **Enter** (2 times)
Type **address**
Press **Enter** (2 times)
Type **20**
Press **Enter** (2 times)
Type **city**
Press **Enter** (2 times)
Type **10**
Press **Enter** (2 times)
Type **state**
Press **Enter** (2 times)
Type **5**
Press **Enter** (2 times)
Type **zip**
Press **Enter** (2 times)
Type **5**
Press **Enter** (2 times)

Your screen should look like Figure 9. Note that dBASE IV automatically converts the field names you type into uppercase letters. The program also automatically generates the next field number and fills in Character for the Field Type and N for the Index column. If you want to change these default values, you can either type a different value or press the Space Bar to cycle through the possible selections. Whenever you type an entry that completely fills the allotted space, dBASE IV beeps and jumps to the next entry. This happened when you typed FIRST_NAME, which is 10 characters long, the maximum length of a field name.

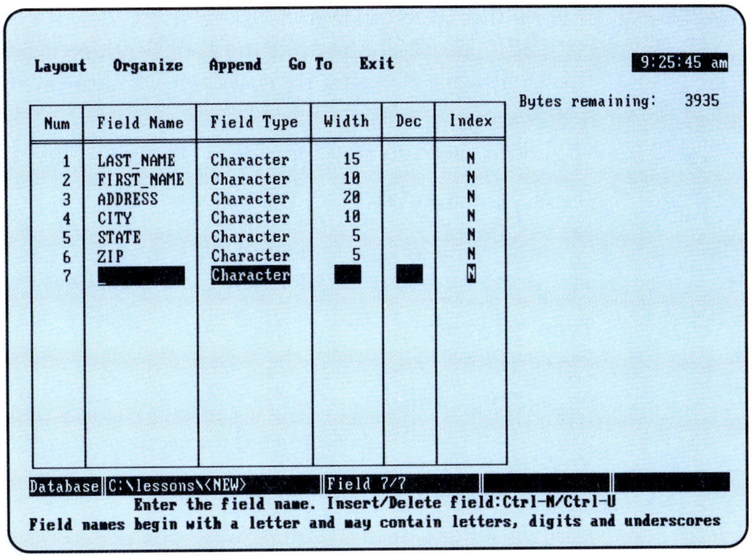

Figure 9 The Completed Data Base Design Screen

Step 5: Check the Table

Check your table against Figure 9. To correct a mistake, move the cursor to the erroneous entry and then retype it. You can move from column to column by pressing the Enter key. You can go from row to row by pressing Up Arrow or Down Arrow. You can move from character to character by pressing Left Arrow or Right Arrow.

Step 6: Exit the Data Base Design Screen

When you have completed and checked your work, you can leave the Data Base Design screen. Several methods are available:

- Activate the Exit menu and choose the Save Changes and Exit option or the Abandon Changes and Exit option.
- Press Enter when the cursor is at the first empty Field Name column after the last defined field.
- Press Ctrl-End or Ctrl-W.
- Press Escape to abandon the design.

Beginners usually find that selecting an option from a menu is the easiest way to remember what to do, even if it is not the quickest. Activate the Exit menu and choose Save Changes and Exit:

Press **Alt-E**
Type **s**

A box will appear in which dBASE IV displays the prompt

```
Save as :
```

The program is asking for the name under which you want to save the data base file. Enter a valid DOS file name without an extension:

Type **`mailing`**
Press **Enter**

Then dBASE IV will create the new file MAILING.DBF and return to the Control Center. The extension DBF stands for Data Base File.

Practice

1. Invoke the Help system. Execute the Contents option and select the topic entitled "Files." Then select the topic entitled "Create Database Files." Read the Help boxes on this topic. When you are finished, return to the Control Center.
2. Highlight the <create> option in Data panel and execute it:

   Press **Up Arrow**
   Press **Enter**

   The program will present a new Data Base Design screen.

   Type **total**
   Press **Enter**

   Observe how dBASE IV presents the next choice for Field Type each time you press the Space Bar and read the description in the message line:

   Press **Space Bar** (6 times)

   Return to the Control Center without saving the data base design:

   Press **Alt-E**
   Type **a**
   Type **y**

Lesson 4: Entering Data Base Records

All you have done so far is define the structure of a new data base file; it does not have any data in it yet. You now face the somewhat tedious task of entering the data.

Step 1: Highlight the Data Base File

The Control Center should be on your screen. The highlight bar should be in the Data panel. If MAILING is not highlighted, do this:

Press **Down Arrow**

Step 2: Execute the Data Command

When you want to examine, enter, or edit data, you execute the Data command by pressing the F2 key.

Press **F2**

Step 3: Examine the Data Entry Form

The dBASE IV program will present the Edit screen shown in Figure 10. The menu bar at the top contains three titles: Records, Go To, and Exit. A blank data entry form appears below the menu bar. A **form** displays the fields of an individual record on the screen. The default format of a dBASE IV form has a separate line for each field. The field names are listed along the left edge of the screen. Beside each field name is reverse video block where you enter the data for that field. The width of the block reflects the field width you specified when you

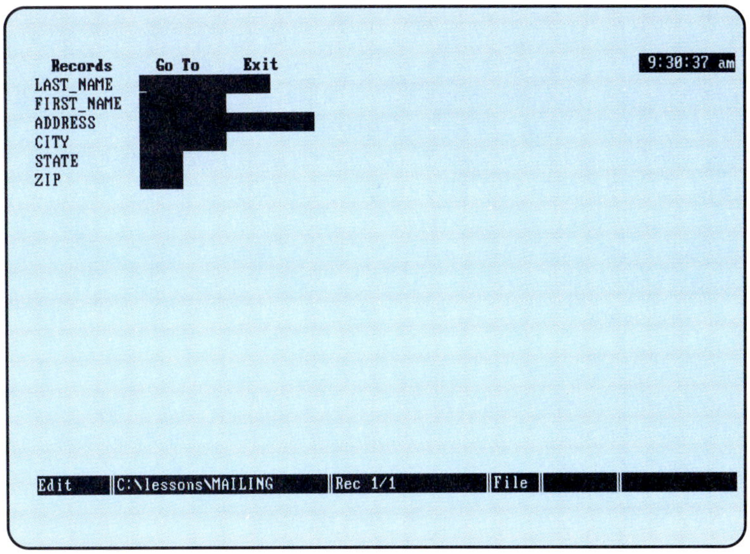

Figure 10 The Blank Data Entry Form on the Edit Screen

designed the data base file. The status bar near the bottom of the screen indicates that you are using the Edit screen, your current file is C:\LESSONS\MAILING.DBF, and you are working on record 1 of 1 so far.

Step 4: Enter the Data for Record 1

Refer to the Paddle and Portage mailing list in Figure 7. Follow these directions to enter the data for the first record:

Type **Skubic**
Press **Enter**
Type **Mike**
Press **Enter**
Type **321 Gregory**
Press **Enter**
Type **Champaign**
Press **Enter**
Type **IL**
Press **Enter**
Type **61820**

Don't be alarmed when dBASE IV beeps and seemingly erases what you have just typed. Because the ZIP field is five characters wide and you have typed exactly five characters, the program automatically enters that field, stores the record, advances to the next record, and beeps to signal what it has done.

Step 5: Check the Record for Errors

This automatic advance feature is handy for entering records one after another, but it requires you to go back to the record you have just entered to check its accuracy.

Press **Page Up**

The completed form for the first record will appear on your screen as shown in Figure 11. Check the data for accuracy. To correct a mistake, use the arrow keys

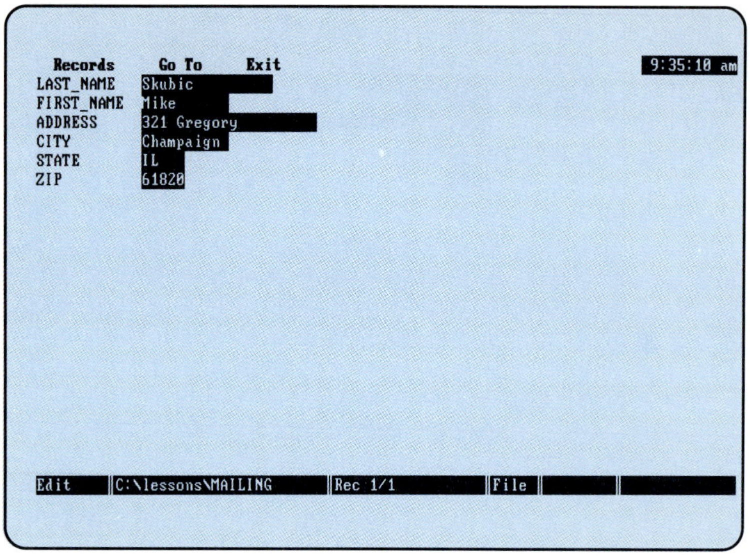

Figure 11 The Completed Data Entry Form for Record 1

to move the cursor and then retype the entry. You can use the Backspace and Delete keys to erase characters. By default, typeover mode is turned on. You can switch to insert mode by pressing the Insert key. Then you can insert new characters into an entry at the current cursor location. Pressing the Insert key again toggles back to typeover mode. When you are sure the record is correct, advance again to the next record:

Press **Page Down**

The program will display the prompt

```
Add new records? (Y/N)
```

Answer Y for Yes:

Type **y**

The program will present the blank data entry form for record number 2 on the screen.

Step 6: Enter the Remaining Records

Now enter the rest of the Paddle and Portage mailing list records from Figure 7. You might prefer to check each record for errors before you type the last digit of the ZIP code field. Then you can avoid having to go back to the previous record, check for errors, advance to the next record, and answer the prompt about adding new records.

After you enter the last record (Carrie Calhoon's) and dBASE IV advances to the next blank record, move back to the previous record:

Press **Page Up**

This will prevent a blank record from being saved as the last record in your data base file. You should have 25 records in MAILING.DBF.

Step 7: Terminate Data Entry

As you enter each record, dBASE IV adds it to the MAILING.DBF data base file. When you are finished entering records, you can either press Ctrl-End or execute the Exit option from the Exit menu to save your work and return to the Control Center.

Press **Ctrl-End**

The Control Center will appear on your screen again.

Practice Execute the Data command:

Press **F2**

Use the Page Up key to examine the forms of the records you have entered. When the first record (Mike Skubic's) is on the screen, return to the Control Center:

Press **Escape**

Lesson 5: Examining an Existing Data Base

Now that you have a complete data base, you can examine its contents. One of the major advantages of a data base management package is the flexibility with which you can retrieve previously stored information. A great many different ways to access data bases are available with dBASE IV. In this lesson, we will look at a method that works well with small data bases like the Paddle and Portage Canoe Outfitters' mailing list.

Step 1: Select the Data Base File

The first step is to tell dBASE IV the data base file you want to examine. If you have already been working with the file, as we have been with MAILING.DBF, you can skip this step. Otherwise, you would highlight the name of the file in the Data panel of the Control Center screen. Then you would press Enter to select the file, and press Enter again to tell dBASE IV that you want to open it.

Step 2: Display the Data Base Design

You may want to look at the record structure of a data base you have never seen before or one that you have not worked with for a while. The Design command, invoked by pressing Shift-F2, lets you review the design of a data base.

Press **Shift-F2**

The Data Base Design screen will appear with the Organize menu activated. Deactivate the menu to examine the screen:

Press **Escape**

Your screen should look like Figure 9 again. When you are finished examining the data base design, activate the Exit menu and select the Abandon Changes and Exit option:

Press **Alt-E**
Type **a**

The program will return to the Control Center.

Step 3: Use the Browse Screen

The Data command, which is invoked by pressing the F2 key, has two functions. It activates either the Edit screen or the Browse screen. The Edit screen, as you learned in the previous lesson, lets you enter and examine each record in its own form. The Browse screen lets you see data in a **table,** which presents a record in each row and a field in each column. You simply press the F2 key again to switch from the Edit screen to the Browse screen, or from the Browse screen to the Edit screen. For example, activate the Edit screen:

Press **F2**

Now, switch to the Browse screen:

Press **F2**

Figure 12 shows the result. If your table shows only the last record, use the Page Up key to move to the beginning of the file. In fact, you can move to any record, field, or character in the data base file. The following list summarizes the cursor movement keys available on either the Browse screen or the Edit screen. Try each of them.

Keypress	*Cursor Movement*
Right Arrow	Right one character
Left Arrow	Left one character
Down Arrow	Down one row
Up Arrow	Up one row
Page Down	Next screen
Page Up	Previous screen
End	End of field (Edit) or record (Browse)
Home	Start of field (Edit) or record (Browse)
Tab	Next field
Shift-Tab	Previous field
Enter	Next field
Ctrl-Right Arrow	Start of next word or field
Ctrl-Left Arrow	Start of previous word or field
Ctrl-PgDn	Last record in file
Ctrl-PgUp	First record in file

Move back to the first field of the first record:

Press **Ctrl-PgUp**
Press **Home**

Practice

1. Switch to the Edit screen:

   Press **F2**

   Now try each cursor movement keypress listed in this lesson.
2. Return to the Control Center. Display the data base design of MAILING.DBF.
3. Return to the Control Center. Display the Browse screen for MAILING.DBF. Use the Page Down key to examine all the records, then return to the Control Center again.

Figure 12 The Browse Screen

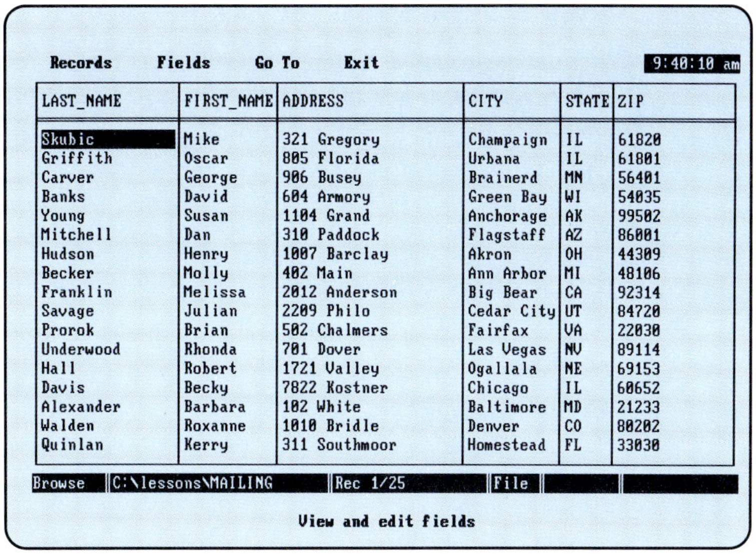

Records   Fields   Go To   Exit   9:40:10 am

LAST_NAME	FIRST_NAME	ADDRESS	CITY	STATE	ZIP
Skubic	Mike	321 Gregory	Champaign	IL	61820
Griffith	Oscar	805 Florida	Urbana	IL	61801
Carver	George	906 Busey	Brainerd	MN	56401
Banks	David	604 Armory	Green Bay	WI	54035
Young	Susan	1104 Grand	Anchorage	AK	99502
Mitchell	Dan	310 Paddock	Flagstaff	AZ	86001
Hudson	Henry	1007 Barclay	Akron	OH	44309
Becker	Molly	402 Main	Ann Arbor	MI	48106
Franklin	Melissa	2012 Anderson	Big Bear	CA	92314
Savage	Julian	2209 Philo	Cedar City	UT	84720
Prorok	Brian	502 Chalmers	Fairfax	VA	22030
Underwood	Rhonda	701 Dover	Las Vegas	NV	89114
Hall	Robert	1721 Valley	Ogallala	NE	69153
Davis	Becky	7822 Kostner	Chicago	IL	60652
Alexander	Barbara	102 White	Baltimore	MD	21233
Walden	Roxanne	1010 Bridle	Denver	CO	80202
Quinlan	Kerry	311 Southmoor	Homestead	FL	33030

Browse | C:\lessons\MAILING | Rec 1/25 | File

View and edit fields

Lesson 6: Adding New Records

Most data bases are continually being changed as people use them. For example, as Paddle and Portage Canoe Outfitters gains more customers, new records will have to be added to the mailing list data base file. Adding new records is one of the most common data base operations.

Step 1: Select the Data Base File

At this point, you should be at the Control Center. Before you can add new records, you must tell dBASE IV the data base file you want to add to. If you have already been working with the file, as we have been with MAILING.DBF, you can skip this step. Otherwise, you would highlight the name of the file in the Data panel of the Control Center screen. Then you would press Enter to select the file, and press Enter again to tell dBASE IV that you want to open it.

Step 2: Activate the Edit Screen

Adding new records to an existing data base is essentially the same process as entering records to a new data base. Execute the Data command to activate the Edit screen:

Press **F2**

Step 3: Move to the Last Record

New records are always added after the last record. Move to the last record in the data base file:

Press **Ctrl-PgDn**

Step 4: Advance Past the Last Record

Whenever you try to advance past the last record in a data base file, dBASE IV will ask you if you want to add new records (see Figure 13). Advance to the next record and answer yes to the prompt:

Press **PgDn**
Type **y**

Step 5: Enter the Record

A blank data entry form will appear on the screen. Simply enter the data for the new record:

Type **Eaton**
Press **Enter**
Type **Candy**
Press **Enter**
Type **2314 Sunset**
Press **Enter**
Type **Rantoul**
Press **Enter**
Type **IL**
Press **Enter**
Type **61866**

Step 6: Terminate Data Entry

As soon as you finish typing the ZIP code, dBASE IV will beep and store the record. A blank data entry form for the next record will appear on the screen. If you have more than one new record to add, you can continue entering them. In our case, only one record is to be added. So, move back to the record you just entered, terminate data entry, and return to the Control Center:

Press **PgUp**
Press **Ctrl-End**

Instead of pressing Ctrl-End, you can also select Exit from the Exit menu.

Practice Activate the Edit screen. Move to the last record in the file. Advance past it. This time, answer no to the prompt asking if you want to add new records. Return to the Control Center.

Lesson 7: Modifying Existing Records

What if a customer moves? His or her record will have to be modified to reflect the change of address. Updating the contents of existing records is another very common data base operation.

Step 1: Select the Data Base File

At this point, you should be at the Control Center. Before you can modify existing records, you must tell dBASE IV the data base file you want to change. If you have already been working with the file, as we have been with MAILING.DBF,

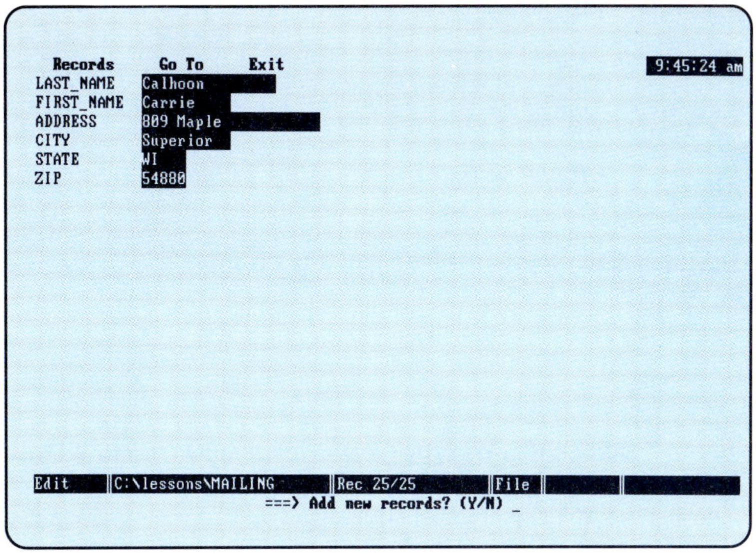

Figure 13 The Add New Records Prompt on the Edit Screen

you can skip this step. Otherwise, you would highlight the name of the file in the Data panel of the Control Center screen. Then you would press Enter to select the file, and press Enter again to tell dBASE IV that you want to open it.

Step 2: Activate the Edit Screen

Records can be modified from either the Edit screen or the Browse screen. Let's use the Edit screen. Execute the Data command to activate the Edit screen:

Press **F2**

Step 3: Select the Record

Just as dBASE IV remembers the data base file on which you are working, it also keeps track of the record. Whenever you are using a data base, an invisible pointer is always aimed at a particular record. This current record is the one listed in the status bar after the label *Rec.* The number before the slash is the current record, and the number after the slash is the total number of records in the data base file.

Before you can change a record, you must have its entry form on the Edit screen or see its line on the Browse screen. In a later lesson, you will learn how to tell dBASE IV to locate a specific record. You can, of course, locate a particular record by visually scanning through the data base. This process, however, can be inconvenient and time consuming, especially with large data bases. For this lesson, let's just modify the current record, which should be Candy Eaton's record.

Step 4: Edit the Data

Once the record to be changed is on the screen, you can move the cursor to any field and make corrections. Follow these directions to change the address in Candy Eaton's record:

Press **Down Arrow** (2 times)
Type **1458 Clearwater**

Press **Enter**
Type **Gary**
Press **Delete** (3 times)
Press **Enter**
Type **IN**
Press **Enter**
Type **46401**

The program will display the prompt

```
Add new records? (Y/N)
```

Answer no:

Type **n**

Note the use of the Delete key to erase existing characters from the field. Three other keypresses can be used to erase characters from a field or other entry. The following table lists the keys you can use to erase characters while editing text.

Key	*Action*
Delete	Erases character at current cursor position
Backspace	Erases character to left of cursor
Ctrl-T	Erases characters from cursor to beginning of next word
Ctrl-Y	Erases characters from cursor to end of field or entry

Step 5: Save the Changes

When you are finished changing records, you can either press Ctrl-End or execute the Exit option from the Exit menu to save your work and return to the Control Center.

Press **Ctrl-End**

Practice

1. Activate the Browse screen:

   Press **F2** (2 times)

   Change Candy Eaton's street address to 1459 Clearwater. Save the change and return to the Control Center.
2. Activate the Edit screen:

   Press **F2** (2 times)

   Change Candy Eaton's street address back to 1458 Clearwater. Save the change and return to the Control Center.

Lesson 8: Deleting Records

Occasionally, records must be completely removed from a data base. In the Paddle and Portage Canoe Outfitters example, customers might not come back for many years or they may not want to receive newsletters in the mail. From time to time, the mailing list data base will have to be purged of these inactive records.

Step 1: Select the Data Base File

At this point, you should be at the Control Center. Before you can delete existing records, you must tell dBASE IV the data base file you want to delete from. If you have already been working with the file, as we have been with MAILING.DBF, you can skip this step. Otherwise, you would highlight the name of the file in the Data panel of the Control Center screen. Then you would press Enter to select the file, and press Enter again to tell dBASE IV that you want to open it.

Step 2: Activate the Edit Screen

Records can be deleted from either the Edit screen or the Browse screen. Let's use the Edit screen. Execute the Data command to activate the Edit screen:

Press **F2**

Step 3: Select the Record

The next step is to locate the record you want to remove. For this lesson, let's just delete the current record, which should be Candy Eaton's record.

Step 4: Mark the Record For Deletion

Records are deleted in two stages: first you mark them for deletion, then you remove them permanently later. This two-stage process allows you to change your mind before records are permanently deleted. Activate the Records menu and select the option Mark Record For Deletion (see Figure 14):

Press **Alt-R**
Type **m**

The record is not actually removed, but the indicator *Del* appears on the right side of the status bar at the bottom of the screen to show that this record is marked for deletion.

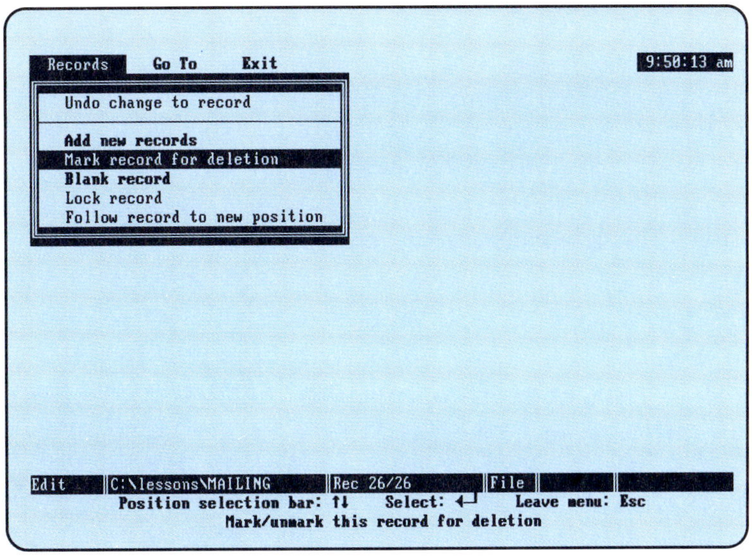

***Figure 14** The Mark Record for Deletion Option*

Step 5: Mark Another Record For Deletion

If you have other records to remove, you can mark them for deletion as well. Move to the preceding record, Carrie Calhoon's, and mark it for deletion too:

Press **Page Up**
Press **Alt-R**
Type **m**

Step 6: Remove a Deletion Mark

Suppose you change your mind about deleting Carrie Calhoon's record. You can simply tell dBASE IV to clear the deletion mark. Activate the Records menu and select the option Clear Deletion Mark (see Figure 15):

Press **Alt-R**
Type **c**

The deletion mark will be removed and Carrie Calhoon's record will be restored.

Step 7: Save the Changes

When you are finished marking records for deletion, you can either press Ctrl-End or execute the Exit option from the Exit menu to save your work and return to the Control Center.

Press **Ctrl-End**

Step 8: Permanently Remove the Marked Record

Records marked for deletion are permanently removed from the data base file by displaying the Data Base Design screen, selecting the Erase Marked Records option from the Organize menu (see Figure 16), and confirming the deletion. Before you perform this step, however, you should make sure you really want

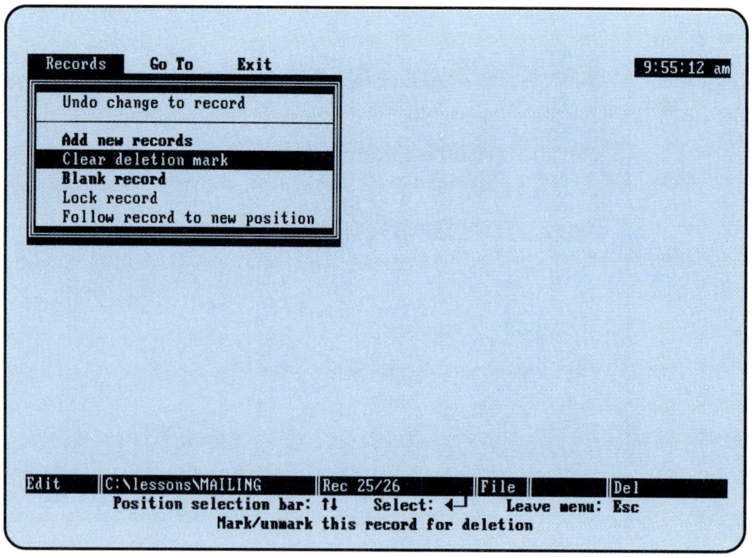

Figure 15 The Clear Deletion Mark Option

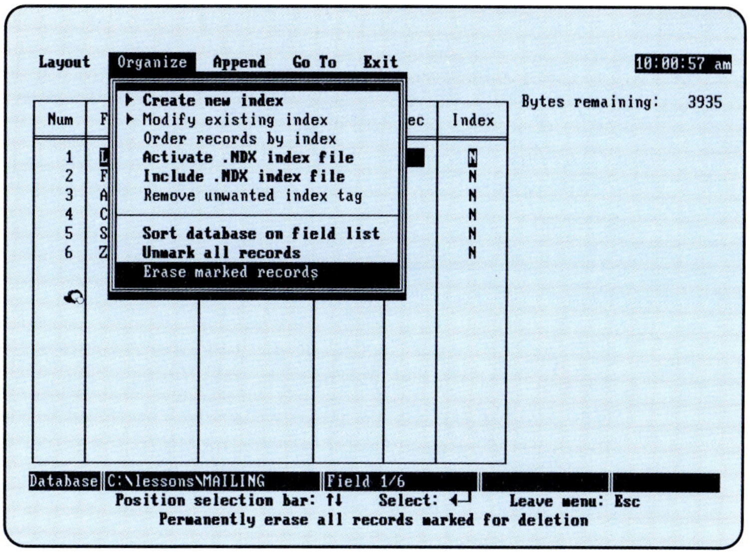

Figure 16 The Erase Marked Records Option

to remove the records marked for deletion. You will not be able to get them back afterwards. Follow these directions to permanently remove Candy Eaton's record:

Press **Shift-F2**
Type **e**
Type **y**

The program will execute a PACK procedure that removes all records marked for deletion, reclaims the disk space used by the deleted records, and renumbers the remaining records. When dBASE IV is finished, save the changes and exit the Data Base Design screen to return to the Control Center:

Press **Alt-E**
Type **s**
Press **Enter**

Practice

1. Activate the Browse screen to confirm that Candy Eaton's record has been removed while Carrie Calhoon's record has been retained.
2. In this lesson you learned that a record can be marked for deletion or a deletion mark can be cleared by selecting an option from the Records menu on the Edit or Browse screen. A shortcut exists for performing both of these operations.

   Press **Ctrl-U**

   This keypress will mark the current record for deletion. Note the *Del* indicator on the right side of the status bar. To clear the deletion mark, repeat the keypress:

   Press **Ctrl-U**

   When you are finished, return to the Control Center.

Lesson 9: Finding Records

If a data base file is small, you can easily find records on the Browse screen. This method, however, is too slow and tedious for large data bases. Fortunately, dBASE IV provides other ways to find records. You can locate a specific record by its record number, or you can find records containing data that match certain search criteria.

Step 1: Select the Data Base File

At this point, you should be at the Control Center. Before you can find records, you must tell dBASE IV the data base file you want to search. If you have already been working with the file, as we have been with MAILING.DBF, you can skip this step. Otherwise, you would highlight the name of the file in the Data panel of the Control Center screen. Then you would press Enter to select the file, and press Enter again to tell dBASE IV that you want to open it.

Step 2: Activate the Browse Screen

Records can be found from either the Edit screen or the Browse screen. Let's use the Browse screen. Execute the Data command to activate the Browse screen:

Press **F2**

If the Edit screen appears, press the F2 key again.

Step 3: Go To the First or Last Record

The Go To menu of the Browse and Edit screens lets you quickly reach particular records in a data base file. Activate the Go To menu:

Press **Alt-G**

Your screen should look like Figure 17. The first two options in the Go To menu let you go to the first or last record in the data base file. Go to the first or top record:

Type **t**

Selecting Top Record from the Go To menu achieves the same result as pressing Ctrl-PgUp. Now try the Last Record option from the Go To menu:

Press **Alt-G**
Type **L**

Carrie Calhoon's record will become the current record.

Step 4: Go To a Particular Record Number

The Record Number option of the Go To menu lets you advance to a particular record number. This option is useful if you happen to know the number of a record you want to find. In most cases, however, you probably won't know the exact record number. Nevertheless, the Record Number option can be handy for moving to an approximate position in a data base file. For example, use the

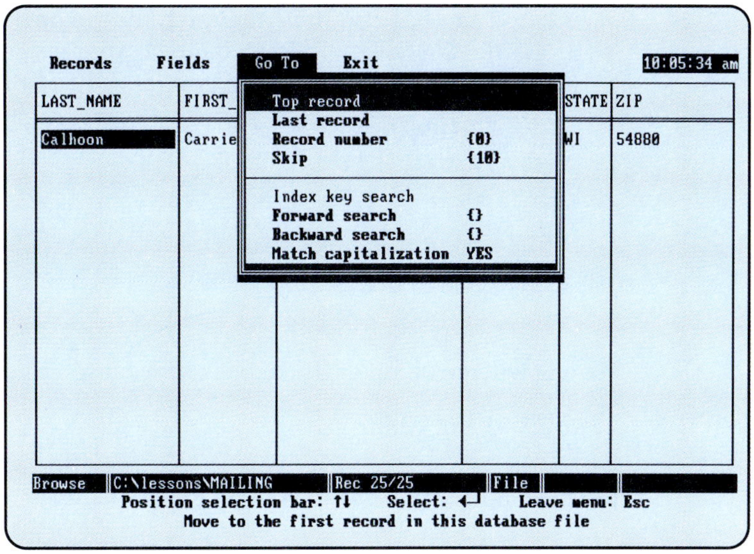

Figure 17 The Go To Menu

Record Number option of the Go To menu to advance to record number 12, which is at about the middle of the MAILING.DBF file:

Press **Alt-G**
Type **r**
Type **12**
Press **Enter**

Rhonda Underwood's record will be highlighted on the Browse screen. The status line will reveal that the current record number is now 12 out of 25.

Step 5: Skip Forward or Backward

The Skip option of the Go To menu lets you jump forward or backward a given number of records. The default number is 10. Activate the Go To menu and select the Skip option:

Press **Alt-G**
Type **s**
Press **Enter**

Record number 22, Sally Weaver's record, will be highlighted. You can skip backward by specifying a negative number of records.

Press **Alt-G**
Type **s**
Type **-10**
Press **Enter**

The program will skip backward to record number 12.

Step 6: Search for a Particular Record

In most cases, you will not remember record numbers. Furthermore, browsing is an inefficient way to search large data bases. Fortunately, dBASE IV lets you find records that contain specific data. Suppose you want to find Jim Diamond's record. You can tell dBASE IV to search for the record that contains "Diamond" in the LAST_NAME field. Move to the beginning of the file, move to the LAST_NAME field, activate the Go To menu, and select the Forward Search option:

Press **Ctrl-PgUp**
Press **Home**
Press **Alt-G**
Type **f**

The program will display the prompt

```
Enter search string:
```

Here is where you enter the name you want to find.

Type **`Diamond`**
Press **Enter**

Jim Diamond's record will be highlighted. Activate the Go To menu again:

Press **Alt-G**

Note the last option in the menu, Match Capitalization. This option is set to YES, which means that dBASE IV will locate only exact matches. If you had entered "diamond" instead of "Diamond" as the search string, the program would have failed to find Jim Diamond's record. You can turn off the Match Capitalization option if you want dBASE IV to ignore the case of letters when searching for data.

The Backward Search option of the Go To menu is like Forward Search, except that it searches from the current record to the beginning of the file. For example, find the nearest preceding record that contains "Chicago" in its CITY field:

Press **Tab** (3 times)
Press **Alt-G**
Type **f**
Press **Home**
Press **Ctrl-Y**
Type **`Chicago`**
Press **Enter**

Becky Davis's record will become the current record. Note that the highlight bar and cursor must be in the field you want to search before you execute the search procedure.

Step 7: Search for a Group of Records

Suppose you want to see the records of all customers from Wisconsin. Follow these directions:

Press **Tab**
Press **Ctrl-PgUp**
Press **Alt-G**
Type **f**
Press **Home**
Press **Ctrl-Y**
Type **`WI`**
Press **Enter**

The program will advance to David Banks's record, the first record that contains "WI" in its STATE field. Execute the Find Next command to advance to the next matching record:

Press **Shift-F4**

Sally Weaver's record will become the current record. Execute the Find Next command again:

Press **Shift-F4**

The program will jump to Carrie Calhoon's record. Execute Find Next once more:

Press **Shift-F4**

The program will wrap around to the beginning of the file and jump to David Banks's record again.

You can also move backward through the group of records that match the search criterion. Try the Find Previous command:

Press **Shift-F3**

The program will jump back to Carrie Calhoon's record.

Step 8: Use the Wildcard Characters ? and *

Two special characters, called **wildcard characters,** can be used in search strings. These characters, ? and *, act like the DOS global file name characters. The question mark (?) matches any single character and the asterisk (*) matches any group of characters.

Suppose you want to find all records from states that begin with the letter *A*. Follow these directions:

Press **Ctrl-PgUp**
Press **Alt-G**
Type **f**
Press **Backspace** (2 times)
Type **A?**
Press **Enter**

The program will advance to Susan Young's record, which has AK in the STATE field. Use the Find Next command to see the other matching record:

Press **Shift-F4**

Dan Mitchell's record, which has AZ in the STATE field, will become the current record.

The asterisk will match any number of characters. Suppose you want to see the records of all customers whose last names begin with W. Follow these instructions:

Press **Ctrl-PgUp**
Press **Home**
Press **Alt-G**
Type **f**
Press **Backspace** (2 times)
Type **W***
Press **Enter**

The program will advance to Roxanne Walden's record. Find the next matching record:

Press **Shift-F4**

Sally Weaver's record will become the current record.

Practice

1. Use the Go To menu to move to the first record in the data base.
2. Advance to record number 15.
3. Use the Backward Search option to find Brian Prorok's record.
4. Find the records of all customers whose first name ends with the letter *e*.

Lesson 10: Modifying the Data Base Design

Occasionally, you need to change the design of a data base file. You might have to change the name, type, or width of a field; add new fields; or delete existing fields. All of these operations can be performed with dBASE IV.

Step 1: Display the Data Base Design Screen

At this point, the Browse screen should still be on your computer. Return to the Control Center and then execute the Design command to display the Data Base Design screen:

Press **Alt-E**
Type **e**
Press **Shift-F2**
Press **Escape**

Step 2: Change a Field Name

Suppose you want to change the name of the ZIP field to ZIP_CODE. Simply move to the ZIP field and edit the name:

Press **Down Arrow** (5 times)
Press **Right Arrow** (3 times)
Type **_CODE**

The field is now named ZIP_CODE. Whenever you change a field name, however, you must activate the Layout menu and select Save This Database File Structure. If you don't execute this option, the data in the former ZIP field will not be copied into the new ZIP_CODE field and you will have to re-enter all of the ZIP codes.

Press **Alt-L**
Type **s**
Press **Enter**

The program will display the prompt

```
Should data be COPIED from backup for all fields? (Y/N)
```

Answer yes:

Type **y**

The program will then ask if you are sure you want to save the changes. Answer yes again:

Type **y**

Step 3: Change a Field Width

You might have noticed that the width of the STATE field is 5, but all state abbreviations are only two letters. This discrepancy wastes three bytes per record. Although three bytes per record may not sound like much, it could add up to a significant waste of disk space if the data base grows very large. Move the cursor to the Width column of the STATE field, and change the 5 to a 2:

Press **Up Arrow**
Press **Tab** (2 times)
Type **2**
Press **Enter**

The width of the STATE field is now 2.

Step 4: Add a New Field

You can also add new fields to your data base design. As an example, let's add a numeric field to MAILING.DBF. This new field will be called CHARGES and will hold the customer's charges for the last trip outfitted by Paddle and Portage. Follow these instructions to add the CHARGES field:

Press **Home**
Press **Down Arrow** (2 times)
Type **charges**
Press **Enter**
Press **Space Bar**
Press **Enter**
Type **7**
Press **Enter**
Type **2**
Press **Enter**

Your screen should look like Figure 18. Note that you had to specify a value for the Dec column because CHARGES is a numeric field.

Step 5: Save the Changes

Any time you modify the data base design, you must save the changes you have made. Activate the Exit menu and select the Save Changes and Exit option:

Press **Alt-E**
Type **s**

The program will ask if you are sure you want to save the changes. Answer yes:

Type **y**

The program will then copy your data to a file with the new data base design, and return to the Control Center.

Figure 18 The CHARGES Field Added to the Record

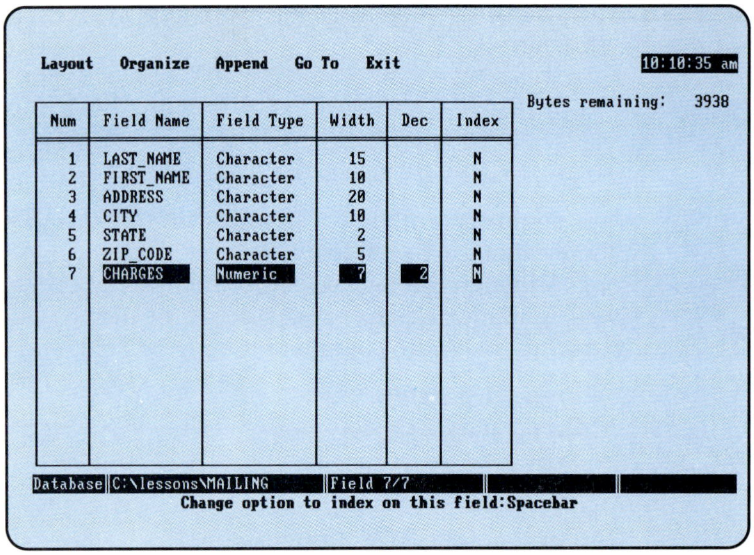

Step 6: Examine the Modified Data Base File

Examine the form of your modified data base file. Execute the Data command twice to display the Edit screen and then move the to first record:

Press **F2** (2 times)
Press **Ctrl-PgUp**

Your screen should look like Figure 19. Note that the CHARGES field is empty except for the decimal point.

Figure 19 The Modified Entry Form Showing the CHARGES Field

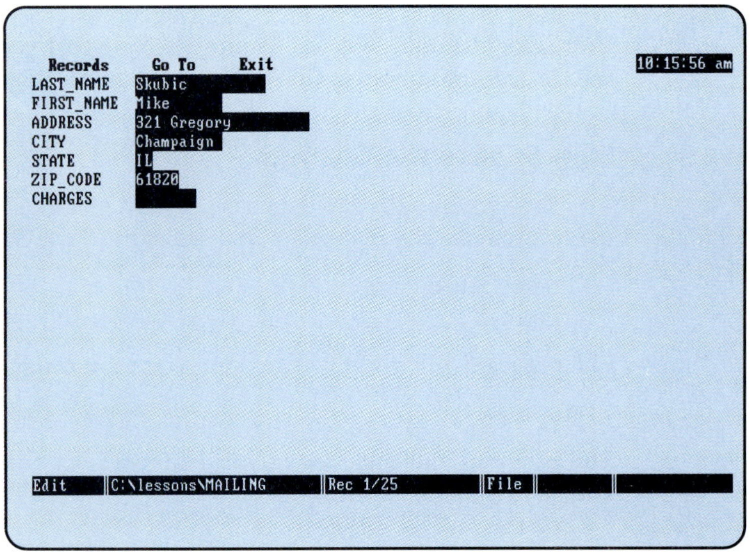

Step 7: Enter the New Field Contents

You have added a new field to the data base design, but you still have to enter the new data. Follow these directions to enter the CHARGES data for Mike Skubic's record:

Press **Down Arrow** (6 times)
Type **245.25**

The program will beep and advance to the next record. Now enter the values from the following table into the CHARGES fields of the remaining records.

Last Name	*Charges*	*Last Name*	*Charges*
Griffith	125.00	Davis	457.75
Carver	55.00	Alexander	125.00
Banks	250.00	Walden	250.00
Young	100.00	Quinlan	250.00
Mitchell	25.00	Irving	175.50
Hudson	375.50	Diamond	350.00
Becker	150.00	Kelley	475.00
Franklin	225.25	Garret	125.50
Savage	125.00	Weaver	250.75
Prorok	235.00	Tudor	120.00
Underwood	75.00	Jenkins	225.25
Hall	115.00	Calhoon	150.00

Practice

1. Move to the beginning of the file and activate the Browse screen. The CHARGES field will not fit on the screen completely. Move the cursor to the CHARGES field and the screen will scroll to reveal the entire width of the column.
2. Exit the Browse screen and return to the Control Center. Activate the Data Base Design screen:

   Press **Shift-F2**

   Activate the Layout menu and highlight the option Save This Database Structure. Invoke the Help system and read about this option. When you are finished, return to the Control Center.

Lesson 11: Sorting the Data Base

One of the most common operations performed on data bases is sorting them into some particular order. Records are stored in a data base file in the order in which they are entered. This order is reflected by the record number assigned to each record. The records of MAILING.DBF were entered in no particular order. Let's sort them according to the contents of the LAST_NAME field. In this case, LAST_NAME will be the **key,** the field used to sort the records of the data base file.

Step 1: Select the Data Base File

At this point, you should be at the Control Center. Before you can sort records, you must tell dBASE IV the data base file you want to sort. If you have already been working with the file, as we have been with MAILING.DBF, you can skip this step. Otherwise, you would highlight the name of the file in the Data panel of the Control Center screen. Then you would press Enter to select the file, and press Enter again to tell dBASE IV that you want to open it.

Step 2: Display the Data Base Design Screen

Execute the Design command to display the Data Base Design screen:

Press **Shift-F2**

The program automatically activates the Organize menu when you display the Data Base Design screen of an existing data base file (see Figure 20).

Step 3: Select the Sort Option

The Organize menu should already be on the screen. Select the option Sort Database On Field List:

Type **s**

Step 4: Specify the Keys

You specify the keys on which to sort the records and the types of sorting to use in the box that appears (see Figure 21). In many cases, just one key will be necessary. You can, however, specify up to ten keys. If you specify more than one key, the sorting is done successively on each key. For example, you might sort a very large mailing list first by state, then by city, then by last name, and then by first name. The records would be arranged alphabetically by state, then by city within each state, then by last name and first name within each city.

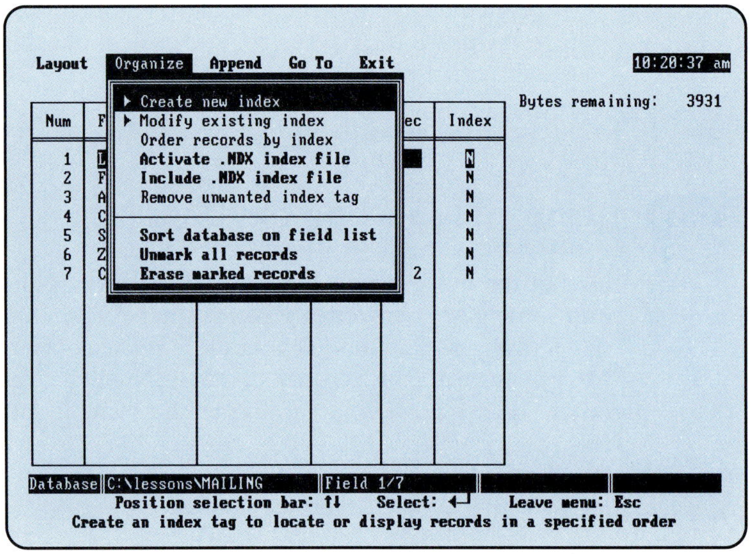

Figure 20 The Organize Menu

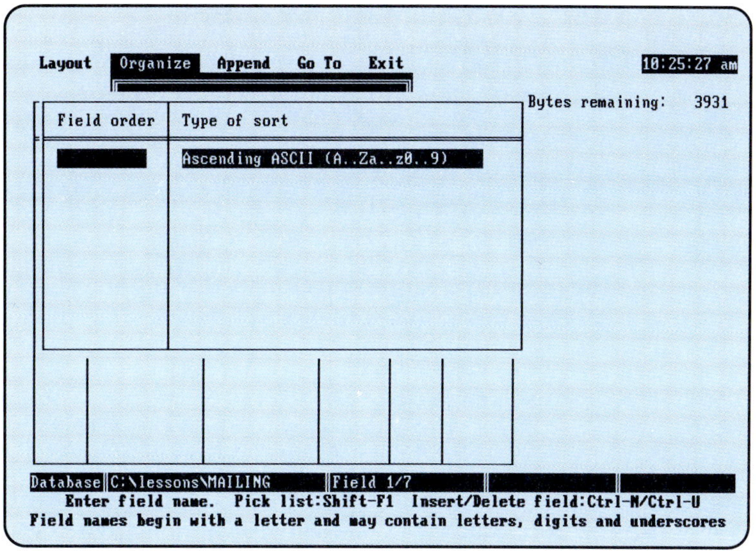

***Figure 21** The Sort Key Box*

Four different types of sorts are available: ascending ASCII, descending ASCII, ascending dictionary, and descending dictionary. Ascending ASCII is the default type of sort. ASCII stands for American Standard Code for Information Interchange. It is the scheme by which computers encode letters and punctuation marks as numbers. An ascending ASCII sort arranges records by key field contents from 0 to 9 and then alphabetically from A to Z, and it distinguishes between uppercase and lowercase letters. Descending ASCII arranges records in the opposite order, from 9 to 0 and Z to A. Ascending and descending dictionary sorts are not case sensitive. For example, if you choose descending dictionary, all records beginning with the letters *a* or *A* will appear before records beginning with *b* or *B*.

In our simple mailing list data base, you need only sort by LAST_NAME and you can use an ascending ASCII sort. Enter the field name of the key and save your specification:

Type **last_name**
Press **Ctrl-End**

Step 5: Specify the New File Name

The program will display the prompt

```
Enter name of sorted file:
```

When dBASE IV sorts a file, it actually creates a new file with the records arranged in the proper order. You will have two versions of the same data base file. So, you must enter a new file name for the sorted data base.

Type **by_name**
Press **Enter**

A new file named BY_NAME.DBF will be created containing the same records as MAILING.DBF, but the records will be sorted by LAST_NAME.

Step 6: Examine the Sorted File

Return to the Control Center, highlight BY_NAME in the Data panel, and activate the Browse screen to examine the sorted file:

Press **Alt-E**
Type **a**
Press **Down Arrow**
Press **F2**

The records will appear in alphabetical order by LAST_NAME as shown in Figure 22. Page down to see the rest of the records, then go back to the first record:

Press **Page Down**
Press **Page Up**

Practice

Return to the Control Center, display the Data Base Design screen, and highlight the Sort Database On Field List option from the Organize menu. Invoke the Help system and read the Sort Data box. When you are finished, return to the Control Center.

Lesson 12: Indexing the Data Base

Sorting a data base file that has many records is a relatively slow process. It can also take up a lot of disk space because a new copy of the entire file is produced. Several versions of the same data base, each sorted in a different way, can occupy a significant portion of a disk. Another disadvantage of sorting is the problem of updating multiple files. An address change, for example, would have to be made to every sorted version of the same data base file.

Indexing is a convenient alternative to sorting that rearranges record numbers instead of entire records. When you index a data base file, dBASE IV does not

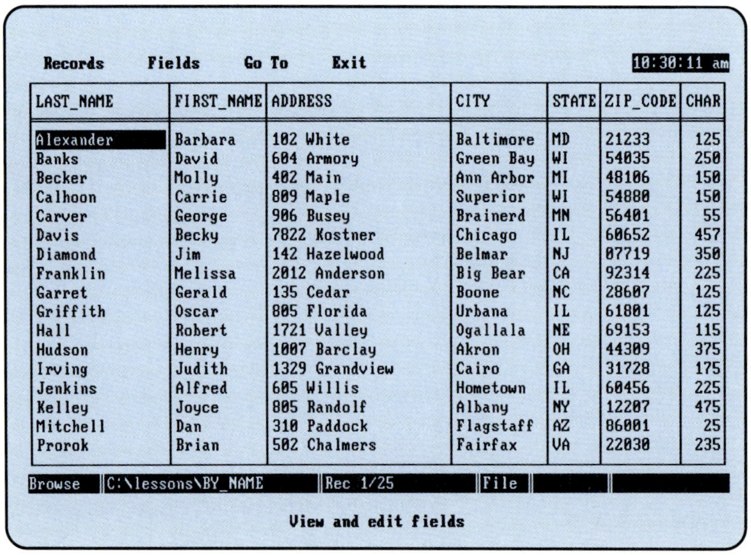

Records Fields Go To Exit 10:30:11 am

LAST_NAME	FIRST_NAME	ADDRESS	CITY	STATE	ZIP_CODE	CHAR
Alexander	Barbara	102 White	Baltimore	MD	21233	125
Banks	David	604 Armory	Green Bay	WI	54035	250
Becker	Molly	402 Main	Ann Arbor	MI	48106	150
Calhoon	Carrie	809 Maple	Superior	WI	54880	150
Carver	George	906 Busey	Brainerd	MN	56401	55
Davis	Becky	7822 Kostner	Chicago	IL	60652	457
Diamond	Jim	142 Hazelwood	Belmar	NJ	07719	350
Franklin	Melissa	2012 Anderson	Big Bear	CA	92314	225
Garret	Gerald	135 Cedar	Boone	NC	28607	125
Griffith	Oscar	805 Florida	Urbana	IL	61801	125
Hall	Robert	1721 Valley	Ogallala	NE	69153	115
Hudson	Henry	1007 Barclay	Akron	OH	44309	375
Irving	Judith	1329 Grandview	Cairo	GA	31728	175
Jenkins	Alfred	605 Willis	Hometown	IL	60456	225
Kelley	Joyce	805 Randolf	Albany	NY	12207	475
Mitchell	Dan	310 Paddock	Flagstaff	AZ	86001	25
Prorok	Brian	502 Chalmers	Fairfax	VA	22030	235

Browse C:\lessons\BY_NAME Rec 1/25 File

View and edit fields

Figure 22 The BY_NAME Data Base on the Browse Screen

change the order of the records and record numbers in the original file. Instead it creates an **index file** that contains two columns of data. One column contains a reference to each record by one or more key values. The other column lists each record number. Suppose you index the MAILING.DBF file by LAST_NAME. The following table shows part of the contents of the index file.

Index Field Data	Record Number
Alexander	15
Banks	4
Becker	8
Calhoon	25
Carver	3
Davis	14
Diamond	19

The last names are arranged in alphabetical order, but the record numbers refer to the order of the records in the original file, MAILING.DBF. Only key data and record numbers are stored in the appropriate order in an index file. The original data base file remains intact and contains the rest of the data.

With large data bases, an index file is usually much smaller than the data base file from which it is created. Indexing a file is therefore faster than sorting a file because less data are copied. As an analogy, think of a library as a data base. Each book on the shelf is like a record. A card catalog is like an index file. Each card in the card catalog just lists data that identify the book, such as title, author, subject, and call number. The call number is like the book's record number. Suppose you want to find books by the author's last name. Which would you rather rearrange: the books themselves or the cards in the card catalog? What if you want to find books by title and subject too? You can maintain several card catalogs with cards arranged differently, yet have just one set of books arranged by call number on the shelves.

As an example, let's index MAILING.DBF by ZIP_CODE.

Step 1: Select the Data Base File

At this point, you should be at the Control Center. Before you can index records, you must tell dBASE IV the data base file you want to index. Highlight MAILING in the Data panel and tell dBASE IV that you want to open this file:

Press **Down Arrow**
Press **Enter**
Press **Enter**

Step 2: Display the Data Base Design Screen

Execute the Design command to display the Data Base Design screen:

Press **Shift-F2**

The program automatically activates the Organize menu when you display the Data Base Design screen of an existing data base file (see Figure 20).

Step 3: Change Index Setting to Y

The Organize menu should already be on the screen with the Create New Index option highlighted. The easiest way to index a file with dBASE IV, however, does not require you to use this menu. Deactivate the menu to see the full Data Base Design screen:

Press **Escape**

To index the data base file on the basis of ZIP codes, simply move to the Index column of the ZIP_CODE field and change the setting from N to Y:

Press **Down Arrow** (5 times)
Press **Tab** (3 times)
Type **y**

Step 4: Save the Change

Save the altered data base design and return to the Control Center:

Press **Alt-E**
Type **s**
Type **y**

The file MAILING.DBF will be indexed on the basis of ZIP codes.

Step 5: Examine the Indexed File

Activate the Browse screen and move to the first record to examine the indexed file:

Press **F2**
Press **Ctrl-PgUp**

The records will appear ordered by ZIP_CODE as shown in Figure 23. Page down to see the rest of the records, then go back to the first record:

Press **Page Down**
Press **Page Up**

Practice

1. Index MAILING.DBF on the basis of LAST_NAME instead of ZIP_CODE:

   Press **Escape**
   Press **Shift-F2**
   Press **Escape**
   Press **Tab** (3 times)
   Type **y**
   Press **Down Arrow** (4 times)
   Press **Tab** (3 times)
   Type **n**
   Press **Alt-E**
   Type **s**
   Type **y**

2. Activate the Browse screen to examine MAILING.DBF indexed by LAST_NAME. When you are finished, return to the Control Center.

Figure 23 The Records Indexed by ZIP_CODE

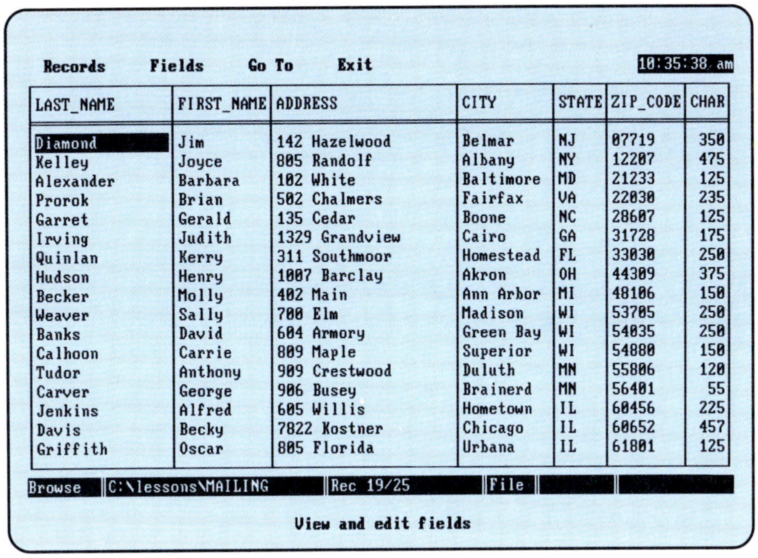
Records Fields Go To Exit 10:35:38 am

LAST_NAME	FIRST_NAME	ADDRESS	CITY	STATE	ZIP_CODE	CHAR
Diamond	Jim	142 Hazelwood	Belmar	NJ	07719	350
Kelley	Joyce	805 Randolf	Albany	NY	12207	475
Alexander	Barbara	102 White	Baltimore	MD	21233	125
Prorok	Brian	502 Chalmers	Fairfax	VA	22030	235
Garret	Gerald	135 Cedar	Boone	NC	28607	125
Irving	Judith	1329 Grandview	Cairo	GA	31728	175
Quinlan	Kerry	311 Southmoor	Homestead	FL	33030	250
Hudson	Henry	1007 Barclay	Akron	OH	44309	375
Becker	Molly	402 Main	Ann Arbor	MI	48106	150
Weaver	Sally	700 Elm	Madison	WI	53705	250
Banks	David	604 Armory	Green Bay	WI	54035	250
Calhoon	Carrie	809 Maple	Superior	WI	54880	150
Tudor	Anthony	909 Crestwood	Duluth	MN	55806	120
Carver	George	906 Busey	Brainerd	MN	56401	55
Jenkins	Alfred	605 Willis	Hometown	IL	60456	225
Davis	Becky	7822 Kostner	Chicago	IL	60652	457
Griffith	Oscar	805 Florida	Urbana	IL	61801	125

Browse C:\lessons\MAILING Rec 19/25 File

View and edit fields

3. Close the file MAILING.DBF:

   Press **Enter**
   Press **Enter**

   Now, open it again. Highlight MAILING in the Data panel and then do this:

   Press **Enter**
   Press **Enter**

   Activate the Browse screen to examine the file. It does not appear to be indexed. What happened? When you close an indexed file or exit dBASE IV and then open that file again, you must explicitly tell the program to order the records by the index. Display the Data Base Design screen, select the Order Records By Index option, and display the Browse screen again:

Press	**Escape**
Press	**Shift-F2**
Type	**o**
Highlight	**LAST_NAME**
Press	**Enter**
Press	**Alt-E**
Type	**a**
Press	**F2**

   The file should again appear indexed by LAST_NAME.

Lesson 13: Generating Reports

You have learned how to use the Browse and Edit screens to examine all or part of a data base on your computer display. The dBASE IV program also provides a wide choice of printing options for producing reports. A **report** is simply a listing of the contents of a data base printed on paper. You can print an unformatted list of all the records in a file or selectively print only certain fields and records. Mailing labels, preprinted forms, and custom-formatted reports can all

Real World

Computerizing the City Clerk

In May, 1986, the city clerk's office in Torrance, California, was given a computer terminal hooked up to the city's Digital VAX 11/780 mainframe. Within 24 hours the staff had tossed their pencils out the window and created and installed five data base programs. They were in the world of computers.

How did it happen so fast? Deputy City Clerk Dora Hong, relying on her self-taught knowledge of data base management programming, simply coached the staff members individually. She worked on dBASE syntax structure from the dot prompt on a blank screen, ignoring menu applications.

Hong's pupils were such fast learners that within three months, they had indexed the city council legislative history up to the most recently approved minutes, indexed the city's deeds, and created a new system of records storage based on a "box filing system." Since then, additional terminals have been installed.

There have been long-term benefits as well. First, according to Hong, the data base program has saved the office enormous amounts of time, particularly in summarizing, indexing, and searching for and retrieving information. It once took nearly a week to summarize, categorize, and file city council legislative history, she said. Now that can be done in less than two hours.

In addition, human filing error has been virtually eliminated, staff assignments can be made more flexibly, and staff morale has increased, according to Hong. Service to city departments and the city council has improved because information is indexed and can be quickly and accurately retrieved.

Source: Dora Hong, "Database Management System Benefits City," *The Office*, October 1988, pp. 117–120.

be created with dBASE IV. In this lesson you will learn how to produce a Quick Report of the Paddle and Portage Canoe Outfitters mailing list. The next chapter will present more advanced printing options.

Step 1: Select the Data Base File

At this point, you should be at the Control Center. Before you can create a report, you must tell dBASE IV the data base file you want to print. If you have already been working with the file, as we have been with MAILING.DBF, you can skip this step. Otherwise, you would highlight the name of the file in the Data panel of the Control Center screen. Then you would press Enter to select the file and press Enter again to tell dBASE IV that you want to open it.

Step 2: Prepare the Printer

Make sure the printer is connected to the computer and turned on. Also, make sure that paper is loaded and aligned to the top of a new page. Finally, make sure that the printer's On Line light is lit. (If it isn't, press the On Line button.)

Step 3: Execute the Quick Report Command

The Quick Report command organizes and prints data from the current data base file. It is an easy way to print a complete report from the Control Center without having to design the report layout yourself. The output is similar to what you

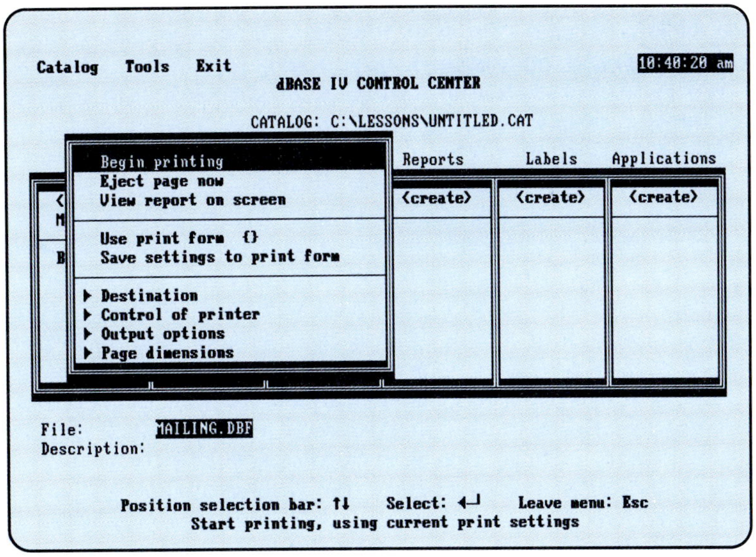

Figure 24 The Print Menu

see on the Browse screen without dividing lines. Execute the Quick Report command:

Press **Shift-F9**

Step 4: Print the Report

The Print menu will appear on your screen as shown in Figure 24. You can begin printing immediately. Select the Begin Printing option:

Type **b**

The output from the printer should look like Figure 25. Note that the records have been printed in indexed order by LAST_NAME. Also note that dBASE IV automatically totaled the numbers in the CHARGES column.

Practice Use the Quick Report command to print the BY_NAME data base file.

Summary

- *Starting dBASE IV.* Switch to the desired subdirectory and enter **dbase** from the DOS prompt.
- *Using the Control Center.* Press F10 to activate the menu bar. Highlight menu options with the arrow keys. Activate a menu by holding down the Alternate key and typing the menu title's first letter. Execute a menu option by highlighting it and pressing Enter or typing the first letter. Deactivate a menu by pressing Escape. Invoke Help by pressing F1.
- *Designing a data base file.* Select the <create> option from the Data panel and enter each field's name, type, and width.
- *Entering data base records.* Activate the Edit screen by pressing F2 and enter the data for each field. Terminate data entry by pressing Ctrl-End.

***Figure 25* Quick Report of MAILING.DBF Indexed by LAST_NAME**

Page No. 1
08/10/89

LAST_NAME	FIRST_NAME	ADDRESS	CITY	STATE	ZIP_CODE	CHARGES
Alexander	Barbara	102 White	Baltimore	MD	21233	125.00
Banks	David	604 Armory	Green Bay	WI	54035	250.00
Becker	Molly	402 Main	Ann Arbor	MI	48106	150.00
Calhoon	Carrie	809 Maple	Superior	WI	54880	150.00
Carver	George	906 Busey	Brainerd	MN	56401	55.00
Davis	Becky	7822 Kostner	Chicago	IL	60652	457.75
Diamond	Jim	142 Hazelwood	Belmar	NJ	07719	350.00
Franklin	Melissa	2012 Anderson	Big Bear	CA	92314	225.25
Garret	Gerald	135 Cedar	Boone	NC	28607	125.50
Griffith	Oscar	805 Florida	Urbana	IL	61801	125.00
Hall	Robert	1721 Valley	Ogallala	NE	69153	115.00
Hudson	Henry	1007 Barclay	Akron	OH	44309	375.50
Irving	Judith	1329 Grandview	Cairo	GA	31728	175.50
Jenkins	Alfred	605 Willis	Hometown	IL	00450	225.25
Kelley	Joyce	805 Randolf	Albany	NY	12207	475.00
Mitchell	Dan	310 Paddock	Flagstaff	AZ	86001	25.00
Prorok	Brian	502 Chalmers	Fairfax	VA	22030	235.00
Quinlan	Kerry	311 Southmoor	Homestead	FL	33030	250.00
Savage	Julian	2209 Philo	Cedar City	UT	84720	125.00
Skubic	Mike	321 Gregory	Champaign	IL	61820	245.25
Tudor	Anthony	909 Crestwood	Duluth	MN	55806	120.00
Underwood	Rhonda	701 Dover	Las Vegas	NV	89114	75.00
Walden	Roxanne	1010 Bridle	Denver	CO	80202	250.00
Weaver	Sally	700 Elm	Madison	WI	53705	250.75
Young	Susan	1104 Grand	Anchorage	AK	99502	100.00
						5055.75

- *Examining a data base.* Press Shift-F2 to see the Data Base Design screen. Press F2 to see the Edit screen or Browse screen.
- *Adding new records.* Activate the Edit screen or Browse screen, advance past the last record, and enter the data for the new records.
- *Modifying records.* Activate the Edit screen or Browse screen and change the data.
- *Deleting records.* Activate the Edit screen or Browse screen and select the Mark Record For Deletion option from the Records menu. Activate the Data Base Design screen and select the Erase Marked Records option to permanently remove marked records.
- *Finding records.* Activate the Edit screen or Browse screen and use the Go To menu.
- *Modifying the data base design.* Press Shift-F2, make the changes, and select Save This Database File Structure from the Layout menu.

- *Sorting a data base.* Press Shift-F2, select the Sort option, specify the keys, and specify the new file name.
- *Indexing a data base.* Change the Index entry of the Data Base Design screen to Y for the field on which the file is to be indexed.
- *Generating reports.* Press Shift-F9 to activate the Print menu and select the Begin Printing option to produce a Quick Report.

Key Terms

As an extra review of this chapter, try defining the following terms.

catalog
data base
field
file
form
index file
indexing
key
menu bar
message line
navigation line
record
report
status bar
table
wildcard character

Multiple Choice

Choose the best selection to complete each statement.

1. A data base file is a collection of
   (a) rows. (b) columns.
   (c) records. (d) bits.
2. The dBASE IV menu system is called the
   (a) dot prompt. (b) Help system.
   (c) status bar. (d) Control Center.
3. Which keys do you press to activate the Exit menu?
   (a) Alt-Escape (b) Alt-E
   (c) Escape (d) F1
4. Which key do you press to invoke the Help system?
   (a) F1 (b) F10
   (c) Escape (d) Alternate
5. Which of the following terms is not a valid field type?
   (a) Character (b) Numeric
   (c) Time (d) Memo
6. Which type of field would you use to store Social Security numbers?
   (a) Character (b) Numeric
   (c) Float (d) Logical

7. What is the maximum size of a dBASE IV record?
   (a) 254 bytes (b) 1000 bytes
   (c) 2500 bytes (d) 4000 bytes
8. Which of the following characters is not allowed in field names?
   (a) A (b) 5
   (c) underscore (_) (d) space
9. Which key do you press to display the Edit screen or Browse screen?
   (a) F1 (b) F2
   (c) F9 (d) F10
10. Which screen lets you see the contents of several records at the same time in a table format?
    (a) Edit screen (b) Browse screen
    (c) Data Base Design screen (d) Control Center screen
11. Which key(s) do you press to jump immediately to the first record in a data base file?
    (a) Home (b) Up Arrow
    (c) Ctrl-Tab (d) Ctrl-PgUp
12. Which menu must you use to permanently remove records marked for deletion?
    (a) Records on the Edit or Browse screen
    (b) Organize on the Data Base Design screen
    (c) Exit on the Edit or Browse screen
    (d) Exit on the Data Base Design screen
13. How do you add new records to an existing data base?
    (a) Press the Insert key.
    (b) Advance past the last record.
    (c) Select Append from the Fields menu.
    (d) Press F1.
14. How would you jump forward ten records on the Browse screen?
    (a) Press Page Up.
    (b) Select Skip from the Go To menu.
    (c) Select Jump from the Records menu.
    (d) Select Forward Search from the Go To menu.
15. Which keypress does not delete characters?
    (a) Delete (b) Backspace
    (c) Ctrl-D (d) Ctrl-Y
16. Which Browse screen menu lets you quickly reach particular records in a data base file?
    (a) Records (b) Fields
    (c) Go To (d) Exit
17. Which wildcard character will match any number of characters?
    (a) ? (b) *
    (c) & (d) $

18. Record numbers are assigned to records on the basis of
    (a) the order in which they were entered.
    (b) the key field.
    (c) the index expression.
    (d) the field width.
19. Which method of organizing a large data base file is usually slow and takes up a lot of disk space?
    (a) indexing (b) sorting
    (c) printing (d) searching
20. Which key(s) execute the Quick Report command and activate the Print menu?
    (a) F1 (b) F2
    (c) Shift-F3 (d) Shift-F9

Fill-In

1. The dBASE IV package cannot be run unless you have a ______ disk or are connected to a local area network.
2. The Control Center is the ______ system of dBASE IV.
3. The menu bar contains the ______ of the currently available menus.
4. One way to activate a menu is to hold down the ______ key and type the first letter of the menu title.
5. You can close a menu and make it disappear by pressing the ______ key.
6. The ______ option lets you retrace your steps through the Help system.
7. A record is a sequence of ______.
8. A byte is equivalent to a single ______.
9. The ______ field type is for counting or exact calculations.
10. A ______ displays the fields of an individual record on the screen.
11. When you are finished entering records, you can either press ______ or execute the Exit option from the Exit menu to save your work.
12. The Data command, which is invoked by pressing the F2 key, activates either the ______ screen or the ______ screen.
13. Whenever you try to advance past the last record in a data base file, dBASE IV will ask you if you want to ______ records.
14. Records can be modified from either the ______ screen or the ______ screen.
15. Records are first ______ for deletion before they are permanently removed from a data base file.
16. If you are at the beginning of a file, you can use the ______ Search option from the Go To menu to find records that contain specific data.
17. The Find Next command, executed by pressing ______, advances to the next record that matches the search criteria.
18. Wildcard characters can be used in search strings to find records containing data with one or more ______ in common.
19. When dBASE IV sorts a file, it actually creates a new ______ with the records arranged in the proper order.
20. A convenient alternative to sorting is ______, which rearranges record numbers instead of entire records.

Short Problems

1. If you are not already running dBASE IV, switch to the LESSONS subdirectory and start the program. Highlight MAILING in the Data panel of the Control Center and tell dBASE IV that you want to use this file.
2. Execute the Data command to display the Browse screen. Move to the last record in the file.
3. Activate the Go To menu and perform a Backward Search to find George Carver's record.
4. Move to the beginning of the MAILING data base file and then move to the STATE field. Activate the Go To menu and perform a Forward Search to find the records of all customers who live in Illinois. Use the Find Next command to view each of these records.
5. Move to the beginning of the MAILING data base file and then move to the CITY field. Activate the Go To menu and perform a Forward Search to find the records of all customers who live in cities that begin with the letter C. Use the Find Next command to view each of these records.
6. Exit the Browse screen and then display the Data Base Design screen. Execute the Order Records by Index option from the Organize menu. Select the LAST NAME index. Activate the Exit menu and select Abandon Changes and Exit. Examine the MAILING data base file on the Browse screen. When you are finished, return to the Control Center.
7. Select the MAILING file in the Data panel and tell dBASE IV that you want to close this file. Then select the BY_NAME file from the Data panel and tell dBASE IV that you want to use this file. Activate the Browse screen to examine the file.
8. Modify Oscar Griffith's address so that it reads "810 Florida" and then return to the Control Center.
9. Index the BY_NAME data base file by STATE. Examine the data base on the Browse screen.
10. Print a Quick Report of the BY_NAME data base indexed by STATE.

Long Problems

1. Create a data base file containing information about your collection of LP records, cassette tapes, and compact discs. Include fields for the title, artist, type of media (LP, tape, or CD), amount paid, and year released. Use a Numeric field for the cost. Index the data base by artist. Print a Quick Report to calculate the total value of your collection.
2. Create a data base file containing your personal property inventory. Include fields for item, serial number, location, date purchased, and amount paid. Use a Date field for the date purchased and Numeric field for the amount paid. Print a Quick Report to calculate the total value of your property.
3. Create an "electronic Rolodex" with dBASE IV. Design and enter the records of a data base file to hold the information you keep in your personal address/phone book. Include fields for name, address, city, state, ZIP code, and phone number. If you like, you can also include fields for work address and phone, birth dates, anniversaries, and any other information you keep. Index the data base by name and print a Quick Report.

4. Suppose you are a teaching assistant for this course. Create a data base file to keep track of grades. Include fields for each student's name, Social Security number, class, section, classroom, meeting day and time, homework grades, test grades, and final letter grade. Make up and enter at least twenty records.
5. Create a data base file that contains information about all of the courses you have taken throughout your college career. Include fields for course title, course number, semester or quarter and year taken, hours or credits earned, instructor, and school (if you have attended more than one).
6. Create a data base file for keeping track of your (or your family's) car expenses. Use a separate record for each month of the year. Include fields for month, taxes, insurance, repairs, gas, oil, parking fees, tolls, speeding tickets, car washes, and any other expenses you can think of.
7. Create a data base file containing your academic schedule for this semester or quarter. Use a separate record for each class. Include fields for class, day, time, building, room, and instructor. Print a Quick Report of your class schedule.
8. Create a data base file that stores information about your textbooks, reference books, and personal books. Include fields for title, author, publisher, copyright date, and cost. Print a Quick Report of your data base.
9. Use a current reference such as *The World Almanac* to create a data base file of information about the fifty states. Include fields for state name, capital city, population, and area in square miles.
10. Don't put away your copy of *The World Almanac* yet. Modify your states data base file so that it includes the names of the governor and the two U.S. senators for each state.

CHAPTER 15

INTERMEDIATE dBASE IV

In This Chapter

Getting Started
Lesson 1: Using Memo Fields
Lesson 2: Creating a Simple View Query
Lesson 3: Creating a Relational Data Base
Lesson 4: Linking Files
Lesson 5: Creating an Update Query
Lesson 6: Using Calculated Fields
Lesson 7: Summarizing Data
Lesson 8: Designing Custom Forms
Lesson 9: Designing Custom Reports
Lesson 10: Creating Mailing Labels
Lesson 11: Using Applications
Lesson 12: Using the Catalog Menu
Lesson 13: Using the Tools Menu

Preview

In Chapter 14 you learned the basics of dBASE IV, the top-selling microcomputer data base management package. This chapter continues your exploration of dBASE IV, focusing on slightly more advanced topics.

After studying this chapter, you will know how to

- use memo fields.
- create view queries.
- create relational data bases.
- link files.
- create update queries.
- use calculated fields.
- summarize data.
- design custom forms.
- design custom reports.
- create mailing labels.
- use applications.
- use the Catalog menu.
- use the Tools menu.

Getting Started

You've already learned how to start dBASE IV and use its most basic features and commands. This chapter assumes you have completed all of the lessons and exercises in Chapter 14. Furthermore, it assumes that you have a computer with a hard disk and dBASE IV installed on it in a subdirectory named DBASE. A DOS path should be set up so that you can run dBASE IV from within any subdirectory. You should have a subdirectory named LESSONS in which to store your data base files.

Lesson 1: Using Memo Fields

Most data base fields contain a single number, word, or phrase. The Memo field type, however, allows you to include a block of text in a data base record. Memo fields can be used to store explanatory notes, descriptions, comments, or other free-form information. For example, you could use a Memo field in a bibliographic data base to record your notes about each book. Actually, the text itself is not stored in the Memo field. It is kept in a separate file. The Memo field tells dBASE IV which file contains the text. As an example, let's create a Memo field for the Paddle and Portage Canoe Outfitters data base to list the compliments or complaints made by each customer.

Step 1: Select the Data Base File

If you are not already running dBASE IV, switch to your LESSONS subdirectory and start the program:

Type **cd \lessons**
Press **Enter**
Type **dbase**
Press **Enter**
Press **Enter**

The Control Center screen should be visible, with the highlight bar in the Data panel. Tell dBASE IV that you want to use the MAILING data base file:

Highlight **MAILING**
Press **Enter**
Press **Enter**

Step 2: Add a Memo Field to the Design

To add a Memo field to an existing data base file, you must modify the data base design. Execute the Design command to display the Data Base Design screen:

Press **Shift-F2**
Press **Escape**

Move past the last field in the record and insert a new Memo field named COMMENTS:

Press **Down Arrow** (7 times)
Type **comments**
Press **Enter**
Type **m**
Press **Up Arrow**

Your screen should look like Figure 1. Note that dBASE IV automatically sets the width of a Memo field to 10 bytes. Remember that a Memo field itself does not actually hold any text. It holds only a pointer to a separate, but related file that contains the text. Now, save the changes you have made and return to the Control Center:

Press **Alt-E**
Type **s**
Press **Enter**

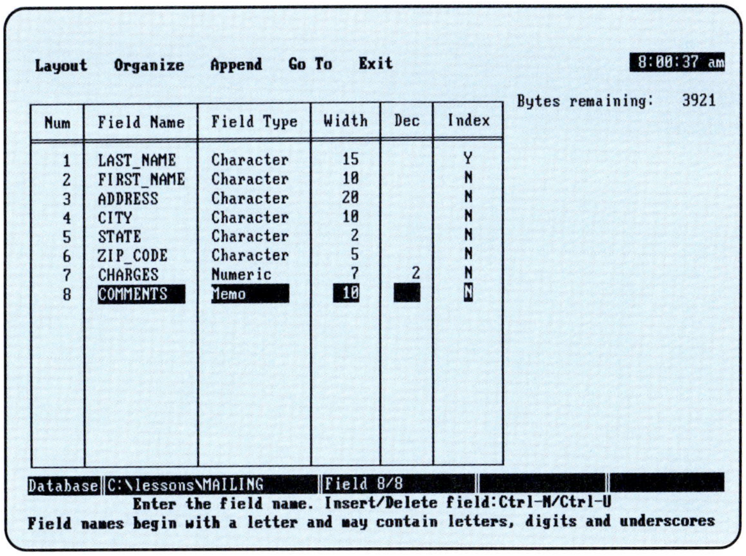

Figure 1 Memo Field Added to the Data Base Design

Step 3: Add Data to the Memo Field

Execute the Data command to display the Edit screen:

Press **F2**

If the Browse screen appears, repeat the command to switch to the Edit screen. Move to the first record in the data base file:

Press **Ctrl-PgUp**

Your screen should look like Figure 2. The COMMENTS field contains the word "memo" in lowercase letters. This word is called a **memo marker.** It indicates whether the file associated with the Memo field contains any text. If the word "memo" appears in lowercase letters, the Memo field file is empty. If it appears entirely in uppercase letters, the Memo field file contains text. The memo marker allows you to see if a Memo field file contains text without having to open it.

At this point, all the COMMENTS fields in the MAILING data base file are empty. To enter text in a Memo field file, move the cursor to that field and open it by pressing Ctrl-Home.

Press **Down Arrow** (7 times)
Press **Ctrl-Home**

The dBASE IV program activates its word-wrap editor, shown in Figure 3. This editor works like a simple word processor. It allows you to enter, edit, and to some extent format text in Memo fields and dBASE IV programs. (You will learn about dBASE IV programs in the next chapter.) A ruler line appears below the menu bar across the top of the screen. The left bracket ([) indicates the left margin, and the right bracket (]) indicates the right margin. The dots indicate character positions, the triangles indicate tab stops, and the numbers indicate inch measurements. By default, the line width in Memo fields is set to 65 characters. Word wrap will occur automatically as you type. You can press the arrow keys to move the cursor and the Backspace and Delete keys to erase characters. The Insert key toggles between the insert and typeover modes. Insert mode is turned on by

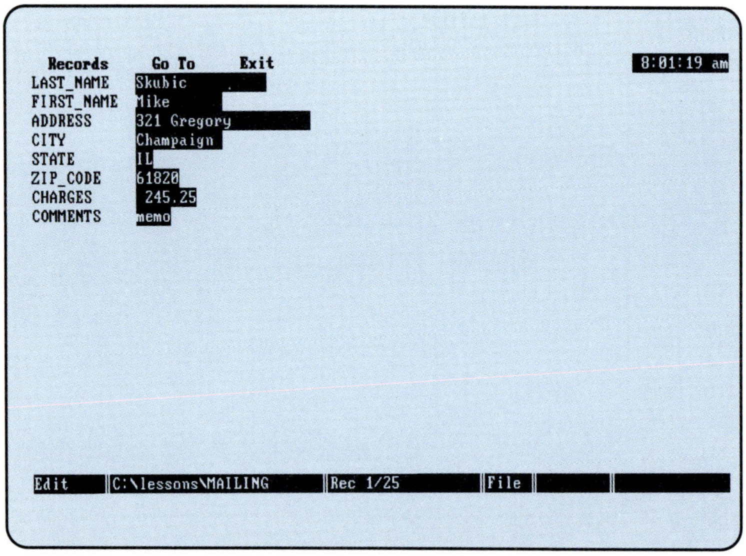

Figure 2 The COMMENTS Field Containing the Memo Marker

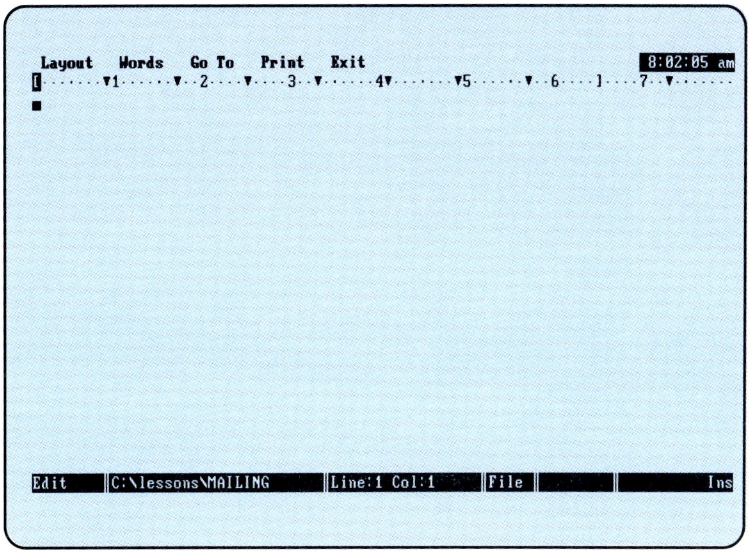

Figure 3 The Word-Wrap Editor

default and is indicated by the abbreviation "Ins," which appears at the right side of the status bar. The Enter key begins a new paragraph. Type the following text, without pressing the Enter key, into the COMMENTS field of Mike Skubic's record:

> **Mike feels that the Beaver canoe is a bit unstable when it is not fully loaded. He likes the nylon Duluth packs. He prefers the Beef Stromboli to the Chicken Stew 'N Dumplings. Next trip, he would like to try a route that does not go through the Silver Falls portage.**

Check your work against Figure 4. If you have made any mistakes, correct them by using the arrow keys to move the cursor and the Delete or Backspace key to erase characters. When you are finished entering or editing text in the Memo field, press Ctrl-End or select the Save Changes and Exit option from the Exit menu.

Press **Alt-E**
Type **s**

The program will return to the Edit screen showing Mike Skubic's record. Note that the memo marker is now "MEMO" in uppercase letters, which indicates that the COMMENTS field contains text.

Step 4: Examine an Existing Memo Field

You cannot see the contents of a Memo field on the Edit screen. Try the Browse screen:

Press **F2**
Press **End**

The result is the same. Only the memo marker "memo" or "MEMO" appears in the COMMENTS field on the Edit or Browse screen. To see the contents of a Memo field, you must move to that field and activate the word-wrap editor.

Press **Ctrl-Home**

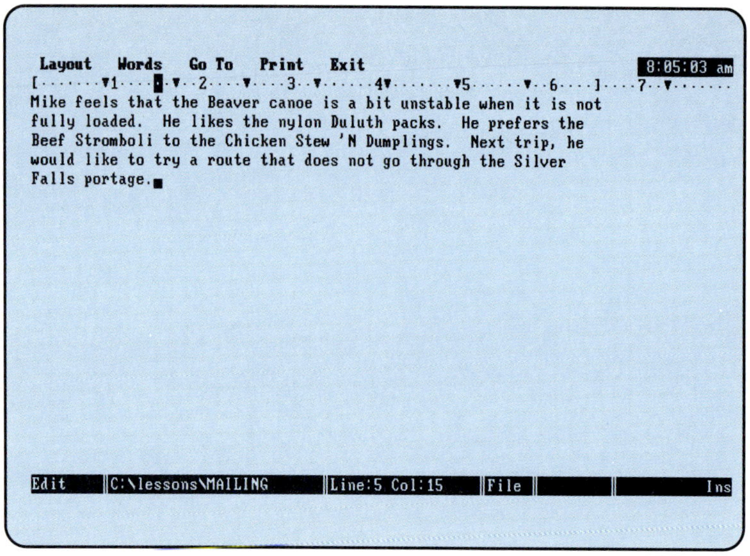

Figure 4 The Completed COMMENTS Field Contents

Your screen should look like Figure 4 again. Now you can read or change the contents of the current record's COMMENTS field. Return to the Browse screen:

Press **Alt-E**
Type **a**

Practice

1. Switch to the Edit screen. Advance to Oscar Griffith's record and enter the following text in the COMMENTS field.

   Oscar loves the Beaver canoe. He prefers the canvas Duluth packs, despite their additional weight. He likes all of the Trail Food.

   Save the text and return to the Edit screen.
2. Activate the word-wrap editor again and change "loves" to "hates." Save your work and return to the Edit screen.

Lesson 2: Creating a Simple View Query

In dBASE IV, a **query** is a set of instructions that lets you retrieve, display, organize, or edit data. Two types of queries can be created: view queries and update queries. A **view query** is used to display selected data on the screen. An **update query** is used to add, modify, or delete data in a data base file. Both view queries and update queries can be saved for future use. They are powerful tools for organizing and managing data. In this lesson, you will create and use a simple view query. You will learn to use update queries in a later lesson.

Step 1: Execute <create> in the Queries Panel

A view query accepts one or more data base files as input and creates a view as output. In this context, a **view** is an arrangement of data on the screen. Let's create a simple view query that will display the records of all the customers who

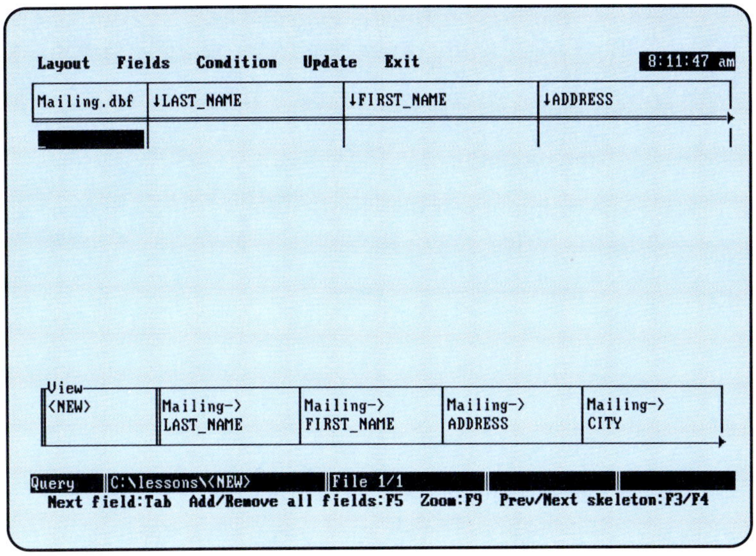

Figure 5 The Query Design Screen

live in Wisconsin. MAILING should be your current data base file. Return to the Control Center, move into the Queries panel, and select the <create> option.

Press **Escape**
Press **Right Arrow**
Press **Enter**

Step 2: Examine the Query Design Screen

The program will present the Query Design screen, shown in Figure 5. Query-by-Example, or QBE, is the approach used by dBASE IV on this screen. QBE is an interactive query language designed to make it easy to tell the data base manager how to retrieve data. The menu bar across the top of the screen contains five titles: Layout, Fields, Condition, Update, and Exit. Just below the menu bar is a **file skeleton,** which is a graphic representation of a data base file. The file skeleton shows the name of the current data base file and the names of all of its fields. You can enter instructions for dBASE IV in the spaces below the names in the file skeleton. Another skeleton is shown near the bottom of the screen above the status bar. This is the **view skeleton,** a graphic representation of the fields that will be presented in the view created by the view query.

Step 3: Move to the STATE Field

Our simple view will present the records of all the customers who live in Wisconsin. Move the highlight bar and cursor to the STATE field:

Press **Tab** (5 times)

The file skeleton will scroll as necessary to reveal the fields to the right.

Step 4: Enter the Filter Condition

A **filter condition** is an expression that determines which records are selected for the view. The simplest type of filter condition is an expression that specifies the characters, numbers, or other values to be matched. For example, to select the records of customers who live in Wisconsin, enter "WI" in the space beneath the STATE field name. Note that specific text must be enclosed in quotation marks.

Type **"WI"**
Press **Enter**

The program will search MAILING.DBF for the records that contain "WI" in the STATE field.

Step 5: Display the View on the Browse Screen

You can see the view you have created by displaying the Edit or Browse screen. Execute the Data command to display the Browse screen:

Press **F2** (2 times)

If the Edit screen appears, execute the Data command again. The Browse screen will present only the records of customers from Wisconsin (see Figure 6).

Step 6: Save the View Query

Suppose you want to be able to use the view query you have created again later. You can save it on your disk and use it at any time without having to redefine it. Return to the Query Design Screen, save the changes, enter a name for the query file, and exit back to the Control Center.

Press **Alt-E**
Type **t**
Press **Alt-E**
Type **s**
Type **wi**
Press **Enter**

The dBASE IV program will return to the Control Center. Note that the file named WI.QBE, which contains the view query you just created, appears in the Queries panel (see Figure 7).

Figure 6 The Browse Screen Displayed by the View Query

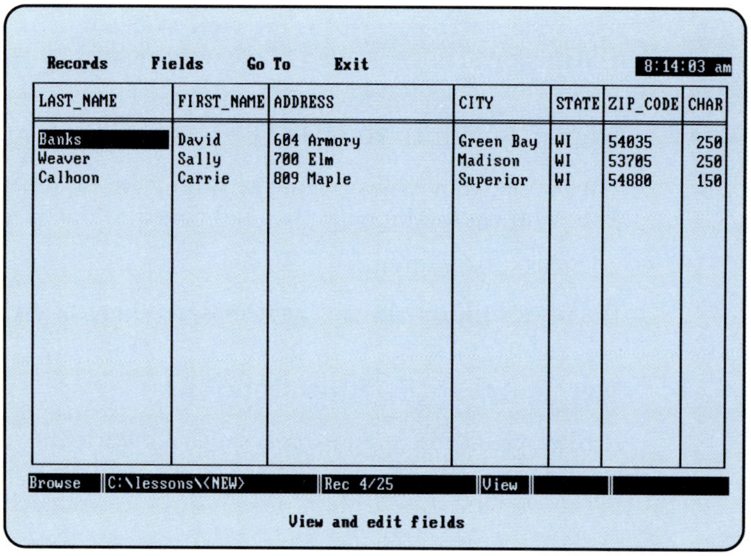

Figure 7 WI.QBE Added to the Queries Panel

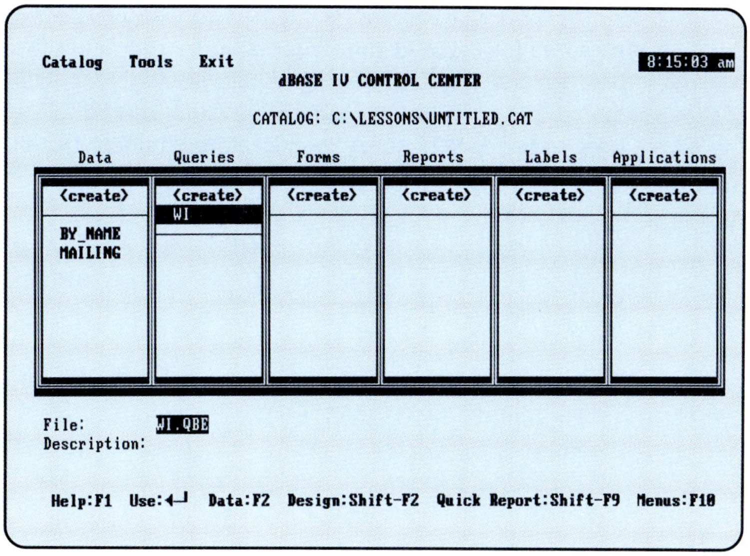

Step 7: Use an Existing View Query

It is easy to use an existing view query file. Move into the Queries panel and highlight the view query file you want. Since WI.QBE is the last file you used, you don't have to go through these steps now. Simply execute the Data command to display the Edit or Browse screen:

Press **F2**

The program will use the view query instructions you have saved to present only the records of customers from Wisconsin. When you are finished examining the screen, return to the Control Center:

Press **Escape**

Practice

Create a view query that presents the MAILING records of customers whose first names begin with the letter *J*. Move the cursor beneath the FIRST_NAME field in the Query Design screen and do this:

Type **like "J*"**
Press **Enter**

The word "like" is a filter condition operator that specifies a pattern match instead of an exact match. Execute the Data command to display the Browse screen. When you are finished, return to the Control Center without saving the view query you have created.

Lesson 3: Creating a Relational Data Base

A **relational data base** is a data base that includes two or more files with at least one field in common. For example, Paddle and Portage Canoe Outfitters might want to keep its mailing list information separate from its accounting information. Right now, the MAILING data base file contains the CHARGES field. A better arrangement would be to put the CHARGES data in a separate data base file along with the customers' names and other accounting information. The two separate files would then be related by the fields they have in common: LAST_NAME and FIRST_NAME. In this lesson, you will learn how to use a view query to derive one data base file from another. The next lesson will teach you how to use a view query to extract information from two separate data base files that are related by at least one common field.

Step 1: Select MAILING.DBF

Move back into the Data panel of the Control Center and select the MAILING data base file:

Press	**Left Arrow**
Highlight	**MAILING**
Press	**Enter**
Press	**Enter**

Step 2: Create a New View Query

Move into the Queries panel and select the <create> option:

Press	**Right Arrow**
Press	**Enter**

The program will present a new Query Design screen containing MAILING.DBF in the file skeleton and all of the MAILING fields in the view skeleton.

Step 3: Remove the Unwanted Fields from the View

By default, all the fields from MAILING are included in your view. But you want to create a new data base file named ACCOUNT.DBF that will contain only three fields from the MAILING data base file: LAST_NAME, FIRST_NAME, and CHARGES. Later you will remove the CHARGES field from the MAILING data base file and add a new field named BALANCE to the ACCOUNT data base file.

In this step, you will tell dBASE IV which MAILING fields you want to remove from your view. This can be done by moving the highlight bar into each field, then selecting the Remove Field From View option of the Fields menu. Follow these directions to remove the ADDRESS, CITY, STATE, ZIP_CODE, and COMMENTS fields from the view:

Press	**Tab** (3 times)
Press	**Alt-F**
Type	**r**
Press	**Tab**
Press	**Alt-F**
Type	**r**
Press	**Tab**
Press	**Alt-F**
Type	**r**
Press	**Tab**
Press	**Alt-F**
Type	**r**
Press	**Tab** (2 times)
Press	**Alt-F**
Type	**r**

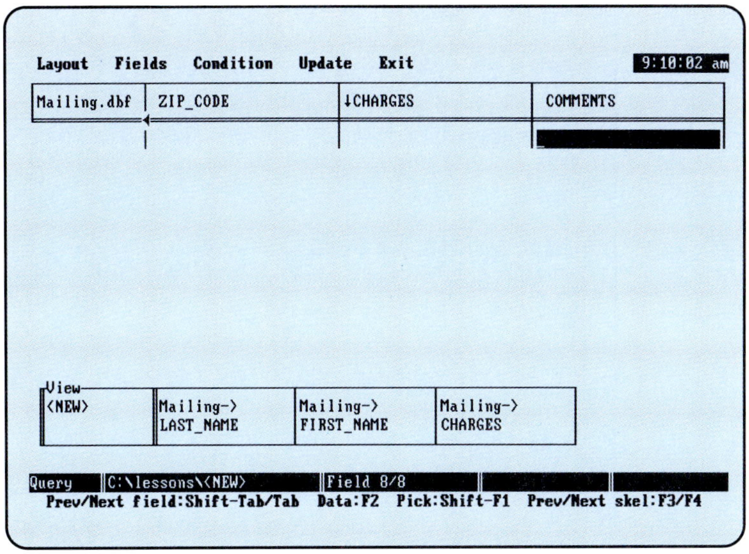

Figure 8 The View Skeleton Containing Only Three Fields

Your screen should look like Figure 8. Examine the view skeleton near the bottom of the screen. It contains only three fields from the MAILING data base file: LAST_NAME, FIRST_NAME, and CHARGES.

Step 4: Sort the Records in the View

Although this step is not absolutely necessary, it will arrange the records in the view in a predictable order. Since you are going to create a new data base file for the records anyway, sorting them in the view will not take up any more disk space. Move the highlight bar back to the LAST_NAME field, select the Sort On This Field option from the Fields menu, and select the Ascending ASCII sort order:

Press **Home**
Press **Tab**
Press **Alt-F**
Type **s**
Press **Enter**

The program will enter the sorting operator Asc1 in the space below the LAST_NAME field in the file skeleton. This operator tells dBASE IV to sort the records in ascending ASCII order when it creates the view.

Step 5: Examine the View

Now you can execute the Data command to display the Browse screen and see the view you have created.

Press **F2**

Figure 9 shows the result. The records are sorted by LAST_NAME. Each record contains three fields: LAST_NAME, FIRST_NAME, and CHARGES.

Figure 9 The View with Records Sorted by LAST_NAME

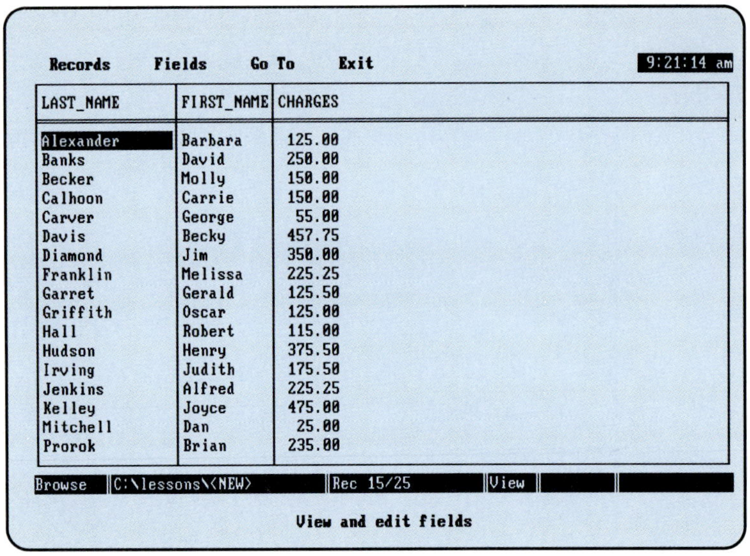

LAST_NAME	FIRST_NAME	CHARGES
Alexander	Barbara	125.00
Banks	David	250.00
Becker	Molly	150.00
Calhoon	Carrie	150.00
Carver	George	55.00
Davis	Becky	457.75
Diamond	Jim	350.00
Franklin	Melissa	225.25
Garret	Gerald	125.50
Griffith	Oscar	125.00
Hall	Robert	115.00
Hudson	Henry	375.50
Irving	Judith	175.50
Jenkins	Alfred	225.25
Kelley	Joyce	475.00
Mitchell	Dan	25.00
Prorok	Brian	235.00

Step 6: Create a Data Base File from the View

A view is just an arrangement of data on the screen. You must tell dBASE IV to create a new data base file named ACCOUNT.DBF from the view you have created. Return to the Query Design screen, select the Write View As Database File option from the Layout menu, and enter the name of the new data base file:

Press **Alt-E**
Type **t**
Press **Alt-L**
Type **w**
Type **account**
Press **Enter**

The program will create a new data base file named ACCOUNT.DBF that has the same design and contents as the view. You do not need to save the view query, so abandon the changes and exit to the Control Center:

Press **Alt-E**
Type **a**
Type **y**

Step 7: Remove CHARGES From MAILING.DBF

From now on, the ACCOUNT data base file will contain accounting information for Paddle and Portage Canoe Outfitters, so you can remove the CHARGES field from the MAILING data base file. Move back into the Data panel, highlight MAILING, and execute the Design command to display the Data Base Design screen:

Press **Left Arrow**
Press **Shift-F2**
Press **Escape**

Now, highlight the CHARGES field and remove it from the record structure:

Press **Down Arrow** (6 times)
Press **Ctrl-U**

Tell dBASE IV to save the change you have made and return to the Control Center:

Press **Alt-E**
Type **s**
Type **y**

Step 8: Add a New Field to ACCOUNT.DBF

Let's make your relational data base more interesting by adding another field to the ACCOUNT file. This new field, named BALANCE, will hold the amount still owed by the customer. The existing field, CHARGES, holds the total charges, paid or unpaid.

Highlight the ACCOUNT file in the Data panel of the Control Center and execute the Design command to display the Data Base Design screen:

Highlight **ACCOUNT**
Press **Shift-F2**
Press **Escape**

Move past the last field in the record structure and specify the new field:

Press **Down Arrow** (3 times)
Type **balance**
Press **Enter**
Type **n**
Type **7**
Press **Enter**
Type **2**
Press **Home**

Your screen should look like Figure 10. Save the modified data base design and return to the Control Center:

Press **Alt-E**
Type **s**
Type **y**

Step 9: Add Data for the BALANCE Field

Now that you have created a new field named BALANCE in the ACCOUNT data base file, you can add the data for each customer. Execute the Data command twice to display the Edit screen and move to the first record in the file:

Press **F2** (2 times)
Press **Ctrl-PgUp**

Move the cursor to the BALANCE field and enter Barbara Alexander's data:

Press **Down Arrow** (3 times)
Type **55**
Press **Enter**

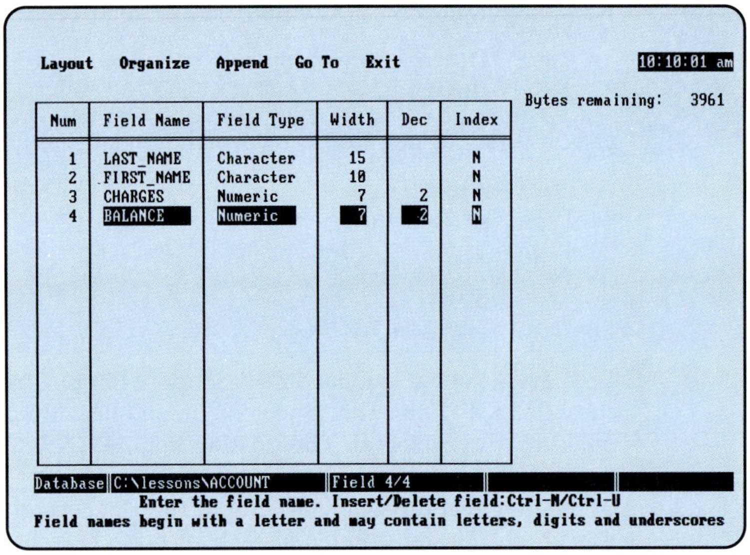

Figure 10 The BALANCE Field Added to ACCOUNT.DBF

The program will advance to the next record. Use the following table to enter the BALANCE figures for the remaining records:

Last Name	Balance	Last Name	Balance
Banks	0.00	Jenkins	0.00
Becker	50.00	Kelley	175.00
Calhoon	25.00	Mitchell	0.00
Carver	0.00	Prorok	0.00
Davis	200.00	Quinlan	50.00
Diamond	0.00	Savage	25.00
Franklin	100.00	Skubic	0.00
Garret	0.00	Tudor	0.00
Griffith	0.00	Underwood	0.00
Hall	0.00	Walden	0.00
Hudson	75.50	Weaver	0.00
Irving	100.00	Young	50.00

Return to the Control Center when you are finished.

Practice

1. Display the Browse screen and check your data entries against the previous table. Correct any errors you made. Return to the Control Center.
2. Create a view that displays only the records of customers who have not paid all of their charges. Move into the Queries panel and select the <create> option to display the Query Design screen. Move the highlight bar to the BALANCE field. Tell dBASE IV that you want to see the records of customers whose BALANCE figures are greater than zero:

   Type **0**
   Press **Enter**

   Display the Browse screen to see the view you have created. When you are finished, exit the Query Design screen without saving the view query and return to the Control Center.

Lesson 4: Linking Files

If two or more files have at least one field in common, you can create a view that links the files and displays data from any of them. Suppose you want to see the last names, addresses, ZIP codes, and balances of customers who have not yet paid all of their charges. You can easily retrieve this information from MAILING.DBF and ACCOUNT.DBF with a view query.

Step 1: Create a New View Query

At this point, ACCOUNT.DBF should be your current data base file. From the Control Center, move the highlight bar to the <create> option in the Queries panel, then display the Query Design screen:

Press **Enter**

Step 2: Add MAILING.DBF to the Query

The file skeleton for ACCOUNT.DBF is near the top of the screen. In order to retrieve data from MAILING.DBF as well, you must display its file skeleton on the screen. Activate the Layout menu and select the Add File to Query option:

Press **Alt-L**
Type **a**

A menu box will appear containing the names of the available data base files.

Highlight **MAILING.DBF**
Press **Enter**

The file skeleton for MAILING.DBF will appear on the screen below the file skeleton for ACCOUNT.DBF (see Figure 11).

Figure 11 Two File Skeletons on the Query Design Screen

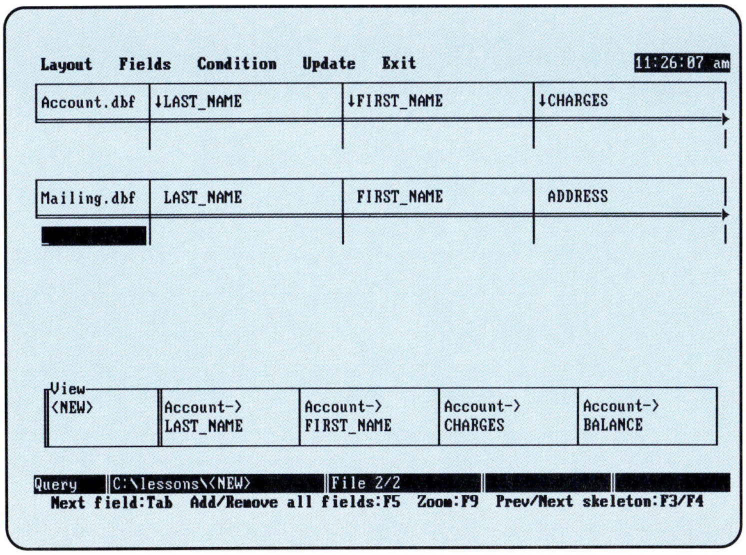

Step 3: Remove All Fields from the View Skeleton

You want only the LAST_NAME, ADDRESS, ZIP_CODE, and BALANCE fields included in the view. The easiest method in this case is to remove all of the fields from the view skeleton and then selectively add the fields you want. Right now, the highlight bar is in the MAILING.DBF file skeleton. You can move to the previous file skeleton by pressing F3 to execute the Prev command, or move to the next file skeleton by pressing F4 to execute the Next command. Move to the ACCOUNT.DBF file skeleton:

Press **F3**

All the fields from ACCOUNT.DBF are currently included in the view skeleton near the bottom of the screen. With the highlight bar beneath the file name, execute the Field command to remove all of the ACCOUNT.DBF fields from the view skeleton:

Press **F5**

The view skeleton will disappear.

Step 4: Add the Desired Fields to the View Skeleton

Now you can add just the fields you want, in the order you want, to the view skeleton. Move the highlight bar beneath the LAST_NAME field in the ACCOUNT.DBF file skeleton and select the Add Field to View option from the Fields menu:

Press **Tab**
Press **Alt-F**
Type **a**

A view skeleton will appear with LAST_NAME from ACCOUNT.DBF as the first field. Follow these directions to add the ADDRESS, ZIP_CODE, and BALANCE fields:

Press **F4**
Press **Tab** (3 times)
Press **Alt-F**
Type **a**
Press **Tab** (3 times)
Press **Alt-F**
Type **a**
Press **F3**
Press **Tab** (3 times)
Press **Alt-F**
Type **a**

The view skeleton now contains LAST_NAME from ACCOUNT.DBF, ADDRESS and ZIP_CODE from MAILING.DBF, and BALANCE from ACCOUNT.DBF (see Figure 12).

Step 5: Enter the Filter Condition

You want to see only those records of customers who have a balance greater than zero. This filter condition can be specified with an expression that contains a **relational operator,** a symbol or word that specifies how items are to be compared. The highlight bar should be beneath the BALANCE field.

Type >**0**
Press **Enter**

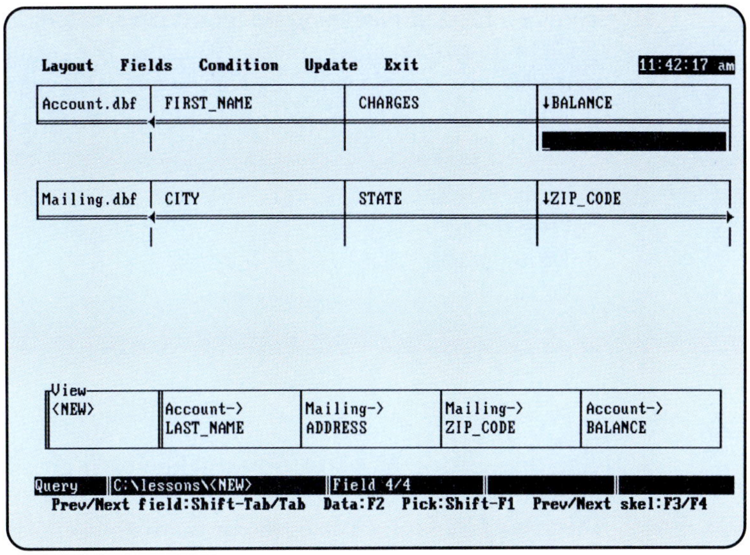

Figure 12 Fields from Different Files in the View Skeleton

The expression *>0* tells dBASE to retrieve only those records with a value greater than zero in the BALANCE field.

Several relational operators are available in addition to > (greater than). The following table lists dBASE IV relational operators.

Operator	Description
>	greater than
<	less than
=	equal
<> or #	not equal
>=	greater than or equal
<=	less than or equal
$	contains
Like	pattern search
Sounds Like	Soundex search

The $ operator is used to retrieve records that contain a specified substring. For example, suppose you want to retrieve all records that contain "New" as part of the contents of the CITY field. You can use the expression *$"New"* as the filter condition.

The Like operator is used to specify search strings that contain wildcard characters (* and ?). For example, the expression *Like "A*"* will find any word or phrase beginning with an uppercase A.

The Sounds Like operator performs Soundex searches. A **Soundex search** finds words that sound like the word you specify. For example, the expression *Sounds Like "jerry"* will find the names Jeri, Jerri, Gerry, and Geri, as well as Jerry.

Step 6: Link the Files

Before you can examine the view, you must link the two data base files by the field they share. This is done by placing the same example variable in the common field, known as the **link field.** An **example variable** is a place holder for the value of a field. It may be up to ten characters long, but must begin with a letter and cannot contain any embedded blanks. For example, you could use the word "name" as an example variable. Follow these directions to enter the same example variable in the LAST_NAME fields and link the ACCOUNT.DBF and MAILING.DBF files:

Press **Home**
Press **Tab**
Type **name**
Press **F4**
Press **Home**
Press **Tab**
Type **name**
Press **Enter**

Note that linking files works best when each possible value in the link field is unique. In our simple example, no two last names are the same, so we can use LAST_NAME as the link field. In the real world, however, a large mailing list data base would probably contain records of several people with common last names, such as Jones or Smith. Such data bases are usually designed with a field for a unique identification number, such as a customer number or Social Security number. This unique field would be included in every related data base file and used as the link field.

Step 7: Examine the View

Execute the Data command to display the Browse screen and examine the view you have created:

Press **F2**

Figure 13 shows the result. The records are sorted by LAST_NAME because the records in ACCOUNT.DBF are sorted by LAST_NAME. The data in the LAST_NAME and BALANCE fields are from ACCOUNT.DBF; the data in the ADDRESS and ZIP_CODE fields are from MAILING.DBF.

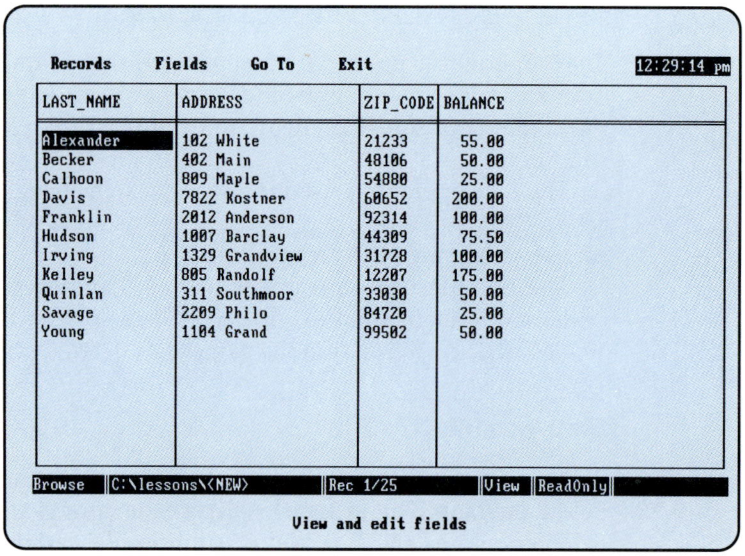

Figure 13 The View Linking MAILING.DBF and ACCOUNT.DBF

Step 8: Save the View Query

You may want to use the view query you have created again. Return to the Query Design screen and save the query in a file named WHO_OWES.QBE:

Press	**Alt-E**
Type	**t**
Press	**Alt-E**
Type	**s**
Type	**who_owes**
Press	**Enter**

The program will return to the Control Center.

Practice Create a view query that links MAILING.DBF and ACCOUNT.DBF and displays the LAST_NAME, CITY, and CHARGES fields. Examine the view you have created. Return to the Control Center without saving the query to disk.

Lesson 5: Creating an Update Query

An update query allows you to make changes to selected records throughout an entire data base file. You can also use an update query to mark certain records for deletion.

Update queries are often used to make corrections to selected records. For example, suppose you consistently entered an incorrect abbreviation in the STATE field for a particular state. You could correct all the mistakes at once with an update query.

Selected records throughout an entire data base also can be marked for deletion with an update query. You could, for instance, mark all records with "WI" in the STATE field for deletion.

An update query is frequently used to make a consistent change to selected fields throughout a data base. Suppose Paddle and Portage Canoe Outfitters charged a five percent late-payment fee to customers who had not paid all of their charges after a certain period of time. Let's create an update query to increase the value in the BALANCE field by five percent for all customers with a balance greater than zero.

Step 1: Select the Data Base File

The data you want to change is in the ACCOUNT data base file. The Control Center should be on your screen. Tell dBASE IV that you want to use the ACCOUNT data base:

Move	to the Data panel
Highlight	**ACCOUNT**
Press	**Enter** (2 times)

Step 2: Create a New Update Query

Move into the Queries panel and select the <create> option:

Press	**Right Arrow**
Highlight	**<create>**
Press	**Enter**

The program will present a new Query Design screen, with ACCOUNT.DBF in the file skeleton and all of the ACCOUNT fields in the view skeleton.

Step 3: Move to the Field to be Changed

BALANCE is the field to be changed. Move the highlight bar beneath BALANCE in the file skeleton:

Press **Tab** (4 times)

Step 4: Specify the Update Operation

Now you can tell dBASE IV which update operation you want to perform. Activate the Update menu and select the Specify Update Operation option:

Press **Alt-U**
Type **s**

Figure 14 shows the menu that appears on the screen. Four update operations are available: Replace, Append, Mark, and Unmark. The Replace operation substitutes values in a field for all or selected records. The Append operation adds selected records to the current data base file. The Mark operation marks records for deletion based on a condition. The Unmark operation is the opposite of the Mark operation. To increase all of the values in the BALANCE field by five percent, you would use a Replace operation:

Type **r**

The program will display a box saying that changing the view query to an update query will delete the view skeleton. In other words, the view skeleton is not needed for an update query, because an update query does not produce a view. An update query changes the records in the original data base file stored on the disk. Tell dBASE IV that you want to proceed with creating an update query:

Type **p**

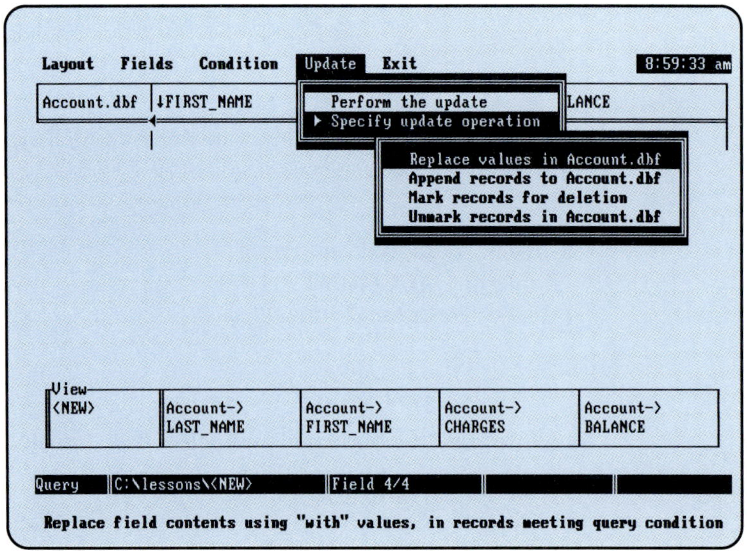

Figure 14 The Specify Update Operation Menu

The view skeleton will disappear. Now you can enter a replacement instruction in the BALANCE field of the file skeleton that will increase each nonzero value by five percent. This instruction must begin with the word "with" followed by an expression. Other conditions may then follow to select the records to be updated. Follow these directions:

Type **`with balance * 1.05`**
Press **Down Arrow**
Type **> 0**
Press **Enter**

Your screen should look like Figure 15.

Step 5: Perform the Update

So far, you have just specified the update operation. Now tell dBASE IV to actually perform the update operation. Activate the Update menu and select Perform the Update:

Press **Alt-U**
Type **p**

When dBASE IV is finished updating the file, it will prompt you to press any key to continue.

Press **Enter**

Step 6: Examine the Data Base File

To see the changes you have made, execute the Data command to display the Browse screen and move to the beginning of the file:

Press **F2**
Press **Ctrl-PgUp**

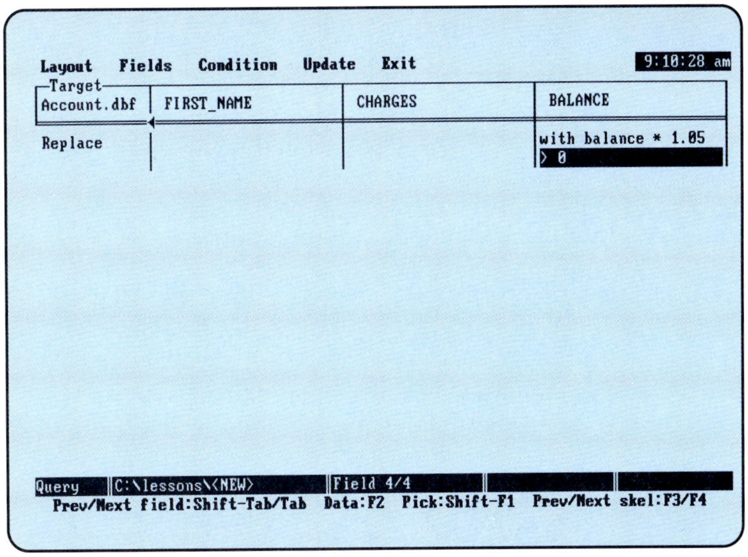

Figure 15 The Update Operation Specified

Figure 16 After Performing the Update Query

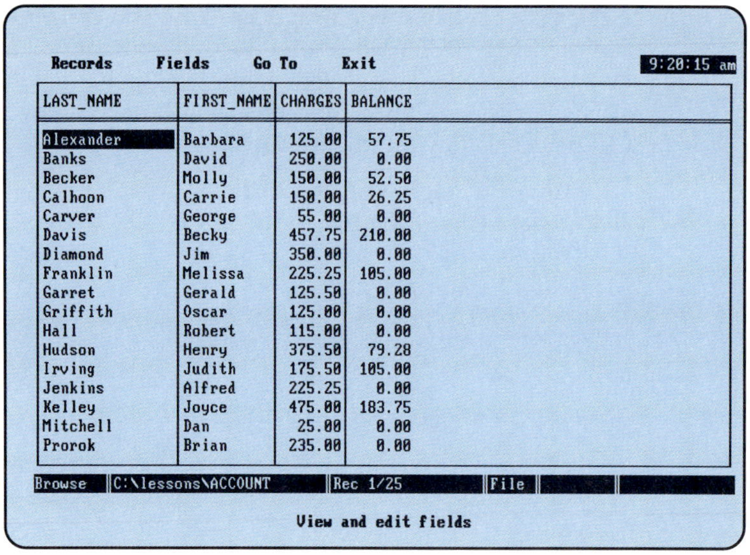

LAST_NAME	FIRST_NAME	CHARGES	BALANCE
Alexander	Barbara	125.00	57.75
Banks	David	250.00	0.00
Becker	Molly	150.00	52.50
Calhoon	Carrie	150.00	26.25
Carver	George	55.00	0.00
Davis	Becky	457.75	210.00
Diamond	Jim	350.00	0.00
Franklin	Melissa	225.25	105.00
Garret	Gerald	125.50	0.00
Griffith	Oscar	125.00	0.00
Hall	Robert	115.00	0.00
Hudson	Henry	375.50	79.28
Irving	Judith	175.50	105.00
Jenkins	Alfred	225.25	0.00
Kelley	Joyce	475.00	183.75
Mitchell	Dan	25.00	0.00
Prorok	Brian	235.00	0.00

Your screen should look like Figure 16. All of the nonzero BALANCE values have been increased by five percent. For example, Barbara Alexander's balance was $55.00. Now it is $57.75, $2.75 more (five percent of $55.00).

Step 7: Save the Update Query

The update query you have created is one that Paddle and Portage will want to use again. Return to the Query Design screen, save the update query in a file named LATE, and then exit to the Control Center:

Press **Alt-E**
Type **t**
Press **Alt-E**
Type **s**
Type **late**
Press **Enter**

The program will create a file named LATE.UPD on the disk and return to the Control Center (see Figure 17). Note that the names of update query files are preceded by an asterisk (*) in the Queries panel.

Practice

Run the LATE update query again:

Highlight **LATE** (in the Queries panel)
Press **Enter** (2 times)
Type **y**

Examine the ACCOUNT file on the Browse screen. The nonzero balances have been increased by five percent again. Return to the Control Center.

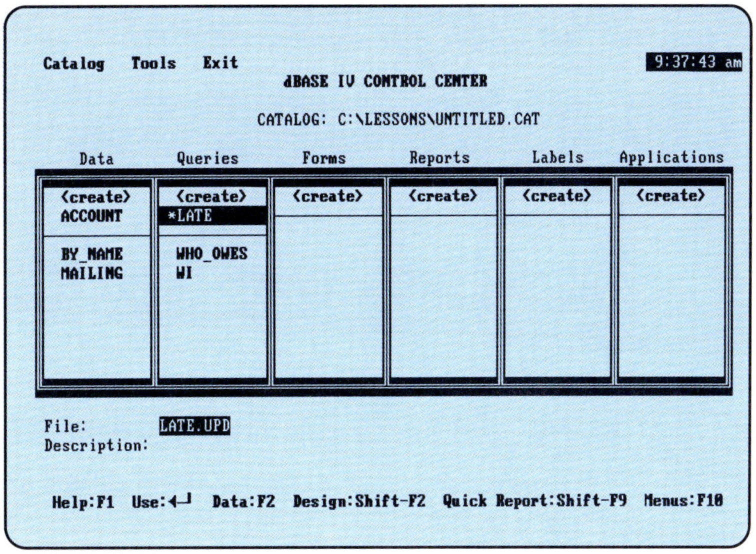

Figure 17 LATE.UPD Saved in the Queries Panel

Lesson 6: Using Calculated Fields

A **calculated field** contains the result of an expression instead of a value entered directly in a data base file. Calculated fields are not stored in data base files, but they can be created in views, forms, and reports. For example, suppose you want to see how much each Paddle and Portage customer has paid toward his or her balance so far. This exact information is not stored, but it can be calculated from the CHARGES and BALANCE fields in ACCOUNT.DBF. Let's create a view query that includes a calculated field named PAID, which shows how much each customer has paid so far.

Step 1: Select the Data Base File

The data you want to manipulate is in the ACCOUNT data base file. The Control Center should be on your screen. Tell dBASE IV that you want to use ACCOUNT.DBF:

Move	to the Data panel
Highlight	**ACCOUNT**
Press	**Enter** (2 times)

Step 2: Create a New View Query

Move into the Queries panel and select the <create> option:

Press	**Right Arrow**
Highlight	**<create>**
Press	**Enter**

The program will present a new Query Design screen with ACCOUNT.DBF in the file skeleton and all of the ACCOUNT fields in the view skeleton.

Step 3: Create the Calculated Field

Activate the Fields menu and select Create Calculated Field:

Press **Alt-F**
Type **c**

The program will display the calculated field skeleton between the file skeleton and the view skeleton. Enter the expression to perform the calculation:

Type **charges - balance**
Press **Enter**

Your screen should look like Figure 18.

Step 4: Add the Calculated Field to the View

You must tell dBASE IV to include the calculated field you have just created in the view. Activate the Fields menu and select Add Field to View:

Press **Alt-F**
Type **a**

The program will prompt you to enter a name for the calculated field.

Type **paid**
Press **Enter**

The calculated field, now named PAID, will be added to the right end of the view skeleton.

Step 5: Examine the View

Execute the Data command to display the Browse screen and examine the view you have created:

Press **F2**

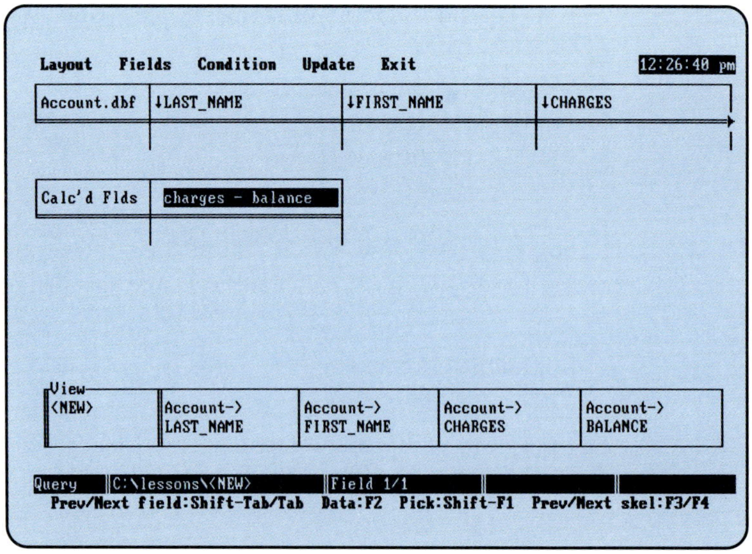

Figure 18 A Calculated Field

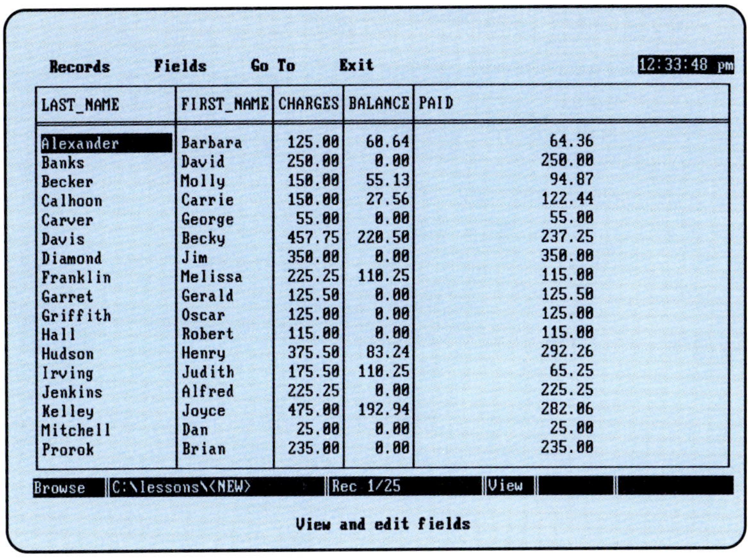
Records Fields Go To Exit 12:33:48 pm

LAST_NAME	FIRST_NAME	CHARGES	BALANCE	PAID
Alexander	Barbara	125.00	60.64	64.36
Banks	David	250.00	0.00	250.00
Becker	Molly	150.00	55.13	94.87
Calhoon	Carrie	150.00	27.56	122.44
Carver	George	55.00	0.00	55.00
Davis	Becky	457.75	220.50	237.25
Diamond	Jim	350.00	0.00	350.00
Franklin	Melissa	225.25	110.25	115.00
Garret	Gerald	125.50	0.00	125.50
Griffith	Oscar	125.00	0.00	125.00
Hall	Robert	115.00	0.00	115.00
Hudson	Henry	375.50	83.24	292.26
Irving	Judith	175.50	110.25	65.25
Jenkins	Alfred	225.25	0.00	225.25
Kelley	Joyce	475.00	192.94	282.06
Mitchell	Dan	25.00	0.00	25.00
Prorok	Brian	235.00	0.00	235.00

Browse C:\lessons\<NEW> Rec 1/25 View

View and edit fields

***Figure 19** The View Showing the Calculated Field*

Figure 19 shows the result. For each record, the contents of the PAID field is calculated by subtracting the value in the BALANCE field from the value in the CHARGES field.

Step 6: Return to the Control Center

You do not need to save this view query, so exit the Browse screen and return to the Control Center:

Press **Alt-E**
Type **e**
Type **n**

Practice Create a view of ACCOUNT.DBF that includes a calculated field named LATE_FEE. Calculate the contents of LATE_FEE by multiplying the contents of BALANCE by 0.05. Display the Browse screen to examine your work. When you are finished, return to the Control Center without saving the view query.

Lesson 7: Summarizing Data

Suppose you want to add up all of the charges and all of the balances in the ACCOUNT data base file. The dBASE IV program provides several **summary operators,** also called **aggregate operators,** for performing such tasks in view queries. Five summary operators are available: SUM, AVG (or AVERAGE), MIN, MAX, and CNT (or COUNT). SUM adds up the values in a column of fields. AVG computes the arithmetic mean of a column of fields. MAX presents the maximum value and MIN presents the minimum value. CNT computes the number of values in a column of fields. Let's use the SUM operator in a view query to add up the values in the CHARGES and BALANCE fields in ACCOUNT.DBF.

Step 1: Select the Data Base File

The data you want to sum is in the ACCOUNT data base file. The Control Center should be on your screen and ACCOUNT should already be the current file. If it is not, you would tell dBASE IV that you want to use ACCOUNT.

Step 2: Create a New View Query

Move into the Queries panel and select the <create> option:

Press	**Right Arrow**
Highlight	**<create>**
Press	**Enter**

The program will present a new Query Design screen with ACCOUNT.DBF in the file skeleton and all of the ACCOUNT fields in the view skeleton.

Step 3: Enter the Summary Operators

You must place the summary operator you want to use in the column of the appropriate field. Move to the CHARGES field and enter the SUM operator:

Press	**Tab** (3 times)
Type	**sum**
Press	**Enter**

Now enter the summary operator in the BALANCE column as well:

Press	**Tab**
Type	**sum**
Press	**Enter**

Your screen should look like Figure 20.

Figure 20 A Summary Operator

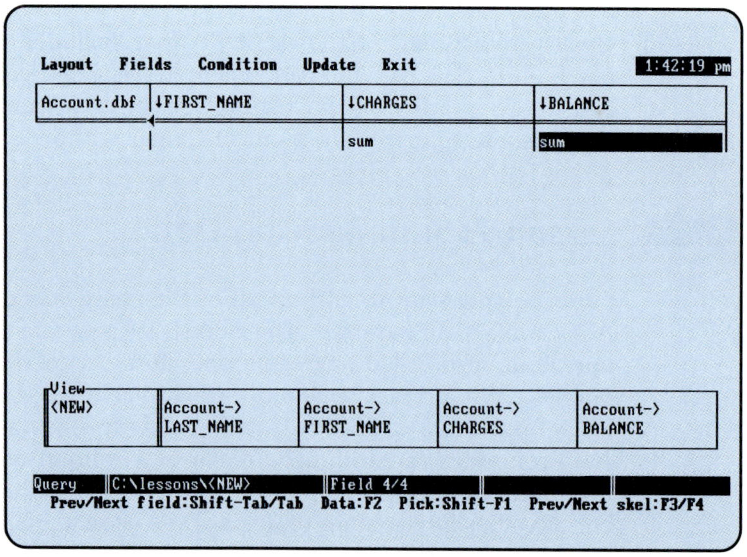

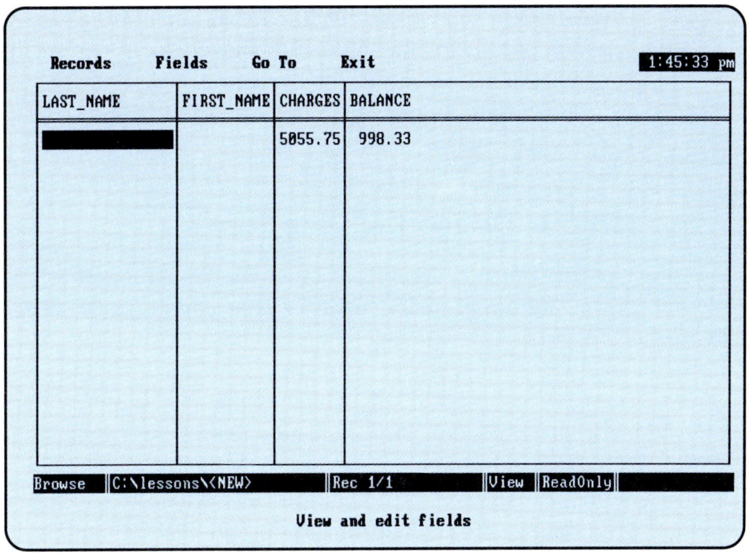

Figure 21 The Summary Values

Step 4: Examine the View

Execute the Data command to display the Browse screen to see the view you have created:

Press **F2**

Figure 21 shows the result. The program shows only the summary values in the appropriate columns. No records are displayed, and all the other fields are blank.

Step 5: Return to the Control Center

You do not need to save this view query, so exit the Browse screen and return to the Control Center:

Press **Alt-E**
Type **e**
Type **n**

Practice

Create a view of ACCOUNT.DBF that computes the average of the CHARGES field and presents the maximum outstanding balance. Display the Browse screen to examine your work. When you are finished, return to the Control Center without saving the view query.

Lesson 8: Designing Custom Forms

You have learned how to display the contents of a data base file or a view on either the Browse screen or the Edit screen. The Browse screen is convenient for looking at a group of records at once. Its format is always a table; each row represents a record, and each column represents a field. The Edit screen is convenient for entering or modifying one record at a time. Unlike the Browse screen table, however, the form on the Edit screen can be redesigned. You can arrange the fields in different positions, draw boxes and lines for emphasis, include explanatory text, omit certain fields for simplicity, and add calculated fields to create custom forms. A well-designed form can facilitate data entry and reduce errors. As an example, let's create a new data base file named CHECKING to maintain Paddle and Portage Canoe Outfitters' checking account.

Step 1: Design the Data Base

At this point, you should be at the Control Center. Move the highlight bar into the Data panel. Tell dBASE IV that you want to create a new data base file:

Highlight **<create>**
Press **Enter**

The program will present a new Data Base Design screen. The CHECKING data base file will have six fields: NUMBER, DATE, DESCRIP, PAYMENT, DEPOSIT, and CLEARED. The NUMBER field will hold the check number. DATE will record the date of the payment or deposit. DESCRIP will hold a description of the transaction. PAYMENT will hold the amount paid or DEPOSIT will hold the amount deposited. CLEARED is a Logical field that will indicate whether the check has cleared. Fill in the field names, types, and widths shown in Figure 22. Check your work and correct any errors you make. When your screen matches Figure 22, save the data base design:

Press **Alt-E**
Type **s**
Type **checking**
Press **Enter**

The program will return to the Control Center.

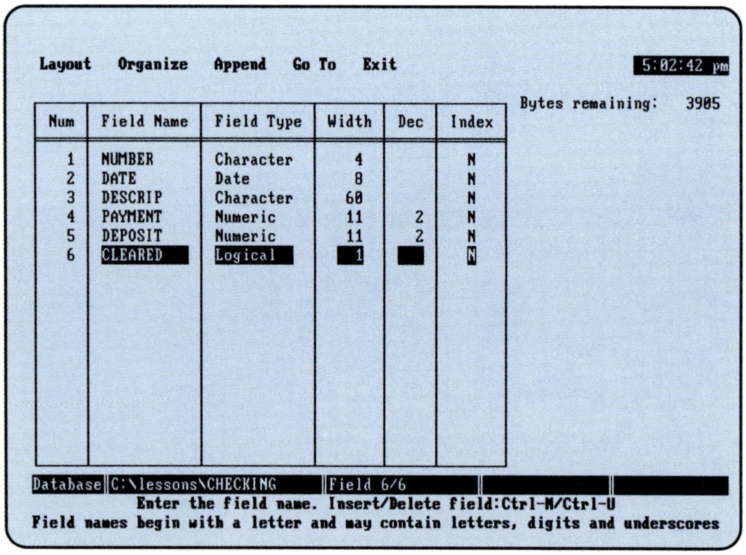

Figure 22 The Data Base Design for CHECKING.DBF

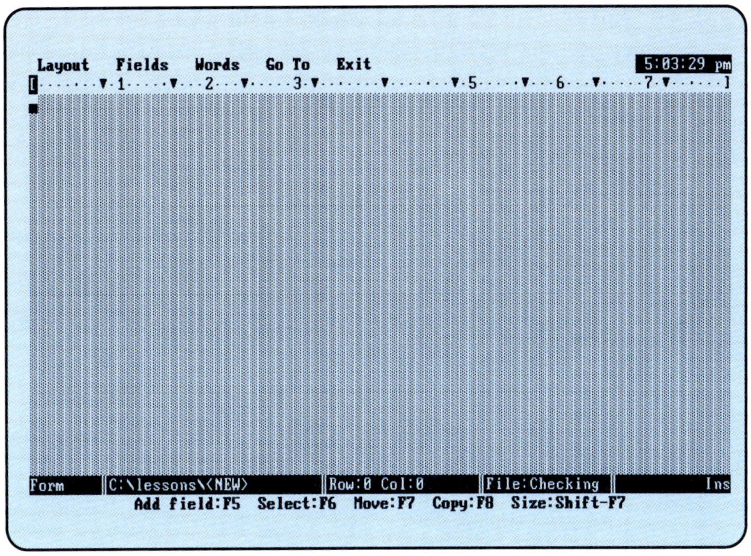

Figure 23 The Form Design Screen

Step 2: Display the Form Design Screen

Before you enter any data for this data base file, you are going to design a custom form. Move the highlight bar to the Forms panel and select the <create> option:

Press	**Right Arrow** (2 times)
Highlight	<**create**>
Press	**Enter**

The Layout menu will be activated automatically. You do not need it right now, so make it disappear:

Press **Escape**

Your screen will look like Figure 23. The Form Design screen has a menu bar, ruler line, shaded work surface, status bar, and message line. A blinking block cursor is in the upper left corner. Note that the status bar reports the current row and column of the cursor.

Step 3: Lay Out the Names and Fields

You can move the cursor to any position on the screen and type a descriptive name. Then you can activate the Fields menu, select the Add Field option, and select a field from the data base file. Follow these directions to lay out the name and field for NUMBER:

Move	the cursor to row 6, column 10
Type	**Number:**
Press	**Space Bar**
Press	**Alt-F**
Type	**a**
Type	**n**
Press	**Enter**
Press	**Ctrl-End**

The bright bar filled with Xs is the **field template.** It represents the width and contents of a data field to be displayed in the form. The Xs stand for characters; the number of Xs indicates the field width. Follow these directions to lay out the rest of the fields:

Move	the cursor to row 6, column 34
Type	**`Date:`**
Press	**Space Bar**
Press	**Alt-F**
Type	**a**
Type	**da**
Press	**Enter**
Press	**Ctrl-End**

Move	the cursor to row 6, column 60
Type	**`Cleared:`**
Press	**Space Bar**
Press	**Alt-F**
Type	**a**
Type	**c**
Press	**Enter**
Press	**Ctrl-End**

Move	the cursor to row 9, column 10
Type	**`Payment:`**
Press	**Space Bar**
Press	**Alt-F**
Type	**a**
Type	**p**
Press	**Enter**
Press	**Ctrl-End**

Move	the cursor to row 9, column 50
Type	**`Deposit:`**
Press	**Space Bar**
Press	**Alt-F**
Type	**a**
Type	**dep**
Press	**Enter**
Press	**Ctrl-End**

Move	the cursor to row 12, column 10
Type	**`Description of Transaction:`**

Move	the cursor to row 13, column 10
Press	**Alt-F**
Type	**a**
Type	**des**
Press	**Enter**
Press	**Ctrl-End**

At this point, your screen should look like Figure 24. In the field templates, 9s represent numeric data, "MM/DD/YY" stands for a date, and "L" refers to a Logical value (True or False).

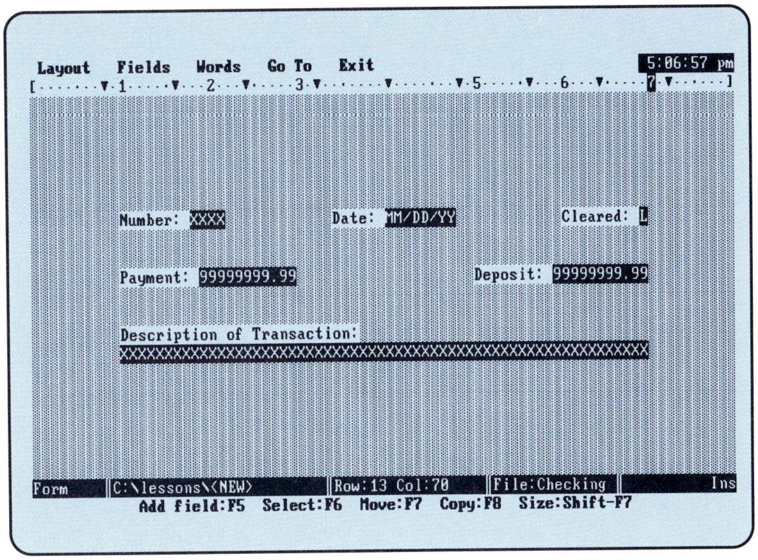

Figure 24 The Names and Fields Laid Out

Step 4: Draw a Box

The Box option of the Layout menu lets you draw a box on the form. Boxes are often used to visually group related information or just to make the form appear more attractive. Follow these directions to draw a double-line box around the fields in your form:

Move the cursor to row 4, column 8
Press **Alt-L**
Type **b**
Type **d**
Press **Enter**
Move the cursor to row 15, column 71
Press **Enter**
Press **Home**

Your screen should look like Figure 25.

Step 5: Enter a Title

How about a title for the form?

Move the cursor to row 4, column 14
Type **`Paddle and Portage Canoe Outfitters Checking Account`**

Step 6: Save the Form

You are now finished designing the form. Save it in a file named CHECKING and return to the Control Center:

Press **Alt-E**
Type **s**
Type **`checking`**
Press **Enter**

The program will generate the form and create a file named CHECKING.SCR in the Forms panel of the Control Center.

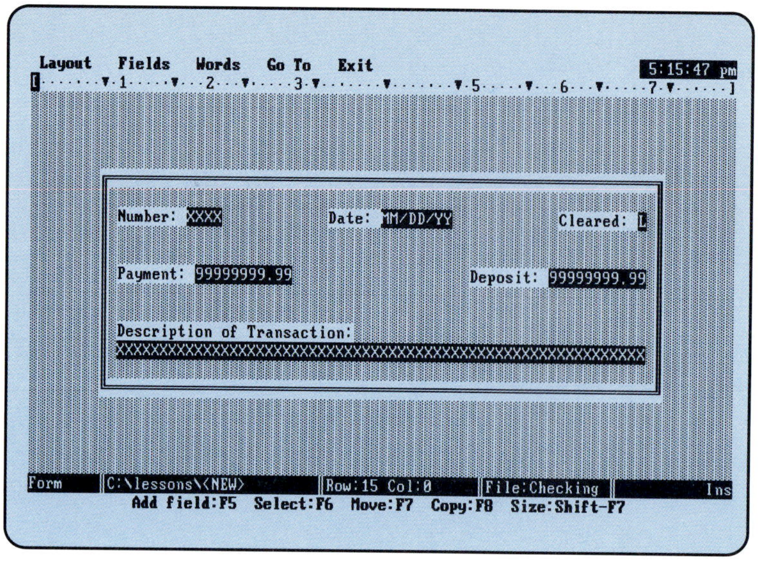

***Figure 25** A Box Around the Form*

Step 7: Use the Form

To use a form for data entry or modification, first highlight its name in the Forms panel. The CHECKING form should already be highlighted. Execute the Data command to display the Edit screen:

Press **F2**

The program will display a blank data entry form on the screen. Follow these directions to enter data into the form:

Type **001**
Press **Enter**
Type **010191**
Type **f**
Press **Enter**
Type **25000**
Press **Enter**
Type **Initial deposit to open account**

Your screen should look like Figure 26. Now return to the Control Center:

Press **Alt-E**
Type **e**

Practice

1. Display the Edit screen again and add a second record to the CHECKING data base file using the customized form. Make up the data for a payment record.
2. Execute the Design command to display the Form Design screen:

   Press **Shift-F2**

   Move the cursor to the PAYMENT field template. Activate the Fields menu, select Modify Field, and then select Template:

   Press **Alt-F**
   Type **m**
   Type **t**

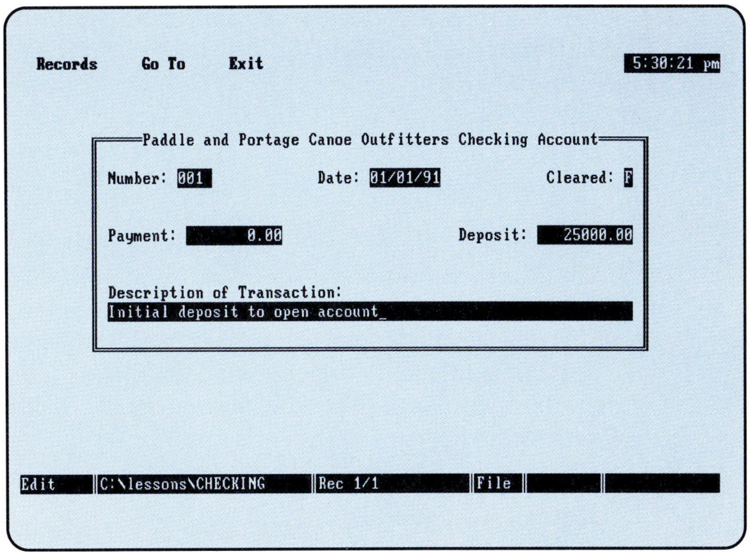

Figure 26 The Form on the Edit Screen

Tell dBASE IV to display the contents of the PAYMENT field as a currency value:

Press **Home**
Press **Ctrl-Y**
Type **$999,999.99**
Press **Enter**
Press **Ctrl-End**

Repeat the procedure for the DEPOSIT field. Then save the changes, return to the Control Center, execute the Data command to display the Edit screen, and see the result. When you are finished examining your work, return to the Control Center.

Lesson 9: Designing Custom Reports

You can use a report to print data you have stored with dBASE IV. In the previous chapter, you learned how to use the Quick Report command (Shift-F9) to print the contents of a data base file in a table format. Quick Report is easy to use, but it is not very flexible. It does not give you much control over the placement of fields on the page and does not let you add explanatory text. One way to select and arrange the fields in a report is to create a view query and then print a Quick Report from the view. But this still limits you to an inflexible, table-style report. The best way to produce customized output from your data base files is to design reports. If you design your own reports with dBASE IV, you can

- group related data together.
- print fields exactly where you want them.
- control pagination.
- perform calculations and summary statistics on data.
- insert custom headings and other text.
- insert data into text to create form letters.

As an example, let's create a custom report that prints output from both MAILING.DBF and ACCOUNT.DBF by using the WHO_OWES view query you created in Lesson 4.

Step 1: Select the View Query File

Custom reports are generated directly from a data base file or from a view query. If you want a report to present data from more than one file, you must create a view that links the files. In Lesson 4, you created the WHO_OWES view query, which displays the names, addresses, and balances of customers who still owe money to Paddle and Portage Canoe Outfitters. You will create a custom report from this view. First, select the view query file. Move the highlight bar into the Queries panel.

Highlight	**WHO_OWES**
Press	**Enter**
Type	**u**

The program will make WHO_OWES.QBE the current file.

Step 2: Display the Report Design Screen

Now move the highlight bar into the Reports panel.

Press	**Right Arrow** (2 times)
Highlight	**<create>**
Press	**Enter**

The program will present the Report Design screen and automatically activate the Layout menu (see Figure 27).

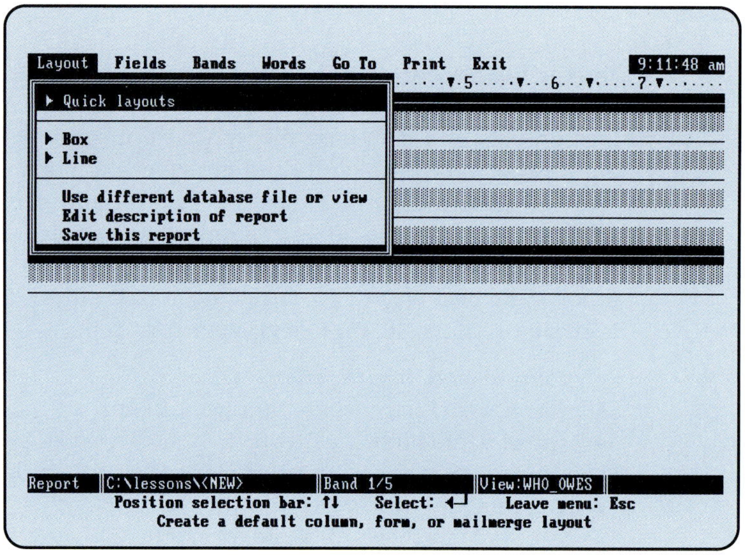

Figure 27 The Report Design Screen with Layout Menu

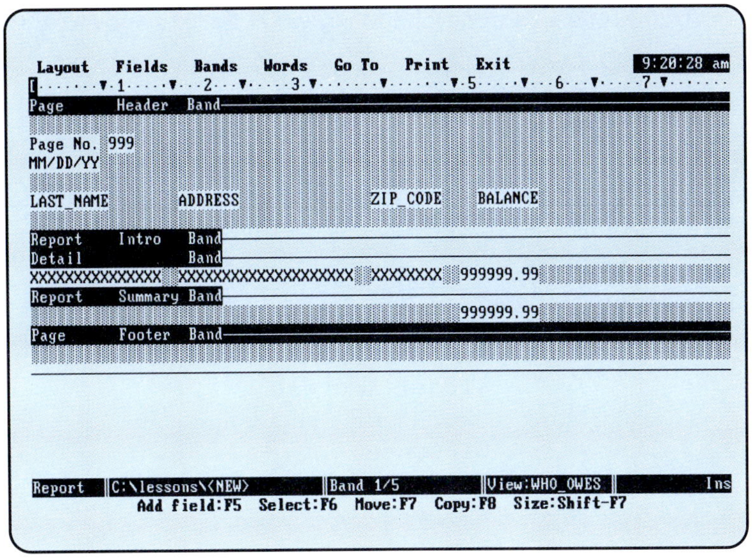

Figure 28 The Quick Layout

Step 3: Create a Quick Layout

It is often easiest to generate a default report layout, then modify the design to suit your specific needs. Select the Quick Layouts option from the Layout menu, then select the Column Layout option:

Type **q**
Type **c**

The program will create the report design shown in Figure 28.

Step 4: Examine the Report Design Screen

The work surface of the Report Design screen is divided into report bands. A **report band** is a logical piece of a report design. The Page Header Band contains information printed at the top of every page of the report. In this case, the Page Header Band includes the page number, the date, and a heading for each data column. The Report Intro Band contains text that appears only at the beginning of a report. You might use the Report Intro Band to print a cover letter explaining the report. The Report Intro Band in your report is empty right now. Next is the Detail Band, which presents the actual data from the records in the data base file or view. The Report Summary Band contains information that appears at the end of a report, such as concluding remarks or final totals. In this case, the Report Summary Band contains a calculated field for the total outstanding balances. Finally, the Page Footer Band contains information printed at the bottom of every page. Your Page Footer Band is empty, but it could be used to print a running title or the page number.

Step 5: Modify the Page Header Band

Let's spruce up the report layout. If "Ins" appears in the status bar at the right edge of the screen, turn off insert mode:

Press **Insert**

Type a running title to appear at the top of every page of the report:

Move the cursor to line 1, column 17
Type **Paddle and Portage Canoe Outfitters**
Move the cursor to line 2, column 20
Type **Outstanding Customer Balances**

Now change the column headings in the Page Header Band as follows.

Move the cursor to line 4, column 0
Type **Customer**
Press **Space Bar**
Move the cursor to line 4, column 17
Type **Street Address**
Move the cursor to line 4, column 39
Type **ZIP Code**
Move the cursor to line 4, column 51
Type **Balance**

Draw a horizontal line beneath the column headings. Follow these directions to activate the Layout menu, select the Line option, select the Single Line option, and specify the endpoints:

Press **Alt-L**
Type **L**
Type **s**
Move the cursor to line 5, column 0
Press **Enter**
Move the cursor to line 5, column 58
Press **Enter**

Step 6: Modify the Report Summary Band

You do not need a Report Intro Band, and the default Detail Band is fine. Let's draw a line below the last record in the table and type a name for the total outstanding balances.

Press **Home**
Move the cursor into the Report Summary Band
Move the cursor to line 0, column 0
Press **Enter**
Press **Up Arrow**
Press **Alt-L**
Type **L**
Type **s**
Press **Enter**
Move the cursor to line 0, column 58
Press **Enter**
Move the cursor to line 1, column 22
Type **Total Outstanding Balances**
Press **Home**

Your screen should look like Figure 29.

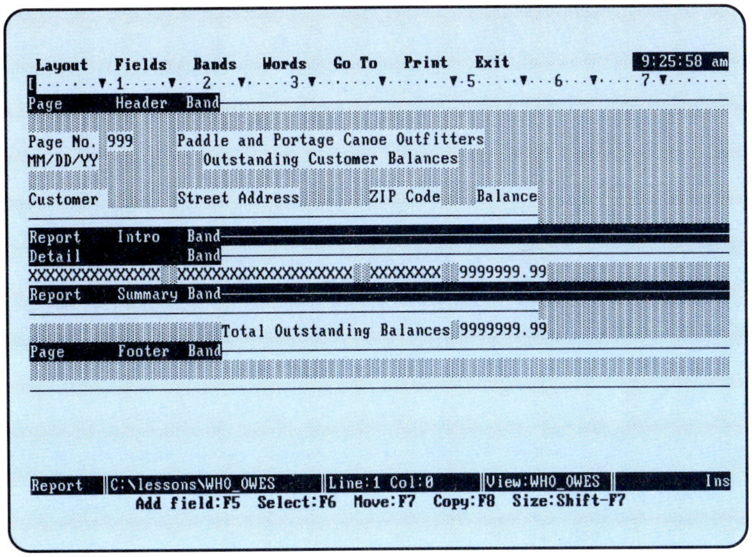

Figure 29 The Completed Report Design

Step 7: Save the Report Design

The report design is complete. Save it so that it can be used again. Activate the Exit menu, select Save Changes and Exit, and name the report file WHO_OWES:

Press **Alt-E**
Type **s**
Type **who_owes**
Press **Enter**

The program will return to the Control Center.

Step 8: View the Report on the Screen

Before you print a report, you can view it on your screen. First, highlight the name of the report you want to see in the Reports panel of the Control Center. This is already done. Tell dBASE IV that you want to use the highlighted report file:

Press **Enter**

The program will present a menu with three options: Print Report, Modify Layout, and Display Data. Select the Print Report option:

Type **p**

The program will then present the Print menu. Select the View Report On Screen option:

Type **v**

Your screen will look like Figure 30. Except for the bottom line, the screen shows how the report will look when it is printed. When you are finished examining the screen, return to the Control Center:

Press **Escape**
Press **Enter**

Figure 30 The Custom Report Viewed on the Screen

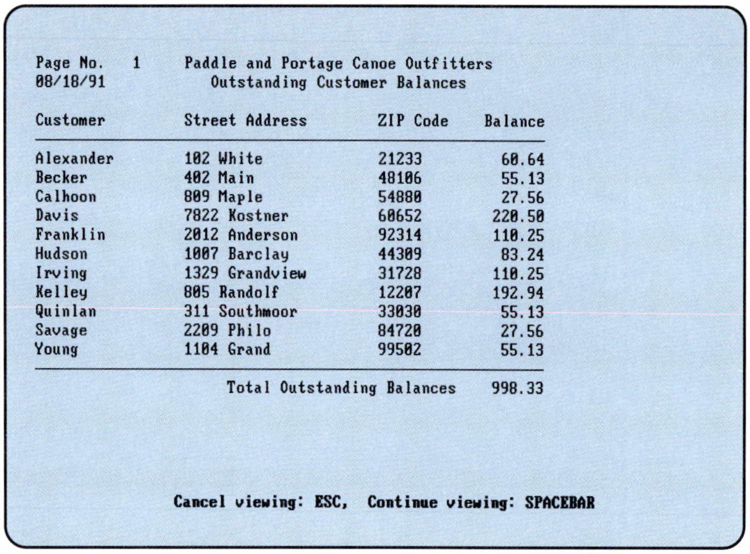

Page No. 1 Paddle and Portage Canoe Outfitters
08/10/91 Outstanding Customer Balances

Customer	Street Address	ZIP Code	Balance
Alexander	102 White	21233	60.64
Becker	402 Main	48106	55.13
Calhoon	809 Maple	54880	27.56
Davis	7822 Kostner	60652	220.50
Franklin	2012 Anderson	92314	110.25
Hudson	1007 Barclay	44309	83.24
Irving	1329 Grandview	31720	110.25
Kelley	805 Randolf	12207	192.94
Quinlan	311 Southmoor	33030	55.13
Savage	2209 Philo	84720	27.56
Young	1104 Grand	99502	55.13
	Total Outstanding Balances		998.33

Cancel viewing: ESC, Continue viewing: SPACEBAR

Step 9: Prepare the Printer

Make sure the printer is connected to the computer and turned on. Also, make sure that paper is loaded and aligned to the top of a new page. Finally, make sure that the printer's On Line light is lit. (If it isn't, press the On Line button.)

Step 10: Print the Custom Report

To print an existing custom report from the Control Center, move the highlight bar into the Reports panel and highlight the name of the report you want to print. This is already done. Tell dBASE IV that you want to use the highlighted file, select Print Report, and select Begin Printing:

Press **Enter**
Type **p**
Type **b**

The report will be output on your printer.

Practice

Modify the WHO_OWES report design so that the Balance figures and total are presented in a financial format. Follow these directions:

Move the cursor to the BALANCE field template
Press **Alt-F**
Type **m**
Type **p**
Type **f**
Press **Ctrl-End** (2 times)

Repeat this process for the TOTAL field template. When you are finished, activate the Print menu and view the report on the screen. Save the modified report layout and return to the Control Center.

Lesson 10: Creating Mailing Labels

Data base management packages are often used to maintain mailing lists and print mailing labels. Fortunately, dBASE IV makes it easy to create and print mailing labels from the records stored in a data base file. As an example, let's print mailing labels for Paddle and Portage Canoe Outfitters from MAILING.DBF.

Step 1: Select the Mailing List Data Base File

First, select the data base file from which you want to create the mailing labels. Move the highlight bar into the Data panel.

Highlight	**MAILING**
Press	**Enter**
Press	**Enter**

Step 2: Display the Label Design Screen

Now, tell dBASE IV that you want to create a mailing label:

Press	**Right Arrow** (4 times)
Highlight	<**create**>
Press	**Enter**

The program will display the Label Design screen, shown in Figure 31.

Step 3: Select the Label Dimensions

The dBASE IV program is already set up to handle the most popular label sizes and arrangements. The default size is $\frac{15}{16}$ by $3\frac{1}{2}$ inches by 1. The 1 refers to one label across the page. Let's tell dBASE IV to create the same size label but to put

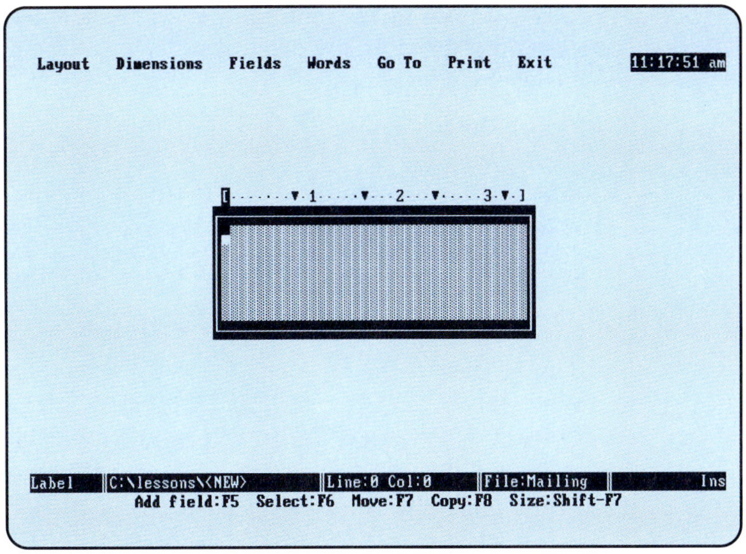

Figure 31 The Label Design Screen

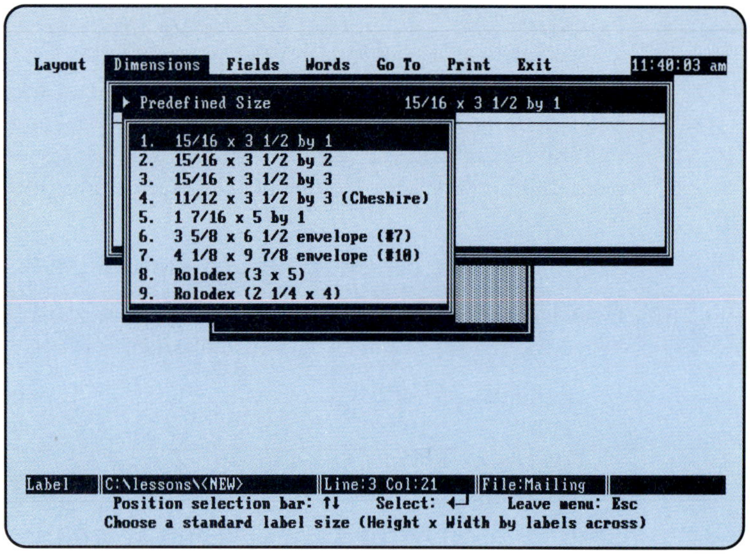

Figure 32 The Predefined Size Menu

two labels across the page. Activate the Dimensions menu and select the Predefined Size option:

Press **Alt-D**
Type **p**

Figure 32 shows the menu of predefined label sizes that will appear on the screen. The first option is the default size. Select the second option to print two standard-size labels across a page:

Type **2**

The program will return to the Label Design screen.

Step 4: Add the Fields

The work surface in the center of the screen is where you design the layout of your mailing labels. Follow these directions to place the fields of MAILING.DBF on the label work surface:

Press **Down Arrow**
Press **Alt-F**
Type **a**
Type **f**
Press **Enter**
Press **Ctrl-End**

Press **Space Bar**
Press **Alt-F**
Type **a**
Type **L**
Press **Enter**
Press **Ctrl-End**

Press **Home**
Press **Down Arrow**

Figure 33 The Completed Label Design

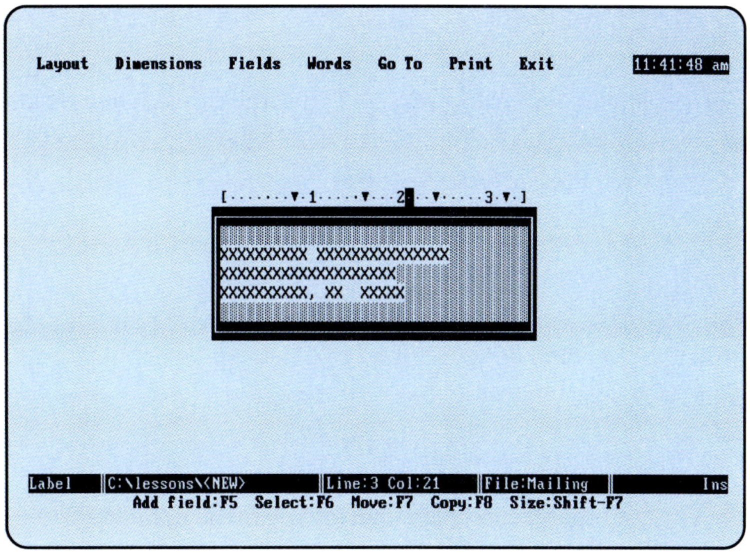

Press **Alt-F**
Type **a**
Type **a**
Press **Enter**
Press **Ctrl-End**

Press **Home**
Press **Down Arrow**
Press **Alt-F**
Type **a**
Type **ci**
Press **Enter**
Press **Ctrl-End**

Type **,**
Press **Space Bar**
Press **Alt-F**
Type **a**
Type **s**
Press **Enter**
Press **Ctrl-End**

Press **Space Bar** (2 times)
Press **Alt-F**
Type **a**
Type **z**
Press **Enter**
Press **Ctrl-End**

All the necessary fields have been placed on the mailing label. Your screen should look like Figure 33.

Step 5: Save the Label Design

Paddle and Portage Canoe Outfitters will want to use this mailing label design over and over again, so you should save it in a disk file named MAILING.LBL. Activate the Exit menu and select Save Changes and Exit:

Press **Alt-E**
Type **s**
Type **mailing**
Press **Enter**

The program will generate a file named MAILING.LBL and return to the Control Center.

Step 6: View the Labels on the Screen

The file MAILING.LBL is already selected in the Labels panel of the Control Center. Follow these directions to view the labels on the screen:

Press **Enter**
Type **p**
Type **v**

Your screen should look like Figure 34. View the rest of the labels:

Press **Space Bar**

After each screen, press the Space Bar to continue. When you have seen all of the labels, dBASE IV will return to the Control Center.

Step 7: Prepare the Printer

Make sure the printer is connected to the computer and turned on. Also, make sure that paper is loaded and aligned to the top of a new page. If you were really printing labels, you would insert blank label sheets instead of ordinary paper

Figure 34 The Mailing Labels Viewed on the Screen

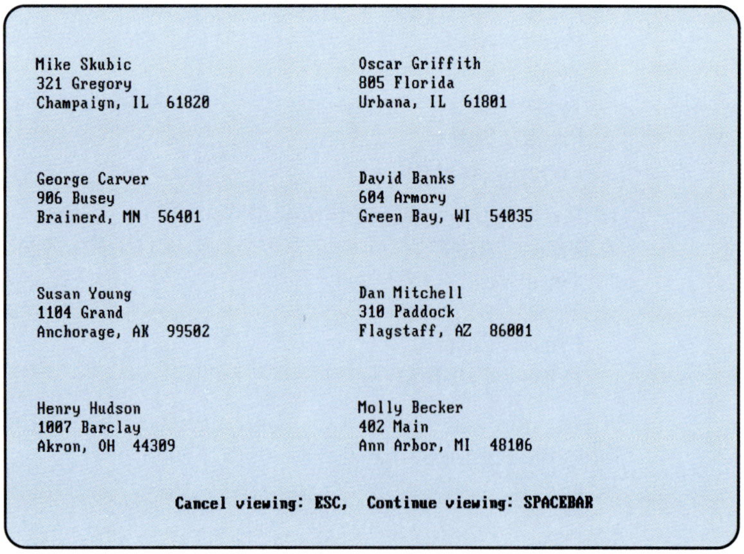

into the printer. Finally, make sure that the printer's On Line light is lit. (If it isn't, press the On Line button.)

Step 8: Print the Labels

To print labels from the Control Center, move the highlight bar into the Labels panel and highlight the name of the label design you want to use. This is already done. Tell dBASE IV that you want to use the highlighted file, select Print Label, and select Begin Printing:

Press **Enter**
Type **p**
Type **b**

The labels will be output on your printer.

Practice Activate the Label Design screen for MAILING.LBL and change the label dimensions to $^{15}/_{16} \times 3\frac{1}{2} \times 1$. Save the modified label design. View the labels on the screen, then print them. Return to the Control Center.

Lesson 11: Using Applications

The dBASE IV package has a powerful built-in programming language. In the next chapter, you will learn how to use the dBASE language to create programs that can perform several separate tasks with a single command. Large programs created with the dBASE language are sometimes called applications. The Applications panel of the Control Center is a place where you can put dBASE applications and other programs. Then you can conveniently select and run these programs from the Control Center. As an example, let's create a very simple dBASE program and store it in the Applications panel.

Step 1: Select the <create> Option

Unless some programs have already been created and stored in the Applications panel, your Applications panel should be empty. You can create a new application. Move to the Applications panel in the Control Center.

Highlight **<create>**
Press **Enter**

The program will present a box with two options: dBASE Program and Applications Generator. The first option activates the word-wrap editor, a text editor that you can use to type in a dBASE program. The second option activates the **Applications Generator,** an easy-to-use tool for creating a customized data base system without programming. Select the first option to activate the editor:

Press **Enter**

The word-wrap editor will appear on your screen (see Figure 35).

Step 2: Type the dBASE Program

In the word-wrap editor, you can type in a dBASE program. As an example, let's create a simple program that will contain only one command: Browse. The Browse command tells dBASE IV to present the Browse screen and display the contents

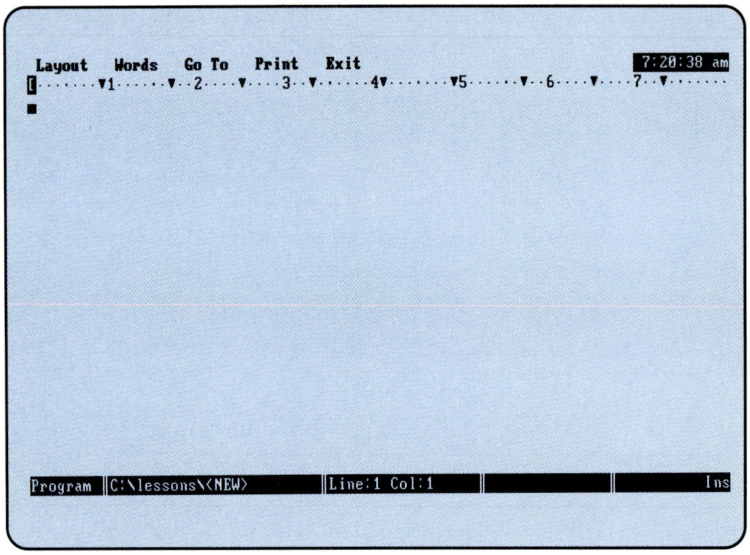

Figure 35 The Word-Wrap Editor for Typing a dBASE Program

of the current data base file in a table. If no data base file is active, the Browse command will prompt you to enter a file name. Type the Browse command into the word-wrap editor, save the program under the name BROWSE, and return to the Control Center:

Type **browse**
Press **Alt-E**
Type **s**
Type **browse**
Press **Enter**

The dBASE IV program will create a file named BROWSE.PRG and return to the Control Center. You should see BROWSE listed in the Applications panel (see Figure 36).

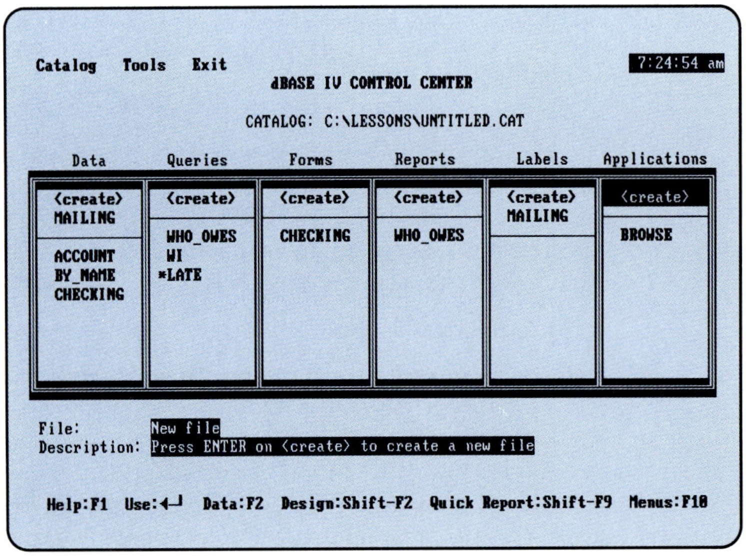

Figure 36 BROWSE Listed in the Applications Panel

Step 3: Run a dBASE Application

To run the program you have created, highlight BROWSE in the Applications panel, press Enter, and select the Run Application option:

Press **Down Arrow**
Press **Enter**
Type **r**
Type **y**

The BROWSE program will be compiled and executed. If no data base file is currently selected, the program will prompt you for a name. If it asks, do this:

Type **mailing**
Press **Enter**

The program will then present the Browse screen, just as if you had pressed F2 to execute the Data command. Obviously, the BROWSE program you have created is very simple and unnecessary, but it illustrates how you can create and run an application from the Control Center. Return to the Control Center:

Press **Alt-E**
Type **e**

Practice Use the word-wrap editor to create an application named EDIT that will contain the single dBASE IV command Edit. Run the application from the Control Center. What does it do? Use the Escape key to return to the Control Center when you are finished examining the screen.

Lesson 12: Using the Catalog Menu

Examine the Control Center screen. By now you have studied and used all of the panels: Data, Queries, Forms, Reports, Labels, and Applications. In this lesson, you will learn more about the Catalog menu. The next lesson will examine the Tools menu. The Exit menu, which you have already used, contains only two options: Exit to Dot Prompt and Quit to DOS. You will learn about the dot prompt in the next chapter. You have already used the Quit to DOS option.

Step 1: Activate the Catalog Menu

Display the Catalog menu on your screen:

Press **Alt-C**

Your screen should look like Figure 37.

Step 2: Examine the Catalog Menu

As you work with dBASE IV, it is likely that you will create many data base files, queries, forms, reports, applications, and other files. Catalogs can help you organize and identify your files. A dBASE IV catalog is simply a list of file names, locations, and descriptions. You decide which files to put in a catalog and which catalog you want to use. Although both dBASE IV catalogs and DOS subdirectories are used to organize files, they are different. A subdirectory contains files on your disk. A catalog merely lists files. When you delete a file from a subdirectory, it

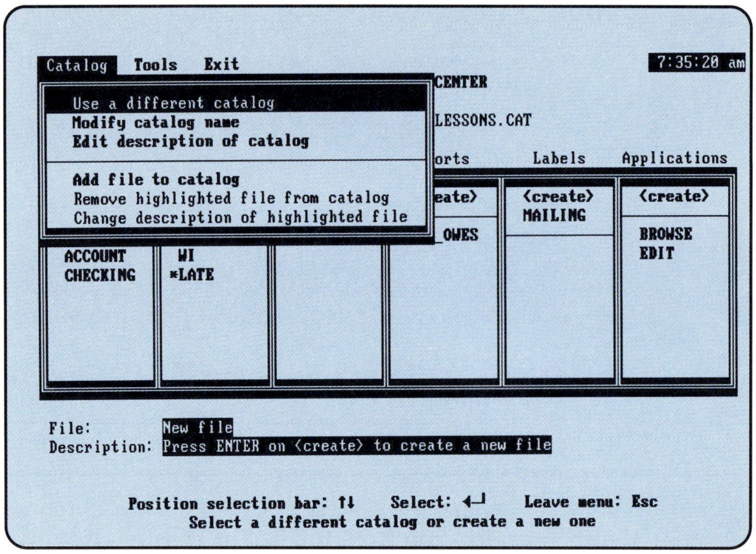

Figure 37 The Catalog Menu

is removed from the disk. When you remove a file from a catalog, its name is removed from the catalog, but the file can still remain on the disk. Catalogs are often used to group all the files needed for a particular job, office, department, or person. You can have as many different catalogs as you want. The purpose of catalogs is to shorten the lists of files that appear in the panels of the Control Center.

Step 3: Select Use a Different Catalog

When you start dBASE IV, the Control Center automatically loads the catalog you used last. If you have not created any catalogs yet, dBASE IV will create the first catalog for you. This initial catalog is named UNTITLED.CAT, and it contains all of the dBASE IV files in your current directory. The first option in the Catalog menu lets you create a new catalog or select an existing catalog.

Type **u**

The program will present a menu with the <create> option and a list of the available catalogs. Select <create> to create a new catalog, or select the name of the existing catalog you want to use. Return to the Catalog menu:

Press **Escape**

Step 4: Select Modify Catalog Name

The second option in the Catalog menu lets you change the name of an existing catalog.

Type **m**

The program will prompt you for a new name for your current catalog, which should be UNTITLED.CAT.

Press **Home**
Press **Ctrl-Y**
Type **lessons**
Press **Enter**

Your catalog will now be called LESSONS.CAT. Activate the Catalog menu again:

Press **Alt-C**

Step 5: Select Edit Description of Catalog

The third option in the Catalog menu lets you create or change the description of a catalog.

Type **e**
Type **`Microcomputer Applications Lessons`**
Press **Enter**

This catalog description will now appear whenever you choose the Use a Different Catalog option. Activate the Catalog menu again:

Press **Alt-C**

Step 6: Select Add File to Catalog

The fourth option of the Catalog menu lets you add a file to the current catalog. Each panel of the Control Center can contain up to 200 files.

Type **a**

The program will present a list of the files in the current subdirectory that are relevant to the current Control Center panel. You simply choose the files you want to include. Return to the Catalog menu:

Press **Escape**

Step 7: Select Remove Highlighted File From Catalog

The fifth option in the Catalog menu lets you remove the highlighted file from the catalog. It also lets you delete the file from the disk. If no file is highlighted in the current panel, you cannot select this option. As an example, let's remove and delete the EDIT file that you created in the Practice exercise of the previous lesson.

Press **Escape**
Highlight **EDIT** (in the Applications panel)
Press **Alt-C**
Type **r**
Type **y**
Type **y**

EDIT will be removed from the Applications panel and deleted from the disk.

Step 8: Select Change Description of Highlighted File

The last option in the Catalog menu lets you create or change the description of the currently highlighted file. This description will then appear on the Control Center screen below the panels. Follow these directions to create a description for BROWSE in the Applications panel:

Highlight **BROWSE** (in the Applications panel)
Press **Alt-C**
Type **c**
Type **`Sample application to execute Browse command`**
Press **Enter**

The program will return to the Control Center screen. Note the file description that now appears below the panels.

Practice Create a file description for each file in all panels of your Control Center screen.

Lesson 13: Using the Tools Menu

The Tools menu of the Control Center provides a number of options that perform useful functions within dBASE IV. Let's briefly examine the options of the Tools menu.

Step 1: Activate the Tools Menu

Display the Tools menu on your screen:

Press **Alt-T**

Your screen should look like Figure 38.

Step 2: Select Macros

The Macros option of the Tools menu lets you create, modify, and use keyboard macros. A **keyboard macro** records keystrokes that you plan to use over and over again. After you create a macro, you can play back the recorded keystrokes automatically. Macros can save time by reducing a long sequence of repetitive keystrokes to just a few keystrokes.

Type **m**

The program will display a menu that lets you record, modify, and play back macros. Macros can be a time-saving feature, but we won't discuss them further in this chapter. Return to the Tools menu:

Press **Escape**

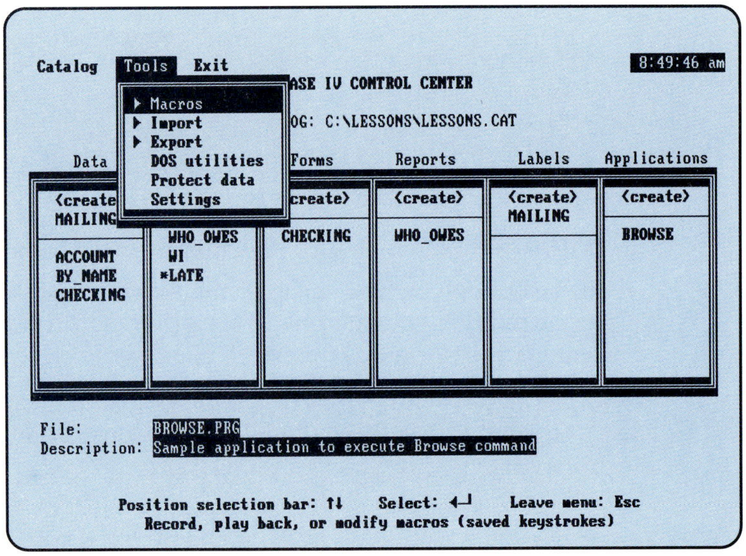

Figure 38 The Tools Menu

Step 3: Select Import

The Import option of the Tools menu lets you read data created by some programs other than dBASE IV.

Type **i**

A menu of program names will appear on the screen. These are the programs from which you can import data. For example, you could select Lotus 1-2-3 to create a dBASE IV data base file from a worksheet file with a .WK1 extension. Return to the Tools menu:

Press **Escape**

Step 4: Select Export

The Export option of the Tools menu lets you create data files that can be read by programs other than dBASE IV.

Type **e**

A menu of programs and data file formats will appear on the screen. Most data base, spreadsheet, and word processing packages can read files created with a format from this list. Return to the Tools menu:

Press **Escape**

Step 5: Select DOS Utilities

The DOS utilities option presents a screen that contains its own menu bar and a directory listing.

Type **d**

Figure 39 shows the result. The directory listing that appears on your screen will depend on the files in your current subdirectory. The menus available on the DOS Utilities screen provide many options for managing disk files. Some of these options duplicate operations that can be performed from DOS, such as deleting, copying, and renaming files. Many of the options available from the DOS Utilities menus, however, go beyond DOS. They are similar to the functions available with a DOS shell. Return to the Tools menu:

Press **Escape**
Type **y**
Press **Alt-T**

Step 6: Select Protect Data

The Protect Data option of the Tools menu lets you assign passwords to your data files.

Type **p**

This feature can be used to control access to sensitive information. It is most often used on local area networks and on computers used by many different people to prevent unauthorized access to dBASE IV and private data files. You should not use Protect Data unless you are familiar with dBASE IV security measures. Return to the Tools menu:

Press **Escape**

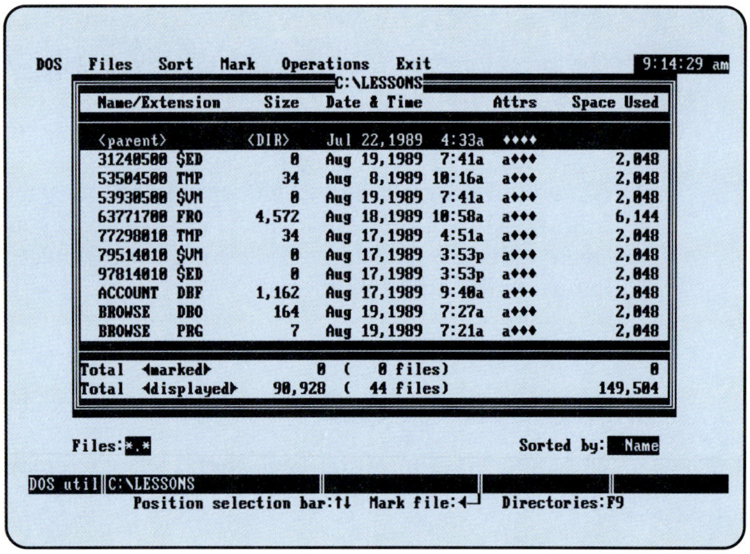

Figure 39 ***The DOS Utilities Screen***

Step 7: Select Settings

The Settings option of the Tools menu lets you customize the way dBASE IV displays and handles data.

Type **s**

The Settings screen contains a menu bar with three options: Options, Display, and Exit. The Options menu is automatically invoked when you select the Settings option. It lets you set certain default dBASE IV options. Now examine the Display menu:

Press **Right Arrow**

The Display menu lets you change the colors assigned to different parts of dBASE IV if you have a color monitor. Return to the Control Center:

Press **Escape**

Practice

1. Activate the Tools menu and select the DOS Utilities option. Use the Down Arrow key to highlight BY_NAME.DBF in the directory listing. Activate the Operations menu and select the Delete option to delete this file. Delete BY_NAME.MDX too. Return to the Control Center.
2. Activate the Control Center's Exit menu and select the Quit to DOS option.

Summary

- *Using memo fields.* A memo field must be specified in the data base design. To enter text in a memo field, move the cursor to that field and press Ctrl-Home.
- *Creating view queries.* Execute the <create> option in the Queries panel and enter filter conditions in the file skeleton.
- *Creating relational data bases.* A relational data base includes two or more files with at least one field in common.

- *Linking files.* You must link files to create a view that displays data from more than one file. The files are placed on the Query Design screen and an example variable is placed in the common field to link the files.
- *Creating update queries.* Activate the Update menu from the Query Design screen and specify the update operation.
- *Using calculated fields.* Calculated fields can be created in views, forms, and reports to present values computed from data fields.
- *Summarizing data.* Summary operators can be used in view queries to compute the sum, average, minimum, maximum, or count of a data field.
- *Designing custom forms.* Execute the <create> option in the Forms panel and lay out the names and fields on the Form Design screen.
- *Designing custom reports.* Execute the <create> option in the Reports panel and complete the desired report bands on the Report Design screen.
- *Creating mailing labels.* Execute the <create> option in the Labels panel and lay out the fields on the Label Design screen.
- *Using applications.* Execute the <create> option in the Applications panel to use the word-wrap editor or Applications Generator to produce a dBASE program.
- *Using the Catalog menu.* Activate the Catalog menu to help you organize and identify your dBASE IV files.
- *Using the Tools menu.* Activate the Tools menu to create keyboard macros, import and export files, use the DOS utilities, protect data, and select default dBASE IV settings.

Key Terms

As an extra review of this chapter, try defining the following terms.

Applications Generator
calculated field
example variable
field template
file skeleton
filter condition
keyboard macro
link field
memo marker
query
relational data base
relational operator
report band
Soundex search
summary (aggregate) operator
update query
view
view query
view skeleton

Multiple Choice

Choose the best selection to complete each statement.

1. Which type of data base field would you use to hold a half page of text?
   (a) Character
   (b) Logical
   (c) Memo
   (d) Text

2. Which key(s) do you press to activate the word-wrap editor to enter or view the contents of a Memo field?
   (a) Home (b) Ctrl-Home
   (c) Enter (d) Ctrl-Enter
3. What type of query would you use to correct a consistent error made throughout an entire data base?
   (a) link query (b) Soundex query
   (c) update query (d) view query
4. Which skeleton lists the fields that actually will be displayed by a query?
   (a) calculated field skeleton (b) file skeleton
   (c) link field skeleton (d) view skeleton
5. A data base that includes two or more files with at least one field in common is called a
   (a) common data base. (b) flat-file data base.
   (c) query data base. (d) relational data base.
6. What is a symbol or word that specifies how two items are to be compared?
   (a) example variable (b) link field
   (c) logical operator (d) relational operator
7. Which of the following filter conditions would retrieve all the records that contain the substring "old" anywhere in the specified field?
   (a) $"old" (b) Like "old*"
   (c) Sounds Like "old" (d) = "old"
8. Which operation is not available for an update query?
   (a) Alphabetize (b) Mark
   (c) Replace (d) Unmark
9. Which type of field is not actually stored in a data base file, but can be created in views, forms, and reports?
   (a) calculated field (b) character field
   (c) float field (d) numeric field
10. Which of the following terms is **not** a summary operator available for use in view queries?
    (a) AVG (b) SQRT
    (c) MAX (d) SUM
11. Which screen is redesigned when you create a custom form?
    (a) Browse screen (b) Edit screen
    (c) View screen (d) Help screen
12. Which symbol represents the contents of a character field in a field template?
    (a) L (b) MM/DD/YY
    (c) 9 (d) X
13. Custom reports are generated directly from a data base file or from a(n)
    (a) entry form. (b) mailing label.
    (c) update query. (d) view query.
14. Which report band specifies the placement of the data fields in a report?
    (a) Report Intro Band (b) Detail Band
    (c) Report Summary Band (d) Page Footer Band

15. What is the default predefined size for mailing labels?
    (a) $^{15}/_{16} \times 3\frac{1}{2} \times 1$
    (b) $^{15}/_{16} \times 3\frac{1}{2} \times 3$
    (c) $3\frac{5}{8} \times 6\frac{1}{2}$
    (d) Rolodex (3×5)
16. Which Control Center panel lists dBASE programs created with the word-wrap editor or Applications Generator?
    (a) Applications
    (b) Labels
    (c) Reports
    (d) Forms
17. Which menu is not available on the Control Center screen?
    (a) Catalog
    (b) Tools
    (c) Field
    (d) Exit
18. In dBASE IV, a list of file names, locations, and descriptions is called a
    (a) catalog.
    (b) menu.
    (c) tool.
    (d) subdirectory.
19. Which Tools menu option would you use to record and play back keystroke sequences?
    (a) Macros
    (b) DOS Utilities
    (c) Protect Data
    (d) Settings
20. Which Tools menu option would you use to see a directory listing and delete a file?
    (a) Macros
    (b) DOS Utilities
    (c) Protect Data
    (d) Settings

Fill-In

1. The ______ field type allows you to include a block of text in a data base record.
2. A ______ is a set of instructions that lets you retrieve, display, organize, or edit data.
3. A ______ is an arrangement of data on the screen.
4. Query-by-Example or QBE is the approach used by dBASE IV on the ______ Design screen.
5. A ______ condition is an expression that determines which records are selected for a view.
6. A relational data base includes two or more files with at least one ______ in common.
7. A ______ search finds words that sound like the word you specify.
8. Files are ______ by placing the same example variable in the common field.
9. An ______ query allows you to make changes to selected records throughout an entire data base file.
10. A ______ field contains the result of an expression instead of a value entered directly into a data base file.
11. The ______ operator can be used in a view query to add up the values in a column of fields.
12. The Form Design screen can be used to customize the form presented on the ______ screen.

13. A field ______ represents the width and contents of a data field on the Form Design, Report Design, and Label Design screens.
14. The work surface of the Report Design screen is divided into report ______.
15. You can specify the size of a mailing label design by activating the ______ menu.
16. Programs written in the dBASE IV programming language can be created and run from the ______ panel on the Control Center screen.
17. A dBASE IV ______ is a list of file names, locations, and descriptions.
18. The Use a Different Catalog option in the Catalog menu allows you to load an existing catalog or ______ a new catalog.
19. The ______ menu of the Control Center contains options for importing and exporting dBASE IV files.
20. The Protect Data option of the Tools menu lets you assign ______ to your data files.

Short Problems

1. Add the following text to the COMMENTS field of Dan Mitchell's record in the MAILING data base file:

   Dan would like us to supply a full-size axe instead of a small hatchet for chopping firewood.

   Return to the Control Center.
2. Create and perform a view query of ACCOUNT.DBF that will display the FIRST_NAME, LAST_NAME, and CHARGES fields of all customers who have balances equal to zero. Save the view query in a file named PAID and return to the Control Center.
3. Create and perform a view query of MAILING.DBF that will display only the cities, states, and ZIP codes, sorted by city. Examine the Browse screen and then return to the Control Center.
4. Create and perform an update query to change each "WI" to "WS" in the STATE field of MAILING.DBF. Use the following replacement instruction in the STATE field:

   "WI", with "WS"

   Note that the comma is necessary and it must be outside the quotation mark. Examine the modified data base file on the Browse screen. Return to the Query Design screen. Change the "WS" entries back to "WI" entries and perform the update again. Return to the Control Center without saving the update query.
5. Create and perform an update query to mark all MAILING.DBF records with "IL" in the STATE field for deletion. Examine the altered file on the Browse screen. Highlight a record of a customer from Illinois. Note that the record still appears on the Browse screen, but it is marked for deletion as indicated by the "Del" in the status bar. Now modify your update query to unmark all of the records of customers from Illinois. Perform the update. Return to the Control Center without saving the update query.
6. Modify the CHECKING form to automatically enter today's date in the DATE field. Place the cursor on the DATE field, activate the Fields menu, select

Modify Field, select Edit Options, and then select Default Value. Follow these instructions:

Type **date()**
Press **Enter**
Press **Ctrl-End** (2 times)

Now use what you have learned to assign the initial value .F. to the CLEARED field. (A period must be entered before and after the F.) Execute the Data command to display the form, and add a new record to see the results of your modifications. Return to the Control Center.

7. Make up and add at least ten records to the CHECKING data base file.
8. Create a custom report of the CHECKING data base file. Use the Quick Layouts option of the Layout menu. Summary fields that will add up the payments and deposits will be created automatically by dBASE IV. Modify the summary field for PAYMENT to name it PSUM. Modify the summary field for DEPOSIT to name it DSUM. Create a new calculated field in the Report Summary Band named BALANCE. Enter this expression to compute the BALANCE: DSUM − PSUM. Save the report in a file named BALANCE. Print the report or view it on the screen. When you are finished, return to the Control Center.
9. Design a custom data entry form for the MAILING data base file.
10. Activate the DOS Utilities option of the Tools menu. Then execute the Help command to read more about this feature.

Long Problems

1. In Long Problem 1 of the previous chapter, you created a data base file of information about your collection of LP records, cassette tapes, and compact discs. Create a custom data entry form, a useful view query, and a custom report for this data base file.
2. In Long Problem 2 of the previous chapter, you created a data base file containing your personal property inventory. Create a custom data entry form, a useful view query, and a custom report for this data base file.
3. In Long Problem 3 of the previous chapter, you created an "electronic Rolodex" with dBASE IV. Create a custom data entry form, a useful view query, and a custom report for this data base file. In addition, print mailing labels of all your records.
4. In Long Problem 4 of the previous chapter, you created a data base file to keep track of student grades. Create a custom data entry form, a useful view query, and a custom report for this data base file.
5. In Long Problem 5 of the previous chapter, you created a data base file of information about the courses you have taken in your college career. Create a custom data entry form, a useful view query, and a custom report for this data base file.
6. In Long Problem 6 of the previous chapter, you created a data base file to keep track of car expenses. Create a custom data entry form, a useful view query, and a custom report for this data base file.
7. In Long Problem 7 of the previous chapter, you created a data base file containing your academic schedule. Create a custom data entry form, a useful view query, and a custom report for this data base file.

8. In Long Problem 8 of the previous chapter, you created a data base file of information about your books. Create a custom data entry form, a useful view query, and a custom report for this data base file.
9. In Long Problems 9 and 10 of the previous chapter, you created a data base of information about the fifty states. Create a custom data entry form, a useful view query, and a custom report for this data base file.
10. Design a relational data base of your own choosing made up of two separate files linked by a common field. Create custom data entry forms for your files. Enter at least twenty records for each file using the forms you have created. Generate and save a useful view query that links the files and presents information from both. Design and print a custom report based on the view query you have created. Try to use what you have learned about summary and calculated fields.

CHAPTER 16

ADVANCED dBASE IV

In This Chapter

Getting Started
Lesson 1: Accessing the Dot Prompt
Lesson 2: Examining a Data Base File
Lesson 3: Entering and Modifying Records
Lesson 4: Deleting Records
Lesson 5: Sorting and Indexing
Lesson 6: Finding Data
Lesson 7: Relating Files
Lesson 8: Using Other dBASE IV Commands
Lesson 9: Using dBASE IV Functions
Lesson 10: Creating a dBASE IV Program
Lesson 11: Using the Applications Generator
Lesson 12: Using SQL Commands

Preview

Chapters 14 and 15 taught you most of what the average user needs to know about dBASE IV. This chapter proceeds to more advanced data base management topics. You may not need all of the commands and features presented in this chapter, but many of them can make your work easier, quicker, and less tedious. Learning more about dBASE IV can help you maintain more complex and powerful data base systems.

After studying this chapter, you will know how to

- access the dot prompt.
- examine a data base file from the dot prompt.
- enter and modify records from the dot prompt.
- delete records from the dot prompt.
- sort and index a file from the dot prompt.
- find data from the dot prompt.
- relate files from the dot prompt.
- use other dBASE IV commands.
- use dBASE IV functions.
- create a dBASE IV program.
- use the Applications Generator.
- use SQL commands.

Getting Started

You've already learned how to start dBASE IV and use its basic features and commands. This chapter assumes you have completed all of the lessons and exercises in Chapters 14 and 15. Furthermore, it assumes that you have a computer with a hard disk and dBASE IV installed on it in a subdirectory named DBASE. A DOS path should be set up so that you can run dBASE IV from within any subdirectory. You should have a subdirectory named LESSONS in which to store your data base files.

Lesson 1: Accessing the Dot Prompt

In the previous two chapters you learned how to use the Control Center, the menu-system interface of dBASE IV. The Control Center is easy to learn and convenient, and it lets you perform most basic data base management tasks. Advanced users, however, sometimes prefer to use the **dot prompt,** the command-line interface of dBASE IV. Instead of choosing options from menus, you can enter commands directly at the dot prompt, named for the dot (.) that appears on the screen. Using dot prompt commands requires more knowledge of dBASE IV, but it is faster, more flexible, and allows access to features not available from the Control Center. Learning dot prompt commands is a prerequisite to dBASE programming, because dBASE programs are made up of commands that are very similar to dot prompt commands. They might seem a little cryptic at first, but once you learn them, dot prompt commands are a quick and efficient way to harness the full power of dBASE IV.

Step 1: Start dBASE IV

If you are not already running dBASE IV, switch to your LESSONS subdirectory and start the program:

Type **cd \lessons**
Press **Enter**
Type **dbase**
Press **Enter** (2 times)

The Control Center will appear on your screen.

Step 2: Exit to the Dot Prompt

The Control Center is automatically activated when you start dBASE IV. Switch to the dot prompt by selecting the Exit to Dot Prompt option from the Exit menu:

Press **Alt-E**
Type **e**

Your screen will look like Figure 1. The dot prompt and a blinking cursor appear at the lower left of the screen, just above the status bar. You enter dBASE commands at the dot prompt, just as you enter DOS commands at the DOS prompt.

Step 3: Enter a Dot Prompt Command

Let's start with a simple example. The dBASE IV command DIR is similar to the DOS command DIR. It displays a list of the data base files in your current directory. To execute a dot prompt command, type it and press the Enter key:

Type **dir**
Press **Enter**

Figure 2 shows the result. After the command is executed, the information scrolls up the screen and a new dot prompt appears.

Figure 1 The Dot Prompt Screen

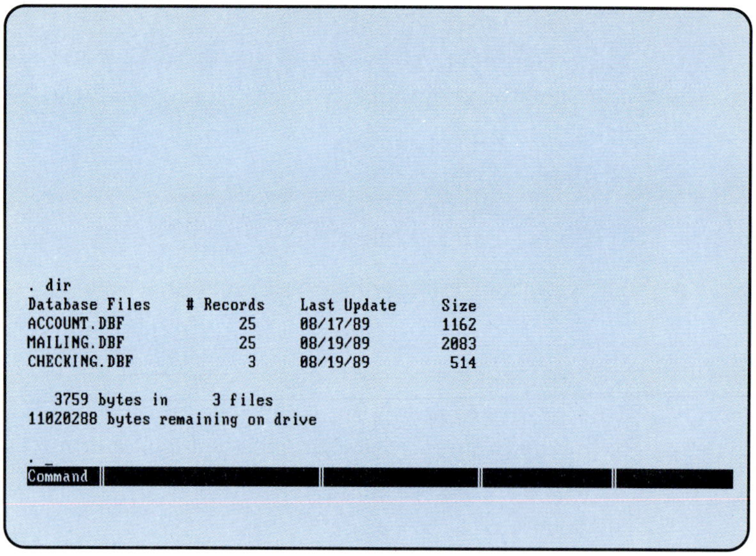

Figure 2 The DIR Dot Prompt Command

Note that you may enter dot prompt commands in uppercase or lowercase letters. Only the first four letters of any command are necessary. A command such as DISPLAY, for example, could be executed by entering just "disp." If you make a mistake before you press the Enter key, you can use the Backspace key to erase characters and retype them. You can press the Left Arrow key or the Right Arrow key to move the cursor within the line, press the Insert key to insert characters, press the Delete key to delete characters, or press the Escape key to erase the entire command.

Step 4: Try an Invalid Command

You don't have a menu of options when using the dot prompt. It is possible, therefore, to enter an invalid command. If you enter a command that dBASE IV does not understand or a command that is missing required information, the program will display a prompt box with three choices: Cancel, Edit, and Help. For example, try an invalid command:

Type **xxx**
Press **Enter**

Your screen will look like Figure 3. The Cancel option will clear the command line. The Edit option will return to the command line so you can modify what you typed and try the command again. The Help option invokes the help system. Cancel the command:

Press **Enter**

Step 5: Get Help

If you enter an invalid command, you can get help by choosing the Help option from the prompt box. You can also press the F1 key, just as you do from the Control Center. Another way to get help is to execute the HELP command. Type

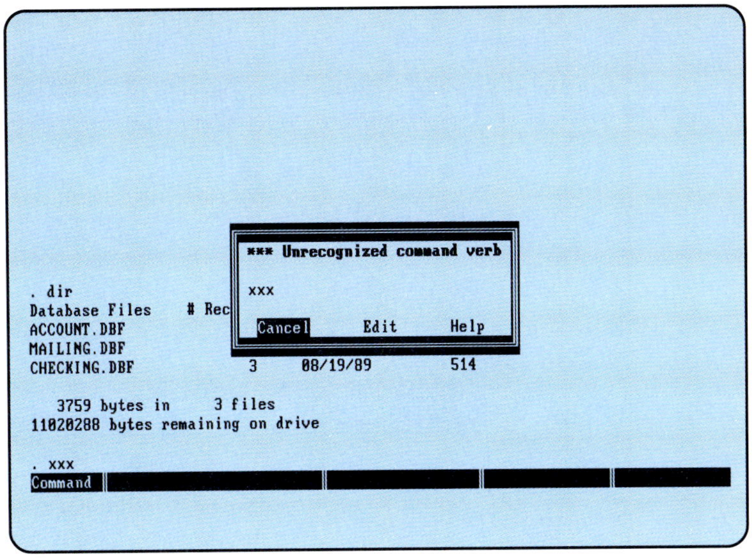

Figure 3 An Invalid Dot Prompt Command

the command you want to learn about after typing "help." For example, to get help about the DIR command:

Type **help dir**
Press **Enter**

The help box containing information about the DIR command will appear on your screen (see Figure 4). When you are finished reading the help box, return to the dot prompt:

Press **Escape**

Step 6: Clear the Screen

When you use the dot prompt, dBASE IV merely scrolls the screen up in response to each command. After several commands, your screen can get cluttered. Fortunately, you can use the CLEAR command to erase the screen.

Type **clear**
Press **Enter**

The screen will be erased.

Step 7: Return to the Control Center

Many seasoned dBASE IV users switch back and forth between the Control Center and the dot prompt. You can return to the Control Center from the dot prompt by executing the ASSIST command.

Type **assist**
Press **Enter**

The Control Center will appear on your screen. Now go back to the dot prompt:

Press **Alt-E**
Type **e**

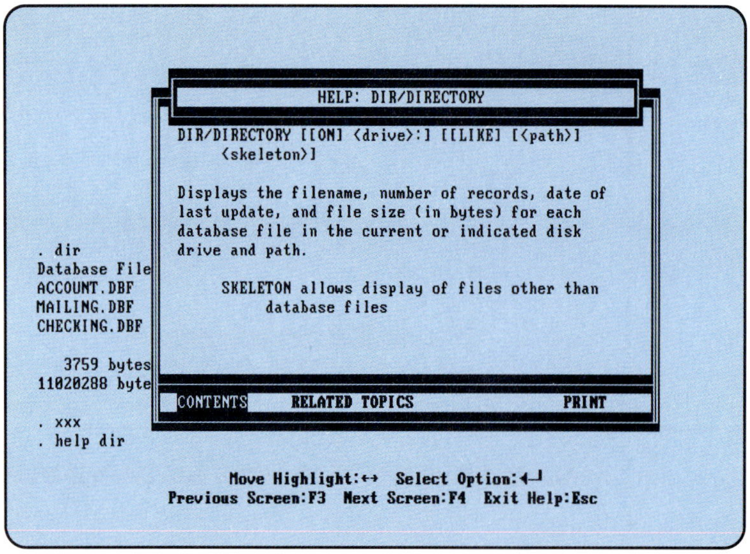

Figure 4 Help from the Dot Prompt

Step 8: Quit from the Dot Prompt

You don't have to return to the Control Center to exit dBASE IV. The QUIT command closes all open files, terminates the dBASE IV session, and returns to DOS.

Type **quit**
Press **Enter**

You should see the DOS prompt on your screen.

Practice

1. Start dBASE IV and activate the dot prompt.
2. Execute the HELP command to read about the QUIT command. Return to the dot prompt.
3. Switch to the Control Center from the dot prompt, then activate the dot prompt again.

Lesson 2: Examining a Data Base File

Every operation that can be performed from the Control Center can also be performed with dot prompt commands. For example, let's use dot prompt commands to open the MAILING data base file and examine its contents.

Step 1: Open a Data Base File

The USE command opens an existing data base file. Once a file is open you can use other dot prompt commands to examine the contents of the file or manipulate its data. Tell dBASE IV that you want to use MAILING.DBF:

Type **use mailing**
Press **Enter**

The program will make MAILING.DBF the current data base file, as revealed in the status bar. The current record is 1 of 25.

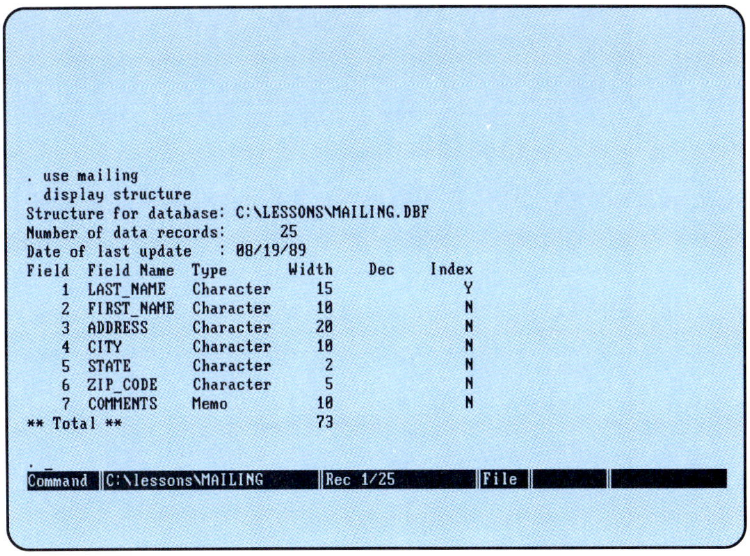

Figure 5 The DISPLAY STRUCTURE Command

Step 2: Display the Structure of the File

Suppose you want to see the names, types, and widths of the fields in the current data base file. The DISPLAY STRUCTURE command will present this information on the screen.

Type **display structure**
Press **Enter**

Your screen should look like Figure 5.

Step 3: Display All of the Records

You can use a variation of the DISPLAY command to see all the records in a data base presented one screen at a time. Execute this command:

Type **display all**
Press **Enter**

Your screen should look like Figure 6. Examine the remaining records:

Press **Enter** (2 times)

The LIST command is similar to the DISPLAY command, except that it scrolls the screen, if necessary, without pausing. For example, try the LIST ALL command:

Type **list all**
Press **Enter**

All the records will be listed on the screen without pauses.

Step 4: Move the Record Pointer

A unique record number is assigned to each record in a data base file. As you work with a file, dBASE IV keeps track of the current record number by means of the **record pointer.** When you open a file, the record pointer is set to the first record. Certain dot prompt commands change the record pointer. Displaying all

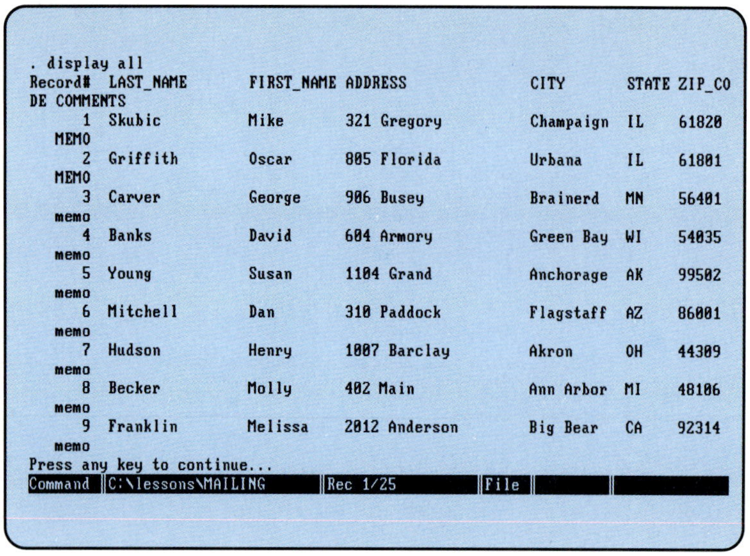

```
. display all
Record#  LAST_NAME         FIRST_NAME ADDRESS              CITY         STATE ZIP_CO
DE COMMENTS
      1  Skubic            Mike       321 Gregory          Champaign    IL     61820
   MEMO
      2  Griffith          Oscar      805 Florida          Urbana       IL     61801
   MEMO
      3  Carver            George     906 Busey            Brainerd     MN     56401
   memo
      4  Banks             David      604 Armory           Green Bay    WI     54035
   memo
      5  Young             Susan      1104 Grand           Anchorage    AK     99502
   memo
      6  Mitchell          Dan        310 Paddock          Flagstaff    AZ     86001
   memo
      7  Hudson            Henry      1007 Barclay         Akron        OH     44309
   memo
      8  Becker            Molly      402 Main             Ann Arbor    MI     48106
   memo
      9  Franklin          Melissa    2012 Anderson        Big Bear     CA     92314
   memo
Press any key to continue...
Command  C:\lessons\MAILING          Rec 1/25          File
```

***Figure 6* The DISPLAY ALL Command**

the records, for example, moves the record pointer from the first record to the end of the file. Examine the status bar. The EOF/25 means that the record pointer is now at the end of the file, past the last record. The GO command lets you change the record pointer. Move the record pointer to record number 12:

Type **go 12**
Press **Enter**

Move the record pointer to the last record in the file:

Type **go bottom**
Press **Enter**

Now move the record pointer to the first record in the file:

Type **go top**
Press **Enter**

Step 5: Display a Particular Record

You can see the contents of the current record with the DISPLAY command.

Type **display**
Press **Enter**

This command displays all of the fields in the record. You can tell dBASE IV to display only specific fields. Try this command:

Type **display last_name, city**
Press **Enter**

The program will display only the contents of LAST_NAME and CITY in the current record.

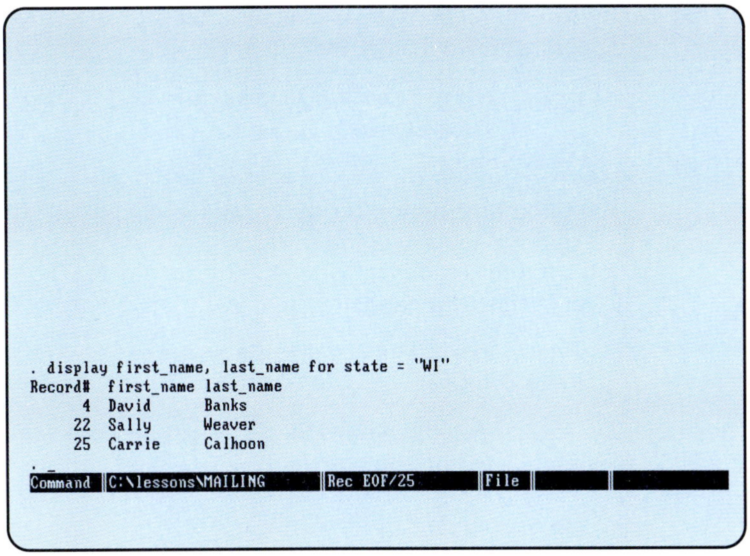

Figure 7 A Group of Records Displayed

Step 6: Display a Group of Records

The DISPLAY and LIST commands can be followed by the word "FOR" and a condition to present the records that fulfill that condition. For example, suppose you want to see the names of all customers from Wisconsin. Execute this command:

Type **display first_name, last_name for state = "WI"**
Press **Enter**

Figure 7 shows the result.

Step 7: Use the Logical Operators

More complex searches can be specified by using logical operators. A **logical operator** modifies the TRUE or FALSE result of one or two conditions. Three logical operators are available:

.NOT.	Changes TRUE to FALSE and FALSE to TRUE
.AND.	Produces TRUE only if both conditions are TRUE
.OR.	Produces FALSE only if both conditions are FALSE

Note that the periods before and after the logical operators are necessary for dBASE IV to identify them in expressions. Let's try each of the logical operators. Suppose you want to see the last names of all customers who do *not* live in Wisconsin. Execute this command:

Type **list last_name for .not. state = "WI"**
Press **Enter**

The program will list only those last names from records in which the contents of the STATE field is not WI.

You can use the .AND. logical operator when you want to fulfill two conditions. Suppose you want to see the records of customers who live in Hometown, Illinois. A large data base might have records from several towns named Hometown in different states. Execute this expression to list only those records of customers from Hometown, Illinois:

Type **list last_name for state = "IL" .and. city = "Hometown"**
Press **Enter**

The program should present the last name Jenkins from record number 24.

The .OR. logical operator is used to fulfill either of two conditions. Suppose you want to see all the last names of customers who live in Illinois or Wisconsin. Execute this command:

Type **list last_name for state = "IL" .or. state ="WI"**
Press **Enter**

You should see the names Skubic, Griffith, Banks, Davis, Weaver, Jenkins, and Calhoon listed on the screen.

Step 8: Copy a List of Records to a Text File

By default, the LIST command presents data base records on the screen. It can also be used to copy data base records to an ordinary text file. This text file then can be read by any text editor or word processing program, or printed from DOS. Suppose you want to create a text file called NAMES.TXT from the MAILING data base. Execute this command:

Type **list first_name, last_name to file names.txt**
Press **Enter**

The names will be listed on your screen and also copied to a text file called NAMES.TXT in your current directory.

Step 9: Print a List of Records

The LIST command can also be used to copy data base records to the printer. Suppose you want to print the list of first names and last names in MAILING.DBF. Make sure your printer is turned on, on line, and loaded with paper. Then execute this command:

Type **list first_name, last_name to printer**
Press **Enter**

The names will be printed just as they appeared on the screen. Using LIST in this manner is a quick and easy way to obtain simple printed output. You can design and produce a custom report from the Control Center if you need a more sophisticated printout.

Step 10: Close a Data Base File

Several methods are available to close a data base file when you are finished working with it. You can execute the USE command without providing a file name:

Type **use**
Press **Enter**

The current data base file, in this case MAILING.DBF, will be closed. Another way to close a file is with the CLOSE command. The CLOSE command may be used when you have more than one file opened at a time. For example, execute this command to close all opened data base files:

Type **close databases**
Press **Enter**

Another way to close the current data base file is to open a different data base file. The current data base file will be closed automatically. For example, execute these commands:

Type **use account**
Press **Enter**
Type **use mailing**
Press **Enter**

The first USE command opens ACCOUNT.DBF. The second USE command closes ACCOUNT.DBF and opens MAILING.DBF.

Practice

1. Open the ACCOUNT data base file.
2. Display the current record.
3. Move the record pointer to record number 10, then display the current record.
4. Display all of the records in the file.
5. List only the LAST_NAME and BALANCE fields of all the records in the file.
6. Close the ACCOUNT data base file.

Lesson 3: Entering and Modifying Records

Entering and modifying records from the dot prompt is similar to entering and modifying records from the Control Center.

Step 1: Open the Data Base File

If the data base file you want to modify is not already open, you must open it. Tell dBASE IV that you want to use the MAILING data base file:

Type **use mailing**
Press **Enter**

Step 2: Add a Record

The APPEND command lets you add new records to the end of a new or existing data base file.

Type **append**
Press **Enter**

As Figure 8 shows, a blank data entry form will appear on the screen in which you can add a new record to the end of the current data base file. From this point, the procedure is the same as entering a new record from the Control Center. Follow these directions to enter a new record:

Type **Eaton**
Press **Enter**

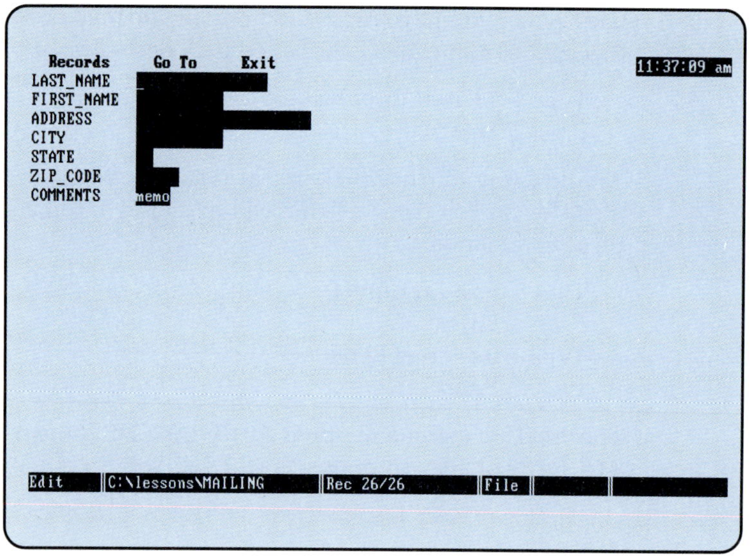

Figure 8 A Blank Data Entry Form Presented By the APPEND Command

Type **Candy**
Press **Enter**
Type **2314 Sunset**
Press **Enter**
Type **Rantoul**
Press **Enter**
Type **IL**
Type **61866**
Press **Ctrl-Home**
Type **Candy prefers the nylon Duluth packs.**
Press **Ctrl-End**

If you have more records to add, you can press Enter, Tab, Down Arrow, or Page Down and answer "Yes" to the prompt to add new records. After you have entered all your new records, save the last record and return to the dot prompt:

Press **Ctrl-End**

Step 3: Edit an Existing Record

Several methods can be used to update and maintain a data base file from the dot prompt. The EDIT command lets you modify one record at a time. It activates the same Edit screen available from the Control Center. For example, execute this command:

Type **edit**
Press **Enter**

The program will display the Edit screen containing the current record, in this case Candy Eaton's record. You can modify the record by editing the contents of any field. Follow these directions to change the address in Candy Eaton's record:

Press **Down Arrow** (2 times)
Type **`1458 Clearwater`**
Press **Enter**
Type **`Gary`**
Press **Delete** (3 times)
Press **Enter**
Type **`IN`**
Type **`46401`**

If you want to change another record, you can press the Page Up or Page Down key to move within the file and display it on the Edit screen. Or, you can return to the dot prompt, move the record pointer to the record to be changed, and then execute the Edit command again. When you have finished editing a record, press Ctrl-End to save the record and return to the dot prompt.

Press **Ctrl-End**

Step 4: Display the Browse Screen

Another way to view, add, or edit records is to activate the Browse screen from the dot prompt. Execute the BROWSE command and move to the beginning of the file:

Type **`browse`**
Press **Enter**
Press **Ctrl-PgUp**

The result is the same as if you had activated the Browse screen from the Control Center. Return to the dot prompt without making any changes:

Press **Escape**

Step 5: Update Records

The REPLACE command lets you make a specific change to selected records throughout a data base file. Suppose you wanted to change all the "WI" abbreviations to "WS" in the STATE field. Execute the following command:

Type **`replace all state with "WS" for state = "WI"`**
Press **Enter**

Observe what you have done:

Type **`list for state = "WS"`**
Press **Enter**

Figure 9 shows the result. All the records that had "WI" in the STATE field now have "WS" in the STATE field.

Practice

1. Replace each "WS" with "WI" in the STATE field of the records in the MAILING data base file.
2. Activate the Browse screen to check your work. Return to the dot prompt when you are finished.

Figure 9 The REPLACE Command

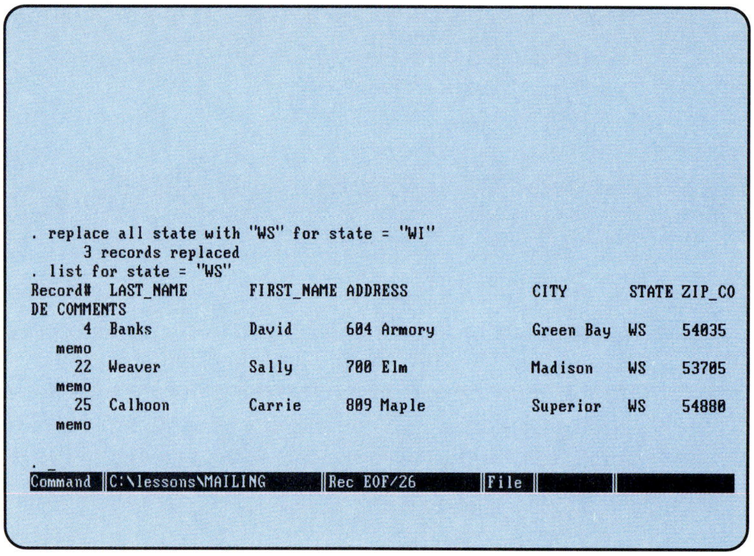

Lesson 4: Deleting Records

Records can be deleted from a data base file when they are no longer needed. Use the DELETE command from the dot prompt to mark one or more records for deletion. You can use the RECALL command to unmark records marked for deletion. The PACK command permanently removes the records marked for deletion in the current data base file.

Step 1: Locate the Record to be Deleted

Unless otherwise specified, the DELETE command marks the current record for deletion. Suppose you want to delete Candy Eaton's record. The first step is to move the record pointer to her record. If you don't remember the exact record number, you can use the LOCATE command to find it.

Type **`locate for last_name = "Eaton"`**
Press **Enter**

The program will report the record number and move the record pointer to that record.

Step 2: Execute the DELETE Command

After the record to be removed has been located, execute the DELETE command to mark the record for deletion.

Type **`delete`**
Press **Enter**

The program will report that one record has been deleted.

If you know the record number of the record to be deleted, you can specify it after the DELETE command and skip Step 1. For example, the following command could also be used to mark Candy Eaton's record for deletion:

```
delete record 26
```

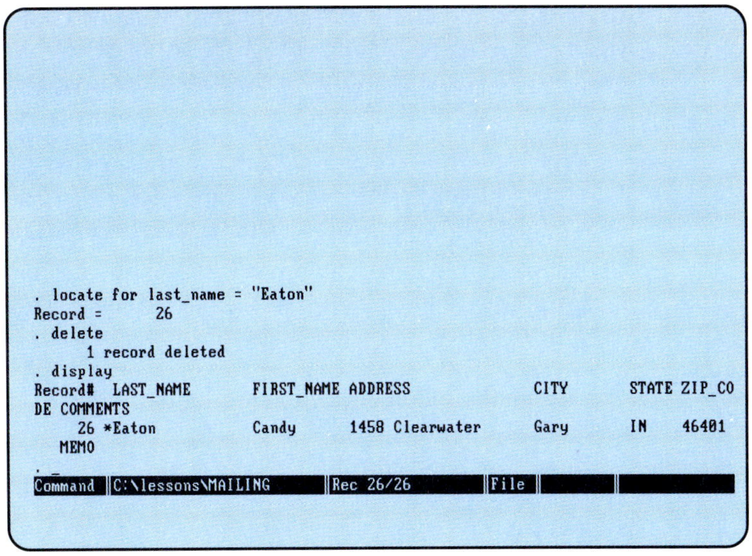

Figure 10 A Record Marked For Deletion

Step 3: Display the Record

The DELETE command does not actually remove a record from the data base file. It only marks the record for deletion. The record pointer remains in the same position. You can confirm the action of the DELETE command by displaying the record marked for deletion.

Type **`display`**
Press **Enter**

As Figure 10 shows, Candy Eaton's record is displayed with an asterisk (*) after the record number, which indicates that the record is marked for deletion.

Step 4: Recall a Deleted Record

Suppose you change your mind about deleting Candy Eaton's record. A record marked for deletion can be reinstated in the data base file with the RECALL command. You can recall the current record, a particular record number, a group of records, or every record marked for deletion in the data base file. Recall Candy Eaton's record:

Type **`recall`**
Press **Enter**

The program will report that one record has been recalled. To confirm that Candy Eaton's record has been reinstated, execute the DISPLAY command:

Type **`display`**
Press **Enter**

The record will be displayed without an asterisk following the record number.

Step 5: Permanently Remove Deleted Records

Suppose you really do want to remove Candy Eaton's record from MAILING.DBF. Mark it again for deletion:

Type **`delete`**
Press **Enter**

The PACK command permanently removes all records marked for deletion. After you execute this command, the data cannot be retrieved. Obviously, you should use the PACK command with caution. Go ahead and permanently remove the record marked for deletion:

Type **pack**
Press **Enter**

The dBASE IV program will reconstruct the MAILING data base file, removing all records marked for deletion. It will also update any associated index files. The record pointer will be placed at the beginning of the file.

Practice

1. Execute the following command to mark the records of customers from Wisconsin for deletion:

   Type **delete for state = "WI"**
   Press **Enter**

2. Reinstate all records marked for deletion:

   Type **recall all**
   Press **Enter**

Lesson 5: Sorting and Indexing

Data base files can be sorted and indexed easily from the dot prompt.

Step 1: Sort a Data Base File on One Field

The SORT command creates a new data base file in which the records from the current file are arranged in the specified order. Suppose you want to create a new data base file named BY_NAME.DBF that contains the records of MAILING.DBF arranged alphabetically by last name. Execute this command:

Type **sort to by_name on last_name**
Press **Enter**

To check your work, open BY_NAME.DBF and list its contents:

Type **use by_name**
Press **Enter**
Type **list**
Press **Enter**

The records of BY_NAME.DBF are arranged alphabetically by the contents of the LAST_NAME field.

Step 2: Sort a Data Base File on Several Fields

You can sort a data base file on more than one field. For example, you may want a file arranged by city, last name, then first name. Execute this command:

Type **sort to by_city on city, last_name, first_name**
Press **Enter**

Now, examine your work:

Type **use by_city**
Press **Enter**
Type **list**
Press **Enter**

The records are first arranged by the contents of the CITY field, then by LAST_NAME and FIRST_NAME within each city.

Step 3: Index a File

Indexing also arranges the records of a data base in a specified order. Rather than creating a new data base file, however, indexing creates an index file of field values and record numbers. Indexing is faster and usually takes up less disk space than sorting. In addition, index files are automatically updated whenever you make a change to the original data base file. Indexing is better than sorting if you often want to view your records in a particular order.

Two indexing methods are available in dBASE IV. The first method stores one index per index file, which is identified by the extension NDX. This is the method that was used with dBASE III PLUS and earlier versions of dBASE. You can still use this method of indexing in dBASE IV to remain compatible with earlier versions of the package. A better method of indexing, however, has been introduced with dBASE IV. This new method uses **multiple index files,** each of which can contain up to 47 separate indexes and is identified by the extension MDX. A default multiple index file is always opened with a data base file when you execute the USE command. Each individual index within a multiple index file is identified by its own unique tag. A **tag** is essentially the name of an index within a multiple index file.

In a previous chapter, you indexed the MAILING data base file by LAST_NAME. The multiple index file for MAILING.DBF, which is MAILING.MDX, already contains one index with the tag LAST_NAME. Suppose you want to index MAILING.DBF by STATE as well. Execute these commands:

Type **use mailing**
Press **Enter**
Type **index on state tag state**
Press **Enter**

A new index, tagged STATE, will be created and added to the multiple index file MAILING.MDX. The STATE index arranges the records of MAILING.DBF alphabetically by state.

Step 4: Activate an Index Tag

The default multiple index file of a data base file is automatically opened when you execute the USE command to open the data base file. No index tag, however, is automatically activated. Records are initially displayed in record number order, the order in which they were entered. You must use the SET ORDER command to rearrange the records on the basis of a tag in the multiple index file. Suppose you want to see the records of MAILING.DBF listed in STATE order. Execute these commands:

Type **set order to tag state**
Press **Enter**
Type **list**
Press **Enter**

Figure 11 Records Indexed By STATE

```
   13 Hall         Robert     1721 Valley       Ogallala    NE   69153
memo
   19 Diamond      Jim        142 Hazelwood     Belmar      NJ   07719
memo
   12 Underwood    Rhonda     701 Dover         Las Vegas   NV   89114
memo
   20 Kelley       Joyce      805 Randolf       Albany      NY   12207
memo
    7 Hudson       Henry      1007 Barclay      Akron       OH   44309
memo
   10 Savage       Julian     2209 Philo        Cedar City  UT   84720
memo
   11 Prorok       Brian      502 Chalmers      Fairfax     VA   22030
memo
    4 Banks        David      604 Armory        Green Bay   WI   54035
memo
   22 Weaver       Sally      700 Elm           Madison     WI   53705
memo
   25 Calhoon      Carrie     809 Maple         Superior    WI   54880
memo

.
Command ||C:\lessons\MAILING     ||Rec EOF/25     ||File ||
```

When the screen stops scrolling, it will look like Figure 11. The records are arranged alphabetically by state abbreviation.

Practice

1. Activate the LAST_NAME tag and list the records of MAILING.DBF in alphabetical order by last name:

   Type **`set order to tag last_name`**
   Press **Enter**
   Type **`list`**
   Press **Enter**

2. You can create an index based on two or more fields. Suppose you want to index a file by state and then by city within each state. Change the existing STATE tag:

   Type **`index on state + city tag state`**
   Press **Enter**
   Press **Enter**

   To see the result, execute these commands:

   Type **`set order to tag state`**
   Press **Enter**
   Type **`list for state = "IL"`**
   Press **Enter**

   Note that the four records from Illinois are now arranged alphabetically by city name.

Lesson 6: Finding Data

Several dot prompt commands are available to help you find specific records within a data base file.

Step 1: Search with the LOCATE Command

The LOCATE command finds records based on the criteria you specify. You have already used this command in Lesson 4 to find Candy Eaton's record. Try it again, but this time use a more specific condition to find Brian Prorok's record:

Type **locate for last_name = "Prorok" .and. first_name = "Brian"**
Press **Enter**
Type **display**
Press **Enter**

The LOCATE command always begins its search at the top of the file, regardless of the current record pointer position. Note that the LOCATE command does not display the record; it merely advances the record pointer.

Step 2: Search for Several Records with LOCATE

The LOCATE command can be used to find several records that meet specified criteria. Suppose you want to see the records of all customers whose last names begin with the letter *W*. Execute these commands:

Type **locate for last_name >= "W"**
Press **Enter**
Type **display**
Press **Enter**

To continue searching for other records that begin with *W*, execute the CONTINUE command:

Type **continue**
Press **Enter**
Type **display**
Press **Enter**
Type **continue**
Press **Enter**
Type **display**
Press **Enter**
Type **continue**
Press **Enter**

When no more records are found, dBASE IV will display the message

```
End of LOCATE scope
```

Step 3: Use the SEEK Command

If a file is indexed and you want to search for records on the basis of the contents of a tag field, the SEEK and FIND commands are faster than the LOCATE command. Activate the LAST_NAME index tag:

Type **set order to tag last_name**
Press **Enter**

Suppose you want to see Dan Mitchell's record. Execute a SEEK command followed by a DISPLAY command:

Type **seek "Mitchell"**
Press **Enter**
Type **display**
Press **Enter**

The SEEK command advances the record pointer to the record that contains "Mitchell" in the field on which the file has been indexed. SEEK is much faster than LOCATE, especially in large data base files, because it uses an index.

Step 4: Use the FIND Command

The SEEK command can be followed by an expression of the same data type as the index field. The FIND command works even faster than the SEEK command because you can specify a character string not enclosed in quotes. For example, execute this command to see Susan Young's record:

Type **find Young**
Press **Enter**
Type **display**
Press **Enter**

Step 5: Set a Filter Condition

Many dBASE IV commands let you specify the word "FOR" followed by a condition that specifies the records you want to manipulate. Essentially, the FOR clause acts as a filter to select only certain records. The SET FILTER command allows you to specify a condition that selects records to be acted on by all subsequent commands. For example, suppose you want to work with only the records of customers from Illinois. Execute the following commands:

Type **set filter to state = "IL"**
Press **Enter**
Type **go top**
Press **Enter**

The GO command is necessary because you must move the record pointer after issuing a SET FILTER command for the filter to take effect. Any command you enter now will affect only those records with "IL" in the STATE field. For example, try this command:

Type **display all**
Press **Enter**

Your screen should look like Figure 12.

Step 6: Set Fields

The SET FILTER command limits the action of subsequent commands to a specified set of records. The SET FIELDS command can be used to limit the action of subsequent commands to a specified set of fields. Suppose you are interested only in the LAST_NAME, FIRST_NAME, and CITY fields. Execute this command to set the fields you want to use:

Type **set fields to last_name, first_name, city**
Press **Enter**

Now, list all of the records:

Type **list**
Press **Enter**

Figure 13 shows the result. The SET FILTER command limits the records to only those from Illinois, and the SET FIELDS command limits the fields to LAST_NAME, FIRST_NAME, and CITY.

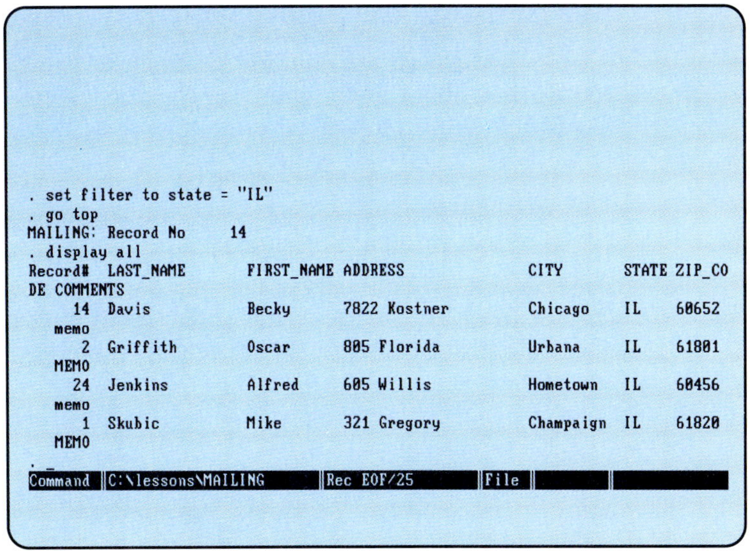

Figure 12 The SET FILTER Command

Step 7: Turn Off Filter and Fields

You can turn off a previous SET FILTER or SET FIELDS command by entering the command again without specifying a condition or list of fields. Execute these commands to include all records and fields in subsequent actions:

Type **set filter to**
Press **Enter**
Type **set fields to**
Press **Enter**

Execute the LIST command to confirm that all records and fields are now available:

Type **list**
Press **Enter**

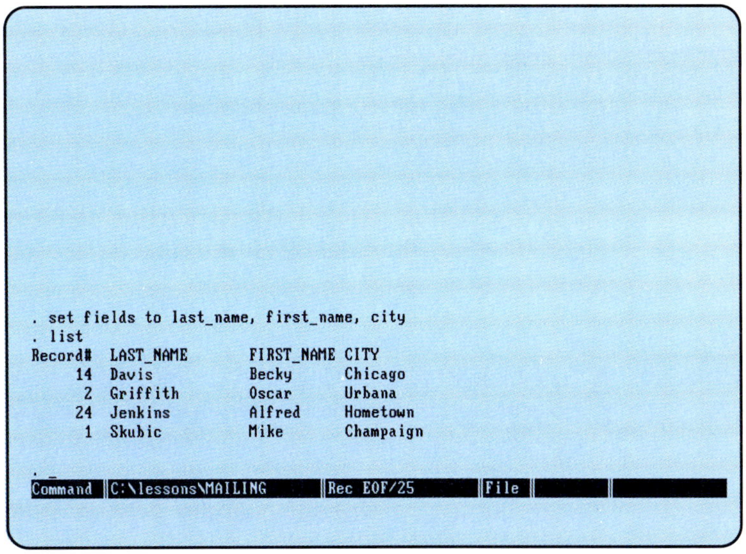

Figure 13 The SET FIELDS Command

Step 8: Create or Modify Query Files

For more advanced data-finding capabilities, you can use view queries, which you learned about in the previous chapter. To create a new query file named EXAMPLE.QBE from the dot prompt, execute the CREATE QUERY command:

Type **`create query example`**
Press **Enter**

The Query Design screen will appear. Here you can specify conditions in the file skeleton and specify fields in the view skeleton just as you did in the previous chapter from the Queries panel of the Control Center. Let's not create a new query file. Exit the Query Design screen and return to the dot prompt:

Press **Alt-E**
Type **a**
Type **y**

You can also modify an existing query file from the dot prompt. Use the DIR command to list the view query files in your current directory:

Type **`dir *.qbe`**
Press **Enter**

Tell dBASE IV that you want to modify the file WHO_OWES.QBE:

Type **`modify query who_owes`**
Press **Enter**

The program will display the Query Design screen containing the view query WHO_OWES. You could now modify the design. Let's leave it alone and return to the dot prompt:

Press **Alt-E**
Type **a**
Type **y**

Step 9: Use an Existing Query File

Once a view query has been designed, you can execute the SET VIEW command from the dot prompt to use it. Suppose you want to see the WHO_OWES view, which presents data from the ACCOUNT.DBF and MAILING.DBF files. Execute these commands:

Type **`set view to who_owes`**
Press **Enter**
Type **`list`**
Press **Enter**

Figure 14 shows the result. Only information from customers who have a balance greater than zero will be presented.

Practice

1. The CLEAR ALL or CLOSE ALL command can be used to close all open files. Execute either command, then open ACCOUNT.DBF. Set a filter condition to specify only those records with nonzero balances, and list all the records on the screen.
2. Tell dBASE IV to display only the LAST_NAME and BALANCE fields, and list the records again.

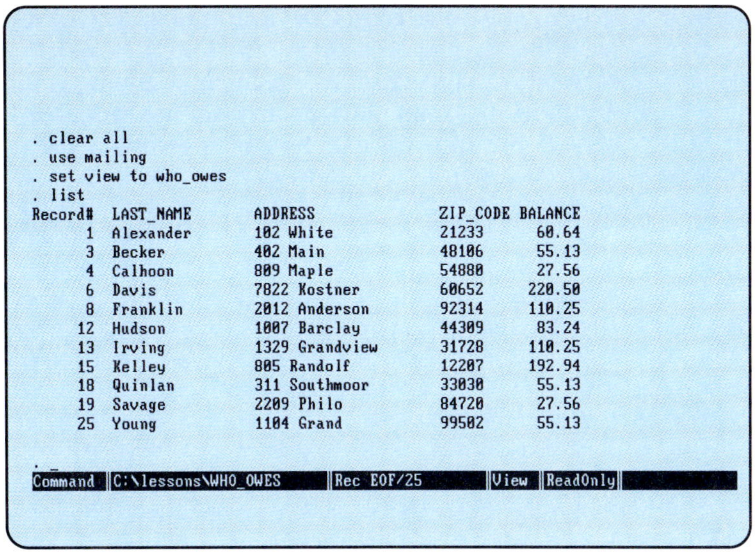

Figure 14 The SET VIEW Command

3. Turn off the SET FILTER and SET FIELDS commands, and list the records again. Execute the CLEAR ALL command to close all open files.

Lesson 7: Relating Files

The dBASE IV program is a relational data base manager that can access and share information from several files at once. This ability to **relate** files allows you to create large, efficient, and flexible data base systems. In the previous chapter you learned how to link two files in a view query and display information from both. This lesson explores how you can relate multiple files from the dot prompt.

Step 1: Use Multiple Work Areas

A dBASE IV **work area** is a place in memory that holds an open data base file. Ten work areas are available. They are referred to by the numbers 1 to 10, by the letters A through J, or by the name of the file currently open in the work area. A number, letter, or name that refers to a work area or data base file is called an **alias** in dBASE IV. Open the MAILING data base file:

Type **`use mailing`**
Press **Enter**

Unless you specify otherwise, a file opened with the USE command will be placed into work area 1. Only one data base file can be open at a time in any work area. In this case, the first work area can be referred to by any of these aliases: 1, A, or MAILING. The ALIAS function can be used to find out the default alias of the current work area. For example, execute this command:

Type **`? alias()`**
Press **Enter**

The program will tell you that MAILING is the alias of the current work area. You will learn more about dBASE IV functions in a subsequent lesson. Basically, a **function** is a predefined expression that returns a value. Functions must be followed by open and close parentheses. The question mark command (?) displays the value of an expression.

At this point, the MAILING data base file is loaded into work area 1. The dBASE IV program always starts out in work area 1. Execute this command to open the ACCOUNT data base file in work area 2:

Type **use account in 2**
Press **Enter**

The program opens the file ACCOUNT.DBF in work area 2, but does not actually switch to that work area. Both MAILING and ACCOUNT are now open in different work areas. The SELECT command is used to change to a different work area. For example, try these commands:

Type **select 2**
Press **Enter**
Type **? alias()**
Press **Enter**

Any command you now execute refers to work area 2. Display the structure of the current file:

Type **display structure**
Press **Enter**

Your screen should look like Figure 15. Now change back to the work area that contains the MAILING data base file:

Type **select mailing**
Press **Enter**

The program will switch to work area 1, which can also be referred to by its aliases, A and MAILING.

Figure 15 MAILING in Work Area 1 and ACCOUNT in Work Area 2

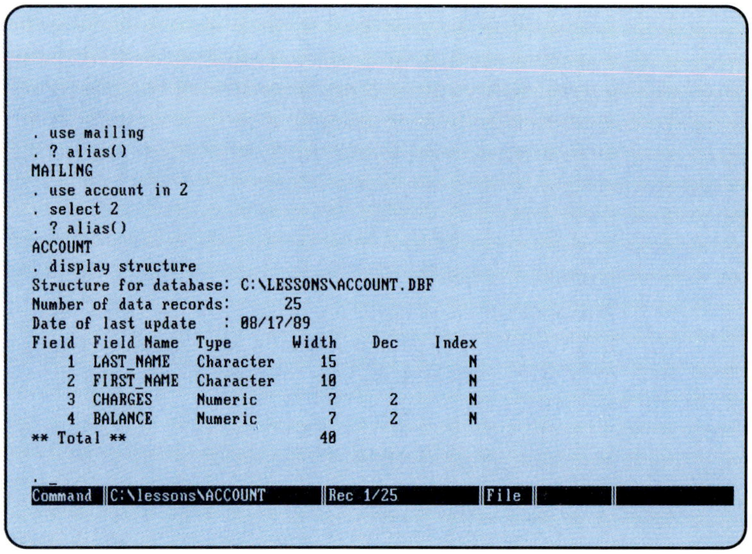

Step 2: Index the Files

Before you can relate files, the files must have a field in common and they should be indexed on that field. The MAILING data base file is already indexed by LAST_NAME. Follow these directions to index the ACCOUNT file by LAST_NAME and activate the index tags in both files:

Type **set order to tag last_name**
Press **Enter**
Type **select account**
Press **Enter**
Type **index on last_name tag last_name**
Press **Enter**
Type **set order to tag last_name**
Press **Enter**
Type **select mailing**
Press **Enter**

Step 3: Execute the SET RELATION Command

After you have opened and indexed multiple files, you can execute the SET RELATION command to relate them. Execute this command:

Type **set relation to last_name into account**
Press **Enter**

Two files in a relation are often called parent and child files. The **parent file** is the more general file that looks up the information. The **child file** is the more specific file that contains the information. In this case, MAILING.DBF is the parent, and ACCOUNT.DBF is the child. More complex data bases can have multiple child relations, in which a parent file may have active links with several child files. Chains of relations are also possible. For example, a parent file can look up information in a child file, which in turn is a parent file that looks up information in another child file.

Step 4: List Fields from Multiple Files

Now that the two files are related, you can access data from both of them. You must, however, precede field names from the related file with the alias of that file and a pointer symbol (->). The pointer symbol is made up of a dash (-) and a greater than sign (>). Suppose you want to list the last names, cities, and balances of the customers. Execute this command:

Type **list last_name, city, account->balance**
Press **Enter**

The dBASE IV program will list the contents of LAST_NAME and CITY from MAILING, along with the matching contents of the BALANCE field from ACCOUNT (see Figure 16).

Step 5: Save the Relation Conditions

You can store the relationship you have established in a special view file with the CREATE VIEW FROM ENVIRONMENT command.

Type **create view balances from environment**
Press **Enter**

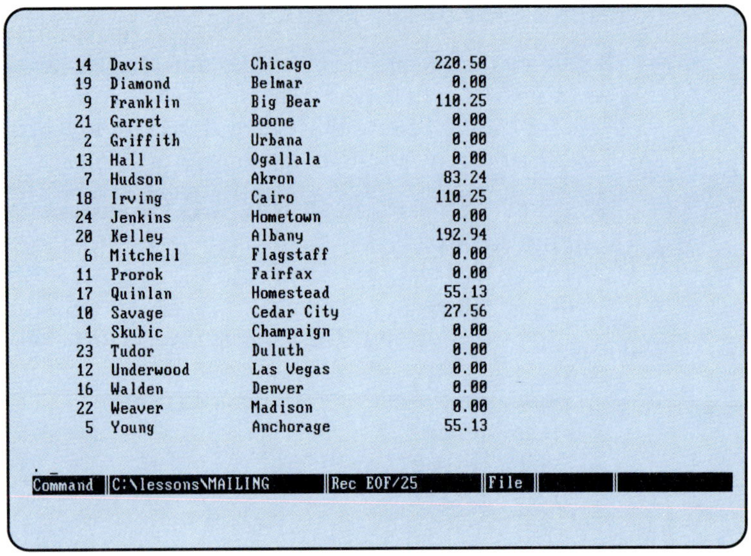

```
14 Davis       Chicago     220.50
19 Diamond     Belmar        0.00
 9 Franklin    Big Bear    110.25
21 Garret      Boone         0.00
 2 Griffith    Urbana        0.00
13 Hall        Ogallala      0.00
 7 Hudson      Akron        83.24
18 Irving      Cairo       110.25
24 Jenkins     Hometown      0.00
20 Kelley      Albany      192.94
 6 Mitchell    Flagstaff     0.00
11 Prorok      Fairfax       0.00
17 Quinlan     Homestead    55.13
10 Savage      Cedar City   27.56
 1 Skubic      Champaign     0.00
23 Tudor       Duluth        0.00
12 Underwood   Las Vegas     0.00
16 Walden      Denver        0.00
22 Weaver      Madison       0.00
 5 Young       Anchorage    55.13

Command ║C:\lessons\MAILING ║Rec EOF/25 ║File ║
```

Figure 16 Fields Listed from MAILING and ACCOUNT

The program will create a file named BALANCES.VUE that remembers all currently open files, relations, filters, and field lists. To use the view file sometime later, you would execute this command:

```
SET VIEW TO BALANCES
```

Practice

1. List the contents of the LAST_NAME and STATE fields from MAILING, and the CHARGES field from ACCOUNT.
2. Execute the CLEAR ALL command to close all files. Tell dBASE IV that you want to use the BALANCES.VUE view file. Then list the last names, ZIP codes, and balances of all the customers with a balance greater than zero. Note that you must specify the alias ACCOUNT before both instances of the field name BALANCE. When you are finished, execute the CLEAR ALL command to close all files.

Lesson 8: Using Other dBASE IV Commands

The dBASE IV language includes more than 145 different commands, not including the 77 variations of the SET command. The *dBASE IV Language Reference* manual that explains these commands is several hundred pages long. Obviously, we cannot cover every dBASE IV command here. This lesson, however, briefly illustrates a few additional dBASE IV commands. See the Command Summaries appendix at the end of this book for a comprehensive list of dBASE IV commands.

Step 1: Use the ? Command

The ? command displays the value of one or more expressions. It is often used to display the result of a function. You have already seen how ? is used with the ALIAS function. Follow these directions to see other examples of the use of the ? command:

Type **? date()**
Press **Enter**

Type **? time()**
Press **Enter**

Step 2: Use the ACCEPT Command

The ACCEPT command prompts a user for a keyboard entry and stores the input in a character memory variable. A **memory variable** is a place in RAM that temporarily holds a data value. It is given a name and can contain a value used to perform a calculation, comparison, or other operation. Unlike the data values stored in the record fields of a data base file, the data values stored in memory variables are lost when you quit dBASE IV. The ACCEPT command, which reads a character value and assigns it to a memory variable, is used primarily in dBASE IV programs. Execute the following command to have dBASE IV prompt the user for his or her name and assign this name to a memory variable named M_NAME:

Type **accept "Enter your name: " to m_name**
Press **Enter**

The program will prompt you to enter your name. Type your name and press the Enter key. Now, use the ? command to display the value stored in M_NAME:

Type **? m_name**
Press **Enter**

Step 3: Use the CREATE Command

The CREATE command is used to design a new data base file from the dot prompt. It activates the Data Base Design screen, in which you enter the field names, types, and widths of your records. Suppose you want to create a new data base file named CUSTOMER. Execute this command:

Type **create customer**
Press **Enter**

Follow these directions to specify the fields and save the structure:

Type **last_name**
Press **Enter** (2 times)
Type **15**
Press **Enter** (2 times)
Type **first_name**
Press **Enter**
Type **10**
Press **Enter** (2 times)
Type **address**
Press **Enter** (2 times)
Type **20**
Press **Enter** (2 times)
Type **city**
Press **Enter** (2 times)
Type **10**
Press **Enter** (2 times)
Type **state**
Press **Enter** (2 times)
Type **2**

Press **Enter** (2 times)
Type **zip**
Press **Enter** (2 times)
Type **5**
Press **Enter**
Press **Alt-E**
Type **s**
Press **Enter**

A new, but still empty data base file named CUSTOMER.DBF will be created.

Step 4: Use the APPEND FROM Command

The APPEND FROM command is used to copy records from an existing file, which does not have to be a dBASE IV file, to the current data base file. It is often used to import data from other programs, such as previous versions of dBASE and Lotus 1-2-3. Let's use the APPEND FROM command to copy the records from MAILING.DBF into the new CUSTOMER file:

Type **append from mailing**
Press **Enter**

The records from MAILING.DBF will be copied to CUSTOMER.DBF. Confirm this by executing the LIST command:

Type **list**
Press **Enter**

Step 5: Use the AVERAGE Command

The AVERAGE command computes the arithmetic mean of the numbers stored in the specified fields and records. Suppose you want to see the average outstanding balance of customers who have a balance greater than zero. Execute these commands:

Type **use account**
Press **Enter**
Type **average balance for balance > 0**
Press **Enter**

The result should be 90.76, as shown in Figure 17.

Step 6: Use the COPY Command

The COPY command creates a new file by duplicating all or part of the current data base file. It is often used to prepare data for use in programs other than dBASE IV. Suppose you want to create a Lotus 1-2-3 spreadsheet file from the current data base file. Execute this command:

Type **copy to account type wks**
Press **Enter**

The program will create a Lotus 1-2-3 file named ACCOUNT.WKS, with records converted to worksheet rows and fields converted to worksheet columns. The field names are written as column headers in the new file.

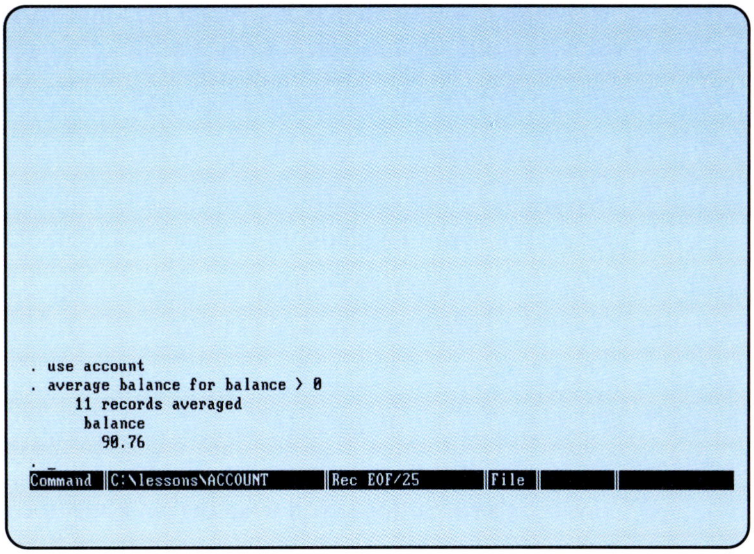

Figure 17 The AVERAGE Command

Step 7: Use the COUNT Command

The COUNT command adds up the number of records in the current file that match the specified conditions. Suppose you want to know how many customers have balances greater than zero. Execute this command:

Type **count for balance > 0**
Press **Enter**

The program should count 11 records.

Step 8: Use the DO Command

The DO command executes a dBASE program. For example, in the previous chapter you created a short dBASE program named BROWSE.PRG that simply executes the BROWSE command. Execute this program from the dot prompt:

Type **do browse**
Press **Enter**

The BROWSE.PRG program will be compiled and executed. When it is finished, you should see the Browse screen. Return to the dot prompt:

Press **Escape**

Step 9: Use the ERASE Command

The ERASE or DELETE FILE command removes a file from the disk. It is similar to the DOS ERASE or DEL command. Suppose you want to delete the file ACCOUNT.WKS. Execute this command:

Type **erase account.wks**
Press **Enter**

The file will be deleted from the disk immediately, with no confirmation prompt, so you should use the ERASE command with caution.

dBASE IV commands that accept a file name can usually be entered with a ? in place of the file name to display a menu of file names from which to choose. For example, execute this command:

Type **erase ?**
Press **Enter**

The program will present a menu of all the files in the current directory (see Figure 18). If you highlight a file name and press the Enter key, that file will be deleted. Return to the dot prompt without erasing another file:

Press **Escape**

Step 10: Use the INSERT Command

The APPEND command adds a new record to the end of the current data base file. The INSERT command adds a new record to the data base file just after the current record. Suppose you want to add a new record with a record number of 10 to the current file. Move the record pointer to record 9 and execute the INSERT command:

Type **go 9**
Press **Enter**
Type **insert**
Press **Enter**

A blank data entry form will appear in which you can enter the data for the new record number 10. Let's not change the data base file. Abandon the INSERT command:

Press **Escape**

Step 11: Use the STORE Command

The STORE command creates one or more memory variables and initializes their contents. Suppose you want to create a memory variable named M_TOTAL and initially store the value 0 in it. Execute this command:

Type **store 0 to m_total**
Press **Enter**

Another way to achieve the same result is to do this:

Type **m_total = 0**
Press **Enter**

You can see the contents of a memory variable by using the ? command.

Type **? m_total**
Press **Enter**

Step 12: Use the SUM Command

The SUM command adds up the contents of the specified fields and records. Suppose you want to see the sum of all charges. Execute this command:

Type **sum charges**
Press **Enter**

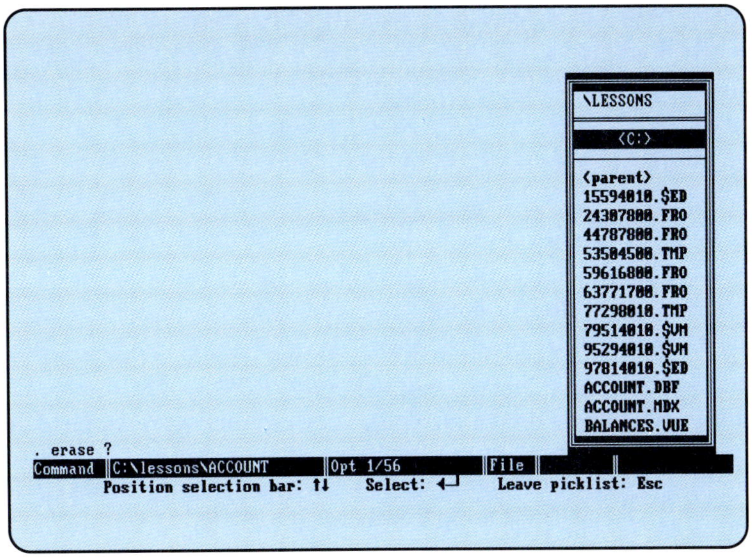

Figure 18 A Menu of File Names

You can use the SUM command to assign a value to a memory variable too. Execute this command to compute the sum and store it in the memory variable M_TOTAL:

Type **`sum charges to m_total`**
Press **Enter**

Now, display the value of M_TOTAL:

Type **`? m_total`**
Press **Enter**

Practice

1. Compute the average of the CHARGES field in the ACCOUNT data base file and store the result in a memory variable named M_AVG.
2. Count the number of records in ACCOUNT.DBF with CHARGES greater than $100.

Lesson 9: Using dBASE IV Functions

A **function** is a predefined expression that returns a data value of a specific type. Functions are often used as parts of other expressions to perform calculations and manipulate text strings. Many dBASE IV functions are similar to functions found in spreadsheet packages, such as Lotus 1-2-3, and programming languages, such as BASIC and Pascal. The dBASE IV package has more than 125 built-in functions. Obviously, we cannot cover them all. This lesson presents only a few examples of dBASE IV functions. See the Command Summaries appendix at the end of this book for a more comprehensive list of dBASE IV functions.

Step 1: Use the ALIAS Function

The ALIAS function returns the alias name of a specified work area. Execute the following commands:

Type **clear all**
Press **Enter**
Type **use account**
Press **Enter**
Type **? alias()**
Press **Enter**

The ALIAS function returns the name ACCOUNT and the ? command presents the name on the screen. Note that the function name is followed by parentheses. Some functions require one or more expressions to be supplied within the parentheses. Other functions, such as ALIAS, do not require any expressions. All function names must be followed by parentheses, even if they require no expressions and the parentheses are empty.

Step 2: Use the DATE Function

The DATE function returns the current date. Execute this command:

Type **? date()**
Press **Enter**

The program will present the current date in the form mm/dd/yy.

Step 3: Use the DISKSPACE Function

The DISKSPACE function returns a number that represents the number of bytes available on the default disk drive. Execute this command:

Type **? diskspace()**
Press **Enter**

The number returned is the amount of free space on the disk in bytes.

Step 4: Use the EOF Function

The EOF function returns a logical value (.T. for TRUE or .F. for FALSE) if the record pointer is past the last record in the file. Execute these commands:

Type **go bottom**
Press **Enter**
Type **? eof()**
Press **Enter**
Type **skip**
Press **Enter**
Type **? eof()**
Press **Enter**

The GO BOTTOM command moves the record pointer to the last record in the file, so the result of EOF() is .F. or FALSE. The SKIP command advances the record pointer one position, past the last record in the file. Then the result of EOF() is .T. or TRUE.

Step 5: Use the INT Function

The INT function truncates any numeric expression to create an integer value. For example, execute this command:

Type **i_value = 10 + int(25.45)**
Press **Enter**
Type **? i_value**
Press **Enter**

The first command is an example of using a function in an expression. The 25.45 is truncated to produce 25, which is added to the 10. The result displayed by the ? command is 35.

Step 6: Use the TRIM and LEN Functions

The dBASE IV language includes many functions that work with strings of characters. For example, the TRIM function removes the trailing blanks from a character string, and the LEN function returns the number of characters in a string. These two functions are often used together. Suppose you want to determine the length of the name in the LAST_NAME field of the first record in the current data base file. Execute these commands:

Type **go 1**
Press **Enter**
Type **? len(trim(last_name))**
Press **Enter**
Type **display**
Press **Enter**

The last name in the first record is Alexander, so the value returned by the LEN function is 9.

Step 7: Use the RECCOUNT, RECNO, and RECSIZE Functions

The RECCOUNT function returns the number of records in the current data base file. The RECNO function returns the record number of the current record. The RECSIZE function returns the number of bytes occupied by a record in the current data base file. Try these functions:

Type **? reccount()**
Press **Enter**
Type **? recno()**
Press **Enter**
Type **? recsize()**
Press **Enter**

Step 8: Use the ROUND Function

The ROUND function rounds a number to a specified number of decimal places. For example, try this command:

Type **? round(162.34789,2)**
Press **Enter**

The number after the comma in the parentheses is the number of decimal places, so the result is 162.35. Your screen should look like Figure 19.

Figure 19 dBASE IV Functions

```
. ? eof()
.T.
. i_value = 10 + int(25.45)
        35
. ? i_value
        35
. go 1
ACCOUNT: Record No       1
. ? len(trim(last_name))
         9
. display
Record#  LAST_NAME         FIRST_NAME CHARGES BALANCE
      1  Alexander         Barbara     125.00   60.64
. ? reccount()
        25
. ? recno()
         1
. ? recsize()
        40
. ? round(162.34789,2)
      162.35
. _
Command ‖C:\lessons\ACCOUNT      ‖Rec 1/25        ‖File ‖
```

Practice

1. The SQRT function returns the square root of the specified number. Use this function to display the square root of 144.
2. The MEMORY function returns the amount of unused memory in kilobytes (1024-byte units). Use this function to display the amount of RAM you have free.
3. Use the TIME function to display the current time.
4. Use the VERSION function to display the dBASE version you are running.

Lesson 10: Creating a dBASE IV Program

A dBASE IV program is a sequence of commands stored in a text file that can be compiled and executed. It is similar to a DOS batch file or a program in a standard programming language, such as BASIC or Pascal. When you use the dot prompt, you enter a command, and it is executed immediately. When you create a dBASE program, you enter all the commands needed to perform some task into a text file. The commands are not actually executed by dBASE IV until you run the program later. The commands, functions, and expressions of dBASE IV make up a language as sophisticated as a standard programming language such as BASIC or Pascal. Obviously, we cannot cover all aspects of dBASE IV programming here. This lesson, however, will show you how to create a simple dBASE IV program.

Step 1: Design the Program

Suppose you want to create a program that will ask the user for a state abbreviation and then list on the screen the full names and addresses of all customers from that state in the MAILING data base file. The first step would be to design the program by deciding which dBASE IV commands are needed to complete this task. You would probably have to study dBASE commands further to design such a program yourself. In this lesson the program has been designed for you.

Step 2: Activate the Editor

A dBASE IV program can be entered into a text file with the word-wrap editor. Close all files and start up the editor to create a program file named STATE.PRG:

Type **`clear all`**
Press **Enter**
Type **`modify command state`**
Press **Enter**

The word-wrap editor screen will appear. Notice that the status bar indicates that you are editing a program named STATE.

Step 3: Enter the Program

Figure 20 shows the completed program. Type your program from the figure. When you are finished, check the program carefully against Figure 20 and correct any mistakes you made.

The program works as follows. The CLEAR command clears the screen. SET TALK OFF suppresses the messages that dBASE IV normally displays at the bottom of the screen. The SET PATH command establishes the internal path to the MAILING data base file. The next command creates a memory variable named M_STATE and stores an empty string in it. The USE command opens MAILING.DBF, and the ORDER clause activates the LAST_NAME index. The ACCEPT command prompts the user for input and stores the entry in the memory variable M_STATE. The UPPER function in the next line converts the entry to uppercase letters. The DO WHILE command repeats the sequence of instructions up to the ENDDO statement as long as the length of the entry in M_STATE is greater than zero. The SCAN command processes the records in the data base file, selecting only those in which the contents of the STATE field is equal to the contents of M_STATE. The ? commands display the contents of the specified fields for each selected record. ENDSCAN indicates the end of the sequence of commands to be performed for each selected record. The second ACCEPT command and

Figure 20 The Completed STATE Program

```
Layout   Words   Go To   Print   Exit                                3:44:25 pm
clear
set talk off
set path to \lessons
m_state = ""
use mailing order last_name
accept "Enter two-letter state abbreviation: " to m_state
m_state = upper(m_state)
do while len(m_state) > 0
   scan for state = m_state
      ?
      ? first_name, last_name
      ? address
      ? city, state, zip_code
   endscan
   ?
   accept "Enter two-letter state abbreviation: " to m_state
   m_state = upper(m_state)
enddo
clear all
set talk on
Program  C:\lessons\STATE        Line:20 Col:12                            Ins
```

M_STATE assignment statement repeat the request for user input and convert the state abbreviation to uppercase letters. The CLEAR ALL command closes all files, and the SET TALK ON command turns on dBASE IV messages again.

In simpler terms, the program will ask the user for a state abbreviation and then present the names and addresses of all customers from that state. It will repeat this process until the user presses the Enter key without entering a state abbreviation.

Step 4: Exit the Editor and Save the Program

To save your work, activate the Exit menu and select Save Changes and Exit:

Press **Alt-E**
Type **s**

The dot prompt will again appear on your screen.

Step 5: Run the Program

Execute the DO command to compile and run your dBASE IV program:

Type **do state**
Press **Enter**

Enter a state abbreviation:

Type **il**
Press **Enter**

Your screen should look like Figure 21. Note that it does not matter if you use lowercase, uppercase, or a combination of both for the state abbreviation. Enter a different state abbreviation:

Type **Wi**
Press **Enter**

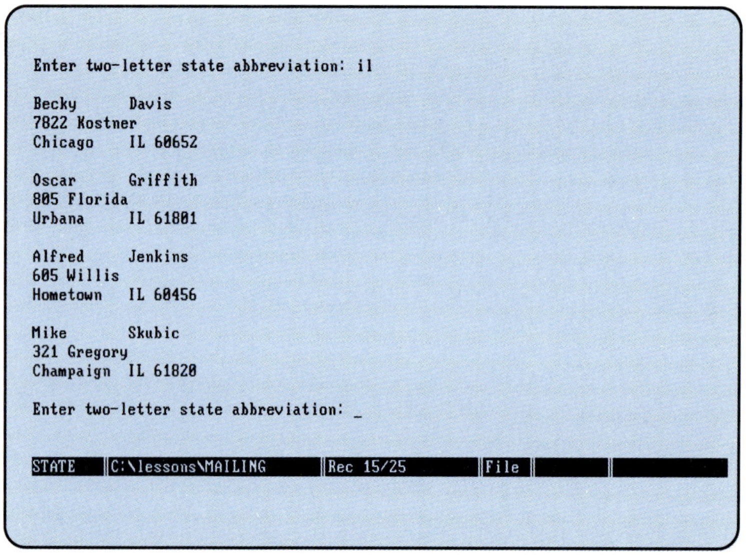

***Figure 21** Running the STATE Program*

You can try as many states as you like. When you are finished, simply press the Enter key without typing a state abbreviation:

Press **Enter**

The STATE program will terminate and return to the dot prompt.

Practice

Execute the STATE program again. Enter an invalid state abbreviation, such as XX. What happens? Try a state for which no records have been entered in MAILING.DBF, such as Massachusetts (MA). Return to the dot prompt when you are finished.

Lesson 11: Using the Applications Generator

The Applications Generator is a sophisticated tool that lets you create custom menu-driven data base systems without programming. Basically, you tell the Applications Generator what you want dBASE IV to do and it automatically creates the dBASE IV program that will perform those tasks. You can then run the new application as is or modify it by adding or changing dBASE commands. The Applications Generator is most often used to set up specialized menus that simplify data base management tasks for a particular individual, department, company, or organization. For example, let's use the Applications Generator to set up a simple mailing list management system for Paddle and Portage Canoe Outfitters.

Step 1: Return to the Control Center

The Applications Generator can be activated from either the dot prompt or the Control Center. Close all files and return to the Control Center:

Type **clear all**
Press **Enter**
Type **assist**
Press **Enter**

Step 2: Activate the Applications Generator

Move the highlight bar to the Applications panel, select the <create> option, and select the Applications Generator option:

Press **Right Arrow** (5 times)
Press **Enter**
Type **a**

The program will display the Application Definition screen shown in Figure 22.

You can also activate the Applications Generator from the dot prompt by entering the command CREATE APPLICATION followed by the name of the new application file.

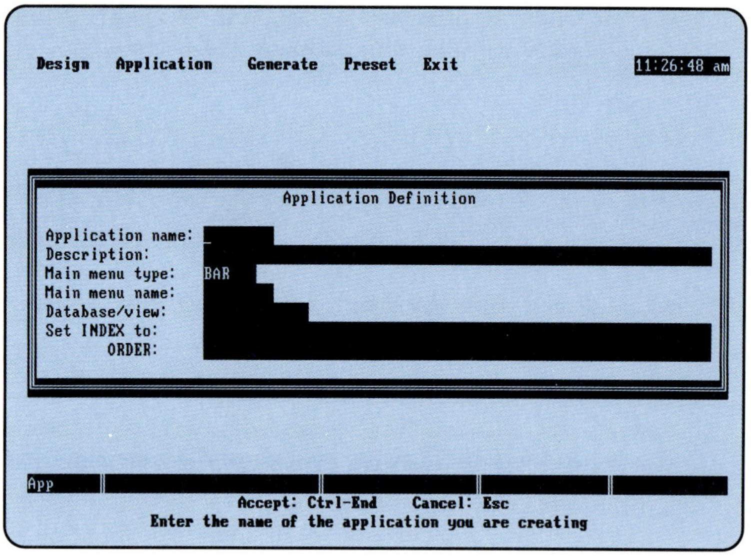

Figure 22 The Application Definition Screen

Step 3: Complete the Applications Definition Screen

Follow these directions to complete the Applications Definition screen:

Type **`mailing`**
Press **Enter**
Type **`Paddle and Portage Mailing List System`**
Press **Enter**
Press **Space Bar**
Press **Enter**
Type **`options`**
Press **Enter**
Type **`mailing`**
Press **Enter**
Type **`mailing.mdx`**
Press **Enter**
Type **`last_name`**
Press **Enter**
Press **Ctrl-End**

The program will present the Applications Generator screen shown in Figure 23.

Step 4: Create a Quick Application

The Applications Generator has many features that let you create specialized menu-driven data base systems. We cannot cover all of its options. We can, however, demonstrate an easy way to create an application that will allow users to perform the most common data base operations. Activate the Application menu and select the Generate Quick Application option:

Press **Alt-A**
Type **g**

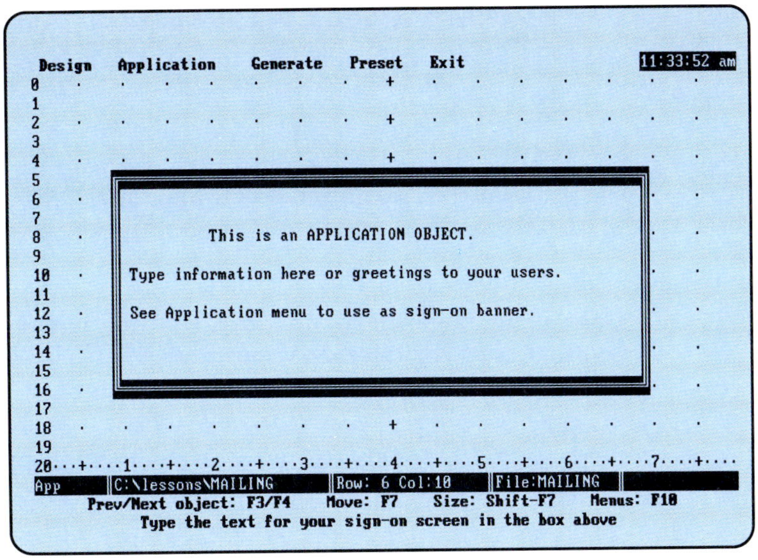

Figure 23 The Applications Generator Screen

The program will display the Quick Application screen, shown in Figure 24. Specify MAILING as the Label Format File, then return to the Applications Generator screen:

Press **Tab** (3 times)
Type **mailing**
Press **Enter**
Press **Ctrl-End**
Type **y**

A few minutes will pass as the Applications Generator creates the dBASE program file. When it is finished, it will ask you to press any key.

Press **Enter**

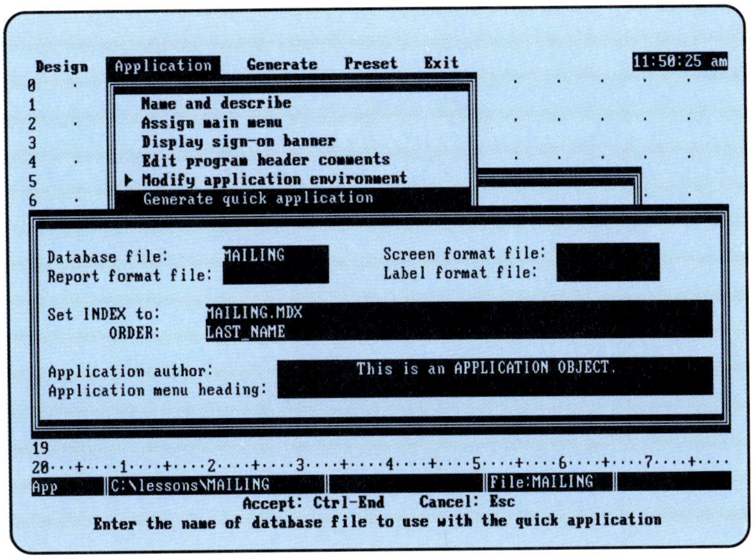

Figure 24 The Quick Application Screen

Step 5: Return to the Control Center

Activate the Exit menu and select the Save All Changes and Exit option:

Press **Alt-E**
Type **s**

The program will return to the Control Center.

Step 6: Use the Application

A new application named MAILING will appear in the Applications panel of the Control Center. Tell dBASE IV that you want to run this application:

Highlight **MAILING**
Press **Enter**
Type **r**
Type **y**

The first time you try to run a new application, dBASE IV will compile it, which can take a few minutes. dBASE IV will then load and run the application. Your screen should look like Figure 25. For a dBASE IV novice, this application is easier to use than the Control Center or the dot prompt for managing the Paddle and Portage Canoe Outfitters mailing list data base. For example, select the Browse Information option:

Type **b**

The Browse screen will appear. Press Escape or select the Exit option from the Exit menu to return to the MAILING application:

Press **Escape**

Now try the Mailing Labels option:

Type **m**

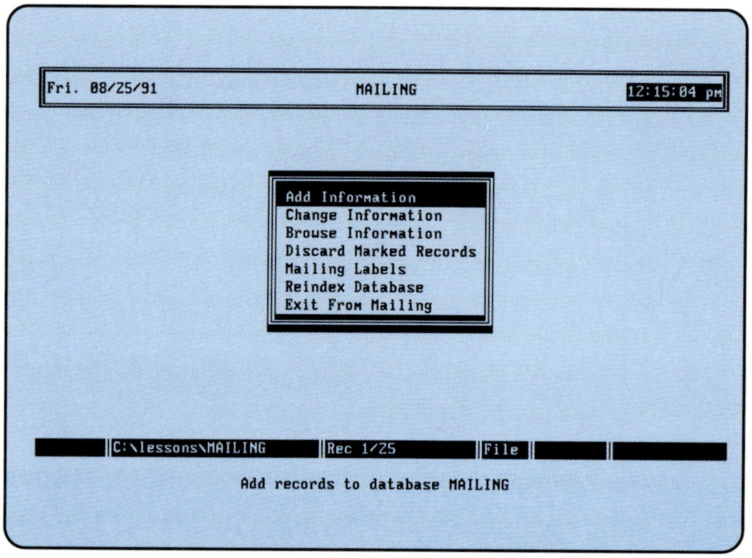

Figure 25 The MAILING Application Menu

The MAILING application will list the fields and allow you to change the record pointer position. Press the Escape key to generate mailing labels for all the records.

Press **Escape**

A new menu will pop up that lets you select where to send the labels. Select the Screen option:

Type **s**

The labels will be "printed" on your screen. You could actually print them on paper by choosing the Printer option instead of the Screen option. Press any key to return to the MAILING application:

Press **Enter**

Step 7: Return to the Control Center

When you are finished using the MAILING application, return to the Control Center by selecting the Exit From Mailing option:

Type **e**

Practice

1. Switch to the dot prompt and run the MAILING application. *Hint:* use the DO command followed by the name of the application.
2. Try every option in the MAILING menu except Mailing Labels. Select the last option to return to the dot prompt, and then switch to the Control Center.

Lesson 12: Using SQL Commands

SQL stands for Structured Query Language. It is a standardized language for managing relational data bases, developed from research conducted at IBM in the 1970s. SQL has since been adopted by many companies as the standard language for mainframe and minicomputer data base systems. In the mid- to late 1980s, several publishers of microcomputer data base software also began to support SQL so that their customers could better standardize data base applications across mainframe, minicomputer, and microcomputer systems. The dBASE IV package allows you to use SQL commands instead of or in addition to dBASE commands. Although SQL consists of fewer than thirty commands, it is an advanced topic. We cannot thoroughly cover SQL data base management here. Nevertheless, we can briefly illustrate SQL by using its commands to create a simple data base.

Step 1: Switch to the Dot Prompt

If you are not already at the dot prompt, activate the Exit menu from the Control Center and select Exit to Dot Prompt:

Press **Alt-E**
Type **e**

Step 2: Turn On Interactive SQL Mode

Like the dBASE language, SQL can be used interactively from a prompt, or its commands can be entered into a file to be run as a program. The easiest and quickest way to learn SQL is to start by executing commands interactively. You must turn on the SQL mode, however, before you can enter SQL commands in dBASE IV. This is done with the SET SQL ON command.

Type **set sql on**
Press **Enter**

The status bar will say SQL at the left side, and the dot prompt will change to the SQL prompt, which looks like this:

```
SQL.
```

Step 3: Create a New Data Base

As an example, let's create a simple data base for Paddle and Portage Canoe Outfitters that keeps track of their canoes. In SQL, the CREATE DATABASE command creates a new data base. Create a new data base named CANOES:

Type **create database canoes;**
Press **Enter**

Note that each SQL command must end with a semicolon. The program will respond

```
Database CANOES created
```

Step 4: Activate a Data Base

You must activate a data base before you can issue any SQL commands to define or access data. The START DATABASE command activates an existing data base.

Type **start database canoes;**
Press **Enter**

Step 5: Create a New Table

The **table** is the basic component of an SQL data base. A table consists of rows and columns. A **row** is like a dBASE record and a **column** is like a field. Each intersection of a row and a column contains a data value. Our example data base will have only one table. Each row will refer to an individual canoe. Three columns will store the data values for each canoe: a unique ID number, the date purchased, and the price paid. The CREATE TABLE command is used to define a new table. It lists the table name and each column name and data type. Execute this command:

Type **create table bought (id char(3), bought date, paid numeric(7,2));**
Press **Enter**

This SQL command tells the data base manager that the BOUGHT table will have three columns. The ID column will hold character data up to three characters long, the BOUGHT column will hold dates, and the PAID column will hold numeric data up to seven digits long (including the decimal point), with two digits to the right of the decimal point.

Step 6: Insert Data Into the Table

The INSERT INTO command is used to enter each row of data into the table. Execute these commands to insert the data for three canoes:

Type **insert into bought values ("001", {10/15/89}, 299.95);**
Press **Enter**
Type **insert into bought values ("002", {07/02/90}, 315.55);**
Press **Enter**
Type **insert into bought values ("003", {04/09/91}, 345.75);**
Press **Enter**

Step 7: Query the Data Base

The SELECT command is used to retrieve data. The simplest form of the SELECT command displays the specified columns from a single table. For example, execute this command:

Type **select id, bought, paid from bought;**
Press **Enter**

Your screen should look like Figure 26.

Step 8: Turn Off SQL Mode

Other SQL commands are available for performing typical data base management chores, such as deleting data, modifying data, modifying tables, relating tables, indexing data, maintaining catalogs, and querying data bases. These topics, however, are beyond the scope of this book. Return to the dBASE IV dot prompt by turning off the SQL mode:

Type **set sql off**
Press **Enter**

Figure 26 SQL Commands

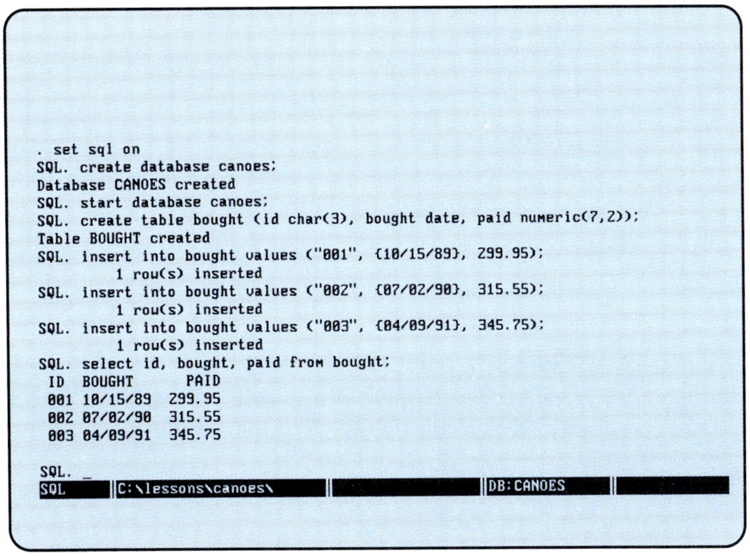

Practice Turn on the SQL mode and execute the HELP command. You can learn more about SQL from the Help facility. Select and read each of the SQL Main Topics. Read about some of the SQL commands. When you are finished, return to the SQL prompt and execute the QUIT command to exit dBASE IV and return to DOS.

Summary

- *Accessing the dot prompt.* Select Exit to Dot Prompt from the Exit menu of the Control Center.
- *Examining a data base.* USE opens a file. DISPLAY and LIST reveal the contents of a file. GO moves the record pointer.
- *Entering and modifying records.* APPEND adds new records. EDIT, BROWSE, and REPLACE let you modify records.
- *Deleting records.* DELETE marks records for deletion and RECALL unmarks them. PACK permanently removes deleted records.
- *Sorting and indexing.* SORT sorts a file. INDEX indexes a file. SET ORDER rearranges records by a tag in the multiple index file.
- *Finding data.* LOCATE finds records. SEEK and FIND are faster commands for searching indexed files. SET FILTER and SET FIELDS let you limit the records and fields found by subsequent commands. SET VIEW activates a view query.
- *Relating files.* Ten work areas are provided for different files. SELECT lets you change work areas. SET RELATION relates two files.
- *Using other dBASE IV commands.* Question mark (?), ACCEPT, CREATE, APPEND FROM, AVERAGE, COPY, COUNT, DO, ERASE, INSERT, STORE, and SUM are other commonly used dBASE IV commands.
- *Using dBASE IV functions.* A function is a predefined expression that returns a data value of a specific type. ALIAS, DATE, DISKSPACE, EOF, INT, TRIM, LEN, RECCOUNT, RECNO, RECSIZE, and ROUND are a few commonly used dBASE IV functions.
- *Creating a dBASE IV program.* MODIFY COMMAND activates the word-wrap editor for entering a program. Commands are simply entered into the file to be run later with the DO command.
- *Using the Applications Generator.* From the Control Center, move to the Applications panel, select the <create> option, and select the Applications Generator option.
- *Using SQL commands.* From the dot prompt, execute SET SQL ON. CREATE DATABASE, START DATABASE, CREATE TABLE, INSERT INTO, and SELECT are commonly used SQL commands.

Key Terms

As an extra review of this chapter, try defining the following terms.

alias	parent file
child file	record pointer
column	relate
dot prompt	row
function	table
logical operator	tag
memory variable	work area
multiple index file	

Multiple Choice

Choose the best selection to complete each statement.

1. What is the command-line user interface of dBASE IV?
   (a) Control Center (b) dot prompt
   (c) Applications Generator (d) Presentation Manager
2. To execute a dot prompt command, simply type it and press
   (a) Enter. (b) Ctrl-End.
   (c) Space Bar. (d) F1.
3. Which command returns to the Control Center from the dot prompt?
   (a) ASSIST (b) CLEAR
   (c) CONTROL (d) SQL
4. Which dot prompt command opens an existing data base file?
   (a) ACCEPT (b) LOAD
   (c) OPEN (d) USE
5. Which dot prompt command presents all of the records without pausing?
   (a) COPY ALL (b) DISPLAY ALL
   (c) LIST ALL (d) SHOW ALL
6. Which dot prompt command moves the record pointer?
   (a) ASSIST (b) DO
   (c) GO (d) USE
7. Which of the following operators is not a valid logical operator?
   (a) .AND. (b) .OR.
   (c) .NOT. (d) .SUM.
8. Which dot prompt command lets you add new records to the end of a new or existing data base file?
   (a) ADD (b) APPEND
   (c) CONTINUE (d) CREATE
9. Which dot prompt command lets you make a specific change to selected records throughout a data base file?
   (a) BROWSE (b) EDIT
   (c) LOCATE (d) REPLACE

10. Which dot prompt command permanently removes all records marked for deletion in the current data base file?
    (a) ERASE (b) DELETE
    (c) PACK (d) RECALL
11. Which dot prompt command rearranges records on the basis of a tag in the multiple index file?
    (a) ACCEPT (b) IMPORT FROM
    (c) SET ORDER (d) SORT
12. Which dot prompt command would you use to find a record in a data base file that is not indexed?
    (a) FIND (b) LOCATE
    (c) SEEK (d) SELECT
13. Which dot prompt command lets you specify a condition to select records for all subsequent commands?
    (a) LOCATE (b) SELECT
    (c) SET FILTER (d) SET FIELDS
14. Which dot prompt command lets you change work areas?
    (a) CHANGE (b) EDIT
    (c) REPLACE (d) SELECT
15. Which dot prompt command copies records from an existing file, not necessarily a dBASE IV file, into the current data base file?
    (a) ACCEPT (b) APPEND FROM
    (c) COMPILE (d) CREATE
16. Which dot prompt command executes a dBASE program?
    (a) CONTINUE (b) DO
    (c) GO (d) USE
17. Which function returns a logical value of .T. if the record pointer is past the last record in the file?
    (a) BOF (b) EXP
    (c) EOF (d) LEN
18. Which dot prompt command do you use to create a new program file with the word-wrap editor?
    (a) CREATE APPLICATION (b) DO
    (c) MODIFY COMMAND (d) SELECT
19. Which is a sophisticated tool for creating custom menu-driven data base systems without programming?
    (a) Control Center (b) dot prompt
    (c) Applications Generator (d) Presentation Manager
20. What is the basic component of an SQL data base?
    (a) column (b) file
    (c) record (d) table

Fill-In

1. The ______ dot prompt command closes all open files, terminates the dBASE IV session, and returns to DOS.
2. The DISPLAY ______ command presents the names, types, and widths of the fields in the current data base file.
3. As you work with a file, dBASE IV keeps track of the current record number by means of the record ______.
4. A ______ operator modifies the TRUE or FALSE result of one or two conditions.
5. A record marked for deletion can be reinstated in the data base file by executing the ______ command.
6. The ______ dot prompt command creates a new data base file with records from the current file arranged in the specified order.
7. Sorting is usually slower and takes up more disk space than ______.
8. You must use the SET ORDER command to rearrange records on the basis of a ______ in the multiple index file.
9. If a file is indexed and you want to search for records on the basis of the contents of a tag field, the ______ and ______ commands are faster than the LOCATE command.
10. The FOR clause in many dBASE IV commands acts as a ______ to select only certain records.
11. Once a view query has been designed, you can execute the SET ______ command from the dot prompt to use it.
12. A ______ area is a place in memory that holds an open data base file.
13. Two files in a relation are often called ______ and ______ files.
14. The ______ command displays the value of one or more expressions.
15. The ______ dot prompt command removes a file from the disk.
16. The ______ command adds a new record to the current data base file just after the current record.
17. A memory ______ is a place in RAM that temporarily holds a data value used in a calculation, comparison, or other operation.
18. A ______ is a predefined expression that returns a data value of a specific type.
19. A dBASE IV ______ is a sequence of commands stored in a text file that can be compiled and executed.
20. A standardized language for managing relational data bases, ______ was developed from research conducted at IBM in the 1970s.

Short Problems

1. From your LESSONS subdirectory, start dBASE IV and activate the dot prompt. Display a directory of the available data base files. Open the ACCOUNT data base file. List all of the records in which the BALANCE field is greater than zero.

2. Compute the sum of the CHARGES field and assign it to a memory variable named M_CSUM. Then compute the sum of the BALANCE field and assign it to a memory variable named M_BSUM.
3. Activate the LAST_NAME index tag. Use the FIND command to move the record pointer to Henry Hudson's record and use the DISPLAY command to view it on the screen.
4. Count the number of records in ACCOUNT with a BALANCE greater than $50.
5. The CMONTH function returns the name of the month from a date. Use the CMONTH and DATE functions to display the name of the current month.
6. The RUN dot prompt command executes a DOS command, or any program that can be executed by DOS, from within dBASE IV. Use the RUN command to execute the DOS CHKDSK command without leaving dBASE IV.
7. Execute the DISPLAY STATUS command to see information about your current dBASE IV session.
8. You can activate existing view queries and reports from the dot prompt. Follow these directions:

Type	`set view to ?`
Press	**Enter**
Highlight	**WHO_OWES.QBE**
Press	**Enter**
Type	`report form ?`
Press	**Enter**
Highlight	**WHO_OWES.FRG**
Press	**Enter**

9. Execute the CLEAR ALL command to close all files. Then open the MAILING data base file. Follow these directions to produce mailing labels from the dot prompt:

Type	`label form ?`
Press	**Enter**
Highlight	**MAILING.LBG**
Press	**Enter**

10. Execute the CLEAR ALL command to close all files. Then turn on SQL mode. Execute the SHOW DATABASE command to list available SQL data bases. (Remember to end SQL commands with a semicolon.) Use the START DATABASE command to activate the CANOES data base. Execute the SELECT command to list the ID, BOUGHT, and PAID columns from the BOUGHT table. Then turn off SQL mode.

Long Problems

1. Create a data base to maintain your checking account. Include the following fields: NUMBER, DATE, PAYMENT, DEPOSIT, CLEARED, and DESCRIP. NUMBER and DESCRIP should be Character fields, DATE should be a Date field, PAYMENT and DEPOSIT should be Numeric fields, and CLEARED should be a Logical field. Enter at least ten records. Create a dBASE program that will calculate the current balance by subtracting the sum of the PAYMENT fields from the sum of the DEPOSIT fields.

2. The CLEARED field in your checking account data base is a logical field in which you will enter T for TRUE when you receive the cashed check back from your bank. Create another dBASE program that will reconcile your data base with the monthly statements you receive from your bank. Hint: compute a balance as you did in the first program, but only for those records that have T in the CLEARED field. The resulting balance should then match the balance reported on your monthly bank statement.
3. In Long Problem 3 of the previous two chapters, you created an "electronic Rolodex" with dBASE IV. Use the Applications Generator to create a Quick Application for this data base file.
4. In Long Problem 4 of the previous two chapters, you created a student grades data base. Develop a dBASE program that will automatically generate and update the final letter grade based on a calculation involving the homework grades and test grades.
5. In Long Problem 5 of the previous two chapters, you created a data base of information about the courses you have taken throughout your college career. Create a dBASE program that will compute your grade-point average.
6. In Long Problem 6 of the previous two chapters, you created a data base of car expenses. Develop a dBASE program that will calculate the total car expenses for a year.
7. Switch to the dot prompt. Create a data base file for a video rental store to catalog their selection of movies. Include the following fields: TAPE_NO, TITLE, DATE, and COST. Make up and enter at least ten records. List the records on the screen and to the printer.
8. Use dBASE IV to create a quick reference guide to dBASE IV dot prompt commands and functions. In other words, create a data base with two fields: COMMAND and DESCRIP. Refer to the Command Summaries appendix at the end of this book or the dBASE IV help facility to find out about commands and functions not mentioned in this chapter. Index the data base by the COMMAND field. After your data base is finished, you can quickly get a description of a command or function by searching the COMMAND field.
9. Use the Applications Generator from the dot prompt to create a Quick Application for the ACCOUNT data base file.
10. Create an SQL data base of your own choosing. You might want to reproduce a dBASE IV data base you already have. You may have to use the Help facility within SQL to learn more about SQL to complete your task.

PART 6

SPECIAL APPLICATIONS

Operating systems, word processors, spreadsheets, and data base management systems are clearly the most commonly used microcomputer software, especially in the business world. But these are by no means the only kinds of programs run on today's computer systems. In fact, there is a wealth of additional software to choose from. We now turn our attention to some other important types of microcomputer application software. Chapter 17 explores the ways microcomputers can gain access to other computers both near and far. The creation and presentation of visual images on microcomputers is the topic of Chapter 18. Combining aspects of both word processing and graphics, Chapter 19 presents the fundamentals of desktop publishing. Chapter 20 briefly presents a variety of other notable types of microcomputer software. Finally, Chapter 21 explores the role computers play in our society.

CHAPTER 17

Communications and Networking

In This Chapter

Communications Hardware
- Internal Modem System
- External Modem System
- Other Modem Considerations

Communications Software
- Terminal Emulation
- File Transfer
- Introducing CROSSTALK

Communications Parameters
- Speed
- Data
- Port
- Parity
- Stop
- Duplex
- Emulate
- Mode

Calling a Mainframe Computer
- Determine and Set the Parameters
- Log On to the Mainframe
- Use the Mainframe
- Disconnect

Sending and Receiving Electronic Mail
- Log On to the System
- Send a Message
- Read a Message

Using an On-Line Information Service
- Log On to the System
- Read the News
- Research an Encyclopedia

Calling Another Microcomputer

Local Area Networks
- Hardware
- Topology
- Protocols
- Software
- Using a Network

Preview

As humans, we need to communicate with each other almost as much as we need water, food, and shelter. Ever since the beginning of time, we have sought ways to improve communications. Our distant ancestors adorned cave walls with magnificent paintings depicting hunting expeditions and religious ceremonies. The Babylonians used wedge-shaped symbols impressed in portable clay tablets to record historic events, business dealings, personal correspondence, and even recipes. Written communication advanced much further with the invention of papyrus, parchment, and paper. As society became increasingly more complex, better and faster methods of communication were developed. The electromechanical telegraphs of the nineteenth century could transmit messages over long distances at speeds of about two characters per second. Thanks to electronics, lasers, computers, and satellites, some of today's phone systems are capable of transmitting the equivalent of more than one hundred *million* characters per second. Anyone with a phone can now almost instantly converse with anyone else with a phone almost anywhere on this planet.

Even by itself, a computer is an amazing device. But equip it with a few relatively inexpensive enhancements, and a computer can communicate through the world-wide telephone network to any other similarly equipped computer. An almost infinite supply of information becomes instantly available. This is the potential of microcomputer communications. On a smaller scale, local area networks bring the benefits of program, data, and equipment sharing to closely knit groups of interconnected computers. We'll now turn to the world of computer communications and networking.

After studying this chapter, you will understand

- the basic hardware of microcomputer communications.
- the primary functions of communications software.
- the various software settings that govern microcomputer communications.
- how to call a mainframe computer with a microcomputer.
- how to use an electronic mail facility.
- how to use an on-line information service.
- how to call one microcomputer from another.
- the fundamental components and uses of local area networks.

Communications Hardware

For most of this chapter, we'll be discussing the connection of a microcomputer to some other computer via a telephone line. The hardware and software of local area networks are different and will be covered in the last major section of this chapter. At the most basic level, four primary hardware components are necessary for microcomputer communications:

- a microcomputer.
- a serial interface.
- a modem.
- a telephone line.

Figure 1 illustrates the typical arrangement of a microcomputer communications system. By now, you should have a pretty good idea what a microcomputer is. As we said back in Chapter 2, a *serial interface* is circuitry used to connect a variety of input/output devices to a computer. One bit of data at a time is

Figure 1 Typical Microcomputer Communications System
The typical system consists of a microcomputer and modem connected to a host computer and modem over a telephone line.

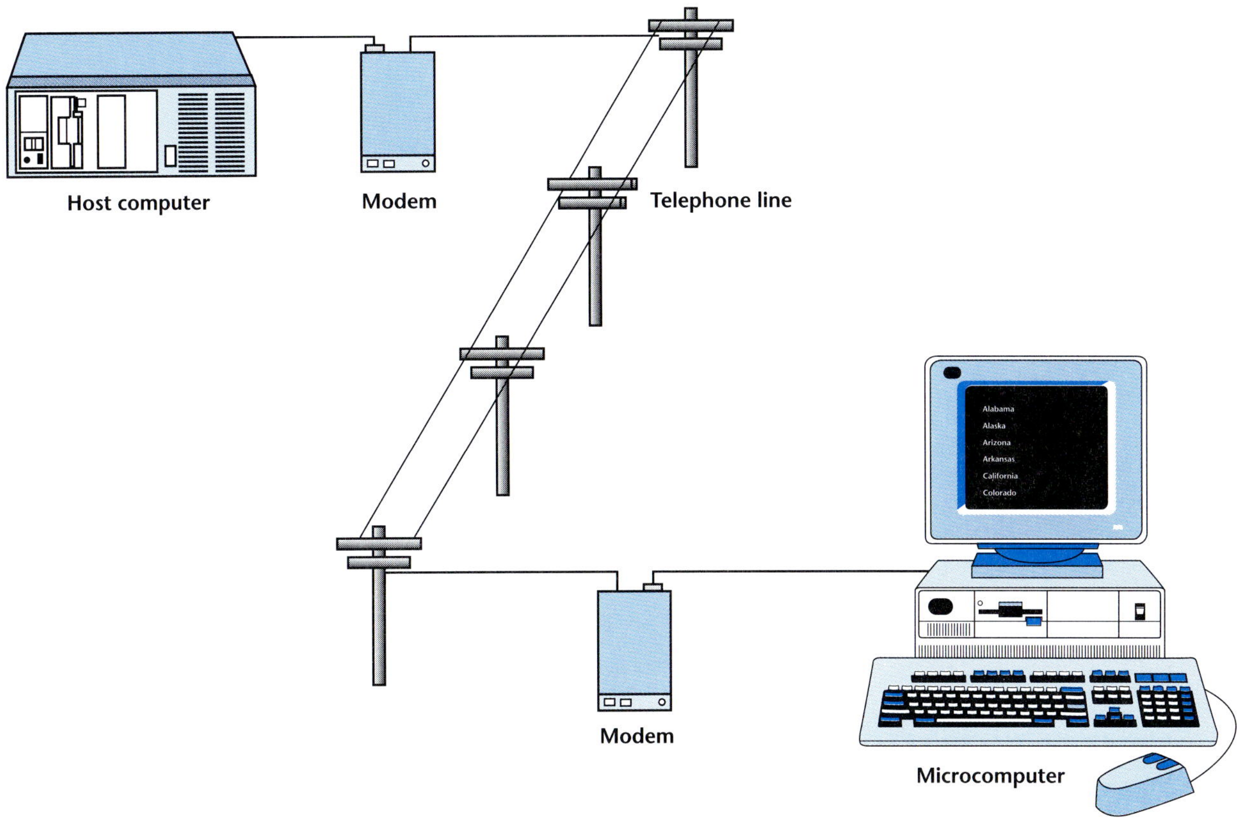

transmitted through a serial interface. The most common type of serial interface is the RS-232 standard, which terminates in a socket with 9 or 25 tiny holes or a plug with as many as 25 pins. As we explained in Chapter 2, a *modem* is a device that converts digital computer data (zeros and ones) into analog electrical signals (continuous voltage levels) that can be transmitted over telephone lines originally designed to carry voices. It also converts analog signals from phone lines back into digital computer data. Finally, a telephone line is necessary to connect the computer to the outside world. In most cases, you'll need a line that terminates in a **modular phone jack**, a socket that accepts the little plastic plug on the end of a telephone cord. At the other end of the telephone line there must be a modem and a computer to answer your call and complete the circuit. The computer you are calling is usually referred to as the **host computer**. Although the host computer may also be a microcomputer, it is frequently a larger, more powerful computer.

Most microcomputer communications systems consist of a microcomputer, a serial interface, a modem, and a telephone line. There are two common modem arrangements, however: the internal modem system and the external modem system.

Insight

Unauthorized Hackers: A Serious Problem?

Hackers are the cat burglars of the information age. When they break into a computer system, however, it's probably because someone left the door open just a crack. Unauthorized access usually is the fault of careless managers who don't see the need for computer security until it's too late.

Any system that uses telephone lines is vulnerable to hackers; one only needs to know a computer system's telephone number to slip into the system. From there, it's only a matter of sneaking past the system's initial security measures.

Invading demonstration accounts is a favorite hacker strategy. Demonstration accounts are used to show potential users the features of a system. From within a demonstration account, it may be possible to gain access to files containing information on working accounts. This can become a problem if the computer administrator has not controlled access to the password and to account files.

Another way to penetrate a system is through the special accounts and passwords that were used when the original system was sent from the computer manufacturer. If the computer system administrator doesn't change or remove them, they can be the keys the hacker is looking for.

Hackers also have been known to steal a legitimate password or account. They may read a password on a screen that someone forgot to clear, or they may see it written down near a terminal. Sometimes, hackers have been able to trick a public network or data base administrator into issuing them a password even though they have unverified credentials.

Unauthorized access to a computer can be a serious problem if computer center administrators ignore the security available to them.

Internal Modem System

An internal modem combines the modem and serial interface components on a single circuit board (see Figure 2(a)). With most microcomputers, an internal modem is an optional device mounted on a circuit board that must be plugged into an expansion slot. Remember, an expansion slot is just a connection inside the computer's system unit into which an additional circuit board can be inserted to increase the computer's capabilities. The internal modem expansion board fits inside the computer, and at the back of the board are one or two modular phone jacks accessible to the outside. If there is only one modular phone jack at the back of the board, a single phone cord goes from the wall jack to the modem. If there are two jacks, one phone cord goes from the wall jack to one of the jacks on the back of the internal modem board, and another cord goes from the other modem jack to a telephone. This arrangement enables you to still use a telephone on the line when you are not using the modem. Figure 2(b) illustrates the internal modem system.

There are both advantages and disadvantages to such an internal modem system. Internal modems are slightly less expensive than external modems because they draw their electrical power right from the computer and require no separate housing. Furthermore, internal modems are especially convenient because they do not take up any additional desk space or electrical sockets. Except for the phone cords, there are no external power or serial interface cables. Two disadvantages to internal modems, however, are that they require an expansion slot and that they are computer-specific, so that, for example, an internal modem for an IBM-compatible computer cannot be used in an Apple Macintosh.

Figure 2 Internal Modem
(a) An internal modem adapter card.

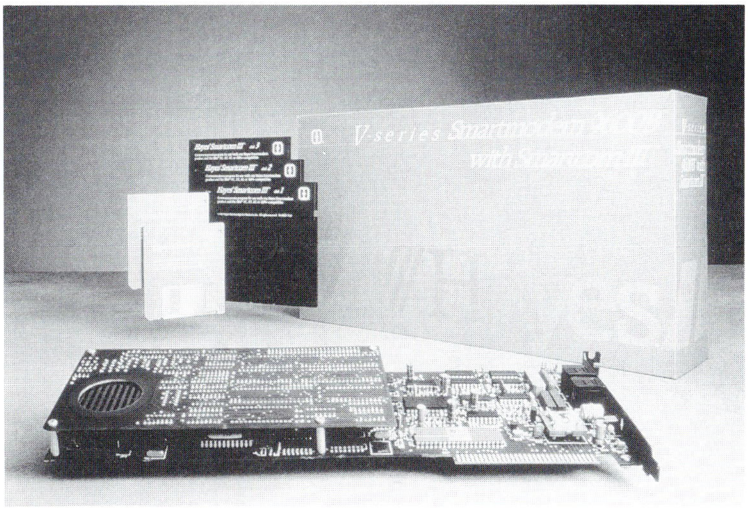

(b) Diagram of internal modem connections.

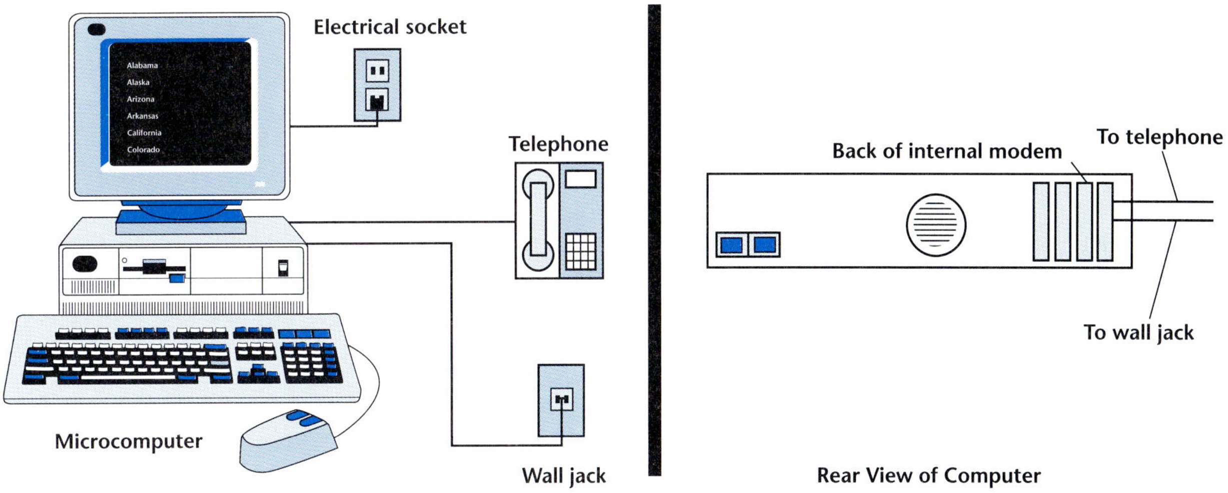

External Modem System

An external modem is built into a box about the size of a paperback book (see Figure 3(a)). It usually requires a separate power supply, consisting of a small adapter to be plugged into an electrical socket. The computer must have a serial interface, either built onto the motherboard or on an expansion board. Also required is a special **modem cable** to connect the external modem to the serial interface socket at the back of the computer. In many cases, the modem cable is computer-specific. Just like an internal modem, an external modem also has one or two modular phone jacks in back. If there are two jacks, one is used for a cord from the wall phone jack and the other is used for a cord to the telephone. Figure 3(b) illustrates an external modem system.

Figure 3 ***External Modem***
(a) An external modem.

(b) Diagram of external modem connections.

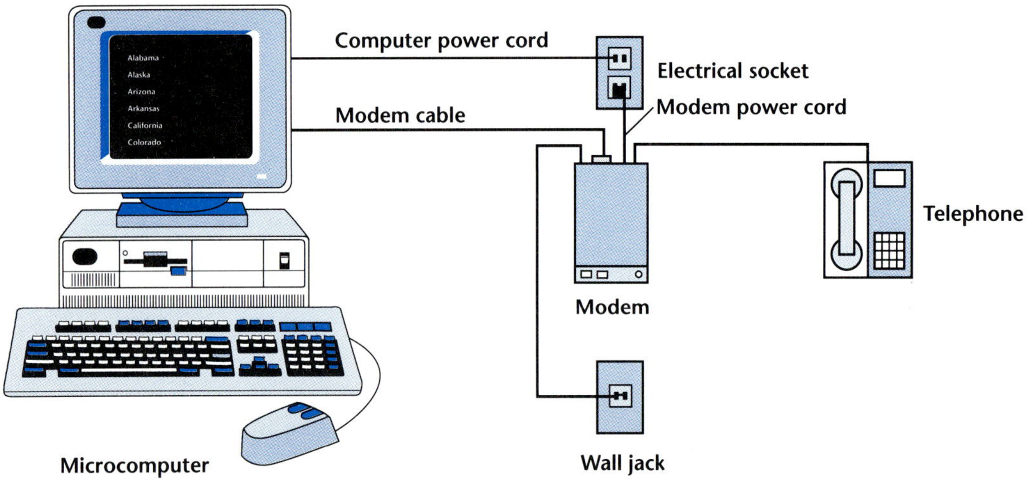

External modems have their advantages and disadvantages too. The main advantage is that an external modem generally can be used with any computer that has a serial interface. This can save you money, for example, if you have both an IBM and an Apple Macintosh computer. Although two different modem cables may be required, it's less expensive to buy two cables and one external modem than an internal modem for each of two different types of computers. Nevertheless, external modems are slightly more expensive than internal modems, they take up desk space, they require an additional electrical socket, and they use an external serial interface cable and power cord. For these reasons, people who only have one computer usually opt for an internal modem.

Other Modem Considerations

In addition to the factors we have just mentioned, there are two other major considerations in the selection of a modem: speed and Hayes compatibility.

Speed Modems are rated by the speed at which they can transmit and receive data over telephone lines. As we said in Chapter 2, this speed is usually expressed in terms of bits per second (bps). Virtually all modern microcomputer modems can transmit data at speeds of at least 300 bps, or about 30 characters per second. Most popular models can achieve speeds of 1200 bps, and many 2400-bps modems also are sold. Typically, faster modems also can transmit and receive data at slower speeds too. For example, a 2400-bps modem also can transmit and receive at speeds of 1200 and 300 bps. Microcomputer modems faster than 2400 bps are on the market, but these are significantly more expensive and may not work with all telephone lines and computers.

Hayes Compatibility The largest microcomputer modem manufacturer in the world is Hayes Microcomputer Products Inc. This company sells more than half of all the 1200 bps modems sold. Its Smartmodem line of microcomputer modems has set a virtual standard in the industry. Consequently, Smartmodems' methods and commands have been adopted by most other microcomputer modem manufacturers. A **Hayes-compatible modem** is one that operates like a Hayes Smartmodem. Smartmodems are rugged, reliable, flexible, and highly controllable. They are, however, at least twice as expensive as most Hayes-compatible clones. For example, while the internal Hayes Smartmodem 1200B sells for about $260, some compatible modems from other manufacturers can be purchased for just under $70.

Hayes compatibility has become especially important because of the widespread acceptance of the way Smartmodems work. Although communications software will generally work with any type of modem, most packages include features specifically designed to work with the Hayes Smartmodem. Thus there are many benefits to selecting a modem that is Hayes compatible. Because of this standardization, setting up microcomputer communications is much easier, especially for novices.

The so-called Hayes standard is, however, subject to change. As technology advances, modem manufacturers have added new features and commands, so that varying degrees of Hayes compatibility now exist among modems from other manufacturers. Some modems recognize only the most basic Hayes modem commands. Others elaborately mimic virtually every feature of the standard Hayes Smartmodem. For most people, the safest bet is to select a modem that is as Hayes-compatible as possible.

Communications Software

Even with a microcomputer, serial interface, modem, and telephone line, you still cannot call up other computers unless you also have communications software. This is a program that performs a variety of essential and convenient communications tasks. It lets you set up your serial interface and modem to work with the host computer you want to call. Then the software lets you dial the host computer's phone number. Once a connection is made, the communications program acts as a vehicle through which you work with the host computer. It provides ways for you to transmit data to and to receive data from the host computer. Many communications programs have programmable features that let you automate frequently performed tasks. When you are finished working with the host computer, the communications program lets you terminate the session, hang up the phone, and return to the operating system.

As it is with most types of software, many communications programs are on the market, each with its own "personality." Some of the most popular communications programs are offered free or for a very nominal cost from hobbyist programmers. There are also quite a few commercial communications packages that provide a wide range of features. One of the best-selling commercial communications programs is CROSSTALK from Microstuf, Inc. There are versions of CROSSTALK for most microcomputers that run CP/M and DOS. As an example, throughout this chapter we'll use CROSSTALK XVI for IBM-compatibles to illustrate some of the important concepts and operations of microcomputer communications. CROSSTALK, and indeed all communications software, performs two basic functions for the user: terminal emulation and file transfer.

Terminal Emulation

Terminal emulation is a feature of communications software that lets you use a microcomputer as a computer terminal. In Chapter 4 we discussed some aspects of multi-user operating systems, which typically allow many people access to the same computer on a time-sharing basis. The type of computer used in this manner is usually a medium-sized minicomputer or a large mainframe computer. Individual users work at their own terminals, which are input/output stations consisting of a keyboard and a display. Terminals may be directly connected to the central computer by a serial interface cable or connected via a modem and telephone line.

A number of popular models of computer terminals manufactured by various companies are on the market. In most cases, different types of terminals can be connected to the same computer. Terminals differ from microcomputers in that they generally don't offer much in the way of computing ability or storage capacity. They basically display incoming characters on the screen and send characters typed at the keyboard to the central computer. The central computer interprets what is typed and acts accordingly. There may, however, be slight differences in the keyboards of different terminals or in the signals that they send to the central computer. Terminal emulation also involves making a microcomputer act just like some particular model of terminal.

For example, one of the most popular types of computer terminal is the DEC VT100, made by Digital Equipment Corporation. By default, CROSSTALK will direct a microcomputer to act like a generic terminal and only use signals common to all computer terminals. You can, however, tell CROSSTALK to make your microcomputer mimic a DEC VT100. Once you do this, your microcomputer will appear just like a DEC VT100 to the host computer you call. Besides the DEC VT100, CROSSTALK can also emulate several other popular terminals.

File Transfer

Terminal emulation is useful, but it only allows your microcomputer to act as a computer terminal. If you already have a microcomputer and need to use other computers, terminal emulation saves you from having to purchase a separate computer terminal. Nevertheless, all you can do is send commands to the host computer and see the results on your screen. The ability to transfer files between computers is what really makes a microcomputer and communications software more useful than a simple computer terminal.

By using CROSSTALK on a microcomputer, you can **capture** incoming data from the host computer and save it in a disk file. This is especially useful if you want to keep a record of part or all of your session with the host computer. In addition, you can tell the host computer to display a particular file on your screen, capture that data, and create an identical file on your microcomputer's hard or floppy disk. Communications programs also may let you directly transfer files from the host computer to your computer without displaying them on your screen. With either method, transferring a file from a host computer to your microcomputer is called **downloading** (see Figure 4(a)). This process allows you to get programs and data from other computers to use with your own microcomputer. Since you can store the downloaded data on your own disk, you are free to edit and manipulate these data in any manner you wish with your own word processor, spreadsheet, data base manager, or other application package.

Similarly, communications programs like CROSSTALK also allow you to transfer files from your microcomputer's secondary storage to the host computer. This is called **uploading** (see Figure 4(b)). There are many reasons for uploading files.

Figure 4 Transferring Files
(a) Downloading. *(b) Uploading.*

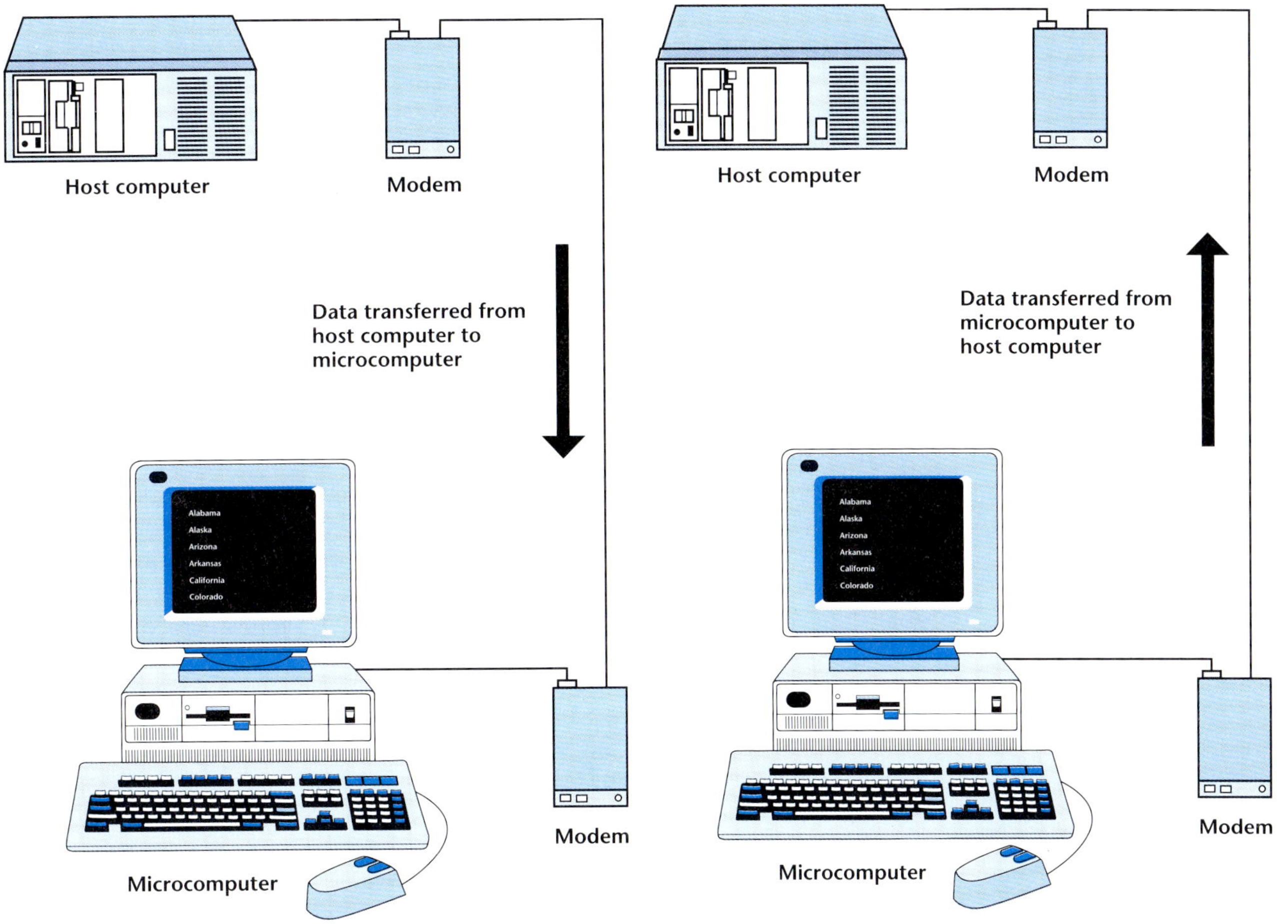

For example, depending on the particular circumstances, there may be significant costs involved in using a host computer. Educational institutions and commercial organizations typically charge by the minute for use of their computers. By preparing files on your own microcomputer before you connect to the host computer, you can save both time and money. Besides, if you had to retype everything you wanted to send to another computer, it would be too tedious and time-consuming to transfer long files.

When you use a communications program like CROSSTALK, you usually can transfer files between any computers that are compatible with that program. The other computer doesn't have to be the same type of computer, nor does it need to be running the same operating system. You don't have to worry about any of the hardware and operating system incompatibilities between the two computers. Ordinary text files consisting of ASCII character codes can almost always be sent between any two computers. Special file transfer techniques are available to correctly send programs between computers, but you can only use downloaded programs that have been designed for your particular microcomputer. For example, there is no problem downloading a text file from an Apple Macintosh to an IBM microcomputer. Nevertheless, although it is technically possible to download a Macintosh program, like MacWrite, from a Macintosh to an IBM computer, that program would not run on the IBM. We'll have more to say about the details of transferring various types of files in the following sections. Right now, let's start up CROSSTALK and see what happens.

Introducing CROSSTALK

For all of the examples and figures in this chapter, we'll be using CROSSTALK XVI Version 3.61 for IBM-compatible microcomputers. This popular program comes on a single diskette with a concise printed manual of about 170 pages. The manual suggests that immediately after purchasing the package you should make a copy of the original CROSSTALK diskette for your daily use. You also can create a subdirectory on your hard disk for CROSSTALK and simply copy the files from the original diskette to this subdirectory. Once you have your working copy and have switched to the proper disk drive or subdirectory, you simply type **XTALK** and press the **Enter** key to start the CROSSTALK program. The initial copyright message pops up on your screen, followed by any one of a number of possible humorous sayings (see Figure 5(a)). After a few seconds' wait to let you appreciate its authors' wit, CROSSTALK displays the Status Screen you see in Figure 5(b).

The Status Screen serves two functions. First, it displays all of CROSSTALK's major options, along with their current settings. Second, it is a menu of some of the available commands. The first two letters of every command on the screen appear in capitalized bright letters. To execute a command, you only have to enter the first two letters of its name. Although you may enter the entire name of a command, this isn't necessary.

In the screen shown in Figure 5(b), CROSSTALK is prompting you to enter the number of a command file to use. A *command file* is simply a list of CROSSTALK commands stored as text in a disk file. CROSSTALK can load a command file from disk into memory and perform the commands it contains just as if you had manually entered those commands from the keyboard. Command files are handy for performing frequently used sequences of commands. For example, if you often call a particular host computer, you can set up a command file to automate the specific operations necessary to make the connection. Several ready-made command files are provided by Microstuf along with CROSSTALK. By

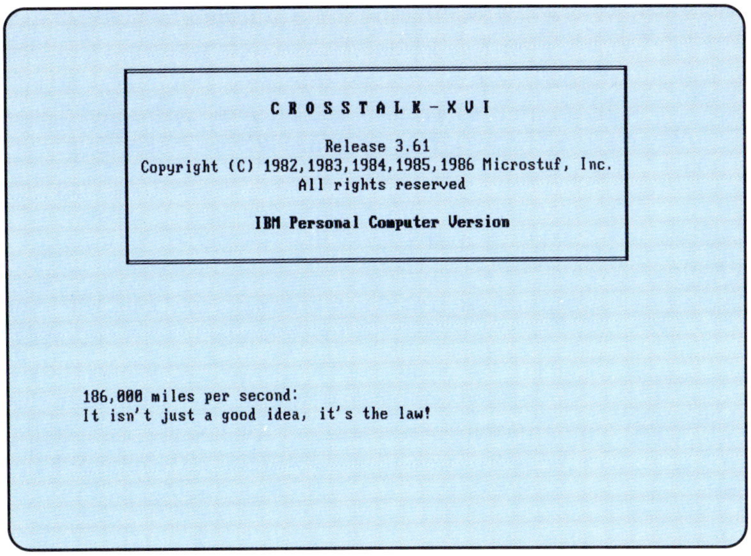

Figure 5 Running CROSSTALK
(a) CROSSTALK copyright screen.

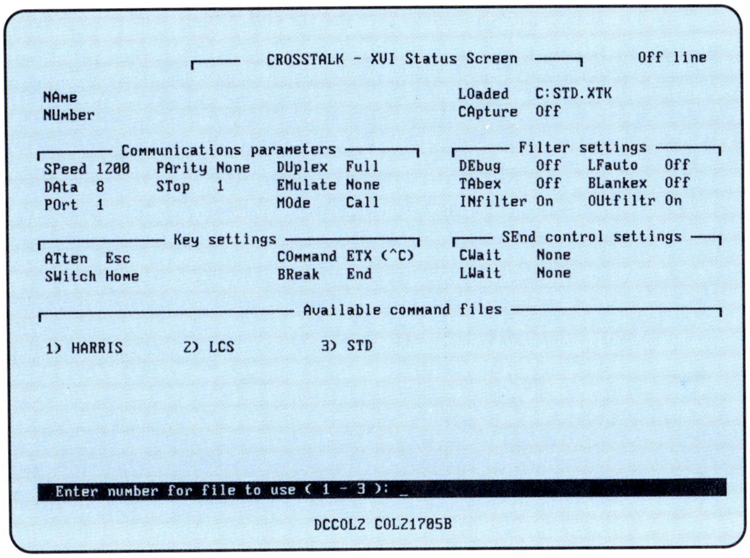

(b) CROSSTALK Status Screen.

default, the one named STD.XTK is automatically loaded into memory and executed whenever you start CROSSTALK. This command file initializes all of CROSSTALK's default settings. Since these default settings are sufficient for now and we don't want to load any other command files, in response to the prompt to enter the number of a file to use, you can just press the **Enter** key.

After you do this, CROSSTALK displays the prompt Command? in the reverse video bar across the bottom of the screen. This is called the *command line,* and it is where you enter CROSSTALK commands. Whenever you see the command line at the bottom of the screen, you know that you can enter a CROSSTALK command. The command line is not present on the screen when you are interacting with a host computer.

Right now, you are not connected to a host computer and the command line is on your screen, so you are free to enter a CROSSTALK command. Although it is not present in the status screen menu, QUit is the command to end CROSSTALK and return to DOS. You can type either **QU** or **QUIT** and then press the **Enter** key to terminate your CROSSTALK session.

Communications Parameters

As you can see from Figure 5(b), the CROSSTALK status screen has many options. The most important are listed beneath the heading **Communications parameters**. These are the settings that specify the technical details of how your microcomputer will communicate with another computer. In one way or another, most communications programs let you specify these settings. Since they are so important, let's go through each of these items one at a time.

Speed

The Speed option indicates the bits-per-second rate at which the modem will transmit and receive data over the telephone line. Since most modems have a range of possible speeds, a communications program must let you specify the transmission rate. The initial default speed for CROSSTALK is 1200 bps. Depending upon the host computer, you may occasionally have to change the speed before you make a connection. While almost all host computers can use 1200 bps, in some instances it may be less expensive to use 300 bps. Faster speeds, however, are more convenient and generally less frustrating. CROSSTALK can operate at speeds of 110, 300, 600, 1200, 2400, 4800, and 9600 bps. The actual speeds you can use depend on your modem and the telephone line. In addition, even faster data transfer rates are available in the latest versions of CROSSTALK for special systems that use very high-speed modems or with computers directly connected with cables. These speeds include 19,200 bps, 38,400 bps, 57,600 bps, and 115,200 bps.

Data

The Data option indicates the number of data bits used by the host computer to represent a single character. This value is sometimes called the *word length* or *character length* of the host computer. There are only two possible values, 7 and 8. The initial default number of data bits is 8. The value you use depends upon the computer you are calling.

Port

Many microcomputers can have more than one serial interface, also called a serial port. Serial ports connect a variety of input/output devices to computers, including modems, some printers, plotters, mice, trackballs, scanners, and graphics tablets. If more than one serial interface is present, the communications program must be told to which port the modem is connected. Serial ports are usually numbered 1, 2, and so on. By default, CROSSTALK assumes that your modem is plugged into serial port 1.

Parity

Parity is a method of error checking used to help ensure that all of the data bits of a character were received correctly after a transmission. Without going into technical details, there are two types of parity: *even* and *odd*. In addition, the parity parameter can also be set to *none*, which shuts off parity error checking. The parity setting you use depends on the computer you are calling. In practice, parity is almost always set to *none*, but a few host computers require even or odd parity.

Stop

The Stop option indicates the number of stop bits used in the transmission of a single character. **Stop bits** mark the end of an individual data character. Again, this depends on the computer you are calling, but as a general rule, one stop bit is used at speeds of 300 bps and greater, and two stop bits are used at 110 bps. Consequently, the Stop option is almost always set to 1.

Duplex

When you use a modem and communications program, your microcomputer acts as a terminal to a host computer. Once the connection is made, the characters you type at your keyboard are sent directly to the host computer. If the host computer operates in **full-duplex** mode, the characters you type are also sent back and echoed on your screen. If the host computer operates in **half-duplex** mode, the characters you type are not echoed back to your screen. The most common setting is full-duplex and so this is what CROSSTALK has as the default. The duplex setting you use also depends on the computer you are calling. If you don't know beforehand whether to use full- or half-duplex, there is an easy way to tell after you make a connection. If you cannot see the characters you are typing, the host computer is probably not echoing your data. In this case, you should set the duplex option to **half**. On the other hand, if you see two of every character you type, the duplex setting should be changed to **full**.

Emulate

The Emulate option lets you tell CROSSTALK to mimic a particular type of computer terminal. This is needed only if the computer you are calling sends special codes to position the cursor and clear the screen. Unless you specify otherwise, most host computers do not assume that you are using a particular model of terminal and so they do not send any machine-specific screen formatting codes. Only standard formatting codes like backspaces, carriage returns, and line feeds will be used. In this case, your microcomputer doesn't need to emulate any particular terminal. So, the default and most commonly used setting for the Emulate option is **none**.

Mode

The Mode option lets you tell CROSSTALK to prepare your modem to either call another computer or wait for a call from another computer. Whenever you call a host computer, there is a modem at the other end of the telephone line that answers your call, as shown in Figure 1. Most people only use their modems to call other computers. To do this, set CROSSTALK's Mode option to **Call**, which is the default setting. You can, however, set up your modem and computer to receive calls from other computers. In this case, set CROSSTALK's Mode option to **Answer**. Once in Answer mode, CROSSTALK simply waits for a call rather than dialing a phone number. With your modem set up to answer calls, your microcomputer can be a host computer. You might use the Answer mode to receive data directly from an associate's computer. Answer mode is also used by people to set up their own computer bulletin board systems, about which we'll have more to say later in this chapter.

Calling a Mainframe Computer

Computer communications can be a somewhat technical subject, with many special terms to describe various options and settings. We could fill this entire book and not cover all the details of transferring information between computers. A better approach is to show you examples of some of the most common uses of microcomputer communications. One of the simplest and most popular microcomputer uses is that of calling a mainframe host computer.

Many businesses, organizations, and schools have their own mainframe computers. At large universities, it's common for individual departments to have their own large computer. The psychology department at the University of Illinois at Urbana-Champaign, for example, has its own Harris H800 mainframe computer. This computer is used by the psychology faculty, staff, and students for many different purposes, including word processing, statistical analyses, programming, administrative duties, and for sending internal memos. Many department members have microcomputers at home or in their offices, but they also need to use the Harris mainframe for some of their work. To give you a fairly representative example, let's go through the process of using CROSSTALK on an IBM-compatible microcomputer to call up this Harris mainframe.

Determine and Set the Parameters

The first step is to gather the information you need to call your particular host computer. In this case, you need to know the phone number, speed, number of data bits, type of parity, and number of stop bits. The Harris computer can communicate at 1200 bps with 8 data bits, no parity, and 1 stop bit. Fortunately, these settings are already the current CROSSTALK default communications parameters. You just have to tell the program the proper phone number and instruct it to make the call. First, make sure CROSSTALK is ready to receive commands by pressing the **Escape** key. To set the phone number, you type the command **NU** followed by a space and then enter the phone number of the computer you want to call. All you have to do to tell CROSSTALK to actually place the call is type **GO** and press the **Enter** key. Assuming your modem is turned on and correctly connected to your microcomputer, CROSSTALK automatically dials the number. You should hear the tones or pulses through the modem's speaker as CROSSTALK dials the phone number and waits for a connection. On the other end of the line, the modem connected to the Harris mainframe answers the call with a special tone. Once the connection has been established, CROSSTALK tells you to proceed.

Log On to the Mainframe

At this point, you need to follow the procedures for logging on to the particular computer you have called. The exact procedures vary from computer to computer. In the case of this particular Harris mainframe computer, the first thing you do is hold down the **Control** key and type a **G**. Then the Harris prompts you to enter your sign-on, which is a special code number followed by your social security number. Next you are prompted to enter your password. When you type a password, most computers don't display the characters on the screen. This is a security measure to help prevent an unauthorized person from looking over your shoulder and seeing your password as you type it. Sign-on numbers are generally assigned by the person who manages the host computer system. Passwords may also be assigned, or you may be able to choose your own password the first time you log on to the computer. Once you have a password for a particular computer, it's important not to forget it. After your sign-on identification and password have been accepted, the computer system greets you and perhaps tells you about any messages or news that await you. Figure 6 shows the microcomputer screen after logging on to the Harris mainframe.

Use the Mainframe

The @ character you see on the screen in Figure 6 is the Harris computer prompt. The mainframe is simply waiting for you to tell it what to do. The reverse-video line at the bottom of the screen is displayed by CROSSTALK and not the host computer. Since you are now connected to the Harris computer just as if you were using a terminal, the characters you type are sent to the Harris computer and its responses appear on your screen. For example, to get on-line help about the Harris computer, you type **HELP** and press the **Enter** key. Figure 7 shows the result.

Of course, our purpose here is not to teach you how to use a particular mainframe computer operated by the psychology department at the University of Illinois. You wouldn't be calling such a computer unless you were authorized and had specific tasks to perform. You would have to read the documentation or perhaps take a special class to learn how to use such a computer. Our purpose has been to use this particular example to illustrate the general process of calling a mainframe computer. Although there are differences between computers, the steps you must take to call most mainframes are similar to those we just outlined.

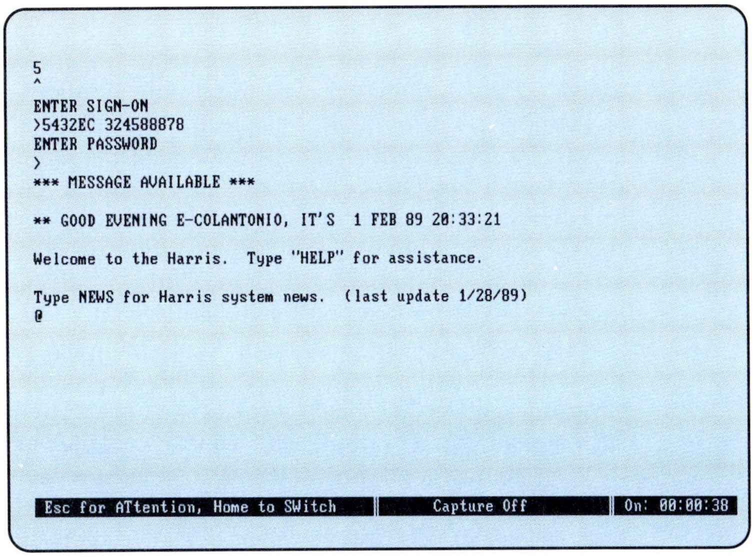

Figure 6 Calling a Mainframe
This shows the screen after logging on to the Harris mainframe.

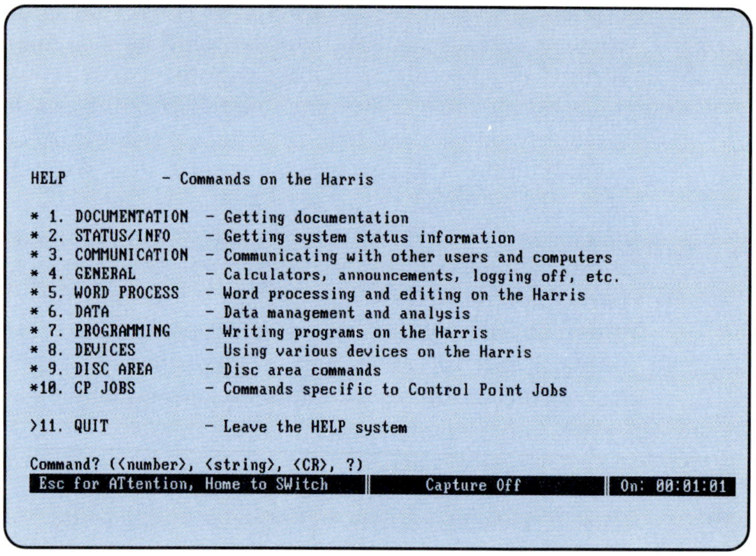

Figure 7 Using a Mainframe
This screen shows the Harris HELP system.

Disconnect

When you are finished working with the mainframe computer, you must sign off, break the connection, and return to CROSSTALK. Most timesharing host computers have a command such as BYE, QUIT, or END that you enter to terminate your current session. When you do this, CROSSTALK senses that the connection has been broken and "hangs up" the phone line. The program then waits for further instructions from you. You can execute other commands, make another call, or enter **QUIT** to stop running CROSSTALK and return to DOS.

Sending and Receiving Electronic Mail

Electronic mail or **E-Mail** is a way to send and receive messages with a computer. It is one of the most useful and most popular applications of computers and communications and is widely used in many businesses today. Basically, electronic mail allows you to send text messages to any other user participating in the system. Messages are saved in private "mailboxes" until users get a chance to call up the system and read their mail. In many cases, you can either enter your messages directly into the electronic mail facility, or upload a text file previously prepared with a word processing package. Messages are sent almost instantaneously. Your correspondents can often read your messages and reply in a matter of minutes if they are currently using the mail facility. Even if a correspondent is not presently logged on to the system, electronic mail can help you avoid the frustration of playing "phone tag," since messages are saved in mailboxes until they can be conveniently read.

Electronic mail can be implemented on almost any computer system or network with multiple users. Many timesharing computer systems have internal electronic mail facilities just for their own users. The Harris mainframe computer system used as an example earlier in this chapter has an electronic mail facility that lets faculty, students, and staff of the psychology department at the University of Illinois send messages to one another. Local area networks, which we discuss later in this chapter, also may have their own electronic mail facilities.

Although these private systems are widely used and extremely popular, there is another whole class of electronic mail facilities. Several companies offer public electronic mail services to anyone who has a microcomputer or terminal and modem. These services allow subscribers to exchange messages by calling a central computer system. Because public electronic mail services are available to anyone willing to subscribe, they greatly enhance your ability to communicate with other computer users all over the world. Many of these public electronic mail services also offer ways to print messages on paper and send them to nonsubscribers via the U.S. Mail, express mail companies, or telegrams. Some can even print paper letters on registered letterheads with reproduced signatures.

One of the most popular public electronic mail services is MCI Mail, offered by MCI Telecommunications Corporation. This particular service has more than 140,000 subscribers. Subscribers pay an initial registration fee of $18 and a mailbox fee of $18 per year. Additional charges are based on the number of minutes spent connected to the system and the lengths of the messages sent. For example, sending an instant electronic message between 500 and 7500 characters in length costs $1.00. Using advanced services and sending printed mail to nonsubscribers also require paying additional fees. Although MCI Mail is somewhat more expensive than the U.S. Postal Service for ordinary letters, it is quicker, more reliable, and it has the advantages of a well-established public electronic mail service that is both easy to use and offers access to a large number of subscribers. To give you an example of electronic mail, let's use CROSSTALK to call MCI Mail to send and receive a message.

Log On to the System

It's a simple matter to subscribe to a service like MCI Mail. All you do is call their toll-free number, and provide your name, address, and credit card number. MCI sends you your user name, user identification number, password, and a starter kit containing instructional manuals and other helpful materials.

After you become a subscriber, you are able to call the MCI Mail system and send and receive messages. This assumes, of course, that there are other subscribers with whom you plan to correspond routinely. The first step in using the MCI Mail service is to call up and log on to the system. MCI Mail has local telephone numbers in more than 50 U.S. cities. They also have a WATS (800) number you can call, but this costs an additional $.10 per minute. Many subscribers call MCI Mail through a public data network such as TYMNET. In brief, a **public data network** is a way to call a distant communications service, such as MCI Mail, from a local telephone number. The terms **packet-switching network** and **value-added network** are also used to describe these facilities. In most cases there are additional connect charges, from $2 to $10 per hour. Nevertheless, using a public data network is still usually less expensive than placing direct long distance calls. TYMNET, operated by McDonnell-Douglas Corporation, is one of the world's largest public data networks with local phone number access to more than 750 U.S. and Canadian cities and more than 70 foreign countries. All you do is call your local TYMNET number with a communications program such as CROSSTALK and tell TYMNET that you want to use MCI Mail.

For example, let's say that you are in Champaign, Illinois, and you want to use MCI Mail. The local TYMNET phone number is 359-1163, which the people at MCI tell you when you subscribe. The default CROSSTALK settings of 1200 bps, 8 data bits, 1 stop bit, and no parity are fine for calling MCI Mail. After starting CROSSTALK and pressing the **Escape** key to get to the command line, you enter **NU 359-1163** to set the phone number and **GO** to dial the number.

CROSSTALK makes the connection and then some random characters appear on the screen while TYMNET senses and matches your communications settings. When these characters stop, you type an **A** to start TYMNET. The public data network responds with:

```
please log in:
```

Now you have to tell TYMNET that you want to use MCI Mail, so you type **MCIMAIL** and press the **Enter** key. TYMNET then connects you with MCI Mail, which asks you to:

```
Please enter your user name:
```

Here you type your first initial immediately followed by your last name, with no spaces or periods, and then press the **Enter** key. MCI Mail then asks for your password, which was assigned to you when you subscribed. After you enter your correct password, MCI Mail greets you, tells you if you have any messages, gives a few brief news headlines, and tells you to press the **Enter** key to continue (see Figure 8(a)). The news headlines are courtesy of Dow Jones/News Retrieval Service, which is also offered through MCI Mail. After you press the **Enter** key again, the main menu appears, as shown in Figure 8(b).

Send a Message

As you can see, MCI Mail's basic menu is quite simple. More information about the various commands can be obtained by entering **HELP**. To send a message to someone, first you enter the **CREATE** command. Messages have the format of an office memo. MCI Mail prompts you with TO:, and you enter the name or identification number of the person to whom you want to send the message. Then you are prompted with another TO:, which lets you send the same message to another person. If you don't want to send the message to anyone else, you just press the **Enter** key. Next, MCI Mail prompts you with CC:, which lets you send a courtesy copy of the message to others who should also see it. If you don't want to send any courtesy copies, you just press the **Enter** key. The com-

Figure 8 Calling MCI Mail
(a) MCI Mail log on.

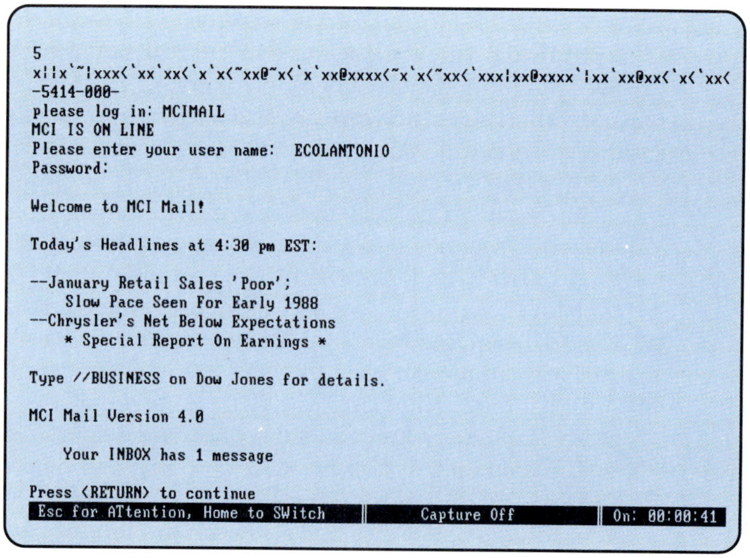

(b) MCI Mail main menu.

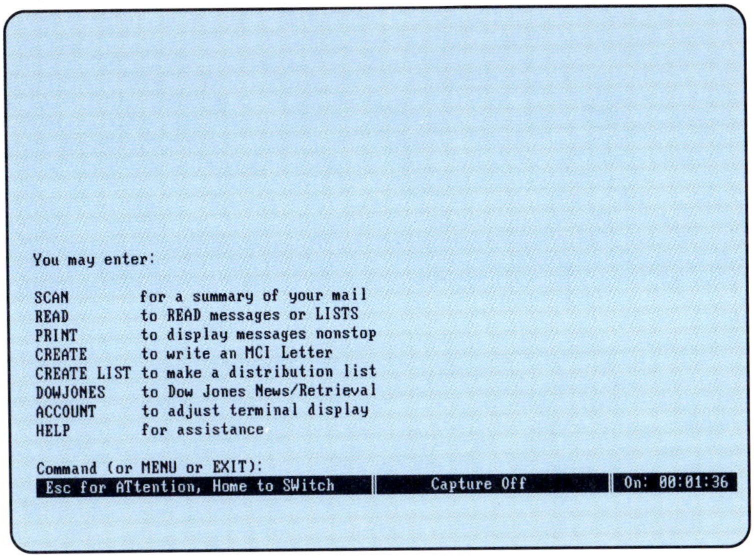

puter then asks for a SUBJECT: and you can enter a few words that describe the topic of your message. Finally, you enter the text of the message itself. Simple mistakes can be corrected with the backspace key and new lines are started by pressing the Enter key. When you're finished typing the message, you enter a single / (forward slash) at the beginning of a new line. Figure 9 shows the screen after entering a sample message.

When you're finished, MCI Mail presents a menu of choices for the first draft of your newly created message (see Figure 10). You can enter **READ** to review your draft before you send it. **EDIT** invokes a built-in text editor that lets you modify the draft. To actually send the message, you enter the **SEND** command. If the recipient is an MCI Mail subscriber, the message is sent as an instant electronic letter. MCI Mail confirms the date and time your message was posted, puts a copy of the message in your "OUTBOX," and returns to the main menu.

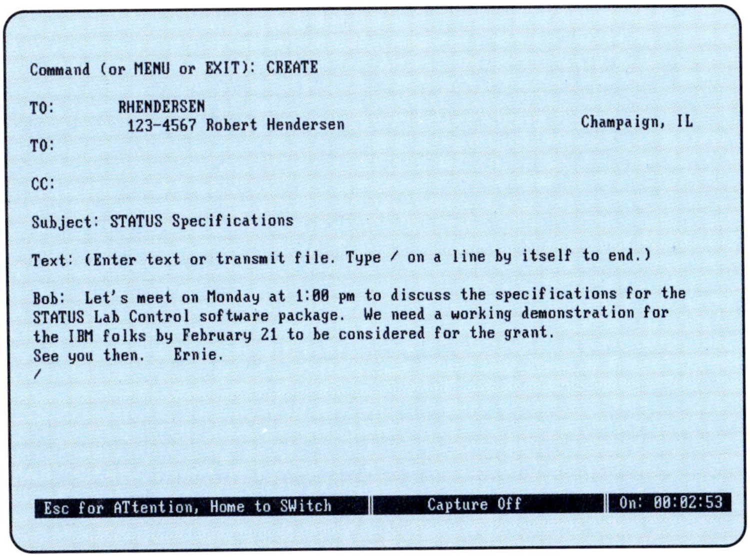

Figure 9 Typing a Mail Message
In MCI Mail, you use the CREATE command to type a new message.

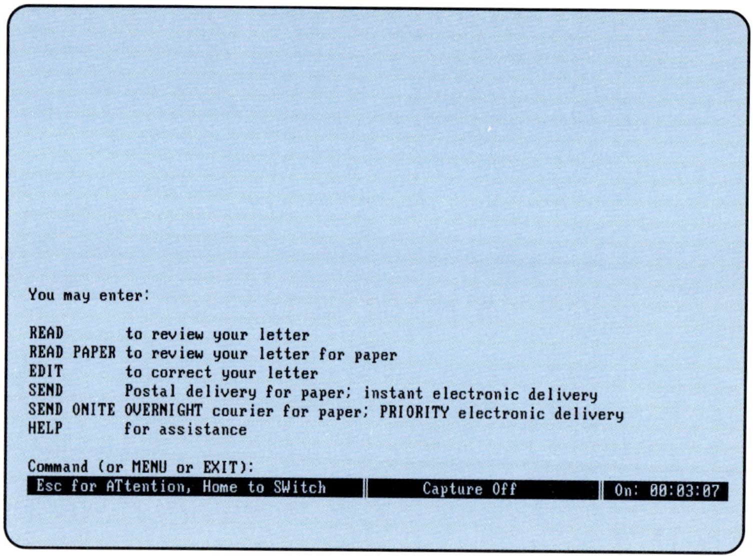

Figure 10 Sending a Message
After you enter a message, MCI Mail presents a menu of options.

Read a Message

Reading a message that someone has sent to you is even easier than sending a message. When you first log on to MCI Mail, the computer tells you if you have any messages in your "INBOX" (see Figure 8(a)). The **SCAN** command lets you see a list of all of your messages. To see messages one by one, you enter the **READ** command from the main menu. This presents the menu shown at the bottom of Figure 11(a). You enter **INBOX** to see any messages that you haven't read yet from other subscribers. Figure 11(b), for example, shows the result of reading an INBOX message. **OUTBOX** displays any messages that you have already sent to others. **DESK** lets you reread messages from others that you have already seen. After you read each new message, MCI Mail gives you a chance to answer the message immediately or simply go on to read the next message.

By turning on CROSSTALK's CAPTURE command just before you read your mail, you can download messages from MCI Mail to a disk file on your microcomputer. These messages can be used with word processing software or printed after you quit CROSSTALK. If you like, you can use CROSSTALK's PRINTER command instead to print your messages directly as they are being displayed on your screen. Simply press the **Escape** key to switch to CROSSTALK's command line and enter the command **PRINTER ON** to duplicate on your printer any text subsequently displayed on your screen. The command **PRINTER OFF** stops sending incoming data to your printer. Many people find that using an electronic mail service from a microcomputer this way helps them manage, organize, and significantly speed up much of their routine correspondence.

Using an On-Line Information Service

A commercial electronic mail facility like MCI Mail is just one of a broad range of on-line communications services available to microcomputer users. There are at least 3000 of these services in the United States alone. Most are specialized on-line data bases aimed primarily at business, academic, and scientific researchers. Others are targeted at more general educational and home markets. These

Figure 11 Reading a Message

(a) Using the READ command.

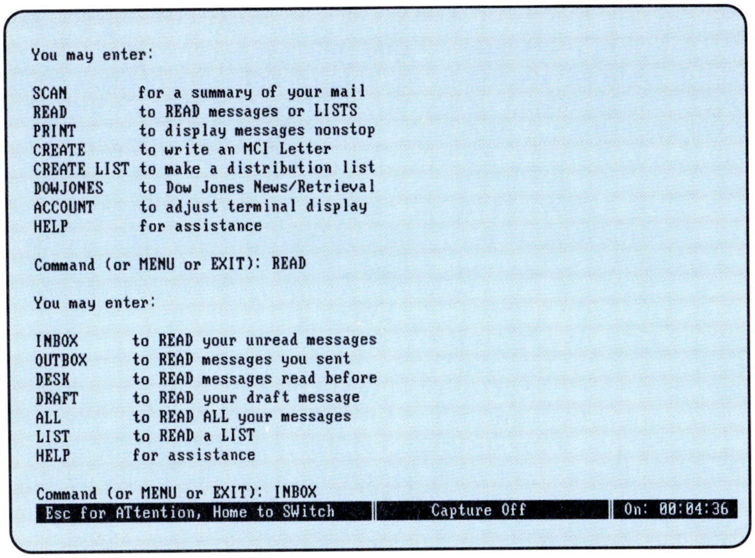

(b) Using the INBOX command.

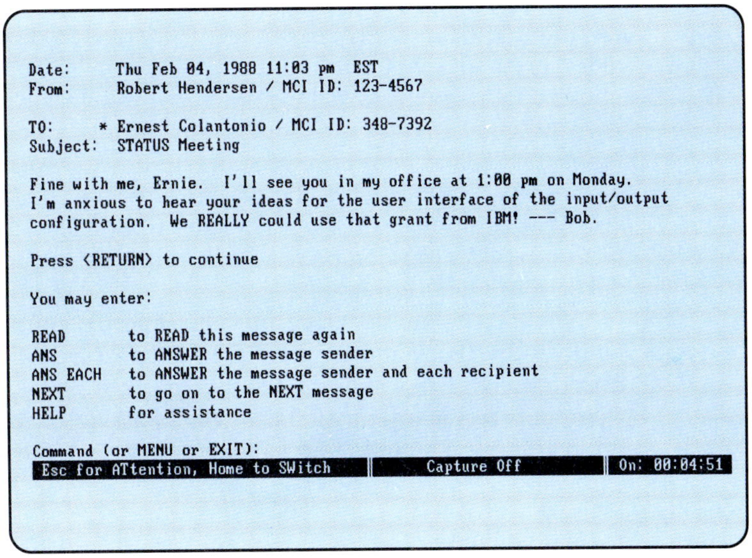

multi-purpose on-line information services support a wide variety of data bases, news, electronic mail, shopping, entertainment, and other miscellaneous facilities. To subscribe, all you need is a microcomputer, a modem, a telephone, and usually a credit card. Without even leaving your home or office, these have-it-all information services let you work, learn, shop, and play. Here are just a few of the capabilities provided by the major on-line information services:

- Gain access to electronic versions of popular encyclopedias.
- Search *Books in Print* and the *Reader's Guide to Periodical Literature*.
- Check the latest weather report for almost any place in the world.
- Read up-to-the-minute news from major wire services.
- Obtain stock quotes and buy and sell stocks.

- Plan your vacation, review airline schedules, and book your tickets.
- Exchange electronic mail.
- "Converse" with other on-line subscribers.
- Obtain free software.
- Get answers to questions about computer hardware and software from other subscribers.
- Browse through electronic shopping malls.
- Read reviews of the latest books, movies, and records.
- Play computer games.
- Join special interest groups.
- Participate in electronic forums.

CompuServe Incorporated, an H & R Block Company, runs the world's largest on-line information service. Established in 1969, today CompuServe has more than 500,000 subscribers. There is an almost dizzying array of individual activities offered by CompuServe, but the major topics include communications and bulletin boards; news, weather, and sports; travel; electronic shopping; money matters and markets; entertainment and games; home, health, and family; reference and education; computers and technology; and business and other interests. CompuServe even has its own magazine for subscribers called *Online Today*, which is published daily in electronic form and monthly in printed form. All this is far from free, however, because CompuServe has a $39.95 one-time registration fee and a $1.50 monthly service fee. It charges $6.00 per hour for using a speed of 300 bps and $12.60 per hour for 1200 bps or 2400 bps. If you use the TYMNET public data network to call CompuServe from a local telephone number, there are additional charges of $10 per hour during "prime time"—regular business hours, and $2 per hour during "standard time"—evenings and weekends. Many of the better services, like the on-line Grolier's *Academic American Encyclopedia*, also have additional surcharges or subscription fees. Nevertheless, on-line information services like CompuServe offer a unique way to greatly expand the potential of your microcomputer.

As a good example of using an on-line information service, let's call CompuServe with CROSSTALK and try a couple of its features. Obviously, we cannot cover every aspect of this abundant resource. Entire books have been written about CompuServe's many possibilities. We'll have to content ourselves with logging on, reading some news, and looking up a topic in the on-line encyclopedia.

Log On to the System

Subscribing and logging on to CompuServe is similar to gaining access to MCI Mail. After you call to subscribe, CompuServe sends you a starter kit that includes your user identification number, password, a manual, and some other handy reference guides. In most major cities, you can reach CompuServe directly with a local phone call through the CompuServe Network for a nominal surcharge of $0.25 per hour. In many other communities, you can reach CompuServe through a public data network such as TYMNET. For example, to call CompuServe via TYMNET, you start with the procedure we outlined in our discussion of logging on to MCI Mail. When you get the *please log in:* message from TYMNET, however, you respond with **CIS02** to access CompuServe. As Figure 12(a) shows, CompuServe then asks for your user identification number and password. CompuServe welcomes you on-line and usually displays some recent news about the system or ads for special services. Eventually, the main or TOP menu appears on your screen, as shown in Figure 12(b).

Figure 12 Calling CompuServe
(a) Logging on.

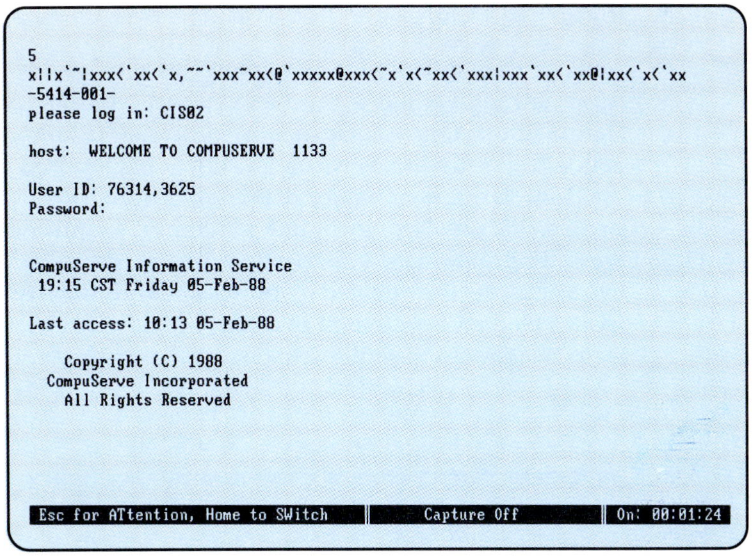

(b) The main or TOP menu.

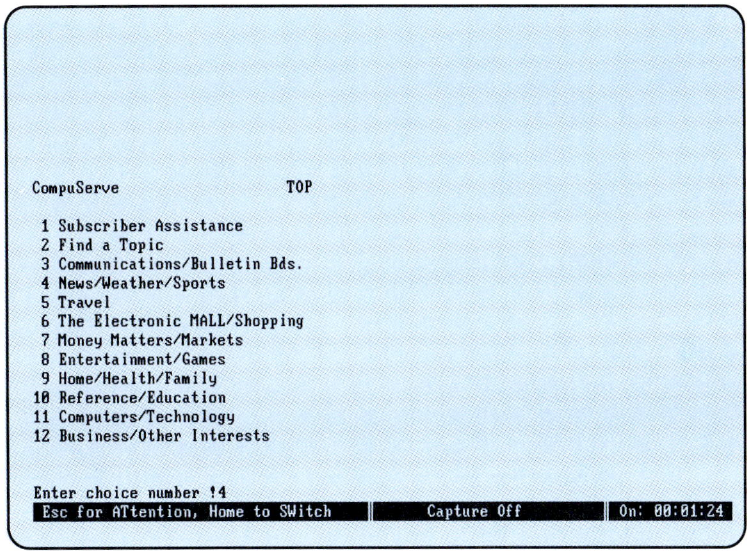

CompuServe uses a combination of menus and direct commands to give you access to its many varied services. The menus are especially nice for beginners because they can be used with very little instruction. There is also an on-line tutorial that teaches new subscribers the basics of navigating through CompuServe's menus. After a while, however, the menus can become tiresome. It begins to seem like most of your time (and money) is spent waiting for menus to scroll across your screen. Since CompuServe has many levels of menus, just reaching the service you want to use can take several minutes. Fortunately, CompuServe also lets you jump directly to any service with the **GO** command, which can save you a great deal of time if you know exactly which feature you want to use. An index of services and "**GO** commands" is given in the CompuServe documentation and is periodically updated in the *Online Today* magazine sent to all subscribers.

Read the News

Some of the most popular on-line features offered by CompuServe present the latest news in various forms. As you can see from CompuServe's Top menu in Figure 12(b), item 4 corresponds to news, weather, and sports. Selecting this option brings up the News menu shown in Figure 13(a). The second item in this list, NewsGrid, is a feature that compiles dispatches from some of the world's largest wire services, including United Press International and The Associated Press. Each news story that arrives in the NewsGrid service—about one every two minutes—is evaluated by professional editors and reporters. The top stories are selected and presented in a list of brief headlines. You can select any one of these headlines to see the actual story. For example, Figures 13(b) through 13(d)

Figure 13 Using NewsGrid
(a) The NEWS menu.

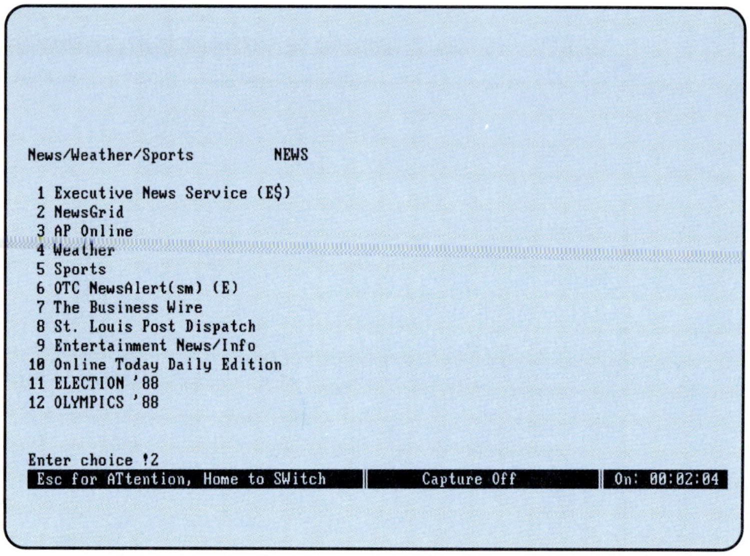

(b) The NewsGrid menu.

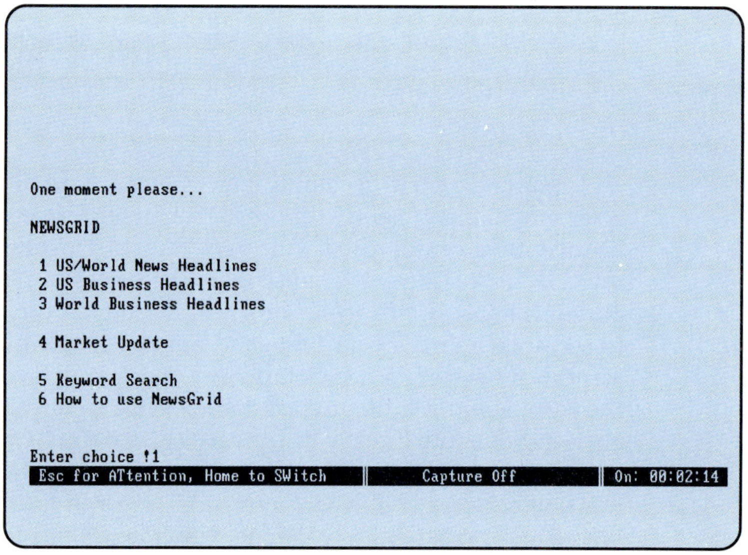

(c) NewsGrid headlines.

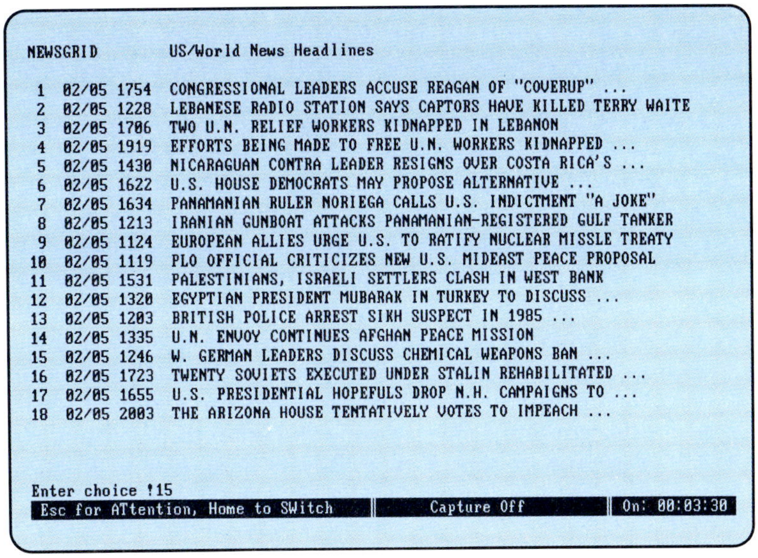

```
NEWSGRID        US/World News Headlines

 1  02/05 1754  CONGRESSIONAL LEADERS ACCUSE REAGAN OF "COVERUP" ...
 2  02/05 1228  LEBANESE RADIO STATION SAYS CAPTORS HAVE KILLED TERRY WAITE
 3  02/05 1706  TWO U.N. RELIEF WORKERS KIDNAPPED IN LEBANON
 4  02/05 1919  EFFORTS BEING MADE TO FREE U.N. WORKERS KIDNAPPED ...
 5  02/05 1430  NICARAGUAN CONTRA LEADER RESIGNS OVER COSTA RICA'S ...
 6  02/05 1622  U.S. HOUSE DEMOCRATS MAY PROPOSE ALTERNATIVE ...
 7  02/05 1634  PANAMANIAN RULER NORIEGA CALLS U.S. INDICTMENT "A JOKE"
 8  02/05 1213  IRANIAN GUNBOAT ATTACKS PANAMANIAN-REGISTERED GULF TANKER
 9  02/05 1124  EUROPEAN ALLIES URGE U.S. TO RATIFY NUCLEAR MISSLE TREATY
10  02/05 1119  PLO OFFICIAL CRITICIZES NEW U.S. MIDEAST PEACE PROPOSAL
11  02/05 1531  PALESTINIANS, ISRAELI SETTLERS CLASH IN WEST BANK
12  02/05 1320  EGYPTIAN PRESIDENT MUBARAK IN TURKEY TO DISCUSS ...
13  02/05 1203  BRITISH POLICE ARREST SIKH SUSPECT IN 1985 ...
14  02/05 1335  U.N. ENVOY CONTINUES AFGHAN PEACE MISSION
15  02/05 1246  W. GERMAN LEADERS DISCUSS CHEMICAL WEAPONS BAN ...
16  02/05 1723  TWENTY SOVIETS EXECUTED UNDER STALIN REHABILITATED ...
17  02/05 1655  U.S. PRESIDENTIAL HOPEFULS DROP N.H. CAMPAIGNS TO ...
18  02/05 2003  THE ARIZONA HOUSE TENTATIVELY VOTES TO IMPEACH ...

Enter choice !15
Esc for ATtention, Home to SWitch | Capture Off | On: 00:03:30
```

(d) NewsGrid story.

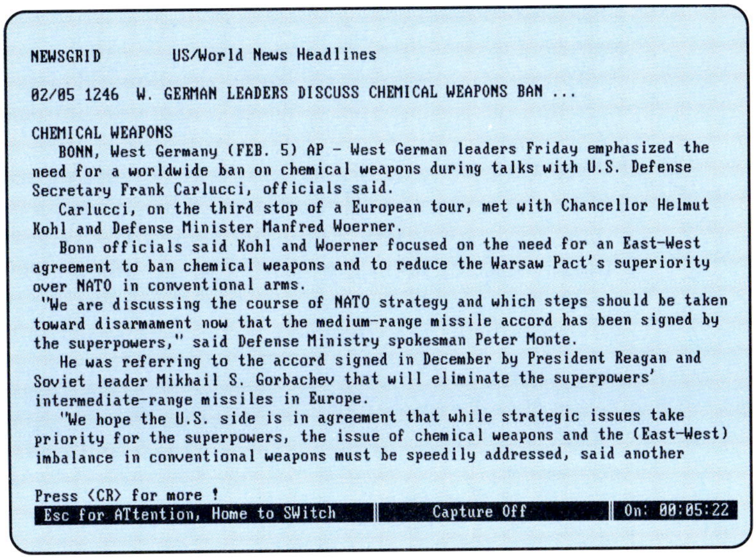

```
NEWSGRID        US/World News Headlines

02/05 1246  W. GERMAN LEADERS DISCUSS CHEMICAL WEAPONS BAN ...

CHEMICAL WEAPONS
   BONN, West Germany (FEB. 5) AP - West German leaders Friday emphasized the
need for a worldwide ban on chemical weapons during talks with U.S. Defense
Secretary Frank Carlucci, officials said.
   Carlucci, on the third stop of a European tour, met with Chancellor Helmut
Kohl and Defense Minister Manfred Woerner.
   Bonn officials said Kohl and Woerner focused on the need for an East-West
agreement to ban chemical weapons and to reduce the Warsaw Pact's superiority
over NATO in conventional arms.
   "We are discussing the course of NATO strategy and which steps should be taken
toward disarmament now that the medium-range missile accord has been signed by
the superpowers," said Defense Ministry spokesman Peter Monte.
   He was referring to the accord signed in December by President Reagan and
Soviet leader Mikhail S. Gorbachev that will eliminate the superpowers'
intermediate-range missiles in Europe.
   "We hope the U.S. side is in agreement that while strategic issues take
priority for the superpowers, the issue of chemical weapons and the (East-West)
imbalance in conventional weapons must be speedily addressed, said another

Press <CR> for more !
Esc for ATtention, Home to SWitch | Capture Off | On: 00:05:22
```

illustrate the process of selecting and reading a NewsGrid story. First you choose the NewsGrid option from the News menu, then you select the type of headlines you want to see, and finally you pick the headline whose story you want to read. When you're finished, you can select other headlines or return to CompuServe's main menu by entering the **TOP** command.

Research an Encyclopedia

It's 2:30 A.M. and you have a term paper due tomorrow in your first class. The school library has been closed for hours. If you're a CompuServe subscriber, all is not lost. Besides, the TYMNET surcharges are less at night. Just boot up the computer, turn on the modem, start CROSSTALK, and call CompuServe. You can probably find something about your topic in the on-line edition of Grolier's

Academic American Encyclopedia. Updated and revised four times each year, this is one of the most current encyclopedic references you're likely to find. It has more than 32,000 articles, fact boxes, bibliographies, and tables. Although there is an additional subscription charge ($7.50 for one month, $29.95 for six months, and $49.95 for one year), many CompuServe subscribers gladly pay to use the Grolier's encyclopedia for help with research, homework, speeches, travel plans, trivia answers, and other reference needs.

As an example, let's look up the word *modem* in the on-line encyclopedia. From CompuServe's Top menu, the quickest way to use the *Academic American Encyclopedia* is to enter the command **GO AAE**. Figure 14(a) shows the menu that appears on your screen. Assuming that you have already subscribed to the encyclopedia service, you select item 2 to look up a topic. CompuServe gives you some brief instructions and then prompts you for the *search term*, as shown in Figure 14(b). This is where you enter the topic that you want to research. To look up *modem*, simply type the word **modem** and press the **Enter** key. Figure 14(c) shows the result.

Calling Another Microcomputer

Electronic mail and on-line information services can be helpful, educational, and fun. Unfortunately, they also can be expensive. You don't have to call up mainframe computers or subscribe to on-line services, however, to make use of microcomputer communications. There are some relatively inexpensive ways to connect one microcomputer to another using a communications program such as CROSSTALK.

For example, you can directly connect two microcomputers without modems or telephone lines. A special cable, called a **null-modem cable**, can be used to connect the serial ports of the two computers. This cable makes each computer "think" that it is hooked up to a modem, when it is really directly connected to another computer. A communications program, such as CROSSTALK, is necessary to transfer files between the two computers. Obviously, connecting two

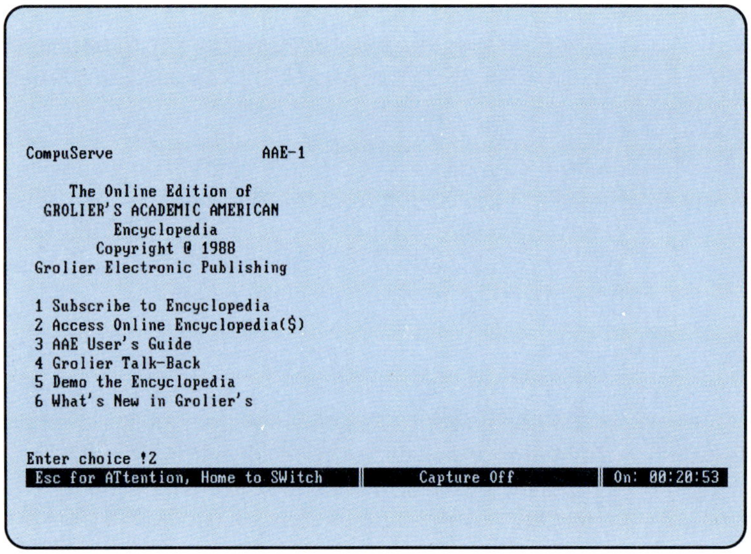

Figure 14 Using an On-line Encyclopedia
(a) CompuServe's Academic American Encyclopedia *menu.*

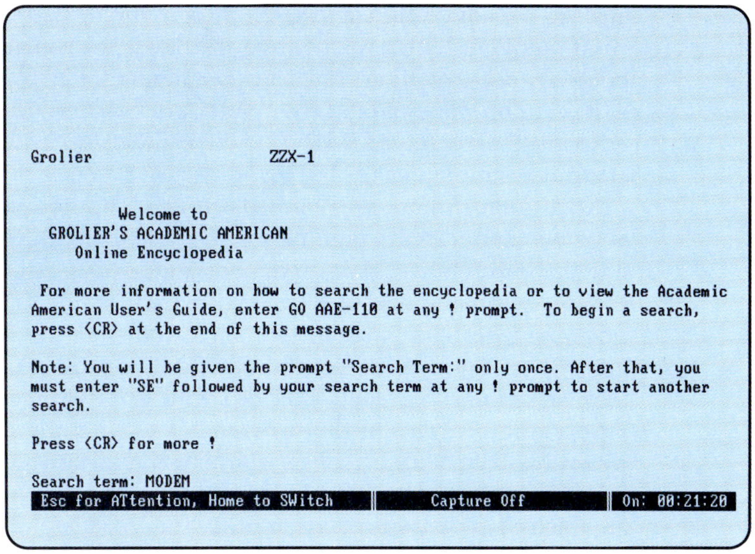

(b) Entering the search term.

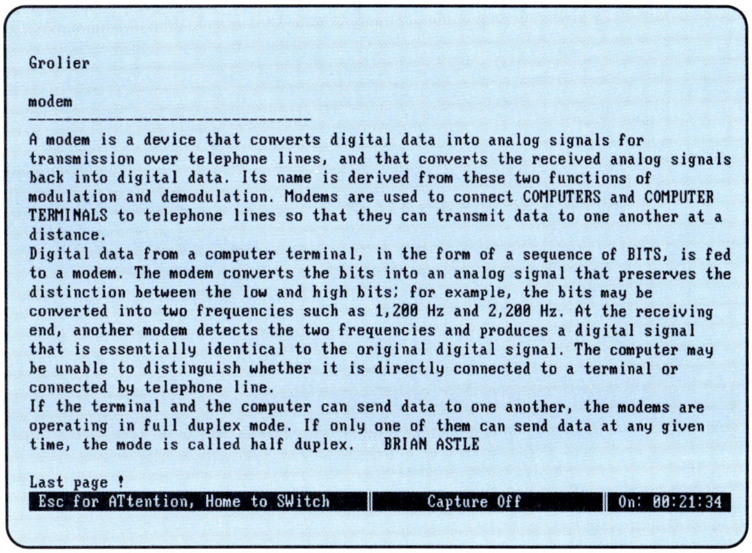

(c) The article on modem.

computers with a null-modem cable is usually restricted to computers in the same room or building. This arrangement is sometimes used with two different types of microcomputers, such as an IBM-compatible and an Apple Macintosh, to transfer files between them.

For more distant microcomputers, you can use modems and the telephone network. Although you can connect different computers running different communications software, the simplest arrangement is to use one microcomputer to call another microcomputer of the same type, with both machines running their own copies of the same communications program. Let's say that you want to send a text file named DOCUMENT.TXT to an associate who lives in another town. You both have IBM-compatible microcomputers and you both have CROSSTALK. First, you call up your associate, agree on which communication parameters to use, and tell her to get her equipment ready to receive a call from your computer. You both say goodbye and hang up your telephones. Your colleague boots up her computer, turns on her modem, starts CROSSTALK, and sets the agreed-upon parameters. Then she puts CROSSTALK into ANSWER mode by entering the command **MODE ANSWER**. CROSSTALK, the modem, and her computer simply wait.

In the meantime, you boot up your computer, start CROSSTALK, and set your communications parameters. By default, CROSSTALK puts your modem and computer into CALL mode. You enter your associate's phone number with the **NU** command and dial the number with **GO**. Your computer calls her computer and her computer answers. To transmit the file DOCUMENT.TXT, you enter the CROSSTALK command **XMIT DOCUMENT.TXT**. Your screen will look something like Figure 15. As you can see from Figure 15, CROSSTALK reports the progress of the file transfer. At the other end of the line, the other copy of CROSSTALK displays a similar screen so your associate can also see the progress of the file transfer. CROSSTALK tells you when the transfer is complete, at which point you can transfer other files, or use the **BYE** command to hang up the phone and break the connection.

If your computer is calling another computer with CROSSTALK, you can also use the RQUEST command to download files. Note that the computer in CALL mode is always in control. The person on the answering end basically just sets up the system and waits for the file transfers.

Local Area Networks

Connecting one microcomputer to another as we have just described is fine for an occasional transfer of files. This procedure is not suitable, however, in situations that require several microcomputers to routinely share data files, programs, and expensive hardware devices such as laser printers, hard disks, and scanners. In these cases, a local area network or LAN is a much better arrangement. As we said in Chapter 2, a local area network allows you to directly connect two or more microcomputers together. Special hardware components and cables are used to link the machines, which are usually located in the same building. Special software is used to control the exchange of files, the execution of shared software, and access to shared hardware devices.

There are many benefits to installing a local area network. Most of these are related to the concept of sharing. Transferring files from one computer to another becomes as easy as copying files between disk drives on the same computer. Even networks that connect different types of computers can easily transfer files. Several users can simultaneously tap into the same data base, which can be kept on a single disk drive. The ability to share data in this manner is a major reason many organizations install networks. If the computers connected to the network are all compatible, software also can be shared. For example, instead of ten copies of dBASE for ten users, a single copy of the network version of dBASE can be run by all users on a network. Although special versions or multi-user licenses may be legally required by the manufacturers of commercial software to be used on a network, this makes distributing updates and installing new packages much simpler. Internal electronic mail is yet another benefit offered by local area networks. This can be a real communications boon to organizations that occupy several offices on different floors of a building. Finally, another major reason for installing a LAN is to share expensive peripheral equipment. For example, a single high-speed, high-quality laser printer can be connected to a network and

Figure 15 Transmitting a File with CROSSTALK
With the sending computer in CALL mode and the receiving computer in ANSWER mode, you can transmit a file with the XMIT command. This screen shows how CROSSTALK reports the progress of the transmission.

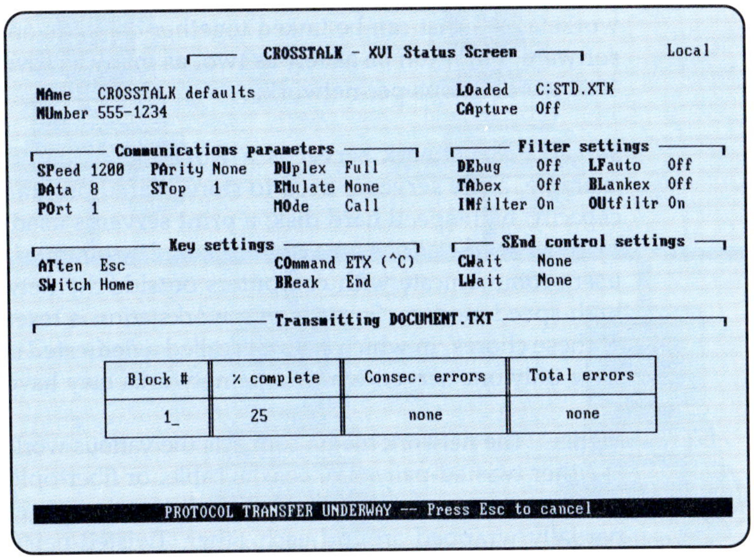

used by several individuals, who get their documents printed on a first-come, first-served basis. A shared laser printer is certainly more economical than a separate one for each user, even if it does take a little longer to get everyone's documents printed.

There are also some disadvantages to local area networks. Each microcomputer may have to be equipped with a special expansion board to be connected to a network. For example, although Apple Macintosh computers come with network circuitry built in, IBM microcomputers require the purchase of an additional network adapter board. Special connection hardware and cables must be purchased and installed in the building. Network software and special versions of application packages may add to the expense. Additional peripheral devices and a high-speed microcomputer to help control the network also may be required. In other words, local area networks can be expensive. The average cost is about $1000 to connect a microcomputer to a network, not including the cost of the microcomputer and any peripheral devices such as printers. Besides the expense involved, networks also can be difficult to set up and maintain. A network expert, skilled in hardware and software installation, is often needed to get the equipment running reliably. In general, networks are much more complex than single-user systems. Finally, installing a local area network can introduce some potential security problems. Special care must be taken to make sure that sensitive data is not shared with unauthorized users.

Hardware

Local area networks consist of several physical components. The key pieces of network hardware include workstations, servers, media, and interfaces. Let's examine each of these.

8. Why might you want to call a mainframe computer with your microcomputer?
9. On what type of computer system can electronic mail be implemented?
10. Which CROSSTALK command can you use to send incoming characters presented on your screen to a printer?
11. What happens when you send an electronic mail message to a fellow subscriber who isn't currently using the system?
12. Why might you use a public data network such as TYMNET to call a communications service such as MCI Mail?
13. List five activities you can do with a major on-line information service.
14. What is the oldest and largest on-line information service?
15. Give two reasons why you might use an on-line encyclopedia such as Grolier's *Academic American Encyclopedia* instead of a printed edition at your local library.
16. List two ways to connect two microcomputers that are not on a local area network.
17. Give three benefits to installing a local area network.
18. What distinguishes a network server from an ordinary network workstation?
19. What is the purpose of a communication protocol?
20. What is the primary purpose of network software?

Multiple Choice

1. Which of the following components is not necessary for distant microcomputer communications?
   (a) serial interface (b) modem
   (c) printer (d) telephone line
2. A disadvantage of internal modems is that they
   (a) are more expensive than external modems. (b) draw their electrical power from the computer.
   (c) require no external cables. (d) are computer specific.
3. Two basic functions of all communications software are
   (a) terminal emulation and file transfer. (b) error detection and file correction.
   (c) data base management and file security. (d) hardware and software sharing.
4. Transferring a file from a host computer to your microcomputer is called
   (a) uploading. (b) downloading.
   (c) polling. (d) emulating.
5. Which of the following is not a communications parameter?
   (a) speed (b) modem
   (c) port (d) parity
6. If you see two of every character you type when using a communications program, which setting should you change?
   (a) duplex (b) port
   (c) speed (d) parity

and complex rules prevent any one user from "hogging" the system. Token-passing is generally used with ring networks. For example the IBM Token-Ring Network is one of the most popular LANs for IBM-compatible microcomputers.

Software

Network software is a set of programs that reside for the most part on a file server. The primary purpose of this software is to move data and messages between the workstations and servers, and to control the sharing of files and hardware devices. In addition, network software also may include electronic mail facilities, enhanced security measures, programs for analyzing network performance, and diagnostic routines for troubleshooting malfunctions.

In many ways, network software is like a supplemental operating system. It controls hardware devices and manages the use of software on a network in conjunction with the microcomputer operating system. In order to understand how network software works we can compare it with software on a stand-alone microcomputer. As Figure 17 illustrates, a stand-alone IBM-compatible microcomputer requires several layers of programs that must work together. At the lowest level are programs that work directly with the hardware. In Chapter 4 we said that these BIOS (Basic Input/Output System) routines act as an interface

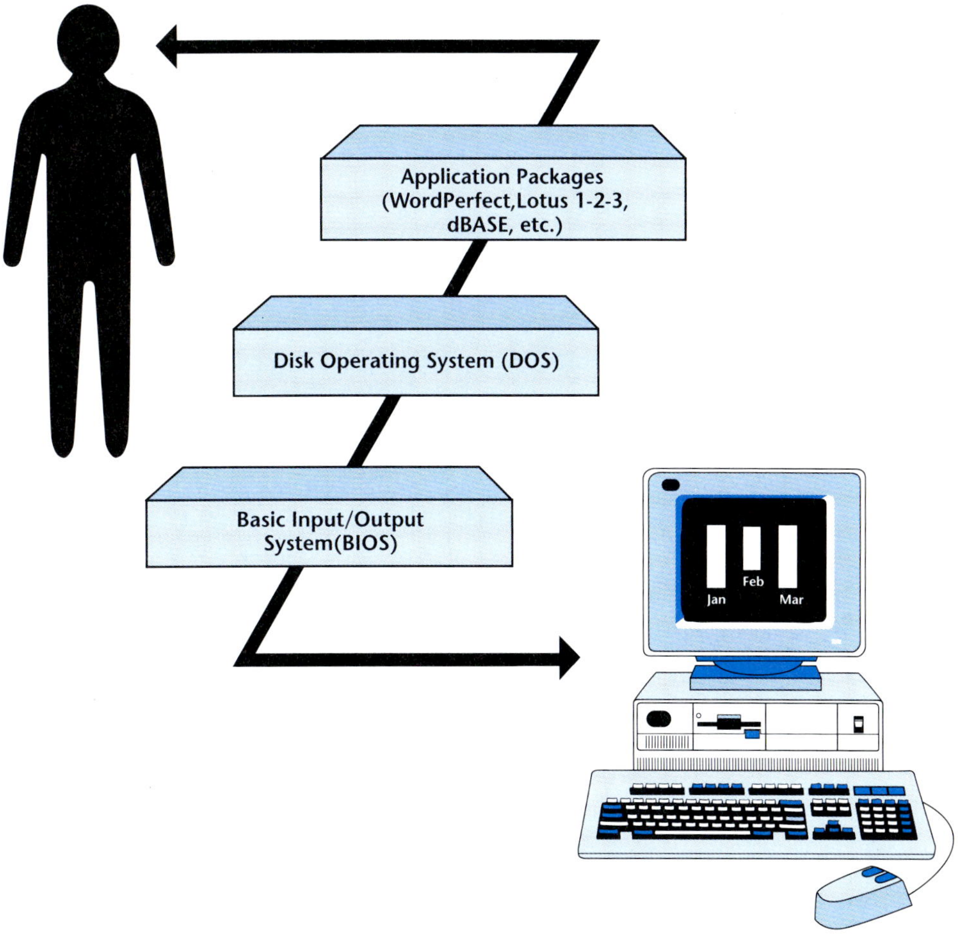

Figure 17 Software Layers on a Stand-alone Computer
An IBM-compatible microcomputer requires several layers of programs that must work together.

Real World

An On-Line Cornucopia

Peggy Berk, a Manhattan communications consultant, starts her day by turning on her modem-equipped computer, dialing into the GTE Telemail network, and reading on her screen any overnight telexes from her clients. Tapping a few keys, she scans the electronic version of *USA Today* before switching to another network to peruse the A.P. and U.P.I. news wires. "I can get along without my morning toast and coffee," she says, "but I can't leave home without going on line first."

Preparing to take a vacation in Jamaica, systems analyst Haig Hovanees logs onto CompuServe, the most popular computer network, calls up Travel Forum, and reads all about the political situation on the Caribbean island. He switches to the electronic *Official Airline Guide*, checks Jamaica flights for departure times, fares, and availability of seats, and makes his plans. Then, turning to his investment portfolio, he taps into the Value Line Database to flick through quarterly results, Standard & Poor's to see earnings forecasts, and Disclosure II to read official reports to the Securities and Exchange Commission. "The system gives me all the information I need to make strategic decisions," says Hovanees. "It's replaced a file cabinet stuffed with newspaper clips."

Across the country, more and more Americans are logging on to computer information and service networks and discovering an ever-enlarging cornucopia at their fingertips. Today anybody with a computer, a modem, and a deep line of credit can buy an airline ticket to Cleveland, rent a Hertz car at the airport, book a room at the Sheraton, buy a novel from Waldenbooks, check the closing prices on Wall Street, and purchase 100 shares of IBM—without ever getting up from the computer.

Source: Philip Elmer-DeWitt, "Calling Up an On-Line Cornucopia," *Time*, April 7, 1986, p. 69.

between the physical components of the computer and the other operating system software and application packages. The next layer consists of the disk operating system (DOS) software that performs more complex activities, such as the logical storage of programs and data in disk files. Finally, the highest level of stand-alone software consists of the application packages used for word processing, spreadsheets, data base management, and other tasks. In each of these layers, software is basically designed for use on a single computer at a time.

Network software on a file server has the same fundamental layers as on a stand-alone machine, but a few more programs and layers are added (see Figure 18). **NETBIOS (NETwork Basic Input/Output System)** routines are added at the lowest level to send data to and receive data from the network adapter board, just as ordinary BIOS routines control the serial and parallel interfaces. Working beside DOS at the next higher level, network server software allows workstations to share disks and peripheral devices, as well as communicate with other workstations. Above DOS and the server software is the **redirector** layer. This software acts as a traffic controller for the data and messages transmitted over the network. Network utilities, menu systems, and security programs make up the next layer of software. These are programs that users can call upon to set up workstations to run on the network, send messages to other workstations, send files to the print server to be printed, gain access to disks and directories on file servers, and see network status reports. Finally, at the top level are application packages like word processors, spreadsheets, and data base managers.

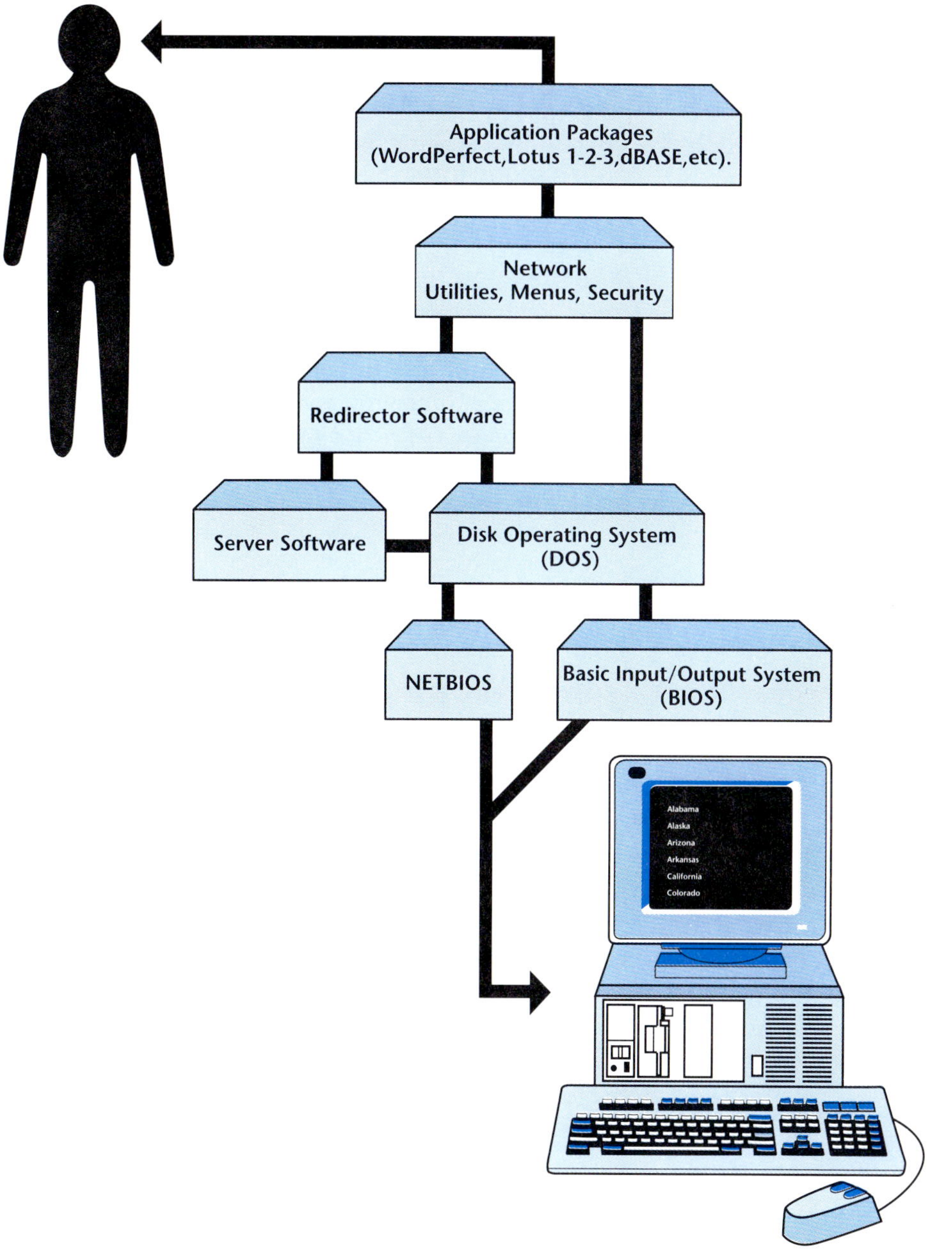

Figure 18 Software Layers on a Network Server
Network software is like a supplemental operating system, adding more programs and layers.

Using a Network

Fortunately, using a local area network is much easier than setting one up or understanding exactly how it works. Network media, interfaces, topologies, protocols, and software layers are generally transparent to the end user. He or she has little or nothing to do with them. Most operating system commands work exactly the same as on a stand-alone computer, except that the user has access to additional disk drives and peripheral devices on a network. For example, a shared hard disk on a file server in a network of IBM-compatible microcomputers is assigned a letter just like the A, B, and C disk drives on a stand-alone machine. The only difference is that shared network hard disks are assigned letters beyond C, such as D, E, F, and so on. So even though your workstation may have only two floppy drives, A and B, it may also have access to hard disk E in one of the file servers. To switch drives, copy files, or run software from the file server, you treat hard disk E just as if it were installed in your own computer. In some cases you may have to use network versions of DOS commands, but they work similarly to ordinary DOS commands. IBM networks, for instance, require you to use the NET PRINT command instead of the regular PRINT command. The NET PRINT command allows you to send a file to a printer that is shared with other network users.

Running application packages on a network is also similar to running them on a stand-alone computer. If users don't share their data files, no special features or procedures are needed to run programs on a network. It doesn't matter whether programs and data are stored on a user's own disk or on a file server's disk. Software manufacturers may require special licenses for multiple workstations to run the same copy of a program at the same time legally. Nevertheless, even non-network versions of programs like WordPerfect and Lotus 1-2-3 run well on a network as long as users work with only their own data files. If two users on a network try to edit the same document with WordPerfect, for example, the work of one of them can be lost. The last person to save the document to the disk will destroy any previous copy saved by someone else.

One of the best reasons for installing a network, however, is to let users share the same data files. Special network versions of software packages are required to let users successfully gain access to the same data files at the same time with no mishaps. Many data base management systems, such as dBASE, are designed to run on networks. These programs employ a variety of file locking, record locking, and security measures to prevent users from destroying each other's data.

Summary

- *The basic hardware of microcomputer communications.* Four primary components are necessary for communications: a microcomputer, serial interface, modem, and telephone line. Two other considerations in the selection of a modem are speed and Hayes compatibility.
- *The primary functions of communications software.* In addition to letting you set up your equipment to call other computers, communications software performs terminal emulation and allows you to download and upload files.
- *The various software settings that govern microcomputer communications.* Several parameters specify the technical details of how your microcomputer will communicate with other computers: speed, number of data bits, which serial port to use, type of parity, number of stop bits, type of duplex, which type of terminal emulation, and whether to call or answer.
- *How to call a mainframe computer with a microcomputer.* First, find out the settings required by the mainframe and, if necessary, change the communications parameters to match. Call the mainframe and enter your sign-on and password. Use the mainframe's facilities; terminate the call when finished.
- *How to use an electronic mail facility.* After subscribing, calling, and logging on to the system, you can send messages to other subscribers and read messages that have been sent to you. Simple menus guide you through addressing your messages, entering the text, and sending them.

- *How to use an on-line information service.* Once you subscribe, many services are at your disposal. After calling and logging on to the system, you can select items from menus or directly enter commands to read the most recent news, research a topic in an on-line encyclopedia, and so on.
- *How to call one microcomputer from another.* Match the communications parameters on both machines. One computer is put into CALL mode and the other into ANSWER mode. The user of the calling computer then dials the answering computer's phone number. The calling computer can then download and upload files from the answering computer.
- *The fundamental components and uses of local area networks.* Networks consist of workstations, servers, media, and interfaces. They allow you to connect two or more microcomputers to share programs, data, and peripheral equipment.

Key Terms

As an extra review of this chapter, try defining the following terms.

bus network
capture
carrier sense multiple access (CSMA)
coaxial cable
communications parameters
communications server
dedicated server
downloading
electronic mail (E-mail)
fiber-optic cable
file server
full-duplex
half-duplex
Hayes-compatible modem
host computer
modem cable
modular phone jack
NETBIOS (Network Basic Input/Output System)
network interface
network media
network server
network software
network workstation
null-modem cable
parity
polling
print server
protocol
public data network (packet-switching network, value-added network)
redirector
ring network
star network
stop bits
terminal emulation
token-passing
topology
twisted-pair wire
uploading

Review Questions

1. List the four basic components of a microcomputer communications system.
2. How is the transmission speed of a modem usually expressed?
3. Why is Hayes compatibility so important in a modem?
4. What are two basic functions performed by all communications software?
5. What is the difference between uploading and downloading?
6. Name one popular communications package for CP/M and DOS microcomputers.
7. List eight communications parameters you can set with most communications software.

8. Why might you want to call a mainframe computer with your microcomputer?
9. On what type of computer system can electronic mail be implemented?
10. Which CROSSTALK command can you use to send incoming characters presented on your screen to a printer?
11. What happens when you send an electronic mail message to a fellow subscriber who isn't currently using the system?
12. Why might you use a public data network such as TYMNET to call a communications service such as MCI Mail?
13. List five activities you can do with a major on-line information service.
14. What is the oldest and largest on-line information service?
15. Give two reasons why you might use an on-line encyclopedia such as Grolier's *Academic American Encyclopedia* instead of a printed edition at your local library.
16. List two ways to connect two microcomputers that are not on a local area network.
17. Give three benefits to installing a local area network.
18. What distinguishes a network server from an ordinary network workstation?
19. What is the purpose of a communication protocol?
20. What is the primary purpose of network software?

Multiple Choice

1. Which of the following components is not necessary for distant microcomputer communications?
   (a) serial interface (b) modem
   (c) printer (d) telephone line
2. A disadvantage of internal modems is that they
   (a) are more expensive than external modems. (b) draw their electrical power from the computer.
   (c) require no external cables. (d) are computer specific.
3. Two basic functions of all communications software are
   (a) terminal emulation and file transfer. (b) error detection and file correction.
   (c) data base management and file security. (d) hardware and software sharing.
4. Transferring a file from a host computer to your microcomputer is called
   (a) uploading. (b) downloading.
   (c) polling. (d) emulating.
5. Which of the following is not a communications parameter?
   (a) speed (b) modem
   (c) port (d) parity
6. If you see two of every character you type when using a communications program, which setting should you change?
   (a) duplex (b) port
   (c) speed (d) parity

7. Which of the following is a security measure that helps prevent unauthorized access to a mainframe computer?
   (a) parity (b) duplex
   (c) password (d) stop bits
8. Which of the following is a popular way to send and receive messages with a computer?
   (a) uploading (b) downloading
   (c) terminal emulation (d) electronic mail
9. A public data network such as TYMNET is often used to call a distant communications service because
   (a) it is more convenient than calling directly.
   (b) it is less expensive than calling long distance.
   (c) it is faster than calling directly.
   (d) it is more accurate than calling long distance.
10. Which of the following is the most popular multi-purpose on-line information service?
   (a) CompuServe (b) GEnie
   (c) MCI Mail (d) Dow Jones/News Retrieval Service
11. Which of the following CompuServe commands is a way to bypass intermediate menus and jump directly to the feature you want to use?
   (a) TOP (b) MENU
   (c) BYE (d) GO
12. Which of the following is an inexpensive way to connect two microcomputers?
   (a) local area network (b) on-line information service
   (c) null-modem cable (d) fiber-optic cable
13. Which of the following arrangements is the best way to link several microcomputers for the purpose of sharing data files, programs, and peripheral devices?
   (a) null-modem cable (b) local area network
   (c) modems and the telephone network (d) on-line information service
14. Which of the following is not a key piece of network hardware?
   (a) network workstation (b) network server
   (c) network media (d) network mouse
15. Which of the following is not a commonly used network protocol?
   (a) polling (b) parity
   (c) carrier sense multiple access (d) token-passing

Projects

1. At 1200 bps, a modem transmits approximately 120 characters per second over the telephone line. A typical single-spaced page of text consists of 50 lines of 60 characters each. How long does it take to transmit one page of text at 1200 bps? Not including figures, each chapter in this book, on average,

is equivalent to about 30 single-spaced typewritten pages. How long would it take to transmit one chapter over the phone line at 1200 bps? Finally, there are 21 chapters in this book. About how long would it take to send all 21 chapters at 1200 bps? Now repeat these calculations with 300 bps and 2400 bps.

2. In this chapter we briefly introduced the CROSSTALK communications package. Do some research to find out more about this type of application software. Compare CROSSTALK with other popular communications programs on the market. Write a short report summarizing what you learn. *PC Magazine, BYTE* magazine, *InfoWorld,* and other computer periodicals are good sources of information and product reviews.

3. Find out more about on-line information services. Compare the features and facilities offered by CompuServe with some other service. Write a brief report with your findings. Which service do you think you would prefer? Why?

4. Does your school, office, or company use a local area network? If you don't personally know of a local area network being used by some organization with which you come in contact, find a magazine or newspaper article about one. Write a brief report describing this "real world" use of a local area network. What kind of a local area network is it? How many workstations are connected together? Why did the organization decide to install the network? How well has the network worked out so far? How much did it cost? Try to answer some of these questions or any others you think are important to get a good understanding of how networks are being put to use in our society.

CHAPTER 18

GRAPHICS

In This Chapter

Graphics Hardware
- Display Adapter
- Monitor
- Input Device
- Hard-Copy Output Device

Graphics Software

Charting Programs
- Types of Charting Programs
- Introducing EnerGraphics
- Creating a Pie Chart
- Creating a Bar Graph

Painting Programs
- Introducing MacPaint
- The MacPaint Screen
- The MacPaint Pointer
- The MacPaint Tools
- Designing a Logo with MacPaint

Drawing Programs
- Introducing MacDraw
- The MacDraw Screen
- The MacDraw Tools
- The MacDraw Menus
- Designing a Desk with MacDraw

Computer-Aided Design Programs
- CAD Features
- Introducing AutoCAD
- Designing a Floor Plan with AutoCAD

Slide Show Programs
- Introducing PC Storyboard
- Creating the Pictures
- Editing the Slide Show
- Presenting the Slide Show

Preview

Computer graphics used to be the domain of scientists and engineers, laboring in their high-tech world of expensive and unwieldy equipment. But now, virtually all modern microcomputers have the potential to produce stunning visual displays. Hardware and software advancements have made computer graphics affordable, effective, easy to use, and even fun. Whether you're a student, artist, author, or executive, computer graphics can help you create pictures to get your point across.

Drawing graphs, charts, and plots by hand is quickly becoming a thing of the past. If you've ever plotted a curve for a science class, drawn a graph for a math class, or constructed a bar chart for a business class, you know the tedium of manual graphics. With the right combination of microcomputer hardware and software, however, you can generally perform such tasks faster, easier, and more accurately than you could by hand. Unless you're a graphic artist, using a computer also produces much more attractive results—on the screen, on paper, on slides, and on overhead transparencies.

Graphs, charts, and plots are structured pictures derived from numerical data. Computer graphics can also help you produce all kinds of free-hand figures and illustrations. For example, some graphics packages let you use a mouse to "draw" or "paint" pictures on the display screen. These programs provide a wide range of sketching, shading, and editing tools. Completed pictures can be saved in disk files and printed or plotted. With a little practice, almost anyone can produce figures, diagrams, and other illustrations for reports, presentations, articles, and books. Besides software for drawing and painting, more specialized graphics packages are available for technical drafting and for producing "slide shows" that run on a computer screen. In this chapter, first we will examine the hardware and then the software of computer graphics systems.

After studying this chapter, you will understand

- the hardware of microcomputer graphics.
- the basic types of microcomputer graphics software.
- how to use a charting program.
- how to use a painting program.
- how to use a drawing program.
- how to use a computer-aided design program.
- how to use a computer slide show program.

Graphics Hardware

Before you can run any graphics software, you must have a computer system that includes several key components. Some computers, such as the Apple Macintosh Plus and Macintosh SE, come complete with all you need to work with graphics. These systems are easy to purchase and set up because they don't require the selection of individual graphics hardware components. In most cases, however, owners must choose from a range of different hardware options to equip their computers for graphics. This is especially true for IBM-compatible microcomputers. Although many different options are available, four basic hardware components are necessary, along with a computer, for a complete graphics system: a display adapter, monitor, input device, and hard-copy output device (see Figure 1). Let's examine each of these in detail.

Figure 1 Graphics Hardware Components
Along with a computer, a complete graphics system must have a display adapter, monitor, input device such as a mouse, and a hard-copy output device such as a printer or plotter.

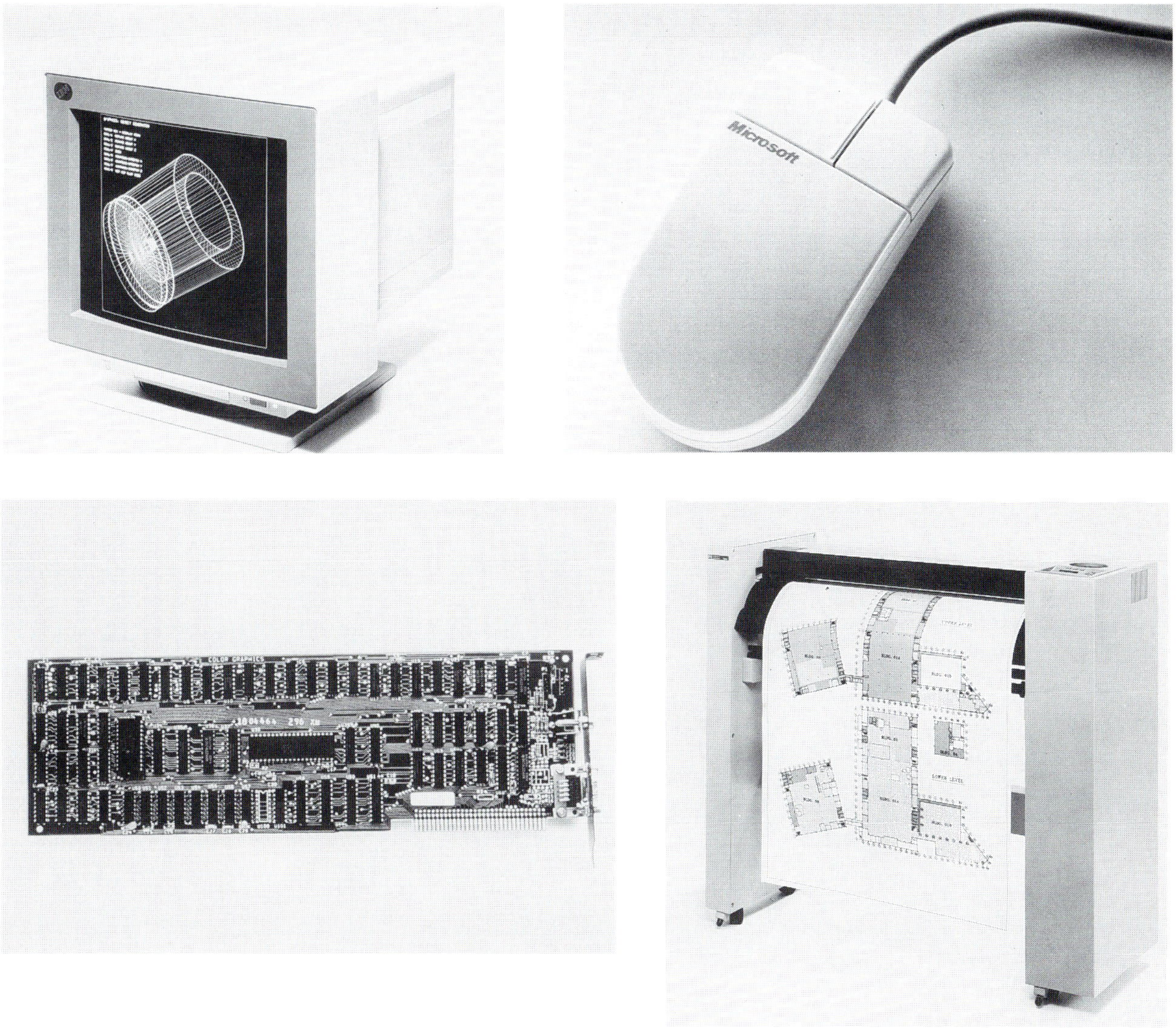

Display Adapter

The single most important part of any graphics system is the display adapter. A display adapter that is capable of producing graphics is sometimes called a **graphics adapter**. As we said in Chapter 2, this is the circuit board that controls the monitor. Sometimes, the display adapter is built onto the computer's motherboard. This is the case in the Apple Macintosh Plus, the Macintosh SE, the Macintosh SE/30, the Macintosh Portable, the Macintosh IIci, and the IBM Personal System/2 microcomputers. In other computers, the display adapter is a completely separate expansion board that fits into one of the expansion slots (see Figure 2). Most of these computers can be equipped with any one of a number of different display adapters. Even computers with a display adapter

Insight

Professional Artists and Microcomputers

Their art may not be destined to grace the galleries of the Louvre, but artists today are producing an astonishing variety of work with microcomputers.

For many years, a good computer graphics system cost more than $20,000 per terminal, not including the hefty price of the mainframe that drove the graphics terminals. The arrival of the microcomputer, with its substantial graphics capabilities, has changed all that. There has been a surge of interest in using the computer for design and even to create drawings and paintings.

Today, many students who are majoring in art and industrial design use computer-aided design (CAD) packages such as AUTOCAD. With a good CAD package, it's possible to develop the design of any complex object by working on smaller subassemblies.

A computer-aided design package is to an artist and designer what the spreadsheet is to the accountant.

built onto the motherboard sometimes can be fitted with an optional circuit board to enhance or upgrade the graphics capability.

Your display adapter determines the video modes that can be used by your software, as well as the type of monitor that you can connect to your system. As we said in Chapter 2, a *video mode* specifies the screen resolution and the colors that can be displayed on the monitor. Screen resolution determines the sharpness and clarity of the images you see. Virtually all microcomputer displays present a matrix of tiny dots, or *pixels*, that are turned off and on in various colors to make pictures. Resolution is expressed in terms of the total number of horizontal and vertical pixels that can be displayed on the screen. Color capability is usually described by the number of different colors that can be on the screen at one time, along with the total number of possible colors to choose from. Some display adapters have only one video mode. The built-in Apple Macintosh SE display adapter, for example, has a screen resolution of 512 horizontal by 342

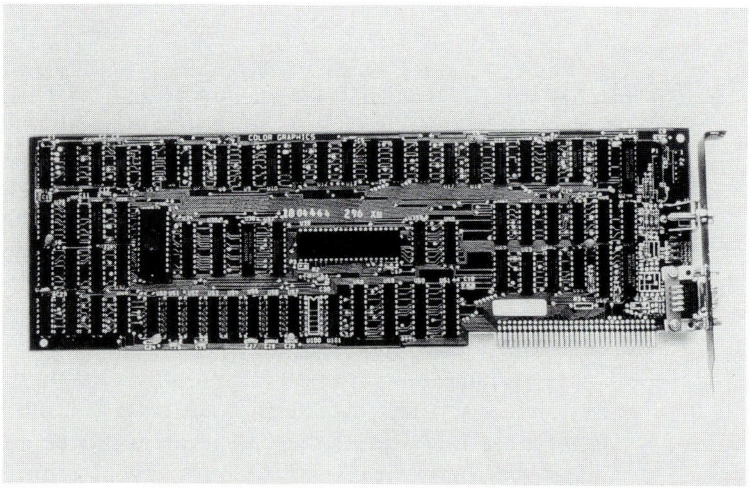

Figure 2 Graphics Adapter *The graphics adapter contains the circuitry that controls the monitor.*

Table 1 IBM Graphics Video Modes and Adapters

Mode	Resolution[a]	Display Adapter[b]	Display Colors[c]
4, 5	320 × 200	CGA EGA MCGA VGA	4 out of 16 4 out of 64 4 out of 262,144 4 out of 262,144
6	640 × 200	CGA EGA MCGA VGA	2 out of 16 2 out of 64 2 out of 262,144 2 out of 262,144
13	320 × 200	EGA VGA	16 out of 64 16 out of 262,144
14	640 × 200	EGA VGA	16 out of 64 16 out of 262,144
15	640 × 350	EGA VGA	Monochrome Monochrome
16	640 × 350	EGA VGA	16 out of 64 16 out of 262,144
17	640 × 480	MCGA VGA	2 out of 262,144 2 out of 262,144
18	640 × 480	VGA	16 out of 262,144
19	320 × 200	MCGA VGA	256 out of 262,144 256 out of 262,144

[a]The Resolution column expresses the total number of horizontal by vertical pixels on the screen.
[b]Display Adapter column abbreviations: CGA = Color Graphics Adapter; EGA = Enhanced Graphics Adapter; MCGA = Multicolor Graphics Array; VGA = Video Graphics Array.
[c]The Display Colors column shows the number of different colors that can simultaneously appear on the screen out of the total number of possible different colors.

vertical pixels and just two "colors," black and white. Most display adapters, however, can operate in a number of different video modes. As Table 1 shows, IBM microcomputer owners have a choice of several different graphics display adapters, most of which can operate in several different video modes.

Monitor

The display adapter and monitor must be perfectly matched to work correctly. Nevertheless, in many instances there are various acceptable combinations. Some display adapters work with a number of different monitors. For example, the IBM Enhanced Graphics Adapter (EGA) can be connected to an IBM Monochrome Display, an IBM Color Display, or an IBM Enhanced Color Display. Some monitors can be connected to a number of different display adapters. These **multiscan monitors** work by changing their resolution to match the display adapter. The NEC MultiSync monitor, for example, can be connected to most of IBM's display adapters as well as the Apple Macintosh II display adapter. Many compatible display adapters and monitors made by other manufacturers can be connected in various combinations. The most important aspect of selecting a monitor is making sure that it works correctly with your display adapter.

Besides matching your monitor to your display adapter, there are three other basic considerations in selecting a monitor: color, size, and sharpness. The first consideration is whether to use a monochrome or a color graphics monitor. Some display adapters can accept either kind. For example, the Video Graphics Array (VGA) display adapter built into the IBM Personal System/2 Models 50, 60, 70, and 80 can be connected to either a black and white monochrome monitor or a color monitor. The monochrome monitor costs around $250—less than half as much as the color monitor. It is the same size and just as sharp, but uses shades of gray to simulate different colors.

Another monitor consideration is the screen size. Measured diagonally, the most common sizes are 9, 12, 14, 16, and 19 inches. In general, the smaller screens appear sharper but present smaller characters and pictures. Larger screens tend to cost more than smaller screens, but this isn't always so. For example, the 12-inch color monitor for IBM Personal System/2 computers costs $90 more than the 14-inch color monitor.

The main reason for this cost difference is the third basic monitor consideration: sharpness. **Dot pitch** is another, more technical term for the sharpness of a monitor. Usually expressed in millimeters, this is the distance between the illuminated centers of any two adjacent dots. The smaller the dot pitch, the sharper the image. The 12-inch IBM color monitor for the Personal System/2 computers costs more because it has a dot pitch of 0.28 mm, while the 14-inch monitor has a dot pitch of 0.41 mm. This makes the images on the larger display somewhat more grainy.

Input Device

Besides the keyboard, many graphics programs require the use of an additional graphics input device. Although the mouse is by far the most common, other types of input devices, such as the trackball and graphics tablet, are also used. As we said in Chapter 2, these input devices allow you to easily move a cursor or pointer anywhere on the screen. A mouse, trackball, or graphics tablet is practically essential for drawing and manipulating objects. Some computers, such as the Apple Macintosh SE, come with a mouse as standard equipment. With many others, a mouse is an option that must be purchased separately. The mouse plugs into a serial interface, into its own special expansion board, or directly into the motherboard. The mouse and similar input devices are basically used to draw and manipulate objects by hand, one at a time.

Another type of input device, the *scanner*, takes a different approach (see Figure 3). As we said in Chapter 2, a page scanner reads in a whole page of text and graphics. The images that are scanned are converted into dots that can be displayed on the screen, manipulated by graphics programs, stored in files, and printed. In addition to full page scanners, some less expensive, hand-held scanners are also now on the market that let you read images in strips two to four inches wide. Scanners are becoming increasingly popular as their prices decrease and as people use graphics and desktop publishing packages more and more.

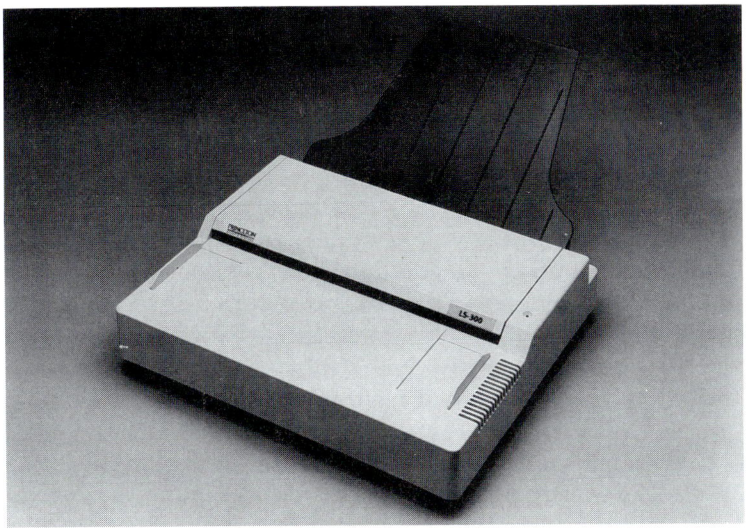

Figure 3 Optical Scanner *A scanner enables a computer to read existing text and graphics from a printed page.*

This method of entering graphical data into computers is suitable for reproducing many different types of images, including photographs, drawings, charts, signatures, and even ordinary text. Although the vast majority of scanners can only copy in black and white, and perhaps some gray tones, there are a few expensive models that can reproduce color images.

Hard-Copy Output Device

Admittedly, some programs use graphics only to present images on a display screen. Computer game, simulation, and slide-show programs are a few examples of this type of software. Nevertheless, most graphics programs are much more useful if they can produce some permanent record of the images they display. So, a hard-copy output device such as a printer, plotter, or film recorder is usually considered an essential component of a complete graphics system.

The most common hard-copy output device for graphics is the ordinary printer. As we said in Chapter 2, the most common type of printer used with microcomputers is the *dot-matrix printer*. This output device is reliable, relatively inexpensive, and easy to operate. Furthermore, dot-matrix printers produce their output on an inexpensive medium—paper. Since all dot matrix printers by definition use dots to create text, most of them have no trouble at all also producing graphics. Some dot-matrix printers can even use multi-color ribbons to produce color pictures. In many cases, the images made by dot-matrix printers are superior to those presented on the display screen, because printers typically have a higher maximum resolution than most monitors. For example, the standard built-in Apple Macintosh display screen has a maximum resolution of 72 dots per inch. The Apple Imagewriter II printer often used with this computer can easily achieve a resolution of 144 dots per inch.

Besides dot-matrix printers, *laser printers* are also frequently used for graphics output. Laser printers are sophisticated devices that can achieve resolutions of at least 300 dots per inch. Besides producing high-quality images, laser printers are also quiet and fast. With a few expensive exceptions, however, laser printers can only print in one color, usually black.

Another fairly common graphics output device is the *ink-jet printer*, which sprays tiny drops of ink on paper to produce images. This less expensive alternative to the laser printer is also quiet and fairly quick. Some of the newest ink-jet printers now on the market can rival laser printers with resolutions of nearly 300 dots per inch. Unlike laser printers, many ink-jet printers can also produce output in several colors.

Plotters use pens instead of a printing mechanism to produce hard-copy output. As a result, they are generally better suited to drafting and map-drawing applications. In addition, most plotters can produce pictures in different colors with different pens. They can even be used to draw on sheets of acetate plastic for use with overhead projectors. Plotters are, however, generally slower than printers.

A more specialized output device used in some graphics systems is the **film recorder** (see Figure 4). Basically, a film recorder turns screen images into 35-mm slides, which can then be shown with an ordinary slide projector. Slides are often more convenient for presenting graphics to large audiences. The film recorder is usually plugged into the computer's display adapter or serial interface. It works by reproducing computer screen images on its own internal screen at one end of an enclosed box. This screen is then photographed with a 35-mm camera mounted on the other end of the box. Generally, film recorders can create images at a higher resolution and with a greater variety of colors than is possible on a computer monitor. The slides produced by film recorders are usually sharper, more detailed, and more colorful. Once the pictures have been taken, the film must be processed at a film lab just like any other 35-mm slides. Costing at least $2000, film recorders are somewhat expensive, but they are well suited to producing high-quality slides for use in presentations and publications.

Graphics Software

Unless you're a programmer, a computer equipped with graphics hardware is of little use without graphics software too. Instead of writing your own programs, you'll probably use commercial software packages to create, display, and print

Figure 4 Film Recorder
A film recorder, such as the Polaroid Palette Plus, turns screen images into 35-mm slides.

charts, pictures, figures, diagrams, and computerized slide shows. Fortunately, an abundance of excellent software is available to help you use your computer as a graphics tool.

Many different kinds of graphics packages are on the market, and new types of programs are being devised all the time. The distinctions between different types of graphics software are sometimes blurred because developers frequently include many diverse features in the same package. Nevertheless, most commonly used microcomputer graphics programs primarily fall into one of the following categories: charting, painting, drawing, computer-aided design, and slide show. For the rest of this chapter, we will examine each one of these categories of graphics software in greater detail. In each case, we will give a specific example of a popular commercial package used on either IBM-compatible or Apple Macintosh computers.

Charting Programs

It's practically impossible to go through a day without seeing at least one chart, graph, or plot. These graphics are very common in newspapers, magazines, books, and television. Countless speakers at presentations, meetings, press conferences, and lectures use charts to help them get their messages across quickly, clearly, and concisely. Graphs have always been valuable for depicting numbers in a more understandable and memorable visual format. Now one of the reasons charts are used so often is the ease with which they can be generated on a computer. All you need is the appropriate graphics hardware and a charting program. A **charting program** produces graphs, plots, and charts from data you enter directly or import from a spreadsheet or data base file. Charting programs typically provide a wide range of different kinds of charts and give you a great deal of control over the charts' final appearance.

Types of Charting Programs

Most types of application packages are capable of producing charts. A few of the most popular kinds of charting programs include:

- *Spreadsheet Enhancement.* Many spreadsheet programs can display and print various graphs. Although some have more advanced features, spreadsheet programs generally are limited to a few different types of graphs and give the user little control over their final format. For many people, this is enough. Other computer users require more elaborate output. Some programs on the market are specifically designed to spruce up the graphs of a particular spreadsheet. For example, 3D-Graphics from Intex Solutions is a program that lets you add depth, instead of just width and height, to Lotus 1-2-3 charts. Spreadsheet enhancement charting programs such as 3D-Graphics can help you easily improve the appearance of your spreadsheet charts at a relatively low cost.
- *Data Base Charting.* Unlike spreadsheets, most data base management systems don't have built-in graphics capabilities. Some graphics packages, however, are designed to work with particular data base systems. DB Graphics from Microrim, for instance, is a charting program specifically for users of dBASE and R:base. This program reads data base files directly to let you create eight different types of color graphs. A data base charting program such as DB Graphics may be the easiest solution for people who need to routinely create graphs from a particular data base management system.

- *Map Making*. Some popular charting programs specialize in generating maps to present data. For example, Atlas Graphics from Strategic Locations Planning is a program for IBM-compatible computers that creates only maps (see Figure 5). Instead of displaying data in bar graphs or pie charts, Atlas Graphics presents information in a map format that can reveal complex geographic relationships. A well-conceived map chart is often better than other graphs for data such as market potential, regional sales performance, and other population statistics. You can enter your own map outlines or purchase additional files that contain regional boundaries for many countries, states, counties, ZIP codes, census tracts, and communities.
- *Dedicated Charting*. Most charting programs on the market offer a wide range of different types of graphs as well as a good deal of control over the graphs' final appearance. These programs are often called *dedicated charting* programs to distinguish them from graphics packages that are integrated with spreadsheets or data base managers. Dedicated charting programs need no other packages to create graphs. Although they can usually accept data files from word processors, spreadsheets, and data base managers, they also take data entered directly from the user. Dedicated charting packages are one of the most popular types of application software, especially in business, government, education, and journalism.

Introducing EnerGraphics

EnerGraphics is a good example of a typical dedicated charting program. Made by Enertronics Research Inc., this popular program was one of the first full-featured charting packages developed for IBM-compatible microcomputers. Despite its many fine competitors, EnerGraphics is still considered to be a top-notch product, especially well suited to creating business graphics. For data analysis, you can create simple pie charts, bar graphs, several types of line plots, and statistical graphs. In addition, EnerGraphics lets you do two- and three-dimen-

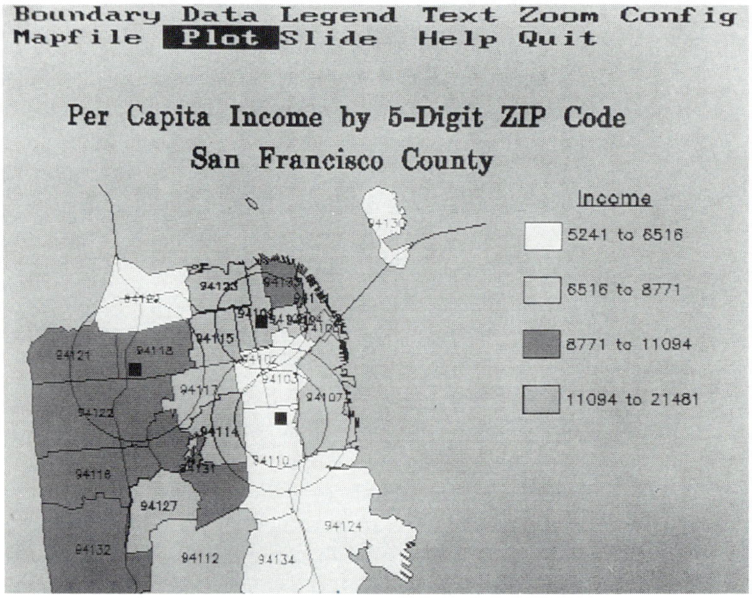

Figure 5 Map-making Program
Some charting programs specialize in making maps, such as Atlas Graphics from Strategic Locations Planning.

sional drawings. This drawing capability can be used to design organizational charts, flowcharts, electrical circuits, mechanical parts, and architectural plans. EnerGraphics also can present your charts in the form of a simple slide show. Let's stick to the basics, however, and see what it's like to use EnerGraphics (version 2.2) to produce a couple of charts.

Installing and running EnerGraphics is quite simple. Most users put the program on a hard disk. After switching to the appropriate disk drive directory, you simply enter **ENG** from DOS to begin. Figure 6 shows the Main menu that appears on your screen.

Creating a Pie Chart

Let's say that you want to create a pie chart showing the cost breakdown of goods manufactured at a cookie factory. There are three components to this cost:

1. Materials = $80 million
2. Labor = $20 million
3. Overhead = $10 million

The first step is to select the Charting option from the Main menu. Since this is the default option, all you have to do is press the **Enter** key. EnerGraphics then displays its Chart menu, shown in Figure 7(a). The available options are listed in the upper right box. To select an option, you can either press the function key that precedes it, or use the arrow keys to position the highlight bar upon it and then press the **Enter** key. For example, you press the **F3** function key to select the Create/Edit Chart option.

The Edit menu then appears on your screen (see Figure 7(b)). Now you select the Create/Edit Data option by pressing the **F1** function key. Next EnerGraphics asks you to specify the type of chart to be created. You can choose a Pie, Bar, Line, or Text chart. Simply type **P** to create a pie chart.

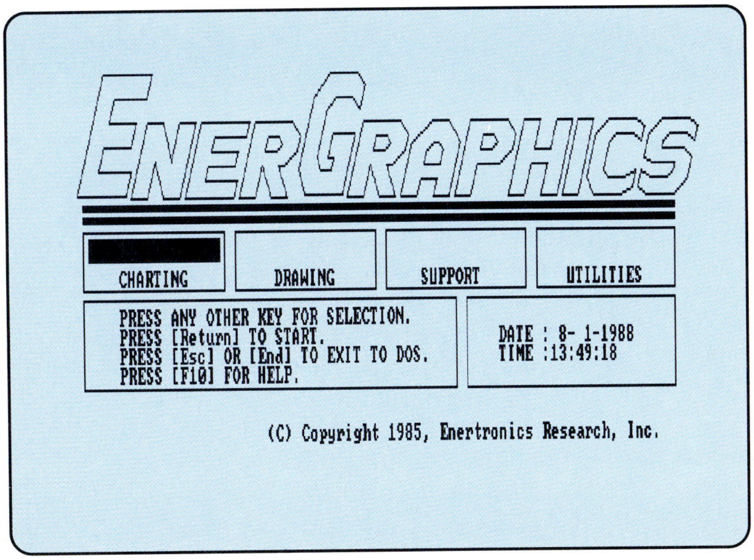

***Figure 6* EnerGraphics Main Menu**
This screen shows the Main menu of the EnerGraphics charting program for IBM-compatible microcomputers.

Figure 7 Creating a Pie Chart

(a) The Chart menu.

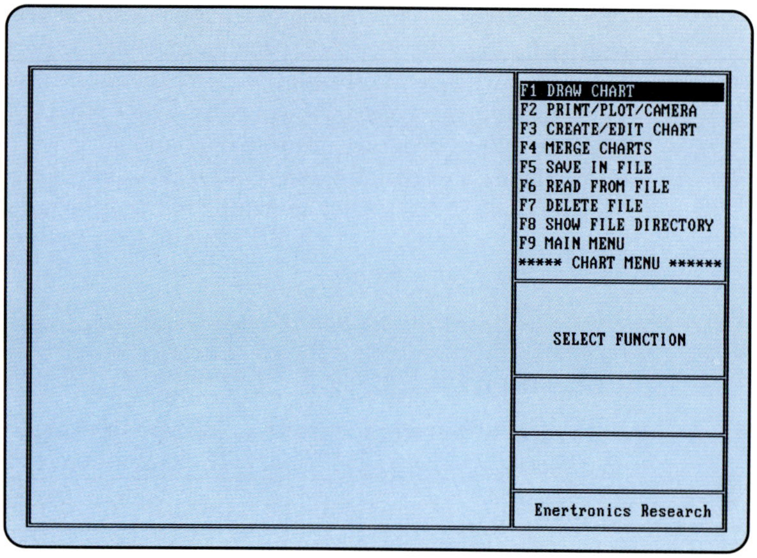

(b) The Edit menu.

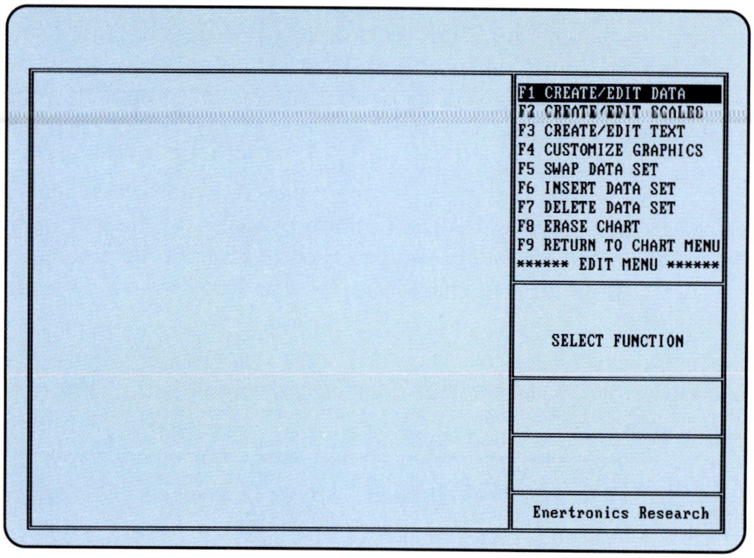

EnerGraphics then presents a screen in which you enter the data and formatting instructions for the pie chart. Figure 7(c) shows this screen after all the information for your pie chart has been entered. For each slice in the pie, you enter its numeric value, its color, its fill pattern, and a number between 0 and 9 that specifies how far the slice should be pulled out, or *offset*, from the rest of the pie. For example, the Overhead slice has a value of 10 ($10 million) and it is to be displayed in color 3 (white or yellow) with pattern 3 (filled in with lines). For emphasis, this slice is given an offset value of 2 so that it will be pulled out from the pie a little more than the other slices.

When you're finished specifying the pie chart slices, you press the **End** key. EnerGraphics then lets you enter a title for the chart, such as **Cost of Goods Manufactured**. Press the **End** key to return to the Edit menu, and then press **F9**

(c) The completed pie chart data table.

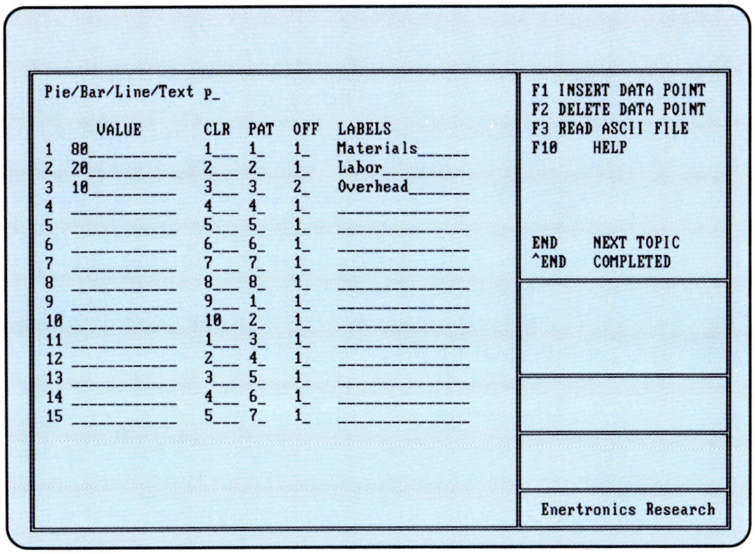

(d) The completed pie chart.

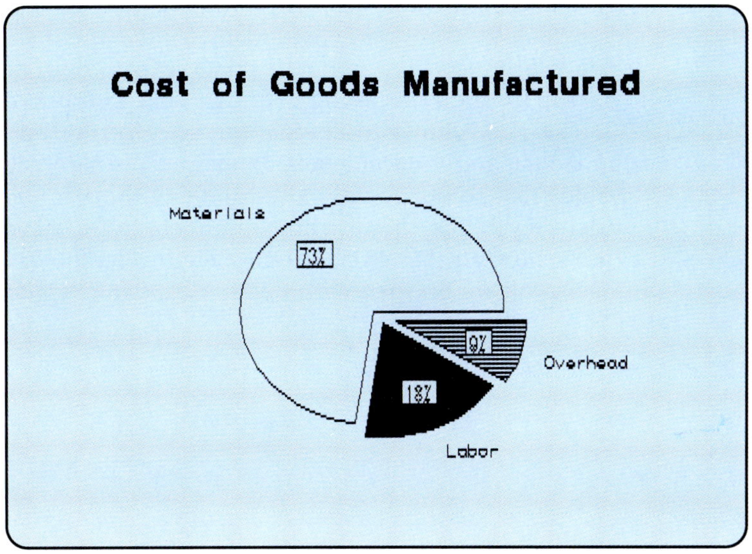

to return to the Chart menu. Now press **F1** to draw the chart. Another screen appears with options for changing certain aspects of the chart's final appearance. For example, you can specify the chart's background color, make the chart three dimensional, or select a frame (border) for the chart. Usually, the default display parameters are fine. EnerGraphics asks if you want to use the default display parameters, and you can answer yes by simply pressing the **Enter** key. Figure 7(d) shows the pie chart that appears on your screen.

When you are finished viewing the chart, you can press any key to return to the Chart menu. At this point, you can print your chart and save it in a disk file. The Chart menu also provides options for loading previously saved charts so that you can view or modify them, and deleting existing charts that are no longer needed.

Creating a Bar Graph

Bar graphs are useful for comparing different sets of data. For example, you could use a bar graph to show the unit sales of two different products, say chocolate chip cookies and peanut butter cookies, for the first six months of the year. In such a graph, the value of the units sold of each cookie for each month is represented by a bar, where the length of the bar corresponds to the magnitude of the value. The bars of each cookie are distinguished by filling them in with different patterns or colors. Let's use EnerGraphics to produce a simple bar graph like the one we've just described.

The first few steps are the same as creating a pie chart. You choose Charting from the Main menu, Create/Edit Chart from the Chart menu, and Create/Edit Data from the Edit menu. When EnerGraphics prompts you for the kind of chart, however, you type **B** for bar chart. The program then allows you to choose from several different types of bar charts. *Normal* is the default type of bar chart, which you can select by pressing the **Enter** key. EnerGraphics then presents a screen in which you enter information about your first data set. Figure 8(a) shows the completed screen for your first data set, which contains the data for chocolate chip cookies. The Legend Entry identifies these bars as representing chocolate chip cookie sales. The Color and Pattern entries specify the appearance of the bars. The Values are the sales figures for each month, and the Labels indicate the names of the months. When you are finished entering the data for chocolate chip cookies, you press **Ctrl-PgDn** to enter the data for peanut butter cookies. Figure 8(b) shows the completed data set screen for peanut butter cookies. When you are finished specifying both data sets, you press the **End** key.

The next step is to specify the scale of the horizontal axis and enter the horizontal and vertical labels. EnerGraphics automatically calculates reasonable values for the horizontal axis scaling. Although you can change these default values if you like, they are fine for our chart. So, all you have to do is enter labels for the horizontal and vertical axes. Figure 8(c) shows the completed Scale screen. When you are finished with this screen, you press the **End** key again.

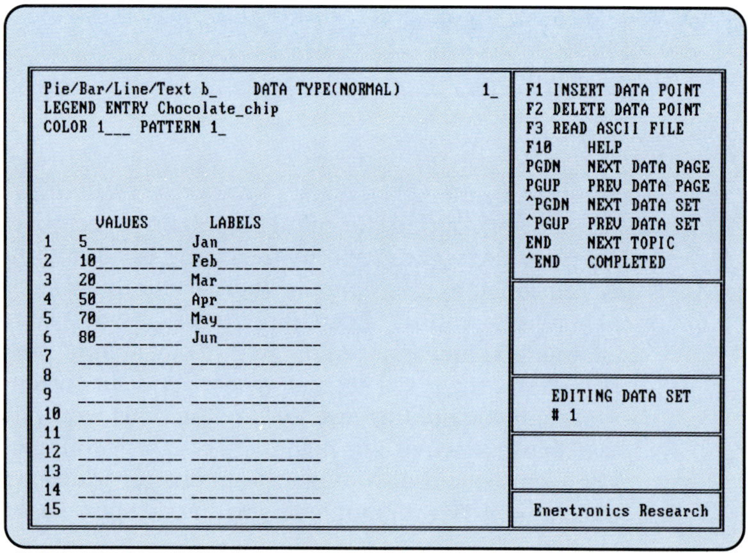

Figure 8 Creating a Bar Chart

(a) The completed data set table for chocolate chip cookie sales.

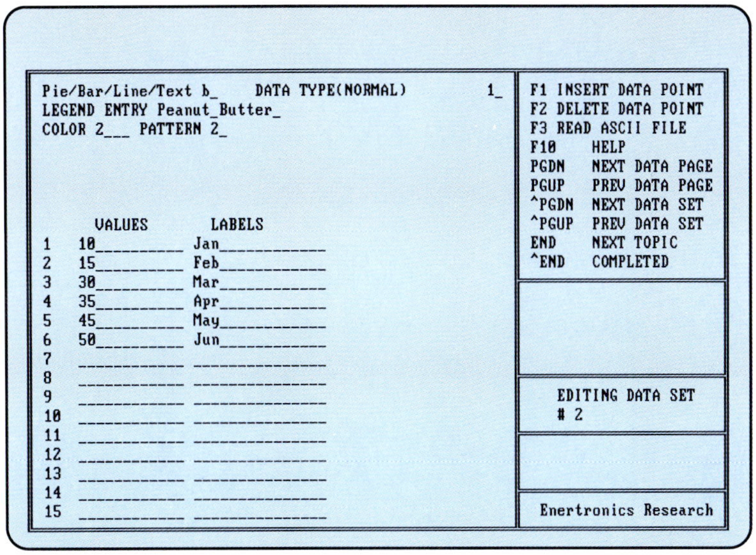

(b) The completed data set table for peanut butter cookie sales.

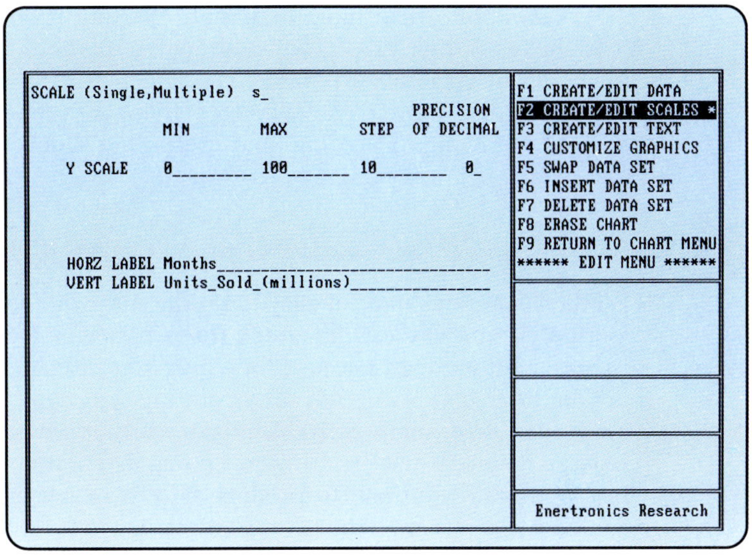

(c) Specifying the scaling and axis labels.

Now you can enter a title for your bar chart. Type **Cookie Sales** and press the **End** key once more. EnerGraphics returns to the Edit menu. Press the **F9** key and the program returns to the Chart menu. Now press the **F1** key to draw the chart. EnerGraphics presents a screen of options that let you alter certain aspects of the chart's appearance. The default values are fine for this graph, so all you have to do is press the **Enter** key. Figure 8(d) shows the chart that appears on your screen.

After viewing the chart, you can press any key to return to the Chart menu. Just like the pie chart, the bar chart can be printed, saved in a disk file, modified, and deleted. When you are finished with EnerGraphics, you can press the **F9** key to return to the Main menu, and then press the **Esc** key to return to DOS.

(d) The completed bar chart.

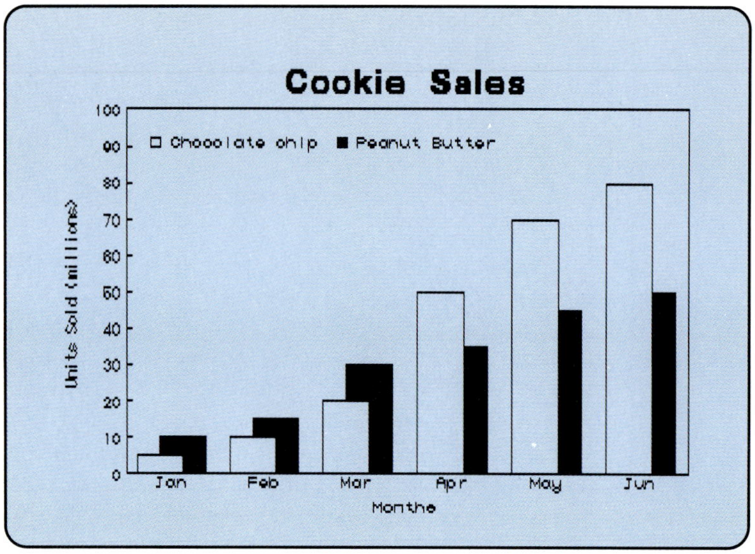

EnerGraphics, like most dedicated charting programs, can do much more than the two simple graphs we've shown in this section. A wide variety of charts can be made with such programs. Their main purpose, however, is to graphically depict data. For more creative images, there are other programs better suited to painting, drawing, designing, and presenting slide shows.

Painting Programs

Painting programs make it easy to produce on your computer screen almost any kind of picture you can imagine. These packages are often described as **pixel-based** or **bit-mapped** because they give you ultimate control over every single dot on the screen. Although early painting programs were considered to be little more than toys, many current versions are impressive design and illustration tools. Artists can use painting programs as another vehicle of expression; the rest of us can use them to produce figures neater and more accurate than we could ever create by hand. For example, some of the figures in this book were first sketched by the author with a painting program before they were redrawn by a professional artist.

Although almost any kind of chart, diagram, figure, and illustration can be produced with a painting program, this type of graphics software is perhaps best suited to free-hand drawing. Several predefined objects like lines, rectangles, and ovals can be incorporated in your creations, but you are by no means limited to these. You can draw your own shapes and use a variety of shading patterns. Many painting programs let you fully utilize the color capabilities of your display adapter and monitor. Sections of the screen and individual objects can be moved, copied, deleted, rotated, and flipped over horizontally or vertically. You can zoom in on parts of the screen to manipulate individual dots and edit images in great detail. Text can be displayed in a wide range of fonts, styles, and sizes. Most painting programs can even import images from full-page or hand-held scanners. Completed pictures can be saved in disk files and faithfully reproduced on paper with a dot-matrix, ink-jet, or laser printer.

Introducing MacPaint

Many painting programs are now on the market for both Apple Macintosh and IBM-compatible computers. One of the first truly popular painting programs was MacPaint for the Apple Macintosh. This program was developed by Bill Atkinson, a software wizard who worked for Apple before becoming an independent consultant. MacPaint was originally sold by Apple, but is currently marketed by Apple's software spinoff, a company named Claris. Originally, a copy of MacPaint was included with every Macintosh at no extra charge. This software, available since the introduction of the Macintosh back in 1984, was probably a major reason many early customers purchased Apple's newest computer in the first place. MacPaint has been continually upgraded and is still one of the most popular of all Macintosh programs, even though you no longer get a free copy with every new computer (it now costs $125).

In many ways, MacPaint is the perfect example of a painting program. It has all the basic features found in most painting programs, yet is well designed and simple to use. In fact, MacPaint is so self-explanatory that most users rarely feel the need to consult the manual, which is only thirty-two pages long (for version 1.5). By experimentation, beginners quickly learn the drawing skills they need to produce pictures. Yet despite its simplicity, MacPaint is a highly flexible program with an impressive set of powerful features. In skilled hands, it can produce striking illustrations like the one you see in Figure 9. As an example of a painting program, let's explore MacPaint and see what it can do.

The MacPaint Screen

On the Macintosh, you start a program by moving the pointer to its icon and **double clicking** (pressing the mouse button twice in rapid succession). Like most painting programs, MacPaint requires a mouse or some other graphics input device such as a trackball or tablet. After the program is loaded into memory, MacPaint presents the screen you see in Figure 10. Although there are differences

Figure 9 MacPaint: A Painting Program
MacPaint is one of the most popular painting programs for Apple Macintosh computers.

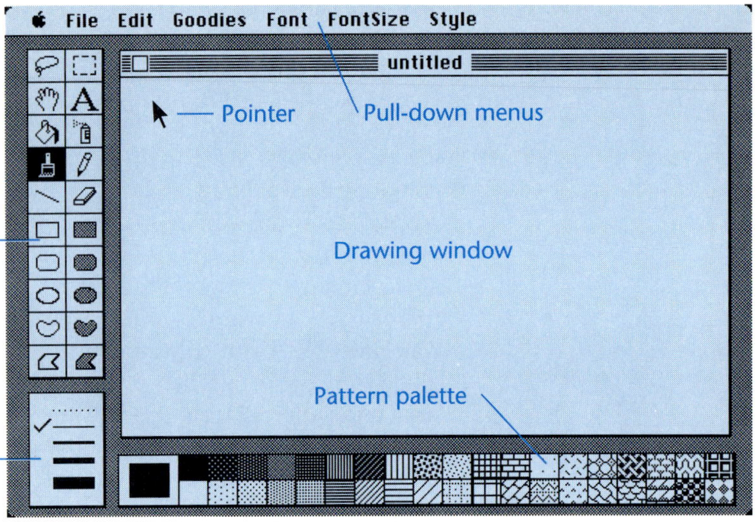

Figure 10 The MacPaint Screen
This shows the MacPaint screen when you first start the program. Note the pull-down menus, tool palette, border palette, pattern palette, and drawing window.

in various painting programs, most of them present a screen similar to this one. The MacPaint screen has five distinct sections:

- *Pull-Down Menus.* With their titles listed across the top of the screen, these menus contain commands for manipulating all or part of your picture. You open a menu by pointing to its title with the mouse and then holding down the mouse button. A menu option is selected by highlighting it with the mouse button held down and then releasing the button.
- *Tool Palette.* At the left side of the screen is a group of boxes filled with symbols. This **tool palette** contains icons that represent tools you can use to draw, add text, move to different parts of the page, and select parts of your picture. The tool shown in reverse video (white on black) is the one currently selected.
- *Border Palette.* Just below the tools, in the lower left corner of the screen, is a group of short line segments. These show the types of lines you can use in your picture. This **border palette** is where you select the thickness MacPaint will use to draw lines and outline shapes. The segment with the check mark beside it shows the current width selection.
- *Pattern Palette.* Along the bottom of the screen is an area known as the **pattern palette**. This shows the patterns you can use with the tools to draw objects and fill in enclosed areas on the screen. The larger box at the left end of the pattern palette shows the pattern that is the current selection.
- *Drawing Window.* This is the large empty area in the center of the screen, the "canvas" where you actually "paint" your picture. The striped bar across the top of the drawing window shows the name of the current picture, which MacPaint refers to as a *document.* Until you specify a name, the picture document is simply labeled *untitled.*

The MacPaint Pointer

Another important item to note on the MacPaint screen is the pointer. Right now, the pointer is the arrow in the upper left corner of the drawing window in Figure 10. It takes on different shapes, depending on which tool you're using. When the pointer is outside the drawing window, it looks like an arrow and is used to make menu, tool, and palette selections. When the pointer is inside the drawing window, it's used to draw and select portions of the picture for manipulation on the screen.

To use a painting program, you must master three basic mouse techniques. The first is simply *moving* the pointer, which is accomplished by rolling the mouse across the desktop in the direction you want to go. The second technique, known as **clicking**, is used to select tools, line widths, and patterns. This involves moving the mouse pointer on top of the item you want to select, and then briefly pressing and releasing the mouse button. **Dragging** is the third mouse action, which is used to pull down menus, outline parts of the picture, move selections, and "stretch" objects. All you do is position the pointer and hold down the mouse button while you move the mouse. When you've reached the final position, you then release the mouse button. These three mouse pointer actions are used over and over when working with a painting program such as MacPaint.

The MacPaint Tools

The twenty tools you see on the screen in Figure 10 are typical features you find in most painting programs. These tools, used in conjunction with the patterns, border widths, and a few menu commands, give you the potential to produce almost any kind of picture you can imagine. There is an endless array of visual effects you can achieve by combining the various MacPaint options. Unfortunately, it still takes skill and patience to create truly artistic work. Nevertheless, the tools provide a way for any user to produce accurate shapes and neat lettering. Before we go on to actually create a picture with MacPaint, let's briefly describe each of the tools, starting with the upper-left corner in Figure 10:

- *Lasso*. Looking like a cowboy's lariat, the lasso is used to encircle irregularly shaped objects and select them to be moved, deleted, or changed in some manner.
- *Selection Rectangle*. This dashed rectangle is stretched to enclose rectangular areas to be manipulated in some fashion.
- *Grabber*. This hand-shaped tool is used to shift the picture document under the drawing window so you can use an entire 8-by-10-inch page.
- *Text*. The letter A symbolizes the tool that is used to enter text into a picture. The font, size, and style of the characters can be chosen from the corresponding pull-down menus.
- *Paint Bucket*. This tool is used to fill an enclosed area with the currently selected pattern.
- *Spray Paint Can*. Simulating the effect of spray painting, this tool is used to gradually shade areas with the currently selected pattern.
- *Paintbrush*. As you move the mouse with the button held down, this tool leaves behind a brush stroke in the currently selected pattern. You can change the shape, size, and slant of the simulated paintbrush by choosing the BrushShape option from the Goodies menu.
- *Pencil*. This tool draws a thin freehand line—black on white backgrounds and white on black backgrounds.
- *Line*. Symbolized by a diagonal line, this tool draws a straight black line in any direction you drag the mouse pointer.
- *Eraser*. Like a magical gum eraser, this tool wipes away anything in its path.
- *Rectangles*. These tools are used to draw sharp-cornered squares and rectangles. The empty one produces just a hollow outline, while the darker tool automatically fills the rectangle with the current pattern.
- *Rounded Rectangles*. These tools draw hollow and filled rectangles with slightly rounded corners.

- *Ovals*. These two tools are used to draw hollow and filled circles and ovals.
- *Freehand Shapes*. The heart-shaped tools are used to create hollow and filled freehand shapes.
- *Polygons*. The last two tools are used to create hollow and filled geometric shapes with multiple straight-line sides.

Designing a Logo with MacPaint

No painting program will make an artist out of you, but a package such as MacPaint can help you create simple, good-looking figures, even if you have little artistic talent. A typical use for MacPaint might be to design a company's logo. Once it's finished, the logo can be saved in a file and used over and over again in other illustrations, charts, diagrams, and letterheads. Let's use MacPaint to create a logo for a fictional software company called E Z Systems.

The logo we have in mind is simple. The name of the company will be displayed in a slightly shaded circle, which is superimposed on a stripe-filled rectangle. The image will be displayed against a drop shadow to give it a three-dimensional look.

The first step is to choose the fill pattern for the rectangle. How about the one with narrow horizontal stripes? To select this pattern, you position the pointer on top of it and click the mouse button. Now you can choose the filled rectangle tool by pointing to its icon in the tools palette and clicking the mouse button. The pointer takes on a plus sign shape when you move it to the drawing window. To create the rectangle, first position the pointer where you want its upper left corner to be. Then hold down the mouse button and drag the mouse diagonally toward the lower right. This opens and "stretches" the rectangle as you drag. Keeping the mouse button pressed down, you can create a rectangle of the desired size. In our case, the rectangle should be about two inches wide and one inch high (see Figure 11(a)).

Next you need to create the circle. The easiest thing to do is to make the circle above, below, or beside the rectangle and then move it on top of the rectangle later. First, you choose the fill pattern for the circle. This time, how about a lightly dotted pattern? Then you select the filled oval tool. Finally, the circle is created like the rectangle—by holding down the mouse button and dragging to open and stretch the shape. The circle should be about 1.5 inches in diameter. Figure 11(b) shows the screen so far.

To move the circle on top of the rectangle, you must first lasso the circle. This is done by selecting the lasso tool and using it to completely enclose the circle. Once you do this, the lasso shrinks to fit the outline of the circle, squeezing out any empty space around the border. The edge of the circle flashes to indicate that it is currently selected. To move it, you position the pointer inside the circle, hold down the mouse button, and drag. The circle should be superimposed over the center of the rectangle, as shown in Figure 11(c).

The drop shadow is next. First you duplicate the circle-rectangle combination by lassoing it, holding down the **Option** key, and moving the new copy aside. Then you select a gray pattern from the pattern pallet and choose the Fill option from the Edit menu. Your screen now looks like Figure 11(d). This time lasso the original circle-rectangle and move it on top of the gray shadow, with a slight offset. Figure 11(e) shows the result.

Finally, you need to type the company name and put it inside the circle. You have a wide range of fonts, sizes, and styles of type to choose from in the Font, FontSize, and Style menus. How about a Geneva font, with a 12-point size, using boldface and shadow styles? Using the AlignMiddle option also from the Style

Figure 11 Designing a Logo with MacPaint

(a) Create a rectangle with horizontal stripes.

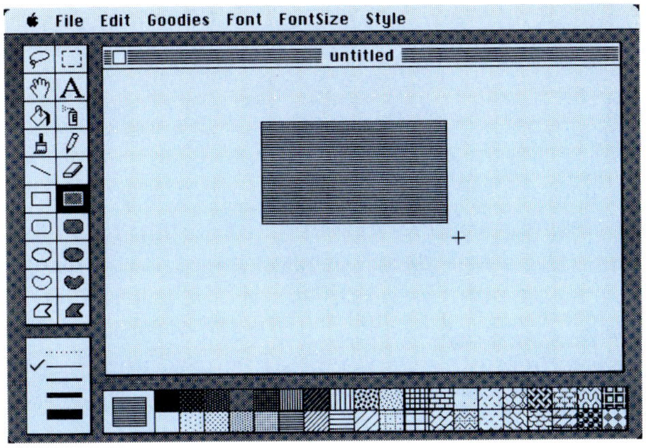

(b) Create a circle filled with a lightly dotted pattern.

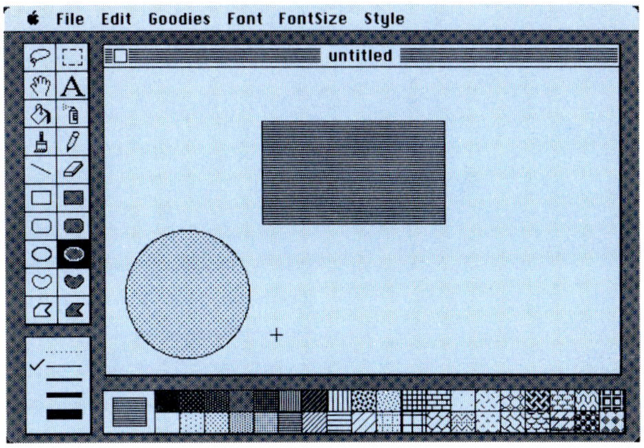

(c) Lasso the circle and move it on top of the rectangle.

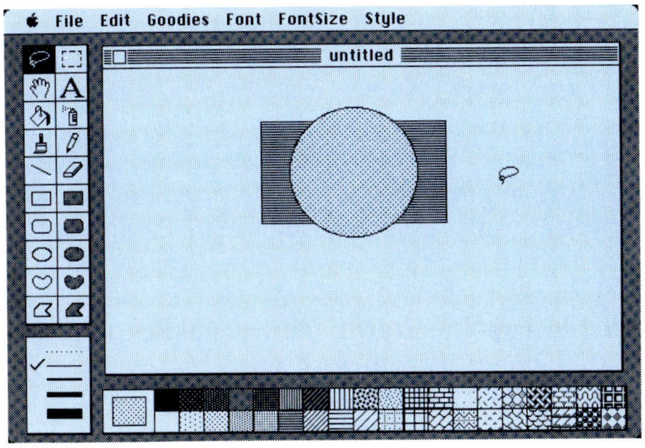

(d) Lasso the circle and rectangle, duplicate them, and select the gray pattern to create the drop shadow.

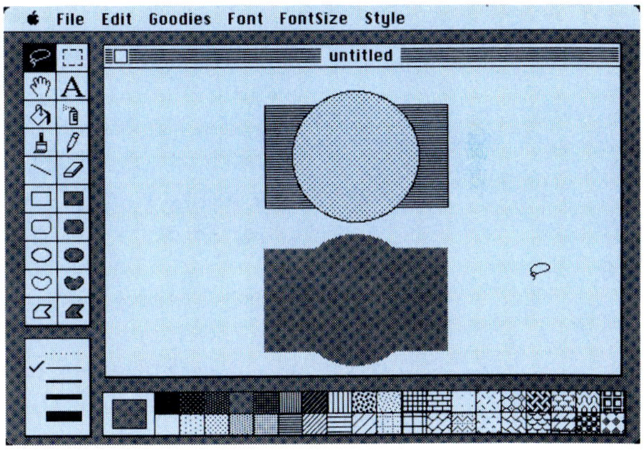

(e) Move the circle and rectangle on top of the drop shadow.

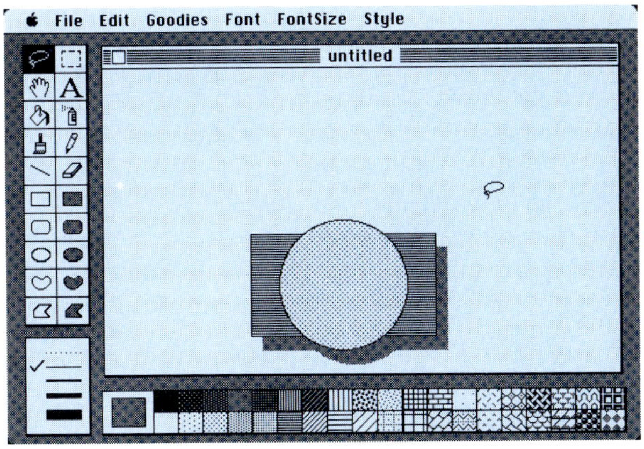

(f) Select the font, size, and style and then enter the text to complete the logo.

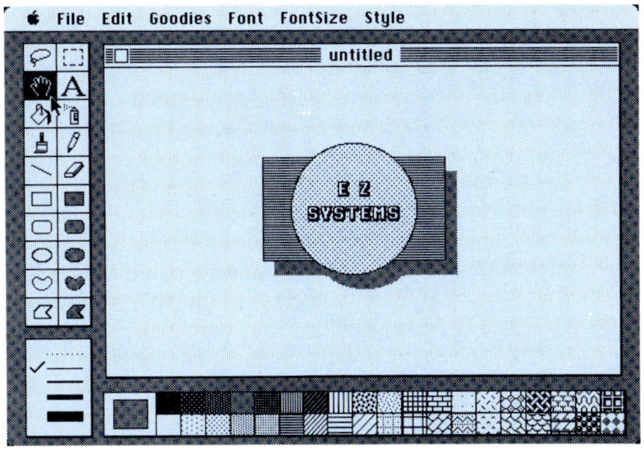

menu will help to center your text. Select the text tool, move the pointer to an empty spot, and click the mouse button. Now type **E Z SYSTEMS**, pressing the **Return** key after the Z. Lasso the text and move it inside the circle. The completed logo is shown in Figure 11(f). The logo can be saved in a disk file with the Save option and printed with the Print option, both of which are in the File menu.

Drawing Programs

Drawing programs differ from painting programs in several important respects. First of all, drawing programs are **object-oriented**, not pixel-based. This means that they let you create and manipulate images comprised of only discrete geometric objects such as lines, curves, rectangles, ovals, irregular outlines, polygons, and text. Drawing programs generally do not include freehand pixel painting features such as brush strokes, paint buckets, spray painting, and erasers. Instead, their features facilitate making very precise scaled drawings. In addition, drawing programs usually take better advantage of high-resolution, hard-copy output devices. For example, although MacPaint reproduces screen images on paper very well, these images have a resolution of only 72 dots per inch, even on a laser printer capable of 300 dots per inch. Drawing programs typically produce sharper output on paper with both dot-matrix and laser printers. Hence they are better suited than most painting programs for architectural renderings, layouts, blueprints, diagrams, charts, maps, mechanical drawings, and other technical illustrations.

In short, drawing programs are good for making structured figures. They are easy-to-use tools for simple drafting applications. Drawing programs let you define on-screen rulers and accurately scale objects to metric or English measurements. Objects keep their individual identities, even if they are partially or completely obscured by other objects. Shapes can be selected, moved, stretched, duplicated, and deleted as needed. An on-screen **grid**, like the squares on graph paper, can be used to keep objects lined up with each other. Many drawing programs can create figures much larger than a single 8-by-10-inch page. Reduction, enlargement, and scrolling features make it easier to work on drawings that are very detailed or too big to fit within a single screen. Although drawing programs don't let you erase parts of an object or edit individual pixels, they do let you change the way objects look by moving them, resizing them, and altering their border and fill patterns.

Introducing MacDraw

Like MacPaint, MacDraw is one of the most popular programs for the Apple Macintosh. Other drawing programs may offer more features, but MacDraw is a simple, yet powerful tool for easily creating precise, complex figures. This software has all the basic features found in most drawing programs. Although it costs more than MacPaint ($195) and is slightly more difficult to master, MacDraw is better suited to creating detailed figures like the one you see in Figure 12. As a good example of a drawing program, let's find out more about MacDraw and use it to design a figure.

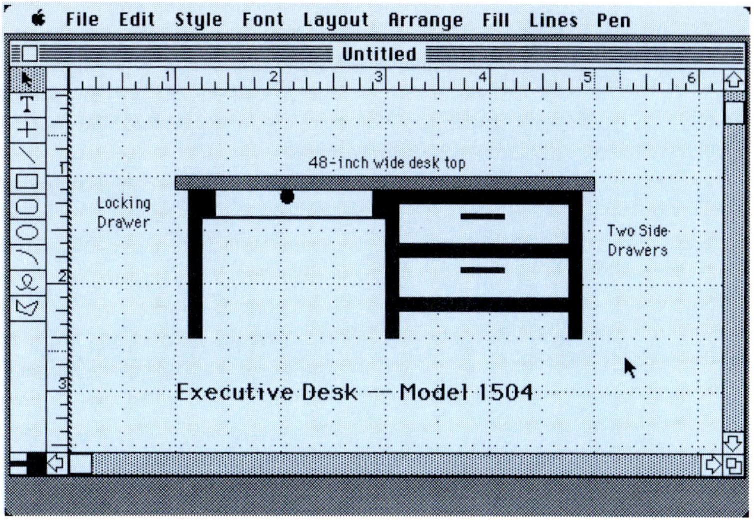

Figure 12 MacDraw: A Drawing Program
MacDraw is one of the most popular drawing programs for Apple Macintosh computers.

The MacDraw Screen

When you start up MacDraw, the program presents a screen like the one you see in Figure 13. It looks a little like the MacPaint screen, but there are some important differences. Figure 13 labels the key items, which include:

- *Pull-Down Menus*. These menus, with their titles listed across the top of the screen, contain commands for controlling how the tools work and manipulating your drawings.
- *Title Bar*. Extending across the top of the drawing window, the title bar shows the name of the current document, and on the left side contains the Close Box, which you can click on to close the current drawing file.
- *Tool Palette*. Along the left side of the screen are the icons that represent your drawing tools. Except for the top one, the selection tool, each of these tools creates a single graphic object. Remember, a graphic object is an individual entity and not a collection of pixels, as is a MacPaint shape. The currently selected tool is shaded.
- *Line/Pattern Box*. This area shows the currently selected line width along with the pen and fill pattern that will affect the next object you draw. The *pen pattern* is the design used to draw lines and borders, while the *fill pattern* is the design used inside solid objects such as rectangles and ovals.
- *Scroll Bars*. Scroll bars are used to move within a document. These MacDraw scroll bars let you see different parts of your drawing by moving it up, down, and sideways behind the window.
- *Size Box*. This little box at the intersection of the scroll bars can be dragged to change the size of your drawing window.
- *Drawing Window*. This is the "drafting table" where you create your drawings. Note the dotted grid lines that are turned on by default to help you precisely size and align your objects.

The MacDraw Tools

As you can see from Figure 13, there are fewer MacDraw tools than there are MacPaint tools. These tools are typical of the ones found in many drawing programs. With the exception of the first, all the tools are used to create or modify

Figure 13 The MacDraw Screen
This shows the MacDraw screen when you first start the program. Note the pull-down menus, tool palette, close box, title bar, line/pattern box, scroll bars, size box, and drawing window.

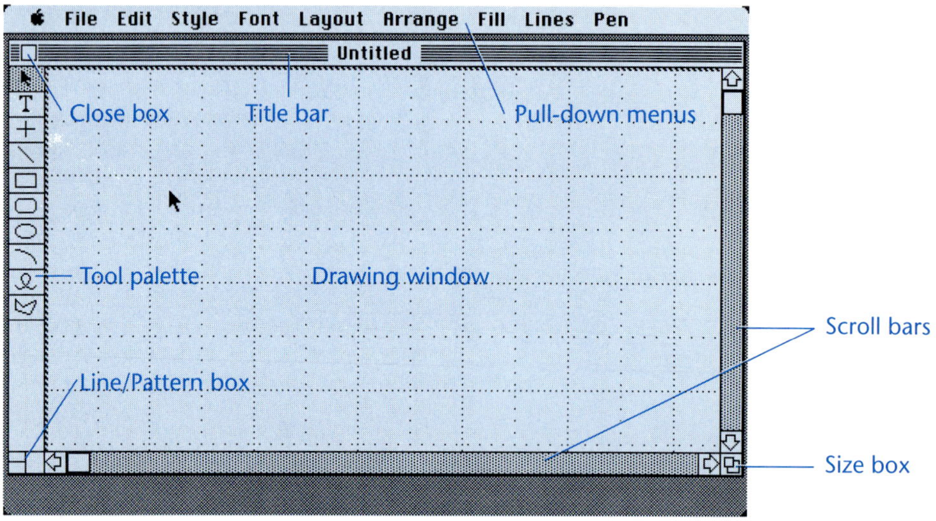

a particular type of geometric object. To select a particular tool, you simply move the pointer on top of its icon and click the mouse button. The currently selected tool is shown in reverse video. Starting from the top of the tool palette, the MacDraw tools include:

- *Selection.* The selection tool, whose icon is shaped like an arrow, allows you to select, move, and resize objects that have already been drawn.
- *Text.* You can create captions, labels, and even entire paragraphs by selecting the text tool, clicking anywhere within the drawing window, and typing. Various character fonts, sizes, and styles can be selected from the Font and Style menus.
- *Perpendicular Line.* This tool allows you to create only perfectly straight horizontal and vertical lines. The lines are drawn with the currently selected line width and pen pattern, as are all lines drawn with any of the tools that create graphic objects.
- *Diagonal Line.* A line can be drawn at any angle with this tool. Although the diagonal line tool can draw perfectly straight horizontal and vertical lines too, this is easier to do with the perpendicular line tool.
- *Rectangle.* This tool lets you create sharp-cornered rectangles and squares. The shapes are made with the currently selected line width, pen pattern, and fill pattern.
- *Round-Cornered Rectangle.* This is just like the previous tool, except that it draws rectangles with rounded corners.
- *Oval.* The oval tool is used to draw ellipses and circles with the currently selected line width, pen pattern, and fill pattern.
- *Arc.* This tool lets you make 90-degree arcs; in other words, quarter circles and ovals.

- *Freehand Shape*. With this tool, you can use the mouse to trace the outline of any irregular shape. But remember, when the freehand shape is finished, it is still considered to be a single graphic object and not a collection of individual dots.
- *Polygon*. The polygon tool is used to create shapes made up of three or more straight-line sides. Like all shapes, polygons are made with the currently selected line width, pen pattern, and fill pattern.

The MacDraw Menus

The pull-down menus whose titles you see at the top of the MacDraw screen are similar to those found in many Macintosh application programs. These menus contain all the available MacDraw commands, each of which performs some necessary or useful action. Figure 14 shows all of the MacDraw menus, including:

- *File*. The commands in this menu allow you to create a new drawing, begin work on an existing drawing, discard the current drawing, save the current drawing in a file, print the current drawing, and quit the MacDraw program.
- *Edit*. This menu contains editing commands that allow you to undo the most recent action; cut, copy, and paste objects from one place to another; and reshape, smooth, and round the outlines of some objects.
- *Style*. The commands in the Style menu allow you to set the character style, alignment, line spacing, and capitalization of text in a caption or paragraph.
- *Font*. This menu allows you to set the typeface and size of characters created with the text tool.
- *Layout*. The Layout menu contains commands for setting up on-screen rulers and grids, as well as enlarging and reducing parts of a drawing.
- *Arrange*. This menu allows you to control the way objects are stacked up, grouped together, and aligned in a drawing. It also contains commands to rotate and create mirror images of existing objects.
- *Fill*. This menu offers thirty-six patterns you can select to fill your shapes and use as the background of captions and paragraphs. A special pattern, called "None," lets you make an object into an empty frame, allowing objects behind it to show through.

Figure 14 The MacDraw Menus
Here are all of MacDraw's pull-down menus.

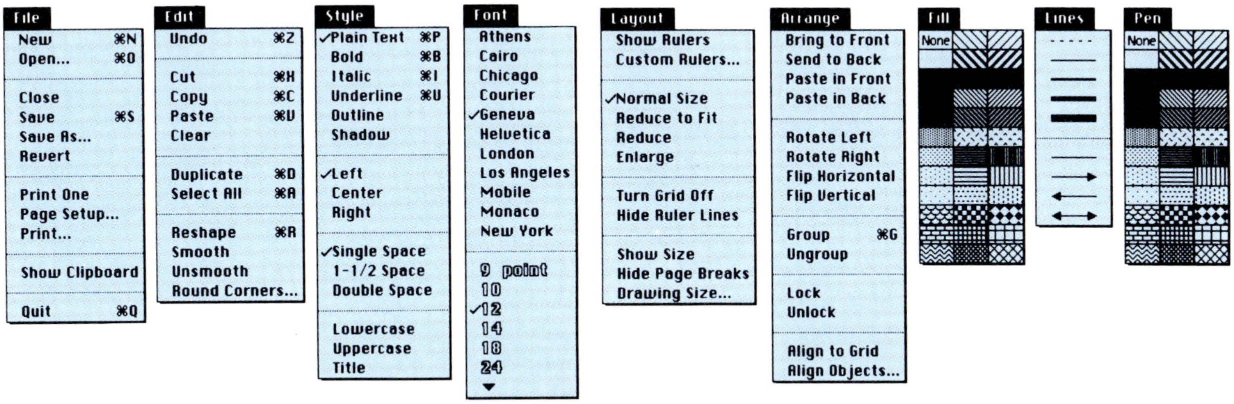

- *Lines*. This menu allows you to select the appearance of lines and the borders of all objects except text.
- *Pen*. The Pen menu offers the same thirty-six patterns as the Fill menu, but it just operates on lines and the borders of objects.

Designing a Desk with MacDraw

Suppose that you work at an office furniture design company, and your task is to sketch the plans for a new desk model. Since the desk plans must be precisely scaled and will be made up of relatively simple shapes, you decide to use MacDraw to create your design. After starting up the program, the first step is to turn on the display of rulers along the top and left sides of the drawing window (see Figure 15(a)). This is done by selecting the Show Rulers option from the Layout menu. By default, the ruler scale is in inches, but you can use the metric system or create your own custom rulers instead. In your case, inches are just fine because you decide that one inch in the drawing will represent one foot in the actual desk. To keep this example simple, we'll just do the front view of the desk.

The desk top is to be four feet wide, so you can represent it in your drawing by a thin rectangle four inches wide. You select the rectangle tool and move the mouse pointer to a convenient starting position, say one inch from the top and one inch from the left. As you move the pointer with the rulers turned on, your exact position in the drawing is precisely indicated by a dotted line in each ruler. Once the pointer is at the desired upper left corner, you hold down the mouse button and drag open the rectangle. After you stretch the rectangle so that it's four inches wide, you release the mouse button. It's easy to do this with accuracy, because objects are automatically aligned to the grid in the drawing window. At this point, your screen looks like Figure 15(b).

Each of the six little black squares you see on the boundary of the rectangle is called a **handle**. When an existing object is selected, you can drag any of its handles to resize it. Handles only appear when an object is selected and do not show up when it is printed. To move an entire object, all you have to do is position the selection tool pointer within the object and drag it anywhere on the screen.

Now you can use rectangles, lines, and any other shapes you need to finish the desk design. Fill patterns can be selected to fill in the shapes. Labels and measurements can be added to annotate the plans. When you're finished, your screen might look something like Figure 15(c). At this point, the drawing can be saved on a disk and printed by using options from the File menu. When it is printed, the drawing will not display any rulers, grid lines, or handles. The lines and text will be as sharp as the printer can manage. On a laser printer, this will look very nice. But even on a dot-matrix printer, drawing programs generally produce crisper output than painting programs.

Computer-Aided Design Programs

Drawing programs such as MacDraw are fine for relatively simple plans, diagrams, and blueprints. Although drawing programs can be used to produce detailed figures, they are not powerful enough for many engineering, architectural, and technical illustrations. For truly complex drafting applications, **computer-aided design**, or **CAD**, packages are much better. They are typically used for drafting plans, blueprints, models, schematics, and other detailed drawings of parts, mechanisms, and buildings. These programs have been used for years

Figure 15 Designing a Desk with MacDraw
(a) Turn on the display of rulers.
(b) Create the desktop with the rectangle tool.
(c) Use rectangles, lines, and other shapes and fill patterns to finish the desk design.

(a)

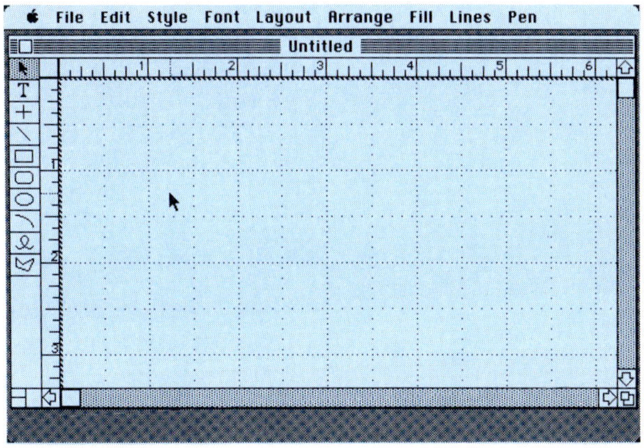

(b)

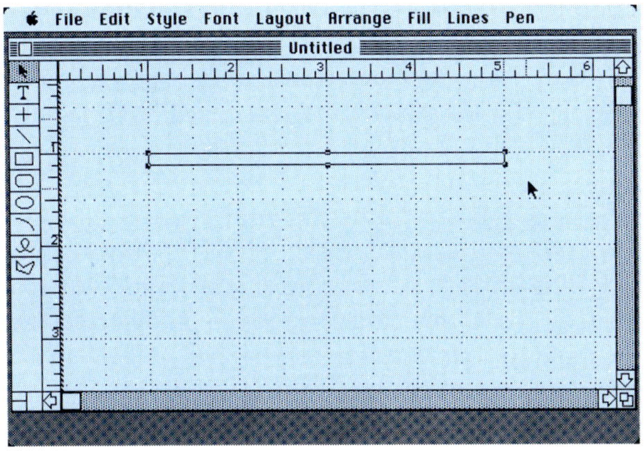

(c)

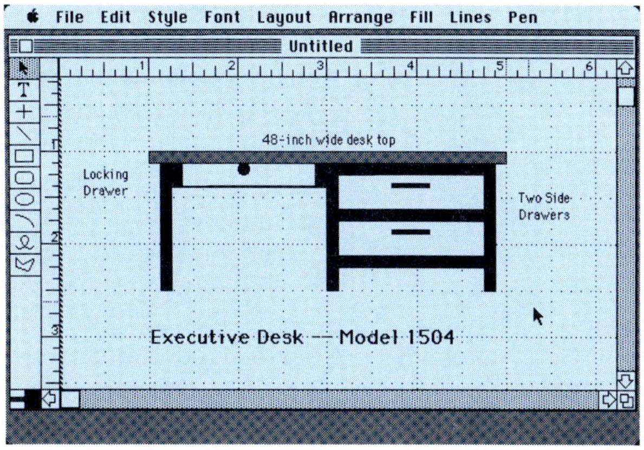

on large computer systems, and have become increasingly popular on microcomputers. Thanks to recent technological advances, microcomputer CAD systems now can do many things that mainframe CAD systems can do, only at a fraction of the cost.

Although CAD programs are generally more difficult to learn how to use than are painting and drawing programs, they still have a wide range of potential users. Mechanical engineers, architects, circuit board designers, civil engineers, surveyors, interior planners, and graphic artists are just a few examples of the many diverse professionals who are using CAD packages. Almost anyone who routinely makes complex, detailed drawings can be helped by a CAD package. Consequently, tens of thousands of CAD hardware and software systems are installed every year.

Besides being more difficult to learn, CAD programs are usually significantly more expensive than painting and drawing programs. For example, while many good painting and drawing programs can be purchased for around $100, many full-featured microcomputer CAD packages cost more than $2000. Although this might seem like a hefty price tag, microcomputer CAD packages are quite a bargain compared to the cost of similar CAD systems for larger computers.

Finally, CAD programs also require more sophisticated hardware components than most painting and drawing programs. To make the best use of a CAD package, you need a powerful microcomputer, a high-resolution color display adapter and monitor, a good mouse or graphics tablet, and a color printer or plotter. Despite their steep learning curve, cost, and hardware requirements, CAD programs are still popular because of their unparalleled ability to create extremely detailed drawings.

CAD Features

Like drawing programs, CAD software is object-oriented. This means that a complicated set of drawing and editing capabilities is used to create and manipulate individual graphic objects, which are sometimes called primitives, elements, or entities. These objects typically include points, lines, curves, arcs, circles, ellipses, rectangles, squares, polygons, and free-form shapes. Some programs also let you draw three-dimensional solids.

You can usually locate objects on the drawing in several different ways. Exact coordinates can be entered at the keyboard, or a mouse or tablet can be used to indicate where objects are to be put. Because precise scaling is so important in most drafting and design applications, good CAD programs let you work in almost any measurement system. For example, when drafting a small mechanical part you can use a centimeter scale, but then switch to feet for an architectural blueprint.

Most CAD packages offer grid and snap features. Like the squares on graph paper, a **grid** is a visual aid for placing objects in the drawing. **Snap** is a feature that automatically aligns objects to the nearest grid lines. Still other drawing aids place axes on the screen, display the current cursor coordinates, and constrain movement to horizontal and vertical directions. You can *zoom in* on objects to get a closer look and *zoom out* to see the big picture. A **pan** feature is usually available to let you move the viewing window up, down, left, or right.

Once objects have been drawn, they must often be edited in various ways. Two CAD editing commands commonly used in drafting are fillet and chamfer. **Fillet** joins two lines to create a rounded corner, while **chamfer** joins two lines with another straight line. Other editing features let you move, copy, erase, rotate, reverse, resize, trim, and fill objects.

For especially complex figures, many CAD programs let you create drawings made up of several layers or levels. A **layer** is like a transparent overlay sheet on a chart: you can create it separately and then superimpose it on top of other layers. Individual layers can be pulled out, viewed, and printed by themselves. Since most CAD programs can also draw in several colors, this layering ability makes them ideal for designing electronic schematics, architectural plans, and other engineering diagrams.

Finally, CAD programs let you save your drawings in disk files and produce accurate reproductions on paper. They typically support a wide range of printers and plotters. Some even work with film recorders to make 35-mm slides directly from the screen.

Introducing AutoCAD

AutoCAD, from Autodesk Incorporated, is one of the most popular microcomputer CAD packages on the market today. With more than 100,000 copies sold, this software is used in some 44 percent of all microcomputer-based CAD installations. Like Lotus 1-2-3 and dBASE, AutoCAD has become a *de facto* standard in the industry. More third-party books, programs, and hardware devices are available for AutoCAD than for any other CAD package. It's a powerful, flexible program against which all other CAD packages are measured.

Originally, AutoCAD was designed for IBM-compatible computers under DOS, but a version is now available for the Apple Macintosh too. The package supports an unusually wide range of display adapters, graphics input devices, printers, and plotters. This comprehensive package is one of the most sophisticated graphics applications you can find on a microcomputer. Expensive and time-consuming to fully master, AutoCAD is clearly not for everyone. Nevertheless, if you have to do detailed drafting projects, like the one you see in Figure 16, then AutoCAD may be just what you need.

Designing a Floor Plan with AutoCAD

As we have said, AutoCAD is a sophisticated software package that is not particularly easy to master. The program has many advanced features and it works quite differently than painting and drawing programs. Although we cannot possibly demonstrate all of AutoCAD's powerful capabilities, we can illustrate a few of its features with a simple example. Since AutoCAD is well suited to many architectural applications, let's use it on an IBM-compatible computer to design the floor plan of a two-bedroom condominium.

Once you turn on your computer, boot DOS, and switch to the proper subdirectory, you start AutoCAD by typing **ACAD** and pressing the **Enter** key. The program then presents its Main menu, which is shown in Figure 17(a). After you enter **1** to begin a new drawing, AutoCAD asks you to supply a name for your drawing. Then the program switches to graphics mode and presents the screen you see in Figure 17(b).

Here is where you create your drawing. The top line on the screen presents status information that indicates you're working on layer 0 and your current cursor coordinates are (0,0). The Root menu, listed along the right side of the screen, displays several options, most of which call up additional submenus. You tell AutoCAD what to do by selecting menu options and entering commands

***Figure 16* AutoCAD**
AutoCAD is a sophisticated computer-aided design package for creating detailed diagrams.

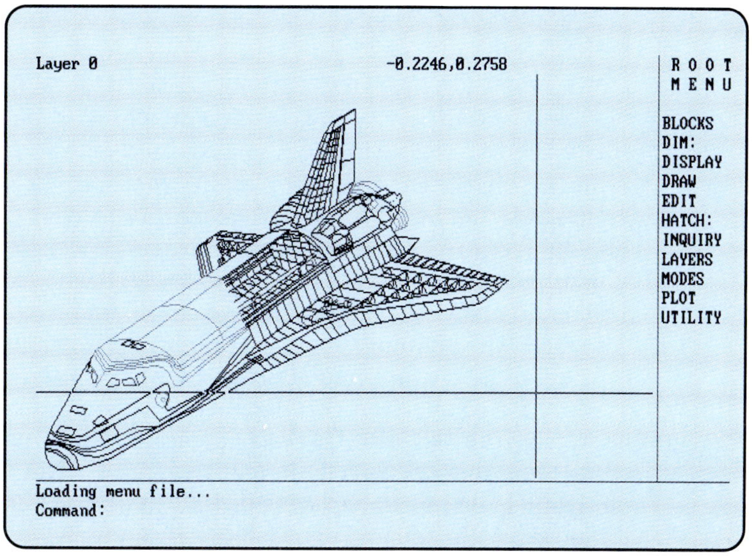

Figure 17 Designing a Floor Plan with AutoCAD
(a) The Main menu.

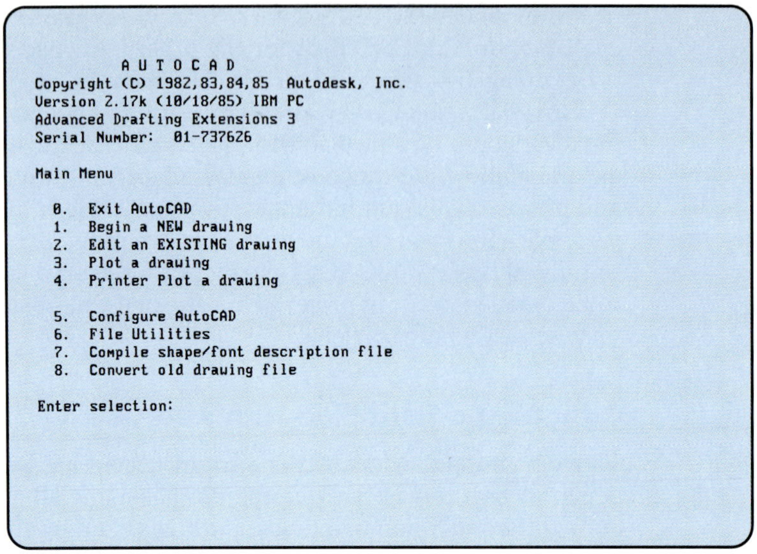

(b) The AutoCAD drawing screen.

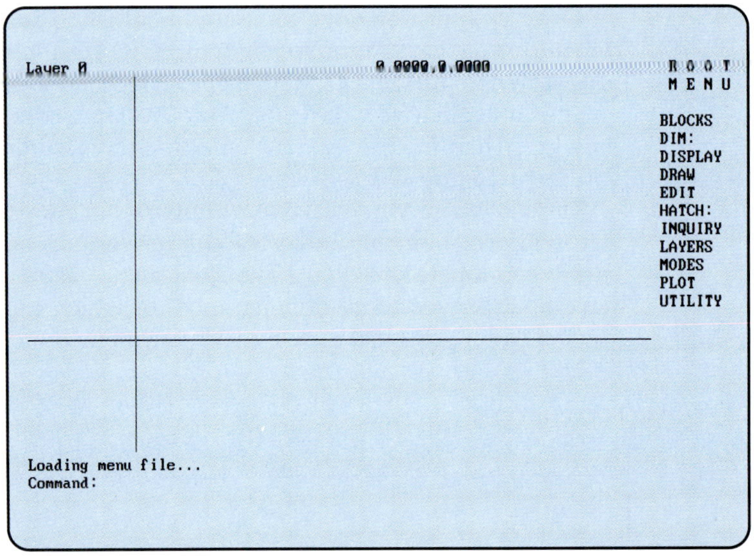

at the keyboard. The three lines at the bottom of the screen are where you enter commands and view AutoCAD's responses to your commands. Finally, the two long lines that intersect on the screen are the **crosshair**; this indicates your current cursor position. Although the crosshair can be moved with arrow keys, it's usually manipulated by using a pointing device such as a mouse, trackball, or graphics tablet. The pointing device is also used to highlight and select menu options.

One of the advantages of using a CAD package is the ease with which you can precisely scale your drawings. For working on large objects, such as buildings, you can tell AutoCAD to use architectural units of measurement. This allows you to work directly in feet and inches. You can also specify how much horizontal and vertical space you need to fit on your screen. Furthermore, you can turn on the grid and snap features to accurately line up your objects. Finally,

(b) :

you can have AutoCAD continuously display your current cursor coordinates in feet and inches at the top of the screen. For example, to specify all of these settings, this is what you do:

1. Select the Utility option from the Root menu, the Units option from the Utility submenu, and the Architectural option from the Units submenu. This tells AutoCAD to measure objects in feet and inches.
2. Select the Limits option from the Root menu and set the lower left corner coordinates to (0′,0′) and the upper-right corner coordinates to (60′,40′). This gives you 40 vertical feet and at least 60 horizontal feet of space on your screen.
3. Select the Display option, then Zoom, and then All. This ensures that your screen is zoomed out all the way to show the full 60-by-40 feet.
4. Select the Modes option, then the Grid option, and then enter **1′**. This turns on a 1-by-1-foot grid.
5. Select the Modes option, then the Snap option, and then enter **1′**. This "snaps" objects to the 1-by-1-foot grid.
6. Hold down the **Control** key and type **D** to turn on the continuous digital readout of your current crosshair position in feet and inches.

(c) Slide

After setting up AutoCAD in this manner, your screen looks like Figure 17(c). Now you can begin drawing your floor plan. Switch to the Draw submenu and select the Trace command. Basically, Trace lets you draw a series of connected fat lines—perfect for floor plan walls. AutoCAD asks for the thickness of the line you want to draw and you can also indicate whether the line is to be filled in or left empty like a thin rectangle. The walls in this plan are 6 inches thick. Solid walls are filled in while window sections are left empty. AutoCAD asks you for a starting point and ending point for each line you draw. You can type coordinates or move the crosshair and press the mouse button to indicate each line's end-points. The grid and crosshair digital readout help you construct rooms that are the right size. Besides the Trace command, you can also use the Line command to draw thin lines, and the Text command to enter labels. Figure 17(d) shows the completed floor plan with the grid turned off.

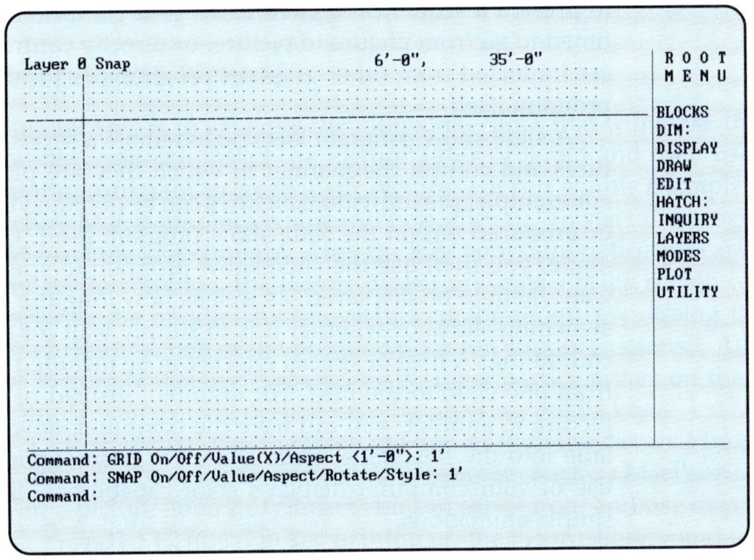

(c) Turning on the Grid and Snap features.

Figure 5 ***Laser Printers***
The three types of laser printers most commonly used with microcomputers for desktop publishing are Hewlett-Packard LaserJets (and compatible printers from other manufacturers), Postscript printers, and QuickDraw printers. Here we show the Hewlett-Packard LaserJet II, the Apple LaserWriter IINTX PostScript printer, and the General Computer Corporation Personal LaserPrinter, which is a QuickDraw printer.

PostScript is a page description language for high-resolution printers and typesetters. Basically, a **page description language** is a specialized computer programming language for defining the size, format, and position of text and graphic elements on a printed page. In other words, a page description language tells a printer how to reproduce a page on paper. PostScript, developed and licensed by Adobe Systems, is one of the most popular page description languages. It's encoded into the hardware of several popular laser printers, including the Apple LaserWriter IINT and IBM's Personal Pageprinter. Starting at around $4000, PostScript printers are rather expensive, but they often include many fonts and provide a great deal of flexibility in the size, shape, and orientation of printed objects. Since PostScript is a *device-independent* language, you can design a document on one system and print it later on another system at a higher resolution. For example, you can rough out your document on a Macintosh and print a draft on a 300-dots-per-inch LaserWriter IINT. When you are finished, you can have your final version printed on an Allied Linotype Linotronic 100 typesetter. This impressive machine, which costs around $35,000, uses the PostScript language to produce output on photographic paper at a resolution of 1270 dots per inch. PostScript laser printers and typesetters can be used with many different types of computers.

Figure 18 ***Cre***
These are the th
or "slides" of o
computer-simul
show.
(a) Slide 1

(b) Slide 2

(c) Slide 3

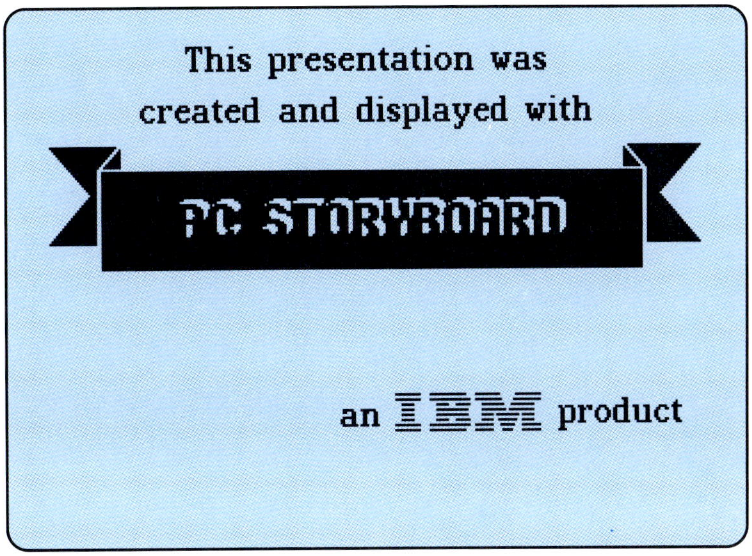

intensity cyan, magenta, and white. The background color is black. The Area setting is Full, which means that the entire screen will be used.

Once you complete the story table, you can press the **F4** function key to try out the show. If you're not satisfied, you can simply go back and change the table to try different options. When you're finished with the slide show, you hold down the **Shift** key and press **F6** to save it on your disk, quit Story Editor, and return to DOS.

Presenting the Slide Show

Although you can use Story Editor to view your slide show as you develop it, the Story Teller program is what you normally use to run a completed slide show. IBM allows you to copy and distribute Story Teller along with your pictures,

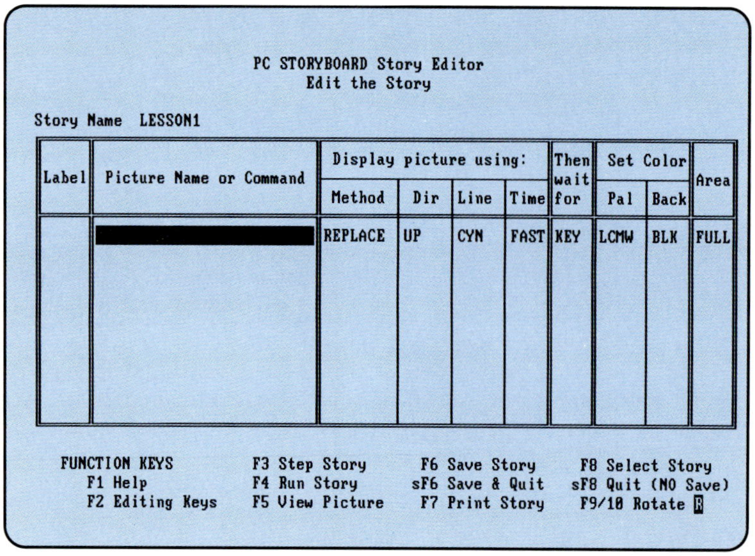

Figure 19 Editing the Story

(a) This table is where you specify how your slide show will progress.

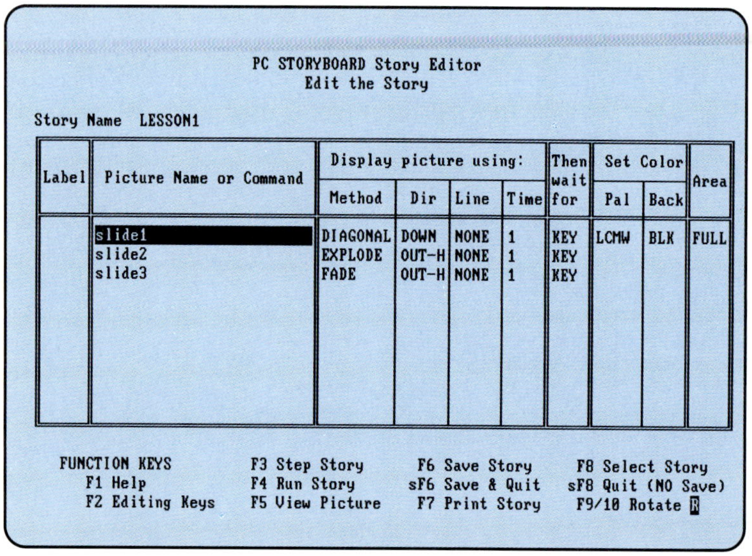

(b) The completed slide show table.

provided each diskette is appropriately labeled to acknowledge IBM's copyright on the program. This makes PC Storyboard handy for making demonstrations and tutorials that will be sold or given away to others.

Running Story Teller is easy. To start our example slide show, simply enter **ST LESSON1**. Story Teller's one drawback is that you get IBM's logo and copyright notice at the beginning of every show. After you press any key, however, this notice disappears and the slide show proceeds. In our example, the screen clears and an invisible diagonal line sweeps across it from top left to lower right, revealing the first slide. Then the program simply waits for you to press a key. When you do, the second slide appears by "exploding" out from the center of the first slide. Press any key again, and the second slide fades into the final slide. Press any key once more, and Story Teller ends and returns to DOS.

Real World

Graphics Gain a Foothold

Managers can be 43 percent more effective if they use computer-generated graphics in their presentations, researcher Gary W. Dickson believes.

Dickson, who is a member of the Minnesota Managerial Graphics Project at the University of Minnesota School of Management, bases his conclusion on more than fifteen experiments with 1500 subjects. "There is tremendous oral and written support of communication using graphics," he said.

Mark Carroll, assistant to the president of Southwestern Bell, produces monthly graphs of customer complaints on his personal computer and updates them daily to quickly spot trends. He converts the graphs into color handouts and overhead transparencies when it's time to present his findings to upper management. "I can paint my message better in pictures than I can in words," he said.

Virginia Johnson, marketing development and training manager at 3M's Audio Visual Division, a sponsor of the Minnesota Project, believes that the creative use of computer graphics makes managers more productive by making meetings more effective. Since managers can spend around 40 percent of their time in meetings, the increased productivity is significant.

Presentation graphics—computer graphics converted to overhead transparencies, color slides, or hard copy with an ink-jet printer, dot-matrix printer, or plotter—is not the only tool that businesses use today. Desktop video is rapidly gaining popularity. Combining the technologies of microcomputer and video, desktop video produces low-cost, high-resolution graphic shows that look like they were produced in a studio.

Ernst & Whinney, a Hartford, Connecticut-based accounting firm, uses the new desktop video technology to pep up its client presentations. The firm uses graphics that dissolve and fade, titles that dance across the screen, and strobe-like effects. "We're presenting the same information," according to L. Ward Holdridge, "but now we're drawing rave reviews."

International Data Corporation reports that U.S. companies will spend $536.4 million a year on business graphics for microcomputers by 1990, which is up from $215.6 million in 1985. Advances in hardware, such as the laser printer, is one reason for the growth. The high expectations of a visually oriented society is another.

Sources: June Rogoznica, "Computer Graphics: Seeing is Believing," *Newsweek Special Advertising Supplement on Business Technology*, November 2, 1987, p. S-10. Karen Berney, "Graphics Come of Age," *Nation's Business*, June 1987, pp. 53–55. Jeffrey Rotfeder, "Now Playing at an Office Near You—Desktop Videos," *Business Week*, June 1, 1987, pp. 85–86.

Summary

- *The hardware of microcomputer graphics.* In addition to the computer, four primary components are necessary: a graphics display adapter, a graphics monitor, a graphics input device, and a hard-copy output device.
- *The basic types of microcomputer graphics software.* Although many packages use graphics, the most popular categories are charting, painting, drawing, computer-aided design, and slide show programs.
- *How to use a charting program.* Charting programs, such as EnerGraphics, let you enter or import data to create all kinds of pie charts, bar graphs, line plots, and statistical graphs.
- *How to use a painting program.* Painting programs, such as MacPaint, are pixel-based tools for creating freehand illustrations.

- *How to use a drawing program.* Drawing programs, such as MacDraw, are object-oriented tools for creating structured figures made up of geometric shapes and text.
- *How to use a computer-aided design program.* CAD programs, such as AutoCAD, are sophisticated drafting tools useful for engineering, architectural, and technical illustrations.
- *How to use a slide show program.* Slide show programs, such as PC Storyboard, let you assemble sequences of computer-generated pictures and control the manner in which they are played back on your screen.

Key Terms

As an extra review of this chapter, try defining the following terms.

border palette
chamfer
charting program
clicking
computer-aided design (CAD)
crosshair
dot pitch
double clicking
dragging
fillet
film recorder
graphics adapter
grid
handle
ink-jet printer
layer
multiscan monitor
object-oriented
painting program
pan
pattern palette
pixel-based (bit-mapped)
slide show program
snap
tool palette

Review Questions

1. What hardware component determines the video modes that can be used by your software as well as the type of monitor that you can connect to your system?
2. List three basic considerations in choosing a monitor.
3. What is by far the most common graphics input device?
4. What hard-copy output device would you use to reproduce screen images on 35-mm slides?
5. List five basic types of graphics software commonly used on microcomputers.
6. List the most popular kinds of charting programs.
7. What types of graphs can you make with most charting programs?
8. What is the basic difference between painting and drawing programs?
9. What is probably the most popular painting program for the Apple Macintosh?
10. What three basic mouse techniques must you master in order to use most painting and drawing programs?
11. List five MacPaint tools and briefly describe their functions.
12. After you create a picture with a painting program, what can you do with it?

13. Why are drawing programs better than painting programs for architectural renderings, layouts, blueprints, diagrams, charts, maps, mechanical drawings, and other technical illustrations?
14. List and briefly describe five of MacDraw's tools.
15. How do you turn on MacDraw's on-screen rulers for precisely measuring objects?
16. How are computer-aided design programs different than drawing programs?
17. List five common CAD features.
18. What is the most popular microcomputer CAD package on the market?
19. Where do the "slides" come from in a computer-generated slide show?
20. List the four component programs of IBM's PC Storyboard package.

Multiple Choice

1. Many modern microcomputers have their display adapter
   (a) built into the monitor. (b) built onto the motherboard.
   (c) plugged into the serial port. (d) connected to a laser printer.
2. Microcomputer displays present a matrix of
   (a) pixels. (b) objects.
   (c) video modes. (d) resolutions.
3. Which of the following is not a consideration in selecting a monitor?
   (a) screen colors (b) screen size
   (c) dot pitch (d) pixel weight
4. Which type of output device turns screen images into 35-mm slides?
   (a) laser printer (b) scanner
   (c) film recorder (d) plotter
5. Which type of charting program would you use to spruce up a graph made with Lotus 1-2-3?
   (a) spreadsheet enhancement (b) data base charting
   (c) map-making (d) dedicated charting
6. Which type of chart would you use to show a cost breakdown?
   (a) pie (b) bar
   (c) line (d) text
7. Which type of chart would you use to compare the sales of two products?
   (a) pie (b) bar
   (c) line (d) text
8. Painting programs are
   (a) bit-mapped. (b) object-oriented.
   (c) dedicated. (d) animated.
9. Which of the following is NOT a commonly used mouse technique?
   (a) clicking (b) double clicking
   (c) skipping (d) dragging

10. Which MacPaint tool would you use to select an irregularly shaped object?
    (a) lasso (b) selection rectangle
    (c) grabber (d) paint bucket
11. Drawing programs are
    (a) bit-mapped. (b) object-oriented.
    (c) dedicated. (d) animated.
12. Which MacDraw menu would you use to cut, copy, and paste objects from one place to another?
    (a) File (b) Edit
    (c) Layout (d) Arrange
13. Which type of graphics package is best for creating very complex engineering, architectural, and technical illustrations?
    (a) charting (b) painting
    (c) drawing (d) computer-aided design (CAD)
14. CAD programs are
    (a) bit-mapped. (b) object-oriented.
    (c) dedicated. (d) animated.
15. Which type of graphics package is best for presenting a sequence of computer-generated pictures?
    (a) charting (b) painting
    (c) CAD (d) slide show

Projects

1. Write a brief report comparing the hardware graphics capabilities of IBM-compatible and Apple Macintosh computers. Be sure to note the resolution and number of colors offered by the various graphics adapters and displays available for each type of computer. Cost is another important consideration. Computer books, magazines, and newspapers are good sources of information.
2. In this chapter, we have presented one particular example of a commercial program for each of the following categories of graphics software: charting, painting, drawing, CAD, and slide show. Find another example of a package in each of these categories and briefly describe the programs you pick in a short report. Try to choose popular programs that run on computers different from our selections. For example, EnerGraphics runs on IBM-compatible computers. Research some other popular charting program that runs on the Apple Macintosh.
3. If you have access to a charting program, use it to reproduce some graph that you've seen in a newspaper, magazine, or textbook. See how many graphs you can find in publications such as *USA Today*, *Newsweek*, *Time*, the *Wall Street Journal*, and *Business Week*.
4. If you have access to a painting, drawing, or computer-aided design package, use it to produce some illustration of your own choosing. You could do the floor plan of your house or apartment, design clothing, sketch something you're planning to build, or just make a creative drawing or abstract design.

CHAPTER 19

Desktop Publishing

In This Chapter

Why Desktop Publishing?

Desktop Publishing Applications

Components of a Desktop Publishing System

- Powerful Microcomputer
- Graphics Display
- Mouse
- Laser Printer
- Scanner
- Word Processing Software
- Graphics Software
- Page Layout Software

Principles of Page Design

Introducing PageMaker

Producing a Newsletter

- Writing and Editing the Text
- Creating or Scanning the Artwork
- Laying Out the Pages
- Printing the Document
- Making Multiple Copies

Preview

Few advances in computer technology have enchanted users like the recent phenomenon of desktop publishing. Perhaps it's because desktop publishing promises to give you total control over your document's final appearance. Now, it seems, you can do without professional typesetters and graphic artists. You can write and edit your own text, draw figures, incorporate photos, design page layouts, and print completed documents on a high-resolution laser printer. Compared to traditional typesetting and printing, desktop publishing is flexible, quick, and inexpensive.

Unfortunately, desktop publishing is also not quite as wonderful as it sounds. First, a substantial hardware investment is necessary. Although a $5000 to $10,000 microcomputer system is much less expensive than full-fledged typesetting equipment, the price tag is still too steep for many potential users. Desktop publishing packages do offer a great deal of flexibility in document design, but you must first learn how to use the software and this can take time. Even if you have the hardware and software for desktop publishing, attractive results are not guaranteed. It also takes talent and skill to design and lay out pages that look good. Professional typesetters and graphic artists can still produce better results than most desktop publishers.

Nevertheless, desktop publishing does fill a very real need for many individuals, businesses, and organizations. There is a huge market for hardware and software that can produce documents that look better than typewritten pages, even if they're not quite as good as true typeset printing. For example, in 1986 an estimated 4000 desktop publishing systems were sold. According to DataQuest, a San Jose, California, market research firm, the 1990 projected sales figure for desktop publishing systems is around 400,000. Even if desktop publishing isn't used at your school or office, it probably will be in the near future. This chapter is a good place to start exploring the dynamic new field of microcomputer desktop publishing.

After studying this chapter, you will understand

- why desktop publishing is so useful and popular.
- the applications of desktop publishing.
- the basic hardware and software components of a desktop publishing system.
- the principles of good page design.
- how to use a desktop publishing system to produce a newsletter.

Why Desktop Publishing?

As Figure 1 shows, on the continuum of document composition, desktop publishing lies somewhere between typewriting and professional publishing. You'll recall that a font or typeface is a set of letters, numbers, punctuation marks, and other symbols with a consistent appearance. Desktop publishing goes beyond typewriting and word processing to offer multiple fonts, proportionally spaced characters, graphics integration, and page layout features. Desktop publishing cannot, however, produce documents that look as sharp as those created by traditional typesetting methods. Nevertheless, desktop publishing provides capabilities that were prohibitively expensive for most microcomputer users just a few years ago.

In the previous chapter, we pointed out the fact that ours is a visually oriented society. Attractive printed materials are an essential component of personal,

Figure 1 Document Composition Continuum
The quality of all four types of document composition is constantly being improved by new hardware and software technology.

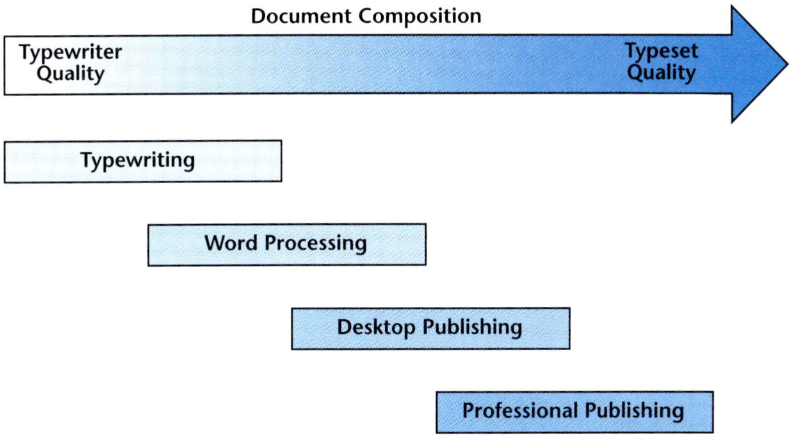

Insight

How Can Desktop Publishing Save a Company Money?

In business, time means money and money means you stay in business. Let's see how desktop publishing fits in.

Imagine that Harry J. Hoodwink owns a small company called Illusions Inc. that makes magicians' supplies. He wants to put out a low-cost yet attractive catalogue of his products. He has two choices in how to produce the catalogue: the conventional typesetting process or desktop publishing.

Using the conventional method, the catalogue's text must be written and edited first. Next, the designer must decide how the catalogue should look. What typeface should be used for the text and headlines? Where should the artwork go?

The designer produces the initial layout by blocking out text and illustrations on a piece of paper, creating a dummy of the material. When the design is complete, the text and headings are set in the typeface chosen. Then the final art must be completed. Finally, the material is pasted together and photographed to produce the negative that will be used to create the printing plate.

If any changes must be made, the text may have to be reset or the art changed in size or scale. The whole process is tedious, expensive, and time consuming. In fact, putting a catalogue together can be prohibitively expensive for a small company.

Using desktop publishing, however, a word processor or part of the desktop publishing system is used to generate the text. Instead of setting type, the graphics capability of the computer translates the text from the word processor into any desired typestyle. Since the text is then in graphics form, it can be moved anywhere on the screen. Line art can also be created with a mouse and moved anywhere as well.

The designed pages are sent to a high-resolution laser printer, and the output is used to produce the printing plates. Revising the catalogue requires simply editing the pages just as you would with a word processor.

Using desktop publishing, Illusion Inc.'s 30-page catalogue can be put together in about a week. If you were Harry J. Hoodwink, which system would you choose?

academic, and business communications. More simply put, the better a document looks, the more likely it is to inform, persuade, or interest the reader. The ability to combine text and graphics in an appealing printed format provides a powerful communications tool.

In a nutshell, desktop publishing is useful and popular because it can cut the costs and reduce the delays associated with producing attractive documents. This is especially true if you have to create near-typeset-quality materials on a regular basis. You may not need to have your work redone by an expensive professional typesetter every time you make minor changes to your text or graphics. In many cases, you can save money and finish quicker by doing the word processing, graphics, page design, page layouts, and printing yourself. Thanks to these savings of time and money, desktop publishing often lets you tackle projects you otherwise couldn't afford to do. For example, limited-distribution newsletters and brochures that would be too expensive to produce by traditional typesetting methods may be economically feasible if done with an in-house desktop publishing system.

Desktop publishing also gives you added control and the freedom to experiment with your document designs. With patience and practice, you can master the skills to entirely produce your own newsletters, brochures, and even books. You can do everything with your own computer without being dependent on others to translate your ideas into finished documents. Many users find it easier to meet deadlines and fine-tune their presentations by doing all the work themselves. By eliminating many tedious and time-consuming page layout chores, desktop publishing allows you to devote more attention to the creative aspects of document design and production.

Desktop Publishing Applications

Newsletters and brochures are probably the first applications that come to mind when you mention desktop publishing to most people. In fact, desktop publishing can be used for almost any printed material that must look good and be produced on time and at minimal cost. Students, consultants, entrepreneurs, retailers, executives, authors, editors, business people, and other professionals use desktop publishing for all kinds of documents. For example, here's a list of just a few common desktop publishing applications:

Advertisements	Posters
Annual reports	Presentations
Books	Product descriptions
Brochures	Proposals
Business cards	Resumes
Business plans	Signs
Catalogs	Software documentation
Magazines	Training guides
Newsletters	User manuals
Newspapers	Workbooks

Components of a Desktop Publishing System

Desktop publishing generally requires a combination of fairly sophisticated hardware and software components. Several of the devices used in desktop publishing are the same as those needed for microcomputer graphics. A powerful microcomputer, a graphics display adapter and monitor, a mouse, and a printer are the minimum necessary equipment. Most desktop publishing systems use laser printers and many include a scanner. Besides word processing and graphics packages, you also need special **page layout software** to enable you to arrange text and graphics on your pages before they are printed. Figure 2 shows a typical desktop publishing system.

Powerful Microcomputer

Desktop publishing involves manipulating both text and graphics on the display screen at the same time. This works best if you have a computer with a fast, powerful microprocessor, and plenty of primary memory and secondary storage. Computers such as the high-end Apple Macintoshes, the IBM Personal Computer AT, and IBM Personal System/2 Models 50, 60, 70, and 80 are a few of the most commonly used desktop publishing machines (see Figure 3). Usually equipped with at least 1 megabyte of memory and a hard disk with a minimum capacity of 20 megabytes, these computers have both the speed and storage necessary for desktop publishing. Many other computers with similar capabilities from various manufacturers are also used.

Figure 2 A Typical Desktop Publishing System
The hardware of a typical desktop publishing system consists of a powerful microcomputer, graphics display, mouse, and laser printer. Some systems also have a scanner as shown here. The software needed for desktop publishing includes a word processing package, graphics packages, and a page layout package.

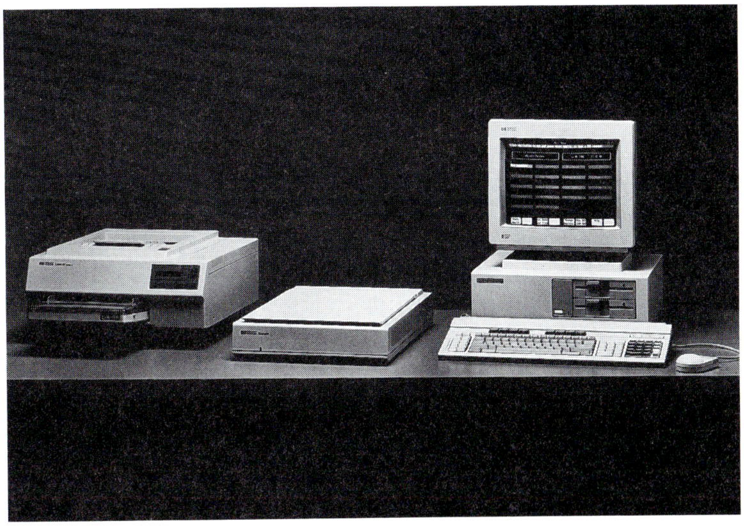

***Figure 3* Microcomputers Used for Desktop Publishing**
Desktop publishing requires a microcomputer with a fast, powerful microprocessor, and plenty of primary and secondary storage. Microcomputers commonly used for desktop publishing include the IBM Personal Computer AT, the IBM Personal System/2 Model 50 (or Model 60, 70, or 80), the Apple Macintosh SE, Apple Macintosh SE/30, and the various Apple Macintosh II models.

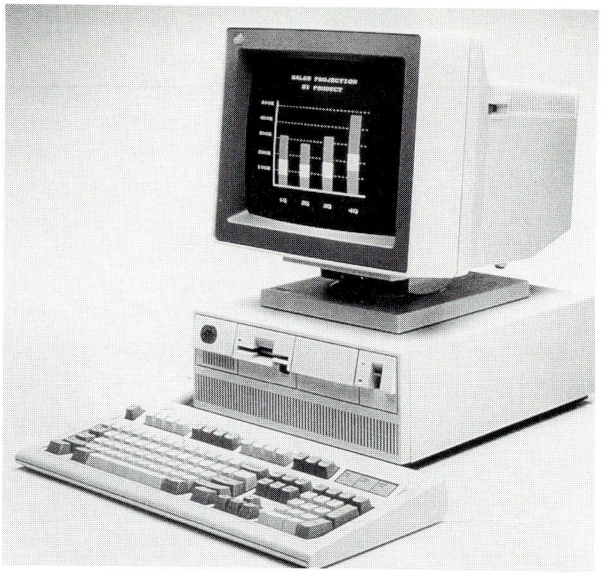

Graphics Display

True desktop publishing is impossible without a high-resolution graphics display adapter and monitor. To be more specific, this means an Apple Macintosh or an IBM-compatible equipped with an Enhanced Graphics Adapter, a Video Graphics Array, a Multicolor Graphics Array, or some other high-resolution graphics adapter. Color capability is not really essential, at least not yet, since only a few high-resolution printers can produce near-typeset-quality output in color. Although desktop publishing is possible on small-screen monitors, many users opt for large-screen models that can legibly display one or two entire pages at once (see Figure 4).

Mouse

Virtually all desktop publishing systems use a mouse or some other graphics input device such as a trackball or graphics tablet; a mouse is by far the most common device. It's used within the desktop publishing software to precisely

Figure 4 Large-Screen Display
Although desktop publishing is often done on microcomputers with small display screens such as the Apple Macintosh SE, a large-screen display is much more convenient because it can show one or two entire pages.

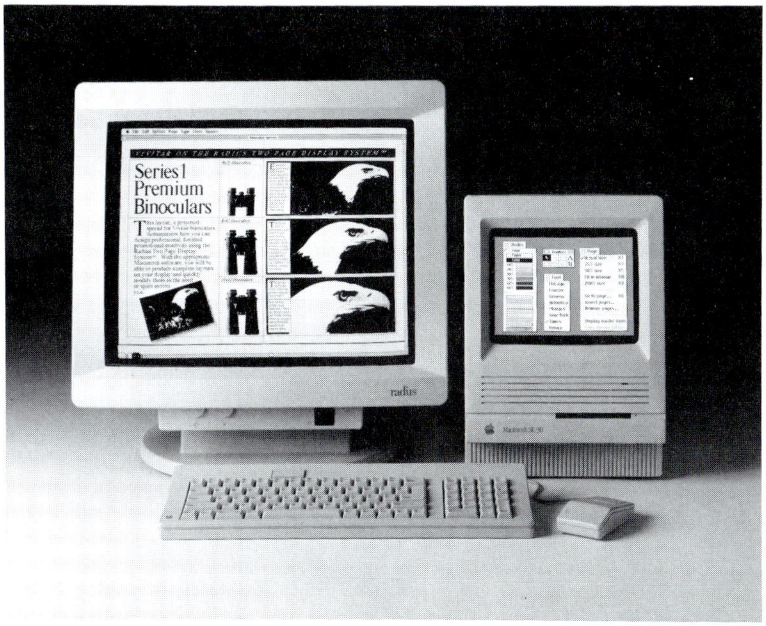

place text and graphics on each page, and also to draw simple objects like lines, boxes, and ovals.

Laser Printer

Although dot-matrix or ink-jet printers are sometimes used, the laser printer is the predominant hard-copy output device for desktop publishing. These quick, quiet printers use photocopier technology to produce text and graphics at resolutions of at least 300 dots per inch. A few color models are now available, but the vast majority of laser printers can produce only black and white output. Typical speeds range from six to twelve pages per minute, for pages that contain only text. Printing graphics is significantly slower. Some laser printers, for example, take more than five minutes to print a page that contains graphics. The three most common types of laser printers used with microcomputers are Hewlett-Packard LaserJets (and their compatible printers), PostScript printers, and QuickDraw printers (see Figure 5).

Hewlett-Packard LaserJets and compatible printers made by other companies are relatively inexpensive laser printers that start at about $1500. They can print both text and graphics at 300 dots per inch and are primarily used with IBM-compatible computers. LaserJet printers can produce various fonts, which must be loaded into the printer's memory from plug-in font cartridges or downloaded from disk files. Each font cartridge contains regular, boldface, and italic letters and symbols in two or three sizes. Font cartridges are convenient, but offer only a limited number of different fonts. For more fonts, you have to buy additional cartridges. Equipping a LaserJet with many fonts can be expensive.

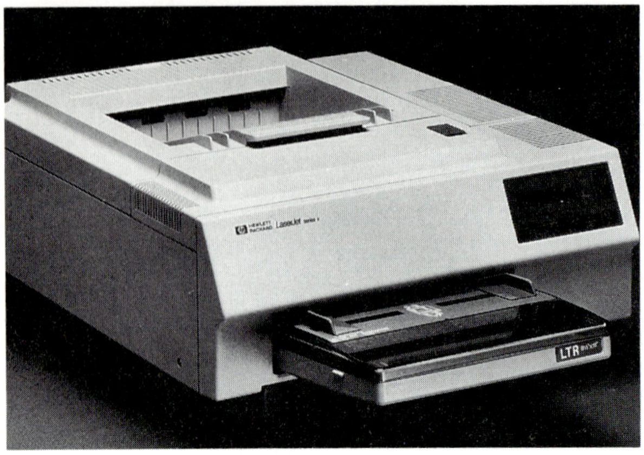

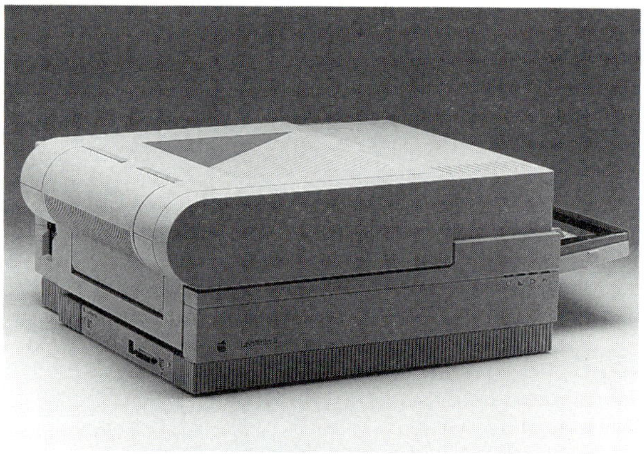

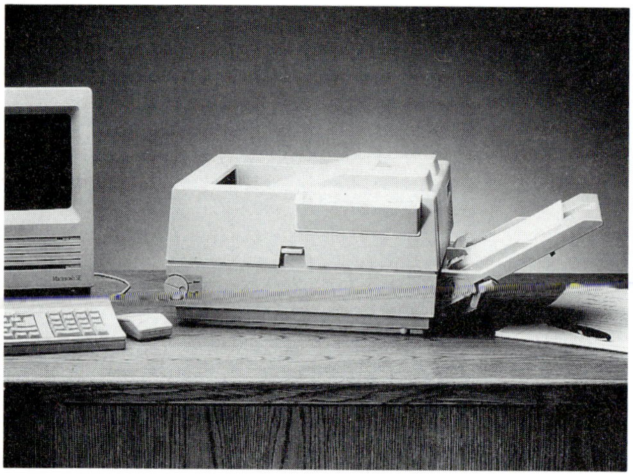

Figure 5 Laser Printers
The three types of laser printers most commonly used with microcomputers for desktop publishing are Hewlett-Packard LaserJets (and compatible printers from other manufacturers), Postscript printers, and QuickDraw printers. Here we show the Hewlett-Packard LaserJet II, the Apple LaserWriter IINTX PostScript printer, and the General Computer Corporation Personal LaserPrinter, which is a QuickDraw printer.

PostScript is a page description language for high-resolution printers and typesetters. Basically, a **page description language** is a specialized computer programming language for defining the size, format, and position of text and graphic elements on a printed page. In other words, a page description language tells a printer how to reproduce a page on paper. PostScript, developed and licensed by Adobe Systems, is one of the most popular page description languages. It's encoded into the hardware of several popular laser printers, including the Apple LaserWriter IINT and IBM's Personal Pageprinter. Starting at around $4000, PostScript printers are rather expensive, but they often include many fonts and provide a great deal of flexibility in the size, shape, and orientation of printed objects. Since PostScript is a *device-independent* language, you can design a document on one system and print it later on another system at a higher resolution. For example, you can rough out your document on a Macintosh and print a draft on a 300-dots-per-inch LaserWriter IINT. When you are finished, you can have your final version printed on an Allied Linotype Linotronic 100 typesetter. This impressive machine, which costs around $35,000, uses the PostScript language to produce output on photographic paper at a resolution of 1270 dots per inch. PostScript laser printers and typesetters can be used with many different types of computers.

QuickDraw laser printers are designed especially for Apple Macintosh computers as lower-cost alternatives to PostScript printers. They are named after the QuickDraw graphics routines built into the hardware of Apple Macintosh computers. Instead of using the PostScript language to specify page layouts, QuickDraw printers use the same built-in system software the Macintosh uses to draw text and graphics on the screen. Two of the most popular QuickDraw printers for the Macintosh are Apple's own LaserWriter IISC and General Computer Corporation's Personal Laser Printer. QuickDraw laser printers have a resolution of 300 dots per inch and typically cost between $1800 and $3000.

Scanner

Although a scanner isn't strictly necessary, it's a popular option in many desktop publishing systems (see Figure 6). As we said in Chapter 2, this device lets you convert photographs and line drawings into computer-readable form. While some scanners can also read text, in desktop publishing systems they're most often used for pictures. Once pictures are stored in disk files, they can be edited with graphics software or inserted directly into page layouts. Many scanners can read 300 dots per inch, matching the output resolution of most laser printers. While this resolution is adequate for many applications, it's still quite grainy when compared to the photographs you see in typeset magazines and books.

Word Processing Software

A word processing program is an essential component of any desktop publishing system. Page layout software does let you enter titles, headers, footers, captions and other incidental text items. Nevertheless, a word processor is still necessary for entering most of the text into a document. Almost any word processor can

Figure 6 ThunderScan
Most scanners are stand-alone desktop models that can cost more than $1000. ThunderScan, on the other hand, is a popular low-price ($249) scanner for the Apple Macintosh that fits into an Apple ImageWriter dot-matrix printer in place of the ribbon cartridge.

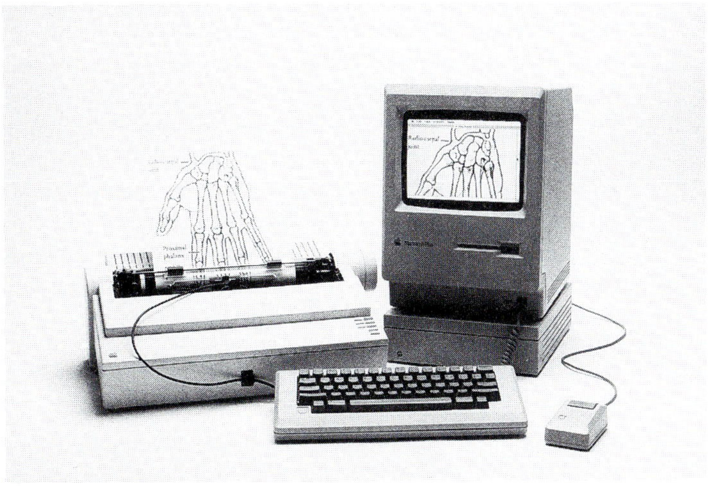

be used in a desktop publishing system, but it's best to use a program with good formatting abilities. If your page designs are simple, you may be able to get by with the desktop publishing features of a high-end word processor. Several what-you-see-is-what-you-get (WYSIWYG) word processing programs can incorporate graphics and snaking and parallel columns. Some use a mouse and a graphics interface, and all can produce near-typeset-quality output on a laser printer. WordPerfect and Microsoft Word are two examples of powerful word processors that can produce final results similar to that of page layout software. If your documents are not elaborate, one of these advanced word processors may be all you need. If your documents are elaborate, however, you'll probably need a page layout program to combine your text and graphics.

Graphics Software

Another component of most desktop publishing systems is some kind of graphics software. After all, one of the major reasons for using a desktop publishing system is to include drawings, diagrams, charts, and photographs in your documents. In some cases, these graphics can be captured by scanning existing images already on paper. With special equipment, it's even possible to capture and store live images from an ordinary video camera. Many of the figures to be included in documents can be produced from graphics software, however. Charting, painting, drawing, and computer-aided design programs can all be used to generate images for desktop publishing. In addition, painting programs can be used to enhance or otherwise manipulate scanned or captured images. Once you store your images, page layout software lets you insert them into your documents.

Page Layout Software

A page layout program is neither word processing nor graphics package, but it lets you integrate products of both of these into a single document. An accurate visual representation of one or two entire pages is depicted on the screen at once. Unlike many word processors, page layout programs generally have WYSIWYG displays. You can specify the number and width of columns on each page. Text from word-processed documents is placed on a page and can be easily arranged into columns. Empty blocks can be left for figures, and previously stored graphics can be placed within these spaces. Most page layout programs let you crop (trim), stretch, or compress graphics to fit within the blank spaces you've reserved. Headings, labels, and captions can be added in any number of fonts, styles, and sizes. Imported text can also be reformatted and rearranged from within the page layout program. **Rules** can be placed to separate columns and offset blocks of text. These dividing lines can be drawn anywhere on a page in a number of different styles and thicknesses. Most page layout programs also can add boxes, ovals, shaded backgrounds, and reversed (white on black) text. Finally, page layout programs are generally not limited to standard letter- or legal-size paper. You can work with documents of almost any size—from small business cards to large 17-by-22-inch newspaper pages. Once your pages have been designed, you can send them directly to your printer from within the page layout program.

Principles of Page Design

Before we see how desktop publishing is used, let's examine the principles that must be your guide. It's easy to get carried away with powerful page layout software. Many beginners make the mistake of employing exotic features just because they're there. Simply having a page layout program won't make you a master of page design. But you don't have to graduate from a school of design to produce attractive pages that communicate clearly. Remember that your goal is to convey a message and not distract the reader. Here are a few basic principles of page design that can help you achieve this goal:

- *Use plenty of white space*. Don't clutter the page. The reader's eye needs a break between text and graphic elements. This is the primary principle of good page design, but it's probably one of the most violated. Just because there's empty space on a page doesn't mean you have to fill it. Be sure to leave adequate margins on all four sides too.
- *Keep objects lined up*. It's important not to let the items in your document wander all over the page. Most page layout packages have horizontal and vertical guides you can use to help keep your objects precisely aligned. Professional page designers use grids to ensure the consistent alignment of margins, columns, and headings.
- *Use graphics sparingly*. Beginners are often so enchanted by their newfound ability to add pictures to their text that they put them everywhere. Don't incorporate figures with abandon just because you like the way they look. It's better to use graphics only when they directly relate to the text. And when you do use pictures, keep them small and simple.
- *Use fonts sparingly*. Here is another case in which more is not better. Although you may have many different fonts available, it's best to restrain your creative urges. Professional designers generally stick to just two typefaces in most simple documents: a sans serif font for headings, and a serif font for the rest of the text. **Serif** typefaces, such as the font used for the body text in this book, have lines crossing and finishing off the main strokes of the characters. **Sans serif** typefaces, like the font used for the headings in this book, are plainer, literally without serifs.
- *Use rules*. Use rules to differentiate parts of a page, but use them sparingly. These dividing lines can make a page appear more inviting and easier to read.
- *Keep your text lines short*. There's a reason why magazines, newspapers, and books often print text in two or three columns across a page. It's difficult for the eye to follow long lines of text, especially if the characters are small. Unless you're using a typeface size larger than 12 points, you should probably use at least two columns, each no wider than four or five inches.
- *Plan your page design first*. Don't jump right into your page layout program without thinking about how you want your final document to look. If you're not a professional page designer, you might try using some existing publication as a model.

Introducing PageMaker

In July 1985, Aldus Corporation released a page layout program called PageMaker for the Apple Macintosh and LaserWriter printer. Many experts mark the real birth of desktop publishing with the introduction of this program. PageMaker set the standard for desktop publishing features by including simple pull-down menus, WYSIWYG page displays, the ability to incorporate text and graphics from many other programs, and support for popular high-resolution laser printers and typesetters. In 1987, Aldus released a version of PageMaker for IBM-compatibles running under the Microsoft Windows operating environment. It is still by far the most popular page layout software for the Macintosh, although Xerox's Ventura Publisher outsells PageMaker for IBM-compatibles.

PageMaker is a leading page layout program, perhaps because it is powerful, easy to learn, and simple to use. Another plus is the fact that PageMaker looks and "feels" almost exactly the same on both Apple Macintoshes and IBM-compatibles. If you learn to use PageMaker on one of these types of computers, you'll have no trouble running it on the other as well. You can even trade PageMaker documents back and forth between Macintoshes and IBM-compatibles. In this chapter, we'll be using PageMaker Version 3.01 for the Macintosh to illustrate some of the principles of desktop publishing.

Producing a Newsletter

The best way to learn about desktop publishing is to see it in action. Perhaps the most common application of desktop publishing is producing newsletters. As an example, let's create a newsletter for a small business. Our fictional business is Paddle and Portage Canoe Outfitters, which rents canoes and camping equipment to people who want to explore the wilderness waters that border Minnesota and Canada. Owned and operated by Becky and Bob Johnson, Paddle and Portage Canoe Outfitters also sells supplies, mainly trail food, and operates an overnight bunkhouse for outgoing and incoming campers. Since canoe outfitting is a seasonal business, the Johnsons send out a newsletter every winter in a subtle effort to get customers to make early reservations. Figure 7 shows the final product—the front and back of the single-sheet newsletter we will produce with PageMaker.

There are five basic steps to creating most documents with a desktop publishing system: writing and editing the text, creating or scanning the artwork, laying out the pages, printing the document, and making multiple copies. Let's go through each of these steps, one by one, for the Paddle and Portage newsletter.

Writing and Editing the Text

PageMaker does let you enter and edit text, but it's not really adequate for typing entire documents. For this you still need a word processing program. Almost any word processing package will do, but it's better to use one specifically endorsed by PageMaker, such as MacWrite or Microsoft Word. If you use a word processor not endorsed by PageMaker, you can only import plain text (without embellishments such as multiple character fonts, styles, and sizes). You'll then have to format all of your text within PageMaker. It's generally easier to set formatting options such as paragraph alignment and character fonts within your word processor, if this is possible. Since MacWrite is fully supported by PageMaker, we'll use it for our newsletter example.

To start MacWrite, you simply position the mouse pointer on the MacWrite icon (pictorial symbol) and press the mouse button. Next, you need to select the formatting options you want to use. In newsletters, paragraphs are usually single-spaced and justified between the left and right margins. You don't have to worry about the exact margins because the paragraphs will be automatically reformed when you place them into their columns later with PageMaker. Single-spacing is already the default line spacing in MacWrite, but you'll have to turn on paragraph justification. This is done by clicking the mouse pointer on the page icon that shows all lines of equal length (see Figure 8).

You also need to decide which character fonts, styles, and sizes to use. Although there are a number of possible choices, it's best to keep things simple. The newsletter will consist of several small sections, with a short headline above each one.

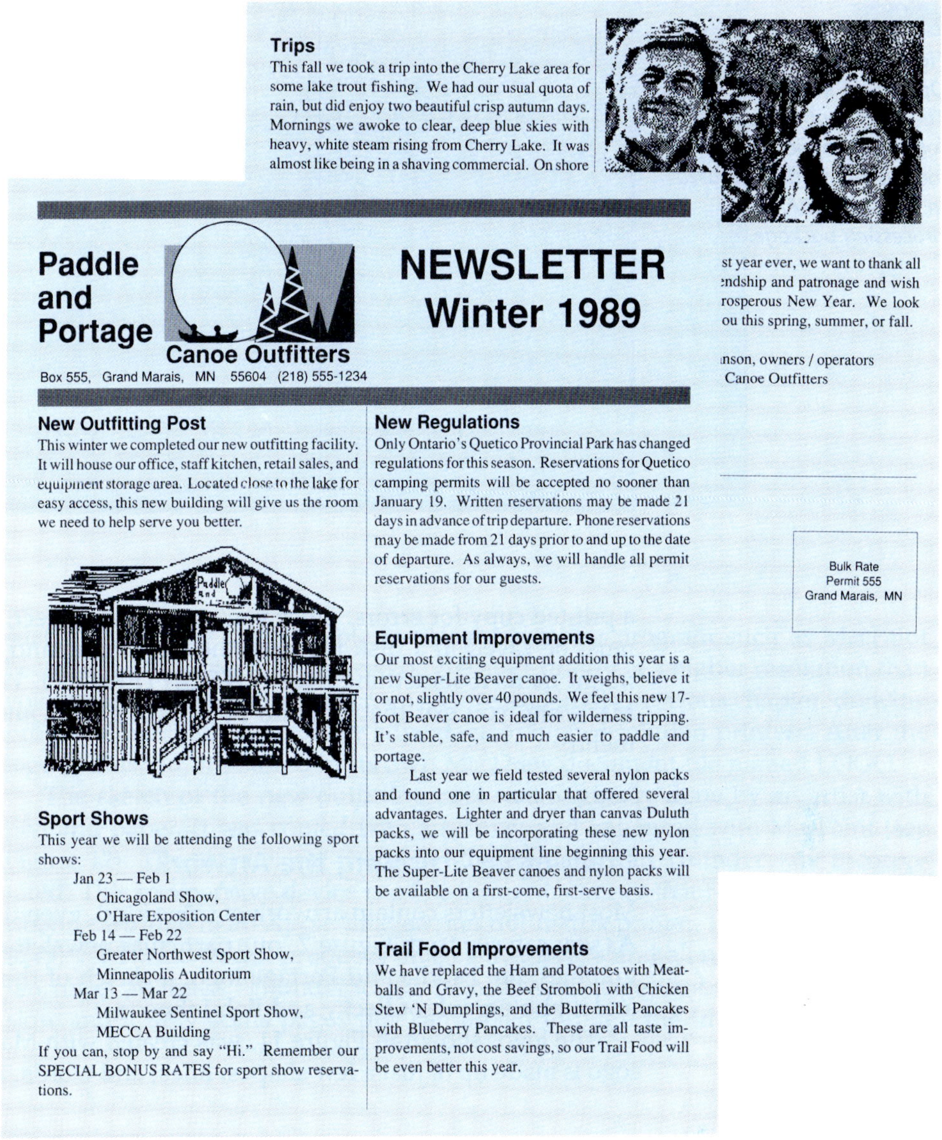

Trips

This fall we took a trip into the Cherry Lake area for some lake trout fishing. We had our usual quota of rain, but did enjoy two beautiful crisp autumn days. Mornings we awoke to clear, deep blue skies with heavy, white steam rising from Cherry Lake. It was almost like being in a shaving commercial. On shore

st year ever, we want to thank all ndship and patronage and wish rosperous New Year. We look ou this spring, summer, or fall.

nson, owners / operators
Canoe Outfitters

Bulk Rate
Permit 555
Grand Marais, MN

Paddle and Portage
Canoe Outfitters
Box 555, Grand Marais, MN 55604 (218) 555-1234

NEWSLETTER
Winter 1989

New Outfitting Post

This winter we completed our new outfitting facility. It will house our office, staff kitchen, retail sales, and equipment storage area. Located close to the lake for easy access, this new building will give us the room we need to help serve you better.

Sport Shows

This year we will be attending the following sport shows:

Jan 23 — Feb 1
Chicagoland Show,
O'Hare Exposition Center
Feb 14 — Feb 22
Greater Northwest Sport Show,
Minneapolis Auditorium
Mar 13 — Mar 22
Milwaukee Sentinel Sport Show,
MECCA Building

If you can, stop by and say "Hi." Remember our SPECIAL BONUS RATES for sport show reservations.

New Regulations

Only Ontario's Quetico Provincial Park has changed regulations for this season. Reservations for Quetico camping permits will be accepted no sooner than January 19. Written reservations may be made 21 days in advance of trip departure. Phone reservations may be made from 21 days prior to and up to the date of departure. As always, we will handle all permit reservations for our guests.

Equipment Improvements

Our most exciting equipment addition this year is a new Super-Lite Beaver canoe. It weighs, believe it or not, slightly over 40 pounds. We feel this new 17-foot Beaver canoe is ideal for wilderness tripping. It's stable, safe, and much easier to paddle and portage.

Last year we field tested several nylon packs and found one in particular that offered several advantages. Lighter and dryer than canvas Duluth packs, we will be incorporating these new nylon packs into our equipment line beginning this year. The Super-Lite Beaver canoes and nylon packs will be available on a first-come, first-serve basis.

Trail Food Improvements

We have replaced the Ham and Potatoes with Meatballs and Gravy, the Beef Stromboli with Chicken Stew 'N Dumplings, and the Buttermilk Pancakes with Blueberry Pancakes. These are all taste improvements, not cost savings, so our Trail Food will be even better this year.

Figure 7 The Finished Newsletter
This is the newsletter we will produce with PageMaker.

How about using 14-point boldface Helvetica type for the headlines, and 12-point plain Times type for the paragraphs themselves? These are commonly used fonts that look nice when printed with the LaserWriter. To select a font, you simply pull down the Font menu, highlight the one you want, and release the mouse button. Similarly, character style and size options are selected from the Style menu. These MacWrite menu selections are shown in Figure 9. You'll have to switch fonts, styles, and sizes several times as you enter titles and then the paragraphs themselves.

Once you've decided on the basic formatting conventions, you simply enter the newsletter's text as shown in Figure 10. Don't worry about the exact final form of the newsletter and don't leave space for figures. All that will be done within PageMaker. When you've finished entering the text, you should go back, check it for errors, and edit it if necessary. Although you don't have to print the document from within MacWrite, you can do so if you find it easier to check over

Figure 20 Placing the Newsletter Text

(a) This screen shows the Text icon, a symbol used to position text on the page.

(b) After you place the Text icon and press the mouse button, the Text icon disappears and the actual text appears.

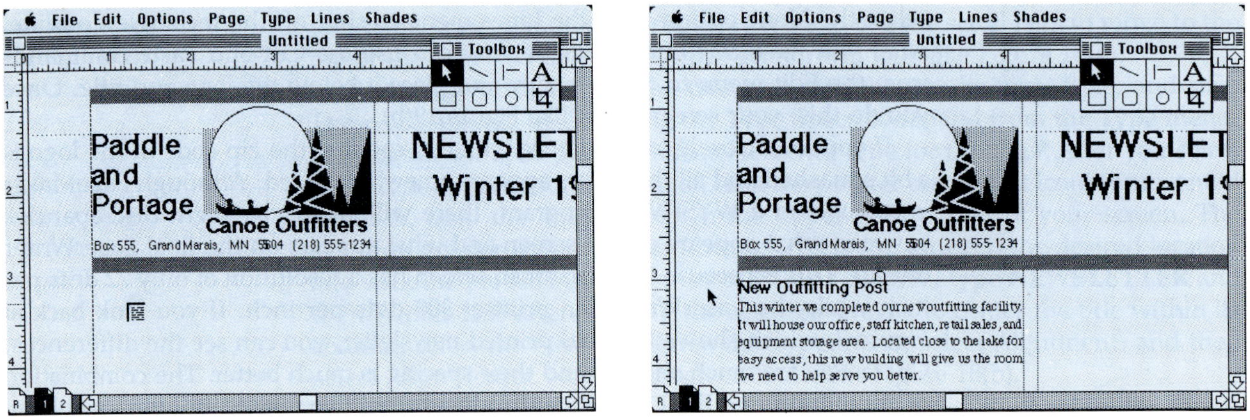

Now let's "zoom out" to get a view of the entire page at once. To do this you select the Fit in Window option from the Page menu. As you can see from Figure 21, this gives you a good idea of what the whole page looks like, even if you can't make out the details. In particular, lines of text are represented by shaded bars instead of the actual characters, which would be too small to distinguish. Converting text to these symbolic bars is called **greeking**; it is done to show the position of text on the screen.

Figure 21 Full-Page View Showing Text Greeking

You can "zoom out" to get a view of the full page, but text becomes too small to read. Page layout programs use greeking to represent text as shaded bars. Greeking allows you to see the position of text on the page, although you can't make out the details.

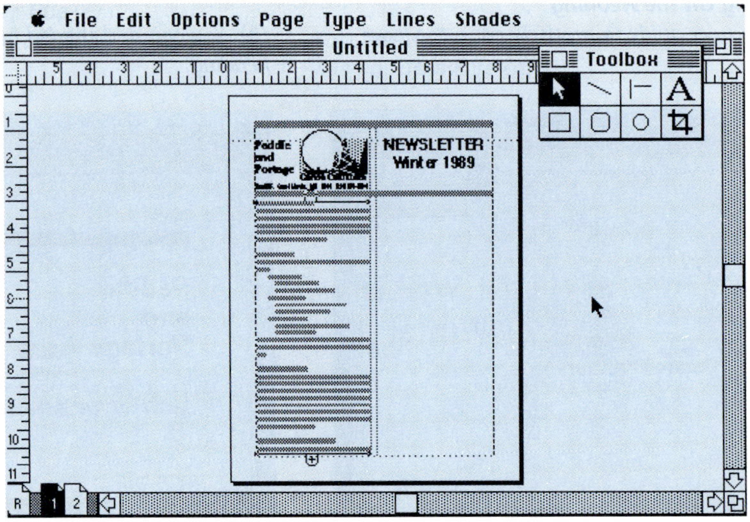

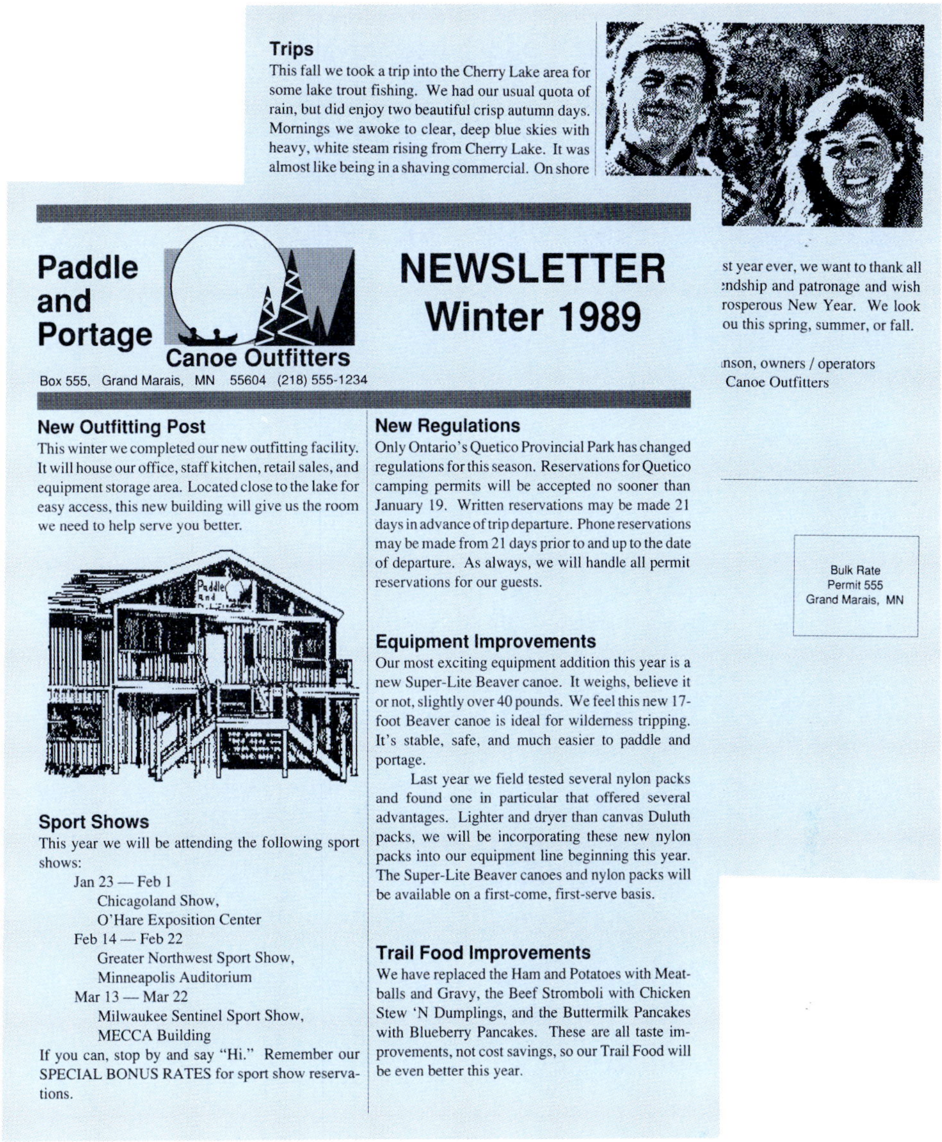

Trips

This fall we took a trip into the Cherry Lake area for some lake trout fishing. We had our usual quota of rain, but did enjoy two beautiful crisp autumn days. Mornings we awoke to clear, deep blue skies with heavy, white steam rising from Cherry Lake. It was almost like being in a shaving commercial. On shore

st year ever, we want to thank all
endship and patronage and wish
rosperous New Year. We look
ou this spring, summer, or fall.

nson, owners / operators
Canoe Outfitters

Bulk Rate
Permit 555
Grand Marais, MN

Paddle and Portage Canoe Outfitters

Box 555, Grand Marais, MN 55604 (218) 555-1234

NEWSLETTER Winter 1989

New Outfitting Post

This winter we completed our new outfitting facility. It will house our office, staff kitchen, retail sales, and equipment storage area. Located close to the lake for easy access, this new building will give us the room we need to help serve you better.

Sport Shows

This year we will be attending the following sport shows:

Jan 23 — Feb 1
Chicagoland Show,
O'Hare Exposition Center
Feb 14 — Feb 22
Greater Northwest Sport Show,
Minneapolis Auditorium
Mar 13 — Mar 22
Milwaukee Sentinel Sport Show,
MECCA Building

If you can, stop by and say "Hi." Remember our SPECIAL BONUS RATES for sport show reservations.

New Regulations

Only Ontario's Quetico Provincial Park has changed regulations for this season. Reservations for Quetico camping permits will be accepted no sooner than January 19. Written reservations may be made 21 days in advance of trip departure. Phone reservations may be made from 21 days prior to and up to the date of departure. As always, we will handle all permit reservations for our guests.

Equipment Improvements

Our most exciting equipment addition this year is a new Super-Lite Beaver canoe. It weighs, believe it or not, slightly over 40 pounds. We feel this new 17-foot Beaver canoe is ideal for wilderness tripping. It's stable, safe, and much easier to paddle and portage.

Last year we field tested several nylon packs and found one in particular that offered several advantages. Lighter and dryer than canvas Duluth packs, we will be incorporating these new nylon packs into our equipment line beginning this year. The Super-Lite Beaver canoes and nylon packs will be available on a first-come, first-serve basis.

Trail Food Improvements

We have replaced the Ham and Potatoes with Meatballs and Gravy, the Beef Stromboli with Chicken Stew 'N Dumplings, and the Buttermilk Pancakes with Blueberry Pancakes. These are all taste improvements, not cost savings, so our Trail Food will be even better this year.

Figure 7 The Finished Newsletter
This is the newsletter we will produce with PageMaker.

How about using 14-point boldface Helvetica type for the headlines, and 12-point plain Times type for the paragraphs themselves? These are commonly used fonts that look nice when printed with the LaserWriter. To select a font, you simply pull down the Font menu, highlight the one you want, and release the mouse button. Similarly, character style and size options are selected from the Style menu. These MacWrite menu selections are shown in Figure 9. You'll have to switch fonts, styles, and sizes several times as you enter titles and then the paragraphs themselves.

Once you've decided on the basic formatting conventions, you simply enter the newsletter's text as shown in Figure 10. Don't worry about the exact final form of the newsletter and don't leave space for figures. All that will be done within PageMaker. When you've finished entering the text, you should go back, check it for errors, and edit it if necessary. Although you don't have to print the document from within MacWrite, you can do so if you find it easier to check over

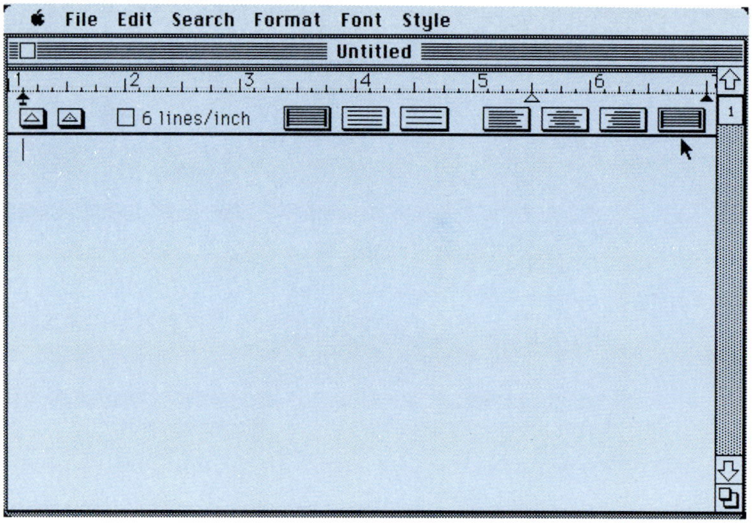

***Figure 8* Formatting Options in MacWrite**
The icons that let you set formatting options are located above the text area in the MacWrite word processing package.

a printed copy for errors. Once you're sure it's correct, the completed document must be saved in a disk file with the Save command from the File menu. You might name it something like NEWSLETTER TEXT. When you're finished with MacWrite, you exit the program by selecting the Quit command from the File menu.

Creating or Scanning the Artwork

Most newsletters contain artwork of some kind, even if it's only a company logo. As you can see from Figure 7, our particular newsletter contains three different graphics: the Paddle and Portage logo, a sketch of the new outfitting building, and a photograph of Becky and Bob Johnson.

The logo, shown in Figure 11, was created with MacDraw. This fairly simple logo is made up of just a few shapes, lines, and words. Using a drawing program

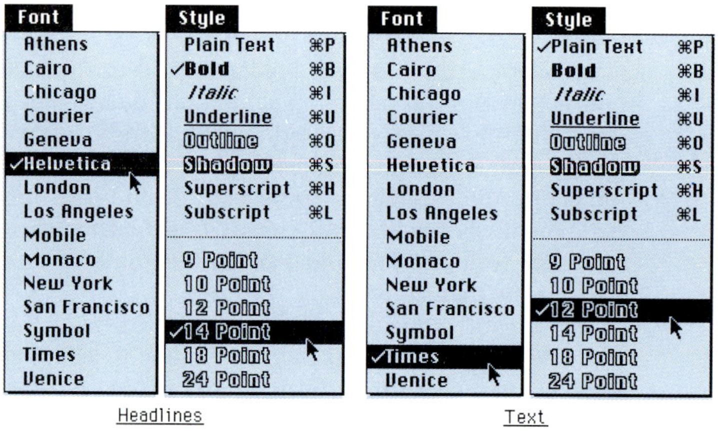

***Figure 9* Character Formatting Settings for Headlines and Text**
Select the 14-point Helvetica font for the headlines and the 12-point Times font for the text in our newsletter.

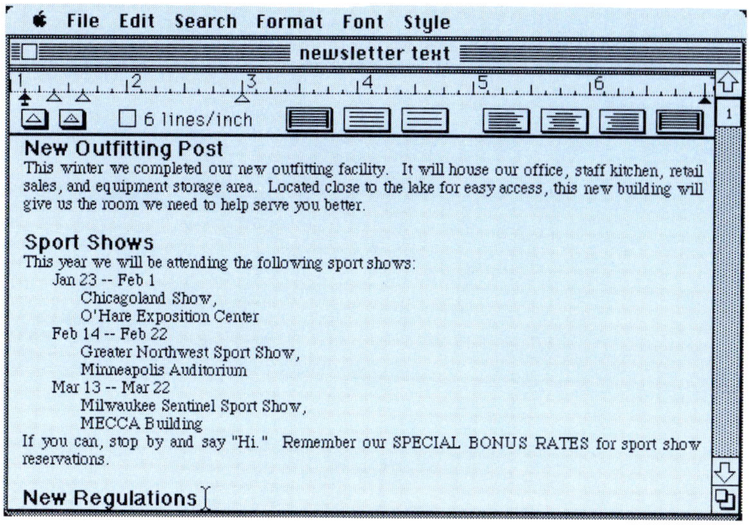

Figure 10 Entering the Newsletter Text with MacWrite
This screen shows the text of the newsletter being created with MacWrite.

such as MacDraw is preferable to using a painting program such as MacPaint because the logo can be produced on the laser printer at a higher resolution than you can see on the computer screen. As we said in the previous chapter, drawing programs generally take better advantage of high-resolution printers. After the logo is finished, it's stored in its own MacDraw document file named LOGO.

The sketch of the new outfitting post was originally done by an artist with pen and paper. It was copied with a scanner and enhanced with MacPaint (see Figure 12). The scanner we used is ThunderScan, from Thunderware Incorporated. This inexpensive device is a full-featured scanner that replaces the printer ribbon cartridge in an Apple Imagewriter dot-matrix printer. It's list price is only $249, yet ThunderScan produces images that rival stand-alone scanners costing ten times as much. ThunderScan's main disadvantages are that it's somewhat slow and it only scans pages that can be fed through the ImageWriter printer.

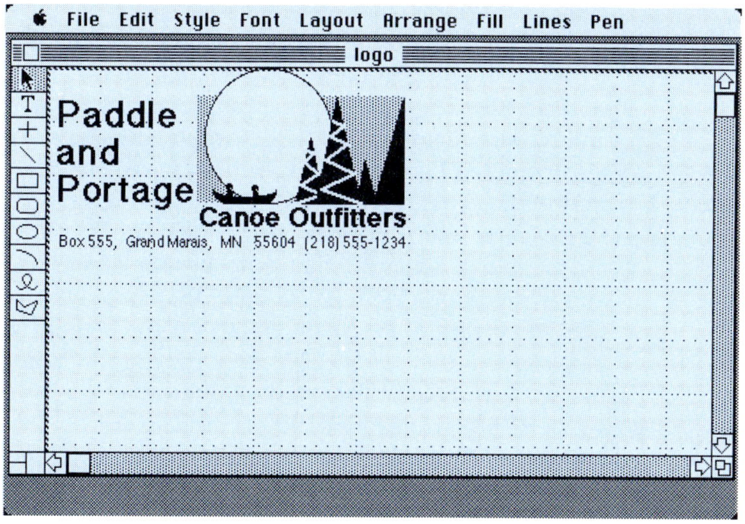

Figure 11 Creating the Logo with MacDraw
This screen shows the Paddle and Portage logo being created with MacDraw.

Figure 12 The Scanned Building Sketch in MacPaint
The sketch of the building was scanned with ThunderScan and stored in MacPaint format.

Once ThunderScan has been installed in an ImageWriter, all you do to scan a picture is insert the original into the printer and run the ThunderScan software. The resulting picture can be adjusted for brightness and contrast, and stored in a number of different graphics file formats. In this particular case, the image was stored in a MacPaint file named BUILDING.

The last graphic in our newsletter is a digitized reproduction of a color photograph of Becky and Bob Johnson. This reproduction was also created with ThunderScan and stored in a MacPaint file named PHOTO (see Figure 13). As you can see from Figures 12 and 13, as well as the finished newsletter in Figure 7, these scanned images are quite grainy. There are several reasons for this graininess. First of all, the original pictures were both rather small. In addition, the scanned copies were kept small to fit in the newsletter. Better results could have been obtained by having the scanner magnify the originals, but then they would be too big for the newsletter. The original photo of Becky and Bob was in color without much contrast. It had to be photocopied to be fed through ThunderScan, which somewhat degraded the image. In addition, storing the images in MacPaint format limits their resolution to 72 dots per inch, even though ThunderScan and the LaserWriter printer can resolve 300 dots per inch.

Without going into technical details, there are ways to improve the results of scanning sketches and photographs, but they involve using advanced techniques and require more storage. For example, images can be saved by ThunderScan in **Encapsulated PostScript (EPS) files**. These are large files containing gray-shade information that can be imported and printed by page layout programs, such as PageMaker, which use the PostScript language. Encapsulated PostScript images are printed in a manner that simulates the grey tones you see in an original black and white photograph. Although EPS files produce better results than MacPaint files, they cannot be easily edited on the screen, since the resolution of most displays is only around 72 dots per inch. Few painting and drawing programs can work with EPS files, so the only way to see your results is to print them on a LaserWriter from your scanner software or from PageMaker. Nevertheless, with patience and the right combination of hardware and software, you can produce scanned images much better than ours that are adequate for many applications.

Figure 13 The Scanned Photo in MacPaint
The photograph of Becky and Bob Johnson was scanned with ThunderScan and stored in MacPaint format.

Laying Out the Pages

The basic text and graphics of the newsletter are finished. The next step is to merge them with PageMaker and add the finishing touches. Starting PageMaker is just like starting MacWrite, except that you click the mouse pointer on the PageMaker icon. The program then presents the screen you see in Figure 14.

Setting Up the Pages Since you are creating a new PageMaker document, you first need to pull down the File menu and execute the New command. PageMaker presents the Page Setup screen, as shown in Figure 15. Here's where you tell PageMaker the size, orientation, and margins of your pages. Our newsletter will be printed on the front and back of a single 8.5-by-11-inch piece of paper. Since we don't need to leave extra space on the inside margin for binding, you should change the inside margin to 0.75-inch, just like the other margins. Furthermore, you should also turn off the Double Sided option because our newsletter will not

Figure 14 PageMaker Startup Screen
This screen appears after you click the mouse button on the PageMaker icon to start up the page layout program.

Figure 15 Page Setup Screen
Here is where you specify page formatting options.

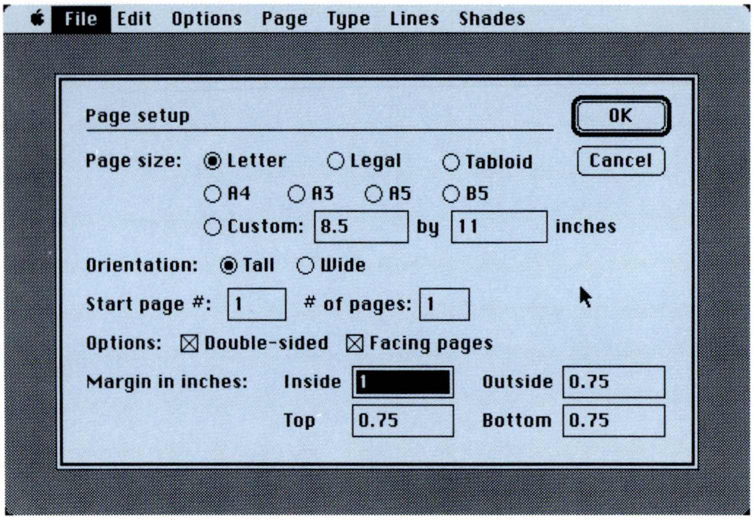

have facing pages like a bound booklet. This is done by simply clicking on the box beside the Double Sided option. When you do this, the X disappears from the box and the Facing Pages option automatically shuts off too. Finally, you should set the number of pages to 2—one page for the front and one page for the back. When you're finished with the page setup specifications, simply click on the OK box.

Turning on Rulers and Column Guides After you finish with the Page Setup screen, PageMaker presents the first blank page of your document, as shown in Figure 16(a). The dotted lines indicate your margins. This particular view is compressed to entirely fit on the screen. PageMaker also can present pages in actual size as well as half as large, three-quarters as large, and twice as large as actual size. The best way to precisely lay out your pages is to activate the on-

Figure 16 Specifying the Columns
(a) This screen shows the first blank page, which initially has no columns.

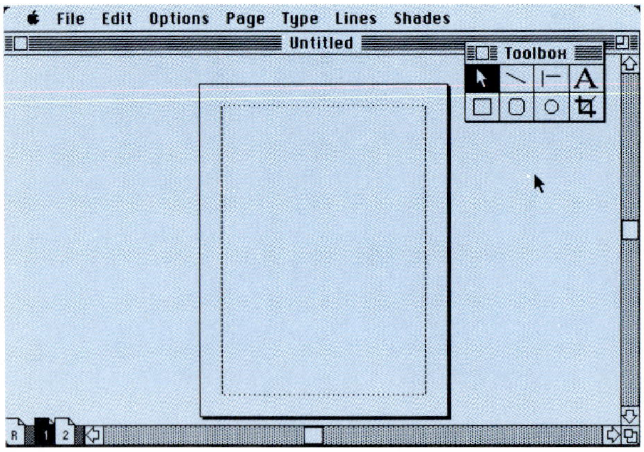

(b) This screen shows the page after the ruler and column guides have been turned on.

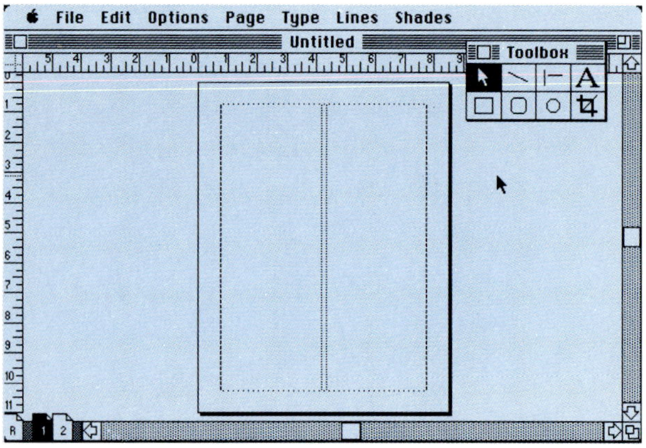

screen rulers. This is done by selecting the Rulers command from the Options menu.

At this point you should also tell PageMaker how many columns you want on your pages. By default, there is only one column showing, but we want two columns in our newsletter. To change the number of columns on a page, you select the Column Guides command from the Options menu and enter **2** for the number of columns. The default space between columns is 0.167 inches, which you can also change if you like, but this distance is fine for our newsletter. After you turn on rulers and specify two columns, your screen looks like Figure 16(b).

Placing the Letterhead Logo The PageMaker screen is like a typesetter's paste-up board, but much more flexible. You use the computer to arrange your pages instead of manually cutting and pasting text and graphics with razor blades, a T-square, and rubber cement. Since the work is done electronically, it's much easier to perfectly align items horizontally and vertically on the page.

The Paddle and Portage logo, which we created with MacDraw, will appear at the top left of the first page of our newsletter. To do this, you select the Place command from the File menu. PageMaker presents a list of both text and graphics documents, and you pick one of these to place on your page. You may have to switch to a different folder or disk to find the document you need. In our case, the MacDraw document is named LOGO. After you select the LOGO document, PageMaker returns to the page screen, but now the mouse pointer has changed to a corner symbol that contains a drawing pen (see Figure 17(a)). This icon represents the logo you just imported. To place it on the page, simply move the icon to the desired location and click the mouse button. The logo can be moved later if you like, but for now let's put it at the upper left corner of the page. As you move close to the corner where the top and left margins meet, the icon "snaps" into place. This is a handy PageMaker feature that helps you precisely align text and graphics to guide lines. After you press the mouse button to place the logo, your screen looks like Figure 17(b).

Figure 17* *Placing the Logo on the Page
(a) This screen shows the Draw icon, a symbol used to position a drawing on the page.

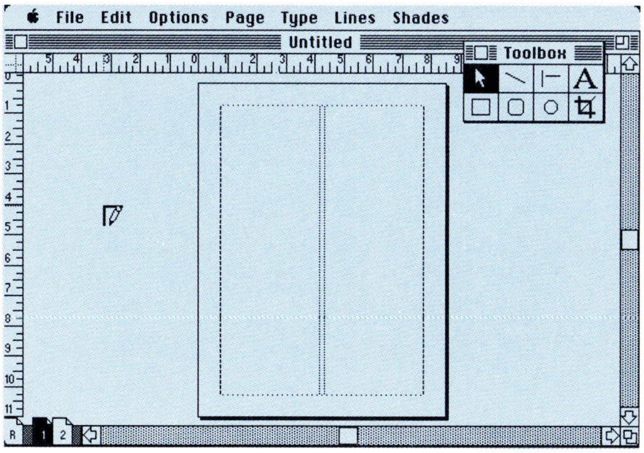

(b) After you place the Draw icon and press the mouse button, the Draw icon disappears and the actual logo appears.

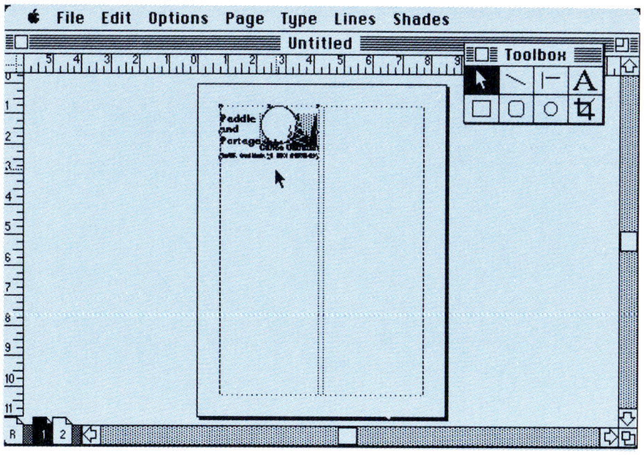

Typing the Newsletter Title Now let's add a title to the newsletter beside the logo. At this point, it's a good idea to switch to a full-size view of the page. This will make it easier to see details, although you'll lose the overall picture of the page. That's all right, however, because you can go back to the miniature view at any time. To switch to actual size, simply pull down the Page menu and select the Actual Size option. You'll probably have to use the scroll bars to move to the top of the page. When you do, your screen will look like Figure 18(a).

Before you actually type the title, you must choose its font, style, and size. These are selected by executing the Type Specs command from the Type menu. How about using 30-point boldface Helvetica type for the title? After you select these type specifications, you then click the pointer on the text icon, represented by an A, from the little toolbox in the upper-right corner of your screen. The selection pointer changes to an I-beam, which you move to the desired location and click the mouse button to insert text. For our title, type **NEWSLETTER** and then **Winter 1989** after pressing the carriage return. To center the title within its column, select the title, pull down the Type menu, select Alignment, and then select Align Center. Now your screen looks like Figure 18(b).

Finishing Off the Heading To spruce things up a little, let's offset our logo and title with two shaded bars. First, we need to shift the logo and title down a bit. Go back to the selection tool by clicking on the pointer icon from the toolbox. Move the pointer anywhere within the logo and click the mouse button again. Handles appear around the logo just like they do when an object is selected in MacDraw. You can now drag the logo around or even resize it by "pulling" on its handles. The title can also be selected and moved in a similar manner.

Before we move them, however, let's use a **ruler guide** to help precisely align the logo and title. This is a dotted line you can pull down from the top ruler or pull sideways from the left ruler. Like margins, these dotted lines won't actually be printed; they just help you keep text and graphics lined up on your pages. PageMaker lets you have up to 40 of these vertical and horizontal alignment guides. Figure 19(a) shows your page after using a horizontal ruler guide to align the text of the logo and title.

Figure 18 Typing the Newsletter Title

(a) It's easier to see details if you switch to the actual-size view of the page.

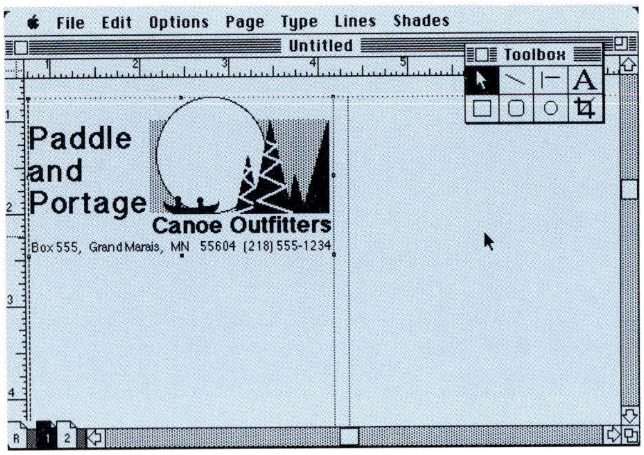

(b) This screen shows the top of the page after the headline has been entered.

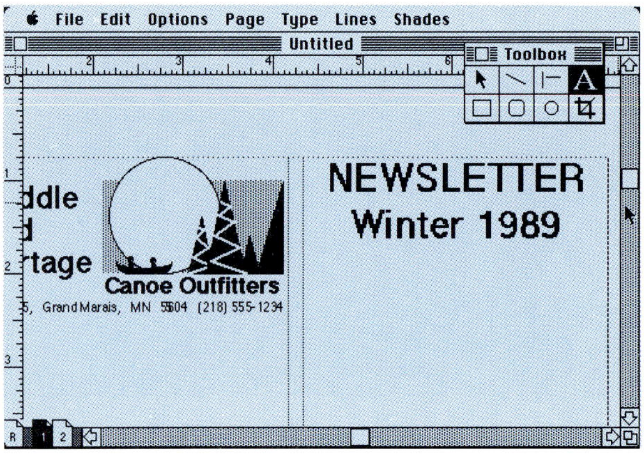

Now let's put a shaded bar above and below the logo and title. For this you need to select the box icon from the toolbox, which is used just like the MacDraw rectangle tool. Place the crosshair cursor at the intersection of the top and left margins, and drag open a thin rectangle all the way over to the right margin. Select the 40 percent shading from the Shades menu to fill in the rectangle, and select the None option from the Lines menu to shut off the rectangle's outline. After you have this one bar made, you can use the Cut and Paste commands from the Edit menu to create a copy and place it below the logo and title. Once you do this, your screen looks like Figure 19(b).

If you look closely at this figure, you can see that the zip code in the logo is a bit squashed and all the letters appear somewhat jagged. Although PageMaker is considered a WYSIWYG program, there will always be slight discrepancies between what appears on the screen and what appears on the final LaserWriter output. This is because the Macintosh screen has a resolution of only 72 dots per inch while the LaserWriter can print at 300 dots per inch. If you look back at Figure 7, which shows the final printed newsletter, you can see the differences. Characters are much sharper and their spacing is much better. The combination of PageMaker and the LaserWriter produces attractive results, but you may have to experiment a little to work out the very fine details that cannot be resolved on the screen.

Placing the Text The next step is to get the actual text of the newsletter and place it on the page. Again execute the Place command from the File menu, but this time select NEWSLETTER TEXT, the MacWrite document we created previously. When you select a word processed document file, PageMaker's pointer turns into a symbol that looks like a tiny page (see Figure 20(a)). Simply place this symbol at the upper-left corner of the area where you want the text to be placed and click the mouse button. The text expands to fill the column, as shown in Figure 20(b). Because MacWrite is fully supported by PageMaker, the formatting conventions you selected when you entered the text are preserved on the page.

Figure 19* *Finishing Off the Heading

(a) You can use a ruler guide to precisely align the logo and headline.

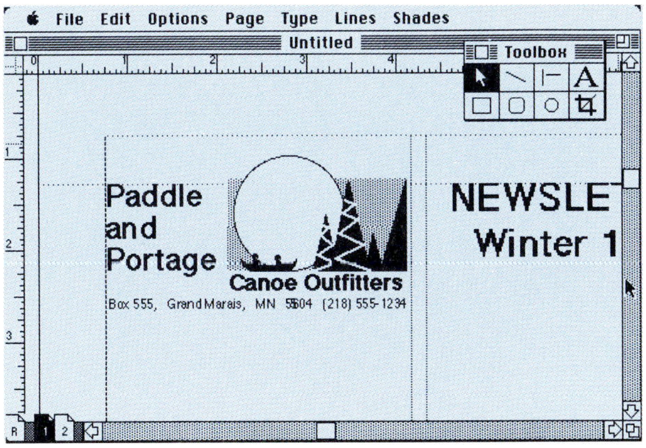

(b) You can add shaded bars above and below the heading.

Figure 20 Placing the Newsletter Text

(a) This screen shows the Text icon, a symbol used to position text on the page.

(b) After you place the Text icon and press the mouse button, the Text icon disappears and the actual text appears.

Now let's "zoom out" to get a view of the entire page at once. To do this you select the Fit in Window option from the Page menu. As you can see from Figure 21, this gives you a good idea of what the whole page looks like, even if you can't make out the details. In particular, lines of text are represented by shaded bars instead of the actual characters, which would be too small to distinguish. Converting text to these symbolic bars is called **greeking**; it is done to show the position of text on the screen.

Figure 21 Full-Page View Showing Text Greeking

You can "zoom out" to get a view of the full page, but text becomes too small to read. Page layout programs use greeking to represent text as shaded bars. Greeking allows you to see the position of text on the page, although you can't make out the details.

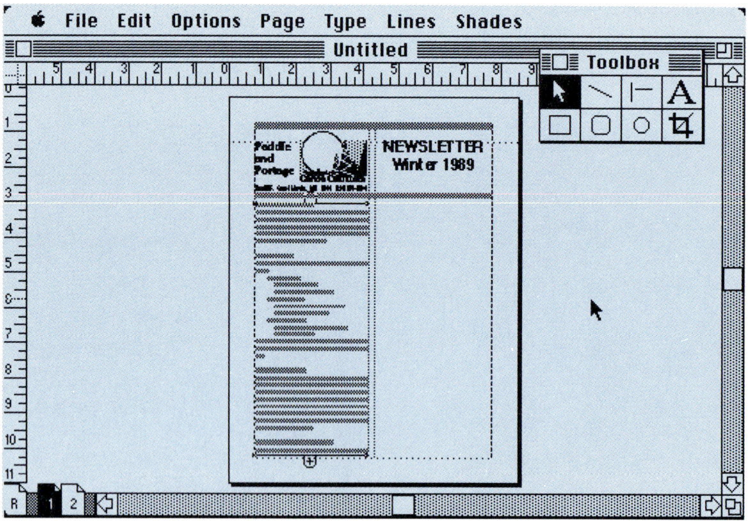

Notice that the top of the text block is indicated by a horizontal line with a loop sticking up from the center (see Figure 21). The bottom of the text block has a similar line, but the loop protrudes down and has a plus sign (+) inside. This plus sign indicates that there is more text in the file waiting to be placed. The loops are like the loops on a window shade—you can "pull" them up or down with the mouse pointer to open up spaces for artwork. For example, the first paragraph of our newsletter text describes the new Paddle and Portage outfitting building. The building sketch is to be inserted after this paragraph, so we need to leave room for it. Simply move the pointer to the bottom loop, hold down the mouse button, and drag the bottom edge of the text block up to a point just below the end of the first paragraph. Then click the mouse pointer on the plus sign in the bottom loop to continue placing text. A little text page icon appears, just like the one that appeared when you began placing text. Move the text icon along the left margin a couple of inches or so below the first paragraph and click the mouse button. As Figure 22 shows, an empty space remains and the text continues below it to the bottom of the column.

PageMaker versions newer than 2.0 can automatically continue text in the next column and on the next page, but you must first select Autoflow from the Options menu. The default text flow mode is Manual, which continues text from wherever you start the text flow to the bottom of the current column. To finish placing the rest of the text in our newsletter, click on the bottom plus sign again and move the page icon up to the top of the right-hand column. Click the mouse button again, and the text fills the column. The plus sign at the bottom of the right-hand column indicates that there is still more text to be placed, and it will have to be placed on the second page.

To switch to the next page, you simply click the pointer on the page symbol with the 2 inside at the lower-left corner of the screen. You'll have to use the

Figure 22 Making Room for the Building Sketch
You can move the little loops at the top and bottom of a text block to open up a "hole" for a picture. This screen shows the space created for the sketch of the new outfitting building.

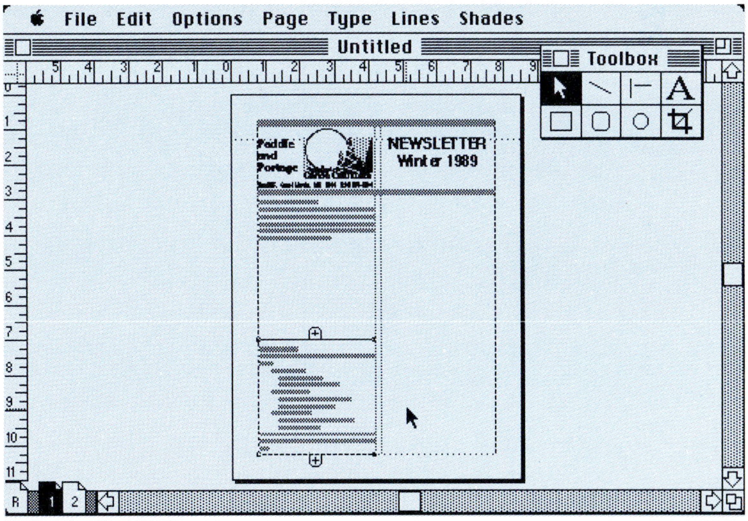

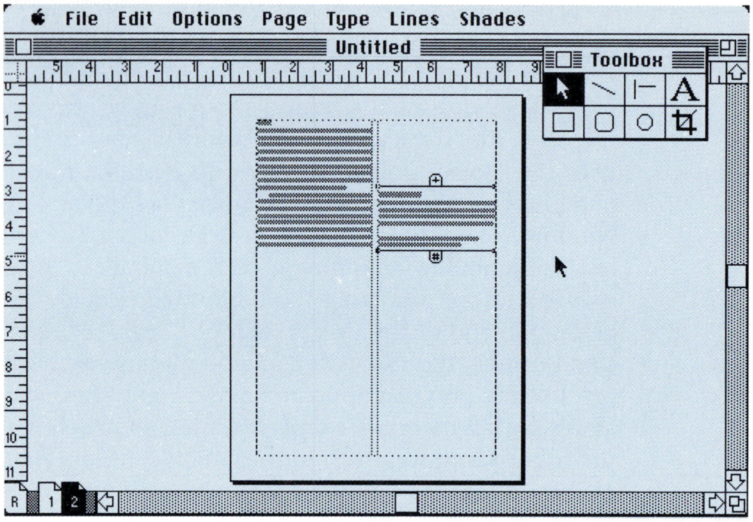

Figure 23 The Second Page of the Newsletter *This screen shows the full-page view of the second page of the newsletter after placing the text.*

Column Guides command from the Options menu to set up two columns on this page too. Then go back to the first page and click on the plus sign in the loop at the bottom of the right-hand column. Switch back to the second page again and now place the text at the top of the left-hand column. The number sign (#) at the bottom of the text block indicates that you finally have all the text placed on the pages. The bottom half of this second page, however, will be reserved for the mailing label. So, move the last text paragraph over to the right-hand column, leaving space above it for our scanned photograph of Becky and Bob. Your second page should now look like Figure 23.

Placing the Sketch and Photo While you're on the second page, you can place the scanned photograph of Becky and Bob in the space you left above the final paragraph. The procedure is just like placing the MacDraw logo, except you choose the MacPaint file named PHOTO, which was created when the photograph was scanned with ThunderScan. If the photo is a little too big to fit into the space you have left for it, you can shrink the photo by dragging its lower-right handle toward the upper left. The second page now looks like Figure 24(b).

To place the scanned sketch of the new outfitting building, go back to the first page. Again, execute the Place command from the File menu, but this time pick the MacPaint document named BUILDING. Move the paint icon into the empty space below the first paragraph in the left-hand column, and press the mouse button to expand the sketch. Again, you may have to slightly adjust the size of the sketch to fit into the space by dragging its lower-right handle toward the upper left. The resulting screen should look like Figure 24(a).

Creating the Mailer At this point, you're almost finished with the page layout. As we said before, this simple newsletter will be put onto a single sheet of paper. The paper will be folded in half and stapled or taped shut. So, the bottom half of the second page must display the mailing information. This consists of the return address in the upper-left corner and the bulk rate mailing permit in the upper-right corner where the postage stamp would normally go. The actual customer addresses will be printed on gummed labels and affixed to the finished newsletters after they are printed.

Figure 24 Placing the Graphics

(a) This screen shows the full-page view after the building sketch has been placed on the first page.

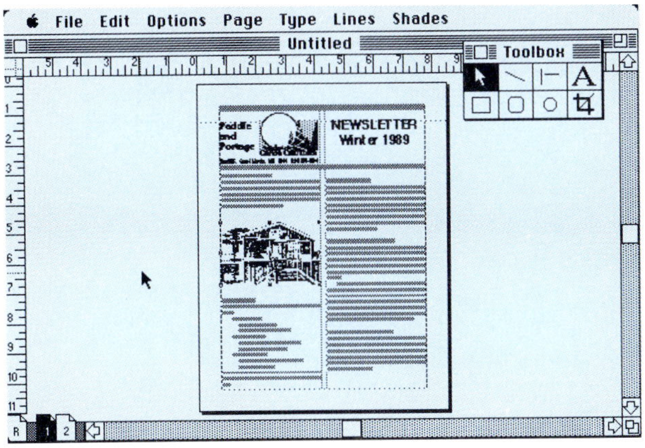

(b) This screen shows the full-page view after the photo has been placed on the second page.

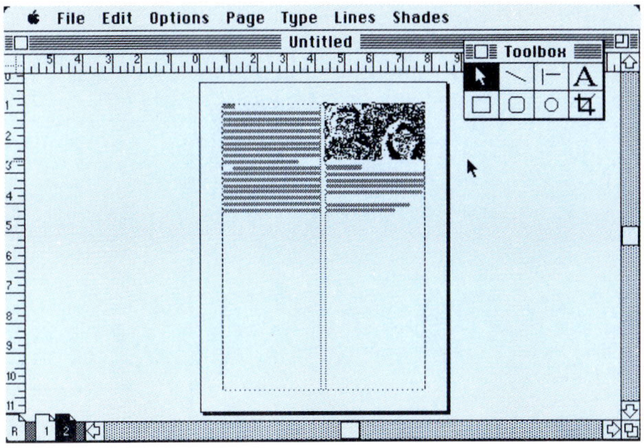

First, you need to draw a horizontal rule across the middle of the second page to indicate where the newsletter is to be folded. Pull down the Lines menu and select the Hairline option. Then select the horizontal and vertical line icon from the toolbox; this is the one to the immediate left of the A text icon. This tool is just like the perpendicular line tool in MacDraw. Move the crosshair cursor to the left page margin, 5.5 inches from the top of the page, as indicated by the vertical ruler. To draw the rule, simply hold down the mouse button, drag open the line all the way to the right margin, and release the button. While you're at it, you might also want to draw vertical hairline rules separating the columns on both pages. At this point, your second page looks like Figure 25(a).

For the return address, we'll use the Paddle and Portage logo. Again execute the Place command from the File menu to put another copy of the logo at the upper-left side of the bottom of the page. This time, however, let's scale it down a little and make it smaller than the logo on the first page. To do this, simply drag the lower-right handle of the logo toward the upper left. The figure will be correspondingly reduced in size.

Finally, you can use the box tool and the text tool to create the bulk rate permit stamp in the upper-right corner of the bottom half of the page. You'll need to switch to an actual-size view of the page to see what you're doing. Feel free to use a ruler guide to help you align the logo and permit on the page. When you're finished, the overall view of the second page should look like Figure 25(b).

Final Adjustments At this point, your newsletter is basically complete. You might, however, want to make some minor adjustments to precisely align text and figures on your pages. Switch to actual-size view or even two times actual size to get a more detailed picture of each page. Feel free to move items around a little. Use ruler guides wherever they might help you align the items. You might even want to use PageMaker's text tool to insert carriage returns and spaces here and there in your text to improve its overall appearance. The time you spend on these details can greatly enhance the final product.

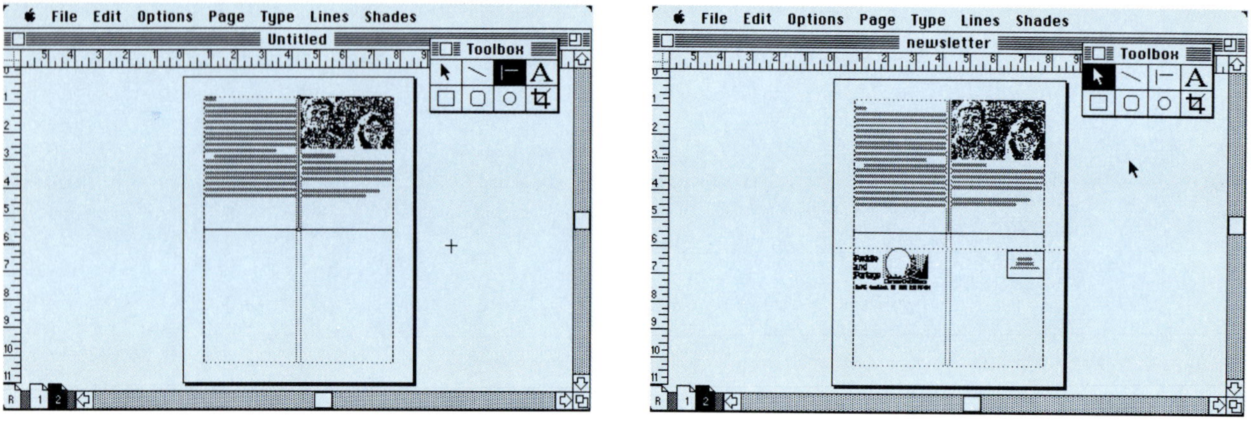

Figure 25 Finishing the Second Page
(a) This screen shows the second page after drawing the horizontal and vertical hairline rules.

(b) This screen shows the completed second page, after the mailing label has been created and the return address logo has been placed.

Printing the Document

When you're satisfied with the way your pages look, it's time to print them. You'll obtain the best results by using a laser printer or a true typesetter. We used the Apple LaserWriter II NTX to produce the final copy of our newsletter, which you see in Figure 7. All you do to print your document from within PageMaker is to execute the Print command from the File menu. Assuming you have a LaserWriter II NTX connected to your Macintosh, PageMaker will display the screen you see in Figure 26. As this screen shows, several options are available for printing on the LaserWriter. For our newsletter, we just used the default options.

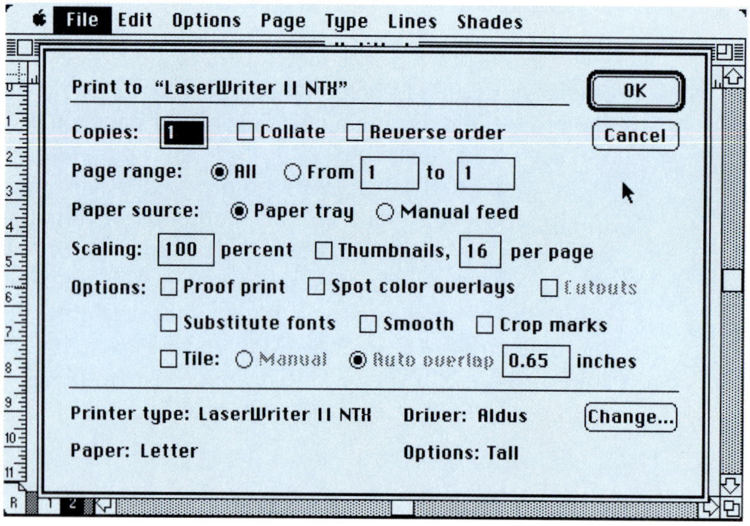

Figure 26 Printing the Newsletter on the Apple LaserWriter II NTX
This is the screen you see after selecting the Print command from PageMaker's File menu, if you have an Apple LaserWriter II NTX printer.

Real World

Desktop Publishing Looks Ahead

"Ultimately, the desktop publishing revolution will have as much impact on business as the telephone and photocopier did in their day."

This bold prediction was made in an industry newsletter editorial by John Sculley, chairman and chief executive officer of Apple Computer, Inc. Sculley's company has a big stake in the desktop publishing market, but he's not the only one who feels this way.

Consider this: U.S. corporations produce more pages a year than all book, magazine, and newspaper publishers combined. More than 80,000 companies in the United States produce technical documentation and many more put out newsletters, brochures, and sales documents. According to a Bell Laboratories study, technical documentation alone will increase at a rate of 500,000 pages per minute worldwide. That's a big potential market.

With desktop publishing technology, businesses can slash their typesetting, camerawork, layout, and pasteup costs, save time, and produce attractive products as well.

GTE Government Systems Corporation in Westborough, Massachusetts, produces about 400,000 pages a year. Using desktop publishing, the company spends about $1.33 per page, which is less expensive than what they could do with a typewriter, according to company officials.

But desktop publishing is not limited to the conventional page. The New York design firm of Carbone-Smolan Associates used desktop publishing to develop informational and directional signs for the Louvre Museum in Paris. Using an Apple Macintosh and LaserWriter printer, the firm prepared models of how the signs would look. As a result, they produced professional-looking documents within a tight time frame.

"It would never have been possible without the Mac," said Key Carbone, a partner in the firm.

Sources: Alex Kozlov, "Desktop Publishing Moves Into the Mainstream," *Newsweek Special Advertising Supplement on Business Technology*, November 2, 1987, p. S18. Mike Higgins, "How Desktop Publishing and LANs Work Together," *The Office*, December 1987, p. 32.

Making Multiple Copies

The term publishing generally refers to preparing and disseminating a document to the public. In most cases, this means making multiple copies of your printed document. If you need just a few copies, say four or five, you can simply have PageMaker print them on the LaserWriter. All you do is enter the number you want in the Copies box when you execute the Print command from the File menu (see Figure 26). If you need lots of copies, it's faster and more economical to use a good plain paper copier or an offset printer. Professional offset printing is probably best for more than a few hundred copies, and it yields better results than an ordinary office copy machine. Print shops that specialize in offset printing can also collate, fold, and bind your documents if necessary.

Summary

- *Why desktop publishing is so useful and popular*. Desktop publishing produces more attractive documents than typewriting and word processing, it cuts costs, it reduces delays, it lets you tackle projects you couldn't otherwise afford to do, and it gives you added control and the freedom to experiment with your document designs.
- *The applications of desktop publishing*. All kinds of documents—advertisements to workbooks—can be produced with a desktop publishing system.

- *The basic hardware and software components of a desktop publishing system.* A powerful microcomputer, a graphics display adapter and monitor, a mouse, a laser printer, a scanner, a word processing program, graphics programs, and a page layout program are all used in desktop publishing systems.
- *The principles of good page design.* These include using plenty of white space, keeping objects lined up, using graphics and fonts sparingly, using rules, keeping your text lines short, and designing your pages before you lay them out.
- *How to use a desktop publishing system to produce a newsletter.* The five basic steps to creating a document with a desktop publishing system are writing and editing the text, creating or scanning the artwork, laying out the pages, printing the document, and making multiple copies.

Key Terms

As an extra review of this chapter, try defining the following terms.

Encapsulated PostScript (EPS) file	QuickDraw laser printer
greeking	ruler guide
page description language	rules
page layout software	sans serif
PostScript	serif

Review Questions

1. What makes desktop publishing an attractive alternative to professional publishing?
2. List five applications of desktop publishing.
3. List the major hardware components of a typical desktop publishing system.
4. What software packages are needed for desktop publishing?
5. What are the three basic laser printer standards used in desktop publishing systems?
6. List five capabilities of page layout software.
7. Which page layout program works almost identically on both Apple Macintosh and IBM-compatible computers?
8. What are the five basic steps to producing a document with a desktop publishing system?
9. Why is it best to use a word processing package explicitly endorsed by your page layout program?
10. Why is a drawing program such as MacDraw better than a painting program such as MacPaint for producing simple graphics to be incorporated into a document and printed on a laser printer?
11. What device would you use to reproduce a photograph or line art for inclusion in a document?
12. Which PageMaker command do you use to import and position text and graphics on a page?
13. What PageMaker feature can be used to help you precisely align text and graphics on your pages?

14. Why is there a slight discrepancy between what you see on your screen and what is ultimately printed on the laser printer?
15. Why is greeking used in full page displays?
16. How do you compress a graphic in PageMaker?
17. How do you draw a rule in PageMaker?
18. How do you print a document in PageMaker?
19. What are two common methods of producing many copies of a document produced with a desktop publishing system?
20. List seven principles of good page design.

Multiple Choice

1. Desktop publishing lies on a continuum between
   (a) file management and data base management.
   (b) charting and computer-aided design.
   (c) typewriting and typesetting.
   (d) word processing and spreadsheets.
2. Which of the following computer components is not strictly necessary for desktop publishing?
   (a) powerful microcomputer
   (b) graphics display adapter and monitor
   (c) high-resolution printer
   (d) modem
3. Which of the following is a device-independent page description language commonly used in laser printers and typesetters?
   (a) PostScript
   (b) LaserJet
   (c) QuickDraw
   (d) Modula-2
4. Which of the following devices might you use to convert photographs and line drawings into computer-readable form?
   (a) laser printer
   (b) scanner
   (c) mouse
   (d) keyboard
5. Page layout software lets you combine the output of
   (a) spreadsheet and data base management packages.
   (b) communications and networking packages.
   (c) word processing and graphics packages.
   (d) project management and accounting packages.
6. Which of the following is *not* a principle of good page design?
   (a) Use plenty of fonts.
   (b) Use plenty of white space.
   (c) Use graphics sparingly.
   (d) Use rules.
7. The first step to creating a desktop published document is usually
   (a) laying out the pages.
   (b) printing the document.
   (c) making multiple copies.
   (d) writing and editing the text.
8. Which of the following types of files contains gray-shade information about a scanned picture?
   (a) ASCII file
   (b) Encapsulated PostScript (EPS) file
   (c) binary file
   (d) EXE file

9. Which of the following techniques is used to represent lines of text that are too small to distinguish individual characters?
   (a) greeking (b) zooming
   (c) clicking (d) justification
10. Page layout programs help you align text and graphics through the use of
    (a) fonts. (b) menus.
    (c) ruler guides. (d) handles.
11. Which of the following PageMaker commands do you use to put text on a page?
    (a) Column Guides command from the Options menu
    (b) Cut command from the Edit menu
    (c) Fit in Window command from the Page menu
    (d) Place command from the File menu
12. Which of the following PageMaker commands do you use to put graphics on a page?
    (a) Column Guides command from the Options menu
    (b) Cut command from the Edit menu
    (c) Fit in Window command from the Page menu
    (d) Place command from the File menu
13. Which of the following output devices achieves the highest resolution?
    (a) dot-matrix printer (b) ink-jet printer
    (c) laser printer (d) typesetter
14. What kind of typeface is commonly used for headings?
    (a) serif (b) sans serif
    (c) pica (d) elite
15. Laser printers produce output at resolutions of at least
    (a) 300 dots per inch. (b) 600 dots per inch.
    (c) 900 dots per inch. (d) 1200 dots per inch.

Projects

1. In this chapter we have used PageMaker to illustrate some principles of desktop publishing. A number of other page layout programs are also used on Apple Macintosh and IBM-compatible microcomputers. Write a brief report that compares one or two of these other programs to PageMaker. Examine features, cost, and support for hardware and software products from other companies. Product reviews in computer magazines and newspapers are a good source of information.
2. What use would you have for a desktop publishing system at school or work? Specifically, what kinds of documents would you produce and why do you think desktop publishing would be better than typewriting or word processing? Do you think these uses would justify the added expense? Write a brief report explaining your position.
3. Is desktop publishing used at your school or office? Try to find an example of an actual desktop publishing system currently used by an individual, business, or organization that you know about and write a brief report about

this system. If you don't personally know of anyone using desktop publishing, try to find an example described in a newspaper or computer magazine such as *Personal Computing*. What kind of computer, word processor, graphics software, page layout program, and printer do they use? What kinds of documents do they produce? Why did they decide a desktop publishing system was necessary? Do they use a scanner? And are they satisfied with their system?

4. If you have access to a desktop publishing system, use it to prepare a document of your choice. You could do an ad, brochure, newsletter, resume, or informal report for one of your classes. If you don't have access to a system, just plan and sketch out your page designs on paper. Be sure to say what your margins would be, how many columns you would have, which fonts you would use, and what kinds of graphics you would include.

CHAPTER 20

SOFTWARE SIDELIGHTS

In This Chapter

Integrated Software
- Advantages of Integrated Software
- Disadvantages of Integrated Software
- Popular Integrated Software Packages

Windowing Environments
- Types of Windowing Environments
- Popular Windowing Environments

DOS Shells

Utilities
- Disk and File Utilities
- Printer Utilities
- Keyboard Utilities

Desk Accessories

On-Line References

Statistical and Math Packages

Project Management Software

Accounting Software

Personal Finance and Tax Programs

Educational Software

Entertainment Software

Hypertext Programs

Artificial Intelligence and Expert Systems

Preview

This chapter covers some of the other important types of microcomputer software on the market today. There is, of course, no way that we can discuss every significant program. Nevertheless, we will introduce many specific examples of popular microcomputer software products, and we hope this will give you an appreciation for the truly amazing variety of microcomputer software packages at your disposal.

After studying this chapter, you will understand

- the advantages and disadvantages of integrated software.
- how a windowing environment can enhance an operating system.
- how a DOS shell can make DOS more user friendly.
- the various types of utility programs available for microcomputers.
- which desk accessories are handy software options.
- that on-line references can save time and effort.
- the availability of statistical and math software for microcomputers.
- how project management software is used as a valuable organizational tool.
- how accounting packages are used by businesses to help with the bookkeeping.
- how personal finance and tax programs can help manage your money matters.
- the range of educational software packages available for microcomputers.
- the vast array of entertaining computer games, simulators, and music programs.
- how hypertext is used to tap into vast stores of information.
- the practical uses of artificial intelligence and expert systems.

Integrated Software

As you know, most people who work with microcomputers use several different types of application software. The most commonly used packages are word processors, spreadsheets, data base managers, communications programs, and graphics programs. In this book we've discussed several programs in each of these categories, but many more programs are on the market. Consumers are presented with a truly bewildering array of software options. Why haven't developers come up with packages that include all five of these major applications? Well, they have, with packages called **integrated software.**

Advantages of Integrated Software

Using integrated software is like one-stop shopping—you can get almost everything you need under one roof. The most important advantage of integrated software is that you learn a single set of consistent menus and commands for a wide range of tasks. In other words, the user interfaces of all included applications are very similar. It generally takes a good deal of time and effort to master any sophisticated application package. But because of its uniform approach to menus and commands, integrated software is usually much easier to learn and use than several separate application programs.

Another advantage of integrated software is its superior ability to transfer data internally among its own individual components. Users can effortlessly share data among the word processing, spreadsheet, data base, communications, and graphics modules. If you were a salesperson, for example, you could download some sales figures from the regional office with the communications program, use the figures to update your data base, transfer the figures to the

Insight

The Future of Software Packages

The crystal ball is cloudy today. The future is a little hard to see.

The truth is that no one knows who will invent the next WordPerfect, Lotus 1-2-3, or dBASE, or what the next breakthroughs will be. The development of microcomputers that are faster, have more memory, and use almost unlimited disk storage has lifted a lot of the constraints on their use already.

One of the most promising areas currently under development is an application of artificial intelligence known as the expert system. An expert system mimics the behavior of a person solving a problem. For example, if the light on your desk isn't lit, you probably go through a series of questions like this:

- Is the light switch on?
- Is the lamp plugged in?
- Is the house fuse blown?
- Is the power out?
- Is the light burned out?
- Is the lamp itself broken, and should it be replaced?

Each of these questions can be answered yes or no. If an answer is yes, there is an action to be taken, such as replacing the bulb or turning on the switch. If the answer is no, you ask another question.

The choice of which question to ask first may be important. Experience suggests that it is fairly unlikely that the lamp itself is broken or that the power is off in the house. It's more likely that the lamp is not plugged in, the switch is off, or the bulb is burned out.

An expert system needs software to produce logical inferences and a large knowledge base to support the particular application. The inference engine needs a fast processor and a large memory, while the knowledge base can require a large disk-storage device. With the powerful new generation of microcomputers, we may have a computerized consultant right at our fingertips.

spreadsheet to generate next quarter's sales projections, produce a bar graph, and insert this graph into a report being prepared with the word processor. All of this can be done in a very straightforward manner with the same integrated package. Although many separate application packages can import and export data to other applications, the procedures are often complicated. By integrating the applications into a single package and using consistent formats for data files, integrated software makes it much easier to manipulate and present data in various ways.

Besides the advantages of consistency and data sharing, integrated software is almost always less expensive than a combination of several individual programs. For example, while an integrated software package may cost $700 or $800, five separate applications might cost $200 to $500 each, for a total of $1000 to $2500.

Disadvantages of Integrated Software

When integrated software was first introduced in the early 1980s, expectations for it were high, but sales have not quite lived up to those expectations. Many users were simply unwilling to give up their familiar stand-alone applications. Although integrated packages are an important software category and are gaining favor in many organizations, they do have two major disadvantages. First, integrated software hampers your ability to choose applications for their individual strengths. For example, while you may really like the spreadsheet in a particular integrated package, you may really dislike the word processor or data base manager. Unfortunately, you're stuck with the entire package, even if you don't need or like certain individual components.

The other main disadvantage to integrated software packages is that they tend to be complex programs that require a good deal of primary memory. Furthermore, some integrated packages are a little slower than smaller stand-alone applications.

Popular Integrated Software Packages

The term *integrated software* has been applied to many packages that include more than one basic application. For example, Lotus 1-2-3 has often been categorized as integrated software because it includes spreadsheet, data base, and graphics capabilities. These days, however, an integrated software package has come to mean one that includes at least word processing, spreadsheet, data base, communications, and graphics capabilities. In addition, integrated software generally includes some programmability, ranging from keyboard macros to a full-fledged, high-level programming language. Several integrated software packages on the market fulfill these requirements, but here are a few of the most popular:

- *Enable.* This package, from The Software Group, is often compared with both Symphony and Framework as one of the leaders in integrated software for IBM-compatible microcomputers (see Figure 1). Of the three, Enable is the most well-balanced package, with an especially powerful data base manager. All of its components are comprehensive and functional.
- *Symphony.* Lotus Development Corporation, maker of 1-2-3, also sells this integrated software package for IBM-compatibles (see Figure 2). As you might expect, Symphony's spreadsheet is one of the best in the business, building on the strong tradition started with Lotus 1-2-3. It also has powerful built-in programming capabilities.
- *Framework III.* Ashton-Tate developed this powerful integrated software package for IBM-compatibles (see Figure 3). The appeal of Framework III is its

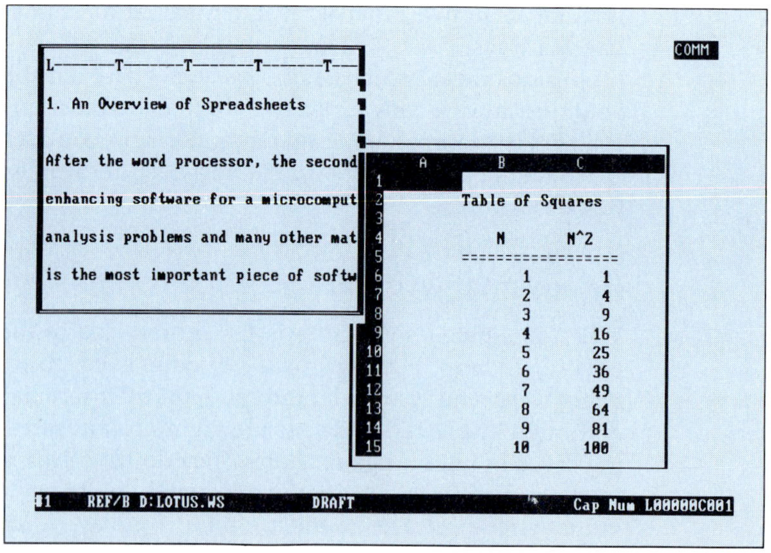

Figure 1 Enable
Enable, from The Software Group, is a well-balanced integrated software package.

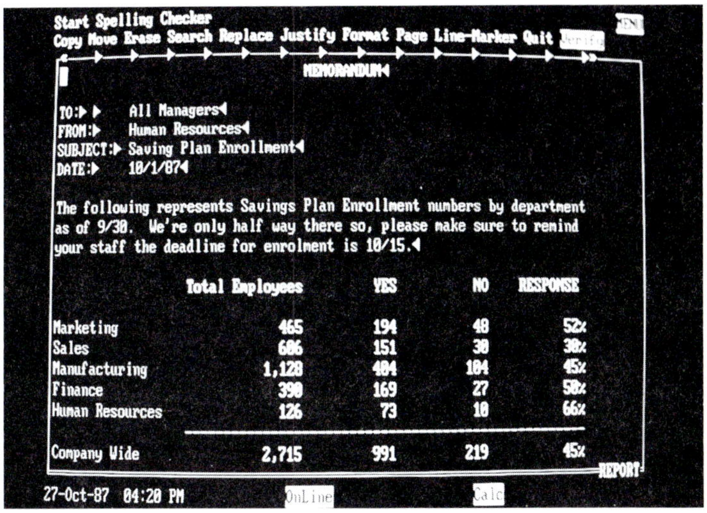

Figure 2 Symphony Symphony, from Lotus Development Corporation, is an integrated software package with especially good spreadsheet capabilities.

superb ability to gather and structure information. The heart of the program is an outline facility. It also has a word processor, spreadsheet, data base manager, and communications module with support for local area networks and electronic mail. Framework III includes its own powerful programming language, called FRED. Like both Enable and Symphony, Framework lists for around $700.

Figure 3 Framework III Framework III, from Ashton-Tate, is an integrated software package with superb capability to gather and structure information.

- *Microsoft Works.* This integrated software package, with versions available for both Apple Macintosh and IBM-compatible computers, is aimed at novice users (see Figure 4). It includes simple word processing, spreadsheet with charting, data base, and communications functions. Although Works cannot boast all of the features found in Enable, Symphony, and Framework III, the Apple Macintosh version is extremely popular. The IBM version of Works lists for around $200, while the Macintosh version lists for $300.

Windowing Environments

Integrated software provides several applications with a consistent user interface and an easy way to share data. Another way to achieve these objectives is to use a **windowing environment.** This is a special type of software that works very closely with the operating system. It allows you to divide your screen into a number of different boxes, or *windows,* and run a separate program in each one (see Figure 5). Since Apple Macintosh computers are by definition window-oriented, the term *windowing environment* is most often used to describe software that enhances or replaces DOS for IBM-compatible computers.

With a windowing environment, you can rapidly switch from one application to the next and easily transfer data among them. Furthermore, you aren't required to abandon your favorite application packages for new ones because most windowing environments generally work with existing software. As a particular windowing environment becomes accepted, however, software developers create special versions of their programs that abide by certain rules specified by that windowing system. Eventually, the windowing environment may lead many independent software developers to adopt a more uniform user interface for their programs. Thus, a windowing environment can provide most of the advantages of integrated software, without forcing you to buy and learn new application packages.

Types of Windowing Environments

In many ways, the capabilities of windowing environments far surpass those of integrated software. First of all, a windowing environment lets you have several programs on your screen at the same time; the actual number of programs may be limited only by the number of windows you can fit on your screen and the amount of memory installed in your computer. You can run almost any program within any window—not just a word processor, spreadsheet, data base manager, communications program, or graphics program. You can even have the same program running separately in two or more different windows. For example, you could create two different windows on your screen, run your word processor separately in each window, and simultaneously edit two different documents. Furthermore, windowing environments often let you cut or copy material from one window and paste it into another window, thereby providing an easy way to transfer data between applications.

If you think this sounds like the single-user, multitasking operating system we described in Chapter 4, you're absolutely right. In fact, many windowing environments are multitasking, which means you can run several programs concurrently. For example, you could print a document from a word processor in one window; at the same time a large and complicated spreadsheet recalculates in another window, while you draw a chart with a graphics program in yet another window. This is true multitasking.

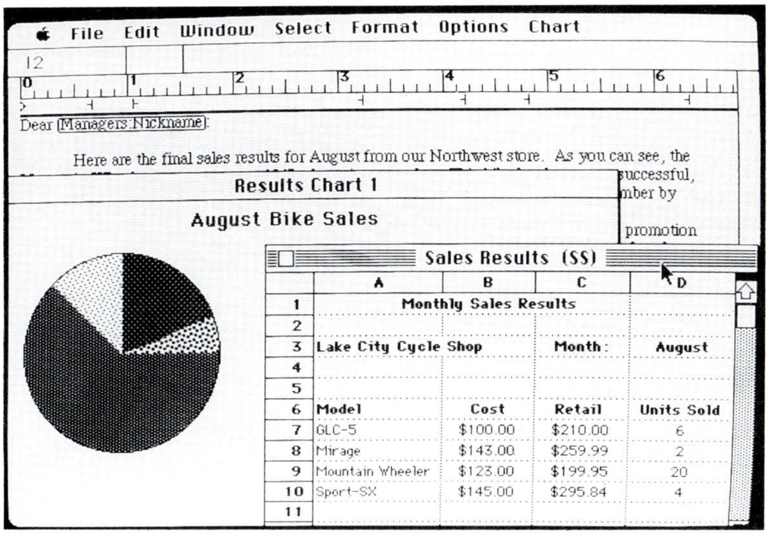

Figure 4 ***Microsoft Works***
Microsoft Works is a popular, relatively low-cost integrated software package aimed at novices.

A few windowing environments, however, are not truly multitasking. These simpler systems allow you to switch between several windows on the screen, but only the program in your current active window is actually running. Each of the other programs on the screen is held in a kind of suspended animation, only to be revived when you switch to that window. So, one way to classify windowing environments is according to whether they are truly multitasking.

The other major distinction between windowing systems is whether they are text-based or graphics-based. The simpler **text-based windowing environment** uses only the standard character set built into the computer. Windows are enclosed in boxes constructed of special line characters. This type of system cannot display graphics within its windows.

A **graphics-based windowing environment,** or **graphical user interface (GUI),** on the other hand, allows you to run programs that deal with pictures and characters of all different sizes, styles, and fonts. It uses a bit-mapped display

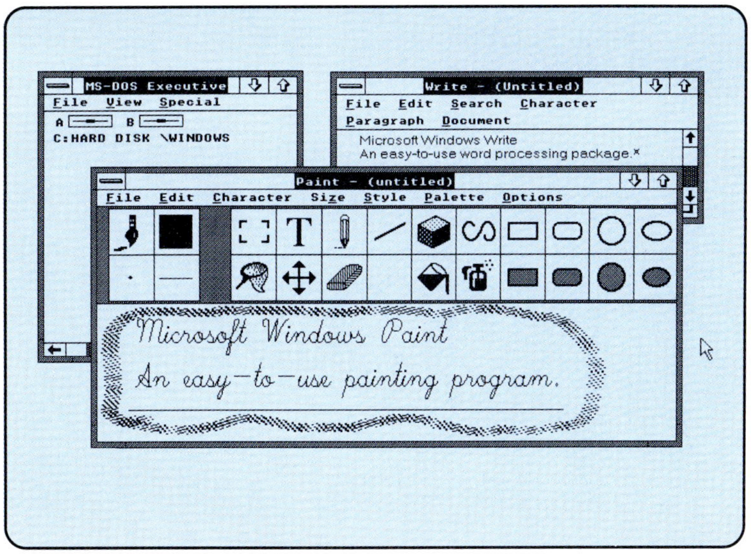

Figure 5 ***Microsoft Windows***
Microsoft Windows lets you run several different programs at the same time.

similar to what you see on an Apple Macintosh screen. Microsoft Windows, shown in Figure 5, is a graphics-based windowing environment for IBM-compatibles. Graphics-based windowing systems are more flexible, yet also more complex, than text-based systems. Consequently, they work best when used on computers that have a powerful microprocessor along with a good deal of memory.

Popular Windowing Environments

A major advantage of a windowing environment is that it offers a way to run a number of different programs on the screen at the same time while allowing you to easily transport data among them. Furthermore, the user interface of a windowing environment is generally menu-based and much easier to learn than ordinary operating system commands. Many windowing environments use graphics and a mouse, both of which help novices as well as experts.

Because of these advantages, there is a definite trend toward graphical user interfaces and away from the DOS style command line in the operating systems of most mid- to high-end microcomputers. It's likely that in the near future most of these machines will come with an operating system that has a built-in GUI, such as the Presentation Manager of OS/2, which we mentioned back in Chapter 4. In the meantime, however, several popular windowing environments on the market enhance existing operating systems. These include:

- *Microsoft Windows.* There is no doubt that Microsoft Windows leads the pack of windowing environments for IBM-compatibles. As Figure 5 shows, this software lets you run several different programs at the same time on the screen in overlapping windows. Microsoft Windows is a true multitasking, graphics-based windowing environment that uses a mouse and several features also found on Macintosh screens, such as icons and scroll bars.
- *DESQview.* This program from Quarterdeck Office Systems is a true multitasking windowing environment for all IBM-compatible computers (see Figure 6). Originally a strictly text-based environment, DESQview can now run most graphics programs in its windows. Unlike Microsoft Windows, DESQview

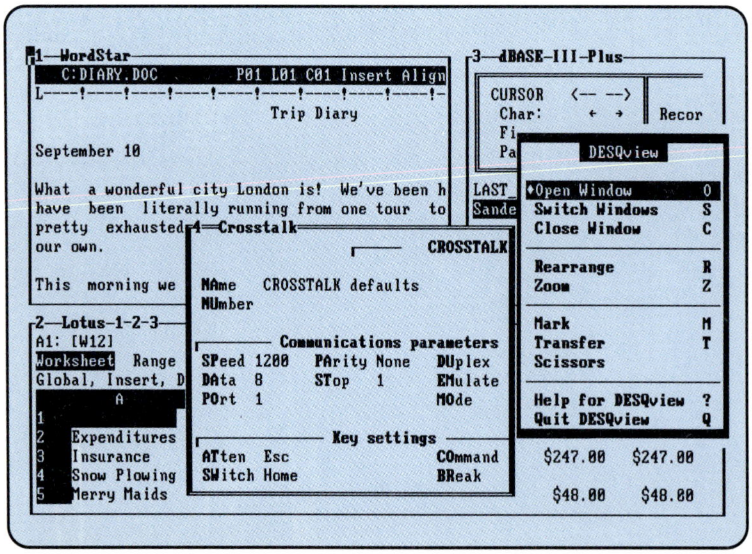

Figure 6 DESQview
Quarterdeck Office Systems' DESQview is a powerful multitasking windowing environment for IBM-compatible microcomputers.

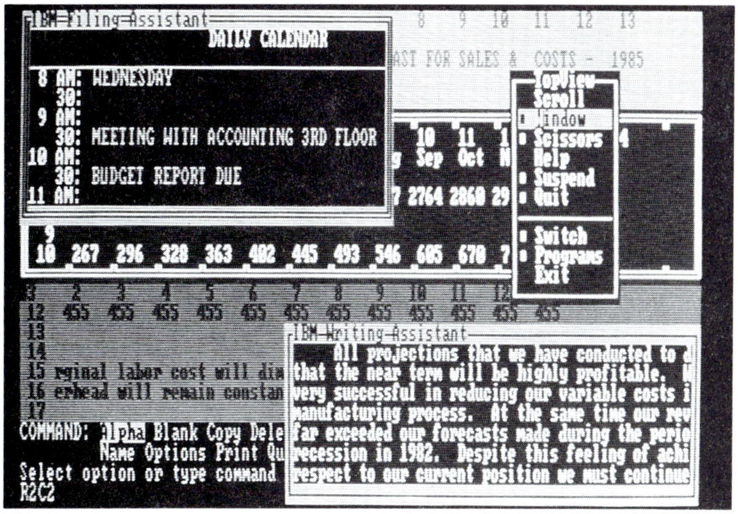

Figure 7 TopView
TopView is a text-based windowing system offered by IBM.

doesn't simulate a desktop with little icons like the Apple Macintosh. Using DESQview is similar to using DOS, except that you can open up several windows on your screen and run a different program in each one. In fact, DESQview can theoretically run up to 255 programs at the same time. Many experts consider DESQview the most elegant windowing environment for DOS computers and claim that its multitasking abilities are superior to those of Microsoft Windows.

- *TopView.* In 1985 IBM released TopView, a true multitasking, text-based windowing environment for its line of personal computers (see Figure 7). TopView was one of the first systems from a big-name manufacturer to let you run several programs concurrently on the same IBM-compatible computer. Although the system successfully handles multitasking, windowing, and switching among applications, TopView is somewhat cumbersome and not particularly easy to use. With the improvements of IBM's new OS/2 multitasking operating system, TopView is probably doomed to quietly fade away.
- *MultiFinder.* The MultiFinder, from Apple Computer, is an enhancement to the Macintosh operating system that adds some multiwindow, multitasking capabilities (see Figure 8). Despite its name, the MultiFinder is not totally multitasking. It does allow you to open up several windows with a different program in each one, but only the program in the currently selected window is fully active. Certain specially designed programs can run in the background, however, and perform unattended, time-consuming tasks such as printing documents, backing up disks, downloading files, recalculating spreadsheets, and sorting data bases. The major advantages of the MultiFinder are that it lets you have several windows open on the screen at the same time and rapidly switch between the programs in these windows.

DOS Shells

A windowing environment is sophisticated software that lets you have several different applications on the screen at the same time. It also can make the underlying operating system easier to use. Microsoft Windows, for example, makes the rather cryptic DOS look and feel somewhat like the user-friendly Apple

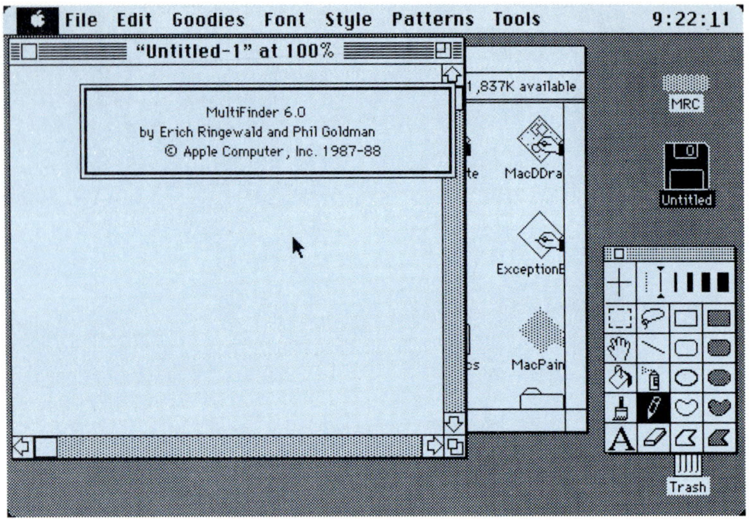

***Figure 8* MultiFinder**
MultiFinder is part of the Apple Macintosh operating system that allows some multitasking capabilities.

Macintosh operating system. In a sense, the windowing environment surrounds the operating system with a software shell that enhances the operating system's user interface. Another popular class of software specializes in this type of enhancement for DOS computers. Such programs are called DOS shells. Basically, a **DOS shell** is a menu-driven addition to DOS that helps you manage your disk files and directories (see Figures 9 and 10). Unlike a windowing environment, a DOS shell generally does not provide multitasking or the ability to transfer data among applications.

The unadorned DOS for IBM-compatible microcomputers has a **command-line interface (CLI).** After booting up, you are faced with a prompt and a blinking cursor that may look like this:

A>_

The screen provides absolutely no hint as to what you should do next. If you're a novice, this barren prompt can be quite intimidating. Even experts have trouble remembering all of the sometimes inconsistent commands for performing various system functions. A DOS shell provides a way to execute most DOS operations from an easy-to-understand menu, instead of forcing you to memorize or look up cryptic commands in a reference manual. It simplifies the task of setting up and moving between disk directories. Most DOS shells also include advanced features that let you view and edit the contents of your files, build your own custom menus for running application packages, set up security systems for computers that are used by different people at different times, and help you manage the immense storage capacity of hard disks. To top it off, most DOS shells are relatively inexpensive, with prices ranging from around $40 to $120.

IBM and Microsoft began including their own DOS shell with DOS, starting with version 4.0. In addition, several DOS shells are currently on the market from other software developers. They all attempt to make DOS easier to use and help you manage your disk files. Besides IBM's and Microsoft's DOS Shell, two of the most popular DOS shells sold today are:

- *XTree Pro.* This is a revamped version of one of the most popular DOS shells on the market to date, Xtree from XTree Company (see Figure 9). The screen it presents shows a chart of all your directories, the first 12 file names in the

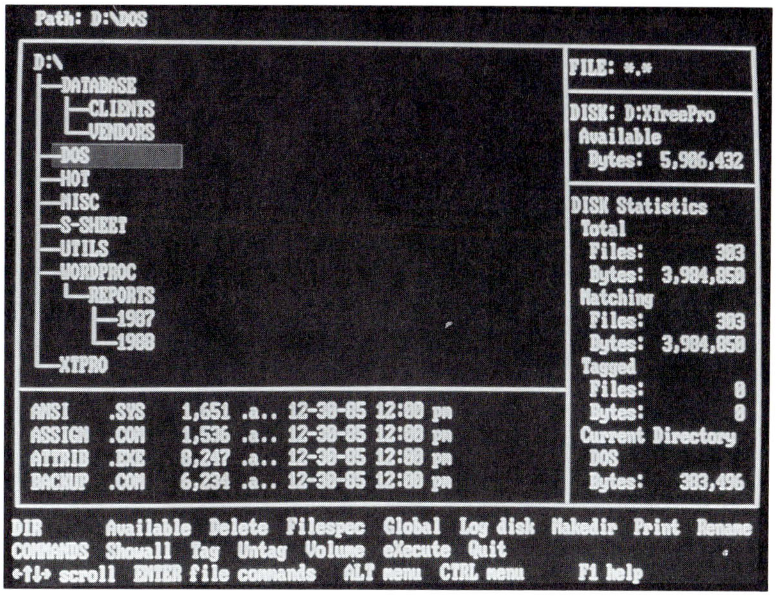

Figure 9 Xtree Pro
Xtree Pro, from Executive Systems, is a popular DOS shell with extensive help facilities.

currently selected directory, statistics about your disk, and a menu of available commands. Xtree Pro lets you easily manipulate files and directories in ways that are difficult if not impossible with DOS alone. The program comes with a text editor similar to WordStar and it allows you to customize the appearance of your Xtree menus. Xtree Pro also has extensive help facilities and a more comprehensive array of features than most DOS shells.

- *Norton Commander.* While the Norton Commander doesn't have every feature found in more comprehensive DOS shells like Xtree Pro, it does its job extremely well. This no-frills DOS shell from Peter Norton Computing is, above all, designed for speed and efficiency (see Figure 10). The program is easy to learn and easy to use, working in ways most people find intuitively obvious. Standard DOS operations are invoked by pressing function keys, which are listed in a menu across the bottom of the screen. The Norton Commander gives you a great deal of flexibility in listing file names on your screen; you can even see the contents of two different directories simultaneously, side-by-side. It has a built-in file viewer and editor that lets you examine and alter the contents of any type of file. Finally, the Norton Commander allows you to easily design your own pop-up menu of up to 20 frequently used programs. To execute any application from this list, you simply select its option.

Utilities

Windowing environments and DOS shells are developed to address perceived deficiencies in existing operating systems. Even the best operating system, however, cannot possibly provide all the functions its imaginative users can dream up. Utilities help fill in the gaps. As we said back in Chapter 3, these are generally small, relatively inexpensive programs designed to perform one or more very specific tasks. Some utilities are included or actually built into the operating system, others are purchased separately to perform tasks that are difficult or impossible to do within a given operating system or application package.

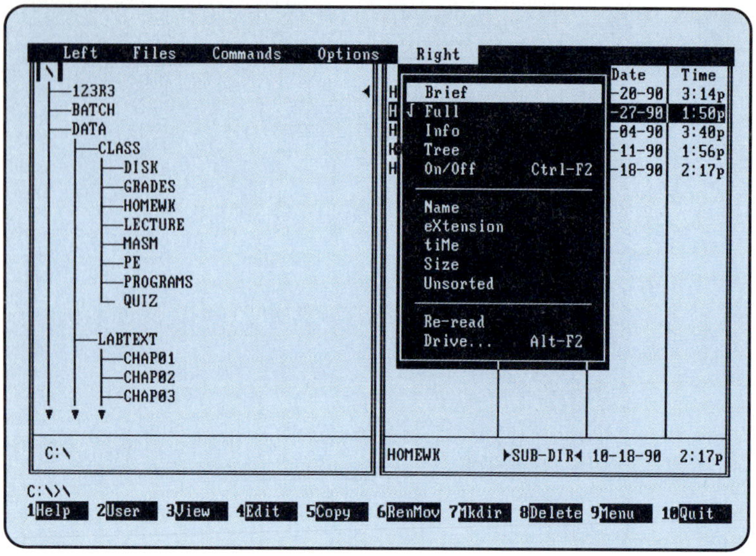

***Figure 10* Norton Commander**
The Norton Commander is a DOS shell from Peter Norton Computing designed for speed and efficiency.

DOS, for example, has no built-in command to recover or "unerase" an accidentally deleted file. To their dismay, many users find they occasionally need just such a facility. Clever software developers have come to the rescue and now there are quite a few utilities available that let you recover deleted files.

Here's another example that relates to an unmet need in a particular type of application package. Many spreadsheet programs cannot print worksheets sideways across several pages of paper. This capability is handy for printing extra-wide spreadsheets, which are commonly used for budgets, income statements, and all kinds of worksheets with many columns. Without the ability to print sideways, the spreadsheet program prints several vertical "stripes" which you must tear apart and tape together horizontally. Fortunately, it didn't take software developers long to invent utilities that let you directly print spreadsheets sideways across several pages. One such program, Sideways, from Funk Software, is shown in Figure 11.

There are literally hundreds, if not thousands, of utility programs available for popular microcomputers such as IBM-compatibles and Apple Macintoshes. These handy little programs address all kinds of problems, deficiencies, and omissions of both operating systems and application software. Some utilities simply provide clever shortcuts and enhancements to help you work faster, better, and smarter. Others are practically necessities that no regular computer user should do without. Although we can't list every type of utility on the market, three of the most popular categories are disk and file utilities, printer utilities, and keyboard utilities.

Disk and File Utilities

Disk and file utilities are programs that help you manipulate, organize, and use your disks and files more easily and efficiently. Within this category alone are many subsets. **File recovery utilities,** such as the Norton Utilities, from Peter Norton Computing, let you reinstate accidentally erased files and restore accidentally reformatted hard disks (see Figure 12). Most of these utilities also include many other handy options for helping you use your computer, including pro-

***Figure 11* Sideways**
Sidways, from Funk Software, is a popular utility that lets you print worksheets across several pages.

cedures to rearrange your directories, view and edit the contents of files, test disks, report file statistics, and locate files and individual sections of text within files.

File compression utilities let you squeeze your files into less disk space by eliminating waste and redundant data. SQZ! Plus, from Turner Hall Publishing, for example, compacts spreadsheet files to about 10 percent of their original size. In other words, SQZ! Plus can pack 10 times more spreadsheet data onto any disk. There are also file compression utilities that work on all kinds of data files, but their space savings are usually not as dramatic as those programs that specialize in one particular type of data file. Even more general file compression utilities, such as NEWSPACE, from Isogon Corporation, can effectively double the data storage capacity of a hard disk.

File transfer utilities let you move data among different types of computers. MacLink Plus from DataViz is a program that can transfer data files between an IBM-compatible and an Apple Macintosh connected with a special cable. Other

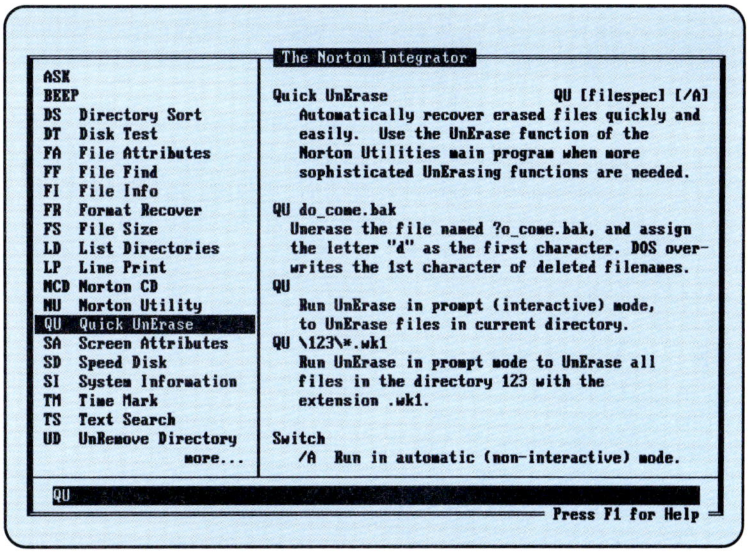

***Figure 12* Norton Utilities**
The Norton Utilities let you recover accidentally erased files and include a host of other handy options.

file transfer utilities can move files between computers that are basically compatible, except for different disk drive formats. Brooklyn Bridge, from White Crane Systems, for instance, lets you transfer files between IBM-compatible computers with incompatible disk drives, such as an IBM Personal Computer that uses 5¼-inch floppies and an IBM Personal System/2 Model 50 that uses 3½-inch floppies.

There are also **file conversion utilities** that can modify files from one application so that they can be used by another application. Software Bridge, from Systems Compatibility Corporation, for example, lets you convert documents among nine different word processing programs without losing formatting features such as underlining, boldfacing, and italics.

Disk copying utilities specialize in duplicating files and disks, especially those that are copy protected. Programs such as Copy II PC for IBM-compatibles and Copy II Mac for the Apple Macintosh from Central Point Software provide file and disk copying procedures that are more efficient and more versatile than those included with the microcomputers' operating systems.

Both DOS and the Macintosh operating system let you make a backup copy of the contents of your hard disk on floppy disks. Periodically making such backup copies is extremely important for preserving your programs and data in case the hard disk malfunctions. These operating system backup procedures, however, are relatively slow and awkward to use, and they typically require a large number of floppy disks. **Disk backup utilities,** such as Fastback Plus, from Fifth Generation Systems, are generally faster, more efficient, easier to use, and require fewer floppy disks than the backup procedures of most operating systems. This particular program is available in different versions for IBM-compatibles and the Apple Macintosh.

Computers spend much of their time reading and writing programs and data on disks. If you hasten these disk accesses, you can significantly decrease the amount of time you spend on certain types of tasks. A host of **disk optimizing utilities** have been developed to help make secondary storage devices operate more efficiently. Some of these utilities, such as Disk Optimizer, from SoftLogic Solutions, reorganize the contents of a disk to achieve maximum performance. As you use a disk, you delete or modify old files and add new files. Pieces of files invariably get broken up and scattered across the disk as the operating system fits new data into whatever unused space it can find. While the operating system always keeps track of these pieces so that your files are kept logically intact, finding the dispersed file segments takes more time. Disk optimizing utilities simply rewrite your file segments in sequence next to each other on the disk so that they can be reached more quickly.

Other utilities, called **disk caching utilities,** take a different approach to speeding up program and data retrieval. Programs such as Super PC-Kwik, from Multisoft Corporation, reserve part of primary memory as an intermediary storage place or **cache** for frequently used software and data. By having your programs automatically use this RAM cache whenever possible, a disk caching utility reduces the number of times your software must directly gain access to disk drives. Since RAM is much quicker than any disk drive, disk caching utilities can noticeably speed up your work.

Printer Utilities

A vast array of different computer printers are on the market. Thanks to standardized parallel and serial interfaces, most printers can be connected to most microcomputers. This can make life difficult for software manufacturers who must develop programs that support many different printers. It's often impossible for any single program, such as a word processor, to take advantage of every feature of every printer. This is especially true of laser printers, which tend to be more complex than other types of printers. As a result, several software developers have come up with printer utilities to help you more fully utilize your printer's potential. SoftStyle's Printworks for Lasers, for example, specializes in letting you use the advanced features of Hewlett-Packard Laserjets and compatible printers with IBM-compatible computers. This program lets you choose fonts, set margins and page lengths, specify how many copies to print, and control many other aspects of page formatting. SoftStyle also sells Printworks for the Mac, a comprehensive control system for Macintosh dot-matrix printers.

Some printer utilities are more specific and attempt to fulfill one particular need, such as printing wide worksheets sideways across one or more pages.

Another type of printer utility reduces or eliminates the wait for your printer to produce documents. A **print spooler** works in the background, sending characters to the printer whenever there's a free moment, while you continue running your application software as usual. Print spooling may slightly slow down the computer, but printing while you work can save a great deal of time in the long run. PrintQ, from Software Directions, is a good example of a printer spooler for IBM-compatible computers. This program intercepts documents bound for the printer, temporarily redirects them to disk storage, and then prints them piecemeal whenever the computer isn't busy doing something else. PrintQ lets you submit any number of documents to be printed without having to wait until the previous print job is finished. You can also print documents in order of priority, print multiple copies of a document, monitor the status of your print jobs, and manage two printers.

Keyboard Utilities

In Chapter 10 we introduced the concept of keyboard macros as they are used in advanced word processors. In Chapter 13 we showed that spreadsheet programs have similar macro capabilities. These macro features allow you to assign frequently used command sequences and long strings of characters to just one or two keypresses. Keyboard utilities, also called *keyboard enhancers,* are utility programs like stand-alone keyboard macro facilities. For example, SuperKey from Borland International, is an IBM-compatible keyboard enhancer that you can use from DOS or within almost any application program (see Figure 13). With this program, commands, names, sentences, paragraphs, and even cursor movements can be recorded and replayed at will by pressing just one or two keys. Since commands and data are often repetitive, many people find that a keyboard utility such as SuperKey can save them a significant amount of typing time and effort.

Desk Accessories

Microcomputers have become high-tech, simulated desktops. We have said before that the Apple Macintosh operating system has taken this concept quite literally, using a desktop image on its screen. The user interfaces of other types of computers are also helping to simulate the activities performed at a desktop. To appreciate the range of activities available, think about how you typically work at a desk. You might be writing a report and suddenly pick up a hand-held calculator to compute some figures. Throughout the day you probably check

Figure 13 SuperKey
Keyboard enhancers, such as SuperKey from Borland International, can help you reduce repetitive typing.

your clock and calendar, jot down some notes, look up addresses, call associates on the phone, and send memos. There are quite a few utilities on the market that let you do all of these tasks and many more with your computer. They are called **desk accessories, desktop organizers,** or simply **pop-up utilities.**

The Apple Macintosh operating system was specifically designed to let you temporarily interrupt your work and use desk accessories. In fact, several desk accessories come built into the operating system. There is an alarm clock, a calculator, a note pad, a graphics scrapbook, and various other operating system utilities. These accessories are available at any time from the Apple menu at the far left side of the menu bar across the top of most Macintosh applications. All you have to do is pull down the Apple menu and select a desk accessory from the list. Your original task is put on hold until you're finished with the desk accessory. Besides those that come with the Macintosh, you can buy additional or enhanced ones from independent software developers. SideKick, from Borland International, for example, is a comprehensive set of desk accessories for the Macintosh that includes a note pad, calculator, communications package, phone directory, automatic phone dialer, appointment scheduler, alarm clock, outline editor, and mini-spreadsheet (see Figure 14).

Desk accessories (including SideKick) are also available for IBM-compatible computers, although they work somewhat differently from the Apple Macintosh packages. DOS requires that such utilities be memory-resident programs. As we said in Chapter 4, a memory-resident program is initially loaded into RAM but remains dormant until it is activated by pressing a special combination of keys. When this is done, your current program is suspended and the computer immediately switches to the memory-resident routine. When you are finished with

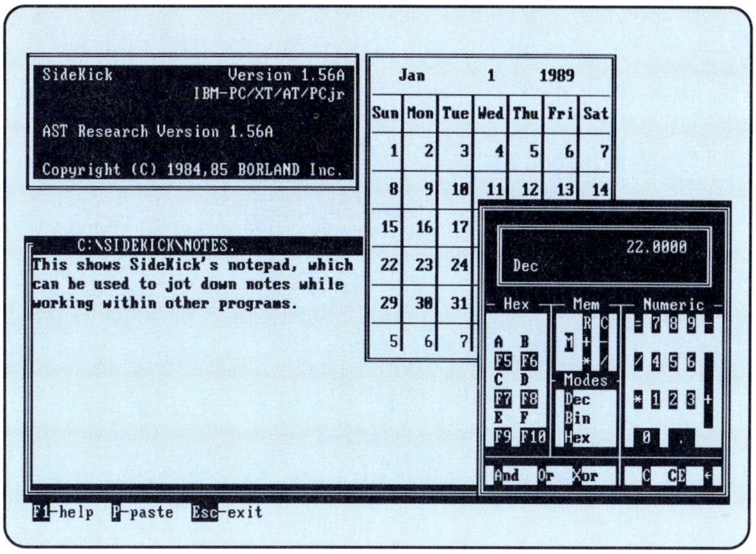

Figure 14 SideKick
SideKick, from Borland International, is one of the most popular sets of desk accessories for both IBM-compatibles and the Apple Macintosh.

the memory-resident utility, it becomes dormant again and you return to your original program.

Many memory-resident utilities have been developed for IBM-compatible computers. Unlike most Macintosh desk accessories, which are stored on a disk until needed, memory-resident programs must be kept in memory if you want to use them. This means that they also consume memory that would otherwise be used for programs and data. DOS was not originally designed to switch rapidly between programs on a routine basis. Unfortunately, confusion and incompatibilities sometimes occur when you try to load and use several different memory-resident programs on the same computer at the same time. Despite the difficulties, clever software developers have created some amazing and very popular memory-resident desk accessories for IBM-compatible computers.

On-Line References

Most application packages now have on-line help facilities that can almost instantly provide, at the touch of a key, more information about how they work. Most word processors now include a spelling checker and many come with an on-line thesaurus. Software developers have expanded and generalized these features to provide a host of stand-alone, on-line reference materials. For example, Webster's New World Combo, from Simon & Schuster Software, is a memory-resident spelling checker, word counter, and thesaurus for IBM-compatible computers (see Figure 15). Because it is memory-resident, Webster's New World Combo can be used within almost any application package. If your word processor doesn't have its own spelling checker and thesaurus, you can use Webster's New World Combo. You can also use these facilities inside your spreadsheet, data base manager, and communications package. Not only are the on-line spelling checker and thesaurus fast and convenient, they also cover impressive numbers of words. The Combo's spelling checker, for example, contains 114,000 words, while the thesaurus has 330,000 synonyms for 20,000 root words. The current list price of Webster's New World Combo is around $90.

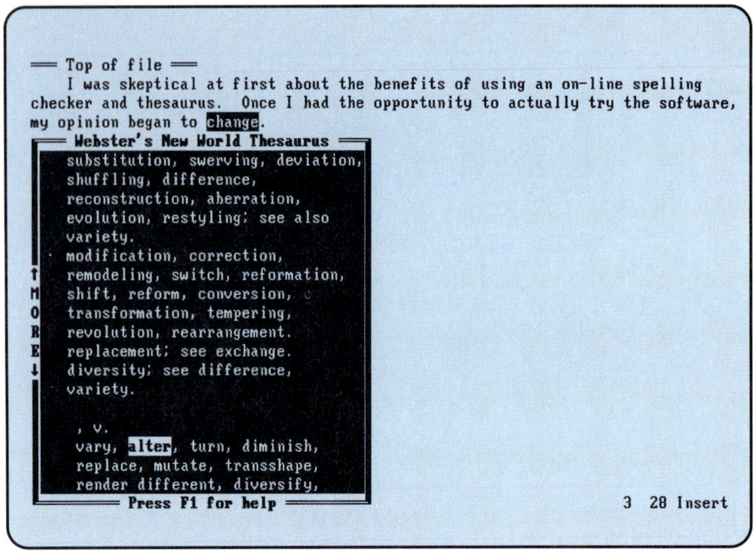

***Figure 15* Webster's New World Combo**
Webster's New World Combo includes a spelling checker, word counter, and thesaurus.

Some software developers have gone beyond the now-common spelling checker and thesaurus to offer many other more sophisticated on-line references. Some of these are quite specific and only cover particular operating systems, programming languages, or application packages. Others are aimed at a more general audience. The Micro Library Series, from Inductel, for example, is a comprehensive set of on-line reference works for IBM-compatibles. Here's what is included in the series:

- Funk & Wagnall's Standard Desk Dictionary
- Lyle Stuart's Concise Dictionary of 26 Languages
- McGraw-Hill's Dictionary of Computers
- Dictionary of Electrical & Electronic Engineering
- Dictionary of Physics
- Dictionary of Chemical Terms
- Dictionary of Biology
- Dictionary of Mechanical & Design Engineering
- US Post Office 5-Digit ZIP Code Directory

The dictionaries are not mere spelling checkers, but rather abbreviated versions of the original reference works that actually contain definitions. The Micro Library Series comes with Inductel's Knowledge Acquisition System software, which allows rapid information retrieval—much more rapid and flexible than a manual search of the actual printed books. These reference works can be purchased individually at prices ranging from roughly $50 to $100. They do, however, consume a great deal of disk space. For instance, the Funk & Wagnall's Dictionary and the Concise Dictionary of 26 Languages come together on 21 floppy disks and require 7.2 megabytes of disk storage. For this reason, some on-line references, such as Microsoft's Bookshelf, come on CD-ROM disks. Although these optical disks can hold more than 500 megabytes of information, they require special disk drives that can cost up to $1000.

Statistical and Math Packages

With all that computers do, it's easy to forget what they do best: work with numbers. Professionals use computers to analyze all kinds of numerical data, from regional sales figures in business reports to rat reaction times in psychological experiments. Statistics is the branch of mathematics concerned with the collection, analysis, interpretation, and presentation of numerical data. Statistical analysis is a critical tool in a variety of fields: the Census Bureau monitors economic and social change, manufacturers maintain product quality controls, public health officials track infectious diseases, agricultural scientists study crop yields, actuaries set insurance premiums, and poll takers gauge public opinion. In fact, the list of those who need statistics is almost endless.

If everyone who needed to do a statistical analysis had to write his or her own software, however, very few analyses would get done. Fortunately, a number of statistical packages that can do these analyses for you are on the market. All you have to do is supply the data, select the particular statistical procedure, and wait for the results. SYSTAT, from the company of the same name, is one example of a popular statistical package for both Apple Macintosh and IBM-compatible microcomputers (see Figure 16). This particular program was modeled after SAS, a major statistical package for mainframe computers. SYSTAT excels at handling large data bases with many different variables. Originally developed by a psychology professor at the University of Illinois, SYSTAT is especially well suited to the advanced statistical techniques used in the behavioral and social sciences.

Besides statistical packages, other types of mathematical software are commonly used by scientists, engineers, and business people. Eureka, from Borland International, for example, is an algebraic equation solver with versions available for both Apple Macintosh and IBM-compatible computers (see Figure 17). This easy-to-use program is a good educational tool for almost any field involving mathematics. Eureka allows you to automatically solve sets of equations and

Figure 16 SYSTAT
SYSTAT is a popular statistical package for both Apple Macintosh and IBM-compatible microcomputers.

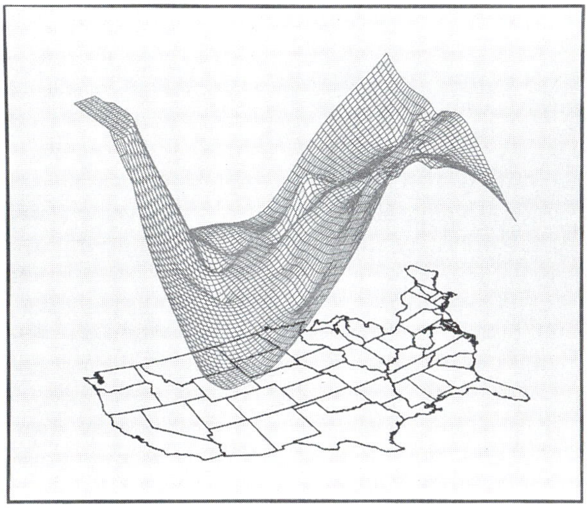

Figure 17 Eureka
Borland International's Eureka is an algebraic equation solver.

graph the results. For instance, let's say that you have the following set of equations and you want to solve them for *x* and *y*:

$$y = x - 1$$
$$x = 2y$$

You simply type these expressions into Eureka's equation window and activate the Solve command. Eureka combines and rearranges the equations to conclude that $y = 1$ and $x = 2$. Furthermore, you could have Eureka plot these two equations and actually see the solution—where the two lines intersect at coordinates (2,1).

Project Management Software

More and more, computers are being used as organizational tools. All kinds of programs are now available for helping you outline, schedule, and chart your thoughts and activities. **Project management software** is one of the most popular and advanced categories of these various organizational programs. The purpose of a project management package is to help you formally plan and control complex undertakings, such as the construction of a new office building, the development of a new product, or the installation of a large computer system. The project management software lets you identify the individual tasks necessary to complete a project and calculate the time, money, and other resources each of these tasks will require.

Modern project management procedures are based on the Critical Path Method (CPM) and Program Evaluation and Review Technique (PERT). The **Critical Path Method (CPM)** is a scheduling method that focuses on the sequence of critical activities that must be performed to complete a project. Critical activities are ones that must start after others are finished, and must be completed before subsequent activities can begin. This sequence of activities is known as the *critical path.*

The **Program Evaluation and Review Technique (PERT)** was originally developed to schedule projects in which the completion times of individual tasks were difficult to estimate. Project schedules were generated for three possible scenarios: pessimistic, optimistic, and most likely. Today, CPM and PERT have become practically synonymous. The term *PERT* is generally used to describe a chart that graphically depicts a project as a network of interconnected activities (see Figure 18). The critical path through this network of activities is usually highlighted in some manner. Virtually all microcomputer project management packages use the critical path method for scheduling and PERT charts to display the relationships between tasks.

The **Gantt chart** is another important tool of project management. Named for Henry L. Gantt, who developed it while working as a consulting engineer for the U.S. government during World War I, the Gantt chart is a horizontal bar graph that shows the major tasks of a project, when each task must be performed, and how long each task will take (see Figure 19). By displaying activities on a time line, a Gantt chart reveals how the duration of individual tasks affects the final completion date of a project. All project management packages produce Gantt charts and many of them use the Gantt chart as their main component.

Almost any undertaking can be better organized through the use of project management techniques. The result can be greater efficiency, higher productivity, better-kept schedules, and significant savings. Realizing the benefits, the U.S. Navy first computerized its project management of the Polaris missile system in the late 1950s. By the 1960s, project management software for mainframe computers was being commercially marketed at prices as high as $200,000. Today, more than a hundred project management programs are available for microcomputers, ranging in price from around $35 to nearly $8000.

One of the most popular microcomputer project management packages is Microsoft Project (see Figures 18 and 19). This $400, IBM-compatible program is especially well suited to organizing small- to medium-sized projects. Microsoft Project has powerful, yet easy-to-use Gantt charting features. The program also lets you create simple PERT charts to show the overall structure of a project. A wide range of customized reports can be printed with Microsoft Project, and

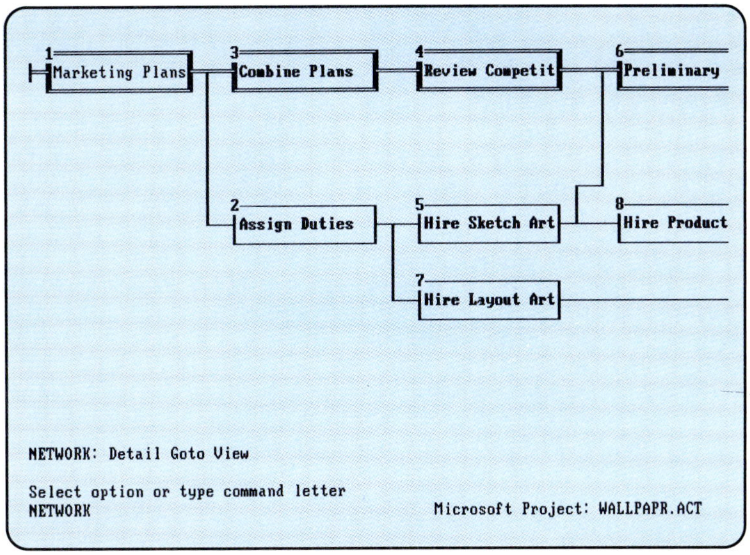

***Figure 18* PERT Chart**
This screen shows a PERT chart produced with Microsoft Project.

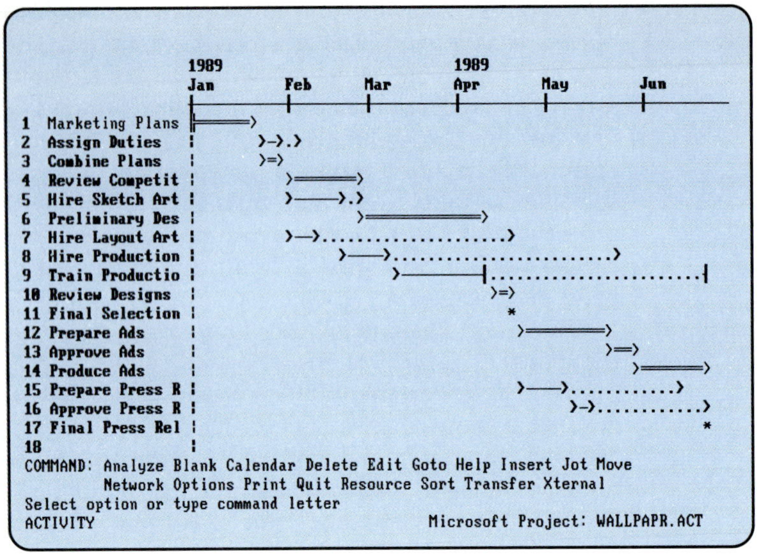

***Figure 19* Gantt Chart**
This screen shows a Gantt chart produced with Microsoft Project.

data can be exported to popular spreadsheet programs such as Lotus 1-2-3. Although it lacks the fancy features found in more expensive programs, Microsoft Project is a capable and straightforward project management system.

Accounting Software

Accounting is the process of recording, analyzing, and reporting business transactions. Accounting information, provided it is accurate and timely, is often the key to success in business, since good decision-making is simply impossible without a systematic record of business transactions. The most efficient way to maintain, manage, and summarize these records is with accounting software.

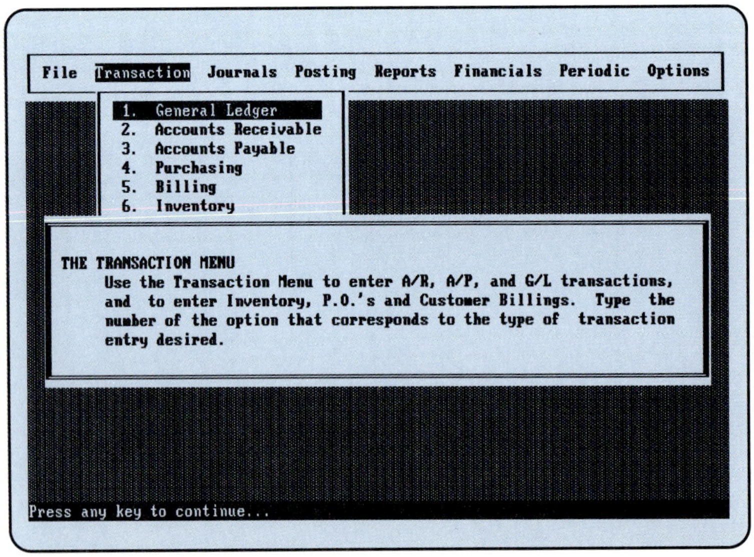

***Figure 20* Dac-Easy Accounting**
Dac-Easy Accounting is one of the most popular accounting packages for IBM-compatible computers.

Accounting software, one of the first commercial uses of computers, has become indispensable in our economy. Virtually all large businesses and many small businesses use computers to help with their bookkeeping.

Traditionally, accounting systems are divided into several subsystems, each of which has a particular function. These subsystems interact with one another to help you enter, classify, store, analyze, summarize, and report the essential financial data of your business. In a computerized accounting system, the subsystems are either separate programs or separate modules within the same program. Specifically, most accounting systems include the following subsystems:

- *General Ledger.* This subsystem is the heart of any accounting system. Basically, the **general ledger** is the main listing of the accounts of a business. Business transactions are recorded in journals. At the end of an accounting period, say a month for example, the totals for each journal are copied or posted to the corresponding accounts in the general ledger. In a computerized system, the general ledger is automatically and continuously updated. The general ledger lets you set up your accounts and constantly monitor all business activities. It gathers data from the other accounting modules and lets you summarize the data in reports such as balance sheets and income statements.
- *Accounts Receivable.* The **accounts receivable** subsystem records all sales of goods and services to customers. It also keeps track of customer credit, payments, and balances. The accounts receivable entries are used to issue statements to customers summarizing their transactions, the total amount owed as of that date, and how long the money has been due. These entries are also used to generate reports that indicate how much money each customer owes and how long it has been outstanding.
- *Accounts Payable.* The **accounts payable** subsystem records the purchases of goods and services from each vendor, that is, from a person or company that sells you something. Besides keeping track of the money due to each vendor, the accounts payable system is also used to generate checks and project the cash balances needed to make the necessary payments. By helping a business pay its bills on time, the accounts payable system makes it easier to take advantage of cash discounts offered by vendors. It also helps monitor and control the cash flow of a business.
- *Inventory Control.* Every business that sells goods must keep running counts of its products and materials on hand. The **inventory control** subsystem helps to track these items, which are continuously being purchased and sold. It also interacts with the general ledger, accounts receivable, and accounts payable systems to keep essential business information up to date. By generating inventory status reports, the inventory control system signals when additional materials should be purchased and helps identify slow-moving products.
- *Purchase Order.* Virtually every business purchases products, materials, and services. In many cases, **purchase orders** must be completed before products and services can be bought. These are printed forms sent to vendors and kept on file to prevent duplicate purchases. The purchase order subsystem can save a great deal of time and help automate the process of acquiring the materials and services needed to run a business. Obviously, the purchase order subsystem must work very closely with the accounts payable subsystem.
- *Billing.* Many businesses that sell goods or services send bills to their customers informing them of the money they owe for their purchases. These bills, called invoices, list each item shipped along with its price and any other terms of the sale. By printing these invoices, the **billing** subsystem provides proof of payment for customers, controls sales taxes, increases cash flow, helps in the packing and shipping of products, and maintains records of each

customer's buying history. As you might expect, the billing subsystem is tied in with the accounts receivable system.

- *Payroll.* Any business with employees can use a payroll system; businesses with many employees simply cannot do without one. Basically, the **payroll** subsystem maintains personnel and pay rate information; generates employee paychecks; computes withholdings and deductions; produces tax reports for federal, state, and local governments; and creates summary reports of employee earnings.

One of the most popular accounting packages for IBM-compatible computers is Dac-Easy Accounting, from Dac Software, Incorporated (see Figure 20). Originally released in 1985, Dac-Easy Accounting has become one of the world's best selling accounting packages. According to Ken Howe, president of Dac Software, the program sells around 25,000 copies each month. This is probably due to the program's functionality, its ease of use, and its low retail list price of just under $100. Dac-Easy Accounting combines the basic general ledger, accounts receivable, accounts payable, purchase order, billing, and inventory control modules, along with a system for budgeting and forecasting. Although it doesn't include a payroll system, this function is available for just under $100 from Dac Software in a separate program called Dac-Easy Payroll. The subsystems all work together and share data to minimize having to make repetitive entries. Furthermore, the programs have pull-down menus and include on-line help facilities. Many small businesses find Dac-Easy Accounting and Dac-Easy Payroll ideal for their bookkeeping needs.

Personal Finance and Tax Programs

For more personal needs, microcomputer software can help you organize your own finances too. Some of the best-selling packages for home computers are personal financial-management programs. Whether you're struggling to balance your checkbook or trying to leverage your investments, a personal finance program can be a useful addition to your software library. One of the most popular, easy to use, and powerful personal financial managers on the market is Andrew Tobias' Managing Your Money, from MECA Ventures (see Figure 21). This program, which sells for about $220, contains financial advice and personal accounting procedures developed by the author of the best-selling book *The Only Investment Guide You'll Ever Need.*

The core of Managing Your Money is a computerized checkbook register to help pay your bills. You can enter details about your checks after writing them, have the program print your checks directly, or use a modem to call Chase Manhattan Bank and have the bank print and mail your checks. But Managing Your Money can do much more than just keep your checkbook balanced. As you enter all of your income and payment records into the program, Managing Your Money automatically updates your budget and tax forms; you can print out budget summaries and sample tax forms at any time. With the Portfolio Manager, you can also keep track of almost any kind of investment, from common stocks to tax-free municipal bonds. On-line help screens provide information about how various types of investment records should be maintained. Your net worth and tax records are automatically updated as you buy and sell investments. With Managing the Market, an $80 add-in option, you have direct access to the Dow

Figure 21** **Managing Your Money
Andrew Tobias' Managing Your Money is one of the most popular personal finance packages.

Jones News Retrieval service for current stock prices. One of the most useful features of Managing Your Money is the Net Worth section, which automatically maintains a breakdown of your net worth by extracting current data from your bank accounts, investments, loans, equity, real estate, insurance, pension plans, and any other holdings. In addition to all of these features, Managing Your Money also includes a simple word processor, a financial calculator, a retirement planner, and sections to help you determine your taxes and insurance needs.

Although personal finance programs can help you estimate your taxes, most cannot produce actual tax forms and schedules for IRS submittal. For that you need more specialized tax-preparation software. Since the federal Tax Reform Act of 1986, this type of software has exploded into widespread use as confused tax payers search for help. One of the best tax-preparation programs is Macintax Taxview (Federal Version), from Softview. This program, which comes in different versions for both the Apple Macintosh and IBM-compatible computers, is easy to use, straightforward, yet surprisingly sophisticated. Macintax Taxview not only follows the structure of IRS tax forms, it exactly duplicates them on your computer screen (see Figure 22). Instead of writing your entries on paper forms, you type them right on the screen. If you need help or want to see the IRS instructions for an entry, you simply point to it and double-click a mouse button. All worksheets, forms, and schedules are automatically linked to each other and the main 1040 form. The $119 program includes support for 30 different forms and schedules and nine worksheets. Furthermore, the IRS has approved all of the forms produced by Macintax for direct submission. So, when you are finished filling out the necessary forms, all you have to do is print them on a dot-matrix or laser printer, sign them, attach your earnings statement and possibly a check, and mail them to the IRS. It almost makes doing your taxes fun.

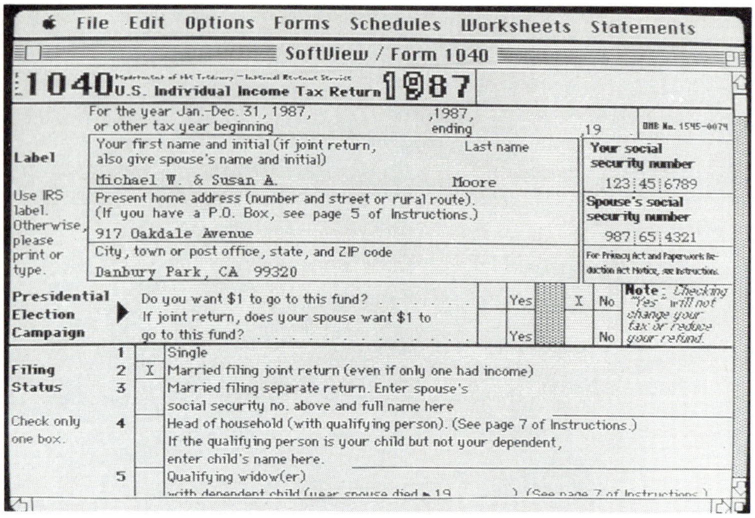

Figure 22 Macintax
Tax preparation software, such as Macintax from Softview, lets you fill out tax forms with your computer.

Educational Software

Besides helping you with specific tasks like managing your finances and preparing your taxes, microcomputers also can teach you various subjects and skills. Educational software packages for microcomputers covering almost every topic imaginable are available. At one end of the spectrum are programs for young children, such as Alphabet Blocks, from Bright Star Technology. This Macintosh program presents an on-screen elf who teaches prereaders the letters and sounds of the alphabet with a clear, digitized voice. At a more advanced level, Broderbund Software's Sensei Physics is a well-designed study aid that covers topics such as vectors, thermodynamics, and the nature of light (see Figure 23). Students learn concepts of physics by designing their own animated experiments. Educational packages such as these are quite effective because they combine graphics, sound, and student participation to make learning both interesting and fun.

Some of the best selling educational packages are those that train specific skills such as typing, math, and foreign languages. The computer's "infinite patience" allows students to work at their own pace until they have reached their desired level of competence. Type!, also from Broderbund Software, is a keyboard training program designed for both classroom and individual use. A special tutorial uses animated hands to show the proper placement of fingers on the keys (see Figure 24). The program is based on extensive research about how people learn to type. Furthermore, Type! provides ample feedback by displaying bar graphs showing speed and accuracy by letter, finger, and hand.

Entertainment Software

Microcomputers can be fun, even if you don't learn anything. An amazing variety of software has been developed with the primary intention of merely providing entertainment. Typically priced below $100, these entertainment packages range from simple childhood diversions such as Tic-Tac-Toe to sophisticated real-life simulations. There are adventure games, strategy games, card games, board games, sports games, parlor games, game show games, pinball games, and

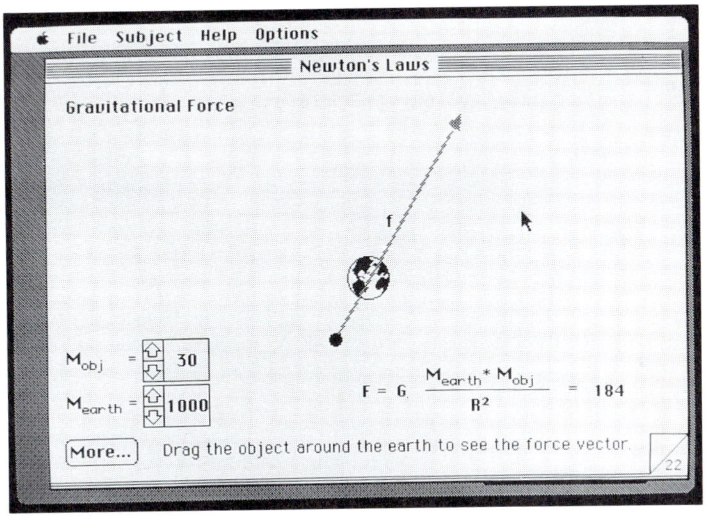

Figure 23 Sensei Physics
Broderbund Software's Sensei Physics is one example of a well-designed, computerized study aid.

arcade "shoot-em-up" games. There are submarine simulators, race car simulators, airplane simulators, jet simulators, and spaceship simulators. There are even musical programs that range from simple computerized pianos to multi-instrument studio synthesizers and professional music composition tools. As impressive as this seems, it's only a brief list of some of the entertainment software you can run on a microcomputer. With the diversity of programs available, it's difficult to single out a few specific products above all others. Nevertheless, and at the risk of offending those whose favorites we don't mention, here are three examples of popular entertainment packages for microcomputers:

- *Flight Simulator.* This $50 "game" is one of the most popular microcomputer programs ever sold (see Figure 25). Originally developed by SubLOGIC Corporation in 1979 for the Apple II computer, Flight Simulator is also sold by Microsoft for IBM-compatibles and Apple Macintoshes. The program has been

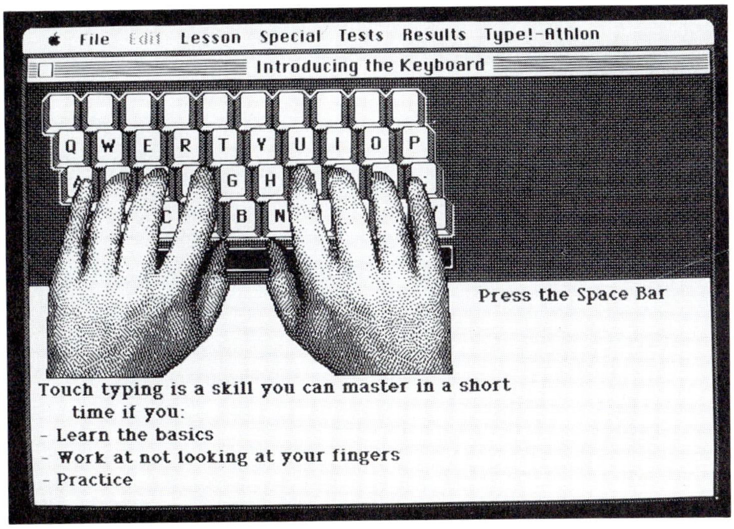

Figure 24 Type!
Also from Broderbund Software, Type! is a keyboard training program.

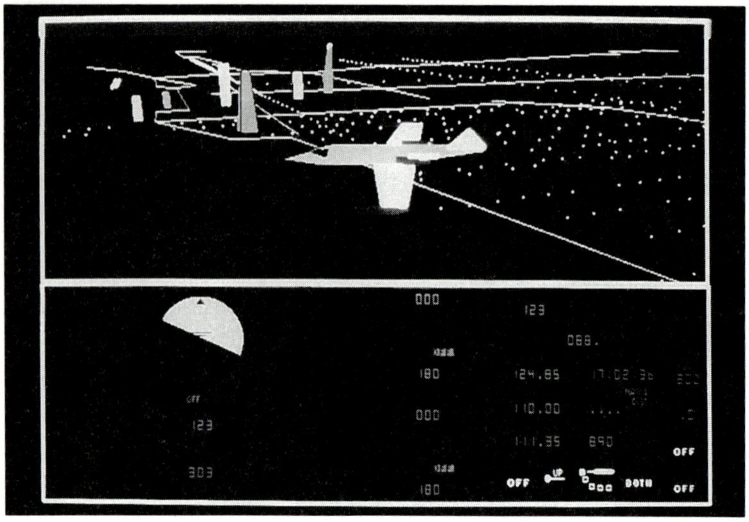

Figure 25 Flight Simulator
Flight Simulator, which lets you see what it's like to fly a small aircraft, is one of the most popular micro-computer programs ever sold.

constantly updated and versions have been developed for most microcomputers, including models from Apple, Atari, Commodore, IBM, and Tandy. With realism approaching that of a $100,000 aircraft simulator, Flight Simulator includes full instrumentation and three-dimensional window displays. The program features more than eighty airports and detailed scenery maps of many U.S. landmarks. For example, you can fly your aircraft past the Statue of Liberty and even between the twin towers of the World Trade Center in New York City. There also is a World War I Ace aerial battle game included for more action-packed fun.

- *Dark Castle.* For the Apple Macintosh, this $40 game is second only to Flight Simulator in popularity. Developed by Silicon Beach Software, Dark Castle is a game in which you are a medieval warrior who has volunteered to go after the Black Knight (see Figure 26). This is no easy task, for you must travel through several treacherous rooms in the Dark Castle. Awaiting you are plague-ridden bats and rats, knife-throwing guards, boulder-rolling and whip-wielding henchmen, vultures, mutants, gargoyles, dragons, the Burning Eye, and magic brooms. Your only defenses are running, jumping, ducking, throwing rocks, and acquiring elixir, the Shield, and the Fireball. You can defeat the Black Knight only by toppling his throne. Dark Castle is a captivating adventure thanks to its exceptional animation and realistic sound effects.
- *Studio Session.* This $90 program, from Bogas Productions, is not nearly as popular as Flight Simulator and Dark Castle. Nevertheless, Studio Session is an excellent example of a music composition package for the Apple Macintosh. It consists of two programs, an Editor and a Player. The Editor allows you to create new songs or modify existing ones, including the 21 sample songs that come with the package. Music for 91 different instruments can be written on as many as six staffs. Each staff is like a separate track of a multi-channel tape deck. The Player plays the music you've written, allowing you to adjust the tempo control and simulated sound meters for the volume level of each track. Although Studio Session can be a serious music composition tool, it is also entertaining and educational.

***Figure 26* Dark Castle** *Silicon Beach Software's Dark Castle is a popular adventure game for the Apple Macintosh.*

Hypertext Programs

In 1963, Ted Nelson was working on a satellite navigation system for the National Aeronautics and Space Administration (NASA). He and his project team needed information about a series of landmarks that would be easy to spot from space. One of the landmarks they chose was Islote Pelado, a small island off the coast of Peru. Although Nelson searched for detailed information about this island, such as how its size changed with the tides, what its color was, and whether its vegetation changed with the seasons, he had little success until a librarian at Stanford's Department of Systematic Biology finally suggested a book called *Birds of the Americas*. Sure enough, a passage in this unlikely book indirectly revealed everything Nelson needed to know about Islote Pelado. It was a classic example of an unstructured approach to information retrieval. These events made an impression on Nelson as he pondered better ways of using computers for information retrieval. In 1965 Nelson coined the term **hypertext** to describe the nonsequential organization and presentation of information with a computer. Today, the word *hypermedia* is sometimes used as a more encompassing term than *hypertext*. **Hypermedia,** like hypertext, refers to the nonsequential organization and presentation of information, but it also includes graphics, audio, and video. Theoretically, a true hypermedia system would allow you to randomly jump from topic to related topic, tapping into any kind of information the computer can digitize and store. Since you can bypass intermediate topics, you need only extract what you specifically want from huge stores of information.

How might you use a hypertext system? Let's say that you need to find out when Illinois became a state for a term paper in U.S. history. You sit down at your computer with hypertext software and begin by retrieving an article about Illinois history. It doesn't take long to determine that Illinois was the twenty-first state and it entered the union on December 3, 1818. In a different part of the same article, you read that the state bird of Illinois is the cardinal. Intrigued, you point to the word *cardinal* and click a mouse button or press a key. A new screen pops up, giving you a choice between several different meanings of the word *cardinal*. You don't particularly want to know about cardinal numbers or officials appointed by the Pope to his council, so you select the option entitled *A Bright-red American Songbird*. Yet another screen appears with an article describing the cardinal. This screen also has options for seeing a full-color picture of the bird and listening to a digitized recording of its call. When you have finished learning about the bird, you can go back to review cardinal numbers, return to Illinois history, or randomly jump to any other topic currently on the screen.

For 20 years or so, computer scientists dabbled with the concepts of hypertext. Then in the mid 1980s, several companies released limited hypertext programs for microcomputers. Today, two of the most noteworthy microcomputer hypertext programs are:

- *Guide.* This program from OWL International was originally created for the Apple Macintosh in 1985, but was adapted in 1987 for IBM-compatibles as well. Although Guide is limited to text and graphics, it does allow you to create your own hypertext documents called Guidelines (see Figure 27). Certain words, phrases, and graphic objects can be designated as "buttons" that provide links to other hidden text and graphics. Priced at less than $200, Guide is a highly functional program that effectively incorporates the basic concepts of hypertext.
- *Hypercard.* This $50 program from Apple Computer for the Macintosh is by far the most well-known hypertext product on the market (see Figure 28). Developed by Bill Atkinson, author of MacPaint, and introduced in August 1987, Hypercard lets you store information on computerized index cards. This information can be in the form of text, graphics, animations, sounds, or digitized voices. Individual index cards are grouped into stacks, usually reflecting some common theme. These stacks can be linked in many different ways, allowing the extremely rapid information retrieval characteristic of hypertext systems. Each index card can hold up to 32 kilobytes of information; the theoretical maximum size of each stack is 500 megabytes. Atkinson estimates that stacks as large as 20 megabytes can be searched in about two seconds. As an even more exciting feature, Hypercard includes its own programming language, called Hypertalk, which is designed especially for nonprogrammers. Using Hypertalk, even novices can build their own customized information systems, called **stackware.** Thousands of stacks have been developed and are currently available commercially and in the public domain. They cover

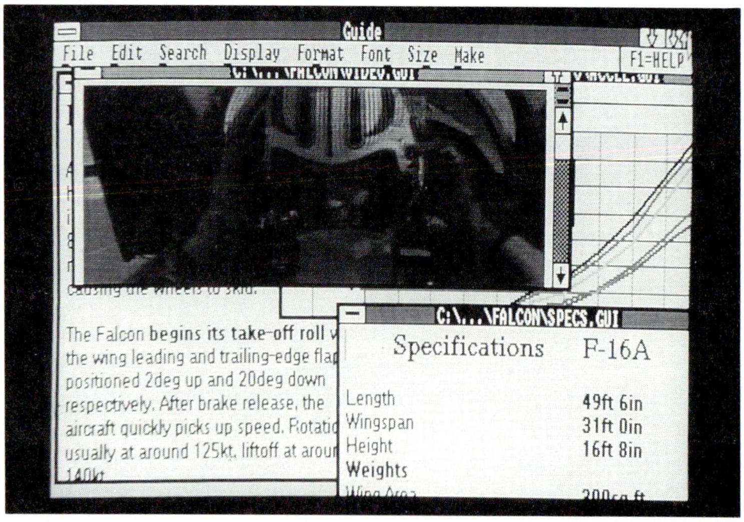

Figure 27 Guide
OWL International's Guide is a basic hypertext package available for both Apple Macintosh and IBM-compatible microcomputers.

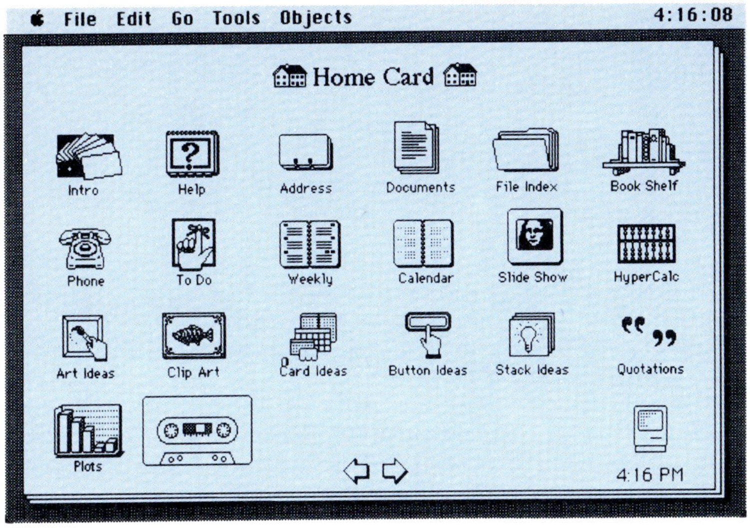

Figure 28 Hypercard
Apple's Hypercard is the leading hypertext package for Macintoshes.

almost every application imaginable, from address books and other traditional data storage facilities, to animated games, illustrated mini-encyclopedias, and educational tutorials.

Artificial Intelligence and Expert Systems

We've all seen computers, robots, and androids on television and in movies that behave just like people. Unfortunately, or perhaps fortunately, this is pure fantasy and it's likely to remain fantasy, at the very least, for a long, long time. Computers and other machines cannot think. Period. Nevertheless, there is an intriguing field of study called **artificial intelligence (AI)** that combines aspects of computer science, mathematics, philosophy, psychology, and linguistics. Since psychologists don't even know for sure what "natural" intelligence is, it's unlikely that computer scientists can develop it artificially. Nevertheless, the main goal of artificial intelligence is to enable computers to mimic certain aspects of human learning and decision making. Artificial intelligence programming techniques have been developed that are now successfully used in a variety of systems, including the following:

- *Natural Language Processors.* Much work is being done to enable computers to understand portions of ordinary human languages such as English. This **natural language processing** has many potential uses, especially in the querying of large data bases. By eliminating the need for users to learn rigid, complex programming languages, natural language processors make computers significantly more accessible. Thanks to artificial intelligence, many natural language systems are currently in use, especially on large mainframe computers.
- *Robots.* A **robot** is a computer-controlled machine that performs mechanical tasks. Techniques of artificial intelligence, including machine learning and automated vision, are currently used in many of today's sophisticated robots. **Machine learning** is a method by which computers can program themselves, through trial and error, to accomplish a particular task. **Automated vision** software allows a computer to distinguish and interpret images from optical

Real World

Breaking the Rules

Ask a dozen people what Hypercard is and you'll probably get a dozen different answers.

One keeps an address book and to-do list in it, one uses it to organize clip art for a newsletter, another runs a personal finance program. One wrote a program that spells out words when his daughter clicks the mouse. Hypercard, it seems, breaks all the rules.

Its producer, Apple, calls it system software, a "personal toolkit that gives users the power to use, customize, and create new information using text, graphics, video, music, voice, and animation."

Hypercard lets people with no programming experience create "stacks" of information that are like stacks of index cards. Each of the cards in the stack can contain text, sounds, and graphics. Using a stack about fishing, a user could get facts about trout and even cause the image of a trout to appear on the screen.

Apple's Chief Executive Officer, John Sculley, believes that Hypercard makes the process of organizing and gaining access to information completely natural and intuitive. "you can discover the contrasts between different subjects that may have no other relationship than your own curiosity," he said.

Hypercard is only the first of a generation of software that defies traditional descriptions. One program, Lotus's Agenda, has been called a "spreadsheet for words," a kind of personal secretary that makes sense of the notes you scribble to yourself on the keyboard. A user can ask to see only items about "Bob" and "butterflies." If Bob collects butterflies, Agenda can link the topics.

Sources: John Schwartz, "Yes, But What Does It Do," *Newsweek,* December 14, 1987, p. 68. Gregg Williams, "Hypercard," *BYTE,* December 1987, p. 109. Keith Ferrell and Selby Bateman, "Out to Change the World: A Conversation with John Sculley," *Compute!,* December 1987, pp. 18–22.

sensors, and is widely used to inspect manufactured items and to guide the actions of robot arms. Robots are now used to manufacture all kinds of products, from automobiles to computers.

- *Expert Systems.* An **expert system** or **knowledge-based system,** is a computer program that contains a collection of facts and a list of rules for making inferences about those facts. The facts and rules usually concern one particular field and are generally contributed by experts in that field. Expert systems use those facts and rules to advise, analyze, categorize, diagnose, explain, identify, interpret, and teach. They attempt to address problems traditionally solved by human experts. A few of the many expert systems now in use are MYCIN, which helps doctors to diagnose infections; PROSPECTOR, which aids geologists in evaluating mineral sites; and TAXADVISOR, which gives estate-planning advice.

Expert systems are among the most useful and marketable products of artificial intelligence. The examples we've just mentioned are quite specific, and many expert systems run only on minicomputers or mainframes. Special artificial intelligence programming languages, such as LISP and PROLOG, are frequently used to develop proprietary expert systems. There is, however, a relatively new class of software that runs on microcomputers and lets nonprogrammers set up their own expert systems. These programs are called expert system shells.

An **expert system shell** greatly simplifies the process of developing an expert system. You supply the facts to create the *knowledge base* and the rules to create

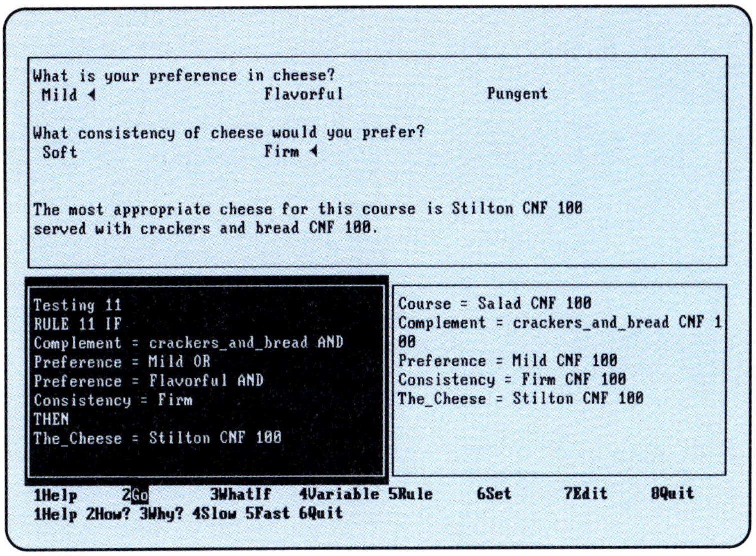

Figure 29 VP-Expert
This screen shows a session from a simple expert system designed with VP-Expert that helps you select cheeses for different courses of a meal.

the *rule base.* The expert system shell contains the *inference engine,* which actually uses your facts and rules to try and answer questions asked by end users, sometimes called clients. If necessary, the inference engine replies with further questions to get additional information. The inference engine then uses simple logic to draw conclusions from the details of a particular situation. Many expert system shells can also explain, with text and graphics, exactly how their conclusions have been reached.

One of the most popular expert system shells for microcomputers is VP-Expert, from Paperback Software International (see Figure 29). At about $150, VP-Expert provides an economical way to develop simple expert systems. The program takes you through all the steps needed to create an expert system, from entering the knowledge base to specifying the details of a typical consultation session with a client. Once you enter the facts that comprise the knowledge base, VP-Expert analyzes the data and automatically derives a preliminary set of rules to govern those data. You can examine this rule base and modify or supplement it as needed. Then the program lets you test the expert system by seeing how it behaves when a client asks a question. Multiple windows take you through a simulated consultation session. One window displays the rules as they are being tested. Another window shows the conclusions that have been reached so far. A third window lists the questions that the client would be asked for more information. In an actual session, the client would have to answer those questions. When the simulated consultation session is finished, VP-Expert displays a graphical tree that shows the complete reasoning path that was followed to reach the conclusions. VP-Expert also lets you assign a *confidence factor* from 0 to 100 to an answer if it's not simply yes or no. Once the expert system has been thoroughly tested in this manner, it is ready for consultation by clients.

Summary

- *The advantages and disadvantages of integrated software.* The advantages of integrated software include the convenience of having a single set of consistent menus and commands, increased ease in transferring data among applications, and less expense in acquiring all the applications. Disadvantages include the inability to choose alternate applications, the requirement for a lot of memory, and possibly slower execution time than with stand-alone applications.

- *How a windowing environment can enhance an operating system.* A windowing environment allows you to have several applications running on your screen at the same time in different windows.
- *How a DOS shell can make DOS more user friendly.* A DOS shell is a menu-driven addition to DOS that helps you manage your disk files and directories.
- *The various types of utility programs available for microcomputers.* Utility programs include disk and file utilities for file recovery, compression, transfer, conversion; as well as disk copying, backup, optimizing, and caching. There are printer utilities for supporting various printers' features, printing spreadsheets sideways, and print spooling. Also, keyboard utilities (keyboard enhancers) provide stand-alone keyboard macro facilities.
- *Which desk accessories are handy software options.* Desk accessories to provide all kinds of useful aids while you are using an application package include calculators, clocks, calendars, note pads, scrapbooks, phone and address books, phone dialers, appointment schedulers, outline editors, and mini-spreadsheets.
- *That on-line references can save time and effort.* Using stand-alone on-line references such as spelling checkers, thesauruses, and other dictionaries is often faster and more convenient than using conventional printed books.
- *The availability of statistical and math software for microcomputers.* Statistical packages help users analyze, interpret, and present numerical data. Other types of math software perform tasks such as automatically solving algebraic equations.
- *How project management software is used as a valuable organizational tool.* Project management packages help users formally plan and control complex undertakings.
- *How accounting packages are used by businesses to help with the bookkeeping.* Accounting software typically includes general ledger, accounts receivable, accounts payable, inventory control, purchase order, billing, and payroll subsystems.
- *How personal finance and tax programs can help manage your money matters.* Personal finance packages contain valuable financial advice and personal accounting procedures. Tax software helps users fill out and print tax forms.
- *The range of educational software packages available for microcomputers.* Packages are available on almost every subject imaginable for young children and adults. Training packages teach specific skills such as typing, math, and foreign languages.
- *The vast array of entertaining computer games, simulators, and music programs.* There are adventure, strategy, card, board, sports, parlor, game show, pinball, and arcade games. There are simulators for different types of vehicles. There are computer programs that synthesize sounds from musical instruments and help you compose music.
- *How hypertext is used to tap into vast stores of information.* Hypertext is a nonsequential method of organizing and presenting information with a computer. The term *hypermedia* is sometimes used to describe hypertext systems that include text, graphics, audio, and video.

- *The practical uses of artificial intelligence and expert systems.* The purpose of artificial intelligence is to endow computers with the ability to mimic certain aspects of human learning and decision making. It is used in natural language processors, robots, and expert systems. Expert systems are computer programs that contain facts and rules, which can be consulted for the answers to specific types of questions.

Key Terms

As an extra review of this chapter, try defining the following terms.

accounts payable
accounts receivable
artificial intelligence (AI)
automated vision
billing
cache
command-line interface (CLI)
critical path method (CPM)
desk accessories (desktop organizers, pop-up utilities)
disk backup utilities
disk caching utilities
disk copying utilities
disk optimizing utilities
DOS shell
expert system (knowledge-based system)
expert system shell
file compression utilities
file conversion utilities
file recovery utilities
file transfer utilities
Gantt chart
general ledger
graphics-based windowing environment (graphical user interface (GUI))
hypermedia
hypertext
integrated software
inventory control
machine learning
natural language processing
payroll
print spooler
program evaluation and review technique (PERT)
project management software
purchase orders
robot
stackware
text-based windowing environment
windowing environment

Review Questions

1. What are the advantages to using an integrated software package?
2. What five applications are usually included in an integrated software package?
3. What can a windowing environment do that an integrated software package cannot do?
4. Name two ways to classify windowing environments.
5. What distinguishes a DOS shell from a windowing environment?
6. List eight types of disk and file utilities.
7. What type of utility lets you print documents while you continue working within an application package?
8. What type of utility lets you assign frequently used command sequences and long strings of characters to just one or two keypresses?
9. List a few examples of commonly used desk accessories.
10. What are the advantages to using a stand-alone spelling checker and thesaurus?
11. Who might be likely to use a statistical package?

12. Name the two types of charts produced by virtually all project management packages.
13. Describe the potential benefits of using project management techniques.
14. What tasks can be performed with a personal finance package?
15. What techniques do many educational packages employ to make learning both interesting and fun?
16. List three basic categories of entertainment software.
17. What type of software allows you to randomly jump from topic to topic, finding any kind of information the computer can store?
18. What kinds of information can be stored with Hypercard?
19. What is the primary goal of artificial intelligence?
20. What type of software lets nonprogrammers set up their own expert systems?

Multiple Choice

1. Which of the following applications is not usually included in integrated software packages?
   (a) word processing (b) spreadsheet
   (c) accounting (d) data base management
2. Which type of software lets you run several different application packages at the same time, with each one in a separate area on the screen?
   (a) integrated software (b) windowing environment
   (c) DOS shell (d) utility
3. Like some advanced operating systems, some windowing environments are
   (a) multiprocessing. (b) multitasking.
   (c) multi-user. (d) networking.
4. A menu-driven addition to DOS that helps you manage your disk files and directories is called a
   (a) DOS shell. (b) DOS utility.
   (c) DOS routine. (d) DOS command.
5. A small program to help you recover an accidentally deleted file is usually classified as a(n)
   (a) operating system. (b) application package.
   (c) programming language. (d) utility.
6. What type of utility might you use to try to fit more files on an existing disk?
   (a) file recovery (b) file compression
   (c) file transfer (d) file conversion
7. What type of utility reduces or eliminates the wait as a printer produces documents?
   (a) print spooler (b) print caching
   (c) print optimizing (d) print backup
8. On IBM-compatible computers running DOS, desk accessories are usually implemented as
   (a) multitasking programs. (b) multiprocessing programs.
   (c) multi-user programs. (d) memory-resident programs.

9. One disadvantage of most on-line reference programs is that they
   (a) are difficult to use.
   (b) are very slow.
   (c) consume a great deal of disk space.
   (d) contain few references.
10. Which type of chart graphically depicts a project as a network of interconnected activities?
   (a) pie chart
   (b) PERT chart
   (c) Gantt chart
   (d) X-Y chart
11. Which type of chart shows the major tasks of a project, when each task must be performed, and how long each task will take?
   (a) pie chart
   (b) PERT chart
   (c) Gantt chart
   (d) X-Y chart
12. Which type of software package would you use to balance your checkbook, maintain a budget, estimate your taxes, and track investments?
   (a) word processing
   (b) data base management
   (c) personal finance
   (d) hypertext
13. The term *stackware* is usually associated with which particular program?
   (a) Guide
   (b) Hypercard
   (c) Lotus 1-2-3
   (d) WordStar
14. What type of software is among the most useful and marketable products of artificial intelligence?
   (a) word processing
   (b) spreadsheet
   (c) expert system
   (d) data base management
15. *Knowledge base*, *rule base*, and *inference engine* are terms that normally refer to what kind of software?
   (a) hypertext
   (b) data base management
   (c) spreadsheet
   (d) expert system shell

Projects

1. We've listed several types of utilities you can buy to supplement the capabilities of an operating system or application package. Try to find five kinds of utility programs not mentioned in this chapter and give a specific example of each one. Computer periodicals such as *PC Magazine*, *BYTE*, *PC World*, *InfoWorld*, *Macworld*, and *MacUser* are good sources of information.
2. Does your school or workplace use any educational software packages? If so, briefly describe the packages and how they are used to instruct students or train workers. If not, try to find two or three specific packages that you think could be used at your school or workplace. List them along with a brief description of their features.
3. A large number of stacks is currently available for Apple's Hypercard program. Research computer periodicals, such as *Macworld* and *MacUser*, to find ten specific examples of commercial or public domain stackware. List them along with a brief description of what they do. Can you think of any other potential uses for hypertext systems?

4. In this chapter we've given a few examples of expert systems that are actually being used. What are some other potential uses of expert systems? What kinds of situations can be broken down into facts and rules? List two or three of your suggested uses and explain how expert systems would be used for these.

CHAPTER 21

Computers and Society: Future Trends

In This Chapter

Computers and Education
- Computer-Assisted Instruction
- Computer-Managed Instruction

Computers and the Arts
- Music
- Art
- Movies

Computers and Medicine
- Training
- Diagnosis
- Imaging

Computers and Government
- The Internal Revenue Service
- The Department of Defense

Computers and Business
- Computer-Aided Design, Engineering, and Manufacturing
- Management Information and Decision Support Systems

Computers and the Workplace
- Job Security
- Performance Monitoring
- Health Concerns
- Ergonomics
- Telecommuting

Computers and the Law
- Hackers
- Viruses
- White-Collar Crime
- Software Piracy
- Copyrights, Licenses, Trademarks, and Patents
- Ethics

Computers and Privacy
- Matching
- Legal Protection
- Security

Computers and the Future
- Microprocessors
- Supercomputers
- Artificial Intelligence
- Neural Networks

Preview

Computers have had a profound effect on our society. Some of the resulting changes are obvious, like the word processors in most offices, the bar-code scanners in most supermarkets, and the automated teller machines in most banks. Other changes brought about by computers are more subtle. Computers are forcing us to rethink our notions of work, crime, privacy, and ethics. In the previous chapters we have explored specific concepts of microcomputer hardware and software. In this chapter we will discuss how computers are being used and abused in our society. We will investigate some of the philosophical issues and concerns that must be addressed to appreciate the true costs and benefits of computerization. Finally, we will look ahead to the computers of the future.

After studying this chapter, you will understand

- how computers are used in education.
- the impact of computers on the arts.
- the uses of computers in medicine.
- how computers are changing the way government operates.
- how computers are used in business.
- the issue of using computers in the workplace.
- the legal problems concerning computers.
- how computers affect our privacy.
- the computer advances to come.

Computers and Education

In the past few years, most schools have acquired computers for use in their instructional programs. More than 90 percent of all U.S. schools have at least one computer. The typical elementary school has six computers, and the typical high school has more than twenty. Computers are even more common at colleges and universities, where students spend more than $1 billion a year on hardware and software. Two broad categories reflect how computers are used in education: computer-assisted instruction and computer-managed instruction.

Computer-Assisted Instruction

Computer-assisted instruction (CAI) uses computers to teach students at their own pace. Interactive lessons are presented that require student participation (see Figure 1). The computer is programmed to provide direct feedback to each student, depending upon his or her individual responses. Computer-assisted instruction is based on the theory that students who proceed at their own pace and participate in lessons with immediate feedback learn quicker and retain information longer. Practice is often the best teacher. Once a concept or skill is introduced, mastery usually proceeds from individual, repeated drill.

Early computer-assisted instruction programs were little more than drill and practice quizzes. Soon, however, teachers began using the computer to challenge and motivate students. Today, sophisticated CAI programs use music, speech, graphics, animation, and other techniques to make learning with a computer interesting and fun. Lessons are often presented as games. The programs are flexible enough to allow students to repeat material they have not yet mastered.

Figure 1 Computer-Assisted Instruction *Computers are used in the classroom to help students master subjects from reading to calculus.*

Computer-assisted instruction is now used for almost every subject imaginable. Computers help toddlers learn to read, high school students master foreign languages, and college students understand calculus, chemistry, and physics.

Computer-Managed Instruction

Computer-managed instruction (CMI) uses computers to help with school administrative tasks (see Figure 2). When combined with computer-assisted instruction, CMI systems allow teachers to track students' progress and to point out their strengths and weaknesses. Computer-managed instruction programs are also used to generate tests, maintain student records, plan bus routes, pay teachers' salaries, keep attendance, keep track of inventory, and make announcements.

Computers and the Arts

Computers are playing an expanding role in all kinds of artistic endeavors. Music, literature, dance, painting, sculpture, photography, and the movie industry have all been affected by the use of computers.

Music

People have used computers to create and play music almost as long as there have been computers. Today, most microcomputers can be equipped with hardware and software to help a musician compose, print, play, and record songs

Insight

How does a Virus Infect a Computer?

Remember your last bout with the flu—the sniffles, headache, fever, aches and pains? The symptoms may be different, but when a computer contracts a virus, the effects can be just as miserable.

Computers are infected when they pick up a virus that some black-hearted soul has secretly planted in an electronic bulletin board or on a floppy disk. Once released, a virus races through computer networks, or is copied from disk to disk, causing all kinds of damage.

Most viruses consist of a few lines of instructions that are tacked onto an innocent program. The instructions usually have three parts. The first, or environmental, component makes the computer tell the virus about its surroundings, including the type of computer and software being used.

The second component directs the computer to insert a copy of the virus into whatever target the creator wants. This so-called "replication component" can cause the virus to spread throughout every program in the computer and then through a mainframe or through electronic mail to other computers in the system. Even backup programs may be infected. Some viruses have a built-in delay that allows them to travel unnoticed through a system.

At the designated time, the virus's third component is activated. This instructs the computer to destroy data, scramble files, disable printers, crash the system, and much more.

An especially devastating virus was created by a Cornell graduate student named Robert T. Morris, Jr. On November 2, 1988, his virus shut down the Defense Department's Arpanet system and penetrated the Milnet network. Morris's virus released subprograms that instructed the computer to make hundreds of copies of the program, guessed the secret passwords of legitimate users, and directed the computer to spread the virus to other computers.

Although intended to be harmless, the Arpanet virus shut down thousands of computers across the country and took days to clear up.

Sources: Philip Elmer-DeWitt, "The Kid Put Us Out of Action," *Time,* November 14, 1988, p. 76. Shawna Vogel, "1988 Disease of the Year: Illness as Glitch," *Discover,* January 1989, pp. 64–66.

Figure 2 Computer-Managed Instruction *Computers help teachers and administrators track students and manage schools.*

***Figure 3* Computer Music**
Computers are commonly used in creating sophisticated music and in recording systems.

(see Figure 3). Digital synthesizers and other electronic musical instruments can be connected to and controlled by computers via the Musical Instrument Digital Interface (MIDI), a communications standard for music. The Apple Macintosh is often used in sophisticated sound-processing systems. Expansion boards are available that can synthesize sound with the same quality as the music on compact discs. Microcomputers also can control multitrack tape recorders and digital mixing boards. A properly equipped Macintosh sound system can record, edit, and play back music with the technical proficiency of a small recording studio.

Art

Many artists now use computer graphics to create stunning visual images (see Figure 4). Virtually any shape can be generated, rotated, expanded, contracted, and otherwise manipulated. Millions of colors are available. Objects can be combined, shaded, and blended together. Three-dimensionality can be depicted by illuminating and shadowing scenes with simulated light from any angle. The artist can experiment infinitely and store his or her most interesting creations on disk. Despite the vitality of this new medium, traditional drawing, painting, and sculpture will not be replaced. Computer art, like photography, has become an art form on its own.

Movies

Film has always been a technological art form. Today, computers are used to edit movies, produce special effects, and create animation (see Figure 5). Many imaginative blockbusters, such as the various *Star Wars, Star Trek, Ghostbusters,*

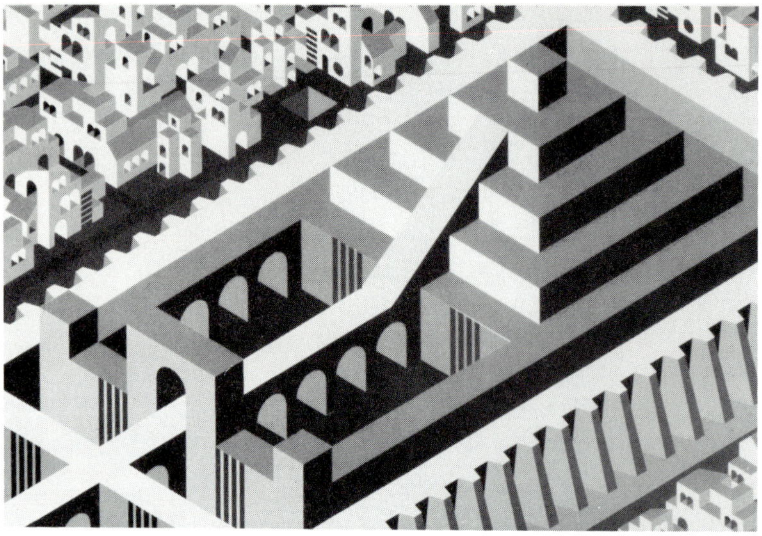

***Figure 4* Computer Art**
Pictures generated with the aid of a computer have become an interesting new art form.

and *Indiana Jones* films, simply would not be possible without computers to catalog scenes, edit segments, synchronize music, integrate special effects, and even generate images.

Computers and Medicine

Computers are now used in many different aspects of the health care industry. The American Medical Association, recognizing the potential benefits of using computers, publishes a journal called *Computers in Medicine* on the subject. Many special interest groups and professional organizations have been formed to explore and promote medical computing. In fact, computers are already hard at work helping doctors learn about, diagnose, and treat our ailments.

***Figure 5* Movies**
This scene from Stephen Spielberg's Young Sherlock Holmes *was generated by a computer.*

Training

Medical students increasingly use computers to help learn material and master skills. Many schools, such as New York University's School of Medicine, provide computer systems that let surgical students perform simulated operations. Sophisticated graphics present three-dimensional views inside the body. The computer can be programmed to test students' skills in handling unexpected complications. The simulated operation and recovery period can be slowed down, speeded up, and rerun to give students considerable practice at a relatively low cost.

Diagnosis

A doctor makes a diagnosis by considering a patient's symptoms and medical history, performing an examination, and when necessary, ordering laboratory tests and imaging procedures. Computers are now used in several facets of medical diagnosis.

Students at the University of Illinois Medical Center in Chicago practice diagnosing illnesses with computer-simulated patients. The computer, however, can also assist doctors in making diagnoses on real patients. Medical data bases and expert systems such as the University of Pittsburgh's CADUCEUS software are used to examine symptoms, recommend laboratory tests, and suggest possible treatments. The CADUCEUS system cross-indexes 500 disease profiles with more than 3000 symptoms. The program, named after the emblem of the medical profession, identifies the relationship between a patient's symptoms and the disease that may be causing them.

Computers also may be used in diagnosis to recognize and interpret visual data. For example, computers can recognize abnormal cells under the microscope. This ability can be applied to automating millions of the blood count and cancer tests performed each year by laboratory technicians.

Imaging

One of the most exciting and beneficial applications of computers in medicine is imaging systems. Various forms of electromagnetic radiation and sound are used to take two- and three-dimensional pictures beneath skin and muscle without surgery (see Figure 6). Computers are necessary to focus, collect, organize, record, and present the scanning beams that let doctors look inside the body.

Computerized axial tomography (**CAT** or **CT**) scanners are essentially three-dimensional X-ray machines. X-rays are shot through the body at many different angles. A computer collects and combines the resulting images into clear, cross-sectional slices of the body. When stacked up, the slices depict internal structures in three dimensions. Shading and color represent different fluids, tissues, organs, and bones. The images can be manipulated electronically to get the best view of the area of interest. CAT scanning provides clearer and more detailed images of soft tissues than ordinary X-ray photographs. This technique also minimizes the amount of X-ray radiation exposure.

Ultrasound scanners avoid potentially damaging radiation by taking pictures with very high-frequency sound waves. Inaudible to the human ear, ultrasound waves are passed into the body, and the reflected echoes are detected and analyzed to build an image. Most modern ultrasound scanners produce moving pictures on a video screen. Considered painless and safe, ultrasound scanners are most often used to take pictures of internal organs and unborn babies.

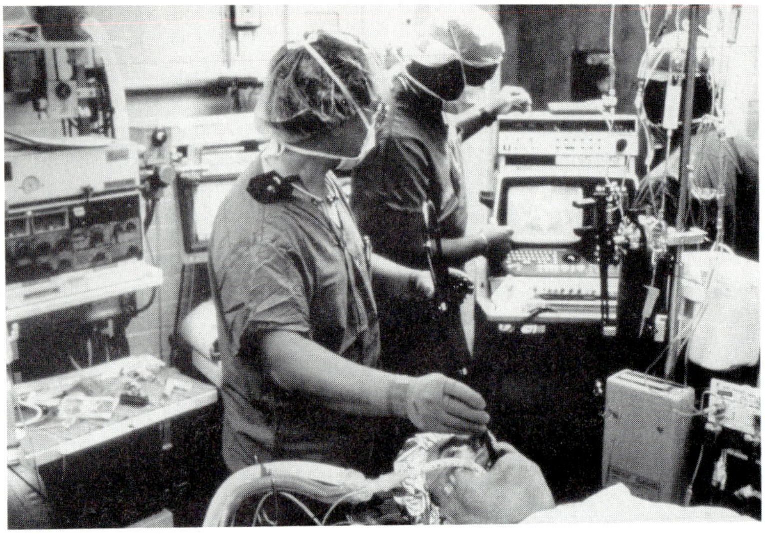

Figure 6 Medical Imaging *Computers allow doctors to look inside the body to help diagnose illness.*

Positron emission tomography (PET) scanning produces images by detecting positively charged particles that are emitted from radioactive substances injected into the bloodstream. The patient is surrounded by an array of detectors linked to a computer that generates images by computing the origin and distribution of the emitted particles. PET scanning is most often used for investigating the brain and detecting tumors.

Magnetic resonance imaging (MRI), also known as nuclear magnetic resonance (NMR) scanning, produces high-quality cross-sectional pictures of the body without X-rays or other radiation. A powerful electromagnet aligns the nuclei (centers) of hydrogen atoms in the body. The nuclei are then knocked out of position with radio waves. The nuclei realign themselves with the magnetic field, producing radio signals that are detected and transformed into computer-generated images. MRI is particularly valuable for studying the brain, spinal cord, heart, blood vessels, eyes, ears, and joints such as the knee. No known risks or side effects of MRI have been established.

Computers and Government

Computers were first developed to help compile census data and perform calculations for the military. Today, the United States government is undoubtedly the largest user of computer hardware and software in the world. In fact, government as we know it simply could not function without computers. Whether they are used to count votes or capture criminals, computers have become indispensable tools for governing nations. Computers have permeated all levels of government, but let's briefly examine the two most obvious users: the Internal Revenue Service and the military.

The Internal Revenue Service

The Internal Revenue Service uses computers to send out tax forms, record and store the data sent in by taxpayers, and track down cheaters and tax evaders (see Figure 7). Each year the IRS must process nearly 100 million tax returns. Records

Figure 7 The IRS
Computers help the Internal Revenue Service collect taxes.

about each taxpayer must be maintained for at least five years. Computers are absolutely essential for collecting and maintaining the Internal Revenue Service's data bases. Tax forms arriving at an IRS regional center are sorted by computers equipped with bar-code readers that can process 30,000 returns per hour. Human employees then examine each form and enter key information, such as the tax bracket and number of exemptions claimed. Another computer checks the forms for math errors and compliance with the tax laws. Eventually, the data ends up on magnetic tape at the IRS National Center in Martinsburg, West Virginia. There, computers further examine the tax returns by comparing the data supplied by employers and banks with the data given by taxpayers. Computers also determine if refunds or additional taxes are due, verify these amounts, and print refund checks.

The Department of Defense

The United States Department of Defense spends more than $2.5 billion each year on computer hardware and software. Like any huge organization, the Defense Department must generate reports, prepare budgets, and maintain data bases. So, many of the military applications of computers are the same as civilian applications: word processing, accounting, and data base management. The military establishment, however, has always sponsored and developed cutting-edge computer technology (see Figure 8). Today, computers are embedded in every advanced military system, from tanks to antimissile satellites.

Computers and Business

Factories and offices have been under tremendous pressure to increase productivity, enhance quality, and compete more effectively with domestic and foreign companies. Business and industry have turned to computers to help achieve these goals.

***Figure 8* The Military**
Computers are an essential component of the nation's defenses.

Computer-Aided Design, Engineering, and Manufacturing

As you learned in Chapter 18, computer-aided design (CAD) is the application of computer graphics to the drafting of parts, mechanisms, or buildings (see Figure 9). Many products, from clothespins to automobiles, are now designed completely using computers. Designers can work faster and more accurately using sophisticated computer graphics systems than they ever could with pencils, pens, T-squares, compasses, and paper. Furthermore, CAD systems offer the flexibility to rotate drawings, zoom in or out, and change scales. Large drawings can be broken down into smaller parts, or parts designed separately can be combined on the screen, printer, or plotter. Completed drawings can be saved on disks for future reference or for use in other projects. Sophisticated CAD

***Figure 9* Computer-Aided Design**
Many companies now use CAD systems instead of traditional drafting techniques to design products.

programs can be tied in with computer-aided engineering and computer-aided manufacturing systems to design, test, and make products completely by computer.

Computer-aided engineering (CAE) allows engineers to simulate and test their designs. Instead of building a physical prototype, an engineer can run a computer simulation to test conditions such as mechanical stress, metal fatigue, and the effects of temperature. General Motors, for example, now uses computer-aided engineering for many automotive parts. The company has found that testing parts by computer is both effective and economical. Before a car is even built, the CAE system can tell what each part will weigh, how strong it will be, and how it will perform.

Computer-aided manufacturing (CAM) uses computers to control the machines that make or assemble products. Many machines used in factories can now be controlled by computers. These include machine tools that cut metal parts, machines that handle materials, such as chemicals and steel, and industrial robots that assemble, weld, or paint parts.

Management Information and Decision Support Systems

A **management information system (MIS)** is computer hardware and software that provide managers with the information they need to do their jobs effectively (see Figure 10). This information includes internal and external data relating to an organization's past and present, as well as projections of what is likely to happen in the future. The purpose of an MIS is to furnish reports within a workable time frame so that managers can make the best decisions concerning the planning, control, and operation of their organization's activities. For example, many large companies use management information systems to generate reports such as profit summaries, cash flow analyses, sales figure presentations, and capital need estimates.

A **decision support system (DSS)** further helps managers by giving them quick answers to interactively asked "what if" questions. Decision support systems provide a basis for judging situations analytically by applying statistical models and mathematical simulation. Unlike management information systems, decision support systems generally deal with relatively unstructured problems, such as those concerning new products, policies, company mergers, and acquisitions. Decision support systems both complement and build on management information systems. Typically interactive, decision support systems are primarily designed to help answer questions with little or no precedent. Management information systems, on the other hand, generally collect, organize, and summarize information to help managers deal with well-structured problems, such as where to locate plants and warehouses, and the preparation of budgets, cost analyses, and sales projections.

Computers and the Workplace

Computers have drastically affected how and where many of us work. Some people have lost jobs, while others have gained jobs, thanks to computers. Computers have made work more pleasant for some and more stressful for others. Do computers adversely affect the health of workers who use them every day? Have computers helped free or confine some workers at home? These are but a few of the issues that have become apparent as computers have moved into the workplace.

Figure 10 Management Information Systems
In today's global marketplace, many managers need computer-based systems to help them get the information they need to run their organizations.

Job Security

The Congressional Budget Office estimates that between 450,000 and 750,000 people lose their jobs each year because of technological advancements (see Figure 11). As many as 4 million manufacturing workers could be displaced by robots by the year 2000, according to researchers at Carnegie-Mellon University. Perhaps 64,000 new jobs will be created in robotics, but these jobs will require highly skilled workers. The same is true for most of the jobs created by high technology. Many of today's blue-collar jobs could be eliminated by 2025.

Computers and robots can free workers from repetitive, difficult, and dangerous tasks. Displaced workers and young people just entering the workplace, however, must be trained in technologically useful skills. Reading, math, and the ability to understand and follow complex instructions are quickly becoming the minimum requirements for finding a job today. Technology and the economy now change so rapidly that most of us will have to receive additional education and training throughout our careers to avoid becoming "obsolete."

Figure 11 Lost Jobs
Many repetitive and dangerous manufacturing jobs are being taken over by computer-controlled robots.

Performance Monitoring

Computers in the workplace usually, but not always, make jobs easier for workers. Some employers use computers to monitor workers' performance (see Figure 12). The Congressional Office of Technology Assessment estimates that 6 million telecommunications, financial service, and airline workers are evaluated on the basis of computer monitoring. For example, a computer may be set up to measure and record the amount of time a worker spends on the phone handling each customer. The worker may be under constant stress to take care of customers in as little time as possible. Unlike a human boss, the computer monitor never goes away. Employers generally praise computerized performance for increasing productivity by providing specific feedback on a worker's strengths and weaknesses. Labor unions, on the other hand, tend to view computer monitoring as a stressful invasion of workers' privacy.

Health Concerns

Computers are in such widespread use that it is prudent to consider the serious health risks, if any, they pose to workers. The major health concerns associated with using computers fall into three categories: radiation, stress, and physical discomfort.

Figure 12 Performance Monitoring
Some employers use computers to evaluate the productivity of workers who handle customers over the telephone.

Since the late 1970s, some people have suggested a connection between the use of CRT screens and the development of cataracts and an increased risk of miscarriages or birth defects. Presumably these problems are caused by low-level radiation emitted by the computer screens. Public concern prompted extensive studies by the U.S. Food and Drug Administration, the Occupational Safety and Health Administration, the National Institute of Occupational Health and Safety, and the Canadian Radiation Protection Bureau. All of these studies found no detectable radiation risk associated with using CRT screens. Using a computer does not seem to cause cataracts, birth defects, sterility, blindness, cancer, or any other serious illness. Although women who work with CRT screens while they are pregnant may be slightly more likely to have miscarriages, these problems may be attributed to statistics, stress, or other office work conditions. In Canada and in some U.S. companies, however, pregnant women who work at CRT screens are routinely assigned to other duties until they have their babies, just to be safe.

Working long hours at a computer can cause stress in some workers. Employers often expect computer workers to be faster, more efficient, and more productive than they were before computers were installed. In reality, employees may feel rushed, isolated, confused, and overworked, especially if their performance is monitored by computer. Some workers think they may lose their jobs if they don't master the computer. Others fear the computer may actually take over their jobs. Serious morale problems can cause stress-related symptoms such as anxiety, depression, indigestion, palpitations, and muscular aches and pains. Employers who ignore worker stress are likely to see increased errors, slowdowns, tardiness, absenteeism, sick leave, and turnovers.

Using a computer for long periods of time can actually cause physical distress, too. Eyestrain, headaches, neck pains, backaches, fatigue, and nausea are common complaints of computer workers. Most of these problems are associated with poorly designed work areas. Glare, noise, heat, cramped space, and improper furniture all contribute to discomfort.

Ergonomics

Ergonomics is the science of designing objects so that they can be most easily, effectively, comfortably, and safely used by people. Ergonomically designed computers, office furniture, and work areas can reduce many of the psychological and physical problems associated with using computers. Many ergonomic improvements have already been made to computers, including detachable keyboards, numeric keypads, adjustable displays, nonglare screens, and rounded mice. In most offices, however, much can be done to improve the furniture and general working environment. Here are some ergonomic recommendations for improving computer work areas (see Figure 13):

- Indirect, recessed lighting fixtures
- Adjustable window blinds or curtains
- Display screen hoods and antiglare glass
- Brighter display screens
- Flatter display screens
- Higher resolution display screens
- Display screens that can be tilted and turned
- Display screens angled 10 to 30 degrees below eye level
- Display screens positioned about 18 to 22 inches from eyes
- Keyboards placed at about elbow height
- Detachable keyboards that tilt from 0 to 15 degrees
- Fully adjustable chairs on casters with lower back rests
- Tilting and swiveling seats
- Upright copy holders
- Acoustical enclosures for noisy printers

Telecommuting

One third of all small businesses started each year are run from the home. An estimated 10 million people in the United States, about 10 percent of the work force, will work at home with computers by the turn of the century, according to the Center for Futures Research at the University of Southern California. Microcomputers, modems, telephones, personal copiers, fax machines, and express mail delivery services have made it possible for many people to work as effectively from home as from a traditional office (see Figure 14). Computer programmers, financial analysts, lawyers, authors, data entry operators, typists, and telephone order takers are a few examples of potential telecommuters.

People who work at home have the flexibility to work odd hours, keep an eye on their kids, save commuting time and expenses, and dress however they like.

*Figure 13 **Ergonomics***
Ergonomically designed computers, furniture, and work areas help reduce stress and physical discomfort. Steelcase, a leading manufacturer of office furniture, has developed the following model of an ergonomic computer workstation.
(a) Seat tilt: 0 to 8 degrees, back rest tilt: 0 to 16 degrees. (b) Seat front edge slope: 0 to 3 degrees. (c) Seat height: 17 to 21 inches. (d) Eye to screen distance: 18 to 22 inches. (e) Vertical viewing angle: 10 to 30 degrees. (f) Screen height: 22 to 33 inches. (g) Screen angle: ± 7 degrees. (h) Keyboard to screen distance: 0 to 7½ inches. (i) Keyboard height: 23 to 32 inches. (j) Keyboard angle: 0 to 15 degrees.

*Figure 14 **Telecommuting***
Thanks to microcomputers, many people now work at home, full or part time, in their own "electronic cottages."

Many telecommuters feel freer, more relaxed, and more productive working at home. Nevertheless, telecommuting has its disadvantages. It's easy to become isolated working at home without the social aspects of a traditional office environment. Career advancement opportunities may be limited. Home workers who aren't self-employed may be paid less and receive fewer benefits than regular employees. Not everyone has the room at home to convert into an office. A substantial initial expense may be required to purchase the microcomputer system, office furniture, and other essentials for setting up a personal workplace. Finally, some people find it difficult to keep their nose to the grindstone when they are at home with no boss around. To balance the advantages and disadvantages, many telecommuters work at home only part time, perhaps two or three days a week. Studies seem to indicate that a mixture of home and office work is the best way for some individuals to meet their psychological, social, and career needs.

Computers and the Law

Computers perform many vital tasks for government, business, and financial institutions. Unfortunately, some computer experts have abused their skills and have used computers mischievously, destructively, or for their own gain. In addition, the widespread use of computers has spawned legal issues never encountered before. New laws and formalized computer ethics are being developed to address these problems.

Hackers

In the early days of computers, many hardware and software advances were made by a group of experts who came to be known as hackers. A **hacker** is a hardware designer or programmer with an obsession for computing. The hacker philosophy is one of sharing, openness, decentralization, and gaining access to computers at almost any cost. These digital explorers are driven by the desire to understand and improve computers. Hackers generally believe that computers and information should be freely available to all who want to use them. Unfortunately, the hacker ethic often ignores notions of security, privacy, trespassing, and the right of a company to make a profit on its computers or software. Hackers have been glamorized as adventurers, visionaries, wizards, and artists. They have also been derided as outcasts, amateurs, pranksters, and law-breakers.

A popular, but mythical, image of the typical hacker can be found in the 1983 movie *WarGames* (see Figure 15). In it, a high school computer whiz who illegally uses the telephone system to find and play networked computer games accidentally breaks into a U.S. Defense Department computer and almost starts World War III. In real life, hackers have been responsible for some expensive, inconvenient, and worrisome computer break-ins. For example, in 1987 a young West German hacker was discovered to have penetrated a U.S Defense Department computer network. For at least five years he had combed sensitive files in search of data on the Strategic Defense Initiative. Although the hacker had accessed only unclassified material, military authorities were not amused.

Viruses

For the most part, hackers are characterized by their search for knowledge or fun or by a desire to improve computer systems. Some people, however, use computers maliciously to perpetrate pranks or outright vandalism. For example, dis-

Figure 15 Hackers
In the movie WarGames, *a fictional hacker who thinks he is playing a new computer game entitled Global Thermonuclear War almost starts World War III.*

gruntled programmers have been known to hide instructions inside software that will purposely destroy data or crash a system long after they are gone. Many techniques have been used to disrupt computer systems. One of the most insidious is the computer virus.

In biological organisms, a virus is an infectious agent that invades cells and instructs them to make copies of itself. A **computer virus** is a hidden program that secretly copies itself from disk to disk and across networks. Typically created by expert programmers, viruses can cause all kinds of mischief. Some viruses are relatively harmless, like the "worm" that spread through IBM's electronic mail network in 1987, flashing a Christmas greeting on all the terminal screens. Other viruses are created specifically to wreak havoc, like the one released at Lehigh University just before Thanksgiving in 1987. The Lehigh virus was hidden in part of the MS-DOS operating system. When a microcomputer was booted from an infected disk, the virus would spread to other disks accessed using a command like TYPE or COPY. After replicating itself four times on other disks, the parent virus would erase every floppy and hard disk in the microcomputer. Meanwhile, each of the four children viruses would infect four other disks before erasing data, and so on.

Viruses are a serious problem, although most computers will never be infected. Fortunately, the risk from computer viruses is now well known, and lawmakers are taking action. On August 1, 1989, a law took effect in Minnesota directed at stopping computer viruses. The Minnesota Computer Virus Crime Bill, the first law like it in the country, expressly prohibits the "intentional distribution of destructive computer programs." Penalties range from a small fine and 90 days in jail to a maximum sentence of ten years in prison and $50,000 in fines for crimes that result in damages of more than $2,500. Maryland and West Virginia have also passed antiviral laws and several other states, including California, are developing similar bills.

Antiviral precautions also can be taken by computer users. For example, only software and disks from well-known sources should be used. Unchecked public-domain and pirated software should be avoided. Software downloaded from less-than-particular electronic bulletin boards should not be trusted. Computers should

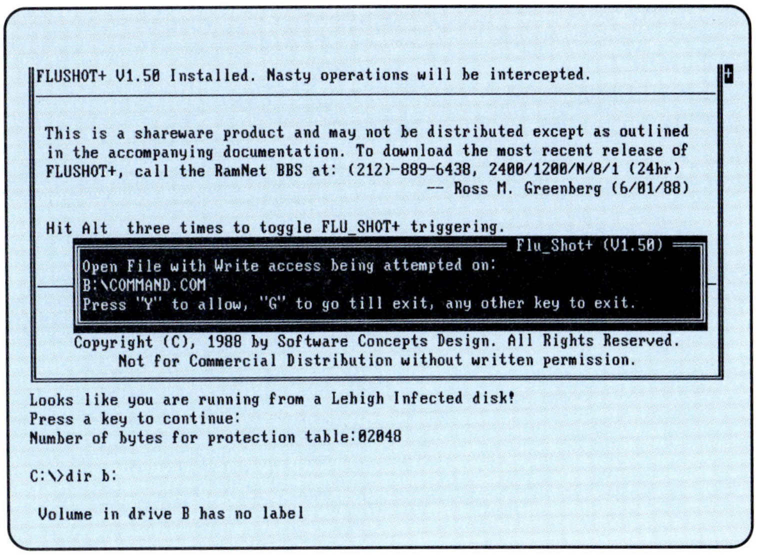

Figure 16 Antiviral Program
Flu-Shot+ is a popular program used to help guard against computer viruses.

not be booted up from borrowed system disks. Backup copies of all software and data should be maintained. Finally, antiviral programs, such as Vaccine and Flu-Shot+, can be used to detect and remove known viruses (see Figure 16). All of these measures can help counter the threat from computer viruses. Unfortunately, practical jokers and saboteurs are constantly inventing new ways to disrupt computer systems.

White-Collar Crime

Although a few hackers and virus programmers may break the law, they generally are not driven by a profit motive. Their crimes may be characterized as misuse of computer services or theft or alteration of programs and data. Another type of computer crime is the theft of hardware or software to be resold. Like any expensive electronic device, computers, especially small computers, are prone to theft if adequate security measures are not taken. Software is even easier to steal than hardware. Theft often occurs from schools where large numbers of microcomputers are available. Basic precautions, such as locking doors, limiting access, and bolting the hardware to the tables, can prevent much computer theft.

A more troublesome type of computer crime is the electronic theft of money. Virtually all large businesses, banks, and other financial institutions in the United States use computers and networks to process their monetary transactions (see Figure 17). Every workday, computer networks in the United States transmit nearly $1 trillion among financial institutions, an amount equal to about 25 percent of the gross national product. About half of all financial transactions in the United States is handled by computers. These enormous amounts of computerized money are an irresistible temptation to some criminals. For example, the average computer crime yields about $500,000, while only $5,000 is taken in the typical armed bank robbery. According to consultants at Ernst & Whinney, a Cleveland accounting firm, $3 billion to $5 billion is stolen each year in the United States in computer-related crimes.

Many instances have been uncovered in which white-collar criminals stole vast amounts of money using computers. In 1975, a computer programmer diverted

Figure 17 Electronic Banking
Applications of computers in banking, such as the estimated 500,000 automated teller machines in the United States, have opened up new opportunities for white-collar crime.

$385,000 from employee accounts in a company investment plan. Each time interest was compounded, he had instructed the computer to divert the fractions of rounded-off pennies to another account. His booty automatically accumulated while he went about his business. Another example of white-collar crime is the case of Stanley Rifkin, a computer consultant hired by Security Pacific Bank of California. Rifkin used his position to obtain information that let him manipulate the bank's electronic funds-transfer system. He instructed the computerized system to transfer $10 million from Security Pacific to a Swiss bank account. Then Rifkin invested the cash in diamonds. He was arrested only after he returned to the United States and bragged about his swindle. One of the largest cases of computer fraud involved the Equity Funding Corporation of America. Some company officials used computers to issue and manage more than 50,000 fake life insurance policies. Over ten years, several hundred million dollars were defrauded from Equity Funding's subsidiary insurance companies.

Software Piracy

One type of computer crime is especially distressing to software publishers. **Software piracy** is the practice of illegally copying software. Most perpetrators don't even realize they are breaking the law. Some individuals copy a commercial program for themselves or a friend without paying the software publisher. Technically, they are violating the publisher's copyright. The legitimate purchaser who allows a copy to be made is violating the software licensing agreement. Some analysts suspect that as many as ten illegal copies exist for every software package lawfully purchased. An industry with sales estimated at $12 billion per year is justifiably concerned about the profits lost to software piracy.

Software usually can be copied easily, quickly, and inexpensively. A program that sells for hundreds or even thousands of dollars can be reproduced with an ordinary computer in a few minutes on several blank diskettes costing as little as 25 cents each. Although the documentation that comes with the program cannot be copied as easily or cheaply, books available in any shopping mall bookstore teach the use of most popular programs.

Software publishers have taken several measures to reduce software piracy. In the late 1970s and early 1980s, many publishers resorted to copy protecting their programs. This technique makes it difficult or impossible for users to make additional copies of a program. Unfortunately, copy protection is usually inconvenient for the legitimate purchaser of a program, who must run the program from a special diskette, keep a key diskette in the floppy drive even if the program is loaded on a hard disk, or follow special procedures when making backup copies. In addition, several inexpensive software and hardware techniques for overriding most copy-protection methods are readily available (see Figure 18). Today, relatively few popular programs are copy protected.

Most software publishers now rely on education, registration, site licensing, and litigation to try to keep software piracy in check. Education involves informing the public that copying commercial software without paying for it is illegal. After all, most people are basically honest and usually will pay for software they use on a regular basis. Individuals and organizations who purchase software are urged to register with the publisher. When a new version of a program is released, most publishers will offer it at reduced rates to registered users. Similarly, many software publishers offer some level of product support over the phone to registered users. Some software publishers offer site licenses to organizations that use many copies of their programs. A **site license** gives the purchaser permission

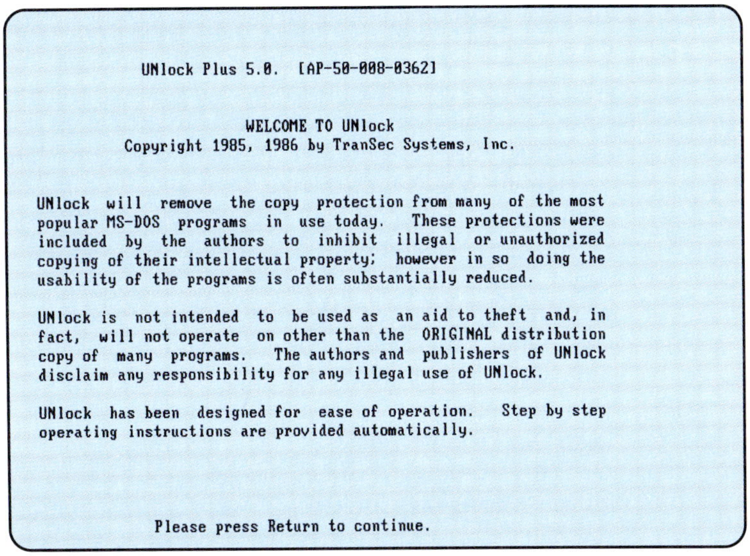

***Figure 18* Overriding Copy Protection**
Some programs, such as UNLock from TranSec Systems, have been designed especially to override other software publishers' copy-protection schemes.

to make copies of software for internal use at a reduced fee for each copy. As a last resort, some software publishers use litigation to stop pirates. Generally, only large organizations that make no effort to control blatant software piracy within their ranks or those companies that actually sell pirated copies for profit are sued.

Copyrights, Licenses, Trademarks, and Patents

Software developers have a number of legal means to protect their intellectual property. Because computer software is based largely on ideas, it is usually copyrighted, like books, plays, and music. In addition, software or parts of programs are sometimes licensed, trademarked, or patented.

Copyright law was originally designed to protect literary and musical works. The Copyright Act of 1980 officially granted computer programs the same protection given to other intellectual property. Under the law, unauthorized copying of software is forbidden unless it is necessary for the normal use of the program or unless it is done to make a single backup copy. Getting a copyright is easy. The work must exhibit the word "Copyright," an abbreviation such as "Copr.," or the copyright symbol ©. The work must also display the year it was created and the name of the copyright holder. Although it is not necessary, the copyright should be recorded by sending a registration form, the registration fee, and a copy of the work to the United States Copyright office. The copyright holder can sue anyone who makes unauthorized copies for damage payments corresponding to lost revenues. For software, a copyright explicitly prohibits duplicating the program code. Under the emerging interpretation of copyright law, a copyright also may be infringed by producing a program that duplicates the total "look and feel" of another program, even if the programming code is completely different. For example, on January 12, 1987, Lotus Development Corporation filed a lawsuit in the Boston Federal District Court claiming that both VP-Planner, published by Paperback Software, and The Twin, from Mosaic Software, infringe on the copyright for Lotus 1-2-3. At the time, these two programs duplicated the 1-2-3 command names, screen arrangement, and other aspects of the popular spreadsheet software. At the time this book was written, the final outcome still had not been decided in the courts.

For some software publishers, copyright law does not provide enough protection. The law puts no limits on the use of copyrighted programs once they are sold. Assuming no other agreements have been made, the purchaser can do whatever he or she wants to do with the program, except copy it. Copyright law does not prevent using, reselling, or even renting purchased software. So, many software publishers use an approach known as **software licensing.** In this, a program is not actually sold, it is licensed. Once the customer reads the license agreement, opens the package, and uses the software, he or she is bound by the license agreement. As Figure 19 shows, a software license agreement typically prohibits the customer from copying the program (except for making a backup copy), using the program on more than one computer at a time, modifying the program, renting the program, or doing anything else the publisher doesn't want done to the program. At this time, it is still not certain whether software licenses represent legal contracts. In practice, most customers treat software as if they own it, just as they do other copyrighted material, such as books, magazines, tapes, and compact discs.

The **trademark** is another legal protection for creative expression. Its use, however, is usually limited to a word, phrase, or graphic symbol representing a company or product. For example, the abbreviation IBM is a trademark of Inter-

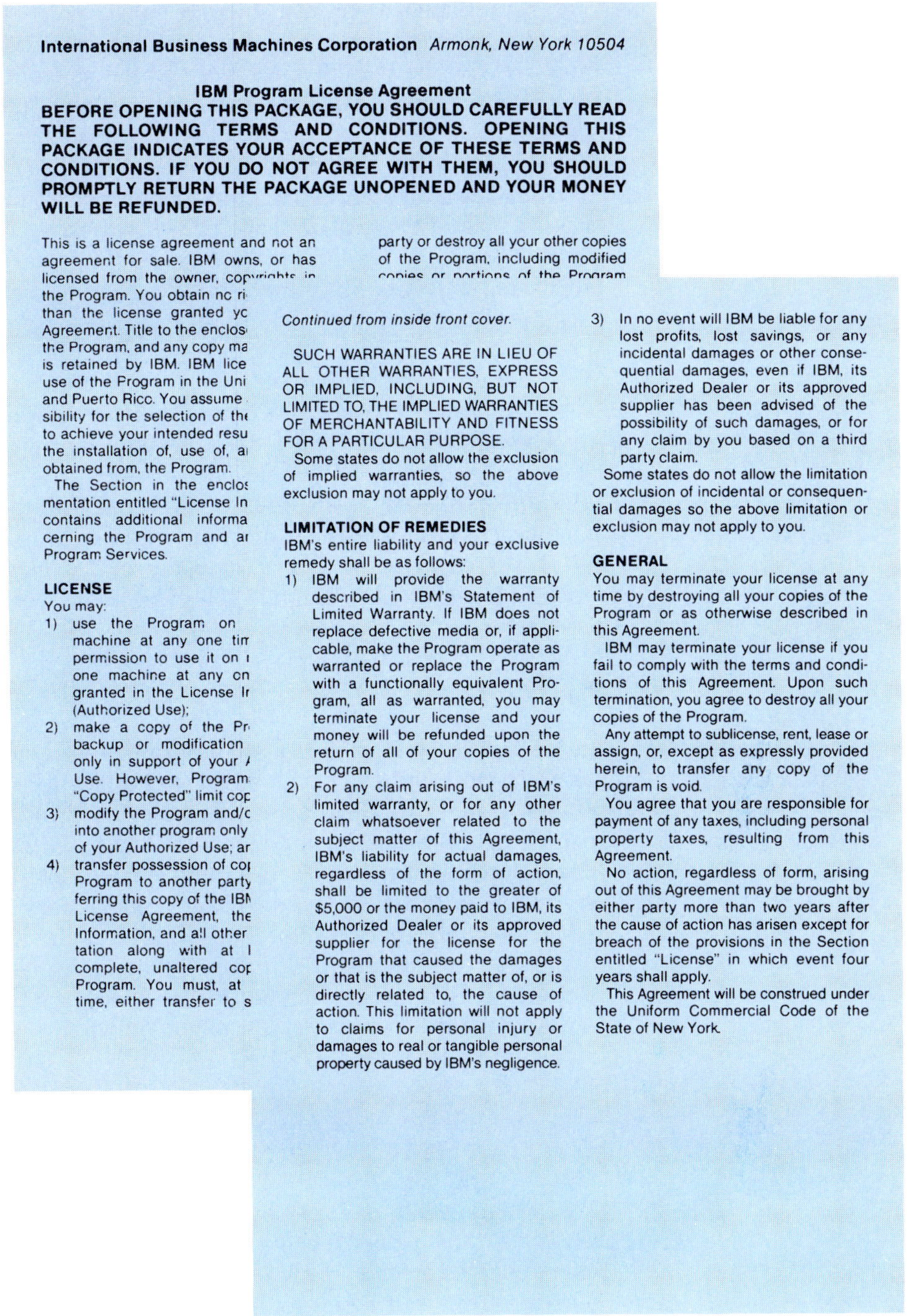
International Business Machines Corporation *Armonk, New York 10504*

IBM Program License Agreement

BEFORE OPENING THIS PACKAGE, YOU SHOULD CAREFULLY READ THE FOLLOWING TERMS AND CONDITIONS. OPENING THIS PACKAGE INDICATES YOUR ACCEPTANCE OF THESE TERMS AND CONDITIONS. IF YOU DO NOT AGREE WITH THEM, YOU SHOULD PROMPTLY RETURN THE PACKAGE UNOPENED AND YOUR MONEY WILL BE REFUNDED.

This is a license agreement and not an agreement for sale. IBM owns, or has licensed from the owner, cop[...] in the Program. You obtain nc ri[...] than the license granted yc[...] Agreement. Title to the enclos[...] the Program, and any copy ma[...] is retained by IBM. IBM lice[...] use of the Program in the Uni[...] and Puerto Rico. You assume [...] sibility for the selection of th[...] to achieve your intended resu[...] the installation of, use of, a[...] obtained from, the Program.

The Section in the enclos[...] mentation entitled "License In[...] contains additional informa[...] cerning the Program and a[...] Program Services.

LICENSE

You may:

1) use the Program on [...] machine at any one tir[...] permission to use it on [...] one machine at any on[...] granted in the License Ir[...] (Authorized Use);
2) make a copy of the Pr[...] backup or modification [...] only in support of your [...] Use. However, Program[...] "Copy Protected" limit cop[...]
3) modify the Program and/c[...] into another program only [...] of your Authorized Use; ar[...]
4) transfer possession of co[...] Program to another party [...] ferring this copy of the IB[...] License Agreement, the [...] Information, and all other [...] tation along with at l[...] complete, unaltered cop[...] Program. You must, at [...] time, either transfer to s[...]

party or destroy all your other copies of the Program, including modified copies or portions of the Program [...]

Continued from inside front cover.

SUCH WARRANTIES ARE IN LIEU OF ALL OTHER WARRANTIES, EXPRESS OR IMPLIED, INCLUDING, BUT NOT LIMITED TO, THE IMPLIED WARRANTIES OF MERCHANTABILITY AND FITNESS FOR A PARTICULAR PURPOSE.

Some states do not allow the exclusion of implied warranties, so the above exclusion may not apply to you.

LIMITATION OF REMEDIES

IBM's entire liability and your exclusive remedy shall be as follows:

1) IBM will provide the warranty described in IBM's Statement of Limited Warranty. If IBM does not replace defective media or, if applicable, make the Program operate as warranted or replace the Program with a functionally equivalent Program, all as warranted, you may terminate your license and your money will be refunded upon the return of all of your copies of the Program.
2) For any claim arising out of IBM's limited warranty, or for any other claim whatsoever related to the subject matter of this Agreement, IBM's liability for actual damages, regardless of the form of action, shall be limited to the greater of $5,000 or the money paid to IBM, its Authorized Dealer or its approved supplier for the license for the Program that caused the damages or that is the subject matter of, or is directly related to, the cause of action. This limitation will not apply to claims for personal injury or damages to real or tangible personal property caused by IBM's negligence.
3) In no event will IBM be liable for any lost profits, lost savings, or any incidental damages or other consequential damages, even if IBM, its Authorized Dealer or its approved supplier has been advised of the possibility of such damages, or for any claim by you based on a third party claim.

Some states do not allow the limitation or exclusion of incidental or consequential damages so the above limitation or exclusion may not apply to you.

GENERAL

You may terminate your license at any time by destroying all your copies of the Program or as otherwise described in this Agreement.

IBM may terminate your license if you fail to comply with the terms and conditions of this Agreement. Upon such termination, you agree to destroy all your copies of the Program.

Any attempt to sublicense, rent, lease or assign, or, except as expressly provided herein, to transfer any copy of the Program is void.

You agree that you are responsible for payment of any taxes, including personal property taxes, resulting from this Agreement.

No action, regardless of form, arising out of this Agreement may be brought by either party more than two years after the cause of action has arisen except for breach of the provisions in the Section entitled "License" in which event four years shall apply.

This Agreement will be construed under the Uniform Commercial Code of the State of New York.

Figure 19 Software License
IBM, like many software publishers, claim to license, rather than sell their programs. Here is the software license agreement that comes with IBM DOS 4.0.

national Business Machines Corporation and 1-2-3 is a trademark of Lotus Development Corporation. To claim a trademark, a company must first make sure no one else is already using it. Then the trademark can be registered with the U.S. Office of Patents and Trademarks. Despite the registration of trademarks, some companies try to exploit the fame of others to sell their products. Even unintentionally using a symbol or name similar to a registered trademark can be cause for litigation. For example, IBM's nickname, Big Blue, is also a registered trademark of the company. SoftDisk Publishing, a 90-employee company in Shreveport, Louisiana, produces a software subscription service called Big Blue Disk. Big Blue Products Incorporated is a small computer reseller in Northport, New York. In 1989 both companies received letters from IBM attorneys demanding they stop using the Big Blue name. At the time this book was published, both companies have refused, but IBM could cause them considerable grief if it decides to wield its wealth and legal might.

A **patent** is an exclusive right to produce or sell an invention for a given time. It is the broadest type of protection but also the most costly and difficult to obtain. Until 1981, the U.S. Office of Patents and Trademarks did not allow patents on computer software. Since then, patents have been allowed for some programming techniques and aspects of user interfaces. For example, in 1988 Xerox was granted a series of patents on the design of certain icons used in screen displays. The patents protect the ornamental design of distinctive Xerox screen symbols such as the wastebasket and floppy disk drive icons. With the patents, Xerox hopes to have "a new form of protection for the look and feel of computer software," according to Daniel Kluth, a patent attorney with Merchant & Gould, a Minneapolis law firm. Xerox is recognized as the company that pioneered graphical user interfaces, now commonly used in the Apple Macintosh, Microsoft Windows, and workstations such as Steve Jobs' NeXT computer. Patents could strengthen Xerox's campaign to collect licensing fees for its graphical user-interface technology.

Ethics

In view of these legal issues, some professional societies and individual companies have sought to develop codes of ethics for those who work with computers. Besides carefully screening potential computer personnel, some companies feel they must educate their employees in the proper use of computers. Professional computing societies, such as the Association for Computing Machinery (ACM) and the Data Processing Management Association (DPMA), have established guidelines of ethical behavior for their own members (see Figure 20). Basically, these guidelines include prohibitions against falsifying data, using company-owned computers for outside activities, gaining unauthorized access to sensitive computer records, illegally copying software or documentation, and divulging trade secrets.

Computers and Privacy

U.S. citizens value their personal privacy and believe they have the right to be left alone. Most people feel that the government and other organizations should not be allowed access to personal data for unauthorized use. Unfortunately, computers can make it easier for snoops to collect, store, and extract all kinds of information about our lives. About 85 federal data bases hold more than 288 million records on at least 114 million people. The FBI's National Crime Information Center maintains more than 10 million criminal history records, which are available to state and local police departments. Who knows how many records are kept and distributed by state and local governments? Around forty states sell the information they collect for driver's licenses and motor vehicle registration to direct-mail firms. This information includes a person's age, sex, Social Security number, and possibly, income range.

Credit corporations, insurance companies, banks, schools, hospitals, utilities, supermarkets, video-rental stores, and other organizations undoubtedly keep

Figure 20 **Computer Ethics**
The Data Processing Management Association (DPMA), the largest society in the field of computer management, has established this code of ethics for its members. (Reprint permission granted. Data Processing Management Association. 1988. All rights reserved.)

Code of Ethics

I acknowledge:

That I have an obligation to management, therefore, I shall promote the understanding of information processing methods and procedures to management using every resource at my command.

That I have an obligation to my fellow members, therefore, I shall uphold the high ideals of DPMA as outlined in its Association Bylaws. Further, I shall cooperate with my fellow members and shall treat them with honesty and respect at all times.

That I have an obligation to society and will participate to the best of my ability in the dissemination of knowledge pertaining to the general development and understanding of information processing. Further, I shall not use knowledge of a confidential nature to further my personal interest, nor shall I violate the privacy and confidentiality of information entrusted to me or to which I may gain access.

That I have an obligation to my employer whose trust I hold, therefore, I shall endeavor to discharge this obligation to the best of my ability, to guard my employer's interests, and to advise him or her wisely and honestly.

That I have an obligation to my country, therefore, in my personal, business and social contacts, I shall uphold my nation and shall honor the chosen way of life of my fellow citizens.

I accept these obligations as a personal responsibility and as a member of this Association. I shall actively discharge these obligations and I dedicate myself to that end.

even more computer files about us than all government agencies combined. For example, the top five credit-rating companies alone have records on more than 150 million people. The information kept in these computer files, if brought together, could paint a surprisingly detailed picture of a person's life. Most individuals have no idea how much personal data has been collected about them, where this information is kept, and who has access to it. No wonder a 1984 Harris Poll found 75 percent of respondents "very" or "somewhat" concerned about their privacy being violated.

Matching

Computers are amazingly efficient at storing, cross-referencing, and retrieving huge quantities of data. These abilities have been put to use by our government and private firms in a practice known as computer matching. Started in the late 1970s as part of an effort to curb welfare fraud, **computer matching** involves comparing records in various data bases to identify individuals who meet overlapping sets of criteria. Some fifteen federal agencies mix and match information from different data bases (see Figure 21). For example, the Veterans Administration uses computer matching to prevent federal employees from receiving excess benefits. The Selective Service System cross-checks draft registrations with Social Security and motor vehicle records to find young men who have not registered. The Education Department uses computer matching to identify federal employees who are delinquent on their student loans. According to the Office of Technology Assessment, more than 2 billion separate records were exchanged in federal computer matching procedures during the period from 1980 to 1984. Every presidential administration since Carter's has sought to expand the use of computer matching to reduce fraud, cheating, and crime.

The U.S. Internal Revenue Service is perhaps the most energetic computer-matching agency. In 1986 the IRS created its debtor master file, which is used to withhold tax refunds from citizens who have defaulted on federal loans. The debtor master file lists more than 750,000 individuals who owe money to the

***Figure 21* Computer Matching**
Many federal agencies use computer matching to track down citizens who cheat, commit fraud, or break the law.

Education Department, the Housing and Urban Development Department, the Veterans Administration, or the Small Business Administration. The IRS even briefly tried buying mailing lists to determine if the spending habits of certain individuals were consistent with their reported income. Although this experiment was discontinued, the IRS continues to expand its use of computer matching. The agency claims that, thanks to such practices, in 1985 alone it recovered $2.5 billion in taxes that otherwise would have been uncollected.

Some analysts fear that the United States is moving toward a national data base with the omnipresent Social Security number as the key. Social Security numbers are already available to at least 125 government and private agencies. Without regulation, many people think that privacy could become even more threatened as technology advances. Fortunately, lawmakers are taking notice. A bill introduced by U.S. Senator William S. Cohen in 1987 would set up official boards to oversee computer matching of federal data bases. The bill is similar to laws regulating the use of government data bases already in effect in European countries such as Sweden, West Germany, and France.

Legal Protection

The U.S. Bill of Rights does not explicitly grant citizens the right to privacy (see Figure 22). This right, however, seems to be implied by several constitutional amendments, most notably the fourth amendment, which states that the "right of the people to be secure in their persons, houses, papers, and effects, against unreasonable searches and seizures, shall not be violated." Since the 1970s, both the federal and state governments have tried to protect the privacy rights of their citizens in the computer age. More than 150 state laws have been passed controlling invasions of privacy. At the federal level, legal protection against invasions of privacy include several important acts of Congress:

- **The Fair Credit Reporting Act of 1970.** This act guarantees citizens the right to inspect and challenge the accuracy of their credit records.
- **The Freedom of Information Act of 1970.** This act guarantees citizens the right to inspect all personal data about them kept by any agency of the federal government unless it would threaten national security or violate another citizen's privacy.

Figure 22 Bill of Rights
The right to privacy is merely implied by the U.S. Constitution in the Bill of Rights, so several acts of Congress and many state laws have been passed to specifically guard citizens' privacy in the computer age.

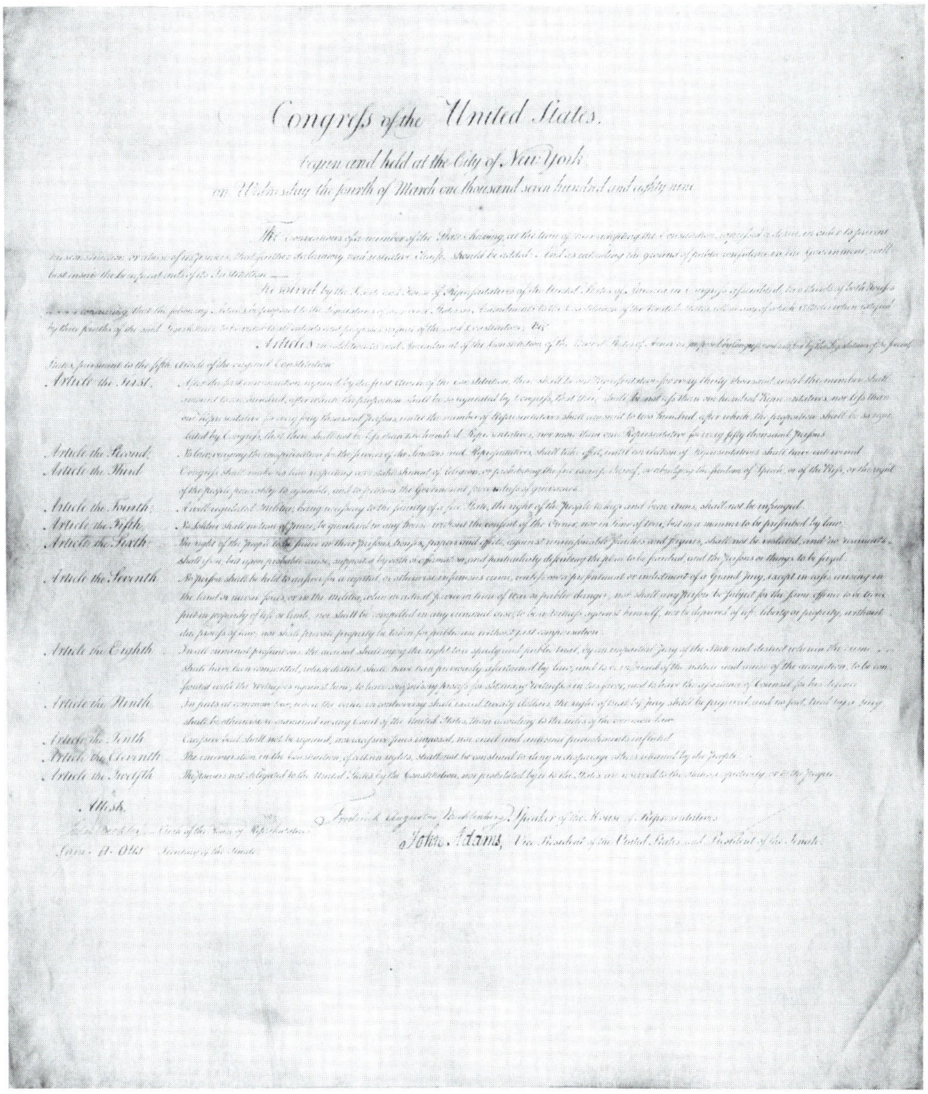

- **The Crime Control Act of 1973.** This act requires federal law enforcement agencies such as the FBI to distribute complete arrest histories, including whether prosecution and conviction followed an arrest, and it allows citizens to inspect and challenge the accuracy of their records.
- **The Education Privacy Act of 1974.** This act guarantees students in federally funded schools the right to keep their academic and behavioral records private, and it allows them to inspect and challenge the accuracy of their records.
- **The Privacy Act of 1974.** This act allows the federal government to collect only "relevant and necessary" information from citizens, who must be informed why the information is needed and how it will be used. Collected information

cannot be used for any but the stated purpose without permission from the citizen. Citizens also have the right to inspect and challenge the accuracy of their records.

- **The Right to Financial Privacy Act of 1978.** This act guarantees citizens the right to inspect and challenge the information about them kept by financial institutions, restricts federal access to these records, and forbids federal agencies from sharing the information they have except for valid law-enforcement purposes.

Security

Organizations can help ensure privacy and reduce computer crime by taking a number of security precautions. Physical access to computers can be controlled by locating them in locked rooms. More elaborate physical access controls may include "smart" identification cards with embedded microchips, combination locks, and video surveillance of computer installations. The most expensive high-tech security systems now use fingerprint matching, retina scanning (see Figure 23), or voice-pattern analysis to restrict access to authorized users. Some computers are equipped with key locks to prevent use by unauthorized personnel.

Access to computer networks, operating systems, application software, data bases, and even individual files can be controlled with log-on or password schemes. Only authorized users are granted the account numbers and passwords that let them use the system. In addition, some computer systems automatically keep access logs that record who has used the system, when they logged on, what they did on the system, and when they logged off. Access logs can help track down unauthorized or criminal use of sensitive computer data.

Another way to protect sensitive data is to use **encryption,** which scrambles information so that it cannot be read without the proper key. The Data Encryption Standard (DES) is a sophisticated method of information protection developed by IBM and adopted by the National Bureau of Standards (NBS) in 1977. The DES was also adopted by the American National Standards Institute (ANSI) in 1980. The National Security Agency has found the DES method of scrambling

Figure 23 Computer Security
One way to prevent violations of privacy and computer crime is to control physical access to computers with locks or sophisticated identification measures, such as this retinal scan entry system.

data to be free from any statistical or mathematical weaknesses. The DES is used by most banks for electronic funds transfers and by most U.S. government agencies, except the military, which uses other encryption methods. To encrypt data with the DES, the user provides a key word, number, or sequence of characters that is seven bytes (56 bits) long. So, there are 2^{56} or 72,057,594,037,927,946 possible keys. A complex mathematical function applies the key to the input data to produce the encrypted output in a procedure that is impossible to work backwards. The only way to unscramble the data would be to try every possible key. Even with today's supercomputers, it would probably take hundreds of years and cost hundreds of millions of dollars to decode data encrypted with the DES. Many data base management packages, such as dBASE IV, and a few stand-alone utilities, such as Privacy Plus, from United Software Security, offer microcomputer users the ability to encrypt their sensitive data files.

Computers and the Future

What is the future of computing? Although it is impossible to predict the future with accuracy, past trends can lead to some educated guesses:

- The time it takes for new technology to be brought to market will continue to decrease.
- The number of computers purchased and put to use will increase.
- Computers will generally be less expensive and more powerful.
- Ergonomics and artificial intelligence techniques will be applied to many new hardware and software products.
- Some areas to watch in the future of computers are microprocessors, supercomputers, artificial intelligence, and neural networks.

Microprocessors

Today's computers will be steadily improved, just as yesterday's computers were. In microcomputers, many of these incremental advances have come from the improvement of microprocessors. For example, in the spring of 1989 both Intel and Motorola introduced their newest high-power microprocessors: the Intel 80486 and the Motorola 68040. The Intel 80486, a member of the same chip family as the 8088 used in the original IBM Personal Computer, is approximately two to four times faster than its closest relative, the 80386 chip. Containing the equivalent of 1,160,000 transistors, the 80486 chip is capable of executing 15 to 20 million instructions per second, yet it can still run all the software created for other members of the 8088 family (see Figure 24). The Motorola 68040 is the newest member of the 68000 microprocessor family, used by Apple in its Macintosh computers. Comparable in power and speed to the Intel 80486, the Motorola 68040 contains 1.2 million transistors. The 68040 can also run software created for its older relatives, the 68000 used in the Macintosh SE, the 68020 used in the Macintosh II, and the 68030 used in the Macintosh IIcx and Macintosh IIci.

Chips such as the Intel 80486 and Motorola 68040 are known as **complex instruction set computer (CISC)** microprocessors because they incorporate many relatively slow instructions especially designed for high-level languages. Intel, Motorola, and other companies have also developed powerful **reduced instruction set computer (RISC)** microprocessor chips, generally used in workstations that run the Unix operating system. RISC chips typically have around 100 simple instructions that execute very quickly. An example is the Intel 80860 RISC pro-

Figure 24 Advanced Microprocessor
Microprocessors, such as the Intel 80486, give today's microcomputers the power of yesterday's mainframes.

cessor introduced in February, 1989. Its engineers claim that the 80860 was designed to be a one-chip version of the Cray 1 supercomputer. In 1976 the Cray 1 sold for $13 million. The 80860 chip is expected to sell for $750 each in quantity and by 1992 the price of a complete 80860 workstation should be below $10,000. The 80860 is estimated to be about 13 times faster than the fastest 80386, the chip used in sophisticated microcomputers such as the IBM Personal System/2 Models 70 and 80. This RISC chip can perform 17 million real-number operations per second, and it includes hardware for three-dimensional graphics processing. The future of computing will be profoundly affected by such powerful and relatively inexpensive CISC and RISC microprocessors.

Supercomputers

Supercomputers are the fastest, most expensive calculating devices ever built. Although you are not likely to own one in the future, supercomputers will affect your life. At a cost of $5 million to $25 million each, the 300 or so supercomputers installed around the world today work at a wide range of tasks, from oil exploration to Hollywood movie making (see Figure 25). Thanks to supercomputer networks, such as the one operated by the National Center for Supercomputing Applications at the University of Illinois, many faculty members, researchers, and students can now access these lightning-fast machines using an ordinary microcomputer and a modem.

The military has always had an insatiable need for high-speed number crunchers for defense research and intelligence uses. Lawrence Livermore National Laboratory alone has eleven of the $20-million supercomputers. The private sector, however, also has realized the benefits of supercomputers. Every day some industry develops a new supercomputer application. Semiconductor manufacturers use supercomputers to cram more transistors onto silicon chips than was ever thought possible. Financial advisers use supercomputers to devise incredibly complex investment strategies. Engineers use them to design a wide range of new products, including cars, jet engines, sailboats, light bulbs, refrigerators, and artificial limbs. Biochemists develop new medicines with supercomputers. Research scientists and mathematicians use supercomputers to simulate structures never

Figure 25 ***Supercomputer Science***
Supercomputers are powerful tools that scientists and mathematicians use to simulate and display complex phenomena.

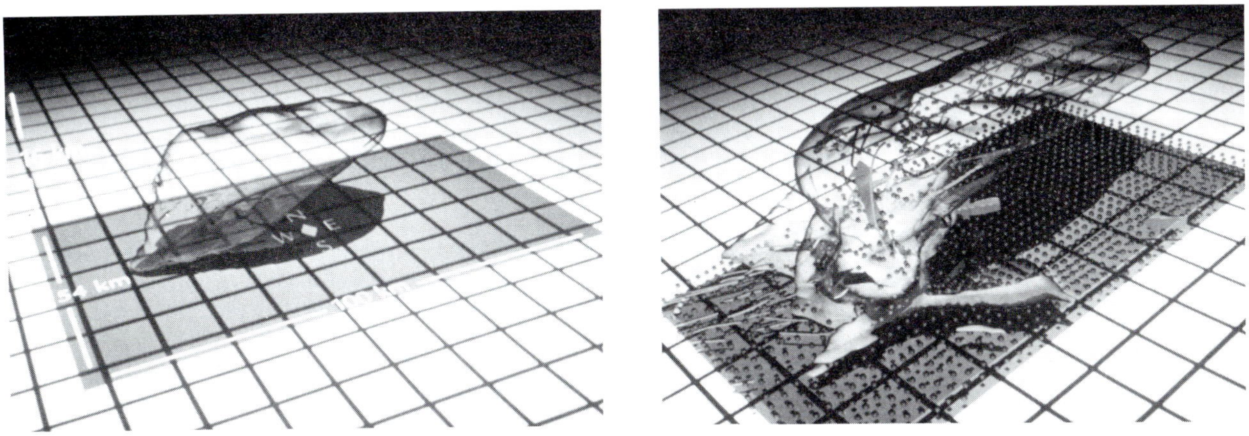

seen by human eyes. Yet as powerful and swift as today's supercomputers are, problems exist that will require a machine 100 times faster. Genetic engineers, particle physicists, robot manufacturers, space scientists, and others will need better supercomputers to make future breakthroughs. Many industry experts believe that supercomputers are essential for tomorrow's economic and technological development.

Artificial Intelligence

Computers, even supercomputers, perform only the tasks for which they have been programmed. For years, however, computer scientists have tried to create systems that mimic the decision-making powers of human beings. That is the elusive goal of artificial intelligence. Although computers still cannot approach the learning and reasoning abilities of a young child, artificial intelligence techniques have been successfully applied in a number of commercial expert systems. At American Express, for example, an expert system is used to approve unusual credit requests for the company's estimated 20 million U.S. cardholders. U.S. intelligence agents routinely consult a terrorism expert system in attempts to anticipate and foil terrorist attacks. Ford Motors has developed an expert system for diagnosing tricky engine problems that dealers can tap into from anywhere in the country. IBM's Diagnostic Expert Final Test (DEFT) system, which analyzes problems with mainframe disk drives, cost the company only $100,000 to develop, yet saves $12 million per year.

Herbert Schorr, who heads IBM's program to commercialize artificial intelligence, claims that we are now in the "second wave" of the information revolution. The first wave was the automation of data processing; the second wave is the automation of decision making. As a result, IBM is one of the world leaders in developing and using expert systems. But even as experts agree that artificial intelligence has improved productivity in many situations, second-wave systems still do not have common sense or awareness of the world outside their narrow

Real World

A Portrait of the Artist

What do Rembrandt, Michaelangelo, and Lillian Schwartz have in common?

They're all artists. Rembrandt, the great Dutch painter, was a master with the brush, the sculptor Michaelangelo with the chisel, and Lillian Schwartz with the log on. She is, in her words, "an artist who uses computers—never a computer artist."

Schwartz may not yet belong with such august company, but her medium—computer art—is rattling the art world. She believes the computer is as important a creative tool as Rembrandt's paint. She has even sold a silkscreen of computer art to the Museum of Modern Art in New York.

The ranks of artists using computers is growing. One artist created 144 red and blue neon fish and uses a computer to control the flashing lights. Others have produced intricate combinations of repetitive lines, or moving sculptures controlled by computers.

Schwartz believes too many artists don't take computer art seriously, even though some pieces command breath-taking prices. (The neon fish cost $50,000.)

Many artists and collectors do have legitimate questions about computer art. Is art that is made by a machine as creative as art conceived by the human mind and then executed by the human hand? Can something that relies so heavily on technology have long-term value? Is there a danger of relying too much on technology and not enough on creativity?

Of course, these questions all border on the philosophical. There are more realistic issues, however. Collectors are worried that after they've spent $2000 for an original computer-generated drawing, it can be reproduced over and over again because it is stored on a disk. And what about the artist who creates a program that "teaches" a computer to draw? After the artist dies, anyone who knows how to operate the computer can produce original art by a dead artist.

Source: Ronald Rosenberg, "Computer as Palette Art Gets Help From Electronics," *The Boston Globe,* July 1, 1989, pp. 21–22.

field of expertise. Nevertheless, computer scientists at Xerox's Palo Alto Research Center and other institutions are planning decision-making systems that will work more like human experts. Will computers ever be developed that are truly intelligent in the human sense? Probably not for the next few centuries. In the meantime, the primitive expert systems we do have are saving U.S. companies millions of dollars.

Neural Networks

An offshoot of artificial intelligence research that might have capabilities beyond expert systems is the field of neural networks. A **neural network** is a type of computer or software simulation loosely modeled after the interconnection of neurons, or nerve cells, in the human brain. Although traditional computers can calculate and perform repetitive data processing much faster than humans, they fail at tasks a child can do, such as recognizing faces and learning to talk and read. Neural networks bypass the necessity of programming the computer to handle every variable in these types of pattern-recognition tasks. Like people, neural networks seem to learn by doing.

For example, a neural network simulation called NetTalk, developed at Johns Hopkins University, can read input text and learn how to pronounce words. Within a week NetTalk developed a 20,000-word vocabulary after being trained with only 1,000 words. NetTalk has 300 processing units that simulate neurons and more than 10,000 connections arranged in three layers. Input letters evoke random outputs. When NetTalk reads the letter *N*, for instance, it might pronounce "ah." Correct responses strengthen the internal connections that formed them and incorrect responses weaken the connections. Eventually, NetTalk learns to pronounce words correctly. The system can generalize its experience to pronounce words it has never encountered before.

Interest in neural networks has been growing rapidly. In the military, neural networks could mean target-recognition systems, self-navigating tanks, and smart missiles that hunt down their targets. In the business world, neural networks could mean computers that can read handwriting, recognize speech, and identify faces. In industry, neural networks could mean better automated vision systems and robotic manufacturing. Neural network research, however, is still in its infancy. According to a study by the Defense Advanced Research Projects Agency (DARPA), neural networks are far from achieving the connectivity of the human brain, which has billions of neurons, each connected to thousands of others. But DARPA projects that by 1994, neural networks could achieve the complexity of a bee's nervous system. Compared to today's computers, bees are pretty smart. After all, they can evade predators, choose routes, and find flowers.

Summary

- *How computers are used in education.* Computer-assisted instruction programs teach students at their own pace, while computer-managed instruction programs help with school administration tasks.
- *The impact of computers on the arts.* Computers are used to compose, play, and record songs. Computer graphics let artists create stunning visual images. Computers also are used to edit movies, produce special effects, and create animation.
- *The uses of computers in medicine.* Computers help train doctors, diagnose illness, and take pictures inside the human body.
- *How computers are changing the way government operates.* The Internal Revenue Service uses computers to collect taxes and the Department of Defense uses them to manage its huge bureaucracy and control its high-tech weapon systems.
- *How computers are used in industry.* Computer-aided design, computer-aided engineering, computer-aided manufacturing, management information systems, and decision support systems help companies increase productivity, enhance quality, and compete more effectively.
- *The issue of using computers in the workplace.* Computers have eliminated many blue-collar jobs and sometimes are used to monitor workers' performance. Health concerns such as radiation, stress, and physical discomforts have been raised, but ergonomics and telecommuting are helping people fit computers more comfortably into their lifestyles.
- *The legal problems concerning computers.* Hackers and computer viruses sometimes can cause serious problems by disrupting computer systems. White-collar criminals use computers to steal vast amounts of money. Software pirates cheat software publishers, who seek to protect their intellectual property with copyrights, licenses, trademarks, and patents. Some professional societies have developed codes of ethics for computer workers.

- *How computers affect our privacy.* Government agencies and private companies are increasing their use of computer matching to identify certain individuals, prompting many federal and local laws ensuring citizens' privacy rights and the security measures taken to safeguard sensitive data.
- *The computer advances to come.* More powerful microprocessors, faster supercomputers, artificial intelligence techniques, and neural networks will profoundly affect the future of computing.

Key Terms

As an extra review of this chapter, try defining the following terms.

complex instruction set computer (CISC)
computer-aided engineering (CAE)
computer-aided manufacturing (CAM)
computer-assisted instruction (CAI)
computer-managed instruction (CMI)
computer matching
computer virus
computerized axial tomography (CAT or CT)
decision support system (DSS)
encryption
ergonomics
hacker
magnetic resonance imaging (MRI)
management information system (MIS)
neural network
patent
positron emission tomography (PET)
reduced instruction set computer (RISC)
site license
software licensing
software piracy
trademark
ultrasound scanner

Review Questions

1. What are two advantages of computer-assisted instruction?
2. What type of computer system helps with school administrative tasks?
3. What communications standard is often used to connect electronic musical instruments to microcomputers?
4. List three uses of computers in movie making.
5. What type of software is CADUCEUS?
6. List four types of medical imaging systems.
7. List two major computer users in the U.S. government.
8. What type of system allows engineers to simulate and test their designs without building a prototype?
9. What type of system uses computers to control the machines that make or assemble products?
10. What type of system provides managers with the reports needed to run their organizations?
11. What type of system helps managers solve unstructured problems with little or no precedent?
12. From the worker's standpoint, what is a disadvantage of computer monitoring?
13. What are three major categories of health concerns associated with computer use?

14. What is the science of designing objects so that they can be most easily, effectively, comfortably, and safely used by people?
15. List three disadvantages of telecommuting.
16. What type of program secretly copies itself from disk to disk and across networks?
17. What is the most lucrative type of computer crime?
18. List four legal means of protecting intellectual property.
19. List three acts of Congress that protect citizens' privacy rights.
20. What method of protecting sensitive data, endorsed by the National Bureau of Standards and the American National Standards Institute, is used by most banks and U.S. government agencies (except the military)?

Multiple Choice

1. Helping students learn at their own pace with immediate feedback is the goal of
   (a) computer-managed instruction (CMI).
   (b) computer-assisted instruction (CAI).
   (c) the Musical Instrument Digital Interface (MIDI).
   (d) computer-assisted engineering (CAE).
2. What imaging method produces high-quality cross-sectional pictures of the body without X-rays or other radiation?
   (a) computerized axial tomography (CAT or CT)
   (b) positron emission tomography (PET)
   (c) optical character recognition (OCR)
   (d) magnetic resonance imaging (MRI)
3. The application of computer graphics to the drafting of parts, mechanisms, or buildings is called
   (a) computer-aided design (CAD).
   (b) computer-aided engineering (CAE).
   (c) computer-aided manufacturing (CAM).
   (d) computer-aided instruction (CAI).
4. According to several exhaustive scientific studies, which of the following is NOT considered a risk of using computers?
   (a) radiation (b) stress
   (c) eyestrain (d) headache
5. Which of the following concepts is NOT part of the hacker ethic?
   (a) sharing (b) openness
   (c) copy protection (d) decentralization
6. Which of the following is NOT an effective precaution against computer viruses?
   (a) copying all software onto your own disks
   (b) using software from only well-known sources
   (c) booting up from only your own system disk
   (d) using antiviral software such as Vaccine

7. Which of the following is NOT an example of software piracy?
   (a) copying a commercial program from a friend
   (b) copying a commercial program to sell to others
   (c) copying a commercial program for backup purposes
   (d) copying a rented commercial program
8. Which type of intellectual property protection is the broadest, but also the most costly and difficult to obtain?
   (a) copyright (b) license
   (c) trademark (d) patent
9. Comparing records in various data bases to identify individuals who meet overlapping sets of criteria is known as
   (a) computer matching. (b) data encryption.
   (c) credit reporting. (d) decision support.
10. Which act of Congress guarantees citizens the right to inspect all personal data about them kept by any agency of the federal government unless it would threaten national security or violate someone else's privacy?
    (a) The Fair Credit Reporting Act of 1970 (b) The Freedom of Information Act of 1970
    (c) The Crime Control Act of 1973 (d) The Privacy Act of 1974
11. Unauthorized or criminal use of sensitive computer data can be tracked down with the help of
    (a) voice-pattern analysis. (b) access logs.
    (c) passwords. (d) neural networks.
12. Which of the following terms describes a method of protecting sensitive information by scrambling it so that it cannot be read without first supplying the proper key?
    (a) encryption (b) password
    (c) log-on (d) retina scanning
13. What type of microprocessor typically has about 100 simple instructions that execute very rapidly?
    (a) complex instruction set computer (CISC) (b) reduced instruction set computer (RISC)
    (c) Intel 8088 (d) Motorola 68000
14. What are currently the most useful and money-saving products of artificial intelligence research?
    (a) computer-assisted instruction software (b) computer-managed instruction software
    (c) expert systems (d) neural networks
15. What type of computer or software, modeled after the human brain, can learn from experience?
    (a) positron emission tomography (b) management information system
    (c) decision support system (d) neural network

Projects

1. Prepare a report about the computer-assisted instruction (CAI) lessons used at your school. If your school has none, research a local college or university that uses CAI. Try to find out what subjects are taught, how many students take CAI lessons, how students like the CAI lessons, and who developed them.
2. Make a list of organizations that you think use a computer to keep personal records about you. Include government agencies, schools, banks, utilities, stores, libraries, and any other parties you can come up with.
3. Further investigate a specific computer virus incident or white-collar crime. Prepare a report that explains why it was done, who did it, and what the outcome was.
4. Are neural networks being used in any commercially available products? Prepare a report that investigates the current, nonresearch uses of neural networks.

APPENDIX A

DATA REPRESENTATION

The CPU in a microcomputer system deals only with the zeros and ones of the binary system, which correspond to the off and on states of an electronic switch. People, however, find data more readable when it is presented as **alphanumeric characters** (letters, numbers, and punctuation marks). This difference raises the problem of how to get from the alphanumeric representations that are convenient for people to the binary zeros and ones that are necessary for computers.

Various number systems and coding schemes have been employed to address this problem. Let's examine the most common ones in use today.

Binary Numbers

The number system we are most familiar with, the decimal system, uses 10 symbols (the digits 0 through 9) to represent numerical quantities; single digits represent quantities smaller than 10, and groups of two or more digits represent quantities larger than 9. A digit's position in a numeral and its value contribute to the overall value of the numeral. Since each position stands for a certain power of 10, the decimal system is said to have a *base* of 10.

The binary system, with a base of 2, uses the symbols 0 and 1 to represent values less than 2, in the same way that the decimal system uses 0 through 9 for values less than 10. Quantities larger than 1 are represented by groups of zeros and ones. The digit positions in these groups represent successive powers of 2, rather than powers of 10. For example, in the decimal system the number 57 is a shorthand expression meaning:

5 7

7 → $(7 \times 10^0) = 7 \times 1 = 7$

5 → $(5 \times 10^1) = 5 \times 10 = 50+$

57

In the binary system, the decimal number 57 is expressed as 111001:

$$1 \quad 1 \quad 1 \quad 0 \quad 0 \quad 1$$

$$(1 \times 2^0) = 1 \times 1 = 1$$
$$(0 \times 2^1) = 0 \times 2 = 0$$
$$(0 \times 2^2) = 0 \times 4 = 0$$
$$(1 \times 2^3) = 1 \times 8 = 8$$
$$(1 \times 2^4) = 1 \times 16 = 16$$
$$(1 \times 2^5) = 1 \times 32 = \underline{32+}$$
$$57$$

Table 1 lists the decimal values of the powers of 2. People who work intimately with computers, such as assembly language programmers, soon become as familiar with these as with the powers of 10. Note that a 10-digit decimal number can represent any of 10 billion values (from 0,000,000,000 through 9,999,999,999), while a 10-digit binary number can represent only 1024 different values (0000000000 through 1111111111). It may clarify this to note that 9,999,999,999 is 1 less than 10,000,000,000 and similarly, 1111111111 is 1 less than 10000000000 (which is 2^{10}, or 1024). It is customary, by the way, not to use commas or spaces when writing binary numbers. Binary numbers can represent fractions and mixed numbers as well as whole numbers (integers). For example, let's examine the decimal number 43.75. Its whole number or integer part is 43; the period is called the decimal

***Table 1* Powers of 2**

Just as the decimal number system uses successive powers of 10 (that is, 1, 10, 100, 1000, ...), the binary number system uses successive powers of 2. Some of these powers and their decimal equivalents are listed here.

2^0 =	1	2^9 =	512
2^1 =	2	2^{10} =	1024
2^2 =	4	2^{11} =	2048
2^3 =	8	2^{12} =	4096
2^4 =	16	2^{13} =	8192
2^5 =	32	2^{14} =	16,384
2^6 =	64	2^{15} =	32,768
2^7 =	128	2^{16} =	64,536
2^8 =	256		

point; its fractional part is 75. Here is how 43.75 breaks down in the decimal system:

$$4\ 3\ .\ 7\ 5$$

$$(5 \times 10^{-2}) = 5 \times \frac{1}{100} = 0.05$$
$$(7 \times 10^{-1}) = 7 \times \frac{1}{10} = 0.70$$
$$(3 \times 10^{0}) = 3 \times 1 = 3.00$$
$$(4 \times 10^{2}) = 4 \times 10 = \underline{40.00+}$$
$$43.75$$

This shows how 43.75 breaks down in the binary system:

$$1\ 0\ 1\ 0\ 1\ 1\ .\ 1\ 1$$

$$(1 \times 2^{-2}) = 1 \times \frac{1}{4} = 0.25$$
$$(1 \times 2^{-1}) = 1 \times \frac{1}{2} = 0.50$$
$$(1 \times 2^{0}) = 1 \times 1 = 1.00$$
$$(1 \times 2^{1}) = 1 \times 2 = 2.00$$
$$(0 \times 2^{2}) = 0 \times 4 = 0.00$$
$$(1 \times 2^{3}) = 1 \times 8 = 8.00$$
$$(0 \times 2^{4}) = 0 \times 16 = 0.00$$
$$(1 \times 2^{5}) = 1 \times 32 = \underline{32.00+}$$
$$43.75$$

In the second case, the period is called the **binary point** (instead of the decimal point). The binary digits to the left of it represent positive powers of 2, and the binary digits to the right of it represent negative powers of 2.

Fixed-Point and Floating-Point Numbers

Computers can handle two main types of numbers: fixed-point numbers and floating-point numbers. A **fixed-point number** is one whose point (decimal or binary) is in a fixed place in relation to the digits. For example, both integers and fractions can be represented as fixed-point numbers. For integers, the point is fixed at the extreme right; for fractions, the point is fixed at the extreme left.

Since the point position is fixed and predefined, it does not have to be stored in memory with the value. A **floating-point number,** also called a **real number,** is one in which the position of the point can vary from number to number. Floating-point numbers can be used to represent quantities that contain both an integer part and a fractional part. You may already be familiar with this concept, which is similar to *scientific notation*. One number is used for the fractional part, called the *mantissa,* and another number is used for the power of the base, or the *exponent*. For example, the number 43.75, which can't be stored as a fixed-point number because it has both an integer part and a fractional part, can be stored as a floating-point number like this:

Mantissa	*Exponent*
4375	2
↑ Decimal point is assumed to be here.	

The decimal point in the mantissa is assumed to be at the extreme left, and thus is not explicitly stored. The exponent indicates that the mantissa (.4375) is to be multiplied by 10^2 to get the actual value ($.4375 \times 10^2 = 43.75$). Most of the time, it is best to have the mantissa shifted all the way to the left, that is, to have a mantissa with no leading zeros. A floating-point number stored in this way is said to be *normalized*.

Fixed-point binary numbers can express either integers or fractions. The binary point is assumed to be at the extreme right in the case of an integer, and at the extreme left in the case of a fraction. Here is the decimal number 43.75 expressed as a fixed-point binary integer and fixed-point binary fraction:

Fixed-point integer 43	*Fixed-point fraction 0.75*
00101011	11000000
↑ Binary point is assumed to be here. (right end)	↑ Binary point is assumed to be here. (left end)

Here is the floating-point number 43.75 (101011.11 in binary) expressed as a mantissa and exponent:

Mantissa	*Exponent*
10101111	00000110
↑ Binary point is assumed to be here.	Integer value only.

Octal and Hexadecimal Numbers

You've probably realized from the few examples given here how unsuited people are to the routine handling of binary numbers. Their length (six digits to represent the decimal value 43) and their monotony (nothing but zeros and ones)

Table 2 Powers of 8 and 16

Octal numbers are based on successive powers of 8. Hexadecimal numbers are based on successive powers of 16.

Powers of 8	Powers of 16
$8^0 = 1$	$16^0 = 1$
$8^1 = 8$	$16^1 = 16$
$8^2 = 64$	$16^2 = 256$
$8^3 = 512$	$16^3 = 4096$
$8^4 = 4096$	$16^4 = 65,536$
$8^5 = 32,768$	$16^5 = 1,048,576$

make dealing with them tedious and error-prone for humans. Two compromises between binary and decimal—the **octal system** (base 8) and the **hexadecimal system** (base 16)—are often used by programmers and other users who work with low-level details of a computer (see Table 2).

The octal system uses eight symbols: 0, 1, 2, 3, 4, 5, 6, and 7. Since 2^3 is equal to 8, the octal system is a convenient shorthand for binary; each octal digit is equivalent to three binary digits. This is illustrated more graphically in the following diagram, which shows how each digit of an octal number can stand for three binary digits:

$7\ 2\ 5\ 0_{(\text{base } 8)}$

$$(0 \times 8^0) = 0 \times 0 = 0$$
$$(5 \times 8^1) = 5 \times 8 = 40$$
$$(2 \times 8^2) = 2 \times 64 = 128$$
$$(7 \times 8^3) = 7 \times 512 = 3584 +$$
$$3752_{(\text{base } 10)}$$

111	010	101	000	← Base 2
7	2	5	0	← Base 8

The hexadecimal number system uses 16 symbols, which are listed in Table 3 with their decimal system equivalents. Although using letters as numbers might seem strange, it is necessary in order to have a single character to represent each value from 10 to 15. Since each hexadecimal digit is equivalent to four binary

Table 3 Hexadecimal Digits
Because it must represent values from 10 through 15 with single characters, the hexadecimal number system uses six letters as "digits."

Base 16	Base 10	Base 16	Base 10
0	0	A	10
1	1	B	11
2	2	C	12
3	3	D	13
4	4	E	14
5	5	F	15
6	6		
7	7		
8	8		
9	9		

digits (2^4 is equal to 16), the hexadecimal system is also a shorthand way to express binary numbers, as illustrated here:

$\text{E A } 8_{\text{(base 16)}}$

$(8 \times 16^0) = 8 \times 1 = 8$

$(10 \times 16^1) = 10 \times 16 = 160$

$(14 \times 16^2) = 14 \times 256 = 3584 +$

$3752_{\text{(base 10)}}$

1110	1010	1000 ←	Base 2
E	A	8 ←	Base 16

The ASCII Coding System

Generally, computers use the binary number system to store and manipulate numeric data. In order to store and represent text in a computer, some scheme must be employed to convert letters, punctuation marks, and special characters to binary numbers. In fact, one way to think of octal numbers is as a set of 3-bit codes that represent the characters 0 through 7. Similarly, the hexadecimal system can be thought of as a 4-bit system for representing the characters 0 through 9 and A through F. These codes can only represent decimal and binary values, however. To represent more than 16 characters, some scheme is required that uses codes of more than 4 bits. Various coding systems have been developed over the years using 6-bit, 7-bit, and 8-bit codes. Of these, the ASCII system is by far the most common.

Table 4 Standard ASCII Codes

Char	Dec	Hex	Binary	Char	Dec	Hex	Binary	Char	Dec	Hex	Binary
NUL	0	00	00000000	+	43	2B	00101011	V	86	56	01010110
SOH	1	01	00000001	,	44	2C	00101100	W	87	57	01010111
STX	2	02	00000010	-	45	2D	00101101	X	88	58	01011000
ETX	3	03	00000011	.	46	2E	00101110	Y	89	59	01011001
EOT	4	04	00000100	/	47	2F	00101111	Z	90	5A	01011010
ENQ	5	05	00000101	0	48	30	00110000	[	91	5B	01011011
ACK	6	06	00000110	1	49	31	00110001	\	92	5C	01011100
BEL	7	07	00000111	2	50	32	00110010	]	93	5D	01011101
BS	8	08	00001000	3	51	33	00110011	^	94	5E	01011110
HT	9	09	00001001	4	52	34	00110100	_	95	5F	01011111
LF	10	0A	00001010	5	53	35	00110101	`	96	60	01100000
VT	11	0B	00001011	6	54	36	00110110	a	97	61	01100001
FF	12	0C	00001100	7	55	37	00110111	b	98	62	01100010
CR	13	0D	00001101	8	56	38	00111000	c	99	63	01100011
SO	14	0E	00001110	9	57	39	00111001	d	100	64	01100100
SI	15	0F	00001111	:	58	3A	00111010	e	101	65	01100101
DLE	16	10	00010000	;	59	3B	00111011	f	102	66	01100110
DC1	17	11	00010001	<	60	3C	00111100	g	103	67	01100111
DC2	18	12	00010010	=	61	3D	00111101	h	104	68	01101000
DC3	19	13	00010011	>	62	3E	00111110	i	105	69	01101001
DC4	20	14	00010100	?	63	3F	00111111	j	106	6A	01101010
NAK	21	15	00010101	@	64	40	01000000	k	107	6B	01101011
SYN	22	16	00010110	A	65	41	01000001	l	108	6C	01101100
ETB	23	17	00010111	B	66	42	01000010	m	109	6D	01101101
CAN	24	18	00011000	C	67	43	01000011	n	110	6E	01101110
EM	25	19	00011001	D	68	44	01000100	o	111	6F	01101111
SUB	26	1A	00011010	E	69	45	01000101	p	112	70	01110000
ESC	27	1B	00011011	F	70	46	01000110	q	113	71	01110001
FS	28	1C	00011100	G	71	47	01000111	r	114	72	01110010
GS	29	1D	00011101	H	72	48	01001000	s	115	73	01110011
RS	30	1E	00011110	I	73	49	01001001	t	116	74	01110100
US	31	1F	00011111	J	74	4A	01001010	u	117	75	01110101
	32	20	00100000	K	75	4B	01001011	v	118	76	01110110
!	33	21	00100001	L	76	4C	01001100	w	119	77	01110111
"	34	22	00100010	M	77	4D	01001101	x	120	78	01111000
#	35	23	00100011	N	78	4E	01001110	y	121	79	01111001
$	36	24	00100100	O	79	4F	01001111	z	122	7A	01111010
%	37	25	00100101	P	80	50	01010000	{	123	7B	01111011
&	38	26	00100110	Q	81	51	01010001	|	124	7C	01111100
'	39	27	00100111	R	82	52	01010010	}	125	7D	01111101
(	40	28	00101000	S	83	53	01010011	~	126	7E	01111110
)	41	29	00101001	T	84	54	01010100		127	7F	01111111
*	42	2A	00101010	U	85	55	01010101				

ASCII (American Standard Code for Information Interchange) is a 7-bit code cooperatively developed by several computer manufacturers whose objective was to produce a standard code for all computers. Their objective has been fulfilled, at least for microcomputers—virtually every such machine marketed today uses some variant of the ASCII code. Although ASCII is officially a 7-bit code (see Table 4) with 128 different characters and control codes, there is an 8-bit version dubbed ASCII-8. In practice, some manufacturers such as IBM also extend standard 7-bit ASCII with another bit to include 128 additional special-purpose characters (see Figure 1).

Table 4 shows the 128 standard ASCII codes. The first column shows the character itself or an abbreviation of a control code. The second column gives the ASCII code for that character or control code in decimal (base 10). The third column gives the same ASCII code in hexadecimal (base 16) and the fourth column gives it in binary (base 2). In some computers, ASCII codes from 0 to 31 are not actually characters that can appear on the screen or be printed. They are control codes for actions such as carriage return, backspace, line feed, form feed, and other signals for coordinating communication between a computer and a display screen, printer, modem, or some other input/output device.

Figure 1 IBM Extended ASCII Codes

This screen shows the extended ASCII code system used by IBM-compatible microcomputers, which includes special characters that appear on the screen for the first 32 ASCII codes, and an additional 128 characters that are encoded by using the eighth (leftmost) bit in an 8-bit byte (normally unused in standard 7-bit ASCII). In this figure, the decimal ASCII code is the three-digit number that appears to the right of each character.

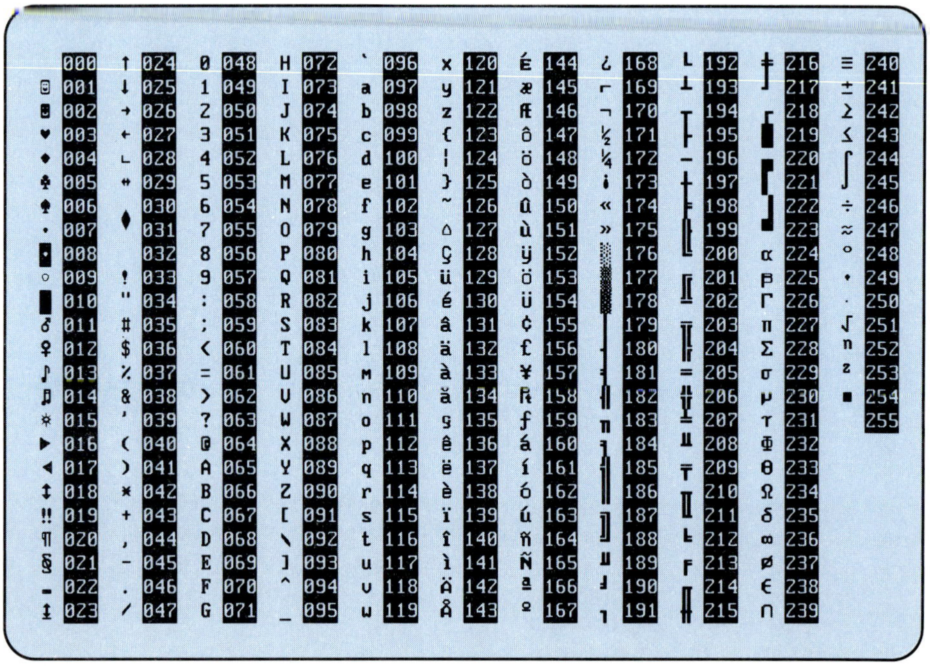

APPENDIX B

SELECTING A SYSTEM

More and more people are buying microcomputers for business and home use. Most companies already have at least one microcomputer, and they are continually acquiring more. Schools at all levels have been purchasing microcomputers for both students and faculty. It's been estimated that at least 20% of all U.S. households will ultimately have some type of microcomputer. Just as most of you will eventually purchase stereo systems, video systems, other high-tech home appliances, and automobiles, it's likely that in the near future you may be investing in a computer system, too. Perhaps you won't be buying a computer for your home, but you might still be involved in the process of selecting a system for your school or work. This appendix offers some guidelines that can help both individuals and organizations in their process of computerization.

Computers are complicated equipment. Although their prices have been steadily dropping, computers still represent a substantial investment for most people. With so many different computer models and an overwhelming array of software packages on the market, unless you're wealthy or are already a computer expert, purchasing a system is no trivial task. The choices you make can have profound effects on the quantity and quality of work you will accomplish with your computer. To make good choices, you need to have a plan.

Selecting a computer system is somewhat like selecting a stereo system or automobile. If you buy on irrational impulses, you risk regretting your decision for years to come. If, on the other hand, you follow a well-thought-out, step-by-step selection process, chances are good that you'll end up with an economical labor-saving system. One such approach involves six basic steps:

1. Learn about computers.
2. Define your needs.
3. Select the software.
4. Select the hardware.
5. Purchase the system.
6. Install the system.

Step 1: Learn About Computers

You need not be a computer scientist to effectively select and use computers. Some basic knowledge, however, can help a great deal. The first step in selecting a system is to become familiar with the capabilities and limitations of computers. In other words, you need to know what computers can and cannot do for you. The chapters in this book are designed to provide you with an understanding of the capabilities and limitations of microcomputers.

Of course, this book can by no means cover all relevant microcomputer topics. Although learning more is not absolutely required, the more you do know the better prepared you'll be to take advantage of what computers have to offer. Fortunately, there are many opportunities for you to learn more about computers. Some of the possibilities include books, periodicals, organizations, shows, courses, conferences, and workshops.

Books

An astonishing number of computer books are available in local bookstores, libraries, and computer stores. Some are quite technical, but many others have been written especially for novices. Some of the most common books you'll find are "How to" books that cover specific computer models or software packages. Others teach programming in certain languages or deal with the philosophical and sociological aspects of using computers. You can even buy books that discuss how to select a computer system.

Periodicals

In 1975, only two magazines were devoted solely to microcomputers. Today, hundreds of microcomputer newspapers, newsletters, and magazines are available. Although books can cover topics in great detail, they're usually somewhat out of date by the time they actually hit the shelves. Newspapers, newsletters, and magazines reveal what's happening in the marketplace *now*. They frequently contain reviews and in-depth evaluations of hardware and software products. Periodicals also contain informative articles and columns that answer questions and provide tips from other computer users. They are crammed with ads from manufacturers, retailers, and mail-order outfits. Many owners have at least one subscription to a microcomputer periodical. Some of the more popular publications include *A+*, *BYTE*, *Infoworld*, *Macworld*, and *PC Magazine*.

In addition to traditional periodicals printed on paper, *disk magazines* have been gaining popularity recently. These publications are issued on floppy disks and are aimed at users of particular computer models. They uniquely provide subscribers with tested programs for business, education, entertainment, and home use.

Organizations

Computer users, it seems, are a very sociable lot. At regular intervals, thousands of folks gather in societies, clubs, and user groups to share computer experiences, help solve each others' problems, and trade software. Although most people don't join such organizations until after they purchase a computer system, joining before buying can be advantageous. Many user groups are centered around a particular computer model or type of popular software. Group members can usually offer advice on where to get the best deals. Joining a computer organization may even qualify you for certain group discounts off the retail prices of selected hardware and software products. Once you have your system, a computer organization can put you in contact with people who have the same hardware and software. These colleagues can be an invaluable source of information because it's likely that they've already solved problems you might be having as a beginning user.

Computer organizations offer fellowship, support, general information, and answers to those tricky questions not answered in any manuals. Many groups have been established since the advent of microcomputers in the mid-1970s. For example, more than 850 groups in the United States serve Apple computer users. Some groups have remained local, small, and dedicated to one particular type of computer, like the Champaign-Urbana, Illinois Apple II Users Group with its 40 or so members. Other groups have grown immense and wield a good deal of influence over the microcomputer industry. The Boston Computer Society, for instance, was founded in 1977 by Jonathan Rotenberg when he was thirteen years old. Today, with about 24,000 members, it's perhaps the nation's largest microcomputer users group. The Boston Computer Society has its own magazine, *Computer Update,* sponsors around 100 monthly events, and has approximately 40 special-interest subgroups, each of which publishes its own newsletter.

Shows

Every year, computer shows are held in various cities across the United States. These events may be sponsored by individual entrepreneurs, manufacturers, retail stores, magazine publishers, or other associations that deal with computers. Although many shows specifically target manufacturers and retailers, others are open to the general computer-buying public. They are typically held in large exhibit halls, with booth space rented to hardware manufacturers, software manufacturers, dealers, distributors, retailers, computer clubs, publishers, and any other organizations that want to sell or advertise products. Admission is often charged. Besides exhibiting new products and services, many shows also offer short talks, seminars, and classes for attendees, frequently given by well-known computer personalities. These shows may last several days and attract thousands of people who come from all over the country.

Computer shows can offer the following opportunities:

- *See new products.* Manufacturers often introduce products at computer shows, so it may be an early chance to see what's new in the market. Furthermore, most shows exhibit a wider variety of products than you can usually find in the typical computer store. It's easy to collect all kinds of brochures, product descriptions, advertisements, and other handouts.
- *Try out products.* Many computer show exhibits are specifically designed to let you "test drive" hardware and software products. This may be your only chance to get hands-on experience with an item before you actually buy it.
- *Buy products.* Frequently, computer shows allow exhibitors to sell their products directly to consumers. At some shows, you can buy anything from a single diskette to an entire microcomputer system. Prices are generally less than retail and it's possible to get some good bargains at computer shows, especially as closing time nears.
- *Learn more.* As we mentioned before, many computer shows sponsor lectures and seminars. Subjects may include very specific topics, such as how to use a particular feature of a software package, or more general matters, such as the role of microcomputers in our society.

- *Meet people.* Computer shows offer excellent opportunities to come into contact with other people who have similar interests. You may meet just one person at a booth looking for the same product, or you may discover an entire users group that you want to join. The people you meet can offer advice, answer questions, and share some of their computer experiences with you.
- *Talk to manufacturers.* Since many hardware and software manufacturers send representatives to computer shows, you may get an opportunity to ask questions, get more information, or even complain about a particular product.

Courses

For people who seek a more structured approach to learning about computers, a wide variety of formal courses is offered to both students and the general public. Traditional educational institutions, like high schools, community colleges, and universities, hold classes aimed primarily at those seeking diplomas. Many community colleges and university continuing education and extension services also offer computer courses for non-degree students. Classes range from simple, non-technical introductions for novices to in-depth studies for those pursuing computer careers. Alternative learning centers, such as those affiliated with local churches, libraries, and park districts, often conduct classes taught by computer experts in their spare time. Although such courses may be less academic than those run by traditional educational institutions, they may be more accessible to the general public. Computer stores often teach courses about particular hardware and software products, but these courses may be limited to customers. Several proprietary (for-profit) schools also offer computer-related coursework. Many accredited home study schools as well as colleges and universities have correspondence courses that teach computer subjects by mail. Finally, some private individuals offer computer courses too. Before you enroll in any course, however, be sure to investigate it thoroughly to determine just what is being offered and how much it will cost.

Conferences and Workshops

Many organizations offer conferences and workshops covering particular computer topics. Some of these events are expensive, intensive training sessions aimed specifically at computer professionals. Others are less technical and attract novice computer users. They typically last from several hours to several days, and are held in various cities across the country.

Step 2: Define Your Needs

Once you have a general picture of what microcomputers can do, you can begin to examine how you might use one. It's important to carefully consider exactly what you want to do with a computer before you purchase anything. Of course, you probably can't anticipate every possible use you'll find for your computer once you get it, but you should have some clearly stated, specific reasons for investing in a system. A good approach is to make a list. Write down, in order of importance, all of the uses you expect to have for a computer. At this stage, try not to think too much about costs, but keep your ideas realistic. As a sample, your list might look something like this:

1. *Word Processing*. For term papers, reports, class notes, and letters.
2. *Record Keeping*. For addresses, phone numbers, personal property inventory, bank account numbers, credit cards, and tax-deductible expenses.
3. *Calculating*. For bills, budgets, and income taxes.
4. *Education*. For math review, foreign language study, college entrance test review, and learning about computer programming.
5. *Entertainment*. For fun with computer games and simulations.

This list is probably fairly typical of the uses a student or other individual might have for a computer at home or school. A business, however, might have a more specific list of computer needs, especially if it is computerizing for the first time, or perhaps considering replacing an existing system. A small business, for example, might have the following uses for a microcomputer system:

1. *General Ledger*. To keep track of financial records and produce reports, such as balance sheets and profit and loss statements, that summarize the financial status of the firm.
2. *Accounts Receivable*. To keep track of the money owed to the company and when payments are due.
3. *Accounts Payable*. To keep track of money the company owes to its suppliers.
4. *Payroll*. To calculate each employee's gross pay, withhold taxes, subtract deductions, print paychecks, and maintain necessary payroll records.
5. *Inventory*. To monitor the goods on hand and make sure enough are in stock for production and customer requests.
6. *Mailing List*. To prepare direct mailing of ads and notices.
7. *Word Processing*. To create letters, reports, newsletters, and memos.
8. *Personnel Files*. To hold information for insurance, retirement, and governmental regulations.

Step 3: Select the Software

Now comes perhaps the most difficult step in acquiring a computer system: selecting the software. First of all, from the user's standpoint, software is much more important than hardware. Software is what makes the computer accomplish useful work. Without programs, computer hardware is utterly worthless. It's likely that you'll pay much more for all the software you'll eventually buy than the hardware. If you have a stereo system, this probably doesn't surprise you, since most people have more money invested in records, tapes, or compact discs than they originally paid for the stereo components. Shopping for software is also more difficult than shopping for hardware, because there is so much more software on the market than hardware. Some software companies sell only by mail, so it may be difficult to obtain information about their programs. A thorough evaluation of software requires using it in your own particular situation for a substantial amount of time. This may be difficult, if not impossible, to do by running a program at a single sitting in your local computer store. Finally, because software usually has a smaller profit margin than hardware, computer salespeople may not be as enthusiastic or helpful about selling a program as they would an entire computer system.

All those difficulties aside, it really is possible, even for novices, to make good software selections. First, go back to your list of computer uses. For each item, come up with at least three different software packages. Here you'll need some of those learning resources we talked about previously. Perhaps the best source of possible selections may be people you know from school, work, clubs, user groups, or computer shows. See if you can arrange to try a potential software selection for an extended period of time. Perhaps a friend or relative has a computer and software you can use. If your school has a computer lab, you may be able to use it at times when classes aren't in session. Many school labs have software you can check out and run on a computer at your own pace.

Probably the best source of information comparing various software packages are computer magazines. Most have reviews of new software products; some even devote entire issues to comparing all the major competitors in a particular application. The publications extensively test each package by using it for a predetermined set of activities, and then quantitatively rate how each one does. Often, the reviewers will conclude with one or more "editor's choices," and give their reasons for selecting these packages as the best of the lot. Scanning the magazine stands and going through back issues in the library are excellent ways to find out more about specific application packages.

As you begin to compile your list of potential software selections, make your own evaluations and rank the packages, if possible. As you talk to people and read product reviews, note the following characteristics of good software:

- *Competent.* Capable of performing an important job well.
- *Easy to Learn.* Can be mastered with moderate effort in a reasonable amount of time.
- *Easy to Use.* Intrudes as little as possible between the user and getting the job done.
- *Tolerant.* Gently and sensibly handles errors made by the user.
- *Layered.* Simple and self-evident on the outside for beginners, and progressively more complex and powerful as internal features are mastered.
- *Flexible.* Can be adapted to handle variations in its basic task.
- *Compatible.* Works well with other software by using standard conventions and being able to share files.
- *Well-Documented.* Comes with clearly written, correct instruction and reference manuals designed with both novices and experts in mind.
- *Supported.* Backed by its manufacturer, which conscientiously fixes errors, provides updated versions, and answers users' questions.
- *Reasonably-Priced.* Provides value comparable to its cost.

Once you complete this process, you'll have a list of computer uses ordered according to your priorities, within which will be sublists of potential software packages ranked by preference. You're not ready to buy anything yet, and you haven't singled out the exact packages you'll eventually get, but you have a pretty good idea of the field of contenders.

Step 4: Select the Hardware

By seriously considering software first, the selection of hardware is much easier. The idea is to choose hardware that can run the software packages you've selected. This helps you put together a system that really matches your needs.

Computer

Some of the software packages you've selected have versions that run on different computers, but many will only work on a single machine. This is where you begin to determine the most important hardware decision facing you: which computer to get. Although there are hundreds of different companies making microcomputers, the great majority of machines fit into one of just a few categories. Today, these categories are IBM and IBM-compatible computers, Apple Macintoshes, Apple II computers, and all others. This is not to belittle all those "other" computers. There are quite a few great machines with large numbers of devoted users. However, there's no doubt that the microcomputers in the first three categories far outnumber all the rest, especially in businesses, offices, and schools.

IBM and IBM-Compatible Computers IBM is the recognized leader in the microcomputer industry. They sell more microcomputers than any other single manufacturer. People who prefer other computers may not concede that IBM sells the "best" computers, but the fact remains that they sell the most. Although IBM no longer manufactures members of its original Personal Computer line (PC Jrs, PCs, PC Portables, XTs, and ATs), millions of these machines remain in use and some dealers are still selling new ones. The current IBM Personal System/2 line of computers improves on the previous models while still being able to run all the old software. IBM computers tend to be solidly-built, reliable machines that have been traditionally popular in the business world. Even though IBM computers might be a bit more expensive than comparable machines from other manufacturers, they have been getting more price-competitive lately. It's been said that "no manager ever got fired for buying IBM."

A true **IBM-compatible** computer is one that can run all the software and accept all the expansion boards and peripheral units that IBM microcomputers can use. Because IBM chose standard parts, published detailed design descriptions in technical references, and used an operating system designed and also sold by Microsoft, it was relatively easy for other manufacturers to produce compatible computers. Although there may still be some exceptions, most IBM-compatibles produced today do a very good job of mimicking the way IBM computers work. Many such "clones" offer more advanced features at a significantly lower price than IBM computers. Some IBM-compatible manufacturers, such as COMPAQ, have become highly-respected microcomputer industry leaders in their own right. Many well-established computer and electronic companies, like Tandy and Zenith, have expanded their lines to include IBM-compatible machines. In addition, quite a few mail-order firms, such as Dell Computer Corporation and Northgate Computer Systems, sell IBM-compatibles that they construct themselves from standard components. In fact, many more IBM-compatibles are sold today than IBM microcomputers.

Although IBMs and IBM-compatibles have their critics, selecting such computers has many advantages. American businesses have over $80 billion invested in IBM and IBM-compatible computers. This includes over 72 million software and hardware products, and hundreds of millions of hours of training. Books, magazines, and user groups devoted solely to IBM-compatible computers abound. Chances are good that you can find experts nearby to help you if you have problems. Most IBM and IBM-compatible systems can be easily expanded if you need to add more capabilities later.

Apple Macintosh Computers In the early days of IBM microcomputers, many people considered them to be powerful and expandable, but not particularly easy to set up and use. Apple, building on their great success with the Apple II line, decided to address these concerns and build a computer "for the rest of us." In 1984, Apple introduced the Macintosh. Easy to learn and fun to use, the Macintosh has changed the way people perceive computers. Today's models preserve the philosophy of simplicity, yet have become more powerful and expandable. The Macintosh is becoming increasingly popular in businesses, especially for word processing, graphics, and desktop publishing applications. Many individuals and schools are also purchasing Macintoshes in ever greater numbers. Hundreds of software packages and a variety of optional peripherals are now available for this machine.

Apple II Computers The original Apple II computer was introduced in 1977. Since then, several million of the Apple II family (including the Apple II+, Apple IIe, Apple III, Apple IIc, and Apple IIGS) have been sold. These computers have done very well in elementary and secondary schools. The Apple II's share of sales in this market is currently around 50%, although some schools are turning more toward Macintoshes and low-cost IBM-compatibles. Apple II computers have also been quite popular as home computers and were common in businesses before the introduction of the IBM Personal Computers. At least 10,000 software packages run on Apple II computers and a wide variety of expansion devices and peripherals are available. Although this family of computers is not as powerful and fast as Macintoshes and IBM-compatibles, they are still viable machines with a large number of devoted users.

Memory

In the early days of microcomputers, RAM was expensive and most machines could have no more than 64K. This situation has changed dramatically. Many microcomputers now have the potential to use up to 4 gigabytes of RAM, and memory chips are less expensive. For many people, the memory that comes with the computer will be sufficient for most of their needs. For example, most IBM microcomputers now come with at least 640K standard and all Macintoshes come with at least one megabyte installed. On other machines, you'll have to make sure you get enough memory to run the application packages you've selected. Since most software manufacturers state how much memory is required for their programs, figuring out how much memory to buy should be fairly simple. If you can, try to choose a computer system that can accept more RAM than you may initially need. Then if you later purchase software that requires more memory, you can add more RAM to upgrade your system.

Disk Drives

When it comes to secondary storage, you have several choices to make. The first one is whether you need the high capacity and rapid data access of a hard disk. This depends on the types of applications you'll run and the quantity of data you'll be working with. Some application packages require a hard disk. Others don't actually require one, but would work much better and faster with a hard disk. If the application programs you run and the data files you'll work with won't each fit on a single floppy disk, you probably need a hard disk. If you're not sure if you want to invest the extra few hundred dollars in a hard disk, make sure that you get a computer system that can accommodate a hard disk if you decide to add one later.

The other most common secondary storage decisions involve what kind and how many floppy drives to get. The 5¼-inch diskette drives are still more common, less expensive, and use less expensive floppies than 3½-inch drives. However, many computers, like the Macintosh and IBM Personal System/2 computers, come with only 3½-inch disk drives standard. Most software is now distributed on either type of disk. Each type of floppy drive has its advantages, but your major concern should be whether you can trade diskettes with colleagues, co-workers, and friends. It's best to get the same type of diskette drives as people with whom you'll be frequently exchanging programs and data. If you do get a hard disk, one floppy drive will probably be sufficient. However, if you often need to copy entire diskettes, it might be worth investing in two drives. In systems without hard disks, having two floppy drives is the most practical arrangement.

Display

With some computers, you have no choice as to what kind of display to get. The Apple Macintosh Plus and Macintosh SE, for example, come with a built-in 9-inch monochrome graphics display. On most computers, however, you have a choice among several alternatives. Older and less-expensive computers give you a choice among monochrome text, monochrome graphics, and color graphics monitors. Many newer microcomputers, like the IBM Personal System/2 series, support only graphics monitors, but you do have a choice between monochrome and color. To complicate matters more, many computers can accept several different display adapters, each of which may support several video modes.

To resolve your display dilemma, first look at your software selections. If you want to run software that uses graphics, you'll need a graphics display. On the other hand, if you're *positive* that you'll only be working with text, you may want to opt for a less expensive monochrome text monitor. Although in most cases color is not absolutely necessary, many people find that color monitors are more pleasant to work with, despite the added expense. If you are planning to use software that manipulates detailed graphics, you'll need a high-resolution display. As with most hardware selections, try to choose a system that can be upgraded later, if possible. Your needs may expand and prices may fall to a point where you would like to invest in a more sophisticated display. It's much easier and less expensive to replace a display adapter and monitor than an entire computer system.

Printer

Literally hundreds of microcomputer printers are on the market. Before you choose a particular model, you must first decide on what type of printer you need. Most microcomputer users have 9-pin dot-matrix printers. These printers can do graphics and can print fairly rapidly in draft mode, yet also have a more attractive, but much slower, near-letter-quality mode. If you will be printing letters on bond or letterhead paper, be sure to look for models that can easily accept single sheets as well as the fan-fold, pin-feed computer paper most dot-matrix printers use. For true letter quality, you might want to get a daisy-wheel printer. These printers produce text that looks just like that from typewriters, but they are quite slow. Applications that produce very high-quality text and graphics may require a 24-pin dot-matrix printer or perhaps even an expensive laser printer. Before you make your final decision on any printer, be sure to see samples of the text and graphics it can produce. Also consider the cost of supplies like paper, ribbons, toner cartridges (for laser printers) and additional typefaces.

Other Peripherals

A wide range of optional peripheral devices can be connected to a microcomputer. In your selection of a system, you should try to choose initially only those devices that will be absolutely necessary. You can always add more peripherals later, provided that you've chosen a system that can be expanded. If you'll be accessing remote computers, you'll need to select a modem. Many graphics applications require the use of a mouse. Some computer games use joysticks or trackballs. Examine your software selections carefully to make sure that you understand exactly what hardware devices are necessary.

Specifications and Benchmarks

In the preceding sections, we've briefly described the hardware you need to select. But, how do you pick the exact models to buy? Just as in making software selections, one method is to look carefully at what people around you have purchased. Some experts have even suggested that you get a system exactly like another one you have access to, perhaps at school, work, or a friend's. This way, you can become familiar with the components before you buy, and after you get your system, you have access to an exact duplicate in case your system isn't working. Although it definitely helps to have access to a similar system, if you only buy what someone else has, you're depending a great deal on their judgment, which may or may not be better than your own.

Another method of selecting hardware is to read reviews published in computer and consumer magazines. Just like software reviews, hardware reviews compare and evaluate actual products. For computers, hardware reviews can provide in-depth information about how they are constructed and how they work. For devices like displays, printers, and modems, reviews can compare models quantitatively and tabulate their features. Be forewarned, however, that these reviews are often saturated with specifications and benchmarks.

Specifications are a detailed list of the exact components, options, and capabilities of a particular hardware device. Microcomputer specifications typically list the manufacturer, exact size, microprocessor, coprocessors, system clock speed, amount of standard RAM, total possible RAM, amount of ROM, disk drives and capacities, number and type of expansion slots, number and type of interfaces, retail list price, and many other details. Sometimes, specifications include measures of performance. For example, many printer specifications include the number of characters printed per second. Although specifications can be one way to compare different devices, they may be misleading. Performance measurements are often made under ideal conditions. So, a printer advertised at 200 characters per second, may not actually be that fast when printing a document from your word processor, especially if it contains underlining, boldface, and italics.

A **benchmark** is an objective, reproducible measure of hardware or software performance, typically the amount of time it takes to run a standard program or process a particular set of data. Just like specifications, benchmarks are one way to compare hardware, but they can also be misleading. For example, a common benchmark for computer performance is one cycle of a calculation known as the *Sieve of Eratosthenes*. This is a method of finding prime numbers (numbers only evenly divisible by themselves and 1) that has been adapted to computers. Although benchmarks such as these may be useful for measuring the time required for certain very specific kinds of computer operations, they provide little or no information about ease of use, reliability, maintainability, the amount of manufacturer support for a product, or other equally important attributes. Sometimes, magazines like *BYTE* and *PC Magazine* develop their own benchmarks for reviewing products. Although these benchmarks are designed to measure performance under typical conditions, they may still not reflect how fast your software will run on your machine. Benchmark results, like specifications, should be taken with a grain of salt.

Step 5: Purchase the System

After selecting your hardware, you may have to go back and modify your list of software packages so that you have ones that will all run on the machine you've chosen. Before you even think of buying anything, you should have a fairly complete list of the exact software and hardware products you'll need. Since most product reviews and ads contain prices, you should also have a good notion of how much all this will cost. This is the time to look at your budget and make some realistic choices. You may not be able to afford all the software packages and optional peripherals you want to get. Fortunately, some of these purchases can be postponed. If you've listed your selections by priority, you can initially buy only those most essential items.

When to Buy

For many people, the most disconcerting circumstances of microcomputer shopping are the rate at which technology advances and how quickly prices can drop. Computer newspapers and magazines are filled with rumors, educated guesses, and pre-release previews about new products and upgrades to existing ones. Most manufacturers, it would seem, are constantly on the verge of releasing a computer, peripheral, or software package that will render every preceding product hopelessly obsolete. Even worse, what you pay $4,000 for this year may cost less than $1,000 two years from now. This perpetual anticipation can immobilize some potential computer shoppers.

Unfortunately, you must simply accept the facts that whichever hardware and software you choose, prices will drop and new versions will be released. There may be some prudence in waiting one or two months if a product is about to be released that will truly meet your needs. However, production often lags behind the demand for new products and it's sometimes best not to be one of the first owners of a brand-new piece of hardware or software. New technology, such as automobiles, stereos, hardware, and software, frequently has unsuspected flaws. It's nearly impossible to detect all of the potential problems in a complex product that's being rushed out of the factory into a highly competitive marketplace. Although it's tempting to be one of the first to get the latest hardware or software, you may wind up as a guinea pig whose complaints contribute to the design of Version 2.0.

In most cases, the time to buy is *now*. If you truly need a computer, you probably can't afford to wait months for the release and delivery of a brand-new product. A great deal of hardware and software is currently available that will provide years of valuable service, even if new versions are released after your purchase. Assuming you've done your homework and selected a system that fulfills your requirements, it shouldn't matter that less expensive, more powerful alternatives will eventually be released. Even if your computing needs grow, you can most likely expand your current system later. Someday, you may even want to select a completely new system, but in the meantime you will have a computer that can help you now.

Where to Buy

Nowadays, computer hardware and software can be purchased from a variety of sources. The outlet you select often depends upon such factors as how much you know about computers, how much money you want to save, how soon you need a system, whether you're buying a well-established brand name product, and whether you're buying hardware or software. You can purchase a computer system from computer stores, department stores, school stores, manufacturers, mail-order firms, and used equipment dealers.

Computer Stores Local retail outlets that specialize in computers, such as Computerland and Radio Shack Computer Centers, are the traditional source of hardware and software products for many shoppers, especially novices. Salespeople are usually knowledgeable and can help a great deal in putting together a system that meets your needs. Most computer stores can also service your hardware should it need repair after the purchase. Many items are in stock or can be ordered and obtained in a few days. Unfortunately, many computer stores sell only a few brands. Although the brands tend to be from a select group of well-established manufacturers, your choices may be somewhat limited at a computer store. Items are usually sold at retail list prices, but there may be occasional sales or discounts given to certain groups of people. It may cost a bit more to buy a computer or peripheral device at a computer store, but dealers are nearby, accessible, and stand behind the hardware they sell.

Despite the additional cost, it often makes sense to buy hardware from a computer store. There is less advantage, however, to buying brand name software from a computer store. Software doesn't break down in the sense that hardware does, so a computer store technician can't repair a program. For most software packages, any problems or questions you have must usually be taken directly to the manufacturer. Although computer store salespeople may be able to answer some of your software questions, they simply can't be experts on every program they sell. In many cases, brand name software can be purchased for less from other sources.

Department Stores Sometimes, retail department stores like Sears, Target, and Service Merchandise sell computers and software. List prices are usually discounted and you can get items immediately if they are in stock. Unfortunately, department store salespeople may not be very knowledgeable about computers. Furthermore, each store typically only carries a single computer brand. In most cases, service after the sale may only be obtained from the original manufacturer. However, if you're fairly knowledgeable about computers and a local department store has exactly what you want, you may be able to get a good bargain.

School Stores If you're a student, faculty, or staff member of a college or university and in the market for a computer system, you may be in luck. Many schools have special deals with computer hardware and software manufacturers enabling them to offer products to qualified buyers at substantial savings. Hardware and software may be sold through a university bookstore, student union, educational consortium, or local computer center at discounts of up to 50% for students, faculty, and staff. Computer manufacturers like Apple, IBM, Hewlett-Packard, and Zenith often make deals with schools to sell their equipment at very low prices. In many cases, sales agents are knowledgeable and schools may also have their own service centers.

Manufacturers Sometimes, there's no dealer in the area that sells the computer you want. Or, you may qualify for a volume discount by wanting to purchase a number of systems all at once. In such situations it may be advantageous to go directly to the manufacturer of a particular hardware or software product. Unless you're purchasing in volume, you'll probably pay the list price and it may take several days or weeks for the item to be shipped to you. However, at least you know that you're going directly to the source and eliminating the middleman. Some large manufacturers, like IBM, may even have a local office through which you can purchase products and get equipment serviced after the sale.

Mail-Order Firms In the past, computer mail-order firms have had a somewhat less than prestigious reputation. With very few exceptions, that reputation is no longer justified. In fact, the seventh largest domestic microcomputer manufacturer, Dell Computer Corporation, is strictly a mail-order firm. This particular company even offers an optional next-day, on-site service contract for most major metropolitan areas and unlimited access to technicians over toll-free phone lines. Although most mail-order firms may not be this accommodating, a great many individuals, schools, and businesses buy computer hardware and software through the mail. Mail-order buying can save you money, and, in this day of overnight package delivery, can also be very convenient.

Still, the rule is "let the buyer beware" when it comes to mail-order purchasing. Ordering hardware over the phone can be daunting to computer novices. Many mail-order firms put together their own computers from standard components. These computers can be fantastic machines, but unless you know exactly what you're doing, it's probably best to stick to established brand names. Although, as we said, some mail-order firms offer repair service, most of them don't. Many advertise technical support over the phone, but it can sometimes be difficult to get through and have your questions answered politely, quickly, and accurately. Make sure that any mail-order firm you do choose has been in business for awhile.

Buying brand name software through the mail, however, offers several advantages. Discounts are usually substantial and the package you get in the mail is identical to what you would get from your local computer store or directly from the manufacturer. Large mail-order firms may have many items in stock and can often deliver them the next day via an overnight carrier for a modest extra charge.

Used Equipment Dealers A recent market study showed that most people buying new computers have owned at least one computer before. What's happening to all those computers that are being replaced? Some are winding up at used computer dealers. As the microcomputer industry ages, more and more used computer stores are opening. Sometimes you can find real bargains at such stores but, like buying a used car, purchasing a pre-owned computer or hardware component can be somewhat risky. Many of the machines in used computer stores are obsolete. They may still be quite useful, but it might be difficult to get parts, service, and software for computers no longer in production. If, on the other hand, a used computer is being sold because its owner simply upgraded to a more powerful system, there may be no reason not to buy it as long as it's been thoroughly tested and guaranteed by the dealer.

Step 6: Install the System

You've chosen and purchased your software and hardware. The system was delivered today and now it's at home still in the boxes. What do you do? Well, first open all the boxes and get out the instructions. Make sure all the components, cables, disks, and other items are there. Follow the directions and set up the machine. Some computers come with tutorial programs you can run to teach you the basics of using the hardware and running the operating system. Besides being entertaining, these tutorials are usually quite informative and well worth the time. Once you feel comfortable with the fundamentals, you can follow the instructions to install your software on your computer. Don't be surprised if you have problems or if things don't work exactly as the tutorials and manuals indicate. Reread the instructions and try again. If you're still having problems, call your dealer or the manufacturer's customer service department. If you still can't get your system running, you may have an honest-to-goodness defect and will have to return your system.

Once you do get your system up and running, try out all of the hardware and software components as soon as possible. Read your warranties and mail in the cards that register you with the manufacturers as a new owner. Not only will this validate your warranties, it will also put you on mailing lists so that you can get information about new versions and upgrades. At this time you might be thinking about insurance and service contracts. If your computer system represents a substantial investment to you, and you come to need it on a daily basis, you'll want make sure that it's insured and that you can get it repaired if it breaks down.

Finally, consider the surroundings in which you set up your system. A sturdy, roomy table or desktop and a well-designed, comfortable chair are musts if you expect to use your computer system for hours at a time. Keep your system clean and free from dust, spills, food crumbs, and other foreign materials. Try to keep any cooling vents unobstructed so that your system won't overheat. Unplug your hardware when not in use and try not to run it during electrical storms. Computer equipment, like other electronic devices, can be easily damaged or even destroyed by electrical surges caused by lightning or other power line disturbances. It might be prudent to plug all of your equipment into a **surge protector**. This is a relatively inexpensive device with a main switch, several electrical sockets, and circuitry to rapidly cut off power when a voltage surge occurs. Careful installation of your computer system can help ensure its reliability and usefulness for years to come.

APPENDIX C

SOFTWARE INSTALLATION

Most operating systems and application packages must be **installed** on your computer before you can use them. This typically involves running a special installation or setup program included with the software. Installation programs often create a new subdirectory on your hard disk, copy the files from the floppy disks included with the package to that subdirectory, and let you specify what kind of hardware you have. At most school microcomputer labs, this has already been done for you by the attendants. If you own a computer, however, you will probably have to install any new software you purchase yourself. The documentation that comes with the software should explain, step-by-step, how to run the installation program and answer any questions that may be asked about your hardware and software. Let's briefly go over the steps necessary to install the software discussed in this book: PC-DOS and MS-DOS Version 3.30, IBM DOS 4.00, MS-DOS 4.01, WordPerfect Version 5.0, Lotus 1-2-3 Release 2.01, Lotus 1-2-3 Release 2.2, Lotus 1-2-3 Release 3.0, and dBASE IV Version 1.0.

PC-DOS and MS-DOS Version 3.30

MS-DOS 3.30 and PC-DOS 3.30 are very similar. The MS-DOS package comes with two manuals entitled *MS-DOS User's Guide* and *MS-DOS User's Reference*. The first one contains the instructions for installing the system. The package can be purchased on either 3½-inch, 720K floppy disks, or 5¼-inch, 360K floppy disks. The 5¼-inch package comes with two disks, one labeled *Startup* and the other *Operating*.

Although the DOS 3.30 *Startup* diskette can be copied to another diskette to routinely boot up the computer from drive A, many people install the operating system on their hard disk C, if they have one. To install DOS 3.30 on a hard disk, follow these steps:

1. Insert the DOS 3.30 Startup disk into drive A.
2. Turn on the computer. If it is already on, press **Ctrl-Alt-Del** to reboot.

3. If the hard disk is not formatted (e.g., if you have a brand new computer), enter **format c: /s**. WARNING: Do not use this command if your hard disk is already formatted, or you will lose all files stored on it.
4. If the hard disk is already formatted with a previous version of DOS, enter **sys c:** instead of using the FORMAT command.
5. Enter **copy command.com c:** to copy the command processor to the hard disk.
6. If a subdirectory named DOS already exists on the hard disk, enter **del c:\dos*.*** to delete its contents. If such a subdirectory does not exist, enter **md c:\dos** to create it.
7. Enter **copy *.* c:\dos** to copy all the files from the Startup diskette to the DOS subdirectory on the hard disk.
8. Take the Startup diskette out of drive A, replace it with the Operating diskette, press **F3**, and press **Enter** to repeat the previous command and copy all of the files from the Operating diskette to the DOS subdirectory on the hard disk.
9. Remove the diskette from drive A, store all your original DOS diskettes in a safe place, and press **Ctrl-Alt-Del** to reboot your computer from the hard disk with DOS 3.30.
10. Enter **path c:\;c:\dos;** to set up the search paths for the root directory and the DOS subdirectory. You can add other search paths on the end of this command if you like. Ideally, this path command should be put in your AUTOEXEC.BAT file.

IBM DOS Version 4.00

The IBM DOS 4.00 package comes with two short manuals entitled *Getting Started with Disk Operating System Version 4.00* and *Using Disk Operating System Version 4.00*. The first one contains the instructions for installing the system. The package can be purchased on either 3½-inch, 720K floppy disks or 5¼-inch, 360K floppy disks. You should get the package with disks that match your floppy drive A. The 3½-inch package comes with two disks, one labeled *Install* and the other *Operating*. The 5¼-inch package comes with five disks labeled *Install, Select, Operating 1, Operating 2,* and *Operating 3*.

Although DOS 4.00 can be installed on floppy disks to boot up the computer from drive A, most people install the operating system on their hard disk C, if they have one. To install DOS 4.00 on a hard disk, follow these steps:

1. Insert the DOS 4.00 Install disk into drive A.
2. Turn on the computer. If it is already on, press **Ctrl-Alt-Del** to reboot.
3. After the copyright screen appears, press **Enter** and follow the instructions given by the installation program, which is called Select.
4. When you are finished with the installation program, remove the DOS floppy disk from drive A, store all your DOS disks in a safe place, and press **Ctrl-Alt-Del** to reboot your computer from the hard disk with DOS 4.00.

MS-DOS Version 4.01

The MS-DOS 4.01 package comes with three manuals entitled *MS-DOS User's Guide, MS-DOS User's Reference*, and *MS-DOS Shell User's Guide*. The first one contains the instructions for installing the system. The package can be purchased on either 3½-inch, 720K floppy disks or 5¼-inch, 360K floppy disks. You should get the package with disks that match your floppy drive A. The 3½-inch package comes with two disks, one labeled *Install* and the other *Operating*. The 5¼-inch package comes with six disks labeled *Install, Select, Operating 1, Operating 2, Operating 3*, and *Shell*.

Although MS-DOS 4.01 can be installed on floppy disks to boot up the computer from drive A, most people install the operating system on their hard disk C, if they have one. To install MS-DOS 4.01 on a hard disk, follow these steps:

1. Insert the MS-DOS 4.01 Install disk into drive A.
2. Turn on the computer. If it is already on, press **Ctrl-Alt-Del** to reboot.
3. After the copyright screen appears, press **Enter** and follow the instructions given by the installation program, which is called Select.
4. When you are finished with the installation program, remove the DOS floppy disk from drive A, store all your DOS disks in a safe place, and press **Ctrl-Alt-Del** to reboot your computer from the hard disk with MS-DOS 4.01.

WordPerfect Version 5.0

When you purchase WordPerfect Version 5.0, you get a softcover book entitled *WordPerfect Workbook*, and a three-ring reference manual. Also included are various keyboard templates and a quick reference card. The 5¼-inch package contains twelve floppy disks:

- *WordPerfect 1* and *WordPerfect 2*. These disks hold the files that make up the main WordPerfect program.
- *Fonts/Graphics*. This disk holds the WordPerfect character sets, fonts, clip art images, and screen capture utility.
- *Learning*. This disk contains the Install program that lets you set up WordPerfect on your computer and the on-line tutorial program that teaches you to use the package.
- *Printer 1* through *Printer 4*. These disks contain printer drivers, the files needed to use WordPerfect with many different kinds of printers.
- *PTR Program*. This disk holds PTR, a program that lets you create a driver for a printer not included on the Printer disks.
- *Speller*. This disk holds the spelling checker dictionary and Spell, a utility that lets you add words to or delete words from the dictionary and create specialized user dictionaries.
- *Thesaurus*. This disk holds the thesaurus program.
- *Conversion*. This disk holds Convert, a program that converts files from selected programs, such as WordStar and MultiMate, to WordPerfect format and vice versa.

To install WordPerfect on a hard disk, follow these steps:

1. Turn on your computer and boot up DOS.
2. Insert the WordPerfect Learning diskette into drive A.

3. Type **a:** and press **Enter** to switch to drive A.
4. Type **install** and press **Enter.**
5. Answer the questions and follow the directions given by the Install program.
6. Remove the Learning diskette from drive A.
7. Now you have to run WordPerfect to install and select your printer driver. Type **wp** and press **Enter** to start WordPerfect.
8. Hold down the **Shift** key and press the **F7** function key to activate the Print menu.
9. Type **s** to choose the Select Printer option.
10. Type **2** to select the Additional Printers option.
11. Type **2** to select the Other Disk option, put the Printer 1 diskette into drive A, type **a:**, and press **Enter**. (If you have a dot-matrix printer, you can save time by inserting the Printer 3 diskette instead.)
12. Press **Up Arrow** or **Down Arrow** to highlight the name of your printer or of a model that works similarly. If you can't find your printer in the list, put a different Printer diskette into drive A, type **2** to select the Other Disk option, type **a:**, and press **Enter.**
13. After you have highlighted your printer, type **1** to choose the Select option and then press **Enter.**
14. Keep pressing the **F7** key until you return to the editing screen. Now you can continue using WordPerfect or press **F7** again to return to DOS.
15. Remove the Printer diskette from drive A and put away all of your original WordPerfect diskettes in a safe place.

Lotus 1-2-3 Release 2.01

When you purchase Lotus 1-2-3 Release 2.01, you get three softcover manuals entitled *Getting Started*, *Tutorial*, and *Reference*. Also included are various keyboard guides and a quick reference card. The 5¼-inch package contains six floppy disks:

- *System Disk.* This disk holds the actual 1-2-3 program, along with a program called Lotus that lets you switch between 1-2-3 and the other programs included with it.
- *PrintGraph.* This disk holds a separate program called PrintGraph that allows you to print your 1-2-3 graphs. Depending on your printer's ability, this program lets you control colors, fonts, and the layout of your graphs.
- *Utility Disk.* This disk contains the Install program that lets you set up 1-2-3 to use a printer and display graphs, and the Translate program that lets you transfer data between 1-2-3 and other application packages.
- *Install Library Disk.* This disk contains files used by the Install program to set up 1-2-3 to run with various monitors and printers.
- *A View of 1-2-3.* This disk holds View, an onscreen tutorial program to help you learn about 1-2-3.
- *Backup System Disk.* This is simply a backup copy of the System Disk, in case you damage or lose the original.

To install Lotus 1-2-3 on a hard disk, follow these steps:

1. Turn on your computer.
2. Type **md \123** and press **Enter** to create a new subdirectory named 123 on your hard disk.

3. Type **cd \123** and press **Enter** to switch to the subdirectory you've just created.
4. Insert the System Disk into drive A.
5. Type **copy a:*.*** and press **Enter.**
6. After the contents of the floppy disk have been copied into the 123 subdirectory, remove the disk from drive A.
7. Repeat Steps 4 through 6 for all the remaining floppy disks included with the package, except the Backup System Disk.
8. Type **install** and press **Enter.**
9. Press **Enter** after reading the introductory screen.
10. The Install program displays the Main menu on the screen. Press **Enter** to select the First-Time Installation option from the menu and follow the directions to answer questions about your monitor and printer.
11. When you finish the First-Time Installation, select the Exit Install option.
12. Put your original Lotus 1-2-3 floppy disks away in a safe place.

Lotus 1-2-3 Release 2.2

When you purchase Lotus 1-2-3 Release 2.2, you get two softcover manuals entitled *Reference* and *Setting Up 1-2-3, Tutorial, Quick Start, and Sample Applications.* Also included are various keyboard templates and two booklets: *Upgrader's Handbook* and *Quick Reference.* The 5¼-inch package contains twelve floppy disks:

- *System Disk.* This disk holds the actual 1-2-3 program, along with a program called Lotus that lets you switch between 1-2-3 and the other programs included with it.
- *Help Disk.* This disk holds the on-line help facility, which lets you get information about a topic while you are using 1-2-3.
- *PrintGraph Disk.* This disk holds a separate program called PrintGraph that allows you to print your 1-2-3 graphs. Depending on your printer's ability, this program lets you control colors, fonts, and the layout of your graphs.
- *Install Disk.* This disk holds the Install program that lets you set up 1-2-3 to use a printer and display graphs.
- *Install Library Disk.* This disk contains files used by the Install program to set up 1-2-3 to run with various monitors and printers.
- *Translate Disk.* This disk holds the Translate program that lets you transfer data between 1-2-3 and other application packages.
- *Sample Files Disk.* This disk holds worksheet files that you use while following instructions in the Tutorial, Quick Start, and Sample Applications sections of the manual.
- *Allways Setup Disk.* This disk holds the Allways spreadsheet publishing add-in program, which lets you format worksheets and graphs.
- *Allways Disk 1* through *Allways Disk 4.* These disks contain font files and device driver files for Allways.

To install Lotus 1-2-3 Release 2.2 on a hard disk, follow these steps:

1. Turn on your computer.
2. Insert the System Disk in drive A and close the door.
3. Type **a:** and press **Enter** to switch to the disk in drive A.
4. Type **init** and press **Enter** to start the Initialization program.

5. Follow the directions to complete the Initialization program, recording your name and company's name on the System Disk.
6. Type **c:** and press **Enter** to switch back to the hard disk.
7. Type **md \123** and press **Enter** to create a new subdirectory named 123 on your hard disk.
8. Type **cd \123** and press **Enter** to switch to the subdirectory you've just created.
9. Make sure the System Disk is in drive A.
10. Type **copy a:*.*** and press **Enter.**
11. After the contents of the floppy disk have been copied into the 123 subdirectory, remove the disk from drive A.
12. Repeat Steps 9 through 11 for the remaining floppy disks included with the package, except the Allways disks.
13. Type **install** and press **Enter.**
14. Press **Enter** after reading the introductory screen.
15. The Install program displays the Main menu on the screen. Press **Enter** to select the First-Time Installation option from the menu and follow the directions to answer questions about your monitor and printer.
16. When you finish the First-Time Installation, select the Exit Install option.
17. Put your original Lotus 1-2-3 floppy disks away in a safe place.

Lotus 1-2-3 Release 3.0

Lotus 1-2-3 Release 3.0 can run only on IBM-compatible computers that have an 80286, 80386, or 80486 microprocessor, a hard disk drive, and at least one megabyte of memory. When you purchase Lotus 1-2-3 Release 3.0, you get a three-ring manual entitled *Reference* and four booklets: *Setting Up, Tutorial, Upgrader's Handbook,* and *Quick Reference.* Also included are various keyboard templates. The 5¼-inch package contains four high density (1.2-megabyte) floppy disks:

- *1-2-3 System Disk.* This disk holds the actual 1-2-3 program.
- *Install Disk.* This disk holds the Install program that lets you set up 1-2-3 on your computer.
- *Drivers Disk.* This disk contains files used by the Install program to set up 1-2-3 to run with various monitors and printers.
- *Font Disk.* This disk holds the various fonts available in 1-2-3 Release 3.0.

To install Lotus 1-2-3 Release 3.0, follow these steps:

1. Turn on your computer.
2. Insert the Install Disk in drive A and close the door.
3. Type **a:** and press **Enter** to switch to the disk in drive A.
4. Type **install** and press **Enter** to start the Install program.
5. Follow the directions to complete the Install program.
6. Put your original Lotus 1-2-3 floppy disks away in a safe place.

dBASE IV Version 1.0

The dBASE IV program can be installed only on computers that have a hard disk drive. When you purchase dBASE IV, you get several booklets and manuals: *Getting Started with dBASE IV, dBASE IV Change Summary, Introduction to the Dot Prompt, Network Installation, Learning dBASE IV, Using the Menu System, Using the dBASE IV Applications Generator, Language Reference, Quick Reference,* and *Advanced Topics.* Also included are various keyboard templates. The 5¼-inch package contains fourteen floppy disks:

- *Installation Disk.* This disk holds the program that lets you install dBASE IV on your computer.
- *System Disk #1* through *System Disk #9.* These disks contain the actual dBASE IV program.
- *Samples Disk #1* through *Samples Disk #3.* These disks hold files that are used as examples in the manuals.
- *Tutorial Disk.* This disk contains the on-line tutorial program, which teaches the basics of using dBASE IV.

To install dBASE IV, follow these steps:

1. Turn on your computer.
2. Insert the Installation Disk in drive A and close the door.
3. Type **a:** and press **Enter** to switch to the disk in drive A.
4. Type **install** and press **Enter** to start the Installation program.
5. Follow the directions to complete the Installation program.
6. Put your original dBASE IV floppy disks away in a safe place.

APPENDIX D

COMPUTER CAREERS

The job outlook for computing careers is bright, thanks to the spread of computers into almost every part of our lives. Restaurant managers use computers for billing and inventory control, accountants work with computer spreadsheets to prepare their clients' tax returns, and engineers design new cars with computers. All of these computers need to be programmed, operated, and maintained. This requires an ever growing army of computer specialists.

You don't necessarily need a college degree in computer science to work with computers today. For example, computer and peripheral equipment operators and data entry keyers (also called data entry operators), two of the hottest careers in the present job market, can receive training in many high schools, public and private vocational schools, business schools, and community colleges.

This appendix, however, will concentrate on the kinds of jobs in computing that require some advanced training or a college degree and involve close work with computers themselves. First, we will look at national employment trends and where computer careers fit into the picture. Then, we'll focus on some specific occupations that you might want to consider. Finally, we will discuss some of the elements of writing an effective résumé and how to make a job interview successful. At the end of the appendix, we include a list of companies to contact for further information about careers in computing.

The Job Outlook

According to the latest government projections, the nation's economy is expected to generate more than 21 million jobs between 1986 and 2000. The U.S. Bureau of Labor Statistics is predicting that computer-related occupations will be among the fastest growing through the year 2000. Many of these jobs will be in the computer hardware and software industry.

During the 1970s and up through the mid-1980s, computer hardware and software manufacturers were popping up everywhere. Then the boom began to fade as the computer industry inevitably began to mature. New companies, such as Steven Jobs' NeXT Corporation, did spring up in the 1980s, but many of the marginal companies died out. The earnings of the industry giants, IBM, Digital Equipment Corporation, and Wang, slacked off or dropped. Slowed growth, decreasing profits, and more international competition are the hallmarks of a maturing industry. Despite this, the government still expects healthy growth in the computer industry, largely because of the booming demand for personal computers by business and private consumers. And even though future technological advances probably won't be as revolutionary as the development of the silicon chip or microcomputer, according to the U.S. Labor Department, emphasis is already shifting from production to research and development as the maturing continues.

Career Choices

Computing jobs are similar from one industry to the next, although salaries can vary considerably. A recent survey, for example, shows that a management information systems/data processing (MIS/DP) specialist in education or a research organization will probably earn less than his or her counterpart working for a large public utility. (The MIS/DP specialist provides managers with the data they need to make informed decisions.) The survey, sponsored by the Data Processing Management Association, also found that salaries vary by region as well. Compensation is currently the best in the Pacific, northeastern, and mountain states, the worst in north central and southern states. Table 1 shows the average salaries of the various professions examined in the survey.

The jobs in computing that we will discuss can be clustered into four main groups: analysts and programmers, computer operators, service technicians, and sales and marketing jobs. We will examine one or more jobs in each category in detail, including the type of work that is done, the qualifications needed, and the outlook for the future.

Analysts and Programmers

When a problem or a new challenge arises in business, systems analysts, programmers, and applications software designers may be called on for help. Analysts and programmers design and write the programs that computers use. Applications software designers create new applications programs to meet specific needs.

Systems Analyst

Companies hire systems analysts to plan and develop computer systems or develop computer applications to meet their specific needs. Many work for banks, manufacturers, insurance companies, and the government. When a data processing problem arises, systems analysts begin by discussing it with management, and then design a system to solve the problem. After gaining management approval, they determine the hardware and software needed, prepare specifications for programmers, and help them debug the system. Most systems analysts specialize in one field, such as science, business, or engineering, because the work is so complex. A growing number of them work with computer networks.

Systems analysts must be able to think logically and have good analytical skills. Employers almost always require systems analysts to have a college degree

Table 1 Average Salaries in the MIS/DP Field

Position	Average Salary
Applications Programming Section Head	$55,100
MIS Manager	54,938
Telecommunications Supervisor	49,740
Data Processing Manager	47,500
Computer Operations Manager	44,013
Systems Analysis Supervisor	42,000
Lead Systems Analyst	41,100
Lead Data Base Specialist	38,378
Information Center Supervisor	37,296
Senior Systems Analyst/Applications Programmer	34,000
Intermediate Systems Programmer	32,470
Senior Telecommunications Specialist	32,012
User Support/Liaison/Coordination Supervisor	31,742
Data Processing Trainer	29,874
Senior Communications Specialist	28,264
Intermediate Applications Programmer	27,500
Data Input/Output Control Supervisor	27,396
Lead Computer Operator	22,000
Data Entry Supervisor	21,008
Senior Documentation Specialist	20,940
Data Input/Output Control Secretary	19,700
Junior Peripheral Equipment Operator	16,820
Data Entry Clerk Typist	16,000
Data Input/Output Control Clerk	14,420
Junior Data Entry Operator	13,270

and be familiar with programming languages. For some very complex work, graduate degrees are preferred. Most employers look for someone with a background in accounting or business management for work in business, and for someone with a background in applied mathematics, engineering, or the physical sciences for work in scientific fields. Degrees in computer or information science or in data processing often give an applicant an edge. Most people entering this field have worked previously as computer programmers, engineers, or managers.

As uses for computers increase, so will the demand for systems analysts. Factory automation, advances in telecommunications, and the increasing availability of computers to small businesses will contribute to the demand. The U.S. Bureau of Labor Statistics predicts about a 75 percent increase in jobs for systems analysts through 2000. The annual salary for a systems analyst starts at about $24,000 and can range up to $49,500. The average salary is $35,765.

Computer Programmer

Computers must have detailed, logical instructions written in a language they can understand. Computer programmers write these instructions using computer languages such as BASIC, Pascal, or C. The programmer writes a specific program for the problem, tests it, and then prepares an instruction manual for whoever is to run the program. Some programs are relatively simple, others are highly complex and require a great deal of precise, logical work.

Ordinarily, a computer programmer's work begins after a systems analyst has defined the problem and compiled a detailed description of steps the computer must follow. Some organizations combine the two positions into a programmer-analyst.

Computer programming is taught at many public and private vocational schools, community colleges, and universities. Because there are so many qualified applicants, employers have higher and higher standards for the people they hire. Generally, employers in scientific fields prefer to hire people with degrees in computer or information science, mathematics, engineering, or other sciences. Business employers look for people who have had courses in programming or business. It helps to have some background in accounting, inventory control, or similar areas. Since programming is so exacting, programmers must have a great deal of mental stamina. They must be able to think logically and to work accurately.

By 2000, there should be about 335,000 new jobs for computer programmers, according to government figures. Job prospects are brightest for college graduates who are familiar with several programming languages, particularly languages used in computer networking and data base management. Work experience also helps. Employers often prefer applicants who have taken part in college internship or work-study programs. The starting salary for a computer programmer is about \$21,800; the top salary is about \$44,300; the average is about \$30,000.

Systems Programmer

Systems programmers create, test, and document software for a computer's operating system and compilers, as well as for its networking and data communications programs. These specialized programmers also advise systems analysts who are developing new systems or modifying old ones. They often help software designers who discover problems with their programs and may help repair a system that is brought down because of a problem with its operating system. Because computers are in use during the day, the systems programmer occasionally may have to work at night and on weekends.

A bachelor's or associate's degree in computer science with an emphasis on assembly language, compiler design, and operating systems is important for this job. Experience is also important. A systems programmer should have at least two years' experience as an applications programmer. Employers are looking for proven technical aptitude and a working knowledge of systems software. Since night or off-peak work may be required, applicants should be able to work long periods in relative isolation.

Because of the hours and isolation on the job, and because so much specialized experience is required, there is a shortage of qualified applicants. People who are interested in becoming systems programmers have time to survey the job field while they are gaining the experience needed. Because the applicant pool is so small, the job outlook for systems programmers is especially bright.

Applications Software Designer

An applications software designer (engineer) is a specialized programmer who creates computer application programs to handle specific customer needs, such as inventory control or product design. Applications programmers work for all kinds of firms. Many are found in companies that write and sell software, such as Microsoft, where they may work in testing and compatibility or even field support and customer training. Some may work for large companies that need specialized applications.

A bachelor's degree with an emphasis in computer or information science is important, and a master's in this area is helpful in many instances. Two to four years of experience in programming is required to specialize in this field. Software designers need top-notch programming skills and the ability to work under pressure.

The job outlook for software designers, as it is for all programmers, is excellent. Employment for programmers is expected to grow much faster than the average for all occupations through 2000.

Computer Operator

Large organizations that rely on mainframe computers need people to operate them or enter data. The details and outlook for these jobs vary widely, so we will mention several only briefly. Generally, these jobs require a high school diploma and some specialized training in community colleges or private institutions.

Two of the fastest-growing jobs in this area include data entry operators and peripheral electronic data processing operators. The U.S. Labor Department is predicting that by 2000, there could be 43,000 new jobs for data entry operators, a 51 percent increase. The field of peripheral electronic data processing operation is expected to provide 70,000 new jobs by 2000.

Other jobs in this area include EDP (electronic data processing) clerks and tape and media librarians, who maintain the computer tapes and written documentation.

Computer Service Technician

As computers become more widely used, more people will be needed to maintain them. Job openings in computer repair and servicing should increase dramatically in the next several years. According to the U.S. Labor Department, there should be about 125,000 new jobs for data processing equipment repairers alone by 2000, an 80 percent increase.

Computer service technicians, often called field or customer engineers, maintain and repair customer equipment and install new computer systems. They may be called on to clean a disk drive, run a diagnostic program to pinpoint a problem and then make repairs, or lay cable for a new computer network. Some are expert at specific repairs or specialize in one brand or type of machine, others work with problems in the computer's internal programming. Most technicians work for wholesalers or computer manufacturers, others for institutions and private companies that have their own computer systems.

Most employers hire computer service technicians who have a high school diploma and one to two years of post-high school training in basic electronics, data processing equipment maintenance, or electrical engineering. This training could come from a college or from a public or private vocational school. Training in basic electronics in the Armed Forces also is acceptable. Applicants must have good human relations skills as well, because they spend so much time listening to customers' complaints, answering questions, and giving technical advice.

The U.S. Bureau of Labor Statistics predicts that employment prospects for computer service technicians will grow much faster than the average for all occupations through the year 2000. Technicians who can repair and maintain several different models or makes of computers or who can work with highly complex systems should have the edge in employment. The salary range for a computer service technician varies widely—from about $15,300 to $42,000, depending on experience. The average annual salary is about $29,000.

Sales and Marketing

There is a growing need for people who understand computer hardware and software and can explain things clearly to customers. The demand for technical writers, who produce product documentation, has been consistently high. In addition, as the computer industry matures, companies are placing more emphasis on sales and on recruiting and training qualified salespeople.

Computer Sales

A computer salesperson has to understand the strengths and weaknesses of different systems, as well as how systems operate and which ones are compatible. A salesperson working for a computer retail outlet has to deal with the products of many different companies and with large-scale clients planning to make significant investments. He or she must be able to put together the most reasonably priced and best-suited system for a client, while ensuring a profit for his or her employer.

Retail salespeople usually work on a commission basis in addition to their regular salary. Companies often set annual sales quotas and offer bonuses as incentives.

Salespeople in retail stores don't necessarily need a college degree. They must understand data processing, however, and have a sound technical proficiency from college or vocational courses. Hands-on experience with a variety of systems is important. Communication and selling skills are essential, and experience in sales and marketing is often required.

Although competition is increasing and employers' standards are getting higher all the time, the job prospects in the field of computer sales are excellent.

Marketing Representative

Marketing or customer support representatives are trained salespeople who work in one geographical region selling new equipment and servicing old accounts. They commonly work for computer manufacturers or distributors rather than for retailers. Market representatives must be able to offer proposals to potential clients and also understand the technical aspects of the company's equipment.

Marketing representatives generally must have a degree in marketing with training in computer science or a bachelor's degree in computer science or electrical engineering with a strong background in business and marketing.

Marketing representatives often work on a commission basis or a salary plus commission basis. Because of the competitive nature of the industry, good marketing representatives are always in demand.

Looking for a Job

Besides checking the want ads in the Sunday paper and in professional publications, how do you go about looking for a job? There are a number of other sources. First, consult your school's placement advisor. He or she has access to a variety of employment information and can help you with any questions you may have about your job search. You may also want to attend a job fair, which can offer instant interviews and the chance to talk to several different companies in one day.

Joining a local data processing organization, such as a branch of the Data Processing Management Association (DPMA), will give you the opportunity to make valuable professional contacts. Also consider joining the American Society for Information Science (ASIS), which operates a placement service for its members.

Contact the nearest branch of the U.S. Office of Personnel Management (OPM) for a list of government agencies with openings and also ask for Standard Form 171, the government-wide application form. You may also consider registering with an employment agency. Their help may be expensive, but their success rate reportedly averages 90 to 92 percent.

The Résumé

Getting a diploma or degree is only half the battle. Once it's in hand and you know what type of work you would like, you must sell yourself to an employer. Having an effective résumé is critical. A résumé not only lists your qualifications, it presents an important first impression of what you are like. There are several things to keep in mind when putting together an effective résumé.

Try to keep it concise, yet include enough detail so the employer can assess your qualifications. Don't describe yourself as "having directed the flow of goods through a multimillion dollar corporation" if you were actually an inventory clerk for a local chain store. This is not the place for a snazzy sales pitch. Always be truthful.

Include your career goal only if you are very certain or it is very specific. You should avoid stating a salary requirement since it can be limiting.

Emphasize your academic background. Pay special attention to career-related course work, programming languages learned, types of hardware used, and programs written. Include only higher-level and relevant classes. List your grade point average only if it's impressive.

There are several ways to list your previous work experience, but the two most common ways are by job or by function. When listing a job, start with the most recent and work backward. Include the dates of employment, name and address of your employer, the nature of your job, and the position you held. Then describe your specific duties and accomplishments. When listing by function, list your fields of specialization or types of work.

Include all your previous work experience, even if it has nothing to do with computers. Employers often consider continuous employment an attribute. Try to play up internships, summer or apprenticeship programs in your field, however. If you spent a summer working as a product specialist intern for IBM, add information about this to your résumé. Include involvement in school or community activities as well, but only if they relate to your career or if they demonstrate your commitment and leadership.

Avoid controversy and filler. Listing work for a special interest group or political party may not always be in your best interest. Use good judgment.

Add the sentence, "References are available upon request" to the end of your résumé and bring your references with you when you are called in for an interview. If you have a particularly eye-catching reference, such as Steven Jobs for instance, do include it on your résumé, however. Be sure to get the permission of anyone you want to use as a reference.

Leave out personal data that is not directly related to the job. It is illegal for employers to discriminate on the basis of age, sex, race, physical disability, or military service. Don't include anything of this nature or you may be putting yourself and your prospective employer in a difficult position. Photographs are unwise unless requested. If they are requested, ask yourself why.

Have your résumé professionally typeset or produced on a letter-quality printer (a laser printer is recommended), and then printed or photocopied on attractive, heavy-stock paper. Stay away from gimmicks, such as purple paper or silver ink.

The Cover Letter

Send a brief cover letter with your résumé. It should supplement your résumé by demonstrating what makes you special, interesting, and worth interviewing.

In the first paragraph, explain why you are writing. If you are responding to an ad or placement office suggestion, state your interest in the position and how you heard about the job. If you are not responding to an ad or job tip, say that you are "inquiring about employment possibilities."

The second paragraph should tell why you should get this job and should also explain your career goals. Sell yourself in a controlled way. Use terms like "enthusiastic and dedicated," "responsible individual," and "eager to share my skills."

For example, explain how your work as a part-time inventory clerk at Megabyte Warehouse, Inc. gave you experience with working under pressure and acquainted you with a large company's shipping procedures. Be polite and respectful, yet self-assured. Finally, don't forget a closing paragraph.

The Interview

Let's say that your prospective employer likes your résumé and cover letter and has called you in for a job interview. All interviews are different, but there are ways to prepare yourself for them. (Most usually last about thirty minutes.)

First of all, be on time. Dress neatly and conservatively to project a good image and to demonstrate your respect for the job and the interviewer. Don't smoke, even if you normally do and the interviewer does. Don't chew gum. If the interview takes place over lunch, don't drink alcoholic beverages and don't eat anything messy.

Try to relax. Be cheerful, not giddy, positive and assertive, but not aggressive or dishonest. Remember to be courteous to the receptionist, the secretary, the office manager, the personnel director, the department head, and the vice president alike. You never can tell who influences whom.

It's very important to do your homework; that is, know what the job entails and how you qualify. Know the general salary range for the position (consult the Bureau of Labor Statistics publications) so you can say how much money you want. A range, such as "low or mid-twenties," is usually acceptable, but be ready with a specific figure as well. Try not to be vague or humorous in your response. Have your references' names, addresses, and phone numbers with you.

Practice a good response to the often-asked questions, such as "What can you contribute to the company?", "What do you see yourself doing five years from now?", and "Tell me about yourself." Have some questions ready about the job or the company. Don't rehash your résumé, except to make a pertinent point. Do bring extra copies of your résumé with you.

As you are leaving, assure the interviewer of your continued interest, ask when a decision will be made, thank him or her, and shake hands.

Write a formal thank-you letter as soon as you get home, re-affirming your interest, suggesting how your skills clearly meet the position's needs, and expressing your enthusiasm about joining the organization.

The Marketplace

We've given you some general information about employment trends, the kinds of jobs available in computing, and how to go about looking for a job. You may want more details about specific jobs, employment qualifications, and products, however. The following list includes the names and addresses of some of the largest manufacturers of computers and peripherals, as well as some other major employers who manufacture automobiles, aircraft, and electronic equipment:

Apple Computer
Professional Staffing
20525 Mariani Avenue
MS-9C
Cupertino, CA 95014

Ashton-Tate
Human Resources Department
20101 Hamilton Avenue
Torrance, CA 90502-1319

AT&T Information Systems
Mr. Robert Bohan
50 Boston Post Road
Orange, CT 06477

Bendix Allied Corporation
Manager—Employer Relations
Allied Signal Automotive
World Headquarters
20650 Civic Center Drive
Southfield, MI 48086

Boeing Company, Incorporated
P.O. Box 3707
MS 31-11
Seattle, WA 98124
Attn: Personnel

Control Data Corporation
Human Resources Department
8100 34th Avenue South
Minneapolis, MN 55440

Data General Corporation
4400 Computer Drive
Westborough, MA 01580

Digital Equipment Corporation
Corporate Employment
150 Coulter Drive
Concord, MA 01752

Ford Motor Company
The American Road
Dearborn, MI 48121
Attn: Central Placement Office

General Dynamics Corporation
Electronics Division
Human Resources P.O. Box 85227
San Diego, CA 92138-5227

General Motors Corporation
EDS Staffing
700 Tower Drive
P.O. Box 7019
Troy, MI 48007-7019

Grumman Corporation
1111 Stewart Avenue
Bethpage, NY 11714
Attn: New Graduate Department

Hewlett-Packard Company
3000 Hanover Street
Palo Alto, CA 94304
Attn: Computer Staffing

Honeywell, Inc.
Honeywell Plaza
Minneapolis, MN 55408

IBM
IBM Employment Office
12 Water Street
White Plains, NY 10601

Intel Corporation
P.O. Box 58119
Santa Clara, CA 95052-8119

Lockheed Electronics Corporation
1501 U.S. Highway 22
Plainfield, NJ 07061

Lotus Development Corporation
Human Resources Department
55 Cambridge Parkway
Cambridge, MA 02142

McDonnell-Douglas Corporation
5701 Pitella Avenue
Cypress, CA 90630
Attn: Personnel

Memorex Corporation
Front Lobby
461 South Milipites Boulevard
Milipites, CA 95035

Microsoft
16011 North East 36th Way
P.O. Box 97017
Redmond, WA 98073-9717

Motorola Corporation
1301 East Algonquin Road
Schaumburg, IL 60195

NCR Corporate Personnel
1700 South Patterson Boulevard
Dayton, OH 45479

Raytheon Corporation
Employment Department
141 Spring Street
Lexington, MA 02173

RCA Corporation
Personnel
Building 2-2
Front and Cooper Streets
Camden, NJ 08102

Rockwell International
Employment Division
3370 Miraloma Avenue
Anaheim, CA 92803

Storage Technology Corporation
2270 South 88th Street
Louisville, CO 80028

Tandy Corporation
500 One Tandy Center
Fort Worth, TX 76012

Texas Instruments, Inc.
P.O. Box 655474
MS 67
Dallas, TX 75265

3M
3M Center
Staffing Department
Building 224-IW-02
St. Paul, MN 55144-1000

TRW, Inc.
Human Relations Department
1900 Richmond Drive
Cleveland, OH 44124

UNISYS Corporation
World Headquarters
One Unisys Place
Detroit, MI 48232
Attn: Corporate Personnel

United Technologies Corporation
Personnel
United Technologies Building
One Financial Plaza
Hartford, CT 06101

Wang Laboratories, Inc.
Corporate Headquarters Building
One Industrial Avenue
Lowell, MA 01851
Attn: Personnel

Sources

Steven Langer, "Compensation in the MIS/DP Field: A Summary of Results of the Sixth Annual Survey," Inside DPMA, July, 1989, p. 12.

"Computer and Mathematics-Related Occupations," reprinted from the *Occupational Outlook Handbook,* 1988-89 edition, U.S. Department of Labor, Bureau of Labor Statistics, pp. 6-12.

George T. Silvestri and John M. Lukasiewicz, "A Look at Occupational Employment Trends to the Year 2000," *Monthly Labor Review,* U.S. Department of Labor, September 1987, pp. 46-47, 56-58.

Valerie A. Personick, "Industry Output and Employment Through the End of the Century," *Monthly Labor Review,* U.S. Department of Labor, September 1987, p. 34.

APPENDIX E

OS/2

A single-user, single-tasking operating system, such as DOS, allows only one program to be run at a time. A multitasking operating system can run more than one program concurrently, or seemingly at the same time. It can juggle the execution of several programs by rapidly switching the attention of the central processing unit among tasks so it seems as if the programs are running simultaneously.

IBM and Microsoft joined forces in 1987 to create OS/2 (Operating System/2), a single-user, multitasking operating system for high-end IBM and IBM-compatible microcomputers that use the Intel 80286, 80386, or 80486 microprocessor. For example, OS/2 will run on an IBM PC AT and IBM PS/2 Models 50, 60, 70, and 80. It will not, however, run on machines that use the 8088 or 8086 chips, such as the original IBM PC, PC XT, or IBM PS/2 Model 25.

This long-awaited operating system more fully utilizes the power of the 80286, 80386, and 80486 chips in ways that DOS never could. OS/2 is a complex operating system that allows programs direct access to almost 16 megabytes of memory and provides true multitasking. Some of the features found in OS/2 make it similar to operating systems designed for minicomputers and mainframes costing hundreds of thousands of dollars. Although it requires a new generation of application packages to make full use of this power, OS/2 can run most existing DOS programs in its **DOS Session,** sometimes called the **DOS Compatibility Box.** This is a special environment that can run a single DOS application at a time. Other applications designed especially for OS/2 can be run concurrently as separate tasks while a DOS program executes in the DOS Session.

IBM OS/2 Standard Edition 1.0, the first version of OS/2, was released with only a basic command-line interface. Subsequent versions of OS/2, however, include a graphical user interface called the **Presentation Manager.** The Presentation Manager, which is similar to Microsoft Windows (see Figure 1), is itself a separate screen group that can run multiple programs. It lets you run programs and choose options with a mouse-directed pointer. Although the simple command-line interface is fine for full-screen programs that do not use graphics, the Presentation Manager is much better for graphics applications.

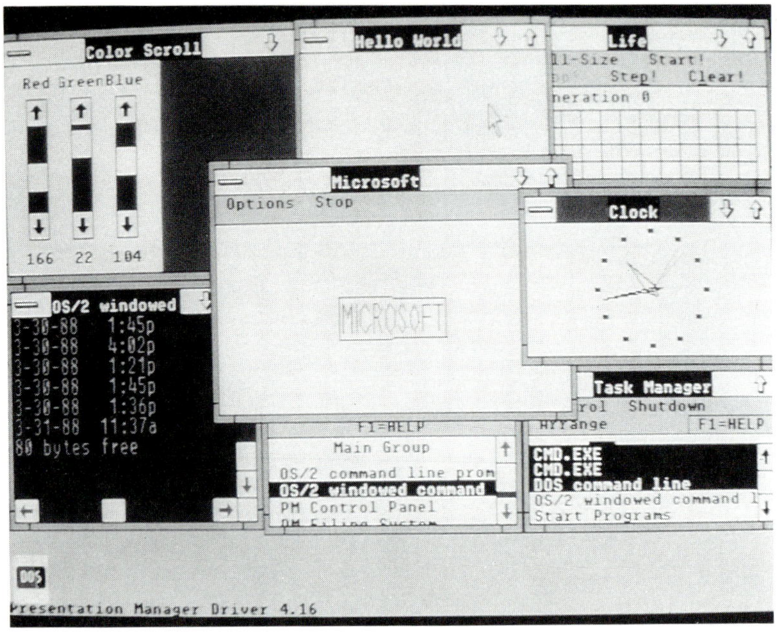

Figure 1 Presentation Manager
The OS/2 Presentation Manager is a graphical user interface similar to Microsoft Windows.

A disadvantage of OS/2 is that because it is a new operating system fewer applications are available for it than DOS. It is also more expensive and requires more sophisticated hardware than does DOS. The minimum hardware configuration for OS/2 is an 80286 microprocessor, 2.5 megabytes of memory, a 1.2- or 1.44-megabyte diskette drive, and a hard disk with at least 5 megabytes of free space. To use the Presentation Manager, you also need a graphics adapter and monitor. The typical OS/2 computer has an 80386 microprocessor, 4 megabytes of memory, at least a 60-megabyte hard disk, a Video Graphics Array (VGA) display adapter, and a mouse.

On the plus side, OS/2 does provide some compatibility with the huge base of existing DOS applications. It also has the potential to run extremely powerful application software. IBM and Microsoft expect that OS/2 will become the standard operating system of the 1990s for high-end IBM-compatible computers.

Installation

Most OS/2 files are stored on the original diskettes in a compressed format, so you cannot use the COPY command to move them to your hard disk. With the computer turned off, you must put the installation diskette in drive A, turn on the computer, and follow the instructions that appear on the screen. The installation process consists of setting up certain subdirectories and copying and expanding files to the hard disk from the OS/2 diskettes. The entire process takes about 20 minutes.

The OS/2 installation process will replace any version of DOS you have on your hard disk, but will not change any other files. You can create a DOS bootup diskette if you still need to use DOS. Like DOS, OS/2 has a CONFIG.SYS file in which you specify configuration parameters. In addition, the Presentation Manager uses a file named OS2.INI to hold certain configuration parameters.

Starting OS/2

To boot up a computer with OS/2 installed on the hard disk, you simply turn it on. The Start Programs window and mouse pointer will appear on the screen. In addition, several icons may appear at the bottom of the screen. These icons represent programs that are loaded and running, but not currently displayed in a window. For example, you may have an icon that looks like a black square with the word DOS in it. This icon represents the DOS Session. The OS/2 print spooler is represented by an icon that looks like a printer. The icon at the lower right that looks like a screen with windows represents the OS/2 Task Manager.

Getting Help

OS/2 has an on-line help facility that you can invoke by pressing the F1 function key or by clicking on the word Help in the Start Programs window with the mouse pointer. After you select Help, the mouse pointer will change to an hourglass icon. You must wait when you see the hourglass because the program is busy and will temporarily ignore mouse and keyboard input. In a moment, the mouse pointer will revert to an arrow and the help screen for Start Programs will appear. The OS/2 help screens are context-sensitive, which means that they always relate to the window or action that was active when Help was invoked. You can also bring up an index to read about other help topics.

Windows

All Presentation Manager windows have certain features in common. The vertical scroll bar along the right side of the window allows you to move up or down through the text by clicking on the arrows or dragging the slider box. Buttons may appear to let you get more information or escape from the window. Select a button by clicking on it or pressing a key that corresponds to it. The default button, which has a highlighted border, can also be selected by pressing the Enter key. You can move a window to a different place on the screen by pointing to its title, pressing the mouse button, dragging the mouse pointer, and releasing the mouse button. You can change the size of a window by pointing to a border or corner, pressing the mouse button, dragging the mouse pointer, and releasing the mouse button.

The File System

The Presentation Manager File System graphically depicts the arrangement of subdirectories and files on your hard disk. It also provides all of the file operations you can perform from the DOS command line. The File System is started by double-clicking on the "File System" entry in the Start Programs window. The File System window will appear and display the directory tree of the disk, usually C:\, from which you booted OS/2. You can see the directory structure of a disk in another drive, such as A or B, by clicking on its icon near the top of the window. If the directory tree does not fit completely on the screen, you can use the vertical scroll bar to move up and down. To see the contents of a subdirectory, simply click on its name. A window will open that lists the files in that subdirectory. The File System uses icons to identify the types of files displayed in a directory window. For example, icons that look like file-drawer folders represent subdirectories, rectangular icons represent executable files or programs, and icons that resemble a page of paper with a turned-down corner represent documents, data files and other types of files. You can run a program by double-clicking on its icon.

The File System has many features for managing files. The titles of its various menus appear across the top of the window: File, Options, Tree, Arrange, Window, and Exit. When you are finished with the File System, you can leave it without actually terminating it. Point to the square in the upper left corner of the window and press the mouse button to pull down the System menu, then select the Minimize option. This will compress the File System into an icon at the bottom of the screen. The File System is still loaded and running, but not displayed in a window.

The Full-Screen Command Line

Sometimes you don't need the Presentation Manager's sophisticated graphical interface. For example, you may want to start your word processor to create a new file simply by entering the name of the program. You can use OS/2's command-line interface instead of the Presentation Manager. Click on the OS/2 Full-Screen Command Prompt option in the Start Programs window. OS/2 will present a screen that looks almost like ordinary DOS. The screen is produced by the program CMD.EXE, which is the OS/2 equivalent of COMMAND.COM, the DOS command processor.

Screen Groups and Sessions

OS/2 allows you to run a number of programs concurrently, but you have only one **physical console**: the display and keyboard. Only one program can communicate with the physical console at a time. OS/2 makes sure that the application you choose is the only program controlling the physical console. Each other program communicates with its own **virtual console**, which is like a pretend display and keyboard.

Each application runs in its own screen group, also called a session. When you switch from one session to another, OS/2 gives control of the physical console to the new session. An application that has control of the physical console is running in the **foreground;** all other applications are running in the **background.**

OS/2 lets you have one Presentation Manager session, one DOS Session, and as many as twelve full-screen command line sessions all running concurrently.

In the Presentation Manager session, you can run as many as sixteen Presentation Manager programs and sixteen windowed text sessions concurrently. The File System, for example, is a Presentation Manager program that runs in the Presentation Manager session. A windowed text session is like the full-screen command-line, except it is in its own window instead of occupying the entire screen. You can create a windowed text session to execute commands such as DIR and CHKDSK. Several Presentation Manager programs and windowed text sessions can share the display screen, but only one can be in the foreground at a time and respond to your keyboard and mouse actions.

The DOS Session runs a special version of DOS that can run most, but not all DOS applications. The DOS Session can run only one DOS application at a time, and this application must be run in the foreground. A program in the DOS Session cannot run in the background. Double-click the DOS icon at the bottom of the screen to invoke the DOS Session. Press Ctrl-Escape to exit the DOS Session.

As we said before, a full-screen, command-line session is invoked by selecting the OS/2 Full-Screen Command Prompt option in the Start Programs window. Close a command-line session by executing the EXIT command from the OS/2 prompt or by pressing Ctrl-Escape.

The Task Manager

The OS/2 Task Manager can be used to switch to a program, rearrange program windows, and shut down a program or the entire system. Press Ctrl-Escape to invoke the Task Manager. The Task Manager is a convenience. You don't have to use it to switch between or close windows. For example, you can switch between sessions without using the Task Manager by pressing Alt-Escape.

APPENDIX F

COMMAND SUMMARIES

MS-DOS Version 4.01

DOS Keys

Keypress	Description
Ctrl-Alt-Del	Reboots DOS.
Ctrl-Break	Cancels a command.
Ctrl-PrtSc	Echoes to the printer.
Enter	Processes a command.
Esc	Cancels the current line.
Pause	Pauses screen scrolling (Enhanced keyboards).
Ctrl-Num Lock	Pauses screen scrolling (PC and AT keyboards).
Print Screen	Prints the contents of the screen (Enhanced keyboards).
Shift-PrtSc	Prints the contents of the screen (PC and AT keyboards).
F1	Retypes one character from the previous command.
F2	Retypes previous command up to the specified character.
F3	Retypes all of the previous command.
F4	Deletes previous command up to the specified character.
F5	Saves current command as if it were the previous command.
F6	Inserts an end-of-file code (Ctrl-Z).
Del	Skips over a character from the previous command.
Ins	Switches insert/overwrite mode in the command line.
>	Redirects output.
>>	Redirects and appends output.
<	Redirects input.
|	Pipes output.

DOS Commands

These conventions are used in the list of DOS commands that follows.

Command Format Conventions	
[ ]	optional command switch or parameter, such as [/a]
or	either/or choice, such as DEL **or** ERASE
...	optional repetition of the previous item as necessary
italics	name or value you must enter, such as the following:
drive:	disk drive name, such as A: or B:
path	directory name, such as \WP\LETTERS\WORK
filename	file name, including extension, such as JIM.DOC
pathname	path plus a *filename*, such as \WP\LETTERS\WORK\JIM.DOC
(Internal)	indicates an internal (resident) DOS command.
(External)	indicates an external (transient) DOS command.
(No Network)	indicates a command that does not work over a network.

You can specify a drive and/or path before any external command in the table below.

DOS Command	Formats and Description
APPEND	APPEND [/x] [/e] [;] **or** APPEND [*drive:*]*path*[;[*drive:*][*path*]...] **or** APPEND [*path*] [/x:[off **or** on]] [/path:[off **or** on]] Specifies the paths to be searched for files with extensions other than BAT, COM, and EXE. (External) /x — Searches for BAT, COM, and EXE files, too. /e — Stores appended paths in the DOS environment. /path — If on, searches for files in the appended paths even if the files have drive or path prefixes.
ASSIGN	ASSIGN [*x* [=] *y*] ... Reassigns a disk drive letter to another drive. (External)
ATTRIB	ATTRIB [+r **or** -r] [+a **or** -a] [*drive*:]*pathname* [/s] Changes a file's read-only or archive attribute. (External) +r — Turns on read-only attribute. -r — Turns off read-only attribute. +a — Turns on archive attribute. -a — Turns off archive attribute. /s — Processes files in subdirectories.
BACKUP	BACKUP [*drive1:*][*path*][*filename*] [*drive2*:] [/s] [/m] [/a] [/f:*size*] [/d:*date*] [/t:*time*] [/L:[[*drive:*][*path*]*filename*]] Backs up one or more files from one disk to another. (External)

DOS Command	Formats and Description
BACKUP *(continued)*	/s — Backs up subdirectories. /m — Backs up only changed files. /a — Adds files without erasing backup disks. /f: — Formats target disks if necessary; *size* indicates type of disk (160K, 180K, 320K, 360K, 720K, 1.2M, or 1.44M) /d: — Backs up only those files modified on or after *date*. /t: — Backs up only those files modified on or after *time*. /L: — Makes a backup log entry in the specified file.
BREAK	BREAK [off **or** on] Turns Ctrl-Break off or on for certain operations. (Internal)
CD or CHDIR	CD **or** CHDIR [*path*] Switches between subdirectories or displays the current directory. (Internal)
CHCP	CHCP [*nnn*] Displays or changes the current code page, where *nnn* is the code page. (Internal)
CHKDSK	CHKDSK [*drive:*][*pathname*] [/f] [/v] Displays a disk and memory status report and checks for errors. (External) (No Network) /f — Fixes lost cluster chains on the disk. /v — Displays the name of every file on the disk.
CLS	CLS Clears the screen. (Internal)
COMMAND	COMMAND [*drive:*][*path*] [*device*] [/e:*nnnnn*] [/p] [/c *string*] Starts a new command processor. (External) /e: — Specifies the environment size, where *nnnnn* is the size in bytes. /p — Keeps the secondary command processor in memory. /c — Performs the commands specified in *string* and then returns to the primary command processor.
COMP	COMP [*drive:*][*pathname1*] [*drive:*][*pathname2*] Compares the contents of two sets of files. (External)
COPY	COPY [*drive:*]*pathname1* [*drive:*][*pathname2*] [/v] [/a] [/b] **or** COPY [*drive:*]*pathname1* [/v] [/a] [/b] [*drive:*][*pathname2*] **or** COPY *pathname1* + *pathname2* ... *pathnameN* Duplicates one or more files. Also appends files. (Internal)

DOS Command	Formats and Description
COPY *(continued)*	/v Turns on the verify switch. /a Copies ASCII files. /b Copies binary files.
CTTY	CTTY *device* Changes the console (terminal) to another device. (Internal)
DATE	DATE [*mm-dd-yy*] Displays or sets the date. (Internal)
DEL or ERASE	DEL **or** ERASE [*drive:*] *pathname* [/p] Removes one or more files from a disk. (Internal) /p Prompts user before each deletion.
DIR	DIR [*drive:*][*pathname*] [/p] [/w] Lists the files on a disk or in a subdirectory. (Internal) /p Pauses after each screen. /w Displays a wide listing.
DISKCOMP	DISKCOMP [*drive1:*] [*drive2*] [/1] [/8] Compares two diskettes. (External) (No Network) /1 Compares just the first sides. /8 Compares just the first 8 sectors of each track.
DISKCOPY	DISKCOPY [*drive1:*] [*drive2:*] [/1] Duplicates an entire floppy disk. (External) (No Network) /1 Copies only one side.
DOSSHELL	DOSSHELL Starts the DOS Shell. (Batch File)
EXE2BIN	EXE2BIN [*drive:*]*pathname1* [*drive:*]*pathname2* Converts EXE files to BIN or COM files. (External)
EXIT	EXIT Exits the COMMAND.COM program. Also, returns to the DOS Shell from the DOS prompt. (Internal)
FASTOPEN	FASTOPEN [*drive:*[=*n*][...]] /x **or** FASTOPEN [*drive:*[=(*n*,*m*)][...]] /x **or** FASTOPEN [*drive:*[=([*n*],*m*)][...]] /x Speeds up disk access by storing directory and file names and locations in a memory cache. (External) (No Network) *n* The number of files FASTOPEN will work with (10–999). *m* The number of file extent entries (1–999). /x Puts the cache in expanded memory.
FDISK	FDISK Partitions a hard disk. (External) (No Network)
FIND	FIND [/v] [/c] [/n] "*string*" [[*drive:*][*pathname*] ...] Searches for a text string in one or more files. (External)

DOS Command	Formats and Description	
FIND *(continued)*	/v	Displays all lines *not* containing the string.
	/c	Displays only the number of lines that contain the string.
	/n	Precedes each line with its line number in the file.
FORMAT	FORMAT *drive:* [/1] [/4] [/8] [/n:*sectors*] [/t:*tracks*] [/v[:*label*]] [/s] **or** FORMAT *drive:* [/1] [/b] [/n:*sectors*] [/t:*tracks*] **or** FORMAT *drive*: [/v[:*label*]] [/f:*size*] [/s] Prepares a disk for use. (External) (No Network)	
	/1	Formats only one side.
	/4	Formats a 360K disk in a 1.2M drive.
	/8	Formats 8 sectors per track.
	/n:	Specifies the number of sectors.
	/t:	Specifies the number of tracks.
	/v:	Specifies the disk name (volume label).
	/b	Leaves room for the DOS hidden system files.
	/s	Creates a bootup disk.
	/f:	Specifies the disk size (160K, 180K, 320K, 360K, 720K, 1.2M, 1.44M)
GRAFTABL	GRAFTABL [*xxx*] **or** /status **or** [?] Enhances the display of graphics characters on a Color Graphics Adapter. (External)	
	xxx	The code page id number.
	/status	Displays the active character set.
	?	Displays instructions for using GRAFTABL.
GRAPHICS	GRAPHICS *type* [*profile*] [/r] [/b] [/lcd] [/printbox:*id*] Allows printing of graphics screens. (External)	
	/r	Prints black on the screen as black on the page.
	/b	Prints the background in color.
	/lcd	Uses aspect ratio of LCD screens.
	/printbox	Selects the printbox size.
JOIN	JOIN [*drive: drive:path*] **or** *drive*: /d Treats a disk drive as if it were a subdirectory. (External) (No Network)	
	/d	Unjoins a previous JOIN.
KEYB	KEYB [*xx*[,[*yyy*],[[*drive:*][*path*]*filename*]]] [/ID:*nnn*] Loads a keyboard-translation table for a country, where *xx* is a two-letter country code and *yyy* is the code page that defines the character set. (External)	
	/ID:	Specifies the keyboard in use to be *nnn*.
LABEL	LABEL [*drive:*][*label*] Creates or changes a disk's name (volume label). (External) (No Network)	

DOS Command	Formats and Description
MD or MKDIR	MD **or** MKDIR [*drive:*]*path* Creates a new subdirectory. (Internal)
MEM	MEM [/program **or** /debug] Displays a memory report. (External) /program Displays programs in memory. /debug Displays technical information.
MODE	MODE [*device*] [/status] **or** MODE LPT*n*[:][*c*][,[*l*][,r]] **or** MODE LPT*n* [cols=*c*] [lines=*l*] [retry=r] **or** MODE COM*m*[:]*b*,[,*p*[,*d*[,*s*[,r]]]] **or** MODE COM*m* baud=*b* [data=*d*] [stop=*s*] [parity=*p*] [retry=r] **or** MODE *display, n* **or** MODE [*display*], *shift* **or** MODE CON[:] [cols=*m*] [lines=*n*] **or** MODE CON[:] rate=*r* delay=*d* **or** MODE *device* codepage prepare=((*yyy*)[*drive:*][*path*]*filename*) **or** MODE *device* codepage select=*yyy* **or** MODE *device* codepage refresh **or** MODE *device* codepage [/status] **or** MODE LPT*n*[:]=COM*m*[:] Establishes settings for various input/output devices. See the *MS-DOS User's Reference* for detailed information. (External)
MORE	MORE < *source* **or** *source* | MORE Accepts input and presents it one screen at a time as output. (External)
NLSFUNC	NLSFUNC [[*drive:*][*path*]*filename*] Specifies country-specific language and code page. (External)
PATH	PATH [*drive*:[*path*][;[*drive*:][*path*]...] **or** PATH [;] Tells DOS where to search for BAT, COM, and EXE files, or displays the current path. (Internal)
PRINT	PRINT [/d:*device*] [/b:*size*] [/u:*value1*] [/m:*value2*] [/s:*timeslice*] [/q:*qsize*] [/t] [*drive:*][*pathname*] [/c] [/p] Prints a text file. (External) /d: Specifies the device name. /b: Specifies the size of the internal buffer in bytes. /u: Specifies the number of clock ticks PRINT will wait for a printer. /m: Specifies the number of clock ticks PRINT can take to print a character. /s: Specifies the timeslice for background printing.

<table>
<tr><th>DOS Command</th><th colspan="2">Formats and Description</th></tr>
<tr><td>PRINT
(continued)</td><td>/q:</td><td>Specifies the number of files allowed in the print queue.</td></tr>
<tr><td></td><td>/t</td><td>Deletes all files in the print queue.</td></tr>
<tr><td></td><td>/c</td><td>Removes the preceding file and all following files from the print queue.</td></tr>
<tr><td></td><td>/p</td><td>Adds the preceding file and all following files to the print queue.</td></tr>
<tr><td>PROMPT</td><td colspan="2">PROMPT [[*text*][$*character*]...]
Changes the format of the DOS prompt. (Internal) The *character* may be one of the following:</td></tr>
<tr><td></td><td>q</td><td>The = character.</td></tr>
<tr><td></td><td>$</td><td>The $ character.</td></tr>
<tr><td></td><td>t</td><td>The current time.</td></tr>
<tr><td></td><td>d</td><td>The current date.</td></tr>
<tr><td></td><td>p</td><td>The current directory.</td></tr>
<tr><td></td><td>v</td><td>The DOS version number.</td></tr>
<tr><td></td><td>n</td><td>The default drive.</td></tr>
<tr><td></td><td>g</td><td>The > character.</td></tr>
<tr><td></td><td>l</td><td>The < character.</td></tr>
<tr><td></td><td>b</td><td>The | character.</td></tr>
<tr><td></td><td>_</td><td>The Enter key.</td></tr>
<tr><td></td><td>e</td><td>The Escape key.</td></tr>
<tr><td></td><td>h</td><td>The Backspace key.</td></tr>
<tr><td>RD or RMDIR</td><td colspan="2">RD **or** RMDIR [*drive*:]*path*
Removes an empty subdirectory. (Internal)</td></tr>
<tr><td>RECOVER</td><td colspan="2">RECOVER [*drive*:][*path*]*filename* **or**
RECOVER *drive*
Reconstructs damaged files or disks. (External) (No Network)</td></tr>
<tr><td>RENAME or REN</td><td colspan="2">RENAME **or** REN [*drive*:][*path*]*filename1 filename2*
Changes the name of one or more files. (Internal)</td></tr>
<tr><td>REPLACE</td><td colspan="2">REPLACE [*drive*:]*pathname1* [*drive*:][*pathname2*] [/a] [/p] [/r] [/s] [/w] [/u]
Updates a set of files. (External)</td></tr>
<tr><td></td><td>/a</td><td>Adds new files to the target instead of replacing existing ones.</td></tr>
<tr><td></td><td>/p</td><td>Prompts user before replacing each file.</td></tr>
<tr><td></td><td>/r</td><td>Replaces read-only files.</td></tr>
<tr><td></td><td>/s</td><td>Searches all subdirectories.</td></tr>
<tr><td></td><td>/u</td><td>Replaces only older files.</td></tr>
<tr><td></td><td>/w</td><td>Prompts user before beginning.</td></tr>
<tr><td>RESTORE</td><td colspan="2">RESTORE *drive1*: [*drive2*:][*pathname*] [/s] [/p] [/b:*date*] [/a:*date*] [/e:*time*] [/L:*time*] [/m] [/n]
Restores files backed up with the BACKUP command. (External)</td></tr>
<tr><td></td><td>/s</td><td>Restores subdirectories.</td></tr>
<tr><td></td><td>/p</td><td>Prompts the user before restoring read-only files or files that have been changed.</td></tr>
</table>

DOS Command	Formats and Description	
RESTORE *(continued)*	/b:	Restores only files modified on or before *date*.
	/a:	Restores only files modified on or after *date*.
	/e:	Restores only files modified at or earlier than *time*.
	/L:	Restores only files modified at or later than *time*.
	/m	Restores only files modified since the last backup.
	/n	Restores only files that no longer exist on the target disk.
SELECT	SELECT menu Installs DOS. SELECT is usually executed by inserting the MS-DOS Install diskette in drive A and pressing Ctrl-Alt-Del. (External)	
SET	SET [*string* = [*string*]] Displays or changes the contents of the DOS environment. (Internal)	
SHARE	SHARE [/f:*space*] [/L:*locks*] Permits file sharing and locking on network systems. (External)	
	/f:	Specifies the storage space used to record file sharing information.
	/L:	Specifies the number of locks to allow.
SORT	[*source*] | SORT [/r] [/+*n*] **or** SORT [/r] [/+*n*] *source* Accepts input, arranges it in order, and writes it out. (External)	
	/r	Reverses the sort (Z–A, 9–0).
	/+*n*	Sorts the file according to the character in column *n*.
SUBST	SUBST [*drive*: *drive*:*path*] **or** SUBST *drive:* /d Treats a subdirectory as if it were a disk drive. (External) (No Network)	
	/d	Cancels a previous substitution.
SYS	SYS *drive*: Installs hidden system files on a properly formatted disk. (External) (No Network)	
TIME	TIME [*hour*:*minute*[:*second*][.*centisecond*]]] Displays or sets the time of day. (Internal)	
TREE	TREE [*pathname*:] [/f] [/a] Displays the directory structure of a disk. (External)	
	/f	Displays the names of the files in each directory.
	/a	Uses only characters that can be output on any display or printer.

DOS Command	Formats and Description
TYPE	TYPE [*drive*:]*filename* Displays a text file on the screen. (Internal)
VER	VER Displays the DOS version number. (Internal)
VERIFY	VERIFY [off **or** on] Turns verification off or on when copying files. (Internal)
VOL	VOL [*drive*:] Displays the disk name (volume label). (Internal)
XCOPY	XCOPY [*drive*:]*pathname* [*drive*:][*pathname*] [/a] [/d:*date*] [/e] [/m] [/p] [/s] [/v] [/w] **or** XCOPY *drive*:[*pathname*] [*drive*:][*pathname*] [/a] [/d:*date*] [/e] [/m] [/p] [/s] [/v] [/w] Duplicates files faster and more flexibly than COPY. (External) /a Copies files that have their archive bit set. /d: Copies files modified on or after *date*. /e Copies subdirectories, even if they are empty. /m Same as /a, but turns off archive bit. /p Prompts user before copying each file. /s Copies subdirectories, unless they are empty. /v Turns on the verify switch. /w Waits before copying files.

Batch File Command	Formats and Description
CALL	CALL [*drive*:][*path*]*batchfile* [*argument*] Invokes *batchfile* from within the current batch file. The *argument* is the command in the current batch file that will be run following *batchfile*. (Internal)
ECHO	ECHO [off **or** on **or** *message*] Turns screen messages off or on, or displays *message*. (Internal)
FOR	FOR %%*c* in *set* do *command* **or** FOR %*c* in *set* do *command* Sets up a repeating loop in a batch file to perform a command for a set of files. The character *c* represents a variable name, the *set* is a set of files, and the *command* is a DOS command or program. (Internal)
GOTO	GOTO [:]*label* Transfers execution in a batch file to the line after *label*. (Internal)

Batch File Command	Formats and Description
IF	IF [not] errorlevel *number command* **or** IF [not] *string1* = = *string2 command* **or** IF [not] exist *filename command* Executes a command based on the result of a condition. (Internal)
PAUSE	PAUSE [*message*] Temporarily suspends the execution of a batch file until the user presses a key. (Internal)
REM	REM [*comment*] Identifies a batch file comment or remark. (Internal)
SHIFT	SHIFT Sets up more than nine batch file parameters. (Internal)

CONFIG.SYS Command	Formats and Description
BREAK	BREAK = [off or on] Turns Ctrl-Break off or on for certain operations.
BUFFERS	BUFFERS = *n*[,*m*] [/x] Sets the number of disk buffers. *n* — The number of disk buffers (1–99). *m* — The maximum number of sectors that can be read or written in one input/output operation (1–8). /x — Sets the maximum number of disk buffers to 10,000 or the largest number of buffers that will fit in memory, whichever is less.
COUNTRY	COUNTRY = *xxx*[,[*yyy*][,[*drive*:]*filename*]] Changes country-specific information. *xxx* — The country code. *yyy* — The code page for the country. *filename* — The file containing country information.
DEVICE	DEVICE = [*drive*:][*path*]*filename* [*argument*] Installs a device driver.
DRIVEPARM	DRIVEPARM = /d:*number* [/c] [/f:*factor*] [/h:*heads*] [/i] [/n] [/s:*sectors*] [/t:*tracks*] Defines parameters for block devices such as disk and tape drives. /d: — Specifies the physical drive number (0–255). /c — Indicates that the drive can sense if its door has been opened. /f: — Specifies the device type or form factor (0–7).

CONFIG.SYS Command	Formats and Description
DRIVEPARM *(continued)*	/h: Specifies the maximum head number (1–99). /i Specifies an electrically-compatible 3½-inch disk drive. /n Specifies a nonremovable block device. /s: Specifies the number of sectors per track (1–99). /t: Specifies the number of tracks per side (1–999).
FCBS	FCBS = *x,y* Allows access to file control blocks. *x* The number of files that can be open at one time. *y* The number of files that DOS cannot close automatically.
FILES	FILES = *x* Specifies the maximum number of open files (*x*).
INSTALL	INSTALL = [*drive*:][*path*]*filename* [*parameters*] Installs RAM-resident features. The *filename* must be FASTOPEN.EXE, KEY.EXE, NLSFUNC.EXE, or SHARE.EXE.
LASTDRIVE	LASTDRIVE = *x* Specifies the last accessible drive, where *x* is the drive letter (A–Z).
REM	REM *comment* Allows a comment or remark to be entered in the CONFIG.SYS file.
SHELL	SHELL = [*drive*:][*path*]*filename* [*parameters*] Begins execution of the top-level command processor.
STACKS	STACKS = *n,s* Supports the dynamic use of data stacks. *n* The number of stacks (0–64). *s* The size of each stack (0–512).

WordPerfect Version 5.0

Cursor Movement Commands

Up one line	Up Arrow
Down one line	Down Arrow
Left one character	Left Arrow
Right one character	Right Arrow
Left one word	Ctrl-Left Arrow
Right one word	Ctrl-Right Arrow
Next tab stop	Tab
End of line	End
Up one screen	Grey Minus (num. keypad)
Down one screen	Grey Plus (num. keypad)
Up one page	Page Up
Down one page	Page Down
Right edge of screen	Home, Right Arrow
Left edge of screen	Home, Left Arrow
Beginning of Line (Before Text)	Home, Home, Left Arrow
Beginning of Line (Before Codes)	Home, Home, Home, Left Arrow
Beginning of document	Home, Home, Up Arrow
End of document	Home, Home, Down Arrow
Go to specified page	Ctrl-Home

Insert and Delete Commands

Switch insert/typeover mode	Insert
Insert hard return	Enter
Insert page break	Ctrl-Enter
Insert hard space	Home, Space Bar
Delete character or block	Delete
Delete character left of cursor	Backspace
Delete word at cursor	Ctrl-Backspace
Delete word left	Home, Backspace
Delete word right	Home, Delete
Delete to end of line	Ctrl-End
Delete to end of page	Ctrl-PgDn

Function Key Commands

Cancel last command	F1
Temporarily return to DOS	Ctrl-F1
Invoke Setup Menu	Shift-F1
Invoke thesaurus	Alt-F1
Search forward for text	F2
Invoke spelling checker	Ctrl-F2
Search backward for text	Shift-F2
Global search and replace	Alt-F2
Invoke Help facility	F3
Split screen into windows	Ctrl-F3
Switch to other window	Shift-F3
Reveal hidden formatting codes	Alt-F3

Indent paragraph	F4
Move, copy, or delete text	Ctrl-F4
Center paragraph	Shift-F4
Turn on block marking	Alt-F4
Invoke List Files menu	F5
Save or load ASCII text file	Ctrl-F5
Invoke Date/Outline menu	Shift-F5
Invoke Mark Text menu	Alt-F5
Boldface text	F6
Align text to tab stop	Ctrl-F6
Center text	Shift-F6
Align text flush right	Alt-F6
Exit menu, document, or program	F7
Create footnotes	Ctrl-F7
Invoke Print menu	Shift-F7
Invoke Math/Columns menu	Alt-F7
Underline text	F8
Invoke Font menu	Ctrl-F8
Invoke Format menu	Shift-F8
Invoke Style menu	Alt-F8
End-of-field merge code (^R)	F9
Invoke Merge/Sort menu	Ctrl-F9
Invoke Merge Codes menu	Shift-F9
Incorporate graphics	Alt-F9
Save current document	F10
Define new keyboard macro	Ctrl-F10
Retrieve existing document	Shift-F10
Invoke macro	Alt-F10

Alphabetical List of Features

In the table below, the Keypresses column lists the keys to press and characters to type to invoke the feature. For example, to invoke the Advance feature (to advance the printer), press **Shift-F8**, type **4**, then type **1**.

Feature	Keypresses
Advance	Shift-F8, 4, 1
Appearance Attributes	Ctrl-F8, 2
Automatic Reference	Alt-F5, 1
Automatically Format and Rewrite	Shift-F1, 3, 1
Backup	Shift-F1, 1
Base Font	Ctrl-F8, 4
Beep Options	Shift-F1, 5, 1
Binding	Shift-F7, B
Block	Alt-F4
Block Protect (Block on)	Shift-F8
Boldface	F6
^C (Text from Keyboard)	Shift-F9, C
Cancel	F1
Cancel Print Jobs	Shift-F7, 4, 1
Cartridges and Fonts	Shift-F7, S, 3, 5

Feature	Keypresses
Case Conversion (Block on)	Shift-F3
Center	Shift-F6
Center Page Top to Bottom	Shift-F8, 2, 1
Colors/Fonts/Attributes	Shift-F1, 3, 2
Columns (Text and Parallel)	Alt-F7
Compose	Ctrl-2
Concordance	Alt-F5, 5, 3
Conditional End of Page	Shift-F8, 4, 2
Control Printer	Shift-F7, 4
Copy File	F5, Enter, 8
Create Directory	F5, =
ˆD (Date)	Shift-F9, D
Date Code	Shift-F5, 2
Date Format	Shift-F5, 3
Date Text	Shift-F5, 1
Date/Outline	Shift-F5
Decimal/Align Character	Shift-F8, 4, 3
Define (Mark Text)	Alt-F5, 5
Delete Directory or File	F5, Enter, 2
Display All Print Jobs	Shift-F7, 4, 3
Display Pitch	Shift-F8, 3, 1
Display Setup	Shift-F1, 3
Document Comments	Ctrl-F5, 5
Document Compare	Alt-F6, 6, 2
Document Format	Shift-F8, 3
Document Summary	Shift-F8, 3, 4
DOS Text File Retrieve	Ctrl-F5, 1, 2
DOS Text File Save	Ctrl-F5, 1, 1
Double Underline	Ctrl-F8, 2, 3
ˆE (End of Record)	Shift-F9, E
Edit Table of Authorities	Alt-F5, 5, 5
Endnote	Ctrl-F7, 2
Endnote Placement Code	Ctrl-F7, 3
Exit	F7
Extra Large Print	Ctrl-F8, 1, 7
ˆF (Field)	Shift-F9, F
Fast Save	Shift-F1, 4
Figure (Graphics)	Alt-F9, 1
Filename on Status Line	Shift-F1, 3, 4
Fine Print	Ctrl-F8, 1, 3
Flush Right	Alt-F6
Footers	Shift-F8, 2, 4
Footnote	Ctrl-F7, 1
Force Odd/Even Page	Shift-F8, 2, 2
Format	Shift-F8
Forms	Shift-F7, S, 3, 4
ˆG (Start Macro)	Shift-F9, G
Generate (Mark Text)	Alt-F5, 6
Generate Tables	Alt-F5, 6, 5
Generic Word Processor Format	Ctrl-F5, 3
Go (Start Printer)	Shift-F7, 4, 4

Feature	Keypresses
Go to DOS	Ctrl-F1, 1
Graphics	Alt-F9
Graphics Quality	Shift-F7, G
Graphics Screen Type	Shift-F1, 3, 5
Headers	Shift-F8, 2, 3
Help	F3
Horizontal Line (Graphics)	Alt-F9, 5, 1
Hyphenation	Shift-F8, 1, 1
Hyphenation Zone	Shift-F8, 1, 2
Indent Paragraph	F4
Indent (Center) Paragraph	Shift-F4
Index Define	Alt-F5, 5, 3
Index Mark	Alt-F5, 3
Initial Settings (Format)	Shift-F8, 3, 2
Initial Settings (Setup)	Shift-F1, 5
Italics	Ctrl-F8, 2, 4
Justification	Shift-F8, 1, 3
Kerning	Shift-F8, 4, 6, 1
Keyboard Layout	Shift-F1, 6
Language	Shift-F8, 4, 4
Large Print	Ctrl-F8, 1, 5
Line Draw	Ctrl-F3, 2
Line Format	Shift-F8, 1
Line Height	Shift-F8, 1, 4
Line Numbering	Shift-F8, 1, 5
Line Spacing	Shift-F8, 1, 6
List Define	Alt-F5, 5, 2
List Mark (Block on)	Alt-F5, 2
List Files	F5, Enter
Location of Auxiliary Files	Shift-F1, 7
Look	F5, Enter, 6
Macro	Alt-F10
Macro Define	Ctrl-F10
Margin Release	Shift-Tab
Margins Left/Right	Shift-F8, 1, 7
Margins Top/Bottom	Shift-F8, 2, 5
Mark Text	Alt-F5
Master Document Condense	Alt-F5, 6, 4
Master Document Expand	Alt-F5, 6, 3
Master Document Subdocument	Alt-F5, 2
Math/Columns	Alt-F7
Menu Letter Display	Shift-F1, 3, 7
Merge	Ctrl-F9, 1
Merge Codes	Shift-F9
Move	Ctrl-F4
Move Block (Block on)	Ctrl-F4, 1
Move Page	Ctrl-F4, 3
Move Paragraph	Ctrl-F4, 2
Move Rectangle (Block on)	Ctrl-F4, 3
Move/Rename (List Files)	F5, Enter, 3
Move Sentence	Ctrl-F4, 1

Feature	Keypresses
Move Tabular Column (Block on)	Ctrl-F4, 2
^N (Next Record)	Shift-F9, N
Name Search (List Files)	F5, Enter, N
New Page Number	Shift-F8, 2, 6
Normal Text (Attributes off)	Ctrl-F8, 3
Number of Copies	Shift-F7, N
^O (Display Message)	Shift-F9, O
Other Directory	F5, Enter, 7
Outline	Shift-F5, 4
Outline (Attribute)	Ctrl-F8, 2, 5
Overstrike	Shift-F8, 4, 5
^P (Primary File)	Shift-F9, P
Page Format	Shift-F8, 2
Page Numbering	Shift-F8, 2, 7
Paragraph Number	Shift-F5, 5
Paragraph Numbering Definition	Shift-F5, 6
Paper Size/Type	Shift-F8, 2, 8
Password	Ctrl-F5, 2
Print	Shift-F7
Print Block (Block on)	Shift-F7, Y
Print Color	Ctrl-F8, 5
Print Full Document	Shift-F7, 1
Print List Files	F5, Enter, 4
Print Page	Shift-F7, 2
Printer Command	Shift-F8, 4, 6, 2
Printer Settings	Shift-F7, S, 3
^Q (Stop Merge)	Shift-F9, Q
^R (End of Field)	Shift-F9, R
Redline	Ctrl-F8, 2, 8
Redline Method	Shift-F8, 3, 3
Remove Redline/Strikeout	Alt-F5, 6, 1
Repeat Value	Escape
Replace	Alt-F2
Replace, Extended	Home, Alt-F2
Retrieve Block (Move)	Ctrl-F4, 4, 1
Retrieve Document	Shift-F10
Retrieve List Files	F5, Enter, 1
Retrieve Rectangle (Move)	Ctrl-F4, 4, 3
Retrieve Tabular Column (Move)	Ctrl-F4, 4, 2
Reveal Codes	Alt-F3
Rewrite	Ctrl-F3, 0
Rush Print Job	Shift-F7, 4, 2
^S (Secondary File)	Shift-F9, S
Save	F10
Screen	Ctrl-F3
Search Forward	F2
Search Forward Extended	Home, F2
Search Backward	Shift-F2
Search Backward Extended	Home, Shift-F2
Select Printer	Shift-F7, S
Setup	Shift-F1

Feature	Keypresses
Shadow	Ctrl-F8, 2, 6
Shell	Ctrl-F1
Side-by-side Column Display	Shift-F1, 3, 8
Size Attribute	Ctrl-F8, 1
Small Caps	Ctrl-F8, 2, 7
Small Print	Ctrl-F8, 1, 4
Sort	Ctrl-F9, 2
Spell	Ctrl-F2
Split Screen	Ctrl-F3, 1
Stop Printing	Shift-F7, 4, 5
Strikeout	Ctrl-F8, 2, 9
Style	Alt-F8
Subscript	Ctrl-F8, 1, 2
Superscript	Ctrl-F8, 1, 1
Suppress (Page Format)	Shift-F8, 2, 9
Switch	Shift-F3
^T (Send to Printer)	Shift-F9, T
Tab Align	Ctrl-F6
Tab Set	Shift-F8, 1, 8
Table (Graphics)	Alt-F9, 2
Table of Authorities Define	Alt-F5, 5, 4
Table of Authorities Edit Full Form	Alt-F5, 5, 5
Table of Authorities Full (Block on)	Alt-F5, 4
Table of Authorities Short Form	Alt-F5, 4
Table of Contents Define	Alt-F5, 5, 1
Table of Contents Mark (Block on)	Alt-F5, 1
Text Box (Graphics)	Alt-F9, 3
Text In (List Files)	F5, Enter, 5
Text In In/Out	Ctrl-F5
Text Quality	Shift-F7, T
Thesaurus	Alt-F1
Thousand's Separator	Shift-F8, 4, 3
Type Through	Shift-F7, 5
^U (Rewrite Screen)	Shift-F9, U
Undelete	F1
Underline	F8
Underline Spaces/Tabs	Shift-F8, 4, 7
Units of Measure	Shift-F1, 8
User-Defined Box (Graphics)	Alt-F9, 4
^V (Insert Merge Code)	Shift-F9, V
Vertical Line (Graphics)	Alt-F9, 5, 2
Very Large Print	Ctrl-F8, 1, 6
View Document	Shift-F7, 6
Widow/Orphan Protection	Shift-F8, 1, 9
Window	Ctrl-F3, 1
Word/Letter Spacing	Shift-F8, 4, 6, 3
Word Search	F5, Enter, 9
Word Spacing Justification Limits	Shift-F8, 4, 6, 4
WordPerfect 4.2 Format	Ctrl-F5, 4

Lotus 1-2-3 Release 2.2

Lotus 1-2-3 Keys

Keypress	Description
/	Activates the Main menu.
Enter	Completes an entry.
Backspace	Erases preceding character.
Delete	Deletes character at cursor.
Insert	Switches INSERT/OVERWRITE mode.
Escape	Exits a menu; erases entry in control panel.
Home	Moves to cell A1.
Left Arrow	Moves left one cell.
Right Arrow	Moves right one cell.
Up Arrow	Moves up one cell.
Down Arrow	Moves down one cell.
Ctrl-Left Arrow	(BIG LEFT) Moves left one screen.
Shift-Tab	Moves left one screen.
Ctrl-Right Arrow	(BIG RIGHT) Moves right one screen.
Tab	Moves right one screen.
Page Up	Moves up one screen.
Page Down	Moves down one screen.
End, Right Arrow	Moves right to intersection of a blank and a nonblank cell.
End, Left Arrow	Moves left to intersection of a blank and a nonblank cell.
End, Up Arrow	Moves up to intersection of a blank and a nonblank cell.
End, Down Arrow	Moves down to intersection of a blank and a nonblank cell.
F1	(HELP) Activates the help facility.
Alt-F1	(COMPOSE) Creates international and graphics characters.
F2	(EDIT) Changes to EDIT mode.
Alt-F2	(STEP) Turns on STEP mode, which executes macros one step at a time for debugging.
F3	(NAME) Displays a menu of range names.
Alt-F3	(RUN) Displays a menu to select the name of the macro to run.
F4	(ABS) Changes the type of cell addressing.
Alt-F4	(UNDO) Cancels the previous change.
F5	(GOTO) Moves to a particular cell address.
Alt-F5	(LEARN) Turns macro learn feature on and off.
F6	(WINDOW) Switches to other split-screen window.
F7	(QUERY) Repeats most recent Data Query command.
F8	(TABLE) Repeats most recent Data Table command.
F9	(CALC) Recalculates all worksheet formulas.
F10	(GRAPH) Displays the most recently specified graph.

Lotus 1-2-3 Release 2.2 Menu Commands (Levels 1 and 2)

Command	Description
/WG	Worksheet Global Specifies the default settings applied to all cells for items such as numeric format, label alignment, column width, recalculation method, cell protection, and the display of zero values.
/WI	Worksheet Insert Adds blank rows or columns to an existing worksheet.
/WD	Worksheet Delete Removes rows or columns from an existing worksheet.
/WC	Worksheet Column Specifies settings for column width and column hiding.
/WE	Worksheet Erase Completely erases the entire worksheet.
/WT	Worksheet Titles Freezes rows and/or columns so they can always be seen.
/WW	Worksheet Window Allows use of two horizontal or vertical windows.
/WS	Worksheet Status Displays information about memory, global settings, and hardware.
/WP	Worksheet Page Inserts a printer page break into the worksheet.
/WL	Worksheet Learn Specifies the learn range where macro instructions will be stored in LEARN mode.
/RF	Range Format Sets the numeric format for a range of cells.
/RL	Range Label Aligns existing labels in a range of cells.
/RE	Range Erase Removes the contents of a range of cells.
/RN	Range Name Creates or deletes cell range names.
/RJ	Range Justify Rearranges words in a column to fit within a specified width.
/RP	Range Protect Prevents changes and deletions to a range of cells.

Command	Description
/RU	Range Unprotect Allows changes and deletions to a range of cells.
/RI	Range Input Restricts cell pointer movement to unprotected cells.
/RV	Range Value Converts formulas to their computed values in a range of cells.
/RT	Range Transpose Reorders a range of cells, switching rows and columns.
/RS	Range Search Locates strings in labels and/or formulas within a specified range.
/C	Copy Creates a copy of existing cell contents.
/M	Move Moves a range of cells to another place in the worksheet.
/FR	File Retrieve Loads a worksheet from a disk into memory.
/FS	File Save Copies a worksheet from memory to a disk file.
/FC	File Combine Copies, adds, or subtracts values from one worksheet to another.
/FX	File Xtract Extracts and saves part of one worksheet in another file.
/FE	File Erase Removes one or more files from a disk.
/FL	File List Displays the names of files on a disk.
/FI	File Import Imports data from a text file into the worksheet.
/FD	File Directory Changes the current disk drive directory.
/FA	File Admin Recalculates linked formulas, shares files on a network, or creates a table of information about the files on a disk.
/PP	Print Printer Sends a worksheet directly to the printer.
/PF	Print File Sends a worksheet to a file to be printed later.

Command	Description
/GT	Graph Type Specifies the type of graph to be created.
/GX	Graph X Specifies the range of cells for the X-axis labels.
/GA	Graph A Specifies the first range of cells to be used as data for the graph.
/GB–/GF	Graph B–Graph F Specify additional data ranges.
/GR	Graph Reset Cancels graph settings.
/GV	Graph View Displays the current graph on the screen.
/GS	Graph Save Stores the current graph in a disk file so it can be printed later.
/GO	Graph Options Specifies various options for enhancing a graph's appearance.
/GN	Graph Name Creates, uses, deletes, or resets a graph name.
/GG	Graph Group Specifies all graph data ranges at once, when the X and A through F data ranges are in consecutive columns or rows of a range.
/GQ	Graph Quit Exits from the Graph submenu.
/DF	Data Fill Enters a sequence of numbers into a range of cells.
/DT	Data Table Tabulates the effects of changing values in formulas.
/DS	Data Sort Rearranges rows of cells in a specified order.
/DQ	Data Query Searches for, copies, extracts, or removes specified rows of cells.
/DD	Data Distribution Creates a frequency distribution of the values in a range of cells.
/DM	Data Matrix Multiplies and inverts matrices of cells.
/DR	Data Regression Fits a line to a set of data points.

Command	Description
/DP	Data Parse Breaks up long labels into individual cell entries.
/S	System Allows the use of DOS commands while working with 1-2-3.
/AA	Add-In Attach Loads an add-in program, such as Allways, into memory.
/AD	Add-In Detach Removes an attached add-in program from memory, freeing the memory it occupied.
/AI	Add-In Invoke Activates an attached add-in program.
/AC	Add-In Clear Removes all attached add-in programs from memory, freeing the memory they occupied.
/AQ	/Add-In Quit Returns to READY mode from the Add-In menu.
/Q	Quit Ends 1-2-3 and returns to DOS.

Lotus 1-2-3 Functions

Function	Format and Description
@@	@@(*location*) Returns the contents of the cell at *location*.
@ABS	@ABS(*x*) Calculates the absolute value of *x*.
@ACOS	@ACOS(*x*) Calculates the arc cosine of *x*.
@ASIN	@ASIN(*x*) Calculates the arc sine of *x*.
@ATAN	@ATAN(*x*) Calculates the arc tangent of *x*.
@ATAN2	@ATAN(*x*,*y*) Calculates the four-quadrant arc tangent of *y*/*x*.
@AVG	@AVG(*list*) Averages the values in *list*.
@CELL	@CELL(*attribute*,*range*) Returns information about an *attribute* for the first cell in *range*.

Function	Format and Description
@CELLPOINTER	@CELLPOINTER(*attribute*) Returns information about an *attribute* for the current cell.
@CHAR	@CHAR(*x*) Returns the character that corresponds to Lotus International Character Set code *x*.
@CHOOSE	@CHOOSE(*offset*,*list*) Returns value or string in *list* specified by *offset*.
@CLEAN	@CLEAN(*string*) Removes control characters from *string*.
@CODE	@CODE(*string*) Returns the Lotus International Character Set code for the first character in *string*.
@COLS	@COLS(*range*) Counts columns in *range*.
@COS	@COS(*x*) Calculates the cosine of *x*.
@COUNT	@COUNT(*list*) Counts the nonblank cells in *list*.
@CTERM	@CTERM(*interest*,*future-value*,*present-value*) Calculates the number of compounding periods for an investment *present-value* to grow to a *future-value*, given a fixed periodic *interest* rate.
@DATE	@DATE(*year*,*month*,*day*) Calculates the date number for *year*, *month*, and *day*.
@DATEVALUE	@DATEVALUE(*string*) Calculates the date number for a *string* that looks like a date.
@DAVG	@DAVG(*input*,*field*,*criteria*) Averages value in a *field* of a data base (*input* range) that meet criteria in *criteria* range.
@DAY	@DAY(*date-number*) Calculates the day of the month in *date-number*.
@DCOUNT	@DCOUNT(*input*,*field*,*criteria*) Counts nonblank cells in a *field* of a data base (*input* range) that meet the criteria in *criteria* range.
@DDB	@DDB(*cost*,*salvage*,*life*,*period*) Calculates depreciation allowance of an asset using the double-declining balance method.
@DMAX	@DMAX(*input*,*field*,*criteria*) Finds the largest value in a *field* of a data base (*input* range) that meets the criteria in *criteria* range.

Function	Format and Description
@DMIN	@DMIN(*input,field,criteria*) Finds the smallest value in a *field* of a data base (*input* range) that meets the criteria in *criteria* range.
@DSTD	@DSTD(*input,field,criteria*) Calculates the population standard deviation of values in a *field* of a data base (*input* range) that meet the criteria in *criteria* range.
@DSUM	@DSUM(*input,field,criteria*) Sums values in a *field* of a data base (*input* range) that meet the criteria in *criteria* range.
@DVAR	@DVAR(*input,field,criteria*) Calculates the population variance of values in a *field* of a data base (*input* range) that meet the criteria in *criteria* range.
@ERR	@ERR Returns the error value.
@EXACT	@EXACT(*string1,string2*) Returns 1 (true) if *string1* and *string2* are the same; returns 0 (false) otherwise.
@EXP	@EXP(*x*) Calculates the value of *e* (2.718282) raised to the power *x*.
@FALSE	@FALSE Returns the logical value 0 (false).
@FIND	@FIND(*search-string,string,start-number*) Returns the number of the first occurrence of *search-string* in *string*, beginning with *start-number*.
@FV	@FV(*payments,interest,term*) Calculates the future value of a series of equal *payments*, given a periodic *interest* rate and number of payment periods (*term*).
@HLOOKUP	@HLOOKUP(*x,range,row-offset*) Returns the contents of the cell in *row-offset* of the horizontal lookup table (*range*).
@HOUR	@HOUR(*time-number*) Calculates the hour (0–23) in *time-number*.
@IF	@IF(*condition,x,y*) Evaluates *condition* and returns *x* if *condition* is 1 (true), *y* if *condition* is 0 (false).
@INDEX	@INDEX(*range,column-offset,row-offset*) Returns the value in the cell located at *column-offset* and *row-offset* in *range*.
@INT	@INT(*x*) Returns the integer portion of *x*, without rounding.

Function	Format and Description
@IRR	@IRR(*guess,range*) Calculates the internal rate of return for a series of cash flows in *range,* based on the percentage *guess.*
@ISAAF	@ISAAF(*name*) Returns 1 (true) if *name* is a defined add-in @function; otherwise it returns 0 (false).
@ISAPP	@ISAPP(*name*) Returns 1 (true) if *name* is an attached add-in @function; otherwise it returns 0 (false).
@ISERR	@ISERR(*x*) Returns 1 (true) if *x* is the value ERR; otherwise it returns 0 (false).
@ISNA	@ISNA(*x*) Returns 1 (true) if *x* is the value NA; otherwise it returns 0 (false).
@ISNUMBER	@ISNUMBER(*x*) Returns 1 (true) if *x* is a value or a blank cell; otherwise it returns 0 (false).
@ISSTRING	@ISSTRING(*x*) Returns 1 (true) if *x* is a string; otherwise it returns 0 (false).
@LEFT	@LEFT(*string,n*) Returns the first *n* characters in *string.*
@LENGTH	@LENGTH(*string*) Counts the characters in *string.*
@LN	@LN(*x*) Calculates the natural logarithm (base *e*) of *x.*
@LOG	@LOG(*x*) Calculates the common logarithm (base 10) of *x.*
@LOWER	@LOWER(*string*) Converts all letters in string to lowercase.
@MAX	@MAX(*list*) Returns the largest value in *list.*
@MID	@MID(*string,start-number,n*) Returns *n* characters from *string,* beginning with the *start-number* position.
@MIN	@MIN(*list*) Returns the smallest value in *list.*
@MINUTE	@MINUTE(*time-number*) Calculates the minute (0–59) in *time-number.*
@MOD	@MOD(*x,y*) Returns the remainder (modulus) of *x*/*y.*

Function	Format and Description
@MONTH	@MONTH(*date-number*) Calculates the month (1–12) in *date-number*.
@N	@N(*range*) Returns the entry in the first cell of *range* as a value.
@NA	@NA Returns the value of NA (Not Available).
@NOW	@NOW Calculates the date and time numbers that correspond to the current date and time.
@NPV	@NPV(*interest,range*) Calculates the net present value of a series of future cash flows (*range*), discounted at a fixed, periodic *interest* rate.
@PI	@PI Returns the value of π (pi), calculated at 3.1415926536.
@PMT	@PMT(*principal,interest,term*) Calculates the payment needed to pay off a loan (*principal*), given the *interest* rate and number of payment periods (*term*).
@PROPER	@PROPER(*string*) Capitalizes the first letter of each word in *string*.
@PV	@PV(*payments,interest,term*) Calculates the present value of a series of equal *payments*, discounted at a periodic *interest* rate and given a number of payment periods (*term*).
@RAND	@RAND Generates a random number between 0 and 1.
@RATE	@RATE(*future-value,present-value,term*) Calculates the periodic interest rate necessary for the investment *present-value* to grow to *future-value*, given the number of compounding periods (*term*).
@REPEAT	@REPEAT(*string,n*) Repeats *string* *n* times.
@REPLACE	@REPLACE(*string1,start-number,n,string2*) Replaces *n* characters in *string1* beginning at *start-number* from *string2*.
@RIGHT	@RIGHT(*string,n*) Returns the last *n* characters from *string*.
@ROUND	@ROUND(*x,n*) Rounds the value *x* to *n* decimal places.
@ROWS	@ROWS(*range*) Counts the number of rows in *range*.

Function	Format and Description
@S	@S(*range*) Returns the entry in the first cell of *range* as a label.
@SECOND	@SECOND(*time-number*) Calculates the seconds (0–59) in *time-number*.
@SIN	@SIN(*x*) Calculates the sine of *x*.
@SLN	@SLN(*cost,salvage,life*) Calculates the straight-line depreciation allowance of an asset for one period.
@SQRT	@SQRT(*x*) Calculates the square root of *x*.
@STD	@STD(*list*) Calculates the population standard deviation of the values in *list*.
@STRING	@STRING(*x,n*) Converts the value *x* to a string with *n* decimal places.
@SUM	@SUM(*list*) Calculates the sum of the values in *list*.
@SYD	@SYD(*cost,salvage,life,period*) Calculates the sum-of-the-years'-digits depreciation allowance of an asset for a specified *period*.
@TAN	@TAN(*x*) Calculates the tangent of *x*.
@TERM	@TERM(*payments,interest,future-value*) Calculates the number of payment periods in the term of an investment necessary to accumulate *future-value*, given *payments* of equal value, when the investment earns a periodic *interest* rate.
@TIME	@TIME(*hour,minute,second*) Calculates the time number for *hour, minute*, and *second*.
@TIMEVALUE	@TIMEVALUE(*string*) Calculates the time number for a *string* that looks like a time.
@TRIM	@TRIM(*string*) Removes the leading, trailing, and consecutive spaces in *string*.
@TRUE	@TRUE Returns the logical value 1 (true).
@UPPER	@UPPER(*string*) Converts all letters in *string* to uppercase.
@VALUE	@VALUE(*string*) Converts the number entered as *string* to its numeric value.

Function	Format and Description
@VAR	@VAR(*list*) Calculates the population variance of the values in *list*.
@VLOOKUP	@VLOOKUP(*x*,*range*,*column-offset*) Returns the contents of the cell in *column-offset* of the vertical lookup table *range*.
@YEAR	@YEAR(*date-number*) Calculates the year, an integer from 0 (1900) to 199 (2099), in *date-number*.

dBASE IV Version 1.0

dBASE IV Keys

Keypress	Description
Right Arrow	Move right one position.
Left Arrow	Move left one position.
Down Arrow	Move down one row.
Up Arrow	Move up one row.
Page Down	Move down one screen.
Page Up	Move up one screen.
End	Move to end of field or record.
Home	Move to beginning of field or record.
Backspace	Delete previous character.
Tab	Move to next field.
Shift-Tab	Move to previous field.
Enter	Move to next field.
Escape	Abandon changes and exit.
Delete	Delete selected item.
Insert	Toggle insert/overwrite mode.
Ctrl-Right Arrow	Move to beginning of next word or field.
Ctrl-Left Arrow	Move to beginning of previous word or field.
Ctrl-PgDn	Move to last record.
Ctrl-PgUp	Move to first record.
Ctrl-Home	Move into memo field.
Ctrl-End	Save changes and exit.
Ctrl-Enter	Save changes and remain.
F1	(HELP) Invoke help facility.
Shift-F1	(PICK) Display list of items to choose from.
F2	(DATA) Switch to Browse or Edit screen.
Shift-F2	(DESIGN) Display the design screens.
F3	(PREV) Move to previous field, object, or page.
Shift-F3	(FIND PREV) Locate previous occurrence of search string.
F4	(NEXT) Move to next field, object, or page.
Shift-F4	(FIND NEXT) Locate next occurrence of search string.
F5	(FIELD) Add field to layout or skeleton.
Shift-F5	(FIND) Find specified search string.
F6	(SELECT) Select contiguous text and fields.
Shift-F6	(REPLACE) Replace search string with another string.
F7	(MOVE) Move selected text and fields.
Shift-F7	(SIZE) Change size of design elements and column widths.
F8	(COPY) Copy selected text and fields.
Shift-F8	(DITTO) Copy data from corresponding field of previous record into current field.
F9	(ZOOM) Enlarge or shrink memo fields, condition boxes, data fill-ins, and file skeletons.
Shift-F9	(QUICKRPT) Print a Quick Report.
F10	(MENUS) Access menus for current screen.
Shift-F10	(MACRO) Access macros prompt box.

Control Center Menus

Catalog	Use a different catalog
	Modify catalog name
	Edit description of catalog
	Add file to catalog
	Remove highlighted file from catalog
	Change description of highlighted file
Tools	Macros
	Import
	Export
	DOS utilities
	Protect data
	Settings
Exit	Exit to dot prompt
	Quit to DOS

Browse Screen Menus

Records	Undo change to record
	Add new records
	Mark record for deletion/Clear deletion mark
	Blank record
	Lock record
	Follow record to new position
Fields	Lock fields on left
	Blank field
	Freeze field
	Size field
Go To	Top record
	Last record
	Record number
	Skip
	Index key search
	Forward search
	Backward search
	Match capitalization
Exit	Exit
	Transfer to Query Design
	Return to (object) Design

Edit Screen Menus

Records	Undo change to record
	Add new records
	Mark record for deletion/Clear deletion mark
	Blank record
	Lock record
	Follow record to new position

Go To	Top record Last record Record number Skip Index key search Forward search Backward search Match capitalization
Exit	Exit Transfer to Query Design Return to (object) Design

Data Panel Menus

Layout	Print database structure Edit database description Save this database file structure
Organize	Create new index Modify existing index Order records by index Activate .NDX index file Include .NDX index file Remove unwanted index tag Sort database on field list Unmark all records Erase marked records
Append	Enter records from keyboard Append records from dBASE file Copy records from non-dBASE file
Go To	Top field Last field Field number
Exit	Save changes and exit Abandon changes and exit

Queries Panel Menus

Layout	Add file to query Remove file from query Create link by pointing Write view as database file Edit description of query Save this query
Fields	Add field to view Remove field from view Edit field name Create calculated field Sort on this field Include indexes

Condition	Add condition box Delete condition box Show condition box
Update	Perform the update Specify update operation
Exit	Save changes and exit Abandon changes and exit Return to (module)

Forms Panel Menus

Layout	Quick layout Box Line Use different database file or view Edit description of form Save this form
Fields	Add field Remove field Modify field Insert memory variable
Words	Style Display Position Modify ruler Hide ruler Enable automatic indent Add line Remove line Insert page break Write/read text file
Go To	Go to line number Forward search Backward search Replace Match capitalization
Exit	Save changes and exit Abandon changes and exit

Reports Panel Menus

Layout	Quick layouts Box Line Use different database file or view Edit description of report Save this report

Fields	Add field Remove field Modify field Change hidden field
Bands	Add a group band Remove group Modify group Group intro on each page Open all bands Begin band on new page Word wrap band Text pitch for band Quality print for band Spacing of lines for band Page headings in report intro
Words	Style Display Position Modify ruler Hide ruler Enable automatic indent Add line Remove line Insert page break Write/read text file
Go To	Go to line number Forward search Backward search Replace Match capitalization
Print	Begin printing Eject page now View report on screen Use print form Save settings to print form Destination Control of printer Output options Page dimensions
Exit	Save changes and exit Abandon changes and exit

Labels Panel Menus

Layout	Use different database file or view Edit description of label design Save this label design
Dimensions	Predefined size Width of label Height of label

	Indentation Lines between labels Spaces between label columns Columns of labels
Fields	Add field Remove field Modify field
Words	Style Display Position Modify ruler Hide ruler Enable automatic indent Add line Remove line Insert page break Write/read text file
Go To	Go to line number Forward search Backward search Replace Match capitalization
Print	Begin printing Eject page now Generate sample labels View labels on screen Use print form Save settings to print form Destination Control of printer Output options Page dimensions
Exit	Save changes and exit Abandon changes and exit

Applications Panel Menus

Layout	Modify a different program Edit description of program Save this program
Words	Style Display Position Modify ruler Hide ruler Enable automatic indent Add line Remove line Insert page break Write/read text file

Go To	Go to line number Forward search Backward search Replace Match capitalization
Print	Begin printing Eject page now Line numbers Use print form Save settings to print form Destination Control of printer Output options Page dimensions
Exit	Save changes and exit Abandon changes and exit Run program Debug program

Selected Dot Prompt Commands

See the *dBASE IV Language Reference* manual from Ashton-Tate for a complete listing of all dBASE IV dot prompt commands.

Command	Formats and Description
? or ??	? **or** ?? *expression* Displays the value of an expression.
@	@ *row,col* [SAY *expression*] [GET *variable*] Displays an expression or accepts information at the given screen row and column.
ACCEPT	ACCEPT [*prompt*] TO *variable* Prompts the user for keyboard entry.
APPEND	APPEND [BLANK] Adds a new record to the end of the active data base file.
APPEND FROM	APPEND FROM *filename* [FOR *condition*] Copies records from *filename* and adds them to the end of the active data base file.
ASSIST	ASSIST Activates the dBASE IV Control Center.
AVERAGE	AVERAGE *field* [*scope*] [FOR *condition*] [WHILE *condition*] Computes the arithmetic mean of a numeric field.
BROWSE	BROWSE [*record-number*] [FIELDS *field-list*] [*scope*] [FOR *condition*] [WHILE *condition*] Activates the Browse screen.

Command	Formats and Description
CANCEL	CANCEL Stops the execution of a command file and returns to the dot prompt.
CLEAR	CLEAR [ALL **or** FIELDS **or** GETS **or** MEMORY **or** MENUS **or** POPUPS **or** TYPEAHEAD **or** WINDOWS] Erases the screen and positions the cursor in the lower left corner. Can also close data base files; release memory variables, field lists, windows, popups, and menus; and empty the type-ahead buffer.
CLOSE	CLOSE [ALL **or** ALTERNATE **or** DATABASES **or** FORMAT **or** INDEX **or** PROCEDURE] Closes files.
CONTINUE	CONTINUE Searches for the next record in the active data base file that meets the condition specified by the most recent LOCATE command.
COPY FILE	COPY FILE *filename* TO *filename* Duplicates any file.
COPY MEMO	COPY MEMO *memo-field-name* TO *filename* [ADDITIVE] Copies the information from a single memo field to another file.
COPY STRUCTURE TO	COPY STRUCTURE TO *filename* [FIELDS *field-list*] Copies the structure of the active data base file to a new file, but does not copy any records.
COPY TO	COPY TO *filename* [FIELDS *field-list*] [*scope*] [FOR *condition*] [WHILE *condition*] Duplicates all or part of an active data base file, creating a new file.
COPY TO	COPY TO *filename* STRUCTURE EXTENDED Creates a new data base file whose records have the structure of the current file.
COUNT	COUNT [TO *variable*] [*scope*] [FOR *condition*] [WHILE *condition*] Counts the number of records in the active data base file that meet the specified conditions.
CREATE	CREATE *filename* Activates the data base design screen.
CREATE LABEL	CREATE LABEL **or** QUERY **or** VIEW **or** REPORT **or** SCREEN *filename* Activates the label, query, report, or forms design screen.

Command	Formats and Description
DELETE	DELETE [*scope*] [FOR *condition*] [WHILE *condition*] Marks records in the active data base file for deletion.
DIR	DIR [*drive:*][*filename*] Displays a directory of data base files or other files if an extension is specified.
DISPLAY	DISPLAY **or** LIST [*scope*] [*field-list*] [FOR *condition*] [WHILE *condition*] Displays one or more records from the active data base file.
DISPLAY HISTORY	DISPLAY **or** LIST HISTORY Displays a list of commands that have been executed and are stored in the history buffer.
DISPLAY MEMORY	DISPLAY **or** LIST MEMORY Displays all active memory variables.
DISPLAY STATUS	DISPLAY **or** LIST STATUS Displays information about the current dBASE IV session.
DISPLAY STRUCTURE	DISPLAY **or** LIST STRUCTURE Displays the data base structure.
DO	DO *program-filename* [WITH *parameter-list*] Starts execution of a dBASE IV command file.
EDIT	EDIT **or** CHANGE [*record-number*] [FIELDS *field-list*] [*scope*] [FOR *condition*] [WHILE *condition*] Activates the Edit screen.
FIND	FIND "*string*" Searches an indexed data base file for the first record with an index key that matches *string*.
GO	GO **or** GOTO [BOTTOM **or** TOP] [[RECORD] *record-number*] [IN *alias*] Positions the record pointer to the specified record in the active data base file.
HELP	HELP [*dBASE-IV-keyword*] Activates the help facility.
IMPORT FROM	IMPORT FROM *filename* [TYPE] PFS **or** DBASEII **or** FW2 **or** RPD **or** WK1 Creates a dBASE IV data base file from a PFS:FILE form, dBASE II file, Framework II file, RapidFile file, or a Lotus 1-2-3 worksheet.
INPUT	INPUT [*prompt*] TO *variable* Prompts the user for input from the keyboard.
INSERT	INSERT [BLANK] [BEFORE] Inserts a new record after the current record, or before if BEFORE is specified.

Command	Formats and Description
JOIN	JOIN WITH *alias* TO *filename* FOR *condition* [FIELDS *field-list*] Creates a new data base file by merging specified records and fields from two open data base files.
LABEL FORM	LABEL FORM *label-filename* [*scope*] [FOR *condition*] [WHILE *condition*] [SAMPLE] [TO PRINTER] [TO FILE *filename*] Use specified label format file to display, print, or write labels to a disk file.
LOCATE	LOCATE [FOR] *condition* [*scope*] [WHILE *condition*] Searches the active data base file for a record that matches the specified condition.
MODIFY COMMAND	MODIFY COMMAND **or** FILE *filename* Starts the word-wrap editor for creating and editing dBASE program and format files.
PACK	PACK Permanently removes records marked for deletion from the active data base file.
QUIT	QUIT Closes all open files, terminates the dBASE IV session, and returns to DOS.
RECALL	RECALL [*scope*] [FOR *condition*] [WHILE *condition*] Reinstates records that are marked for deletion in the active data base file.
REINDEX	REINDEX Rebuilds all active index files in the current work area.
RELEASE	RELEASE [*variable-list*] [ALL] Removes all or specified memory variables.
RENAME	RENAME *old-filename* TO *new-filename* Changes the name of a file.
REPLACE	REPLACE [*scope*] [FOR *condition*] [WHILE *condition*] *field* WITH *expression* ... Replaces the contents of specified fields with new values.
REPORT FORM	REPORT FORM *filename* [*scope*] [FOR *condition*] [WHILE *condition*] [TO PRINTER **or** TO FILE *filename*] Prints a report from the active data base file.
RUN	RUN **or** ! *DOS-command* Executes the specified DOS command or program from within dBASE IV.
SEEK	SEEK *expression* Searches for the first record in an indexed data base file with a key that matches *expression*.

Command	Formats and Description
SELECT	SELECT *work-area-name* **or** *alias* Chooses a work area in which to open a data base file.
SET	SET Displays a menu for setting most parameters of dBASE IV.
SKIP	SKIP [*expression*] [IN *alias*] Moves the record pointer forward or backward in a data base file.
SORT TO	SORT TO *filename* ON *field1* [/A] [/C] [/D] ... [ASCENDING **or** DESCENDING] [*scope*] [FOR *condition*] [WHILE *condition*] Creates a new data base file in which the records of the active data base file are sorted in the specified order.
SUM	SUM *field* [*scope*] [FOR *condition*] [WHILE *condition*] Computes the sum of a numeric field.
USE	USE [*database-filename*] [IN *work-area*] Opens an existing data base file.
ZAP	ZAP Removes all records from the active data base file.

Selected dBASE IV Functions

See the *dBASE IV Language Reference* manual from Ashton-Tate for a complete listing of all dBASE IV functions.

Function	Format and Description
ALIAS	ALIAS([*work-area-number*]) Returns alias name of a work area.
ASC	ASC(*string*) Returns the decimal ASCII code of the first character of *string*.
BOF	BOF([*alias*]) Indicates the beginning of the file.
CDOW	CDOW(*date*) Returns the day of the week from *date*.
CEILING	CEILING(*x*) Calculates the smallest integer greater than or equal to *x*.
CHR	CHR(*x*) Converts ASCII code *x* to a character.

Function	Format and Description
CMONTH	CMONTH(*date*) Returns the name of the month from *date*.
COL	COL() Returns the current column position of the cursor on the screen.
CTOD	CTOD(*string*) **or** {*string*} Converts *string* to a date type variable.
DATE	DATE() Returns the current date as a character string in the format mm/dd/yy.
DAY	DAY(*date*) Returns the day-of-the-month number from *date*.
DBF	DBF([*alias*]) Returns the name of the data base file in use in the currently selected work area.
DELETED	DELETED([*alias*]) Returns logical true (.T.) if the current record in the specified work area is marked for deletion; otherwise, returns false (.F.).
DISKSPACE	DISKSPACE() Returns the number of bytes available on the default drive.
DTOC	DTOC(*date*) Converts *date* to a character string.
EOF	EOF([*alias*]) Returns true (.T.) if the end of the file has been reached; otherwise, returns false (.F.).
FIELD	FIELD(*field-number* [, *alias*]) Returns the field name of *field-number* from the file structure of the data base file.
FILE	FILE(*filename*) Returns true (.T.) if *filename* exists on the selected disk; otherwise, returns false (.F.).
FLOOR	FLOOR(*x*) Returns the largest integer less than or equal to *x*.
FOUND	FOUND([*alias*]) Returns true (.T.) if the previous FIND, LOCATE, SEEK, or CONTINUE command was successful; otherwise, returns false (.F.).
INKEY	INKEY([*n*]) Returns an integer representing the most recent key pressed by the user.

Function	Format and Description
INT	INT(*x*) Truncates *x* to an integer.
LEN	LEN(*string* **or** *memo-field*) Returns the number of characters in *string* or *memo-field*.
LIKE	LIKE(*pattern, string*) Returns true (.T.) if *string* matches *pattern*; otherwise, returns false (.F.).
LUPDATE	LUPDATE([*alias*]) Returns the date of the last update to the specified data base file.
MEMLINES	MEMLINES(*memo-field*) Returns the number of lines contained in *memo-field*.
MEMORY	MEMORY([0]) Returns the number of kilobytes of RAM currently unused.
MLINE	MLINE(*memo-field, line-number*) Extracts a line from *memo-field*.
MONTH	MONTH(*date*) Returns the month number from *date*.
PCOL	PCOL() Returns the current column position on the printer.
PRINTSTATUS	PRINTSTATUS() Returns true (.T.) if the printer is ready to accept output; otherwise, returns false (.F.).
PROW	PROW() Returns the current row on the printer.
RECCOUNT	RECCOUNT([*alias*]) Returns the number of records in the specified data base file.
RECNO	RECNO([*alias*]) Returns the current record number of the specified data base file.
RECSIZE	RECSIZE([*alias*]) Returns the size of a record in the specified data base file.
ROUND	ROUND(*x, decimal-places*) Rounds *x* to the specified number of *decimal-places*.
ROW	ROW() Returns the row number of the current cursor position on the screen.

Function	Format and Description
SEEK	SEEK(*expression* [,*alias*]) Evaluates *expression* and attempts to find it in the master index of the data base file. Returns true (.T.) if the index key is found; otherwise, returns false (.F.).
SELECT	SELECT() Returns the number of the highest unused work area.
SOUNDEX	SOUNDEX(*string*) Returns a four-character code representing the phonetic or sound-alike match to *string* when the exact spelling is not known.
SQRT	SQRT(*x*) Returns the square root of *x*.
STR	STR(*x* [,*length*] [,*decimal-places*]) Converts the number *x* to a character string.
TIME	TIME() Returns the current time as a character string in the format hh:mm:ss.
TRIM	TRIM(*string*) **or** RTRIM(*string*) Removes all trailing blanks from *string*.
VERSION	VERSION() Returns the dBASE IV version number in use.
YEAR	YEAR(*date*) Returns the year number from *date*.

GLOSSARY

absolute reference a cell address that does not change when it is moved or copied
access arm a mechanical extension in a disk drive that moves the read-write head toward or away from the center of the disk
account a file containing financial information
accounting package software that manages an organization's finances
accounts payable the accounting subsystem that records the purchases of goods and services from each vendor
accounts receivable the accounting subsystem that records all sales of goods and services
action line in dBASE III PLUS, the line above the status bar that shows the command generated by the current Assistant operation
active cell see *current cell*
Ada a powerful, comprehensive high-level programming language applicable to a wide range of problems
adapter see *expansion board*
address a unique identifying number for a storage location in memory
address file see *secondary merge file*
aggregate operator see *summary operator*
alias in dBASE, a number, letter, or name that refers to a work area or data base file
allocation unit in DOS, a group of contiguous sectors, also known as a cluster
alphanumeric characters letters, numbers, and punctuation marks
alternate operating environment see *windowing environment*
American Standard Code for Information Interchange (ASCII) the code used by most microcomputers for representing text in binary form
application see *application software*
application generator see *fourth generation language*
application package see *application software*
application software a program or set of programs that applies the computer to useful tasks like helping you write letters, figure taxes, maintain mailing lists, and draw charts
Applications Generator in dBASE, an easy-to-use tool for creating a customized data base system without programming
archive attribute the file attribute that indicates if a file has been changed since it was last saved with the DOS BACKUP command
artificial intelligence (AI) a field of study combining aspects of computer science, mathematics, philosophy, psychology, and linguistics whose main goal is to mimic human learning and decision making
ascending order the arrangement of numbers from smallest to largest, and of text alphabetically from A to Z
ASCII file see *text file*
assembler a program that translates assembly language instructions into the binary numbers of machine language
assembly language a programming language that substitutes meaningful abbreviations for the numerically coded instructions of a machine language
Autokey macro A VP-Planner Plus macro created by recording keystrokes
automated vision a type of software that allows computers to distinguish and interpret images from optical sensors
automatic hyphenation a word processing feature that uses a set of built-in rules to split words at the ends of lines when necessary without confirmation from the user
automatic recalculation the ability of a spreadsheet program to immediately update the entire worksheet whenever the contents of a cell are changed

background in OS/2, where an application that does not have control of the physical console is running
backup an extra copy of vital programs or data; to make such a copy
balance sheet a report that summarizes the assets, liabilities, and capital of a business
bar graph a chart in which numeric values are represented by evenly spaced, thick vertical lines
BASIC (Beginners' All-purpose Symbolic Instruction Code) a simple, interactive programming language originally designed to teach students about computer programming
Basic Input/Output System (BIOS) on some computers, the hardware interface that controls physical components such as disk drives, monitor, keyboard, and printer

batch file a text file that lists operating system commands to be performed automatically when the name of the batch file is entered
batch processing using batch files to reduce several frequently used operating system commands to just one command to save time and effort
batch processing commands a special set of internal DOS commands, such as CALL and ECHO, that add power and flexibility to batch files
benchmark an objective, reproducible measure of hardware or software performance
Bernoulli box see *Bernoulli disk drive*
Bernoulli disk drive a secondary storage device that combines the advantages of both floppy and hard disk drives
billing the accounting subsystem that prepares and records invoices
binary file a file that contains programs or data that are not encoded as ASCII characters
binary point the period that separates the whole part from the fractional part of a mixed binary number
bit the basic unit of data processing; a single binary digit, 0 or 1, off or on
bit-mapped see *pixel-based*
bits per second (bps) unit of modem transmission speed
block a contiguous section of text—can consist of a single character up to an entire document
booting up initially loading and executing the operating system
border palette a menu of line thicknesses used to draw lines and outline shapes
branching altering the order in which batch file commands are executed using IF and GOTO commands
briefcase computer see *laptop computer*
browse to casually scan the records of a data base
bug an error or problem in a computer program
built-in dictionary an automatic proofreading feature that looks for spelling errors
bus a set of wires and connectors that link the CPU to memory and other computer components
bus network a topology in which each workstation is connected to a single cable running past all the workstations
byte a contiguous group of eight bits; the amount of memory it takes to store a single character or a numeric quantity from 0 to 255

C a concise, yet powerful programming language frequently used for the development of system software and application packages
cache an intermediary storage place
calculated field a field that contains the result of an expression instead of a value entered directly in a data base file
capture to gather incoming data from a host computer and save it in a disk file
carrier sense multiple access (CSMA) a protocol that requires each network workstation to listen before sending messages or data
catalog in dBASE, a list of files
cathode ray tube (CRT) a display that uses an electronic gun to paint images on a phosphor-coated glass screen
cell the box at the intersection of a row and a column in a worksheet
cell address a designation that specifies a cell's exact location within a worksheet
cell pointer the highlighted cell that marks the current location in a worksheet
cell reference see *cell address*
central processing unit (CPU) the part of a computer that performs calculations, logic, and control operations
chaining executing a batch file as the last command in another batch file
chamfer a CAD feature that joins two lines with another straight line
character formatting specifying the way individual letters or words are presented
charting program a program that produces graphs, plots, and charts from data entered directly or imported from a spreadsheet or data base file
chassis a metal and plastic frame that houses all of the internal components of a computer
child file the more specific file in a relation that contains the information to be looked up by the parent file
chip see *integrated circuit chip*
circular reference the result of a formula in a cell being either directly or indirectly dependent on the value in that very same cell
clicking moving the mouse pointer on top of an item to be selected and briefly pressing and releasing the mouse button
clipboard a temporary storage area for copying data
clone a computer that works just like, or very similar to, another computer
coaxial cable a center conductor surrounded by a shield or wire braid, used for cable television and local area networks
COBOL a high-level programming language introduced in 1960 especially for business data processing
code in WordPerfect, a hidden formatting indicator generated when you press a key such as Enter or Tab, or execute a command that changes a document's appearance, such as Center or Bold
code page a conversion table that tells DOS how to translate data stored as numeric values into letters, numbers, punctuation, and other symbols to be displayed or printed
color graphics monitor a monitor that can display both text and graphics in more than one color
column a field in an SQL table
column-wise recalculation the order of worksheet recalculation that begins with cell A1 and proceeds down column A, goes on to cell B1 and proceeds down column B, and so on

combining see *merging*
command a directive that is issued to a program
command-line interface (CLI) a user interface, such as DOS without the DOS Shell, that presents a prompt and accepts commands instead of using menus, icons, and windows
comment out temporarily shut off a command in a program or batch file by inserting a comment in front of it on the same line
communications package software that lets a computer transfer messages, programs, and data to other computers
communications parameters the settings that specify the technical details of how a computer will communicate with another computer
communications server a network workstation that lets users communicate with computers outside the network via serial ports and a high-speed modem
compact disc read-only memory (CD-ROM) an optical disk drive that allows access to previously recorded data, but not storage of any new data
compiler a program that translates high-level language instructions into machine language
complex instruction set computer (CISC) a microprocessor, such as the Intel 80486 or Motorola 68040, that incorporates many relatively slow instructions especially designed for high-level languages
computer an electronic device that performs calculations and processes data into information
computer-aided design (CAD) a type of software package for drafting complex plans, blueprints, models, schematics, and other detailed drawings of parts, mechanisms, and buildings
computer-aided engineering (CAE) a system that allows engineers to simulate and test their designs on a computer before they are built
computer-aided manufacturing (CAM) a system in which a computer controls the machines that make or assemble products
computer-assisted instruction (CAI) a system that uses computers to teach students at their own pace
computer graphics the presentation of images such as figures, charts, graphs, maps, diagrams, and other pictures on a display screen
computer-managed instruction (CMI) a system that uses computers to help with school administrative tasks
computer matching a technique that involves comparing records in various data bases to identify individuals who meet overlapping sets of criteria
computer virus a hidden program that secretly copies itself from disk to disk and across networks, often causing mischief or outright destruction of data
computerized axial tomography (CAT or CT) a computer-controlled, three-dimensional X-ray machine
context-sensitive the ability of a help facility to display information specifically relevant to the current activity
Control Center the menu system of dBASE IV
control panel the space on the screen that displays cell information, menus, messages, and the operating mode
coprocessor integrated circuit chip designed to perform a specialized task for the main microprocessor
copy-and-paste a word processing operation in which a section of text is reproduced in another location
copy-protection a way to prepare diskettes so that it is difficult or impossible to copy them with ordinary operating system commands
CP/M a single-user, single-tasking generic microcomputer operating system sold by Digital Research
criteria requirements that a record must fulfill to be retrieved by a search or query
Critical Path Method (CPM) a scheduling method that focuses on the sequence of critical activities that must be performed to complete a project
crosshair two lines that intersect on the screen to indicate the current cursor position
current cell the cell marked by the cell pointer, where you can enter data or initiate commands
cursor a small, blinking underscore or box that marks the position where characters will appear on the screen when typed
cut-and-paste a word processing operation in which a section of text is moved from one location to another

daisy-wheel printer a printer with solid, raised characters embossed on the ends of little arms arranged like the spokes of a wheel, for producing slow, but letter-quality output
data numbers, text, pictures, and sounds that are to be processed into information; in a spreadsheet program, data can be numbers, labels, or formulas
data base an organized collection of one or more files of related data
data base management package software that lets you organize large quantities of information, such as mailing lists and inventories
data bus the pathway connecting the microprocessor to memory
data encryption a security method that encodes information so that it can be read and changed only by authorized users who know the password
data entry form a listing of each field in a record, accompanied by an empty box for each field's contents
debug to remove the errors from a computer program
debugger a program that helps to detect errors in software under development
decision support system (DSS) a computer system that helps managers make decisions by applying statistical models and mathematical simulation
dedicated server a network workstation reserved solely as a file, printer, or communications server
dedicated word processor a microcomputer system expressly designed and solely used to prepare, store, and print documents

de facto standard a standard that emerges from many manufacturers voluntarily making products that will work together

default predefined settings for certain features (margins, line spacing, column widths, etc.) that a software package uses automatically if the user does not explicitly establish settings

default drive the disk drive where DOS will look for programs and data files unless otherwise specified

delete to remove, erase, or destroy one or more pieces of information

delimiter a space, comma, semicolon, equal sign, or tab

descending order the arrangement of numbers from largest to smallest, and of text alphabetically from Z to A

desk accessory a utility program that provides commonly used desk functions such as a calculator, calendar, or address book

desktop computer the most common type of microcomputer, small enough to fit on top of a table or desk

desktop organizer see *desk accessory*

desktop publishing using a computer and laser printer to produce near-typeset-quality documents

desktop publishing package software that combines the results of word processing and graphics to produce near-typeset-quality documents

device controller a set of chips or a circuit board that operates a piece of computer equipment such as a disk drive, display, keyboard, mouse, or printer

device driver a file that contains the programming code needed to attach and use a special device, such as a nonstandard disk drive, memory board, mouse, monitor, or printer

digitizer see *graphics tablet*

direct access medium storage medium, such as magnetic disk, that allows data items to be retrieved in any order

direct-connect modem see *external modem*

directory a list of the files stored on a disk; another term for subdirectory

disk a medium used by computers to store information, consisting of one or more flat surfaces on which bits are recorded magnetically or optically

disk backup utility a program that facilitates making backup copies of a hard disk on floppy disks

disk buffer an area of memory DOS uses to temporarily hold data being read from or written to a disk

disk caching utility a program that reserves part of memory as an intermediary storage place to speed up the retrieval of frequently used software and data

disk copying utility a program that specializes in duplicating files and disks, especially those that are copy protected

disk drive a computer system component that reads and writes programs and data on disks

diskette see *floppy disk*

Disk Operating System (DOS) see *PC-DOS*

disk optimizing utility a program that makes secondary storage devices operate more efficiently

display output screen on which the computer presents text and graphic images

display adapter a circuit board or set of chips that controls a monitor

display-only field see *read-only field*

document the paper output of a word processor

documentation the user manual or technical information about a computer or software package

document file a collection of text created by a word processing program in such a way that the text includes embedded formatting codes

DOS a generic name for PC-DOS and MS-DOS

DOS Compatibility Box see *DOS Session*

DOS environment a special area of memory, like a scratch pad for DOS, that some programs use to hold variables, values, and text

DOS prompt a symbol that identifies the current default drive and indicates that DOS is waiting for a command

DOS Session the special environment in OS/2 that can run a single DOS application at a time

DOS shell a menu-driven addition to DOS that helps manage disk files and directories

DOS Shell the DOS shell developed by IBM and Microsoft and included with DOS versions 4.0 and newer

dot-matrix printer a common type of printer that constructs character images by repeatedly striking pins against the ribbon and paper

dot pitch the distance between the illuminated centers of any two adjacent dots on a display screen

dot prompt the dBASE command-line interface

dot prompt command a dBASE command entered in response to the dot prompt and not selected from a menu

double clicking pressing and releasing a mouse button twice in rapid succession

downloading transferring a file from a host computer to your computer

draft mode the fastest print mode in which low-quality characters are formed by a single pass of the printhead

dragging holding down the mouse button while moving the mouse—used to pull down menus, outline parts of a picture, move selections, and stretch objects

drive specifier a disk drive letter immediately followed by a colon

edit to make changes in a file

electronic mail (E-mail) a way to send and receive messages with a computer

electronic typewriter an electric typewriter with a built-in microprocessor

Encapsulated PostScript (EPS) file a graphics file containing gray-shade information that can be imported and printed by page layout programs that use the PostScript language

encryption a method of protecting sensitive data by scrambling it so that it cannot be read without the proper key

end user see *user*

endnote a numbered comment or explanation similar to a footnote, except that it appears at the end of the document instead of at the bottom of each page

erasable optical disk drive a disk drive that uses optical disks that can be written to and read from any number of times

ergonomics the science of designing objects so that they can be most easily, effectively, comfortably, and safely used by people

example variable in dBASE IV, a place holder for the value of a field entered in the link field to link two data base files

expansion board a circuit board that plugs into an expansion slot

expansion card see *expansion board*

expansion slot an internal connector that allows you to plug an additional circuit board into the motherboard; an extension of the bus

expert an experienced computer user

expert system a computer program that contains both a collection of facts and a list of rules for making inferences about those facts

expert system shell microcomputer software that contains an inference engine and lets nonprogrammers set up expert systems by supplying (1) their own facts to create knowledge bases and (2) rules to create rule bases

exponent in scientific notation, the number indicating the power of ten to be multiplied by the mantissa

exporting writing data in a format that can be accepted by a different program

extension the second part of a DOS file's name

external command a DOS command that is kept in disk storage and temporarily loaded into memory only when needed or specifically requested

external modem a modem built into its own separate housing

fiber-optic cable glass filaments that transmit data in the form of extremely rapid pulses of light generated by lasers, used for high-speed local area networks

field a group of related characters in a data base record; a single data item, such as a number, character, word, or phrase

field template in dBASE, a representation of the width and contents of a data field to be displayed in a form

file a collection of information kept in secondary storage and loaded into primary memory when needed by a program; in a data base, a group of related records

file attribute a characteristic of a file, such as read-only or archive

file compression utility a program that squeezes files into less disk space by eliminating waste and redundant data

file control block (FCB) a data structure used by early versions of DOS to manage open files

file conversion utility a program that modifies files from one application so that they can be used by another application

file locking allowing only one person or program to use the same file at the same time on a network

filename the primary part of a DOS file's name

file recovery utility a program that can reinstate accidentally erased files, restore reformatted hard disks, or perform other useful file operations

file server a network workstation used to store shared program and data files on a large-capacity, high-speed hard disk

file sharing allowing two or more people or programs to use the same file at the same time on a network

file skeleton a graphic representation of a data base file

file specification the combination of a disk drive specifier, a filename, and an extension

file transfer utility a program that can move data among different types of computers

fillet a CAD feature that joins two lines to create a rounded corner

film recorder a graphics output device that turns screen images into 35-mm slides

filter a DOS command (FIND, MORE, or SORT) that normally reads input from the keyboard, changes it in some way, and then displays it as output on the screen

filter condition in dBASE, an expression that determines which records are to be selected for a view

Finder a part of the Apple Macintosh operating system that allows users to run application programs, set up disks, and organize, copy, and delete files

firmware low-level, system software stored in ROM chips, such as the BIOS

first line indent a format in which only the first line of the paragraph is moved in from the left margin

fixed currency format a worksheet format in which two places are to the right of the decimal point, thousands are separated by commas, and each number is preceded by a dollar sign

fixed disk drive see *hard disk drive*

fixed-point number a number whose decimal or binary point is in a fixed place in relation to the digits

flat-file data base manager a program that works with one file of structured data at a time

floating-point number a number in which the position of the decimal or binary point can vary

floor model a powerful, expensive microcomputer with a system unit larger than that of the typical desktop computer and designed to accommodate more add-in hardware components

floppy disk an inexpensive, flexible magnetic medium for storing computer programs and data that can be removed from the disk drive when not in use

floppy disk drive a disk drive that accepts floppy disks

font a set of letters, numbers, punctuation marks, and other symbols with a consistent appearance

footer one or more lines of text printed at the bottom of every page
footnote a numbered comment or explanation at the bottom of a page
foreground in OS/2, where the application that has control of the physical console is running
form a screen or printout that shows the fields of an individual record
formatting initializing a disk so that files can be stored on it
formula an expression that instructs a spreadsheet program to perform calculations or other manipulations on numbers, labels, or the contents of cells
FORTRAN one of the first high-level programming languages, designed to fulfill the computational needs of scientists, engineers, and mathematicians
fourth generation language (4GL) the most abstract type of programming language, designed to make it as easy as possible for users to tell a computer what to do
free-form data base manager a program designed to handle narrative text and irregular pieces of data, such as paragraphs, pages, articles, notes, discussions, and instructions
full-duplex a communications mode in which the characters sent to the host computer are echoed back to the terminal's screen
function a ready-made procedure that performs tedious, complex, or often-used computations or other manipulations
function keys on an IBM-compatible computer, the keys on the left side or top of the keyboard labeled F1 through F10 or F12, used to perform common operations

game adapter a circuit board or set of chips that allows the use of joysticks or trackballs
Gantt chart a horizontal bar graph that shows the major tasks of a project, when each task must be performed, and how long each task will take to perform
general ledger the main listing of the accounts of a business
generic operating system an operating system that can be adapted to almost any type of computer
gigabyte (G) 1,073,741,824 bytes
global pertaining to or acting upon an entire document, spreadsheet, or data base file
global delete the ability to remove all those records that meet certain criteria
global filename character the * (which matches any group of characters) or the ? (which matches any single character) used in a DOS file specification to indicate names with one or more characters in common
global modify the ability to change all those records that meet certain criteria
global search and replace changing a word or phrase automatically throughout an entire document
graphical user interface (GUI) a sophisticated, easy-to-use system that includes pull-down menus, icons, windows, and a simulated desktop
graphics any kind of graphs, plots, drawings, and other images not restricted to text characters
graphics adapter a display adapter that can produce graphics
graphics-based windowing environment a windowing environment that can work with programs that display pictures and characters of all different sizes, styles, and fonts
graphics package software that can produce graphs, plots, drawings, pictures, or charts
graphics tablet a flat surface on which the user draws with a stylus, pen, or some other pointing device
greeking representing text too small to be distinguished by tiny characters or shaded bars to show its position on a page
grid criss-crossed lines used to keep objects lined up with each other on the screen; a visual aid for placing objects in a drawing

hacker a hardware designer or programmer with an obsession for computing
half-duplex a communications mode in which the characters sent to the host computer are not echoed back to the terminal's screen
hand-held computer the smallest type of microcomputer, smaller than a paperback book and weighing less than a pound
handle a little black square on the boundary of a selected object, used to drag or resize the object
hanging indent a format in which all lines of a paragraph except for the first are moved in from the left margin
hard disk a circular platter of rigid aluminum or glass covered with a thin magnetic coating for storing computer programs and data
hard disk drive a disk drive that contains one or more hard disks
hard hyphen a hyphen created by pressing the - key
hard page break in WordPerfect, a division between two pages that is manually generated by pressing Ctrl-Enter
hard return in WordPerfect, a new line or paragraph begun by pressing the Enter key
hard space in WordPerfect, a blank created by pressing the Space Bar
hardware the physical components of a computer system
Hayes-compatible modem a modem that operates like a Hayes Smartmodem
head crash the result of a disk drive's read-write head colliding with a minute obstruction or hitting the surface of a disk
header one or more lines of text printed at the top of every page
headword in WordPerfect, a word that can be looked up in the thesaurus

hexadecimal system base 16 number system
hidden column a worksheet column that exists and contains data, but is not displayed or printed
hidden file a special file used by DOS or some other program that does not appear in the disk directory
hierarchical a method of organizing files into rank-ordered groups
high-level language an abstract programming language that facilitates the expression of complex data processing operations
host computer the computer being called by another computer
hypermedia the nonsequential organization and presentation of information, including graphics, audio, and video
hypertext the nonsequential organization and presentation of information with a computer
hyphenation the division of certain words at the ends of lines to improve the appearance of text

IBM-compatible a microcomputer that works just like, or in some ways better than, an IBM microcomputer, and can run the same software
icon a small pictorial symbol that represents a file, a file folder, an action to be performed, or a program to be run
importing reading and, if necessary, translating data originally created with some other program
income statement a report that summarizes the revenues and expenses of a business for a given period of time
incremental backup a backup procedure that copies only those files that have been changed since the last backup
indenting moving text away from the margin toward the center of the page
index file a file that contains record numbers listed in a particular order
indexing a way to reorder the records of a data base without actually duplicating the data in a new file or rearranging the actual records in the original file
information a more organized and useful form of input data
ink-jet printer a printer with a mechanism for squirting tiny droplets of ink to form text and graphics on paper
input any data or information entered into a computer
insertion point another term for *cursor*; where text is inserted with a word processing package
insert mode a typing mode in which all characters typed at the current cursor location push aside existing text to the right
installed when a software package is copied to a hard or floppy disk and set up to be run
instruction set a limited collection of low-level tasks a computer can do with a single instruction
integrated circuit chip a thin slice of semiconductor material, such as pure silicon crystal, impregnated with carefully selected impurities, commonly used in computers and many other electronic devices
integrated software a software package that includes word processing, spreadsheet, data base, graphics, and communications capabilities
intelligent recalculation see *smart recalculation*
interface a connection between a computer's CPU and an external device operated under its control
internal command an essential or frequently used DOS command that is kept in memory
internal modem a modem built onto an expansion board or directly onto the motherboard
interpreter a program that translates and runs one high-level language instruction at a time as it is entered into a computer
interrupt a signal that suspends the current program to tell the CPU that some critical event has occurred
inventory control the accounting subsystem that tracks products and materials on hand
invoice a bill sent to a customer
iteration a way to obtain an approximate result to an indirect circular reference in a worksheet by recomputing the formulas a number of times

journal a chronological listing of transactions
joystick a vertical lever that can be tilted in any direction to control a cursor or steer a simulated vehicle
justified a type of text alignment in which text is flush to both the left and right margins

key a field used to sort or index the records of a data base
keyboard the primary input device with which you enter data and tell a computer what to do
keyboard macro see *macro*
keyboard template a plastic or cardboard guide that fits over or near the function keys on the keyboard listing the most common keyboard commands
kilobyte (K) 1,024 bytes
knowledge-based system see *expert system*

label in a DOS batch file, a place for a GOTO command to branch to; in a spreadsheet program, any kind of text, such as a heading, title, name, address, or note in a worksheet cell
label macro a macro created by entering the labels that represent the keystrokes to be performed when the macro is run
label prefix character a special character (', ^, ", \) that tells the program that the following item is a label and not a number or formula, and indicates how to align labels within cells or if a character is to be repeated within a cell
laptop computer a full-fledged microcomputer squeezed into a 4- to 15-pound housing smaller than most briefcases
laser printer a high-quality printer that uses tightly focused beams of light to transfer images to paper

layer a CAD feature like a transparent overlay sheet that can be created separately and superimposed on top of other layers

learn feature in Lotus 1-2-3, a way to create a macro by recording keystrokes

learn mode an easy-to-use method of defining a macro by recording keystrokes

learn range in Lotus 1-2-3, the single-column range of cells where keystrokes will be recorded for a macro definition

left indent a format in which all lines of a paragraph are moved in from the left margin

letter-quality like the output of a good electric typewriter

light pen a rod used to point at or draw on a computer display screen

line editor a simple program that can only work with a single line of text at a time

line graph a plot that represents each data value by a point at an appropriate distance above the horizontal axis and connects the points by line segments

line height in WordPerfect, the distance between lines of printed text

link field a common field that connects two data base files

linker a program that combines the output files of programming language translators into a single executable program file

liquid crystal display (LCD) a flat-panel screen that presents black characters against a grey background, commonly used in watches, clocks, calculators, and hand-held and laptop microcomputers

load to copy a program or data file from disk into memory

local area network (LAN) several microcomputers connected together within the same building, or nearby buildings, to share hardware, software, and data

locked cell see *protected cell*

logged the current disk drive or directory

logical formula in a worksheet, a formula that compares values and produces a result of 1 for true or 0 for false

logical operator in dBASE, an operator (.AND., .OR., or .NOT.) that modifies the true or false result of one or two conditions

log-in to enter the assigned group name, user name, and password to gain access to a system

Lotus Access System a program called Lotus that lets you start 1-2-3 or any of the other programs that come with the Lotus 1-2-3 package

machine language the only programming language that can be directly used by a computer, consisting of binary numbers that represent CPU instructions, memory addresses, and data

machine learning a method by which computers can program themselves, through trial and error, to accomplish a particular task

macro a sequence of keystrokes that can be recorded, stored, and replayed

magnetic disk a semipermanent storage medium that can be erased and written over and over again

magnetic resonance imaging (MRI) a medical scanning method that produces high-quality cross-sectional pictures of the body without X-rays or other radiation

magnetic tape a long strip of thin plastic covered with a magnetic coating

magnetic tape drive a secondary storage device that uses magnetic tape to hold programs and data

mail-merge a word processing or data base feature that lets you combine a master document with a data file of names and addresses to create personalized form letters

mainframe a big, powerful, fast, expensive computer

management information system (MIS) a computer system that provides managers with the information they need to do their jobs more effectively

mantissa in scientific notation, the decimal part of the number that is to be multiplied by the power of ten indicated by the exponent

manual hyphenation a hyphenation method that requires you to confirm the splitting of each word as you scroll through the document

manual recalculation a feature that causes the formulas in a worksheet to be recalculated only when explicitly directed to do so

many to many link a type of link that connects multiple records to other multiple records in data base files

master document a document containing text and special commands to be mail-merged with a data file

master index file the index file that specifies the order in which all records will be displayed unless otherwise specified

megabyte (M) 1,048,576 bytes

megahertz (MHz) a unit of frequency equal to one million cycles per second

memo marker in dBASE IV, an indicator that appears in a record to show if the associated memo field contains any text

memory a computer's internal storage for temporarily holding programs and data

memory-resident a type of program that allows a user to temporarily suspend an activity and switch to another one under a single-tasking operating system such as DOS

memory variable in dBASE, a place in RAM that temporarily holds a data value

menu a list showing options available in a program

menu bar a list of the names of pull-down menus across the top of the screen

menu pointer the highlighted block that shows the command that will be invoked if you press the Enter key

merging combining two worksheets into one

message line in dBASE, a line near the bottom of the screen that displays messages

Micro Channel Architecture the high-performance bus (underlying circuit) design of IBM's Personal System/2 Models 50 through 80 microcomputers

microcomputer a small computer that uses a single microprocessor chip as its central processing unit
microcomputer standard a generally accepted set of rules by which hardware and software operate
microprocessor a central processing unit made up of a single integrated circuit chip
million instructions per second (MIPS) a unit of computer performance that represents the execution of computer instructions
minicomputer a medium-sized computer that simultaneously serves several users or controls complex equipment
minimal recalculation a spreadsheet program feature that increases speed by recalculating only those cells that have changed, and the cells that depend on them, since the worksheet was last recalculated
mixed reference a cell address that is half-relative and half-absolute, in which either a row or column is absolute, but not both
mnemonic an easy-to-remember abbreviation for a computer operation, such as ADD
mode indicator the highlighted block in the upper right corner of the control panel that describes the current operating mode, such as READY or MENU
modem a device that allows a computer to transmit and receive programs and data over ordinary phone lines
modem cable a cable that connects an external modem to a serial interface socket at the back of a computer
modular phone jack a socket that accepts the little plastic plug on the end of a telephone cord
monitor a computer display screen (see *display*)
monochrome graphics monitor a single-color screen that can display both text and graphics
monochrome text monitor a single-color screen that displays sharply-defined characters, but no graphics
motherboard the main circuit board of a computer
mouse an input device consisting of a small box with one or more buttons that is slid across the tabletop to manipulate objects on the screen, draw, and select menu options
MS-DOS see *PC-DOS*
multidimensional spreadsheet a spreadsheet program that allows every cell in a worksheet to be connected to corresponding cells in other worksheets
MultiFinder an addition to the Apple Macintosh operating system that allows some multitasking capabilities and lets users run application programs, set up disks, and organize, copy, and delete files
multifunction board an expansion board that includes several add-on options, such as memory, a real-time clock, a game adapter, a display adapter, and serial and parallel interfaces
multiple index file in dBASE IV, a file with an extension of MDX that can contain up to 47 separate indexes of a data base file
multiprocessing the ability to run several programs simultaneously by using more than one processing unit
multiscan monitor a monitor that can change its resolution to match a number of different display adapters
multitasking the ability to run more than one program concurrently

natural language processing getting computers to understand portions of ordinary human languages such as English
natural recalculation the order of worksheet recalculation that updates a cell only after evaluating any cells on which it depends
navigation line in dBASE, a line near the bottom of the screen that lists some of the available keystrokes
near letter-quality (NLQ) a dot-matrix print mode that produces attractive output by having the printhead make two or more passes over each character
nesting in DOS, using the CALL command to invoke one batch file from within another batch file without ending the first batch file
NETBIOS (Network Basic Input/Output System) low-level programs that send and receive data to and from the network adapter
network computers connected to share hardware, software, and data
network adapter a sophisticated expansion board that connects a microcomputer to a local area network
network interface the adapter and connector that link a workstation to a network
network media the cables that connect network workstations
network server a network workstation that handles special chores
network software a set of programs, mostly on the file server, that moves data and messages between the workstations and servers, and controls the sharing of files and hardware devices
network workstation an ordinary microcomputer used to run software, transfer files, and send messages on a network
neural network a type of computer or a software simulation loosely modeled after the interconnection of neurons, or nerve cells, in the human brain
newspaper-style columns text that continues from the bottom of one column on the left to the top of the next column to the right on the same page
nonprocedural language see *fourth generation language*
novice a beginning computer user
null-modem cable a cable for directly connecting the serial ports of two computers
number a numeric quantity, such as 100, 52.34, or 0.05
numeric formula in a worksheet, a mathematical expression that calculates using numeric values and produces a numeric result
numeric keypad on an IBM-compatible computer, the area on the right side of the keyboard arranged like the number keys on a calculator

object code software that has been translated into machine language
object-oriented a package that lets you create and manipulate images made up of only discrete geometric objects such as lines, curves, rectangles, ovals, irregular outlines, polygons, and text
octal system base 8 number system
one-to-many link a type of link that connects a single record in one file to multiple records in one or more other files
one-to-one link a type of link that connects a single record in one file to a single record in another file
on-line connected to and controlled by the computer
on-line help information about how a program works that you can display on the screen, without your having to look it up in a printed reference manual
on-line information service a service that allows computers equipped with a modem to retrieve vast quantities of information and communicate with other users
on-line reference a program such as a spelling checker, thesaurus, or user manual that you can use while running another program
open style in WordPerfect, a style that has just a beginning code, often used to set formats for an entire document
operand a number on which an operation is to be performed
operating system a set of programs that controls a computer's hardware and manages the use of software
operation code (opcode) the part of a machine language instruction that indicates which operation is to be performed
operator a symbol that represents an action to be performed in a formula, such as + or *
optical disk drive a secondary storage device that uses a laser to read or write data on a plastic disk
optimal recalculation see *minimal recalculation*
orphan the first line of a paragraph that appears at the bottom of a page
OS/2 a single-user, multitasking operating system, developed by IBM and Microsoft, for IBM and IBM-compatible microcomputers that use the Intel 80286, 80386, and 80486 microprocessors
output any information produced by the computer; the computer's responses to your input
overwrite mode a typing mode in which characters typed at the current cursor location replace existing characters

packet-switching network see *public data network*
page break a division between two pages
page description language a specialized computer programming language for defining the size, format, and position of text and graphic elements on a printed page
page formatting specifying the general organization of an entire page of text
page layout software a package for arranging text and graphics on pages before they are printed
painting program a pixel-based program for producing pictures on a computer screen
paired style in WordPerfect, a style that has a beginning and ending code
palette the total number of colors to choose from in a particular video mode
pan a CAD feature that lets you move the viewing window up, down, left, or right
paragraph formatting specifying the appearance of individual blocks of text
parallel columns text that continues in the same column on the next page
parallel interface a connection that transmits data, an entire byte at a time, between a computer and an external device, such as a printer
parallel port see *parallel interface*
parameter an entry that designates possible alternate actions
parent file the more general file in a relation that looks up the information in the child file
parity a method of error checking used to help ensure that all of the data bits of a character were received correctly after a transmission
partition a separate section of a hard disk that may contain its own operating system
Pascal a general-purpose, high-level language originally designed to teach students the principles of good programming
patent an exclusive right to produce or sell an invention for a given time
path a drive specifier followed by a list of subdirectory names, separated by backslashes, that describes the route to a particular subdirectory
pattern palette a menu of patterns that can be used with drawing tools to create objects and to fill in enclosed areas on the screen
payroll the accounting subsystem that maintains personnel information, generates paychecks, computes tax withholdings, and creates summary reports of employee earnings
PC-DOS a single-user, single-tasking operating system developed by Microsoft for IBM microcomputers
pel see *pixel*
personal computer see *microcomputer*
physical console the display and keyboard
pie chart a graph that represents values as wedges of a circle, used to show the parts of a whole
piping a DOS feature, symbolized by the | (vertical bar), that takes the output of one command, which would normally go to the display screen, and feeds it as input to another command
pixel picture element; a tiny dot on a computer display
pixel-based a package that has control over every dot on the screen
plotter an output device that uses one or more pens to draw on paper
point a typographical measure equal to about 1/72-inch

pointer movement keys keys that you press to move the cell pointer

polling a protocol in which a controlling workstation sends messages to other workstations on the network, asking each one in turn if it has any messages or data to transmit

pop-up menu a list of options that appears on the screen only when a user issues a special command

pop-up utility see *desk accessory*

portable computer a microcomputer about the size of a small suitcase, designed to be moved, but not used, in transit

positron emission tomography (PET) a medical scanning technique that produces images by detecting positively charged particles emitted from radioactive substances injected into the bloodstream

PostScript a page description language for high-resolution printers and typesetters

power supply a refined source of electrical power for a computer that contains a transformer to lower and regulate the voltage level

power user see *expert*

Presentation Manager the graphical user interface of OS/2

primary file in WordPerfect, the text of a form letter containing special mail-merge codes

primary key the field on which records are sorted first

primary storage a computer's internal memory

print buffering see *print spooling*

printer a device for producing permanent copies of computer output on paper

printer setup string a group of special control codes directing the printer to turn on such options as compressed print

print queue a list of files to be printed in the background

print server a network workstation used to control a printer shared by other workstations on a network

print spooler a utility program that reduces or eliminates waiting for a printer to produce documents

print spooling the ability to print one document while working on another

procedure file see *batch file*

ProDOS a single-user, single-tasking proprietary operating system for the Apple II family of microcomputers

program a sequence of step-by-step instructions that tell a computer what to do

Program Evaluation and Review Technique (PERT) a scheduling method for tasks whose completion times are difficult to estimate

programmable data base manager a relational or flat-file data base manager that includes its own programming language or works with a standard programming language such as BASIC, C, COBOL, FORTRAN, or Pascal

programmer a person who creates computer programs

programming language a set of symbols and rules that direct the operations of a computer

project management software a package that helps to formally plan and control complex undertakings

prompt a symbol or statement that indicates the computer is waiting for a response from the user

proportional spacing allotting different amounts of space for different characters

proprietary hardware or software, with tightly controlled patents or copyrights, that cannot be legally duplicated without being licensed by the originator

proprietary operating system an operating system designed specifically for a single model or line of computers

protected cell a cell that cannot be altered, deleted, or moved unless its protection is first turned off

protocol a set of rules that govern how computers communicate

public data network a way to call a distant communications service from a local telephone number

pull-down menu a list of options that appears when the list's title or symbol is selected from the top of the screen

query a search for records that meet one or more specific criteria; in dBASE, a set of instructions to retrieve, display, organize, or edit data

Query-by-Example (QBE) a highly interactive query language that makes it easy for a user to extract information from a data base

query file in dBASE III PLUS, a special type of file that filters a data base to display or print only those records that meet specific criteria

query language a specialized set of commands for rearranging or extracting data from data bases

QuickDraw laser printer a laser printer designed especially for Apple Macintosh computers as a lower-cost alternative to PostScript printers

RAM cache a part of memory specially reserved for data that must be frequently retrieved

RAM disk an area of memory that is set up to simulate a disk drive

RAM resident see *memory resident*

random access memory (RAM) storage in which all addresses are equally accessible; the portion of a computer's primary storage used to hold programs and data temporarily

range a block of adjacent cells in a worksheet, indicated by the address of the upper left cell, two periods, and the address of the lower right cell

read-only attribute the file attribute that determines if a file can be written, modified, or deleted

read-only field a data base field whose contents can be viewed but not altered

read-only memory (ROM) permanent primary storage that is encoded with programs and data at the factory, retains its contents when the power is turned off, and can be read and used but never erased, changed, or augmented

read-write head a tiny electromagnet on a disk drive's access arm that can create or erase minuscule magnetic spots on the disk directly below

real number see *floating-point number*

real-time clock a built-in clock that keeps the date and time-of-day for a computer

record an array of related fields that contains all the data about a particular person or object

record buffer in Lotus 1-2-3 Release 3.0, a 512-byte area of memory that stores the most recent keystrokes

record feature in Lotus 1-2-3 Release 3.0, a way to create a macro by copying keystrokes saved in the record buffer

record locking preventing the deletion or modification of an individual record currently being used by another person on the same network

record number a unique number assigned to each record in a data base file

record pointer in dBASE, an invisible pointer that keeps track of the current record

redirection changing the normal source or destination of information processed by a DOS command by using the >, <, or >> symbols

redirector a layer of software that acts as a traffic controller for the data and messages transmitted over a network

reduced instruction set computer (RISC) a microprocessor that has a relatively small number of simple instructions that all execute very quickly

reformatting erasing and reinitializing a previously formatted disk

register a storage compartment inside the CPU for temporarily holding numbers that are currently being manipulated

relate to link two or more data base files

relational data base a data base that includes two or more files with at least one field in common

relational data base manager a program that allows you to create, maintain, reorganize, and print structured data from more than one file at a time

relational operator a symbol or word that specifies how items are to be compared

relative reference a cell address that pertains to a cell's position relative to the current cell, and changes when the cell is moved or copied

replace a word processing feature used to automatically substitute one word or phrase for another throughout a document

replaceable parameter a special code inserted into a batch file that allows the user to pass information to the batch file while it is running

report a printed listing of the contents of a data base

report band in dBASE IV, a logical piece of a report design

resident routine see *internal command*

resolution the sharpness of a display screen

ring network a topology in which each workstation is connected to a single cable that runs past all of the workstations, with the two ends of the central cable hooked together

robot a computer-controlled machine that performs mechanical tasks

root directory the main directory on every DOS disk

row a record in an SQL table

row-wise recalculation the order of worksheet recalculation that begins with cell A1 and proceeds across row 1, then row 2, and so on

ruler guide in a page layout program, a dotted line that helps keep text and graphics aligned

ruler line a line that shows the positions of the margins and tab stops

rules dividing lines placed to separate columns and offset blocks of text

running head the same title printed on every page

sans serif a kind of plain typeface without serifs

scanner an input device that can read text and/or graphics from paper and enter it directly into the computer

scatterplot see *XY graph*

scroll bar an on-screen tool used to allow movement within a document, usually found in word processing packages with graphics interfaces

scrolling the upward movement of text on a display screen

search a word processing feature used to locate a name or topic within a document

secondary key the field on which records are sorted second, after the primary key

secondary merge file in WordPerfect, the data file that contains the names and addresses for a mail-merge

secondary storage storage that supplements primary storage by providing a place to keep programs and data when they are not needed

sector a division of a disk track

semiconductor a substance that conducts electricity poorly at low temperatures, but well at high temperatures, and is used to make integrated circuit chips

sequential access medium storage medium, such as magnetic tape, on which data items can be retrieved only in the order in which they were recorded

serial interface a connection that transmits bytes of data, one bit at a time, between a computer and an external device, such as a modem

serial port see *serial interface*

serif a kind of typeface that has lines crossing and finishing off the main strokes of the characters

service program low-level program in the BIOS or DOS that can be invoked by other software to perform hardware-related tasks

shared word processor a word processing system on a large, multiuser computer

single-tasking the simplest type of operating system that accommodates a single user and runs a single program at a time

site license permission to make copies of software for internal use at a reduced fee for each copy

slide show program a program that allows you to present a sequence of pictures on a computer screen, either automatically timed or directly controlled
Small Computer System Interface (SCSI) a connection that provides high-speed access to peripheral devices such as hard disks
smart recalculation the ability of a spreadsheet program to automatically update only those cells, if any, that are affected when a new entry is made
snaking columns see *newspaper-style columns*
snap a CAD feature that automatically aligns objects to the nearest grid lines
soft hyphen a hyphen generated by the auto-hyphenation feature
soft page break a division between two pages automatically generated by the word processing software
soft return a new line begun by the word wrap feature
soft space an extra blank generated by a word processing program to justify text
software a program or set of programs that tells a computer system what to do
software licensing a legal agreement in which a program is not actually sold, but licensed to a user with limits on what can be done with the program
software piracy the practice of illegally copying software
sorting arranging items in some particular order
Soundex search a search technique that finds words that sound like the specified word
source a disk or file to be copied
source code software in an assembly language or a high-level language before it is translated into machine language
specifications a detailed list of the exact components, options, and capabilities of a particular hardware device
speech synthesizer an output device that either mimics human speech or constructs it out of prerecorded sounds
spelling checker see *built-in dictionary*
spooling multitasking technique that prints files in the background while the computer is used for other work
spreadsheet see *worksheet*
spreadsheet package software that helps you manipulate tables of numbers
stack a data structure used by the CPU, operating system, or application program as a temporary storage area
stacked bar graph a variation of the basic bar graph that shows components and total amounts for each category by dividing each bar into sections
stackware information systems created with the Hypertalk language of Apple's Hypercard program
star network a topology in which an individual cable is run from a central server to each workstation
startup directory the disk drive and directory automatically used to store and retrieve worksheet files unless otherwise specified
static menu a list of options that usually remains on the screen in a fixed position
status bar in dBASE, a line near the bottom of the screen that displays information about the operation you have chosen
status line in WordPerfect, the line at the bottom of the screen that displays messages and warnings
stop bits bits that mark the end of an individual data character transmission
string combination operator the & (ampersand), which joins two labels
Structured Query Language (SQL) a standardized language for extracting information from a relational data base
style in WordPerfect, a collection of formatting codes and possibly text that can be created, saved, and inserted into documents to automate formatting and provide a consistent appearance to documents
style sheet a collection of formatting instructions that can be saved in a file and applied to different documents
subdirectory a group of files on a disk organized under a single name
submenu a menu that is activated by selecting an option from a higher-level menu
summary operator in dBASE IV, an operator for performing operations in view queries such as SUM, AVERAGE, and COUNT
supercomputer an extremely fast mainframe
supermicro see *workstation*
supermini a powerful minicomputer with capabilities similar to those of some mainframes
surge protector a device that rapidly cuts off the electricity when a voltage surge occurs
switching drives telling DOS to use a different disk drive as the default
symbolic addressing the assignment of meaningful names, such as TOTAL, to computer memory locations
system board see *motherboard*
system call see *service program*
system clock a crystal, oscillating several million times per second, that synchronizes the internal operations of the microprocessor and other computer components
system prompt see *DOS prompt*
system software the software that handles the many details of managing a computer system
system unit in many microcomputers, the box that houses the central processing unit, control circuitry, expansion boards, memory, and disk drives

table a screen that displays a record in each row and a field in each column; the basic component of an SQL data base
tag in dBASE IV, the name of an index in a multiple index file
target a disk or file copy to be created
telecommute to work at home using a microcomputer or a terminal connected to a computer at the office
teleconference an electronic forum that allows computer users who share special interests to communicate and hold on-line meetings

template a general-purpose, ready-made worksheet in which the user fills in the blanks or changes selected entries

terminal a computer input/output station consisting of a keyboard and a display

terminal emulation a communications software feature that lets you use a microcomputer as a computer terminal

text area in WordPerfect, the area on the screen where you enter text and edit a document

text-based windowing environment a windowing environment that uses only the standard character set built into the computer and that cannot work with graphics programs

text file a file, also known as an ASCII file, that contains only ordinary letters, numbers, and punctuation marks

time-sharing an operating system that rapidly switches among several users at fixed intervals of time

token-passing a protocol that uses a control signal called a token that determines which workstation is allowed to transmit messages or data

tool palette a menu of icons for drawing, adding text, moving about, and selecting parts of a picture created with a painting or drawing program

topology the way hardware components are arranged in a network

touch screen an input device built into or over a display screen that uses infrared light beams or an electrically conductive surface to identify the position of a finger as it points to the screen

track a ring on a disk where data can be stored

trackball a box that contains a protruding ball that can be freely rotated in any direction and is often used as an alternative to a mouse

trademark a legal protection for creative expression, usually limited to a word, phrase, or graphic symbol representing a company or product

transient routine see *external command*

Transputer a special microprocessor that can be connected with other Transputers to construct a fast, powerful multiprocessing computer

twisted-pair wire two wires that have been partially wrapped around each other, used for ordinary telephone lines and inexpensive local area networks

typeface see *font*

ultrasound scanner a medical imaging device that uses very high-frequency sound waves

undo a feature that lets you cancel your most recently performed operation

UNIX a multiuser, multitasking generic operating system originally developed at AT&T's Bell Laboratories

update query in dBASE IV, a query used to add, modify, or delete data in a data base file

uploading transferring a file from your computer to a host computer

upwardly compatible the ability of a new software product to handle every official command that worked with previous versions of it

user a person who runs software on a computer to accomplish some task

user friendly easy-to-learn; can be used by people who don't have a lot of computer experience

user interface how a user directs the actions of software and how the software responds to these requests

utility a small, specific program that adds handy features to a particular operating system or application package

value-added network see *public data network*

very high level language see *fourth generation language*

video mode a combination of screen resolution and number of colors that can be used at one time

view in dBASE, an arrangement of data on the screen

view file in dBASE III PLUS, a file that displays data from two or more data base files

view query in dBASE IV, a set of instructions that displays selected data on the screen

view skeleton in dBASE IV, a graphic representation of the fields that will be displayed by the view query

virtual console a simulated display and keyboard used by programs that run in the background under OS/2

voice recognition system an input device that can recognize a finite number of isolated sounds, words, and phrases

volume label in DOS, the name of a disk

widow the last line of a paragraph that appears at the top of a page

wildcard character in WordPerfect and dBASE, the * (which represents any group of characters) or the ? (which represents any single character) used in search and replace operations

what-you-see-is-what-you-get (WYSIWYG) a feature in which a document is printed on paper exactly as it appears on the screen

window a boxed-in area on the screen that shows the activity of a particular software program

windowing environment system software that lets you divide your screen into a number of different boxes and run a separate program in each one

word processing a common computer application that allows you to produce documents, such as letters and reports, with a computer

word processing package a software package used to create, enter, edit, format, store, and print documents

word wrap a word processing feature that automatically begins new lines when necessary without the user having to press the Enter key (carriage return)

work area in dBASE, a place in memory that holds an open data base file

worksheet a table of columns and rows of numbers, text labels, and formulas used in a spreadsheet package for the manipulation of numerical, financial, and accounting data

workstation a small, yet powerful computer generally used by only one person at a time, traditionally used by scientists and engineers for drafting, design, and map-making

write once, read many (times) (WORM) an optical disk drive that allows users to record data once, and then only read it thereafter

write-protection a diskette feature that can be used to prevent the contents from being erased or altered

write-protect notch a small rectangle cut out of one side of a 5¼-inch diskette that can be covered with a gummed tab to write-protect the disk

write-protect switch a tab on a 3½-inch diskette that can be slid to open a little hole in the disk's plastic case, thereby write-protecting the disk

XY graph a plot that shows the relationship between two or more variables

PHOTO CREDITS

Chapter 1
1 IBM; 2 Northwestern Life Insurance; 3 WordPerfect Corp.; 4 University of Illinois; 12(a) IBM, (b) Apple Computer, Inc., (c) Toshiba America, Inc.; 13 Memorex; 14 Tandy Corp.; 15 NEC America, Inc.; 16 Compaq Computer Corp.; 17 IBM; 18 IBM; 19 Apple Computer, Inc; 20 IBM; 21 IBM; 22 Apple Computer, Inc.; 23 Sun Microsystems, Inc.; 24 Digital Equipment Corp.; 25 IBM; 26 Cray Research, Inc.

Chapter 2
1 Thom O'Connor; 2 IBM; 3 Intel Corp.; 6 BASF; 7 TEAC Corp. of America; 9 Seagate Technology; 11 Tallgrass Technologies; 12 IOMEGA Corp.; 14 SONY Corp. of America; 15 IBM; 16 Apple Computer, Inc.; 17 IBM; 18 Apple Computer, Inc.; 19 AST Research, Inc; 20(b) IBM; 21(b) Brother International Corp.; 22(b) Hewlett-Packard Co.; 23(b) Hewlett-Packard Co.; 24 Hewlett-Packard Co.; 25 Hayes Microcomputer Products, Inc.; 26 Apple Computer, Inc.; 27 Wico Corp.; 28 IBM; 29 IBM; 30 CalComp; 31 Princeton Graphic Systems.

Chapter 4
10 Microsoft Corp.; 12 Apple Computer, Inc.

Chapter 5
8 IBM.

Chapter 17
2(a) Hayes Microcomputer Products, Inc.; 3(a) Hayes Microcomputer Products, Inc.

Chapter 18
1(a) IBM, (b) Microsoft Corp., (c) Hewlett-Packard Co.; 2 IBM; 3 Princeton Graphic Systems; 4 Polaroid Corp.; 5 Strategic Locations Planning, Inc.

Chapter 19
2 Hewlett-Packard Co.; 3(a&b) Apple Computer, Inc., (c) IBM; 4 Radius, Inc.; 5(a) GCC Technologies, (b) Apple Computer, Inc., (c) Hewlett-Packard Co.; 6 Thunderware, Inc.

Chapter 20
2 Lotus Development Corp.; 3 Copyright © 1988, Ashton-Tate Corp. All rights reserved. Reprinted by permission. Framework is a registered trademark and Framework III is a trademark of Ashton-Tate; 4 Microsoft Corp.; 7 IBM; 9 XTREE Co.; 11 Funk Software, Inc.; 13 Borland International; 16 Systat, Inc.; 17 Borland International; 21 MECA Ventures, Inc.; 22 SoftView, Inc.; 23 Broderbund Software, Inc.; 24 Broderbund Software, Inc.; 25 Microsoft Corp.; 27 OWL International, Inc.

Chapter 21
1 Radio Shack, a division of Tandy Corp.; 2 IBM; 3 IBM; 4 Dicomed; 5 © Pixar. Photo by Fred Ward/ Black Star. Knight from "Young Sherlock Holmes"; 6 Hewlett-Packard Co.; 7 Photography by Milt and Joan Mann—CAMERAMANN INTERNATIONAL; 8 Sanders Associates, a Lockheed Co.; 9 Calcomp; 10 Apple Computer, Inc.; 11 Chrysler Corp.; 12 Hewlett-Packard Co.; 14 Apple Computer, Inc.; 15 Photofest; 17 NCR Corp.; 21 Photography by Milt and Joan Mann—CAMERAMANN INTERNATIONAL; 22 The Granger Collection; 23 EyeDenify, Inc.; 24 Intel Corp.; 25 Research: Robert Wilhelmson, Harold Brooks, Brian Jewett, Crystal Shaw, Louis Wicker. Visualization: Matthew Arrott, Mark Bajuk, Colleen Bushell, Jeffery Yost.

Appendix E
1 Microsoft Corp.

INDEX

Absolute reference, 579, 580
Access arm, 50
Accounting packages, 105, 898–900
Accounts payable, 899
Accounts receivable, 899
Ada, 18, 98
Adapter, *see* Expansion board
Address, 46
Address file, *see* Secondary merge file
Address lines, 44
Adobe Systems, 852
Aggregate operators, *see* Summary operators
Aldus Corporation, 855
Alias, 735
Allen, Paul, 96, 109
Allied Linotype Linotronic 100 typesetter, 852
Allocation units, 162
Alphabet Blocks, 902
Altair 8800, 96
Alternate operating environment, *see* Windowing environment
American Express, 945
American Medical Association, 920
American National Standards Institute (ANSI), 942
Analog signals, 71–72
Analytical engine, 98
Andrew Tobias' Managing Your Money, 900–901
Apple Computer, 23, 25, 56, 136, 144, 871
  Apple II, 23, 25
  Apple III, 25
  A/UX, 134
  floppy disks, 49–50
  graphics, 806
  history, 23, 25–26
  Hypercard, 906, 908
  Imagewriter, 859–860
  keyboard, 59–60
  LaserWriter, 852, 853
  Lisa, 25, 134
  MultiFinder, 134–135, 885
  network, 793
  ProDOS, 134
Apple Macintosh, 25–26, 44, 72, 91, 111, 938
  desk accessories, 891–892
  graphics monitor, 62
  Portable, 74
  system described, 134–136
Application generators, *see* Fourth generation languages
Application interface, 128
Application packages, applications, *see* Application software
Applications Generator, 699
Application software, 18, 100, 105–106, 128
  communications and networking, 103
  data base management, 102
  desktop publishing, 104
  graphics, 103
  spreadsheets, 101–102
  word processing, 100
Archive attribute, 214
Artificial intelligence (AI), 106, 907–908, 945–946
Arts, computers and, 917–920, 946
ASCII (American Standard Code for Information Interchange), 212, 774
ASCII file, 212
Ashton, Alan, 329
Ashton-Tate, 78, 607, 610, 611, 880
Assembler, 94
Assembly languages, 93–94
Associated Press, 788
Association for Computing Machinery (ACM), 938
AT&T, 132, 133, 136
Atari, 44
Atkinson, Bill, 821, 906
Atlas Graphics, 814
AutoCAD, 8, 832–836
Autodesk Incorporated, 832
Automated vision, 907–908
Automatic hyphenation, 403–404
Automatic recalculation, 575
A/UX, 134

Babbage, Charles, 98
Backup, 51, 53–54
Bad sectors, 162
Bar graph, 510–515, 818–820
BASIC (Beginners' All-Purpose Symbolic Instruction Code), 18, 86, 96, 613
Bastian, Bruce, 329
Batch file, 249–251
Batch processing commands, 252–261
Battery pack, 40–41
Bell Laboratories, 98, 132, 133
Berk, Peggy, 798
Bernoulli, Daniel, 54
Bernoulli box, *see* Bernoulli disk drive
Bernoulli disk drive, 54–55
Big Blue, 937, 938
Big Blue Disk, 938
Big Blue Products Incorporated, 938
Billing, 899–900
Bill of Rights, 940
Binary file, 212
BIOS (Basic Input/Output System), 127–128, 797–798
Bit, 43–44
Bit-mapped, *see* Pixel-based
Bits per second (bps), 72
Block, 306–310
Bogas Productions, 904
Books in Print, 785
Booting up, 147–150
Border palette, 822
Borland International, 891, 892, 895
Branch, 92
Branching, 256
Bricklin, Dan, 23, 101
Briefcase computers, *see* Laptop computers
Bright Star Technology, 902
Broderbund Software, 902
Brooklyn Bridge, 890
Bus, 44, 63
Business, computers and, 923–925
Business Week, 144
Bus network, 794
Byte, 44
BYTE magazine, 607

C, 18, 98, 132, 133
Cache, 890
CADUCEUS, 921
Calculated field, 679–681
Canadian Radiation Protection Bureau, 928
Canion, Joseph R. (Rod), 144
Capability, computer for, 7
Capture, 773
Carbone, Key, 871
Carbone-Smolan Associates, 871
Card, *see* Expansion board
Carnegie Mellon University, 5, 926
Carrier sense multiple access (CSMA), 796
Carroll, Mark, 841
Catalog, 612

Cathode ray tube (CRT), 60, 928
Cell, 463
 address, 463
 pointer, 464
 reference, *see* Cell address
Central Point Software, 890
Central processing unit (CP), 14, 41, 42, 43, 44
Centronics Data Computer Corporation, 65
Centronics standard, 65, 66
Chaining, 253
Chamfer, 832
Character length, *see* Word length
Charting programs, 813–820
Chassis, 38
Child file, 737
Chips, microprocessor, 78
Chronicle of Higher Education, 4
Circular reference, 577
Clarion Professional Developer, 99
Claris, 821
Clicking, 823
Clones, 24
Coaxial cable, 794
COBOL (Common Business Oriented Language), 18, 86, 98, 613
Code, 354–356
Code page, 268
Cogent Research, 125
Cohen, William S., 940
Color graphics monitor, 62–63
Column, 754
Column-wise recalculation, 576
Command file, 774
Command line, 775–776
Command-line interface (CLI), 886
Commands, 106–107, 151
Comment out, 259
Commodore, 44
Commodore VIC-20, 31
Communication, computers for, 10
Communications packages, 18, 103
 hardware, 766–771
 parameters, 776–778
 software, 771–776
Communications server, 794
Compact Disc Read-Only Memory (CD-ROM), 55–56
Compaq, 5, 44, 109
Compaq Computer Corporation, 24, 144
Compaq Portable 386, 21
Compiler, 96
Complex instruction set computer (CISC), 943, 944
CompuServe, 10, 786–790
Computer-aided design (CAD), 830–836, 924–925
Computer-aided engineering (CAE), 925
Computer-aided manufacturing (CAM), 925
Computer-assisted instruction (CAI), 916–917
Computer graphics, 61
Computerized axial tomography (CAT or CT), 921
Computer-managed instruction (CMI), 917
Computer matching, 939–940
Computers
 comparison of types of, 26–28
 desktop, 21–22
 floor models, 22
 hand-held, 19–20
 laptop, 5, 20
 mainframes, 29
 minicomputers, 28–29
 portable, 21
 reasons for studying, 4–8
 supercomputers, 30–31
 typical system, 13–19
 uses of, 8–13
 workstations, 28
Computers in Medicine, 920
Computer virus, 918, 931–933
Conference on Data Systems Languages (CODASYL), 98
Confidence factor, 909
Congressional Budget Office, 926
Congressional Office of Technology Assessment, 927, 939
Context-sensitive, 475
Control lines, 44
Control panel, 464
Coprocessors, 42–43
Copying files, 168–172
Copy-protection, 178–179
Copyright, 936
Copy II Mac, 890
Copy II PC, 890
CP/M (Control Program/Monitor), 129–130
Cray 1 supercomputer, 944
Cray Research, 31
Cray X-MP and Y-MP, 31
Crime Control Act (1973), 941
Criteria, 540
Critical Path Method (CPM), 896, 897
Crosshair, 834
CROSSTALK, 772, 774–776, 789–792
Current cell, 464
Cursor, 110, 289

Dac-Easy Accounting, 900
Dac-Easy Payroll, 900
Dac Software, Incorporated, 900
Daisy-wheel printers, 68
Dark Castle, 8, 904
Dartmouth College, 96
Data, 15, 463
Data base, 29, 102, 617
Data base charting, 813
Data base management packages, 18, 102, 607
Data bus, 44–45
Data Encryption Standard (DES), 942–943
Data lines, 44
Data Processing Management Association (DPMA), 938
DataQuest, 846
DataViz, 889
Davis, Frederic E., 144
dBASE IV, 607, 943
 advanced, 713–756
 beginning, 609–649
 intermediate, 657–706
DB Graphics, 813
Decision support system (DSS), 925
DEC VT100, 772
Dedicated charting, 814
Dedicated server, 794
De facto standard, 22
Default drive, 149, 160–161
Defense, Department of, 98, 918, 923, 931
Defense Advanced Research Projects Agency (DARPA), 947
Demodulation, 72
Desk accessories, 891–893
Desktop computers, 21–22
Desktop organizers, *see* Desk accessories
Desktop publishing packages, 18, 104, 845–871
 applications, 848
 components of, 849–854
 layout with, 861–869
 principles of, 854–871
DESQview, 884–885
Device controller, 40
Device driver, 262
Device-independent language, 852
Diagnosis, computers for, 921
Dickson, Gary W., 841
Dictionaries, 894
Digital Equipment Corporation, 29, 78, 132, 136, 772
Digital Productions, 31
Digital Research, 129
Digital signals, 71, 72
Digital VAX 11/780 mainframe, 648
Digitizer, *see* Graphics tablet
Direct access medium, 53
Direct-connect modem, *see* External modem
Disk backup utilities, 890
Disk buffer, 262
Disk caching utilities, 890
Disk copying utilities, 890
Disk drive, 15, 39
 See also Secondary storage
Disk drive controllers, 64

Disk Optimizer, 890
Disk optimizing utilities, 890
Display adapter, 64, 807–809
Displays, 15, 60
  color graphics monitors, 62–63
  monochrome graphics monitors, 61–62
  monochrome text monitors, 60–61
Document summary, 345
DOS (Disk Operating System), 109, 130–131, 145, 798
  advanced, 241–277
  command summary, 183
  Compatibility Box, 131
  environment, 270
  intermediate, 189–234
  prompt, 149
  Shell, 272–277, 885–887
  using, 146–183
  versions, 145–146
Dot-matrix printer, 66–68, 811
Dot pitch, 810
Dot prompt, 714–718
Double clicking, 821
Double-density floppy disk, 49
Double-sided floppy disk, 49
Dow Jones News Retrieval Service, 782, 900
Downloading, 773
Draft mode, 66
Dragging, 823
Drawing programs, 826–830
Drexel University, 13
Duplex mode (full/half), 777

Education, computers and, 13, 916–917
Educational packages, 105, 902
Education Department, 939, 940
Education Privacy Act (1974), 941
Electronic mail (E-mail), 780–784
Employment, *see* Workplace
Enable, 880, 881
Encapsulated PostScript (EPS) files, 860
Encryption, 942–943
Endnote, 418–420
End user, *see* User
Energraphics, 8, 814–820
Enertronics Research Inc., 814
Enhanced Graphics Adapter, 809–810, 850
Entertainment packages, 105, 902–904
Equity Funding Corporation of America, 934
Erasable optical disk drive, 56
Erasing files, 175–177
Ergonomics, computers and, 929
Ernst & Whinney, 841, 933
Esber, Edward M., Jr., 78
Ethics, computers and, 938
Eureka, 895–896
Example variable, 673–674
Expansion board, 39, 63, 64–65
Expansion slot, 39, 63
Expert, 19
Expert system(s), 106, 907–909, 945–946
  shell, 908–909
Exponent, 567
Extension, 154
External commands, 151
External modem, 72–73

Fair Credit Reporting Act (1970), 940
Fan, 41
Fastback Plus, 890
FBI, National Crime Information Center of, 938
Fiber-optic cable, 794
Field, 421, 617
Field template, 686
Fifth Generation Systems, 890
File, 102, 617
  attribute, 214
  compression utilities, 889
  control block (FCB), 263
  conversion utilities, 890
  locking, 271
  recovery utilities, 888–889
  server, 794
  sharing, 271
  skeleton, 663
  transfer, 772–774
  transfer utilities, 889–890
Filename, 154
Fillet, 832
Film recorder, 812
Filter, 245–246
Filter condition, 663
Finder, 134, 135
Firmware, 127
First line indent, 365
Fixed disk drive, *see* Hard disk drive
Flight Simulator, 903–904
Floor models, 22
Floppy disk, 17, 39
Floppy disk connector, 41
Floppy disk drive, 39, 48–51
Flystra, Daniel, 101
Font, 846, 851
Food and Drug Administration (FDA), U.S., 10, 928
Footer, 413–415
Footnote, 418–420
Ford Motors, 945
Form, 622
Format, 163–168
Formula, 463
Forrester's Professional Automation Report, 131
FORTRAN (Formula Translator), 18, 98
Fourth generation languages (4GLs), 98–100
Framework III, 880–881
Frankston, Bob, 23, 101
FRED, 881
Freedom of Information Act (1970), 940
Fryar, Carolyn, 499
Full-duplex, 777
Fun, computers for, 7–8
Function, 466–467, 743–746
Funk & Wagnall's Standard Desk Dictionary, 894
Funk Software, 888
Future, computers and, 943–947

Game adapter, 64
Gantt, Henry L., 897
Gantt chart, 897
Gates, 42
Gates, William H., III, 96, 109
General Computer Corporation, 853
General ledger, 899
Generic operating systems, 129, 133
Ghostbusters, 919–920
Giga, 47
Gigabyte (G), 47
Global file name characters, 155, 174, 176
Global search and replace, 302
Government, computers and, 922–923
Graphical user interface (GUI), 111–112
  See also Graphics-based windowing environment
Graphics, 15, 18, 103
  adapter, 807–809
  computer, 61
  and desktop publishing, 854
  displays, 850
  hardware, 806–812
  monitors, 61–63
  objects, 832
  software, 812–813
  tablet, 76
Graphics-based windowing environment, 883–884
Greeking, 400, 866
Grid, 826, 832
Grolier's *Academic American Encyclopedia*, 786, 789–790
GTE Government Systems Corporation, 871
Guide, 906
Guidelines, 906

Hackers, 768, 931
Haider, R., 7
Half-duplex, 777
Hand-held computers, 19–20
Handle, 830
Handler, Gary D., 136
Hanging indent, 366
Hard copy, 66
Hard disk, 51
Hard disk controller, 40
Hard disk drive, 39, 51–53
Hard page break, 323
Hard return, 293
Hard spaces, 318
Hardware, 15–17
control of, by operating systems, 118–119
interface, 127–128
Harris H800 mainframe computer, 778–780
Harvard Business School, 101
Hayes-compatible modem, 771
Hayes Microcomputer Products Inc., 771
Head crash, 52
Header, 413–415
Headword, 357
Health concerns, computers and, 927–929
Helvetica type, 857, 864
Henderson, Robert, 8–9
Hertz, 46
Hewlett-Packard LaserJets, 851, 891
Hidden files, 162
Hierarchical system, 194
High-density floppy disk, 49
High-level languages, 94
machine-independent, 94
problem-oriented, 94
procedure-oriented, 94
Hodel, Donald, 12
Holdridge, L. Ward, 841
Hollins College, 6
Hong, Dora, 648
Host computer, 767
Housing and Urban Development Department, 940
Hovanees, Haig, 798
Howe, Ken, 900
Hypercard, 12, 906–907, 908
Hypermedia, 905
Hypertalk, 906
Hypertext packages, 105, 905–907
Hyphenation, 402–405

IBM (International Business Machines), 44
Convertible, 8, 9
Diagnostic Expert Final Test (DEFT) system, 945
DOS, 109, 112, 130–131
Enhanced Keyboard, 60
and FORTRAN, 98
history, 23–25
mainframe, 29
microcomputers, 62, 94, 96
OS/2, 131–132
Personal Computer, 8, 9, 15, 23–24, 25, 42, 61, 87, 91, 460
Personal Pageprinter, 852
Personal System/2, 15, 22, 24–25, 31, 38–41, 47, 57, 63, 72, 78, 944
TopView, 885
trademark, 936–938
IBM-compatibles, 24
Icon, 26, 59, 111, 135
Illinois, University of, 7, 8–9, 31, 778, 895
Medical Center, 921
National Center for Supercomputing Applications at, 944
Imaging, computers for, 921–922
INBOX, 784
Incremental backup, 204–205
Indenting, 364–367
Index file, 645
Indexing, 644–645
Indiana Jones, 920
Inductel, 894
Inference engine, 909
Information, 15
Information management, computers for, 9
Ink-jet printers, 68, 812
INMOS Limited, 125
Input, 15, 41–42
Input/output devices, 810–812
Instruction set, 87
Integrated circuit chip, 42
Integrated software, 105, 878–882
Intel 8080, 129
Intel 8088, 42, 44, 87, 93
Intel 80486, 78, 943
Intel 80860, 943–944
Intel Corporation, 129
Interface(s), 65
application, 128
hardware, 127–128
parallel, 65–66
serial, 65
Small Computer System (SCSI), 66
user, 128
Interior, Department of the, 12
Internal commands, 151
Internal modem, 72
Internal Revenue Service (IRS), 901, 922–923, 939–940
International Data Corporation, 133, 841
Interpreter, 96
Interrupts, 127
Intex Solutions, 813
Inventory control, 899
Isogon Corporation, 889
Iteration, 575, 577–578

Jobs, Steven, 23, 25, 56, 938
Job security, computers and, 926
Johns Hopkins University, 946
Johnson, Virginia, 841
Joystick, 73

Kapor, Mitch, 460
Kaypro, 5
Kelly Services, 499
Kemeny, John, 96
Key, 421, 539, 641
Keyboard, 17, 57–60
enhancers, *see* Keyboard utilities
macro, 704
template, 291–292
utilities, 891
Kildall, Gary, 129–130
Kilo, 47
Kilobyte (K), 47
Kluth, Daniel, 928
Knowledge Acquisition System, 894
Knowledge base, 908
Knowledge-based system, *see* Expert system(s)
Kurshan, Barbara, 6
Kurtz, Thomas, 96

Label, 257, 463
Label prefix character, 464
Laptop computers, 5, 20
Laser printers, 68–70, 811, 851–853
LaserWriter, 855, 857, 860, 865, 871
Lashlee, Hal, 607
Law, computers and, 931–938
Lawrence Livermore National Laboratory, 944
Layer, 832
Learn feature, 588–590
Learning, computers for, 4–5
Learn range, 588–589
Left indent, 365–366
Legal protection, computers and, 940–942
Lehigh University, 932
Letter-quality, 68
License, 936
Lichtenberger, Mark, 6
Light pen, 74–75
Line graph, 523–528
Line height, 319–320
Link field, 673

Liquid crystal display (LCD), 19, 60
LISP, 908
Local area network (LAN), 65, 103, 792–800
  hardware, 793–794
  protocols, 796–797
  software, 797–798
  topology, 794–795
  using, 799–800
Logical formula, 492
Logical operator, 721–722
Looping, 92
Los Alamos Scientific Laboratory, 30
Lotus Development Corporation, 457, 460, 880, 936
  Agenda, 908
  trademark, 937
Lotus 1-2-3, 86, 109–110, 457, 813, 880, 898, 936
  advanced, 555–599
  beginning, 459–500
  intermediate, 509–546
Lovelace, Countess Augusta Ada, 98
Lyle Stuart's Concise Dictionary of 26 Languages, 894

McDonnell-Douglas Corporation, 781
MacDraw, 826–830, 858–859, 863–865, 868–869
  designing desk with, 830
  menus, 829–830
  screen, 827
  tools, 827–829
McGraw-Hill's Dictionary of Computers, 894
Machine languages, 92–93
Machine learning, 907
Macintax Taxview, 901
Mackay, Stan, 287
MacLink Plus, 889
MacPaint, 821–826, 859, 860, 868, 906
  designing logo with, 824–826
  pointer, 822–823
  screen, 821–822
  tools, 823–824
Macro, 436–438, 584–588, 704
MacUser magazine, 144
MacWrite, 774, 856–858, 861, 865
Magnetic disk, 15–17
Magnetic resonance imaging (MRI), 922
Magnetic tape, 53
Magnetic tape drive, 53–54
Mail-merge, 438
Mainframes, 29
  calling, 778–780
Management information system (MIS), 925
Managing the Market, 900
Managing Your Money, 900–901
Mantissa, 567
Manual hyphenation, 403
Manual recalculation, 575–576
Map making, 814
Masica, Sue, 12
Math packages, 105, 895–896
MCI Mail, 781–784
MCI Telecommunications Corporation, 781
MECA Ventures, 900
Medicine, computers and, 920–922
MedSIG (Medical Special Interest Group), 10
Mega, 47
Megabyte (M), 47
Megahertz (MHz), 46
Memo marker, 660
Memory, 15, 38–39, 46, 64
Memory-resident programs, 120–121
Memory variable, 739
Menu, 26, 107
  bar, 110, 612
  pointer, 469
  pop-up, 108–110
  pull-down, 110
  static, 107–108
Merchant & Gould, 938
Message line, 613
Micro Channel Architecture, 25
Microchips, 78
Microcomputer(s), 13, 849
  calling another, 790–792
  defined, 14–15
  hardware, 15–17
  internal structure of, 38–41
  software, 17–18
  standards, 22–26
  types of, 19–22
  users, 18–19
Micro Library Series, 894
Microprocessor, 14–15, 41–42, 943–944
  data bus size of, 44–45
  register size of, 43–44
  speed of, 45–46
  structure of, 42–43
Microrim, 813
Microsoft Corporation, 24, 96, 109, 903
  Bookshelf, 894
  Excel, 460
  and MS-DOS, 109
  operating system, 109, 130, 131
  and OS/2, 131–132
  Project, 897–898
  Windows, 91, 884, 885, 938
  Word, 854
  Works, 882
Microstuf, Inc., 772
Million instructions per second (MIPS), 27–28
Minicomputer, 28–29
Minimal recalculation, 575
Minnesota Computer Virus Crime Bill, 932
Mixed reference, 579, 581–582
Mnemonics, 93
Mode indicator, 464
Modem (modulator/demodulator), 70–72, 767, 771
  cable, 769
  direct-connect, *see* Modem, external
  external, 72–73, 769–770
  Hayes-compatible, 771
  internal, 72, 768
Modular phone jack, 767
Modulation, 72
Molecular Editor, 13
Monitors, 60–63, 809–810
  See also Display
Monochrome graphics monitor, 61–62
Monochrome text monitor, 60–61
Morris, Robert T., Jr., 918
Mosaic Software, 936
Motherboard, 38
Motorola microprocessor chips, 134
Motorola 68030, 78
Motorola 68040, 943
Mouse, 17, 59, 850–851
Movies, computers and, 919–920
MP/M, 129
MS-DOS (Microsoft Disk Operating System), 130
Multicolor Graphics Array, 850
MultiFinder, 134–135, 885
Multifunction board, 65
Multiple index files, 729
Multiprocessing, 123–125
Multiscan monitors, 810
Multisoft Corporation, 890
Multitasking operating systems, 121–122, 123, 145
Multiuser, single-tasking operating systems, 122, 123
Music, computers and, 917–919
Musical Instrument Digital Interface (MIDI), 919
MYCIN, 908

NASA, 607, 905
National Bureau of Standards (NBS), 942
National Institute of Occupational Health and Safety, 928
National Security Agency, 30–31, 942–943
Natural language processing, 907
Natural recalculation, 577
Navigation line, 613

Near letter-quality (NLQ), 66–68
NEC MultiSpeed HD, 20
NEC MultiSync monitor, 810
Nelson, Ted, 905
Nesting, 254
NETBIOS (NETwork Basic Input/Output System), 798
NetTalk, 946–947
Network, 26–27, 103, 125–126
  adapter, 65
  interface, 794
  media, 794
  neural, 946–947
  server, 794
  software, 797–798
  topology, 794–796
  workstation, 794
  See also Local area network
Net Worth, 900–901
Neural network, 946–947
NewsGrid, 788–789
NEWSPACE, 889
Newspaper-style columns, 415–417
New York Times, 12
New York University School of Medicine, 921
NeXT, Incorporated, 56
NeXT computer, 56–57, 938
Nonprocedural languages, *see* Fourth generation languages
Northwestern Mutual Life, 6
Norton Commander, 887
Norton Utilities, 888–889
Novice, 18–19
Nuclear magnetic resonance, *see* Magnetic resonance imaging
Null-modem cable, 790–791
Number, 463
Numeric formula, 491–492

Object code, 94
Object-oriented, 826
Occupational Safety and Health Administration, 928
Office of Patents and Trademarks, U.S., 937, 938
On-line information services, 10, 784–790
On-line references, 105, 893–894
Online Today, 786, 787
Only Investment Guide You'll Ever Need, The, 900
Opcode, *see* Operation code
Open style, 444
Operand, 93, 492
Operating system, 88–89, 118
  Apple Macintosh system, 134–136
  components, 126–128
  controlling hardware by, 118–119
  CP/M, 129–130
  crashing of, 119
  DOS, 130–131
  generic, 129, 133
  interacting with users of, 120
  managing software by, 119–120
  OS/2, 131–132
  ProDOS, 134
  proprietary, 26, 129, 134, 135
  types of, 120–126
  UNIX, 132–134
Operation code, 92–93
Operator, 492–495
Optical disk drive, 55–57
Optimal recalculation, *see* Minimal recalculation
Orphan, 405–407
OS/2, 131–132, 145, 884
OUTBOX, 783–784
Output, 15, 41–42
OWL International, 906

Packet-switching network, *see* Public data network
Pac Man, 8
Page description language, 852
Page layout software, 849, 854
PageMaker, 855–871
Painting programs, 820–826
Paired style, 444
Palette, 63, 822, 827, 838
Pan, 832
Paperback Software International, 909, 936
Parallel columns, 415–417
Parallel interface, 65–66
Parallel port, *see* Parallel interface
Parallel processing, 124
Parameter, 166
Parent file, 737
Parity, 777
Partition, 265–267
Pascal, 18, 86, 96–98, 613
Pascal, Blaise, 96
Patent, 938
Path, 194–195
Pattern palette, 822
Pawluk, Hal, 607
Payroll, 900
PC-DOS (Personal Computer Disk Operating System), 130, 145
PC Storyboard, 837–840
PDP minicomputers, 132
Pel, *see* Pixel
Performance monitoring, computers and, 927
Peripherals, 65, 73–79
Personal computers, 14
  See also Microcomputers
Personal finance packages, 105, 900–901
Peter Norton Computing, 887, 888
Peterson, Pete, 329
Pie chart, 520–523, 815–817
Piping, 246
Pittsburgh, University of, 921
Pixel, 62, 808
Pixel-based, 820
Plotter, 70, 812
Point, 412
Pointer, 110
Pointer movement keys, 478
Polling, 796
Pop-up menu, 108–110
Pop-up utilities, *see* Desk accessories
Portable computers, 21
Portfolio Manager, 900
Positron emission tomography (PET), 922
PostScript printers, 851, 852
Power supply, 39
Power user, *see* Expert
Presentation, computers for, 12
Presentation Manager, 132, 884
Primary file, 440–443
Primary key, 539
Primary storage, 38–39, 46
  RAM, 46–47
  ROM, 47
Printer(s), 17, 66
  daisy-wheel, 68
  dot-matrix, 66–68, 811
  ink-jet, 68, 812
  laser, 68–70, 811, 851–853
  utilities, 890–891
Printhead, 66
PrintQ, 891
Print queue, 233, 398
Print server, 794
Print spooler, 891
Privacy, computers and, 938–943
Privacy Act (1974), 941–942
Privacy Plus, 943
Prodex, 9
ProDOS, 134
Productivity, computers for, 6–7, 8–9
Program, 15, 86–87
Program Evaluation and Review Technique (PERT), 896, 897
Programmer, 17
Programming languages, 18, 86, 91–92
  assembly, 93–94
  fourth generation, 98–100
  high-level, 94–98
  machine, 92–93
Project management packages, 105, 896–898
PROLOG, 908
Prompts, 107
  DOS, 149

Proportional spacing, 318
Proprietary operating systems, 26, 129, 134, 135
PROSPECTOR, 908
Protocol, 796–797
Public data network, 781
Pull-down menu, 110
Purchase orders, 899

QDOS (Quick and Dirty Operating System), 131
Quarterdeck Office Systems, 884
Query, 540, 662–665
QuickDraw laser printers, 851, 853

RAM resident programs, *see* Memory-resident programs
Random access memory (RAM), 46–47
Range, 467
Ratliff, Wayne, 607
Reader's Guide to Periodical Literature, 785
Read-only attribute, 214
Read-only memory (ROM), 46, 47
Read-write head, 50
Read-write memory, *see* Random access memory (RAM)
Real-time clocks, 64
Rebooting, 119, 150–151
Recalculation, 575
  automatic, 575
  column-wise, 576
  manual, 575–576
  minimal, 575
  natural, 577
  row-wise, 576
Record, 421, 617
Record buffer, 590–591
Record feature, 590–592
Record pointer, 719–720
Redirection, 242–245
Redirector, 798
Reduced instruction set computer (RISC), 943–944
Register, 43–44
Relate, 735
Relational data base, 665–670
Relational operator, 672–673
Relative reference, 579–580
Replaceable parameter, 252–253
Report, 647–648
Report band, 691
Resident routines, *see* Internal commands
Resolution, 61
Response time, 122
Rifkin, Stanley, 934
Right to Financial Privacy Act (1978), 942
Ring network, 794
Ritchie, Dennis, 98, 132
Robots, 907–908
Root directory, 194
Row, 754
Row-wise recalculation, 576
RS-232C standard, 65, 66
Rule base, 909
Ruler guide, 864
Ruler line, 317–318
Rules, 854

Sachs, Jonathan, 460
Sans serif typefaces, 855
SAS, 895
Scanner, 76–77, 810–811, 853
Scatterplot, *see* XY graph
Schorr, Herbert, 945
Schwartz, Lillian, 946
Screen groups, 131
Sculley, John, 871, 908
Search term, 790
Seattle Computer Products, 131
Secondary key, 539
Secondary merge file, 438–440, 441–443
Secondary storage, 47–48
  Bernoulli disk drives, 54–55
  floppy disk drives, 48–51
  hard disk drives, 51–53
  magnetic tape drives, 53–54
  optical disk drives, 55–57
Sector, 164
Security, computers and, 942–943
Security Pacific Bank of California, 934
Selective Service System, 939
Semiconductor, 42
Sensei Physics, 902
Sequential access medium, 53
Serial interface, 65, 766–767
Serial port, *see* Serial interface
Serif typefaces, 855
Service programs, 127
Shabbacoff, Phil, 12
Sheppard, John, 10
SideKick, 9, 892
Sideways, 888
Silicon Beach Software, 904
Simon & Schuster Software, 893
Single-density floppy disk, 49
Single-sided floppy disk, 48
Single-user, multitasking operating system, 121–122
Single-user, single-tasking operating system, 120–121
Site license, 935–936
Slide show programs, 836–840
Small Business Administration, 940
Small Computer System Interface (SCSI), 66
Smalltalk, 134
Smartmodem, 771
Smith, Allan, 13
Snap, 832
Social Security, 939, 940
Soft-Disk Publishing, 937–938
SoftLogic Solutions, 890
Soft page break, 323
Soft return, 292
Soft spaces, 318
SoftStyle's Printworks, 891
Softview, 901
Software, 17–18, 86–87
  managing, by operating systems, 119–120
  See also Application software; System software
Software Arts, 101
Software Bridge, 890
Software Directions, 891
Software Group, 880
Software licensing, 936
Software piracy, 934–936
Sony, 55
Sorting, 420–422
Soundex search, 673
Source, 169
Source code, 94
Southern California, University of, 929
Speaker, 40–41
Speech synthesizer, 78–79
Spooling, 232
Spreadsheet enhancement, 813
Spreadsheet packages, 18, 101–102
SQZ! Plus, 889
Stack, 264
Stacked bar graph, 528–531
Stackware, 906–907
Star network, 794
Star Trek, 607, 919–920
Star Wars, 919–920
Static menu, 107–108
Statistical packages, 105, 895–896
Status bar, 617
Status line, 289
Stop bits, 777
Strategic Locations Planning, 814
String combination operator, 492, 494
String formula, 492
Structured Query Language (SQL), 610, 753–756
Studio Session, 904
Style, 443–446
Subchassis, 38
Subdirectory, 151, 153, 194–198
SubLOGIC Corporation, 903
Summary operators, 681, 682
Sun Microsystems, 28
SuperCalc5, 460
Supercomputers, 30–31, 944–945
SuperKey, 891
Supermicro, *see* Workstations
Superminis, 28–29

Super PC-Kwik, 890
Switching drives, 160–161
Symbolic addressing, 93
Symphony, 880, 881
SYSTAT, 895
System board, *see* Motherboard
System calls, *see* Service programs
System clock, 45–46
System file, 135
Systems Compatibility
 Corporation, 890
System software, 17, 88
 operating systems, 88–89
 utilities, 89–90
 windowing environments, 91
System unit, 15–16

Table, 626, 754
Tag, 729
Tandy, 44, 109, 904
 PC-6 Pocket Computer, 20
Target, 169
Tasks, 120
Tate, George, 607
TAXADVISOR, 908
Tax packages, 105, 900–901
T800-20 Transputer chip, 125
Telecommuting, 71, 929–931
Teleconferences, 10
Template, 564–565
Terminal, 122
Terminal emulation, 772
Text area, 290
Text-based windowing
 environment, 883
Text file, 179
Thesaurus, 893
Thompson, Ken, 132
3D-Graphics, 813
ThunderScan, 859–860, 868
Thunderware Incorporated, 859
Time-sharing, 122
Time slices, 122
Tobias, Andrew, 900
Token-passing, 796–797
Tool palette, 822
Topology, 794–796
TopView, 885
Toshiba T3100, 17
Touch-screen, 75–76
Trackball, 73–74
Trademark, 936–938
Training, computers for, 921
Transient routines, *see* External
 commands
Transputer, 125
Turner Hall Publishing, 889
Twin, The, 936
Twisted-pair wire, 794
TYMNET, 781–782, 789
Type!, 902
Typeface, *see* Font

Ultrasound scanners, 921
United Press International, 788
United Software Security, 943
UNIX, 131, 132–134, 136, 145
Update query, 662
Uploading, 773–774
Upwardly compatible, 146
User, 18–19
 interacting with, of operating
 systems, 120
User friendly, 19, 106
User interface, 106, 128
 commands, 106–107
 graphical (GUI), 111–112
 pop-up menus, 108–110
 prompts, 107
 pull-down menus, 110
 static menus, 107–108
US Post Office 5-Digit ZIP Code
 Directory, 894
Utilities, 89–90, 887–891

Vaccine and Flu-Shot+, 933
Value-added network, *see* Public
 data network
VAX 8200, 29
Very high-level languages, *see*
 Fourth generation
 languages
Veterans Administration, 939, 940
Video Graphics Array, 810, 850
Video mode, 63, 808
View, 662
View query, 662
View skeleton, 663
Virus, computer, 918, 931–933
VisiCalc, 23, 101
Voice recognition systems, 77
Volume label, 224–226
VP-Expert, 909
VP-Planner, 936
Vulcan, 607

WarGames, 931
Webster's New World Combo, 893
Western Freezers, 9
White-collar crime, 933–934
White Crane Systems, 890
Widow, 405–407
Wild-card characters, 345, 637
Window, 26, 91, 882
Windowing environment, 91,
 882–885
 graphics-based, 883–884
 text-based, 883
Windows Presentation Manager,
 132
Wirth, Niklaus, 96
Word length, 776
WordPerfect, 8, 283, 854
 advanced, 395–448
 beginning, 285–330
 intermediate, 337–385
WordPerfect Corporation, 283, 287,
 329
Word processing, 6–7, 100
 and desktop publishing,
 853–854
WordStar, 887
Word wrap, 292
Work area, 735–736
Workplace, computers and, 6,
 925–931
Worksheet, 463
 See also Spreadsheet packages
Workstations, 28
Wozniak, Stephen, 23
Write Once, Read Many (WORM),
 56
Write-protection, 177
Write-protect notch, 177–178
Write-protect switch, 178
Wubker, Ron, 9
WYSIWYG (What-You-See-Is-
 What-You-Get), 854, 865

XENIX, 134
Xerox, 938
 8010 Star Information System
 of, 25–26, 134
 Palo Alto Research Center of,
 25, 134, 946
 Ventura Publisher of, 855
XTree Company, 886
XTree Pro, 886–887
XY graph, 531–535

Zenith, 44
Zilog Z80 chips, 129
Zoom in/out, 832

MS-DOS® 4.01											
Ctrl–Alt–Del Reboot Ctrl–Break Cancel Ctrl–Print Screen Echo Print Screen Print Enter Process cmd. Esc Cancel line Del Skip char. Ins Toggle insert D.C. Heath	Retype one character from previous command F1	Retype previous command up to specified character F2	Retype all of previous command F3	Delete previous command up to specified character F4		Save current command as previous command F5	Insert End–of–file code Ctrl–Z F6	F7	F8		F9	F10

Cut here

WordPerfect® 5.0												
for IBM Personal Computers Delete to End of Ln/Pg End/Pg Dn Delete Word Backspace Go To Home Hard Page Enter ◄Margin Release Tab Screen Up/Down –/+ (num) Soft Hyphen – Word Left/Right ←/→ © WordPerfect Corp. 1988 D.C. Heath	Shell Thesaurus Setup Cancel F1	Spell Replace ◄Search ►Search F2	Screen Reveal Codes Switch Help F3	Move Block ►Indent◄ ►Indent F4	Ctrl Alt Shift	Text In/Out Mark Text Date/Outline List Files F5	Tab Align Flush Right Center Bold F6	Footnote Math/Columns Print Exit F7	Font Style Format Underline F8	Ctrl Alt Shift	Merge/Sort Graphics Merge Codes Merge R F9	Macro Define Macro Retrieve Save F10

Cut here

Lotus 1–2–3® R. 2.2												
/ Main menu Enter Process entry Esc Exit menu Home Go to A1 Ctrl← Left screen Ctrl→ Right screen D.C. Heath	COMPOSE HELP F1	STEP EDIT F2	RUN NAME F3	UNDO ABS F4	Alt	LEARN GOTO F5	WINDOW F6	APP1 QUERY F7	APP2 TABLE F8	Alt	APP3 CALC F9	APP4 GRAPH F10

Cut here

dBASE IV® 1.0												
Enter Next field Tab Next field Shift–Tab Previous field Esc Abandon Ctrl–End Save & exit Ctrl–Enter Save & remain Ctrl–PgUp First record Ctrl–PgDn Last record D.C. Heath	PICK HELP F1	DESIGN DATA F2	FIND PREV PREV F3	FIND NEXT NEXT F4	Shift	FIND FIELD F5	REPLACE SELECT F6	SIZE MOVE F7	DITTO COPY F8	Shift	QUICKRPT ZOOM F9	MACRO MENUS F10